Fifth Edition

LABOR RELATIONS LAW

BENJAMIN J. TAYLOR
University of Oklahoma

FRED WITNEY
Indiana University

PRENTICE-HALL, INC., *Englewood Cliffs, New Jersey 07632*

Library of Congress Cataloging-in-Publication Data

TAYLOR, BENJAMIN J.
    Labor relations law.

    Bibliography: p.
    Includes indexes.
    1. Collective labor agreements—United States.
2. Labor laws and legislation—United States.
I. Witney, Fred, (Date). II. Title.
KF3408.T35 1987   344.73'0189   86–22554
ISBN 0-13-519661-2   347.304189

Editorial/production supervision and interior design: Marcia Rulfs
Cover design: Ben Santora
Manufacturing buyer: Harry P. Baisley

Printed in the United States of America
10 9 8 7 6 5 4 3 2 1

ISBN 0-13-519661-2   01

Prentice-Hall International (UK) Limited, *London*
Prentice-Hall of Australia Pty. Limited, *Sydney*
Prentice-Hall Canada Inc., *Toronto*
Prentice-Hall Hispanoamericana, S.A., *Mexico*
Prentice-Hall of India Private Limited, *New Delhi*
Prentice-Hall of Japan, Inc., *Tokyo*
Prentice-Hall of Southeast Asia Pte. Ltd., *Singapore*
Editora Prentice-Hall do Brasil, Ltda., *Rio de Janeiro*

TO THE MEMORY OF E. B. McNATT
Professor of Economics Emeritus
University of Illinois

Teacher—Counselor—Friend

CONTENTS

PREFACE   *xv*

I
Introduction to
Collective Bargaining

1   NATURE AND DEVELOPMENT
     OF COLLECTIVE BARGAINING   *1*

     The Nature of Collective Bargaining.   The Mainsprings of Unionism.
     The Extent and Significance of Collective Bargaining.   The Legal Climate.

II
Legal Suppression
of Collective Bargaining

2   LABOR UNIONS:
     UNLAWFUL COMBINATIONS   *9*

The Early Union Movement: Its Socioeconomic Content.
Conspiracy Doctrine Applied to Unions.   The Case Against the Unions.
Characteristics of the Conspiracy Trials.   In Defense of Labor Unions.
The State of Affairs Before Commonwealth v. Hunt.
Labor Unions Declared Lawful Organizations in 1842.
Commonwealth v. Hunt: *Its Significance.*
From the Conspiracy Doctrine to the Labor Injunction.

3   NATURE AND USE OF
THE LABOR INJUNCTION   *22*

The Nature of Injunctions.   Forms of Injunctions.
The Injunction in Labor Disputes.
The Concept of "Property" in Labor Injunction Cases.   Abuses of Injunctions.
The Yellow-Dog Contract and the Labor Injunction.

4   THE STRUGGLE FOR
A LABOR ANTITRUST POLICY   *40*

Application of Sherman Act to Labor Unions.
Economic Issues in Danbury Hatters *Doctrine.*
Labor's "Magna Charta" or "Enigma"?
Rule of Reason: Development of a Double Standard.
The Bedford Stone *Decision: Effect on Union Tactics and Completion of the Double Standard.*

III

Government
Encouragement to
Collective Bargaining

5   CONTROL OF
THE LABOR INJUNCTION   *68*

The Changing Economic and Political Scene.
Early Regulation of the Labor Injunction.
Early Labor Injunction Legislation: Court Attitudes.
"One Picket per Entrance."
Labor Injunction Control Legislation Held Unconstitutional.
"Holmes and Brandeis Dissenting."
Norris–La Guardia.   Area of Industrial Freedom.
Concept of "Labor Dispute."   The Passing of the Yellow-Dog Contract.
Labor Injunction: Procedural Limitations.
Judicial Construction of Norris–La Guardia.
The Impact of Norris–La Guardia.

6 ANTITRUST PROSECUTION
SINCE NORRIS-LA GUARDIA   *100*

Norris–La Guardia and Labor Protection.
Labor Dispute Defined Broadly in Norris–La Guardia. Judicial Reaction.
The Apex Doctrine Nullifies Effect of Coronado Decision.
Labor Unions and the Sherman Act: Present Application.
Consequences of Supreme Court Action.

7 THE LOGIC OF
GOVERNMENT PROTECTION   *118*

The Problem. Patterns of Antiunion Conduct: Industrial Espionage.
Patterns of Antiunion Conduct: Attack on Union Leadership.
Patterns of Antiunion Conduct: Strikebreaking Tactics.
Patterns of Antiunion Conduct: Company Unions. Need for Public Control.

8 PRECURSORS OF
THE WAGNER ACT   *135*

The Beginnings of Legislative Support.
The Early Laws: Yellow-Dog Contracts and Discrimination Unlawful.
Attitude of the Judiciary. Events of World War I. Railroad Legislation.
Railway Labor Act Amended in 1934. National Industrial Recovery Act.
Section 7 (a): Nature and Enforcement. Passage of the Wagner Act.

9 THE WAGNER ACT   *161*

The Socioeconomic Rationale of the Wagner Act.
State of Affairs Before Jones & Laughlin.
The Jones & Laughlin Decision.
Substantive Provisions: Unfair Labor Practices.
Substantive Provisions: The Principle of Majority Rule.
Unfair Labor Practice Procedure.
Unfair Labor Practice Charge.
Formal Proceedings.
The Wagner Act Record. Representation Procedure. Industrial Democracy.
Wagner Act During World War II. Results of the Wagner Act.

10 THE TAFT-HARTLEY ACT:
GENERAL OBSERVATIONS   *199*

The Shift in Government Policy.
Factors Resulting in Passage of Taft-Hartley. Taft-Hartley Provisions.
Union Unfair Labor Practices. The Rights of Employees as Individuals.
The Rights of Employers. National Emergency Strikes.
Other Taft-Hartley Provisions. Operation of Taft-Hartley.
Enforcement Procedures. Changing NLRB Personnel and Policies.
Union Political Activities. Taft-Hartley Amendments.

JURISDICTION OF THE NATIONAL

11   LABOR RELATIONS BOARD   *246*

Self-Imposed Restrictions.
Federal Preemption: Legislative Aspects of Taft-Hartley.
Federal Preemption: The Supreme Court.   Coverage of Hospital Employees.
Taft-Hartley and Bankruptcy Code: Bildisco and Its Aftermath.
Congressional Response.
Agricultural Workers.

IV
Control of
Collective Bargaining

12   ELECTION POLICIES OF THE NLRB   *283*

Employer Free Speech Under the Wagner Act.
Construction of Taft-Hartley Provisions.   Captive-Audience Problem.
Names-and-Addresses Policy: The Excelsior Doctrine.
Bargaining on the Basis of Authorization Cards: The Gissel Doctrine.
Power of the NLRB to Order Bargaining: Categories of Unfair Labor Practices.
Employer Election Petitions.   Decertification Elections.
Runoff Elections.

CONTROL OF

13   THE BARGAINING UNIT   *325*

The Bargaining Unit: Its Nature.   Influence of the Wagner Act.
Establishment of the Bargaining Unit: Wagner Act Experience.
Pressure for Bargaining-Unit Limitations.
Treatment of Craft Bargaining Units.   Craft Workers Under Taft-Hartley.
Forepeople Under the Wagner Act.
Supervisors Under Taft-Hartley.   Managerial Employees Other Than Supervisors.
Plant Guards.   Plant-Guard Organization Problems Under Taft-Hartley.
Professional Workers.   "Extent of Organization."   Coordinated Bargaining.

CONTROLS ON

14   THE SUBSTANCE OF BARGAINING   *366*

Union Security: A Controversial Issue.
Taft-Hartley and the Union Shop.   Section 14 (b) and Right-to-Work Laws.
Union Security Under the Railway Labor Act.
Union Shop and Union Political Activities.
The Agency Shop in Right-to-Work Law States.
The Agency Shop Under Taft-Hartley.   Legal Control of the Checkoff.
Controls Over Good-Faith Bargaining.   The Collyer Doctrine: Deferral to Arbitration.

15   ENFORCEMENT OF THE COLLECTIVE
      BARGAINING AGREEMENT   424

Internal Enforcement Procedure: The Grievance Procedure.
Control of the Grievance Procedure: Wagner Act Experience.
Grievance Procedure Under Taft-Hartley.
Duty of Fair Representation: Employee Recourse Through NLRB.
When Direct Negotiations Fail: Arbitration.
Arbitration and the Supreme Court: From Westinghouse *to* Lincoln Mills.
The "Trilogy" Cases.   Norris–La Guardia Influence on No-Strike Provisions.
Sinclair *Reversed by* Boys Markets.
Metropolitan Edison: Discipline of Union Officers.
Dual Jurisdiction of Arbitrators and NLRB.
Bargaining Obligation of Successor Employer.   Successor Employer Obligations.

V

Collective Bargaining:
Area of
Industrial Conflict

16   STRIKES, LOCKOUTS,
      AND PICKETING   465

Recapitulation.   Economic Striker Rights.   Landrum-Griffin Revision.
Jurisdictional Strikes: Illegal Under Taft-Hartley.
Strikes Against NLRB Certification.
Lockout Rights of Employers.   Employee Conduct on the Picket Line.
Fines Against Union Members Working During a Strike.
Concept of "Concerted Activity": Meyers Industries.
Recognitional and Organizational Picketing.

17   SECONDARY BOYCOTT PRESSURES   507

Legal Status Under Taft-Hartley.   Ally Doctrine.
Definition of Persons and Individuals.   Common-Situs Picketing.
Roving or Ambulatory Situs.   Consumer Secondary Boycotts.
Hot-Cargo Agreements.   Construction and Clothing Industry Exemption.

18   STATE PICKETING POLICY AND
      THE U.S. SUPREME COURT   538

The Thornhill *Doctrine: Basic Meaning.*
Stranger Picketing and the Free-Speech Guarantee.
The New York Cases: Absence of Labor Dispute Not Controlling.
Peaceful Picketing Not Protected by the Guarantee of Free Speech.
Free-Speech and Private Property Rights.

19 NATIONAL EMERGENCY LABOR DISPUTES

556

Characteristics of National Emergency Disputes.
Difficulties in Identifying Emergency Disputes. Economic Effect of Strikes.
Taft-Hartley Procedures. The Last-Offer Vote Record.
Settlement Record During the Injunction Period.
Constitutionality of Taft-Hartley Provisions. Railway Labor Act Emergency Provisions.
Government Policy in the Railroad Industry.
Compulsory Arbitration and Collective Bargaining.
Suggested Alternatives to Existing Emergency Procedures Eliminate Interference.
Suggested Alternatives to Existing Emergency
Procedures: Labor-Management Advisory Committee Proposal.
Statutory Strikes. Seizure. Partial Injunction. Choice of Procedures.

VI
Additional Areas of
Government Control

20 LABOR-MANAGEMENT REPORTING AND DISCLOSURE ACT OF 1959

584

Background of Regulation of Internal Union Affairs.
Bill of Rights of Members of Labor Organizations. Equal Rights.
Freedom of Speech and Assembly. Dues, Initiation Fees, and Assessments.
Protection of the Right to Sue. Safeguards Against Improper Disciplinary Action.
Enforcement of the "Bill of Rights." Reports to Secretary of Labor.
Reports by Unions. Conflict-of-Interest Reporting. Employer Reports.
Labor Relations Consultants. Control of Trusteeships.
Conduct of Union Elections. Election Provisions.
Financial Safeguards for Labor Organizations.

21 LABOR RELATIONS IN THE PUBLIC SECTOR

627

Basis of Denial of Government Employee Bargaining.
Collective Bargaining Among Federal Employees.
The Postal Service. Federal Reserve System.
Civil Service Reform Act of 1978: Title VII.
Grievance and Arbitration Procedures. Unfair Labor Practices and Their Resolution.
Contract Negotiation Impasses. Collective Bargaining at the State and Local Levels.
Status of State Laws. The Right to Strike. Union Security Practices.
Resolution of Disputes. Arbitration.

22 DISCRIMINATION IN EMPLOYMENT OPPORTUNITY

652

Evolution of Racial Discrimination Policy.
Equal Employment Opportunity: Essential Features of Title VII.

The Equal Pay Act and Comparable Worth.
Arbitration and Title VII Rights.   Religious Discrimination.   National Origin.
Affirmative Action Programs.   Preferential Treatment.
Equal Employment Opportunity and Labor Unions.
Age Discrimination.

23   EVOLUTION AND PROBLEMS OF LABOR RELATIONS LAW   *690*

Issues with Policy Implications.
Equal Employment Opportunity.
General Views.

A   THE SHERMAN ANTITRUST ACT   *697*

B   THE CLAYTON ACT   *699*

C   THE NORRIS–LA GUARDIA ACT   *701*

D   THE WAGNER ACT   *706*

E   LABOR MANAGEMENT RELATIONS ACT, 1947   *714*

F   THE LANDRUM-GRIFFIN ACT   *745*

G   CIVIL SERVICE REFORM ACT OF 1978   *769*

     EQUAL EMPLOYMENT OPPORTUNITY ACT AMENDING CIVIL
     RIGHTS ACT OF 1964: TITLE VII—EQUALITY EMPLOYMENT
H   OPPORTUNITY   *797*

     BIBLIOGRAPHY   *815*

     INDEX OF CASES   *827*

     GENERAL INDEX   *845*

PREFACE

This book is intended for either undergraduate or graduate liberal arts and business school curriculums and for business and union people with little legal background. It stresses the institutional framework in which the government structure of collective bargaining is cast. Though the book is not intended for lawyers, members of the legal profession and law school students might find it useful to gain an appreciation and an understanding of the impact of government in the field of labor relations. The study deals with the major trends in the law of collective bargaining, the reasons for these trends, and their consequences on the overall functioning of collective bargaining.

The law of labor relations has little meaning in the absence of an understanding of the dynamics of labor relations. Consequently, attention has been devoted to the labor relations environment in which the legal structure operates. Moreover, where appropriate, there is economic analysis of the problems resulting from the efforts of government to define the rights, duties, and obligations of labor unions and employers in the area of labor relations and collective bargaining. In this manner, it is hoped that the reader will be in a better position to evaluate public policy in labor relations.

The structure of the book strikes a balance between the development of the law of collective bargaining and current problems of labor relations. Through Part III an analysis is made of the general sweep of events from 1806 through the Wagner Act era. Parts IV and V highlight the effects of Taft-Hartley and subsequent amendments on the operation of labor relations. Part VI deals with the essential features of the Landrum-Griffin Act, labor relations in the public sector, and problems of minority workers and women. Included are texts of major federal labor statutes and a summary at the end of each chapter.

The difficulty of labor relations law, but also its challenge and attraction, is that the law is ever changing and developing. This, of course, is the justification for the new edition. Because the basic structure of the past editions has proved successful it remains unchanged. What *is* new are doctrines established by the National Labor Relations Board and the courts since the publication of the last volume. In keeping with the goal of the first four editions, not all the changes are treated; we have concentrated on major developments of outstanding significance.

Indeed, there have never been as many fundamental changes in national labor policy between publications of previous editions of this book. In part this is attributable to the Reagan appointed NLRB which has reversed many important decisions of its predecessors. The fifth edition of LABOR RELATIONS LAW examines such controversial cases as *Milwaukee Spring, Meyers Industries, Gourmet Foods, St. Francis Hospital, United Technologies,* and *Pattern Makers League.*

In addition to Reagan Board generated cases, the fifth edition of LABOR RELATIONS LAW addresses many "red letter" cases. Examples include *Bildisco, W. R. Grace, Ellis* v. *Railway Clerks,* and *Bowen* v. *U.S. Postal Service.*

Further highlights of this edition include a discussion of the federal courts' response to the *comparable worth* doctrine (Ch. 23). Major developments in *public sector organization* and *collective bargaining* are examined (Ch. 21). All Taft-Hartley Act chapters have been revised and updated. And Chapter 20, "Labor Management Reporting and Disclosure Act of 1959 (Landrum-Griffin)," explores legal developments in employers' use of labor consultants and otherwise deals with fresh developments in this area.

The authors are grateful for the reception by the faculty and students of the past editions. As before, we believe the volume is amenable for a one-semester course. Depending on the interests of the particular faculty member and the background of the class, the course could be limited to certain areas treated in the volume, which is written in a manner providing flexibility to adapt to particular faculty and student needs. No textbook, regardless of its merits, can be successful without quality teaching. This is particularly true in labor relations law, what with its swift and continuously changing character. Indeed, the teacher has the difficult and challenging task of keeping students aware of developments since the publication of the volume. Even before this book reaches the students, the NLRB and the courts will inevitably have changed former policies and added new dimensions to the law of labor relations. Only the teacher can handle these developments in the classroom. Lastly, the authors intend that all general masculine pronoun references be interpreted as referring to both males and females.

As always, we are indebted to more people than we can thank. We owe an everlasting debt to the late Dr. E. B. McNatt, who provided indispensable assistance in the preparation of the original volume. Dr. Dale Yoder gave encouragement and perceptive help in this as well as in the past editions. We are particularly grateful to Dr. P. A. Brinker and Dr. Donald Wolf for their help in preparing the revised chapter on secondary boycotts and public employees, respectively. As before, our families have suffered the greatest costs of all. We are most grateful for their patience.

BENJAMIN J. TAYLOR
FRED WITNEY

CHAPTER ONE

NATURE AND DEVELOPMENT OF COLLECTIVE BARGAINING

THE NATURE OF COLLECTIVE BARGAINING

Collective bargaining is the joint determination by employees and employers of the problems of the employment relationship. Such problems include wage rates and wage systems, hours and overtime, vacations, discipline, work loads, classification of employees, layoffs, and worker retirement. The advent of collective bargaining does not give rise to these problems. Rather, they are intrinsic to the industrial relations environment, and exist with or without unionization. In the absence of the organization of workers, the employer solves these problems on a unilateral basis. The framework in which they are settled will be conditioned by the employer's conceptions of fairness, attitudes toward maximization of profit, social responsibility, and knowledge of current labor market conditions. Collective bargaining means that the employer does not unilaterally determine all the conditions of employment. Through this vehicle, the employer and the representatives of his or her workers attempt to reach a meeting of minds on wages, hours, and other terms and conditions of work. If the parties fail to reach a satisfactory adjustment, the result can be an interruption of production. Collective stopping of work by workers constitutes a strike. The interruption is termed a lockout if the employer controls the timing and duration of the work stoppage. However, the threat of a strike or lockout, and the stoppage itself, are the prods that stimulate management and unions to find a peaceful solution to the problems of employment. Indeed, the strike is an integral part of the collective bargaining process. Without it, collective bargaining does not function effectively as the vehicle of joint determination of the issues of the employment relationship.

Although collective bargaining embraces a wide variety of the problems of employment, the process by no means solves each and every issue of employment. At any one stage in the development of the socioeconomic environment, certain problems of employment appear ill suited for the collective bargaining process. For example, few people fifty years ago would have argued that pensions constituted a proper subject for collective bargaining. As the socioeconomic environment changes, the content of bargaining likewise becomes altered. Moreover, at any one time there are a variety of employment issues that cannot be solved through the framework of collective bargaining. This does not mean that unions should not be consulted in areas that appear beyond collective bargaining. Progressive managements see the value of taking the union into their confidence on issues that can be solved only imperfectly, if at all, through collective bargaining. In this way, the cooperation of the labor organization is fostered, and the general prosperity of the firm advanced. Few collective bargaining systems require management to consult with the union prior to the investment of new capital in the business. However, since such investment could affect the economic status of its workers, the firm might profit from consultation with their representatives concerning plans for expansion. Workers are becoming increasingly aware of the impact of foreign investment and production on their jobs.

Collective bargaining systems, moreover, cannot provide the answer to each human problem of employment. Many of them must still be disposed of through common sense and fair dealing. Despite the broad character of collective bargaining, the process simply cannot resolve the myriad of human employment problems. Collective bargaining is highly elastic in character. It can accommodate the most difficult of employment problems. But the very nature of collective bargaining makes the process unwieldy for the solution of each and every human problem within the employment relationship. Collective bargaining is ostensibly *collective* in nature. It deals with the problems common to large groups of workers. It can provide for wage systems, but the process will not resolve the question of whether or not John Jones can leave the job two hours early to take his wife home from the hospital. Of course, the union will protect workers who receive arbitrary treatment from management. But this is a negative or defensive mechanism. Human problems should be resolved positively and in a manner that will meet the standards of justice and industrial efficiency. This can best be accomplished outside the formalized structure of collective bargaining.

A balanced view of collective bargaining aids in the understanding of its limitations and potentialities. It cannot solve every human employment problem. Nor does it provide the solution for each and every economic problem confronting the firm, the industry, or the nation. For example, collective bargaining cannot solve the problem of depression-type unemployment. However, union-management relations, of which collective bargaining is a part, can fulfill a much wider mission than is assigned to collective bargaining in contemporary society. In the last analysis, collective bargaining is essentially a negative and protective institution. It limits the authority of management, imposes obligations on employers, and assures workers of a series of industrial rights. These, of course, are the historical and traditional purposes of unions.

There is, however, a much wider area in which union-management relations can operate. This area embraces the issues vital to the economic prosperity of the firm, industry, and nation. Matters of plant layout, sales and distribution, plant locale, investment, method of acquisition of new capital, pricing, and the like are commonly regarded as foreign to union-management solution. No labor contract, for example, can effectively provide for the method by which a firm should raise $500,000 of needed emergency capital. The economic conditions of the particular time must determine such a decision. However, to say that such issues are beyond collective bargaining does not imply that they are beyond union-management dealings. Indeed, consultation between management and unions over such business problems would probably increase the long-run overall harmony of the relationship. Such collective *dealings* (not collective *bargaining*), if conducted in good faith, should do much to advance the productive potential of American industry and American manpower.[1] To expand these dealings would mean a more mature approach to the economic problems of the firm, the industry, and the nation.

THE MAINSPRINGS OF UNIONISM

The union is the vehicle of collective bargaining. What affects the growth and effectiveness of unions conditions the overall vitality of the collective bargaining process. This does not mean that the development of unionism and of collective bargaining proceeds at the same rate. For a time there can be unions without collective bargaining. Such a condition can arise when employers refuse to recognize unions or to negotiate labor contracts even after employees have organized labor unions. However, in the long run, unions and collective bargaining are two sides of the same coin, because unions go out of existence if they are not successful in gaining collective bargaining recognition and obtaining contracts. If unions are weak and of ephemeral character, collective bargaining will not be much of a factor in the society. Consequently, the forces surrounding collective bargaining are those that stimulate unionism. What then are the mainsprings of the union movement?

The contemporary economic environment operates to render ineffective the effort of the worker to improve his or her economic status through individual bargaining. Characteristics of modern industry (including features such as large-scale production, concentration of ownership, and the divorce of ownership from management) have encouraged workers to utilize collective action to improve their standard of living. It is the totality of the economic environment that has served to stimulate the development and growth of the labor movement.

Before the rise of the modern factory system, there was little need for collective bargaining in the United States. When agriculture constituted the nation's leading pursuit, most people owned their own tools and in effect acted as their own employers. This applied not only to agricultural workers but also to workers who performed duties in the small handicraft shops prevalent during the early days of the United States. The need for collective bargaining arises when the worker sells his or her labor to another person. Its need is intensified when a nation's economy is organized around companies so large that the individual worker loses importance to the enterprise.

Shortly after the turn of the present century, industry replaced agriculture as the nation's top pursuit. The small handicraft shop gave way to the modern industrial facility, which in some cases employed several thousands of workers. By the beginning of World War I, the vast majority of the nation's labor force was employed in industry. In 1950, out of a labor force of about 63 million, approximately 46 million were employed in nonagricultural industrial facilities and only about 8.5 million earned their livings on farms.

By the mid 1980s, the total civilian labor force had increased to over 105 million. Nearly 95 million people are engaged in nonagricultural employment. Manufacturing accounts for slightly over 20 million workers. Government and services combined, however, provide employment to over 34 million people. Only slightly more than 3 million are employed in agriculture. This change has resulted in many political, sociological, and economic problems.

Still, the mere fact that the American economy shifted from agriculture to industry and is now shifting to services and government employment does not automatically mean the rise of the union movement. The fundamental prerequisite for the emergence of a permanent union movement rests in the development of a permanent working class. In addition, it is necessary that workers recognize the limited alternatives available to them in labor markets. A stable and permanent union movement emerges when workers recognize that their status as workers is not a temporary phenomenon and that they will experience a rising standard of living only insofar as they are able to maintain employment. Periodic rises in the unemployment rate and relatively slow wage advances make union membership attractive to some workers.

This principle of union growth is underscored by American experience. For many years, workers themselves were not greatly interested in collective bargaining: such was their attitude, even though the American economy was shifting from agriculture to industry. Why was this the case? While American industry was expanding at a rapid rate and the western frontier was still relatively unexploited, the opportunities for upward occupational mobility for workers and their children were abundant. As a matter of fact, before the exhaustion of the western frontier, a good number of workers were able to push west to begin their own enterprises. All of this meant that many workers believed that their period of service as industrial workers was only an interlude until they found the opportunity to start up their own businesses. As long as this attitude prevailed, there was no definite working-class consciousness, and a permanent labor movement was precluded. However, with the maturing of American industry and the declining opportunities of the western frontier, workers became aware that the opportunities for them or their children to advance from the ranks of the employees to the proprietor class were remote. They learned that the attitudes of vested economic interests toward new competition, the large amounts of capital needed to finance a new venture of even modest size, and the growing concentration of ownership of American industrial facilities all served to block elevation to the proprietor class. These forces produced a permanent working-class philosophy. The result was a permanent union movement.

It is not only the institutional arrangement of modern industry that stimulates workers to organize into unions. The structure of the contemporary labor and product markets adds to the propensity for unionism. The development of national and international markets provides the framework for wage-cutting. Employers in some industries compete vigorously for sales on the basis of lower prices. To protect profit margins and still garner the lion's share of the product market, employers are under constant pressure to reduce wages or to increase productivity. This is particularly true in industries in which labor costs represent a sizable percentage of total costs. Moreover, the opportunity for wage-cutting becomes greater in periods of severe unemployment. Labor unions represent the worker's adjustment to this feature of the economic environment. To resist the downward pressure on wages, some workers organize labor unions.

The pressure of economic life requires the complete organization of industries. Once a union gains a foothold in an industry, it is compelled to organize most of its firms. To do otherwise is to invite the demise of the labor organization. Nonunion firms, operating with lower labor standards, may be able to undersell their organized rivals. Such a state of affairs, if unchecked, would eventually result either in the elimination of the union or in the bankruptcy of the firms organized. Clearly, the structure of labor, product, and service markets provides a mainspring toward unionization and, of equal importance, widespread organization.

The economic side of collective bargaining is by no means the only stimulus for unionism. It is, of course, possible that unions may provide their members with better pay, vacations, paid holidays, pensions, and the like. However, workers form labor unions not only for economic considerations, but also because of psychological and social factors. Not all results of unions find their way into the pay envelope. Workers want to have a voice in the determination of things of importance in the bargaining unit. Personal dignity attaches to the extent to which they accomplish this objective.

THE EXTENT AND SIGNIFICANCE OF COLLECTIVE BARGAINING

Although little need existed for trade unionism prior to the industrialization of the nation, the rate of growth of the organized labor movement did not keep pace with the country's industrial development. Neither has labor organization in the services and government employment areas proceeded at the same rate. By 1920, about 30 million people were engaged in nonagricultural pursuits. In contrast, the number of workers in trade unions numbered about 5 million. From 1794, the year in which the first union was formed in the United States, until the New Deal period, the figure of 5 million represented the top level of union membership. Union membership declined to less than 3 million during the severe economic depression of the early thirties.

After 1935, union membership increased at a rapid pace. By 1950, approximately 15 million workers were members of labor unions, as compared with the 3 million of 1933. Though union membership as a percentage of the labor force declined to about 21 percent by 1985, compared to 30 percent in the middle 1950s, the fact remains that in that year, approximately 23 million employees were in unions and associations. However, reference to the mere numbers of the labor movement does not provide an accurate standard for evaluating its importance.

Union policy and activities in the highly organized sectors affect not only these particular industries, but also the operation of the entire economy. The modern economy is a highly integrated machine. Anything of importance that takes place in one area of the economy will produce effects throughout industry. Union wage policy in basic steel, for example, could cause repercussions throughout the entire economy. No particular segment of industry is isolated from the effects of changes in wages, costs, and prices in any significant branch of industry. Since labor unions operate in the most vital parts of the nation's economy, they exert an important influence on the entire economic structure.

THE LEGAL CLIMATE

The progress of organized labor during the New Deal period was no accident. It resulted partly from the operation of a legal environment that fostered unionism. New Deal labor laws outlawed employer antiunion practices that for years had stifled unionization. No longer was government an ally to management during labor disputes. A contributory factor making for union progress in the New Deal period was the revival of business activity. However, the growth of unionism was rooted also in the favorable legal environment as well as in improved economic conditions.

The legal climate is one of the principal factors conditioning the effectiveness and the scope of collective bargaining. Unionism flourishes under a favorable legal climate and is retarded in a hostile legal environment. Labor history reveals that public policy toward collective bargaining has not been uniform. When this policy has been favorable, a rapid rate of growth of the labor movement has ensued. The reverse has been the case when the legal environment has been unfavorable. A purpose of this book is to sketch the salient features of the development of the law of collective bargaining. What course the law of labor relations takes in the future will largely determine the position of collective bargaining in our nation. Only through an accurate knowledge of the roots of the law of collective bargaining can we intelligently influence its future development.

In analyzing the character of labor relations law, a careful examination must be made of several sources of that law. Important decisions of the judiciary must be considered. For many years, the courts determined the elements of the law of collective bargaining. The judiciary charted the legal boundaries of union con-duct. Subsequently, statutory law became more important than the common law as a determinant of the content of labor relations law. However, the influence of the courts on the character of labor law is still of great importance. The Supreme Court of the United States, the custodian of the federal Constitution, possesses the power to review all legislation in the light of the standards of the nation's basic document. It has the authority to invalidate statutory law, including labor legislation, on the grounds of conflict with the Constitution. Upon many occasions, the high court utilizes its power of judicial review to strike down legislation calculated to strengthen the union movement. In other ways as well, the Supreme Court plays an important role in shaping the structure of labor relations law.

Action of the legislative branch of government merits close attention. Labor relations legislation ultimately became of paramount importance in the story of the development of organized labor. Since 1932, Congress has enacted four major labor relations laws which have set the course of federal labor policy. These laws—Norris–La Guardia, the Wagner Act, Taft–Hartley, and Landrum-Griffin—will provide the framework for much of our subsequent discussion. Important decisions of labor agencies, such as the National Labor Relations Board (NLRB), must also be considered. Labor boards are indeed an important source of labor law. Thus, the NLRB interpretation of the Wagner Act and Taft-Hartley largely determines the practical application of these laws. The fact that adminis-trative rulings of labor boards are reviewable by the courts does not detract from their importance in the shaping of labor relations law.

Finally, the executive branch of government as a source of labor law must receive attention. Acting within their legal areas of operation, the President of the United States and the governors of the states influence the labor relations envi-ronment. During war periods the President historically becomes a particularly important figure in the labor arena. Also, the executive branch of government becomes important when the President or the governors intervene in important strikes. Another important example of executive action occurred in 1962 when President Kennedy issued Executive Order 10988, which provided a measure of protection for federal employees to engage in collective bargaining. The Civil Service Reform Act of 1978 provided for statutory protection of those rights instead of dependence on executive order.

The efforts of Congress and state legislatures to promote unionization have frequently been thwarted by the judiciary. The legislative branch of govern-ment would have protected the right of employees to self-organization and collec-tive bargaining. However, until 1937, the Supreme Court refused to sanction such legislation, declaring such efforts of Congress and state legislatures to be unconstitutional. Indeed, one of the most interesting aspects of labor relations law is this tussle between the judiciary and the legislative branches of government on the labor issue. Why this lag between the judiciary and the legislative branches occurred will subsequently become evident. Moreover, the effect of this conflict on the development of the union movement will be highlighted.

As never before, a careful analysis of the law of labor relations is necessary.

Collective bargaining is in the spotlight. Almost every day the newspapers detail organizational efforts of unions, strikes, and employer responses to union tactics. An understanding of the development and current posture of the law influencing the labor relations environment is required if the nation is to deal intelligently with one of its most important problems.

SUMMARY

Collective bargaining involves the joint determination of work conditions by workers and employers. The process is one part of union-management relations, and there exists the possibility that collective dealings (not *collective bargaining*) between unions and employers in areas regarded normally as beyond collective bargaining may constitute the proper structure for negotiations. Such may be the case in public employment.

Unionism represents the adjustment by workers to the problems of modern industrialism. Since unionism serves the economic, psychological, and social needs of workers on the job, the labor union remains a persistent and vital institution in contemporary society. The progress of unions has not been uniform. Their growth has been influenced by socioeconomic and legal factors. The importance of the labor union movement is not measured by mere reference to the absolute number of workers in labor unions. Indeed, if membership in all associations that use union tactics is totaled, the import of unionization may be more impressive than is often thought.

This book is concerned with the legal framework in which the collective bargaining process operates. To understand this framework, reference must be made to statutes, court decisions, and rulings by administrative agencies such as the NLRB. Such an investigation is of vital significance, for the power of government can aid or hinder labor organizations.

DISCUSSION QUESTIONS

1. What is meant by the term "collective bargaining"?
2. Under what conditions did collective bargaining start in the U.S.?
3. How important is the number of workers who are union members for an assessment of union strength and influence in the economy?
4. Is the judiciary as important today as it was before 1937 as a determinant of the content of labor relations law?

NOTES

1   See Alexander R. Heron, *Beyond Collective Bargaining* (Palo Alto: Stanford University Press, 1948).

CHAPTER TWO

LABOR UNIONS:

UNLAWFUL COMBINATIONS

THE EARLY UNION MOVEMENT:
ITS SOCIOECONOMIC CONTENT

The United States ranked second only to Great Britain in industrial activity in the first half of the nineteenth century. The trend of the future was set during this period even though agriculture remained the nation's leading occupation. In 1820, of all workers gainfully employed, about 72 percent earned their livings on the nation's farms. Manufacturing and the mechanical arts accounted for only about 12 percent of U.S. workers. However, the trend was definite and unmistakable. By 1860, the number of workers gainfully employed in agriculture had decreased to about 60 percent, while manufacturing and the mechanical arts accounted for about 18 percent.[1] Indeed, the rapid rise of manufacturing after 1800 is one of the outstanding features in the development of the nation's economy. By 1860, the gross value of manufactured products was around $1,800 million.[2] This was ten times the estimated figure for 1810. In the nation's irresistible march to industrialism, household manufacturing became a casualty. By 1860, the factory had generally replaced the household as the locale for manufacturing. The factory turned out cheaper and better products than could be produced in the home. The machine required the factory environment for its effective utilization. Factory methods were first applied to metal and iron products, food, and furniture. The increase in cotton manufacturing was typical of what was to occur in other industries. In 1808, there were only 8,000 spindles in all the nation. In 1860, more than 5 million spindles were in operation. One writer reported that by 1850, "it had become possible for rich and poor alike to dress adequately and attractively in cloth of American manufacture."[3]

The rise of the factory system in this period did more than serve as a harbinger of American industrial greatness. It produced a distinct labor class and thereby created the basis for modern labor problems: the adjustment of workers to the economic and social problems of industrialism. In the colonial era, a male worker at least normally passed through the stages of apprentice and journeyman, and eventually became an independent master craftsman. In this role, the functions of laborer, employer, capitalist, merchant, and entrepreneur were performed. However, as the factory system arose, the economy took on its contemporary characteristic of specialization of function. This meant that an increasing number of workers were destined to remain "hired hands" throughout their lives.

As the market for the products of industry widened under the stimulus of an ever-improving transportation system, the economic position of the laboring class was changed. The products made in one locality competed with those turned out in other areas. When employers found that they were being undersold by rival producers, they frequently reduced wages to wipe out the price differential and still maintain profit margins. As a matter of fact, many of the strikes in the early 1800s were protests against wage-cutting. For example, in Manayunk, Pennsylvania, a textile manufacturing town, there was a strike in 1828 against a 25 percent reduction in pay. Commons in this connection declared, "Even at the old prices, it was said, a spinner could make only 'from $7.50 to $8.50 per week for himself [sic] by working the full period of twelve hours daily, and in doing this he actually earned for his employers from $40 to $50 per week.' "[4] Indeed, low wages were the lot for many of the newly created working class. This was particularly true in the New England textile factories which employed large numbers of women and children, groups notorious for their weak bargaining power. In some cases, whole families were employed in the factories, but their earnings were low. Thus, four members of a family worked a total of 93 days between April 25 and May 19, 1832, for a net return of $18.30.[5]

Other conditions of work in the early factories also reflected competitive pressures of product markets. Hours of work were long relative to current standards, frequently ranging from twelve to fourteen per day. The lack of provisions for the prevention of accidents was not yet a public issue. Little attention was paid to the establishment of healthy working conditions. In short, in the race to create profitable enterprises, the early factory owners generally had little time to pay attention to the welfare of their employees. Thus, one historian, speaking on the lot of labor in the 1800–1850 period, concludes: "Although the factory system from the beginning brought to society in general increased leisure and many conveniences the value of which can scarcely be measured, the people whose sweat and toil made these changes possible profited little."[6]

The search for profits and the exploitation of new markets occupied the major proportion of the new factory owner's time. Riches stimulated the desire for still more riches. That the worker shared but little in the fruits of the newly created industrial system was of little concern to the predominantly agriculturally-oriented public. Many publicly endorsed the philosophy of Alexander Hamilton, who once declared, "All communities divide themselves into the few and the many. The first are rich and well born and the other, the mass of people who seldom judge or determine right."[7] Social responsibility was not to become an important element of the American industrial system until industry grew to a more secure position in the economy. The precedent for labor unrest was set by the uncertainties of firm and industry survival due to fierce domestic and international competition. The framework for the labor-management strife of contemporary society was erected at the dawn of American industrialism.

CONSPIRACY DOCTRINE APPLIED TO UNIONS

Stimulated by a more rapid rate of socioeconomic change, some workers formed labor unions to protect their interests. The American labor movement dates from the early part of the nineteenth century, though ephemeral organizations and sporadic worker protests occurred previously. In the early 1800s, organizations of a more permanent character were formed to provide workers with a shield of protection from the consequences of the new industrialism.

Efforts at organization of the early unions were confined largely to the skilled workers of the shoemaking, weaving, hatmaking, and printing trades rather than among the less skilled factory workers. This feature of labor union development is easily explained. It is commonly accepted that the conditions of the factory workers were much worse than those of the skilled craft workers. But many factors operated to forestall the organization of the hired hands of the newly created factories. These workers, unlike the craft workers, were very easily replaced due to their surplus. Training for their jobs was practically unnecessary, as evidenced by the large number of children who successfully held down factory jobs. Moreover, a high proportion of factory workers were women and children, groups which for many reasons were not readily organizable at that time. Many factory workers did not possess the necessary insight into the socioeconomic forces released by the growing industrial society. This is not surprising, for many of these workers were uprooted from the farms and had had little opportunity except for the most meager type of education. Although the evidence is not clear, one could say with a degree of certainty that a sizable proportion of the early factory workers was illiterate. The craft workers, of more worldly experience, quickly understood the necessity of effective organization of labor to meet the problems of the new structural arrangement of industry. This is not to say that the factory workers did not protest against working conditions. On the contrary, they participated in many strikes, most frequently carried out against wage-cutting. However, these strikes were poorly managed and generally unsuccessful. No union can maintain itself for long when it cannot strike successfully. Thus the early attempts at unionization by unskilled factory workers were usually unsuccessful. Indeed, it was not until the birth of the Congress of Industrial Organizations (CIO) in 1935 that the nation's factory workers organized on a successful and permanent basis. Even then, their success was due to a more favorable government policy, which was not present in earlier years.

Of the early unions, the shoe and bootmakers' organizations were by far the most aggressive. Many of the other unions had a sporadic existence, the craft workers banding themselves together to carry out periodic strikes and then dissolving after the strikes were terminated. In contrast, the shoemakers' unions had a permanent existence during the early period. The Philadelphia shoemakers, for example, organized in 1792 and maintained their organization permanently for many years. So successful were these shoemakers' unions that shoemaker employers' associations were established, which had in part as their objective the neutralization of the craft workers unions. For a time, employers resorted to economic pressure tactics calculated to defeat the labor unions. Among their most effective weapons was the employment of replacements willing to work for wages below the scale demanded by unionists.

In 1806, some employers struck upon a new method to deal with the shoemakers' unions. They sought the aid of the courts. This procedure—the solicitation of government aid in labor disputes—remains to this day a persistent element in the industrial relations pattern. It is noteworthy that the precedent was established as early as 1806.

In that year, the Philadelphia shoemaker employers charged that unions were conspiracies. As conspiracies, they contended, labor unions were unlawful combinations. A conspiracy, generally defined, is the combination of two or more persons who band together to prejudice the rights of others or of society. Under the doctrine of conspiracy would fall, for example, the plot of a group of people who work together to bring about conviction of an innocent person. Likewise, the conspiracy doctrine would apply to the action of a group that plotted to overthrow an established government. Before conspiracy can be charged, it must be shown that the group has caused or will cause an injustice to other people or to society. An interesting characteristic about the conspiracy doctrine is that conspirators can be indicted and found guilty before they commit any overt act. For example, it is a crime to plot the murder of a person even if the evil plan is not executed. Another feature of importance is that an action by one person, though legal, becomes illegal when carried out by a group. This characteristic of the conspiracy doctrine had particular significance in the labor union conspiracy cases.

How did the employers attempt to prove that labor unions were conspiracies and hence unlawful organizations? How did unions, according to this point of view, prejudice the rights of others or of society? How did employers support the contention that by regulating wages labor unions caused "great damage and prejudice of other artificers, and journeymen in the said act and occupation of a (shoemaker), to the evil example of others, and against the peace and dignity of the Commonwealth of Pennsylvania"?[8]

THE CASE AGAINST THE UNIONS

Employers based their case against the unions partly on the economic doctrines of the classical school of economics. It was to be expected that the people responsible for the prosecution of unionists would be influenced by the economic doctrines of their times.[9] However, the pure elements of classical theory were not realized in practice. This placed a greater burden on the labor factor than was commonly assumed. Resistance by labor to such philosophies resulted because full employment was not the norm of operations.

Control of wages by unions, it was argued, "is an unnatural, artificial means of raising the price of work beyond its standard, and taking an undue advantage of the public."[10] It was contended that the increase of wages by union pressure led to higher prices of commodities. This in turn was supposed to result in the reduction of demand for products, causing unemployment in the community. The net effect of the union, therefore, was to cause injury to the community, to damage commerce and trade, and to prejudice the rights of all workers. So ran the general argument of the prosecution.

In addition, it was argued that nonunion workers were injured by the refusal of unionists to work beside them. It was contended that "a master who employs fifteen or twenty hands is called upon to discharge that journeyman who is not a member of the body; if he refuses they all leave him whatever may be the situation of his business."[11]

In the early trials, much was made of the fact that labor unions had been declared unlawful in England by both common law and statutory legislation.[12] Prosecutors urged that English law had in fact established a precedent for American courts. In his charge to the jury, the presiding judge in one conspiracy case declared that "the common law of England . . . must be deemed to be applicable. . . ."[13] In other words, the American courts should be bound by the doctrines and laws prevailing in England. The prosecution conceded, however, that workers as individuals had the right to take action to increase their wages. Individual bargaining for higher wages, even individual quitting of work because of dissatisfaction with working conditions, was legal. The charge was that the combining of workers to force higher wages constituted illegal conduct. On many occasions, the principle of conspiracy law was cited, whereby "what may be lawful in an individual, may be criminal in a number of individuals combined, with a view to carrying it into effect."[14] In this connection, the prosecution in the first conspiracy case, in 1806, declared:

> Let it be well understood that the present action is not intended to introduce the doctrine that a man [sic] is not at liberty to fix any price whatsoever upon his own labor. Our position is that no man [sic] is at liberty to combine, conspire, confederate, and unlawfully agree to regulate the whole body of workmen in the city. The defendants are not indicted for regulating their own individual wages, but for undertaking by a combination to regulate the price of the labor of others as well as their own.[15]

In summary, the charge against unions was that (1) labor organizations are conspiracies because they injure society and prejudice the rights of individuals; and (2) unions were declared unlawful in England and English law is a compelling precedent for American courts. These factors led one of the judges in the very first conspiracy case to remark that "a combination of workmen to raise their wages may be considered in a twofold point of view: one is to benefit themselves . . . the other is to injure those who do not join their society. The rule of law condemns both."[16]

CHARACTERISTICS OF THE CONSPIRACY TRIALS

Between 1806 and 1842, there were seventeen trials in which labor unions were charged with conspiracy. Of these, shoemakers' unions were involved nine times. In all cases, the unionists were charged with engaging in a criminal conspiracy. This meant that if convicted, the defendants could have been imprisoned. However, the penalties that were assessed were in the form of small fines. In passing sentence, judges threatened a more serious penalty for second offenses. The effect of the judgments was to discourage union activities.

A Philadelphia court decided the first conspiracy case against a union in 1806. Later trials were held in Pittsburgh, Baltimore, Buffalo, Hudson, and New York. The doctrine established in the Philadelphia case spread to the other cities. Courts always pay close attention to decisions developed in other judicial jurisdictions. Had the Philadelphia court ruled labor unions to be lawful associations, it is likely that few, if any, prosecutions would have taken place in other cities.

The worker defendants in the conspiracy cases were tried by juries. An analysis of the composition of the juries reveals that the jurors were representative of the merchant and employer groups. For example, in the first conspiracy trial, three of the jurors were grocers, two made their living as innkeepers, one was a tavernkeeper, and the others respectively were designated as "merchant," "hatter," "tobacconist," "taylor," and "bottler." In the early days of our nation, property qualifications were generally a prerequisite for jury duty. Workers, who held little or no property, were generally excluded from jury service. This feature undoubtedly influenced the outcome in the conspiracy trials. In addition, the decisions were influenced, not only by the social and economic predilections of the jurors, but by the general background of the judges presiding at the trials. Some of the judges made little effort to conceal their antiunion feelings. For example, one judge, while making his charge to the jury, declared, "If these evils [organization of workers in labor unions] were unprovided for by the law now existing, it would be necessary that laws should be made to restrain them."

IN DEFENSE OF LABOR UNIONS

Competent legal counsel defended the workers brought to trial in the conspiracy cases. Their preparation was such that they could make a thorough presentation of the workers' position. Arguments offered by the defense counsels reflected modern thinking on collective bargaining. The workers involved in the conspiracy cases had the benefit of learned and articulate counsel. Their conviction under the conspiracy doctrine was not attributable to lack of ability on the part of their defense lawyers. Workers through their lawyers argued that labor unions did not produce the evils so vividly portrayed by the prosecution. No empirical data or evidence was presented to bear out the prosecution's arguments, it was contended. It was also argued that collective action undertaken by workers to raise wages did not set in motion economic forces that resulted in hardship to the community. Defense counsels vigorously, but in vain, pointed to the positive contributions that labor unions could make to the economic and social life of the community. According to the defendants, English law did not apply to American courts, for by the Revolution, we divorced ourselves from British rule and "have shaken off the supremacy of English law."[17]

Furthermore, the defense objected to being tried under common law. It was argued that no statute or action by the legislative branch of government outlawed labor unions. Accordingly, why should a court outlaw this form of association when the legislature, the representative branch of government, had not seen fit to take this action? Freedom of action, it was further contended, applied not only to business people in the conduct of their economic activities, but applied equally to workers who sought to advance their position in the economy by collective action. The doctrine of liberty was not reserved for any particular economic group; instead, it equally embraced workers, farmers, and merchants. These arguments, presented in a most lucid and convincing manner, failed to sway the courts, for when the juries were polled, labor unions were indicted as unlawful associations. It seemed for a time that there was no place for unions in American economic life.

THE STATE OF AFFAIRS BEFORE <u>COMMONWEALTH</u> V. <u>HUNT</u>

In spite of the conspiracy cases, workers continued to form labor organizations. Although the negative legal environment was "effective . . . in checking the early trade societies," Selig Perlman, a foremost labor historian, reported that the early trade union movement was retarded even more by the industrial depression that set in after the conclusion of the Napoleonic Wars.[18] By 1836, there were several hundred local trade unions established in leading industrial cities of the East. The structure of the labor movement was taking on a more modern appearance. By 1842, city centrals had been formed in practically every eastern city in which local trade unions operated. National labor organizations also made their appearance during the years in which the courts applied the conspiracy doctrine to organized labor. In addition, the first federation of labor unions in the United States was established in this period. The National Trades' Union, as this federation was called, was organized in New York City in 1834. At its first convention, delegates appeared from many of the local unions and city centrals operating in New York,

Philadelphia, Boston, Brooklyn, Poughkeepsie, and Newark. The federation sought to unite in one organization every local union, city central, and national labor union in the nation. The National Trades' Union had a striking resemblance to the present national federation, the AFL-CIO. Along with every other unit of the organized labor movement, it was swept away in the depression of 1837.

Thus, many workers organized labor unions even though the courts had declared their associations unlawful. Apparently, some workers felt that they had too much to gain from their labor unions to disband them because of the declaration of unlawfulness. It may be that workers believed that collective action was the prerequisite for the satisfactory settlement of their employment grievances. As a matter of fact, employees in this period did protest against many economic and political conditions.[19] In addition, significant changes were taking place in political philosophy. The more liberal philosophy of Jackson and Jefferson was displacing the basically conservative doctrines of Alexander Hamilton. More attention was being given to the rights and liberties of individuals. Some writers in this period stressed that liberty and freedom in economic affairs were not the monopoly of any group, but rather the common heritage of all citizens regardless of occupational status. The poor as well as the wealthy could take action to implement their right "to life, liberty, and the pursuit of happiness." Many workers interpreted the emphasis on liberty "and the rights of man" as a philosophical justification for organization and collective bargaining. Moreover, employees probably felt that they were not violating a law by organizing labor unions. No legislative branch of government had embodied into statutory law the doctrines established by the courts in the conspiracy cases.

The totality of economic and political forces encouraged the formation of labor unions. Many workers believed that intolerable conditions of employment could be erased only through the process of organization and collective bargaining. They interpreted the liberal political writings of the period as the philosophical justification for collective bargaining. In such a context, the application of the conspiracy doctrine to labor unions appeared incongruous. So incensed were the workers against the courts that in 1836 in New York and Washington mass protest demonstrations were held. During these demonstrations two judges, who had previously convicted unionists as criminal conspirators, were burned in effigy.[20]

LABOR UNIONS DECLARED LAWFUL ORGANIZATIONS IN 1842

Such were the prevailing circumstances when Chief Justice Shaw of the Supreme Judicial Court of Massachusetts handed down his decision in the celebrated case, *Commonwealth* v. *Hunt*.[21] Before the case received Justice Shaw's attention, a lower court had found a group of shoemaker unionists guilty of conspiracy. The workers were convicted in the lower court because they refused to work for an employer who hired a shoemaker not a member of their union. The indictment was that the action of the unionists interfered with the right of the nonunion shoemaker to practice his trade. Shaw struck sharply and repeatedly at the conception that labor unions are evil organizations. He did state that, like any other organization, a labor union may exist for a "pernicious" and "dangerous" purpose. But he emphatically affirmed that labor unions may also exist for a "laudable" and "public-spirited" purpose. Rather than inflicting injury on society, he contended, a union may advance the general welfare of the community by raising the standard of life of the members of the union. In this connection, Shaw pointed out that labor organizations "might be used [by workers] to afford each other assistance in times of poverty, sickness, or distress; or to raise their intellectual, moral, and social conditions; or to make improvements in their art."

For a union to be indicted and convicted under the conspiracy doctrine, Shaw contended, it must be shown that the objectives of the union were unlawful, or that the means employed to gain a lawful end were unlawful. Unless this could be proved, a labor organization had to be considered a lawful association. In the case at hand, Shaw held that the prosecution did not prove that the conspiracy doctrine should have been applied to the labor union. In addition, the Chief Justice pointed out that not all union members were responsible if some of the body engaged in unlawful acts. In such a case, the law should only result in the conviction of the guilty party, not of the other members of the association. The fact that labor unions may adopt measures "that may have a tendency to impoverish another; that is, to diminish his gains and profits" did not constitute a reason for indictment of the organization. Accordingly, Shaw held that union members may agree not to work for an employer who hired workers not members of their association. By the same token, he implied that the action of workers to raise their wages by collective bargaining did not justify the application of the conspiracy doctrine. Though such action could reduce employer profits or even increase prices of commodities, the ultimate purpose of collective bargaining was to advance the welfare of members of the union, a purpose that Shaw implicity supported.

COMMONWEALTH V. HUNT: ITS SIGNIFICANCE

Commonwealth v. *Hunt* was a landmark in the development of the law of industrial relations. Its effect was to dissolve the identity between the conspiracy doctrine and labor unions. Labor organizations taken by themselves were declared lawful, and unionists were no longer to be regarded as criminals in the eyes of the courts. In general, most other courts, though not bound by the Massachusetts decision, followed the doctrine established by Shaw. *Commonwealth* v. *Hunt* did not, however, mean that the courts were to withdraw from the area of industrial relations. Shaw did not advocate the complete removal of the conspiracy doctrine from the affairs of labor unions. In fact, after *Commonwealth* v. *Hunt,* the conspiracy doctrine was still utilized to proscribe particular labor union activities. The courts continued to scrutinize the affairs and operations of labor unions. Where the court in a particular labor case felt that a union was seeking an unlawful objective, or using unlawful means to gain a lawful objective, judicial action was undertaken to harass the labor organization. In 1806, the year in which the conspiracy doctrine was first applied to labor unions, the courts invaded the field of industrial relations. To this day they continue to influence profoundly the direction and character of labor relations.

FROM THE CONSPIRACY DOCTRINE TO THE LABOR INJUNCTION

As noted, the courts continued to apply the conspiracy doctrine to labor unions even after Shaw handed down his decision in the celebrated Massachusetts case. Although the conspiracy cases after 1842 did not involve the legal status of labor unions per se, the courts made use of the doctrine to restrain a number of union activities. Professor E. E. Witte of the University of Wisconsin reported there were actually more labor conspiracy cases in the second half of the nineteenth century than in the first half.[22] During the period from 1863 to 1880 alone, labor unions were involved in eighteen conspiracy trials. In one of these cases, decided by the Supreme Court of New Jersey in 1867, the facts were essentially the same as those in *Commonwealth* v. *Hunt.*[23] A group of employees had formed a labor organization, a rule of which was that its members could not work alongside nonunion workers. The unionists took action against an employer to force him to dismiss two nonunion employees. The New Jersey court was not bound by Shaw's decision in *Commonwealth* v. *Hunt.* Nevertheless, the New Jersey court concurred "entirely . . . with the principles embodied in the opinion" of the Massachusetts case, but still held that the New Jersey case was "clearly distinguishable."

After 1880, the courts made use of the conspiracy doctrine in labor disputes only infrequently. This development, however, did not result from a shift in the basic attitude of the courts toward collective bargaining. Subsequent years were to underscore the antipathy of the judiciary to the efforts of workers to better their economic position through collective action. Neither did this change in court policy result from a shift in employers' attitude. They still sought the aid of the judiciary in their conflicts with organized labor. Finally, the conspiracy doctrine did not fade away because of the slackening of the organizational efforts of workers. Organized labor in the second half of the nineteenth century made significant progress. The Knights of Labor,[24] a militant labor organization that sought to organize "men and women of every craft, creed, and color," was formed in 1869. By 1886, the Knights of Labor claimed a membership of 700,000, representing the high-water mark of union membership in the United States since the first labor organization was formed in 1794. The organization engaged in many successful strikes, particularly on the railroads controlled by that great financier of the period, Jay Gould. After 1886, the Knights of Labor declined rapidly, but in its place arose the American Federation of Labor. Even in the period of its infancy, the AFL gave promise of an organization well equipped to expand and implement the process of collective bargaining.

Some employers utilized economic pressure, which often erupted into open violence between the competitive groups. During and after strikes, organized employees were often confronted with serious obstacles in their collective bargaining activities. For example, in the famous Homestead strike of 1892, the Carnegie Steel Corporation hired 300 men from the Pinkerton Detective Agency to serve as strikebreakers.[25] Before the conflict was over, at least a dozen of the workers and detectives had been killed and scores were injured. In this framework of opposition to collective bargaining, it was to be expected that antiunion employers would seek the aid of the courts. The conspiracy doctrine, of course, could be utilized to discourage the spread of trade unionism. Prosecution of workers in conspiracy trials, however, was a rather cumbersome affair. Some of the trials lasted several days and during this time unionists could continue to damage the position of employers. It was increasingly more difficult to procure witnesses to offer testimony against worker defendants. Of even greater importance was the trend toward jury sympathy to worker organizations seeking to raise their economic standards through collective bargaining. Jury requirements were becoming liberalized, with the result that workers might be called upon to help decide labor conspiracy cases. In addition, some jurors, aware of the spread of industrialization and the growth of large corporations, were prone to side with unionists. It was necessary to seek a new legal weapon to discourage unionism. The technique had to meet the requirements of speed, simplicity, and definiteness. Above all, if employers were to resist organization of their firms, it was mandatory to remove the labor dispute from the jurisdiction of a potentially sympathetic jury. All these requirements were met by the labor injunction.

SUMMARY

The application of the conspiracy doctrine to labor unions was an important factor in employers' resistance to the spread of the American labor union movement. Employers, concerned with the vitality of the early union movement, enlisted the courts as an ally in their challenge to organized labor. The courts proved a vehicle for use by employers resisting organization of their employees. Juries convicted unionists as criminal conspirators who, unless restrained, would do evil to the community. This conclusion was reached by assuming that the economy would function best if it were free of organizations that placed unnatural restrictions upon it. Such an assumption was then, as now, open to debate.

Commonwealth v. *Hunt* was a landmark labor law case because it dissolved the identity between the conspiracy doctrine and labor unions. However, by 1842, the year in which the case was decided, employers and judges were casting around for a more effective legal device to contain unions than the cumbersome and uncertain conspiracy trial. Moreover, union activities were still subject to the conspiracy doctrine after *Commonwealth* v. *Hunt,* even though unions themselves were regarded as legal institutions.

DISCUSSION QUESTIONS

1. Should employers be free to make any decision they might choose that involves issues over wages, hours, or other terms and conditions of employment?

2. Why did skilled craft workers organize earlier than did unskilled workers?

3. Explain the origin, nature, and use of the conspiracy doctrine. What impact did it have on union attempts to organize workers?

4. Was the conspiracy doctrine less important after 1842 than before? What factors influence your answer?

NOTES

1   Chester W. Wright, *Economic History of the United States* (New York: McGraw-Hill Book Company, 1949), p. 331.

2   *Ibid.,* p. 319.

3   James A. Barnes, *Wealth of the American People* (New York: Prentice-Hall, Inc., 1949), p. 224.

4   John R. Commons and Associates, *History of Labour in the United States* (New York: The Macmillan Company, 1926), p. 418.

5   Barnes, *op. cit.,* p. 288.

6   *Ibid.,* p. 285.

7   Charles A. Beard and Mary Beard, *The Rise of American Civilization* (New York: The Macmillan Company, 1927), p. 316.

8   John R. Commons and Eugene A. Gilmore, *A Documentary History of American Industrial Society,* III (Cleveland: The Arthur H. Clark Company, 1910), p. 64.

9   *The Wealth of Nations* by Adam Smith, commonly recognized as the leading spirit of the classical school of economics, had just appeared in 1776.

10   Commons and Gilmore, *op. cit.,* III, p. 228.

11   *Ibid.,* III, p. 70.

12   For a treatment of the application of English law to labor unions in this early period, see James M. Landis and Marcus Manoff, *Cases on Labor Law* (Chicago: The Foundation Press, 1942), pp. 1–28.

13   Commons and Gilmore, *op. cit.,* III, p. 384.

14   *Ibid.,* III, p. 69.

15   *Ibid.,* III, p. 68.

16   *Ibid.,* III, p. 233.

17   *Ibid.,* III, p. 261.

18   Selig Perlman, *A History of Trade Unionism in the United States* (New York: The Macmillan Company, 1929), p. 7.

19   Grievances of workers in this period included the length of the working day, imprisonment for theft, the Pennsylvania compulsory military system under which rich people could avoid military duty, the failure of legislatures to enact machine lien laws to protect

workers' wages in the event of employer bankruptcy, lack of free public education for the children of workers, and the general political and economic inequity between the workers and the rich.

20   E. E. Witte, "Early American Labor Cases," *Yale Law Journal,* XXXV (1926), p. 827.

21   *Commonwealth of Massachusetts* v. *Hunt,* Massachusetts, 4 Metcalf 3 (1842).

22   "Early American Labor Cases," *supra.*

23   *State of New Jersey* v. *Donaldson,* 32 NSL 151 (1867).

24   For an interesting account of the Knights of Labor, see T. V. Powderly, *The Path I Trod* (New York: Columbia University Press, 1940). Powderly was the second "General Master Workman" of the Knights of Labor.

25   Perlman, *op. cit.,* p. 134.

NATURE AND USE
OF THE LABOR INJUNCTION

The use of the labor injunction in labor disputes constitutes one of the most controversial issues in the area of industrial relations law. Representatives of management and organized labor sharply disagree on the use of the injunction in employer-employee conflicts. Parties not directly affiliated with either management or labor have added to the controversy by contributing divergent views on the subject. Jurists, scholars, legislators, and even lay people from time to time have condemned or praised the labor injunction. Fundamental to the controversy is that the labor injunction provides the basis for court entry into labor disputes. To some, court intervention in labor disputes is undesirable. They claim that the use of the injunction in labor disputes not only has interfered with the right of workers to collective bargaining, but has caused no end of disturbance in labor-management relations. Some contend that the state of industrial relations is improved to the degree that the court's power to issue the injunction is circumscribed. Opponents of the labor injunction further claim that the collective bargaining process is strengthened and promoted, and that management and labor representatives will be more prone to reach a rapid and peaceful settlement of their controversies when they become aware that the courts are powerless to determine the outcome of labor disputes.

On the other hand, there are those who argue that the use of the labor injunction is necessary to protect the employer from the "lawlessness of labor unions." They claim that its withdrawal from the field of labor-management relations would encourage the irresponsibility of organized labor. In addition, supporters of the labor injunction urge that it be retained to protect the public interest from unions, which, they argue, threaten the health and safety of the community.

Passage of the Norris–La Guardia Anti-Injunction Act did not eliminate controversy over the labor injunction.[1] The issue was tossed to the forefront by passage of the Taft-Hartley Act. Some people, mostly labor leaders, criticized this legislation on the ground that it once again stimulated the use of the injunction in labor disputes. The injunction controversy largely prevented any change in the law during the first session of the 81st Congress. When it became apparent that any revision of Taft-Hartley would nonetheless include the procedure, representatives of unions lost interest in attempts to change the law. Organized labor was not interested in legislation that would empower the courts to restrain union activities during labor disputes through the issuance of injunctions.

This chapter will trace the development of the use of injunctions in labor disputes. The objective is to gain a better understanding of the instrument to facilitate an appraisal of its worth as a technique of government control of labor relations. In later chapters, we shall deal with the character of legislation passed to curtail the use of injunctions in labor disputes, and we shall determine how Taft-Hartley and Landrum-Griffin influence the injunction's use in employer-employee conflicts.

THE NATURE OF INJUNCTIONS

An injunction is a court order directing a person—and, if necessary, his or her associates—to refrain from pursuing a course of action. In a comparatively small number of cases, the court may order affirmative action on the part of the people affected by the decree. Injunctions are issued in nonlabor cases as well as under circumstances where employer-employee relations are involved. More recently, injunctions have been used to restrain the circulation of libelous, indecent, or seditious material. During the Prohibition era, the instrument was employed to enforce laws forbidding the sale of liquor. In the great majority of injunction cases, however, in labor and nonlabor cases alike, the protection of property rights is the issue. In labor cases, the issue of property rights is involved almost exclusively. Where the union seeks to obtain an injunction against employers, the property issue is not involved, of course. Experience shows that unions have made little use of the injunction. Up to 1931, employers obtained 1,845 injunctions against unions, while unions obtained only 43 against employers.[2] The National Labor Relations Board, however, has stepped up the use of injunctions against employers in recent years.

A special sort of court issues injunctions. In general, we think of a court in terms of a judge, jury, witnesses, cross-examination, and the like. This type of court is the familiar court of law, or trial court. In contrast, the court that issues injunctions is termed an "equity court." The distinguishing feature of an equity court is that the judge alone decides the case under controversy. There are no juries in equity courts. In cases involving injunctions, the judge alone decides whether or not one shall be issued. This is true in both labor and nonlabor cases.

In injunction cases, the judge alone decides all issues of fact and law. No jury influences the outcome of the proceedings. A person who violates an injunction is held in "contempt of court." It is essential to note that the judge who issues the injunction determines whether the injunction has been violated. Severe penalties can be inflicted on violators of injunctions, including the payment of heavy fines and imprisonment. One may question the entire injunction procedure. Is not the power of the judge of sweeping character? May not the judge abuse his or her power? Is it proper for the same person to act as judge, jury, and executioner of justice? As a matter of fact, the injunction is a valuable part of our judicial system. An equity court can protect property before any injury to that property occurs. A trial court may award money damages to owners of property only after the damage to the property takes place. The equity court is preventive whereas the trial court is remedial. Of course, where the judgment of one person is the sole standard of reference, there is always possibility of abuse. Even while admitting this feature, however, one would hesitate to condemn the entire injunction procedure.

Suppose two owners of adjoining coal mines disagree on the property line separating their respective mines. One owner proceeds to mine the coal in the disputed area. If later proceedings reveal that the person who mined the coal did not in fact own the area in dispute, serious, if not irreparable, damage has been caused to the other person's property. The injured party may, of course, sue for damages. But the person would be greatly grieved if events proved that the wrongdoer had no funds to pay the damages awarded by a jury. The injunction procedure would have prevented these unhappy circumstances. The injured party could have applied for an injunction, and the court probably would have ordered that no coal mining take place until the dispute over the property line had been settled. A court of law could not have served the cause of justice in this illustration. The injunction gives swift and definite protection to property. In its absence, the property in the illustration would suffer damage that even money obtained in a subsequent lawsuit could probably not remedy. Injunctions are issued when in their absence irreparable damage to property would occur, leaving the property owner with no adequate remedy in a law court to compensate for threatened injury.

FORMS OF INJUNCTIONS

A person who seeks an injunction will support his or her case at the outset with a series of sworn statements or affidavits. A court will be petitioned to issue an immediate order to prevent injury to property. The plaintiff will contend that the matter is of such urgency that time does not permit a thorough investigation of the circumstances. There is no time for a full hearing, the questioning of witnesses, or other time-consuming judicial procedures. Frequently, the courts will heed the request of the plaintiff and issue what is termed a *temporary restraining order.* The purpose of this decree is to preserve the status quo until a full investigation is made of the circumstances. Temporary restraining orders are in effect injunctions. They prevent a person or persons from pursuing some contemplated course of action. Penalties for violating a temporary restraining order could be just as severe as those imposed for disobedience of a more permanent type of injunction. In addition, it should be noted that the temporary restraining order is issued before the merits of the case are determined. The defendant or defendants are not provided with an opportunity to present their side.

In issuing the temporary restraining order, a judge does not claim that the plaintiff is right and the defendant wrong. Rather, the order is issued to preserve the status quo in order that property might not be irreparably damaged before the merits of the case can be determined. The justification for the temporary restraining order is that the relative position of the parties will not be injured by the maintenance of the status quo. For example, in the coal illustration, the position of the parties would not have been affected materially by the issuance of a temporary restraining order. After the merits of the case were fully determined, the coal would still have been intact for the use of the victor in the injunction proceedings.

When a temporary restraining order is issued, the judge at the same time sets a date for a hearing. Under some circumstances, courts will not issue a temporary restraining order. Instead, upon plaintiff's application for equity relief, a judge may set a date for a hearing. In either case, the court will direct that a hearing be held shortly after the temporary restraining order is issued or application for injunctive relief filed. The court is aware that the interests of the defendant may be injured by the temporary restraining order. Consequently, justice demands that the defendant be given an opportunity to present his or her case soon after the court issues the temporary restraining order. Defendants, of course, have a better opportunity to be treated fairly if the court refuses to issue a temporary restraining order and instead orders a hearing to determine the facts of the case. However, courts frequently do issue a temporary restraining order, particularly under circumstances where irreparable damage to property appears imminent.

On the basis of the hearing, the court may dissolve or modify the temporary restraining order if one has been issued previously. If it is dissolved, this action ends the matter. The defendant may then carry out the line of conduct that the temporary restraining order prohibited. On the other hand, as a result of this hearing, the court may issue a second form of injunctive relief—the *temporary injunction.* The temporary injunction is a more permanent form of injunction than the temporary restraining order. However, the full merits of the case are still not determined when this form of injunction goes into effect.

The reason for this involves the nature of the hearing prior to the issuance of the temporary injunction. It is true that the defendant may present affidavits and offer objections to the arguments of the plaintiff. Still, the full judicial procedure is not in operation. Witnesses are ordinarily not called, and no elaborate investigation of the case is made. There may be little opportunity for cross-examination, most important for testing the credibility of evidence. Both sides may be represented by counsel, but the judge still must determine "where the truth lies amid the contradictions of the affidavits presented by the contending parties, without opportunity to see or question any of the witnesses."[3] Despite these considerations, the temporary injunction demands the full obedience of the parties affected by the decree. Violators will be punished. Even if future investigation proves the defendant right and the plaintiff wrong, the defendant may still be punished if the temporary injunction is violated.

The final form of injunction is the *permanent injunction.* This form is issued after a full hearing on the merits of the case is held. Witnesses are called, questioned, and cross-examined. At this point the defendant has the opportunity to present a full case. The judge has had the opportunity to study carefully all documents and testimony in the proceeding. The hearing on the permanent injunction may result in the termination of the temporary injunction, or in the issuance of a permanent injunction. If a permanent injunction is issued, the defendants are permanently enjoined from engaging in certain action. The defendant may appeal the decision of the judge if there is a higher court available. However, the terms of the lower court's permanent injunction must be obeyed during the appeal proceedings.

THE INJUNCTION IN LABOR DISPUTES

This brief description of the general injunction procedure provides a basis for discussion of the use of injunctions in labor disputes. Labor injunctions in the United States were frequently employed after 1895. The chief reason for this was that the Supreme Court in that year decided the celebrated *Debs* case,[4] upholding the constitutionality of the labor injunction. One might speculate on the course of industrial relations had the high court held the use of the instrument to be unconstitutional. Such a circumstance would have had a most profound influence on the whole process of collective bargaining, industrial relations, and the development of labor unions.

The *Debs* case was indeed a landmark in the field of labor law. The case grew out of a dispute between the Pullman Car Company and the American Railway Union. In 1894, the workers of the Pullman Car Company struck in protest against a cut in wages and the discriminatory discharge of a number of union leaders. When it became apparent that the union could not win its strike by direct action, the workers through their union officers requested the railroads to boycott the use of Pullman sleeping cars. This the railroads refused to do. As a result, the union induced a series of strikes against the railroads.

Such strikes immediately involved the government of the United States. The railroads are used in interstate commerce,[5] carry the mails of the United

States, and from time to time haul personnel and equipment of the armed forces of the United States. As a result, officers of the United States government requested and obtained an injunction ordering the union, including its officers, to cease striking against the railroads. Eugene V. Debs, president of the union, and a number of other officers of the union were subsequently imprisoned for violating the terms of the injunction. The case was eventually appealed to the Supreme Court of the United States. In affirming the use of injunctions in labor disputes, the Supreme Court brushed aside the contention that the proper arm of government to suppress or control the action of the strikers was the executive branch, stating: "Is the army the only instrument by which rights of the public can be enforced and the peace of the nation preserved?" And the Court continued in this vein when it declared that "the right to use force does not exclude the right of appeal to the courts for judicial determination and the exercise of all their powers of prevention." Not only may labor disturbances or union activities be restrained by local police officers, state militia, federal troops, and the like, but the high court of the United States held that the injunction process may likewise be properly employed.

With the constitutionality of the labor injunction affirmed, the instrument became a potent factor in labor-management controversies. Professor Witte reported that prior to 1931, state and federal courts issued a total of 1,845 labor injunctions.[6] Data on the number of injunctions issued after that year are largely unavailable until 1947. As will be pointed out, Congress and some states enacted legislation in 1932 regulating the use of injunctions in labor disputes. In light of this development, the number of injunctions issued in labor disputes from 1932 to 1947 decreased sharply. However, the injunction sections of the Taft-Hartley Act, along with Landrum-Griffin in 1959, stimulated the increased use of the instrument. From August 23, 1947, the date on which the Taft-Hartley Act became effective, until June 30, 1949, there were 69 instances in which injunctions were sought against labor unions under the terms of the law. From 1950 through 1966, the National Labor Relations Board petitioned for 2,405 injunctions involving labor disputes. Not all of these were directed against unions, but union actions accounted for a majority.[7]

THE CONCEPT OF "PROPERTY" IN LABOR INJUNCTION CASES

As noted, injunctions are issued in labor disputes for the purpose of protecting property from "irreparable damage." It is therefore of considerable importance to determine the meaning of "property" for labor injunction purposes. If the term is defined narrowly, the opportunity for employing the labor injunction will be reduced. Conversely, if property is construed broadly, the possibilities for its use will be increased proportionately. The courts have attached a meaning to property that broadens the concept significantly. For purposes of court proceedings, the term includes much more than tangible items, such as machinery, land, buildings, physical goods, and the like. Courts in the United States have consistently held that the concept includes intangible items as well. The right to do business falls squarely within the meaning of the property concept. Likewise, the liberty to hire workers and sell goods to customers is included within the definition. In short, the freedom to run a business in a profitable manner falls within the boundaries of the concept.

The courts did not develop this definition of property merely to provide the basis for the labor injunction. This wide interpretation of the property doctrine was an integral part of American law long before the first labor injunction was issued. It was to be expected, therefore, that the courts would apply this concept of property to labor disputes. It is not difficult to see how the broad definition of the property concept would affect labor disputes. If a labor union interferes with the free access of an employer to labor and commodity markets, it is considered that there is damage to property. Should a strike, picketing, or a boycott decrease the opportunities for profitable operation of the business, an injury to property is deemed to arise. "Irreparable damage" to property can be inflicted, not only by violent destruction of physical items, but also by union activities calculated to interfere with the carrying out of business.

Some people contended that the courts were in error in applying the broad concept of property to labor disputes.[8] To support their views, they pointed to the practice in England. For injunction purposes, courts in England generally limited property to include only physical items. But the point of importance is that the restricted meaning of property applies to labor and nonlabor cases alike.[9]

The argument has been raised that a more restricted definition of the term *property* would make the injunction in labor disputes appear more just. This argument holds that only property in its tangible form should be used as the basis for labor injunctions. This contention rests on impracticable grounds. The broad concept of property is ingrained in the very marrow of judicial thought. It is extremely doubtful that legislation aimed in a contrary direction could stand the test of constitutionality. In the *Debs* case, for example, the Supreme Court failed to distinguish between the authority of the judiciary to protect the right to control and use property and its right to protect injury to physical property. The implication is that the courts may extend protection to property under both circumstances. With more significance than the constitutional question, this viewpoint fails to recognize the basic objections to the labor injunction. The mere limitation of the property concept to include only physical objects would not result in the disappearance of these objections. The broad concept of property provides for the wider application of the labor injunction, but the wide concept in itself did not stimulate the historical abuses growing out of the use of the injunction in labor disputes. What has been the accusation against the labor injunction? Why do these objections proceed from a more fundamental basis than that of how the mere concept of property has been as applied to labor cases?

ABUSES OF INJUNCTIONS

Several abuses of the injunction process were common before the passage of the Norris–La Guardia Act. Some were more the result of the circumstances of the times than of any conscious attempt to usurp power on the part of the judiciary.

Judges as Legislators

One abuse of the injunction was the legislative character of court action. Through its power to issue injunctions, the judiciary literally enacted legislation. Before a law is passed by Congress or a state legislature, there is ordinarily much debate on the measure. Public hearings are held on the more important of the proposed laws wherein any citizen has the right to be heard. Some citizens may object to a particular law enacted by a legislative body, but one can be assured that the legislation was passed by the collective judgment of the people elected to represent their interests.

When judges issued labor injunctions, their only standard of reference was their own social and economic predilections. No jury acted in injunction proceedings. In labor disputes, the judge alone decided whether an objective or activity of a labor union was lawful or unlawful. Judges outlawed many union activities. Strikes engaged in for certain purposes were stamped out by the labor injunction. Some judges forbade the calling of strikes when they deemed their purposes unlawful. The "fairness" or "justice" of the strike's purpose is not the issue here. The point of importance is that the injunction procedure provided the courts with the power to determine the legal and illegal boundaries of union activities. In the absence of legislation, the courts acted in labor disputes as the legislative branch of government. Clearly, the economic and social attitudes of judges influenced their decisions. Every labor dispute had its social and economic ramifications. The manner in which judges interpreted their environment had an important bearing on whether or not an injunction would be issued. In equity cases, the judge alone, motivated by his own beliefs, attitudes, and prejudices, decided the issues. The decisions did not indicate dishonesty or unfairness of the judiciary, but rather reflected their legal training, their social environment, and their lack of knowledge of industrial relations. Whatever the reason, the result was to favor the interests of the property-owning group at the expense of labor groups.

The Blanket Injunction

In the past, labor injunctions frequently made illegal acts that, standing alone, were lawful. Such injunctions were also applied to persons other than those immediately involved in a dispute. Even at the present time, anti-injunction laws notwithstanding, some injunctions have this effect. Labor injunctions in many cases have been directed against "all other persons whomsoever" who might have aided workers in a labor dispute.[10] This meant that an injunction was applied to persons other than those immediately involved in the controversy. People not directly concerned with the dispute, but nevertheless sympathetic to workers engaged in union activities, could not undertake action to support them. For example, such persons could have been enjoined from contributing money for strike relief when a court had previously declared a strike illegal. In addition, the labor injunction frequently outlawed activities which in themselves were legal. Thus the decrees often made it unlawful for workers and their sympathizers to "interfere in any way whatsoever" to further a labor dispute. Such language failed to make a distinction between activities commonly regarded as unlawful, such as violent destruction of property, and patterns of conduct commonly regarded as lawful, such as the exercise of the right to free speech. In 1911, the Supreme Court upheld an injunction that forbade anyone from speaking or writing to further a labor union activity.[11]

Sweeping or "blanket" terms such as "all other persons whomsoever" and "interfering in any way whatsoever" produced serious consequences. Lawful acts were made illegal. Both participants and nonparticipants in the dispute were affected. Injunctions containing such all-inclusive terms could violate basic civil liberties guaranteed in the Constitution of the United States. Moreover, those terms were fundamentally devoid of definite meaning. One rule which could have been followed in injunction cases was that the terms of the injunction should be clear. There was very little clarity in terms such as "whatsoever" and "whomsoever." The average person would scarcely have known under what circumstances he or she could have violated a court order. For example, did a church violate the terms of a *blanket injunction* because it provided free meals to workers who participated in a strike ruled unlawful by the courts? The matter grew more serious because of the enforcement procedure of injunctions. When the judge who issued the injunction subsequently interpreted and enforced it, the problem reached a magnitude disproportionate to its importance.

The Status Quo in Labor Disputes

A temporary restraining order and temporary injunction are issued for the purpose of maintaining the status quo between the parties to the injunction proceedings. Their effect is to stop at once action by the defendant, until a hearing and investigation can be conducted to determine fully the merits of the dispute. Justification of the procedure rests on the premise that the relative position of the parties will not be affected by the temporary injunction proceedings. If subsequent court investigations prove that the conduct of the defendant is not unlawful, the injunction is supposed to be terminated. The defendant should then be free to carry out the action she or he was pursuing, or had intended to pursue before the court interfered. On the other hand, if the temporary restraining order or the temporary injunction had not been issued, the defendant might have caused "irreparable damage" to the property of the plaintiff.

This line of reasoning, though generally valid in nonlabor injunction proceedings, did not apply to labor disputes. Temporary injunction proceedings, regardless of the outcome of subsequent court action, had the effect of discriminating against the labor union. Events in labor disputes move swiftly. The ultimate outcome of strikes, then as now, could be determined in a few days. Interference with strike activities through the injunction process made it difficult for the union to carry the strike to a successful termination.

Temporary injunction proceedings had a far-reaching effect on the general public. Public opinion tended to turn against the strikers once the court order was issued. Regardless of the merits of the cases and notwithstanding the eventual outcome of the full injunction proceedings, the court orders branded the workers as lawbreakers. Newspapers unfriendly to organized labor exploited the legal proceedings. Editorial and news commentators could use the court order as a basis for condemning the purpose of the strike and the conduct of the workers. Labor unions had a difficult task in winning a strike when general public opinion condemned the undertaking.

Injunction proceedings also lessened the chance of winning a strike by directing the energies of union leadership to the courtroom. In some cases the proceedings were conducted far from the locality of the strike. The strategy was to strip the rank and file of its leadership. Time spent in court proceedings endangered the success of strikes. In addition, the expense of combating injunctions was often considerable. Money paid out for lawyers' fees was not available for publicity, strike relief, or the purchase of food for strikers and their families.

Perhaps the greatest effect of the labor injunction was to dampen the enthusiasm of workers for the strike. They became fearful and confused by the court's intervention in the dispute. This was particularly so when the workers were engaged in their first strike or when they were relatively new to the labor union movement. The injunction procedure in labor disputes was a rather complex affair. Usually, workers did not understand such legal action and as a consequence, the strike effort deteriorated.

These observations repudiate the contention that the status of the parties remained the same during the period in which the temporary restraining order or the temporary injunction was in effect. If an order stimulated fear and confusion among the workers, resulted in the dissipation of union funds, directed the energies of union leadership from the strike to the courtroom, and tended to turn public opinion against the strike, one can scarcely argue that the status quo between the parties had been maintained. Instead of protecting the employer's property against irreparable damage, temporary injunction proceedings could result in irreparable damage to the union's position. This was the usual result of injunctions, regardless of the outcome of later court proceedings.

Time Lags in Injunction Proceedings

Studies indicate that the courts made frequent use of the temporary restraining order. Frankfurter and Greene[12] reported that the temporary restraining order was involved in more than one-half of all federal labor injunction cases during 1901–1928.[13] Of the 118 officially reported federal labor injunction proceedings in this period, 70 involved the temporary restraining order. In 49 of the 118 cases, the courts actually issued the temporary restraining order.[14] In 45 labor injunction cases in the clothing trades in New York City between 1910 and 1927, the courts issued 26 temporary restraining orders.[15] Professor Witte, however, reported that in Massachusetts, in 234 applications for injunctions from 1898 to 1916, temporary restraining orders were issued in only 29 cases.[16] The defendant had no opportunity to present a case in temporary restraining order proceedings. The order was issued on the application of the plaintiff. Thus, in labor cases in which temporary restraining orders were issued, the union had no opportunity to answer the charges of the employer.

As noted, courts normally order a hearing concurrent with the issuance of the temporary restraining order. At this hearing, the defendant has an opportunity to present a case. However, from the date the temporary restraining order is issued until the hearing is held, the order is in force and has to be obeyed by the defendants in the dispute. Obviously, the interests of labor unions would be protected by a speedy hearing after the temporary restraining order was issued. A long delay would cause irreparable damage to the labor union. If a court enjoined a strike for any prolonged length of time, the strike was likely to be permanently broken regardless of further injunction proceedings. In nonlabor injunction cases, the lapse of time between the issuance of the temporary restraining order and the hearing ordinarily took from five to ten days. In the absence of injunction control legislation, the time lag in labor injunction cases was much longer. One study showed that out of 42 cases in which temporary restraining orders were issued, the intervening period was less than a month in only 16 cases. In one unusual case, the period was one year.[17] Recognizing the inherent unfairness of such a long delay, subsequent labor injunction legislation limited the time between the issuance of temporary restraining orders and the hearings.

A hearing on a temporary restraining order could result in the order's modification, continuance, or termination. If a court felt that activities of a labor union should continue to be restrained, a temporary injunction would be issued. Actually, the hearing on the temporary restraining order did not offer a great amount of protection to the labor union. The union could offer counteraffidavits to challenge the allegations of the employer. But in general at these hearings, "the usual safeguards for sifting fact from distortion or imaginings—personal appearance of witnesses and cross-examinations by opposing counsel—[were] lacking."[18] Thus, the hearing was of dubious value to labor organizations, and equally so when a court denied the application for a temporary restraining order and would instead direct a hearing to determine whether a temporary injunction should be issued.

Even today, the full injunction procedure is rarely exhausted in labor cases. Labor unions generally contest a temporary restraining order. But the bulk of labor cases terminate with the issuance of the temporary injunction. Unions rarely continue injunction proceedings to the point where the court decides whether to issue a permanent injunction, or to dissolve or modify the temporary injunction. The reason for this is that frequently the strike is broken or some other settlement of the dispute is made before the full injunction procedure is exhausted.

It is only at the final stage of the injunction proceedings that the merits of the case are fully determined. At this level, witnesses appear, and there is the opportunity for cross-examination. But these safeguards are worthless in labor injunction cases, for labor unions find little practicable value in exhausting the injunction procedure. These considerations moved Frankfurter and Greene to remark that

> in theory the final injunctive decree alone is an adjudication on the merits, tempo-rary restraining orders and temporary injunctions are nominally provisional. In fact, however, the restraining order and temporary injunction usually register the ultimate disposition of a labor litigation, which seldom persists to a final decree. Lack of resources may frustrate pursuit on the litigation, or as is often the case, the strike has ended before the final stage is reached and ended not infrequently as a result of the injunction.[19]

Quality of Evidence in Injunction Proceedings

Judges issue injunctions only after considering evidence. This is equally true in labor and nonlabor cases. The character of the evidence presented is the real issue in the issuance of the labor injunction. "Character" does not mean the *amount* of evidence. Employers and unions alike support their positions with a considerable quantity of evidence. The challenge relates to the quality of the evidence. Affidavits constitute the chief—if not the exclusive—form of evidence that courts consider before ruling whether or not temporary restraining orders or temporary injunctions are to be issued.

Experience with the labor injunction has demonstrated that the affidavits submitted in labor cases are in large measure unreliable. One judge reflected this point of view when he stressed the "utter untrustworthiness of affidavits" and further asserted, "Such documents are packed with falsehoods, or with half-truths which in such a matter are more deceptive than deliberate falsehoods."[20] In some early cases, courts decided injunction proceedings on the basis of affidavits sworn to by private detectives hired by employers to break strikes and unions. Such evidence, according to a former Justice of the Supreme Court, is particularly untrustworthy. He declared in this connection that "all know that men who accept such employment commonly lack fine scruples, often willfully misrepresenting innocent conduct, and manufacturing charges."[21]

The point of importance is not that one side is basically more honest than the other in labor injunction proceedings. Both parties color their cases to suit their needs. This is to be expected. The chief objection is that the court must make an important decision, affecting the liberty and life of many people, on the basis of evidence that is often untrustworthy. On the basis of this conflicting evidence, the court must make its decision. One judge squarely pointed up the difficulty of the problem when he stated, "I confess my inability to determine with any satisfaction from an inspection of inanimate manuscript questions of veracity. In disposing of the present rule, I am compelled to find, as best I may from two hundred thirty-five lifeless, typewritten pages of conflicting evidence, the facts which must determine respondents' guilt or innocence on the quasi-criminal charge of contempt."[22]

Some people brush aside the importance of the issuance of labor injunctions on the basis of evidence of this character. It is contended that the labor union will be reimbursed for damages resulting from an injunction issued on the basis of employer evidence subsequently proved false. Actually, equity proceedings do recognize the possibility of injury to a defendant where an injunction is issued on the basis of unworthy evidence of the plaintiff. To provide for this possibility, the court will normally require the plaintiff to post a bond along with an application for an injunction. If an injunction is issued on the basis of the plaintiff's evidence and if the full injunction procedure reveals the plaintiff's evidence to be false, the court will award proceeds from the bond to the defendant. This award is supposed to compensate the defendant for damages occurring from the injunction proceedings.

Such an award has little bearing in labor injunction cases. The bond is not forfeited in any injunction case until the permanent injunction is denied. It has been pointed out that unions generally do not find it practicable to exhaust this procedure. In labor cases, the temporary restraining order or the temporary injunction is usually the final stage of injunction proceedings. The injury that occurred to a labor union in an injunction proceeding cannot be measured in dollars and cents. Much of the damage inflicted on unions by the labor injunction is of an intangible character. No monetary value can be placed on items such as loss of potential or actual membership, loss of prestige, undermining of the union, and the like. In actual labor injunction cases, some courts did not even require the posting of bonds, or they set the amount of bonds at very low levels. In the light of these factors, "it [was] not surprising that the recovery on the bond in labor cases [was] almost unknown."[23] Through 1928, unions were awarded damages in only three cases. And these awards only compensated the unions for court costs and attorney fees, not for the damages they actually sustained.

THE YELLOW-DOG CONTRACT AND THE LABOR INJUNCTION

Organized labor in 1917 felt the full impact of the labor injunction on the right to self-organization and collective bargaining. In that year, the Supreme Court of the United States handed down the celebrated *Hitchman* decision.[24] The Court held that the labor injunction could be employed to enforce the *yellow-dog contract*.[25] The yellow-dog contract was a device utilized by antiunion employers to stop the progress of the union movement. Its chief characteristic was the promise of a worker not to join a labor union while in the hire of an employer. A typical yellow-dog contract was involved in the *Hitchman* case:

> I am employed by and work for the Hitchman Coal & Coke Company with the express understanding that I am not a member of the United Mine Workers of America, and will not become so while an employee of the Hitchman Coal & Coke Company; that the Hitchman Coal & Coke Company is run non-union and agrees with me that it will run non-union while I am in its employ. If at any time I am employed by the Hitchman Coal & Coke Company I want to become connected with the United Mine Workers of America, or any affiliated organization, I agree to withdraw from the employment of said company, and agree that while I am in the employ of that company I will not make any efforts amongst its employees to bring about the unionizing of that mine against the company's wish. I have either read the above or heard the same read.[26]

The yellow-dog contract was first used in the 1870s by the stone manufacturers when combating the Molders' Union.[27] The Supreme Court in 1908[28] and in 1915[29] declared unconstitutional a federal and state statute designed to outlaw the use of these agreements. An analysis of this development is reserved for a later chapter.[30] However, the instrument did not come into widespread use until after the *Hitchman* decision. The yellow-dog contract was used mainly when unionization was attempting to gain a foothold. It is difficult to state to what degree the union movement was retarded by the utilization of the instrument. One may be safe in concluding, however, that when it was employed, the progress of unionization was seriously retarded. Though the device was used most extensively in the bituminous coal mines of West Virginia, Tennessee, and Kentucky, the yellow-dog agreement served to hinder the progress of collective bargaining and unionization in the coal, shoe, glass, full-fashioned hosiery, clothing, metal trades, and the commercial printing industries.

Some may wonder why workers signed such agreements. Perhaps some signed because they were opposed to collective bargaining in principle and preferred to work in a nonunion shop. Another possible reason was that such contracts were signed under the force of economic necessity. Workers with families to support and no other employment opportunities would be expected to execute the agreement. It was largely a question of "sign or starve."

Such circumstances throw a considerable amount of doubt on the Supreme Court's declaration that the workers involved in the *Hitchman* case "voluntarily made the agreement and desired to continue working under it." Was it actually true, notwithstanding the language of the Court, that the yellow-dog contracts won the "unanimous approval of [the] employees"? Were these individual contracts really signed "with the free assent" of the employees?

On the face of it, the Court was correct in the belief that the contracts were "voluntarily made," but a deeper penetration of the problem leads to a different conclusion. A contract does not appear to be "voluntarily made" when one of the parties has no actual liberty to refuse to execute the agreement. One would expect a more profound analysis of the problem from a court of equity. Justice Pitney, who delivered the majority decision of the court in the *Hitchman* decision, remarked in this very case that "a court of equity . . . looks to the substance and essence of things and disregards matters of form and technical nicety." It appears that the Court failed to fulfill this worthwhile function when it concluded that the workers had actual liberty to refuse to sign the yellow-dog contract.

In the minority opinion, joined in by Justices Brandeis, Holmes, and Clarke, recognition was made of the realities of the proceedings. These men were aware that the inquiry of "the substance and essence of things" required a more practical view of the matter. In this respect the minority opinion, written by Brandeis, states: "If it is coercion to threaten to strike unless plaintiff consents to a closed union shop, it is coercion also to threaten not to give one employment unless the applicant will consent to a closed non-union shop. The employer may sign the union agreement for fear that labor may not be otherwise obtainable; the workman may sign the individual agreement for fear that employment may not be otherwise obtainable."

Additional economic circumstances surrounded the *Hitchman* case. In 1907, the United Mine Workers of America, the defendant in the *Hitchman* decision, was organizing the miners in the states of Pennsylvania, Maryland, Virginia, and West Virginia. The union had successfully organized the mines in the so-called Central Competitive Area, which included the states of Illinois, Indiana, Ohio, and western Pennsylvania. Labor standards in the Central Competitive Area, however, were threatened by the unorganized mines of the eastern states. Unionized mines could not be expected to compete with the nonunion mines where labor standards were lower. Owners of unorganized mines could afford to sell coal more cheaply on the market than could the operators of the organized mines. Thus, the United Mine Workers of America were vitally concerned with organizing the eastern mines and raising labor standards. The very existence of the union depended on organizing the nonunion mines. Either this would be accomplished or the union in effect would be required to go out of business. Stimulated by these pressing circumstances, the United Mine Workers Union began an intensive organizing campaign in West Virginia. The Supreme Court was aware of these economic factors when it declared in the *Hitchman* case that "the plain effect of this action was to approve a policy which, as applied to the case, meant that in order to relieve the union mines of Ohio, Indiana, and Illinois from the competition of the cheaper product of the nonunion mines of West Virginia, the West Virginia mines should be organized." Apparently, the high court was fully conscious of these economic circumstances; nevertheless, this knowledge did not control its decision.

The union knew of the yellow-dog contracts at the Hitchman mine in West Virginia. Nonetheless, a labor organizer induced many of the miners to agree to join the union. Both the majority and minority of the Court made much of the difference of the terms "to join actually" and "to agree to join." Actually, the organizer did not "join up" miners who had signed the yellow-dog agreement. He merely requested them to agree to join. After a miner agreed to join, his name was written into a book. The plan of the union was first to gain the support of a majority of the miners, and then to call a strike at these mines. At the time of the strike, the union probably would have issued union cards and the miners would then be actual members of the union. Brandeis argued in this connection that "there is evidence of an attempt to induce plaintiff's employees to *agree* to join the union; but none whatever of any attempt to induce them to violate their contract." The majority of the Court held that no practical difference existed between "agreeing to join" and "actually joining." In this respect, the Court was perfectly correct. Its shortcoming lay in the fact that it did not extend its "practical" view of things to the broader implications of the *Hitchman* case. When it served its purpose, the Court employed practical reasoning and looked to the "substance and essence of things"; but, at the point of decision, the Court abandoned this procedure and interpreted the facts and law of the case in a most narrow and technical fashion.

In reaching its decision, the Court held that the union attempted to "subvert the system of employment at the mine by coverted breaches of the contract of employment known to be in force there." The contract, reasoned the Court, was voluntarily made by the workers and the employer. The right to freedom of contract is a liberty enjoyed by all. This right, as "any other legal right," is entitled to protection. By inducing a breach of contract, the labor organization was interfering with the right to contract. Hence the Court was constrained to enjoin the organization from further interference with the right to contract. The injunction was a proper remedy, and consequently this instrument was to be employed to protect and make effective the yellow-dog contract. Such was the reasoning of the Court. Not only was the yellow-dog agreement legal, but the Supreme Court was prepared to implement it through the injunctive process. What this meant to collective bargaining and unionization was indeed profound. Faced with an organization campaign, the employer made the execution of the yellow-dog contract a condition of employment. In periods of less than full employment, workers would be economically coerced into the agreement. The employer then applied for an injunction restraining any person who might encourage workers to join a union. Any disobedience to the injunction was punishable as contempt of court.

The *Hitchman* decision was the low-water mark of the attitude of the Court toward collective bargaining and unionization. Not until 1932 was the effect of this decision eradicated. Its reversal came not by a change of attitude in the courts, but by action of the legislative branch of government. From 1917 until 1932, the courts were a potent force against attempts to unionize. Not content with the fact that the bargaining power between employers and employees was inherently unequal, the Supreme Court in the *Hitchman* decision made the balance even less equal. The *Hitchman* doctrine clearly demonstrated the hostility of the courts to collective bargaining. It served clear notice that the courts were available to restrict union efforts at organization.

SUMMARY

The injunction is issued by equity courts. Normally, it is an order that directs a person and (where pertinent) his or her associates to refrain from pursuing a certain course of action. The application of the injunction to labor disputes stifled the growth and effective operation of unions. Through the injunction, the courts denied to workers the opportunity to resort to collective action to improve their economic lot. In the *Debs* case, the Supreme Court upheld the constitutionality of the labor injunction. The result was the widespread use of the instrument in labor disputes. Many union activities necessary for the effective operation of unionism were restrained by the courts. The judiciary served well the interests of the antiunion employer. The effects of the labor injunction on unionism were varied. However, organized labor felt the full impact of the labor injunction when the Supreme Court held that the instrument could be utilized to enforce the yellow-dog contract. The indiscriminate use of the injunction in labor disputes occurred along with the rapid progress of American industrialism. The courts via the injunction slowed down the drive toward collective action until society reacted to limit the legislative character of the courts.

DISCUSSION QUESTIONS

1. What is meant by a labor injunction? Explain how it was introduced in the United States.

2. Describe the various forms and procedures of injunctions.

3. What was the primary significance of the *Debs* case?

4. In what way did the concept of property affect issuance of injunctions?

5. Five abuses of injunctions have been identified. Discuss each type of abuse thoroughly.

6. Why did the courts approve of yellow-dog contracts? How could they have been important to employers?

NOTES

1   47 Stat. 70 (1932).

2   Edwin E. Witte, *The Government in Labor Disputes* (New York: McGraw-Hill Book Company, 1932), p. 234.

3   *Ibid.,* p. 92.

4   *In re Debs,* Petitioner, 158 U.S. 564 (1895).

5   The Constitution of the United States, Article I, Section 8, provides the federal government with the power "to regulate commerce . . . among the several states. . . ."

6   Witte, *op. cit.,* p. 84. The use of the labor injunction was first noted in the 1880s. However, its utilization became widespread after the constitutional question was settled.

7   *National Labor Relations Act of 1949, Senate Report to Accompany S. 249,* 81st Congress, 1st sess., p. 8; National Labor Relations Board, *Annual Reports,* 1949–1966.

8   See J. P. Frey, *The Labor Injunction* (Cincinnati: Equity Publishing Company, 1927). Also Witte, *op. cit.,* pp. 105–106.

9   The injunction was first used in labor disputes in England in 1868. Since that time, its application to labor disputes has been very infrequent there. One reason for this is the more restricted meaning attached to the property concept in England. In this connection,

see Charles O. Gregory, *Labor and the Law* (New York: W. W. Norton & Company, 1946), p. 97.

10   The Supreme Court in the *Debs* case sustained an injunction the terms of which forbade "all other persons whomsoever" from encouraging the strike.

11   *Gompers* v. *Bucks Stove and Range Company,* 221 U.S. 418 (1911). This case is discussed in more detail in Chapter 4.

12   Felix Frankfurter and Nathan Greene collaborated to bring out the definitive study dealing with the abuses of the labor injunction. It is called *The Labor Injunction* (New York: The Macmillan Company, 1930). At the time the book was written, Frankfurter was a professor of law at Harvard University. President Roosevelt subsequently appointed him to the Supreme Court of the United States. Undoubtedly, *The Labor Injunction* was a powerful force making for the enactment of labor injunction control legislation.

13   Felix Frankfurter and Nathan Greene, "The Labor Injunction," *Encyclopedia of the Social Sciences,* VIII, p. 654.

14   Frankfurter and Greene, *op. cit.,* p. 64, Appendix 1.

15   P. F. Brissenden and C. O. Swayzee, "The Use of Injunctions in the New York Needle Trades," *Political Science Quarterly,* XLIV (1929), pp. 548, 563.

16   Witte, *op. cit.,* p. 90.

17   *Ibid.,* p. 90.

18   *Encyclopedia of the Social Sciences, op. cit.,* p. 655.

19   *Ibid.,* p. 654.

20   *Great Northern Railway Company* v. *Brosseau,* 286 Fed. 416 (1923).

21   Justice McReynolds in *Sinclair* v. *U.S.,* 279 U.S. 749 (1929).

22   *Long* v. *Bricklayers' Union,* 17 Pa. Dist. R. 984 (1929).

23   Witte, *op. cit.,* p. 91.

24   *Hitchman Coal Company* v. *Mitchell,* 245 U.S. 229 (1917).

25   For a general treatment of the yellow-dog contract, see Joel Seidman, *The Yellow-Dog Contract* (Baltimore: Johns Hopkins Press, 1932).

26   *Hitchman Coal Company* v. *Mitchell, op. cit.*

27   Harry A. Millis and Royal E. Montgomery, *Organized Labor* (New York: McGraw-Hill Book Company, 1945), p. 511.

28   *Adair* v. *U.S.,* 208 U.S. 161 (1908).

29   *Coppage* v. *Kansas,* 236 U.S. 1 (1915).

30   See Chapter 8.

CHAPTER FOUR

THE STRUGGLE FOR
A LABOR ANTITRUST POLICY

During the first thirty years of the twentieth century, industry became the dominant feature of American economic life. By 1930, nonagricultural occupations accounted for about 80 percent of the labor force. The number of workers attached to manufacturing increased over the thirty-year period from about 4.5 million to more than 8 million. In 1900, the total value of goods produced by industry was $11 billion. By 1930, the figure had increased to $70 billion. The nation was business-oriented. Many believed that business, if left alone, would insure steady employment, an increased standard of living, and in general a better life. Calvin Coolidge once remarked that "the business of the United States is business."[1] Few would deny that the current American position of world industrial leadership largely reflects the emphasis that public policy has traditionally placed on encouraging and strengthening competition.[2] The problem for debate —at the turn of the century as now—was how best to encourage and strengthen competition.

The early part of the twentieth century was an era of declining competition and increasing concentration of control of American industry. As markets became more fully exploited, business leaders rapidly saw the advantages of cooperation over competition. The result was the establishment of price agreements, trusts, pools, and trade associations. Each and every one of these devices was fashioned to stamp out competition between rivals. When the economic environment permitted, the business community renounced rigid competition as the regulator of industrial life for the greater certainty of cooperative control by the few. The elimination of competition meant the growth of huge and powerful corporations more capable of plotting their own destinies without the interdependencies occasioned by competition among many small firms.

The situation can thus be described:

> Throughout the twentieth century the limitations upon economic opportunity and
> the concentration of economic power have increased rapidly in the United States.
> Economic individualism and personal freedom have declined. The language of free
> competition remains, but free competition has been circumscribed. Orthodox eco-
> nomics still speaks of *laissez faire,* but business itself has restricted the mechanism
> through which the principles of *laissez faire* can operate.[3]

The dominance of big business in American life did not go unnoticed. By
the latter part of the nineteenth century, the public became somewhat concerned
over the concentration of ownership into fewer hands. Business groups had
formed huge trusts and combinations, the purpose of which was to monopolize
the production and sale of vital products. Combinations operated in basic industries such as oil, sugar, tobacco, whiskey, and shoemaking machinery. The goal
of the combinations was to eliminate competition. Once competition was stifled,
it was a relatively simple matter to establish price levels that would maximize
profit. To realize this objective, combinations regulated the rate of output, established market territories, imposed penalties on violators of combination policy,
and eliminated outside sources of competition. Congress enacted the Sherman
Antitrust Act in 1890 to eliminate monopolistic control of the nation's economy.[4]
Predatory monopolistic practices endangered the traditional character of American economic life. Hence the law reflected the faith of the nation in free competition. It suggested that the American system of free enterprise did not exist for
a few industrial giants. Rather, an economic system was to be maintained in which
the small producer was to have an opportunity to enter into the economic affairs
of the nation. The Sherman Act was based on the belief that competition, and not
monopoly, advanced the interests of the nation.

APPLICATION OF SHERMAN ACT TO LABOR UNIONS

Whatever the effect of the antitrust laws on the business structure, the fact
remains that their operation retarded the development of trade unionism. After
the passage of the Sherman Act, labor unions felt its impact on many occasions.
Unions were to learn that the law limited a variety of vital union activities. The
prosecution of labor unions under the antitrust provisions stimulated controversy, centering on the fact that Congress made no specific reference to labor
unions in the Sherman Act. Sections 1 and 2 of the law state:

> Every contract, combination, . . . or conspiracy, in restraint of trade or commerce
> among the several States, . . . is . . . illegal . . . every person who shall monopolize,
> or attempt to monopolize, or combine or conspire with any other person or per-
> sons, to monopolize any part of the trade or commerce among the several States
> . . . shall be guilty of a misdemeanor.

Central to the controversy was the fact that the two key sections did not specifically exclude unions. The question of importance was whether the words "combination" or "person" referred to unions as well as to business enterprises. Did Congress, by not mentioning unions, intend by omission that unions were to be excluded from the operation of the statute? Much has been written on this controversy. One representative study concluded that the intent of Congress was to exclude unions from the scope of the statute.[5] On the other hand, another study supported the opposite point of view.[6] Examination here on the intent of Congress would be of little practical value. The controversy was eventually resolved by the Supreme Court of the United States. It would be a barren academic exercise to inquire whether or not the Court was correct in holding labor unions subject to the Sherman Act. The fact is that the Court for many years applied the Sherman Act to unions. It is of greater importance to examine the manner in which the antitrust laws affected labor unions. What economic circumstances were involved in the application of the Sherman law to labor union cases? What labor union activities were restrained by action of the high court? How did the application of the Sherman law to labor organizations affect the development of the union movement?

Sherman Act Penalties

Before considering these problems, however, it is necessary to spell out the penalties provided for in the Sherman Act. Congress provided adequately for the enforcement of the law. The penalties were to apply equally to labor unions and to business enterprises convicted under the statute. The statute provides for three methods of enforcement. First, violators are guilty of a misdemeanor. Thus, the courts may punish violators on conviction of the statute "by fine not exceeding five thousand dollars, or by imprisonment not exceeding one year, or by both."[7] Second, the Sherman law empowers the district attorneys of the United States "to institute proceedings in equity to prevent and restrain such violations." This means that the federal government may enforce the law by the injunction process. Finally, the law provides for damage suits against violators. Section 7 of the law states that "any person who shall be injured in his business or property by any other person or corporation, by reason of anything forbidden or declared to be unlawful by this Act, may sue therefor in any circuit court of the United States . . . and shall recover threefold the damages by him sustained, and the costs of the suit, including a reasonable attorney's fee." It is noteworthy that Section 7 provides for damages that are three times the actual damage caused by the violation. Such a provision could serve as a deterrent to anyone aware of the possibility of such a judgment.

Earliest Union Conviction Under Antitrust

Prosecution of labor unions under the Sherman Act started shortly after its enactment. In 1893, a federal court in Louisiana applied the antitrust statute to labor unions for the first time.[8] A group of unions in New Orleans engaged in a sympathetic strike, the purpose of which was to further the position of a drayers union's strike. The lower court declared that one of the results of the strike was "the forced stagnation of commerce that flowed through New Orleans." It was held that the action of the workers restrained trade within the meaning of the Sherman Act. In handing down its decision, the court brushed aside the contention that unions were excluded from the terms of the antitrust law. On this score, the court held that although the statute had its origin in the "evils of massed capital," the intent of Congress was to "include combinations of labor, as well as capital: in fact, all combinations in restraint of commerce, without reference to the character of the persons who entered into them." The court issued an injunction that forbade further strike action. It is noteworthy that the injunction was the procedure utilized to enforce the Sherman Act in the first instance wherein the statute was applied to labor unions.

More commonly, the Sherman Act in 1893–1894 was applied to a series of strikes involving the railroad industry.[9] In one of these early cases, a federal district court suggested that any railroad strike was a violation of the Sherman Act. The court declared that

> in any conceivable strike upon the transportation lines of this country, whether main lines or branch lines or branch roads, there will be interference with and restraint of interstate or foreign commerce. This will be true also of strikes upon telegraph lines, for the exchange of telegraphic messages between people of different states is interstate commerce. In the presence of these statutes . . . it will be practically impossible hereafter for a body of men to combine to hinder and delay the work of the transportation company without becoming amenable to the provision of these statutes.[10]

This was a very important judicial observation. If every railroad strike restrained trade within the meaning of the Sherman Act, railroad employees could not engage in a lawful strike. The district judge referred to all strikes. He did not distinguish between those conducted peacefully and those carried out violently. There was no inquiry into the purpose of the strike. If this doctrine had been established in law, it would have profoundly affected the character of industrial relations and collective bargaining in the railroad industry, and quite possibly in industry in general.

In re Debs

The *In re Debs* case in 1895 provided the Supreme Court the opportunity to decide the applicability of the Sherman law to railroad strikes.[11] The high court upheld an injunction restraining the Pullman strike. However, the Court did not rule on the applicability of the Sherman Act to labor disputes. Before the Supreme Court reviewed the *Debs* case, some circuit courts of appeal had approved injunctions in the Pullman strike, basing their action mainly on the Sherman law. For example, one court declared that "on July 2, 1890, Congress enacted a law that enlarged the jurisdiction of the federal courts and authorized them to apply the restraining power of the law for the purpose of checking and arresting all lawless interference with . . . the peaceful and orderly conduct of railroad business between the States."[12] Another court held that "it may be conceded that the controlling, objective point, in the mind of Congress, in enacting this statute, was to suppress what are known as 'trusts' and 'monopolies.' But, like a great many other enactments, the statute is made so comprehensive and far-reaching in its express terms as to extend to like incidents and acts clearly within the expression and spirit of the law."[13]

When the *Debs* case finally reached the attention of the Supreme Court, the injunction was sustained, as noted, but the Court based its action on the power of the federal government to regulate and promote interstate commerce. In this respect, the Supreme Court declared: "We enter into no examination of the act of July 2, 1890 [Sherman Antitrust Act], upon which the Circuit Court relied mainly to sustain its jurisdiction. It must not be understood from this that we dissent from the conclusions of that court in reference to the scope of that act, but simply that we prefer to rest our judgment on the broader ground."[14] A railroad strike of the Pullman variety, which involved a great deal of violence, was unlawful with or without the Sherman law. The Supreme Court upheld the injunction on the powers of the federal government to regulate interstate commerce, and not on the basis of the Sherman Act.

ECONOMIC ISSUES IN <u>DANBURY HATTERS</u> DOCTRINE

Labor unions may have drawn some comfort from the *Debs* case on the ground that the Supreme Court did not specifically hold the Sherman law applicable to labor unions. Thirteen years later, however, organized labor suffered a severe legal defeat in an antitrust case. In 1908, the Supreme Court of the United States decided the famous *Danbury Hatters* case,[15] and held that the Sherman law applied to labor unions. To the present time the *Danbury Hatters* case remains a landmark in the law of collective bargaining.

The United Hatters of North America, the labor organization involved, claimed in 1908 a membership of about 9,000. The union was affiliated with the American Federation of Labor. In those days, the AFL possessed a total membership of approximately 1,400,000. The United Hatters in the early 1900s was in the process of organizing the felt hat industry. Out of the 82 firms manufacturing hats, the union had successfully organized 70. In the organized firms, management recognized the union as the bargaining agent of the workers. Wages, hours, and other conditions of employment were determined through collective bargaining.

Collective bargaining did not operate in the nonunion shops. Conditions of work there were not subject to negotiation. As a result, labor standards in the nonunion shops were presumably lower than those in the organized firms. These circumstances provided a distinct competitive advantage to the nonunion firms. Operating with nonunion labor, employers could sell hats more cheaply than those marketed by organized firms, since the unorganized firms had greater flexibility in adjusting wage costs. The organized firms were not capable of withstanding the competition of the more viable nonunion firms for any prolonged length of time. The United Hatters recognized the necessity of organizing the nonunion plants in order to place the burden of competition on other variables than wages. Labor standards in the unionized firms were threatened to the extent that the national union was in danger of disintegration. Survival for the union meant the standardization of employment conditions throughout the entire industry. Such an objective could not be attained short of the organization of each firm in the hat industry. The competitive advantages enjoyed by the nonunion firms, based on lower labor standards, could be erased only by expanding the collective bargaining process to the entire hat industry.

In 1902, the United Hatters undertook the task of organizing Loewe & Company, located in Danbury, Connecticut. The union requested that the company recognize it as the bargaining representative of its employees. Union officials further requested that only union members be permitted to work in the firm. The company refused the demands of the union. As a result, the union called 250 workers out on strike. The organizational strike fell short of its objective since the number of strikers constituted only a minor percentage of the entire workforce. In addition, the company found replacements for the striking workers and was able to operate successfully. The organizational strike alone was not enough to achieve the union goal.

Faced with such circumstances, the United Hatters resorted to indirect economic pressure. It instituted a nationwide boycott against the products of Loewe & Company. Through widespread publicity, the union induced retailers not to handle the firm's hats. Similar pressure was placed on wholesalers. In addition, the general public was requested not to purchase any item from retailers or wholesalers handling Loewe's products. Under such pressures, many retailers and wholesalers ceased doing business with the company. Eventually the cooperation of the American Federation of Labor was attained. The AFL promoted the boycott by giving it wide publicity in leaflets, labor papers, and the daily press. Labor organizers toured the nation inducing unionists and dealers not to purchase Loewe's hats. The boycott was very successful. In one year, the company claimed a loss of $85,000.

In the summer of 1903, the company sued the United Hatters and its members for damages under the Sherman law. After a circuit court of appeals found the union not in violation of the statute, the company appealed the case to the Supreme Court of the United States. On February 3, 1908, the Court handed down its decision. It held that the United Hatters and its members had violated the Sherman law. The boycott implemented by the union had the effect of restraining trade within the meaning of the Sherman law. On this score the Supreme Court declared:

The combination described in the declaration is a combination "in restraint of trade or commerce among the several states" in the sense in which those words are used in the act . . . and [this] conclusion rests on many judgments of this court, to the effect that the act prohibits any combination whatever to secure action which essentially obstructs the free flow of commerce between the States, or restricts in that regard, the liberty of a trader to engage in business.

The *Danbury Hatters* doctrine resulted in increased prosecution of labor unions under the Sherman law. Now that the Supreme Court held the law applicable to labor unions, a new weapon was available to combat trade unionism.

In addition, the doctrine established the principle that individual union members were responsible for the actions of their officers. On January 5, 1915, approximately seven years later, the Supreme Court sustained a judgment of $252,000 against the United Hatters and its members. Justice Holmes, who wrote the opinion for the Court, declared that since "members paid their dues and continued to delegate authority to their officers unlawfully to interfere with the plaintiffs' interstate commerce in such circumstances that they knew or ought to have known, and such officers were in the belief that they were acting in the matters within their delegated authority, then such members were jointly liable."[16] The practical significance of the 1915 decision was that rank-and-file members as well as the union and its officers had been held liable for the payment of the judgment. It is noteworthy that the Taft-Hartley Act, enacted in 1947, though providing for a variety of ways in which labor organizations can be sued for damages, provides that damages can be recovered only from the assets of the unions and not from union members.

The *Danbury Hatters* doctrine also outlawed secondary boycott activity. A *secondary boycott* may be defined as the pressure placed on one business unit to force the firm to cease doing business with another business enterprise. It will be recalled that the United Hatters exerted pressure on the retailers and wholesalers to force them to cease trading with Loewe & Company. This action of the United Hatters fell within the secondary boycott category. The outlawing of secondary boycott action of unions resulted in a decline of effectiveness of the collective bargaining process. A broad and effective mode of economic action was no longer legally available to labor organizations. The struggle for recognition in the *Danbury Hatters* case demonstrated that the resort to the secondary boycott could have been the only alternative to the extinction of the union and of collective bargaining throughout the industry. The Supreme Court, however, was not persuaded by the economic circumstances that stimulated the action of the United Hatters. It was not sensitive to the fact that the boycott was instigated as a last resort in an effort to establish a bargaining relationship with the United Hatters. Essentially, the high court was of the opinion that "the liberty of a trader to engage in business" was equal to the liberty of workers to move to other economic endeavors to improve their standard of life if a particular pursuit was deemed unsatisfactory.

LABOR'S "MAGNA CHARTA" OR "ENIGMA"?

Organized labor vigorously condemned the *Danbury Hatters* doctrine. It was denounced in labor papers, leaflets, and at labor gatherings. Union leaders missed
no opportunity to protest against the action of the Supreme Court. They objected
to prosecution of organized labor under a statute that they considered had been
enacted to curtail business monopolies. Organized labor did more than merely
denounce the *Danbury Hatters* doctrine. They resolved to change it. They were
unsuccessful in attempts to obtain Supreme Court opinions favorable to the
collective bargaining process. Supreme Court justices hold life tenure, if desired,
and as a consequence were relatively insulated from whatever political pressures
unions could bring to bear. Unions became aware that political action to influence
elective officials was the only effective weapon at their disposal. If the Supreme
Court held labor unions subject to the Sherman law, the proper course of action
was to try to change the law to preclude prosecution of labor unions under the
antitrust statute. This, of course, put unions into the political arena.

The American Federation of Labor became involved in politics at the
beginning of the twentieth century. Legislation designed to promote a more
favorable legal environment for collective bargaining was introduced regularly at
sessions of Congress and state legislatures. Later discussion, however, will reveal
that the courts nullified state laws favorable to organized labor.[17] On the federal
level, it was reported that

> "the labor bills were passed by the House of Representatives at several sessions
> of Congress, but invariably failed in the Senate. About 1904, owing to the activity
> of the National Association of Manufacturers and related organizations, labor
> influence was decreased in the House. The Federation resolved that it could no
> longer remain a purely economic organization. It was obliged to seek influence in
> elections."[18]

The *Gompers* Decision

After the *Danbury Hatters* decision, handed down in 1908, union efforts to
influence elections were intensified. Reportedly, "in 1908 the method of 'questioning' was applied to the candidates of the two great parties, and the Democratic party was endorsed. At the elections of 1910 and 1912 the Democrats were
again endorsed."[19] Stimulated to political activity by the Supreme Court's construction of the Sherman law, the labor movement in 1911 was further motivated
to intensify its efforts. In that year, the Supreme Court handed down the famous
Gompers decision.[20] The Bucks Stove and Range Company refused to bargain or
to recognize the Molders & Foundry Workers Union of North America, an affiliate
of the American Federation of Labor. As a result, the AFL placed the name of
the company in the "We Don't Patronize" list of its publication, the *American
Federationist.* The effect of the advertisement was to decrease the sales of the

company's stoves. In addition, retail stores that handled Bucks' stoves were boycotted, and some retailers, to protect their own interests, refused to do business with the stove company. An injunction was obtained by the company against the officers of the AFL. Samuel Gompers, founder and first president of the AFL, along with the Federation, violated the injunction. The *American Federationist* continued to carry the company's name in the "We Don't Patronize" list.

For disobedience to the injunction, Gompers and two other AFL officers were sentenced to jail for terms ranging from six months to one year. The case was appealed to the Supreme Court. On purely technical grounds, the contempt charges against the union officials were dismissed. But the Supreme Court held that a boycott promoted by words and printed matter violated the Sherman Antitrust Act. The fact that the AFL spread the boycott by the exercise of speech and the use of printed matter did not make the action of the union officers any less unlawful. In this connection, the Court declared:

> The court's protective and restraining powers extend to every device whereby property is irreparably damaged or commerce is illegally restrained. To hold that the restraint of trade under the Sherman Anti-Trust Act . . . could be enjoined but that the means through which the restraint was accomplished could not be enjoined, would be to render the law impotent.

The Supreme Court of the United States relegated the constitutional guarantee of free speech and press to a secondary right in labor cases involving the Sherman law. A boycott restraining trade within the meaning of the Sherman law was unlawful, and trade unionists who promoted such a boycott by either spoken or written words violated the Sherman law. They could not plead immunity on the ground that the exercise of free speech and press is protected by the Constitution of the United States.

The *Gompers* decision pushed unions toward greater efforts to influence election results. Unions intensified their political activities. In the congressional elections of 1908 and 1910, the unions managed to influence the election of some candidates who pledged their support to organized labor. In 1912, organized labor pledged its support to Woodrow Wilson for the presidency on the basis of campaign pledges approved by the AFL. In that year, Woodrow Wilson was elected President, and the Democratic party showed majorities in both houses of Congress. For the first time in twenty years, the Democratic party controlled the executive and legislative branches of the national government. The Democratic party acted swiftly to fulfill its obligations to organized labor. In October 1914, the Clayton Act became law.[21] Organized labor thought the Act was calculated to provide unions relief from the Sherman Antitrust Act. In the following section, the provisions of the Clayton Act that were applicable to labor organizations will be discussed, along with an assessment of the political intent of the Congress and President Wilson regarding the Clayton Act amendments to the Sherman Act.

Clayton Act Enigma

The celebrated Section 6 of the Clayton Act dealt with the application of antitrust statutes to labor unions. It provided the following modifications of the Sherman Act:

> That the labor of a human being is not a commodity or article of commerce. Nothing contained in the anti-trust laws shall be construed to forbid the existence and operation of labor, agricultural, or horticultural organizations, instituted for the purpose of mutual help, and not having capital stock or conducted for profit, or to forbid or restrain individual members of such organizations, from lawfully carrying out the legitimate objects thereof; nor shall such organizations, or the members thereof, be held or construed to be illegal combinations or conspiracies in restraint of trade, under the anti-trust laws.

Labor leaders drew great comfort from Section 6. It stated that "the labor of a human being is not a commodity or article of commerce." It provided that "nothing contained in the anti-trust laws shall be construed to forbid the existence and operation of labor organizations." In addition, Section 6 proclaimed that labor organizations and their members shall not be held to be "illegal combinations or conspiracies in restraint of trade, under the anti-trust laws." There was a great celebration in the ranks of organized labor. Unionists felt that the courts no longer could apply the antitrust laws to labor unions. Samuel Gompers, president of the American Federation of Labor, jubilantly declared that Section 6 was labor's "Industrial Magna Charta upon which the working people will rear their construction of industrial freedom."[22]

Close consideration of Section 6 makes one wonder why labor leaders felt so jubilant about the Clayton Act. It is doubtful that President Wilson ever intended to exempt labor or any other group from the Sherman Act. He may have intended, during the campaign, to support government impartiality in labor disputes, but changed his mind after the election. One writer has argued that labor obtained minor gains during the early days of the administration, such as the Sundry Civil Appropriation Bill, which prevented the Justice Department from using appropriated funds for prosecuting labor violations under the Sherman Act.[23] However, such surface gains proved meaningless in reality since, for example, there was no law to keep the Justice Department from using other funds to prosecute unions. By 1913, the President was attempting to end the animosity between his administration and the business community, which had developed during the 1912 campaign. At the same time he wanted to strengthen the antitrust provisions of the Sherman law in order to foster greater competition in the economy. The President was not to be deterred from his drive to obtain stronger laws against business monopolies. At the same time, labor unions could not be ignored in the drive for better control over monopolies.[24] The political realities in the Congress would not have permitted both a stronger monopoly control law and a total exemption of unions from the antitrust provisions. Section 6 of the

Clayton Act had the approval of organized labor when it was first introduced in the House, but union leaders later decided that the provision was not what they desired and sought amendment. There was no further support from the President, since he considered that the campaign pledges made to labor had been fulfilled. Indeed, the President and leaders of the House resisted union pressures for outright exemption from the Sherman law.[25]

Labor pressures in the House led to an attachment to Section 6 that stated:

> Nor shall such organizations, or the members thereof, be held or construed to be illegal combinations or conspiracies in restraint of trade, under the anti-trust laws.

Some of the House leaders, along with organized labor, interpreted this amendment to mean union exclusion from the provisions of antitrust laws. It is probable that the "Magna Charta" statement of Gompers stemmed from this construction. However, this interpretation was not accepted by President Wilson or the Committee on the Judiciary.[26] No general agreement was reached in the House on either the labor exemption controversy or the meaning of the injunction section. The President, along with the House and Senate, agreed that Section 6 did grant unions the right to exist, but Congress could not agree upon the interpretation of either Section 6, the exemption of labor from antitrust prosecution, or Section 20, the controversy over the power of the courts to issue injunctions. Therefore, "to him [Wilson] must go much of the responsibility for the failure of the Clayton Act to satisfy labor's demands."[27]

Organized labor wanted complete exemption from the antitrust laws. This could have been accomplished by a very simple provision: "Nothing contained in the antitrust laws shall be construed to apply to labor organizations." But Congress and the President did not intend to exempt unions from the antitrust laws, and the proposal was rejected. If that had been its intention, Congress would have adopted the proposal. Instead, a relatively meaningless provision was enacted. Indeed, the President was convinced that the Clayton Act merely granted unions the legal right to exist. Some of the early testimony of Gompers before Congress indicated that winning such a right was his major objective. In the *Danbury Hatters* and *Gompers* decisions, the Supreme Court did not hold unions subject to the antitrust laws because labor was considered a commodity or an article of commerce. Unions were held to have restrained trade within the meaning of the Sherman Act because their boycott activities interfered with the interstate shipment of hats and stoves. The first sentence of Section 6 therefore did not change labor law. It was an empty phrase devoid of practical importance. Additional statements in Section 6 likewise should have made organized labor suspicious of the Clayton Act. Courts since 1842 held labor unions in themselves to be lawful organizations. In antitrust cases, the Supreme Court did not deny that employees had the right to form labor unions. As a consequence, the statements "nothing contained in the antitrust laws shall be construed to forbid the existence and operation of labor organizations" and "nor shall such organizations or the members thereof, be held or construed to be illegal combinations or conspiracies in restraint of trade, under the antitrust laws" added nothing new to labor law. Labor unions were lawful organizations before the passage of the Sherman law, and they were lawful organizations after the Sherman Antitrust Act was passed. Add to these phrases the statement that unions may "lawfully carry out the legitimate aspects thereof," and Section 6 appears worthless as a protective measure to labor unions. Who but the courts were to spell out when unions were lawfully carrying out their legitimate objectives? That was the crux of the problem in the Sherman Act antitrust cases. The Supreme Court declared that the implementation of a boycott by a labor union did not constitute a lawful activity under the Sherman law. All Section 6 did in this respect was to affirm the right of the courts to decide the questions of lawful and unlawful union activities and objectives.

Not only was the Clayton Act to prove worthless to labor unions, but their position was made much worse by the measure. Under the Sherman law, only the government could obtain an injunction for the enforcement of that law. Employers had no right to obtain an injunction against a union on the ground of violation of the antitrust statute. They could sue unions for treble damages, but employers were not permitted to obtain injunctions under the 1890 law. The Clayton Act changed these circumstances. It provided that private parties as well as law-enforcement officers of the federal government could obtain injunctions in antitrust cases. This meant that the ability of employers to obtain injunctions against unions was considerably increased. If the government was not inclined to proceed against unions in injunction proceedings under the antitrust laws, employers after 1914 could petition the courts for injunctions themselves. Subsequently, unions were required to contest numerous antitrust injunction suits originating from employer action. One writer stated:

> Of a total of 64 proceedings of all kinds brought against labor under the Sherman Act after the passage of the Clayton Act, 34, or more than one-half, were private injunction suits. The law may thus be said to have more than doubled the chances that labor activities would be hampered by the Sherman Act. This is indeed a curious, though probably the most important consequence of a law which labor greeted as its great charter of industrial freedom.[28]

Actually, the changes of 1914 proved an enigma to organized labor.

RULE OF REASON: DEVELOPMENT OF A DOUBLE STANDARD

The major purpose for the enactment of the Sherman Act was to deal with growing business monopolies. It will be recalled that labor unions were not excluded from the provisions of the antitrust laws despite the confusion that stemmed from the legislative history of both laws. It remained for the Supreme Court to construe the degree to which the laws would be applied to both business and labor cases. The *rule-of-reason doctrine* was established and applied in business cases, but ignored in nearly all labor cases. This prompted Justice Brandeis in a 1927 case to imply that a double standard had been developed between business and labor.[29] This section deals with the development of the double standard by focusing on the major business and labor cases that clearly point out the double treatment under the law.

Rule of Reason: Application to Business

In one of the first business cases arising under the Sherman law,[30] the Supreme Court served notice that the antitrust laws were not to prevent the growth of big business. The American Sugar Refining Company purchased the stock of independent refineries and as a result controlled 98 percent of all cane sugar refining capacity of the country. The Court held that the control of an industry gained by the purchase of stock did not restrain interstate commerce within the meaning of the Sherman law. In 1904, however, the Court ordered the dissolution of a railroad monopoly created through the purchase of stock.[31] A combination of two independent railroads was effected through stock acquisition manipulations. The Northern Securities Company, a holding company formed to effect the transaction, gained control of the Northern Pacific Railway and the Great Northern Railway. The roads had been competing with parallel lines, that served the northwestern states from St. Paul and Duluth to Seattle and Portland. In ordering the combination to dissolve, the Supreme Court held that the effect and purpose of the monopoly suppressed competition and restrained trade within the meaning of the antitrust law.

Those who supported the underlying philosophy of the Sherman law were pleased with the *Northern Securities Company* decision. They believed that the Supreme Court intended to interpret the antitrust statutes in a manner that would cut down industrial giants. The Supreme Court did not maintain a hard line, however, for in 1911, it established the celebrated rule-of-reason doctrine in the *Standard Oil* and *American Tobacco* decisions.[32] In those cases, the Supreme Court distinguished between "reasonable" and "unreasonable" restraint of trade. Combinations that reasonably restrained commerce were not unlawful under the Sherman Act. Only those that unreasonably restrained trade were unlawful. Not *every* combination that suppressed competition was to be dissolved, but only those that unreasonably stamped out competition.

By introducing the rule-of-reason doctrine into the construction of the Sherman law, the Supreme Court precluded any possible objective interpretation of the statute. The terms *reasonable* and *unreasonable* admit no precise definition. Obviously, the construction to be placed on the terms could vary with different persons. What may be reasonable to one individual may be unreasonable to another. In the *Standard Oil* and *American Tobacco* cases, the Supreme Court did rule that the monopolies unreasonably restrained commerce. The Standard Oil

Company in the early 1900s refined between 85 to 90 percent of the country's oil.[33] On its part, the American Tobacco Company controlled, at the time of the case, about 97 percent of the production of domestic cigarettes and had a monopoly over most of the supply of other tobacco items, such as cigars, smoking tobacco, and snuff.[34]

The application of the rule of reason in subsequent antitrust cases, however, brought different results. In a case involving the United States Steel Corporation, the Supreme Court did not find a violation of the Sherman law.[35] Prosecution of the company was sought on the basis of monopolization under Section 2, not restraint of trade under Section 1. The decision was reached not to prosecute, despite the fact that the steel corporation had been organized as a holding company in 1901 for the purpose of acquiring the stock of independent operating companies. By 1920, the corporation controlled at least 50 percent of steel production in the nation. In addition, "from 1901 to 1911, when the government proceedings were instituted, there had been no price competition in the steel industry."[36] It was reported that "every stage in the production of iron and steel from the mining of ore and the manufacture of coke to the production of pig iron, as well as the manufacture of rails, bars, plates, sheets, tubes, rods, and other finished products, are under the control of the holding company."[37] Despite the facts presented, the Supreme Court ruled that the United States Steel Corporation was not in violation of the antitrust law. This was quite a contrast to the *Northern Securities* case.

In 1913, the Court likewise refused to apply the Sherman law to a shoe machinery combination.[38] The United Shoe Machinery Company, the defendant in the case, produced about 90 to 95 percent of all shoe machinery used in the nation. Four independent companies were united into one combination by the corporation. Promoters of the combination openly avowed their intent to control the entire production of shoe machinery equipment. This combination discouraged its customers' use of any machine not controlled by the United Shoe Machinery Company. On the one occasion when the combination was threatened with competition, the assets of the would-be competitor were bought up by the combination.[39] Faced with this situation, the Supreme Court held that the combination merely effected a reasonable restraint of trade.

By now it appeared that the Supreme Court construed the term "reasonable" in a very broad manner. In addition, the Supreme Court, in a series of decisions, held that price and production control effected by trade associations did not violate the antitrust statute.[40] In this connection the Court declared:

> Persons who unite in gathering and disseminating information in trade journals and statistical reports on industry, who gather and publish statistics as to the amount of production of commodities in interstate commerce, and who report market prices, are not engaged in unlawful conspiracies or restraint of trade merely because the ultimate result of their efforts may be to stabilize prices or limit production.[41]

Thus the rule of reason protected trade associations, even though the net result of their activities resulted in artificial control of prices and production. After 1927, the application of the rule of reason in business cases was varied. The Court tended to rule illegal such activities as price fixing, market allocations, and the like without regard to the reasonable or unreasonable effect doctrine.

Rule of Reason: Application to Labor Organizations

Neither the passage of the Clayton Act nor the development of the rule-of-reason doctrine in business antitrust cases alleviated the position of labor unions under the Sherman law. In 1921 the Supreme Court of the United States had its first opportunity to deal with the application of the antitrust law to labor unions following enactment of the Clayton Act and the establishment of the rule of reason doctrine.[42] The Court decided the case squarely on the precedent of the *Danbury Hatters* and *Gompers* decisions. Labor's so-called Magna Charta pronouncement and the rule of reason did not influence the Court in its interpretation of congressional intent to apply the Sherman law to organized labor.

The 1921 case involved the International Association of Machinists, then an affiliate of the American Federation of Labor, and the Duplex Printing Press Company of Battle Creek, Michigan. At that time, there were only three other companies manufacturing printing presses in the United States. All four firms were in active competition with each other. From 1909 until 1913, the machinists' union was successful in organizing all the firms with the exception of the Duplex Company. In the shops in which the union had won recognition, employers recognized the eight-hour day, established a minimum-wage scale, and generally complied with other employment practices demanded by the union. On the other hand, the Duplex Company, which refused to recognize the union, operated on a ten-hour-day basis, refused to establish a minimum-wage scale, and disregarded the standards of work demanded by the union. Operating with lower labor standards, the Duplex Company represented a formidable competitive threat to the organized firms. So severe was this competition that two of the organized firms notified the union that they would be obliged to terminate their agreements with it unless their competitor, the Duplex Company, also entered into an agreement with the union and thereby raised its labor standards. Organization of the Duplex Company was the prerequisite for standardization of labor costs and uniformity of competitive conditions within the industry.

Aware of the soundness of the argument of the organized firms, the International Association of Machinists attempted to organize the Duplex Company. Since the company refused to negotiate with the union on a voluntary basis, the IAM called an organizational strike. The strike proved totally unsuccessful because only a fraction of the workers responded to the strike call of the union. Out of the 250 employees of the Duplex Company, eleven engaged in the strike.

The union had two alternative courses of action. Either it could terminate its contract in the organized plants, thereby ending collective bargaining in the industry, or it could resort to economic action calculated to force the Duplex Company to recognize the organization. The union chose the latter course of conduct. Union action took the form of a secondary boycott directed against the products of the Duplex Company. Since New York City represented one of the most important markets for the products of Duplex, the International Association of Machinists aimed to prevent sale of the company's presses in the New York area. To accomplish its objective, the union implemented an elaborate program that included ordering members of the union located in New York not to install or repair Duplex presses; notifying a trucking company usually employed by Duplex customers to haul the presses not to do so; and warning customers not to purchase or install Duplex presses. These activities were designed to eliminate the Duplex Company from the New York market with the effect of encouraging Duplex customers to purchase presses manufactured by companies with which the union had contracts. The economic circumstances surrounding the *Duplex* case were strikingly similar to those involved in the *Danbury Hatters* affair. And, as in the latter case, the Court held that the action of the union violated the terms of the Sherman law. In the opinion of the Court, there was no mention of the rule of reason that guided decisions in antitrust cases involving business enterprises.

Subsequent to the *Duplex* decision, the Court utilized the rule of reason doctrine in one case to find lawful a union activity that had the effect of restraining commerce.[43] Involved in the case with the labor organization was an employers' association, the National Association of Window Glass Manufacturers. This association was composed of firms that produced handmade glass. The union was the National Association of Window Glass Workers, which represented the workers engaged in the handmade glass industry. As the result of the advent of the automatic glass machine, the supply of handmade glass workers, a highly skilled craft, decreased by such an amount that there were not enough craftworkers to run all the handmade glass plants on a full-time basis. An industry-wide agreement was executed between the labor organization and the employers' association. To solve the labor supply problem, the contract provided that half the factories would operate between September 15, 1922, and January 27, 1923, and the remaining half between January 29, 1923, and June 11, 1923.[44] After reviewing the economic factors involved in the case, the Court concluded that "we see no combination in unreasonable restraint of trade in the arrangement made to meet the short supply of men." With the exception of this one case, the Court never again utilized the rule of reason in labor cases.

The Court, though ignoring the rule of reason doctrine in the *Duplex* case, could scarcely bypass completely the Clayton Act. As stated previously, however, the law was interpreted in a fashion that afforded no relief to unions in antitrust cases. With respect to Section 6 of the Clayton Act, the Court in *Duplex* declared:

> There is nothing in the section to exempt such an organization or its members from accountability where it or they depart from its normal and legitimate objects and engage in an actual combination or conspiracy in restraint of trade. And by no fair

or permissible construction can it be taken as authorizing any activity otherwise unlawful, or enabling a normally lawful organization to become a cloak for an illegal combination or conspiracy in restraint of trade as defined by the antitrust laws.

Thus the courts still claimed the power to determine whether or not a labor organization was "lawfully carrying out legitimate objects." Nothing in the Clayton Act, the Supreme Court contended, denied this right to the judiciary. As a consequence, the Court ordered an injunction stamping out the secondary boycott instigated by the International Association of Machinists. The *Duplex* decision meant that the position of organized labor under the Sherman law remained unchanged. Secondary boycott activities were still unlawful. The right to do business was still paramount to the right of workers to self-organization and effective collective bargaining.

After the decision was rendered, organized labor went before the Supreme Court of the United States in six antitrust cases.[45] Before 1921, the federal courts applied the antitrust statutes only to railroad strikes and union secondary boycott activities. After 1921, and the *Duplex* decision, courts applied the Sherman law to ordinary factory and coal strikes. The double standard between business and labor cases was to be developed further in the *Coronado* and *Bedford* cases.

The *Coronado* Doctrine: Continued Development of the Double Standard

In the early part of the twentieth century, the United Mine Workers of America was confronted with a serious economic problem. The gains it had won through collective bargaining were threatened by the operation of nonunion mines. Intensive competition characterized the bituminous coal industry; unionized mines paying comparatively high wages and maintaining union standards of employment could not compete on even terms with nonunion mines operating with lower labor standards and lower costs. This differential, the union recognized, could only be erased by organization of the nonunion mines. Previously, we noted how the judiciary hindered the United Mine Workers from carrying out its objective by enforcing the yellow-dog contract with the labor injunction.[46] Union efforts in the mines were further checked by the application of the Sherman law to its organizational activities. The *Coronado* cases were the outgrowth of union efforts to expand organization in the coal industry in the face of employer opposition.

The Coronado Coal Mine was controlled by the Bache-Denman Coal Company, a corporation that controlled several coal mines in Sebastian County, Arkansas. In the spring of 1914, the company decided to operate its properties on an open shop and nonunion basis. This decision was made despite the fact that the United Mine Workers of America had valid contracts with the coal companies controlled by Bache-Denman, including one with the Coronado Mine. To implement its decision, Bache-Denman closed down a number of unionized mines and planned to open them on a nonunion basis. Aware of the possibility of violence, the company, while the mines were shut down, laid plans to operate them as open shops. Such preparation included the hiring of guards from the Burns Detective Agency, the purchase of rifles and ammunition, eviction of union members from company houses, and the stretching of cable around the mines. The coal company was aware of the threat of violence when the decision was reached to operate the mines on a nonunion basis. In this connection, Bache said, "To do this means a bitter fight, but in my opinion it can be accomplished by proper organization."[47]

Workers at the Coronado Mine expected the same pattern of action as at other mines of the Bache-Denman Coal Company. To forestall such action, the workers at the Coronado Mine struck, but the company refused to submit to union demands and during the strike attempted to operate the Coronado Mine with nonunion workers. On April 6, 1914, about a month after the strike had begun, a union committee, along with a large crowd of union miners and sympathizers, visited the superintendent of the Coronado Mine with the intention of persuading the company to restore operations on a union basis. The company refused once again. As a result, the crowd injured a number of nonunion employees, ran the guards off the premises of the mine, and flooded the mine, causing the cessation of all operations.

Violence erupted on July 17 when the unionists, equipped with rifles, attacked the mine in force. After a few hours, the guards and nonunion employees were driven from the premises. Several of the nonunion employees were murdered. By the end of the day, the entire mine was destroyed by dynamite and fire. A dialogue between the parties, which is a substantial attribute in an established collective bargaining relationship, was not available to alleviate the conflict.

Almost immediately the operators brought suit against the Mine Workers Union charging a violation under the Sherman law. They claimed that the union had caused $740,000 in damages, but asked for a judgment three times this sum, since the Sherman law provides for treble damages. After prolonged litigation in the lower federal courts, the Supreme Court of the United States decided the first *Coronado* case on June 5, 1922, or about eight years after the strike took place.[48] The Supreme Court denied the company the damages it requested and ruled that the United Mine Workers of America had not violated the Sherman law. In reaching this conclusion, the Court held that "coal mining [was] not interstate commerce, and the power of Congress [did] not extend to its regulation as such." Since coal mining was not considered interstate commerce, the Sherman law, a federal statute, had no application to a strike effected in a coal mine. Owners of the coal company contended that the antitrust law applied because 75 percent of the output of their mines was delivered outside the state of Arkansas. This argument was rejected by the Court on the basis that the entire production of the Bache-Denman mines, 5,000 tons weekly, constituted an infinitesimal portion of the nation's entire coal production, about 10 to 15 million tons weekly.

The acts of violence during the strike were deplored by the Court, but it held that such unlawfulness in itself does not establish the jurisdiction of the Sherman law over a situation in which, in the absence of violence, the Act would not apply. Moreover, the Court was not convinced that the operation of the mine on a nonunion basis would have resulted in the sale of more coal by virtue of lower prices based upon lower labor costs. In this connection, it declared that the company would not lower the price of coal, but "would probably pocket the profit" that a reduction of wages would make possible.

However, the main ground for the Court's decision in the *Coronado* case was that the company did not prove that the union intended to monopolize or restrain interstate commerce within the meaning of the Sherman law. It was not sufficient to show that a strike may have indirectly reduced the amount of coal in commerce, but proof had to be adduced that the unionists had conspired to restrain trade or suppress competition. This type of evidence, the Court contended, had not been produced by the plaintiff. The real purpose of the Coronado strike was well publicized. The United Mine Workers of America was on a campaign to stop nonunion coal from competing with union-mined coal. Since the Bache-Denman Coal Company had taken action inconsistent with the union program, the union had retaliated with a strike to implement its economic program. The Court recognized this, for in the *Coronado* opinion it declared that union leaders were stimulated "to press their unionization of nonunion mines not only as a direct means of bettering the conditions and wages of their workers but also as a means of lessening interstate competition for union operators which in turn would lessen the pressure of those operators for reduction of the union scale or the resistance to an increase."

The awareness of the general economic program of the Mine Workers Union, however, did not determine the *Coronado* decision. The Court held that no evidence had been produced to demonstrate that the strike itself was stimulated by a plot to suppress competition within the meaning of the Sherman law. If the union had in fact conspired to eliminate the marketing of nonunion coal, and hence to restrain trade, the company had not proven it. If the company could prove that the union had intended to eliminate the sale of nonunion products, the company, the Court suggested, would win the case. This observation was an invitation to the company to hunt for such new evidence, and the company undertook a search for it. That the search was fruitful was demonstrated in 1925 in the second *Coronado* case.[49] This time, the high court held that the 1914 strike at the Coronado Mine had violated the Sherman law. It reversed its 1922 decision on the ground that the company had now supplied "the links lacking at the first trial."

The company secured as a witness a former officer of the union who had been involved in the 1914 strike. This witness had been the secretary of the local union engaged in the strike, and worked as a checkweigher in the mine. He, along with others, was tried and imprisoned for engaging in the bloody 1914 strike. In his testimony, he claimed that the union undertook to prevent coal mined at the Coronado Mine while the strike was in progress "from getting into the market."

He further testified that union officers and union members engaged in the Coronado strike had instigated the acts of violence because they were aware that "if Bache coal, scab-dug coal, got into the market it would only be a matter of time until every union operator in the country would have to close down his mine, and scab it, because the union operators could not meet Bache competition." This testimony convicted the union, for the Court now held, in direct contrast to its position in 1924, "that the purpose of the destruction of the mines was to stop the production of nonunion coal and prevent its shipment to markets in states other than Arkansas, where it would by competition tend to reduce the price of the commodity and affect injuriously the maintenance of wages for union labor in competing mines."

An additional bit of new evidence also influenced the change on the part of the high court. As noted, in the first *Coronado* case, the estimate of the output of the Bache-Denman mine had been placed at 5,000 tons weekly. In the second case, the company adduced evidence that supported its claim that the action of the union prevented the production of 5,000 tons of coal daily. The company proved to the satisfaction of the Court that this larger figure justified the application of the Sherman law to the labor dispute. It is significant to note, however, that, despite the larger production estimate, the Court did not declare outright that coal mining constituted interstate commerce. Many years later, the Supreme Court was again to rule that mining was not interstate commerce. Actually, the amount of coal in question was not too important in the *Coronado* case. When the Court concluded that a conspiracy had existed to reduce the amount of coal in commerce, the conviction of the labor union was assured. This same verdict would have been handed down, no doubt, regardless of the amount of coal in question.

The effect of the *Coronado* decision was to deter the organizational campaign of the Mine Workers Union. After the decision, many nonunion operators, following the precedent of the Bache-Denman Coal Company, brought suit against the union when faced with organizational campaigns. Uniformly, the complaint was always that the union conspired to suppress competition within the meaning of the Sherman Act by eliminating from commerce coal produced under nonunion conditions. Records indicate that the United Mine Workers of America was a defendant in antitrust proceedings more frequently than any other labor organization.[50] Not only did the *Coronado* decision stand as an obstacle to the efforts of the Mine Workers Union to organize the coal industry, but it served to dampen efforts of the entire labor movement. The Court held that unions, though unincorporated, could be sued as a body in the federal courts. It was not necessary for a plaintiff to proceed against each member of the union. The union as a body could be attacked in damage suits.

Of much greater significance, the *Coronado* doctrine shed doubt on the legality of any important strike. It is of importance to note that secondary boycott activities were not involved in the *Coronado* affair. Under the *Danbury Hatters* doctrine, repeated in the *Gompers* case, the Court applied the Sherman law because of the implementation of secondary boycott activity. In contrast, the union was convicted in the *Coronado* case because of a strike directed against the company immediately involved in the dispute. Organized labor was aware that every major strike had the effect of reducing the amount of products in commerce. The Supreme Court in the *Coronado* case declared that when the intent of those preventing "the manufacture of production is shown to be to restrain or to control the supply entering and moving in interstate commerce, or the price of it in interstate markets, their action is a direct violation of the Antitrust Act." So sweeping was this declaration that union leaders feared that any strike for any purpose that diminished the amount of products in interstate commerce would be unlawful under the Sherman law. Should a strike result in reduction of the supply of goods in commerce, all that remained to convict under the Sherman law would be to adduce evidence that the strikers "intended" to suppress interstate trade. To prove such intent, as the *Coronado* case indicated, would not be a very difficult task. Thus the testimony of a single witness was the chief ground for the conviction under the Sherman law of the union and workers involved in the *Coronado* affair. The decision generated uncertainty in the ranks of organized labor. Every important strike could be subject to the jurisdiction of the Sherman law by virtue of the sweeping implications of the *Coronado* doctrine.

In 1924, in another case, the legal atmosphere surrounding the application of the Sherman law to strikes against employers immediately involved in a labor dispute was somewhat clarified. In the spring of 1920 the United Leather Workers Union attempted to organize five Missouri corporations engaged in the manufacture and sale of leather goods and trunks. After the companies refused to bargain collectively, the labor organization called its members out on strike. Picket lines were thrown up at each of the factories for the purpose of persuading nonstriking workers to join in the strike and to force the company not to hire replacements for the strikers. Some of the tactics employed by the union to stop production in the plants were not lawful, but the record indicates that the strikers did not resort in any manner to the excess of lawlessness displayed by the workers in the *Coronado* case. In any event, the union was successful in curtailing the operation of the factories, and the companies charged that the effect of the strike and the publicity prevented the manufacture and shipment of the products of their factories in interstate commerce. As a result, the companies claimed that the union restrained trade within the meaning of the Sherman law.

Here indeed was a test case involving the application of the Sherman law to a strike instigated against employers directly involved in a labor dispute. The union did not engage in secondary boycott activities, nor was the strike conducted in a context of lawlessness exemplified in the *Coronado* affair. Before the Supreme Court took jurisdiction of the case in 1924, lower federal courts dealt with the case. In November 1920, a district court judge issued a permanent injunction under the terms of the Sherman law, stamping out the strike. The judge held that the union injured the interstate commerce of the companies within the meaning of the Act.[51] Upon appeal, the Eighth Circuit Court upheld the ruling of the district court judge by a 2–1 vote. The majority of the circuit court of appeals held that "the natural and inevitable effect of the prevention by the defendants of the making of the plaintiffs of the articles they had made interstate contracts to sell, make, and deliver, was the prevention of their performance of their contracts and the prevention or partial prevention of their interstate commerce, and this result was so evident and unavoidable that the defendants could not have failed to know, to propose, and to intend that this should be the result."[52] In short, any strike for any purpose was unlawful under the Sherman law, provided that the strike reduced the amount of goods in commerce. Particular evidence to show intent of the workers to restrain commerce, as was required in the *Coronado* case, was not essential for conviction under the Sherman law, for intent could be inferred from the action of the strikers. In effect, the district and circuit courts held that workers who struck and suppressed interstate commerce could not keep from knowing the result of their action.

Had the Supreme Court of the United States upheld the position of the lower court, the right of workers to strike would have been circumscribed to the degree of rendering their fundamental economic weapon virtually useless. But the Supreme Court in a 6–3 decision reversed the judgment of the lower federal courts. The majority of the Supreme Court concurred with the dissenting judge in the circuit court of appeals who, in speaking of the majority opinion, had declared: "The natural, logical, and inevitable result will be that every strike in any industry or even in any single factory will be within the Sherman Act and subject to federal jurisdiction provided any appreciable amount of its products enters into interstate commerce." In commenting on this statement, the majority of the high court declared, "We cannot think that Congress intended any such result in the enactment of the Antitrust Act." The Supreme Court overruled the lower federal court on the ground that the employers produced no evidence to indicate that the workers intended by their strike and picketing to restrain commerce. Even though the effect of their activities caused the reduction in the supply of products for interstate commerce, the Court contended, "The record is entirely without evidence or circumstances to show that the defendants in their conspiracy to deprive the complainant of their workers were directing their scheme against interstate commerce."[53] Thus, six members of the Supreme Court prevented the application of the Sherman law to every important strike. It is interesting to note that thirteen federal judges handled the *Leather Workers* case. Six held that the Sherman law outlawed every strike of any consequence. In short, the *Coronado* doctrine dramatized the Supreme Court's double standard in its extreme form.

THE BEDFORD STONE DECISION: EFFECT ON UNION TACTICS AND COMPLETION OF THE DOUBLE STANDARD

In 1927, organized labor felt the full measure of the double standard constructed under the Sherman law, for in that year, the Supreme Court of the United States handed down the famous *Bedford Stone* decision.[54] This decision was a landmark in labor cases arising under the antitrust statutes. If organized labor sensed a new direction in decisions because of the *Leather Workers* decision, this attitude changed when the high court handed down its ruling in the *Bedford Stone* case. That decision, perhaps more than any other labor antitrust case, demonstrated to organized labor that the Sherman provisions provided a potent weapon to combat unionism and collective bargaining.

Arrayed against each other in the *Bedford Stone* case were an association of employers and an international labor union. The employers' association was composed of twenty-four corporations engaged in the business of quarrying and fabricating limestone in the Bedford-Bloomington area in Indiana. Their combined investment was about $6 million, and their annual aggregate sales amounted to approximately $15 million, more than 75 percent in states other than Indiana. Together, the twenty-four corporations produced about 70 percent of all the cut stone in the nation. The local employers' association was affiliated with a national employers' organization, called the International Cut Stone & Quarryers Association. Thus the highly solvent employers in the *Bedford Stone* case banded together for their mutual benefit into an effective local employers' association, which was affiliated with a national employers' organization and dominated the cut stone industry of the nation. On the other hand, the labor organization, the Journeymen Stone Cutters Association, had a total membership of 5,000 members in fifty local unions. The union jurisdiction extended to workers employed in quarries and affiliated quarry facilities and covered workers who installed cut stone in buildings.

Before 1921, the Bedford-Bloomington quarry operators recognized the Journeymen Stone Cutters Association as the bargaining agent of the workers employed in their quarries. As a result, stone was quarried under collective bargaining conditions. In 1921, however, the employers' association refused to extend the trade agreement, and in its place set up a series of company-dominated unions. Later discussion will reveal that company-dominated unions do not perform the functions of collective bargaining. An effective union cannot serve the interests of employers and employees at the same time.[55] Company-dominated unions, under the influence of management, are not free to protect basic employment interests of workers. In spite of the protests of the Journeymen Stone Cutters Association, the operators resumed production under nonunion conditions. The Indiana quarries had to be organized once again, or the Journeymen Stone Cutters Association would for all intents and purposes disintegrate as a labor organization, since the Indiana area was the most important stone-producing region in the nation.

Stimulated by such considerations, the Journeymen Stone Cutters Association enacted a clause in its constitution that forbade its members to handle stone "cut by men working in opposition" to the labor organization. In other words, the members decided not to work with nonunion cut stone. This rule was implemented in states and cities in which the Bedford-Bloomington operators sold stone to building contractors. Customers of these operators were persuaded not to purchase Indiana stone, for they were aware that, once purchased, the stone would not be installed in buildings by union members. For example, a building contractor in New York would hesitate to purchase nonunion Indiana stone when he knew the members of the Stone Cutters Association would refuse to install the product.

The tactics of the Stone Cutters Association were essentially the same as those employed by the labor organization involved in the *Duplex* affair. Both unions implemented a secondary boycott to force antiunion employers to recognize labor unions. Pressure was exerted on firms for the purpose of forcing them to cease doing business with companies directly involved in the labor dispute. Such pressure constitutes a secondary boycott. So impressed was the Court with the similarity of the *Bedford Stone* case to the *Duplex* decision that it declared, "with a few changes in respect to the product involved, dates, names, and incidents, which would have no effect upon the principle established, the opinion in *Duplex Company* v. *Deering* might serve as an opinion in this case."

The Court was correct in establishing this similarity from the point of view of the weapon employed by the unions. Upon closer examination, the analogy is not as clear-cut as indicated by the majority opinion, since in the *Duplex* case the union marshalled its forces against only one employer, while in the *Bedford Stone* affair the union was arrayed against an employers' association of great wealth and power. In any event, the Court, in the *Bedford Stone* case, held that the conduct of the union violated the antitrust act because "the strikes . . . preventing the use and installation of petitioners' products in other states, necessarily threatened to destroy and narrow petitioners' interstate trade by taking from them their customers."

Double Standard Implied

Organized labor suffered a reversal with the Supreme Court's decision in the *Bedford Stone* case. Before the Court reviewed the case, a district court and a circuit court of appeals refused to restrain the activities of the labor union. The high court's knowledge that the Stone Cutters Association was pitted against a powerful employers' association did not affect the decision. The union conduct was peaceful, and no violence of any sort occurred in connection with the boycott. As a matter of fact, the union did not even engage in picketing. The sole activity of the workers was to refuse to handle nonunion stone for the purpose of defending their union against a powerful and wealthy employers' association. In addition, the union did not deter contractors from purchasing stone not quarried in the Bloomington-Bedford region. The boycott was instituted against nonunion stone, and there was no interference with the liberty of contractors to purchase union-made stone. The Court ruled that the union's action constituted an "unreasonable restraint of . . . commerce within the meaning of the Antitrust Act . . . ," despite the character of the application of the rule of reason in business cases. Brandeis dissented vigorously from the majority on this issue and made it clear that the double standard had been fully developed and that its development stopped just short of prohibiting strikes entirely. Justice Brandeis declared:

> If, on the undisputed facts of this case, refusal to work can be enjoined, Congress created by the Sherman Law and the Clayton Act an instrument for imposing restraints upon labor which reminds of involuntary servitude. The Sherman Law was held in *United States* v. *United States Steel Corporation* . . . to permit capitalists to combine in a single corporation 50 percent of the steel industry of the United States dominating the trade through its vast resources. The Sherman Law was held in *United States* v. *United Shoe Machinery Co.* . . . to permit capitalists to combine in another corporation practically the whole shoe-machinery industry of the country, necessarily giving it a position of dominance over shoe manufacturing in America. It would, indeed, be strange if Congress had by the same Act willed to deny to members of a small craft of workingmen the right to co-operate in simply refraining from work, when that course was the only means of self-protection against a combination of militant and powerful employers. I cannot believe that Congress did so.[56]

With the *Bedford Stone* decision, the pattern of the application of the Sherman law to labor unions was completed. A law enacted presumably to check the growth of "big business" was more restrictive to union organization. It served as a fertile ground for the labor injunction and provided the basis for damage suits against labor unions. Secondary economic activity by unions when the alternative was disintegration of the labor organization was deemed unlawful. Such action was no less unlawful when its implementation was on a peaceful basis. The judiciary was prepared to coerce free workers into "involuntary servitude," even though the refusal to work had as its fundamental purpose the raising of standards of living of workers by establishing, retaining, or widening the collective bargaining process. Strikes against employers directly involved in a labor dispute were likewise unlawful when proof could be adduced that the "intent" of the union was to suppress the amount of goods in commerce. The rule of reason doctrine, which proved of enormous benefit to business, did not alleviate the stern application of the Sherman law to labor unions. One standard was set for business enterprises and another for labor unions. In addition, the high court brushed aside as unimportant the powerful economic and social forces that surrounded labor disputes in antitrust cases. Economic and social realism was rejected in favor of the standard of cold and legal formalism. This narrow legal approach invariably resulted in a restriction of the collective action that was intended to improve union members' economic and social status in life.

SUMMARY

The period around the turn of the twentieth century was one in which big business and monopolistic organization characterized the economic system. Congress became concerned with this turn of events and passed the Sherman Antitrust Act in 1890 and the Clayton Act in 1914 to legislate the nation's economy into a competitive pattern. The effort largely failed in terms of regulation of firm size, but had a stronger effect upon the activities of labor organizations. The application of the antitrust laws to organized labor made secondary boycotts illegal. This proved restrictive to union efforts to organize. The integration and interdependency of the economy made the secondary boycott a first-rate union weapon. The inability to use the weapon decreased union power to influence the outcome of economic struggles.

Out of the application of the antitrust laws to union activities arose several landmark labor cases: *Danbury Hatters, Gompers, Duplex, Coronado,* and *Bedford Stone.* A comparison of these cases with business cases such as *E. C. Knight, Northern Securities, Standard Oil,* and *United States Steel* makes it clear that the Supreme Court developed a double standard in the application of antitrust provisions to the two groups. On the one hand, the Supreme Court in effect held that unionism was incompatible with the antitrust statutes. On the other hand, it ruled that the rule of reason would be applied in each business case to determine if there had been a reasonable or unreasonable restraint of interstate trade. The Sherman Act, passed primarily to check big business, was more effective in the control of labor's collective bargaining process.

DISCUSSION QUESTIONS

1. Trace the development of the application of Sherman Act provisions to labor unions prior to 1908. What implication did these early cases have for the right to strike?

2. Compare the rules of *In re Debs* and *Danbury Hatters.* How did each case affect union growth and development?

3. What did labor expect from the Clayton Act, and what did that Act actually allow?

4. Explain the rule of reason, its application to business, and its application to unions.

5. Compare the *Coronado* cases to the *Bedford Stone* decision. In your comparison, show the similarities and differences in the surrounding circumstances.

NOTES

1   Reported in Thomas C. Cochran and William Miller, *The Age of Enterprise* (New York: The Macmillan Company, 1943), p. 324.

2   Reuben E. Slesinger, *National Economic Policy: The Presidential Reports* (Princeton, N.J.: D. Van Nostrand Co., Inc., 1968), p. 98.

3   Cochran and Miller, *op. cit.,* p. 356.

4   Sherman Anti-Trust Law, 26 Stat. 209, Act of July 2, 1890. On October 15, 1914, Congress enacted the Clayton Act, 38 Stat. 780, which in part purports to make the Sherman law more effective relative to the checking of monopoly control of industry.

5   Edward Berman, *Labor and the Sherman Act* (New York: Harper & Brothers, 1930).

6   A. T. Mason, *Organized Labor and the Law* (Durham, N.C.: Duke University Press, 1925).

7   A 1955 amendment raised the maximum fine to $50,000.

8   *United States* v. *Workingmen's Amalgamated Council,* 54 Fed. 994 (1893).

9   Berman, *op. cit.,* p. 64.

10   *Waterhouse* v. *Comer,* 55 Fed. 149 (1893).

11   *In re Debs,* Petitioner, 158 U.S. 564 (1895).

12   *United States* v. *Agler,* 62 Fed. 24 (1897).

13   *United States* v. *Elliott,* 64 Fed. 27 (1898).

14   *In re Debs, op. cit.*

15   The official name is *Loewe* v. *Lawlor,* 208 U.S. 274 (1908). However, this landmark case is commonly referred to as the "Danbury Hatters" case, for the factory in question was located in Danbury, Connecticut. In 1915 the dispute was tried once more in the Supreme Court. The second case is officially cited as *Lawlor* v. *Loewe,* 235 U.S. 522 (1915).

16   *Ibid.*

17   See Chapter 8.

18   J. R. Commons and Associates, *History of Labour in the United States* (New York: The Macmillan Company, 1926), p. 531.

19   *Ibid.,* p. 532.

20   *Gompers* v. *Bucks Stove and Range Company,* 221 U.S. 418 (1911).

21   38 Stat. 780 (1914).

22   Edwin E. Witte, *The Government in Labor Disputes* (New York: McGraw-Hill Book Company, 1932), p. 68.

23   Dallas L. Jones, "The Enigma of the Clayton Act," *Industrial and Labor Relations Review,* X, No. 2, January 1957, p. 31.

24   *Ibid.,* p. 207.

25   *Ibid.,* p. 209.

26   *Ibid.,* pp. 211–212.

27   *Ibid.,* p. 221.

28   Berman, *op. cit.,* p. 103.

29   *Bedford Cut Stone Company* v. *Journeymen Stone Cutters Association,* 274 U.S. 37 (1927).

30   *United States* v. *E. C. Knight,* 156 U.S. 1 (1895).

31   *Northern Securities Company* v. *United States,* 193 U.S. 199 (1904).

32   *Standard Oil Company of New Jersey* v. *United States,* 221 U.S. 1 (1911). *United States* v. *American Tobacco Company,* 221 U.S. 106 (1911).

33   Milton Handler, *Cases and Materials on Trade Regulations* (Chicago: The Foundation Press, 1937), p. 388.

34   *Ibid.,* p. 401.

35   *United States* v. *United States Steel Corporation,* 251 U.S. 417 (1920).

36   Handler, *op. cit.,* p. 424.

37   *Ibid.,* p. 422.

38   *United States* v. *United Shoe Machinery Company,* 227 U.S. 32 (1913).

39   Myron W. Watkins, "Trusts," *Encyclopedia of Social Sciences,* XV, p. 117.

40   See Handler, *op. cit.,* pp. 256–385, for a discussion of the legal and economic aspects of trade associations.

41   *Maple Flooring Manufacturers Association* v. *United States,* 268 U.S. 563 (1925).

42   *Duplex Printing Press Company* v. *Deering,* 254 U.S. 443 (1921).

43   *National Association of Window Glass Manufacturers* v. *United States,* 263 U.S. 403 (1923).

44   Berman, *op. cit.,* p. 150.

45   *Ibid.,* p. 118.

46   See Chapter 3.

47   *United Mine Workers* v. *Coronado Coal Company,* 259 U.S. 344 (1922).

48   *Ibid.*

49   *Coronado Coal Company* v. *United Mine Workers of America,* 268 U.S. 295 (1925).

50   Berman, *op. cit.,* p. 119.

51   *Herbert and Meisel Trunk Company* v. *United Leather Workers International Union,* 268 Fed. 662 (1920).

52   *United Leather Workers International Union* v. *Herbert and Meisel Trunk Company,* 284 Fed. 446 (1922).

53   *United Leather Workers International Union* v. *Herbert and Meisel Trunk Company,* 285 U.S. 457 (1925).

54   *Bedford Cut Stone Company* v. *Journeymen Stone Cutters Association, op. cit.*

55   See Chapter 7.

56   *Bedford Cut Stone Company* v. *Journeymen Stone Cutters Association, op. cit.*

CHAPTER FIVE

CONTROL OF
THE LABOR INJUNCTION

THE CHANGING ECONOMIC AND POLITICAL SCENE

As demonstrated, the legal climate surrounding the collective bargaining process in the period 1806–1932 was restrictive. Theoretically, unions were lawful organizations, workers were legally free to join unions, and the right to strike as such was lawful. In practice, however, the courts controlled the right of workers to join unions and the liberty of labor organizations to engage in activities designed to make collective bargaining effective. The use of the injunction in labor disputes proved a most formidable obstacle to the expansion and implementation of trade unionism. Frequently, labor unions had the economic strength to deal with the antiorganizational activities of employers, but fell before the labor injunction. When the courts held that the yellow-dog contract could be implemented by the labor injunction, the position of unions in an economic struggle was diminished immeasurably. The anomalous condition existed wherein workers legally free to join labor unions were prevented from doing so. Courts enforced the yellow-dog arrangement, which enabled employers to maintain shops closed to union workers. These same courts frequently outlawed union tactics calculated to obtain shops closed to nonunion labor. The wide application of the Sherman law to labor unions likewise operated to constrain the union movement. Union action aimed to enforce bargaining demands against employers was deemed unlawful under the antitrust laws. In their interpretation of the Sherman law, the courts took the position that workers had the right to collective bargaining only insofar as there was no infringement of the right to do business. This right of employers was considered more important than the liberty of workers to engage in action that would make collective bargaining work. For a time it appeared that all strikes of major proportions would be unlawful. That this condition did not result was attributable to the judgment of a few members of the Supreme Court. Had the composition of this Court been a shade different, it is likely that all strikes that suppressed the shipment of goods in interstate commerce would have been deemed unlawful. In the light of all this evidence, it can scarcely be denied that courts served well the interests of antiunion employers. The judiciary proved to be a willing ally to employers in labor-management disputes. As a result, the level of union membership in 1930 amounted to only about 3 million.[1]

Court limitations of worker rights to collective bargaining might have continued indefinitely had it not been for the economic collapse of the 1930s. The depression in this period constituted the most severe economic debacle ever suffered by the nation. Unemployment totaled about 25 percent of the labor force. Widespread bankruptcy of business enterprises and bank failures characterized the period. Foreclosures of firms, repossession of personal property, and loss of homes added to the difficulties of the nation. Fear and deprivation characterized the American people. Never before in the history of the nation was the faith of the people at such low ebb.

About 15 million people tramped the streets looking for work. Life savings disappeared in the whirlwind of financial ruin. Farmers did what they could to save their land, but farm after farm went on the auctioneer's block. Measures were supported to declare moratoriums on foreign debts, and the nation debated the possibility of applying the same principle to its own debtors, who were losing their homes, farms, and other worldly possessions. Rightly or wrongly, the average American identified the misery of the depression with business, perhaps because of the emphasis that had been placed on the role of capital in economic growth by students of the economic order.

The effects of the economic collapse could be multiplied indefinitely. School terms were reduced, and some schools and colleges even closed their doors. As educational appropriations were severely cut by economy-minded and debt-fearing legislators, teachers' salaries were usually decreased as far as possible. In Chicago, teachers worked for months without pay, many walking to and from school, not even having the pennies for carfare. More than one Chicago teacher went without lunch, still trying to do the job in the face of a bankrupt city government. At the college level, conditions were not much better. Scholars who had devoted their life to research and university-level instruction found themselves without jobs, or with salaries cut to such a degree that life was barely possible. Other professional groups suffered in equal or even worse fashion. People had no funds to purchase the services of musicians, lawyers, artists, or architects. These people, like industrial workers, tramped the streets looking for whatever work could be found. Disease increased, since money was not available for adequate—to say nothing of preventive—medicine. Ten thousand veterans of World War I marched on Washington in 1932, demanding immediate payment of their bonuses. They were dispersed with tanks, gas bombs, and bayonets. At that time, the national government was not politically capable of instituting a fiscal and monetary policy to deal with such disturbances in the economy.

Many aspects of the culture reflected the changes in social thought. The realities of the depression gave a new direction to literature and the arts. Books of social significance, such as *The Grapes of Wrath* and *Union Square,* claimed the public's attention. Such plays as *Waiting for Lefty* and *Of Mice and Men* highlighted the growing concern of the people with the imperfections of the economic order. The motion picture industry reflected somewhat the changing social thought. *The Grapes of Wrath* was filmed. *The River* and *The Plough That Broke the Plains* portrayed America in film. Depression-stimulated student organizations on college campuses concerned themselves with problems of social and economic significance. Opposition to birth control was largely overcome as an increasing number of parents doubted the wisdom of rearing families in an unfavorable economic environment. Thus the depression reached even to the structure and composition of family life. As never before, the economy was subjected to critical intellectual appraisal. One thing was certain: The concept of economic Darwinism was dead. Society recognized that millions of its most fit members could survive only imperfectly in a depression economy. An increasing number of people recognized that institutional defects in the economic environment rather than personal inadequacies caused business failure, unemployment, and poverty.

EARLY REGULATION OF THE LABOR INJUNCTION

Organized labor had had a long history of attempts to curb the use of injunctions prior to the period of turmoil of the 1930s. Political pressure by labor unions to obtain legislative relief from the labor injunction dates from the turn of the century. Impressed with the effects of the instrument in labor disputes, organized labor worked diligently to curtail the power of the courts to intervene in labor-management controversies. The spearhead of this legislative assault was the American Federation of Labor, the only national federation of labor unions still in existence prior to the C.I.O. in 1935. Organized labor learned through experience the impact of the injunction on the collective bargaining process. Labor leaders pointed to the abuses of the instrument, asserting that the judiciary served as a potent ally to employers in labor disputes. These abuses and their implications in industrial relations were examined in Chapter 3.

The American Federation of Labor conducted its legislative campaign on national and state levels. Its objective was to engineer the passage of state and federal legislation designed to provide protection from the equity power of the courts. This was a logical and necessary approach, for both state and federal courts issued labor injunctions. State control of the labor injunction antedated federal regulation. Thus it was on the state level that organized labor first succeeded in influencing the enactment of anti-injunction legislation. The rewards, however, were not destined to endure. Prior to October 15, 1914, the date on which Congress enacted the Clayton Act (which in part regulated the labor injunction), only six states had passed legislation restricting the power of the state courts to issue injunctions in labor disputes. These states were California (1903), Oklahoma (1907), Massachusetts (1911), Kansas, Arizona, and Montana (1913).[2] The California and Oklahoma laws provided that acts that are not criminal when committed by a single person shall not be subject to injunction when engaged in by a number of persons involved in a labor dispute. Massachusetts provided that its state courts could not enjoin peaceful picketing. The purpose of the Montana law was to prohibit discrimination against workers in equity proceedings. It provided that standards developed by the courts for the issuance of injunctions in nonlabor disputes should apply equally to labor disputes. In addition, the Oklahoma and Massachusetts laws granted persons involved in contempt cases the right to trial by jury.

Arizona and Kansas enacted legislation that closely resembled the injunction sections of the Clayton Act. The efforts of Arizona and Kansas may be regarded as the first genuine attempts to regulate by law the use of injunctions in labor disputes. While the laws of California, Oklahoma, Massachusetts, and Montana purported to control specific aspects of the labor injunction, Arizona and Kansas fashioned legislation calculated to remove the courts from this area of industrial relations. The laws of these two states prohibited judicial interference by injunction in controversies involving employers and employees when these controversies grew out of a dispute that concerned terms or conditions of employment. Such legislation removed the prerogative of the judiciary to declare what is lawful and unlawful in the carrying out of labor disputes. This restriction on the equity function of the courts marked a significant innovation in labor relations law. The judiciary had taken upon itself the full right to determine the legitimate boundaries of labor union activity. Arizona and Kansas had endeavored to check the courts from exercising such sweeping power in the area of industrial relations. It was legislation of this character that the American Federation of Labor championed and hoped to have enacted by all states and the federal government.

Although the first visible results of its efforts appeared in state legislation, the American Federation of Labor consistently attempted to promote the passage of a federal anti-injunction labor law. Indeed, the use of the injunction in labor disputes, along with the prosecution of unions under the Sherman law, stimulated the entrance of organized labor into national politics. To induce the passage of favorable national legislation, organized labor openly supported candidates sympathetic to its legislative program, and worked for the defeat of the "antilabor" politician. To this day, the union movement follows essentially this same political program, the foundation of which was laid down in the early 1900s. Organized labor had reason to believe that its efforts to obtain national anti-injunction legislation had borne fruit on October 15, 1914, for on this date Congress enacted the Clayton Act. Previously, we saw that labor's jubilation over the antitrust provisions of the Clayton Act was premature. A careful analysis of this act's Section 6 reveals that its terms added nothing new to the law of industrial relations. Actual experience with the law disclosed that the prosecution of labor organizations under the Sherman Act continued unabated.

The rejoicing of labor with respect to the injunction sections of the 1914 law appeared to be on firm ground. In general, the terms regulating the equity power of the federal courts in labor disputes seemed clear enough. The Clayton Act provided that the federal courts could not restrain employees involved in a labor dispute from engaging in peaceful picketing; from carrying out a strike in a peaceful manner; from engaging in a peaceful boycott; from attending any place where such employees may lawfully be; and from peacefully assembling in a lawful manner and for lawful purposes. These prohibitions are contained in Section 20 of the Clayton Act.[3] The terms "peaceful" and "lawful" defy objective construction and the Supreme Court was free to insert its own definition of what these terms meant. Patterns of union conduct previously interfered with by the federal courts were not immunized against the labor injunction.

Other sections of the Clayton Act closely regulated the procedure of issuing injunctions in labor disputes. Under circumstances wherein Section 20 did not operate to protect activities of labor unions, such as picketing attended with violence, the Clayton Act spelled out the procedure that had to be followed by the federal courts. A temporary restraining order could not be granted without notice to the labor union unless irreparable injury to property appeared imminent, for which injury there was no adequate remedy in law. In addition, a temporary restraining order issued without notice to the labor organization must by its terms expire within a period of ten days after issuance. No preliminary injunction could be issued without notice to the trade union. Persons accused of violation of injunctions might, if they desired, be tried by jury. Employers applying for an injunction had to post a bond for the indemnification of a union for court costs and damages if subsequent events proved that the organization had been wrongfully enjoined or restrained. Finally, the Clayton Act provided that every injunction or temporary restraining order must set forth in reasonable detail the specific acts to be enjoined.

Since on the one hand, the Clayton Act forbade completely under certain circumstances the issuance of labor injunctions, and on the other hand, outlined carefully the procedure to be followed in the issuance of injunctions, unions felt, —mistakenly—that the law adequately protected organized labor. Inspired by its apparent success on the federal level, organized labor then concentrated on the task of obtaining the passage of state anti-injunction laws. Once again, the record reveals that its efforts were only moderately rewarded. Although the American Federation of Labor advocated legislation patterned after the Clayton Act in every state legislature in the nation, only five states prior to 1921 enacted laws duplicating the terms of the federal anti-injunction statute.[4] No progress on the state level was made after 1921. The basic reason for this was that the Supreme

Court of the United States declared the Arizona law unconstitutional. The action of the high court reduced the incentive to work for the passage of state anti-injunction laws. Of what use would it be to enact such laws if they could not stand the test of constitutionality? Since the role of the Supreme Court in shaping the character of labor injunction control legislation is of conclusive importance, attention must be directed to the reaction of the courts to such statutes.

EARLY LABOR INJUNCTION LEGISLATION: COURT ATTITUDES

The Clayton Act, as noted, did not operate to preclude the application of the Sherman law to labor unions. Once the Supreme Court took this position, it affirmed the use of the labor injunction to restrain unions found in violation of the antitrust statutes. This was the essence of the *Duplex* decision of 1921 and of the *Bedford* doctrine of 1927. Thus, the principle was laid down that the injunction provisions of the Clayton Act were not operative if the judiciary found that labor unions had restrained trade within the meaning of the Sherman law. As a consequence, antitrust laws served as a basis for the issuance of labor injunctions for many years.

In addition, in 1917, the Supreme Court affirmed the use of the injunction to make effective yellow-dog contracts. Despite the provisions against the use of labor injunctions in the Clayton Act, the high court in the *Hitchman* decision held that the equity power of the judiciary could be properly employed to implement agreements in which workers agreed not to join labor unions as a condition of employment. As a matter of fact, the Court did not make any reference to the Clayton Act in the *Hitchman* case, even though the terms of that law may have been reasonably construed to prohibit the issuance of labor injunctions in yellow-dog cases. The fundamental intent of the Clayton Act was to check the power of the federal courts to intervene by injunction in labor disputes that grew out of controversies that concerned terms and conditions of employment. A controversy as to whether or not workers could form labor organizations for the purpose of collective bargaining fell squarely within the meaning of the injunction sections of the Clayton Act. In addition, Section 20 of the Clayton Act forbade the use of the injunction in labor disputes where the effect of the instrument would enjoin persons from "communicating information" or "from attending at any place where such persons may lawfully be." Even granted that the term "lawfully" is subject to no precise definition, the courts may have been guided by the intent of the legislation, as demonstrated in Chapter 4. Of course, this approach was precluded when the Supreme Court chose to hold that interference with a yellow-dog contract transgressed rights vouchsafed in the Constitution.

The high court was required to resolve an additional question. What about the application of the Clayton Act to cases in which violations of the antitrust statutes or yellow-dog contracts were not involved? Would the Court now construe the statute in a manner that provided a degree of protection to labor unions against the labor injunction? The answer to this question was found in the *American Steel Foundries* and *Truax* cases.

"ONE PICKET PER ENTRANCE"

In spite of the broad restrictions on the issuance of injunctions in labor disputes, the Supreme Court in the 1921 *American Steel Foundries* case[5] interpreted the law in a manner that sharply limited the application of injunctions to labor-management controversies. The high court construction of the Clayton Act in this case meant that the Act was to leave unchanged the law of industrial relations. This was subsequently recognized by the Court when it declared that the injunction sections of the Clayton Act "were merely declaratory of what had always been the law and the best practice in equity."

As a result of a strike over wages, a labor organization had picketed a plant. The company obtained an injunction from a federal district court that stamped out all picketing. On review of the case, the Supreme Court modified the order, but limited union picketing to one picket per entrance of the factory. On this score Chief Justice Taft declared: "We think that the strikers and their sympathizers engaged in the economic struggle should be limited to one representative for each point of ingress and egress in the plant or place of business and that all others be enjoined from congregating or loitering at the plant or in the neighboring street by which access is had to the plant. . . ." Although these pickets (the Court termed them "missionaries") were to have the right of observation, communication, and persuasion, they could not approach nonstriking workers in groups, and their communication to these workers could not be abusive, libelous, or threatening. In addition, the Court held that a picket acting alone could not obstruct an unwilling listener by "dragging his step." It is noteworthy that the Court was concerned not only with the number of pickets but also with their conduct on the picket line.

A further limitation was attached to the picketing activities of labor unions. According to the Court, the Clayton Act provisions protected the activities only of employees of an employer on strike, or of ex-employees who might reasonably be expected to return to work for the employer. Other workers directly involved in a labor dispute, who were not in the present or past employment of the company but who might still have had a real economic interest in the working conditions of the firm, could not lawfully picket. This doctrine, it will be recalled, was first laid down in the *Duplex* case wherein Section 20 of the Clayton Act did not operate to make lawful union activities carried on by employees in one city to bring economic pressure against an employer located in another city. On this point, the Court in the *Duplex* case declared, "Congress had in mind particular industrial controversies, not a general class war." Following the *Duplex* decision, a narrow construction was placed on the Clayton Act in the *American Steel Foundries* case.

Unions learned that the Clayton Act would not prevent the intervention of court injunctions in labor disputes. Regardless of the purpose of union economic pressure and notwithstanding the peacefulness of picketing, the Supreme Court was not prepared to construe the Clayton Act as providing a greater area of freedom to labor unions than posting one picket per entrance to a plant. Even though the Court was careful to point out that "each case must turn on its own circumstances," the doctrine established in the *American Steel Foundries* case was followed by many courts. After this case, the courts almost always limited the number of pickets that could be utilized in a labor dispute.

LABOR INJUNCTION CONTROL LEGISLATION HELD UNCONSTITUTIONAL

Shortly after the *American Steel Foundries* case, the Supreme Court ruled on the lawfulness of a state labor injunction control law. In the *Truax* case,[6] the high court held unconstitutional the Arizona labor injunction law. Previously, the Supreme Court of Arizona had approved its state law. Despite the construction of the state court, the Supreme Court of the United States held that the Arizona law had violated the due process clause of the Fourteenth Amendment to the Constitution.[7]

Facts of the case disclose that the employees of a restaurant located in Bisbee, Arizona, became involved in a labor dispute with their employer over conditions and terms of employment. Since the employer refused to yield to their demands, some of the workers went on strike. The owners of the restaurant managed to operate without the strikers and, to retaliate, the striking employees carried on a vigorous boycott against the management. So successful was the boycott that the restaurant receipts dropped from $156 to $75 per day. The boycott was carried on by picketing the immediate premises of the restaurant. Although no violence was involved, the pickets carried banners containing statements against the restaurant and its owners, workers, and customers. According to the Supreme Court of the United States, the Arizona statute precluded the issuance of injunctions under circumstances of the *Truax* case. As a result, it held that the statute deprived the restaurant owners of their property without due process of law and accordingly violated the Constitution of the United States. "Property," of course, included the right to operate a business in a profitable manner, and a statute could not stand as a cloak behind which a labor organization could interfere with the employer's right to do business. On this score Chief Justice Taft, speaking for the majority of the Court, declared, "a law which operates to make lawful such a wrong as is described in plaintiff's complaint deprives the owner of the business and the premises of his property without due process, and cannot be held valid under the Fourteenth Amendment." This reasoning was the opposite of that employed by the Arizona Supreme Court in giving its definition of property in the 1918 case. Union actions, it was argued, merely suggested to an owner the advisability of a change in business methods, but in no sense interfered with the methods of conducting business. The economic weapons could be both primary and secondary boycotts and, further, "moral intimidation and coercion of threatening a boycott could be employed."[8] As noted, this liberality was not destined for long life after appeal to the United States Supreme Court.

A second reason for the declaration of unconstitutionality was the claim of the United States Supreme Court that the statute denied employers equal protection of the law. It contended that the Arizona statute provided employees with a right not enjoyed by employers. The Court declared:

> The necessary effect of [the Arizona law] is that the plaintiffs would have had the right to an injunction against such a campaign as that conducted by the defendants, if it had been directed against the plaintiffs, business and property in any kind of a controversy which was not a dispute between employer and former employees. If the competing restaurant-keepers in Bisbee had inaugurated such a campaign against the plaintiff and conducted it with banners and handbills of a similar character, an injunction would necessarily have been issued to protect the plaintiffs in the employment of their property and business.

"HOLMES AND BRANDEIS DISSENTING"

Holmes and Brandeis[9] teamed up to challenge the decision of the majority. Indeed, in many other circumstances, the dissenting opinions of these two men eventually became the holdings of the majority of the Court. On many matters of fundamental importance, the Supreme Court now refers to the dissenting opinions of Holmes and Brandeis. History has demonstrated the wisdom of their views on the utilization of social and economic data in legal proceedings, the proper relationship between the legislative and judicial branches of government, and their overall approach to constitutional matters.

Holmes in the *Truax* case reaffirmed his belief that the legislative power of government should be checked by the judiciary only under rare and unusual circumstances. He always held closely to the principle that state legislatures and Congress should be free from judicial restraint in their attempts to experiment in legislative matters. This position was grounded in the proposition that the legislative arm of government is subject to the direct control of the electorate. Representatives who enact unpopular laws cannot expect reelection. Holmes refused to accept the proposition that the judiciary should constitute a forum for the invalidation of laws passed by popularly elected legislators. Such an attitude squares with the viewpoint of those who would see the democratic process strengthened. The containment of the legislative process by the judiciary could result in the checking of progress. Judges are elected or appointed to their positions for comparatively long periods of time. For example, members of the federal judiciary may hold office for life or, as the Constitution points out, "The

Judges, both of the supreme and inferior Courts, should hold their offices during good Behavior. . . ." This means that the judiciary, insulated against changing personnel, could act as a permanent check against the legislative will of the people. Such a circumstance is clearly demonstrated in the area of labor law.

These considerations were underscored by Holmes in the *Truax* case when he declared that

> there is nothing that I more deprecate than the use of the Fourteenth Amendment beyond the absolute compulsion of its words to prevent the making of social experiments that an important part of the community desires, in the insulated chambers afforded by the several states, even though the experiment may seem futile or even noxious to me and to those whose judgment I most respect.

Brandeis emphasized the principle that the legislative branch of the government could properly limit the equity power of the courts in labor disputes without violating the due process clause of the Constitution. He stressed the fact that injunction control laws represented a reasonable exercise of legislative power and hence did not deprive employers of their property without due process of law. Since experience with the use of the injunction in labor disputes revealed the need for legislative restriction, the enactment of such laws was neither unreasonable nor arbitrary. Changing needs of society require the changing character of legislative approach to social and economic problems. Workers chose to form labor unions to advance their economic welfare. The courts through the injunction process threw the weight of the law on the side of management in labor controversies. Legislators, aware of these circumstances and basing their action on a plethora of data, decided to reduce the role of government in collective bargaining by decreasing the power of courts to intervene.

The fact that many legislative bodies found that regulation of the injunction in labor disputes would serve the public interest was given great weight by Brandeis. He was deeply impressed by the careful accumulation of factual evidence that stimulated the advocacy and passage of injunction control legislation. As a matter of fact, the contribution of Brandeis to the judicial process was his insistence that the courts weigh carefully the circumstances that produced legislation. He encouraged the courts to consider laws in their socioeconomic context and not to pass judgment on the basis of legal niceties or judicial precedent. In this manner, Brandeis breathed life into the law. To him, the law was not a dead, unresponsive, or unchanging institution. Rather, he thought that courts had to be aware of the swiftly moving events in the area of economic and social affairs. A law that might have been arbitrary a century ago at present might be a reasonable legislative approach to a particular problem because of the changing character of the needs of the public. This then was the creed of Brandeis: to penetrate behind the complex and intricate apparatus of the law and attach controlling weight to empirical data showing the necessity for legislation. That Brandeis was fully aware of the numerous abuses growing out of the use of the injunction in labor disputes is amply demonstrated by his statement in the *Truax* case. He declared that in labor injunction proceedings,

> an alleged damage to property, always incidental and at times insignificant, was often laid hold of to enable the penalties of the criminal law to be enforced expeditiously without that protection to the liberty of the individual which the Bill of Rights was designed to afford; that through such proceedings a single judge often usurped the functions not only of the jury but of the police department; that in prescribing the conditions under which strikes were permissible and how they might be carried out, he usurped also the powers of the legislature; and that incidentally he abridged the constitutional rights of individuals to free speech, to a free press and to peaceful assembly.

As for the "equal protection" argument of the majority of the Court, Brandeis contended that a state legislature might regulate the use of the labor injunction without violating the equal protection clause of the Constitution. Such a conclusion was grounded in the commonplace legal principle that the states may set up reasonable classifications for legislative purposes. A classification between employers and employees, according to Brandeis, appeared reasonable, and consequently, to deny the use of the injunction to protect property rights in employer-employee disputes did not violate the equal-protection section of the Constitution, even though the same property rights would be protected by the injunction when parties did not stand in an employer-employee relationship. Thus Brandeis felt that the Arizona law neither denied employers the equal protection of the law, nor deprived them of their property without due process of law. A labor injunction control law constituted a valid exercise of the legislative power of the states, for such a law was designed to correct a condition deemed evil by the collective judgment of the people of the commonwealth.

NORRIS–LA GUARDIA

The action of the Supreme Court checked any progress in the area of injunction control legislation. For about a decade, no state attempted to regulate the use of the labor injunction. In addition, state supreme courts, following the precedent of the U.S. Supreme Court, construed those state anti-injunction labor laws passed after the Clayton Act in such a manner as to render them impotent. Since the rate of issuance of labor injunctions continued unabated, organized labor still desired legislative relief. The problem, however, was to fashion a law that would effectively limit the equity power of the courts in labor disputes *and* stand the test of constitutionality.

A congressional committee appointed a panel of experts to help in the drafting of legislation that would remove the abuses of the labor injunction, stand the test of constitutionality, and generally serve the cause of justice. In 1927, an anti-injunction bill was presented to the public for debate. In March 1932, the bill was finally passed by overwhelming majorities in both houses of Congress and shortly afterward was signed by President Hoover. This bill was popularly termed the Norris–La Guardia Federal Anti-Injunction Act. What was the nature of this law, and how was it received by the judiciary?

Norris–La Guardia: Underlying Theory

Congress justified the Norris–La Guardia Act by pointing to the need for collective bargaining in modern society. This consideration is clearly stated in the provision of the law that spells out the public policy of the United States with respect to employer-employee relations. This section begins by pointing out that under prevailing economic conditions, developed with the aid of government authority for owners of property to organize in the corporate and other forms of ownership association, the individual unorganized worker is commonly helpless to exercise actual liberty of contract and freedom of labor. Such a statement was supposed to reflect the current industrial environment, suggesting that a job to a worker is infinitely more important than is a single worker to a modern corporation. The law assumed that business enterprise would not be greatly disturbed if any single worker quit because of dissatisfaction with working conditions. On the other hand, a job was seen to be of crucial importance to the worker and the family. To insure a flow of income, the individual worker might continue to work under conditions that he or she felt were unsuitable, and would be more prone to hold jobs regardless of working conditions when there were no alternative job opportunities. Under such conditions, it would be extremely difficult, if not impossible, to argue that a worker needed a job less than a corporation needed a single worker. Consequently, the law found that there existed no liberty of contract between single workers and employers in modern industry, as was assumed in litigated cases prior to 1932. If there was no actual liberty of contract, the single worker had little or no freedom in selling his or her labor, having to hold a job regardless of working conditions. This is not to say that some workers did not quit jobs because of dissatisfaction with working conditions. Nor did these considerations deny the fact that some enterprising workers prepare themselves for better jobs by study and training. Despite these qualifications, the fact remains that in modern society, the typical individual worker tends to hold a job as long as the employer permits.

Workers tend to raise their bargaining strength by forming labor unions. An employer, though not greatly disturbed when one worker leaves employment, must be vitally concerned when all workers cease working. Regardless of the rate of output, some costs of operation continue unabated. Production stoppage could result in the inability to fill orders and even in a permanent loss of customers. Since employers are aware that collective action of workers could result in the effective use of the strike, causing economic loss to the firm, they must listen with some degree of respect to the complaints and suggestions of organized workers. In short, by organizing into labor unions, workers are in a better position to sell their services in a manner that can be more in accordance with their conception of the standards of justice and fairness.

The Norris–La Guardia Act recognized the helplessness of the individual worker in the employment relationship. It suggested that the formation of labor unions could correct the inherent inequality of bargaining power between employers and employees. Finally, it affirmed that U.S. public policy sanctions collective bargaining and approves the formation and effective operation of labor unions.

Purpose of Norris–La Guardia Act

Thus, the basic purpose of the Norris–La Guardia Act is easily understood. Collective bargaining is endorsed by the public policy of the United States. Consequently, logic would appear to demand that Congress implement this policy by checking a condition that had historically operated to retard the growth and effective operation of the union movement. The fundamental purpose of Norris–La Guardia is to circumscribe sharply the power of the courts to intervene in labor disputes.

Since experience had shown that the injunction constituted the means by which the courts had entered the area of labor-management relations, Congress checked the prerogative of the courts to issue labor injunctions. The regulation of the injunction was incidental to the main purpose of Congress: to insulate industrial relations from the influence of the courts. If the facts had indicated that the courts had interfered in labor-management relations in other ways, the approach of Congress might have been different. From the 1880s, however, the history of labor relations had revealed that the injunction constituted the *modus operandi* of the judiciary. Hence, the law found that regulation of the equity power of the courts was the proper approach to the problem.

It was the manner in which the courts wielded their power that stimulated congressional action. If evidence had revealed that the use of the injunction did not place government on the side of employers in labor disputes, there of course would have been no necessity for an anti-injunction law. However, close attention was directed to the abuses growing out of the labor injunction. These factors led to an unmistakable conclusion: The use of the injunction placed the power of government on the side of management in labor disputes. The statute indicated that justice is advanced when government remains impartial. Accordingly, the judiciary had to behave as a neutral, not as an ally, in labor disputes. These considerations would have been equally valid if the injunctive power of the courts had been utilized to make government an ally of trade unions in labor disputes. Regulation of the injunction under these circumstances would have been just as necessary as under the conditions that actually prevailed.

Norris–La Guardia did not provide labor unions with any new legal rights. It merely allowed them a greater area in which to operate free from court control. Naturally, this circumstance facilitated immeasurably the ability of labor unions to act as effective collective bargaining agencies. It is true that Norris–La Guardia encouraged the growth of the labor movement. The fact remains, however, that this growth was nurtured by the government only to the degree that Norris–La Guardia checked the power of the courts to interfere in labor-management disputes. The Act did not require workers to join unions, nor did it stop employers from preventing the development and operation of unions by methods other than the use of the injunction. Its underlying objective was to set up an area for industrial conflict in which the courts were forbidden to tread.

AREA OF INDUSTRIAL FREEDOM

Of all the abuses growing out of the use of the injunction in labor disputes, perhaps the outstanding one was that the courts had the power to make industrial relations law. Labor leaders denounced in no uncertain terms a procedure that permitted the judiciary to usurp the power of the legislature. In particular, they protested against an arrangement that empowered the courts to decide the lawful and unlawful areas of labor union activities. The cry of organized labor—"government by injunction!"—arose from the authority of the courts to decide by themselves, regardless of the existence of the legislative arm of government, the licit and illicit in industrial relations.

Such an arrangement served to raise the courts to a position of preeminence in the area of labor-management relations. By virtue of their authority to issue injunctions in labor disputes, the courts wielded a most extraordinary power over labor relations. The manner in which they exercised this power is a matter of public record. Overwhelming evidence indicates that the equity power of the courts served the interests of the employer in labor disputes. In light of these considerations, and if the philosophy of the Norris–La Guardia Act is understood, it should be clear why the law set up a system of self-determination for labor unions. Congress stripped the federal courts of the power to restrain certain forms of union conduct. Regardless of the objective of the labor union in carrying out these activities, the authority of the federal courts to restrain such conduct was neutralized. In short, Congress immunized certain union conduct from the review of the courts. What are these activities that are insulated against court intervention?

Section 4 of Norris–La Guardia begins by declaring that no federal court shall have the power to issue any form of injunctive relief in any case involving a labor dispute, the effect of which would prohibit any person or persons participating or interested in such a dispute from doing, whether singly or in concert, any of a series of acts. The first of these acts immunized from court review is the right of workers to cease or to refuse to perform any work. Hence, this provision is designed to deny federal courts the opportunity to interfere with the right of workers to strike. Illustrations were offered that revealed that some courts stamped out strikes when judges did not approve of the purpose for which the strikes were carried out. For example, many courts restrained strikes for union security. Under the terms of Norris–La Guardia, the federal courts could not substitute their own judgment for that of workers where strikes were concerned. Judges could not restrain any strike, regardless of its objective. This does not mean that strikes are never carried out for a purpose that is clearly antisocial. That such is the case is evidenced by the fact that some public-spirited labor leaders have advocated the outlawing of certain types of strikes. The point of importance here is that Norris–La Guardia deprived judges of the power to utilize their own standards of reference to decide the lawfulness or unlawfulness of strikes. If strike control was deemed necessary in the public interest, this curtailment was supposed to be the work of the legislative branch of government. This was considered a superior approach to one in which judges, basing their decisions on their own socioeconomic outlook, were empowered to limit the right of workers to strike.

Under the protection of the Norris–La Guardia Act, labor unions could provide workers engaged in a labor dispute with strike-relief funds or with anything else of value. In the past, some judges had forbidden labor unions from providing strikers with strike-relief funds. Such a condition, of course, decreased a union's chance to win a strike. Workers on strike soon exhaust what savings they may have accumulated while at work. During a strike, the worker still must meet household expenses, insurance policy premiums, medical bills, rent, and the like. Some unions attempt to ease this burden by providing strikers with modest strike benefits. In most cases, the sum is only a fraction of what the worker would have earned at the job. However, the money is of considerable importance in such a circumstance, even if it means nothing more than improving the morale of the strikers. When unions supplement strike-relief funds with food tickets or with food itself, the lot of the striker is improved. Norris–La Guardia meant that federal courts could no longer deny labor organizations the right to perform these functions.

Section 4 also checked the power of the courts to restrain the right of workers to picket or to give publicity to labor disputes. The law facilitated the ability of workers to win labor disputes by broadening considerably the lawful area of union publicity activities. No federal court could restrain picketing activities of unions as long as violence or fraud was not present. A comparison between the picketing sections of the Clayton Act and Norris–La Guardia is worthwhile. In the former law, there was no mention of the term *picketing* or words denoting a similar meaning. The Norris–La Guardia Act, however, specifically stated that nonviolent and fraud-free "patrolling" to publicize a labor dispute could not be enjoined. In the *American Steel Foundries* case, the Supreme Court had held that the Clayton Act protected workers' picketing only to the extent of "one picket per entrance." In establishing this point of view, the Court no doubt was persuaded in part by the fact that the Clayton Act avoided use of specific language to protect picketing activities. Norris–La Guardia prevented such a limited construction of its provisions by utilizing the term "patrolling."

The law also permitted workers engaged in labor disputes to advise and urge other employees to join the conflict. Frequently, some workers refuse to go out on strike even though a labor union may officially proclaim one. The position of the strikers would be greatly abetted if all workers joined the strike; for where all workers strike, the employer normally cannot produce at all, or can operate only at a very low rate of production. In the past, courts were very careful to protect nonstrikers from the overtures of the workers engaged in the conflict. The decision of the Supreme Court in the *American Steel Foundries* case highlights this proposition. The effect of Norris–La Guardia was to provide more freedom to unions and their members to encourage all workers to strike. The action of the union in this respect is limited by the general restrictions in Section 4. Thus, whenever a union urges nonstrikers to join in the conflict, such a campaign must be free from violence or fraud.

Section 4 further forbade the issuance of a labor injunction when it would keep a union from aiding any person participating in or interested in any labor dispute who was being proceeded against, or was prosecuting, any action or suit in any state or federal court. Thus, the resources of a labor organization could be utilized to defend members of the union, or the union itself, in court proceedings. Sometimes, as an outgrowth of a labor dispute, legal action is taken against the officers of the union. Under such conditions, the organization may decide to come to the support of its officers and provide them with the services of expert and expensive legal talent. After Norris–La Guardia, such an activity could no longer be enjoined by a federal labor injunction. Furthermore, under the protection of Norris–La Guardia, labor unions could conduct meetings or assemble peacefully to promote the interests of their members. There had been evidence that some courts actually forbade workers from holding peacefully conducted meetings. An injunction that produced such a result could cause irreparable damage to a labor organization involved in a labor dispute. During the course of a strike, a union frequently holds meetings involving all or a portion of the membership to discuss items of strike strategy or to vote on the issues of the conflict. Norris–La Guardia meant that the federal court could no longer restrain the right of a union to conduct such meetings.

To underscore the guarantees already discussed, Congress added a general provision to Section 4. It stated that no court could issue an injunction to prevent workers from agreeing with each other to do any of the acts allowed in Section 4. This section was intended to prevent the application of the conspiracy doctrine to those activities removed from the scope of the labor injunction. An act engaged in by one worker no longer could be ruled unlawful when carried out by a group of workers. It was noted previously that the conspiracy doctrine operated to make group action unlawful even though the same activity would be lawful if carried out by one person. This general "anti-conspiracy" clause of Section 4 is actually rather superfluous. The general intent of the Norris–La Guardia Act would in any case prevent the application of the conspiracy doctrine to labor activities protected from the injunction. However, in its zeal to block court intervention in labor disputes, Congress wrote this provision into Section 4. It wanted to be doubly sure that the right of workers to strike, give publicity to labor disputes, hold meetings to promote their interests, or come to the aid of their fellows by providing them with legal aid or strike benefits would not be circumscribed by the judiciary.

CONCEPT OF "LABOR DISPUTE"

It is clear that Congress immunized a variety of trade union activities from the application of the federal injunction. By checking the power of the courts, the Norris–La Guardia Act expanded the freedom of action of labor unions. In addition, the law protected labor union activities on a much broader basis, extending beyond a labor dispute involving an employer and his or her own employees. The guarantees of the law not only extended to such a limited situation, but its immunities also operated when the disputants did not stand in a proximate relationship of employer and employee. In short, for purposes of Norris–La Guardia, a *labor dispute* included any controversy concerning terms of employment or concerning the representation of employees in collective bargaining, regardless of whether or not the disputants stood in the proximate relation of employer and employee.[10] By adopting a broad definition of a labor dispute, Congress expanded considerably the limits to which unions could lawfully operate. This conception of a labor dispute squared with the realities of modern industrial life. It recognized that the successful operation of collective bargaining frequently requires the implementation of union pressure on an industry-wide or craft basis. Moreover, it recognized that the brunt of union organizational activities of a plant may fall to workers other than those directly employed by the firm. No other concept of labor dispute would have made the anti-injunction law an effective check against the labor injunction. As an illustration, the Seventh Circuit Court of Appeals ruled in 1977 that a union group that used the name of an employer it sought to organize was protected from an injunction by Norris–La Guardia. The group called itself the Great America Service Trades Council, AFL-CIO, and ran an advertisement in a newspaper addressed to applicants and potential applicants asking them to report to the council's office to sign a bargaining authorization card. The company claimed the union infringed on its registered trademark of "Great America" and asked for an injunction in federal district court, which was granted. The court of appeals reversed the decision, holding that the union's action was a legitimate one of trying to organize workers and that the use of the company's name was to facilitate this aim.[11]

THE PASSING OF THE YELLOW-DOG CONTRACT

The Norris–La Guardia Act effected still another important change in the law of industrial relations. It declared that yellow-dog contracts are not enforceable in any court of the United States. In this manner, the architects of Norris–La Guardia nullified the effect of the *Hitchman* decision, the case in which the Supreme Court upheld the validity and enforceability of the yellow-dog contract. Thus fifteen years elapsed before organized labor was released from the yellow-dog contract. Just as important is the observation that such relief came not from a change of attitude of the judiciary but from action of the legislative branch of government.

If one is aware of the effects of the yellow-dog contract on the collective bargaining process, it should be easy to understand why the instrument was declared unenforceable by Norris–La Guardia. No other single measure could exceed the effectiveness of a yellow-dog contract when enforced by an injunction. Section 3 of the law condemned the yellow-dog contract as inconsistent with the public policy of the United States. Norris–La Guardia identified public policy as support and endorsement of the collective bargaining process. Since the yellow-dog contract conflicts with such public policy, Congress denied federal courts the authority to enforce such promises.

It is noteworthy that the Norris–La Guardia Act did not outlaw the yellow-dog contract. It only made the federal courts unavailable for the enforcement of the instrument. In later years, however, the National Labor Relations Board (NLRB) held that an employer engages in an unfair labor practice if he or she demanded that employees execute such agreements. Thus the yellow-dog contract, the most complete of all antiunion measures, was laid to rest by action of Congress. No federal court is available for the enforcement of a contract, the terms of which require that a worker give up employment on joining a union, nor can an employer require such agreements of employees.

LABOR INJUNCTION: PROCEDURAL LIMITATIONS

Nothing could be more inaccurate than to conclude that the Norris–La Guardia Act forbade under every circumstance the issuance of federal injunctions in labor-management controversies. Certainly the law circumscribed sharply the power of courts to intervene in labor disputes. On the other hand, Congress did not prohibit altogether the issuance of labor injunctions. If a labor-management controversy does not fall within the labor dispute concept, the exercise of the equity power of the federal courts is not precluded. Despite the broad definition of labor dispute in Norris–La Guardia, there are circumstances in which a labor-management conflict does not fall within the scope of the law.[12] Injunctions can also be issued when union activities involve fraud and violence. Since the law does not distinguish between tangible property and the right to do business under proper conditions, the federal courts may protect by injunction both forms of property. Before any injunction can be issued, however, Norris–La Guardia sets up certain standards that must be adhered to by the federal courts.

Temporary Restraining Orders.   In the first place, the law set up several restrictions bearing on the issuance of temporary restraining orders. The authors of Norris–La Guardia were well aware of the abuses growing out of the use of the temporary restraining order. The law provided that a hearing must take place to determine whether or not the temporary restraining order should be issued. At such hearing, the defendants in the case must be provided with the opportunity to challenge the allegations of the complainant. On the other hand, Norris–La Guardia recognized the possibility that the issuance of the temporary restraining order without such a hearing might be the only procedure whereby property could be protected from substantial and irreparable injury. For example, there would be no time to notify the defendant and hold a hearing if workers were inflicting serious damage to an employer's plant or machinery. Such circumstances demand that court intervention take place without delay. Under such pressing circumstances, a court could issue a temporary restraining order without a hearing, and the complainant must adduce testimony under oath the character of which, if sustained, would justify the court in issuing a temporary injunction upon the basis of a hearing participated in by the defendant.

If a temporary restraining order is issued in the absence of a hearing, the order by its own terms must expire within five days. This time limit was included to prevent the possibility of a temporary restraining order remaining in effect for a prolonged period. As noted, some courts, without requiring a hearing, issued temporary restraining orders that remained in force for long periods of time. When this occurred, the labor union suffered irreparable injury. The full injustice of this practice came to light when subsequent investigation proved the union innocent of the crimes alleged by the complainant. Such a possibility was precluded under the Norris–La Guardia Act by virtue of the five-day limitation.

The law set up another limitation on the issuance of temporary restraining orders. It provided that no temporary restraining order could be issued except upon condition that the complainant submit a bond with the court to recompense those enjoined for any loss, expense, or damage caused by the erroneous issuance of such an order. The amount of the bond was to be fixed by the court. In this manner, Norris–La Guardia recognized that until a full investigation was made of a case, there was always the possibility that the defendants might be unjustly enjoined. If the court restrains a labor union from a course of conduct on the basis of employer-filed evidence and if subsequent investigation proves the evidence to be invalid, Norris–La Guardia provides for some compensation for the union.

Even though the posting of a bond may serve to deter employers from requesting temporary restraining orders based on false evidence, the fact remains that the baseless enjoinment of the labor union may result in irreparable damage to the organization, regardless of the subsequent recovery of money damages. Thus real protection of unions from the labor injunction is derived from other provisions of Norris–La Guardia, and only seemingly from the bond-posting requirement. Yet this feature makes for better injunction procedure than prevailed in the period before the Norris–La Guardia Act, when many courts failed to require the posting of any bond or set the figure at a very low level. Courts resorted to this practice even though the posting of bonds of reasonable amounts was required in nonlabor cases.

Temporary and Permanent Injunctions.   Congress also established a series of standards to guide the federal courts in the issuance of temporary and permanent injunctions. Norris–La Guardia provided that no court could issue these forms of injunctive relief unless a hearing was held. Before the passage of the anti-injunction law, the courts held hearings prior to the issuance of temporary injunctions. However, the character of the hearing required by the terms of the Norris–La Guardia Act differed sharply from the typical hearing conducted prior to enactment. Under Norris–La Guardia, if an injunction was sought, witnesses had to be produced to support allegations in the complaint. Thus, federal courts could no longer issue temporary injunctions on the basis of mere sworn affidavits, a procedure proven inequitable in the pre–Norris–La Guardia period. In addition, the union had to be permitted to produce witnesses to challenge the allegations. Both sides had to be allowed the opportunity to cross-examine witnesses. Thus, the law gave the court a better basis to determine the facts of the case. An injunction issued after such precautions most likely is justified. It is important to note that these requirements apply equally to temporary and permanent injunction proceedings.

Federal courts may not grant injunctive relief unless the facts indicate that in the absence of the injunction, substantial and irreparable injury to property will result. Moreover, prior to the issuance of a temporary or permanent injunction, the court must be satisfied that greater injury will be inflicted upon the complainant by the denial of relief than will be inflicted upon the defendant by the granting of relief. This provision recognized that a labor union might suffer from the issuance of an injunction. It further recognized that an employer might be injured in the absence of an injunction. Only after the court balances these relative injuries may it exercise its equity power in labor disputes. Of course, the problem must be resolved largely on a subjective basis. In any event, the requirement of balancing the relative damages to the disputants was supposed to serve the cause of justice.

In addition, under the terms of Norris–La Guardia, the court prior to the granting of equity relief must be satisfied that the complainant has no adequate remedy at law. This means that no injunction will be issued against a labor union if the court finds that the employer may recover damages resulting from unlawful union activity in trial court proceedings. Considerations that would prompt a court to find that an employer has no adequate remedy at law include: (1) financial irresponsibility of the labor union; (2) the fact that an employer would be required to file a multiplicity of suits to recover damages; and (3) the possibility that it would be difficult to obtain a jury that would not be sympathetic to the labor union. The latter factor would be important in a community that is a stronghold of unionism—the so-called "union town."

Still another finding of fact must be made by the court before Norris–La Guardia sanctions the granting of a temporary or permanent injunction. The facts must reveal that local police officers charged with the duty to protect the complainant's property are unable or unwilling to furnish adequate protection. This provision threw the responsibility for the protection of property on the local community. Many people would agree that such protection is the primary concern of local police officers. If the local police force is capable of providing such protection, it is undesirable for the federal government to exercise its authority in labor disputes. Most labor-management disputes have a local setting. It appears that local control of the matter will advance the long-run cause of industrial relations harmony. Local police officers frequently know personally the people involved in the dispute. Such law enforcement officers, as a result of this personal relationship, can frequently contain violence by resort to mere moral suasion. However, provided the other requirements of Norris–La Guardia are satisfied, federal courts may issue injunctions in labor disputes when local protection of property is lacking.

Elimination of the Blanket Injunction.   Previous discussion revealed that one of the most flagrant abuses growing out of labor injunctions involved the blanket injunction. The chief characteristic of this abuse relates to the all-inclusive scope of the court order. Courts enjoined lawful as well as unlawful acts and directed injunctions at people not committing unlawful acts as well as those engaging in such conduct. The blanket injunction resulted from the courts' utilization of catchall phrases. Unions found that the task of winning labor disputes was made difficult, if not impossible, when they were confronted with the blanket injunction.

Authors of Norris–La Guardia took these considerations into account when the provisions of the law were written. To eliminate the blanket injunction, the law required that all injunctions issued by federal courts had to be specific in their terminology. Persons or organizations enjoined in the carrying out of unlawful conduct had to be specified by name. This provision eliminated the use of the typical ambiguous phrase, frequently found in the labor injunction before Norris–La Guardia: "all other persons whomsoever." In addition, the federal courts now had to state clearly the unlawful acts to be enjoined. Thus, the law required that the labor injunction prohibit only "specific acts as may be expressedly complained of in the bill of complaint filed" as a result of a labor dispute. This standard eliminated the catchall phrase: "in any way interfering with the operation of the complainant's business." Such vague clauses were frequently contained in injunctions issued prior to the passage of Norris–La Guardia. The law recognized that in the course of some labor disputes, some actions of unionists and their sympathizers might be unlawful while others might be lawful. The purpose of requiring specific wording by courts in injunctions was to eliminate only the performance of illegal conduct. The requirement for specific terminology applied equally to the temporary restraining order and the temporary or permanent injunction.

Promotion of the Collective Bargaining Process.   Norris–La Guardia rests on the assumption that labor peace can best be achieved through the acceptance in good faith of the collective bargaining process. This feature of the law is best exemplified by its provision denying parties to a labor dispute the opportunity to obtain injunctive relief unless all possibilities of settling their controversies through collective bargaining have been exhausted. In short, the law places the primary responsibility for achieving industrial peace on management and labor. The equity powers of the judiciary are not available to any party to a labor dispute if the court finds that the party has not made reasonable efforts to settle the dispute by direct negotiation. When direct negotiation fails, the disputants are expected to make use, whenever appropriate, of mediation and voluntary arbitration.[13] Good faith in collective bargaining must further be demonstrated by the willingness of the parties to comply with any law controlling the collective bargaining process. For example, a union does not qualify for injunctive relief if it has violated legislation regulating the collective bargaining process. Although labor unions make few applications for injunctions, the fact remains that a labor organization cannot avail itself of the advantages of the equity power of the judiciary when facts indicate that it has not complied with a law applicable to a labor dispute. Under Taft-Hartley, for instance, it is an unfair labor practice for a labor union to refuse to bargain collectively. If a union fails to fulfill this responsibility, the federal courts must act unfavorably on its application for equity relief.

Few people will find fault with this requirement of Norris–La Guardia. It is unwise to make available injunctive relief when facts indicate that the applicant has violated a law applicable to the labor dispute. Successful collective bargaining requires an honest attempt by both sides to reach a peaceful agreement. If any party to a labor dispute fails to bargain in good faith or refuses to comply with laws bearing on the collective bargaining process, it appears reasonable to deny to this party injunctive relief.

Violations of Injunctions.   Two significant innovations for contempt of court proceedings are found in Norris–La Guardia. If a person is charged with contempt of court, the accused has the right to a "speedy trial and public trial by an impartial jury." Previously, it was pointed out that persons charged with contempt before Norris–La Guardia had no right to a jury trial. Such a procedure meant that the same judge who issued an injunction had the power to decide whether that injunction had been violated and what the punishment should be. In many cases, judges abused this prerogative and imposed penalties on highly questionable grounds. Particular abuse resulted when judges were biased against trade unions. After Norris–La Guardia was passed, a person charged with violation of a labor injunction could be tried by a jury of his or her peers. Such an opportunity is denied defendants in a labor injunction proceeding when contempt is committed in the presence of the court or so near thereto as to interfere directly with the administration of justice. But a person charged with contempt of court can request a change of judge if demand for the withdrawal of the judge is made prior to the hearing on the contempt proceeding. Upon the demand for the retirement of a judge, the judge must withdraw from the case and another judge must be designated to conduct the proceeding. Obviously, this provision was inserted in the Norris–La Guardia Act to eliminate from contempt proceedings a judge possessing a strong antiunion bias. Persons charged with the violation of a labor injunction had no such privilege before Norris–La Guardia was passed.

JUDICIAL CONSTRUCTION OF NORRIS–LA GUARDIA

Historical evidence demonstrated that when the equity power of the courts was exercised in labor disputes, the power of government was on the side of employers. Norris–La Guardia was passed to eliminate this condition. By freeing certain union practices from the impact of the injunction and by regulating closely the procedure of issuing injunctions, Congress implemented its desire to neutralize the influence of the courts in labor-management controversies. Despite the law's clear terms, the judicial interpretation of the Norris–La Guardia Act was awaited with high interest, particularly by organized labor and employers. Both were aware of the possibility that the judiciary might nullify the second attempt of Congress to regulate the use of injunctions in labor disputes.

The first indication of the judicial fate of Norris–La Guardia involved the Supreme Court's construction of the Wisconsin anti-injunction law. In 1931, Wisconsin enacted an injunction law that foreshadowed Norris–La Guardia. In many respects, the Wisconsin law was similar to the federal anti-injunction measure. The terms of the state law were just as protective of labor unions as were those subsequently contained in Norris–La Guardia. Consequently, what the Supreme Court had to say about the Wisconsin law would be applicable to Norris–La Guardia. If the Court found the state law unconstitutional, or interpreted it in a manner that would drastically reduce its applicability, the same fate would be in store for the federal anti-injunction law. If, on the other hand, the high court upheld the constitutionality of the Wisconsin law and construed its terms in a liberal manner, the supporters of the federal law would be encouraged.

In addition, the character of the construction of the Wisconsin law would influence profoundly the effectiveness and progress of state anti-injunction laws. Passage of the Norris–La Guardia Act encouraged many state legislatures to enact laws patterned after the federal statute. If the high court treated the Wisconsin law unfavorably, these state laws would be rendered useless. Other states that might have been inclined to enact anti-injunction laws would be discouraged by an adverse construction of the Wisconsin statute. Thus, from the state and federal point of view, the nation awaited with deep interest the Supreme Court construction of the Wisconsin anti-injunction law.

The Tile-Laying Industry Case

The Wisconsin law was tested in 1937 in a case involving the tile-laying industry of Milwaukee.[14] For many years this industry had been in a depressed condition. Lack of building operations had resulted in serious unemployment among tile layers. Severe competition also added to the problems of the industry. Some of the workers of the industry were organized and others were not. Labor standards in the unionized section were higher than those prevailing in the nonunion portion. To protect the union worker, the Tile Layers Union had insisted that each employer with whom it had a contract employ only members of the union. In addition, the union required that no employer work on the job. This requirement was embodied in the following clause contained in each agreement:

> ARTICLE III. It is definitely understood that no individual, member of a partnership, or corporation engaged in the Tile Contracting Business shall work with the tools or act as Helper but that the installation of material . . . shall be done by journeymen members of the Tile Layers Union Local #5.

Obviously, the objective of the prohibition was to provide more jobs for union members. Widespread unemployment among tile layers and the fact that the tile-laying industry contained many employers who hired only a small number of employees induced the union to adopt a program to increase job opportunities for its members. A Mr. Senn became involved in a dispute with the union over the restriction contained in Article III.

Senn was in the contracting business in Milwaukee. His operations were very small. At peak seasons, he employed only two journey tile layers and two helpers. He worked along with his employees and performed on-the-job work normally done by a journey tile layer or helper. The union wanted Senn to become a union contractor, and requested that he sign an agreement that would deny him the opportunity to work personally on the job. He claimed that he would execute a union agreement provided that Article III did not appear in the agreement.

As expected, the union refused such a request. It pointed out the reasons for Article III and further declared that the granting of Senn's request would discriminate against all contractors who signed agreements that included Article III. Since the union could not grant Senn's request, he refused to sign the agreement or to allow his small shop to be unionized. As a result of his refusal, the union picketed his place of business. According to the record, the picketing was peaceful and was conducted without violence. The objective of the picketing was to persuade the public to cease doing business with Senn and to encourage the people of Milwaukee to take their business to employers under contract with the labor union.

The Wisconsin Anti-Injunction law, the statute in question, operated to protect the picketing activities of the union. Senn sought an injunction from the state courts to enjoin further picketing. He claimed that the picketing was injuring his business and that the objective of the union—to require him to refrain from working with his own hands—was unlawful. The state courts of Wisconsin refused his request, pointing to the provisions of the Wisconsin statute forbidding the courts to issue injunctions to enjoin peaceful picketing. Not content with the decision of the state court, Senn appealed his case to the Supreme Court of the United States. He claimed that the Wisconsin law was unconstitutional on the ground that it deprived him of his property without due process of law. As such, the charge against the Wisconsin statute duplicated the one leveled against the Arizona anti-injunction law, which had been held unconstitutional in *Truax* v. *Corrigan.*

By a 5–4 vote, the Supreme Court upheld the constitutionality of the Wisconsin law. Brandeis delivered the majority opinion of the Court. He pointed out that the end sought by the union was not malicious or unlawful, for the union rule was reasonable and "adopted by the defendant out of the necessities of employment within the industry and for the protection of themselves as workers and craftsmen in the industry." Brandeis conceded that the disclosure of the existence of the labor dispute by the union might be annoying to Senn. But, he declared, "such annoyance, like that often suffered from publicity in other connections, is not an invasion of the liberty guaranteed by the Constitution. Unions may request by picketing that the public withhold patronage from an employer 'unfair to organized labor' and bestow it on unionized firms." Brandeis showed the similarity of such union picketing to the advertisements of merchants who compete with one another by means of the press, by circulars, or by window displays. If the latter form of advertising does not violate the Constitution, Brandeis believed that a union publicity campaign, carried on peacefully and truthfully, was likewise lawful.

Other arguments were presented by Brandeis to support the Court's position. Both members of the union and Senn had the right to strive to earn a living. Senn sought to do so through exercise of his individual skill and planning. It was not unlawful if workers by combination sought the same objective. The union did not desire to injure Senn, but the picketing was carried on to "acquaint the public with the facts, and, by gaining its support, to induce Senn to unionize his shop." Brandeis pointed out that Senn had the equal opportunity to "disclose the facts in such manner and in such detail as he deemed desirable, and on the strength of the facts to seek the patronage of the public." In any event, if the effect of the picketing prevented Senn from securing jobs, there was no invasion of constitutional rights, for "a hoped-for job is not properly guaranteed by the Constitution."

Since the means of the union and the end it sought did not violate the Constitution, the Supreme Court held that the Wisconsin law that insulated the union activities from the injunction did not deprive Senn of his property without due process of law. In this connection, Brandeis declared, "If the end sought by the unions is not forbidden by the Federal constitution the state may authorize working men to seek to attain it by combining as pickets, just as it permits corporations and employers to combine in other ways to attain their desired economic ends." The *Senn* decision marked a significant change in attitude on the part of the Supreme Court. Workers could take effective action to achieve their economic objectives. Such a program was not unlawful merely because it inter-fered with the right to run a business. Not only business people could organize for their mutual protection, but workers likewise could join in association and undertake action designed to implement the objectives of their associations. The *Senn* decision, which reflected the Brandeis philosophy, stands as a landmark in industrial relations law. It was the forerunner of a long line of court decisions that constructed a more favorable climate for the operation of effective collective bargaining.

The *Lauf* Doctrine: Wide Application of Norris–La Guardia Assured

One year after the *Senn* decision, the Supreme Court decided the fate of Norris–La Guardia. For a time it appeared that the federal judiciary would repeat the Clayton Act performance and destroy the effectiveness of Norris–La Guardia. In spite of the unmistakable intent and written mandate of Congress, the lower federal courts held that the terms of the Norris–La Guardia Act did not apply to labor disputes when the disputants did not stand in a proximate relationship of employer and employee. Such an interpretation, wholly inconsistent with the terms of the law, if sustained by the Supreme Court, would have destroyed the effectiveness of Norris–La Guardia. It would have allowed a wide basis for the issuance of the labor injunction. The result would have been a nullification of the second attempt of Congress to provide labor unions with a measure of relief from the restraining hand of the judiciary.

For these reasons, all interested parties awaited the Supreme Court's rul-ing in the *Lauf* case with deep interest.[15] Like the tile-laying case, the locale was Milwaukee. Unlike that case, however, the industry was the retail meat markets of the city. The company in the dispute operated five meat markets. About thirty-five employees worked in them. None belonged to Local No. 73 of the AFL Butchers Union, the labor organization in question. The labor union attempted to organize the five stores. The union conducted an extensive picketing program, the objective of which was to condemn the company in the public's eyes as unfair to organized labor. Previously, the company had refused the union demand to compel its workers to join the union as a condition of employment. It contended that its employees had their "own association and were perfectly well satisfied." There was speculation that the company had sponsored the inside union with the objective of keeping it out of a nationally affiliated labor organization.

In any event, the picketing continued, and subsequently the lower federal courts enjoined all picketing activities of the Butchers Union. The terms of the injunction provided that the union and its members were forbidden from (1) in any way picketing the premises of the complainant; (2) advertising, stating, or pretending that the complainant was in any way unfair to said defendants or organized labor generally; and (3) persuading or soliciting any customers or prospective customers of the said complainant to cease patronizing the complainant at its meat market.[16] As noted, the lower federal courts issued the injunction on the ground that the pickets were not employees of the company.

If the Supreme Court had sustained the injunction, Norris–La Guardia would not have afforded much protection to labor unions conducting organizing campaigns. Unions grow through the organization of the unorganized. The job of organizing a nonunion plant is at times very difficult. For this reason, experienced representatives of established international unions frequently spearhead organizational campaigns. Such international representatives are not actual employees of the plants that are being organized. For this reason, the lower federal courts that handled the *Lauf* case enjoined these representatives' activities. It follows from such a doctrine that nationally affiliated unions would not have been able to organize a nonunion area or a plant in which a company-dominated union is operating. Under such a construction of Norris–La Guardia, the public policy expressed in the statute—encouragement of the collective bargaining process—could not have been implemented.

The Supreme Court refused to sustain the ruling of the lower federal courts. It found that a labor dispute existed in the *Lauf* case, even though the disputants did not stand in proximate relationship of employer and employee. Such an interpretation is demanded by the terms of Norris–La Guardia. The members of the Butchers Union had a real economic interest in the outcome of the organizational drive of the nonunion retail meat markets. Higher labor standards prevailing in the union shops were imperiled to the extent that nonunion shops operated. If the Butchers Union did not organize each nonunion shop, it could be expected that union stores, once their collective bargaining contracts expired, would resist the execution of new ones, claiming inability to meet nonunion competition. As a result of these considerations, the Supreme Court held that a labor dispute within the meaning of Norris–La Guardia existed. Since the controversy constituted a labor dispute, the high court ordered dissolved the injunction which restrained the picketing. The Butchers Union was free to picket the nonunion meat markets even though they had no members working in the shops.

The *Lauf* decision affirmed the power of Congress to define and limit the jurisdiction of the federal courts. It demonstrated that Norris–La Guardia was to apply to a wide area of industrial relations. Unions were to be protected in their activities regardless of whether the disputants were in the proximate relationship of employer and employee. The *Lauf* decision served to emphasize the fact that the way was clear for Congress to regulate the collective bargaining process.

The New Negro Alliance: Elasticity of Norris–La Guardia Demonstrated

For the terms of the Norris–La Guardia Act to be applicable, a controversy must grow out of a dispute concerning the terms or conditions of employment, or be concerned with the association or representation of workers for collective bargaining. It is apparent that the protective features of the statute are in operation when there are disputes over wages, hours, working conditions, and the like. A short time after the *Lauf* decision, however, the Supreme Court applied the Norris–La Guardia Act to a controversy that in its technical sense involved neither conditions of employment nor the organization of employees for collective bargaining. The dispute grew from the desire of black people for better treatment with respect to employment opportunities.

Washington, D.C., the nation's capital, was the locale of the dispute involving the application of the Norris–La Guardia Act to a group of black people who attempted to improve their employment opportunities. The Sanitary Grocery Company had opened a branch store in a section of Washington populated by black people. The company refused to employ them in this particular outlet, as well as in other branch stores patronized by black persons. Such discriminatory tactics brought an organized protest from the black community of Washington. The protest issued from the New Negro Alliance, a corporation organized by black people for the advancement and improvement of its members and for the promotion of educational, civic, and charitable enterprises. The Alliance demanded from the Sanitary Grocery Company that it abandon its anti-black policy. It requested that in the normal course of labor turnover, the company employ black persons in the new branch store and others patronized chiefly by black people. The company refused to agree to these requests. As a result, the New Negro Alliance implemented a picketing campaign calculated to depress the business of the company. Workers patrolled in front of the company's stores carrying signs that read: "Do Your Part! Buy Where You Can Work! No Negroes Employed Here!"

A federal district court enjoined all picketing by the Alliance on the ground that there was no labor dispute within the meaning of the Norris–La Guardia Act. Later a circuit court of appeals sustained the decision of the district court. The New Negro Alliance appealed the case to the Supreme Court, claiming that the terms of Norris–La Guardia protected the activities of the Alliance from the injunction. In a split decision, the Supreme Court reversed the decision of the lower court and agreed with the Alliance that its picketing activities were protected by the Norris–La Guardia Act.[17] The minority of the Court, composed of McReynolds and Butler, contended that this was a racial, not a labor, dispute. In addition, they agreed with the lower court that (1) there was no employer-employee relationship; (2) the Alliance was not a trade union but a social organization; (3) the controversy was not a labor dispute within the meaning of Norris–La Guardia, for the Alliance was not attempting to negotiate terms of employment (it was only attempting to substitute black for white labor); and (4) if the Alliance were allowed to picket in this circumstance, its members might picket any private home in which white and non-black servants were employed.

The majority opinion of the Court rested on Section 13 of Norris–La Guardia. It was argued that the "labor dispute" section covered controversies between persons seeking employment and employers, and that the law applied equally when the objective of a dispute was to improve the conditions of workers through the collective bargaining process or to promote employment opportunities for a racial group. As a result of this construction of Norris–La Guardia, the Supreme Court ordered that the injunction against picketing activities of the New Negro Alliance be dissolved.

THE IMPACT OF NORRIS–La GUARDIA

Approval by the Supreme Court of Norris–La Guardia checked the use of the federal labor injunction. The action of the high court also stimulated the passage of state labor injunction control legislation. By 1967, twenty-five states and Puerto Rico had enacted injunction control legislation.[18] The state statutes vary, but all have similarities to Norris–La Guardia. On the other hand, the other twenty-five states have not yet enacted any law regulating the use of the labor injunction. It is likely that labor injunction procedures in these states have improved because of the existence of the federal law. However, the fact remains that the absence of state injunction control legislation provides the springboard for court intervention in labor disputes. Experience has conclusively demonstrated that such intervention has resulted in the placing of government on the side of employers in labor-management controversies. For example, some experience in Ohio indicates that the equity power of the state courts has proven harmful to the growth and effective operation of the collective bargaining process.[19]

If a great deal of labor violence had followed the Norris–La Guardia Act, the legislation would not have been effective. Some people were fearful that this condition would result from the passage of the statute. However, there is no evidence that more violence accompanied labor disputes after Norris–La Guardia than took place before this law was passed. As a matter of fact, some of the U.S.'s most bloody strikes, such as Pullman and Homestead, occurred before 1932. It is noteworthy that in England, labor violence has been less extensive than in the United States. This remains true even though the use of the labor injunction in Great Britain has been comparatively infrequent. It must be emphasized that violence is unlawful with or without injunctions. Overturning of automobiles, beatings, damage to machinery, and the like are not less unlawful because of the nonexistence of the injunction. On the other hand, as remarked previously, it is doubtful that an injunction will prevent violence if workers are bent on it.

One must be careful to distinguish between the violence of labor disputes and the use of organized labor's economic weapons. Implementation of the strike, picketing, and the boycott do not signify labor violence. In fact, Norris–La Guardia was passed to free these normal expressions of collective action from the restraining hand of the judiciary. The point of importance is that the anti-injunction law has not encouraged the carrying out of these trade union functions within a context of lawlessness and violence.

Nor should one point to the growth of the union movement as grounds for the condemnation of Norris–La Guardia. Indeed, the statute was passed to promote the union movement and collective bargaining. By regulating the use of the injunction in labor disputes, Norris–La Guardia provided a legal environment favorable to the growth of the union movement. One may quarrel with the objective of the law, but one scarcely can criticize the legislation because it has accomplished its goal. It is extremely doubtful that the growth of the union movement could have taken place in the absence of an effective law controlling the use of injunctions in labor disputes.

SUMMARY

The Great Depression of the thirties resulted in a profound change in the climate of social thought about the place of unions in contemporary society. As a result, Congress and some state governments passed legislation to provide a more favorable legal structure for the operation of unionism. The Norris–La Guardia Act was the first expression of this new legislative policy. It served to neutralize the power of the courts in labor disputes by regulating the substance and procedure of the labor injunction. Whereas the Clayton Act was interpreted into ineffectiveness by the Supreme Court, Norris–La Guardia was treated favorably by the courts. This was expected, because the judiciary could not very well isolate itself from the forces of social thought.

Congress justified Norris–La Guardia by pointing to the need for collective bargaining in modern society. Since the abuse of the labor injunction operated to forestall unionism, it was proper to pass legislation to deprive employers of the opportunity to utilize the judiciary as an ally in labor-management disputes. The effect of Norris–La Guardia was to provide unions with a larger area in which to carry on their activities without interference by the courts. As such, the law conferred no new rights on workers. It merely neutralized the federal courts in labor disputes. The Supreme Court has been diligent in carrying out the congressional intent even in cases where it considered justice would have been better served by deviation from that intent.

The passage of Norris–La Guardia served to implement its basic objective: the containment of the influence of the courts in labor disputes. Among other things, it deprived the federal courts of the power to enforce the yellow-dog contract; denied them the right to enjoin peaceful and truthful picketing regardless of the purpose of the picketing; forbade courts to enjoin peaceful strikes regardless of the purpose of the strike; and established a carefully drawn-up procedure to regulate the issuance of the injunction in labor disputes when the law did not forbid the instrument. Some states passed "little" Norris–La Guardia acts to protect workers not covered by the national statute.

DISCUSSION QUESTIONS

1. What impact did the Supreme Court's rule regarding Wisconsin's anti-injunction law have on the various states in their attempts to control use of the labor injunction?

2. How did the Supreme Court construct Section 20 of the Clayton Act, and what effect did that have on unions?

3. What was the intent of Congress in the passage of the Norris–La Guardia Act?

4. Explain how Norris–La Guardia dealt with the following issues:

a. court neutrality in labor disputes

b. definition of a labor dispute

c. yellow-dog contracts.

Were important court decisions overturned by Congress in these categories?

5. Congress placed procedural limitations on court issuance of injunctions. When could the courts use injunctions in labor cases under these procedural restrictions?

6. Demonstrate, with reference to appropriate court cases, how the Supreme Court interpreted the Norris–La Guardia Act?

7. How might the provisions of Norris–LaGuardia be applied to nonlabor organizations? Is there adequate court authority to provide an answer to this question?

NOTES

1   Florence Peterson, *American Labor Unions* (New York: Harper & Brothers, 1935), p. 56.

2   Edwin E. Witte, *The Government in Labor Disputes* (New York: McGraw-Hill Book Company, 1932), pp. 270–273.

3   See Appendix B for the exact language of Section 20.

4   These states were Oregon, North Dakota, Utah, Washington, and Wisconsin.

5   *American Steel Foundries* v. *Tri-City Central Trades Council,* 257 U.S. 312 (1921).

6   *Truax* v. *Corrigan,* 257 U.S. 312 (1921).

7   The Fourteenth Amendment to the Constitution states: "Nor shall any State deprive any person of life, liberty, or property, without due process of law; nor deny to any person within its jurisdiction the equal protection of the laws."

8   Benjamin J. Taylor, *Arizona Labor Relations Law* (Tempe: Arizona State University, Occasional Paper No. 2, Bureau of Business and Economic Research, College of Business Administration, 1967), pp. 14–15.

9   For an interesting and stimulating account of the life of Louis Dembitz Brandeis, see A. T. Mason, *Brandeis: A Free Man's Life* (New York: The Viking Press, 1946). On the life of Oliver Wendell Holmes, Jr., see Silas Bent, *Justice Oliver Wendell Holmes* (New York: Vanguard Press, 1932).

10   See Chapter 6 for a discussion of the importance of the concept of labor dispute established in Norris–La Guardia relative to the application of antitrust laws to labor activities. Section 13 of Norris–La Guardia spells out the meaning of "labor dispute." See text of Norris–La Guardia in Appendix C for the exact language of Section 13.

11   *Marriott Corp.* v. *Great America Service Trades Council,* AFL-CIO, No. 76–1453 (CA7, 1977).

12   See, for example, *Carpenters and Joiners Union* v. *Ritter's Cafe,* 315 U.S. 722 (1942). The *Ritter* case is discussed in Chapter 19. The principle of the case is that picketing must

be confined to the industry in which the labor dispute has arisen if the picketing is to be protected from the labor injunction.

13   The nature of arbitration is discussed in Chapter 15.

14   *Senn* v. *Tile Layers,* 301 U.S. 468 (1937).

15   *Lauf* v. *Shinner & Company,* 303 U.S. 323 (1938).

16   Harry A. Millis and Royal E. Montgomery, *Organized Labor* (New York: McGraw-Hill Book Company, 1945), p. 624.

17   *New Negro Alliance* v. *Sanitary Grocery Company,* 303 U.S. 552 (1938). However, in 1950, the Supreme Court upheld a decision of the California Supreme Court that enjoined racial picketing, in *Hughes* v. *Superior Court of California,* U.S. Supreme Court, May 8, 1950. The 1950 decision does not per se overrule the *New Negro Alliance* doctrine because the California case involved the state judiciary. In the *New Negro Alliance* case, the issue centered on the right of the federal courts to enjoin racial picketing. Still, it must be conceded that the 1950 decision represented a wide departure from the principles that the Supreme Court established in the *New Negro Alliance.*

18   United States Department of Labor, *Growth of Labor Law in the United States* (Washington, D.C.: U.S. Government Printing Office, 1967), p. 207.

19   Glenn W. Miller, *American Labor and the Government* (Englewood Cliffs, N.J.: Prentice-Hall, Inc., 1948), pp. 107, 112.

CHAPTER SIX

ANTITRUST PROSECUTION SINCE NORRIS–LA GUARDIA

NORRIS–LA GUARDIA AND LABOR PROTECTION

Norris–La Guardia did more than curb the labor injunction. It served to restrict labor union prosecution under the antitrust laws. Although the terms "Sherman Act" or "antitrust laws" do not appear in Norris–La Guardia, the background of the law reveals that this was the unmistakable intention of Congress. It was enacted to provide unions with the benefits they had hoped for under the Clayton Act. On this score the authors of the statute declared, "The purpose of the bill is to protect the right of labor in the same manner the Congress intended when it enacted the Clayton Act, which act, by reason of its construction and application by the Federal Courts, is ineffectual to accomplish the Congressional intent."[1] Along the same lines, the Supreme Court subsequently affirmed that "the Norris–La Guardia Act was a disapproval of *Duplex Printing Press* v. *Deering* and *Bedford Cut Stone Company* v. *Journeymen Stone Cutters Association* as the authoritative interpretation of Section 20 of the Clayton Act."[2] Thus, the Norris–La Guardia Act granted protection to labor unions from the application of the Sherman Act. How did Norris–La Guardia accomplish this purpose? How did the Supreme Court react to this new effort of Congress? What recent developments indicate a possible change in direction on the part of the Court regarding the extent of permissible union action in the pursuit of its own interests?

LABOR DISPUTE DEFINED BROADLY IN NORRIS–LA GUARDIA

In writing Norris–La Guardia, Congress remedied the labor provisions of the Clayton Act. Section 20[3] of the latter statute prohibited the federal courts from restraining certain activities of unions growing out of a labor dispute. However, in the Clayton Act, Congress failed to define the meaning of *labor dispute.* The judiciary was obliged to define the term. The character of the construction was of paramount importance, for the labor dispute definition determined the practical effects of the Clayton Act. Thus an activity of a union growing out of a labor dispute could not be enjoined. But the very same activity—say, peaceful picketing or an orderly strike—not arising out of a labor dispute was subject to the injunction.[4] The concept of a labor dispute had particular importance for unions involved in antitrust proceedings. The last sentence of Section 20 provided that an activity of a labor union immunized by the statute could not be held to constitute a violation of any law of the United States. For practical purposes, this meant that where Section 20 protects a union activity from a labor injunction, the federal judiciary may not find such conduct to be a violation of any law of the United States, including the Sherman Act. On the other hand, this immunity does not apply when the act of the labor organization does not arise out of a labor dispute as that term has meaning for the purposes of the Clayton Act.

In the *Duplex* decision, it was necessary for the Supreme Court to construe the meaning of labor dispute. Much to the disappointment of organized labor, the Court defined the concept in a very narrow fashion. It held that for a labor controversy to fall within the meaning of a labor dispute for purposes of the Clayton Act, the parties to the dispute had to stand in proximate relationship of employer and employee. It will be recalled that with the exception of the *Coronado* affair, the major antitrust cases resulting in legal setbacks to organized labor centered on secondary boycotts. In a secondary boycott, a union exerts pressure against employers who have no direct controversy with the organization. Labor organizations have often exerted pressure on other firms for the purpose of winning their dispute with the employer with whom the union is embroiled in a controversy. Such was the logic of the secondary boycott activities instigated by unions in the *Danbury Hatters, Bucks Stove, Duplex,* and *Bedford Stone* affairs.

Organized labor hoped the Clayton Act would be interpreted to forbid the issuance of an injunction to restrain secondary boycott picketing. The courts would then have been required to hold that the secondary economic pressure of unions did not violate any federal law, including the Sherman Act. These hopes were not realized; the high court excluded union secondary pressure activities from the protection of Section 20 because the parties to the controversy did not stand in proximate relationship of employer and employee. The limitations in Section 20, the Court said, applied only to disputants in a labor controversy "who are proximately and substantially concerned as parties to an actual dispute respecting the terms or conditions of their own employment, past, present, or prospective." The Court refused to protect union activity directed against firms "wholly unconnected" with a company with which a union has a dispute over conditions of employment except "in the way of purchasing its products in the ordinary course of interstate commerce."

Brandeis vigorously denounced this point of view of the majority of the Supreme Court. He argued that the fundamental purpose of the Clayton Act was to broaden the legitimate area of union activities. Brandeis felt that Section 20 of the Clayton Act protected a secondary boycott from the injunction, and hence from the application of the Sherman Act, for "a statute of the United States declares the right of industrial combatants to push their struggle to the limit of the justification of self interest."

The authors of Norris–La Guardia were well aware of the various constructions placed on the term *labor dispute* by the judiciary. In the absence of legislative action, labor unions could not engage in secondary economic pressure activities, for the parties involved in such disputes do not stand in a proximate relationship of employer and employee. The task of Congress was to write a definition of labor dispute that would nullify the effect of the *Duplex* decision. It was necessary to spell out the concept in a manner that would legalize union secondary boycott activities. To accomplish this objective, Norris–La Guardia defined a labor dispute as any controversy concerning conditions of employment, regardless of whether the disputants stand in proximate relationship of employee and employer.

JUDICIAL REACTION

In spite of the clear terms of Norris–La Guardia, organized labor was fearful that the courts would find some way to nullify the intent of Congress. Union leaders remembered the fate of the Clayton Act. Court construction would determine whether or not the new law was to provide benefits to labor unions. For these reasons, the judicial construction of the law was awaited with much interest. The Supreme Court of the United States interpreted the Norris–La Guardia Act so as to conform with the intent of Congress. Its terms were broad enough, the Court held, to forbid the issuance of labor injunctions to restrain union secondary pressure tactics.

This principle was first established in the *Milk Wagon Drivers Union* case in 1940, and reaffirmed the next year in the more widely known *Hutcheson* decision. The members of the Milk Wagon Drivers Union, an American Federation of Labor affiliate, handled the bulk of the home milk deliveries in Chicago. With the advent of the depression, however, the "vendor system" of milk distribution was established. Under this depression-stimulated method, vendors purchased milk from nonunion dairies and sold the product to retail stores. As a result, the stores were able to sell milk at a price below that prevailing for milk delivered at home. To complicate the whole affair, the vendors organized themselves into a CIO union, but this feature of interunion rivalry did not influence the subsequent decision of the Supreme Court. The members of the Milk Wagon Drivers Union picketed the retail stores that handled milk under the new milk distribution method.

The action of the Milk Wagon Drivers Union constituted a secondary boycott, for pressure was placed on the retail stores not to deal with the vendors, with the intent of encouraging the vendors not to purchase milk from nonunion dairies. Interstate commerce was involved because the Chicago milk area included the state of Wisconsin. After a federal district court refused to enjoin the action of the labor organization, an appeal was made to the Seventh Circuit Court of Appeals.[5] This court reversed the district court and held that the AFL union, by engaging in a secondary boycott, violated the terms of the Sherman Act. Finally, the Supreme Court, in a unanimous decision, held that Norris–La Guardia protected the action of the AFL union, for the union was engaged in a labor dispute within the meaning of the law.[6]

In the *Hutcheson* case, Norris–La Guardia was once more interpreted in a manner that protected union secondary boycott activities.[7] In this matter, an interunion jurisdictional problem was involved. It centered on a controversy involving the United Brotherhood of Carpenters and Joiners of America and the International Association of Machinists. Both these labor organizations were affiliated with the AFL at the time of the conflict. The dispute was over the issue of which of these unions was to install and dismantle machinery in the Anheuser-Busch property in St. Louis.

When the Machinists Union was awarded the job by the company, the Carpenters Union called a strike, picketed the plant, and refused to permit its members to work on new construction taking place on Anheuser-Busch property. In addition, through letters and labor journals, the union called upon its members and friends to refrain from purchasing or selling Anheuser-Busch beer. In a split decision, three jurists dissenting, the Supreme Court held that the action of the Carpenters Union was protected by Norris–La Guardia. Despite the fact that the secondary boycott grew out of a jurisdictional dispute between two unions, the high court held that the terms of Norris–La Guardia were applicable. The controversy was a labor dispute within the meaning of the Act, and for this reason the federal courts were not permitted to restrain the activities of the labor organizations. Not only did the term *labor dispute* include controversies between an employer and his or her own employees, but the term was elastic enough to prohibit prosecution of a union involved in an interunion jurisdictional dispute.

Roberts wrote the dissenting opinion in the *Hutcheson* case contending that Norris–La Guardia did not preclude the application of the Sherman Act to union secondary boycott action. His position was that even though Norris–La Guardia might serve to protect unions against injunctions in such controversies, the union could be sued for damages or tried under the criminal provisions of the Sherman Act. It will be recalled that the Sherman Act provided for its enforcement along three lines—injunction, damage suits, and criminal prosecution. According to Roberts, the fact that the injunction might be prohibited in labor cases did not mean that the other two methods of enforcement could not be employed. He declared that what a reading of the [Norris–La Guardia] Act makes letter clear, is that the prosecution of actions for damages authorized by the Sherman Act, and of the criminal offenses denounced by the Act, are not touched by the Norris–La Guardia Act. By a process of construction never, as I think, heretofore indulged by this court, it is now found that, because Congress forbade the issuing of injunctions to restrain certain conduct, it intended to repeal the provisions of the Sherman Act authorizing actions at law and criminal prosecutions for the commission of torts and crimes defined by the antitrust laws.

Roberts' viewpoint, though on the surface tenable, appears wholly inconsistent with the intent of Norris–La Guardia. It is doubtful that Congress meant to restrain the issuance of injunctions in labor cases arising under the Sherman Act, only to permit unions to be attacked through damage suits and criminal prosecution. If the position of Roberts had prevailed, unions would have lost whatever benefits Congress had intended them to have from the operation of Norris–La Guardia in antitrust cases. Also, the law would have protected secondary boycott activities from the labor injunction, but the government or employers could have proceeded against unions engaging in such conduct by initiating damage suits or criminal prosecutions under the Sherman Act.

The viewpoint of Roberts was brushed aside by the majority of the Court as constituting an erroneous interpretation of the Norris–La Guardia Act. Frankfurter, the jurist who wrote the majority opinion of the Court, contended that Norris–La Guardia reasserted the purpose of the Clayton Act and broadened its terms. If the judiciary had not interpreted the Clayton Act so as to immunize labor union secondary boycott activities, Congress, by expanding the concept of labor dispute in the Norris–La Guardia Act, had certainly meant to forbid the courts to enjoin such union conduct. If a secondary boycott could no longer be enjoined under the Norris–La Guardia Act, such an activity must not violate any law of the United States, including the Sherman Act. Frankfurter pointed out that Section 20 of the Clayton Act immunizes labor unions from prosecution under any federal law when the judiciary may not restrain the conduct of the labor union by the labor injunction. Finally, Frankfurter challenged the view of Roberts that unions could still be subject to damage suits and criminal proceedings under the Sherman Act, even though Norris–La Guardia forbids the issuance of injunctions to restrain a particular pattern of union conduct. On this score, Frankfurter declared:

Congress expressed this national policy and determined the bounds of a labor dispute in an act explicitly dealing with the further withdrawal of injunctions in labor controversies. But to argue, as it was urged before us, that the *Duplex* case still governs for purposes of a criminal prosecution is to say that that which on the equity side of the court is allowable conduct may in a criminal proceeding become the road to prison. It would be strange indeed that although neither the Government nor Anheuser-Busch could have sought an injunction against the act here challenged, the elaborate efforts to permit such conduct failed to prevent criminal liability punishable with imprisonment and heavy fines.

THE APEX DOCTRINE NULLIFIES EFFECT
OF CORONADO DECISION

Organized labor was permitted by the principles affirmed in the *Hutcheson* and *Milk Wagon Drivers Union* cases to undertake economic activities to expand the area of collective bargaining. Doctrines established by the Supreme Court in the *Danbury Hatters, Bucks Stove, Duplex,* and *Bedford Stone* cases were swept away by the impact of Norris–La Guardia. Only the *Coronado* cases appeared as a threat to labor unions in their Sherman Act relationship. In these cases, it will be recalled, the Supreme Court held that a labor union violated the antitrust provisions when it engaged in a strike, the effect and intent of which was to reduce the amount of goods in interstate commerce.

In 1940 the Supreme Court decided the *Apex* case,[8] a proceeding that in many respects duplicated the *Coronado* affair. Similar to the *Coronado* case, a great deal of violence surrounded the strike directed against the Apex Company of Philadelphia. The strike also had the effect of reducing the amount of nonunion goods in interstate commerce. The Apex Company engaged in the manufacture of hosiery, producing annually merchandise valued at approximately $5 million. It shipped in interstate commerce about 80 percent of its finished product. The company operated a nonunion shop, and in April 1937 the hosiery workers' union demanded that the firm recognize the labor organization as the bargaining agent of its workers and employ only union members.

On May 6, 1937, about a month after the company refused to agree to the union's demands, members of the hosiery workers' union employed in the Apex plant, along with other members of the union employed in other hosiery factories in Philadelphia, gathered at the factory. Once more, the union officers demanded that the company operate the plant on a union basis. When this last ultimatum was refused, the officers of the union declared a sit-down strike. Beyond causing damage to plant and machinery, the union prevented the shipment of 130,000 dozen pairs of finished hosiery, of a value of about $800,000. Evidence proved that about 80 percent of this merchandise was scheduled for shipment outside the state of Pennsylvania. The company sued the union under the Sherman Act provisions and a trial court awarded it damages of $237,310. The trial judge, utilizing his prerogative under the antitrust provisions, trebled this figure to a sum exceeding $700,000. In 1940, after extensive litigation in the lower federal court, the case was finally reviewed by the Supreme Court.

The *Apex* decision was awaited with deep interest. After the district court had awarded the Apex Company approximately $700,000 damages, a wave of similar damage suits against labor unions was instituted under the Sherman Act. Professor E. B. McNatt stated:

Two days after the Federal District Court awarded the $711,932 to the Apex Company in Philadelphia, three New England trucking companies filed an antitrust action against the International Brotherhood of Teamsters, asking for $90,000 damages resulting from a strike. And a few weeks later, on May 22, the Republic Steel Corporation filed a similar suit against the CIO and some 700 individuals asking for $7,500,000 treble damages under the Sherman Act for injuries suffered as a result of the Little Steel strike of 1937.[9]

In addition to deciding the outcome for these and other damage suits, the *Apex* decision would determine whether or not the Court would reaffirm the *Coronado* doctrine in a period of "liberalism." Would the Supreme Court, despite the enactment of legislation to encourage collective bargaining, utilize the Sherman Act to outlaw strikes carried out to force companies to recognize and bargain with labor unions?

The issue in the *Apex* case was not whether the action of the union was lawful. As indicated, the Supreme Court spoke of the conduct of the unionists in terms of "lawless invasion of petitioner's plant and destruction of its property by force and violence of the most brutal and wanton character." Clearly, the union's conduct was unlawful. The state courts undoubtedly would have served as a forum in which the union could have been sued for damages. However, the company chose to sue the union for damages under the Sherman Act. Consequently, a fundamental question of the *Apex* case was whether violence made the Sherman Act applicable to a labor dispute, when, in the absence of violence, the statute would not have been applicable. The Supreme Court replied in the negative, for "restraints not within the [Sherman] Act when achieved by peaceful means are not brought within its sweep merely because, without other differences, they are attended by violence."

With this question clarified, the Court then proceeded to determine whether the Apex strike constituted restraint of trade within the meaning of the Sherman Act. Again the Court reached a negative conclusion and ordered the suit against the union dismissed. To support this decision, it declared that labor unions to function effectively must eliminate nonunion competition, and that action undertaken to achieve this objective does not violate the Sherman Act. The Court ruled that the intent of a labor union to eliminate nonunion competition by collective economic action did not violate the Sherman Act since "an elimination of price competition based on differences in labor standards is the objective of any national labor organization. But this effect in competition has not been considered to be the kind of curtailment of price competition prohibited by the Sherman Act."

In addition, the Court declared lawful for purposes of the Sherman Act strikes that have the effect of suppressing the amount of goods in commerce. Labor unions intend to stop production when they strike. Stoppage of production and a strike are one and the same thing. If a firm is engaged in interstate commerce, the amount of such commerce during the strike is reduced. Unions strike, however, not to reduce deliberately the amount of goods in commerce or to influence their price, but to win disputes with companies. As the Supreme Court declared in the *Apex* case, if the lawfulness of strikes resulting in a diminution to commerce were questioned, the Sherman Act would threaten the legality of "practically every strike in modern industry."

Thus the effect of the *Apex* decision was to destroy the doctrine established in the *Coronado* cases. In this connection, it is noteworthy that even though the circumstances of *Apex* and *Coronado* were strikingly similar, the Supreme Court ruled on the action of the hosiery union without specifically overruling the *Coronado* doctrine. Even so, the *Apex* case established the principle that a strike, the effect and the intent of which is to reduce the goods in commerce, does not violate the Sherman Act, provided the strike is carried out for the purpose of furthering the interests of the labor organization.

The position of the Supreme Court in the 1940–1941 antitrust labor cases improved the legal position of organized bargaining agencies. The judiciary no longer utilized the Sherman Act to block organizing activities of unions. Secondary boycotts were deemed lawful, and the antitrust provisions no longer threatened the legality of major strikes undertaken to enforce demands against employers. On the other hand, labor unions were still subject to prosecution under the Sherman Act. In the *Apex* case, the Court reaffirmed the principle that the antitrust statutes do apply to labor organizations. In this connection, it was stated that for thirty-two years, the Court in its efforts to determine the true meaning and application of the Sherman Act had held that its terms "do enclose to some extent and in some circumstances labor unions and their activities."

At present, however, the Sherman Act outlaws union activities only when labor organizations combine with business groups to promote monopoly, and it is illegal for a contractor that the union has no interest in organizing to agree with a labor organization to boycott nonunion subcontractors that the union does have an interest in organizing.[10] The application of this rule is subject to interpretive change, as we shall see later in this chapter. The principle was emphasized in 1945 when the Supreme Court handed down its decision in the *Allen Bradley Company* case.[11] Local No. 3, affiliated with the International Brotherhood of Electrical Workers (AFL), had jurisdiction covering workers engaged in the manufacture of electrical equipment and in the installation of electrical products. Contractors operating in New York City had agreed not to purchase electrical equipment from suppliers not under contract with Local No. 3. This meant that electrical product manufacturers outside of the city were excluded from a profitable market. On their part, manufacturers agreed not to sell electrical products to any contractor unless the contractor employed members of Local No. 3.

After a time, the combination among the three groups proved highly successful to all concerned. The business of New York City electrical manufacturers increased sharply since they did not face any out-of-city competition. Jobs were available for members of Local No. 3 and their wages increased through the tripartite arrangement. Contractors likewise benefited from the arrangement. The effect of the arrangement is further indicated by the fact that the New York manufacturers sold their goods in the protected city market at one price and sold identical goods outside of New York City at a far lower price. All parties to the arrangement thereby benefited. But the tripartite agreement caused much hardship to the consuming public, to those electrical manufacturers denied the opportunity to sell in the New York market, and to electrical workers outside the city.

Such an arrangement, the Court held, violated the Sherman Act. It stated that "Congress never intended that unions could, consistent with the Sherman Act, aid nonlabor groups to create business monopolies and to control the mobility of goods and services." However, it is important to note that if the labor union alone, by strike or boycott, accomplished the same results, the Sherman Act would not be applicable. Thus one jurist of the Court stated, "If the union in this instance had acted alone in self-interest, resulting in a restraint of interstate trade, the Sherman Act concededly would be inapplicable." The violation of the law occurred when the union, manufacturers, and contractors of New York City combined to exclude from use in the city electrical equipment manufactured outside the city of New York. The *Allen Bradley* doctrine did not overrule the principles established in the *Hutcheson* and *Apex* decisions. Unions are free from prosecution under the Sherman Act, provided the Court is convinced that their activities are carried out for the sole purpose of advancing their own interests. The crime of the union in the *Allen Bradley* case was to combine with nonlabor groups for the purpose of monopolizing markets and effecting profits.

LABOR UNIONS AND THE SHERMAN ACT: PRESENT APPLICATION

Additional labor cases before the Supreme Court highlight the broadening of the zone in which labor organizations can apparently violate the Sherman Act. A new era of interpretation of labor union liabilities under the antitrust statutes appears to be developing. Two opinions were handed down on the same day, June 7, 1965, dealing with (1) limitations placed on the marketing hours of employers' products (*Jewel Tea* case)[12] and (2) industry elimination of small employers (*Pennington* cases).[13] A third case *(Connell)* involved using a contractor whom unions had no intent to organize, to get at subcontractors for organizational purposes.[14]

The *Jewel Tea* Case

In the *Jewel Tea* case, collective bargaining negotiations involved a multiemployer association. The 1957 negotiations concluded with the signing of a pact by employers other than Jewel Tea and the National Tea Company to refrain from selling meat between the hours of 6:00 P.M. and 9:00 A.M. Jewel Tea contended that it signed the contract under duress of a union strike.

Jewel Tea brought suit in July 1958, seeking invalidation of the agreement under Sections 1 and 2 of the Sherman Act. It argued that the employer association and union had agreed among themselves that all collective bargaining agreements would contain the same provisions. Further, the company contended it was placed under the duress of a strike vote, since the rest of the industry had signed with the union. It argued that this amounted to a conspiracy to force agreement that meat would not be sold between 6:00 P.M. and 9:00 A.M., with or without union members working. Jewel Tea argued that it had been given no choice in the matter, since a strike would have hampered its competitive position within the region. A federal district court ruled that the union had only acted in its own self-interest, since the record was devoid of evidence of a conspiracy. The court of appeals, however, reversed the trial court and ruled that the agreement was a conspiracy whether it was called an agreement or a contract.

Upon review, the U.S. Supreme Court upheld the trial court, reversing the court of appeals. In a three-way split among the Justices, it held that the parties were required to bargain on subjects intimately tied to wages, hours, and working conditions. The antitrust exemptions applied, since the union action to limit marketing hours had been undertaken in the union's own self-interest. The Court reviewed the history of bargaining in the industry to arrive at its decision. Historically, the union had bargained on both working hours and operation hours of companies. It was reasoned that operations that continued beyond the agreed-upon working hours of union members would require someone other than union members to serve customers. Even if a self-service market was involved, union workers would be required to carry a heavier burden during working hours because of the increased demand to clean the work areas and package meat.

Justice Douglas entered a vigorous dissenting opinion. He argued that the collective bargaining agreement itself was clear proof of a conspiracy between the union and employers to restrain operations in the product market. He saw no difference between an agreement to sell at fixed prices and one to limit the hours during which a store could market its products. In his opinion, the *Allen Bradley* case had foreclosed the expansive view of labor exemption from the antitrust provisions. It was not necessary to review the bargaining history of the industry or to look at the effect that expanding marketing hours to between 6:00 P.M. and 9:00 A.M. would have on the work standards of union members. In effect, he reasoned that any agreement that employers could not make between themselves under antitrust, could not be justified by the existence of a collective bargaining agreement.

The *Pennington* Case

The *Pennington* case was decided by the Supreme Court on June 7, 1965, the same day as the *Jewel Tea* decision. It involved an antitrust suit for treble damages by a small coal-mining employer whose argument stemmed from the National Coal Wage Agreement of 1950. Prior to 1950, the industry had been notorious for its frequent strikes and the government seizure of mines. Relative peace was brought to the industry when the pact was signed in 1950.

An amendment to the 1950 agreement was negotiated in 1958 whereby company signatories agreed to pay 80 cents per ton on each ton acquired if the required 40 cents per ton had not already been paid into the United Mine Workers (UMW) Welfare and Retirement Fund. This clause was to discourage the leasing of coal fields to firms operating under wage standards inferior to those established by collective bargaining. But Pennington argued that the UMW had collusively agreed to support mechanization of the large mines and to impose the terms of the wage agreement on all mines without regard to ability to pay. As support, the plaintiff identified the large investment outlays the union made to mechanize some of the mines.

Additionally, the UMW was accused of prevailing upon the Secretary of Labor to influence a prevailing wage determination under the Walsh-Healey Act that would eliminate small operators from supplying coal to the Tennessee Valley Authority (TVA). It was argued that the small operators could not effectively enter competitive bids if they were forced to pay prevailing union wage rates.

When some of the operators failed to meet their payments to the Welfare Fund, the UMW brought suit for violation of the wage agreement. Several small firms retaliated by bringing suit against the UMW for entering into a conspiracy with the large operators to settle the general problem of overproduction by eliminating the marginal firms.

The Supreme Court upon review remanded the case for retrial in a federal district court in accordance with its decision on the case. It held that not every agreement arising out of collective provisions was exempt from the Sherman Act provisions merely because it involved a mandatory subject for bargaining. Exemption could not be claimed "when it is clearly shown that it [the union] has agreed with one set of employers to impose a certain wage scale on other bargaining units." This position was justified by holding that such an agreement restricted the freedom of unions to "respond to each bargaining situation as the individual circumstance might warrant." Justice White, in a footnote to his opinion for the Court, remarked that a union, if acting unilaterally, could seek to impose uniform wage standards on the entire industry even if it suspected that some marginal operators could not compete if required to pay the union scale. The mere act of attempting to impose a uniform wage standard was not sufficient evidence to uphold a union-employer conspiracy charge. The intent to eliminate marginal firms had to be supported by specific and concrete evidence.

Justice Douglas, in a concurring opinion joined in by two other justices, interpreted the Court's opinion as meaning that an industry-wide collective bargaining agreement was obvious evidence of the existence of a conspiracy with no further investigation required. He also wrote that a union could not agree on a wage scale in excess of the ability of some employers to pay when such agreement was for the purpose of forcing some of them out of business.

Retrial in Tennessee District Court

The 1965 retrial provided the guidelines within which the U.S. district court was required to solve the mining cases. The trial court reviewed the entire history of bargaining in the bituminous coal industry, similar to the *Jewel Tea* review, including the possibility of collusion on TVA bids to determine whether the UMW was guilty of Sherman Act violations. It was found that the union was not in violation of the antitrust law. The trial court held on the basis of the *Hutcheson* case that a union, if acting alone and not in concert with nonlabor groups, was not in violation of the antitrust act. The concurring opinion of Justice Douglas was construed to mean that, to be found illegal, the wage agreement had to exceed the ability of some firms to pay, and even then it had to be made expressly for the purpose of putting some employers out of business. Also, the union investment in some companies did not in itself show collusive bidding. The trial court was convinced that the bids entered by the large companies were justified on the basis of productivity gains. Several studies have verified the validity of this position.[15]

Another Court's View

In 1968, two small coal operators sued the United Mine Workers in a federal district court, charging they could not operate profitably under the terms of a contract imposed on them by the union and Bituminous Coal Operators Association. A jury decided that the UMW had engaged in a conspiracy and intended to contract with the two small companies only on the terms provided in the national agreement. Thus, it was held that the union had forfeited its exemption under the Sherman Act. Triple damages were awarded in the amount of $1,432,500 for one company and $67,500 for the other.

The decision was upheld by a federal appeals court. Unfavorable union treatment in the appellate court prompted the UMW to appeal to the U.S. Supreme Court. Review was denied without comment.

The trial court's action makes it clear that UMW's motives were considered to be different from those of the 1965 case. The jury was convinced that the union had combined with an association of companies to prevent effective competition from a third party.

"Clear Proof" Not Required

The Supreme Court took another run at the antitrust implication of the 1950 Coal Agreement in *Ramsey* v. *Mineworkers*,[16] which was decided in 1971. In this case, the high court took the position that union antitrust liability did not require the meeting of the standard of "clear proof" that is clearly specified in the Norris–La Guardia Act, but required only that parties making a complaint establish their case by a preponderance of the evidence. The Norris–La Guardia Act required that no union shall be liable for acts of its officers who violated the antitrust laws, except on "clear proof" of the officers' "actual participation in or actual authorization of, such acts." In this respect, then, the standard of proof requirement to find unions in violation of the antitrust statutes had been eased.

Eighteen small coal mine operators in Tennessee filed suit in federal district court alleging UMW violation of the Sherman Act. It was charged that the UMW had agreed not to oppose mine mechanization and that, in turn, the large producers with whom the union dealt had agreed to give wage increases and to make royalty payments to the union welfare fund. Basically, the charge was that there was a conspiracy with the large operators to drive the small unmechanized mines out of business by forcing them to pay wages and other benefits that they could not afford. The 1958 Protective Wage Clause Amendment to the 1950 Soft Coal Wage Agreement required the UMW not to enter into wage agreements applicable to employees covered by the contract on any basis other than those specified in the contract. In other words, the agreement was that the union would not permit other employers to sign a collective bargaining agreement with the UMW on terms different from those agreed to by the multiemployer group. The employer group constituted the larger mechanized operators in the industry.

The federal district court in Chattanooga, Tennessee, dismissed the suit. In doing so, the judge interpreted the 1958 amendment in the context of Norris–La Guardia Act language. He decided that the law required "clear proof" not only that UMW officers had actually participated in writing the amendment, but also that the amendment itself constituted a violation of the Sherman Act. In the decision, the judge remarked that under the "preponderance of the evidence" rule that is applied to most antitrust cases, the UMW had implied agreement to an illegal conspiracy, but that when the "clear proof" standard was applied, the UMW was not held to be liable under the antitrust laws. The trial court's opinion was affirmed by an appellate court.

The Supreme Court agreed to review the case. It held that the lower court was in error and remanded the case for retrial. The majority opinion was that the lower courts "read far too much" into the Norris–La Guardia Act's "clear proof" standard, which applies only to showing that union officers had authority to perform allegedly illegal acts. The acts themselves are to be judged on the preponderance of the evidence rule.

Justice Douglas, in dissent, was of the opinion that Congress intended that the "clear proof" standard should be applied broadly in antitrust suits dealing with the unions, and that because the majority of the Court did not agree, their opinion amounted to a drastic rewriting of a part of the Norris–La Guardia Act.

The retrial held later in 1971 resulted in the trial judge instructing the jury that while the agreement between the UMW and the major operators was not in itself illegal, the agreement would on its face be a violation of the Sherman Act if the jury found proof that the agreement had been entered into with the intent of driving some coal mine operators out of business, or with the knowledge that it would have that effect.

The jury returned a "guilty" verdict requiring the UMW and one large company to pay triple damages. The lower court's decision was upheld by an appellate court, and a request for review before the United States Supreme Court was refused without comment. The union and company had asked the high court to decide the ultimate question of whether an agreement is on its face illegal when a union and an employer or group of employers agree to a basic contract that requires the union to insist on the same terms in its negotiations with other employers that have been imposed on the signatory employers.

The *Connell* Case

The *Connell* case, in 1975, involved an employer signing an agreement to subcontract its plumbing and mechanical work only to employers with whom the union had a contract. The contract was signed under protest, and the employer went to federal court to request an injunction to halt enforcement of the agreement on the ground that it was in violation of the antitrust laws. In a 5–4 decision, the Court overruled the Fifth Circuit Court of Appeals, rejecting the NLRB's position that the agreement was not subject to federal antitrust laws. The Court's majority held that the contract constituted a "direct restraint of the business market [with] substantial anti-competitive effects, both actual and potential, that would not follow naturally from the elimination of competition over wages and working conditions." Even the construction industry proviso to Section 8 (e) of the National Labor Relations Act did not privilege the agreement, because, the Court held, the "proviso extended only to agreements in the context of collective bargaining relationships and possibly to common-situs relationships on particular job sites as well."

A key factor in the 5–4 decision was the union's lack of desire to represent the general contractor's employees. The Court then charged the lower courts to decide whether the arrangement violated the antitrust laws. It does not appear that the agreement in *Connell* would have prompted the Court to rule as it did if the union had had an interest in Connell's employees.

Jou–Jou Designs Exemption

A federal appeals court in New York ruled in 1981 that Congress had sanctioned different rules for the garment and construction industries by permitting the use of subcontracting agreements as an organizational weapon.[17] Collective bargaining contracts do not have to exist in order to make the parties exempt from antitrust laws. The actual practice before the court was as follows: a jobber had agreed to farm out garments to shops that were represented by a certain union; the favored shops processed the garments and returned them to the jobber for sale to retailers. The important feature of the rule was that collective bargaining contracts were found unnecessary to exempt the parties from antitrust charges.

CONSEQUENCES OF SUPREME COURT ACTION

The *Allen Bradley* case had made it clear that unions could not act "in combination with non-labor groups" to influence the product market prohibited businesses through the antitrust laws. Unions, therefore, had restrictions placed on their favored Norris–La Guardia Act positions.

The *Pennington* case narrowed the assumption contained in *Allen Bradley* that any union wage agreement with employers was exempt from antitrust. *Pen-*

nington provided that a union could legally agree with an employer or group of employers on wages, hours, and other terms and conditions of employment. However, those agreements are still subject to antitrust prosecution if the union agrees to impose those same provisions on other employers. The trial court left to the jury a question of fact of whether the actual purpose of the national union contract was in fact to drive small producers from the market.

Jewel Tea opened the gate to antitrust action against unions a little wider. The Court held that a jury's or judge's findings of fact could impose antitrust liability on unions, even though the issue involved was one that unions might reasonably believe to be a proper subject for bargaining.

The *Connell* case attacked a previously acceptable and legal union organizing tactic, bringing court surveillance of union organizing activity within the context of the antitrust laws. If a union was not trying to organize a contractor, the Court found in *Connell,* it could compel him to boycott subcontractors that the union desired to organize.

A considerable amount of uncertainty has been thrust upon the legality of multiemployer bargaining because of these Supreme Court rulings. The most serious consequence is that the high court in particular has served notice that the judiciary is going to determine the motives of the parties to collective agreements on subjects of mandatory bargaining. The vigorous dissent of Justice Goldberg in *Pennington* indicates that the judiciary may once again be moving in the direction of setting up its own socioeconomic philosophies over the congressional intent of how collective bargaining should work.

It is possible for both juries and trial judges to determine the motives of unions in seeking uniform contracts throughout an industry by imposing their own philosophies on whether a union acts unilaterally or in collusion with an employer group. To some, mere discussion at the bargaining table of the possible competitive effect of a wage package may be sufficient to prove the existence of a conspiracy. The development of such an application would in effect place the collective bargaining process in approximately the same state in which it existed prior to Norris–La Guardia. It has already been explained that unions do attempt to standardize wage settlements throughout an entire industry. Such a condition has generally accompanied successful union organization in several industries, one of which is coal. Although the UMW has had only limited success in such efforts, it does make continued bids to standardize agreements throughout the areas it represents. Widening the area of judicial action might seriously hinder this UMW effort.

Another possible consequence of these cases is that the collective bargaining process itself could be put in danger. Guy Farmer, former chair of the National Labor Relations Board, "reported that between 80 and 100 percent of the workers covered by union contracts" in several industries are under multiemployer contracts.[18] The concurring opinion of Justice Douglas indicated that both unions and employers are liable when restraint-of-trade violations grow out of such agreements. If the one is found in violation, then the other cannot expect to escape. It is possible that employers will resist entering into multiemployer agreements with unions if marginal firms are permitted to resist signing agreements by bringing charges of collusion in the courts and collecting treble damages levied against both unions and large employers. Such a development would endanger the entire collective bargaining process. As mentioned, unions cannot organize successfully in the absence of a wage standard that they seek to impose on all units in a particular competitive sphere. In *Charles D. Bonanno Linen Service,* a 1982 case, the U.S. Supreme Court supported this union objective. In a 5–4 decision, it held that an employer could not withdraw from a multiemployer bargaining unit because an impasse had occurred at the bargaining table. To permit a unilateral employer withdrawal at that time, the Court reasoned, would "herald the demise of multi-employer bargaining."

The task is to fashion legislation that will protect the interest of the public without endangering the ability of labor unions to act as effective collective bargaining agents. The vehicle to accomplish this worthwhile objective should be in the form of new and proper labor legislation. As a matter of fact, Congress adopted this procedure when it amended the National Labor Relations Act in 1947 and 1959. It has been suggested that measures to amend the existing labor laws dealing with union abuses in the product market may lose support. It is argued that Congress is unlikely to proceed if the Court deals firmly with the subjects of their debate. It may be that political expediency would be furthered by a lack of legislative action if the felt abuses are cleared away by new antitrust applications in the federal courts.

SUMMARY

Other than curbing the labor injunction, Norris–La Guardia at first relieved labor unions from prosecution under the antitrust laws. To accomplish this objective, Congress defined the term *labor dispute* in a very broad fashion. It did this to overcome the basic shortcoming of the Clayton Act. Congress had failed to define the term in that law, and the Supreme Court had thence construed the meaning of labor dispute in a way that deprived unions of any protection in antitrust suits.

Some people felt, however, that the Supreme Court would nullify Norris–La Guardia, so that the position of organized labor would be no better than it was before the Act's passage. These fears proved groundless, for in the *Apex* and *Hutcheson* cases, the Court broadly construed Norris–La Guardia, providing unions with the opportunity to engage in activities calculated to effectuate the collective bargaining process.

Although Norris–LaGuardia legalized union tactics formerly held objectionable under the antitrust laws, the Supreme Court in the *Allen Bradley* decision found that the Sherman Act still applied to unions when they conspired with employers to monopolize markets. Cases decided since 1965 have broadened the base of the antitrust laws so as to cover a wider area of labor activities. A great deal of uncertainty and speculation as to the eventual effect of these decisions has been generated. It seems very possible that the judiciary will take on an expanded role in determining how collective bargaining will work, at least in industries covered by multiemployer contracts.

DISCUSSION QUESTIONS

1. The judiciary was required to define the meaning of labor dispute contained in Section 20 of the Clayton Act. What was the judicial response to the congressional definition provided in Norris–La Guardia?

2. Compare the Supreme Court's *Apex* decision of 1940 to its *Coronado* rule. What standard of union conduct was established by *Apex,* and how durable has it been?

3. Did *Allen Bradley* alter *Apex* standards in any way? Do you agree with the *Allen Bradley* decision? Why or why not?

4. Does the Court permit too much latitude in labor cases as evidenced by its tolerance in the *Jewel Tea* case? Why or why not?

5. Review the facts surrounding the *Pennington* case. Did the Court's decision in *Pennington* constitute a narrowing of its vision in *Apex,* or do you think the decision was consistent with *Apex* and subsequent cases including *Jewel Tea?*

6. With the *Ramsey* v. *Mineworkers* case in mind, do you think the Court's understanding of union responsibility in the labor market is realistic? Support your position with historical and legal facts concerning the responsibilities of unions under collective bargaining.

7. What changes, if any, could be made by labor law amendments to provide more realistic coverage of unions under antitrust legislation? Include in your answer an assessment of union economic power.

NOTES

1   House of Representatives, *Document No. 669,* 72d Congress, 1st sess., p. 3.

2   *United States* v. *Hutcheson,* 321 U.S. 219 (1941).

3   Section 20, Clayton Act, reads as follows: "That no restraining order or injunction shall be granted by any court of the United States, or a judge or the judges thereof, in any case between an employer and employees, or between employers and employees, or between employees, or between persons employed and persons seeking employment, involving, or growing out of, a dispute concerning terms or conditions of employment, unless necessary to prevent irreparable injury to property, or to a property right, of the party making the application, for which injury there is no adequate remedy at law, and such property or property right must be described with particularity in the application, which must be in writing and sworn to by the applicant or by his agent or attorney.

"And no such restraining order or injunction shall prohibit any person or persons, whether singly or in concert, from terminating any relation of employment, or from ceasing to perform any work or labor or from recommending, advising or persuading others by peaceful means so to do; or from attending at any place where any such person or persons may lawfully be, for the purpose of peacefully obtaining or communicating information, or from peacefully persuading any person to work or to abstain from working; or from ceasing to patronize or to employ any party to such dispute, or recommending, advising, or persuading others by peaceful and lawful means so to do; or from paying or giving to, or withholding from, any person engaged in such dispute, any strike benefits or other moneys or things of value; or from peaceably assembling in a lawful manner, and for lawful purposes; or from doing any act or thing which might lawfully be done in the absence of such dispute by any party thereto; nor shall any of the acts specified in this paragraph be considered or held to be violations of any law of the United States."

4   *American Federation of Musicians* v. *Stein*, 218 F. (2d) 679 (1954); cert. denied 348 U.S. 873 (1955).

5   *Milk Wagon Drivers Union* v. *Lake Valley Farm Products*, 108 Fed. (2d) 436 (1939).

6   *Milk Wagon Drivers Union* v. *Lake Valley Farm Products*, 311 U.S. 91 (1940).

7   *Hutcheson, op. cit.*

8   *Apex Hosiery Company* v. *Leader*, 310 U.S. 409 (1940).

9   E. B. McNatt, "Labor Again Menaced by the Sherman Act," *The Southern Economic Journal*, VI, 2 (October 1939), p. 208.

10   *Connell Construction Co., Inc.* v. *Plumbers, Local 100, Plumbers and Steamfitters*, 421 U.S. 616 (1975).

11   *Allen Bradley Company* v. *Local Union No. 3, IBEW*, 325 U.S. 797 (1945).

12   *Local Union 189, Amalgamated Meat Cutters and Butcher Workmen of North America, AFL-CIO* v. *Jewel Tea Company Inc.*, 381 U.S. 676 (1965).

13   *United Mine Workers of America* v. *James M. Pennington*, 381 U.S. 657 (1965); *Pennington* v. *United Mine Workers*, 257 F. Supp. 815 (1966).

14   *Connell Construction Co., Inc., op. cit.* (1975).

15   See Carroll L. Christenson and Richard A. Myren, *Wage Policy Under the Walsh-Healey Public Contracts Act: A Critical Review* (Bloomington, Indiana: Indiana University Press, 1966), pp. 194–198.

16   *Ramsey* v. *Mineworkers*, U.S. Sup. Ct., No. 88 (February 24, 1971).

17   *Jou-Jou Designs, Inc.* v. *Garment Workers, ILGWU*, 643 F 2d 905 (1981).

18   John Scott and Edwin S. Rockefeller, *Antitrust and Trade Regulation Today; 1967*, (Washington, D.C.: The Bureau of National Affairs, Inc., 1967), p.43.

CHAPTER SEVEN

THE LOGIC OF
GOVERNMENT PROTECTION

THE PROBLEM

Commonwealth v. *Hunt* dissolved the identity between the conspiracy doctrine and the labor union. The decision established the lawfulness of labor organizations. However, by no means did the decision impose a respect for the right of workers to self-organization and collective bargaining. Workers were free to join labor unions, but there was no guarantee that they could exercise that right. In this connection, it should also be noted that Norris–La Guardia did not prevent interference with the collective bargaining rights of workers. The law restricted the power of courts in labor disputes, but set up no prohibition on their interfering with workers' rights to engage in collective bargaining activities.

If employers are free to utilize their superior economic strength to prevent the organization and operation of labor unions, the fact that workers have the legal right to self-organization and collective bargaining has little practical value. A right, to be meaningful, must be respected. A democratic system provides for the right to freedom of worship. But if this right were not respected, the right to that freedom would have little practical significance. The same principle applies to the field of industrial relations. Of what value to workers is their right to collective bargaining if they are not free to exercise that right? Should the evidence reveal that there have been practices calculated to prevent workers from the enjoyment of this right, it would appear logical that government should protect the right of workers to self-organization and collective bargaining. Just as government has taken positive action to prevent the nullification of other rights enjoyed by citizens of the nation, it would seem equally valid for government to protect the right of workers to collective bargaining. If, on the other hand, the record indicates that the right of workers to self-organization and collective bargaining has been respected, there is no occasion for government control.

Organs of government have declared that workers have the right to self-organization and collective bargaining. This recognition is grounded in the fact that labor unions fulfill a proper function in our economy. These considerations are underscored in a powerful statement made by former Chief Justice Taft:

> Labor unions are recognized . . . as legal when instituted for mutual help and lawfully carrying out their legitimate objects. They have long been thus recognized by the court. They were organized out of the necessities of the situation. A single employee was helpless in dealing with an employer. He was dependent on his daily wage for the maintenance of himself and family. If the employer refused to pay him the wages he thought fair, he was nevertheless unable to leave the employer and resist arbitrary and unfair treatment. Union was essential to give laborers an opportunity to deal on equality with their employer. They united to exert influence upon him and to leave him in a body in order by this inconvenience to induce him to make better terms with them. They were withholding their labor of economic value to make him pay what they thought it was worth. The right to combine for such a lawful purpose has in many years not been denied by any court.[1]

What remains to be seen is the extent to which the right of employees to self-organization and collective bargaining has been respected. Such an investigation must precede any recommendations for legislation calculated to protect this right of workers.

Several studies have dealt with efforts undertaken to forestall unionization of employees.[2] The most complete study dealing with antiunion tactics was conducted by the La Follette Committee. On June 6, 1936, Congress ordered a full-scale investigation of these antiunion techniques. Senator La Follette of Wisconsin headed the committee authorized to make the study. The committee published 14 volumes of testimony. It conducted 58 days of hearings, at which some 245 witnesses testified. The committee later published a series of summary documents, which organizes and makes more readable the mass of evidence collected at the hearings.[3] Its findings highlight the intensity and thoroughness with which the union movement was challenged.

Care was taken by the committee to insure the accuracy of its reports. In the hearings of the committee, all of which were open to the public, witnesses were summoned from every group having an interest in the proceedings. The committee was careful not to accept at face value testimony of questionable truthfulness unless it could be verified from other sources. Consequently, its findings appear to be of unquestionable accuracy. Space limitations render it impossible to make a thorough report of the group's investigation. However, this volume—and, particularly, this chapter—could not be complete unless some consideration were given to the work of the La Follette Committee. Accordingly, while highlighting the patterns of antiunion conduct, we will direct attention to its results. Under present labor laws, many of the antiunion tactics disclosed by the La Follette group are unlawful. This, however, does not render this investigation any less important. Appreciation of present public policy rests upon the understanding of the factors producing such control.

PATTERNS OF ANTIUNION CONDUCT: INDUSTRIAL ESPIONAGE

The La Follette Committee reported that industrial espionage was a common, if not universal, practice in American industry. The purpose of industrial espionage was to prevent the organization and operation of a labor union. The industrial spy centered his or her work in the local union. A chief function of the spy was to provide the company with the names of union members. In particular, the employer wanted to ascertain the names of the workers most active in the labor union. Such information provided the basis for discharging these workers or otherwise isolating them from other employees. That these lists were used to influence the results of organizing campaigns is underscored by the following testimony of a former member of the National Labor Relations Board:

> I have never listened to anything more tragically un-American than stories of the discharged employees of the Fruehauf Trailer Co., victims of a labor spy. More often men in the prime of life, of obvious character and courage, came before us to tell of the blows that had fallen on him for his crime of having joined a union. Here they were—family men with wives and children—on public relief, blacklisted from employment, so they claimed, in the city of Detroit, citizens whose only offense was that they ventured in the land of the free to organize as employees to improve their working conditions. Their reward, as workers who had given their best to their employer, was to be hunted down by a hired spy like the lowest of criminals, and thereafter tossed like useless metal on the scrap heap.[4]

To obtain membership data, the spy could attend union meetings. A more effective method consisted of election to some official position in the union, such as financial or recording secretary. In this capacity, the spy could learn of every applicant for membership. At times, gathering the names of union members proved difficult. But, as the La Follette Committee reported, "In this, his initial task, the spy must not fail. If need be, therefore, he will bribe janitors or custodians, rifle files or desks, and burglarize offices to secure access to union records."[5]

Obviously, the operation of the industrial spy impaired the effective operation of a labor union. Workers were fearful that participation in union affairs—even the attendance of union meetings—might cost them their jobs. The following bit of testimony highlights this:

> *Senator La Follette:* As a result of your experience, what would you say caused this fear of your organization when they became suspicious that a spy was in their midst?
>
> *Mr. Robertson* (a labor leader): Because they felt to have their membership in our organization known to the company would place their jobs in jeopardy.[6]

Spy D-11, who operated in a plant in Hopewell, Virginia, also pointed out how spy activities result in union disintegration. After the workers of the plant became aware of his operations, he claimed that most of the workers felt "they would get out of the union if they knew just how to go about it."[7]

Industrial spies could cause the destruction of labor unions in ways other than by ascertaining the names on union membership lists. Another effective method was to discredit union leaders in the eyes of the rank and file. A labor union's strength was sapped after the membership lost confidence in its officers. A classic example in this connection was the action of one spy who faked a photograph of the local union president leaning on the bar of a saloon and then preferred charges of drunkenness.[8] In another instance, a spy who managed election to the secretaryship of a local union affiliated with the International Association of Machinists brought charges of embezzlement of union funds against organizers of the union. Subsequently, the charges were proved to be false, but not until the local union had begun to disintegrate.[9] In addition, the spy might attack union officials on the basis of religion or nationality.

The industrial spy frequently assumed the role of an *agent provocateur*. In this role, "he incites the union to violence, preaches strikes, inflames the hot-headed and leads the union to disaster."[10] Many examples of this procedure are available. One spy sat in the meetings of the strike strategy committee of the Dodge Local of the United Automobile Workers in 1936 and urged the use of force and violence.[11] Another spy, operating in Kent, Ohio, in 1936, urged the unionists to dynamite a plant involved in a strike.[12] The strategy of these tactics, of course, was to goad the union into unlawful conduct, the effect being the stimulation of adverse public opinion, legal and military reprisal, and general disintegration of the labor union.

What was the source of supply of labor spies? A large number were furnished by private detective agencies. From 1933 to 1936, the Pinkerton Detective Agency claimed 309 industrial clients; Corporation Auxiliary Company, 499; National Corporation Service, 196; and the Burns Detective Agency, 440. Smaller detective agencies reported serving 497 clients. The La Follette Committee reports, "From motion-picture producers to steel makers, from hookless fasteners to automobiles, from small units to giant enterprises—scarcely an industry that is not fully represented in the list of clients of the detective agencies. Large corporations rely on spies. No firm is too small to employ them." [13] In the period 1933–1937, a total of $9,440,132.12 was expended by American firms to combat unions by means of industrial espionage and strikebreaking.[14]

Frequently, ordinary workers were trapped by detective agencies into spying on the union activities of their fellow workers. In spy jargon, such an individual was known as a "hooked man [*sic*]," an individual engaged in industrial espionage without knowledge that he was reporting to a detective agency or that his reports were going to an employer. Detective agency representatives who lured workers into spy activities were known as "hookers," and the process of entrapping workers to engage in spy activities was referred to as "hooking." Since most workers would refuse to spy on their fellow employees, the hooker used some pretext to induce a worker to write reports for the detective agency. The bait that the hooker usually used was money. A worker in financial difficulties would be an excellent prospect. The hooker might use a variety of pretexts to entrap an innocent worker. An outstanding example was the attempt of a representative of the Pinkerton Agency to hook the chairman of the grievance committee of a United Automobile Workers local. The representative posed as a federal officer to win the confidence of the worker. He asserted that he was an official of the government making an investigation of plant conditions.[15] Other hookers, to win the confidence of workers, posed as representatives of "minority stockholders," the "insurance setup," and the "financial house." One hooker even posed as a representative of a philanthropic agency that was working in the interests of the workers of the plant.

Employers' use of industrial spies was one factor that made government protection of the right to collective bargaining appear reasonable. After industrial espionage was outlawed, the professional detective agencies terminated such activities. For example, after the passage of the National Labor Relations Act, the Pinkerton Agency directed all its branch offices "to discontinue the furnishing of information to anyone concerning the lawful attempts of labor unions or employees to organize and bargain collectively, and not to undertake hereafter to furnish such information."[16] In addition, once industrial espionage was outlawed, the law was generally respected and its use declined. It is important to note, however, that spying terminated only after the passage of legislation. It is unlikely that industrial espionage would have ceased if it had not been outlawed.

PATTERNS OF ANTIUNION CONDUCT: ATTACK ON UNION LEADERSHIP

As in every other organization, the successful functioning of labor unions depends in large part on leadership. How well labor union officials carry out their tasks will determine the success or failure of the trade union. Union leaders must of necessity bear the major burden of organizing drives. They are likewise instrumental in the successful implementation of strikes. In short, union leaders are the driving force of the union movement. If union leadership could be coerced into inactivity, the labor organization itself would become functionless and in time would wither away. Repeated attacks against union leadership could destroy the leadership's effectiveness while discouraging others from assuming the role of the union leader.

The record is clear that union leaders have experienced both physical violence and intimidation. In addition, the record is equally clear that these individuals have been subjected to constant attacks against their character. The purpose of both of these approaches is to reduce the effectiveness of union leaders by frightening them into inactivity. Some people frighten more easily than others. This is as true of the union leader as of any other person. Consequently, it is difficult, if not impossible, to measure objectively the effect of the attacks on union leadership on the union movement. However, available evidence pointing up the character of the attacks would indicate that they have seriously retarded the progress of the union movement.

In Cleveland, on September 21, 1937, at about 11:45 P.M., Vincent Favorito approached his parked automobile. He had just attended a union council meeting. The purpose of the meeting was to deal with problems arising in the "Little Steel" strike of 1937. Before he reached his automobile, Favorito was attacked by three men. He described this attack as follows:

> As I was walking toward my car, approaching my car I was about five feet from it there, I turned off the sidewalk to go to my car which was facing north on West Tenth. The man that was on my right side, the man that was walking toward me, hit me with a blackjack on the back of my head and the fellow that was coming toward me from the back end of my car hit me on the face with a gun, and I felt the man in back of me grapple me by the neck and put his knee on my back, and immediately then something come into my mouth like a gag, we can call it a gag because it was a rag, and I couldn't say a peep; and I was held on both arms by these two men that evidently wanted to knock me out, and didn't do it, and we struggled there. I happened to get loose some way and I get this man here that was in back of me and I throws him over me, but he went right on top of me, and I happened to hit the ground, and him on top of me, and I held him there.
>
> I was afraid that if I would get kicked in the head that it would be the end of me. I held onto him, and while I was holding onto him these other blokes or thugs were hitting me, kicking me, and swearing. While this was going on they also kicked the fellow that was up on top of me and he happened to let go and I hollered. As I hollered my brother-in-law and my sister heard me and come to my rescue.[17]

On December 13, 1936, Charles Doyle, a member of the Steel Workers Organizing Committee, was attacked. The assault took place after Doyle attended a union meeting in the back room of Marie's Grill on South Park Avenue in Buffalo, New York. According to Doyle, he was pounced on by four men after he left the restaurant. He testified to the La Follette Committee that "someone hit me in the mouth from the front with his fist and immediately after that something hit me from behind, right on the ear at the side of the jaw."[18]

Testimony presented before the La Follette Committee also pointed up another attack in Cleveland against a union leader. This victim was Gerald Breads, an employee of the Otis Steel Company. Breads was active in organization work. His testimony is revealing:

> *Mr. Breads:* I was at the Bohemian National Hall on Broadway, I wouldn't know what number it was, it is right there at Pershing Road.
> *Senator La Follette:* When was that?
> *Mr. Breads:* That was on the night July 13, 1937. I had to go to work that night at 11 o'clock so I left that hall about 9 and another fellow by the name of Paul Chocky was with me. We started away from the hall to get the dinky that runs across the Clark Avenue Bridge, and just as we was going across Broadway—

Senator La Follette (interposing): Was this while the strike was on?

Mr. Breads: There was a car pulled away from the curb. I stepped in front of the car and got out in the streetcar tracks and I seen Dewey Jones and another fellow jumping in the car alongside.

Senator La Follette: Did you recognize the other man?

Mr. Breads: I couldn't; no. So I started through the gas station with the idea that if I got on the dinky they wouldn't follow me into there. I had an idea what was going to happen. Before I got to the dinky they had cut me off. Dewey Jones and the other fellow in the back seat jumped out and pulled revolvers on me.

One of them stuck one in the back of my neck and Jones was in front of me holding one in my stomach.

Well, words passed both ways, they called me names and I called them back, I guess, and I asked them what it was all about. They told me to never mind that I would get mine, that I would get what was coming to me, and they wanted to put me in the car and I said no. They tried to force me in the car and shoved me right against the car and the fellow who was riding in the back seat with Jones at the time the car stopped, he grabbed me and shoved me farther in. Then there was nothing I could do but get up on the seat. I don't know what route we took, or where we was, but I come to under the Clark Avenue Bridge, after I got bashed over the head a couple of times with a blackjack and revolver butt, and I was also hit on the arm too.[19]

Rough shadowing was also employed to intimidate union leadership. Rough shadowing was the practice of keeping union leaders under open surveillance. As such, the procedure differed from industrial espionage, which was surreptitious in character. The objective of rough shadowing was to instill fear in the minds of union leaders. It also served the purpose of creating fear in the minds of workers who might have wanted to talk to union leaders. Rough shadowing may have been carried on during strikes, but was most frequently employed during preparation for strikes. One organizer claimed he was followed wherever he went. Another testified that even his home was kept under surveillance. This latter individual, attempting to lose his "shadowers," moved his residence and even changed his name. But this defense measure was only temporarily successful. He testified as follows:

When we started our organizing campaign it was practically impossible to carry on any activity at the headquarters of our union. It was necessary to use our homes as secret places where workers would be able to gather for the purpose of discussing the organizational problems. I lived at the time on the West Side, and about a week after I became a member of the staff several carloads of Republic stool pigeons were parking at my house. They were there from 7 o'clock in the morning until about midnight and they had a special crew on some occasions that remained there overnight. I realized that my home cannot be used any more as a place where workers can be invited to come to talk about labor questions, so I had to move out of there. I also knew if I moved out of that place under my own name they would discover it just as soon. So I moved into another apartment under a different name, under "Stevens," and I was there about 2 weeks and these same people that were shadowing me before discovered the home where I lived and I had to move again, and from "Stevens" I stretched it to "Stevenson," and that is how I used that alias of "Stevenson" in order to make sure that my home will not be discovered.[20]

In addition to physical violence and intimidating tactics, union leaders endured attacks against their character. The purpose of such attacks was to break down the will of union leaders and to destroy the loyalty which connected the rank and file with union leadership. Nothing could be more damaging to a union than the discrediting of union leaders in the eyes of the membership. This objective could be achieved by the circulation of false rumors and stories about union leaders. As is well known, a rumor is difficult to combat. Attacks against the character of a labor leader might take many forms. He might be denounced as a "communist," "foreign element," "agitator," or "labor racketeer." During World War II, notices posted throughout one plant suggested that union organizers were a group of "intimidators" who threatened the "substitution of Nazi-ism for Americanism."[21] In another case, also taking advantage of the wartime environment, the assertion was made that a union was "backed by Germans," the intent being to discourage membership in the labor union.[22]

PATTERNS OF ANTIUNION CONDUCT: STRIKEBREAKING TACTICS

The purpose of strikebreaking was to destroy a union once it was formed. To carry out effective collective bargaining, a labor union must be able to strike successfully. Both the employer and the workers must be aware of this union capability. If a union cannot wage an effective strike, the employer need not pay much attention to its demands. Moreover, workers soon lose respect and interest in such an organization. This does not mean that unions should or do resort to the strike at every opportunity. Mature collective bargaining should diminish the need for industrial warfare. However, to function effectively at any stage of the collective bargaining process, a union must be capable of implementing an effective strike.

In light of these considerations, it should occasion no surprise to learn that employers bent on the destruction of a labor union utilized every possible tactic to break a strike. Crushing the strike dealt an irreparable blow to the labor union. This was particularly true where the issue in the strike was union recognition. Labor unions must first be recognized by employers as collective bargaining agencies before they can bargain collectively over economic issues. Since this is true, tactics were frequently calculated to break union-recognition strikes.

This section points up some procedures that have been used to destroy labor unions by crushing strikes. Again, it must be kept in mind that many, if not all, of these practices are now illegal. This fact, however, does not lessen the need for an analysis of strikebreaking procedures.

There are three major lines of approach to break strikes: (1) the fortification of a plant with munitions and private plant police, the latter hired not to protect property against theft, fire, and the like, but for the purpose of intimidating workers who would strike; (2) the hiring of professional strikebreakers; and (3) the breaking down of strikers' morale by instituting back-to-work movements.

A series of events that occurred in the spring of 1935 in Canton, Ohio, demonstrates the first procedure. The employees of a steel corporation had organized a labor union. The corporation refused to recognize or bargain with the representatives of the union. As a result, the union prepared to strike for recognition. Among other things, this strike illustrated the propensity of workers to resort to economic force when other efforts to gain recognition have failed. It also demonstrated the lack of a procedure to eliminate the need for those strikes called to force recognition of labor unions for collective bargaining purposes.

Aware of the imminence of the strike, the steel corporation made preparations to break it. The La Follette Committee describes the general character of these preparations as follows:

> The police department of [the] steel corporation reached the height of its activity during periods of union organization and in times of strike. As the first line of defense against labor organizations, it mobilized all the paraphernalia of military warfare. Manpower, munitions, and spies were all concentrated, deployed, and maneuvered with the objective of defeating organizing efforts, and of ambushing the union when it undertook the desperate step of calling a strike.[23]

More specific observations demonstrate the elaborate preparations for the strikebreaking. A few days before the strike, the corporation mobilized its plant police from other cities. Thus, fourteen men arrived from Buffalo; nineteen from Youngstown; one man from Chicago; twenty-five from Massillon; and twenty-one from Warren. The munitions arsenal of the corporation was also increased. A day or so before the strike, the corporation purchased sickening gas and gas equipment for $8,804.30.[24] In addition, the company laid in a supply of pipes cut to club length, shotguns, small arms, and tear gas.

This preparation for a strike by a corporation was not an isolated example. The La Follette Committee reported even more extensive preparations, including the setting up of floodlights, the erection of electrically charged barbed wire around plant boundaries, and the use of armored trucks for the transportation of strikebreakers through picket lines. In addition, a corporation aware of an impending strike might work the plant overtime to build up inventory. If the company could fill orders during the course of the strike, it had a better chance to break the work stoppage.

The use of professional strikebreakers figured prominently in the pattern of strikebreaking. There is a considerable difference between the professional strikebreaker and the worker who merely refuses to strike. Workers should have the right to refrain from participating in a strike. If a union calls a strike and some employees refuse to strike, their decision should be respected. Although these workers tend to break a strike, they certainly are not professional strikebreakers. Individuals in this latter category, the La Follette Committee reported, had been supplied by the same agencies furnishing industrial spies.[25] In many cases, the professional strikebreaker possessed a criminal record. Sam "Chowderhead" Cohen, a famous strikebreaker, commenting on his long criminal record, declared, "You see, in this line of work they never asked for no references."[26] The job of the professional strikebreaker was to smash picket lines, to give the appearance that the plant was operating, and to incite violence so that the public authorities would take action against the unionists. For example, the strikebreaker might burn paper in a plant furnace so that the smoke of the chimney would give the appearance of plant production. The driving of empty trucks to and from the plant for the same purpose might also be performed by the strikebreaker. Actually, the professional strikebreaker was frequently incapable of carrying out the actual production duties performed by the ordinary worker. Generally, strikebreakers would merely amuse themselves in the plant to while away the time.

The record shows that the professional strikebreaker frequently provoked violence during strikes. For this reason, these individuals were at times termed *agents provocateurs.* Unionists or strikers recall being spit at by such people. Stones were hurled into picket lines and other disorderly acts executed to incite the strikers to violence. If the strikers were goaded into violent action, the employer could then appeal to the public authorities. Frequently, arrests followed, jail sentences and fines were imposed, and in some cases the state militia or the National Guard were called to the scene of the strike. The presence of these groups was very demoralizing to the unionists. Moreover, action of public authorities against strikers condemned the unionists as lawbreakers in the eyes of the public.

Wages paid to strikebreakers ranged from $5 to $15 per day; at least, these were the wage levels at the time that the La Follette Committee conducted its investigations. As stated, it was rare for strikebreakers to perform the duties of regular workers. Since this was the case, the employer realized no immediate profit from the use of strikebreakers. However, if the employment of these individuals could break a union, the employer presumably would profit in the long run. No union meant no collective bargaining. This in turn meant lower wages and lower labor standards.

Strikebreaking could be accomplished by pointing to the possibility of violence and to the effects of the strike on the business of the community, or by encouraging antilabor newspapers. All of these techniques, as well as others, were included in the celebrated "Mohawk Valley Formula." This organized system of strikebreaking was devised by James H. Rand, Jr., president of Remington Rand. By utilization of this formula, he was able to break strikes in six of his plants. The breaking of the strikes resulted in the destruction of the unions, for in each case the purpose of the strike had been to try to force the company to bargain collectively. Since the formula proved so successful, the National Association of Manufacturers circulated its principles among its members.

The Mohawk Valley Formula was developed in meticulous detail. It represented careful thinking and showed a deep insight into social processes. It serves as one illustration of the extent to which union organization met resistance. Such tactics have since been condemned in the nation's labor laws.

PATTERNS OF ANTIUNION CONDUCT: COMPANY UNIONS

The record of industrial relations indicates that some companies used more moderate procedures to forestall the development and operation of collective bargaining. One such technique consisted of the sponsoring of company unions.[27] The formation of such organizations, often referred to as employee representation plans, was due to the recognition by management of the workers' desire to determine by organized action some of the elements of the employment relationship. Company unions provided for the expression of this deep-seated drive of workers. They also served to channel its implementation in a manner that lessened the threat to decision-making, which some firms consider a managerial prerogative. This was the case because company unions were not independent from the control of management.

Company unions were not part of the labor union movement. They were not affiliated with either the AFL or the CIO. They were limited in membership to the workers in one company or one plant. Since company unions depended on their own resources, they could not utilize the resources, financial and otherwise, of international unions. They did not possess the backing of established and effective affiliates. Unlike regular unions, they could not avail themselves of experienced and capable labor leaders for the purpose of representation.

Collective bargaining implies the existence of labor unions free to act independently from the control of management. The process culminates in the execution of collective bargaining agreements, which are to be respected by both the labor union and the company. In addition, the collective bargaining function sometimes results in a strike. None of these basic features of real collective bargaining is found in company unions. On the contrary, employers dominated company unions by influencing the selection of their officers, supervising their functions, and directing their activities to suit the interests of management. Collective bargaining contracts between company unions and the company did not exist. At most, the activities of company unions consisted of calling minor grievances of workers to the attention of management. Officers of company unions had to take care that these unions did not vigorously prosecute major issues—such as the demand for higher wages, seniority systems, vacations, paid holidays, and the like. Such officers had to be careful how they spoke and acted before management representatives. If they appeared "unreasonable," management might discriminate against them with respect to layoffs, transfers, and promotions. In a regular labor union, union representatives are protected by collective bargaining agreements, and more effectively, by the organization itself.

In still another respect, the company union failed to function as a true collective bargaining agent. In regular labor unions, officers hold their positions as long as they satisfy the rank and file. Union leaders must be responsive to the demands of the membership. To do otherwise would mean jeopardizing their positions. This is essentially true at both the local and international levels. Such responsiveness to the demands of the rank and file does not characterize the company union. Representatives of such an organization, enjoying little or no protection from possible discriminatory reprisal by management, had of necessity to curry the favor and good will of company officials. Since this was the case, company union representatives would prosecute desires of the rank and file only to the extent that their implementation did not conflict seriously with company policy. Such a situation scarcely constitutes true collective bargaining.

Company unions were the creatures of management. If the interests of management would be advanced by their elimination, this could be accomplished without much difficulty. In short, the continuity of company unions depended upon the pleasure of management. Company unions possessed no sovereignty and exerted only that authority bestowed on them by the employer. Since company unions attempted to serve two masters—the company and the workers—such organizations could not function as effective collective bargaining agencies. Labor unions, as defined by national labor policy, must represent and be responsible to their membership. This element was lacking in company unions. Consequently, they fell short of providing effective vehicles through which workers could engage in collective bargaining in accordance with national policy.

At times, an independent local labor organization, free from the control of management, may function at the company or plant level. Such organizations have no affiliation with federations or international unions, but unlike company unions, these independent unions can perform the collective bargaining function. This is true because, though independent from federations or international unions, they are not subject to the control of the company. Such independent labor unions are controlled directly by the membership. Independent unions execute labor contracts, hold regular membership meetings, collect dues, elect their officers independent from the influence of management, and when necessary, call strikes. Independent unions have at times affiliated with the international unions of the AFL-CIO. These international unions have not, of course, issued charters to unions dominated by employers. Before application for such a charter can be considered favorably, the company union has to rid itself of all evidences of employer control. As a matter of fact, in many cases, company unions became regular labor unions by asserting their independence from management.

NEED FOR PUBLIC CONTROL

The foregoing brief discussion, based largely on government documentation, discloses that a variety of techniques have been used to interfere with the formation of labor unions and the exercise of the collective bargaining process. Thus workers have often been denied the right to engage in collective bargaining. Such a right has been recognized by the government as lawful. Indeed, the Norris–La Guardia Act identifies collective bargaining with public policy. If the collective bargaining process was socially desirable, the utilization of antiunion techniques defeated the public purpose. It was necessary that society protect the right of workers to engage in collective bargaining. The alternative would result in an incongruous situation: On the one hand, public policy grants workers the right to self-organization and collective bargaining, and on the other hand, society silently approves by inaction employers' antiunion techniques. Consistency demanded that the government take appropriate action to provide protection to workers in the exercise of their right to collective bargaining. It appeared necessary that the government should either adopt this course of action, or else denounce collective bargaining as an antisocial and unlawful institution.

An additional consideration highlighted the need for public protection of the workers' right to collective bargaining. Even though confronted with hostile opposition, some employees were still determined to engage in concerted activities. To check interference with organizational efforts, workers made use of their economic weapon—the strike. Employees resorted to the strike to force management to recognize their unions, to bargain collectively with their representatives, and to cease interfering with the organization and functioning of their unions. The record of industrial relations demonstrates that workers frequently made use of the organizational strike. During the period 1919–1933, union organizational issues, such as refusal to recognize or bargain with labor unions, alone or in combination with other causes, accounted for 24 percent of all strikes. In 1934, 45.9 percent of all strikes resulted from those causes.[28] It is noteworthy that the Supreme Court of the United States recognized the seriousness of this problem in industrial relations. The Court in 1937 declared: "Refusal to confer and to negotiate has been one of the most prolific causes of strife. This is such an outstanding fact in the history of labor disturbances that it is a proper subject of judicial notice and requires no citation of instances."[29] In a 1967 study, one of the authors found that 94 percent of unfair labor practices filed against employers in one district office of the National Labor Relations Board stemmed from conduct arising directly out of union organizing campaigns.[30] Resistance to union organization, both past and present, seems to be the single most important cause of strife in the labor relations area.

Organizational strikes, like economic strikes (that is, strikes for wages, hours, vacations, and so on), interfere with the effective operation of the national economy. A democratic government, responsive to the needs of the country, is expected to deal with the problem. To reduce the frequency of organizational strikes, the nation could outlaw strikes calculated to force management to permit union organization and collective bargaining. Such an approach obviously would be more appropriate for nations in which freedom of association is more restricted than for a democratic society. Outlawing of organizational strikes would be repugnant to a democracy. If legislation of this character were to stand the test of constitutionality, the law of industrial relations would be turned back considerably. If workers were not permitted to strike for union recognition, the union movement could make little progress, and, indeed, would likely disintegrate into ineffectual units. In such a legal environment, the employer would need only to refuse to bargain with a union. If a labor organization, as a result of such conduct, would dare to strike, the penalties of law would come into operation. It appears clear enough that outlawing of union organizational strikes would result in the eventual destruction of the labor union movement.

Instead of outlawing the organizational strike, the public interest might be better served by legislation prohibiting the causes and abuses of such strikes. Specifically, Congress and state legislatures could forbid resistance to union organizational efforts. In addition, such legislation could require that employers bargain collectively with workers' unions when a majority of employees express such a desire through democratic standards of expression. Due care should be taken to balance the rights of both groups. Laws of this character do not confer any new rights or impose any new restrictions on anyone if properly administered by an impartial agency. Such legislation requires merely the respect of a right already possessed by both groups.

Such an approach would be in the public interest. Strikes for organizational purposes could be made unnecessary. Workers could utilize the remedial processes of the government if there were tamperings with their right to self-organization and collective bargaining. Since the frequency of such strikes should decrease, the public would be relieved from the inconveniences following in the wake of organizational strikes. Moreover, labor history demonstrates clearly that strikes for recognition purposes are usually bitter in character. Such strikes are frequently contested because management and workers are fully aware that the breaking of a recognition strike will result in the elimination of the labor union. The story of industrial relations is replete with instances of the bloody nature of the organizational strike. The circumstances of Memorial Day, 1937 in Chicago highlight the point. Growing out of the context of an organizational strike carried out against a steel corporation, the record reveals a tragic pattern of events. Police attempted to disperse a large group of strikers and their sympathizers, and the result was violence. When the struggle ended, 10 strikers had been killed, 90 other unionists had been injured (30 by gunfire), and 35 of the police had sustained injury.[31]

Another example points up the violence that frequently followed in the wake of strikes undertaken to force management to recognize unions as representatives of their employees. On Monday, February 18, 1935, a union struck against an Ohio rubber company. The La Follette Committee reported that the strike resulted from the labor relations policy of the company, which was "based upon a refusal either to enter into a written agreement with the union of its employees or to recognize that union as exclusive bargaining agent for its employees."[32] The company prepared to break the strike. Industrial spies were hired from professional detective agencies. At the time of the strike, the company had available a guard force of 133 men, a good share of whom were professional strikebreakers. About nine hundred workers were employed in the factory, the result being a ratio of about one guard to seven employees. This led one worker to draw a parallel between the environment of a prison and the company. He complained that a "free-born American citizen trying to work and make a living for my family" had to work in a "plant being infested with guards walking among us. . . ."[33] In addition, a supply of munitions was purchased. For $3,340.69 the company received tear gas and gas equipment, jumper-repeater tear gas rifles, three long-range field guns, and a large supply of shells.[34]

Such preparations were hardly conducive to peaceful strike conditions. As the La Follette Committee reported, "The company had created an explosive situation. The course of its activities preceding the strike can justly be construed as incendiary."[35] Despite the fact that strikers were given instructions "to conduct themselves in an orderly manner," violence characterized the strike from the beginning. When guards started shooting tear gas into the union's picket line, the strikers threw bricks. People not connected with either party were injured by the violence. The mayor of the town testified that some of the guards shot gas shells at some strikers near a school "and some of the school children near at the time got some of the gas."[36]

The strikers subsequently established a rest camp on an empty lot within sight of the factory. Shelter tents and a commissary wagon provided some protection against the winter cold. A few days after the camp was established, the sheriff ordered the strikers to disperse. After the workers refused to break up their camp, the guards en masse "attacked the camp, gassed it, burned the shelter tent, and arrested about 40 strikers as violators of the peace."[37] This illustration further underscores the need for effective laws to protect the rights of all parties concerned in labor disputes.

Not only do workers and the public benefit from such a legislative program, but employers also profit from such an arrangement. As stated, many employers have fully respected the collective bargaining process. Long before the Wagner Act, a good number of companies dealt in good faith with their employees' labor organizations. Many union-recognizing employers competed with companies that resisted the attempts of their workers to bargain collectively. Such a condition resulted in a competitive disadvantage to organized firms. This was usually the case because the nonunion companies could sell products at cheaper prices. Cheaper prices resulted from the lower labor standards of the nonunion firms. In view of these considerations, it could be expected that employers who dealt in good faith with their workers' unions would have welcomed a legal environment facilitating the organization of their nonunion competitors.

Some employers derived another advantage from a legal climate requiring respect of the workers' right to self-organization and collective bargaining. Such an arrangement provided an employer with an opportunity to engage in the collective bargaining process in good faith without losing the esteem of his or her business associates. It is possible that many employers combated labor unions because the *general* attitude of the business group advocated this course of action. In spite of personal inclinations to the contrary, an employer may have followed this line of procedure in order to maintain standing in the group. Employers may have been concerned that should they violate the "code" of their associates, they might suffer social and economic reprisal. In a legal environment with firmly established rules, such an employer could have dealt in good faith with a labor union without fear of ostracism. Such employers would be afforded a valid basis for their actions—in the event that the law had required respect of the workers' right to self-organization and collective bargaining.

In the last analysis, legal protection of the right of workers to self-organization can be defended on the basis of the social desirability of collective bargaining. As long as the process is socially useful, the public interest is served to the degree that the right is respected. It follows therefore that the right of workers to collective bargaining must be protected against the invasions of those who would treat this right with contempt.

SUMMARY

Government inquiry revealed that antiunion companies engaged in many tactics calculated to wipe out effective unionism. These activities were brought to light by many studies, including the celebrated findings of the La Follette Committee. Evidence revealed that spies, strikebreakers, and company unions were utilized in the attempt to destroy labor unions. Some employers attacked union leadership and set up systematic strikebreaking programs, such as the Mohawk Valley Formula, to accomplish the same objective.

Such activities stimulated long and bitter organizational strikes. These strikes would not have been necessary if there had been a recognition of the right of employees to engage in collective bargaining. This, many reportedly refused to do; the result was industrial warfare. It became apparent that legislation was necessary to curb antiunion behavior so that the right of workers to engage in collective bargaining would be protected.

DISCUSSION QUESTIONS

1. Rank the patterns of antiunion conduct reported by the La Follette Committee in the order of the effect that each might have had on worker rights to self-organization and collective bargaining. Support your decisions.

2. How important is it to attempt to eliminate or reduce organizational strikes and other related activities to lesser levels of permissible conflict?

NOTES

1   *American Steel Foundries Company* v. *Tri-City Central Trades Council,* 257 U.S. 184 (1921).

2   For example, see *Report of the U.S. Commission on Industrial Relations,* 11 vols., Washington, D.C., 1916, and *Interchurch World Movement's Study of the Steel Strike of 1919,* with its special reports on espionage and strikebreaking carried on by the United States Steel Corporation. See also books such as *The Labor Spy,* by Sidney Howard and Robert Dunn; *I Break Strikes,* by Edward Levinson; and *Spies in Steel,* by Frank Palmer.

3   *Violations of Free Speech and Rights of Labor, Report of the Committee on Education and Labor,* pursuant to S. Res. 266, 74th Congress. This report will hereafter be cited as La Follette Committee Report.

4   La Follette Committee, *Report on Industrial Espionage,* Report No. 46, Part III, 75th Congress, p. 39.

5   *Ibid.,* p. 62.

6   *Hearings,* Part IV, pp. 1239–1240 (reference to the volumes of the hearings of the La Follette Committee will be designated throughout this chapter as *Hearings*).

7   *Ibid.,* Part VIII, p. 3113.

8   *Ibid.,* Part V, p. 1457.

9   *Ibid.,* Part III, pp. 889–891.

10   La Follette Committee, Report No. 46, *op. cit.,* p. 63.

11   *Hearings,* Part IV, p. 1266.

12   La Follette Committee, Report No. 46, *op. cit.,* p. 63.

13   *Ibid.,* p. 22.

14   *Ibid.,* p. 79.

15   *Hearings,* Part IV, p. 1318.

16   Pinkerton's National Detective Agency, Inc., Order 105—Business Accepting, dated April 20, 1937. Reported in La Follette Committee, Report No. 46, *op. cit.,* p. 122.

17   La Follette Committee, *Private Police Systems,* Report No. 6, Part II, 76th Congress, 1st sess., p. 193.

18   *Hearings,* Part XXVI, p. 11058.

19   *Ibid.,* Part XXVI, pp. 11076–7.

20   *Ibid.,* Part XXVI, p. 10924.

21   *Riecke Metal Products Company,* 40 NLRB 872 (1942).

22   *Fred A. Snow & Company,* 41 NLRB 1292 (1942).

23   La Follette Committee, Report No. 6, *op. cit.,* p. 126.

24   *Ibid.,* p. 128.

25   La Follette Committee, *Strikebreaking Services,* Report No. 6, 76th Congress, 1st sess., pp. 65, 74.

26   R. R. R. Brooks, *When Labor Organizes* (New Haven: Yale University Press, 1937), p. 146.

27   For an authoritative and interesting account of the character and operation of company unions, see Bureau of Labor Statistics Bulletin 634, *Characteristics of Company Unions* (Washington, D.C., 1938).

28   *Monthly Labor Review,* XXXIX (July 1934), 75; XLII (January 1936), 162.

29   *NLRB* v. *Jones & Laughlin Steel Corporation,* 301 U.S. 1 (1937).

30   Benjamin J. Taylor, *The Operation of the Taft-Hartley Act in Indiana,* Indiana Business Bulletin No. 58 (Bloomington, Indiana: Bureau of Business Research, 1967), p. 27.

31   For an account of the Memorial Day tragedy, see La Follette Committee, *The Chicago Memorial Day Incident,* Report No. 46, Part II.

32   La Follette Committee, Report No. 6, *op. cit.,* p. 57.

33   *Hearings,* Part XXI, p. 9218.

34   La Follette Committee, Report No. 6, *op. cit.,* p. 60.

35   *Ibid.,* p. 60.

36   *Hearings,* Part XXI, exhibit 4243, p. 9349.

37   La Follette Committee, Report No. 6, *op. cit.,* p. 62.

CHAPTER EIGHT

PRECURSORS OF
THE WAGNER ACT

THE BEGINNINGS OF LEGISLATIVE SUPPORT

The 1890s were years of transition for the American labor movement. The Knights of Labor was passing into oblivion and the young American Federation of Labor was seeking effective means of gaining social acceptance. The financial panic of 1893 brought with it difficulties in expanding unionism into new areas. It was, however, the prevailing philosophy of the courts that proved the major obstacle to union progress. In 1895, in the *Debs* case, the Supreme Court sanctioned the use of the injunction in labor disputes. This procedure was followed by the courts and enlarged upon for several years, as mentioned in previous chapters. The lower federal courts in the middle 1890s were making widespread use of the Sherman Act to constrain union activities. The executive branch of the government upon occasion intervened in labor disputes. This was the case at both the federal and state levels. For example, in 1894, President Cleveland ordered federal troops to break the Pullman strike called by the American Railway Union. Cleveland took this action despite the protests of Governor Altgeld of Illinois. By 1900, the entire union membership in the nation totaled less than 1 million.

The legislative branch of government was beginning to demonstrate more concern for the union movement. There was a marked lag between the judicial and the legislative branches of government in the development of the law of collective bargaining. The legal aspects of the labor injunction illustrate the principle. State and federal attempts to control the injunction in labor disputes antedated the recognition by the courts that such control was necessary for industrial peace. A similar parallel between these two branches of government is noted with respect to positive legal protection of the right of workers to self-organization and collective bargaining. It may be worthwhile to emphasize the basic reason for such a lag. The tenure of office of the members of the judiciary is more secure than that of the legislators. In addition, many judges receive their commissions by appointment and consequently are removed from the direct control of the electorate. As a result, the legislator is more responsive to the changes in attitude of the people. It took the cataclysmic events of the 1930s plus the "court packing" threat by Roosevelt to change the structure of the Supreme Court to effect judicial approval of the social legislation enacted by Congress and the states.

The first attempts of the legislative branch of government to provide a degree of protection to workers utilizing their right to self-organization and collective bargaining took place in the 1890s. Such efforts antedated labor injunction control legislation by about a decade; they came about fifty years after *Commonwealth* v. *Hunt,* the decision that marked the beginning of judicial approval of labor unions. And, as mentioned, this legislative attempt occurred during a period of almost total judicial control of the collective bargaining process.

THE EARLY LAWS: YELLOW-DOG CONTRACTS AND DISCRIMINATION UNLAWFUL

In the 1890s, fifteen states enacted laws calculated to provide protection of the right of workers to self-organization and collective bargaining: Massachusetts, Connecticut, New York, Pennsylvania, New Jersey, Ohio, Indiana, Illinois, Wisconsin, Minnesota, Kansas, Missouri, California, Idaho, and Georgia.[1] The statutes prohibited employers from discharging employees for joining labor unions and from making the yellow-dog contract a condition of employment. The Indiana law of 1893 is characteristic of these early laws. It provided the following protection:

> It shall be unlawful for any individual, or member of any firm, agent, officer, or employee of any company or corporation to prevent employees from forming, joining and belonging to any lawful labor organization, and any such individual members, agents, officer, or employee that coerces or attempts to coerce employees by discharging or threatening to discharge from the employ of any firm, company or corporation because of their connection with such labor organization, and any officer or employer who exacts a pledge from workingmen that they will not become members of a labor organization as a consideration of employment, shall be guilty of a misdemeanor, and upon conviction thereof in any court of competent jurisdiction shall be fined in any sum not exceeding one hundred dollars ($100), or imprisoned for not more than six (6) months, or both, at the discretion of the court.

Thus, the early laws attempted to eliminate two powerful antiunion weapons. Consideration has already been given to the yellow-dog contract. However, we must emphasize that no single antiunion procedure exceeded the effectiveness of the yellow-dog agreement. Workers could not exercise their right to self-organization and collective bargaining where employees were required to agree not to join labor unions as a condition of employment. Elimination of the effectiveness of the yellow-dog contract was a logical starting place to protect the collective bargaining process. Unlike Norris–La Guardia and some of the modern state anti-injunction statutes, the early laws outlawed the yellow-dog contract and made violators subject to fines and imprisonment if they should demand the execution of such agreements. Under Norris–La Guardia and state laws patterned after it, the method of rendering the yellow-dog contract ineffectual was merely to make the judiciary unavailable for the enforcement of such agreements. In this respect, the early laws may have been more effective than more recent attempts to stamp out the yellow-dog contract. However, when the National Labor Relations Board was created, it held that coercion of employees to execute such agreements constituted an unfair labor practice. Failure to comply with an order of the NLRB could result in contempt of court proceedings.[2]

Discharge of workers because of union activities is another effective weapon to forestall unionization. In modern industry, the worker's job is normally the sole means of support. Without a job, the worker and family are helpless. The fear of loss of job is a prominent factor in the discouragement of union membership. Should a few workers be discharged because of union activities, the remaining workers would possibly have little appetite for union affairs. Workers could scarcely enjoy their right to self-organization and collective bargaining if they were fearful that union activities could terminate their means of livelihood. These factors make the prohibition of discharge of workers for union activities appear feasible.

In 1898, Congress passed the Erdman Act. The purpose of the law was to promote interstate commerce. This objective was to be realized by setting up procedures designed to reduce labor conflict in the nation's railroads. Though the law provided for the mediation and arbitration of labor disputes, our concern at this point is with the provisions of the Erdman law that protected the right of railroad workers to self-organization and collective bargaining. The Erdman law in part resulted from the celebrated *Pullman* strike of 1894. Fundamentally, this strike was caused by the refusal of the Pullman Company to enter into collective bargaining negotiations with its workers. As noted, the strike eventually spread to the railroads themselves. Congress was aware that organizational strikes could again interrupt railroad traffic among the states. Such strikes could result from the demand by the railroads that workers execute yellow-dog contracts, and from the discharge of workers because of union activities. Congress reasoned that if these two antiorganizational practices could be eliminated, the necessity for organizational strikes on the railroads would be reduced. Consequently, the interstate commerce of the nation would thereby be promoted.

As a result of these considerations, the Erdman Act contained the famous Section 10. This section made it a misdemeanor for railroad employers to require any employee or any person seeking employment, as a condition of such employment, to enter into an agreement, either written or verbal, not to become or remain a member of any labor corporation, association, or organization; or to threaten any employee with loss of employment or unjustly to discriminate against any employee because of his membership in such labor corporation, association, or organization.

Similar to the state laws mentioned previously, the Erdman Act outlaws the yellow-dog contract. But the railroad law was more effective than the state laws, for it prohibited railroad employers from discriminating in any way against workers who exercised their right to self-organization and collective bargaining. The state laws prohibited only discrimination by discharge, but permitted other acts to discourage union activities, such as discriminating against union-minded workers with respect to promotions, layoffs, transfers, and the like. Under the Erdman Act, all forms of discrimination against union employees were outlawed.

Compared to modern legislation, the early attempts to protect the rights of workers to self-organization and collective bargaining were ineffective. They did not prohibit the formation of company-dominated unions. Nor did they outlaw methods often used to break strikes and prevent the organization of labor unions. In addition, the early laws did not require that employers recognize their employees' unions and enter into negotiations with these unions. Finally, the method of enforcement of the statutes was ineffective. Enforcement was left entirely to court proceedings. This meant that violators of the law might avoid prosecution. The modern collective bargaining statute places the responsibility for enforcement on an expert administrative agency. This feature, as will be discussed in detail in later chapters, means the effective enforcement of such statutes.

Despite their obvious shortcomings, the early statutes were landmarks of industrial relations law. They reflected a growing awareness of the need for government action if the right of workers to self-organization and collective bargaining was to be effective. The early laws represented a beginning in the effective implementation of the collective bargaining process.

ATTITUDE OF THE JUDICIARY

The modest beginnings of legislative support of the collective bargaining process were rigidly controlled by the courts. The judiciary occasionally failed to give weight to the factors producing legislative action. Many of the state laws were declared unconstitutional by state supreme courts. However, the decisive factor came at the hands of the Supreme Court of the United States. In 1908, the Court invalidated Section 10 of the Erdman Act.[3] Seven years later, the Kansas statute suffered a similar fate.[4] Observers should have expected these decisions. They were handed down in a period in which the Supreme Court was not convinced of the necessity for collective bargaining. The jurists were not impressed with the social and economic factors justifying the attempts of government to protect workers in their employment relationship. The Court's position that the Constitution was to be protected from arbitrary invasions by the legislative branch caused it to rule against legislative action calculated to raise the collective bargaining power of the nation's workers. The record of the Supreme Court in the 1890s and in particular during the first two decades of the present century reveals unmistakably that the judiciary was not convinced that collective bargaining was a needed institution in light of its definition of individual property rights. The judges were determined that the economic welfare of worker groups should not be raised either by legislative action or workers' self-help activities. In their view, economic welfare was determined by the manner in which property was utilized. They feared that interference with the use of property could stifle competition and decrease the welfare of national trade.

In 1895, the Supreme Court sustained the use of the injunction in labor disputes.[5] In 1908, it applied the Sherman Act to labor union activities.[6] This decision set the precedent for subsequent prosecution of unions under the antitrust provisions. Such prosecution, as indicated, retarded the development of the American labor union movement. In 1917, two years after the Kansas attempt to outlaw the yellow-dog contract was held unconstitutional, the Supreme Court held that the yellow-dog contract could be protected by the labor injunction.[7] In 1921, the Supreme Court interpreted the legislative intent of the Clayton Act to hold unconstitutional the efforts of state governments to regulate the labor injunction.

Not only did the Court display this attitude toward labor relations legislation, but it likewise struck down laws designed to protect workers from the inexorable operation of the economic system. Thus, in 1918 and again in 1922, the Court held unconstitutional a congressional measure to control the use of child labor in American industry.[8] In 1923, the high court refused to sustain legislation that established a minimum wage for women employed in industry.[9]

Such was the record of the Supreme Court in the period in which legislative attempts were made to protect the right of workers to collective bargaining. In view of its pattern, one scarcely could have expected the high court to sustain these legislative efforts. And the Supreme Court did not deviate from its established pattern of interpretation of protective labor relations law. Both the *Adair* and *Coppage* decisions were consistent with the overall direction of the Court.

In characteristic fashion, the Supreme Court refused to give serious weight to the economic reasons that justified Section 10 of the Erdman Act. The Court could not see how Section 10 might prevent interruptions to interstate commerce by eliminating the need for strikes that resulted from the interference of railroad employers with the right of workers to self-organization and collective bargaining. In this connection, the Court asked, "What possible legal or logical connection is there between an employee's membership in a labor organization and the carrying on of interstate commerce?" Such a statement reflects the Court's philosophy during this period. Many years elapsed before the judiciary decided that there was both a logical connection and a valid legal relationship between the promotion of interstate commerce and government protection of the right of workers to self-organization and collective bargaining.

Once the Court held that there was no positive relationship between the objectives of Section 10 and the promotion of interstate commerce, it found the section unconstitutional. The Court reached the conclusion that Section 10 deprived both railroad operators and industry workers of their property without due process of law. Freedom to contract is a liberty guaranteed by the Fifth Amendment to the Constitution. Congress may pass no law that deprives people of this liberty. Thus, the Court declared that "such liberty and right embraces the right to make contracts for the sale of one's own labor." From this premise the Court held that workers and employers could agree on the execution of a yellow-dog contract. This was a freedom that could not be circumscribed by the legislature. The railroad employer had the right to establish conditions of employment and the employee had the right "to become or not, as he chose, an employee of the railroad company upon the terms offered to him." In other words, the Court said that if railroad workers did not like the idea of signing a yellow-dog contract, they had the right not to accept employment under such conditions. The implication was that the employee was free to seek other employment. What the Court failed to consider was that workers might have few alternative employment possibilities. Either they worked for the railroad or they were forced to seek another job, which might be an inferior alternative. The facts of economic life might have forced employees to sign the agreement even though they objected vigorously to such an employment agreement. At this time, the Court was more concerned with abstract and formal notions of law than with social and economic reality. Such an approach invariably resulted in harm to the interests of the nation's workers.

That portion of the Erdman Act forbidding the discharge of workers because of union activities was likewise held unconstitutional. The Court did not completely understand the new industrial life. The employer had the right to discharge a worker for union activities in the same way that the individual worker had the right to quit the employment of an employer who persisted in hiring nonunion workers. The Court declared that "in all such particulars the employer and the employee have equality of right, and any legislation that disturbs that equality is an arbitrary interference with the liberty of contract which no government can legally justify in a free land." In short, the Court did not understand that the employer, who possesses infinitely greater economic power than the worker, could use that power to deny workers their right to collective bargaining. It was assumed that there was already balanced power between the two groups. The worker was free to join a labor union. But that "freedom" was not realized if employers could deny workers their right to collective bargaining. If government had decided to protect this right against the arbitrary invasion of employers, it appears that the cause of freedom would have been advanced, not limited. The conduct of the employer would be limited by government only insofar as such restriction permitted the worker to enjoy the exercise of a lawfully recognized right.

In the *Coppage* case, in which the Supreme Court invalidated the Kansas statute, essentially the same arguments that appeared in the *Adair* case were offered. Constant reference was made to the *Adair* opinion to support the *Coppage* decision. The Court utilized the *Adair* decision as a precedent to strike down the Kansas law. Thus, the Court declared in the *Coppage* decision that "this case cannot be distinguished from *Adair* v. *United States.*" Only changes in the formal approach appear in the *Coppage* decision. Since Kansas passed the statute under the authority of its police power, the Court was required to show that the statute had no relationship to the promotion of the general welfare of the people of the state. It accomplished this task by asking, "What possible relation has . . . the Act to the public health, safety, morale, or general welfare?" In the *Adair* case, the Court held that Section 10 of the Erdman Act did not constitute a valid exercise of the power of Congress to promote interstate commerce. In the *Coppage* proceeding, the Court held that the passage of a state law outlawing the yellow-dog contract and prohibiting discharge for union reasons was not "a legitimate object for the exercise of the police power." In a ruling similar to the *Adair* decision, the Court in the *Coppage* case held that the Kansas law deprived both employers and employees of their property and personal liberty without due process of law. In this respect, the Court ruled on the Fourteenth Amendment (the constitutional provision that limits the power of the states) and not the Fifth Amendment (the one that checks the power of the Congress).

Justice Holmes dissented sharply from the viewpoint of the majority of the Court. Holmes, in the *Adair* case, upheld the right of Congress to fashion the public policy of the United States. He felt that there was a reasonable relationship between the promotion of interstate commerce and a law calculated to reduce the need for strikes in the railroads. Holmes felt that the Court, the judicial arm of government, should not overrule Congress, the legislative branch of government, in matters of public policy. He was even less impressed with the argument of the Court that Section 10 of the Erdman Act violated the Fifth Amendment to the Constitution. On this point, he declared that Section 10 "is, in substance, a very limited interference with the freedom of contract, no more. The section simply prohibits the more powerful party to exact certain undertakings, or to threaten dismissal or unjustly discriminate on certain grounds against those already employed." Holmes's dissent in the *Coppage* case rested on his reasoning in the *Adair* proceeding. He made the following simple statement:

in present conditions a workman not unnaturally may believe that only by belonging to a union can he secure a contract that shall be fair to him. If that belief, whether right or wrong, may be held by a reasonable man, it seems to me that it may be enforced by law in order to establish the equality of position between the parties in which liberty of contract begins. Whether in the long run it is wise for the workingmen to enact legislation of this sort is not my concern, but I am strongly of opinion that there is nothing in the Constitution of the United States to prevent it, and that *Adair* v. *United States* . . . should be over-ruled.

This position was representative of Holmes's general attitude toward public policy. He consistently held that Congress and the states should be given wide latitude in legislative matters. The judiciary should respect the opinion of Congress and the state legislatures in matters of public policy. The Constitution should only be employed to check the legislative branch of government when a law flagrantly and unmistakably violated its terms.

EVENTS OF WORLD WAR I

By its position in the *Adair* and *Coppage* cases, the Supreme Court denied to legislative bodies the authority to protect the right of workers to collective bargaining. The effect of these decisions meant that government could not control their bargaining relationships. In a normal peacetime economy, it was the considered opinion of the Court that legislative restraint in the collective bargaining process was necessary.

Had World War I not occurred, it is possible that legislative action in the area of collective bargaining would have been forestalled for many years. However, World War I served to focus the attention of the public on the state of the nation's labor relations policy. The need for uninterrupted production was essential. Any strike for any purpose was seen as detrimental to the interests of the nation. In order to establish a procedure to eliminate wartime strikes, President Wilson called a conference of outstanding representatives of industry and organized labor. At the conference, employers and unions gave a no-lockout and no-strike pledge, not including union-recognition strikes, which remained legal. To settle all labor-management disputes peacefully, the conference recommended the setting up of a war labor board. This proposal was accepted by President Wilson, and on April 8, 1918, the National War Labor Board (NWLB) was established. To guide the operation of the Board, the conference adopted a series of principles agreed to by labor and management representatives. Our concern here is with only one of these principles. This was the declaration by the conference representatives that the War Labor Board should protect employees in their right to self-organization and collective bargaining. The Board was to enforce the following policy: "The right of workers to organize in trade unions and to bargain collectively through chosen representatives is recognized and affirmed. This right should not be denied, abridged, or interfered with by the employers in any manner whatsoever. . . . Employers should not discharge workers for membership in trade unions, nor for legitimate trade union activities."[10]

By adopting this policy, it was hoped that strikes caused by employers' denial of employees' right to self-organization and collective bargaining would be sharply reduced. It is noteworthy that organizational strikes were not outlawed. To have adopted the latter course of action would have meant the disintegration of the union movement.

The National War Labor Board enforced in good faith the right of employees to self-organization and collective bargaining. The Board ordered the reinstatement with back pay of workers who were discharged because of union activities, required employers to bargain collectively with representatives of workers' labor unions, and ordered the polling of workers in elections to determine their choices of bargaining agents.[11] Many of these policies were to be embodied in the celebrated National Labor Relations Act passed by Congress in 1935. Although the National War Labor Board had no express authority to enforce its rulings, Wilson in practice did require compliance with the Board's orders through the exercise of his war powers. For example, Wilson seized the properties of the Western Union Telegraph Company because the carrier had discharged workers who joined unions. Similarly, the Smith & Wesson Arms Company was seized when the firm refused to bargain collectively.[12]

Still another circumstance of World War I served to shape the character of future public policy in industrial relations. With the entry of the United States into World War I, the federal government took over the operation of the nation's railroads. The task of supervising the operation of the railroads was lodged in the Railroad Administration. A director-general headed the agency. Early in 1918, the director-general issued General Order No. 8, which provided that "no discrimination will be made in the employment, retention, or conditions of employment of employees because of membership or nonmembership in labor organizations." In short, General Order No. 8 reestablished the principle of Section 10 of the Erdman Act, and thereby conflicted directly with the doctrine that the Supreme Court had laid down in the *Adair* decision. No one, however, chose to question the right of the federal government to protect collective bargaining rights in the railroad industry during World War I. Of course, the government, not private individuals, operated the roads. This may have had a bearing on any eventual court proceedings involving General Order No. 8.

The Railroad Administration recognized the railway unions as lawful bargaining agents. Of course, since the final determination of the conditions of work rested with the federal government, there was no actual collective bargaining in the industry during the war. Speculation as to whether there can be free collective bargaining in an industry owned or operated by the government continues to this day. It is known that the public, the vast majority of union leaders, and the rank-and-file workers frown on strikes when a plant or industry is owned or operated by the government under conditions of war. Free collective bargaining implies that workers have the moral and legal right to strike. Nevertheless, the Railroad Administration did entertain the demands of the railway unions. In many cases, the administration granted such demands. From this point of view, the railway unions performed an active role in shaping the conditions of work on the railroads during World War I.

Federal protection of the right of workers to collective bargaining during World War I served a dual purpose. In the first place, it demonstrated that a peaceful procedure could be instituted by government to decrease the need for the organizational strike. Such a wartime experiment was a harbinger of future labor relations policy. If protection of the right to collective bargaining during wartime promoted the cause of industrial peace, it appeared equally valid that the same result could follow from such a program during peacetime. In the second place, the favorable government policy toward organized labor during World War I stimulated the growth of the union movement. In 1917, union membership in all labor organizations totaled about 3 million. At the termination of World War I, this figure was 4 million, an increase of 33 percent.

This increase in union membership reflects the profound effect of government policy on the collective bargaining process. It indicates that a favorable legal environment stimulates union growth. After World War I ended, the National War Labor Board was abolished. This meant that once again the worker was left without government protection in collective bargaining relationships. As a result, union membership declined steadily; by 1933, membership was less than 3 million. The decline appears more serious if adjustment is made for the growth of the population and the labor force over the period 1919 to 1933. In 1920, the population of the United States was about 105 million; by 1930, the figure had increased to approximately 123 million. The labor force increased from about 40 million in 1920 to about 47 million in 1930. In the same period, there occurred a noticeable shift in the composition of the labor force. The number of people employed in agriculture declined sharply. In 1920, about 27 percent of the labor force was in agriculture, but in 1930, agriculture accounted for only 21 percent of the labor force. This meant that there was a shifting of workers to occupations more amenable to union organization. The agricultural worker for a variety of reasons was not easily organized. Yet despite the increase and change in the character of the labor force, the level of union membership was no higher in 1933 than it had been in 1917.

The depression of the thirties contributed its share to thwart the progress of the union movement. Labor history does demonstrate that the strength of organized labor, in terms of numbers and bargaining power, is reduced in depression periods. Giving full weight to the depression of the thirties, the fact still remains that the chief factor preventing the growth of the union movement from World War I until the advent of the New Deal was the lack of legislative support. The union movement showed no progress, indeed actually declined in strength, during the relatively prosperous years of the twenties. In these years, the level of unemployment averaged about 5 percent of the labor force. This figure does not represent a condition conducive to a decline in union membership, given the state of technology at the time. But, in spite of the relatively high level of employment, the union movement showed no progress and, if adjustment is made for changes in the size and composition of the labor force, organized labor actually lost ground in the twenties. The average union membership during these years was about 3.5 million.

Contrast this experience with that for the years 1932–1939. By 1939, the union movement claimed about 8 million members. Organized labor made this progress in the face of severe unemployment. Despite all efforts of the government to combat unemployment, the economy still suffered from serious unemployment until the entry into World War II. In 1939, for example, about 17 percent of the labor force was unemployed. Obviously, the better business conditions during the New Deal period as compared with the depression years of 1929–1932 had had something to do with the growth of the union movement, but the most important factor is commonly held to be the positive support given by government to collective bargaining.

Some attribute this lack of progress in the prosperous years of the twenties to deficiencies in union leadership. Granted the importance of vigorous leadership to the union movement, the fact still remains that such leadership may not have arisen precisely because of the uncertainties of the environment. It is more than a coincidence that the split in the union movement occurred during a period in which the organs of government were sympathetic to organized labor. Organization of the mass-production worker by the CIO was a result of favorable government policy. It is difficult to contend that labor leaders of the twenties simply did not see the overall desirability of the organization of the mass-production worker into industrial unions. As a matter of fact, the same union leaders who were responsible for the rise of the CIO were operating in the twenties. But in the twenties, despite the high level of employment, union leaders were not in agreement on the possibility of successfully concluding huge organizing drives. They were aware that efforts to organize the unskilled who did not possess well-entrenched skills would likely result in defeat. Why undertake such a venture if they were doomed to defeat? Clearly, the court experiences of the twenties dictated against such efforts. Industry's open-shop campaign of the period presented insurmountable obstacles to organization because of the relative ease of striker replacement. Moreover, the position of the judiciary on collective bargaining profoundly affected attitudes toward organizing activities. Some employers intensified their resistance to unions to the degree permitted by the organs of government. Rather than feeling that their techniques were antisocial in character, many employers considered that they were performing a public service by destroying the collective bargaining process. The prevailing attitude toward collective bargaining was in all probability a reflection of general public sentiment.

Workers themselves were not isolated from the effects of the legal atmosphere. Some have attributed the decline in union membership in the twenties to the increasing real income of the workers. It is true that real income of workers did increase, but that should not have prevented some progress in the union movement. Workers may have refrained from union activities out of fear of loss of job because of open-shop tactics, because of the effectiveness of the labor injunction, or because of the disrepute of association with a labor union. Those who argue that the lack of progress of the union movement in the twenties resulted from increasing real income do not fully appreciate the profound effect of government on collective bargaining. Since the legal climate operated to prevent the demonstration of effective union leadership, and inasmuch as the legal environment operated to discourage the unorganized worker from union activity, the union movement was bound to lose ground. Moreover, the real-income argument cannot be supported by empirical data. No actual investigation has been made to test the thesis. Social phenomena are not to be explained solely by statistics. On the other hand, the record testifies to the imprisonment and fines imposed on workers for union activity, to the number of strikes broken as a result of the injunction, and to the antiorganizational activities of employers. Finally, the real-income explanation, if extended to its logical conclusion, would mean that there is no need for any labor union movement. From the dawn of history, the worker has experienced a constantly increasing material standard of life. Fundamentally, this progress results from the advancing state of the arts of production. Since this progress is relentless, and if the real-income argument has validity, workers should show little propensity toward union organization. That such is not the case is demonstrated by the union movements of the western democracies.

On the basis of the foregoing observations, the conclusion must be reached that the character of the law of labor relations constitutes a most vital element influencing the growth of the union movement. The condition of the business cycle, the nature of union leadership, and the attitude of employers are of only secondary importance. An analysis of the union movement from World War I through the New Deal period supports this point of view. Given a favorable legal environment, the union movement will expand in numbers and in bargaining strength. Given a restrictive legal environment, the collective bargaining process will lose ground.

RAILROAD LEGISLATION

In 1926, Congress passed the Railway Labor Act.[13] The chief purpose of this law was to establish a variety of procedures, including mediation and voluntary arbitration, to reduce labor conflict in the railroads. These procedures, however, rested on the assumption that workers would be represented by labor organizations. In short, Congress felt that industrial peace on the railroads could be achieved through the collective bargaining process. Accordingly, the Railway Labor Act of 1926 provided that "representatives . . . shall be designated by the respective parties in such manner as may be provided in their corporate organization or unincorporated association, or by other means of collective action, without interference, influence, or coercion exercised by either party over the self-organization or designation of representatives by the other." Briefly, both workers and management were to be free in the selection of their own representatives without interference. Once chosen, these representatives were to confer together to settle labor disputes. Thus, Congress passed a law calculated to protect the railroad worker's right to collective bargaining. The Railway Labor Act of 1926 provided for a greater degree of protection than had Section 10 of the Erdman Act. In the 1926 law, the railroad employers were required to negotiate with the freely selected collective bargaining representatives of their workers. This feature was not included in the Erdman Act.

Previous to the passage of the Railway Labor Act of 1926, the railroads had sponsored a number of company-dominated unions. Attention was given to the ability of these organizations to serve as true collective bargaining agencies. Since they were creatures of the company, they were not considered equipped to represent workers in collective bargaining. After the passage of the statute, the question immediately arose as to their legality. The law did not specifically proscribe company-dominated unions. On the other hand, these organizations did not appear to have received support from the new law. Under its terms, workers were given the right to choose freely their representatives for collective bargaining. A company-dominated union might not fall within this classification.

In 1930, the question of the legality of the company union merited the attention of the Supreme Court of the United States. Once again, the Court was to rule on the constitutionality of the law that protected the right of railroad workers to collective bargaining. The railroads contended that the *Adair* decision, handed down by the Court in 1908, controlled the present proceedings. The Texas & New Orleans Railroad, the railroad involved in the case, refused to recognize or bargain with the Brotherhood of Railroad Clerks, a labor union free from company influence. Instead, the railroad supported the company sponsored and dominated "Association of Clerical Employees—Southern Pacific Line." The union claimed that the railroad was violating the Railway Labor Act of 1926.

In a decision that contrasted in every respect with the *Adair* doctrine, the Supreme Court upheld the constitutionality of the Railway Labor Act of 1926.[14] It ordered the railroad to cease interfering with the right of workers to choose whichever bargaining agents they wished. In this case, the Court held that promotion of the collective bargaining process was of the "highest public interest," for such a procedure would prevent "the interruption of interstate commerce by labor disputes and strikes." In other words, the protection of the right of workers to collective bargaining promoted commerce among the states. The view was held that collective bargaining reduced the need for organizational strikes, and that the collective bargaining process itself provided the means for industrial peace.

With respect to the Railway Labor Act of 1926 violating the "due process" clause of the Constitution, the Court had this to say:

> The Railway Labor Act of 1926 does not interfere with the normal exercise of the right of the carrier to select its employees or to discharge them. The statute is not aimed at this right of the employers but at the interference with the right of employees to have representatives of their own choosing. As the carriers subject

to the Act have no constitutional right to interfere with the freedom of the employees in making their selections, they cannot complain of the statute on constitutional grounds.

In effect, the Supreme Court overruled the *Adair* doctrine. It did not do so in so many words. But for practical purposes, it recognized that the *Adair* decision was no longer applicable in railroad disputes. This was not the last time the Court was to reverse itself on matters of labor legislation. For example, in 1937, in the *West Coast Hotel* case,[15] the Court reversed itself on the matter of minimum-wage laws. From 1923, the Court had held such laws unconstitutional. In 1937, it ruled differently. Precedent is always a major factor in the decision-making process of the judiciary. On the other hand, factors such as changes in court personnel, political pressure, and fundamental changes in the economic and social environment at times overshadow the importance of precedent.

RAILWAY LABOR ACT AMENDED IN 1934

The *Texas & New Orleans Railroad* decision stands as a landmark in the law of industrial relations. For the first time, the Supreme Court of the United States had recognized the authority of government to provide a measure of protection to the right of workers to self-organization and collective bargaining. The decision represented a clear-cut victory for those who contended that the collective bargaining process could not be carried out successfully without government encouragement. Moreover, the decision indicated the possibility of additional legislation to implement the collective bargaining process.

In 1934, Congress strengthened the provisions of the Railway Labor Act. It enacted a series of important amendments to the 1926 law. Some of the new provisions added more protection to the right of workers to self-organization and collective bargaining. Despite the policy and provisions of the 1926 law, the collective bargaining process was not functioning as Congress had intended. An investigation pointed up the following employer practices:[16]

> 1. Carrier officers have participated in or supervised, directly or indirectly, the formation of, and carrier managements have retained a measure of control over constitutions, bylaws, and other governing rules of organizations of their employees.
> 2. Carrier officers have supervised, or taken part in prescribing, the rules governing nominations and elections or other methods of choice of the representatives, committees and officers of such organizations.

Such practices of the railroads meant that their employees were being denied the right to select unions of their own choosing. Since the railroads sponsored company-dominated unions, the collective bargaining procedures provided for in the Railway Labor Act could not operate. The law was grounded in the belief that industrial peace and interstate commerce would be promoted to the degree that the collective bargaining process was utilized. Obviously, the objective of the statute could not be realized when the carriers interfered with the selection of workers' representatives.

Aware of these circumstances and encouraged by the outcome of the *Texas & New Orleans* case, Congress passed the 1934 amendments to strengthen collective bargaining in the railroad industry. Aimed at eliminating employer influence over the selection of workers' representatives for collective bargaining, the 1934 law forthrightly declared that "no carrier shall, by interference, influence, or coercion seek in any manner to prevent the designation by its employees as their representatives of those who or which are not employees of the carrier." It clearly established the right of officers of national unions to represent employees of the carrier. This was accomplished by providing that "representatives of employees for the purpose of this Act need not be persons in the employ of the carrier. . . ." In addition, the law provided that railroad employers were prohibited from using funds to support any employee organization or union representatives. They were also prohibited from deducting wages or collecting dues, fees, assessments, or contributions from employees transferable to labor organizations.

A National Mediation Board was established by the 1934 amendments. The Board was empowered to give meaning to the railroad employees' right to collective bargaining. It was authorized to conduct elections to determine which union the employees desired for collective bargaining purposes. A union receiving the majority of the votes was to be certified as the lawful representative. Railroad employers were required to bargain with the union obtaining certification.

As an adjunct to the law, Congress outlawed the yellow-dog contract on the railroads. This appeared superfluous, for Norris–La Guardia, passed in 1932, had already made the yellow-dog contract ineffectual. However, Congress in its zeal to establish the collective bargaining process in the railroads outlawed the yellow-dog contract to underscore its intent.

To enforce the provisions of the law, Congress provided severe penalties for violations. The law provided for fines up to $20,000, imprisonment, or both, for willful violations of the terms of the Act. It became the duty of the various district attorneys of the United States to prosecute any person who violated the terms of the law. With such severe penalties backing up the clear statement of the law, company-dominated unions, as expected, declined sharply after the passage of the 1934 amendments.[17] Thus, Congress was successful in eliminating employer interference with the right of the railroad employees to self-organization and collective bargaining. As will subsequently be noted, the Wagner Act drew heavily from the philosophy and techniques of the amended Railway Labor Act.

NATIONAL INDUSTRIAL RECOVERY ACT

In 1932, the nation was in the depths of the depression. After the election of Roosevelt, the federal government resorted to a variety of measures to promote recovery. Underlying all these attempts was a common purpose: to increase the purchasing power of the people. The New Deal aimed to promote economic recovery by bolstering the demand for goods. To this end, an extensive public works program was instituted. In keeping with the objective of increasing purchasing power, these projects were financed by government borrowing. An integral part of the scheme was the increase of workers' wages. If wages could be increased, workers would have more money to spend. The resulting increase in expenditures would stimulate employment and promote economic recovery.

The general plan of the New Deal to promote recovery was contained in the National Industrial Recovery Act (NIRA). This law provided for the regulation of production and prices by groups of business people. The theory underlying the NIRA was that such control would provide balance in the economy. Business people in the various industrial facilities of the nation formed groups for the purpose of production and price control. Once formed, the group executed a "code." About 550 such codes were adopted during the NIRA era. The codes provided for industrial self-government by business. Production and prices were not to be controlled by unregulated competition, but through regulations adopted by the parties to the codes. Since such an arrangement violated the Sherman Antitrust Act, the NIRA provided that the antitrust statutes were not to apply to parties to the codes.

Congress required that two provisions pertaining to labor be included in every code. In the first place, each code was required to establish a minimum wage for the workers it covered. This was in keeping with the desire of the New Deal to increase purchasing power. Actually, the average minimum wage established by the codes was about 40 cents per hour. In the second place, the National Industrial Recovery Act required that its Section 7 (a) be included in each and every code. Section 7 (a) provided legal protection for the right of workers to collective bargaining. One reason for 7 (a) was the desire of the New Deal to alleviate the causes of industrial relations warfare. Section 7 (a), as will be shown below, made it mandatory that employers respect the right of employees to self-organization and collective bargaining. It was designed to outlaw practices adopted to frustrate the collective bargaining process. On the other hand, the economic motive of Section 7 (a) cannot be disregarded. Legal protection of collective bargaining would mean stronger unions from the point of view of both numbers and bargaining capabilities. Such a condition might mean effective pressure by labor unions for higher wages. Thus, a strong organized labor movement could serve the basic theory of the New Deal about how to promote economic recovery: by increasing national purchasing power.

From 1933, the year in which the NIRA and Section 7 (a) was passed, until 1935, the year in which the NIRA was declared unconstitutional, union membership increased from 2,973,000 to 3,890,000—almost 33 percent.[18] These figures testify to the importance of labor relations law to the growth of the union movement.

SECTION 7 (a): NATURE AND ENFORCEMENT

Section 7 (a) contained two major principles: (1) that employees shall have the right to organize and bargain collectively through representatives of their own choosing, and shall be free from the interference, restraint, or coercion of employers of labor, or their agents, in the designation of such representatives, in self-organization, or in other concerted activities for the purpose of collective bargaining or other mutual aid and protection; and (2) that no employee and no one seeking employment shall be required as a condition of employment to join any company union or to refrain from joining, organizing, or assisting a labor organization of his or her own choosing.

Thus, for the first time during years of peace, Congress declared that workers throughout industry were to be protected in their collective bargaining activities. In comparison with subsequent labor relations legislation, however, Section 7 (a) contained many fundamental defects. Congress did not provide for a procedure to enforce the policy expressed in the section. Section 7 (a) failed to specify the patterns of antiunion conduct that were illegal. It did not expressly declare that company-dominated unions were unlawful. It did not state that employers were required to bargain collectively with the freely chosen representatives of their employees. Nor did Section 7 (a) forbid discrimination against employees for union activities.

These fundamental defects of Section 7 (a) soon came to light. Employers did not accept the union argument that Section 7 (a) outlawed the company-dominated union. In contrast, organized labor interpreted the section to mean that only regular labor organizations were to represent employees for collective bargaining purposes. The unions interpreted the intent of Congress as sanctioning a wide expansion of the labor union movement. Since Section 7 (a) did not provide for its own enforcement or interpretation, and since employees and employers believed it to mean different things, a wave of strikes occurred during the summer of 1933. These strikes resulted from the intensity of organizational activities. To comply with Section 7 (a), company unions were formed. Organized labor, feeling that these organizations did not reflect the policy of the government, struck for recognition of their own labor unions.

The National Labor Board

Since the wave of strikes impaired the nation's economic recovery, President Roosevelt created the National Labor Board to administer the labor policy of the NIRA. The Board was composed of three union representatives, three industry representatives, and one "impartial" person. It was established on August 5, 1933. At first the Board was successful in its attempts to regulate industrial relations. Almost immediately after its creation, it intervened in a hosiery strike in Berks County, Pennsylvania. More than 10,000 workers were involved in the strike, and every full-fashioned hosiery mill in the county was shut down. The National Labor Board settled the strike on the basis of a procedure known as the "Reading Formula." This formula provided that (1) the strike was to be called off; (2) the striking workers were to be reinstated in their jobs without prejudice or discrimination; (3) an election was to be held under the supervision of the National Labor Board to designate representatives for collective bargaining; and (4) representatives chosen in such elections were to be authorized to negotiate with employers with a view to executing agreements concerning wages, hours, and working conditions.[19] In all but eight of the forty-five mills, workers chose the Hosiery Workers Union as their collective bargaining representative. After the elections were held, a large number of mills in the area still refused to negotiate a contract with the union representatives. The National Labor Board ordered these employers to negotiate written agreements with the unions. Eventually, practically all firms executed collective bargaining agreements with the freely chosen representatives of their workers.

The success of the National Labor Board in the hosiery industry was repeated in other industries. On the basis of the Reading Formula, the Board peacefully settled disputes involving hundreds of thousands of workers in the wool, silk, clothing, street railways, and machine shop industries.[20] The high-water mark of the Board's operations was reached in November 1933. In this month, the number of strikes subsided considerably. On November 22 and 23, the Board conducted the most extensive elections of its existence, involving some fourteen thousand workers in captive coal mines. By November, the Board had established several regional boards. This decentralization permitted the national Board to deal with major controversies and, most important, permitted its members to reflect more carefully on matters of policy. A special study of the National Labor Board states that, for a time, "it seemed that, thanks to the Board's application of 7 (a), an ideal of industrial democracy was in the process of realization in the field of industrial relations."[21] However, by the end of the year, it was apparent that the National Labor Board could not offer adequate remedies for violations of its orders. Since it could not function effectively, the Board did not serve the public interest, for unions resorted to the organizational strike to enforce Section 7 (a).

A series of events operated to weaken the prestige and operating ability of the National Labor Board. The first blow was delivered by the Weirton Steel Company and the Budd Manufacturing Company. Both concerns refused to respect the principles of the Reading Formula. Determined in their positions, the corporations refused to agree to elections to determine the question of union representation. The Weirton Company refused to allow its workers to vote on whether they desired to be represented by the Amalgamated Association of Iron,

Steel and Tin Workers, a regular labor union; or by a union created and sponsored by the company. Despite protests from the federal government, the Weirton Company held an election in which workers merely voted to designate representatives under the company union plan. This open conflict with the National Labor Board seriously impaired the Board's prestige.

By February 1934, mainly as a result of its futile efforts to settle the *Weirton* and *Budd* disputes on the basis of the Reading Formula, the National Labor Board was on the verge of collapse. The example had been set by *Weirton* and *Budd* for others to follow. Orders of the Board were not respected and its authority was disregarded. Because the peaceful procedures of the Board had broken down, the frequency of organizational strikes increased sharply. Workers and employers were both determined to prevail in organizational contests. Since the National Labor Board could not control the situation by holding elections, employees resorted to the strike to gain their objective.

Aware of these circumstances, President Roosevelt attempted to bolster the authority and prestige of the disintegrating National Labor Board. In February 1934, he issued two Executive Orders that increased the power of the Board.[22] These orders provided that the National Labor Board was to conduct elections to determine collective bargaining representatives of workers. If at such an election a majority of workers chose a particular labor union for representation, the employer would be required to recognize and negotiate with this union. If an employer should refuse, the National Labor Board was to refer the case to the Compliance Division of the National Recovery Administration and/or to the office of the Attorney General of the United States. These agencies were to obtain compliance with the orders of the Board.

It appeared at first that the National Labor Board might now function as an effective organization. The intent of the President was clear. He had clothed the Board with status and power. Heretofore the Board had functioned on a more or less informal basis. It developed on its own initiative the Reading Formula, other policies, and its administrative procedures. Moreover, the great defect of the Board lay in its inability to enforce its decisions. Consequently, there was reason to believe that the Executive Orders of February 1934 would correct these shortcomings. This point of view, however, failed to materialize because of the intensity of the organizational conflicts.

Immediately after the President issued the Executive Orders, the "majority principle" laid down by the orders was challenged. It was contended that this principle would deprive nonunion workers of their employment rights, for the National Labor Board held that an employer must bargain with a majority-selected labor union as the exclusive representative of all employees. Unions argued that on the other hand, collective bargaining could not be carried out effectively if employers were free to make private deals with individual workers. If such an arrangement were established, it would not be difficult to undermine a labor union. This could be done by showing favoritism to the nonunion worker. To avail themselves of such benefits, it was argued, some workers might give up their union membership. Any sizable withdrawal from the labor union would mean its collapse. Once this occurred, the employer would then be free to determine employment conditions on a unilateral basis and need no longer show concern for the nonunion worker.

General Johnson and Donald R. Richberg, high-ranking officers of the National Recovery Administration, shared the employer point of view. This proved to be a determining factor in the decline of the National Labor Board. It could not implement the majority principle and assure parties to a dispute that its views were supported by all members of the government. Actually, the National Labor Board refused to heed the viewpoint of Johnson-Richberg; however, their position served to promote confusion in National Labor Board policy.

In March 1934, the National Labor Board suffered another blow to its prestige. During this month, the nation was threatened with an industry-wide automobile strike. The automobile companies refused to recognize an automobile union that was then being organized under the sponsorship of the AFL. To prevent their workers from enjoying the benefits of true collective bargaining, the automobile manufacturers sponsored company-dominated unions. The AFL insisted on a free election to determine the bargaining desires of the automobile workers. The manufacturers refused, and the AFL threatened to close down the nation's major automobile plants.

Such a strike, of course, would have seriously retarded the recovery efforts of the New Deal. The National Labor Board, aware of the implications of a nationwide automobile strike, diligently attempted to settle the dispute on the basis of the Reading Formula. However, the Board failed to effect a settlement. President Roosevelt and Johnson of the National Recovery Administration, then intervened in the dispute. This intervention made it clear to the public that the National Labor Board did not have the authority or the capability to settle important labor controversies. On March 25, 1934, President Roosevelt obtained a peaceful settlement of the dispute. The fact that White House pressure had prevented the strike added further to the impairment of the National Labor Board's status as an effective labor agency.

The National Labor Board never recovered from this blow to its prestige. Employers and unions had little respect for or faith in its procedures. Labor unrest again mounted in intensity as unions became aware of the impotence of the Board. Organized labor, convinced of National Labor Board inadequacies, undertook to enforce 7 (a) through its own economic strength. Organizational strikes occurred during the early summer of 1934 in Toledo, Minneapolis, and San Francisco; and a nationwide steel strike was threatened by the Amalgamated Association of Iron, Steel and Tin Workers.[23] The National Labor Board did not prevent the outbreak of these strikes, nor was it capable of obtaining a settlement once they occurred. Its failure in this respect was inevitable. Its prestige was irreparably damaged by presidential intervention in the automobile dispute.

Finally, on May 29, 1934, the judiciary completed the cycle of Board humiliations. A district court refused to order the Weirton Steel Company to participate in a representation election to permit workers to choose freely their representatives for collective bargaining. Both the Reading Formula and the Executive Orders of February 1934 had underscored the right of workers to make this choice. However, the district court refused to order the collective bargaining election. On the basis of such a judicial ruling, it is not difficult to see why both employers and unions lost confidence in Board procedures.

Public Resolution No. 44:
The First National Labor Relations Board

Congress recognized the shortcomings of the National Labor Board. Its failure stimulated members of Congress, particularly Senator Wagner of New York, to search for more effective protective procedures. Congress was alerted to the danger of relying on an inept agency to preserve industrial peace. Strikes for organizational purposes would continue in number and intensity to the degree that Congress failed to provide for the speedy and adequate enforcement of the free selection by workers of bargaining representatives. If unions had been reluctant to strike for recognition purposes prior to 1933, Section 7 (a) had completely changed this state of affairs. Collective bargaining had become a matter of public policy. The nation's workers were determined to engage in collective bargaining with or without government protection. As a result, 45.9 percent of all strikes in 1934 occurred wholly or in part from organizational issues.[24]

Congress, fully aware of this stream of events, undertook the task of providing workers with adequate machinery to select their bargaining representatives. Senator Wagner of New York led the drive for legislation to accomplish this objective. As early as February 1934, he introduced the so-called Wagner Labor Disputes Act.[25] Later he proposed still another law, the Industrial Adjustment Act, which would have provided even broader protection for the collective bargaining process. Fundamental to Wagner's program was a streamlined method for enforcement. He would have set up a quasi-judicial agency, termed the "National Industrial Adjustment Board," empowering this agency to prevent employer antiunion practices. In addition, the agency was to have the authority to conduct elections enabling workers to select bargaining representatives. Employers would be expected to recognize and negotiate with these representatives. Orders of the Board would be enforceable in the United States circuit courts of appeals. Unlike the ill-defined authority upon which the National Labor Board operated, the Wagner agency would have derived its power from a statute of Congress. Its mandate would have been clearly defined and, to obviate the possibility of disrespect for Board orders, as was the case with the National Labor Board, the Wagner Board could have called upon the courts to enforce its decisions.

Despite the approval of the Wagner program by President Roosevelt, Congress did not enact the Wagner Labor Disputes Act or the Industrial Adjustment Bill. Congress adjourned without passing legislation to govern the nation's labor relations policy. However, the 73d Congress did not adjourn without providing for the replacement of the defunct National Labor Board. For this purpose, Congress on June 16, 1934, passed Joint Resolution No. 44. Three days later the Resolution was approved by the President.

The purpose of Joint Resolution No. 44 was to provide for the interpretation and enforcement of Section 7 (a) of the National Industrial Recovery Act. Unlike the Wagner program, which would have set up a labor board on the basis of legislation independent of NIRA, the National Labor Relations Board, created by Joint Resolution No. 44, was tied to Section 7 (a) of the NIRA. This Board expired with the decision that the National Industrial Recovery Act was unconstitutional.

The National Labor Relations Board appeared more fortified to provide adequate protection to the right of workers to self-organization and collective bargaining than the defunct National Labor Board had been. The spirit in which the NLRB had been created demonstrated the desire of Congress for vigorous legal implementation of collective bargaining. More specifically, the NLRB was empowered to conduct representation elections to permit workers to choose their collective bargaining representatives. In addition, it was authorized to investigate alleged violations of Section 7 (a).

On the other hand, this Board suffered from the defect that had proven fatal to the National Labor Board; that is, the National Labor Relations Board did not have the power to enforce its own orders. Enforcement depended on the action of the Compliance Division of the National Recovery Administration or on the Department of Justice. This proved a serious barrier to the effective operation of the agency. In addition, employer antiunion practices, supposedly prohibited by Section 7 (a), were not spelled out in Joint Resolution No. 44. This meant that the new Board, like its predecessor, had to establish its own principles. Joint Resolution No. 44 in effect placed the responsibility for establishing a national labor relations policy on the shoulders of a government agency. In any matter so important and complicated, it is essential that Congress provide guides for an agency to follow. Section 7 (a) declared in general terms that workers had the right to self-organization and collective bargaining without employer interference. But it did not spell out what constituted "employer interference." For example, as mentioned, it was not clear whether or not company-dominated unions were unlawful.

Vagueness with respect to the scope of authority of the National Labor Relations Board, and the division of responsibility for the enforcement of its decisions constituted the two chief obstacles to effective operation of the agency. In short, Board orders were not respected. The Compliance Division of the NRA did order the removal of the "Blue Eagle" from firms which ignored Board decisions. However, this technique of enforcement proved highly unsatisfactory. Consumers did not particularly care whether a company sported the Blue Eagle, the emblem showing compliance with the overall policy of the NIRA. The Department of Justice likewise did not provide an adequate vehicle for enforcement. The

Board referred thirty-three cases to the Department of Justice. Of these, the department sought only one injunction for enforcement purposes.[26] Sixteen cases were sent back to the NLRB for additional evidence. In three other cases the department exercised its prerogative to overrule the Board and held that no suit was justified. Finally, in the remaining cases, the Department of Justice for one reason or another refused to enforce orders of the Board.

Such an enforcement program did not enhance the prestige of the Board. Employers were not greatly impressed by its orders, for it was apparent that enforcement was a remote possibility. For effective operation, an administrative agency must have the ability to enforce its decisions. Had the NLRB been authorized by Joint Resolution No. 44 to solicit the courts for enforcement orders, the record of the agency would have been more imposing. As it was, the Board held that employers violated Section 7 (a) in eighty-six instances during the first eight months of its operation, but in only thirty-four cases did employers comply with orders of the Board.

PASSAGE OF THE WAGNER ACT

When the 74th Congress assembled for the first time in 1935, Senator Wagner again led a drive for labor relations legislation. He was convinced that the National Labor Relations Board established under Joint Resolution No. 44 did not provide a sound basis for adequate protection of the collective bargaining process. Wagner's bill received support from the American Federation of Labor. President Roosevelt also gave his approval to the measure.

The factor that resulted in the speedy passage of Wagner's proposal, however, was the declaration by the Supreme Court that the entire National Industrial Recovery Act was unconstitutional.[27] As noted, Joint Resolution No. 44 and the National Labor Relations Board created under its terms were rooted in the NIRA. When this law was held invalid, the NLRB had no legal basis for its actions. Since its legislative authority was swept away, the orders of the Board had no legal validity. The Supreme Court's decision in the famous *Schecter* case was handed down on May 27, 1935. After this date, all federal protection of workers' rights to self-organization and collective bargaining terminated. Section 7 (a) and the National Labor Relations Board created under Joint Resolution No. 44 became dead letters.

After the *Schecter* decision, the legislative pace quickened. Senator Wagner pushed for speedy passage of his bill, which by this time was popularly termed the "Wagner Act." House and Senate hearings on the measure were intensified. Members of these committees were well aware of the need for legislation to promote industrial peace. It was apparent that such peace could not be obtained in the absence of a law that would effectively establish the collective bargaining process in American industry. The American Federation of Labor pressed for new legislation. The campaign that the AFL conducted for the passage of the Wagner Act centered on the Section 7 (a) guarantees. Mass meetings to urge the passage of the Wagner Act were held under the sponsorship of the AFL and other labor groups. Organized labor made clear the character of its future political program. It threatened to work for the defeat of each and every senator or representative who opposed the Wagner Act. Never before did organized labor conduct such an all-out campaign to urge the passage of a particular bill.

On June 27, 1935, the Wagner Act was passed by Congress.[28] Its technical name was the National Labor Relations Act, but its popular name, and the one that will be used in this volume, was the Wagner Act. President Roosevelt approved the legislation on July 5, 1935, stating that

> this Act defines, as a part of our substantive law, the right of self-organization of employees in industry for the purpose of collective bargaining, and provides methods by which the Government can safeguard that legal right. It establishes a National Labor Relations Board to hear and determine cases in which it is charged that this legal right is abridged or denied, and to hold fair elections to ascertain who are the chosen representatives of employees. A better relationship between labor and management is the high purpose of this Act. By assuring the employees the right of collective bargaining it fosters the development of employment control on a sound and equitable basis. By providing an orderly procedure for determining who is entitled to represent the employees, it aims to remove one of the chief causes of wasteful economic strife. By preventing practices which tend to destroy the independence of labor, it seeks, for every worker within its scope, that freedom of choice and action which is justly his.[29]

With the passage of the Wagner Act, legislative approval of the collective bargaining process was reasserted. A law had been passed specifically for the purpose of protecting and encouraging the growth of the union movement. The law also set up an agency that appeared well fortified to implement the purpose of the statute. Public policy had changed considerably since the labor conspiracy cases of 1806. Society now declared that collective bargaining was socially desirable. Collective bargaining was to constitute the normal procedure for the establishment of the conditions of employment within American industry. As we shall see, there were many aspects to the Wagner Act, some of them complicated and controversial, but none more important than its social approval of the collective bargaining process.

SUMMARY

For many years, the Supreme Court nullified the efforts of Congress and state legislatures to protect employees in their right to self-organization and collective bargaining. The attitude of the judiciary remained rooted in precedent even though the legislative branch of government recognized that the facts of industrial life had made legal protection of the collective bargaining process a desirable public policy. The Supreme Court had difficulties balancing the constitutional property guarantees, as it interpreted them, with laws passed by Congress. The economic doctrines of the Constitution were subject to interpretation by all three branches of government. But the high court nullified legislative attempts to implement collective bargaining because of the social and economic predilections of the judges who composed the high court. The *Adair* and *Coppage* cases revealed a philosophy not conducive to an understanding of the dynamics of the economic system. Only through speculation could one comment on the attitude of the majority of the electorate in the area of collective bargaining.

Despite such an attitude on the part of the judiciary, Congress passed legislation calculated to protect the right of the nation's railway workers to self-organization and collective bargaining. Part of this legislation was patterned after the principles established by the first National War Labor Board. The National Industrial Recovery Act, passed by Congress to implement economic recovery, attempted to extend federal protection to collective bargaining throughout all industry. This policy was set up in Section 7 (a) of the NIRA. However, this section contained basic defects, which made its effective enforcement impossible. When the Supreme Court held the NIRA unconstitutional, Section 7 (a) became a dead letter. Subsequently, Congress enacted the Wagner Act to protect employees in their right to self-organization and collective bargaining.

DISCUSSION QUESTIONS

1. What was the purpose of the Erdman Act? How did the Supreme Court deal with it? Did the law serve any useful purpose for later consideration?

2. Which labor policy experiences of World War I were later utilized in New Deal legislation?

3. How could the Railway Labor Act of 1926 be ruled on as it was in the *Texas & New Orleans Railroad* case with *Adair* as a precedent?

4. Why would legislation be enacted affecting railroads but not for industry in general?

5. The Railway Labor Act was amended in 1934. Which conditions in 1934 that had not been apparent in 1926 led Congress to make changes in the law?

6. Discuss the economic reasoning behind passage of the National Industrial Recovery Act of 1933.

7. What were the strengths and weaknesses of the National Industrial Recovery Act?

8. Discuss the Court's rationale in its *Schecter* decision. What effect did the decision have on Congress in subsequent legislation?

NOTES

1   *Report of the Industrial Commission on Labor Legislation,* V (Washington, D.C.: U.S. Government Printing Office, 1900), p. 128.

2   National Labor Relations Board, *Rules and Regulations and Statements of Procedure* (Washington, D.C.: U.S. Government Printing Office, 1965), p. 63.

3   *Adair* v. *U.S.,* 208 U.S. 161 (1908).

4   *Coppage* v. *Kansas,* 236 U.S. 1 (1915).

5   *In re Debs,* Petitioner, 158 U.S. 564 (1895).

6   *Loewe* v. *Lawlor* (*Danbury Hatters* case), 208 U.S. 274 (1908).

7   *Hitchman Coal & Coke Company* v. *Mitchell,* 245 U.S. 229 (1917).

8   *Hammer* v. *Dagenhart,* 247 U.S. 251 (1918); *Bailey* v. *Drexel Furniture,* 259 U.S. 20 (1922).

9   *Adkins* v. *Children's Hospital,* 261 U.S. 525 (1923).

10   National War Labor Board, *Report, April, 1918, to May, 1919,* pp. 121–122.

11   *Ibid.,* pp. 53–156.

12   *Ibid.,* p. x.

13   44 Stat. 577 (1926).

14   *Texas & New Orleans Railroad* v. *Brotherhood of Railroad Clerks,* 281 U.S. 548 (1930).

15   *West Coast Hotel* v. *Parrish,* 300 U.S. 391 (1937).

16   *Statement of Federal Co-ordinator of Transportation,* December 8, 1933, pp. 5–7.

17   Twentieth Century Fund, Inc., *Labor and Government* (New York: McGraw-Hill Book Company, 1935), p. 88.

18   Florence Peterson, *American Labor Unions* (New York: Harper & Brothers, 1945), p. 56.

19   National Recovery Administration, Release No. 285, dated August 11, 1933.

20   Lewis L. Lorwin and Arthur Wubnig, *Labor Relations Boards* (Washington, D.C.: Brookings Institution, 1935), p. 100.

21   *Ibid.,* p. 102.

22   Executive Order No. 6580, February 1, 1934; Executive Order No. 6612-A, February 23, 1934.

23   Lorwin and Wubnig, *op. cit.,* p. 115.

24   *Monthly Labor Review,* XLII (1935), p. 162.

25   S. 2926, 73d Congress, 2d sess. (1934).

26   D. O. Bowman, *Public Control of Labor Relations* (New York: The Macmillan Company, 1942), p. 45.

27   *Schecter Poultry Corporation* v. *United States,* 295 U.S. 495 (1935).

28   49 Stat. 449 (1935).

29   *Public Papers and Addresses of Franklin D. Roosevelt* (New York: Random House, 1938–1950), pp. 294–295.

CHAPTER NINE

THE WAGNER ACT

THE SOCIOECONOMIC RATIONALE OF THE WAGNER ACT

The National Labor Relations Act, hereinafter referred to as the Wagner Act, provided a partial answer to changing problems of labor relations. It was a product of modern industrialism, rooted in the growth of big business and the corporate organization of industry. Supporters of the legislation recognized that the modern industrial environment rendered obsolete the concept of individual bargaining as the regulator of industrial relations. Social and economic change brought greater attention to the need for effective collective bargaining. Moreover, the Wagner Act recognized the incongruity of industrial autocracy in the context of political democracy. It appeared to Wagner Act supporters that the extension of the democratic process to the employment relationship was necessary and appropriate if the nation were to remain free and democratic. As Senator Wagner once put it, "Let men know the dignity of freedom and self-expression in their daily lives, and they will never bow to tyranny in any quarter of their national life."[1] The Wagner Act assumed democracy to be an indivisible process. Denial of the implementation of the process in any quarter of society would constitute a threat to free institutions.

The Wagner Act had still another express purpose. It was to act as an economic stabilizer for the nation. As mentioned, the New Deal, of which the statute was an integral part, resulted from the failure of traditional practices to provide the nation with economic prosperity. The theory of the New Deal was that sufficient purchasing power in the hands of the people would constitute one road to a healthy economic life. According to the architects of the New Deal, the nonunion employee did not possess actual liberty of contract. Such an employ-

ment relationship meant that an employer could keep for the firm a disproportionate share of its revenues under conditions of persistent excess supply of labor.
This condition could prolong the downturn stage of the business cycle, for the
purchasing power to buy the commodities and services turned out by industry
might not be available to unemployed consumers. Effective collective bargaining,
according to New Deal policy, provided one way out of the difficulty. Through
collective bargaining, wages would tend to increase, the result being the increase
of effective demand for the products of American industry. One employer
spokesperson supported this approach to economic stability when he declared:

> It became obvious to the management of our company that no mass production
> could long be carried on unless there was increased purchasing power by the great
> masses of people. To us this meant there must be increases in wages and shorten-
> ing of hours. This became the very fixed conviction of our management. The more
> difficult question was as to how this should be accomplished, and we arrived at the
> conclusion that collective bargaining by employer and employee . . . was the only
> means by which, under our system, any adjustment in the equitable distribution of
> income could be accomplished. We realized the difficulty of this method, but we
> felt that if this method did not accomplish the desired end, then the present
> capitalistic system would collapse. . . . There is a further and more selfish reason
> as to why we took the step which we did in co-operating with the organization of
> our plants. We felt that if the present economic system was to continue, it was
> inevitable that in the future there should be the organization of labor, and that real
> collective bargaining would eventually be made effective.[2]

Under the provisions of the Constitution, it was not sufficient for Congress
to declare that the Wagner Act plan would serve the public interest by accomplishing its economic objectives. The national government is one of delegated
powers.[3] This means that Congress had to find specific authority in the Constitution before it could enact a specific law. In the case of the Wagner Act, Congress,
to meet the constitutional obligations, hooked the statute to the power of the
federal government to regulate interstate commerce. Attention has already been
directed to the large number of strikes engaged in by workers to force employers
to accept the collective bargaining process. These strikes were bitterly contested.
Frequently, they resulted in destruction of property, injuries, and even loss of life.
Congress reasoned that such strikes, termed organizational strikes, obstructed
interstate commerce by impairing the flow of raw materials and processed goods
among the states, and causing diminution of employment and wages in such
volume as to impair substantially the market for goods flowing from or into the
channels of commerce. An organizational strike in the telephone and telegraph
industry, for example, would obviously prevent the exchange of goods among the
states. Entrepreneurs rely on the telephone and telegram to effectuate the sale
and purchase of goods. Likewise, an organizational strike in a factory would
obstruct interstate commerce. Unless goods were first produced, they could
scarcely enter the channels of interstate commerce. Finally, organizational strikes
meant that wages of workers and profits of companies were either decreased or

temporarily nonexistent. This resulted in the reduction of the sale and purchase of goods in interstate commerce. If organizational strikes resulted in such obstruction to commerce, the obvious inference was that reduction of the frequency of such strikes would promote trade among the states. The Wagner Act aimed to eliminate the cause of such strikes by outlawing employer antiunion practices.

Congress also believed that legal protection of the right of workers to self-organization and collective bargaining would result in a diminution in the number of nonorganizational strikes. In this connection, the Wagner Act declared that "experience has proved that protection by law of the right of employees to organize and bargain collectively safeguards commerce from injury . . . by encouraging practices fundamental to the friendly adjustment of industrial disputes arising out of differences as to wages, hours, or other working conditions. . . ." By such a statement Congress meant that the collective bargaining process, once firmly established within the economy, could serve as a bridge to industrial harmony. The record of industrial relations testified to the fact that a labor union secure in its status was apt to be more responsible, more responsive to the problems of management, and more reasonable than one whose status was in a constant state of uncertainty. Studies sponsored by the National Planning Association pointing up the causes of industrial peace supported this observation.[4] Management would likewise be more prone to reach a peaceful settlement in a labor dispute when dealing with a strong and secure labor union. If management felt that a union was so weak that it could not possibly withstand a serious challenge to its existence, the company officials could purposely force a showdown. Frequently, the result was unnecessary industrial warfare. Collective bargaining, if it was to serve the cause of industrial peace, presupposed an arrangement in which the contesting parties possessed equality in bargaining power. Should one side be very weak and the other very strong, the possibilities for industrial warfare would be increased.

Beyond this reasoning, Congress could point to the history of industrial relations on the railroads to support the contention that employees had been denied the right of free collective bargaining. Despite the defects of the Railway Labor Act of 1926, the promotion of the collective bargaining process in the railroad industry by law did serve the cause of industrial peace. When Congress passed the Wagner Act, there was no conclusive evidence indicating how the 1934 amendments to the Railway Labor Act of 1926 would function. The amendments were passed on June 30, 1934, and the Wagner Act was enacted one year later. However, in that one year, marked by a great amount of industrial warfare, the railroads were not affected by the wave of strikes. Railroad workers, secure in their right to self-organization and collective bargaining, had no occasion to resort to the organizational strike.

This then was the underlying philosophy of the Wagner Act. Industrial strife was promoted to the degree that employers denied to workers their right to self-organization and collective bargaining. The legal requirements of the Constitution were met by the Wagner Act, for interstate commerce was burdened by strikes resulting from such denial. In addition, Congress placed great faith in collective bargaining as the vehicle for industrial peace. Finally, it was hoped that the effect of economic depressions could be lessened by legal protection of the collective bargaining process, for this might mean more purchasing power for the nation's workers. That is, workers could win more purchasing power if unions possessed the economic power often attributed to them.

On the basis of such observations, Congress set forth the public policy of the United States, proclaiming:

> It is hereby declared to be the policy of the United States to eliminate the causes of certain substantial obstructions to the free flow of commerce and to mitigate and eliminate these obstructions when they have occurred by encouraging the practice and procedures of collective bargaining and by protecting the exercise by workers of full freedom of association, self-organization, and designation of representatives of their own choosing, for the purpose of determining the terms and conditions of their employment or other mutual aid or protection.

Opposition in some quarters was evident almost immediately after passage of the Act. Some employers attempted to prevent the effective operation of the law by seeking injunctions to restrain the activities of the National Labor Relations Board. Court actions were so numerous that the NLRB spent its first months of operation defending itself in court. However, it should be made clear at this point that a majority of employers either supported the Wagner Act provisions or offered no opposition to their implementation.

An event almost unique in the field of federal law stimulated injunctive attack against the NLRB. On September 5, 1935, a few months after the passage of the Wagner Act, the National Lawyer's Committee of the American Liberty League declared that the statute was unconstitutional.[5] This pronouncement was made long before the Supreme Court had had an opportunity to review the legislation. The League pronouncement stimulated widespread violation of the Act's provisions. The National Labor Relations Board, commenting on this, declared:

> During its first months, and before the Board had opportunity even to announce its procedures, an incident occurred which was to stimulate injunction suits against the Board, and even to provide a sample brief for those wishing to attack the act. This was the publication by the National Lawyer's Committee of the American Liberty League, on September 5, 1935, of a printed assault on the constitutionality of the act. This document, widely publicized and distributed throughout the country immediately upon its issuance, did not present the argument in an impartial manner for the use of attorneys. It was not a review of the cases which might be urged for and against the statute. It was not a brief in any case in court nor was it an opinion for any client involved in any case pending. Under the circumstances it can be regarded only as a deliberate and concentrated effort by a large group of well-known lawyers to undermine public confidence in the statute, to discourage compliance with it, to assist attorneys generally in attack on the statute, and perhaps to influence the courts.[6]

Soon after the National Lawyer's Committee circulated its anti-Wagner Act tract, the injunction proceedings began. The Board reported that the process was "like a rolling snowball." In a matter of weeks, the legal attacks against the Board became uniform throughout the nation. Thus "the allegations or pleading filed by an employer in Georgia, for example, would show up in precisely the same wording in a pleading filed in Seattle."[7] Such a procedure testified to the organized nature of the attack against the Wagner Act. The pleas for injunctions were successful. In some cases, the judges did not themselves understand the provisions of the National Labor Relations Act. Some judges, the NLRB reported, had the impression that the Act provided for mediation and arbitration. Others believed it was no more than a law of conciliation. The fact was that there were absolutely no features of conciliation or arbitration in the Wagner Act. In the first few months of the life of the Board, the federal district courts issued twenty injunctions restraining the operations of the NLRB. However, some judges, aware of the fact that NLRB orders could not be enforced except upon review by the circuit court of appeals and the Supreme Court, refused to act favorably upon employer applications for injunctions.

STATE OF AFFAIRS BEFORE JONES & LAUGHLIN

The attack against the Wagner Act, spearheaded by the National Lawyer's Committee, prevented the successful operation of the law. Its administrative agency, the National Labor Relations Board, could not effectively exercise the powers granted it by Congress. Criticized and ridiculed in the daily press, hamstrung by legal proceedings, the NLRB suffered crushing blows to its prestige. Organized labor began to lose faith in the law. Its purpose and provisions were clear enough. On paper it purported to permit employees to form—free from employer influence—labor unions and to utilize their organizations as collective bargaining agencies. In practice, however, it soon became obvious that neither the law nor the NLRB could operate as a protector of collective bargaining rights. With the decrease of workers' confidence in the law, the number of organizational strikes increased. From the summer of 1935 until the spring of 1937, the period of the passage of the Wagner Act, strikes that were at least partly for recognition and organizational issues accounted for about 50 percent of all strikes.[8] Workers were impressed with the declaration by Congress that collective bargaining constituted the national policy of the United States. Their organizational efforts had their roots in the public approval of labor unions. These roots were nourished by the growing recognition of the possible effects of the collective bargaining process in the life of the nation. Citizens were engaged in a search for new answers to the financial ills plaguing the economy. Workers were no longer to be denied their right to self-organization and collective bargaining. If the NLRB could not enforce this right, the employees of the nation might resort to violence. Some regard the relatively large number of organizational strikes in the first years of the Wagner Act as demonstrating the failure of the law. Such an observation is without convincing support. The real reason for this great wave of strikes may have been the ineffective operation of the Wagner Act. Since the law's provisions were not widely accepted at first, employees may have resorted to organizational strikes to seek their objective of recognition of bargaining agents. Outward manifestations of employer resistance to collective bargaining were not checked by the NLRB in court proceedings. Thus, the organizational strike and not the NLRB, an agency largely neutralized through early court proceedings, served to implement the public policy set forth in the Wagner Act.

Only a clear-cut declaration of constitutionality of the Wagner Act by the Supreme Court could effectuate the law. If the Court validated the Act, the legal proceedings against the NLRB would cease. The agency could then devote full energies to the enforcement of the statute. Voluntary compliance to the Wagner Act, indispensable to the successful operation of any law, would increase, since lengthy and costly legal proceedings against the NLRB would prove futile. Under such conditions, the peaceful procedures of the Wagner Act would be substituted for industrial warfare. Labor leaders and workers alike could seek legal remedies for violations of the right to self-organization and collective bargaining. The need for the organizational strike would be reduced, if not virtually eliminated.

The effect of a validation of the Wagner Act by the Supreme Court appeared clear enough. What was doubtful was whether or not the high court would sustain the legislation. Would the Court hold the Wagner Act unconstitutional on the basis of the *Adair* decision? Or would the more recent *Texas & New Orleans* decision control the proceedings? Even the avid supporters of the Wagner Act recognized the strong possibilities for an adverse decision. The Railway Labor Act, sustained in the *Texas & New Orleans* decision, applied only to the railroad industry, whereas the Wagner Act covered all workers engaged in interstate commerce. It was recognized that the Supreme Court might choose to distinguish between a general statute and one very limited in scope.

The composition of the Court was a source of uncertainty to supporters of the Wagner Act. On the Court were Van Devanter, Sutherland, McReynolds, and Butler. Students of the Supreme Court were well aware of the social and economic philosophies of these men. Their philosophies were present in decisions denying the right of government to legislate for the benefit of the working population. The judges believed that the operation of the economic system provided payment to workers in accordance with their worth to their employers. They assumed that the forces of a competitive economy would protect the worker from exploitation. In short, this group believed that the type of economic system described by Adam Smith in 1776 was in operation in the 1930s. These men felt that the government should not protect the weak from the strong, but that workers should exercise their economic prerogatives to effect such protection. Thus, if workers were dissatisfied with the conditions of work determined unilaterally by the employer, they were free to quit and seek employment elsewhere.

Characteristics of the contemporary economy—such as chronic unemployment, concentration of economic power, monopolistic control of product markets, formation of huge corporations, and the inherent disparity of bargaining power between the worker and the company—failed to impress these members of the Supreme Court. It was not generally recognized that Adam Smith had advocated government intervention when necessary to restore competitive conditions to an economy.

Still another factor worried supporters of the Wagner Act. Even granted that the statute as such would be validated, the question still remained as to how far the Court would apply the law. The specific issue was whether or not the law would apply to manufacturing. Approximately 10 million workers were employed in manufacturing in 1935. These workers constituted a highly organizable group. If the Court upheld the Wagner Act but denied its application to manufacturing, the statute would not serve to expand significantly the area of unionization and collective bargaining. On the other hand, the application of the law to manufacturing facilities would result in the protection of the right of self-organization and collective bargaining for a group, which could spearhead an expansion of the union movement. In addition, if manufacturing were included within the scope of the Wagner Act, the Court would establish a precedent that would likely result in the application of the statute to industries such as mining, foresting, fishing, finance, and some sectors of wholesale and retail trade. By denying the application of the law to manufacturing, even though upholding the general constitutionality of the law, the Supreme Court could limit its terms to interstate bus lines, truck and water transportation, and telephone and telegraph systems. The workers involved in these industries constituted a mere fraction of the nation's organizable workers.

In light of judicial precedent, there was some basis to believe that the Supreme Court might hold manufacturing to be beyond the scope of the Wagner Act. In 1894, the Court had held that "commerce succeeds to manufacturing and is not a part of it."[9] In 1936, in the *Carter Coal* case, the Court could not see how regulating the labor relations of a coal company advanced and safeguarded interstate commerce.[10] Although the *Carter Coal* case did not involve the manufacturing industry, the 1936 decision represented a line of reasoning that indicated a limited construction of interstate commerce and caused considerable uncertainty about the future of the Act. Thus, in the *Carter* case, decided after the passage of the Wagner Act, the Court declared:

> mining brings the subject matter of commerce into existence. Commerce disposes of it. A consideration of the foregoing . . . renders inescapable the conclusion that the effect of the labor provision of the [Bituminous Coal Conservation Act], including those in respect of minimum wages, wage agreements, collective bargaining, and the Labor Board and its powers, primarily falls upon production and not upon commerce; and confirms the further resulting conclusion that production is a purely local activity. It follows that none of these essential antecedents of production constitutes a transaction in or forms any part of interstate commerce.

Such language appeared almost to preclude the Court's application of the Wagner Act to manufacturing facilities.

Balanced against the foregoing, some factors served to support the view that the Wagner Act would be sustained and its terms applied to manufacturing. As noted, a great number of organizational strikes occurred after the employees of the nation became aware that the NLRB could not effectively carry out the provisions of the new labor policy. The vast majority of these strikes occurred in the nation's manufacturing facilities. Some of the strikes were unprecedented in scope, intensity, and destruction. They resulted in destruction of property, in physical injury, and in loss of life. Such developments were likely to have an effect on the Supreme Court. Moreover, the Court must have been impressed with the overwhelming reelection of Roosevelt in 1936. The result of the election, in which Roosevelt failed to receive the electoral votes of only Maine and Vermont, served to underscore the people's satisfaction with New Deal policies in that they were willing to experiment in areas previously considered best left alone. It was reasonable to believe that the Court would consider these election results. Finally, the threat of Roosevelt to "pack" the Supreme Court must have had some influence on its members. Impressed by his astounding success at the polls, Roosevelt was reluctant to permit the Supreme Court complete freedom to evaluate New Deal policies. He was determined to satisfy the demands of the people that social legislation be implemented. Accordingly, he proposed legislation that would have minimized the influence of the conservative element of the Supreme Court. Even though Congress refused to enact the law, the attempt undoubtedly left its mark on the members of the Court. Alternatively, it was clear from the legislative history of the Act exactly what Congress intended. This had not been the case in much of the earlier legislation dealing with labor policy.

THE JONES & LAUGHLIN DECISION

Such was the environment in which the Supreme Court ruled on the Wagner Act. The nation was aware of the magnitude of the forthcoming decision and, as perhaps never before, anxiously awaited the high court's decision. Labor hoped for a clear-cut decision of constitutionality, for that would mean legal protection of bargaining rights. Many employers hoped for the opposite ruling, for that would mean little government influence would affect the collective bargaining process. The issue was settled in April 1937 in the case involving the Jones & Laughlin Steel Company.[11] By the slim majority of a single vote, the Supreme Court upheld the Wagner Act and, of equal importance, validated its application to the manufacturing sector of the American economy. On the majority were Chief Justice Hughes and Associate Justices Roberts, Stone, Cardozo, and Brandeis.

As some observers expected, the minority of the Court was composed of Sutherland, McReynolds, Van Devanter, and Butler. Once again, these men affirmed that constitutional prohibitions precluded the government from aiding and encouraging union organizations to establish collective bargaining. The minority group held that employers could utilize any antiunion tactic to defeat the collective bargaining process. The minority held that the *Texas & New Orleans* decision did not apply to a proceeding involving a manufacturing establishment. It was further avowed that the government could regulate the labor relations of the railroads, for this industry was considered a part of interstate commerce. But, it was argued, Congress had violated the Constitution by endeavoring to protect the right of workers to collective bargaining in manufacturing, for this industry was not a part of commerce. In short, whatever happened in the manufacturing industry did not directly affect trade among the states. Should a strike in manufacturing result from the discharge of workers because of union activities, or from the refusal of an employer to bargain collectively, the effect upon commerce was "far too indirect to justify congressional regulation." One may take issue with this point of view. For example, if the steel industry was shut down because of the reluctance of the owners to recognize the steelworkers' union, there would likely be a real and substantial effect upon interstate commerce. The effect would depend upon the extent of stockpiling in anticipation of the work stoppage. In addition, the lack of worker income to expend upon consumer goods would have an indirect effect on commerce. Such a strike, for whatever reason, would mean that there was no steel for shipment between the states. Production is as essential for interstate commerce as are the transportation facilities that carry the goods from one state to another. The breakdown of either production or transportation has an effect on interstate commerce. On the basis of these practical observations, the position of the minority group in the *Jones & Laughlin* decision appears untenable and unrealistic. In any event, the group held that the federal government could not lawfully regulate the labor relations of a manufacturing facility. Manufacturing, these members concluded, was not a part of interstate commerce, and consequently the Constitution prohibited federal control over the steel industry.

This point of view was not shared by the majority of the Court. Chief Justice Hughes, speaking for the Court, declared that strikes in manufacturing facilities, such as in a steel mill, "would have a most serious effect upon interstate commerce." The majority argued that it was proper for Congress to take action to prohibit employers from interfering with the right of workers to bargain collectively because organizational strikes might result in "catastrophic" effects on commerce. In masterful language, Hughes struck at the contention of the minority that the effect of organizational strikes in commerce would be "indirect or remote." Thus, Hughes remarked:

> We are asked to shut our eyes at the plainest facts of our national life and to deal with the question of direct and indirect effects in an intellectual vacuum. Because there may be but indirect and remote effects upon interstate commerce in connection with a host of local enterprises throughout the country, it does not follow that

other industrial activities do not have such a close and intimate relation to interstate commerce as to make the presence of industrial strife a matter of the most urgent national concern. When industries organize themselves on a national scale, making their relation to interstate commerce the dominant factor in their activities, how can it be maintained that their industrial labor relations constitute a forbidden field into which Congress may not enter when it is necessary to protect interstate commerce from the paralyzing consequences of industrial war?

It was by the use of such language that the Supreme Court upheld the Wagner Act's application to manufacturing. The entire theory of the authors of the law was given judicial approval. It was accepted by the Court that not only did organizational strikes involving the railroads or other instruments of commerce burden trade between the states, but work stoppages in manufacturing, resulting from employer antiunion activities, likewise burdened interstate commerce. It was therefore deemed proper for Congress to eliminate the causes of such strikes, because such action protected and promoted interstate commerce.[12]

Beyond dealing with the applicability of the Wagner Act to manufacturing, the Supreme Court directed its attention to another constitutional question. Did the statute violate the due process clause of the Fifth Amendment to the Constitution? Again the majority of the Court upheld the statute. It was held that the procedural provisions of the law adequately protected employers from the arbitrary action of the NLRB. Foremost in this connection, the Court stressed that the judiciary constituted the ultimate source of enforcement authority for the provisions of the law. As will be pointed out below, an employer aggrieved with a decision of the Board has the right to appeal to the courts. Not only was the Wagner Act upheld with respect to the procedural aspects of due process, but the Court held also that the substance of the Wagner Act did not deprive an employer of property or liberty without due process of law. On this point, the majority leaned heavily on the *Texas & New Orleans* decision. Since manufacturing was deemed to fall within the concept of interstate commerce, the railroad decision was applicable. Thus, the Court in the *Jones & Laughlin* decision reaffirmed the principle that law "cannot be considered arbitrary or capricious if it prohibits interference with the right of workers to self-organization."

It is important to stress that even if the Court had held the law applicable to manufacturing, the Wagner Act could have been declared unconstitutional on the basis of interfering arbitrarily and unreasonably with the freedom of employers to run their businesses. However, the Court refused to hold unlawful a statute that protected the right of workers to collective bargaining. Since workers were extended the right to collective bargaining by both the judiciary and legislature, it appeared reasonable and prudent that government should outlaw practices calculated to prevent self-organization and collective bargaining. Such was the conclusion of the Supreme Court.

Thus, on April 12, 1937, the Supreme Court validated the Wagner Act. Not only were its terms consistent with the due-process clause of the Constitution, but the application of the law was to cover general industrial facilities. The

Jones & Laughlin decision represented perhaps the most important pronouncement of the Supreme Court with respect to organized labor. At the time it
constituted one of the most favorable decisions that had yet been made in the
interest of the nation's workers. It made possible the implementation of public
policy promoting collective bargaining.

SUBSTANTIVE PROVISIONS: UNFAIR LABOR PRACTICES

The Wagner Act made collective bargaining a matter of public policy. Section 7
of the statute declared: "employees shall have the right to self-organization, to
form, join or assist labor organizations, to bargain collectively through representatives of their own choosing, and to engage in concerted activities, for the
purpose of collective bargaining or other mutual aid or protection." To make this
right effective, Congress outlawed employer practices that operated to deny
workers the freedom to carry out the collective bargaining function. In short,
Congress was not content merely to state that workers have the right to self-
organization and collective bargaining. It was determined to prohibit any interference with the exercise of that right.

To accomplish the Section 7 objective, Section 8 of the Wagner Act set
forth five *unfair labor practices.* These practices were declared unlawful. Subsequently, attention will be devoted to the methods by which the Wagner Act
provided for remedies when employers violate the terms of Section 8. At this
time, we are concerned with the nature of the unfair labor practice.

Section 8 (a) (1).   This section makes it an unfair labor practice for an employer
to "interfere with, restrain, or coerce employees in the exercise of their rights
under Section 7." Independent interferences with employees' rights may occur
exclusive of any other violation specified by Section 8 (a). The NLRB has held
that violations of Section 8 (a) (1) exist when employees are (1) threatened with
the loss of their jobs or other reprisals; (2) granted wage increases timed to
discourage union membership; and (3) questioned by employers about union
activities under such circumstances as will tend to coerce them in the exercise of
their rights under Section 7.[13] Independent violations have also been declared
when the working places or homes of employees were placed under surveillance
by employers to the extent that reasonable communication regarding organization was restricted. In this regard, the utilization of industrial spies constitutes a
violation. An independent violation has been found when a sales manager, representing the employer, offered a more lucrative job in another city to an employee
if he would drop his union activities.

Although the Wagner Act did not prevent an employer from utilizing
economic power to defeat a strike by peaceful means, the NLRB has ruled that
a firm interfered with the right to self-organization by hiring strikebreakers for
the purpose of provoking violence or creating fear in the minds of employees.
When the NLRB held that the Mohawk Valley Formula, a systematic procedure

for breaking strikes, violated the Wagner Act, it stated, "Those activities were employed to defeat the strike, end the strike, rather than settling it through collective bargaining."[14] Inciting to violence against union organizers and members of labor organizations was also deemed an unfair labor practice. In one case, a company was found to have violated this subsection of the law when a forelady incited violence against a union organizer by suggesting to the employees in her section, "What do you say, girls, we give her a beating?"[15]

Some of the unfair labor practices during World War II had a distinct wartime flavor. A number of employers utilized the wartime environment to interfere, restrain, or coerce workers from exercising their right to self-organization and collective bargaining. A violation of the National Labor Relations Act was found when an employer posted notices throughout the plant suggesting that union organizers were a group of "intimidators" and threatened the "substitution of Naziism for Americanism."[16] Nor was an employer permitted to assert that a union was "backed by Germans" when the intent was to unlawfully discourage membership in the organization. A supervisor implicated his employer in an unfair labor practice by intimating that the company would not ask for occupational army service deferment for an employee if the worker persisted in union activities. Employers were not permitted to distribute "I am an American" buttons to their employees not wearing union buttons. The obvious inference that union members were not loyal Americans evidently prompted the Board's decision. Effecting the arrest of persons distributing union literature in a plant was deemed unlawful, even though the employer argued that the plant was engaged in secret war work and that the persons jailed might have been spies and saboteurs. It was noted that a labor union was organizing the plant's workers when the employer procured the arrest. Nor did the Board sustain the argument that employers could engage in unfair labor practices with impunity because the company was producing materials for the exclusive use of the government. The NLRB further ruled that an employer engaged in an unfair labor practice when it appealed to its workers' patriotism to defeat a union in a bargaining election by drawing a contrast between the hardships endured by men in the armed forces and the attempts of the employees to better their economic position through organization. On the other hand, the Board found no violation of the Wagner Act when union members were discharged because they had violated a Federal Bureau of Investigation domestic security measure. These employees were not permitted to utilize their union status as a bar to dismissal.

During the war period, the NLRB established another source of subsection 1 violation. Wartime wage increases were prohibited unless approved by the National War Labor Board. Consequently, one of the most effective appeals that a trade union could make to maintain its membership was impaired for the duration of the war. To compensate in part for this wartime condition, the NLRB ruled that an employer violated the Wagner Act if it refused to consult with the representatives of its employees' labor organization before filing a wage-increase application with the NWLB.

Section 8 (a) (1) of the Act is so constituted that a violation of any of its subsections by clear implication is of necessity considered interference, restraint, or coercion in the exercise of Section 7 rights. A refusal-to-bargain violation, for example, is not only expressly in violation of Section 8 (a) (5), which makes it an unfair labor practice, but of necessity interferes with the Section 7 right to "bargain collectively through representatives of their own choosing." Any 8 (a) (1) infringements that also violate specific provisions of the Act are considered derivative violations.

Over the years, of course, the NLRB and courts held that much employer conduct did *not* constitute a violation of this provision of the Wagner Act. For example, in 1984, a federal appeals court, upsetting a Board decision, held that an employer in a consumer-oriented business (fast foods) could lawfully ban the wearing of union buttons. In that case, the employer enforced a rule that forbade the wearing of any kind of unauthorized buttons.[17]

Section 8 (a) (2).   "Domination or interference with the formation or administration of a labor organization or contribution of financial or other support to it" is a violation of Section 8 (a) (2). It has already been pointed out that a union that is the creature of an employer does not constitute a proper vehicle for the carrying out of the collective bargaining process. Congress was well aware of this fact and consequently outlawed employer domination of labor unions. The NLRB, however, was required to spell out the circumstances under which an employer dominates a labor organization. Specifically, what are the characteristics of an employer-controlled union?

The Board has found a union to be company-dominated in a case where the employer told its employees that they should establish a union and indicated the form that the labor organization should take. If an employer or its representatives actively solicits members on behalf of a labor organization, such a union is illegal. A union may be company-dominated when the employer provides the union with bulletin boards, a company automobile, and stenographic service or office space.

The Board has held that, by advancing money to employees who were unable to pay membership dues, a company contributed support to a union and the organization was ordered dissolved. Another union was held company-dominated because the employer permitted members of the organization to solicit members for the union on the employer's property during working hours and, most important, with the consent of the employer. In *Highway Trailer Company*,[18] employees were fired and threatened with discharge because of their refusal to join the organization for which the employer had expressed his preference, and consequently the NLRB ordered the organization dissolved.

Other employer practices that indicate that a labor organization is the creature of the company include those instances in which the employer has suggested the form of the constitution; in which a few hand-picked employees have been urged to create the organization; and in which management has been willing and eager to sign agreements with the organization it helped to create.

An important criterion in determining whether a labor organization is company-dominated may be the extent of collective bargaining between the union and management. The NLRB said:

> If the organization did not make any effort to meet with the employer concerned, and other features of the labor organization are indicative of company-domination, the Board may conclude, on the basis of the laxity in petitioning for a meeting on the part of the labor organization, that the employee's organization is the creature of the employer.[19]

Not only is neglecting to meet with management material evidence that the labor organization is company-dominated but, even when conferences do occur, the labor organization in question may be deemed company-dominated if the negotiations "be such as to reveal the employer's domination of the organization."[20]

In a 1983 case, beyond the normal remedy directing the employer to cease and desist recognizing a company-dominated union, the NLRB also ordered the employer and union to rebate to employees all dues and initiation fees collected, plus interest.[21] What generated this unusual order was evidence demonstrating that over a three-year period, the employer had kicked back $68,000 to union officials who referred business to the employer from other contacts the union had with businesses.

To clarify this section, the Board adopted a number of principles to determine whether an organization is independent of employer domination. Thus, if members of the organization hold regular meetings on property other than the company's; if members of the union pay dues; if the union has written agreements with the company; if the organization has contacts with other workers' organizations; if the union has the right to demand arbitration of differences whereby management abandons absolute veto power; then, the NLRB found, the organization is clearly its own master and is free to submit the real wishes of its members to management.

Section 8 (a) (3).   This section makes it an unfair labor practice for employers to discriminate "in regard to hire or tenure of employment on any term or condition of employment to encourage or discourage membership in a labor organization." This clause was directed against the most common and highly effective antiunion weapon—the discharge of workers who are union members or those who would promote the formation of a labor union. By adopting this provision, Congress endeavored to erase fear from the minds of union-conscious workers. Again, the Wagner Act charged the NLRB with the duty of interpreting and carrying out the terms of the provision. What constitutes discrimination? Is transferring an employee to an inferior job because of union activity discrimination within the meaning of the Act? Can union workers ever be discharged? What evidence will the Board consider material in determining whether an employer truly discriminated against workers for union activity?

The most common form of discrimination that the Board declared an unfair labor practice was discharge of an employee for union activity. When the evidence in a case proved that an employee was discharged because of union activity, the Board ordered reinstatement. In most instances, the employer denied that he or she discharged an employee or otherwise discriminated for union activity, and consequently the NLRB would investigate to determine whether there had really been the discrimination prohibited by the Wagner Act. When an employer denied that discharges or other forms of claimed discrimination were within the meaning of the Act, the Board took into account the entire background of the case, reviewing the totality of circumstances to determine the nature of employer action against employees.

Not only will employers usually maintain that they did not discriminate against an employee on the grounds of union activity, but in nearly all cases they will tender some reasons to the Board for discharging an employee. The most common alleged reason given for the discharge is the employer's claim that the worker was inefficient. In determining whether the employee was inefficient or whether this was a subterfuge for dismissal for union activities, the NLRB considers the following facts: (1) length of total employment; (2) experience in the particular position from which the employee was discharged; (3) efficiency ratings by qualified persons; (4) specific acts showing efficiency or inefficiency; and (5) comparison with other employees. Other reasons advanced for discharge include decrease in productivity, insubordination, infraction of company rules, fighting, and swearing. In all instances, the NLRB will determine if the reasons have "color and substance," or whether they are only a convenient pretext designed to defeat the law.

Employers discriminate against employees and thereby engage in an unfair labor practice if they refuse employment to persons because of their former or current membership in a labor organization. Moreover, discrimination can also occur in respect to other conditions of work. In one case, the Board found that a company had discriminated against employees, transferring some workers to a very difficult section of the firm as punishment for their union activities, or with the intention of making them quit. One union man would have had to move twenty to twenty-five cars of rock and dirt, and in so doing would have been forced to work for a month without pay. Another instance of discrimination occurred when an employer transferred a worker to another position in which he had no experience, with the motive of firing him for the inefficient work that would result.

The Board has also construed discrimination to include those instances in which an employer has temporarily laid off employees for union activity. Refusal to reinstate employees because of union activity also is discrimination within the meaning of the Wagner Act. Other forms of discrimination include those cases in which an employer forces an employee engaged in union activities to work the worst shifts; pays more wages to a nonunion employee than to a union employee doing equal work; violates seniority rules; and discharges a man's wife because he is a union member.

A case before the U.S. Supreme Court involved the issue of whether an employer owning several plants, Deering Milliken, had violated the discrimination provisions of the Act when it permanently closed down one of its plants for antiunion reasons.[22] The plant that was shut down was located in Darlington, South Carolina. The Darlington case was first taken before the NLRB as a result of unfair labor practices growing out of a plant shutdown after a vigorous company campaign to resist union organizational efforts. In March 1956, when the organizational campaign was initiated, the company interrogated employees and threatened to close the Darlington plant if the Textile Workers Union won the election. On September 6, 1956, the union prevailed in the Board-held election by a narrow margin. The decision was made to liquidate the plant. Employees were informed by the company that the reason for such a decision was the election result and encouragement was extended for employees to sign a petition disavowing the union. The Board found Darlington in violation of the discrimination provision of the Act. The Board ordered back pay for all employees until they obtained substantially equivalent work or were put on preferential hiring lists at the other Deering Milliken mills. Upon review, the second court of appeals denied enforcement and argued that a company had an absolute right to close out a part or all of its business, regardless of antiunion motives.

The U.S. Supreme Court reviewed the case in 1965 and agreed partially with the court of appeals. It held that a single employer could go out of business completely for whatever reason it chose. But "a discriminatory partial closing may have repercussions on what remains of the business, affording employer leverage for discouraging the free exercise of Section 7 rights among remaining employees of much the same kind as that found to exist in the 'runaway shop' and 'temporary closing' cases."[23] The Court held that "a partial closing is an unfair labor practice under Section 8 (a) (3) if motivated by a purpose to chill unionism in any of the remaining plants of the single employer and if the employer may reasonably have foreseen . . . that effect."[24]

A more specific test was provided by the Court for resolving such cases. It stated:

> If the persons exercising control over a plant that is being closed for antiunion reasons (1) have an interest in another business, whether or not affiliated with or engaged in the same line of commercial activity as the closed plant, of sufficient substantiality to give promise of their reaping a benefit from the discouragement of unionization in that business; (2) act to close their plant with the purpose of producing such a result; and (3) occupy a relationship to the other business which makes it realistically foreseeable that its employees will fear that such business will also be closed down if they persist in organizational activities, we think that an unfair labor practice has been made out.[25]

The Board had ruled only on the basis of the effect the plant closing had had on Darlington employees. The Court test required that a determination be made regarding the effect the closing had had on the employees in other plants owned and operated by the Deering Milliken group. In June 1967, the NLRB held that there was sufficient evidence to support the charge that the shutdown of the Darlington plant was for the purpose, at least in part, of discouraging union membership in other plants owned by Deering Milliken. It also found that the closing had a "chilling" effect on the other plant employees as far as union activity was concerned.

Discrimination with regard to hire or tenure will be found only if employees in other plants are affected by the antiunion behavior of an employer. A decision will have to be made in each case, since a partial closing will not constitute a per se violation of the Act. However, it seems clear that multiplant firms cannot make antiunion decisions in one plant without intending the same result to spill over onto all the others.

In 1983, the Board applied the *Darlington* doctrine under circumstances where a single plant employer had closed a plant permanently in retaliation for the workers filing an unfair labor practice charge.[26] Rejecting the union's argument that the employer had engaged in discrimination under the law, the NLRB held that a single-plant employer had an absolute right to close permanently and go out of business.

Strangely enough, it was not until 1983 that the issue of burden of proof was settled in discrimination cases. In 1980, the NLRB established the *Wright Line* doctrine,[27] in which it held that the General Counsel (whose role will be discussed in the next chapter) need only show by the preponderance of evidence that union activities contributed to a discharge, while the employer had the burden to prove that the discharge would have taken place even if the employee had not engaged in union activities. In the 1983 case, an employee was terminated after he attempted to organize a union. To justify discharge, the employer asserted that the employee was terminated because he had left keys in the bus to which he was assigned and had taken unauthorized coffee breaks. When a supervisor became aware of the employee's union activities, he had threatened to discharge the employee. Sustaining both the Board's reinstatement of the employee and the *Wright Line* doctrine, the U.S. Supreme Court held that the employer had not proven that the employee would have been discharged in the absence of his union activities.[28] The Court found that the employee's infraction of the plant rules was too minimal to warrant discharge.

Before concluding this section on discrimination, it may be of value to point out that an employer under the Wagner Act had the opportunity to discharge or otherwise discipline against its employees for any reason except upon the grounds of union activity. It must not be forgotten that the employer retained the right to discharge an employee for other causes: disobedience, bad work, carelessness, drinking on duty, and so on. The law only forbade an employer from discriminating against a worker solely for membership or activity in a union.

Section 8 (a) (4).   This section also prohibits employers from discharging or otherwise discriminating against an employee because he or she has filed charges or given testimony under the Wagner Act. Thus, Congress provided protection for workers who might bring a charge against an employer alleging violation of the terms of the law. Moreover, since the procedures of the Wagner Act require hearings and court proceedings, it was reasonable to forbid discrimination against workers who would participate in such proceedings. The Board has in the past interpreted such employer behavior as a violation of Section 8 (a) (3) as well.

Section 8 (a) (5).   Finally, Section 8 (a) (5) of the Wagner Act makes it an unfair labor practice for an employer to refuse to bargain collectively with the representatives of the employees. By this provision, Congress intended partly to eliminate the need for the recognition strike. Since employers would be required to bargain collectively, workers would not find it necessary to strike for the recognition of the union. Moreover, this portion of Section 8 constitutes the heart of the Wagner Act, for it was enacted to promote the collective bargaining process once a bargaining unit was established. Once more, the NLRB was required to implement public policy. Specifically, what must an employer do in order to fulfill the legal obligation to bargain collectively? The answer to this problem is embedded in scores of NLRB decisions and orders. A brief analysis of them will reveal the character of employer behavior that satisfies the requirement of the law.

In the first place, if an employer refuses to meet with representatives of the employees, the employer has failed to bargain collectively and so has engaged in an unfair labor practice. Of course, the labor organization must make a proper demand to the employer requesting collective bargaining. A demand to bargain must come from the proper source of the union and must be clearly presented to the representatives of the company who usually deal with matters concerning labor relations. A casual remark is not a sufficient demand, but a request for collective bargaining by registered letter is sufficient.

In practice, employers have advanced various excuses for their refusal to meet or to bargain collectively with representatives of their employees. In various decisions, the Board has held in this respect that an employer is not relieved of the duty to bargain collectively by the outbreak of a strike; by shutting down the factory (lockout); or by asserting that pension demands of the union are not proper subjects for negotiations.

A more definite action of some employers to avoid collective bargaining is evidenced in their attempts to undermine unions by engaging in other unfair labor practices. There is, of course, no duty to bargain if the union does not represent a majority of employees in the appropriate unit. Thus, on occasion employers have attempted to evade their duty to bargain collectively by attempting to destroy the majority status of the union. The Board has ruled, however, that an employer who engages in unfair labor practices resulting in the destruction of the majority status of the labor organization is not relieved of the duty to bargain collectively with the representatives of that union.

Employers must do more than just meet with the representatives and merely go through the motions of bargaining. To satisfy the requirement of collective bargaining, an employer must bargain in "good faith."[29] In defining that term, the Board held that to bargain in good faith, an employer "must work toward a solution, satisfactory to both sides, of the various problems under discussion by presentation of counter-proposals and other affirmative conduct."[30] In another case, the Board declared that "the obligation of the Act is to produce more than a series of empty discussions, [and so] bargaining must mean more than mere negotiations. It must mean negotiations with a bona fide intent to reach an agreement if agreement is possible."[31]

The behavior of the employer at the meeting itself may indicate the desire to bargain in good faith. A conference completely dominated by the employer, with the representatives of the union mere auditors to the proceedings, has been held to constitute evidence that the employer does not desire to bargain collectively. If an employer makes no attempt to offer counterproposals during the meeting, the Board has ruled that such action indicates that the employer refuses to bargain in good faith. "The Board has considered counter-proposals so important an element of collective bargaining that it has found the failure to offer counter-proposals to be persuasive of the fact that the employer has not bargained in good faith."[32]

In a series of decisions, the NLRB has maintained that the nature of the employer's conduct after having been requested to bargain collectively is indicative of whether the employer really desired to negotiate in good faith. An employer does not intend to bargain in good faith when, after being asked to bargain collectively, he or she restrains and interferes with the employees' right to self-organization; when he or she attempts to bargain with individual employees; and when he or she calls a general meeting of its employees, dominates such meetings, and therein attacks the union.

The Wagner Act declared that a labor organization designated by the majority of the employees in a unit appropriate for collective bargaining shall be the exclusive representative of all employees in such unit for the purposes of collective bargaining in respect to rates of pay, wages, hours, or other conditions of work. Thus, the Board held early in its career that an employer engaged in an unfair labor practice by refusing to recognize a union as the exclusive representative of all the employees in the bargaining unit. Not only must an employer recognize a labor organization as the representative of all employees in the appropriate unit, but he or she must also bargain collectively with the union for all the employees in the unit, regardless of whether all are members of the union.

The Board established a rule that if an agreement between a company and a labor organization has been reached through discussion, such an agreement must be embodied in a written contract. In other words, an employer does not fulfill the obligation to bargain collectively—and thereby engages in an unfair labor practice—by refusing to render an agreement reached orally into a written trade agreement. In dealing with the matter, the NLRB declared in one case that "an assertion that collective bargaining connotes no more than discussions designed to clarify employer policy and does not include negotiations looking toward a binding agreement is contrary to any realistic view of labor relations. The protection to organization of employees afforded by the first four subdivisions of Section 8 can have meaning only when the ultimate goal is viewed as the stabilization of working conditions through genuine bargaining and [written] agreement between equals."[33] Eventually, the Supreme Court of the United States upheld this policy of the NLRB.[34]

Although the NLRB imposed upon employers the duty to bargain collectively, the law does not require that the parties must reach an agreement. Consequently, when an impasse in the negotiations between an employer and the representatives of the employees occurs, the employer is not required to continue to bargain collectively. When differences develop between parties over substantive issues and the employer has bargained in good faith, the NLRB has declared that an employer has fulfilled the collective bargaining obligations. If, however, the situation should change and new issues are introduced, the employer must resume the process of collective bargaining.

Board-Developed Union Responsibilities

During the Wagner Act years, the Board administered the unfair labor practice portion of the law in a vigorous manner. By checking employer antiunion practices, the Board gave substantial support to the growth of unions. The results of the Board's work in this direction are recorded later in this chapter. However, as unions grew stronger, the attitude of the public toward them underwent a change. A growing number of people were becoming less tolerant toward organized labor. The changing climate of opinion was in part attributable to the antisocial activities of some unions. In some cases, the growing power of unions was not matched by an increased degree of social responsibility on the part of union leadership.

This changing attitude was felt at the NLRB. Its members were aware of the growing tide of antiunion sentiment in the nation. As a result, the Board's policies in unfair labor practice cases underwent a significant change. It began to search for ways in which the Wagner Act could impose obligations on unions even though the law did not contain any unfair labor practices for unions. There was, however, another factor making for this change in NLRB policy. Undoubtedly, the Board tried to make the statute appear more favorable to employers to forestall sweeping and fundamental changes in the Wagner Act.

There were several ways in which the NLRB utilized the Wagner Act to impose obligations on labor unions. In 1947, the NLRB handed down its decision in the celebrated *Times Publishing* case. In this case, the Board held that an employer was under no obligation to bargain with a labor organization which itself did not bargain collectively in good faith. In establishing this policy, the Board stated:

> The test of good faith in bargaining that the Act requires of an employer is not a rigid but a fluctuating one, and is dependent in part upon how a reasonable man might be expected to react to the bargaining attitude displayed by those across the table. It follows that, although the Act imposes no affirmative duty to bargain upon labor organizations, a union's refusal to bargain in good faith may remove the possibility of negotiation and thus preclude the existence of a situation in which the employer's own good faith can be tested. If it cannot be tested, its absence can hardly be found.[35]

In another case in 1947, the Board held that employees who participated in a strike, whose purpose was to compel an employer to recognize and bargain with the union of the striking employees, rather than with a certified labor organization, were not entitled to reinstatement.[36] Thus, to obtain the protection of the Wagner Act, unions and their members were not permitted to force employers to recognize one union when another organization had been certified for collective bargaining. During World War II, under another set of circumstances, the Board refused to order the reinstatement of strikers. It happened that a union called a strike to force an employer to violate the wage stabilization orders and procedures of the National War Labor Board. The employer discharged the workers, and the NLRB held that they lost their reinstatement right under the Act because the union had engaged in an illegal strike.[37]

SUBSTANTIVE PROVISIONS: THE PRINCIPLE OF MAJORITY RULE

It was necessary that Congress spell out the conditions under which employers are considered to have refused to bargain collectively with the representatives of their employees. Collective bargaining implies negotiations between representatives of management and representatives of employees. Consequently, it was indispensable for the Wagner Act to state the circumstances under which an employer was considered to have refused to bargain collectively. To resolve this problem, Congress adopted the principle of majority rule. For purposes of the Wagner Act, an employer engaged in an unfair labor practice only when he or she refused to bargain with a union selected by a majority of the employees for purposes of collective bargaining. If a labor organization did not possess the support of the majority, an employer was under no legal compulsion to bargain.

Still another principle of industrial democracy was embodied in the Wagner Act. Under its terms, a union selected by a majority of workers had to represent all workers in the bargaining unit, regardless of their membership status. A majority labor organization must bargain equally for members and nonmembers in respect to rates of pay, hours of work, or other conditions of employment. Moreover, if a majority of the workers in a unit vote for a union, it must represent all workers in the unit regardless of whether they voted for the union, voted against it, or failed to vote.

Some have opposed the majority-rule principle on the ground that it violates the rights of minority groups. Suppose 75 percent of the workers in a plant select a labor organization as their bargaining representative. Under the Wagner Act, the union was not only to represent this 75 percent, but also had to bargain for the remaining 25 percent. However, the fact that the labor organization chosen by the majority of workers must represent all workers does not transgress the tenets of democracy. Nothing is further from the truth. In fact, the principle of majority rule implements the democratic way of life. In political life, a Republican elected to the House of Representatives represents the Democratic members of the district as well as the Republicans. In addition, each Democratic member in the district is bound by decisions that the Republican representative might make.

Not only is the principle of majority rule consistent with democracy, but it is justified on the basis of effective collective bargaining. If nonunion workers could make their own employment agreements with their employers, the labor union would soon collapse. It would be easy for employers to favor the nonunion workers. These workers could be paid higher wages, helping to lure other workers out of the organization. If a large number of workers withdrew from the union, the labor organization would soon cease to exist. With the disintegration of a union, an employer would not need to be so considerate of the nonunion worker.

There is still another value attached to the principle of majority rule from the viewpoint of effective collective bargaining. Suppose the workers of a factory choose among five labor organizations. Assume that one union received the support of the majority of employees while the others received a scattering of the workers' support. If the minority unions were given the right to bargain for the workers who voted for them, collective bargaining could hardly be conducted successfully. Such "balkanization" of the bargaining unit would defeat the purpose of a law calculated to make collective bargaining effective. Thus, in this example, there would be five contract negotiation sessions, five grievance committees, and five different chances for the plant to shut down because of disagreement over working conditions. Management as well as workers would suffer under such a system. Membership raiding among the unions would be incessant. Production could hardly be carried out effectively in such an environment. What worth would it be to management or to workers if the company negotiated contracts successfully with four of the unions, only to have the plant shut down because the fifth union called a strike over contract terms?

Thus, it can readily be seen that the principle of majority rule satisfies the requirements of democracy and industrial harmony. Majority rule means the promotion of industrial democracy and orderly collective bargaining. Any other principle of representation would mean ineffective collective bargaining, retardation of the rate of production, and general industrial chaos.

UNFAIR LABOR PRACTICE PROCEDURE*

The National Labor Relations Board was established by Congress to protect the rights prescribed by the Wagner Act. This includes the rights of employees, employers, unions, and the general public. The protection of these rights requires the remedying of unfair labor practices and the conduct of representation elections.

The NLRB responsibilities were not divided under the Wagner Act, but the Taft-Hartley amendments organized the agency into two divisions. One division, consisting of the General Counsel and her or his staff, investigates and prosecutes unfair labor practice cases and conducts representation elections. It is the General Counsel who maintains general supervision over the thirty-three regional offices of the NLRB. In the next chapter, we shall discuss the role of the General Counsel in the operation of Taft-Hartley. A director heads each regional office and has direct supervision over field examiners and attorneys. The chief function of the regional director is to issue complaints for unfair labor practices and to resolve issues involved in election cases. Field examiners investigate unfair labor practice cases and conduct elections, and on behalf of the regional director may conduct hearings involving elections. Attorneys perform the same kind of work as field examiners, but may also appear in court proceedings. One need not be an attorney to serve as a field examiner, and this position offers employment to college graduates interested in labor relations.

The second division is the five-member board that hears and decides the unfair labor practice cases prosecuted by the General Counsel. The Board also hears and decides questions concerning representation elections referred to it by the regional offices.

The NLRB solicits neither unfair labor practices to remedy nor representation elections to conduct. Every case has its origin as a result of a charge or petition filed in one of the regional offices by some individual or organization. Specific procedures guide the administration of the statute from the regional offices through the U.S. Supreme Court.

UNFAIR LABOR PRACTICE CHARGE

An unfair labor practice charge must be filed with the regional office in the area in which the labor dispute occurred and must involve conduct defined by the law as an unfair labor practice.

After the charge is filed by an individual, union, employer, or any other party, the regional office must determine whether the Board has jurisdiction over the enterprise. The Board has established minimum standards indicating the volume of business that must be shown before it can exercise its power. These standards, expressed in terms of gross dollar volume of business or interstate

*The procedures mentioned in this section include changes made by the Taft-Hartley Act.

transactions, differ for various categories of enterprises. Certain employers and employees are excluded from coverage under the Act. Once the jurisdictional dollar standards are met and it is determined that the employer and employees are covered by the Act, an investigation is conducted.

Investigation and Informal Settlement

An investigation is conducted by a field examiner or an attorney, who takes written statements and affidavits from available witnesses. When the investigation is completed, the case may be disposed of by withdrawal, settlement, or dismissal. If the case is not closed by one of these three methods, formal proceedings may be initiated if the regional director issues a complaint.

A charge may be withdrawn if the charging party feels that the case is without merit. Frequently, withdrawal is solicited by the regional office, but the charging party may take the initiative. A withdrawal, however, must be approved by the regional director; approval will be granted as long as it is not contrary to the purposes of the Act.

The regional director will dismiss a charge when evidence of a violation of the Act is lacking. Dismissals result if the charging party refuses to withdraw the charge voluntarily. If the regional director dismisses the charge, a request for review may be filed within ten days with the General Counsel in Washington, who may approve or dismiss the regional director's action in the absence of settlement. The regional director must issue a complaint if her or his action is not upheld by the General Counsel.

Board settlements are methods of closing cases in the regional offices by agreement of the parties, and are frequently obtained after complaints are issued. Board settlements are of two types: all-party and unilateral. Both must be approved by the regional director.

All-party settlements permit the charged party, the regional office, and the party making the charge to bring about remedial action on a voluntary basis. This type of settlement does not involve prolonged formal action.

Unilateral board settlements are entered into without the charging party. This type of settlement is approved by the regional director if she or he considers that the settlement fully remedies the unfair labor practice committed. Often, the charging party may have no objection to the agreement, but may simply not wish to sign because an individual involved in the charge may feel he or she was abandoned. The charging party may object to the regional director's actions and appeal to the General Counsel within ten days, requesting a reconsideration of the case.

Non-Board settlements are those in which the Board is not a formal party to the agreement; the parties have settled their differences privately in a satisfactory manner. The settlement must be submitted to the regional director along with a withdrawal request, but the director is under no obligation to approve it. From 1936 until 1947, the years in which the Board administered the Wagner Act, the agency managed to settle 90.6 percent of all its cases involving unfair labor practice charges on an informal basis.[38] In this period, labor unions and employees filed 43,556 charges with the NLRB, alleging employer violations of the Wagner Act. However, more than 50 percent of these cases were either dismissed by the Board or withdrawn by the filing party. Dismissal or withdrawal of cases resulted when the Board decided there was no violation of the Wagner Act. Thus, these figures disclose that, on the basis of informal procedures, the NLRB dismissed more than 50 percent of all unfair labor practice cases alleging employer violations. These figures contradict allegations that the NLRB proceeded to prosecute every employer charged with violating the law.

In about 37 percent of the unfair labor practice cases filed in 1936–1947, the Board adjusted the disputes to the satisfaction of employers, employees, and labor unions. Again, no formal proceedings were involved in such adjustments. In many cases, during an informal investigation of the case, a field examiner merely advised an employer that he or she was violating the law. Frequently, the employer was not aware of the unlawful conduct and, when advised of it, immediately complied with the law.

The fact that the vast majority of the cases were settled on an informal basis by the NLRB speaks well of the Board, employers, unions, and employees. If a majority of the cases filed with the Board had proceeded to formal hearings, investigations, and court proceedings, the administration of the law could not have been effective. By obtaining voluntary compliance with the law, by dismissing cases outright, and by urging labor unions to withdraw baseless charges, the NLRB was able to function successfully. Moreover, the informal settlement of cases resulted in a considerable saving of time and money for all parties involved in Wagner Act proceedings.

The record established under the Wagner Act continued under Taft-Hartley. For example, in 1981, 43,321 unfair labor practice charges were filed by employers, employees, and unions. Of this number, before formal proceedings started, 33.2 percent were withdrawn, 34.6 percent were dismissed, and 26.5 percent were settled between the parties concerned.[39] In other words, the vast majority of charges was disposed of without formal litigation.

FORMAL PROCEEDINGS

Formal proceedings result if the parties are unable to resolve the dispute informally, or if the regional office feels the violation was flagrant and does not approve the informal settlement. The regional office may also refuse such approval if the charged party was a previous offender, or if the settlement agreed to by the parties does not realistically remedy the unfair labor practice.

The Complaint.   A complaint is issued by the regional office on behalf of the General Counsel; it is a formal charge by the government of violation of federal law. The complaint lists the provisions of the Act allegedly violated and the time and place of the hearing covering the unfair labor practice charges. The charged party must answer the complaint within ten days either by admitting, denying, or explaining the facts alleged in the complaint.

The Hearing.   The hearing is the formal trial and is presided over by an administrative law judge (formerly called trial examiner), an agent of the five-member Board in Washington, not of the General Counsel. It is conducted in accordance with the rules of evidence and procedure that apply in the U.S. district courts. After the hearing, the law judge issues a decision. If a violation is found, the decision includes an appropriate remedy. Any party that disagrees with the law judge's decision may appeal to the Board in Washington within twenty days. The NLRB has full power over the decisions issued by the law judges. It may adopt the decision in whole or in part, or reverse it in whole or in part. In rare cases, the Board may direct the law judge to conduct a new hearing. As required by law, the NLRB must review each administrative law judge's decision appealed to it.

In the majority of cases, a respondent complies with the Board's decision and order. If the respondent does not comply, the Board may seek enforcement of its order through any U.S. court of appeals. Similarly, the party charged with a violation of the unfair labor practice provisions may also appeal the Board's decision to a U.S. court of appeals. Likewise, appeals may be made if the Board reverses a law judge's decision. If there is dissatisfaction with the circuit court decision, requests may be made for review to the U.S. Supreme Court. Once a circuit court order is finalized (by failure to seek review or denial thereof by the Supreme Court), the party charged must obey the Board order or face contempt-of-court proceedings.

Only 9.4 percent of all unfair labor practice cases filed with the Board from 1936 to 1947 involved formal proceedings. These proceedings were necessary when employers refused to comply with the law on an informal basis. They felt that their interests would best be served by not complying with informal recommendations tendered by Board officials. These employers in no sense can be censured, for it was their legal right to exhaust fully the procedures of the Wagner Act before complying with the law. The remarkable fact is that so few employers chose to bring into operation the formal procedures of the law. Undoubtedly those employers—or at least the majority of them—honestly felt that they had not violated the law even though an informal investigation may have pointed in that direction. This record continued and even improved under the Taft Hartley Act. For example, in 1984, only 4.2 percent of unfair labor practice cases involved formal proceedings.[40]

THE WAGNER ACT RECORD

How the Board discharged its responsibility is a matter of public record.[41] In the Wagner Act years of 1936–1947, the NLRB reinstated 76,268 workers who had been discharged because of union activities. Moreover, the Board awarded workers $12,418,000 in back pay. Congress recognized that reinstatement of workers discharged because of union activity without awarding them pay for time lost during their period of discharge would be an empty gesture. Accordingly, the Wagner Act provided that workers discharged because of union activities would be reinstated with back pay. In addition, the NLRB disestablished 1,709 company-dominated unions; ordered employers to post 8,156 notices stating that the company would henceforth comply with the Wagner Act; and on 5,070 occasions ordered employers to bargain collectively. Finally, the Board ordered 226,488 strikers reinstated on their jobs. Many of these workers had struck because of employer unfair labor practices; still others had suffered discrimination at the termination of a strike. It has been a favorite union-busting technique for employers to refuse to reinstate strike leaders in their jobs after a strike ends. These figures stand as a testimonial to a law and an agency dedicated to the promotion of collective bargaining and the union movement. This record underscores the proposition that a main source of criticism of the NLRB during its Wagner Act period resulted from the zeal of the agency to perform its duties in a positive and vigorous manner.

Though organized labor bitterly criticized Taft-Hartley when it was originally enacted in 1947 and continues to oppose certain provisions of the law, the fact remains that under the 1947 law, the NLRB still protects the rights of employees. The innovation of Taft-Hartley was not that it repealed those features of the Wagner Act that protected employees' organizational and collective bargaining rights. As will be seen, the major innovation of Taft-Hartley was to place restrictions on certain union activities. In other words, despite such controls, employees still enjoy the protection that they had under the Wagner Act. For example, under Taft-Hartley in 1984, 6,249 employees were ordered to be reinstated in their jobs after having been unlawfully discharged, and were awarded $39,227,845 in back pay plus interest.[42]

As a matter of fact, in 1979, the Board even made it easier for employees to collect back pay. Reversing a 30-year policy, it ruled that a striker discharged discriminatorily no longer needed to request reinstatement to activate the employer's obligation for back pay.[43] Previously, unlike other unlawfully discharged employees (for example, one who was discharged for union activities), an illegally discharged striker had been compelled to request reinstatement from the employer to trigger the employer's back pay obligation. Under the current policy, all unlawfully discharged employees are treated equally. An employer's back pay obligation starts from the date of unlawful discharge and continues until the employee is offered the opportunity to return to work, whether or not the employee accepts this opportunity.

REPRESENTATION PROCEDURE*

Representation cases must also follow a prescribed procedure before the Board is empowered to intervene and conduct elections. Representation elections, like

*The procedures mentioned in this section include changes made by the Taft-Hartley Act.

unfair labor practices, are initiated by the filing of a petition. The petition may be for the purpose of obtaining initial recognition of a union or it may be to decertify the existing bargaining agent. The regional office is authorized to make an investigation of the petition.

The Investigation.   An investigation is conducted in order to obtain information about the following: (1) whether the employer's operations meet the Board's jurisdictional standards; (2) the appropriateness of the unit of employees for purposes of collective bargaining (employees are grouped into units where similar interests exist); (3) the sufficiency of employee interest in representation by a labor organization (an election will usually be conducted by the Board if at least 30 percent of the employees indicate an interest in representation); and (4) whether the petition was filed at the proper time. An election may not be conducted if a valid election had been held during the preceding twelve-month period.

Representation petitions may be disposed of before a hearing by the same methods used in closing unfair labor practice cases—by withdrawal, dismissal, or settlement. If the petition has merit and no arrangements for a consent election have been made, the parties are entitled to a hearing. The law entitles the parties to a representation hearing, which is a formal proceeding designed to obtain information to aid the regional director in deciding the adequacy of the petition. The regional director must make a decision on the appropriateness of the bargaining unit, the timeliness of the petition, the sufficiency of employee interest, and other pertinent matters. The hearing is not held if the parties enter into a consent election agreement, since the matters that must be resolved in the hearing are by such agreement voluntarily resolved by the parties.

Consent elections have the advantage of being conducted much faster than those that require formal hearings. Also, when the parties consent to an election, the work load of the regional office is reduced. Normally, the regional offices are successful in persuading the parties to accept the consent election. In 1984, of the 5,181 elections conducted, 84 percent were of the consent type.[44] We shall discuss the consent election further in the following chapter.

In hearing cases, the regional director reviews the record of the hearing and resolves eligibility, appropriateness of unit, and other requirements; then either directs an election or dismisses the petitions. The decision may be appealed to the Board in Washington. In 1959, Congress authorized the NLRB to refuse to review decisions of the regional directors, and in 1961, the Board implemented this new power. Thus, the NLRB has the discretion to review or not to review appeals from the regional directors. In fiscal year 1976, decisions of the regional directors were appealed to the Board in about 37 percent of the cases.[45] However, the Board accepted only a comparatively small number (14 percent) of these cases for review. In practice, the NLRB accepts for review only those election cases that present precedent-making issues; those in which the regional directors made grievous errors in applying Board or court policies under the law (not a likely event, given the expertise of the regional directors); or those in which a party charges that the hearing was not conducted in a fair manner. Data for the years after 1976 are not available. However, there is no indication that the NLRB has since elected to review a greater percentage of regional director decisions.

Election Supervision.   Personnel from the regional offices supervise the secret-ballot elections after elections are ordered by the regional director or consented to by the parties. Representatives of both employers and unions are entitled to observe the procedure, and to challenge any employee who applies for a ballot. Challenges must be based on "reasonable cause." When the election results depend on the challenged ballots, the regional director must conduct an investigation and make a decision on the challenged votes.

Employer or union conduct affecting an election may be subject to objections within ten days after the ballots are counted. Such objections must be investigated by the regional director and, if they are found to be justified, an election may be set aside and a new one ordered. This depends on the nature of the issues and the type of consent agreement executed by the parties. Challenges and objections might or might not be resolved on the basis of the investigation without a hearing. Depending on the circumstances, the ultimate decision on challenges or objections will be made by the regional director or the Board.

A representation petition may be withdrawn at any time—before the hearing, after the hearing, or after a second election has been ordered by the regional director or the Board. Once the election has been conducted and all the problems associated with it settled, its outcome must be certified. A certification of representatives occurs when a labor organization wins an election. Following certification of representatives, in the absence of an appeal, an employer is obligated to enter collective bargaining negotiations with the appropriate union. Should the labor organization lose, however, there is no certification of results and the employer is not required to bargain.

INDUSTRIAL DEMOCRACY

During the Wagner Act years of 1936–1947, the NLRB was called upon to determine representatives for collective bargaining in 36,969 cases.[46] Labor unions won lawful bargaining rights in 30,110 instances, and workers voted for "no union" in 6,859 cases. Slightly more than 9 million workers were eligible to vote in representation elections. Of this total, 7,677,135 workers, 84.1 percent, actually cast ballots. Votes cast for labor unions amounted to 6,145,834, and votes against unions numbered 1,531,301. These figures testify to the success of the Wagner Act in establishing an orderly manner for the selection of bargaining representatives. The law substituted the ballot box for industrial warfare. Workers in free secret-ballot elections had the opportunity to select or reject the process of collective bargaining. The Wagner Act established the principle of representative democracy in the nation's industrial life.

Indeed, in December 1976, in an election held in Millers Falls, Massachusetts, some unknown employee cast the *30-millionth* vote in the forty-two-year operation of the NLRB.[47] Speaking of this milestone, Betty Southhard Murphy, then the chair of the Board, stated:

> The statute has stood the test of time. During these four decades, the United States in large measure has achieved industrial democracy under law. The statute has been a key factor in our country's immense economic growth; it has brought an evolution of labor relations from sitdown strikes and violence to a thoughtful bargaining and productive compromise.[48]

To the union movement, however, the significance of the milestone was somewhat diminished because of the decline of union success in NLRB elections. Whereas unions had been selected as bargaining agents in about 80 percent of the polls between 1936 and 1947, their success in elections had declined to the 50 percent range in the 1970s.[49] In fiscal year 1980, unions prevailed in only 45.7 percent of the elections.[50] By 1983, union victories had edged up to 47.7 percent, a figure still far below their success rates in earlier years. There are many causes for this sharp decline in union election victories, including the structural change in the nation's labor force, particularly the growing proportion of white-collar employees and women. For a variety of reasons, unions have had difficulty in organizing these segments of the labor force in the same proportions as they have grown.

In any event, on July 5, 1985, the NLRB celebrated its 50th anniversary. In the past 50 years, it has conducted 345,000 elections involving over 32 million employees.[51] Clearly, national labor policy has established the principle of industrial democracy.

WAGNER ACT DURING WORLD WAR II

The Wagner Act proved particularly beneficial to the nation during World War II.[52] The winning of a modern war requires maximum production. The Wagner Act provided workers with a peaceful and orderly procedure to adjust their organizational controversies. Instead of resorting to the organizational strike, the nation's employees could make use of the offices of the National Labor Relations Board.

Events proved that workers and labor unions utilized the peaceful procedures of the Wagner Act in unprecedented numbers. The NLRB handled a tremendous number of cases during the war period. Three factors accounted for this. In the first place, industry greatly expanded its facilities. As a result, the level of employment reached unprecedented heights. By August 1945, the nation's labor force had reached the level of 66,650,000. This number is compared with 54,230,000 reported for 1939. Moreover, unemployment was nearly wiped out during the war years. Whereas 7,300,000 were unemployed in 1939, there were only 830,000—mostly "unemployables"—idle in August 1945. As might be expected, increased trade union activities followed the expansion of the level of employment. Whereas in 1940, union membership in all the nation's labor force was reported at only 8,500,000, the figure had soared to 13,750,000 in 1944. Such augmentation of union activities constituted the second factor making for the heavy workload of the NLRB during World War II. Finally, this increase was attributable to the confidence of the nation's workers and labor unions in the Wagner Act and in the NLRB. In prewar years, the NLRB had demonstrated its power and effectiveness in protecting the right of workers to self-organization and collective bargaining. As a result, the Board entered its wartime career as an agency that had won the respect and admiration of the nation's workers. Obviously, if unions and workers had held the NLRB in low esteem, they would not have utilized the Wagner Act as the vehicle whereby the right to self-organization and collective bargaining could be implemented.

Evidence indicating the large increase in the work of the NLRB during World War II may be briefly noted. Whereas the Board conducted only 3,386 representation elections or crosschecks during the years 1936–1940, in which 1,225,098 valid votes were cast, during the war years of 1941–1945, the NLRB administered 20,562 elections in which 4,889,627 workers cast valid ballots. In other words, more than 85 percent of all representation elections conducted by the Board during the first ten years of its operation was held in the war period. Workers resorted to the election procedures of the Wagner Act because, as noted, they had faith that once their unions were certified, the NLRB would guarantee that employers would recognize them as collective bargaining agencies. Actually, the NLRB issued 2,796 wartime orders requiring employers to bargain collectively with labor unions chosen by their employees. This figure is slightly in excess of the number of all such orders handed down by the NLRB during the years 1937 to 1941.

The major portion of the Board's activities during World War II involved the certification of bargaining representatives. By 1945, representation cases constituted 75.1 percent of the total of all cases, and unfair labor practice cases accounted for 24.2 percent. In comparison, in 1936, the first full year of the Board's operation, unfair labor practice cases accounted for 81 percent of the total of all cases filed with the Board, whereas representation cases accounted for only 19 percent. These figures indicate that during World War II, employers, instead of interfering with the right of employees to organize and bargain collectively, were more anxious to learn with whom they were required to bargain. The change in the comparative importance of representation cases indicated that after several years of the Wagner Act, employers and employees alike recognized the role of collective bargaining in modern industry. However, it should not be overlooked that 18,187 unfair labor practice cases were filed with the Board during the period 1941–1945. This figure was only 932 less than the number of all unfair labor practice cases filed with the NLRB in the prewar years, 1936–1940. The wartime unfair labor practice cases involved 18,108,433 employees. Consequently, in war as in peace, legal protection of the right of workers to self-organization and collective bargaining is clearly a prerequisite for industrial peace.

Another aspect of wartime labor relations should be stressed. Much of the Board's wartime work involved basic war industries. More than 50 percent of all bargaining elections conducted by the NLRB were held in the nation's crucial war industries, which included those of iron and steel, machinery, food, chemicals, wholesale trade, electrical equipment, textiles, aircraft, and shipbuilding. Approximately 50 percent of all unfair labor practices likewise involved the same nine industries.

Literally millions of the nation's war production workers resorted to the machinery of the NLRB for adjustment of their organizational disputes. War production would have been seriously retarded if employees had not had the opportunity to settle their organizational controversies through the Board's peaceful and democratic procedures. Recognizing the importance of speedy disposition of wartime representation and unfair labor practice disputes, the NLRB streamlined its regulations under which disposition of the cases was made. By granting greater authority to its regional directors and by otherwise accommodating its procedures to the exigencies of war conditions, the NLRB decreased by several months the time required to process its cases. By lawful certification of bargaining agents and through speedy elimination of unfair labor practices, the NLRB hoped to abolish completely the justification for organizational strikes.

RESULTS OF THE WAGNER ACT

Organizational strike experience during World War II is one standard with which to evaluate the results of the Wagner Act. As noted, approximately 50 percent of all strikes that occurred during 1934 to 1936 resulted wholly or in part from organizational disputes.[53] These strikes involved about 43 percent of the workers who engaged in all strikes during this period. In comparison, in 1942, the first full year of U.S. involvement in World War II, organizational controversies wholly or in part caused 31.2 percent of all strikes.[54] In subsequent war years, the organizational strike was of even less comparative importance. In 1943, organizational disputes, alone or in combination with other causes, resulted in 15.7 percent of all work stoppages; in 1944, they caused 16.3 percent of all strikes; and in 1945, they wholly or in part caused 20.5 percent of all work stoppages. From the point of view of the number of workers engaged in strikes during the war years (1942–1945), work stoppages carried out for organizational purposes alone or in combination with other causes involved approximately 18.5 percent of all workers who engaged in strikes during this period. In the light of the organizational strike experience of 1934 to 1936, it is likely that in the absence of the effective operation of the Wagner Act, organizational strikes would have been of greater absolute and comparative importance during World War II.

A comparison of the frequency of organizational strikes during World War I with those during World War II might further indicate the extent to which the Wagner Act was successful in decreasing such work stoppages in World War II. The Bureau of Labor Statistics has faithfully recorded throughout the years the number of strikes resulting from the refusal of employers to recognize their employees' unions. Under the terms of the Wagner Act, an employer engages in an unfair labor practice by refusing to recognize a certified labor organization as the exclusive representative of the workers in the bargaining unit. Accordingly, workers during World War II had little reason to engage in strikes to gain recognition for their labor unions, since their organizations could accomplish this objective by resorting to the peaceful machinery provided by the NLRB. During World War I, when there existed no agency similar to the NLRB, it is reported that 314 strikes and lockouts were caused by employers' refusal to recognize unions in 1917, and 221 such work stoppages took place in 1918. Expressed as a ratio, recognition strikes accounted for approximately 7 percent of all 1917 strikes and lockouts, and such interruptions to production resulted in 6.5 percent of all work stoppages in 1918. On the other hand, the Bureau reports that in 1942, the first full year of World War II, only 169 recognition-caused work stoppages occurred, accounting for only 5.6 percent of all 1942 interruptions. In subsequent years, the record indicates, the recognition strike continued to be of less importance, comparative and absolute, during World War II as compared to its importance in World War I.

Even though the lack of World War I data precludes a comparison of World War I and World War II recognition strikes on a "worker-days-lost" basis, it still appears that World War II employees and trade unions, able to utilize the NLRB procedures, resorted to the recognition strike far less frequently than did World War I employees. It is thus probable that the number of World War II recognition strikes would have been greater had there been no NLRB.

These figures underscore the contention that the Wagner Act was a powerful force making for industrial peace during World War II. They highlight the necessity for an orderly system to provide effective and speedy protection of the right of workers to self-organization and collective bargaining. With the passage of years, it is likely that the Wagner Act would have contributed even more to the elimination of the organizational strike. Workers and unions, aware of the remedies of the NLRB, would have relied more on peaceful legal procedures than on the strike to make the right to collective bargaining effective.

The success of the Wagner Act in decreasing the number of organizational strikes cannot be denied. The trend during World War II removed all doubt on the issue. However, some people contend that the Wagner Act, though decreasing the number of organizational strikes, stimulated strikes for nonorganizational issues—wages, hours, pensions, vacations, and the like. The arguments run along the following lines. Under the protection of the Wagner Act, union membership increased, the union movement expanded into new areas, and general bargaining strength of labor unions sharply increased. These circumstances increased the number of nonorganizational strikes, for under the Wagner Act, unions became a powerful force in the national economy. In other words, the Wagner Act did not promote industrial peace.

Close analysis of this argument will indicate its fundamental defects. In the first place, the Wagner Act was not passed to eliminate all types of strikes. It was enacted to reduce the number of organizational strikes. Unless we are prepared to make fundamental changes in the structure of a free enterprise system, strikes over wages, hours, and conditions of work will always characterize our national life. It is not fair to evaluate the Wagner Act on the basis of the number of all strikes arising during its operation. A valid basis for evaluating its contribution to industrial peace consists of the trend in organizational strikes.

Clearly, the Wagner Act stimulated the growth of the union movement. Union membership increased from about 4 million in 1935 to about 16 million in 1948. Under its protection, the CIO was able to organize the mass production industries on an industry-wide basis. Responding to the challenge of the CIO, the AFL likewise undertook important organizational activities. Obviously, the Wagner Act accomplished its objective of promoting collective bargaining. One may quarrel as to whether or not a large and strong labor union movement is good or bad for society. Whatever the answer to this question, the fact remains that the Wagner Act was very effective in stimulating the growth and strength of organized labor.

Other results of the Wagner Act appear equally impressive. Not only was the statute successful in reducing the number of organizational strikes and expanding the union movement, but the Wagner Act operated to increase greatly the number of effective collective bargaining agreements. In 1946, the last full year of the Wagner Act, the Bureau of Labor Statistics reported that the number of collective bargaining contracts in the nation totaled well over 50,000. In addition, during each year , many of these contracts are rewritten in whole or in part. These figures underscore the contention that industrial peace and not industrial warfare is the result of the collective bargaining process. By far the vast majority of labor contracts are negotiated and signed without resort to the strike. The general public is not usually aware of this fact. Strikes are more often reported than peaceful settlement of agreements. Such a focus on conflict, however, is not unique to labor-management relations.

It is noteworthy that the Wagner Act stimulated an increase in the number of collective bargaining agreements. Moreover, it should be kept in mind that these contracts, once executed, often provided the basis for peaceful industrial relations for the life of the contract. Not only did they provide a peaceful procedure for the day-to-day relationship between employees and employer, but they also served to stabilize labor relations for long periods of time. The biggest hurdle to industrial peace is the execution of the first collective bargaining agreement. Recent Board experience supports such an assertion. After the first contract is achieved, and assuming that a management and a union recognize their mutual problems and aspirations, long-run industrial peace is likely.

SUMMARY

The Wagner Act sought to promote collective bargaining by denying employers the opportunity to interfere with the right of workers to self-organization and collective bargaining. Through this procedure, Congress hoped to provide workers with a measure of social and economic justice, to promote a stable economic system, and to foster industrial peace. The law did not seek to promote strong unions as ends in themselves. Rather, the objectives of the Wagner Act were social in character, extending beyond the advancement of any particular economic group. Since the law effectively stopped antiunion conduct on the part of employers, the reaction of this group to the law was extremely unfavorable. Many employers attempted to nullify the law by enlisting the support of their old ally, the judiciary. However, by a majority of one, the Supreme Court of the United States in the *Jones & Laughlin* case upheld the constitutionality of the Wagner Act. The Court also assured wide coverage of the law by applying its terms to manufacturing.

The substance of the law centered on Section 7, which guaranteed the right of employees to self-organization and collective bargaining. To make this right meaningful, employers were required to bargain collectively with unions chosen by a majority of their employees and were forbidden to engage in other patterns of antiunion conduct. The National Labor Relations Board was established to enforce the Wagner Act. To sound out the collective bargaining desires of employees, the Board was required to conduct elections in appropriate bargaining units. In addition, it was empowered to prevent employer interference with the collective bargaining rights of the workers covered by the law. In recent years, action has been taken to invoke the unfair labor practice provisions of the Act to eliminate racial discrimination.

Under the protection of the Wagner Act, the union movement made phenomenal progress. Union membership increased from about 4 million in 1935 to about 16 million in 1948. The effectiveness of the Wagner Act in this respect stimulated a great deal of employer hostility. However, the Wagner Act remained intact until 1947, the year of Taft-Hartley.

DISCUSSION QUESTIONS

1. What was the economic rationale of Congress in passing the Wagner Act?

2. What public policy statement did Congress set forth in the Wagner Act? Has it changed? Should it change?

3. How was the Wagner Act received by affected parties in the first two years of its existence?

4. What was the specific significance of the *Jones & Laughlin* decision on the Wagner Act? Were there more general applications to the ruling beyond labor relations?

5. Why did five employer unfair labor practices need to be specified in order to accomplish the objective of Section 7? How do the five unfair labor practices clarify the meaning of Section 7?

6. Discuss the significance of the original *Darlington* doctrine. How was the original position changed in the NLRB's *Contris Packing Co.* case in 1983?

7. Do you agree with the principle of majority rule established by Congress in the Wagner Act? What is that principle? How important is it for union organizational successes?

8. Set up an alleged violation of one of the unfair labor practices presented in the chapter. Then trace the procedure necessary to process the case through the procedures of Taft-Hartley.

9. Are there identifiable trends that can be discovered from a review of the Wagner Act record in unfair labor practice cases? In representation cases?

NOTES

1   *New York Times* Magazine Section, May 9, 1937, p. 23.
2   Statement of H. M. Robertson, General Counsel, Brown and Williamson Tobacco Corporation, in Senate Committee on Education and Labor, *Hearings on a National Labor Relations Board*, 74th Congress, 1st sess., 1935, p. 218.
3   See Chapter 8.
4   See *Causes of Industrial Peace Under Collective Bargaining*, National Planning Association (Washington, D.C., 1948–1950).
5   National Labor Relations Board, *First Annual Report*, 1936, p. 46.
6   *Ibid.*, p. 47.
7   *Ibid.*, p. 48.
8   U.S. Department of Labor, Bureau of Labor Statistics, *Monthly Labor Review*, XLII, 162 (1936), p. 1308; XLIV, 1937, p. 1230.
9   *United States* v. *Knight*, 156 U.S. 12 (1894).
10   *Carter* v. *Carter Coal Co.*, 298 U.S. 238 (1936).
11   *NLRB* v. *Jones & Laughlin Steel Corporation*, 301 U.S. 1 (1937).
12   Since the *Jones & Laughlin* decision, the Supreme Court has widely construed the meaning of the interstate commerce clause for the purposes of national labor relations legislation. Decisions of the Supreme Court have empowered the NLRB to exercise jurisdiction over public utilities supplying energy to enterprises engaged in interstate commerce, *Consolidated Edison Company* v. *NLRB*, 305 U.S. 197 (1938); national fraternal organizations, *Polish National Alliance* v. *NLRB*, 322 U.S. 643 (1944); and a local transportation system in an industrial city, *NLRB* v. *Baltimore Transit Company*, 321 U.S. 796 (1944); and a large retail department store, *NLRB* v. *J. L. Hudson Company*, 135 Fed. (2d) 380, certiorari denied by Supreme Court, October 11, 1943; as well as to a charitable hospital, *NLRB* v. *Central Dispensary and Emergency Hospital*, 324 U.S. 847 (1945). The Supreme Court has also held that a firm falls within the authority of the NLRB even if it only exports goods into interstate commerce, *Santa Cruz Fruit Packing Company* v. *NLRB*, 303 U.S. 453 (1938); or only receives goods from other states, *Newport News Shipbuilding and Dry Dock Company* v. *Schauffler*, 303 U.S. 54 (1938). Moreover, in the *Fainblatt* case (*NLRB* v. *Fainblatt*), 306 U.S. 601 (1939), the Supreme Court rejected the criterion that an employer's operations must be large enough to be of great national importance in order to fall within the scope of the

NLRB. It declared that the operation of the NLRB does not "depend on any particular volume of commerce affected more than that to which courts would apply the maxim *de minimis.*" It should be noted here that this broad concept of interstate commerce developed by the Supreme Court for purposes of the Wagner Act applies equally to NLRB operations when it administers the Taft-Hartley law.

13   Benjamin J. Taylor, *The Operation of the Taft-Hartley Act in Indiana* (Bloomington, Indiana: Bureau of Business Research, Indiana University, 1967), p. 3.

14   National Labor Relations Board, *op. cit.,* p. 55.

15   National Labor Relations Board, *Decisions and Orders of the National Labor Relations Board,* VII, 1936, p. 54.

16   *Riecke Metal Products Company,* 40 NLRB 872 (1942).

17   *Burger King* v. *NLRB,* 725 Fed. (2d) 1053 (1984).

18   3 NLRB 591 (1938).

19   National Labor Relations Board, *Third Annual Report,* 1938, p. 115.

20   7 NLRB 877.

21   *Jackson Engineering Co.,* 265 NLRB No. 175 (1982).

22   *Textile Workers Union* v. *Darlington Mfg. Co.,* 380 U.S. 263 (1965).

23   *Ibid.,* pp. 274–275.

24   *Ibid.,* p. 275.

25   *Ibid.,* pp. 275–276.

26   *Contris Packing Co.,* 268 NLRB No. 7 (1983).

27   *Wright Line, Inc.,* 251 NLRB 1083 (1980).

28   *NLRB* v. *Transportation Management Corp.,* 426 US 393 (1983).

29   National Labor Relations Board, *op. cit.,* p. 96.

30   2 NLRB 39 (1937).

31   3 NLRB 10 (1938).

32   National Labor Relations Board, *op. cit.,* p. 97.

33   2 NLRB 39.

34   *H. J. Heinz Company* v. *NLRB,* 311 U.S. 514 (1941). When Congress enacted Taft-Hartley, this principle established by the NLRB during the early years of its administration of the Wagner Act was incorporated into the legislation.

35   *Times Publishing Company,* 72 NLRB 676 (1947).

36   *Thompson Products, Inc.,* 72 NLRB 888 (1947). See Chapter 17 to learn how such strikes are treated under the Taft-Hartley law.

37   *American News Company,* 55 NLRB 1302 (1944).

38   National Labor Relations Board, *Twelfth Annual Report,* 1947, p. 86.

39   National Labor Relations Board, *Forty-sixth Annual Report,* 1981, p. 5.

40   Office of General Counsel, NLRB, *Summary of Operations for Fiscal Year 1984,* January 28, 1985, p.2.

41   National Labor Relations Board, *Twelfth Annual Report,* 1947, pp. 83–90.

42   National Labor Relations Board, *Forty-fifth Annual Report,* 1980, p. 3.

43   *Abilities & Goodwill,* 241 NLRB No. 5 (1979).

44   National Labor Relations Board, *Forty-fifth Annual Report,* 1980, p. 15.

45   National Labor Relations Board, *Interim Report and Recommendations of the Chairman's Task Force of the NLRB for 1976,* November 5, 1976, p. 29.

46   National Labor Relations Board, *Twelfth Annual Report,* 1947, pp. 83–90.

47   *AFL-CIO News,* March 5, 1977.

48   National Labor Relations Board, *Forty-first Annual Report,* 1976, p. 2.

49   *Ibid.,* p. 17.

50   National Labor Relations Board, *Forty-fifth Annual Report,* 1980, p. 16.

51   Commerce Clearing House, *Labor Law Reports,* No. 700, July 19, 1985.

52   See Fred Witney, *Wartime Experiences of the National Labor Relations Board* (Urbana, Illinois: University of Illinois Press, 1949). This study discusses the operation of the Wagner Act during World War II.

53   See U.S. Department of Labor, Bureau of Labor Statistics, *Monthly Labor Review,* XLII, 162 (1936), p. 1308; XLIV, (1937), p. 1230. Although the Wagner Act was approved by Congress on June 27, 1935, and signed by President Roosevelt on July 5, 1935, the statute was not operationally effective until the Supreme Court approved the legislation on April 1, 1937. Consequently, to ascertain the effectiveness of the Wagner Act in reducing organizational strikes, it appears appropriate to disregard 1935 and 1936, although the Act was technically in operation during these two years.

54   U.S. Department of Labor, Bureau of Labor Statistics, *Monthly Labor Review,* LVI, (1943), p. 973.

CHAPTER TEN

THE TAFT–HARTLEY ACT: GENERAL OBSERVATIONS

THE SHIFT IN GOVERNMENT POLICY

On June 23, 1947, Congress overrode a presidential veto and enacted the Taft-Hartley Act.[1] The law was far more controversial than both the Norris–La Guardia and Wagner Acts. This time, however, the positions of management and organized labor were reversed. Management defended the amendments while organized labor denounced congressional action. The controversy began while Congress was debating the law, and it increased in intensity after the law's enactment. With the law's passage, management and labor joined in the battle with renewed vigor. Radio commentators, newspaper journalists, politicians, and students of industrial relations contributed their share to the controversy. The Taft-Hartley Act substantially changed the direction of industrial relations, and its effect was to produce a controversy never before known to follow the passage of a single labor law.

Literally hundreds of articles and tracts have been written on the law. By December 1, 1949, the National Labor Relations Board reported a bibliography on the legislation that included about three hundred items. By no means did the list include all the material written or presented in speeches on the legislation. In scholarly publications, popular magazines, newspaper editorials, company and union tracts, public lectures, and radio debates, the people concerned with labor relations law analyzed the Taft-Hartley Act. If the legislation did nothing else, it underlined the importance of industrial relations law to the functioning of trade unions and the collective bargaining process.

Proponents of Taft-Hartley

Defenders of the legislation generally direct their arguments along the following lines: the law frees workers from the tyrannical hold of "union bosses"; it reduces the monopolistic position of labor unions; it protects the public from catastrophic strikes; it protects management from union abuses; it makes unions legally and financially responsible for their actions; it reduces communism within the union movement; it diminishes the power of "labor dictators"; and it promotes greater equality of bargaining power between management and labor. Additionally, defenders of the law, answering critics, vigorously argued that the Taft-Hartley Act does not "enslave labor"; deprive workers of the legal protection of their right to self-organization and collective bargaining; destroy labor unions; reduce the bargaining power of labor unions; or interfere with the ability of labor to strike for better working conditions. Finally, the supporters of the law claimed that it "equalized" the legal position of employers and unions. The Wagner Act was appraised as one-sided, providing restrictions against unfair labor practices by management, but imposing no restraints on labor unions. Taft-Hartley provided measures against union as well as employer unfair labor practices.

Management groups had argued against the Wagner Act even before the law had been passed. One argument was that labor organizations should be under the same or equivalent limitations and responsibilities as were employers, or else management restrictions should be removed. The argument presented by management groups has been labeled the "doctrine of mutuality."[2] Between the passage of the Wagner Act and the Taft-Hartley amendments, mutuality was generally the basis for proposing amendments. The United States Chamber of Commerce proposed the addition of unfair labor practices of unions in 1937, after the Supreme Court had upheld the constitutionality of the Wagner Act.

Criticism of the Wagner Act was not limited to employer groups. The American Federation of Labor was not satisfied with some of the NLRB's policies and made proposals to change the law. It is important to note that the general public was not confronted by a labor movement united on the desirability of the law. Competition between the AFL and the CIO for members reinforced the public's concern about a lack of union regulation.

A steel corporation, shortly after the passage of the Taft-Hartley Act, supplied each of its employees with a letter defending the law. In part, the tract declared:

> The Taft-Hartley Act is designed to protect the rights of the *individual* worker. During the past few years the abuses of individual workers by some union bosses and some unions have become as great as those by the unscrupulous employers of the past era. The Taft-Hartley Act does *not* weaken the power of the Unions. It is aimed at assuring control of the Unions by the *individual* worker and protecting him [*sic*] from *abuse*—abuse in case he disagrees with his Union leaders.[3]

The same theme of protection of the union member from the labor organization was expressed by representatives in Congress. In this connection, one senator declared: "I want to protect the worker. It seems to me he is the forgotten man. The individual worker is the man in trouble."[4] Only one more statement will be selected from a mountain of material turned out by Taft-Hartley defenders. The Joint Committee on Labor-Management Relations, established under the Taft-Hartley Act and headed in 1948 by former Senator Joseph H. Ball, reported that the law "is working well, without undue hardship upon employers or employees, and promoting the adjustment of labor problems equitably and in a more friendly and co-operative relationship."[5]

Opponents of Taft-Hartley

Organized labor regarded the Taft-Hartley Act in a much different light. Union representatives charged that it curtailed the opportunities for the effective operation of the collective bargaining process. They claimed that the law gave aid and comfort to the employer who shows little or no inclination to bargain collectively. It was charged that the law seriously interfered with the right of labor to strike. On the basis of this assertion, labor leaders denounced the statute as a "slave labor law," a claim that was vigorously denied by the law's supporters. New organizational drives, unions claimed, were made difficult or impossible by features of the statute. In general, labor leaders charged that the statute reduced the opportunities for effective collective bargaining, impaired free collective bargaining, promoted industrial strife, forestalled the expansion of unionism into new areas, and threatened the existence of the American labor union movement.

Selective observations of leading labor officials highlight the positions taken against the Taft-Hartley amendments. On June 20, 1947, the executive board of the CIO declared, "The sponsors of this legislation have attempted to commit the perfect crime. They seek to destroy labor unions, to degrade living standards, to extinguish and to cripple the exercise of basic rights and forever to prevent the great mass of those whose needs are thus to be sacrificed to reaction and privilege from shaking off this yoke of want and depression."[6]

Testifying before the Committee on Labor and Public Welfare, Arthur J. Goldberg, General Counsel of the CIO, declared, "It is my contention that the Taft-Hartley Act is a strikebreaking law, that the Taft-Hartley Act can convert any legal strike into an illegal strike."[7]

Not to be outdone by the CIO, the AFL condemned the Taft-Hartley Act in an equally vigorous manner. During the AFL convention of 1947, the Executive Council of the Federation contended that the statute "seeks to weaken, render impotent, and destroy labor unions. It does so by striking a vital blow at free collective bargaining and substituting a process of government domination over employer-employee relationships."[8]

William Green, president of the AFL, declared, "The Taft-Hartley Act was passed over the strong opposition of labor. Workingmen and unions throughout the nation protested against the passage of this objectionable legislation. This opposition was based upon the knowledge of labor that it was impracticable, unworkable, and violated the common elemental rights of labor. Time and experience have shown that labor was right and the sponsors of the bill were wrong."[9]

The controversy concerning the law highlights the necessity for a careful approach to determining the factors primarily responsible for the new law. To this end, we must be concerned with fact and experience. The controversial questions must be appraised in terms of the record in order to pass judgment on the statute. Is the statute actually a "slave labor" law? Are unions really weakened by the statute? What about the issue of protecting the union member from the labor organization? Is it true that the statute substitutes government control of collective bargaining for free collective bargaining? Does Taft-Hartley seriously interfere with the right to strike? Does the employee still receive adequate protection of the right to self-organization and collective bargaining? These problems and others merit close attention.

FACTORS RESULTING IN PASSAGE OF TAFT-HARTLEY

The Taft-Hartley Act represents a significant change in the climate of industrial relations law. Before proceeding to an analysis of the issues growing out of the application of this statute, it is essential that attention be focused on the factors that partially explain enactment of Taft-Hartley. Laws do not spring from a vacuum; they are the result of definite conditions that give rise to legislative action. At this point, our concern is not to criticize or commend Congress for the enactment of Taft-Hartley, but merely to examine the circumstances that produced the statute. The mere presentation of the environmental framework that resulted in the passage of the legislation does not necessarily mean a stamp of approval on the law. With these qualifications in mind, an examination of some forces which influenced the passage of Taft-Hartley will prove profitable.

Perennial Opposition to the Wagner Act

Some employers and other special-interest groups never accepted the philosophy of the Wagner Act. They were not inclined to feel favorable toward a law that gave effective legal support to the collective bargaining process. The success of the Wagner Act in promoting a strong and expanding union movement served to intensify efforts to destroy the legislation. From the year in which the statute was enacted until the passage of Taft-Hartley, each session of Congress was marked by organized efforts to repeal the Wagner Act.

Actually, opponents of the Wagner Act were successful on the state level long before they managed to alter the federal labor relations policy. As noted in the preceding chapter, the Wagner Act applied only to workers engaged in interstate commerce. Even after the Supreme Court decided to apply the law to manufacturing, millions of workers engaged in activities defined as intrastate received no benefits from the Wagner Act. One writer points out that in 1940, some 13 million nonagricultural workers were in industries not covered by the Wagner Act.[10] This category includes employees of beauty parlors, garages, cleaning establishments, and retail stores. Some state legislatures, aware of this situation, enacted "little Wagner Acts" to provide intrastate workers with legal protection of the right to self-organization and collective bargaining. In 1937, the year in which the Supreme Court validated the Wagner Act, such laws were passed in Utah, Wisconsin, New York, Pennsylvania, and Massachusetts. Rhode Island enacted a "little Wagner Act" in 1941, and the Connecticut legislature passed one in 1945. Except for minor differences, these state laws resembled the national statute. Thus a considerable number of intrastate workers received legal protection of their organizational rights.

Organized labor desired that many more states would pass similar legislation. However, their hopes were not realized. Instead the trend was reversed: in place of laws favorable to unions, many states enacted restrictive labor relations laws. In fact, Wisconsin, Pennsylvania, and Utah repealed their little Wagner acts and passed in their place legislation that provided for general restrictions on the activities of labor unions. In addition, the states of Michigan, Minnesota, Kansas, and Colorado passed legislation that likewise provided for the general regulation of labor unions. All these union-control laws were enacted before Taft-Hartley was passed by Congress. Wisconsin, Pennsylvania, Minnesota, and Michigan adopted such laws in 1939; Kansas and Colorado in 1943; and Utah in the spring of 1947.

The union-control acts of these states bore little resemblance to the Wagner Act. In the place of statutes protecting the right of labor to self-organization and collective bargaining, they provided for the curtailment of the right of employees to strike, picket, boycott, and carry on organizational campaigns. Labor leaders bitterly denounced these laws. For example, Henry Ohl, chair of the Wisconsin Federation of Labor, characterized the new Wisconsin law as the "most astounding and most vicious piece of legislation in my 40 years of experience."[11]

A. J. Biemiller, member of the Wisconsin legislature, likewise criticized the Wisconsin law, claiming that the bill would "strait-jacket" labor and would "allow employers to block the growth of unionism."[12] A Wisconsin newspaper viewed the concern of labor and concluded that "probably never before in the last two decades have labor leaders shown such alarm over a piece of legislation."[13]

Pressure groups that were successful in obtaining union-control laws on the state level also spearheaded the attack on the Wagner Act. The same criticisms voiced against the little Wagner acts were leveled against the Wagner Act and the NLRB. For example, Milo R. Swanton, executive secretary of the Wisconsin Council of Agriculture, the special-interest group that ostensibly effected the passage of the Wisconsin union-control law,[14] appeared before the Senate Labor Committee and presented similar criticisms of the Wagner Act.[15]

Thus, opponents of the Wagner Act type of legislation were successful on the state level prior to the amending of the national law. State union-control laws antedated by many years the amending of the Wagner Act and the enactment of Taft-Hartley. In fact, many of the provisions contained in the 1947 federal labor statute duplicated terms of previously enacted state laws. Such similarities should be expected, for the same pressure groups that accepted neither the philosophy nor the objectives of the Wagner Act worked diligently to assert their philosophy in both state and federal statutes. Organized labor did not present a united effort to forestall such pressures for change.

The Wagner Act: Popular Delusions

Perhaps no other law was so misunderstood by the public as the Wagner Act. It is possible that general misconceptions regarding the Wagner Act constituted an important factor in the enactment of Taft-Hartley. The public did not have much of an opportunity to understand the nature of the Wagner Act, nor of the duties and functions of the NLRB. In general, the law and the Board received bad press. Rulings of the NLRB consistent with the overall philosophy and purpose of the Wagner Act were highly criticized. Little effort was made by any group to relate administrative rulings to the basic philosophy and objectives of the Wagner Act. Board members rarely appeared to explain why the fundamental philosophy of the Wagner Act was consistent with the modern industrial relations environment.

In addition, the public was not adequately informed as to what the Wagner Act did not do. Popular misunderstandings surrounding the law arose. Some people believed that the Wagner Act provided for mediation and conciliation and that the NLRB was a mediation agency. Nothing, of course, was further from the truth. When President Roosevelt approved the Wagner Act on July 5, 1935, he declared that the NLRB "is an independent quasi-judicial body. It should be clearly understood that it will not act as a mediator nor as a conciliator in labor disputes. . . . Compromise, the essence of mediation, has no place in the interpretation and enforcement of the law."[16] Further, the public was not clearly informed that the Wagner Act and the NLRB did not require workers to join labor unions; force agreement between management and labor; establish conditions and terms of employment; or prevent the discharge of employees for any reason other than for labor organization activities. The Wagner Act did not purport to eliminate *all* strikes, but merely *organizational* strikes; and the law did not *require* the closed shop, but merely permitted it when a majority-designated union and employer agreed on such an arrangement through collective bargaining.

The NLRB was portrayed as an agency unique in the federal legislative framework. It was charged that the NLRB acted as prosecutor, judge, and jury in unfair labor practice cases. What the public did not learn was that every Board decision was subject to review by the federal courts, including the Supreme Court of the United States. All federal administrative agencies were organized along the lines of the NLRB. In addition, the vast majority of cases of the NLRB were settled on a voluntary and informal basis without the necessity of proceeding to costly and time-consuming litigation. The public was led to believe that an employer, once charged with an unfair labor practice, had little opportunity to defend herself or himself. It was not widely known that more than 50 percent of all charges alleging employer unfair labor practices were dismissed by the NLRB or withdrawn by the charging party at Board insistence. The debate over the need to amend the Wagner Act was interrupted by World War II. However, even the war years were not devoid of occurrences that conditioned the general public for changes in national labor policy.

Developments During World War II

From January 12, 1942, until June 25, 1943, wartime labor disputes were settled in accordance with the procedures outlined by the President of the United States. With one glaring exception, they proved successful in minimizing the effects of strikes on the operation of the nation's wartime economy. This exception involved the coal strikes that swept the nation during the early months of 1943. The United Mine Workers Union, led by John L. Lewis, defied the NWLB and would not cooperate with it to find a peaceful solution for the coal disputes. Its officers even refused to attend the coal-dispute hearings conducted by the Board. The coal strikes plus the defiant attitude of the officers of the UMW stimulated the passage of the controversial War Labor Disputes Act.[17] This law gave statutory authority to the President to seize war facilities; made it a criminal offense to instigate, direct, or aid a strike in a government-seized plant; gave the National War Labor Board statutory authority and defined its powers; prohibited labor organizations from contributing funds for political purposes; and, finally, outlawed strikes in privately operated war plants unless thirty-day strike notices had been filed and a strike vote had been taken to indicate the strike desires of war workers.

Both William Green, president of the AFL, and Philip Murray, president of the CIO, vigorously condemned the law. They contended that organized labor should not be punished by such legislation because the nation's unions had largely kept the no-strike pledge in good faith. Ultimately, President Roosevelt vetoed the bill, declaring:

> American labor as well as American business gave their "no-strike, no-lockout" pledge after the attack on Pearl Harbor. That pledge has been well kept except in the case of the leaders of the United Mine Workers. For the entire year of 1942, the time lost by strikes averaged only 5/100ths of 1 per cent of the total man hours worked. The American people should realize that fact—that 99 and 95/100 per

cent of the work went forward without strikes and that only 5/100ths of 1 per cent of the work was delayed by strikes. That record has never before been equaled in this country.[18]

Congress, however, was not deterred by the President's arguments. It passed the War Labor Disputes Act over his veto. Actually, from the point of view of wartime production, there was little need for the War Labor Disputes Act. Even before its passage, the President, by virtue of his constitutional war powers, had the authority to seize any plant or facility in the nation when the operation of a firm was threatened or interfered with by a strike. As a matter of fact, at the time Congress was considering the law, the government had already seized the mines involved in the 1943 coal strikes. Once the mines were seized, the miners returned to their jobs and production was resumed. Moreover, the law did not improve on the procedures for the settlement of wartime disputes. On the contrary, by providing for the strike-vote election, Congress actually encouraged wartime strikes.[19] As expected, workers voted to strike in the vast majority of ballots. This did not mean a work stoppage occurred every time a group of workers voted to strike. The effect of a favorable strike vote, however, served as a mandate to strike. Thus it scarcely can be argued that the War Labor Disputes Act promoted the nation's wartime production program. The statute was not needed to insure adherence of American labor to the no-strike pledge. Underlying the War Labor Disputes Act was a definite change in labor philosophy, which in postwar years contributed to the passage of national and state antiunion legislation.

That organized labor largely maintained its wartime no-strike pledge is borne out by the record. The average annual worker-days lost to industry because of work stoppages during the war period, in relation to the number of worker-days worked, was 11/100 of 1 percent. In comparison, an average of 27/100 of 1 percent was lost from total working time because of work stoppages in the years 1935–1939. Whereas the average duration of strikes was twenty-three days in 1939, twenty-one days in 1940, and eighteen days in 1941, the average duration of strikes was much less during the war years. In 1942, the average length of a strike was twelve days; in 1943, it was only five days; and in 1944, five and one-half days.[20] Of course, labor's no-strike pledge would not have been effective had the government failed to establish procedures calculated to adjust wartime disputes fairly and speedily. The overall plan for wartime labor peace was highly successful. In this plan, the National War Labor Board played a leading role. During the war, it settled approximately 18,000 disputes, which involved about 12 million workers. Assured that their disputes would be adjusted fairly and quickly by the NWLB when direct negotiations and mediation failed to result in a solution, the nation's unions maintained the no-strike pledge in good faith. However, strikes that did occur during World War II received widespread public attention and were not forgotten in the postwar period when national labor policy was reconsidered.

Another controversy arose during World War II that cannot be ignored in evaluating factors that led to enactment of the Taft-Hartley Act. "No issue presented to the War Labor Board precipitated more furious debate than union security."[21] Employer representatives contended that a dispute over union security should not be settled by the NWLB. On this point, management declared that it believed, "the board should not accept for arbitration or consideration the issue of the closed shop, requiring a person to become or remain a member of a labor organization if he is to get or hold a job."[22]

Organized labor was just as emphatic in its belief that the Board should settle all disputes, including those arising out of union security. It was argued that if management's position on union security was accepted, workers, *pledged not to strike,* could not take effective action to protect their unions from antilabor conduct. In the light of these considerations, it is understandable why labor "hailed with delight" Roosevelt's decision that *all* disputes, including the union-security controversy, were to be within the jurisdiction of the NWLB.

Roosevelt's decision, however, did not settle the controversy. In fact, the dispute over the issue merely foreshadowed the conflict that was to take place among the union and employer members of the NWLB. Employer representatives of the Board felt the government should not compel workers to join a union in order to work. They stated that "it is contrary to the principles of democratic government for this or any other governmental agency, to make union membership a condition of employment."[23] On the other hand, labor unions urged that the wartime industrial relations environment required the NWLB to direct the inclusion of union-security arrangements in labor agreements. One of the most important phases of the NWLB's work was related to the manner in which it settled the union-security controversy.

No great problem confronted the Board when union-security clauses were contained in labor agreements made before World War II. Under such circumstances, the Board usually ordered the same arrangement to be contained in contracts negotiated during the war years. In short, it directed the continuation of a closed shop or union shop when such an arrangement had previously been included in a labor agreement. Labor unions were delighted with this policy. Since workers pledged not to strike, it is possible that union-security arrangements could have been eliminated in the absence of NWLB policy.

The Board, however, refused to order a closed shop or union shop when such arrangements had not characterized a firm's prewar contracts. This decision, bitterly denounced by labor union leaders, was in keeping with the principle laid down by President Roosevelt that "the Government of the United States will not order nor will Congress pass legislation ordering a so-called closed shop."[24] The Board interpreted the President's statement as extending to the union shop as well as closed shop. However, it did not feel that the President's policy was violated when it directed the continuation of the closed shop and union shop when these union-security arrangements were in effect before World War II.

If the NWLB had refused to grant some form of union security to a labor union that had not enjoyed such an arrangement before World War II, the government would in effect have frozen the open shop where it had existed before Pearl Harbor. Unions argued they would not be protected against members who dropped out of the organization for real or fancied reasons. The latter consideration assumed great significance in the light of the wartime wage stabilization program. A labor union's greatest appeal is the contention that it is able to obtain higher wages. During World War II, increases in wage rates could be obtained only after governmental approval. Some union members, aware of these considerations, might have felt that union membership was not necessary and hence might have dropped out of the organization. This could have been particularly true when the union failed to obtain governmental approval for wage-rate increases.

In short, organized labor felt that the progress of the union movement during World War II turned on the union-security policy of the NWLB. Union leaders were fearful that in the absence of an adequate union-security program, the union movement would become a wartime casualty. The NWLB was impressed by the position of organized labor. In particular, the Board was aware of labor's no-strike pledge. Some form of union security, it felt, was justified to balance the scales. Thus the public members of the Board declared that "the unions for the duration of the war gave up the use of their economic power with which to win increased security and increased wages. The nation should, in equity, provide the unions with a fair protection against disintegration both from the impacts and controls of war. . . ."[25]

Indeed, the NWLB was faced with dilemmas! On one hand was the union's position. On the other was the principle laid down by President Roosevelt. Clearly, it appears of questionable public policy for a government agency to force workers into labor unions. Such a policy appears as unjust as one that would result in the undermining of the union movement. To resolve this most perplexing problem, the NWLB utilized the *maintenance-of-membership arrangement.* This arrangement required that all present and future members of the union must remain members for the duration of the contract as a condition of employment. The NWLB did not invent the maintenance-of-membership arrangement. In 1941, the National Defense Mediation Board, an agency set up to help settle labor disputes in the pre–Pearl Harbor defense period, had made use of the arrangement. Moreover, the National Defense Mediation Board did not itself create the maintenance-of-membership device. Such arrangements were used as union-security measures during the early 1930s in the chemical, meat-packing, and paper and pulp industries. Maintenance of membership, the NWLB reasoned, adequately reconciled the problem of individual freedom and union security. On this point, it declared that the maintenance-of-membership arrangement

> is not a closed shop, is not a union shop, and is not a preferential shop. No old employee and no new employee is required to join the union to keep his job. If in the union, a member has the freedom for 15 days to get out and keep his job.

If not in the union, the worker has the freedom to stay out and keep his job. This freedom to join or not to join, to stay in or get out, with foreknowledge of being bound by this clause as a condition of employment during the term of the contract, provides for both individual liberty and union security.[26]

To add further protection for the individual worker, the NWLB at one time required that maintenance of membership would not be ordered unless a majority of the members of a union voted for the inclusion of a maintenance-of-membership provision in a labor agreement. Such a referendum had to be secret and conducted under the supervision of the Board. This policy closely resembled the union-shop election feature provided by Taft-Hartley and later repealed in 1951. However, the NWLB conducted only one maintenance-of-membership election. An election was held in the *International Harvester* case. Out of a total of 10,751 ballots cast, 9,703, or 91 percent, voted in favor of the union-security arrangement. After this election, the Board dropped the procedure. It declared that "the technique had many disadvantages. It was expensive. When large companies were involved, it was time consuming and required the services of many trained people—far in excess of the Board's small staff. It created disturbances in the plant and interfered with war production."[27]

The principal ground upon which the agency declined to direct maintenance of membership was "union irresponsibility." The chief test for union "responsibility" rested on the degree to which labor unions kept labor's wartime no-strike pledge in good faith. Unions that violated the pledge did not obtain the coveted maintenance-of-membership arrangement. In the first case in which the NWLB refused to order maintenance of membership, the union involved had clearly violated the no-strike pledge. While a renewal of the labor agreement was being negotiated with the company, the union repeatedly threatened to strike. Eventually, the union leaders recommended to the union members that they authorize a strike. This they did, and a strike took place. In denying the union's request for maintenance of membership, the NWLB pointed out that "the fact that the union leaders and membership authorized a strike instead of using peaceful means of settling the question under dispute indicated to the Board that the union was insincere in its no-strike pledge."[28]

By denying maintenance of membership to unions that arbitrarily violated labor's no-strike pledge, the NWLB obviously served the best interests of the nation. As noted, the NWLB awarded maintenance of membership to compensate organized labor for its surrender of the right to strike. Clearly, if a particular labor union violated this pledge and thereby endangered the security of the nation, it had no moral right to union security. In short, the NWLB used maintenance of membership to reward unions that maintained the no-strike pledge. Such a policy aided the nation's wartime production program and served the interests of industrial justice. The public followed the union-security issue during the war period, and its concern was reflected in the eventual passage of state right-to-work laws and the Taft-Hartley Act. Both reflected the expressed concerns with closed- and union-shop arrangements. Debate over the desirability of such arrangements continues to this day.

Responsibility of Organized Labor

When the Wagner Act was passed, the labor movement was weak from the point of view of membership and bargaining strength. However, under the protection of government policy, the union movement grew and prospered. With this growth, it was inevitable that some unions and some union leaders would resort to practices of dubious social value. Some labor leaders, relatively new and inexperienced in their roles as officers, did not discharge their duties judiciously. A few of the older union leaders, aware of their increased power, adopted courses of action that invited public criticism. For example, the coal strikes of early 1943, carried out during a critical period in the nation's war effort, were recalled with disfavor when strikes increased throughout industry in the early postwar period.

With the growing strength of organized labor, the public became more aware of the abuses of the labor movement. Aspects of the closed shop, the boycott, strikes of questionable moral justification, the discrimination of unions against minority groups, restrictions on output, and laxity in the administration of members' dues served to focus critical attention on the union movement. Actually, these features had been part of the union movement long before the passage of the Wagner Act. However, with the growing power of labor unions, these abuses took on greater proportions in the public mind. People basically antiunion in thinking made the most of union shortcomings to point to the general undesirability of unions and collective bargaining.

The critical observer of organized labor is well aware of this area of union conduct. As a matter of fact, this aspect of organized labor is recognized by many union leaders. A labor union publication had this to say about antisocial practices of labor organizations:

> Every national union official, as well as the intelligent membership of organized labor, knows there are some things wrong in the trade union movement. In this respect trade unions differ, and they differ in accordance with their age and history, with the attitude of the industry with which they deal, with the type of their membership, and with respect to other factors.[29]

It is clear that the Wagner Act did not purport to deal with antisocial practices of labor unions. Its purpose was to equalize bargaining power between management and labor. It did not regulate union activities, even those that appeared injurious to the public. This omission was seized upon by opponents of the Wagner Act to brand the law unfair and one-sided. It was charged that the law regulated the activities of employers in the collective bargaining relationship but neglected to deal with any union practices. At the time the statute was enacted, such an argument received little attention. Union abuses were not considered a major problem because the country was more concerned with restoring prosperity. In short, union-control legislation in 1935 was not of major concern. Legislation providing effective protection of the right of workers to self-organization and collective bargaining was essential if the collective bargaining process was to be strengthened and expanded. However, the argument of "one-sidedness" took on a different meaning after the union movement became a powerful factor in the national economy. There was a need for the Wagner Act. Its defect lay in the fact that it was not broadened from time to time to regulate union practices as abuses were recognized.

Organized labor was largely responsible for the failure of Congress to enact amendments to the Wagner Act that would correct outstanding abuses of the union movement. Representatives of organized labor refused to participate in any program calculated to preserve the substance of the Wagner Act, but to outlaw or regulate antisocial union activities as well. Unions wanted no change in the Wagner Act. For many years, their stand-pat policy was effective. Until 1946, the nation sent Democratic majorities to both houses of Congress and reelected Franklin Roosevelt three times, a record unprecedented in American history. Supported by organized labor, the Democratic congresses refused to alter the Wagner Act in any manner whatsoever. From 1935 to 1947, the law remained unaltered.

It may have been politically expedient over the long run for the union leaders to have supported the enactment of periodic amendments to the Wagner Act. Such revisions, made by a sympathetic Congress, would have been moderate in character and designed in such a manner as to eliminate the necessity for sweeping changes with a single statute. Such changes, moreover, would have been directed at specific union abuses and would probably not have been as inclusive as the 1947 amendments.

The Strike Record of 1946

In the elections of 1946, the nation's representatives were aware of many problems growing out of World War II. People identified price control, shortages of consumer goods, and the general postwar inconveniences with the incumbent political party. The public was ready to deal with many of the accumulating problems that had received slight legislative attention because of the pressures of regulating a wartime economy.

Although the candidates fought the 1946 election campaign on a wide front, they made much of the wave of strikes that took place after the termination of World War II. Actually, the strike experience in 1946 was the worst the nation had ever encountered. In that year, 4,985 strikes occurred. Of greater importance, these strikes resulted in an unprecedented 116 million worker-days of lost production. Estimated working time lost because of the 1946 strikes amounted to 1.43 percent. In comparison with the 1946 strike figures, the record for 1945 discloses 4,750 strikes and only 38 million worker-days lost to production, the latter figure resulting in a loss to estimated working time of .47 percent.

The 1946 strike record was considered evidence of inadequacies in the Wagner Act. Actually, no labor law oriented toward free collective bargaining could have prevented the 1946 strike wave because 62.5 percent of all the strikes in this year were caused by disputes between employees and employers over wages, hours, and other working conditions. Since the organizational strike in 1946 accounted for only a fraction of all work stoppages, it was not correct to "blame" the Wagner Act for the 1946 strikes. This statute could be held accountable only from one point of view: it had fostered a labor movement strong enough to take strike action in attempts to achieve collective bargaining objectives.

The 1946 strike wave had its roots in fundamental economic factors. With the end of the war, the hours of work decreased from a wartime average of about 45 per week to a 1946 average of 40.4. Such a reduction of hours meant loss of overtime premiums and a sharp reduction in weekly earnings. To offset the reduction of the average work week, labor unions struck to increase hourly rates. Union pressure for higher wages in 1946 was also stimulated by the inflationary spiral of prices. General postwar shortages, the termination of rationing, reconversion problems, the unprecedented postwar public debt, the liberal credit policy of banks, and the foreign commitments of the United States were all important postwar inflationary factors. When price controls were removed in the summer of 1946, these inflationary forces produced an upward swing in the price level never before experienced in the nation. The cost-of-living index moved from 133.3 on June 15, 1946, to 153.3 on December 15, 1946 (1935–1939 = 100). Thus in a period of six months, the cost of living increased by 15.04 percent. Caught between a reduction of take-home pay and rising prices, labor unions, pledged to protect the standard of living of their members, engaged in widespread strikes for higher rates of pay.

Consideration of the basic causes for the strikes of 1946 raises questions about the argument that the Wagner Act was the factor responsible for their outbreak. But Congress and the public were convinced that new labor legislation would alleviate many of the perceived abuses of organized labor.

After congressional debate, the Taft-Hartley Act was adopted in the House by a 320–79 vote, and the Senate voted in favor of the legislation 68–24. When the law reached the desk of President Truman, he vetoed the legislation. This was expected; in the summer of 1946 he had vetoed the "Case bill," a law that contained many of the provisions embodied in the Taft-Hartley law. While vetoing the Taft-Hartley Act, Truman declared:

> The bill taken as a whole would reverse the basic direction of our national labor policy, inject the Government into private economic affairs on an unprecedented scale, and conflict with important principles of our democratic society. Its provisions would cause more strikes, not fewer. It would contribute neither to industrial peace nor to economic stability and progress. It would be a dangerous stride in the direction of a totally managed economy. It contains seeds of discord which would plague this Nation for years to come.[30]

Despite the action of President Truman, the House and Senate overrode his veto, and Taft-Hartley became the law of the land on June 23, 1947.

Thus Taft-Hartley supplanted the Wagner Act as the expression of the labor policy of the nation. Supporters of the legislation did not hesitate to affirm that the law marked a significant shift in the attitude of government toward collective bargaining. In this connection, Hartley declared that the bill was designed to reverse the basic direction of national labor policy. In fact, that was the primary intention of the authors of the measure.

TAFT-HARTLEY PROVISIONS

The Labor-Management Relations Act (Taft-Hartley) amended but did not displace the Wagner Act. The Wagner Act unfair employer practices were continued virtually word for word in the 1947 law. One significant change was that the closed shop (the arrangement requiring that all workers be union members at the time they are hired) was prohibited. In addition, the freedom of the parties to authorize the union shop (the employer may hire anyone he or she chooses, but all new workers must join the union after a stipulated period of time) was narrowed. Congressional intent in the passage of this amendment was to narrow even more the restrictions against employees with regard to hire or tenure of employment. Greater freedom of choice for employees to determine representation status free from both union and employer interference was intended.

The congressional attitude toward unions was expressed in other important provisions of the Taft-Hartley Act that dealt with the following concerns: (1) union unfair labor practices; (2) the rights of employees as individuals; (3) the rights of employers; and (4) national emergency strikes. In addition, other provisions dealt with internal union affairs, the termination or modification of existing labor contracts, and suits involving unions. In subsequent chapters, these matters will receive full treatment. To establish the general flavor of these features of the law, we will make some general comments about them at this time.

UNION UNFAIR LABOR PRACTICES

Six union unfair labor practices were identified by the Taft-Hartley Act. Labor organizations operating in interstate commerce were to refrain from the following practices: (1) restraining or coercing employees in the exercise of their guaranteed collective bargaining rights; (2) causing an employer to discriminate in any way against an employee in order to encourage or discourage union membership; (3) refusing to bargain in good faith with an employer regarding wages, hours, and other conditions of employment; (4) certain types of strikes and boycotts; (5) requiring employees covered by union-shop contracts to pay initiation fees or dues "in an amount which the Board finds excessive or discriminatory under all the circumstances"; and (6) "featherbedding," the requirement of payment by an employer for services not performed.

Two of the six provisions have perhaps had the greatest influence on collective bargaining—and undoubtedly a salutary one—since the enactment of Taft-Hartley. The first is the ban on union restraint or coercion of employees in the exercise of their guaranteed bargaining rights, which also entails a union obligation to avoid coercion of employees who choose to refrain from collective bargaining altogether. What constitutes such restraint or coercion? The myriad of rulings rendered by the NLRB and the courts since 1947 has at least indicated that such union actions as the following will always run the risk of being found "unfair": communicating to an antiunion employee that the employee will lose her or his job should the union gain recognition; the signing of an agreement with an employer that recognizes the union as exclusive bargaining representative when in fact it lacks majority employee support; picket-line violence; and threats of reprisal against employees subpoenaed to testify against the union at NLRB hearings.

The second Taft-Hartley provision makes it an unfair practice for a union to cause an employer to discriminate against an employee in order to influence union membership. There is a single exception to this prohibition. Under a valid union-shop agreement, the union may lawfully demand the discharge of an employee who fails to pay the initiation fee and periodic dues. Otherwise, however, unions must exercise complete self-control in this area. They cannot try to force employers to fire or otherwise penalize workers for any other reason, whether these reasons involve worker opposition to union policies, failure to attend union meetings, or refusal to join the union at all. Nor can a union lawfully seek to persuade an employer to grant hiring preference to employees who are "satisfactory" to the union. Subject only to the union-shop proviso, Taft-Hartley sought to place nonunion workers on a footing equal to that of union employees.

Another restriction on union practices pertains to union refusal to bargain. This third Taft-Hartley restriction extended to labor organizations the same obligation that the Wagner Act had already imposed on employers. Prior to 1947, it was widely publicized that some unions merely presented employers with a list of demands on a take-it-or-leave-it basis. To many observers, however, the law's inclusion of this union bargaining provision has meant very little. Unions can normally be expected to pursue bargaining rather than attempt to avoid it. Nevertheless, the NLRB has used this provision to some extent in the years since Taft-Hartley to narrow the scope of permissible union action. The Board has, for example, found it unlawful under this section for a union to strike against an employer who continues to negotiate on a multiemployer basis with the goal of forcing it to bargain independently. It has also found that a union's refusal to bargain on an employer proposal for a written contract violates this part of the law. In short, some inequities seem to have been corrected by this good-faith bargaining provision.

The fourth unfair union practice has given rise to considerable litigation. Indeed, of all six Taft-Hartley union prohibitions, the ban on certain types of strikes and boycotts has proven the most difficult to interpret. Even as "clarified" by Congress in 1959, this area remains a particularly difficult one for labor lawyers.

Briefly, Section 8 (b)(4) of the 1947 act prohibited unions from striking or boycotting if such actions have any of the following three objectives: (1) forcing an employer or self-employed person to join any labor or employer organization or to cease dealing with another employer (secondary boycott); (2) compelling recognition as employee bargaining agent from another employer without NLRB certification; (3) forcing an employer to assign particular work to a particular craft.

Particularly in regard to the secondary boycott provision, it does not take much imagination to predict where heated controversy could arise. To constitute a secondary boycott, the union's action must be waged against "another" employer, one who is entirely a neutral in the battle and is merely caught as a pawn in the union's battle with the real object of its concern. But when is the secondary employer really neutral and when is it in fact an ally of the primary employer? The Board has sometimes ruled against employers alleging themselves to be "secondary" on the grounds of common ownership with the "primary" employer and, again, when "struck work" has been turned over by primary employers to secondary ones. But Board and court rulings here have not been entirely consistent.

In its other clauses, too, the Taft-Hartley strike and boycott provisions have led to intense legal battles. When is a union, for example, unlawfully seeking recognition without NLRB certification, and when is it merely picketing to protest undesirable working conditions, a normally legal action? Is a union ever entitled to try to keep within its bargaining unit work that has traditionally been performed by the unit employees? On some occasions, but not all, the Board has ruled that there is nothing wrong with this. The histories of post-1947 cases on these issues constitute a fascinating study in the making of fine distinctions. At least, however, the large incidence of litigation might indicate that the parties have not been totally able to overlook the new rights and responsibilities placed upon them by Taft-Hartley, whatever these might be.

Last—and least in the magnitude of their effect—stand the relatively unenforceable provisions relating to union fees and dues and featherbedding.

The fifth union unfair practice prohibits charging workers covered by union-shop agreements excessive or discriminatory dues or initiation fees. The provision includes a stipulation that the NLRB should consider "all the circumstances" in determining discrimination or excess. Such circumstances, the wording of the Taft-Hartley Act continues, include "the practices and customs of labor organizations in the particular industry and the wages currently paid to the employees affected." Without further yardsticks and depending almost exclusively on the sentiments of individual employees rather than on irate employers for enforcement, this part of the Act has had little practical value. In one of the relatively few such cases to come before it thus far, the Board ruled that increasing an initiation fee from $75 to $250, and thus charging new members the equivalent of about four weeks' wages when other unions in the area charged only about one-eighth of this amount, was unlawful. In another case, it was held that the union's uniform requirement of a reinstatement fee for ex-members that was higher than the initiation fee for new members was *not* discriminatory under the Act.

The sixth and final unfair labor practice for unions has proved even less influential in governing collective bargaining. Taft-Hartley prohibits unions from engaging in featherbedding. The Board has ruled that this provision does *not* prevent labor organizations from seeking *actual* employment for their members, "even in situations where the employer does not want, does not need, and is not willing to accept such services." The NLRB was upheld by the U.S. Supreme Court in 1952 when it ruled that the antifeatherbedding provision applied only if there was payment for services not performed or not to be performed. The high court said that the law leaves to collective bargaining the determination of what work shall be included as compensable services.[31] Mainly because of this interpretation, the antifeatherbedding provision has had little effect. A union would be quite willing to have work performed with the question of need irrelevant. Employer representatives of some industries—entertainment and the railroads, in particular—have succeeded in convincing the public that their unwanted—but performing—workers are featherbedding, but under the current interpretation of the law, such practices are not illegal.

In one rare case, however, the NLRB in 1974 did find a violation of the antifeatherbedding provision, when it ordered a union to reimburse an employer for the wages paid to a steward whom the union forced on the employer for the purpose of checking union cards of drivers who arrived at a construction site.[32] This case stands as an exception to the unenforceability of the law.

THE RIGHTS OF EMPLOYEES AS INDIVIDUALS

In other areas, too, the Act attempted to even the scales of collective bargaining and the alleged injustices of the 1935–1947 period. Taft-Hartley, unlike the Wagner Act, recognized a need to protect the rights of individual employees against labor organizations. It explicitly amended the 1935 legislation to give a majority of the employees the right to refrain from, as well as engage in, collective bargaining activities. It also dealt more directly with the question of individual freedoms—even beyond its previously mentioned outlawing of the closed shop, union coercion, union-caused employer discrimination against employees, and excessive union fees.

Perhaps most symbolically, Taft-Hartley provided that should any state wish to pass legislation more restrictive of union security than the union shop (or, in other words, to outlaw labor contracts that make union membership a condition of retaining employment), the state was free to do so. Some states have enacted legislation to restrict the range of permissible union security. Many states —mainly in the South and Southwest—now have so-called "right-to-work laws."

Advocates of such laws have claimed that compulsory unionism violates the basic American right of freedom of association. Opponents of right-to-work laws have pointed out that among other arguments, majority rule is inherent in our democratic procedure. Thus far, however, there has been an impressive correlation between stands on this particular question and attitudes about the values of unionism in general. Individuals opposed to collective bargaining have favored right-to-work laws with amazing regularity. Pro-unionists seem to have been equally consistent in their attacks on such legislation. It is still unproven that right-to-work laws have had much effect on labor relations in the states where they exist. One study points out, "The general pattern emerges that existing right-to-work laws have generally been unenforceable and have accomplished little."[33] The laws are perhaps considerably more symbolic than they are of real consequence.

Also designed to strengthen workers' rights as individuals was a Taft-Hartley provision allowing any employee the right to present grievances directly to the employer without union intervention. The union's representative was to have a chance to be present at such employer-employee meetings, but the normal grievance procedure, in which the union actively participated, would be suspended. Few employees have thus far availed themselves of this opportunity. Clearly, the action can antagonize the union and, since the employer's action is normally being challenged by the grievance itself, the employee usually prefers to work with the union.

Finally, the Act placed a major restriction on the dues checkoff arrangement. Many employers had been deducting union dues from their employees' paychecks and remitting them to the union. Companies were thus spared the constant visits of dues-collecting union representatives at the workplace; unions had also found the checkoff an efficient means of collection. Under Taft-Hartley, the checkoff was to remain legal, but only if the individual employee had given authorization in writing. Moreover, such an authorization could not be irrevocable for a period of more than one year. This restriction has hardly hampered the growth of the checkoff. Currently, the arrangement is provided for in approximately 80 percent of all labor contracts, compared to an estimated 40 percent at the time of Taft-Hartley passage.

THE RIGHTS OF EMPLOYERS

In a third area, Taft-Hartley circumscribed freedom of action of unions in the quest for industrial relations equity. It explicitly gave employers certain collective bargaining rights. For example, although employers were still required to recognize and bargain with properly certified unions, they had more freedom of expression to their views concerning union organization, so long as there was "no threat of reprisal or force or promise of benefit."

Thus, an employer may now, when faced with a representation election, tell employees that unions are worthless, dangerous to the economy, and immoral. Employers may even, generally speaking, hint that the permanent closing of the plant would be the possible aftermath of a union election victory and subsequent high union wage demands. Nor will an election be set aside if employers play upon the racial prejudices of their workers (should these exist) by describing the union's philosophy toward integration, or if they set forth the union's record in regard to violence and corruption (should this record be vulnerable) and suggest that these characteristics would be logical consequences of the union's victory in its plant—although in recent years the Board has attempted to draw the line between dispassionate statements on the employer's part and inflammatory or emotional appeals.[34] An imaginative employer can in fact now engage in almost any amount of creative speaking or writing for employees' consumption. The only major restraint on employers' conduct is that they must avoid threats, promises, coercion, and direct interference with worker-voters in the reaching of their decisions. Two lesser restrictions also govern: the employer may not hold a meeting with employees on company time within twenty-four hours of an election; and employers can never urge employees individually at their homes or in their offices to vote against the union. The Board has held that employers can lawfully do this only "at the employees' work area or in places where employees normally gather."

Under this section of Taft-Hartley, employers can also (1) call for elections to decide questions of representation (as noted earlier); (2) refuse to bargain with supervisors' unions (the Wagner Act protection was withdrawn for these employees, although they are not prohibited from forming or joining unions *without* the NLRB machinery and other safeguards of public policy); and (3) file their unfair labor practice charges against unions.

Understandably, such changes were received with favor by the employer community.

NATIONAL EMERGENCY STRIKES

Of most direct interest to the general public, but of practical meaning only to those employers whose labor relations can be interpreted as affecting the national health or safety, are the national emergency strike provisions that were enacted in 1947. As in the case of most Taft-Hartley provisions, these remain essentially unchanged to this day.

Sections 206 through 210 of the Act provide for government intervention in the case of such emergencies. If the President of the United States believes that a threatened or actual strike affects "an entire industry or a substantial part thereof" in such a way as to "imperil the national health or safety," he or she is empowered to take certain carefully delineated action. The President may appoint a Board of Inquiry to find out and report the facts regarding the dispute. The Board is allowed subpoena authority and can thus compel the appearance of witnesses. It cannot, however, make recommendations for a settlement. On receiving the Board's preliminary report, the President may apply through the Attorney General for a court injunction restraining the strike for sixty days. If no settlement is reached during this time, the injunction can be extended for another twenty days, during which period employees are to be polled in a secret-ballot election on their willingness to accept the employer's last offer. The Board is then to submit its final report to the President. Should the strike threat still exist after all these procedures, the President is authorized to submit a full report to Congress, "with such recommendations as he [*sic*] may see fit to make for consideration and appropriate action."

By 1985, the national emergency provisions had been invoked on thirty-four occasions. They had not always been effective in bringing about settlements, however. Rees conveys the majority opinion of detached observers in pointing out that "where the fact-finders have been successful in settling disputes it is often because they have been functioning as high-level mediators, commanding more respect from the parties than the mediators ordinarily furnished by government agencies."[35] There is also evidence that the eighty-day "cooling-off" period has sometimes done no more than delay the strike for that length of time. Such was the case in several of the times that injunctions were used. In addition, presidents have tended to avoid using the Taft-Hartley injunction procedures, often because unionists have viewed them as antilabor, as well as because they have not been especially effective in settling disputes. Lyndon Johnson, for example, exhibited a notable reluctance to tap sections 206–210 when basic steel bargaining reached an impasse in the late summer of 1965, achieving settlement extralegally instead, through personal pressure and recommendations. A once controversial issue regarding the national emergency strike provisions is no longer debatable, however. The United States Supreme Court, ruling against the Steelworkers union, found the provisions themselves constitutional in 1959.

OTHER TAFT-HARTLEY PROVISIONS

Other provisions of the Act have also caused union leaders some concern. The 1947 legislation devoted attention to internal union affairs, the first such regulation in American history. Its impetus came not only from the previously cited alleged communist "taints" attached to several unions, but also from the fact that, in the case of a few other labor organizations, lack of democratic procedures and financial irregularities (often involving employer wrongdoing as well) had become glaringly evident. Accordingly, the Act set conditions for unions seeking to use the NLRB's services: (1) all union officers were obligated to file annual affidavits with the Board, stating that they were not members of the Communist Party; (2) certain financial and constitutional information had to be annually filed by unions with the Secretary of Labor; and (3) unions (as well as corporations) could no longer contribute funds for political purposes in connection with any federal election. The affidavit requirement, judged to be ineffective, was repealed in 1959. The other stipulations were allowed to remain in force until that date, when they were only slightly amended and then substantially enlarged upon as further discussion will indicate. Essentially, aside from what unionists vocally termed a nuisance value, the provisions were notable as the first recognition in public policy that some internal regulation of the union as an institution was in the public interest—and as a harbinger of more such regulation to come.

Another Taft-Hartley provision that upset some union leaders involved the termination or modification of existing labor contracts. Applicable to both labor organizations and employers, it requires the party seeking to end or change the agreement to give a sixty-day notice to the other party. The law further provides that during this period, the existing contract must be maintained without strikes or lockouts. In addition, the Federal Mediation and Conciliation Service and state mediation services are to be notified of the impending dispute thirty days after the serving of the notice. Workers striking in violation of this requirement lose all legal protection as "employees" in collective bargaining, although the law also asserts that "such loss of status for such employee shall terminate if and when he is re-employed" by the employer.

In some instances, leaders of labor organizations have found it both difficult and politically unpopular to restrain their constituents from violating this provision. Unionists have also on occasion frankly pointed out that the scheduling prerequisites for striking have deprived their organizations of some economic power, at least insofar as the element of surprise is concerned. Yet many representatives of both parties would undoubtedly agree with Falcone that "these provisions have slowed down the calling of strikes, enabled mediators to intervene before it is too late to help and have generally provided an orderly method for resolving disputes and reaching final settlements."[36] From the point of view of the public interest, it is clearly on this latter basis that the effectiveness of the notice provisions should be judged.

Finally, Section 301 of Taft-Hartley decreed that *"suits for violations of contracts* between an employer and a labor organization representing employees in an industry affecting commerce" could be brought directly by either party in any United States district court. Labor agreements, in short, were to be construed as being legally enforceable for the first time in American history. Damage suits are not calculated to increase mutual trust or offset misunderstandings between the parties in labor relations, however, and unions and management have generally recognized this. Consequently, relatively few such suits have come to the courts in the years since this provision was enacted. Many contracts today in fact contain agreements not to sue, a perfectly legal dodge of Section 301. The remedy of the suit—for employers confronted with union violations of no-strike clauses or for unions faced with management lockout inconsistent with no-lockout provisions, for example—nonetheless remains available for both parties in the absence of any restrictive covenants.

OPERATION OF TAFT-HARTLEY

Agency Reorganization

Before Taft-Hartley, the NLRB was a single agency with control of policy concentrated in the hands of a three-member Board. The Board was then empowered to delegate functions and decentralize operations for efficient administration of the national labor law.

The Congress decided to deviate from the structure that governed all other federal administrative agencies. Unlike these agencies, the Board was to function primarily as a court. It was to be concerned only with general policy to guide operations in the decentralized offices across the country. It was also given responsibility to make decisions on election and complaint cases. Its membership was increased from three to five, but any of its powers could be delegated to any three members. The President of the United States was authorized to appoint members for a term of five years, subject to Senate approval.

In the summer of 1977, President Carter supported labor law reform legislation that, among other things, would have increased Board membership to seven so that cases could be processed more rapidly. As will be discussed later in the chapter, one of the major criticisms of the operation of Taft-Hartley was of the delay in deciding unfair labor practice and election cases. Increasing the Board membership to seven would have allowed the creation of more three-member panels to speed decisions. Even with the five-member Board, many cases were assigned to three-member panels for decisions. The entire Board participates in cases which have exceptional importance, but most decisions are decided by three members. Thus, increasing the membership of the agency would have meant that decisions could be turned out more rapidly.

In October 1977, the House of Representatives enacted the Labor Law Reform Act of 1977. The legislation would have increased Board membership to seven, and would have authorized the NLRB to establish two-member panels to affirm routine administrative law judge decisions in unfair labor practice cases. As will be demonstrated in subsequent portions of this volume, the Labor Law Reform Act of 1977 contained other significant features. However, in the summer of 1978 Senate approval was blocked by a successful filibuster.

Under the Wagner Act, the General Counsel was used by the Board as its legal advisor for directing litigation and supervising Board attorneys, except for the law judges. However, under Taft-Hartley, Congress placed sole responsibility to investigate and prosecute cases with an independent General Counsel, who is appointed by the President with Senate approval for a four-year term. The General Counsel plays a critical and powerful role in the operation of Taft-Hartley. The Board can only decide cases that are generated by the General Counsel. Thus, when the General Counsel refuses to issue an unfair labor practice complaint, the NLRB may not reverse the decision. As a matter of fact, if a charge filed by an employer, employee, or union is dismissed by the General Counsel, the charging party may not have the decision reversed by either the NLRB or the courts. It has been held that the federal courts have no authority to review the day-to-day exercise of the discretion given to the General Counsel in the issuance of unfair labor practice complaints.[37] In other words, should the General Counsel dismiss a charge, the party has no legal forum to appeal to for the reversal of the decision.

Of course, this does not mean that in practice the General Counsel will arbitrarily dismiss complaints. When conduct is arguably in violation of the statute as applied and interpreted by the NLRB and the courts, it is expected that a complaint will be issued. In any event, the role of the General Counsel in the operation of Taft-Hartley cannot be overlooked. Some people may argue that a charging party should have the right to appeal to some legal forum when a General Counsel refuses to issue a complaint. As matters stand now, complaints can be generated only by the General Counsel, and the decision may not be upset by either the NLRB or the courts.

Thus, the NLRB is essentially a court that decides cases only after they are generated by the General Counsel. As noted in the previous chapter, after a complaint is issued, a law judge issues a decision after a hearing. After the law judge issues a decision, it may be appealed to the NLRB. At this point the Board exercises its decision-making power. Should the complaint not be issued, there is no hearing before a law judge, and, of course, no decision which the NLRB can review.

In determining the fundamental reason for the "split personality" in the enforcement of Taft-Hartley, one should recall the bitter criticism leveled against the NLRB during the Wagner Act years. In response to this criticism, Congress desired to reduce the power of the Board by eliminating its investigation and prosecution functions. In any event, unique in federal law, Taft-Hartley is enforced by two separate and independent agencies. At this late date, after nearly four decades, it is not likely that Congress will bring Taft-Hartley into harmony with the way other federal laws are enforced. There is serious doubt as to why Taft-Hartley should be singled out for special treatment in the matter of enforcement.

Quality of Service: Unfair Labor Practice Cases

The procedure involved in the processing of unfair labor practice cases and representation elections was discussed in the previous chapter. Now we are concerned with the quality of the operation of Taft-Hartley. In this regard, one central proposition is of material importance: *The growth of the case load under the law has been no less than spectacular.* Possibly no other federal law has produced such an increase in the number of cases. Consider, for example, the ten-year period between 1970 and 1980. In 1970, the total case load under Taft-Hartley (unfair labor practice charges and election cases) amounted to 33,581.[38] By 1980, the

NLRB case load had increased to 57,381.[39] In 1970, 21,038 unfair labor practice charges were filed and 12,543 election petitions submitted. In 1980, employers, unions, and employees filed 44,063 unfair labor practice charges, and 12,701 election cases were submitted. It is evident that the major source of the increased case load is generated by the filing of unfair labor practice charges.

In assessing the reasons for the tremendous growth in the case load, it would not be accurate to conclude that the increase is attributable to the fact that the law has been broadened to include union activity. Such a reason would explain why the case load increased immediately after Taft-Hartley was enacted, but note that the increase in the number of cases occurred *during* the operation of Taft-Hartley. Undoubtedly, one reason for the increase has been intensified union activity and growing employer resistance to organization. As union membership declined as a percentage of the organizable labor force (from about 33 percent in 1956 to about 17 percent at present) unions, to maintain their position in the nation, have engaged in more vigorous organizational activity. However, employers in many instances have resisted organization. When these two factors are meshed, it is understandable that Taft-Hartley activity would increase so dramatically. Other reasons have been advanced for the phenomena, including greater public awareness of the operation of the law; more labor lawyers who stimulate usage of the law; some new NLRB jurisdiction policies that have served to expand the coverage of the law; the addition of the health-care industry to NLRB jurisdiction in July 1974; and inadequate penalties that encourage additional violations.[40]

Starting in 1982, however, the NLRB case load started to decline, and by 1984, it had decreased to a total of 43,426 cases.[41] Unfair labor practice cases dropped to 34,855 and election cases to 7,770. Added to these were 801 cases filed in categories other than unfair labor practice and election disputes. The case load for 1984 was the lowest total since 1974. Probably the major reason for this decrease was the economic recession of the early 1980s, the worst since the Great Depression. Unions find it difficult to organize during periods of serious unemployment and poor business conditions. When organizational effort slackens, or proves unsuccessful, unions have less need for the services of the NLRB. Another possible factor was the labor movement's disenchantment with the Reagan-appointed Board. On this issue, the *Wall Street Journal* stated: "Some unions are boycotting the conservative Board due to rulings they view unfair."[42] Later on, some of those decisions will be discussed. In any event, only time will tell whether the decline of the case load in the early 1980s represented a permanent condition or only a temporary aberration.

Time Delay

Whatever the future may bring in terms of case load, the NLRB quality of service remains of paramount importance. Pure and simple, the procedures under the law are too slow and reflect the maxim that "justice delayed is justice denied." This is particularly true in unfair labor practice cases, and to a lesser extent in election cases. In fiscal year 1980, it took a median of 484 days, or 16 months, from the time that an unfair labor practice charge was first filed until the NLRB finally issued a decision.[43] By 1983, the latest year for which data are available at this writing, the total elapsed time from filing the charge to the issuance of the Board's decision amounted to a median of 627 days.[44] By far, the longest delay, a median of 194 days, was between the time of the administrative law judge's decision and the time that the NLRB denied a case. In other words, by the time the entire unfair labor practice procedure has been exhausted (charge, complaint, hearing, the administrative law judge ruling, and NLRB disposition of the case), employers, employees, and unions have had to wait over 20 months to learn how Taft-Hartley applied to their case.

With such a long delay, it is easy to understand why the interests of employers, employees, and unions are affected adversely. For example, an employer may be required to pay a huge amount in back pay awards, a punishment particularly harmful to a small employer. Employees discharged in violation of the law must wait an unreasonable length of time before they receive a remedy; and a union's organizational campaign may collapse while waiting for a decision from the NLRB. Commenting on this problem, a House of Representatives Committee stated:

> The National Labor Relations Board is in a crisis. Delays in decision-making at the Board level and a staggering and debilitating case backlog have results in workers being forced to wait years before cases affecting their livelihood and the economic well-being of their families are decided. We have reached a point where legal rights given to employees under the National Labor Relations Act are in jeopardy because of the Board's failure to issue timely decisions. Delays by the Board in deciding cases also impact adversely on employers since a company's potential monetary liability rises while the case is pending before the Board.[45]

Dealing with the Problem

To reduce delay at the NLRB level, the most serious bottleneck in unfair labor practice cases, presidents should not allow vacancies on the Board to remain unfilled for a long period of time. For example, Board Member Howard Jenkins left the agency on August 27, 1983, but Reagan did not replace him until March 1985. Indeed, a major reason for the Board's slowness in 1983 was attributable to the fact that the NLRB was operating shorthanded.[46] Increasing the number of NLRB members to, say, seven or nine would expedite the Board's decisions. To speed up its work, the agency should also establish reasonable timetables for deciding cases. In addition, the Board should take action to curb attorneys who file excessive and frivolous exceptions for the sole purpose of causing delay. As a congressional committee put it: the Board should consider disciplinary action against repeat offenders who seek to abuse the Board's processes.[47]

Though these recommendations and the improvement of other internal procedures would reduce delay, a major change in method is not within the power of the NLRB, but requires approval of Congress. As noted earlier, under Taft-Hartley, the NLRB must review each unfair labor practice administrative law judge decision appealed to it. In 1984, the Board issued more than 1,161 decisions in unfair labor practice and election cases.[48]

For many years, it has been proposed that the NLRB should have the authority to refuse to review any case appealed from the administrative law judge; that is, the decision of the law judge would be final unless the NLRB at its discretion elected to review it. Should Congress approve this change in procedure, it would reduce by about six months the processing of those unfair labor practice cases that the NLRB does not elect to review. Under this kind of authority, the NLRB would review only those cases that would be precedent-making, or those cases decided in a manner inconsistent with the policies established by the Board or the courts. These kinds of cases would represent only a small portion of the cases that the Board now must review. This proposal would also serve to reduce the NLRB backlog of cases, which stood at 1,148 as of September 1, 1984, the highest in the history of the NLRB.[49]

As many NLRB officials had previously recommended, former Chair Betty S. Murphy advocated that Congress provide the Board with the authority to refuse to review all unfair labor practice cases appealed to the agency. She said that the present system of automatic review is not "a good use of the taxpayers' money."[50]

At this writing, Congress has still refused to enact the necessary legislation. Congress' refusal appears strange, because as we have learned, since 1959, the NLRB has had the power to refuse to review election cases referred to it from decisions of regional directors. Whatever the reason for the refusal of Congress to treat all kinds of cases in the same way, it is not in the public interest to force the NLRB to review every unfair labor practice case appealed to it.

The time delay becomes still more serious when Board decisions are appealed to the courts. After the NLRB issues a decision, a dissatisfied party may appeal to a federal court of appeals, and then may elect to have the U.S. Supreme Court review the case. When this occurs, the long delay between the filing of the unfair labor practice charge and the ultimate decision of the federal courts is increased significantly. It is not unusual for the courts to take several years before they dispose of a case. Compounding this problem is that many NLRB decisions are appealed to the courts. Between 1936 and 1976, circuit courts of appeals acted on 6,208 NLRB issues.[51] As the Board stated:

> The National Labor Relations Board conducts the most extensive litigation in the United States courts of appeals of any Federal agency.[52]

In a typical year, about 50 percent of all NLRB unfair labor practice decisions are appealed to the courts.[53] In fiscal year 1984, the federal appeals courts issued 259.

Normally, NLRB decisions are sustained by the federal courts. On the average, they have been sustained in whole or in part in about 85 percent of the cases. One explanation for this excellent batting average, however, is that the NLRB is selective in the cases that it allows to be appealed to the courts. In other words, the agency generally will select only cases that have a reasonable opportunity for success.

Quality of Service: Election Cases

As noted in the previous chapter, in about 80 percent of all election cases, the parties consent to an election. They voluntarily agree to a settlement of the controversial issues involved in an election, such as the jurisdiction of the NLRB, the eligibility of employees to vote in an election, the scope of the bargaining unit, the time and place of the election, and other matters. At times, the parties consent to an election, but reserve the right to raise these issues *after* the election takes place. These elections are called *consent-stipulated* elections. Like a consent election, however, the consent-stipulated election is held without a hearing or an order directing the election. The 80 percent figure includes both consent and consent-stipulated elections. Frequently, however, there is no need for a party to raise the issue to which it stipulated because of the results of the election. For example, an employer would probably not question the right of a few employees to vote in the poll if the union wins by a very large majority. On the other hand, the employer probably will raise the issue if the union wins the election by a few votes. But if the union should lose the election, there would be no need whatsoever for the employer to raise the issue.

When the consent election is used, the poll is conducted within a short time after the election petition is filed. With this type of election, there is no problem of long delay. In 1984, consent elections were held an average of 47.6 days after the filing of the election petition.[54] However, when the parties refuse to consent to an election, the problem of time delay becomes more significant. Formal hearings must be held concerning the controversial issues involved in an election. A field examiner or regional attorney conducts the hearing, and evidence is supplied by the parties who are normally represented by attorneys. After the hearing is held, the regional director must resolve the controversial issues. Only then will the election be directed. *Directed elections* are held about seventy-five days after the filing of the petition.[55] This interlude could favor either the employer or the union, depending upon the circumstances prevailing in a given situation. If the union needs more time to try to convince employees to vote for it, delay time would be in its favor. On the other hand, if the employer needs more time to undermine the majority status of the union, delay would favor the employer.

Fairness to all concerned would demonstrate that elections be held as quickly as possible after a petition is filed, while recognizing the rights of employers and unions to raise legitimate issues. As noted earlier, Congress took a big step in this direction when in 1959 it authorized the NLRB to refuse to review the decisions of regional directors in election cases. Starting in 1961, the Board took advantage of this authority and delegated to the regional directors the power to make the final decisions in all matters in controversy. For example, regional directors have the final authority to decide which employees would be eligible to vote when this issue is in conflict between the parties. Before 1961, the NLRB was compelled to review all decisions of the regional directors, just as now the Board is compelled to review all decisions of administrative law judges in unfair labor practice cases. When the Board was required to review all decisions of the regional directors before an election could take place, it is easy to understand why there was often an interminable delay before the poll was conducted. In some cases, a year or more would elapse between the filing of the election petition and the holding of the election. Of course, even under the present situation, there could be long delays when the NLRB elects to review a decision of a regional director. In those cases, elections are held in approximately 230 days.[56] However, as stated, the NLRB agrees to review only a small portion of the cases appealed to it by a party dissatisfied with a regional director's decision.

In August 1977, the Board adopted a new rule that speeds up the processing of the cases that it elects to review. Before that time, an election could not be held until the Board had resolved all the controversial issues. Under the new rule, the election can be held as scheduled, but to protect the interests of all concerned, the ballots are impounded and not counted until the NLRB has issued its decision.

In other words, directed elections take place much faster than was the case before 1961. Apparently this has not made much difference to unions. Their success at the polls has declined steadily over the years. In 1958, unions won 61 percent of elections, but the figure dropped to 55 percent in 1972, 50 percent in 1976,[57] and as noted in Chapter 9, 47.7 percent in 1983.[58] It would appear that the problems of new organization are far more serious than simply the delay in holding NLRB elections. In a particular case, however, delay could hurt a union in an election by giving an employer more opportunity to undermine the majority status of a union.

It would be in the interest of all concerned to hold directed elections as quickly as possible. This objective could be accomplished by proceeding to an election promptly after the filing of a petition and before a hearing takes place. Then, after the election, a dissatisfied party could raise issues that might result in a decision by a regional director or the NLRB to set aside the results of an election and order a new one, or even to rule that another election not take place. By cutting out the hearing that now must automatically take place, a new procedure would allow the election to be held promptly after the filing of a petition. Under such circumstances, the regional director could establish the ground rules of the election. Should a party be dissatisfied with the determinations, a protest could be made after the election.

Not only would the elimination of automatic hearings before elections improve the speed with which polls are conducted, but it would prevent a party from demanding a hearing just to delay an election. At times employers or unions invoke the hearing for that purpose, raising frivolous issues in the hearing. As matters stand now, it would require approval from Congress to eliminate the compulsory preelection hearing. On this issue, a blue-ribbon Task Force, appointed by then-NLRB-Chair Murphy to improve the quality of service of the agency, said:

> The Task Force is informed that recommendations have been made to Congress that the statute be amended to permit elections without hearings in certain situations. The Task Force sees no way that such elections can be directed under the present statute, and therefore any recommendations by the Task Force would be beyond its jurisdiction.[59]

In the summer of 1977, President Carter proposed passage of the Labor Law Reform Act of 1977. As reported in the *Wall Street Journal* on July 19, 1977, Carter "pledged to fight in Congress for the passage of the controversial labor law revisions . . . to make union organizing easier." One feature of the legislation was designed to cut down the delays in elections by imposing strict deadlines on the NLRB. Under the Carter program, the Board would have been mandated to conduct an election within fifty days when a petition is filed by 30 to 50 percent of the employees in the bargaining unit. The time limit was to be reduced to twenty-five days should the petition have been filed by a majority or more of the employees. Should an election case present exceptionally complex or novel issues, the Board could set a time limit of seventy-five days.

In October 1977, the House of Representatives enacted the measure, but in the summer of 1978, the Senate failed to pass it because of a filibuster carried on by the law's opponents. Although Carter supported the legislation, and although organized labor had helped to elect him and a Democratic Congress, the bill was not enacted into law. Only two votes in the Senate were lacking to end the filibuster. As further discussion will clarify, the proposal was highly controversial, provoking a bitter struggle between the labor movement and the business community. The election of Ronald Reagan as President in 1980, with reelection in 1984, and a Republican controlled Senate vigorously opposed by the labor movement with few exceptions, notably the Teamsters, caused unions to lose all hope in the foreseeable future for improvement in Taft-Hartley.

ENFORCEMENT PROCEDURES

Taft-Hartley provides four kinds of remedies for violations of its provisions. The first is the remedial order designed to make the position of wronged parties the same as it was before the violation. Remedial measures include cease-and-desist orders when unfair labor practices are found, the posting of notices on employer property or in union halls, and the payment of back wages in discriminatory discharge cases.

The second sanction is imposed by courts for contempt of an injunction or restraining order. Taft-Hartley provided for injunctions or restraining orders under three types of conditions. One required the General Counsel to seek an injunction to restrain unlawful strikes or boycotts after an investigation revealed apparent union violations. However, the General Counsel did not actively pursue this duty until well into the 1960s. The reason was a fear of obtaining a preliminary injunction to halt union action and then learning later that the move was not justified. It will be recalled that injunctions can seriously impede unions to the point of making some impotent—particularly, small, relatively powerless labor organizations. More recently, the General Counsel has given more attention to this duty. The second condition provides that the General Counsel might seek a restraining order requiring compliance with the law while a case is pending before the Board. This is not required, but the General Counsel may do so. The purpose is to eliminate flagrant violations of the Act until Board orders can be invoked to deal with the situation. The third permits the Board to seek an injunction from a circuit court of appeals to enforce its order. The petitioned court may grant the injunction if it agrees with the order. The fourth statutory provision for an injunction permits the Attorney General to seek an injunction in national emergency strikes or lockouts.

The third kind of sanction provided by Taft-Hartley permits the loss of employee rights. For example, employees could lose their rights if they engaged in strikes prior to the end of the sixty-day waiting period required for contract renegotiations.

Still a fourth type of penalty called for fines or imprisonment when certain provisions of the Act were violated. These offenses were limited to violations of the statutory ban on political contributions of union member dues to candidates in federal elections; employer and union violations of the checkoff of union dues restrictions; and interference with NLRB agents in the performance of their duties. Later on, we shall be concerned with union activities in federal elections, and with the checkoff as a bargaining issue. However, criminal penalties, imprisonment, or fines are not authorized for employer or union commission of unfair labor practices.

Unions argue that the remedies and penalties under Taft-Hartley are inadequate. They say that employer violations of the law are encouraged because of knowledge of the weak penalties. In 1976, Sol Stetin, president of the Textile Workers of America, said:

> The flagrant union-busting actions by southern textile manufacturers demonstrated that the intent of the law could be frustrated at relatively little cost by employers who refused to accept collective bargaining.
> Nowhere is the evidence of cold-blooded and illegal anti-union activity by an employer more shocking, more preponderant, more repeatedly proven before the NLRB and the courts than in the case of J. P. Stevens.[60]

To deal with this situation, unions have urged stiffer penalties against employers who frequently and flagrantly violate the law. In past years, Congress refused to enact the recommendations of organized labor. Under the proposed

Labor Law Reform Act of 1977, the NLRB would have been required to seek a court order to reinstate immediately an employee illegally discharged for union activities during an organizational campaign. Thus, the employee would not have to wait until the entire procedure of the law is exhausted. In addition, to make it more expensive for employers to violate the law and deter discharges during organizational campaigns, the employee so discharged would have received double back pay when the NLRB directed his or her reinstatement.

Speedy reinstatement of employees discharged for union activities during an organizing campaign by a court order would eliminate the long delays which have taken place in some cases. Perhaps the classic example of this situation was involved in the illegal closing of the Darlington, South Carolina, mill of the Deering-Milliken textile chain. In the previous chapter, we learned that the mill was shut down illegally after the Textile Workers Union won an election. The shutdown occurred in 1956, which resulted in 556 employees losing their jobs. Though the NLRB and the U.S. Supreme Court ordered back pay for these employees, they did not receive any compensation until August 1981, twenty-five years after the illegal closing of the plant. At that time, the former employees or their heirs (about 100 had died in the interim) received $5 million to distribute among them.[61]

Under the Carter-supported Labor Law Reform Act of 1977, an employer found to have willfully violated a final order of the NLRB or a federal court might have been barred from obtaining contracts from the United States government for up to three years. An exception could have been made for national defense reasons. With respect to J. P. Stevens, Textile Workers' President Stetin noted that although this company had violated the law on repeated occasions, it received contracts from the federal government for more than $100 million.

Since the Labor Law Reform Act of 1977 was not enacted into law, some states passed statutes that dealt with employers who repeatedly violated Taft-Hartley. Such employers were forbidden to sell products or services to the state for a period of up to three years. Under the Wisconsin statute, for example, employers who had three adverse rulings by the NLRB that were affirmed by federal appeals courts within a five-year period could not do business with the state for three years. However, a federal appeals court held that the Wisconsin statute could not apply to employers covered by the federal law, on the grounds that otherwise the balance between federal and state jurisdiction would be upset.[62] In May 1985, the U.S. Supreme Court agreed to review the case to determine whether Taft-Hartley preempted the state laws. In the next chapter, we shall deal with the doctrine of federal preemption nullifying state laws that conflict with federal law. If this principle of federal law is recognized by the Court, it is not likely that the Wisconsin statute will prevail.

In November 1983, a congressional committee reported favorably on a bill that would have denied for three years federal government contracts to employers who willfully violated orders of the National Labor Relations Board.[63] However, the bill received no further consideration and was not enacted.

"Make-Whole" Controversy

As noted previously, an employer engages in an unfair labor practice under Taft-Hartley by refusing to bargain collectively. When this occurs, the normal NLRB remedy is to direct the employer to comply with the law and bargain with the union. However, this kind of remedy might be of no practical value, since an employer may continue in the illegal conduct. In addition, such a Board order does not remedy the losses to employees who were placed at a disadvantage because of the employer's illegal conduct. These considerations prompted a union to request from the NLRB a more meaningful remedy to enforce the national policy.

In *Ex-Cell-O*, [64] an employer refused to bargain collectively for a long period of time after the union was victorious in a representation election. The union requested that the NLRB order the employer to pay to the employees the wages and fringe benefits that they would arguably have obtained through collective bargaining had the employer bargained in good faith. An administrative law judge agreed with the union. In March 1967, two years after the union had been certified as the legal bargaining agent, he stated:

> Employers who promptly comply with their obligations are placed at an economic disadvantage and flouters of the national policy are financially rewarded. These results are completely antithetical to the purposes of the law and call for a remedy which will help restore the situation to that which would have existed but for the unfair labor practices.

Accordingly, the judge not only ruled that the firm must bargain with the union, but also directed that it compensate the employees for the money value of the improved wages and benefits that it would be reasonable to conclude that the union would have been able to secure through collective bargaining except for the firm's refusal to bargain. To compute the amount due the employees, the law judge was prepared to compare the wages and benefits received in the plant in question with those prevailing in other plants owned by the company in the area, whose employees were covered by labor agreements negotiated by the same national union. To implement such a "make-whole" remedy, other formulas for computation could be devised.

In other words, the objective of the law judge's decision was to take the profit out of stalling in collective bargaining, making it expensive for a firm to refuse to bargain in good faith. Whatever delight the employees and union received from this decision was short-lived, however, because three years later, the NLRB, by a 3–2 vote, held that it did not have the statutory power to grant such relief. Though the Board unanimously found that the employer had violated the law by his refusal to bargain collectively, the majority (which included by this time two Nixon appointees) held that it could not compel employers to put into effect wage increases that they had not agreed to make. What makes the majority decision somewhat questionable is that all five Board members stated that they were in "complete agreement that the customary remedies the NLRB imposes are inadequate." Also, as the minority members stressed, the NLRB under Taft-Hartley in Section 10 (c) has the power "to take such affirmative action . . . as will effectuate the policies of this Act." It would seem that under proper circumstances a "make-whole" remedy would be proper to effectuate the law's policy for the promotion of collective bargaining.

Though the NLRB refused to order a "make-whole" remedy in *Ex-Cell-O,* some courts apparently believe that the Board has the legal power to do so. In *Tiidee Products,* a federal appeals court remanded a case to the Board and instructed the agency that it had ample power to issue a "make-whole" remedy to "provide meaningful relief for employees unlawfully denied the fruits of collective bargaining."[65] Also, another federal court held in *J. P. Stevens*[66] that the Board has the power to direct the remedy. In remanding the case to the NLRB to determine whether its narrow remedy was proper in light of the illegal conduct of the company, the court stated that

> although the courts will not lightly interfere with Board orders, the Board is under a complimentary obligation to set forth in valid fashion the relationship between the case and the remedy it orders.

Perhaps one reason for the remand is that J. P. Stevens was notorious for its illegal conduct in combating unions. Thus:

> J. P. Stevens is now in its 12th step in a long chain of litigation, each marked by a separate NLRB order to the company and each involving new problems arising against the background of the preceding step, but all of them relating to the basic controversy over unionization of the Company's numerous plants throughout the South.[67]

However, in October 1980, J.P. Stevens and the Clothing and Textile Workers negotiated a labor agreement covering ten of the corporation's eighty plants and 3,500 of its 30,000 production employees. This constituted the first realistic victory in the union's seventeen-year struggle against the corporation.[68]

In any event, despite the judgment of the courts that the Board has the authority under Taft-Hartley to direct a "make-whole" remedy, the NLRB at this writing still refuses to do so. In January 1972, the Board again refused to direct the remedy in the *Tiidee* case remanded to it by the federal court.[69] To support its position, the NLRB relied heavily upon the United States Supreme Court decision in *H. K. Porter.*[70] In that case, the court ruled that the NLRB did not have the power to compel parties to adopt any contractual provision. Thus, the Board believed that by directing a "make-whole" remedy, it would in effect be writing contractual language. However, as the appeals court stated in *Tiidee,* the remedy does not require the inclusion of contract terms in a labor agreement, but does serve to compensate employees for past illegal conduct of the employer. When a labor agreement was actually negotiated, the parties would be free to adopt whatever wage structure results from the collective bargaining process. The idea of the "make-whole" remedy is to award damages to employees to compensate them for previous illegal employer conduct.

In the Labor Law Reform Act of 1977, mentioned earlier, the NLRB would have been authorized to implement the "make-whole" remedy. Under this proposed legislation, should the Board find that an employer illegally refused to bargain collectively for a first contract, it would have been empowered to compensate employees by the following formula: an amount equal to the average wage negotiated at similar plants where collective bargaining proceeded lawfully. The data needed to determine the amount are regularly compiled and published by the Bureau of Labor Statistics.

CHANGING NLRB PERSONNEL AND POLICIES

The National Labor Relations Board was created by Congress for the purpose of administering the National Labor Relations Act in accordance with public policy. Public policy in 1935, as now, was declared

> to eliminate the causes of certain substantial obstructions to the free flow of commerce and to mitigate and eliminate these obstructions when they have occurred by encouraging the practice and procedure of collective bargaining and by protecting the exercise by workers of full freedom of association, self-organization, and designation of representatives of their own choosing, for the purpose of negotiating the terms and conditions of their employment or other mutual aid or protection.[71]

The main functions of the agency in achieving that purpose are (1) to prevent and remedy unfair labor practices of both employers and labor organizations; and (2) to conduct secret-ballot elections to determine whether workers desire to be represented by labor organizations.

The National Labor Relations Board in its capacity as a quasi-judicial agency has been subject to criticism because of changing interpretations placed on the broad legal principles contained in the national labor laws. Charges cast at the Board for preferential treatment of some groups have been an occupational hazard in its nearly fifty years of existence.

Sources of criticism against the Board have not been limited to any single group. Academicians as well as labor, management, and the general public have all expressed opinions regarding the changing character of federal labor policy. Neil Chamberlain, for example, wrote that "one cannot speak of federal labor policy with definiteness since a policy which is enunciated today may be modified a year from today."[72] The reasons given for changes in policies were (1) changing Board membership, (2) a realization that some policies are ineffective in practice, and (3) changing social norms. Each of the reasons enumerated, however, may be considered as reflecting the philosophies of Board members, with policy changes coinciding with changing membership.

In succeeding chapters, as we deal with the NLRB, there will be numerous examples of how the Board has changed its policies. At this time, we merely mention that policies have changed, sometimes by full circle, and explain that the reason for the change in policy results from the changes in the composition of Board membership.

Contrary to popular conception, there is no statutory political test for Board membership. Naturally, however, presidents tend to appoint persons who share their general economic and labor relations philosophies. As one study stated:

> . . . no adequate empirical evidence has previously been reported that shows that once appointed, Board members acted in a biased manner. The results of our study strongly suggest that the presidential appointment process has a substantial influence on the adjudication of ULP [unfair labor practice] complaints. Interpretation of the facts and law governing union-management relations is therefore dependent in part on the make-up of the Board.[73]

In the Eisenhower era, the Board was described as quite reluctant to restrict employers in their free-speech policies during election campaigns as well as in other unfair labor practices. On the other hand, the Kennedy and Johnson boards have been more restrictive of employer activities.

Labor organizations were highly critical of Board policies during the Eisenhower and Nixon years. In 1955, the CIO said:

> Americans have long been accustomed to believe that under our form of government the law is supreme. The record of the Labor Board under Republican auspices now strikingly reveals how often those who "interpret"—and not the Congress—actually make the law.[74]

Employers have also taken exception to various policies. Both employers and unions approach labor relations from ideological standpoints. Due to the changing character of the five-person Board in Washington, it has long been recognized that both groups are politically oriented toward a policy of generating pressures to attempt to influence decisions. Thus, even if one group had favorable experiences during one political administration, it may have unfavorable ones during the next. So long as Board decisions are partially political, one must expect a political evaluation of the effectiveness of agency administration from the parties who have a continuous relationship with it.[75]

Criticisms by some employer groups have gone far beyond the usual attitude of "keeping the pressure on" in order to influence policies. The Subcommittee on Separation of Powers, a part of the Senate Judiciary Committee, investigated the NLRB to determine how well it had performed its role. The Chamber of Commerce and the National Association of Manufacturers at one time led a campaign both to rewrite the nation's basic labor laws and to abolish the National Labor Relations Board. It was proposed that the functions now performed by the Board be transferred to either a labor court or to federal district courts. The campaign was so intense that in 1965, the Chamber of Commerce and the NAM appointed a committee of 150 lawyers to draft changes in the National Labor Relations Act. The finished product was a 167-page report circulated under the title "Labor Management Relations Act."[76]

The general charge made against the Board by the pressuring employer groups is that policy is made by the five members, who are allegedly not responsive to Congress or the people, but to labor unions. In this regard, employers charge, the interests of the American worker are not served, but only the interests of labor union leaders are promoted.

There were several specific charges levied at the Board in support of attempts to eliminate it. The Senate Subcommittee chair, Sam J. Ervin, contended that court review of Board actions was too limited to eliminate erosion of the congressional intent in formulating statutory provisions.[77] As a result, it developed policies that have little relevance to statutory language. Ervin remarked:

> Language defining bargaining rights, the duty to bargain, and the class of topics which are subject to bargaining has been "interpreted" by the Board in such a way that the statutory phrases now mean more than Congress intended or would have wished, or could have imagined.[78]

With the election of Reagan in 1980 and his reelection in 1984, the NLRB was again criticized, but this time by organized labor. Almost unique in the history of the Board, Reagan was able to appoint all five members, including Chair Donald Dotson, a former management attorney. Stung by what it believed to be many unfair decisions, the labor movement pulled out all stops in its attack against the agency. Speaking at a labor law session, a union attorney described the Reagan-appointed members as "pirates" who had taken over the National Labor Relations Board and "are steering it on an anti-worker course."[79] Another veteran labor attorney, for 31 years the general counsel of the International Ladies Garment Workers Union, said:

> . . . we are dealing with a board whose tilt to Management is the most pronounced in my experience.[80]

Lane Kirkland, president of the AFL-CIO, suggested the repeal of the Taft Hartley Act and abolishment of the NLRB on the grounds that unions would be better off without them.[81]

That the Reagan Board had reversed former policies is, of course, nothing new. Perhaps what was new involved the comparative rapidity and the large number of reversals. As former Board Member Zimmerman said:

. . . never in the history of the Labor Board have so many major established principles been overruled as in 1984 when a new majority began its revision course.[82]

At the appropriate places in this volume, we shall highlight some of the more controversial policies adopted by the Reagan Board. Though the federal courts, including the U.S. Supreme Court, generally sustained Reagan Board policies, it has not always prevailed. In a 1986 case, *NLRB* v. *Food and Commercial Workers* (Docket No. 84–1493, February 26, 1986), the high court unanimously held nonunion employees do not have the right to vote in union affiliation elections. Union members voted to affiliate with a national union, exluding nonunion employees from the election. Since they were excluded, the Reagan board refused to compel the employer to bargain with the union. Pointing out the policy meddled with the union's internal affairs, the Court said: "We hold that the Board exceeded its authority under the Act in requiring that nonunion employees be allowed to vote for affiliation before it would order the employer to bargain with the affiliated union."

Some of the actions of the Reagan NLRB, however, did not necessarily deal with major policy reversals, but only with the routine handling of cases. In 1975–1976, a Board appointed entirely by Nixon and Ford found for the employer in 29 percent of all contested unfair labor practice and election cases. In the Carter years, the figure dropped to 27 percent. In 1983 and 1984, the Reagan Board found for the employer in 60 percent of all cases.[83] Of course, despite this apparent management tilt, the Reagan Board would assert that its administration of the law was correct, and that in fact its predecessors did not enforce the law in a proper manner.

Indeed, needless to say, Dotson has defended the NLRB policies adopted during his tenure as chair. He has said that the goal of the Reagan Board was to return Taft-Hartley law to the middle ground that it occupied before the advent of the Carter Board.[84] Dotson sharply criticized labor leaders, the media, and a large segment of the academic community for not recognizing that the Reagan appointees were "reinstating some doctrines that had been Board law for over thirty years prior to the Carter . . . changes."

Inconsistent NLRB and judicial decisions may be based to some extent on philosophical and political differences, but they also stem from the interpretive difficulties in the laws themselves. In this regard, Justice Felix Frankfurter wrote in a 1957 case:

> The judicial function is confined to applying what Congress enacted after ascertaining what it is that Congress enacted. But such ascertainment . . . is nothing like a mechanical endeavor. It could not be accomplished by the subtlest of modern "brain" machines. Because of the infirmities of language and the limited scope of science in legislative drafting, inevitably there enters into the construction of statutes the play of judicial judgment within the limits of the relevant legislative

> materials. Most relevant, of course, is the very language in which Congress has expressed its policy and from which the Court must extract the meaning most appropriate.[85]

The Board, out of necessity, must behave in the same fashion as it considers how cases fall within the broad congressional language and extracts the meaning most appropriate to fit the situation at hand. The answer to the controversy over changing Board personnel and as a result changing policies cannot be resolved to the point of pleasing all who criticize the agency. It may well be that the Board's responsiveness to political changes could be eliminated somewhat by a permanent NLRB membership. A permanent membership similar to the tenure policy of the federal judiciary, independent of the national political climate and staffed consistently with impartial members, could result in more consistent policies and procedures and thus more equitable treatment of those coming into contact with the agency. Elimination of the NLRB and shifting its function either to a labor court or to the federal courts appears to be an inferior alternative either to maintaining the agency intact as it is or shifting to permanently tenured members.

UNION POLITICAL ACTIVITIES

For many years, unions under both the Railway Labor Act and the National Labor Relations Act took the position that they had the right to assist candidates for federal office. Business corporations were financially prohibited from making direct contributions to federal election campaigns by the Federal Corrupt Practices Act of 1925.[86] The same restriction was placed on unions for the first time in the War Labor Disputes Act of 1943, which was in effect until the end of World War II. Nevertheless, the CIO organized the Political Action Committee (PAC) in July 1943, and received its initial financing from the treasuries of international unions. Thereafter, PAC was financed by contributions from CIO membership. Expenditures to "get out the vote" were made, but direct contributions to candidates were not made. A Senate Special Committee on Campaign Expenditures reported in 1945 that there had been no clear-cut violation of the law because only "expenditures" had been made, which were not the same as "contributions." The Senate Committee majority was not of the opinion that expenditures should be prohibited by amending the Corrupt Practices Act. The House Campaign Expenditures Committee in 1946 was of the opposite opinion.

Congress took a position on union contributions and expenditures in 1947 when it passed the Taft-Hartley Act. Section 304 made it unlawful for corporations and unions to make either contributions or expenditures in connection with a variety of federal election functions. However, the legislative history of Section 304 revealed that voluntary contributions from members to a separate political organization would not be unlawful. The section was written for the purpose of prohibiting unions from using member dues for political activities. Senator Taft's view prevailed that the First Amendment protected the voluntary right of individuals to engage in political functions.

Federal Election Campaign Act of 1971: The *Pipefitters* Case

Congress clarified its position again in 1971 in a new statute. Two sections, 205 and 610, were important in the interpretation of union rights to contribute or expend funds in federal election campaigns.

Representatives Crane and Hansen offered amendments to Section 610 that in their views would codify court decisions interpreting what unions or corporations could do in connection with a federal election. The use of voluntary money expended or contributed through COPE, the AFL-CIO's Committee on Political Education, was not at issue. The basic difference between the two amendments involved the use of dues money for political endeavors. The Crane amendment would have forbidden the political use of dues money required of members for employment or union membership. The Hansen amendment, which prevailed and was written into law, had the effect of expanding unions' use of dues for political activities. It permitted the use of funds from a union's general treasury to establish, administer, and solicit contributions for political funds. In 1972, the U.S. Supreme Court in *Pipefitters* construed the Federal Election Campaign Act of 1971 as an expansion of statutory authority for unions to expend general dues money for political purposes.[87] A local union established a political fund contributed to by its members on an apparently voluntary basis. However, it used members' dues to establish and administer the fund. On this basis, lower federal courts held that the union violated the 1971 law. However, the high court in *Pipefitters* reversed the lower court, and established the following guidelines:

> 1. Voluntary political funds are legal so long as the contributions from members are segregated from union funds.
> 2. Contributors must not be coerced and must know that the fund is to be used for political purposes.
> 3. Union funds may be used to solicit, establish, and administer political funds. The fund need not be a separate entity from the union, but it must be segregated from the general treasury.
> 4. Political contributions and expenditures must not be made from dues and assessments paid by members as a condition of employment or union membership, or from union commercial transactions.

It would appear that on balance, the new election law as applied by the U.S. Supreme Court had strengthened the capability of organized labor to engage in the political arena. However, in Chapter 14 it will be pointed out that union members may claim a proportional return of their dues expended by a union for political activities when they are compelled to be union members as a condition of employment. That is, they are entitled to that portion of their dues used by a union for political purposes to which they object.

In January 1976, the U.S. Supreme Court clarified the application of federal election laws.[88] In effect, the Court held that it is unconstitutional under the First Amendment to forbid union leaders and management representatives as *individuals* to spend their personal funds during an election. They can air their personal views as loudly, as often, and as expensively as they like. On the other hand, the Court ruled that it is not unconstitutional for Congress to place limits on the size of donations intended to aid formal campaign committees. In May 1976, Congress spelled out the limits of these donations, which restrict contributions from any person, including a union or an employer, to a particular candidate for federal office or to the candidate's authorized committees. The limit was placed at $1,000. However, a multicandidate political group, such as the AFL-CIO COPE, or a similar organization established by employers, may contribute up to $15,000 to a national political committee and up to $5,000 to other political committees.

In March 1985, the U.S. Supreme Court held that the $1,000 limit did not apply to independent political committees operating during presidential elections.[89] Independent political action committees are those not directly affiliated with or authorized by a presidential candidate and that spend money without consulting the candidate. Holding that the $1,000 limit violated the First Amendment guarantee of free speech, the high court opened the door for unlimited donations to and expenditures by independent political action committees in presidential campaigns. Even before the U.S. Supreme Court had lifted the $1,000 restriction, political action groups ignored the law, with conservative groups spending $13 million to help elect Reagan in 1980 and $15.3 million for his reelection in 1984.[90] In contrast, independent groups spent only $49,000 for Carter in 1980 and $621,247 for Mondale in 1984. If the objective of the federal election laws was to curb spending in political elections, they have not been very successful, to say the least. It is common knowledge that millions of dollars are spent to elect political candidates.

In June 1978, the U.S. Supreme Court increased the capability of unions to engage in political activities in a different way. It held in *Eastex* that employees have the right to distribute material dealing with political issues in a plant during nonwork time and in nonworking areas. Employees distributed pamphlets opposing a proposed "right to work" amendment to the Texas Constitution and attacked Nixon for vetoing a proposed increase in the minimum wage. The employer was prepared to discipline the employees for distributing the pamphlets. Ruling that such discipline would violate the employees' right under Taft-Hartley to engage in activities for mutual aid and protection, the Court reasoned:

> '[M]utual aid or protection'. . . protects employees from retaliation by their employers when they seek to improve working conditions through resort to administrative and judicial forums, and . . .employees' appeals to legislators to protect their

interests as employees are within the scope of the clause. To hold that activity of this nature is entirely unprotected, irrespective of location or the means employed, would leave employees open to retaliation for much legitimate activity that could improve their lot as employees.[91]

Chief Justice Warren E. Burger and Justice William H. Rehnquist dissented because they believed that:

Congress never intented to require the opening of private property to the sort of political advocacy involved in this case.

In 1981, a federal appeals court held, however, that an employer could lawfully forbid employees from distributing a leaflet that specifically endorsed candidates for political office. It held that the Supreme Court's intention was for the problems presented in *Eastex* to be decided on a case-by-case basis.[92]

TAFT-HARTLEY AMENDMENTS

The Taft-Hartley Act remained in force for twelve years before controversy over its provisions resulted in congressional amendment in 1959. The amendments were contained in Title VII of a broader piece of legislation known officially as the Labor-Management Reporting and Disclosure Act of 1959, or more popularly the Landrum-Griffin Act. The first six titles of Landrum-Griffin deal with control of union affairs. The six labor reform measures will be dealt with in a later chapter. Our first concern in this volume is with the controversial provisions of Taft-Hartley that led to the Title VII amendments.At appropriate places in later chapters we shall indicate policies adopted in Landrum-Griffin to change Taft-Hartley.

SUMMARY

Public policy toward organized labor has changed significantly over the years. As demonstrated both previously and in the current chapter, public policy has consecutively practiced repression, strong encouragement, and modified encouragement coupled with detailed regulation. It seems a safe prediction not only that further shifts in this public policy can be expected but that these changes—as was not always the case in earlier times—will depend for their direction on the acceptability of current union behavior to the American public.

This latter point is particularly important to the unionists of today. Especially since 1937, when it held the Wagner Act wholly constitutional, the Supreme Court has permitted the legislative branch of government a wide latitude to shape public policy. Congress and the state legislatures are judicially free to determine the framework of labor law. To most citizens, such a situation is only as it should be. The judiciary is expected to interpret law, not to legislate it. It is generally expected that actions of the legislative branch should be voided only when the particular statute clearly and unmistakably violates the terms of the Constitution. In recent years, the electorate and not the courts have decided public policies toward labor, and the public has become much more critical of union behavior. Such a development has the effect of forcing labor organizations to become increasingly conscious of the images they project.

Every law since Norris-La Guardia has expanded the scope of government regulation of the labor-management arena. Legislative control over collective bargaining started in 1932, when the judiciary was limited in the use of injunctions to deal with labor disputes. In 1935, Congress was concerned primarily with restricting employer conduct. The legislative branch attempted to balance the scales in collective bargaining in 1947 by placing limitations on union conduct, and in 1959, it acted again by enacting legislation to deal with internal union affairs. Each time Congress has reviewed its enacted labor laws, it has increased the scope of regulation of collective bargaining. Future legislation can be expected to move further in the direction of government intervention into the collective bargaining process.

DISCUSSION QUESTIONS

1. How valid do you consider the pro and con arguments over the Taft Hartley Act? What facts can be cited to support each position?

2. Evaluate the union unfair labor practices contained in Taft-Hartley from the standpoint of need arising out of abuses, clarity as to Congressional purpose, and effectiveness in interpretation and enforcement.

3. How did Taft-Hartley intend to protect the rights of employees as individuals against unions?

4. What rights did employers need to have in the 1947 law in order to make relations with unions more equitable?

5. Compare the organizational structure of the NLRB under the Wagner Act to that under the Taft-Hartley Act.

6. Assess the NLRB's record under Taft-Hartley. How efficient is the Board? Do the data imply an antiunion bias?

7. Are the remedies for Taft-Hartley violations adequate or inadequate? Name each remedy and support your answer for each. Include the "make-whole" controversy in your discussion.

8. How have some states responded to repeat violators of Taft-Hartley provisions? How effective are those responses?

9. How serious is political bias in NLRB policies as it is related to changing Board personnel?

10. Political Action Committees (PACs) have been heavily criticized. What is permissible to PACs that was prohibited prior to passage of the Federal Election Campaign Act of 1971?

NOTES

1   Act of June 23, 1947, Public Law 101, 80th Congress, Chapter 120, 1st sess. The official name of this law is the Labor-Management Relations Act, 1947. However, throughout this volume it will be referred to by its popular name—Taft-Hartley.

2   Julius Rezler and S. John Insalata, "Doctrine of Mutuality: A Driving Force in American Labor Legislation," *Labor Law Journal,* XVIII, 5 (May 1967), p. 261.

3   From the personal files of the author.

4   *Hearings before the Committee on Labor and Public Welfare,* U.S. Senate, 80th Congress, 1st sess., on S. 55 and S. J. Res. 22, Part I, p. 73.

5   *Report of the Joint Committee on Labor-Management Relations,* Senate Report No. 986, Part I, March 15, 1948, p. 2. Title IV of Taft-Hartley created a joint committee to study and report on basic problems affecting friendly labor relations and productivity. This committee is officially termed the Joint Committee on Labor-Management Relations. It is composed of seven members of the Senate Committee on Labor and Public Welfare and seven members of the House of Representatives Committee on Education and Labor. The chair of the first committee was Joseph H. Ball, who was defeated in 1948 for reelection as senator from Minnesota. The vice-chair was Fred A. Hartley. The composition of this first committee, appointed shortly after the passage of the law, though bipartisan, was dominated by supporters of Taft-Hartley. As indicated below, the minority group of the committee did not share the view of the majority on the operation of Taft-Hartley.

6   Congress of Industrial Organizations, *Taft-Hartley and You.*

7   *Hearings before the Committee on Labor and Public Welfare,* 81st Congress, 1st sess. on S. 249, Part I, p. 436.

8   U.S. Department of Labor, Bureau of Labor Statistics, *Monthly Labor Review,* XLV (1947), p. 529.

9   *Hearings before the Committee on Labor and Public Welfare, op. cit.,* Part IV, p. 1837.

10   Charles C. Killingsworth, *State Labor Relations Acts* (Chicago: The University of Chicago Press, 1948), p. 3.

11   *Green Bay Post Gazette,* February 17, 1939.

12   *Ibid.,* March 2, 1939.

13   *Ibid.,* February 20, 1939.

14   Wisconsin Employment Relations Board, *First Annual Report,* 1938, p. 2.

15   Bureau of National Affairs, *Labor Relations Reporter,* Washington, D.C., IV (1939), p. 507.

16   National Labor Relations Board, *First Annual Report,* 1936, p. 9.

17   57 Stat. 163. The law was popularly termed the Smith-Connally Act.

18   Bureau of National Affairs, *op. cit.,* XII (1943), p. 632.

19   The strike-vote election procedure of the War Labor Disputes Act was discussed in the previous chapter.

20   Bureau of National Affairs, *op. cit.,* XVII (1946), p. 604.

21   National War Labor Board, *Termination Report,* Washington, D.C., I (1946), p. 81.

22   *Ibid.,* p. 90.

23   *Ibid.,* p. 90.

24   *Ibid.*, p. 82.

25   *Humble Oil & Refining Company,* 15 War Labor Reports 380 (1944). The Bureau of National Affairs, a private publishing house, compiled all of the decisions of the National War Labor Board during World War II. It included these decisions in 28 volumes called the *War Labor Reports.* Consequently, cases of the NWLB cited in this chapter as well as in the next refer to these volumes. For example, 15 War Labor Reports 380 means that the *Humble Oil & Refining* case will be found in the 15th volume of the War Labor Reports, p. 380.

26   *The Little Steel Cases,* 1 War Labor Reports 324 (1942).

27   National War Labor Board, *op. cit.,* p. 84.

28   *Ibid.*, p. 96.

29   International Association of Machinists, *The Truth About the Taft-Hartley Law and Its Consequences to the Labor Movement,* Washington, D.C., (April 1948), p. 29.

30   *Congressional Record,* LCII, p. 5703.

31   *American Newspaper Publishers Association* v. *NLRB,* 345 U.S. 100 (1952).

32   *J. R. Stevenson Corp.,* 212 NLRB 968 (1974).

33   Raymond L. Hilgert and Jerry D. Young, "Right-to-Work Legislation—Examination of Related Issues and Effects," *Personnel Journal,* December 1963, p. 559.

34   See, particularly, the excellent article by Derek C. Bok, "The Regulation of Campaign Tactics in Representation Elections Under the National Labor Relations Act," *Harvard Law Review,* LXXIII, 1 (November 1964), for a fuller discussion of these and various related organizational campaign legislative matters.

35   Albert Rees, *The Economics of Trade Unions* (Chicago: The University of Chicago Press, 1962), p. 39.

36   Nicholas S. Falcone, *Labor Law* (New York: John Wiley & Sons, Inc., 1963), p. 275.

37   *United Electrical Contractors Association* v. *Ordman,* 366 F. (2d) 776 (CA 2, 1966); cert. denied 385 U.S. 1026 (1966).

38   National Labor Relations Board, *Thirty-fifth Annual Report,* U.S. Government Printing Office, Washington, D.C., (1970), p. 7.

39   National Labor Relations Board, *Forty-fifth Annual Report,* U.S. Government Printing Office, Washington, D.C., (1980), p. 1.

40   Bernard Samoff, "The Case of the Burgeoning Load of the NLRB," *Labor Law Journal,* XXII, 10 (October 1971), pp. 611-630.

41   Office of General Counsel, NLRB, *Summary of Operations, Fiscal Year 1984,* p.1.

42   *Wall Street Journal,* February 13, 1985.

43   National Labor Relations Board, *op. cit.,* p. 294.

44   Committee on Government Operations, 98th Congres, 2nd Session, House Report 98–1141, October 4, 1984, "Delay, Slowness in Decisionmaking, and the Case Backlog at the National Labor Relations Board," p. 7.

45   *Ibid.*, p. 4.

46   Donald L. Dotson, "Processing Cases at the NLRB," *Labor Law Journal,* XXXV, 1 (January 1984), p. 3.

47   Committee on Government Operations, *op. cit.,* p. 6.

48   *Ibid.*, p. 9. This figure is for the first 11 months of 1984. In 1982, the Board issued a total of 1,546 decisions. Later data are not available at this writing.

49   *Ibid.*, p. 7.

50   *Wall Street Journal,* July 6, 1976.

51   National Labor Relations Board, *Forty-first Annual Report,* 1976, p. 253.

52   *Ibid.*, p. 21.

53   Frank N. McCulloch and Tim Bornstein, *The National Labor Relations Board* (New York: Frederick A. Praeger, Inc., 1974), p. 117.

54   Office of General Counsel, NLRB, *op. cit.*, p. 3.

55   National Labor Relations Board, *Interim Report,* November 5, 1976, p. 7.

56   National Labor Relations Board, Statistical Services Staff, Letter, June 24, 1981.

57   National Labor Relations Board, *Forty-first Annual Report,* 1976, p. 17.

58   Chapter 9, p. 203.

59   National Labor Relations Board, *Interim Report, op. cit.*, p. 7.

60   *AFL-CIO News,* March 26, 1976, p. 8.

61   U.S. Department of Labor, Bureau of Labor Statistics, *Monthly Labor Review,* CIV, 3 (March 1981), p. 76. See also *AFL-CIO News,* July 23, 1977, and Commerce Clearing House, *Labor Law Reports,* No. 486, August, 1981.

62   *Wisconsin Department of Industry, Labor and Human Relations* v. *Gould,* CA-7, Nos. 84-1115 and 84-2075, December 13, 1984.

63   H.R. 1743, 98th Congress, Labor Law Debarment Act, Commerce Clearing House, *Labor Law Reports,* No. 608, November 4, 1983, p. 3.

64   185 NLRB 107 (1970).

65   *IUE* v. *NLRB (Tiidee Products),* 426 F. (2d) 1243 (1970).

66   *Textile Workers Union* v. *NLRB (J. P. Stevens),* CA DC No. 71–1469, February 1, 1973.

67   Department of Labor, Bureau of Labor Statistics, *Monthly Labor Review,* XCVI, 5 (May 1973), p. 54.

68   U.S. Department of Labor, Bureau of Labor Statistics, *Monthly Labor Review,* CIV, 1 (January 1981), p. 19.

69   194 NLRB 1234 (1972).

70   *H. K. Porter Co.* v. *NLRB,* 397 U.S. 99 (1970).

71   49 Stat. 449 (1939).

72   See Don R. Sheriff and Viola M. Kuebler, eds., *NLRB in a Changing Industrial Society,* Conference Series No. 2 (Iowa City: College of Business Administration, The University of Iowa, 1967), p. 43.

73   William N. Cooke and Frederick H. Gautschi III, "Political Bias in NLRB Unfair Labor Practice Decisions," *Industrial and Labor Relations Review,* XXXV, 4, (July 1982), p. 549.

74   "Economic Outlook," *Congress of Industrial Organizations, Department of Education and Research,* XVI, 2 (February 1955), p. 16.

75   Benjamin J. Taylor, *The Operation of the Taft-Hartley Act in Indiana,* Indiana Business Information Bulletin 58 (Bloomington, Indiana: Bureau of Business Research, Indiana University, 1967), p. 88.

76   *Congressional Record* (Washington, D.C.: Government Printing Office, August 2, 1968), p. S10118.

77   *Congressional Record* (Washington, D.C.: Government Printing Office, September 5, 1968), pp. S10288–89.

78   *Ibid.*

79   *AFL-CIO News,* October 27, 1984.

80   *Wall Street Journal,* January 25, 1984.

81   *Wall Street Journal,* January 6, 1984.

82   *AFL-CIO American Federationist,* XLII, 5 (July 6, 1985), p. 5.

83   *AFL-CIO News,* June 1, 1985, p. 3.

84   Commerce Clearing House, *Labor Law Reports,* No. 692, May 24, 1985.

85   *Local 1976 Carpenters Union* v. *NLRB,* 357 U.S. 93 (1957).

86   Section 313, 43 Stat. 1074.

87   *Pipefitters Local Union No. 562* v. *United States,* 407 U.S. 385 (1972).

88   *Buckley* v. *Voleo,* U.S. Sup. Ct. Nos. 75–436, 75–437, January 30, 1976.

89   *Federal Election Commission* v. *National Conservative Political Action Committee,* No. 83-1032, March 18, 1985.

90   *Wall Street Journal,* March 19, 1985.

91   *Eastex Inc.* v. *NLRB,* 437 U.S. 556 (1978).

92   *United Automobile Workers* v. *National Labor Relations Board,* CA DC, Case No. 79-2539, March 3, 1981.

CHAPTER ELEVEN

JURISDICTION OF THE NATIONAL LABOR RELATIONS BOARD

At this point, we are concerned with the jurisdiction of the NLRB. If the agency refuses to take jurisdiction over a case, the Taft-Hartley law is not available to the employer, the union, or the employees involved in the dispute. Only when the NLRB exerts jurisdiction does the law comes into play. Also, unlike many other federal agencies, the General Counsel and the NLRB do not take the initiative to start the operation of the law. To activate the provisions of the law, an unfair labor practice charge or an election petition must be filed.

Early in its career, the NLRB decided that it would not deal with all cases which fall within the area of interstate commerce. As a federal agency, created by a federal law, the NLRB has the constitutional authority to take jurisdiction over any case which falls within the area of interstate commerce. However, because of budget considerations, soon after the NLRB was established, it refused to take cases that had only a minimal effect on commerce between the states. With a growing case load and a staff limited in numbers by insufficient appropriations, the agency decided to concentrate upon cases that had a more important relationship to interstate commerce. Later on, the Board decided to restrict its jurisdiction further, which resulted in the further curtailment of the operation of national labor policy.

It is the purpose of this chapter to review the evolutionary nature of the Board's self-imposed jurisdictional restrictions, the question of state control of labor relations in areas abnegated by the Board, and the impact of Landrum-Griffin in resolving the gray area of labor relations left by Board and Supreme Court actions. We shall also be concerned with other jurisdictional problems, including a 1974 amendment to Taft-Hartley that brought nonprofit health care facilities within the coverage of the law.

SELF-IMPOSED RESTRICTIONS

The Wagner Act bestowed upon the NLRB authority to assume jurisdiction over unfair labor practices and questions of representation "affecting commerce."[1] Section 2 (7) described the phrase so broadly that the Supreme Court held the jurisdictional authority of the Board to be coextensive with the reach of Congress under the commerce power.[2] It will be recalled that the *Jones & Laughlin Steel Corporation* case decided the constitutionality of the Wagner Act and at the same time extended the commerce power of Congress to include the production process as well as distribution. The reach of Congress did not apply to manufacturing processes as late as 1935, when the National Industrial Recovery Act was ruled unconstitutional.[3] Once the Wagner Act was upheld, it was the duty of the Board "to eliminate the causes of certain substantial obstructions to the free flow of commerce. . . ."[4] The Board's authority was established more clearly in a 1939 Supreme Court case, when the Court held that it was obvious that it was the intent of Congress "to exercise whatever power is given to it to regulate commerce."[5]

This broad power of the NLRB to extend coverage of national labor policy to all possible situations was, however, never utilized. Authority of the agency to choose its own area of operation was approved by the courts; that is, the Board's jurisdiction did not depend on the volume of commerce involved in a particular situation. The NLRB had discretion as to what cases it would accept. Therefore, businesses having very little effect on interstate commerce, as defined by the Board, were omitted from the national regulatory power of the agency on a case-by-case basis.

From its start, the NLRB experienced a significantly growing case load. Between 1937 and 1941, the Board case load expanded from 4,400 cases to 9,100.[6] Increased demands on the Board led it to decline jurisdiction of labor disputes on a case-by-case basis. The extent that it declined to accept labor cases depended partly on the backlog of cases in process. The purpose given for such action, however, was that the policies of the Act would not be furthered if it accepted cases in which an employer's operation did not have a substantial impact upon interstate commerce.[7] The Board argued that the determining factor in establishing jurisdiction was the extent of interference a labor dispute might have on commerce.

Even before the Wagner Act was declared constitutional, the Board had to come to grips with the problem of jurisdiction. In its first year of operation, it communicated to the public that under certain conditions, retail trade or other purely local businesses did not fall within federal jurisdiction.[8]

The immediate postwar period, 1945–1947, was a particularly troublesome one for NLRB operations. The nation was in the process of changing to peacetime production of consumer goods; union organizational drives were more active than during the war years; unions were attempting to achieve gains they had foregone because of the war effort; and employer resistance to unions was rising rapidly. The Board's case load swelled to about fourteen thousand by 1947.

Despite the increased demand for NLRB services, staff size was 800 in 1945, 990 in 1946, and only 720 in April 1947.[9] Because of insufficient appropriations during 1945–1947, jurisdictional control over marginal companies was declined on the grounds of their activities in interstate commerce. But in reality, lack of an adequate budget was the major reason why the Board declined jurisdiction over these cases.

The Taft-Hartley Act, passed in 1947, left the jurisdictional provisions of the 1935 law virtually unchanged. The new Act brought with it a difference in opinion between the Board and the General Counsel regarding the extent of Board obligation to assert jurisdiction over cases declined in the Wagner Act era. The result was that the Board did expand its control for a short period, but declined to do so on a permanent basis. The case-by-case method of asserting jurisdiction generated considerable uncertainty among some businesses and industries as to their status under the 1947 law.[10]

Publication of Jurisdictional Standards

Controversy over the uncertainties of Board behavior in providing interested parties protection from prohibited activities led to publication of some general guidelines clarifying Board jurisdictional policies in October 1950. The Board declared that it would take jurisdiction over firms clearly affecting commerce regardless of the channel from which the effect came. Included in the category of declared responsibility were public utility and transit companies, multistate firms meeting certain dollar standards of interstate commerce, and establishments affecting national defense.[11] But the guidelines established in 1950 were destined for a short life.

A further curtailment of the Board's jurisdiction was first revealed in a series of NLRB releases of Board member statements and subsequent decisions in the fall of 1953 and during the first part of 1954. Mr. Guy Farmer, then chair of the Board, in a speech after assuming office stated:

> I think perhaps the time has come to accept the proposition that it is not necessary or even desirable for the Federal Government to step into every labor dispute however insignificant it might be. It has always seemed to me, without engaging in any debate of the relative merits of state versus federal rights, that, regardless of the legal scope of the commerce clause the Federal Agencies should, as a matter of self-restraint, impose limits on their own power and thus provide the opportunity for local problems to be settled on a local basis by the citizens of the communities in which these problems arise.[12]

In other words, the Board, dominated by President Eisenhower appointees, justified its retrenchment of jurisdiction on philosophical grounds rather than on those of limited budget and manpower, as previously was the case.

In July 1954, the Board published a revised version of its 1950 jurisdictional dollar guidelines. Under the new "yardsticks," as the dollar standards are often called, many small business firms and their employees were removed from Taft-Hartley protection. The volume of business an enterprise had to sell to firms in other states to qualify for coverage was raised from $25,000 to $50,000. Purchases from out-of-state-based firms by an enterprise seeking coverage were also raised from the 1950 level of $50,000 to a new high of $1 million. Trucking companies operating in intrastate commerce but linked to trade between the states under a franchise arrangement were required to do at least a $100,000 volume of business per year before Taft-Hartley would apply. Radio and television stations qualified only if their annual dollar volume of business totaled at least $200,000. A newspaper whose annual revenue fell below $500,000 per year was no longer subject to the law. Prior to 1954, the Board had not established a dollar limit for radio, television, or newspaper establishments whose operations affected commerce. Additionally, the Board declared that public utility and transportation systems would be subject to Taft-Hartley only if they grossed $3 million per year. There was considerable contraction of independent and chain retail store coverage, as well as of many firms affecting national defense.[13]

Not all Board members agreed with the new jurisdictional standards. A minority dissented vigorously from the self-imposed restrictions of 1954. Labor and management groups entered the debate along with academicians. The most heated aspect of the debate centered on the authority of states to exercise jurisdiction over those business enterprises in interstate commerce denied coverage under federal law by the Board. One reason given for raising the jurisdictional standards in 1954 was the expectation that states would take the initiative by enacting state labor relations laws. However, fourteen years later, only seventeen states and Puerto Rico had done so.[14]

The reasons the Board gave for decreasing federal authority over enterprises in interstate commerce were (1) the desire for states to regulate the area of labor relations abnegated by it, and (2) its own wish to encourage renewed state labor legislation patterned after the Taft-Hartley Act. It also appears that the Board assumed that states had authority to exercise control over the rejected areas.

FEDERAL PREEMPTION: LEGISLATIVE ASPECTS OF TAFT-HARTLEY

When Congress passed the Taft-Hartley law, the national lawmakers were aware of the supremacy of federal law within interstate commerce. Aware of this state of affairs, but still desiring to provide the states with authority to deal with some labor relations problems within interstate commerce, Congress spelled out with precision those areas in which it desired state regulation to prevail. Perhaps the best illustration of the congressional approach to the federal-state jurisdictional problem involves the manner in which union security is treated in the national law. Whereas the federal law only outlaws the closed shop, the states under express provision of Taft-Hartley may prohibit any form of compulsory union membership.[15] At the time that Congress was considering the passage of Taft-Hartley, several states had already prohibited all forms of union security. Since Congress was determined to preserve this state jurisdiction, it relinquished federal supremacy in this area of industrial relations. In the absence of such a clear statement of federal policy, Congress feared that state law prohibiting union security would have been invalidated because of federal supremacy in matters affecting commerce. In this connection, the House Labor Committee declared:

> Since by the Labor Act Congress preempts the field that the act covers insofar as commerce within the meaning of the act is concerned . . . the committee . . . has provided expressly . . . that laws and constitutional provisions of any state that restrict the right of employers to require employees to become or remain members of labor organizations are valid, notwithstanding any provision of the National Labor Relations Act.[16]

Other areas of Taft-Hartley spell out additional points on which Congress desired the states to control labor relations within interstate commerce. The meticulousness with which these areas are indicated lends additional support to the idea that, in the absence of national legislation to the contrary, the states were forbidden to operate within interstate commerce once the federal government had occupied the field by the enactment of constitutional legislation. Thus the federal labor law required that parties who were seeking to modify or terminate collective bargaining contracts had to give notice of this fact not only to the Federal Mediation and Conciliation Service but also to any state agency that performed mediation services.[17] The director of the Federal Mediation and Conciliation Service was ordered to avoid attempting to mediate disputes that have only a minor effect on interstate commerce if state or other conciliation services were available to the parties.[18] In addition, the director of the federal mediation agency was empowered to establish suitable procedures for cooperation with state and local mediation agencies.[19] Under authority of another provision of the Taft-Hartley law, employers could sue unions in either federal or state courts for injuries suffered as a result of union action declared illegal in the national law.[20] Obviously, it was in these areas of labor relations that Congress desired the states to have concurrent jurisdiction with the national government. Congress recognized that the doctrine of national preemption would operate to exclude such state regulation of industrial relations within interstate commerce in the absence of clear and specific authority extended by the national government.

Not only did the Taft-Hartley law establish a system of concurrent federal-state jurisdiction within interstate commerce over certain specified areas of industrial relations, but it also provided that the NLRB, under certain limited conditions, could cede jurisdiction to state boards in unfair labor practice cases. This authority was given by Section 10 (a) of the law.[21] This provision of the statute has crucial importance in the determination of the question of whether the states may lawfully occupy the area of interstate commerce vacated by the NLRB.

Section 10 (a) empowered the NLRB to prevent any person from engaging in any unfair labor practice affecting interstate commerce. It further provided that this power of the Board "shall not be affected by any other means of adjustment or prevention that has been or may be established by agreement, law, or otherwise." With the single exception that the law established a limited procedure whereby the NLRB could cede jurisdiction to the states, this section of Taft-Hartley showed the determination of Congress to reserve for the national labor agency full and exclusive power to enforce the terms of the national labor statute. No other enforcement agency, federal or state, regardless of the circumstances under which a case arose, had any power to implement the provisions of the Taft-Hartley law. This was the clear and unmistakable meaning of Section 10 (a). With this one exception, Congress was anxious to insure the uniform application of national labor policy throughout interstate commerce. Uniform national labor policy within interstate commerce could not be realized if Congress had permitted a variety of federal and state courts or labor agencies to interpret and apply national labor policy. If Congress had allowed a variety of enforcement channels of the Taft-Hartley law to exist, there might have been as many different versions of its meaning as there are law-enforcement forums within the nation. It was this state of affairs that Congress desired to avoid in 1947.

The determination of Congress to insure the uniform application of the federal law within interstate commerce was not lessened by the limited circumstances under which the NLRB could cede jurisdiction of unfair labor practice cases to state agencies. In the first place, Section 10 (a) clearly specified that the only way in which the federal agency could cede jurisdiction to the states was "by agreement." This meant that the Board could not cede jurisdiction to the states merely by declaring that it would not exercise its authority over a certain category of cases. Unless an agreement was entered into by the NLRB with state agencies, Section 10 (a) prohibited state exercise of control over labor relations within interstate commerce. Such an agreement was not implied merely by a decline of jurisdiction by the NLRB. Agreement was possible only if the state law to be applied was identical with the federal law in both language and application stemming from interpretation.

Obviously, the reason why Congress included the consistency test within Taft-Hartley was to provide for the uniform application of national labor policy within interstate commerce. The objective of uniformity could not have been realized if federal and state law treated the same set of circumstances in an unlike manner. If the consistency standard had not been included in the federal law, a situation could have arisen in which activities unlawful under federal law could be lawful under state law. It was this kind of confusion that Congress meant to avoid when it established the barrier to NLRB jurisdictional cession to the states. In this connection, the Senate Labor Committee, which reported the Taft-Hartley law in 1947, stated: "The provision which has been added to this subsection permits the National Labor Relations Board to allow State labor-relations boards to take final jurisdiction of cases in border-line industries (that is, border line insofar as interstate commerce is concerned) provided the state statute conforms to national policy."[22]

In 1975, the restrictions contained in Section 10 (a) prompted the Board to refuse to cede jurisdiction to the state of Minnesota in cases involving non-profit hospitals. (Below is a discussion of the general problem of Taft-Hartley application to nonprofit hospitals.) Minnesota, which had a law covering that industry, petitioned the Board to cede jurisdiction in this area. The Board refused because of differences between Taft-Hartley and the state law. Under the Minnesota law, strikes and lockouts were prohibited, and binding arbitration was required when nonprofit hospitals and employees had reached an impasse in collective bargaining. As will be seen, no such restrictions were contained in federal law.[23]

FEDERAL PREEMPTION: THE SUPREME COURT

On several occasions, even before Taft-Hartley, the U.S. Supreme Court had invalidated state laws when they conflicted with national labor legislation. In 1943, Florida enacted a union regulation law that, among other things, required that union officials obtain a license before operating within the state.[24] To satisfy the requirements for the license, a union official had to prove that he or she was a citizen of the United States, had resided in the United States for ten years, had not been convicted of a felony, and was of good moral character. The law also required that the applicant pay a fee before obtaining the license. In 1945, the Supreme Court held that the statute was invalid to the extent that it applied to interstate commerce, on the grounds that it circumscribed the full freedom of choice that employees are given in the selection of bargaining representatives under national labor law.[25] In this connection the Court declared that "the full freedom of employees in collective bargaining which Congress envisioned as essential to protect the free flow of commerce among the states would be, by the Florida statute, shrunk to a greatly limited freedom." Thus the state of Florida could not use a state law to deprive workers of rights protected by the Wagner Act.[26]

The application of the principle of federal supremacy over state law within interstate commerce also involved a case dealing with bargaining rights of foremen and women.[27] In May 1943, the NLRB held that it would no longer extend the protection of the Wagner Act to foremen or women in the exercise of their collective bargaining rights. Specifically, the Board ruled that supervisors no longer constituted units appropriate for collective bargaining within the meaning of the national law. Under this policy, unions of supervisors could not be certified by the NLRB for collective bargaining purposes. However, while this NLRB policy was in effect, the New York State Labor Relations Board afforded the full protection of the New York State Labor Relations Act to foremen and women. Consequently, a union of supervisors, denied access to the NLRB, petitioned and obtained a certification from the state labor agency for purposes of collective bargaining. When this case was heard by the Supreme Court of the United States, the state of New York argued that a state had the authority to act until federal power was actually exercised over the particular employees. However, the Court rejected this argument, declaring that "the State argues for a rule that would enable it to act until the federal board had acted in the same case. But we do not think that a case-by-case test of federal supremacy is permissible here. The federal board has jurisdiction of the industry in which these particular employers engaged and has asserted control of their labor relations in general." The Supreme Court held that the state board did not have the power to permit supervisors to become a bargaining unit under a state labor law because the federal law had denied them this right. Thus the decision demonstrated that a state could not endow employees covered by national labor law with rights not consistent with federal law.

In two cases involving state regulation of the right to strike, the Supreme Court again implemented the doctrine of federal supremacy in the field of labor relations. In both cases it held that the state laws interfered with the right of workers to strike as protected by the federal law. Accordingly, the Court invalidated these state laws to the degree that they applied to firms and employees covered by the Taft-Hartley law.

One of these cases involved the provision of the Michigan state labor law, which required a strike-vote election before a work stoppage could legally take place.[28] Under the Michigan law, a strike was not lawful unless authorized by a majority of the workers within a bargaining unit. In short, the Michigan statute made the lawfulness of a strike turn on the outcome of a strike poll. The second case dealt with the Wisconsin Public Utility Anti-Strike Law.[29] This statute outlawed strikes and lockouts in public utilities and substituted a system of compulsory arbitration to resolve disputes between employers and unions within the public utility field. Decisions of the arbitrators, subject to review by the courts, were binding upon the parties.

In 1948, the Supreme Court held that the Wisconsin Employment Relations Board did not have jurisdiction over a representation proceeding involving the bargaining representative of employees of a telephone company.[30] The company was engaged in interstate commerce within the meaning of federal legislation. However, a union involved in the case filed a petition with the state board requesting the agency to determine the collective bargaining representative. On the point of determination of bargaining representatives, there was no essential conflict between the federal and Wisconsin laws. The NLRB and the state agency were both equipped to dispose of the problem. Still, the Supreme Court held that the Wisconsin board could not deal with the question of representation in industries that fall within the area of interstate commerce. The fact that the NLRB had not taken jurisdiction of the controversy did not lessen the Court's determination to reserve for the national labor agency the jurisdictional area granted to it by national legislation enacted pursuant to the United States Constitution.

The principle of national preemption of the control of labor relations within interstate commerce was the basis for a Supreme Court decision involving unfair labor charges against an employer and a labor organization.[31] In this case, a union had utilized a variety of coercive techniques on a worker to force him to join the organization. He refused and the employer ultimately discharged him. The tactics of the union and the employer's discharge of the worker constituted unfair labor practices under the Wisconsin Labor Relations Act. Accordingly, the Wisconsin Employment Relations Board ordered reinstatement of the employee, and the Wisconsin Supreme Court subsequently enforced the action of the state board. Ultimately, the Supreme Court of the United States reversed without opinion the ruling of Wisconsin's labor agency and Supreme Court. The United States Supreme Court merely cited the *Bethlehem Steel*[32] and *La Crosse Telephone*[33] decisions as the authority for its ruling in the case. Undoubtedly, the conduct of the union and the employer would have been illegal under the Taft-Hartley law. Still, the United States Supreme Court, mindful of the distribution of power between federal and state governments, did not permit the similarity between federal and state legislation to determine its decision.

In 1953, the Supreme Court handed down its decision in the *Garner* case,[34] and once again ruled that states were without authority to assume jurisdiction over labor relations disputes that fall within the area of the NLRB. Involved in this case was picketing by a labor organization that violated the laws of Pennsylvania. Without question, the picketing was also unlawful under the Taft-Hartley Act. A Pennsylvania court held that the union conduct violated the Pennsylvania Labor Relations Act and enjoined the picketing. However, the Supreme Court of Pennsylvania upset the ruling of the lower court on the grounds that the labor dispute fell within the exclusive jurisdiction of the NLRB. The United States Supreme Court upheld the high court of Pennsylvania, declaring that in enacting the Taft-Hartley law, "Congress did not merely lay down a substantive rule of law to be enforced by any tribunal competent to apply law generally to the parties. It went on to confide primary interpretation and application of its rules to a specific and specially constituted tribunal and prescribed a particular procedure for investigation, complaint and notice, and hearing and decision, including judicial relief pending a final administrative order."

In 1976, the U.S. Supreme Court again upheld the supremacy of national labor policy.[35] The case involved Wisconsin labor relations law. An employer and a union both tried to put economic pressure on each other during the months of negotiations for a new contract. Within this context, a union membership meeting voted unanimously to require members to refuse overtime work until a new agreement was reached. The employer filed an unfair labor practice charge against the union alleging that the activity violated Taft-Hartley. A regional director found that the union tactic did not violate the federal statute and dismissed the charge. Then the employer filed charges under the Wisconsin law, and the state agency and two state courts held that refusal to work overtime violated the state statute.

When the U.S. Supreme Court reviewed the case, it held that Wisconsin could not outlaw the union activity in question, because the activity was not regulated under Taft-Hartley. In other words, when union, employee, or employer conduct is not regulated by federal law, a state may not outlaw such activity. To find otherwise, the high court said, would frustrate federal labor relations policy.

Given these judicial precedents, a 1984 U.S. Supreme Court decision dealing with the 1977 New Jersey Casino Control Act was somewhat surprising. Determined to prevent organized crime from infiltrating the casino industry, the state law imposed qualifications on union officials representing casino industry employees. Not eligible to serve as union officers were those with a criminal record, or with ties to organized crime. By a 4–3 vote, two justices not participating, the high court held the state statute did not conflict with the Taft-Hartley provision under which employees have the right to elect officers of their own choosing.[36] It said that where a state is confronted with crime, corruption, and racketeering, "more stringent state regulation of the qualifications of union officials was not incompatible with the national labor policy as embodied in Section 7."

In any event, despite this aberration, probably justified because of unique circumstances, the U.S. Supreme Court has uniformly held that states could not take jurisdiction of labor disputes falling within the scope of the national law.

The *Guss* Case and the "No Man's Land"

The *Garner* case served notice that the Supreme Court did not look with favor upon state control of labor disputes falling within the scope of national labor legislation. However, it did not conclusively resolve the federal-state jurisdictional problem. Finally, in 1957, the Supreme Court clearly excluded the states from asserting control over cases declined by the NLRB. In the light of the language of Taft-Hartley and court precedent, it was only logical to expect such a decision of the high court.

In *Guss* v. *Utah Labor Relations Board,* the Court held that when the Board had jurisdiction, even if it refused to exercise it, states could assert their own laws only when the NLRB ceded jurisdiction under Section 10 (a) of the National Labor Relations Act.[37] It will be recalled that Section 10 (a) required states to apply law identical to that of the federal statute. Not a single state qualified to accept cases on conditions prescribed by Section 10 (a). Denial of state jurisdiction meant the creation of a "no man's land" within which labor relations were subject to neither federal nor state regulation.

The implications of the no man's land were several. First, when the agency declined jurisdiction, it meant that bargaining elections could not be conducted by use of Board machinery to determine whether collective bargaining representatives would be chosen. No method was available to the parties to resolve any conflict arising out of organizational issues. One of the basic purposes of national law is to eliminate organizational strikes. The failure to assert control over some firms would result in strikes seeking to force recognition.

Second, the decision had the effect of allowing employers and unions to engage in activities illegal under national labor law without fear of intervention by either the NLRB or the states. Employers could discharge workers for union activities, refuse to bargain with a majority union, and sponsor company-dominated labor organizations. On the other hand, unions were free to engage in such illegal activities as secondary boycott strikes, jurisdictional strikes, and strikes for closed shops, and could refuse to bargain in good faith without fear of restraint. Indeed, when employers and unions recognized that no law would apply, it could be said that they were actually being encouraged to engage in conduct that would otherwise be proscribed under law.

The Supreme Court was aware of the importance of its decision. It pointed out possible alternative solutions to the no-man's-land problem. One was congressional enactment of appropriate legislation. Another was that the Board could reassert its jurisdiction by reevaluating its dollar-volume guidelines.

The *Guss* decision created an immediate response from both Congress and the NLRB. In July 1958, Congress increased the Board's operating budget to permit a lowering of its dollar standards for the purpose of reducing a portion of the no-man's-land area. As a result, the Board revised its jurisdictional standards in October 1958. The policies set forth in 1958 remain in effect at the present time.[38]

Despite the efforts of the Congress and Board, a gray area remained, since many employers, unions, and employees engaged in interstate commerce were still outside the scope of national labor policy. Congressional action on the no man's land was certain, since the controversy was not stilled by the greater budget and Board reevaluation of jurisdictional policies.

Impact of Landrum-Griffin: Title VII

In 1959, Congress attempted to deal with the no-man's-land problem. It enacted an amendment to Section 14 of Taft-Hartley. Two courses of congressional action were available to fill the gap. Congress could require the NLRB to take jurisdiction of all cases defined legally as falling within interstate commerce. Or it could permit states to exercise jurisdiction over those cases declined by the Board. As early as January 1958, President Eisenhower had recommended greater state control, and his preference was known to Congress.

Section 14 (c) of the 1959 Landrum-Griffin amendments to Taft-Hartley contained the final decision made from among the alternatives facing the legislators. The section was designed to deal with the no man's land. It reads:

(c) (1) [The NLRB is empowered, under certain conditions, to decline jurisdiction] where, in the opinion of the Board, the effect of such labor dispute on commerce is not sufficiently substantial to warrant the exercise of its jurisdiction. . . . (2)

> Nothing in this Act shall be deemed to prevent or bar any agency or the courts of any State or Territory (including the Commonwealth of Puerto Rico, Guam, and the Virgin Islands), from assuming and asserting jurisdiction over labor disputes over which the Board declines, pursuant to paragraph (1) of this subsection, to assert jurisdiction.[39]

Thus under the new law, the NLRB at its discretion could decline to assert jurisdiction over any case when in its judgment the effect of the labor dispute on commerce was not sufficient to warrant the exercise of its jurisdiction. State courts and agencies had the authority to take jurisdiction of cases the Board declined. Nothing in the new law required the states to take jurisdiction over these disputes. The law was merely permissive in this respect, not compulsory. It is not likely, however, that a state having a general labor relations law similar to Taft-Hartley will decline jurisdiction. But in states without such a law, the no-man's-land problem still exists.

The Board could also expand its jurisdiction to reach all cases falling within the area of interstate commerce. To the extent that the federal agency should expand its jurisdiction, the states' rights to intervene in interstate commerce would correspondingly decline. Though the Board could lawfully increase the scope of its jurisdiction, it could not reduce its authority beyond that which was in force as of August 1, 1959. It is also important to note that under the new law, the Board was authorized to decline jurisdiction over an entire industry. Congress provided this power to the Board because the Supreme Court in 1958 had ordered the agency to take jurisdiction over the hotel and motel industry.[40] Before this time, the Board had refused to handle cases involving this industry. After the Supreme Court decision, the Board has exerted jurisdiction over motels and hotels, provided the enterprise receives at least $500,000 in gross revenue in a year.[41]

Problems flowed from the congressional policy on jurisdiction. How could the parties determine whether the NLRB would take jurisdiction over a particular case? Could the states apply state law, or could they pick and choose in this respect?

A party involved in a labor dispute can follow two procedures to determine whether the NLRB will accept or decline jurisdiction over a particular case. It can refer to the Board's published standards, which express in money volume the categories of cases the Board will take.[42] Perhaps a more definitive method is to seek an advisory opinion from the NLRB on whether it will take a particular case. The agency made such a procedure available shortly after the passage of the new law.[43] Such advisory opinions, however, deal exclusively with the issue of jurisdiction and will not relate to the merits of the dispute. In addition to the parties involved in a labor dispute, the Board will accept requests for advisory opinions from state courts and labor agencies. Advisory opinions may be filed only if a proceeding is currently pending before an agency or court. In general, the request for an opinion is expected to contain the general nature of the business of the employer involved in the dispute, and present relevant data on commerce. The Board permits the party filing the request for an advisory opinion to withdraw it at any time before the Board issues the instrument.[44]

In regard to the body of law to be applied by a state court or labor agency, it is clear that state law may be applied. A Senate version would have required the states to apply only federal law in all cases affecting interstate commerce. The Conference Committee, however, rejected the Senate proposal so that state law may be applied.[45]

As expected, states having state labor relations laws apply state law, though there is no express prohibition in the 1959 amendment against their applying federal law. Since state laws differ in content and are subject to different construction by state agencies and courts, the principle and value of uniformity expressed in Section 10 (a) no longer apply. In some competitive categories, depending upon circumstances, this state of affairs could be harmful to employees and employers. Such a situation is a defect of the 1959 amendment. It permits different labor relations policies within interstate commerce. Employers operating under a strict state law would face a competitive disadvantage over employers in a state with a weak or no organizational law. Likewise, inequitable treatment of employees from one state to another exists. As noted, another defect of the 1959 amendment is that many states do not have labor relations laws. In those states, the no-man's-land problem is still in effect. In the light of these observations, it would be proper to conclude that Congress did not deal effectively with the problems resulting from NLRB entrenchment of jurisdiction. More impressive, to this day Congress has not acted to correct the obvious shortcomings of the 1959 amendment.

Other Jurisdictional Problems

Making use of its authority to decline jurisdiction over all cases within an industry, a power conferred upon it in the 1959 amendment, the Board refused to assert jurisdiction over horse and dog racing,[46] and over a local doctor's medical practice.[47] In 1979, reversing an earlier policy, the Board asserted jurisdiction over condominiums and cooperative apartments with a gross annual revenue of at least $500,000.[48]

At one time, the agency refused jurisdiction over private colleges and universities.[49] In 1970, it reversed this policy in *Cornell University*,[50] and currently such educational institutions are covered by the law. To be covered by Taft-Hartley, the private institution must gross at least $1 million in annual revenue. The modesty of this amount assures that the vast majority of private universities and colleges now fall under the jurisdiction of the NLRB. Not only are nonacademic employees covered by this policy, but faculty members may also use the NLRB to aid them in organizational and collective bargaining efforts.[51] Also, Taft-Hartley applies to private elementary and secondary schools. Provided that a school grosses $1 million annually, the NLRB will take jurisdiction whether or not the school operates for private profit. However, public schools and universities are still excluded from the coverage of the federal law. This is the case because ever since the passage of the Wagner Act, public employees have been excluded from the coverage of the law. Thus, state action is required to provide the legal basis for collective bargaining in public schools.

In 1980, however, the U.S. Supreme Court dealt a devastating, if not fatal, blow to the organizational and collective bargaining rights of faculty members employed by private colleges and universities.[52] What probably came as a shock to some faculty members was that by a 5-4 vote the majority held that the faculty members are "managerial employees" and hence excluded from the scope of the law. They are managerial employees, said the majority, because they effectively recommend the hiring, promotion, salary, and tenure of the faculty; standards of admission; curriculum; grading system and graduation requirements; and participate in the hiring of deans and other administrative officers. In a sharp dissent, Justice Brennan said that faculty members play an entirely different role compared with managers in business in that a faculty exercises "its decision making power in its own interest rather than the interest" of the administration of a university. In other words, Brennan charged that the majority did not understand the role of faculty members within a university.

In any event, where *Yeshiva* applies, university administrators have no obligation to recognize or bargain with a faculty-designated bargaining agent, and presumably, unless prevented by tenure rules, may lawfully discharge a faculty member for participating in union activities. Such a state of affairs undoubtedly will reduce the growth of collective bargaining in academe, though public universities are not covered by the decision. Only one hope was held out by the decision. Buried in a footnote, the majority said there may be "institutions of higher learning unlike Yeshiva where the faculty are entirely or predominantly managerial." In other words, a determination would be made on a case-by-case basis. In a 1985 case, for example, the Board held that faculty members were not managerial employees because they did not effectively formulate and effectuate school policies. Unlike at *Yeshiva,* said the agency, faculty members' recommendations were frequently overruled by the institution's administration.[53]

Though hopes for its passage are very doubtful, in 1984, legislation was proposed in Congress stipulating that faculty members are employees under Taft-Hartley. Should that law ever be enacted, *Yeshiva* would be nullified.

In another major reversal of policy, the NLRB in 1976 declared that it would take jurisdiction of *nonprofit, noncommercial, and charitable institutions.*[54] For over thirty years, the NLRB had declined jurisdiction over such institutions and, indeed, had affirmed that policy as recently as 1974.[55] A majority of the Board held that the statutory basis for the exclusion disappeared when in July 1974, Congress amended Taft-Hartley to provide coverage to nonprofit hospitals, a matter that will be discussed in the next section of this chapter.

Under the new policy, nonprofit enterprises are no longer automatically excluded from the coverage of the law.[56] Institutions such as the Chicago Lighthouse for the Blind are included under the new policy.[57] Under compelling circumstances, however, the Board is prepared to make exemptions, as in *Goodwill Industries*. The Board held that collective bargaining could undermine the goal of Goodwill of hiring handicapped persons for rehabilitation purposes. Higher wages, the Board reasoned, could lead to the hiring of more productive workers and a reduction in Goodwill's work force of handicapped people. Aside from these rare instances, employees of charitable institutions now have the same protected legal right to organization and collective bargaining as employees in commercial and profit-making firms. A charitable institution's gross revenue must be sufficient, however, to meet the dollar standards established by the Board in order to come within its jurisdiction. In *Rhode Island Catholic Orphan Asylum,* the 1976 precedent case, the institution grossed more than $250,000, sufficient to meet the dollar standard for institutions of that type. In *Chicago Lighthouse for the Blind,* the enterprise earned more than $50,000 per year by performing certain subcontracted work for companies located outside the state of Illinois. In short, under the current policy, a charitable institution that meets the dollar standards established by the Board will not automatically be excluded from its jurisdiction just because it provides a worthy social service.

In 1973, the Board declined all cases arising in law firms.[58] It held that law firms had a minimal degree of impact on interstate commerce, and apparently believed that unionization of its employees could compromise the confidentiality between the law firm and its clients. Once again the Board changed its policy, and in 1977, held that law firms as a class will no longer be excluded from its jurisdiction.[59] Reversing its position, the Board said:

> Since it is clear that law firms, as a class, do have a substantial impact on interstate commerce, we shall assert jurisdiction over them.

A major factor that induced its change of position about the relationship of law firms to interstate commerce was a U.S. Supreme Court decision in 1975 that law firms are covered by the antitrust laws.[60]

Though the precedent case, *Foley, Hoag & Eliot,* involved an election petition filed by clerks and messengers, it appears that attorneys working in large law firms who consider themselves employees rather than managers or owners could use the NLRB for organizational and collective bargaining purposes. Whenever it could be established in a particular case that law firm employees are engaged in confidential activities, the NLRB will probably exclude them from the bargaining unit. However, in 1980, the Board refused to exclude the nonlegal staff members of a law firm just because they had access to the firm's confidential material.[61]

Before 1977, the Board had consistently refused to apply Taft-Hartley to foreign banks and other commercial enterprises operating in the United States when they were owned by a foreign government. The issue arose again in the Chicago branch of the State Bank of India, Bombay. At that time, the NLRB reversed its former policy, directing an election among the American citizens working for that bank.[62] To justify this change, the Board stressed that in 1976, Congress had enacted the Foreign Sovereign Immunities Act, which reduced the immunity of foreign commercial enterprises operating in the United States. The NLRB said that this new law manifested a congressional intent to deny "sovereign immunity to a foreign state's private or commercial acts" occurring within the United States. Since under the 1976 law, such enterprises are subject to American federal and state court jurisdiction, the Board believed that it would not be consistent to continue its former policy. Thus, American citizens working for foreign enterprises have gained legal protection of their organizational and collective bargaining rights and are no longer, in the words of the union involved, "second-class citizens."

In short, in the case of law firms, charitable institutions, foreign-operated enterprises, and private educational institutions, the Board in the 1970s shifted its position in favor of extending coverage. It is noteworthy that so far there has been no class of cases in which the Board has declined jurisdiction after it originally asserted jurisdiction. Thus, the NLRB has elected to broaden the coverage of Taft-Hartley rather than to restrict it.

For one class of employees, by a 5-4 vote in 1981, the U.S. Supreme Court specifically approved a Board policy expanding coverage of Taft-Hartley. In *Hendricks County Rural Electric Membership Co.*, the Board held that confidential employees are not generally exempt from Board jurisdiction. Excluded are only employees who have access to confidential matters directly relating to labor relations, such as the secretary of an industrial relations manager. Other employees who have access to confidential matters not directly relating to labor relations, such as the secretary of a purchasing manager, are covered by Taft-Hartley. For exclusion, in other words, an employer must show that the employee has access to information relating directly to labor relations matters.

In another highly controversial area, though not involving a change in policy, the NLRB held that it would exert jurisdiction over church-operated commercial enterprises.[63] Like some other religious bodies, the Christian Science Church operates a variety of profit-making commercial enterprises. In the precedent case, the church argued that it should be exempt from the coverage of Taft-Hartley because of the First Amendment to the Constitution calling for the separation of church and state, and further claimed that the profits that it earned from its commercial ventures were used to further the cause of religion. Rejecting these arguments, the NLRB directed an election among employees who worked in the commercial enterprises run by the church.

In other religion-related matters, the Board assumed jurisdiction over private schools operated by the Roman Catholic Church.[64] Though the Board recognized that the schools' admission policies were set to attract future priests, the evidence demonstrated that the schools operated primarily as college preparatory schools with the same curriculum and extracurricular activities as other private and public high schools. Also, it noted that only 16 percent of the graduating class in the year preceding the Board's decision had entered seminary colleges. It would seem, however, that if a religious body operates a school for solely religious instruction, the Board would probably not apply Taft-Hartley.[65]

In 1979, however, the U.S. Supreme Court by a 5-4 vote in *Catholic Bishop of Chicago*[66] reversed the Board and ruled that lay teachers employed by church-operated schools are not covered by Taft-Hartley. Writing for the majority, Chief Justice Warren Burger said that Congress had never intended the NLRB to have jurisdiction over such schools. He believed that the exercise of such jurisdiction would automatically raise serious First Amendment issues entangling the NLRB in religious matters. Therefore, he said, Congress must authorize Board authority over parochial schools by adopting specific language. In other words, Taft-Hartley would have to contain a provision that expressly stipulated that the NLRB had jurisdiction. Since the law does not contain such a provision, the majority of the Court concluded that the Board does not have jurisdiction over parochial schools. In the absence of an "affirmative intention" expressed by Congress, Burger reasoned, the Court should refuse to construe the law in a manner that "could in turn call upon the Court to resolve difficult and sensitive questions arising out of the guarantees of the First Amendment religion clauses."

Justice Brennan, writing for the minority in a vigorous dissent, argued that the majority had invented a "canon of statutory construction" solely for deciding this case. Never before, he said, had the Court required the affirmative expression of Congress in providing the NLRB with jurisdiction over particular categories of employers. For example, as noted, the Board has asserted jurisdiction over private universities, charitable institutions, law firms, foreign government enterprises, and church-operated commercial enterprises, although Taft-Hartley does not expressly authorize the Board to take jurisdiction over them. Brennan also argued that where Congress had intended to exempt NLRB jurisdiction, it did so by specific exclusionary language, as with government employees, agricultural labor, railroads and airlines, supervisors, and, at one time, nonprofit hospitals. He also stressed that when Taft-Hartley was enacted, Congress had turned down a proposal which would have exempted religious institutions—a clear expression of congressional intent.

So far, however, the NLRB has not applied *Catholic Bishop of Chicago* to church-related colleges and universities, holding the doctrine applied only to parochial elementary and secondary schools.[67] Also not covered by it are church-operated child care centers[68] and religious hospitals.[69] The Board held that employees of these institutions are covered by Taft-Hartley because religious indoctrination was not their fundamental purpose, as is the case with parochial elementary and secondary schools.

In any event, whatever the merits may be of *Catholic Bishop of Chicago*, as in *Yeshiva*, the U.S. Supreme Court has sharply restricted the application of Taft-Hartley, denying many employees legal protection of their unionization and collective bargaining activities. As a possible consequence, there could be industrial strife. Albert Shanker, president of the American Federation of Teachers, said that if denied the protection of the NLRB, such employees could strike to force their employers into collective bargaining arrangements.[70]

A few other jurisdictional matters are of general interest. Under current policy, the Board asserts jurisdiction over professional baseball, and presumably over other professional sports;[71] over symphony orchestras with an annual revenue of at least $1 million;[72] and over the gambling industry, rejecting the contention of owners of a casino in Nevada that gambling in that state is essentially local in character.[73] In addition, labor unions as employers fall within the jurisdiction of the NLRB.[74] Under this policy, union representatives and office employees have been able to form unions of their own to bargain collectively with the union employers.

In a particularly interesting case, the NLRB in 1976 refused jurisdiction over the employees of a business conducted by an Indian tribe on its reservation.[75] It held that Indian tribes are sovereign entities insofar as activities on their reservations are concerned, and that the tribal council is equivalent to a government for purposes of NLRB jurisdiction. This decision may come as a surprise to Indians who have difficulty in other matters with the United States government!

In a comparatively more recent and important case, the U.S. Supreme Court held in 1984 that Taft-Hartley applied to illegal aliens.[76] When the Sure-Tan Company's illegal aliens formed a union, the employer in retaliation reported them to the Immigration and Naturalization Service. To avoid deportation, some of them quit their jobs and voluntarily left the United States. Such employer conduct, the high court ruled, amounted to a constructive discharge in violation of Section 8(a)(3) of the law forbidding discrimination against employees for union activities. At this writing, however, the issue of a proper remedy remains unresolved. How can the NLRB direct the reinstatement of employees who are illegal aliens and who fled the country? To deal with this problem, plus the issue of back pay, the Supreme Court remanded the case to the NLRB to fashion a proper remedy. It will be interesting to learn how the Board deals with this problem.

COVERAGE OF HOSPITAL EMPLOYEES

In 1967, the NLRB departed from its policy of declining jurisdiction over proprietary (profit-making) hospitals. In the *Butte Medical Properties* case, the Board established a new standard for profit-making hospitals that are privately owned.[77] Jurisdiction is asserted if such hospitals have gross revenues of at least $250,000 per year.

The Board justified its action by noting that state regulation of privately owned hospitals is limited in the sphere of labor relations. Also, national health insurance companies and the federal government make considerable payments to proprietary hospitals for providing health protection. These payments were deemed to have a considerable impact on interstate commerce. Interstate commerce is also affected by substantial purchases of supplies and services from out-of-state sources.

Privately owned nursing homes, operating for a profit, were also placed under the National Labor Relations Act if the employer receives at least $100,000 in annual gross revenue.[78] The Board justified its action by applying the same reasoning used in the *Butte* case. Nonprofit hospital employees did not enjoy coverage of the national labor law. The Act denied coverage of such employees unless a part of the net earnings went to the benefit of any private shareholder or individual.

The original language of Taft-Hartley and the 1967 change in Board jurisdictional policy over proprietary hospitals placed noncovered employees at a distinct bargaining disadvantage. The lack of parity in the bargaining rights of employees within the industry posed potentially explosive circumstances.

The relative wage and benefit discrepancies between hospital workers and those in other sectors were sufficient to ignite work stoppages. However, differential assertion of Board jurisdiction over essentially identical employees added a new dimension to the entire process of collective bargaining. Civil rights organizations placed increased pressures on nonprofit and public hospitals to conform to the same labor relations standards that the NLRB imposed on firms over which they did assert jurisdiction. Bitter strikes resulted from the differential federal policy of guaranteeing bargaining rights for some hospital employees, but not for others.

These considerations prompted Congress to reevaluate the policy of exempting employees of nonprofit hospitals from the coverage of Taft-Hartley. In July 1974, it amended the law and brought within the jurisdiction of the NLRB almost 2 million employees who worked in about 3,300 nonprofit hospitals. Now, with legal protection of their bargaining rights, most of these employees are organized. One consequence of the new legislation is that recognition strikes are no longer necessary in the health-care industry. This serves the public interest, since formerly many long and bitter strikes were undertaken by nonprofit hospital employees because hospital management refused to recognize their unions. The 1974 amendment does not cover government-operated hospitals. It applies only to the private sector. Labor relations in state-operated hospitals is covered by state law, and federal hospitals are covered by federal law. (In a subsequent chapter, we will treat the problem of the public sector.)

Since hospitals supply a critical public service, under this new legislation, unions representing employees in both proprietary and nonprofit hospitals are required to give ninety days notice before terminating or seeking to modify labor agreements, thirty days more than Taft-Hartley requires in other industries. In addition, a hospital union may not lawfully strike or picket unless it gives ten days notice. This provision was adopted to give hospital management an opportunity to make arrangements for the continuity of patient care. Furthermore, a labor dispute in a health-care institution is automatically subject to mediation by the Federal Mediation and Conciliation Service. Moreover, unlike its authority in other industries, the agency is empowered to appoint a fact-finding board to make recommendations to settle hospital labor disputes.

Problems of Application

With the passage of the amendment, the NLRB was faced with a series of problems in its application. In 1975, it held that it would apply the same dollar jurisdictional standards to nonprofit health-care establishments as it had previously adopted for profit-making units.[79] As noted, this was $250,000 for hospitals and $100,000 for nursing homes and related facilities. Thus, the same dollar standards for jurisdictional purposes apply to all health-care establishments regardless of whether or not they are operated for profit.

Bargaining Units

A much more complicated problem involved the establishment of appropriate bargaining units for employees who work in hospitals. Of course, this problem had existed even when the NLRB took over jurisdiction of profit-making hospitals. The problem became much more extensive, however, when Congress brought 6,260 nonprofit hospitals under the jurisdiction of the NLRB. In addition, the legislative history of the 1974 amendment provided instructions to the Board with regard to hospital bargaining units. The Senate Committee Report said that "due consideration should be given by the Board to prevent proliferation of bargaining units in the health care industry."[80] In other words, Congress did not believe it to be in the public interest to have a multitude of small and narrow bargaining units within a hospital. In carrying out the congressional mandate, the Board principally grouped hospital employees in terms of their community of interests, training, educational background, professional status, and bargaining history. This was not an easy task, because at times, a particular group on the basis of some of these criteria could reasonably fall within the category of another group.

Before the advent of the Reagan NLRB, six separate bargaining units had been established in the health-care industry. These were registered nurses,[81] physicians employed by a hospital (other than residents and interns),[82] other professional employees,[83] technical employees,[84] clerical employees,[85] and general service and maintenance employees.[86] In this way, the previous Board believed, it had struck a reasonable balance between the congressional mandate against proliferation of bargaining units and the desires of employees, based upon their community of interests, to select their own bargaining agent. Under that policy, if all employees within a health-care institution were organized, there could be a maximum of six bargaining units. On the other hand, the collective bargaining rights of one group did not depend upon the organization of other classifications. For example, a bargaining unit composed of registered nurses could be established even though other groups remained nonunion.

In a sharp reversal of policy, the Reagan Board abolished the previous system of bargaining units.[87] Instead of the "community of interest" test, it held that a separate bargaining unit would be established in the health-care industry only if there was a "disparity of interests" greater than that required in other industries. However, the decision did not establish a standard or guideline demonstrating how a group of health-care employees could prove it has a disparity of interests sufficient to distinguish it from other groups. It would seem that the new policy might be applied to establish only two bargaining units within a health-care institution—professional and nonprofessional. If this does in fact result, organization within hospitals will be far more difficult, since it is normally easier to unionize comparatively small groups of employees.

Predictably, the Reagan Board's decision was sharply criticized by the labor movement, but praised by health-care management and employer groups. Union representatives complained that the new policy was "outrageous, destroying ten years of legal precedent," and represented a "naked political attack on hospital workers' right to organize."[88] In contrast, the other side supported the new decision, charging that the previous policy was "contrary to the intent of Congress," and stating that the new policy appeared to be "a victory for the hospital."[89]

Hospital Interns and Resident Physicians

Board decisions on the hospital bargaining-unit problem were frequently reached by majority and not unanimous vote. Depending upon changes in Board personnel, the character of its bargaining unit policies may change. One particular Board policy may be upset in the future. In *Cedars-Sinai Medical Center*,[90] a majority of the Board sparked an unusual amount of controversy and general interest when it held that hospital interns and resident physicians have no rights under Taft-Hartley. It held that such persons are not "employees" within the meaning of the law, but rather students pursuing a graduate medical education. Though interns and residents are paid for their work and devote a great deal of their time to patient care, the Board held that the law does not apply to them. Currently, there are about 12,000 interns and 20,000 resident physicians working in the nation's private hospitals. For those who believe that collective bargaining is necessary to improve the conditions of their employment, the Board's decision created a great deal of resentment. The leader of a group of interns and residents promoting collective bargaining said that the Board

> has publicly affirmed that the profits of hospital employers are more important than the welfare of workers or the sick.[91]

During the 1976 congressional hearings concerning NLRB operations, Representative Frank Thompson of New Jersey, who authored the 1974 hospital amendment, said that the law should be changed to eliminate *Cedars-Sinai Medical Center.* He feared that residents and interns might strike for union recognition. In bitter criticism of the Board policy, he said:

> And the doctors and interns had to strike for recognition. Now they will appeal that, but the basis of their appeal, I am afraid, is a terribly difficult one. They would have to establish the Board was arbitrary, so that might lead us to amending the act. I discussed this yesterday with my distinguished ranking member and friend Mr. Ashbrook. He is as upset about that decision as I. The Board is human and like all humans, including myself, you make mistakes. Perhaps not as many as I make, but I think to call interns and residents "students" was a very definite mistake and can lead to extreme difficulty in that industry.[92]

However, a bill that would have brought residents and interns within the scope of the law, nullifying *Cedars-Sinai Medical Center*, was defeated in the House of Representatives.[93] Also, a federal appeals court held that the NLRB policy did not violate its authority under Taft-Hartley.[94]

Special Rules for Health-Care Industry

In a later chapter, we shall discuss the right of unions to solicit employees for membership on employer property, and the corollary right of the employers to ban union solicitation on their premises. However, the NLRB established a special set of rules for hospitals, recognizing that a health-care institution is different from a business in general. Hospital management can forbid the right of employees to solicit or distribute union literature on behalf of a union in patient-care areas even if the activity occurs during nonworking time.[95] Thus, in order to avoid disturbing patients, hospitals may forbid all such union activity in patient rooms and other patient-care areas such as X-ray, operating, and therapy rooms. On the other hand, the NLRB invalidated a hospital rule that forbade union solicitation in cafeterias and visitors' lounges. It held that even though patients have access to these areas, the possibility of disruption of patient care would be remote. In addition, the NLRB held that off-duty employees have the right to solicit on behalf of a union outside the premises of a hospital. Thus, an off-duty employee had the right to distribute union literature on a rear loading dock and in the front driveway.[96]

In July 1977, the Tenth Circuit Court of Appeals held that hospitals were authorized to ban union solicitation in both patient-care and patient-access areas, such as hallways, elevators, cafeterias, and waiting rooms. In this case, *St. John's Hospital* v. *NLRB,* the court held that it was "specious" to draw a distinction between patient-care areas and patient-access areas. Unlike the Board, it said that union solicitation in patient-access areas could have an upsetting effect on patients.

Later on, however, the U.S. Supreme Court held that a hospital may not arbitrarily ban union solicitation on all of its premises. In June 1978, the Court held in *Beth Israel Hospital*[97] that a hospital may not forbid distribution of union literature and solicitation in a cafeteria unless it can show that such activities disturb patients. In that case, only 1.56 percent of the cafeteria's patrons were patients. In *Baptist Hospital*[98] the Court modified a no-solicitation rule that had applied to virtually the entire premises of a hospital. Holding that such a rule unreasonably interfered with organizational rights, the Court held that a union could solicit members in areas in which there were no patient rooms, such as cafeterias, gift shops, and lounges located on the lobby floor. On the other hand, the hospital was permitted to ban solicitation in corridors and lounges located on floors occupied by patients. Apparently, for those locations, the hospital had presented sufficient evidence to show that patients would be adversely affected by union activity.

Although these two decisions do not resolve the entire problem with finality, it is safe to say that a health care institution may not arbitrarily forbid union solicitation in all areas to which patients have access. For a no-solicitation rule to be valid, the burden is on the hospital to prove that union activity in such areas would not be in the best interests of the patients. The presumption is that a ban in non-patient rooms or care areas is unlawful without a showing that such activity is likely to disrupt patient care or disturb patients.[99]

Recall that before employees may strike or picket, the union must give ten days' notice to the hospital. With one exception, to be noted below, the Board has applied that requirement in a literal fashion. In one case, a union complied with the notice requirement and was picketing the hospital. Four union officers of another union joined the picket line to show sympathy. They picketed for only one and one-half hours on one day during a strike that lasted over two weeks. Despite the fact that the sympathy pickets did not place any additional union pressure on the hospital, the Board held that the union that had provided the sympathy pickets had violated the ten-day notice requirement.[100] In another case, the Board held that the prepicketing notice was applicable even though a union was picketing at the site of the construction of a new hospital. At that time, of course, there was no immediate adverse impact upon the institution's ability to provide health-care services. But the picketing was nevertheless found illegal because the union had failed to submit the notice. The NLRB was clearly saying that the requirement "was to be read literally."[101] In *Laborers, Local 1057,* however, a federal appeals court reversed this obviously unrealistic policy.

Hospital employees who strike or picket without filing the ten days' notice may be discharged by the hospital. It does not matter whether the employees are represented by a union, or whether a union had knowledge of their illegal conduct. The General Counsel dismissed the charges filed by such discharged employees, who had claimed that they were engaging in protected activity under Taft-Hartley.[102]

On the other hand, the General Counsel refused to find that a union violated the ten days' notice requirement in a case where a hospital had committed flagrant and massive unfair labor practices during and after an NLRB election. Though the union filed a notice, it did not meet the technical requirements of the notice, such as stating precisely when picketing and striking would begin. In holding that the union had not violated the notice requirement, the General Counsel stated:

> Although the Union literally breached the [notice] provisions of the Act by striking and picketing after serving upon the Employer and the FMCS a notice which lacked the specificity requirements, the failure to strictly comply with the requirements were deemed excused by the Employer's serious and flagrant unfair labor practices against which the strike and picketing were meant as a protest.[103]

The General Counsel said further that the legislative history of the 1974 amendment demonstrated that unions would not be held to the notice requirement when a hospital commits serious or flagrant unfair labor practices.

These observations demonstrate the way the NLRB and the General Counsel have handled problems growing out of the 1974 amendment. They meet these issues as they arise, and this is by no means the end of the story. It will be interesting to learn how the Board deals with these issues—one hopes in a sound way, because the labor relations program in the health-care industry is vital to the public interest.

TAFT-HARTLEY AND BANKRUPTCY CODE: BILDISCO AND ITS AFTERMATH

Here we address a special kind of jurisdictional problem—the relationship between Taft-Hartley and the U.S. Bankruptcy Code. In question is the determination of which statute prevails when the two conflict. The issue was joined in a case involving a small New Jersey building supply distributor, Bildisco and Bildisco. It had a labor agreement with the Teamsters Union that was scheduled to expire in April 1982. Significantly, the contract provided that it was binding on the parties "even though bankruptcy shall supervene."

While the labor agreement was in force, the employer, without bargaining with the union, refused to pay scheduled wage increases, stopped paying the agreed-upon health and pension contributions on behalf of the workers, and refused to turn over union dues that were deducted from the workers' paychecks. Acting favorably on an unfair labor practice charge filed by the union, following its traditional policy, the National Labor Relations Board held that the employer violated Taft-Hartley.[104] The employer was found guilty of an unfair labor practice because it had unilaterally changed the terms of a labor agreement, and had failed to bargain with the union before making the changes. From its inception, national labor policy has protected the integrity of labor agreements. Neither employer nor union may unilaterally alter the terms of a labor agreement.

In January 1980, long before the contract was due to expire, Bildisco had filed a voluntary petition for bankruptcy under Chapter 11 of the Bankruptcy Code. Under Chapter 11, a company continues to operate with court protection from creditor lawsuits while it tries to work out a plan to pay its debts. Under these circumstances, the employer is called "debtor-in possession," normally operating the enterprise with the same management personnel under bankruptcy court supervision. In the proceeding before a bankruptcy court, Bildisco received permission to reject the total collective bargaining agreement. On appeal by the union, a federal district court upheld the decision of the bankruptcy court. By this time, the NLRB had held that the employer had violated national labor policy. Thus, when the case was appealed by the NLRB and the union, the federal appeals court was faced with two conflicting decisions: the NLRB had held that Bildisco had violated Taft-Hartley; but the bankruptcy court, upheld by the district court, permitted the employer to reject the entire labor agreement. Upholding the lower court decision, the federal appeals court held that Bildisco had the right to abrogate the labor agreement.[105] In other words, the appeals court ruled that when the two federal statutes in question conflict, the Bankruptcy Code prevails over Taft-Hartley.

Such was the setting as the U.S. Supreme Court was prepared to issue its decision after receiving the appeal from the NLRB. To say the least, the labor relations community awaited this decision by the high court with deep interest. Much more was at stake than the small New Jersey building supply firm. In 1983, Wilson Foods had filed for bankruptcy and immediately cut employees' wages by 40 to 50 percent.[106] In the same year, Continental Air Lines had also filed for bankruptcy under Chapter 11 and had immediately cut wages by about 50 percent.[107] In both cases, strikes occurred, but the firms were able to operate.

On February 22, 1984, in one of the most significant labor cases in modern times, the Supreme Court issued its decision, upholding the decision of the federal appeals court.[108] By a 5–4 vote, the high court held that an employer could abrogate a labor agreement *immediately upon filing for bankruptcy under Chapter 11.* The employer did not have to wait for a bankruptcy court for permission: mere filing of the petition was sufficient to get rid of the labor agreement.

The second major issue determined by the Court equally shocked the labor movement. By unanimous decision, the Court established standards to guide bankruptcy courts when faced with the problem of determining whether an employer could permanently eliminate a labor agreement. In this respect, the high court ruled that all an employer need show is that the agreement "burdens" the chances for survival under Chapter 11. No requirement was placed on the employer to show that the labor agreement made the difference between survival or extinction of the firm. Indeed, no showing was required to establish whether the contract was the critical factor or even a major reason for the employer's financial difficulties. A firm's financial problems could result from a variety of factors, including the rate of interest, inept management, failure to modernize a facility, poor marketing, insufficient advertising, or changes in consumer demand for a product or service. Obviously any labor agreement burdens an employer in the sense that a low wage is less burdensome than a higher wage. But in arriving at a decision as to whether a contract may be permanently eliminated, a bankruptcy judge had only to determine whether the employer made a "reasonable" effort to negotiate a less burdensome contract. If the employer and union were not able to do that, the bankruptcy court may still cancel the contract.

Obviously, these standards would not make it difficult for employers to use Chapter 11 to be free of labor agreements. Indeed, one bankruptcy lawyer termed the standards as "cosmetic," sending a strong signal to bankruptcy courts to permit employers to abrogate labor agreements.[109]

Thus, the upshot of *Bildisco* was that an employer would not commit an unfair labor practice by filing under Chapter 11 for bankruptcy and immediately abandoning a labor agreement. The contract could be lawfully eliminated even before a bankruptcy judge had given the employer permission to nullify the contract. In short, the high court held that when Taft-Hartley and the Bankruptcy Code conflicted, the latter statute prevailed. National labor policy was to be subordinated to an employer's use of the bankruptcy statute to break labor agreements.

Needless to say, the labor movement and the business community differed widely in their reactions to *Bildisco.* Unions feared that almost any employer, even those whose financial situations were not critical, could use this decision to break labor agreements and get rid of unions at the same time. Unions do not have a viable role to play in the absence of a labor agreement. Thus:

> The Supreme Court decision drew immediate expressions of shock and dismay from labor leaders and officials, who viewed it as a weapon to aid employers in ousting unions or pressuring them to accept unwarranted concessions on wages, benefits, and work rules. AFL-CIO President Lane Kirkland said, "We're disappointed in the decision and we will pursue a legislative remedy . . . ."
>
> William Winpisinger, president of the International Association of Machinists, described the decision as simply "outrageous . . . ."[110]

Just as vigorously, the business community hailed the decision. Representatives of management were fulsome in their praise for *Bildisco.* As reported in the *Wall Street Journal* on February 24, 1984,

> . . . a Cleveland bankruptcy lawyer and former federal bankruptcy judge, contends that all labor-intensive companies will have to consider filing for bankruptcy as a result of the Supreme Court decision.
>
> "The officers and directors of any company will be more inclined to consider the bankruptcy alternative as a management tool to answer some of the problems of a troubled company, he said. "It's gotten to the point where management almost has to consider it."
>
> [An] Atlanta lawyer . . . was more direct. "For smaller companies that have been beaten up by unions over the last 10 years," he said, "it may be a way of getting even."

[Another said] "Chapter 11 is not pleasant, . . . It's sort of like going through open heart surgery and brain surgery at the same time. However, the reality is that it is now clear that the option (Chapter 11) is available. If a contract with a union won't allow a company to exist and make a profit, that company doesn't have to wither away."

CONGRESSIONAL RESPONSE

On February 22, 1984, the very same day that *Bildisco* was announced by the Supreme Court, the labor movement mounted a massive campaign to nullify *Bildisco* through congressional action. Only twice before in labor history, when Taft-Hartley was enacted in 1947 and Landrum-Griffin in 1959, had organized labor marshalled such a vigorous legislative campaign. Although labor failed in the prior two instances, this time it was successful in persuading Congress to enact legislation in its favor. As part of a general revision of the Bankruptcy Code, Congress provided the labor movement protection from the *Bildisco* decision.[111] Congress enacted the new law on June 29, 1984, only four months after the Supreme Court action, and it was signed by Reagan on July 10, 1984.

To be sure, under the current legislation, employers can still use the Bankruptcy Code to modify or nullify a labor agreement. This was clearly demonstrated when in July 1985, Wheeling Pittsburgh Steel Corporation received permission from a bankruptcy court to reduce the wages and benefits that had been provided in a labor agreement negotiated with the United Steelworkers of America. When Wheeling Pittsburgh reduced wages, the workers struck the plant, underscoring the proposition that employees have the legal right to strike when an employer reduces contractual benefits after bankruptcy court proceedings.

However, unlike the situation in *Bildisco,* an employer's opportunity to abandon labor agreements had been sharply restricted. In the first place, no longer may an employer unilaterally repudiate a labor agreement when filing a petition for bankruptcy. A contract can be abolished only when permission is granted by a bankruptcy judge. After filing such petition, but before requesting the bankruptcy court to reject a contract, the employer must propose to the union modifications in the labor agreement necessary to keep the firm in business. The company must provide the union with relevant information, financial reports, and the like, so that the union can intelligently evaluate the proposal. Also, the proposal must be fair and equitable to all concerned. For example, if employees are required to take a wage cut, a similar sacrifice must be made by management personnel. In other words, all concerned—employees, management, creditors, and stockholders—must sacrifice equitably. If the firm's proposal is not fair and equitable to all parties, the company will not be permitted to modify or repudiate the labor agreement. After the employer makes a proposal, he or she must bargain with the union in good faith to reach a mutually satisfactory modification of the labor agreement.

If the parties cannot agree on contractual matters, the employer may then request a bankruptcy court to alter or nullify the contract. However, before providing relief, the bankruptcy judge must comply with strict standards—far more effective than those established in *Bildisco.* Before authorizing the employer to modify or repudiate the contract, the bankruptcy court must make sure that the employer made an equitable proposal to the union and bargained in good faith, and that the proposal was rejected by the union without good cause. Only when these conditions are fulfilled may the bankruptcy judge permit the employer to modify or abrogate the collective bargaining agreement, provided the court believes that the balance of the equities involved in a case clearly requires nullification or rejection.

Thus, the new law removes many of the consequences of the Supreme Court decision. Indeed, the AFL-CIO commented that it is "pleased with the measure," which it termed a "vast improvement over what the Supreme Court left us with."[112] No longer may bankruptcy law be used as a license to break labor agreements.

AGRICULTURAL WORKERS

Agricultural workers are excluded from the protection of Taft-Hartley and have been since 1935, when the Wagner Act was passed. Repeated attempts have been made by the labor movement to include agricultural workers under Taft-Hartley, but the Congress has not done so. Several states have enacted legislation to deal with labor relations in agriculture.

Arizona Law

A few states, notably Arizona and California, have tried to fill the gap created by national labor policy. However, the Arizona law, passed in 1972, rather than protecting the right of farm workers to organize and bargain collectively, weakens their position. Under the Arizona law, harvest-time strikes are limited.[113] An employer is authorized to apply to a state court for a restraining order to halt for ten days a strike during the harvest season. Representation elections are authorized, but once an election is directed, the union is limited in its opportunity to communicate with the workers. What is more serious, eligibility to vote in the election is in effect decided by the employer. These election procedures are in complete variance with the practices established by the NLRB under federal law. In addition, the law makes illegal consumer secondary boycotts when their purpose is to endorse, encourage, or force an employer to recognize or bargain with a union. Under the law, there are important restrictions on the ability of a union to negotiate a meaningful labor agreement. The law makes it unlawful for a union to negotiate a grievance procedure covering discharge or suspension of employees; a successor-employer clause; a seniority system; or a hiring hall. Unions may not negotiate provisions to deal with the issue of mechanization and displacement of workers by technology. In the light of the provisions of the law, it should occasion no surprise to learn that it was supported by the employer groups, and

> there has been little organizing in Arizona, because the United Farm Workers Union is very critical of the law, believing it makes organizing efforts futile.[114]

In 1977, the United Farm Workers of America, headed by Caesar Chavez, challenged the constitutionality of the Arizona law in federal court as being in violation of the United States Constitution guarantees of free speech, equal protection of the law, and due process.[115] Objective analysis of the law, and comparing it with national labor policy, would require agreement with Chavez' observations that the Arizona law makes it difficult, if not impossible, for farm workers to organize and bargain collectively in a meaningful way.

In April 1978, the Phoenix federal district court supported Chavez, holding that the Arizona law was unconstitutional in its entirety.[116] In particular, the court referred to the following areas of the law: legislated delays in election proceedings; inability of unions to communicate with employees at the employer's facility; proscription on the union capability to provide consumer publicity; denial of trial by jury resulting from compulsory arbitration; and imposition of vague and ambiguous criminal sanctions. In summarizing the decision, one study said:

> Overall, the court stated that the law was flawed by undue restrictions and perverted the right of workers to organize and bargain.[117]

In June 1979, the U.S. Supreme Court reversed the district court.[118] However, this decision dealt specifically with only a single provision of the law—representation election proceedings. The Court held that the ineffectiveness of the election processes was not unconstitutional, stating:

> . . .Arizona was not constitutionally obliged to provide a procedure pursuant to which agricultural employees, through a chosen representative, might compel their employers to negotiate. That it has undertaken to do so in a niggardly fashion, then, presents as a general matter no First Amendment problems.

With respect to the other provisions, the high court said that the federal district court had been premature in its determination that they were unconstitutional. First they had to be applied by the Arizona Agricultural Employment Relations Board and tested in the Arizona courts. Though they might have been interpreted and applied in an unconstitutional manner, the Court found that those provisions on their face did not violate the federal Constitution.

California Law

In contrast with Arizona, California in June 1975 enacted a farm labor law that was patterned somewhat after Taft-Hartley, but that recognized the special problems of the agricultural industry. The law was adopted after many weeks of conferences held between the governor of the state, Edmund G. Brown; representatives of the Teamsters and the United Farm Workers of America; and agricultural business interests. The Chief Counsel of the United Farm Workers of America said it was a "good bill," and a representative of the employer group declared that "it isn't a perfect bill, but it is workable and fair."[119]

Unlike the Arizona law, the California farm measure permitted strikes during harvest time (the only time that a farm strike would have any meaning) by a union that has won a bargaining election and has been certified by the California Agricultural Labor Relations Board. Consumer secondary boycotts were permitted by certified unions. Strikes for recognition were illegal because the law had provided for meaningful secret elections to determine whether farm workers desire to be represented in collective bargaining. Thus, California's 250,000 farm workers in the state's $9-billion-a-year farm industry had the opportunity to decide for themselves which union, if any, they desired to represent them in collective bargaining. Also, such elections were to be held within seven days after an election petition was filed, a procedure that recognized the migrant nature of farm labor. The elections were to be held when 50 percent or more of a grower's peak labor force is employed. In contrast, under the Arizona law, elections did not need to be held during the peak period, which permitted a minority of workers to determine the representation issue for the majority. Another difference is that under the Arizona law, elections did not need to be held expeditiously after an election petition was filed. If an election was delayed long enough, it would not make much difference whether a union won since the harvest season could be almost over.

Some serious problems developed in the application of the California law. So many elections were conducted during the first five months of its operation that the state's Agricultural Labor Relations Board ran out of money. During this period, the agency conducted 429 elections involving about 40,000 farm workers.[120] A former member of the Board said:

> We had no idea we were going to have so many elections and all these unfair labor practice charges. Almost all the elections were challenged.[121]

Thus, between February 7, 1976, and the summer of that year, when additional funds were made available, the Board ceased functioning, did not hold elections, and stopped processing unfair labor practice charges.[122] It was as if the NLRB had ceased all operations for many months.

Another problem involved a highly controversial issue, the right of union representatives to enter the premises of an employer for organizational purposes.

Soon after the law went into operation, the Agricultural Labor Relations Board held that organizers could lawfully enter the premises of an employer's land at specified times and places and in limited numbers. This property-access policy was bitterly opposed by the growers, who contended that it deprived them of their property rights in violation of the California and U.S. constitutions. When the issue was tested in the courts, the Supreme Courts of California and the United States refused to upset the property-access rule.[123] The U.S. Supreme Court upheld the California court's decision on the grounds that a substantive federal question was not involved.[124]

In an effort to make sure that a state board composed of different members would not change the property-access rule, the United Farm Workers developed Proposition 14, placing the law on the November 1976 ballot as a constitutional amendment. The proposal also included a provision that would guarantee continuous funding for the Agricultural Labor Relations Board. However, California voters rejected Proposition 14 by a wide majority.[125] Since the referendum failed, the state board, despite the courts' decisions, can abolish the property-access rule, and the funds for the operation of the law depend upon the discretion of the California legislature.

The problems of the Agricultural Labor Relations Board were eased considerably when in 1977 the Teamsters and the United Farm Workers called a truce in their jurisdictional battle. For over ten years, these two unions had fought each other to represent California's 250,000 farm workers. They raided each other's membership and undermined existing labor contracts, and their battle was at times marked by violence. A good share of the Board's work involved elections in which the two organizations were on the same ballot; dealt with objections to election results filed by the losing union; and concerned unfair labor practice charges filed by the rival organizations against each other. Such bitter rivalry not only hindered the organization of new members, but also placed the employer in the middle of the jurisdictional fight. In this light, it came as a welcome relief when the two organizations agreed to a truce in which the Chavez union would have jurisdiction over the farm workers in the fields and the Teamsters over the workers in the packing sheds and the truck drivers. One employer probably reflected the sentiment of all concerned when he said:

> The workers will feel more peaceful and secure. The growers will no longer feel as though they are in a fight between the Palestine Liberation Organization on one hand and the Israelis on the other. The general public ought to feel better, and it'll make the job of the Agricultural Labor Relations Board much easier.[126]

If the goal is to provide labor relations stability in the agricultural industry, protecting the legitimate rights of unions, workers, and employers, a federal labor policy is needed. Only in that way would there be uniformity of treatment of all groups and recognition of the public interest. It would seem that Congress should recognize its responsibilities to the industry.

Summary

The NLRB decision to decline jurisdiction over cases has created a no man's land in the area of labor relations. In the *Guss* case, the U.S. Supreme Court held that the states could not take jurisdiction over a case that fell within the area of interstate commerce. Though Congress attempted to close the gap in 1959, the effort has not dealt adequately with the problem. Currently, only seventeen states and Puerto Rico have enacted laws similar to Taft-Hartley. In the majority of states, however, the no-man's-land problem still exists, as does the uncertainty as to the kind of law that will be applied by the states in the area abnegated by the NLRB. In the last analysis, what the 1959 law has done is to destroy the principle of uniformity of labor relations law in the area of interstate commerce without doing very much to assure that all employers, employees, and unions engaged in interstate commerce have the opportunity to resort to a lawful forum in disputes covered by the Taft-Hartley Act.

In the 1970s, by NLRB decision and legislative action, the coverage of the law was extended to groups previously excluded. However, the U.S. Supreme Court in *Yeshiva* and *Catholic Bishop of Chicago* sharply restricted the jurisdiction of the Board. At this writing, Congress still has not placed agricultural workers under Taft-Hartley. To fill this gap, a few states, particularly Arizona and California, established special legislation to deal with the problem. Whereas in general, the California law represents a fair and balanced policy, the one in Arizona operates to restrict rather than to encourage collective bargaining.

Discussion Questions

1. What general effect did the NLRB have on Taft-Hartley coverage when it voluntarily declined jurisdiction over certain cases even though it had statutory authority to deal with the cases?

2. How have the courts generally dealt with the problem of supremacy of national labor policy when states have passed conflicting laws? Is there an apparent conflict between the Supreme Court's *Guss* and *Brown* cases?

3. What is the importance of the *Yeshiva* case? Are all faculty members effectively eliminated from Taft-Hartley coverage?

4. What is the current status of NLRB jurisdiction over the following: law firms? church operated commercial enterprises? church related colleges and universities? illegal aliens?

5. How does the NLRB's *St. Francis Hospital* case dealing with permissible bargaining units in hospitals deviate from past Board policies? What are the possible implications of the new policy for organizing new units with hospitals?

6. What was the Supreme Court's decision in the *Bildisco* case? What is currently permissible under the Bankruptcy Code regarding alteration of collective bargaining agreements?

7. How well have the states responded to fill the gap left by Taft-Hartley's exclusion of agricultural workers from its coverage?

NOTES

1   National Labor Relations Act, Sections 9 (c) and 10 (a), 49 Stat. 449, 453 (1935).

2   *NLRB* v. *Jones & Laughlin Steel Corporation*, 301 U.S. 1 (1937).

3   *Schecter Poultry Corporation* v. *United States*, 295 U.S. 495 (1935).

4   National Labor Relations Act, Section 2 (7).

5   *NLRB* v. *Fainblatt*, 306 U.S. 601, 607 (1939).

6   Stephen S. Bean, "Federal-State Jurisdiction: An Analysis," in *Symposium on the Labor-Management Reporting and Disclosure Act of 1959*, ed. Ralph Slovenko (Baton Rouge, Louisiana: Claitor's Bookstore Publishers, 1960), p. 660.

7   *Yellow Cab & Baggage Company*, 17 NLRB 469 (1939).

8   National Labor Relations Board, *First Annual Report*, U.S. Government Printing Office, Washington, D.C., 1936, p. 135.

9   Harry A. Millis and Emily C. Brown, *From the Wagner Act to Taft-Hartley* (Chicago: The University of Chicago Press, 1950), pp. 60–61.

10   *Ibid.*, p. 401.

11   The dollar standards established in 1950 were reported in National Labor Relations Board, *Sixteenth Annual Report*, U.S. Government Printing Office, Washington, D.C., 1951, p. 16, as follows:

"Enterprises producing or handling goods destined for out-of-state shipment, or performing services outside the state in which the firm is located valued at $25,000 a year;

"Enterprises furnishing goods or services of $50,000 a year or more to concerns [dealing in commerce];

"Enterprises with a direct inflow of goods or materials from out-of-state valued at $500,000 a year;

"Enterprises with an indirect inflow of goods or materials valued at $1,000,000 a year;

"Enterprises having such a combination of inflow or outflow of goods or services that the percentages of each of these (foregoing) categories, in which there is activity, taken together adds up to 100."

12   NLRB Release R-428, October 21, 1953.

13   Fred Witney, "NLRB Jurisdictional Policies and the Federal-State Relationship," *Labor Law Journal*, VI, January 1955, p. 4.

14   As of October 1968, labor relations laws could be found in Colorado, Connecticut, Hawaii, Kansas, Maryland, Massachusetts, Michigan, Minnesota, New Jersey, New York, North Dakota, Oregon, Pennsylvania, Rhode Island, Utah, Vermont, Wisconsin, and Puerto Rico. See "State Laws," *Commerce Clearing House Labor Law Reporter*, October 18, 1968.

15   Section 14 (b) of Taft-Hartley provides that nothing in the federal labor law "shall be construed as authorizing the execution or application of agreements requiring membership in a labor organization as a condition of employment in any State or Territory in which such execution or application is prohibited by State or Territorial law."

16   House Report No. 245 on H.R. 3020, 80th Congress, 1st sess., p. 44.

17   Section 8 (d) (3).

18   Section 203 (b).

19   Section 202 (c).

20   Section 303 (b).

21   Section 10 (a) of Taft-Hartley provides that "the Board is empowered, as herein-after provided, to prevent any person from engaging in any unfair labor practice [listed in Section 8] affecting commerce. This power shall not be affected by any other means of adjustment or prevention that has been or may be established by agreement, law, or otherwise: Provided, that the Board is empowered by agreement with any agency of any State or Territory to cede to such agency jurisdiction over any cases in any industry [other than mining, manufacturing, communications, and transportation except where predominantly local in character] even though such cases involve labor disputes affecting commerce, unless the provision of the State or Territorial statute applicable to the determination of such cases by such agency is inconsistent with the corresponding provision of this Act or has received a construction inconsistent therewith."

22   Senate Report No. 105 on S. 1126, 80th Congress, 1st sess., 1947, p. 26.

23   *State of Minnesota,* 219 NLRB 1095 (1976).

24   Laws of Florida, 1943, Chapter 21968, p. 565.

25   *Hill* v. *Florida,* 325 U.S. 538 (1945).

26   Though this case arose under the Wagner Act, the principle set forth by the Supreme Court would, of course, have full application to Taft-Hartley.

27   *Bethlehem Steel Company* v. *NYSLRB,* 330 U.S. 767 (1947).

28   Public and Local Acts, Michigan, Section 423.9 (a), 1949; Michigan Statutes Annotated, Section 17.454 (1) (Cum. Supp. 1949).

29   Wisconsin Statutes, 1947, Chapter 11.50.

30   *La Crosse Telephone Corporation* v. *WERB,* 336 U.S. 18 (1948).

31   *Plankinton Packing Company* v. *WERB,* 338 U.S. 953 (1950).

32   *Bethlehem Steel, op. cit.*

33   *La Crosse Telephone Corporation, op. cit.*

34   *Garner* v. *Teamsters Union,* 246 U.S. 485 (1953).

35   *Lodge No. 76, IAM* v. *Wisconsin Employment Relations Commission,* 96 S. Ct. 2548 (1976).

36   *Brown* v. *Hotel and Restaurant Employees, Local 54,* 104 Sup. Ct. 3179 (1984).

37   353 U.S. 1 (1957).

38   "1. *Nonretail enterprises:* $50,000 outflow or inflow, direct or indirect. Outflow and inflow may not be combined, but direct and indirect outflow or direct and indirect inflow might be combined to meet the $50,000 requirement. 2. *Office buildings:* Gross revenue of $100,000 or more of which $25,000 or more is derived from organizations that meet any of the standards. 3. *Retail concerns:* $500,000 gross volume of business. 4. *Instrumentalities, links, and channels of interstate commerce:* $50,000 from interstate (or linkage) part of enterprise, or from services performed for employers in commerce. 5. *Public utilities:* $250,000 gross volume or meet nonretail standards. 6. *Transit systems:* $250,000 gross volume. Taxicab companies must meet the retail standard. 7. *Newspapers and communications systems:* $100,000 gross volume for radio, television, telegraph, and telephone; newspapers, $200,-000 gross volume. 8. *National defense:* Substantial impact on national defense. 9. *Business in the Territories and the District of Columbia:* The standards apply in the territories; all firms in the District of Columbia are covered. 10. *Associations:* Treated as single employer." National Labor Relations Board, 24th Annual Report, 1959.

39   Labor Management Reporting & Disclosure Act, Section 14 (c) (1959).

40   *Hotel Employees Local 255* v. *Leedom,* 358 U.S. 99 (1958).

41   *Floridian Hotel of Tampa,* 124 NLRB 261 (1959).

42   See National Labor Relations Board, *Twenty-third Annual Report*, 1958, pp. 8–12, for a discussion of these standards.

43   New NLRB *Rule to Meet Amended Act,* 45 *Labor Relations Reporter* 49 (1959).

44   Address of Stuart Rothman, NLRB General Counsel, before the Association of State Labor Relations Agencies, Detroit, Michigan, November 18, 1959.

45   Conference Report, House Report No. 1147, 86th Congress, 1st sess., 1959, p. 37.

46   *Centennial Turf Club, Inc.,* 192 NLRB 698 (1971).

47   *Alameda Medical Group, Inc.,* 195 NLRB 312 (1972).

48   *30 Sutton Place Corp.,* 240 NLRB No. 94 (1979).

49   *Columbia University,* 97 NLRB 424 (1951).

50   183 NLRB 329 (1970).

51   *Fordham University,* 193 NLRB 134 (1971).

52   *NLRB* v. *Yeshiva University,* 444 U.S. 672 (1980). This decision generated sharp criticisms among faculty groups. See, for example, John William Gercacz and Charles E. Krider, "NLRB v. Yeshiva University: The End of Faculty Unions?"*Wake Forest Law Review,* XVI, 6 (December 1980), pp. 891–914; American Association of University Professors, "The Yeshiva Decision," *Academe,* Bulletin of the AAUP, LXVI, (May 1980), pp. 188–197.

53   *The Cooper Union for the Advancement of Science and Art,* 273 NLRB No. 214 (1985).

54   *Rhode Island Catholic Orphan Asylum,* 224 NLRB 70 (1976).

55   *Ming Quong Children's Center and Social Services Union, Local 535,* 210 NLRB 899 (1974).

56   National Labor Relations Board, *Forty-first Annual Report,* Washington, D.C., 1976, p. 23.

57   225 NLRB 46 (1976).

58   *Bodle, Fogel, Julber, Reinhardt & Rothschild,* 206 NLRB 512 (1973).

59   *Foley, Hoag & Eliot,* 229 NLRB 80 (1977).

60   *Goldfarb* v. *Virginia State Bar,* 421 U.S. 773 (1975).

61   *Kleinberg, Kaplan, Wolf, Cohen, and Burrows, P.C.,* 253 NLRB No. 54 (1980).

62   *State Bank of India,* 229 NLRB 137 (1977).

63   *First Church of Christ Scientist in Boston,* 194 NLRB 1006 (1972).

64   *Catholic Bishop of Chicago,* 220 NLRB 359 (1975).

65   *Association of Hebrew Teachers of Metropolitan Detroit,* 210 NLRB 1053 (1974).

66   *NLRB* v. *Catholic Bishop of Chicago,* 440 U.S. 490 (1979).

67   *Barber-Scotia College, Inc.,* 245 NLRB No. 48 (1979).

68   *St. Louis Christian Home,* 251 NLRB No. 195 (1980). Enf. *NLRB* v. *St. Louis Christian Home,* CA-8, No. 80-2031, November 11, 1981 and *The Salvation Army of Massachusetts Dorchester Day Care Center,* 271 NLRB No. 37 (1984).

69   *St. Elizabeth Community Hospital,* 259 NLRB No. 156 (1981). Enf. *St. Elizabeth Community Hospital* v. *NLRB,* CA-9, No. 82-7098, June 22, 1983.

70   *Wall Street Journal,* March 22, 1979.

71   *American League of Professional Baseball Clubs,* 180 NLRB 190 (1970).

72   NLRB, *Rules and Regulations,* Section 103.2 (March 7, 1973).

73   *El Dorado, Inc.,* 151 NLRB 579 (1965).

74   *Office Employees International Union, Local 11* v. *NLRB,* 353 U.S. 313 (1957).

75   *Fort Apache Timber,* 226 NLRB 63 (1976).

76   *Sure-Tan, Inc.* v. *NLRB,* 460 U.S. 1021 (1984).

77   *Butte Medical Properties, d/b/a Medical Center Hospital,* 168 NLRB 52 (1967).

78   *University Nursing Home,* 168 NLRB 53 (1967).

79   *East Oakland Community Alliance,* 218 NLRB 1270 (1975).

80   Senate Report 93–76, 93d Congress, 2d sess. 5 (1974).

81   *Mercy Hospitals of Sacramento,* 217 NLRB 765 (1975).

82   *Montefiore Medical Center,* 235 NLRB No. 29 (1978).

83   *Dominican Santa Cruz Hospital,* 218 NLRB No. 182 (1975).

84   *Barnert Memorial Hospital Center,* 217 NLRB 775 (1975).

85   *St. Joseph of the Peace,* 217 NLRB No. 135 (1975).

86   *Newington Children's Hospital,* 217 NLRB No. 134 (1975).

87   *St. Francis Hospital,* 271 NLRB No. 160 (1984).

88   *AFL-CIO News,* August 18, 1984 and October 13, 1984.

89   *Wall Street Journal,* August 17, 1984.

90   223 NLRB 251 (1976).

91   *Wall Street Journal,* March 23, 1976.

92   *Oversight Hearings on the National Labor Relations Board,* Hearings Before Subcommittee on Labor-Management Relations, Committee on Education and Labor, House of Representatives, 94th Congress, 2d sess., May 5, 1976, p. 845.

93   H.R. 2222, 96th Congress.

94   *Physicians National House Staff Association* v. *Fanning,* CCA DC, Case No. 78–1209, July 11, 1980.

95   *St. Johns Hospital and School of Nursing, Inc.,* 222 NLRB 1150 (1976).

96   *Tri-County Medical Center,* 222 NLRB 1089 (1976).

97   *Beth Israel Hospital* v. *NLRB,* 98 S. Ct. 2463 (1978).

98   *NLRB* v. *Baptist Hospital,* 99 S. Ct. 2598 (1979).

99   *St. John's Hospital & School of Nursing,* 222 NLRB 1150 (1976).

100   *Hospital and Healthcare Employees, District 1199,* 222 NLRB 212 (1976).

101   National Labor Relations Board, Washington, D.C.: *Forty-first Annual Report,* 1976, p. 24.

102   Office of the General Counsel, "NLRB General Counsel's Monthly Report on Health Care Institution Cases," Release No. 1385, March 27, 1975, p. 2.

103   *Ibid.,* p. 6.

104   *Bildisco and Bildisco,* 255 NLRB No. 154 (1981).

105   *NLRB* v. *Bildisco,* 682 F. 2d 72, CA-3, 1982.

106   *Monthly Labor Review,* CVI, 9, (1983), p. 40.

107   *Monthly Labor Review,* CVI, 11, (1983), p. 73.

108   *NLRB* v. *Bildisco and Bildisco,* 465 U.S. 513 (1984).

109   *Wall Street Journal,* February 23, 1984.

110   *Monthly Labor Review,* April 1984, p. 48.

111   Public Law 98-353.

112   *AFL-CIO News,* June 30, 1984.

113   Karen S. Koziara, "Agricultural Labor Relations in Four States—A Comparison," *Monthly Labor Review,* U.S. Department of Labor, Bureau of Labor Statistics, C, 5 (May 1977), p. 16.

114   *Ibid.,* p. 17.

115   *AFL-CIO News,* January 29, 1977.

116   *United Farm Workers National Union* v. *Babbitt,* 449 F. Supp. 449 (DC Ariz 1978).

117   Harold C. White and William Gibney, "The Arizona Farm Labor Law: A Supreme Court Test,"*Labor Law Journal,* XXXI, 2 (February 1980), p. 97.

118   *United Farm Workers National Union* v. *Babbitt,* 99 S. Ct. 2301 (1979).

119   *Wall Street Journal,* May 30, 1975.

120   W. H. Segur and Varden Fuller, "California's Farm Labor Elections: An Analysis of the Initial Results," *Monthly Labor Review,* U.S. Department of Labor, Bureau of Labor Statistics, XCIX, 12 (December 1976), p. 29.

121   *Wall Street Journal,* October 12, 1976.

122   Segur and Fuller, *op. cit.,* p. 25.

123   *Agricultural Labor Relations Board* v. *Superior Court,* 546 P. (2d) 687 (1976).

124   *Pandol & Sons* v. *Agricultural Labor Relations Board of California,* 429 U.S. 802 (1976).

125   Segur and Fuller, *op. cit.,* p. 30.

126   *Wall Street Journal,* January 21, 1977.

CHAPTER TWELVE

ELECTION POLICIES
OF THE NLRB

Establishment of a unit appropriate for collective bargaining, to be discussed in Chapter 13, is important for the purpose of carrying out the basic objective of the national labor legislation. Prior to mutual agreement on the part of the parties or a determination of the appropriate unit by the regional director, and immediately prior to the actual poll, unions and employers are usually engaged in organizational campaigns attempting to sway workers either toward union membership or away from it. The campaign usually becomes more intense after the Board is petitioned to hold an election. The drive to enlist workers into unions is made both prior to petitioning the NLRB to conduct a representation election and thereafter, to maintain or increase the proportion of workers who agree to cast ballots for the union when the poll is actually held. Unions seek to have bargaining authorization cards signed, which demonstrate the potential strength of the labor organization at the polls. At least 30 percent of an appropriate unit must sign bargaining authorization cards before the NLRB considers there to be sufficient interest in collective bargaining to justify holding an election. It is considered that such a percentage raises a question of representation. Unions, on the other hand, normally try to obtain signed cards from approximately 55 percent or more of the unit before they consider their chances at the poll adequate to petition for an election. The basic reason for needing this larger percentage is that once employers enter election campaigns, many workers often decide against supporting a union by the date secret ballots are cast. Some employers recognize unions and commence to bargain on the strength of the bargaining authorization cards signed by employees. Others refuse to accept such cards as evidence of employee desires. Since the enactment of the Wagner Act in 1935, the Board has had the responsibility of insuring the rights of employees to engage in collective bargaining through representatives of their own choosing. Such a guarantee requires the development of a set of principles to govern the election conduct of unions and employers so as to provide maximum freedom for employees to choose or not to choose bargaining representatives. In short, the NLRB has the responsibility to reconcile the legal rights of employees to organize with the constitutional right of employers to free speech. Absolute freedom does not exist for either group. This chapter will deal with the election policies developed by the Board and courts since 1935. Both administrative rules and statutory requirements are considered as they have developed and changed to the present time.

EMPLOYER FREE SPEECH UNDER THE WAGNER ACT

Wagner Act Policies

During the early Wagner Act years, the economic position of employers was considered so superior to that of labor unions that employers were forbidden to take part in organizing campaigns.[1] In handing down its first decisions, the Board contended that any words of employers during organizing campaigns, whether written or oral, constituted a force more powerful than peaceful persuasion. Thus employers were ordered to remain "neutral." The early rules were developed when both unions and the Board were in their infancy. Neither was very strong and employers often posed a formidable force when they defied union organizational efforts. Unemployment was widespread and the least employer utterance was often all that was required to frustrate employee efforts to organize into unions.

It did not take the Board and the U.S. Supreme Court long, however, to begin a search for criteria that would reveal which factors should be used to determine the coercive potential of employer communication, and for methods of equalizing the opportunities for employers and unions to present oral arguments to employees.[2] Absolute restriction on the right of employers to speak during preelection campaigns was difficult to justify in a society with constitutional guarantees of freedom of speech.

In 1940, particularly, the courts were struggling to find a workable free speech policy to guide employer activities during preelection campaigns. In one well known case, *Thornhill* v. *Alabama,* the Supreme Court in dealing with employee picketing rights held that "the dissemination of information concerning fact of a labor dispute must be regarded as within the area of free discussion that is guaranteed by the Constitution."[3] The statement by the Court was an indicator of what was to come in employer free speech cases. The Sixth Circuit Court of Appeals in another case ruled that "the right to form opinions is of little value if it may not be communicated to those immediately concerned."[4] Obviously, the courts were driving toward the establishment of guidelines that would permit employers to enter preelection representation campaigns, while at the same time remaining careful to insure employees their legal right to choose voluntarily representatives for collective bargaining.

The U.S. Supreme Court in a 1941 decision was confronted with the issue of determining employer rights to free speech under the First Amendment to the Constitution.[5] The *Virginia & Electric Power Company* case established the basic premise upon which the NLRB and the courts were to continue their attempts to structure free representation elections with balanced rights for all concerned parties. The Court in its decision made it clear that a per se approach to forbidding employer speech was not acceptable, and stated:

> The employer . . . is as free now as ever to take any side it may choose on this controversial issue. But, certainly, conduct, though evidenced in part by speech, may amount, in connection with other circumstances, to coercion within the meaning of the Act. And in determining whether a course of conduct amounts to restraint or coercion, pressure exerted vocally by the employer may no more be disregarded than pressure exerted in other ways.

Employer speech therefore was not necessarily considered coercive. Infringement of the rights of employees attempting to organize had to be evaluated in view of the totality of circumstances in each case. In a string of Board cases prior to Taft-Hartley enactment, it was established that employers could speak out if their words fell short of coercion, threats, or promises of economic benefits for employees who rejected unionization. For example, antiunion speeches could not be delivered to captive audiences.[6] A captive audience occurs when workers are ushered into a common meeting place on company time and property to listen to their employer on a subject determined solely by the employer. In the absence of a captive meeting, however, an employer was permitted to predict a decline in jobs if the union won the election. In still another case concerning employer speech, the Board ruled that "the consequences it prophesied from unionization carried no connotation that its own economic power would be used, if necessary, to make its prophecy come true."[7] Obviously, the NLRB was having difficulty in early cases in attempting to provide employees with the greatest possible freedom to determine their collective bargaining desires.

One writer has argued that the totality-of-conduct doctrine was in the process of development throughout the period 1941–1948.[8] The totality-of-conduct doctrine refers to an attempt to review actions within the totality of all circumstances. For example, a speech that seems harmless on the surface may in fact carry with it implied threats of which employees are very much aware because of some other recent event. In the *American Tube Bending* case, decided in 1943, the Board dealt with an employer's remarks to employees on company property regarding a forthcoming election. After delivering a captive-audience speech, the employer followed up by sending letters to workers on the same issue. The Board ruled that neither the speech nor the letters was coercive, but that such employer activity had in fact interfered with employee free choice in the selection of bargaining representatives. The Second Circuit Court disagreed and reversed the Board decision.[9] By 1947, in *United Welding Company,* the NLRB held that employers could send letters to individual employees for the purpose of communicating their own views regarding the issues at hand.[10] The context within which employers were permitted to respond to union organizational efforts was a difficult problem for the Board. The difficulty extends to this day, as we shall see shortly.

The issue of employer participation in election campaigns was before Congress on at least two separate occasions. The House of Representatives appointed a Special Committee to Investigate the National Labor Relations Board; this committee published its results in 1940.[11] Among other things, it recommended protection of employer expressions of opinion if these were not accompanied by acts of coercion. Legislation did not develop, however, because of the nation's concern with the war. Congressional hearings over employer free speech during representation election campaigns continued after World War II during debates over the Taft-Hartley Act. The Senate was generally of the opinion that the totality of conduct should determine the degree of employer participation in preelection campaigns. Senate Report 105 of the 80th Congress proposed that "if . . . under all the circumstances [there is] no threat . . . of reprisal or force, or offer . . . of benefit . . ." employers should be permitted to express their views to employees or to answer union propaganda. Alternatively, the House of Representatives was not of the opinion that the totality-of-conduct doctrine should be controlling. It argued that there should be no rule restricting employer free speech. If a speech was in itself coercive, then it was not privileged. Otherwise it should not be restricted.

If the view of the House had prevailed, the nature of the employer's speech itself would have controlled the resulting decision. A course of past conduct that restricted employee union activities could not be considered an integral aspect of any preelection campaign culminating in a final employer speech. The speech in and of itself might be relatively harmless unless the content was correlated to past events for interpretation. Section 8 (c) of Taft-Hartley finally emerged from the debates. It states:

> The expressing of any views, argument, or opinion, or the dissemination thereof, whether in written, printed, graphic, or visual form, shall not constitute or be evidence of an unfair labor practice under any of the provisions of this Act, if such expression contains no threat of reprisal or force or promise of benefit.

It seems obvious that the law provides for many privileges in the area of free speech. One Board member remarked that the Taft-Hartley provision barred the agency "from even considering such statements in weighing the significance of other conduct." The National Association of Manufacturers wrote that the provision, if given a literal construction, "obviously would impose a harsher rule of evidence even than existed under common law rules in criminal cases."[12] It remained, however, for the Board and the courts to determine the substantive issues.

CONSTRUCTION OF TAFT-HARTLEY PROVISIONS

General Shoe Doctrine

The NLRB in a very early case following Taft-Hartley enactment ruled an election invalid in its significant *General Shoe* ruling because an employer read an "intemperate" statement to the employees.[13] It should be observed that the Board did not base its decision for ordering a new election on unfair labor practices. It held:

> Conduct that creates an atmosphere which renders improbable a free choice in an election may invalidate the election even though such conduct may not constitute an unfair labor practice. . . . In election proceedings, it is the Board's function to provide conditions as nearly ideal as possible, to determine the uninhibited desires of the employees.[14]

The Board made clear that the criteria applied in a representation proceeding to determine whether certain activities interfered with elections need not be the same as those applied in unfair labor practice cases. The majority argued that Congress applied its provisions only to unfair labor practice situations. Representation cases were intended to be treated differently, and as such, the Board's own administrative standards were relevant in fulfilling the basic objectives of extending to employees freedom of choice in selecting bargaining representatives. In *General Shoe,* the Board said that its purpose was to establish "laboratory conditions" wherein employees could express their desires in elections free from events that would prevent them from making a free choice. Perhaps "laboratory conditions" was a poor term to use because the realities of industrial relations are not the same as the conditions that prevail in a pristine scientific laboratory, where all variables are controlled. As the following discussion will disclose, however, the Board over the years has strived to set up these "conditions as nearly ideal as possible." One problem was that as the composition of the Board's membership changed, the "laboratory conditions" were viewed differently.

Even though the Board had established its desire to set elections aside when it considered that conditions had been inadequate for employees to make their selection, unions contended that the *General Shoe* doctrine provided inadequate remedies once their majority position had been undermined during the campaign. Labor unions argued that they should be certified as bargaining representatives on the basis of having gathered 50 percent of bargaining authorization cards signed within a bargaining unit when employer behavior resulted in union election losses. Their argument was based on the victory experience rate for subsequent elections after the setting aside of elections. They were not nearly as likely to win second elections as they were the first ones. The Board came to accept this argument in 1949, a special case of agency control over preelection behavior that will be treated later in this chapter.

The Board applied the *General Shoe* doctrine when it believed that preelection conduct had interfered with the right of employees to make a free choice and set elections aside, even though such conduct did not constitute an unfair labor practice. What the parties said to the employees had not contained threats of reprisal or promise of benefit. Nor had the parties engaged in conduct that violated that portion of Taft-Hartley guaranteeing the right of employees to engage in or refrain from union activities free from interference, restraint, or coercion. As a matter of fact, the employer conduct involved in *General Shoe* was not deemed an unfair labor practice, but the election was nevertheless set aside on the grounds that employer conduct had created "an atmosphere calculated to prevent a free and untrammeled choice by the employees."

In applying the *General Shoe* doctrine, the Board has held that an election is invalid when an employer assembles employees at the focal point of his or her authority, such as calling employees into an office of a supervisor for the purpose of urging them to reject the union.[15] As a later case demonstrates, however, the Board will not automatically invalidate an election on these grounds without evaluating the facts of a particular case. In one instance, an employer interviewed virtually all employees, not as individuals, but in small groups of five or six. The Board noted that there was no reason for any worker to believe he or she had been singled out. The place of the interviews was the office of the general manager. However, employees had previously visited with the general manager in his office to discuss grievances and obtain loans. Thus the Board said that the office and the general manager "had no special impact of awe." Also, the general manager's office was apparently the only place available to the employer for the interviews. Finally, the evidence demonstrated that the general manager's remarks to the employees were temperate and noncoercive in nature. Under these circumstances, the Board held that the election that the union had lost would not be set aside.[16] In other words, interviewing employees at the focal point of an employer's authority may or may not invalidate an election. It depends upon the size of the group interviewed; where the interview takes place; the position in the company of the interviewer and his or her past relationship to the employees; and the character of his or her remarks.

When company officials visited employees' homes to urge them to reject the union, the NLRB upset the election results.[17] On the other hand, unions may visit employees in their homes during election campaigns, and such conduct does not invalidate an election.[18] Though this might appear unfair, the Board reasoned that unions, unlike employers, do not have power over the employees' tenure of employment and working conditions.

General Shoe was also applied when an employer within twenty-four hours of an election made a speech to a massed assembly of employees on company time.[19] In setting aside an election under these circumstances, the Board said in *Peerless Plywood* that

> such a speech because of its timing, tends to create a mass psychology which overrides arguments made through other campaign media and gives an unfair advantage to the party, whether employer or union, who in this manner obtains the last most telling word.

(See below for a detailed treatment of the captive-audience problem.) However, this twenty-four-hour policy does not prevent an employer or union from making last-minute appeals to employees by other modes of communication, such as distribution of campaign literature.[20] Also, the Board in a split decision held that the twenty-four-hour rule is not violated when an employer's representative speaks to an individual or small group of employees telling them they do not need a union and should reject the union in the election.[21] The two dissenting members believed that the employees in this case were "captive." The employees were spoken to at their work stations. They knew that all other employees had been similarly addressed. Therefore, the "mass psychology" to which *Peerless Plywood* alludes was probably operative. An employer, said the two dissenters, should not be permitted to achieve indirectly what that decision directly forbids.

Under certain circumstances, the Board will set aside an election because of the conduct of a third party; that is, of people other than the representatives of the employer or the union engaged in activities that the Board believed cast substantial doubt on the employees' opportunity to express freely their choice in an election. In one such case, the Chamber of Commerce, the local newspaper, and the bank made it clear that the union was not welcome. The newspaper ran a front-page editorial that said in effect that if the union came in the employer involved in the election would leave. The bank deferred making loans and told applicants that it would talk further about loans if the mill remained nonunion.[22] Concluding that such third-party conduct had created a general atmosphere of fear and confusion, even though there was no clear indication that the employer was responsible, the Board directed a new election after the union lost the first one. On the basis of the same principle, the Board invalidated an election won by a union. Between the filing of the petition and the day of the election, events occurred that had created fear and confusion. There was extensive damage to property, anonymous telephone threats to eligible voters, a bomb threat, and unruly conduct on the picket line. No credible evidence attributed these events to the union involved in the election, but nonetheless the Board invalidated election results on the grounds that the general atmosphere at the time of the election had made a rational and uncoerced choice impossible.[23]

The third-party principle cuts both ways. It may be used to set elections aside when unions win or lose at the polls. The results will be invalidated even though probative evidence does not establish that the objectionable conduct was attributable to the union or employer involved.

General Shoe has also been applied when an employer or a union initiates racial propaganda in an election campaign calculated to inflame racial prejudice of employees and deliberately designed to overemphasize and exacerbate racial feelings by irrelevant and inflammatory appeals. More will be said about this issue

in a later chapter. We mention it here to show that at times the use of inflammatory and irrelevant racial propaganda might be the basis for setting aside an
election after a union lost[24] or won it.[25] In the former case, among other things,
just before an election was held in Georgia, an employer mailed to its employees
a picture showing a closeup of an unidentified black male dancing with an unidentified white woman. In the latter case, union campaign literature urged employees, most of whom were black, to act upon race as a factor in the election.

As will be discovered more fully below, the Board held in *Excelsior Underwear*[26] that an employer must file with a regional director a voter eligibility list
containing the names and addresses of all eligible voters within seven days after
an election is directed or the parties consent to an election. Such a list will then
be turned over to the union. Should the employer fail to comply with this policy,
and if the union loses the election, the Board may direct a new one.

In the past, the Board applied the *General Shoe* doctrine when employers
and unions materially misrepresented the facts involved in an election. This
policy was established in 1962 in *Hollywood Ceramics.* [27] In this case, the agency said
that it would set aside elections

> where there has been misrepresentation or other similar campaign trickery, which
> involves a substantial departure from the truth, at a time which prevents the other
> party or parties from making an effective reply, so that the misrepresentation,
> whether deliberate or not, may reasonably be expected to have a significant impact
> on the election.

In other words, the Board then believed that deliberate and substantial lies
should not be used in a campaign, particularly when the falsehood was brought
into the campaign at the last minute so that the other party could not effectively
answer it, and when the falsehood could reasonably be expected to influence the
results of the poll. In one case, an employer created a false impression of the
bargaining results of the union in another plant owned by the same employer.
In effect, he told the employees that the union had given up a Christmas bonus
without getting anything in return. Since this declaration was made shortly before
the election, in too short a time for the union to reply, the Board held that the
employer conduct was sufficiently material to set aside the election.[28] Another
employer told a group of employees if the union won the election

> the right and the freedom of each of you to come in and settle matters will be gone.

Setting aside the election, which the union lost, the NLRB held that the employer
had materially misrepresented the employees' statutory right to present their own
grievances to the employer.[29] (See Chapter 15 for a discussion of employees'
rights to present grievances to the employer on an individual basis.) Like employers, unions have also felt the sting of this policy. In one such case, an employer
claimed lack of profit during the campaign. To counter, the union said that the

NLRB requires $50,000 profit by an employer before it will conduct an election. This, of course, was a lie, and the Board upset the election that the union had won.[30] Another union had its election victory set aside in part because it sent employees campaign literature that said that an employer who commits an unfair labor practice

> can be fined up to $5,000 and possibly imprisoned up to one year, or both.[31]

This was an egregious misrepresentation of the law, because Taft-Hartley does not stipulate criminal penalties for anyone, employers or unions, who commits unfair labor practices.

To be sure, the Board has had difficulty in administering the "truth-in-campaign" doctrine. There were frequently tough questions to be determined in its application. For example, did the statement contain a complete lie or was it only an exaggeration or mere election propaganda? If a lie, did the other party have sufficient time to reply? Should employees have known better than to believe the lie? Did the lie reasonably impair the outcome of the election? Though these are weighty questions, the doctrine was rooted in the belief that the standards of conduct of an NLRB election should not sink to the level sometimes associated with political elections. Employees should have the opportunity to vote in an election without being influenced by the "big lie," particularly when at stake are the employees' job protection and working conditions, as well as the interests of the employer and union.

In April 1977, by a 3–2 vote, the Board held that it would "no longer probe into the truth or falsity" of statements made during an election campaign.[32] The particular item involved in the case, *Shopping Kart Food Market,* was the misrepresentation of the employer's profit. A union agent said the firm's profit was $500,000 when the truth of the matter was that profits totaled only $50,000. In the majority's view, employees are

> mature individuals who are capable of recognizing campaign propaganda for what it is and discounting it.

It also justified the new policy by stating that investigating the truth of campaign statements produced a "host of ill effects" including

> extensive analysis of campaign propaganda, restriction of free speech, variance in application as between the board and the courts, increasing litigation, and a resulting decrease in the finality of election results.

The minority said they were

> unwilling to permit the parties to campaign, without challenge, on the basis of misrepresentation and distortion of issues so directly related to the economic security of workers.

The third edition of this text contained the following:

> In short, with the knowledge by the parties that the campaign statements will not be policed, it follows that we can expect an escalation of distortions, lies, and other deceit in election campaigns. It would seem that the party who tells the biggest lies would have an edge. Some employees may not have the "maturity" spoken of by the majority. Also, even mature people may not have the capability to recognize a lie if it is told in plausible terms. Though the previous policy had its difficulties and disadvantages, some would argue that employees have the right to be protected against deliberate lies in the effort to swing their votes. This view may still prevail because *Shopping Kart Food Market* was adopted by only a single vote.

This prophecy proved correct, but only until August 1982! In December 1978 in *General Knit of California,*[33] as a result of a change of one member,[34] the NLRB reversed *Shopping Kart.* And after President Reagan appointed two new members, in *Midland National Life Insurance,* again by a 3–2 vote, the Board resurrected *Shopping Kart.* So, in five years, the NLRB changed policy three times on this issue.

Threats

Recall that Section 8 (c) of Taft-Hartley, popularly called the "free speech" provision, places a limitation on what may be told employees during an election campaign. Statements are not privileged if they contain a threat "of reprisal or force or promise of benefit." Should either an employer or a union violate these standards of communication, the Board will set aside an election. Under these circumstances, such conduct also constitutes an unfair labor practice because under Taft-Hartley, employees may not be restrained or coerced in the exercise of their right to engage in or refrain from union activities. Understandably, the determination of whether or not statements are privileged or contain threats or promises is one of the most difficult problems that confronts the Board. The line between them cannot be drawn with precision. Upon occasion, the Board has shifted its policies on some of the kinds of statements made to employees, and what complicates this vexatious problem is that at times the courts have not agreed with the NLRB. Since the Board and the courts have found it difficult to deal with this issue, the task of the authors becomes even more difficult. To illustrate the kinds of statements that fall within the threat and promise categories, some guidelines are presented.

When an employer threatens employees with economic retaliation should a union prevail in the poll, the Board has directed a new election. In one such instance, employer representatives made outright threats of plant closure and loss of employee benefits. It is material that in this case the threats were made to only four employees out of 3,000 in the unit, but the Board still ordered a new election because statements made during election campaigns are the subject of discussion and reflection among the electorate.[35]

The following employer statement was also considered a threat:

> . . . if by chance the union were to be voted into this shop, there is no doubt in my mind, because of the terrific demands they are making . . . there will be a strike. Somismo will not be able to cope with that problem; there will be a strike; whether we go out of business or not I am not saying right now. . . . I want to say that the demands of the union cannot and will not be met.[36]

Another employer conveyed to employees the belief that should the union win the election, the company would divert production to a nonunion plant which it also owned. In speeches to the employees, it was intimated that the nonunion status of the plant was responsible for rising employment, and that its continued nonunion status was necessary to avoid a possible drop in employment in the future. In setting aside the election, the Board held that the employer's preelection statements constituted a thinly veiled threat to provide more and better job opportunities at nonunion plants than at organized plants.[37] Also held as a threat was an employer's statement read to assembled employees that the interference of a union would only hinder the company's economic recovery and delay the recall of laid-off employees.[38] The Board noted that the employer did not explain why this would occur nor establish that these adverse economic effects would result from matters beyond employer control.

On the other hand, an election will not be set aside when an employer simply predicts the economic consequences of collective bargaining, provided the statement is made in such a way so as not to instill fear in the employees that they will lose their jobs or suffer loss of benefits. The U.S. Supreme Court said that the employer may make

> a prediction as to the precise effect he believes unionization will have on his company. In such a case, however, the prediction must be carefully phrased on the basis of objective facts to convey an employer's belief as to the demonstrably probable consequences beyond his control.[39]

In this regard, the NLRB explained that an employer

> is permitted to present his partisan views of the economic conditions of the company and its competitive position in the industry, as long as these are presented in a noncoercive manner.[40]

Thus, in one case, during the election campaign, a union indicated that it intended to demand a $3- to $4-an-hour wage increase. Shortly before the election, the employer expressed to the employees concern for the company's competitive position should the union receive such a high wage increase. The NLRB rejected the union's petition for a new election, reasoning that the employer was making a prediction of the economic consequences of unionization, and in such a way as not to threaten the employees with reprisal.[41]

In addition, an employer has the lawful right to express the opinion that a union would not be in the interests of the employees. Such statements, provided that they are made in nonthreatening language, have not resulted in the invalidation of elections. In one such case the employer's director of industrial relations circulated a letter to the employees which stated that it was his

> sincere belief that if this union were to get in here it would not work to your benefit but to your serious harm.[42]

Since the letter did not threaten employees with retaliation, the Board refused to direct a new election.

At times, however, an employer's statements have been held to be a threat, such as when the employer in effect tells the employees that it would be futile for them to vote for a union. In this kind of case, the employer tells the employees that he or she will bargain with the union because the law demands it, but will not really attempt to bargain in a meaningful manner. In one such case, an employer compared the legal duty to bargain with a "horse" being led to "water." He said:

> As I mentioned to you before, I am not inclined to be forced to do anything. It is a free country, I am a free man, and I believe that I ought to be able to do what I believe I have to do and, that is, I'll bargain; but it's like leading a horse to water. When he's got his head underwater, you don't know for sure he is drinking, but then you've got to practically drown the horse before he drinks enough water, before you bring him out.
>
> The length of negotiations has to do with how long do you hold the horse's head under the water. Finally he wants a drink of water and he comes up, so he talks for a little bit, a little while, and goes back and forth. And, as I pointed out, a lot of it is for show.

Holding the statement to be a threat, the Board said that it included the intent of the employer to engage in sham bargaining.[43] In another instance, the plant being organized was part of a multiplant corporation. Before the election, the employer told the voters that even if the union won the election, their benefits would only be the same as the employees in the other plants. While setting aside the election, which the union lost, the Board said the statement indicated union representation would be a futility, and that in no event would a union improve working conditions.[44]

In the light of the preceding observations, it should be obvious that the Board faces a very difficult problem in determining when an employer makes a noncoercive prediction of economic consequences resulting from collective bargaining over which the company would have no control should the plant be organized, and when an employer makes an outright threat of economic retaliation should the union win the election. It is equally difficult to establish when an employer offers a noncoercive opinion as to the desirability of unionization or when he or she unlawfully instills in the employees' minds that it would be futile for them to vote for a union because despite the union, the company does not intend to bargain in good faith. Though the Board and the courts have established some guidelines, the agency must make the determination in the light of the facts of a particular case. As the NLRB said:

> In making this evaluation, the Board treats each case on its facts, taking an *ad hoc* rather than a *per se* approach to resolution of the issues.[45]

Certainly the line between privileged statements and threats cannot possibly be drawn to fit every set of particular facts.

Needless to say, the perception of privileged statements and threats, as well as of lawful or unlawful announcements of benefits to influence elections (as treated below) depends to a great extent on Board personnel. It should come as no surprise to learn that the Reagan Board has permitted the employer more tolerance in these matters than have its predecessors. Consider, for example, the Reagan Board's reversal of policy dealing with employer interrogation of employees before elections. During organizational campaigns, employers at times question individual employees to learn about union matters, including the employees' sympathy to the union. When the NLRB first addressed this issue, it held that interrogations of any individual employee was per se unlawful as being inherently coercive.[46] Later on, in 1954, the Board abandoned the per se approach, holding that it would find such interrogation as unlawful only when it was coercive in light of the circumstances of a case.[47] In 1980, the Board returned to the per se rule, finding that questioning of individual employees was coercive regardless of circumstances.[48] In the 1980 case, the employer had questioned an active supporter of the union, but had not actually threatened the employee. However, the NLRB said

> the coercive impact of these questions is not diminished by the employees' open union support or by the absence of attendant threats.

In 1984, with the Reagan appointees in place, the NLRB abolished the per se rule, saying

> it completely disregarded the circumstances surrounding an alleged interrogation and ignored the reality of the work place.[49]

In *Rossmore House,* the employer had questioned an active and known supporter of the union and made inquiries about the organizational campaign and other union matters. Finding that the questions were not threatening, and that they implied no promise of benefit, the Reagan Board held the employer's conduct was lawful. Donald Zimmerman, a holdover member from the previous Board (no longer a member at this writing) dissented, saying the majority had ignored the fact that employers sometimes use subtle coercion, and that even known union supporters may be intimidated by such coercion. Zimmerman was particularly concerned that under the new policy, without an explicit threat or promise of benefit, the interrogation of an open union supporter would not be considered to have violated the law under any circumstances. In any event, under current policy, the Board will determine the lawfulness of individual employee interrogation by considering a variety of factors, such as the background of the incident, the nature of the information sought, the identity of the questioner, whether the employee is an open union supporter, and the place and method of interrogation. In 1985, a federal appeals court upheld the NLRB policy established in *Rossmore House*. [50]

At times unions have also seen election victories set aside because they, the unions, threatened employees. In one of these instances, the NLRB held that the union had shown objectionable conduct prior to the election by threatening two employees that if they did not join the union, they would not work. [51] A labor organization was also found to have interfered with an election when one hour before the election was held, a union agent threatened that any employee who helped the employer in a strike would be "made an example of," and said that an employee who "worked both sides of the fence" during the last strike was still in the hospital. [52]

Announcement of Benefits

With respect to the proscription against making promises during an election campaign, a federal court remarked:

> Interference is no less interference because it is accomplished through allurements rather than coercion. [53]

In order to persuade employees to reject a union, employers at times promise benefits and even at times put benefits into effect during an election campaign. If the Board finds that such conduct is designed to interfere with the free choice of employees, a new election will be ordered should the union suffer defeat at the poll. The test is the timing of the announcement of the benefits. If no factor other than the approach of the election is involved, the Board has held that the benefit was announced to influence the employees' vote. Thus, the Board stated:

> As a general rule, an employer, in deciding to grant benefits while a representation election is pending, should decide that question as he would if a union were not

in the picture. On the other hand, if an employer's course of action is prompted by the Union's presence, then the employer violates the Act whether he confers the benefit or withdraws them because of the union.[54]

This means that it is not a per se violation of the law for the employer to announce a benefit while an election is pending. However, the burden is on the employer to show that factors governed the timing of the announcement independent of the election.[55] In one case, valid business considerations motivated a wage increase, and the final decision to put it into effect was made before the union filed its election petition. Under these circumstances, the NLRB upheld the results of an election in which the union lost.[56] In another instance, the employer was obligated to increase benefits pursuant to his contract with the Tennessee Valley Authority. Even though the increase in benefits occurred while an election was pending, the Board did not invalidate the election because the increase was not motivated by the pending poll.[57] Though an employer may not tell employees that they will lose their present benefits if they elect the union, an employer may lawfully imply that present benefits are not guaranteed, but are negotiable.[58] A union told the employees that present benefits are "guaranteed" and that employees "can only gain" from collective bargaining. The NLRB held that the employer did not interfere with the outcome of the election, which the union lost, when it told the employees that they could actually lose wages and benefits because of the uncertainties at the bargaining table.

On the other hand, the Board has frequently invalidated election results when the employer could not show that any factor other than the scheduled election was the reason for the announcement of the benefits. Elections have been set aside when the employer during the election campaign said that the company would be more generous in granting benefits if the union were not there;[59] announced a profit-sharing plan to the employees prior to the election;[60] granted salary increases when they were not given at any other of the employer's plants besides the one in which the election was conducted, and contrary to past practice;[61] and promised a hospitalization plan to be put into effect after the election was held.[62]

Though the opportunities for employers to announce benefits during an election campaign are restricted, a union may make almost any promise to the employees. In one campaign, a union promised the employees that there would be a labor agreement containing many benefits, including protection against discharge; pension and dental plans; a credit union; and certain purchases that employees could make at a discount. The employer protested the union victory in the election, citing the union's making unlawful promises of benefits. The Board upheld the election on the grounds that employees generally know that a union cannot secure benefits automatically by winning an election but must seek to get them in collective bargaining. It said that the union promises amounted to campaign propaganda, which had already been ruled permissible.[63]

In other words, the Board distinguishes between an employer's promises and those a union makes, because the employer has the power to put benefits into effect unilaterally, whereas the union does not. As the Board said:

> Union promises of the type involved in the case were deemed to be easily recognized by employees to be dependent on contingencies beyond the union's control and do not carry with them the same degree of finality as if uttered by an employer who has it within his power to implement promises or benefits.[64]

If, however, a union has the power to put a benefit into effect should it win an election, a promise of a union could upset an election. This issue was squarely raised in a case where the union promised those employees who signed union-authorization cards that they would not be required to pay the $10 initiation fee if the union won the election. Though the NLRB ruled that this was not an unlawful promise within the meaning of Section 8 (c) of Taft-Hartley,[65] the Supreme Court held to the contrary, finding that the promise was not authorized and setting aside the election, which the union had won by a vote of 22–20. Rejecting the Board's view that the promise to waive the initiation fee was not based on the commitment of the employee to vote for the union, the high court said in *Savair Manufacturing,* the precedent case:[66]

> Whatever his true intentions, an employee who signs a recognition slip prior to an election is indicating to other workers that he supports the union. His outward manifestation of support must often serve as a useful campaign tool in the union's hands to convince other employees to vote for the union, if only because many employees respect their co-workers' views on the unionization issue. By permitting the union to offer to waive an initiation fee for those . . . signing a recognition slip prior to the election, the Board allows the union to buy endorsements and paint a false portrait of employee support during its election campaign. . . . We do not believe that the statutory policy of fair elections . . . permits endorsements, whether for or against the union, to be bought and sold in this fashion.

Subsequent to the Supreme Court decision, however, the Board held in *Lau Industries* that it would not invalidate an election won by the union when it promised to waive the initiation fees of all workers, regardless of whether they had signed authorization cards before the election.[67] In *Savair Manufacturing,* the promise was made only to those employees who had signed authorization cards. The Board believed that the promise in *Lau Industries* was lawful because it was extended to all eligible voters.

Other Reasons for Setting Aside Elections

A company may not conduct an election on its own among employees after an election petition has been filed with the NLRB.[68] The NLRB reasoned that such an employer poll did not serve any legitimate purpose that could not be better served by the pending Board election. A company may conduct its own poll among employees, however, provided that an election petition has not been filed, and provided further that the employer makes it clear to the employees that the purpose of the poll is only to ascertain the truth of a union's claim of majority status, and provided that employees are given assurances against reprisal and are polled by secret ballot.[69]

Should an employer place employees under surveillance, the NLRB will set aside an election. This occurred in one case when a supervisor five times drove past a union meeting attended by about thirty employees.[70] Obviously, the purpose of the spying was to find out who was attending the meeting. Also, when employees are discharged unlawfully during the campaign period, the Board will automatically set aside the results of an election. In one such case, an employee was discharged on the date upon which the election petition was filed. After the union lost the election, the Board ordered a new one on the grounds that discharge for union activities put fear and confusion into the minds of the employees.[71] Finally, as will be demonstrated below, there are some conditions under which the Board will set aside an election after the employer uses the captive-audience meeting and does not extend an equal opportunity to the union.

CAPTIVE-AUDIENCE PROBLEM

Bonwit Teller Doctrine

The captive-audience rules of the Board, in its attempts to provide a balanced opportunity for unions and employers to conduct their campaigns, have been particularly troublesome. Not only has the NLRB had to deal with the involuntary assembling of employees on company property during working time, but it has also had to apply no-solicitation and no-distribution rules invoked by companies to regulate work and nonwork activity on company premises. Bans against solicitation and distribution restrict oral attempts to encourage workers to join a union or passing out literature for the same purpose. Captive-audience policies are complex, and a variety of approaches have been taken by the NLRB in attempts to equalize employer and union rights. The complexity of the issues requires separate treatment of some of the evolving Board doctrines.

The captive-audience doctrine has been subject to considerable change as NLRB membership has shifted over the years. In a 1946 case before Taft-Hartley enactment, the Board dealt with employer meetings with employees on company premises prior to an election.[72] The Board ruled that a captive audience gave the employer an undue amount of control over the election and constituted an unfair labor practice. However, the Second Circuit Court of Appeals modified the Board order somewhat and argued that "we should hesitate to hold that he [the employer] may not do this on company time and pay provided a similar opportunity to address them were accorded the union."[73] The case obviously suggested providing equal time for the union's reply. The NLRB did not have time to work out the details involving equal time to reply to captive-audience speeches before the Taft-Hartley Act was passed. For example, it was not clear whether unions were to be afforded equal time on the company's premises and on company time, or if some other method of reaching employees was to be devised.

The *Babcock & Wilcox* case went before the Board in 1948, after Taft-Hartley passage. It provided that the mere use of captive audiences could no longer form the sole basis for a ruling of unfair labor practices.[74] The decision was based on the Taft-Hartley provision dealing with employer free speech.[75] Union victories at the polls started to decline almost immediately. In fiscal year 1947, union election victories amounted to 81.4 percent of cases reaching the election stage; by 1951, their victories had declined to only 71 percent of elections. Such a record may or may not reflect the impact of the captive-audience doctrine. It may well reflect the nature of the bargaining units that unions were attempting to organize by 1951. Possibly the units that were easier to organize were reflected in the 1947 victories, with union efforts centered on more difficult, smaller units by 1951. Whatever the reason, union victories started declining at about the same time the Board announced an easing of employer speech restrictions.

An equal opportunity for unions to reply to employer speeches under captive-audience conditions was also rejected by the NLRB in a 1950 case.[76] A new dimension to the captive-audience doctrine was added the following year in the *Bonwit Teller* case.[77] Like many other department stores, Bonwit Teller enforced a privileged no-solicitation rule, which forbade its employees to urge other employees to join the union on the company's premises on either work or non-work time, such as during lunch periods and coffee breaks. Department stores have the right to enforce such a rule, and employees who violate it are subject to discharge. The Board and courts have permitted department stores and similar public-access businesses to enforce such a rule because it was recognized that union solicitation on company premises, particularly on selling floors, even on nonwork time, could interfere with sales. On the other hand, other types of businesses may not enforce a privileged no-solicitation rule. In *Republic Aviation Corporation,* the U.S. Supreme Court held that in firms in which there is no public access, such as a factory, employees have the right to solicit union membership on nonworking time.[78] Under such circumstances, the Court held that the denial to employees of the right to engage in such activities on nonwork time constituted an unfair labor practice.

Thus, Bonwit Teller enforced a privileged no-solicitation rule, but at the same time used the captive audience in an effort to persuade its employees to reject the union in the coming election. It also denied the union the opportunity of equal time to address the employees in a similar meeting. The union lost the election and filed an unfair labor practice charge. The Board ruled differently than it had in *Babcock & Wilcox,* holding that an unfair labor practice violation had occurred because the employer had not provided the union an equal opportunity to rebut the employer's statements. The Board further ruled that when a company can lawfully enforce a privileged no-solicitation rule, it cannot use a captive audience unless it provides an equal opportunity for the union to reach employees. In short, the NLRB introduced the equal opportunity doctrine in any industry where a company can enforce a privileged no-solicitation rule.

After *Bonwit Teller*, which was sustained by a federal circuit court of appeals,[79] the Board extended the equal opportunity doctrine to industry in general. It ceased to distinguish between department stores, which could lawfully enforce a privileged no-solicitation rule and other companies, which could not. Thus, when an auto parts company and one that manufactured pottery used the captive audience, the Board invalidated the elections, which the unions lost, because the firms had not afforded equal time to the unions to respond under the same circumstances.[80] As noted, such firms, unlike department stores, could not forbid union solicitation on company property on nonworking time. In short, prior to the 1952 national elections, the Board held that the captive audience could not be used by any employer unless the company granted equal time to the union to reply on company time. No longer would the test be whether or not a company could lawfully enforce a privileged no-solicitation rule.

Livingston Shirt and Current Policy

After Eisenhower was elected President in 1952, he appointed new members to the Board. One of the first important decisions of the new members was to upset the equal opportunity doctrine. In *Livingston Shirt*,[81] the new Board held that a union was not entitled to equal time to reply to an employer's antiunion speech delivered to a captive audience. In defending its position, the Eisenhower Board said:

> If the privilege of free speech is to be given real meaning, it cannot be qualified by grafting upon it conditions which are tantamount to negation.

Apparently, it meant by this that the employer's right to free speech was in effect destroyed by giving the union an equal opportunity to respond. Recognizing that the union would have the opportunity to reply, the employer might have decided not to use the captive audience. This reasoning is debatable, since it is still in the power of the employer to use or not to use the captive audience. If a company elects to use this right, the question is whether the right to free speech is in effect destroyed if the other side of the story is told under equal circumstances. Also, the Board justified its decision by pointing out that the union had other ways to communicate with employees, such as solicitation on nonwork time (if an employer cannot enforce a privileged no-solicitation rule); visiting employees in their homes and writing them letters (provided that it has their names and addresses); holding a union organizational meeting; taking out advertisements in newspapers; and distributing leaflets at the plant gates. Another method is to use union organizers (nonemployees of the firm) at the company premises to hand out union literature and to speak to employees. This method may be limited by the employer, however, because the U.S. Supreme Court later held that employers could forbid outside organizers from the premises, including the parking lots, if by reasonable effort the union could use other available opportunities to communicate with employees.[82]

Whether or not these alternative methods available to unions measure up to the effectiveness of the employers' use of the captive audience is debatable. Whereas all employees must attend a captive-audience meeting arranged by the employer, attendance at a union organizational meeting is voluntary, and it is not likely that all employees would attend. Probably union organizers would argue that these alternative methods of communication, singly or collectively, do not balance the right of employers to address all the employees in a group on company time.

It should be noted that the Board did not exclude all opportunities for unions to reply to captive audiences. In *Livingston Shirt,* it said that the union had this opportunity if the employer had in effect

> either an unlawful no-solicitation rule, prohibiting union access to company premises on other than working time, or a privileged no-solicitation rule, broad but not unlawful because of the employer's business.[83]

At about the same time that the Board denied unions the equal opportunity to address captive audiences, it held in *Peerless Plywood*[84] that an employer could not use the captive audience within a twenty-four-hour period before an election. The rationale of this policy has already been presented, and it need not be repeated here. If the Board was concerned, however, with protecting the right of free speech of employers, *Peerless Plywood* appears somewhat inconsistent, despite the Board's rationale. If free speech is to be protected, it does not seem appropriate on that basis to put a time limitation on it.

Equal Time and Employer Unfair Labor Practices

In 1958, the U.S. Supreme Court sustained the *Livingston Shirt* doctrine, but seemed to hold in abeyance a definitive rule as to whether the union should have an equal opportunity to reply to an employer captive-audience speech when the employer has committed unfair labor practices.[85] The issue arose in *Montgomery Ward & Co., Inc.,*[86] in which case the decision of the NLRB was eventually sustained by a federal circuit court of appeals.[87] In this instance, the employer made a captive-audience speech and denied equal opportunity to the union. The company also enforced an unlawful no-solicitation rule that prohibited employees from soliciting union members in nonworking areas during nonwork time. Also, in the captive-audience meetings, the employer made coercive speeches. The NLRB set aside the election and held that the union should have been given equal opportunity to reply because the employer had "created a glaring imbalance in organizational communication."

It would appear that the NLRB is prepared to direct that unions be afforded equal time to address captive audiences when the employer uses this device as an antiunion weapon and commits unfair labor practices. In *Elson Bottling*,[88] the employer made threatening speeches at captive-audience meetings. He also solicited employees to withdraw from the union. Because of these unfair labor practices, the Board directed the employer to provide the union with the opportunity to make a one-hour speech to assembled employees on company time. It believed that equal time was justified because its customary remedial orders to stop the employer unfair labor practice would not be sufficient. Thus, it said:

> The possibility is strong that but for [employer's] unlawful conduct the Union would ultimately have secured the additional support it needed here to achieve majority status. We shall require that, upon the request of the union, the employer shall make available to the union and its representatives, at a mutually agreeable time within three months of this decision, suitable facilities such as are customarily used for employee meetings so that the union may speak to the employees assembled on company time.[89]

As a result of J. P. Stevens' long history of unfair labor practices, the NLRB ordered the company to permit the union equal time to respond to any captive audience address by the employer.[90] The unfair labor practices of J. P. Stevens were so pervasive that the Board also directed a series of extraordinary remedies, including posting, mailing, publishing and reading of compliance notices with copies signed by the company president, board chairperson and directors, and by the highest management officials at the plant, union access to bulletin boards for one year, and access of union organizers to nonwork areas of the plant.

When Employees Ask Questions

In sum, there are limited circumstances under which a union is guaranteed an equal opportunity to reply when the employer uses the captive audience as part of an antiunion campaign. Under current law, it would have this opportunity when the employer enforces an unlawful no-solicitation rule; under a privileged no-solicitation rule of the kind permitted in retail department stores, prohibiting solicitation on nonworking time in areas open to the public; and apparently under special circumstances where employers commit serious unfair labor practices. Other than these conditions, an employer may use the captive audience without giving the union equal opportunity to reply. Should the union lose an election, it will not be set aside just because the employer denied the union this opportunity.

In 1975, the Board moved further to protect the right of employers to hold captive-audience meetings. At the start of one such meeting, held by the J. P. Stevens Company, twenty-two employees got up and asked questions. When the employees refused to sit down and cease asking questions, the employer discharged them. By majority vote, the Board upheld the discharges on the grounds that they viewed the conduct of the employees as a plot to disrupt the meeting with questions that were "loaded, loud, and distracting."[91] In a previous case, the Board had held that an employer could not discharge a single employee who got up toward the end of a captive-audience address to ask a question.[92] In sharp dissent, the minority in the second case stated that J. P. Stevens'

> entire course of conduct in the latter stages of the union campaign clearly reflected its desire to chill concerted partisan activity by inquisitive employees rather than to insure the unencumbered presentation of its speeches.

And:

> There is not a scintilla of evidence of a conspiracy to heckle or otherwise interrupt respondent's speakers so as to prevent an effective presentation of the speech. Nor is there testimony of an agreement among employees, explicit or implicit, to ask disruptive questions.

Needless to say, the discharged workers' union, the Textile Workers, bitterly criticized the Board's decision. Its president, Sol Stetin, said:

> The NLRB has in effect turned its back on workers who had the courage to stand up and challenge company propaganda during the course of a "captive audience" meeting. It now appears to be a crime for pro-union workers to exercise their right of free speech.[93]

Labor Law Reform Act of 1977

The bitter controversy over the equal time doctrine received congressional attention. As mentioned previously, President Carter supported legislation to reform Taft-Hartley. Some of the features of the Labor Law Reform Act of 1977 were treated in previous chapters. Of importance here is that, under the proposed legislation, the NLRB would have been directed to set up procedures to assure workers an equal opportunity to hear from both sides at captive-audience meetings.

A novel addition was incorporated in the House version, enacted in October 1977, but blocked in the Senate in the summer of 1978 by a filibuster. It would have permitted employers to campaign against unions in union halls. Probably this innovation would not have benefited employers because the union members could always elect to be absent when the employer representative speaks. Unlike a captive-audience meeting, held on company property and time, union members are not forced to attend a union meeting.

NAMES-AND-ADDRESSES POLICY:
THE EXCELSIOR DOCTRINE

In 1966, the unions tried once again to persuade the NLRB to provide them equal time when employers used the captive audience. By this time, the Board consisted of members who were appointed by presidents Kennedy and Johnson. The unions felt that with this kind of membership, the Board would return to the policy of equal time that had been in effect before the 1952 national elections, reversing *Livingston Shirt.* However, the Board refused to do this, and it sustained the right of employers to use the captive audience without giving unions equal time.[94]

At the same time that the NLRB refused to authorize equal time for unions, it adopted its names-and-addresses policy in its *Excelsior* rule.[95] Under this policy, within seven days after an election is scheduled, the employer must supply to NLRB regional directors the names and addresses of employees eligible to vote. This is called the "Excelsior" list. The regional director then furnishes the list to the union. Such a list must be furnished in all elections, consent or directed, and whether or not the employer uses the captive audience. In effect, the Board said to the unions, "we will not give you equal time to respond at captive audiences, but we will make available to you the names and addresses of the voters." It was a sort of compromise decision that the NLRB believed would balance the scales.

It will be recalled that the Supreme Court in 1941 implied that Board policies regarding elections should be evaluated in the context of all the circumstances involved.[96] It also called for balanced rights for all parties involved in labor disputes. The NLRB recognized that management possessed another avenue for communicating with employees that was not available to unions. Employers had in their possession the names and addresses of all workers included in the bargaining unit involved in the contest. Possession of such a list made it relatively simple to mail out propaganda dealing with union organizational attempts. Literature could be mailed out in the form of a regular weekly or monthly newsletter to employees, or as a special mailing enabling management to present its views on representation elections. Obviously, the greater accessibility of management to its employees placed unions at a distinct disadvantage in attempting to present views to prospective supporters.

In *Excelsior,* the Board stated that equal access to the names and addresses of eligible bargaining-unit voters "insure[s] the opportunity of all employees to be reached by all parties" even though unions may have other avenues by which they "might be able to communicate with employees." Employers may not decide for themselves whether a need for such a list exists.[97] Board policy requiring employers to file eligible voter names and addresses with regional directors was justified on the basis that Congress entrusted the NLRB alone to establish procedures and policies to conduct fair elections. Merely because employers had only been required to file employee names in the past did not preclude the agency from requiring employers to furnish addresses. In addition, it was argued that the names and addresses of all registered voters are general public information in public elections. Also, such information is required by law when proxy battles occur for corporation control. During proxy contests, stockholder names and addresses must either be supplied to the contestants, or management must mail campaign materials for the other parties. The Landrum-Griffin Act of 1959 also held that all candidates for union office had a right to have the union distribute campaign literature to all members.[98] In the past, the Board had only required filing a list of eligible voter names. The list of names was then made available to all parties involved in election proceedings. In some cases, unions were able to find out the addresses of persons on the lists, but certainly not all of them.

Knowledge of addresses in addition to names had the effect of increasing employee ability to make a determination either for or against representation, since greater communication is thus possible. The reason given by the NLRB for its decision was that an opportunity for both sides to reach all employees "is basic to a fair and informed election." Employer refusal to supply such information to the regional directors would be grounds for setting aside elections, if requested by unions.

The *Excelsior* doctrine gave unions a more effective organizational tool. Knowledge of employees' names and addresses made it easier for unions to visit employees in their homes and to send them literature. However, it is debatable whether *Excelsior* actually balances the impact of the employer's use of the captive audience. To some employees, reading is painful, and some may resent home visits by union organizers. Oral communication to all employees assembled on company time would probably in most cases outweigh home visits and the reading of literature. Also, given the wide distribution of an employer's labor force, particularly in large cities, it would be difficult to canvas all the employees involved in a pending election.

One consequence of the names-and-addresses policy was probably not anticipated by the Board. Knowing that the union will have this information, employers undoubtedly use the captive audience more frequently than in the past. When the Board rejected the union's petition for equal time when the employer uses the captive audience, and instead announced the names-and-addresses policy, it said that it would delay considering the reversal of *Livingston Shirt* until such time as the effects of the new policy became known. If the NLRB meant by this to determine the relative success of unions in elections, the names-and-addresses policy has not done the unions much good. In 1966, unions won 61 percent of the elections in which they were involved.[99] By 1979, this figure had dropped to below 50 percent.[100]

After a great deal of litigation in the lower federal courts, in 1969 the U.S. Supreme Court sustained the NLRB names-and-addresses policy.[101] The Court said the NLRB has

> wide discretion to ensure the fair choice of bargaining representatives. The requirement that companies furnish worker lists to unions furthers the free-choice objective of encouraging an informed employee electorate by allowing unions the right of access to employees that management already possesses.

Thus the Board now has clear authority to require employers to provide a list of names and addresses of employees for union use in connection with representation elections. The requirement is viewed as a part of the NLRB order directing that an election be held.

BARGAINING ON THE BASIS OF AUTHORIZATION CARDS: THE GISSEL DOCTRINE

A Board policy that has generated considerable criticism, particularly from management groups, involves orders requiring employers to bargain with unions even though election results do not favor unions. One section of the law enumerating employer unfair labor practices requires an employer to bargain collectively with a union designated as representative by a majority of employees in an appropriate unit. To determine whether a union is the choice of a majority of employees, the Board conducts elections. If the union wins a validly conducted election, the employer is required to bargain with it. But an election is not always necessary before an employer is required to bargain. This is called the *Gissel* doctrine.

The Board policy requiring employers to bargain with a union based on a bargaining authorization-card count was established in 1949 in response to unfair labor practices that had destroyed a union's card-based majority. The *Joy Silk Mills* case involved employer conduct such as the promise of benefits about one week before the election, interrogation of employees concerning how they would vote, and implied threats of reprisal if the union won the election or if employees voted for the union.[102] On the basis of employer unfair labor practices in the *Joy Silk Mills* case, the Board refused to order a new election, but instead ordered the company to bargain with the union. The order to recognize and bargain was based on the evidence that the union had represented a majority of employees in the unit prior to employer interference, restraint, and coercion, which had deprived the union of the margin of votes necessary to win at the poll.

In still another case, decided in 1964, the Board overturned some prior decisions regarding election policies.[103] The *Bernel Foam* case involved an employer refusal to bargain upon request when the union offered to prove it represented a majority of employees in the unit. The employer insisted upon a Board election as proof, but in the meantime, engaged in conduct designed to induce employees to repudiate the union. After the union lost the election it filed unfair labor practice charges. The company defended itself on the basis of a past Board rule requiring that a union could not file unfair labor practices after elections were held if it had had knowledge of such practices prior to proceeding to the poll.[104] The NLRB overruled the previous policy on the ground that such a choice was difficult and dubious for a union to make, particularly since the choice was created by employer unlawful conduct. Thus a union that participates in an election despite employer refusals to bargain may, after losing the election, file refusal-to-bargain charges based on employer preelection conduct. Three circuit courts subsequently approved the NLRB's decision.[105] The U.S. Supreme Court extended its approval in 1969, which will be discussed subsequently.

As the law now stands, there are three distinct ways by which unions may obtain Board certification without winning elections. First, there is the *Joy Silk* type of case. This involves unfair labor practices occurring concurrent with a refusal to honor union requests to bargain, destroying the labor organization's card-based majority. Unlike the actual *Joy Silk Mills* case, no election is held in this type of bargaining order. The mere existence of unlawful employer behavior is sufficient to justify a Board order to bargain with the labor organization.

Second, there is the *Bernel Foam* type of case. This type of case involves unfair labor practices existing concurrent with a refusal to bargain, with the result that a union's card-based majority is destroyed. In cases of this nature, an election has been held and lost by the union, but the NLRB still compels collective bargaining. The NLRB justifies such a remedy on the basis that illegal employer action prior to a poll calculated to eliminate the union advantage is not appropriately remedied by forcing a labor organization to go through another campaign. There is no effective way of restoring a union to the same position it was in prior to the illegal conduct and as such, a bargaining order is the only appropriate remedy, especially since unions usually lose the second or third election.

The third type of case is somewhat easier to understand. It is called a *Snow*-type case by the Board and involves only a refusal-to-bargain violation. No election has been held in these situations. The violation requiring Board bargaining orders is that in which the employer initially recognized the union on a demonstration that it represented a majority of employees in an appropriate unit, but subsequently reneged without a valid excuse. The validity of employer arguments for withdrawing union recognition after it is extended is subject to Board determination on the basis of the entire record. In 1970, the Board reaffirmed this policy.[106] In response to questions of the union representatives, the employer in this case had "agreed that the union represented a majority and agreed he would recognize the union." Subsequently, the employer reneged, and advised the union to seek an election. Under these circumstances, the NLRB held that the company had violated its obligations under the law and ordered the employer to bargain.

Before the Nixon Board became established, there was another way in which a union could gain bargaining rights without an election. Under these circumstances, the employer had not engaged in any unfair labor practice to destroy the union's majority status. The company had merely refused to recognize or bargain with the union based upon a majority of signed union membership cards. However, the previous Board had held that a bargaining order would be issued if the employer had knowledge of the union's majority status outside the cards.[107] For example, it could gain this knowledge by observation of its employees on a picket line during a strike. The Nixon Board reversed this policy.[108] It held that a bargaining order would not be issued solely on the basis of authorization cards. In *Linden Lumber Division, Summer & Co.,* a strike took place after the employer refused to recognize the union. Thus, the employer had opportunity to determine from events outside the cards that the union had majority support. Nevertheless, the Board held that an employer

> should not be found guilty of a violation of Section 8 (a) (5) (refusal to bargain collectively) solely on the basis of its refusal to accept evidence of majority status other than the results of a Board election.

In 1974, the U.S. Supreme Court upheld the Board's policy by a 5–4 vote.[109] In practice, this means that the Board will not direct an employer to bargain with a union on the basis of authorization cards showing that the union has majority support, even if the employer has knowledge independent of the cards of the majority status of the union, provided that the employer has not engaged in unfair labor practices calculated to destroy the union's majority. Under these circumstances, the union must test its majority status in an election. In the minority view of the Court, however, the union should not be required to go through the election with its inevitable delays, prolonging the time for collective bargaining, because, as they stated:

> The language and history of the act clearly indicate that Congress intended to impose upon an employer the duty to bargain with a union that has presented convincing evidence of majority support, even though the union has not petitioned for and won a Board-supervised election.

Most would agree that a secret election conducted by the NLRB is the best way to determine the desire of employees for collective bargaining. However, when an employer engages in serious unfair labor practices, and by this conduct makes a fair election unlikely, the Supreme Court of the United States stated in *Gissel* that authorization "cards may be the most effective—perhaps the only—way of assuring employee choice."[110] In other words, the question arises as to why an employer should be rewarded for illegal acts. If employers believe the authorization-card method to be undesirable, all that they have to do to avoid it is to obey the law. In the absence of serious unfair labor practices, the NLRB will use the election as the sole method of determining the employer's obligation to bargain collectively. It should be noted that the Board has issued *Gissel* bargaining orders sparingly. It has not issued such bargaining orders in a reckless fashion. Thus, between 1962 and 1975, the Board conducted 114,301 elections and issued 63,185 bargaining orders—the number of elections that the unions won. In contrast, for the same period of time, the Board issued only 1,405 bargaining orders based upon the *Gissel* doctrine, or only .02 percent of the number of the other barganing orders.[111] This experience prompted a former chair of the NLRB, Betty S. Murphy, to say:

On both an absolute and a relative basis, requiring an employer to bargain on authorization cards is the exception rather than the rule, and in the overwhelming majority of instances union bargaining rights are established pursuant to secret-ballot elections conducted by the Board.[112]

At this writing, the frequency of *Gissel*-type barganing orders has not increased. The NLRB continues to use them only under exceptional conditions.

POWER OF THE NLRB TO ORDER BARGAINING: CATEGORIES OF UNFAIR LABOR PRACTICES

In any event, the authorization-card method has whipped up a storm of controversy that to this day has not subsided. It contains two major elements: the NLRB power to order bargaining on the basis of authorization cards, and the reliability of the authorization cards. Some argue that, under Taft-Hartley, the NLRB is limited to the use of the election as the sole method upon which to base a bargaining order. However, the Supreme Court in *Gissel* decided by an 8–0 vote that the law does not provide that the election is the sole method by which employees may select a union to represent them. It stated that it

was recognized that almost from the inception of the Wagner Act a union could establish majority status by other means as here by possession of cards signed by the majority of the employees authorizing the union to represent them for collective bargaining purposes.

After establishing the legal basis for bargaining orders based upon authorization cards, the Court determined the circumstances under which they may be used for this purpose. It established three categories of unfair labor practices that may be committed during an organizational campaign.

First Category of Unfair Labor Practices

In this category are those acts that were so "pervasive" and "atrocious" as to call for an order even without inquiry into the union's card-based majority position. In other words, a bargaining order could at that time have been issued under these circumstances, even though the union had not obtained the signatures of a majority of the employees in the bargaining unit. The Court apparently believed that when the employer commits flagrant and atrocious unfair labor practices, most employees would be fearful of signing cards.

However, in 1979, the NLRB held that despite such "pervasive and atrocious" unfair labor practices, it would not direct bargaining where the union had not succeeded in obtaining a majority of the employees to sign authorization cards.[113] To justify this new policy, a Board majority said that a bargaining order presented "a substantial risk of imposing a union on nonconsenting employees."

Instead of a bargaining order in these cases, the Board directed a series of remedial steps designed to dissipate the effects of the employer's numerous violations of the law: post and mail to employees and publish in local newspapers notices of the employer's illegal conduct; the president of the company in the presence of a Board agent was to periodically read the notices to assembled employees on company time; and the company was to permit union organizers access to the plant as prescribed by the Board order.

In 1982, for the first time, by a 3–2 vote, the NLRB in *Conair Corporation* granted bargaining rights to a union even though the union had not succeeded in securing a majority of the bargaining unit's authorization cards.[114] In that case, the employer had engaged in massive unfair labor practices during the organizational campaign, including the discharge of union members, threats of plant closure, and promises of additional benefits to employees should the union lose the election. Unanimously the Board agreed that the employer had committed numerous outrageous and pervasive unfair labor practices over a period of nine months, involving every level of management from the highest executive officers to low-level supervisors.

To justify its decision, the majority stated:

> . . . [t]his case is the "exceptional" type envisioned in *Gissel* which warrants the issuance of a remedial bargaining order "without need of inquiry into majority status on the basis of cards or otherwise." Under these exceptional circumstances we find that a remedial bargaining order is the only way to restore to employees their statutory right to make a free and uncoerced determination whether they wish to be represented in collective-bargaining by a labor organization.

In 1984, the Reagan Board reversed *Conair,* holding in *Gourmet Foods* that "under no circumstances" will it order bargaining with a union that did not demonstrate majority support, regardless of the character of employer unfair labor practices.[115] To rule otherwise, the Board said, would thwart the employees' right to select a union of their own choosing. Claiming it did not have the authority to issue a nonmajority bargaining order, the NLRB said the majority rule principle must be maintained even in those "exceptional cases" where an employer committed massive unfair labor practices.

In evaluating *Gourmet Foods,* it should be noted the U.S. Supreme Court had said in *Gissel* that a bargaining order should be issued without inquiry into the union's card-based majority when an employer's unfair labor practices were "pervasive and atrocious." At that time, the high court seemingly implied the NLRB had the authority to issue bargaining orders under those conditions, recognizing that in such a plant environment, employees would be intimidated against signing authorization cards in the first place. In 1980, the federal appeals court in Philadelphia held the NLRB had the authority to issue nonmajority bargaining orders.[116] In contrast, in 1981, the District of Columbia federal court of appeals doubted whether the Board had such authority.[117]

Eventually the U.S. Supreme Court may determine specifically whether the Board has the authority to issue nonmajority bargaining orders. However, even if the court ruled in the affirmative, this would not mean the NLRB would be compelled to do so, because the agency issues such orders on its own discretion.

Second Category of Unfair Labor Practice

It was in the second category that the Supreme Court placed those unfair labor practices that show a "lesser showing of misconduct." Under these circumstances, the Court held that at some point in its campaign, the union must have demonstrated that it had the support of a majority of the employees. In other words, before a bargaining order would be issued under this category, the employer must be engaged in serious unfair labor practices and the union must have had a card-based majority. In *Apple Tree Chevrolet*[118], for example, a majority card-based bargaining order was issued. Whereas 35 employees had signed union-authorization cards, only 27 voted for the union in the election. During the election campaign, the employer engaged in a variety of unfair labor practices, including preelection announcement of benefits, threats, and interrogation. In a rather creative effort, the employer also used a psychologist who met with employees in small groups to identify their complaints. After receiving the psychologist's report, the employer met with employees to announce that changes would be made. Given the other unfair labor practices, the Board found this tactic to have "a strong coercive effect on the employees' freedom of choice." It also held its effect to be "long lasting, if not permanent."

Though the Reagan Board refuses to issue nonmajority bargaining orders, it has applied *Gissel* to the second category of unfair labor practices. For example, in a 1984 case, a union at one point in its organizational campaign was supported by the majority of the employees. Later on, it lost majority status, but the Reagan Board nonetheless issued a bargaining order, calling the employer's treatment of employees "sadistic."[119] Representative of the employer's conduct was an incident in which the two employees, one of them 62 years old, were directed to transfer a large pile of steel pipe from the yard to storage racks in the shop. They picked up one length of pipe, each supporting one end, but were instructed to carry two lengths at a time. On successive trips they were told to take three, then four lengths at a time. When the 62-year-old employee complained that his heart was pounding, the employer asked if he was quitting. The employee responded that he was not, and suggested that he could carry two pipes at a time, but not four. Nonetheless, the employer returned to the shop, shouted that the employee had quit, and handed him his paycheck.

In addition, the Board found that after the union's demand for recognition, the employer had interrogated employees regarding their union sympathies, threatened to close the shop if they won union representation, required the employees to sign letters renouncing the union, and promised and granted various benefits. The other known union supporter was also discharged.

Third Category of Unfair Labor Practices

In the third category, the Court placed those minor employer violations that are likely to have a minimal impact on elections. Under these circumstances, the NLRB will not issue a bargaining order.

Validity of Authorization Cards

In opposition to the authorization-card method as the basis for bargaining orders, some argue that these cards are not reliable indications of employees' desires for collective bargaining. Indeed, a federal appeals court stated that

> it would be difficult to imagine a more unreasonable method of ascertaining the real wishes of employees than a "card check" unless it were an employer's request for an open show of hands.[120]

In this respect, it is argued that union organizers coerce employees to sign the cards; employees do not understand what they are signing; group pressure will prompt employees to sign; and union organizers will misrepresent the purpose of the card by telling employees that they are being used only to obtain an election from the NLRB and not for the purpose of authorizing the union to represent them in collective bargaining. As expected, the NLRB has established standards relating to the validity of the cards.[121] To count, a card must plainly state that the employee authorizes the union to represent him or her in collective bargaining. In 1983, a federal appeals court held that a dual-purpose card authorizing the union both to represent employees in collective bargaining and to request an election is valid, provided the union organizer does not tell employees the sole purpose of the card is only to get an election.[122] In short, despite the language on the face of the card, the card will not be counted if it can be proved that the employee was told the card would be used solely for the purpose of obtaining an election. Should the union organizer use coercive tactics, the card will not be deemed valid. As to the employee's intelligence, the Board stated that

> to assume that the employee does not understand what he is signing as long as he can read would be to downgrade his intelligence.[123]

Upon review of these standards, the Supreme Court held that they were sufficient to protect against abuse in the signing of authorization cards. It stated that when cards are obtained in conformance with the NLRB standards, there need be no fear of misrepresentation, and added that "employees should be bound by the clear language of what they sign."

In short, the Supreme Court endorsed the policy of issuing bargaining orders based upon authorization cards. It held that such a remedy is proper when employer illegal conduct makes it unlikely that a fair election could be held. In the absence of such a remedy, the Court stated that the employer could continue to delay or disrupt the election process and put off indefinitely his obligation to bargain; and any election held under these circumstances would not be likely to demonstrate the employees' true, undistorted desire.

It is important to understand that should the Board or the federal courts find that authorization cards do not meet the standards for validity, the union will not receive bargaining rights, regardless of how serious employer unfair labor practices may be. In one case, a federal appeals court held the cards invalid when the union had used trickery to obtain them. Each employee was told that all other employees had signed the card. Since that was not true, the court refused to direct bargaining, saying it did not matter that the employer had engaged in unlawful preelection conduct.[124]

Another point of interest is that the NLRB will not turn over to employers authorization cards signed by employees. In one case, a company said it needed the cards to challenge their validity in an effort to show there was not sufficient support for the union to justify an election. The company argued that it had the right to the cards under the Freedom of Information Act. While upholding Board policy, a federal appeals court ruled that the law did not apply because disclosure would invade the privacy of the employees.[125] It stated:

> We would be naive to disregard the abuse which could potentially occur if employers and other employees were armed with this information. . .

The appeals court found that the "inevitable result" of disclosure "would be to chill the rights of employees."

In other words, if the employer learned the names of employees who had signed cards, the court implies that they could be discharged. Under these circumstances, employees would be fearful to sign union-authorization cards. Though the issue arose in a regular representation election case, the policy would also be applicable in cases involving the *Gissel* doctrine.

Trading Port Doctrine: Retroactivity of Bargaining Orders

In 1975, the NLRB made even more meaningful bargaining orders based upon *Gissel*. Until that year, the obligation of the employer to recognize and bargain collectively began on the date that the bargaining order was issued.[126] However, it was recognized that a great deal of time elapsed from the time that the employer began a campaign of unfair labor practices until such time as the Board issued a bargaining order. As noted in a previous chapter, it takes more than a year from the time that an unfair labor practice charge is filed until such time as the Board issues a decision. More delay occurs when appeals are made to the federal courts. During this period of time, the employer could profit from illegal conduct. As the *Wall Street Journal* remarked:

That allows some guilty employers to freely continue the unfair practices and ignore the union while NLRB and court appeals continue. In this way an employer can "buy time" . . . and gain the benefits of presumably lower labor costs during the interval.[127]

To stop such tactics, the NLRB in *Trading Port*[128] held that the legal obligation of the employer to bargain with the union began on the date that its unfair labor practice started. Under this policy, it would be much more costly for an employer to engage in unfair labor practices calculated to destroy the majority status of a union. This new retroactive feature of a bargaining order allows a union to try to win backdating of any wage increases or other gains it achieves in collective bargaining that follow the Board's order to bargain. It can lawfully demand such retroactive concessions from the time an employer started its unfair labor practices.

In the precedent case, *Trading Port,* the Board order to bargain was handed down in July 1975. However, the company had started its unfair labor practices in September 1973. In August of that year, the union had signed up 42 of the 49 employees. The company then started a massive and flagrant campaign of unfair labor practices, including threats to close the business. In December 1973, the election was held, but the employer illegal conduct resulted in the union losing the election by 25 to 3. Not only did the NLRB direct the employer to recognize and bargain with the union, but it held that the obligation of the company to bargain had started in September 1973. The NLRB stated that an employer's bargaining obligation

> should commence as of the time the employer has embarked on a clear course of unlawful conduct or has engaged in sufficient unfair labor practices to undermine the union's status.

Subsequently, in October 1976, a federal court of appeals sustained *Trading Port* in *Ann Lee Sportswear, Inc.*[129] As noted, if an employer desires to be free from a *Gissel*-type bargaining order, as found in *Trading Port,* all the company has to do is to obey the law. If it does not, and seeks to destroy a union's majority status by engaging in unfair labor practices, it could be faced with a very costly remedy.

EMPLOYER ELECTION PETITIONS

During the first few years of experience with the Wagner Act, employers, regardless of the circumstances, were denied the opportunity to petition the NLRB for representation elections. Widespread discontent over such treatment was expressed in terms of unequal treatment between management and unions. In 1939, the Board permitted employers to petition for elections only when they were faced with two unions seeking recognition in the same bargaining unit.

The Taft-Hartley Act permits employers to file representation petitions even though only one union demands recognition for collective bargaining purposes. However, an employer cannot petition for an election before recognition is requested. This restriction not only prevents unions from requesting recognition before they in fact represent a majority of the bargaining unit, but it also keeps employers from obtaining elections before unions are ready to test their strength at the polls. Union attempts to enlist employees in its ranks often take a prolonged period of time. To permit management to petition for an election at any time it desires during a campaign could destroy union organizational activities for a period of one year. The Board will hold only one election in any twelve-month period, unless the one held was set aside due to unfair labor practice violations or under the *General Shoe* doctrine. The twelve-month ban on elections could become an effective antiunion device without restrictions on employer election requests. During the course of a year, a union can disintegrate. Nor are employers permitted to seek the same result by soliciting employee signatures on election petitions requesting that representation elections be held.[130]

As it has with all other forms, the Board has significant control over employer election petitions. It is required to investigate petitions filed to determine whether "a question of representation exists." An employer's right to seek an election is not a guarantee that the company will obtain an election every time it seeks one. The investigation provides the basis for the Board to reject an employer petition for an election at the close of the first anniversary of an incumbent bargaining agent when it is for the purpose of harassment. However, the employer's right to petition for an election at the close of a year on occasion reveals that a union is aware of its minority standing, and it may withdraw from the election. There is no requirement for a labor organization to subject itself to an election if it is unable to run even a close race in a poll. Withdrawal of an incumbent union from election proceedings, of course, relieves an employer from bargaining obligations.

When neither the employer nor rival unions petition for an election, the NLRB holds that the employer may lawfully recognize one of the unions and execute a labor agreement, provided the union recognized represents a majority of the employees in the barganing unit. In the precedent case on this issue, handled by the agency in 1983, the employer recognized one of the rival unions based upon an authorization-card check conducted by a neutral party.[131]

DECERTIFICATION ELECTIONS

The Taft-Hartley Act establishes machinery whereby unions may be decertified.[132] Under its provisions, an NLRB certification is valid for only one year. After that time, employees within the bargaining unit can petition the Board for a decertification election. The Board will conduct such a poll when 30 percent of the employees sign a petition requesting a decertification election. If a labor union is defeated in such a referendum, it loses bargaining rights within the unit. In addition, once the Board conducts a decertification election, there can be no additional elections within the bargaining unit for one year. The statute permits only one election per year for certification purposes in a particular bargaining unit. Thus the defeat of a union in a decertification election relieves the employer from all legal obligation to bargain collectively for at least twelve months. During this period it is entirely possible that the union might completely disintegrate, thereby precluding collective bargaining on a permanent basis. The election must be free of unfair labor practices to obtain this result.

The decertification election provides employees with the opportunity to get rid of a union in which they no longer have confidence. One could hardly quarrel with this right of employees. On the other hand, the decertification procedure should be viewed in combination with the "free speech" provision of the law. Employers who desire to avoid collective bargaining can be expected to campaign vigorously for the defeat of the union. They may use the captive audience, or any other lawful method, to seek the demise of the union. Once a decertification petition is filed, the same rules apply as in the original representation election.[133]

On the other hand, the NLRB has announced policies that limit employer conduct with regard to decertification elections. An employer may not file a decertification petition. Nor can it help employees file such a petition or induce them to file for decertification. Also, an employer may not conduct a poll of any employees after the expiration of the labor agreement so as to plant a seed for a union decertification movement. In one case, the election was secret, and the employer promised that there would be no reprisals. Nevertheless, the NLRB held that the poll was unlawful because the employer did not have a good-faith doubt that employees still wanted a union.[134] In addition, a decertification petition will be dismissed if it is filed while proceedings are being held to deal with employer unfair labor practices.[135] However, an employer may answer employee questions concerning the procedures involved in obtaining a decertification election. When presented with such a question, an employer told the employee to write to the NLRB Regional Director. Holding the action of the employer to be legal, the Board said the company had only provided the employee with "mere ministerial aid."[136] Also, an employer may lawfully promise employees that the status quo in employment conditions will be maintained if the union loses the election.[137]

Unions lose a majority of decertification elections. In the first two years of Taft-Hartley operation, unions lost bargaining rights in 144 out of 229 decertification elections conducted. In 1981, unions lost representation rights in 75 percent of the 856 decertification elections conducted. However, the total loss of union members amounted to only 27,527.[138] In the same year, although victorious in only 43 percent of the representation elections conducted, unions earned bargaining rights or continued as representatives for 165,232 employees. Given this experience, contrary to some who regard the increase in the number of decertification elections as a symptom of the demise of the labor movement, one writer concludes:

> . . . it is clear that decertification contests are still not a significant burden to most unions.[139]

In 1982, the NLRB adopted a new policy that may increase the chances of unions to prevail in decertification elections.[140] Prior to *Dresser Industries,* employers were permitted to cease bargaining with a union after a decertification petition had been filed.[141] Under the new policy, the employer must continue to bargain with the incumbent union, even if a valid decertification petition has been filed. Should the union be able to negotiate a labor agreement satisfactory to the majority of the employees, it may win the decertification election. Of course, when the employer is determined to get rid of the union, it will adopt a hard posture at the bargaining table, thwarting the opportunity of the union to negotiate a successful contract.

A union member who files a decertification petition may be disciplined by a union. The worker may be expelled from membership, but he or she cannot be subject to a fine.[142] The rule permitting expulsion is an exception to general Board attempts to protect the integrity of Board processes. For example, the United States Supreme Court agrees that it is unlawful to discipline a member for filing unfair labor practices against a union.[143] But the Board held that a decertification petition was a special situation justifying an exception to the general rule for two reasons. Expulsion or suspension is permitted because (1) the petition threatens the very existence of the union as an institution, and (2) as a matter of self-defense, the union cannot allow a member to lead an antiunion campaign while retaining the right to attend union meetings, obtain knowledge of union strategy, and even vote on union affairs. Expulsion is probably of little consequence to a member who files a decertification petition, but permitting fines in such cases would be punitive especially since fines are enforceable in the courts in accordance with a 1967 Supreme Court decision.[144]

RUNOFF ELECTIONS

At times more than one union is on the election ballot. After the election, it may be determined that no union received the majority of votes but, on the other hand, neither did a majority of employees vote to reject *all* unions in the election. Under these circumstances, it is necessary to conduct a runoff election.

Under the Wagner Act, the NLRB shifted its policy several times to deal with this problem. When Taft-Hartley was enacted, Congress stipulated that the top two choices are to be placed on the ballot. If the nonunion option ranks in the top two at the original poll, it must go on the ballot in the runoff election. On the other hand, the nonunion choice will be dropped from the ballot should two unions be designated as the top two choices. This type of election is not frequent, with the number amounting to only 155 in fiscal year 1980.

SUMMARY

It has been demonstrated that the NLRB has considerable responsibility for creating an election atmosphere that provides employees with the greatest range of freedom to select or reject collective bargaining representation. The agency attempts to balance employee-employer rights to engage in preelection campaigns by establishing policies in the context of a totality of circumstances. Board policies as developed to date have been evolutionary in nature and not radical, despite periodic changes in Board personnel and legislative enactment. Sole responsibility to establish effective representation election policies and to develop remedies for violations of such rules has been given the NLRB by Congress. The U.S. Supreme Court reviews Board actions in the last resort, but generally supports the agency in its implementation of congressional enactments. The high court does require a convincing articulation of Board-established rules in carrying out its legislative charge. Limitations may be placed on employer and union preelection activities to the extent that free elections are advanced by doing so. Though the *Gissel* doctrine remains controversial, the Supreme Court permits bargaining orders based upon authorization cards. The Board requires that unions receive equal time to respond to employer captive-audience speeches under certain circumstances; and that names and addresses of eligible bargaining-unit voters be filed with regional directors within seven days after election orders or agreements. The effort to establish the *General Shoe* laboratory conditions continues to be a major problem, complicated by changing NLRB membership that results in some shifting policies.

Employers have been extended the right to petition for elections after they are confronted with a request for recognition. Decertification elections are also possible for employees disenchanted with union representation. Unions lose about 75 percent of these elections, but the total loss of membership is minimal. Runoff elections are also provided to determine employee preferences in selecting bargaining representatives. The top two choices of initial polls are currently carried over to the runoff election.

Election policies and procedures remain in a state of change. The Board and courts continue their search for workable policies that will insure the rights of all parties to election proceedings.

DISCUSSION QUESTIONS

1. Trace the development of employer free speech policy in election campaigns to the Taft-Hartley Act. How did the Taft-Hartley Act handle the controversy over employer participation in election campaigns?
2. What is the essential essence of the *General Shoe* doctrine?

3. Compare the Board's *Shopping Kart* and *General Knit* cases. How might frequent policy shifts affect the parties to an election?

4. What is current Board policy regarding employer interrogation of individual employees concerning union matters during organizational campaigns? Is the policy threatening or potentially coercive in employee exercise of organizational rights? Are unions ever in a position to make threats in violation of employee rights?

5. Explain the problems associated with captive-audience rules of the Board. Has the names-and-addresses policy alleviated the burden on the Board to provide unions equal time to reply when captive audiences have been held?

6. Explain the doctrine established by *Gissel*. Evaluate the undetermined and controversial feature of *Gissel* concerning the authority of the Board to issue nonmajority bargaining orders.

7. What are some of the problems with bargaining authorization cards?

8. When may an employer petition the Board to conduct an election? Do you see advantages or disadvantages to this right?

9. How might *Dresser Industries* affect union decertification election results? How have unions fared historically in such elections?

10. Do employees have ample choice in runoff elections? Does Taft-Hartley present the possibility that a minority union may be certified because of the requirements for runoff elections?

NOTES

1   *Wickwire Brothers,* 16 NLRB 16 (1936).

2   John E. Drotning, "Employer Free Speech: Two Basic Questions Considered by the NLRB and Courts," *Labor Law Journal,* XVI, 3, (1965), p. 131.

3   310 U.S. 88 (1940).

4   *Ford Motor Company* v. *NLRB,* 114 F. (2d) 905 (1940).

5   *NLRB* v. *Virginia Electric & Power Company,* 314 U.S. 469 (1941).

6   *Clark Brothers Company, Inc.* v. *NLRB,* 163 F. (2d) 373 (1947).

7   John M. Stochaj, "Free Speech Policies," *Labor Law Journal,* VIII, 8 (August 1957), p. 532.

8   Drotning, *op. cit.,* p. 134.

9   *NLRB* v. *American Tube Bending,* 134 F. (2d) 993 (1943), cert. denied 320 U.S. 768 (1943).

10   *United Welding Company,* 72 NLRB 954 (1947).

11   House of Representatives, Special Committee to Investigate the National Labor Relations Board, *Intermediate Report,* House Report No. 1902, 76th Congress, 3d sess., 1940, Part I, p. 83.

12   *National Association of Manufacturers Law Digest 66* (1947).

13   *General Shoe Corporation,* 77 NLRB 124 (1948).

14   *Ibid.*

15   *Economic Machinery Company,* 111 NLRB 947 (1955).

16   *NVF Company, Hartwell Division,* 210 NLRB 663 (1974).

17   *The Hurley Co.*, 130 NLRB 282 (1961).

18   *Plant City Welding and Tank Co.*, 119 NLRB 962 (1957).

19   *Peerless Plywood Co.*, 107 NLRB 427 (1953).

20   *General Electric Co.*, 161 NLRB 618 (1966).

21   *Electro-Wire Products*, 242 NLRB No. 144 (1979).

22   *James Lees and Sons Co.*, 130 NLRB 1290 (1961).

23   *Al Long, Inc.*, 173 NLRB 447 (1968).

24   *Sewell Manufacturing*, 138 NLRB 66 (1962).

25   *NLRB* v. *Schapiro & Whitehouse, Inc.*, 356 F. (2d) 675 (1966).

26   156 NLRB 1236 (1966).

27   140 NLRB 221 (1962).

28   *Bausch & Lomb, Inc.*, 185 NLRB 262 (1970).

29   *Lof Glass, Inc.*, 249 NLRB No. 57 (1980).

30   *Southwest Latex Corp.*, 175 NLRB 1 (1969).

31   *Monmouth Medical Center* v. *National Labor Relations Board*, CCA 3, Case No. 78-1832, August 20, 1979.

32   *Shopping Kart Food Market*, 228 NLRB 190 (1977).

33   239 NLRB No. 101 (1978).

34   The new member at that time was John C. Truesdale. See his article "From *General Shoe* to *General Knit:* A Return to *Hollywood Ceramics,"Labor Law Journal*, XXX, 2 (February 1979), pp. 67-79.

35   *Standard Knitting Mills, Inc.*, 172 NLRB 1122 (1968).

36   *Somismo, Inc.*, 133 NLRB 131 (1961).

37   *General Electric Co.*, 215 NLRB 520 (1975).

38   *Honeywell, Inc.*, 225 NLRB 79 (1976).

39   *NLRB* v. *Gissel Packing*, 395 U.S. 575 (1969).

40   *TRW, Inc.*, 169 NLRB 21 (1968).

41   *Testing Service Corp.*, 193 NLRB 332 (1971).

42   *Ohmite Manufacturing Co.*, 217 NLRB 435 (1975).

43   *Donn Products, Inc.* and *American Metals Corp.*, 229 NLRB 9 (1977).

44   *American Telecommunications Corp.*, 249 NLRB No. 149 (1980).

45   National Labor Relations Board, *Thirty-eighth Annual Report*, U.S. Government Printing Office, Washington, D.C., 1973, p. 73.

46   *Standard-Coosa-Thatcher Co.*, 85 NLRB 1358 (1949).

47   *Blue Flash Express, Inc.*, 109 NLRB 391 (1954).

48   *PPG Industries*, 251 NLRB 1146 (1980).

49   *Rossmore House*, 269 NLRB No. 198 (1984).

50   *Hotel and Restaurant Employees, Local 11*, CA–9, No. 84–7353, May 18, 1985.

51   *Lyons Restaurant*, 234 NLRB No. 10 (1978).

52   *Sciosa Home and Industrial Disposal Service*, 266 NLRB No. 22 (1983).

53   *Western Cartridge Co.* v. *NLRB*, 134 F. (2d) 240 (CA 7, 1943).

54   *The Great Atlantic & Pacific Tea Co., Inc.*, 166 NLRB 27 (1967).

55   *Performance Measurements Co., Inc.*, 148 NLRB 1657 (1964).

56   *Meir's Wine Cellars, Inc.*, 188 NLRB 153 (1971).

57   *Tennessee Auger Co.*, 169 NLRB 914 (1968).

58   *Ludwig Motor Corp.*, 222 NLRB 635 (1976).

59   *The Borden Manufacturing Co.*, 193 NLRB 1028 (1971).

60   *Hineline's Meat Plant, Inc.*, 193 NLRB 867 (1971).

61   *American Hoist and Derrick Co., Industrial Brownhoist Division,* 184 NLRB 551 (1970).

62   *Cadillac Overall Supply Co.,* 148 NLRB 1133 (1964).

63   *Smith Co.,* 192 NLRB 1098 (1972).

64   National Labor Relations Board, *Thirty-seventh Annual Report,* U.S. Government Printing Office, Washington, D.C.,1972, p. 74.

65   *Dic-Amco, Inc.,* 163 NLRB 1019 (1967).

66   *Savair Manufacturing Co.,* 414 U.S. 270 (1973).

67   *Lau Industries,* 210 NLRB 182 (1974).

68   *NLRB* v. *My Store, Inc.,* 345 F. (2d) 494 (CA 7, 1965); *Phillips Manufacturing Co.,* 148 NLRB 1420 (1964).

69   *Struksnes Construction Co., Inc.,* 165 NLRB 1062 (1967).

70   *Wall Colmonoy Corp.,* 173 NLRB 40 (1968).

71   *Ponn Distributing, Inc.,* 203 NLRB 482 (1973).

72   *Clark Bros. Company,* 70 NLRB 802 (1946), 163 F. (2d) 373 (1947).

73   *Ibid.*

74   *Babcock & Wilcox,* 77 NLRB 577 (1948).

75   It will be recalled that Section 8 (c) provided that "the expressing of any views, arguments, or opinion, or the dissemination thereof, whether in written, printed, graphic, or visual form, shall not constitute or be evidence of an unfair labor practice under any of the provisions of this Act, if such expression contains no threat of reprisal or force or promise of benefit."

76   *Sands Corrugated Paper Machinery Company,* 89 NLRB 1363 (1950).

77   *Bonwit Teller, Inc.,* 96 NLRB 608 (1951).

78   *Republic Aviation* v. *NLRB,* 324 U.S. 105 (1956).

79   *Bonwit Teller, Inc.* v. *NLRB,* 197 F. (2d) 640 (CA 2, 1952).

80   *Metropolitan Auto Parts,* 99 NLRB 401 (1952); *Onondaga Pottery Co.,* 100 NLRB 1143 (1953).

81   107 NLRB 400 (1953).

82   *NLRB* v. *Babcock & Wilcox,* 351 U.S. 105 (1956).

83   See also National Labor Relations Board, *Nineteenth Annual Report,* U.S. Government Printing Office, Washington D.C., 1954, p. 75.

84   107 NLRB 427 (1953).

85   *NLRB* v. *United Steelworkers (Nutone, Inc.),* 357 U.S. 357 (1958).

86   145 NLRB 846 (1964).

87   *NLRB* v. *Montgomery Ward & Co., Inc.,* 339 F. (2d) 889 (CA 6, 1965).

88   155 NLRB 714 (1965).

89   A federal court of appeals modified this order of the NLRB. It held that the union would have equal time to reply should the employer make captive-audience speeches during future election campaigns. *NLRB* v. *H. W. Elson Bottling Co.,* 379 F. (2d) 223 (CA 6, 1967). However, it is significant that the court ruled that unions have the opportunity to reply to captive-audience meetings under a particular set of employer unfair labor practices.

90   *J. P. Stevens and Co.,* 245 NLRB No. 20 (1979).

91   *J. P. Stevens,* 219 NLRB 850 (1975).

92   *Prescott Industrial Products Co.,* 205 NLRB 51 (1973).

93   *AFL-CIO News,* August 23, 1975.

94   *General Electric,* 156 NLRB 1247 (1966).

95   *Excelsior Underwear, Inc.,* 156 NLRB 1236 (1966).

96   *NLRB* v. *Virginia Electric & Power Company, op. cit.*

97   *Swift & Company,* 162 NLRB 6 (1967).

98   Section 481 (c).

99   National Labor Relations Board, *Thirty-first Annual Report,* U.S. Government Printing Office, Washington D.C., 1966, p. 20.

100   National Labor Relations Board, *Forty-fourth Annual Report,* U.S. Government Printing Office, Washington D.C., 1979, p. 3.

101   *NLRB* v. *Wyman-Gordon,* 394 U.S. 759 (1969).

102   *Joy Silk Mills, Inc.,* 85 NLRB 1236 (1949); 185 F. (2d) 732 (1950), cert. denied 341 U.S. 914 (1951).

103   *Bernel Foam Products Company,* 146 NLRB 1277 (1964).

104   *Aiello Dairy Company,* 110 NLRB 1365 (1954).

105   National Labor Relations Board, *Thirtieth Annual Report,* U.S. Government Printing Office, Washington, D.C., 1965, pp. 129–130.

106   *Redmond Plastics, Inc.,* 187 NLRB 487 (1970).

107   *Wilder Manufacturing,* 185 NLRB 175 (1970).

108   *Summer & Company, Linden Lumber Division,* 190 NLRB 718 (1971).

109   *Summer & Co., Linden Lumber Division* v. *NLRB,* 419 U.S. 301 (1974).

110   *NLRB* v. *Gissel Packing Company,* 395 U.S. 575 (1969).

111   *Oversight Hearings on the National Labor Relations Board,* Hearings Before Subcommittee on Labor-Management Relations, Committee on Education and Labor, House of Representatives, 94th Congress, 1st sess., October 23, 1975, p. 127.

112   Max S. Wortman, Jr. and Nathaniel Jones, "Remedial Actions of the NLRB in Representation Cases: An Analysis of the *Gissel* Bargaining Order," *Labor Law Journal,* XXX, 5 (May 1979), pp. 281-88.

113   *United Dairy Farmers Cooperative Association,* 242 NLRB No. 179 (1979).

114   261 NLRB No. 178. For a criticism of the doctrine see Robert P. Hunter, *"Conair: Minority Bargaining Orders Usher in 1984 at NLRB,"* *Labor Law Journal,* XXXIII, 9, (September 1982), p. 571.

115   *Gourmet Foods,* 270 NLRB No. 113 (1984).

116   *United Dairy Farmers Cooperative* v. *NLRB,* 663 F. 2d 1054 (CA 3, 1980).

117   *Teamsters Local 115* and *Flavor Delight, Inc.* v. *NLRB,* 640 F. 2d 1054. Cert. denied 102 Sup. Ct. 141 (1981).

118   237 NLRB No. 103 (1979).

119   *MMIC, Inc.,* 270 NLRB No. 51 (1984).

120   *NLRB* v. *S. S. Logan Packing Co.,* 386 F. 2d 562 (CCA 4, 1967).

121   *Cumberland Shoe Corporation,* 144 NLRB 1268 (1964); *Levi Strauss & Company,* 172 NLRB 57 (1968); *McEwen Manufacturing Company,* 172 NLRB 990 (1968).

122   *NLRB* v. *Keystone Pretzel Bakery, Inc.,* CA 3, No. 81-2067, December 29, 1982.

123   On this basis, the Board invalidated cards signed by Spanish-speaking employees. It determined that the employees could not speak, write, or read English (*Gate of Spain Restaurant,* 192 NLRB 1091 [1971]).

124   *NLRB* v. *Roney Plaza Apartments,* CCA 5, Case No. 77-3481, July 2, 1979.

125   *Pacific Molasses Co.* v. *NLRB,* 577 F. (2d) 1172 (CCA 5, 1978).

126   Indeed, in *Steel-Fab* (212 NLRB 363 [1974]), the Board held that when it issued a *Gissel*-type bargaining order, it would no longer find that the employer refused to bargain collectively in violation of Section 8(a)(5) of the Act. Though the Board said that *Steel-Fab* marked a major change in legal theory, it believed that there would be no practical change in the scope of effectiveness of its remedial orders.

127   *Wall Street Journal,* July 22, 1975, p. 4.

128   219 NLRB 298 (1975).

129   *Ann Lee Sportswear, Inc.* v. *NLRB*, CA 5, Case No. 75–1719, October 29, 1976.

130   *Serv-Air, Inc.* v. *NLRB*, 401 F. 2d 363 (1968).

131   *Great Southern Construction, Inc.*, 266 NLRB No. 69 (1983).

132   Section 9 (c) (1) (A).

133   William A. Krupman and Gregory I. Rasin, "Decertification: Removing the Shroud," *Labor Law Journal*, XXX, 4, (April 1979), pp. 231–34.

134   *Mid-Continent Refrigerated Service Co.*, 228 NLRB 649 (1977).

135   *Big Three Industries*, 201 NLRB 197 (1973).

136   *Kono-TV-Mission Telecasting*, 163 NLRB 1005 (1967).

137   *El Cid, Inc.*, 222 NLRB 1315 (1976).

138   National Labor Relations Board, *Forty-sixth Annual Report*, U.S.Goverment Printing Office, Washington D.C., 1981, p. 18.

139   Joseph Krislov, "The Increase in Union Decertification Elections," U.S. Department of Labor, Bureau of Labor Statistics, *Monthly Labor Review*, CII, 11 (November 1979), p. 31.

140   *Dresser Industries, Inc.*, 264 NLRB No. 145 (1982).

141   *Telautograph Corp.*, 199 NLRB 892 (1972).

142   *International Molders & Allied Workers Local No. 125*, 178 NLRB 25 (1969).

143   *NLRB* v. *Industrial Union of Marine and Shipbuilding Workers of America*, 391 U.S. 418 (1968).

144   *NLRB* v. *Allis-Chalmers Manufacturing Company*, 388 U.S. 175 (1967).

CHAPTER THIRTEEN

CONTROL OF
THE BARGAINING UNIT

THE BARGAINING UNIT: ITS NATURE

Each collective bargaining contract covers a certain group of workers. When a labor contract is being negotiated, the representatives of labor and management are careful to spell out its terms to the affected workers. Workers covered by the agreement are said to constitute the bargaining unit. For example, in a contract between the United Steelworkers of America and Carnegie-Illinois Steel Corporation, the scope of the bargaining unit was set up in the following terms: "... this Agreement applies to all individuals occupying production, maintenance and hourly rated non-confidential clerical jobs employed in and about the Company's steel-manufacturing and by-product coke plant." Excluded from the bargaining unit, however, were those "individuals occupying salaried, watchmen, guard, confidential clerical or supervisory positions of foreman level and above." The significance of being part of the bargaining unit should be obvious. All workers within the bargaining unit have their conditions of work determined through the collective bargaining process. On the other hand, workers excluded from the unit are not represented by the labor union. They must adjust their employment problems on an individual basis, or they may constitute a separate bargaining unit under certain conditions. At times, both management and the union are in full agreement that certain workers shall be excluded from the bargaining unit (in the above illustration, both the steel company and the union agreed that forepeople should not be included). Agreement is not always possible: employees such as those labeled craft or professional may feel that membership in a separate unit would enhance their bargaining positions. The NLRB has had to decide the basic criteria for the creation of separate bargaining units.

INFLUENCE OF THE WAGNER ACT

Before passage of the Wagner Act, representatives of labor and management had full authority to determine the scope and character of the bargaining unit. It was their exclusive responsibility to decide problems relating to coverage of the labor agreement. This condition was altered after the passage of the National Labor Relations Act in 1935. The Wagner Act required that employers bargain collectively with unions selected by a majority of workers in the bargaining unit. This meant that the NLRB, the administrative agency of the Wagner Act, was required to poll workers to determine whether a majority of workers in a bargaining unit wanted a certain union to represent them in collective bargaining. Prior to the holding of such referendums, however, the NLRB set up the bargaining unit. All workers included were eligible to vote in the representation election. If a majority of workers participating in such a referendum cast ballots for a particular labor organization, the NLRB would normally certify this union as the representative of all workers in the bargaining unit. Should the labor union and the employer eventually negotiate a labor contract, the workers in the bargaining unit would be covered by it. Thus establishment of the bargaining unit by the NLRB serves a dual purpose: (1) it determines which workers are eligible to vote in a representation election; and (2) it sets up the group of workers to be covered by a labor contract resulting from negotiations with a certified labor organization.

ESTABLISHMENT OF THE BARGAINING UNIT: WAGNER ACT EXPERIENCE

Under the Wagner Act, the NLRB had a considerable degree of freedom in the establishment of the bargaining unit. Congress merely instructed the Board to set up a bargaining unit that would be appropriate for the purposes of collective bargaining. Such a unit, according to the Wagner Act, should be of such character as would "insure to employees the full benefit of their right to self-organization and collective bargaining." Beyond this mandate, the Wagner Act placed no restrictions on the NLRB. The agency was permitted to establish whatever unit it believed would further the cause of effective collective bargaining. To this end, the NLRB was free to set up units along craft, employer, or industrial lines. In a particular case, the NLRB might hold that collective bargaining would be furthered by the establishment of a craft unit. Under other circumstances, Board members might elect to establish an industrial unit. Whatever the character of the unit, the Board had to be convinced that the workers included in the unit constituted an appropriate group for the purposes of collective bargaining.

Character of Guides Utilized by the NLRB

The foregoing indicates that the NLRB originally possessed a considerable amount of power in the establishment of the bargaining unit. However, the Board early in its career established a series of guides to be employed. These guides had a common denominator: the setting up of a unit that would effectuate the collective bargaining process. In other words, the NLRB did not utilize its power in a capricious or arbitrary manner. Its decisions were related to the particular circumstances in each situation. Upon many occasions, the Board declared that it would not apply "rigid rules to determine the appropriate unit in each case."[1] Instead, the Board held that the "appropriate unit in each case must be determined in the light of the circumstances in the particular case."[2]

The character of the guides that the Board established was related to its fundamental objective: establishing units that would make the collective bargaining process effective. Factors that the agency considered in setting up units included (1) the history, extent, and type of organization of employees in a plant; (2) the history of their collective bargaining; (3) the history, extent, and type of organization and the collective bargaining of employees in other plants of the same employer, or of other employers in the same industry; (4) the skill, wages, work, and working conditions of employees; (5) the desires of employees; (6) the eligibility of employees for membership in the union or unions involved in the election proceedings and in other labor organizations; and (7) the relationship between the unit or units proposed and the employer's organization, management, and operation of the plant.[3]

The Board exercised a considerable degree of freedom in its selection of bargaining-unit guides. Moreover, it employed them on a relatively consistent basis. In the vast majority of cases the bargaining unit was set up with a minimum amount of friction among labor unions, employers, and the Board. If the Board had been capricious in its actions or utilized inappropriate guides, one would expect the setting up of bargaining units to have stimulated a great deal of controversy among the parties to NLRB proceedings. As a matter of record, the Board during 1936–1947 settled about three-fourths of all cases involving the issue of the bargaining unit on an informal basis.[4] In other words, the Board, the employers, and the unions involved in these cases were of the same judgment as to the character of the bargaining unit.

Establishment of the Bargaining Unit: Controversial Issues

In bargaining-unit cases settled on an informal basis, the NLRB generally played the role of observer. All parties recognized the appropriateness of a particular collective bargaining unit. Under informal circumstances, the Board merely approved a grouping that appeared logical to all concerned. However, in the cases that were decided only after formal action, the power of the NLRB to set up the bargaining unit assumed significant proportions. When differences of opinion among employers, unions, or the Board were involved, the agency finally resolved the dispute. Action of the NLRB in setting up the unit was conclusive and normally not reviewable in the courts.[5]

Controversy regarding the establishment of the bargaining unit could arise from several sources. Suppose an employer desires a unit that, if set up, would relieve the company of any legal obligation to bargain with employee-designated representatives. Assume also that the enterprise is multiplant in character. The labor union has organized only one plant. It petitions the Board for certification. If the Board sets up a unit encompassing all the plants, the union likely will not win a representation election, since the unorganized employees will overbalance the organized group. On the other hand, the labor union would stand a better chance of winning the representation election if the bargaining unit was limited to the plant already organized by the union.

Conflict between craft and industrial unions constituted another basis for friction in the determination of bargaining units. This issue was kept before the public's eye by the American Federation of Labor, a federation composed of unions essentially craft in character. The AFL charged that the NLRB favored the industrial unions of the CIO. (It will be recalled that the AFL and the CIO did not merge until 1955.) Such favoritism, the AFL contended, resulted in the loss of power and membership of AFL-affiliated labor unions. The basis for the AFL grievances against the NLRB is described in the following illustration.

Suppose a group of twenty-five electricians, members of the International Brotherhood of Electrical Workers (AFL), worked in a factory that employed 1,000 production workers. Suppose the NLRB set up a plant-wide bargaining unit. Such a unit would include the twenty-five craft workers. In a bargaining election, the production workers voted overwhelmingly for a CIO industrial union—say, the United Steelworkers of America. Under such circumstances, the industrial union would have been certified by the NLRB. It would have become the legal representative of all workers in the bargaining unit, production workers and electricians alike. The employer would bargain with the industrial union only, and would not be required to recognize the craft organization as the bargaining agent of the twenty-five electricians. If the industrial union obtained a union-shop arrangement, the problem would become more crucial. Such a condition would require that the electricians join the CIO union, pay dues to it, and, as a condition of employment, maintain their membership in good standing. The electricians might feel that their interests were not properly considered in negotiations with the employer, or that the CIO union was more concerned with the welfare of the larger group of production workers.

A final source of controversy relating to the establishment of the bargaining unit centered on the question of whether certain groups should be certified for collective bargaining purposes. Defining the bargaining unit is a prerequisite for election and certification purposes. In the absence of certification, a group of workers could not enjoy legal protection of their right to collective bargaining. Under these circumstances, it is doubtful that the workers can obtain a collective bargaining contract. Therefore, attempts were often made to prevent the Board from setting up bargaining units containing certain classifications of workers.

The problem of the appropriateness of units containing certain groups of workers became particularly serious during World War II. Some employers contended that replacements for workers who had left for duty with the armed forces did not constitute units appropriate for the purposes of collective bargaining. These employers felt that replacements had no standing under the Wagner Act because their services would not be required once industry reconverted to peacetime activities. Rejecting this argument, the Board held that wartime replacements could constitute appropriate bargaining units.[6] A contrary ruling would have denied millions of wartime workers the opportunity to participate in the collective bargaining process.

Despite the objections of some employers, the NLRB in a 1942 case held that instructors employed to train groups of new wartime employees were to be included in the same bargaining unit as production workers.[7] In still another case, a group of instructors hired to train army and navy personnel in the operation of war materiel produced by a company were considered eligible for inclusion in a unit for purposes of collective bargaining. Despite the fact that these instructors carried out their training duties in an area located many miles from the company's major plant, the NLRB held that they could constitute an appropriate bargaining unit. Another controversy centered around a group of nurses. An employer urged that a number of nurses, employed by the company for first-aid purposes, should be included in a production workers' bargaining unit. However, the Board classified them into a separate unit on the ground that the nurses constituted a well-defined professional group with interests and conditions of work dissimilar from the production workers.

Finally, the position of forepeople and plant guards under the Wagner Act whipped up a storm of controversy. Employers argued that these two groups did not constitute units appropriate for the purposes of collective bargaining. In contrast, thousands of these employees felt that their economic positions would be advanced if they worked under the protection of collective bargaining contracts. They were aware that it would be much easier to obtain such agreements if the NLRB would certify their unions for purposes of collective bargaining. To this end, they objected to the employer point of view and urged the NLRB to rule that they might be properly classified into collective bargaining units. The manner in which the Board resolved the foreperson and plant guard problem generated considerable controversy over Board action under the Wagner Act.

The Weight of the Evidence

Members of the NLRB were well aware of the significance of their authority to set up the appropriate bargaining unit. As the foregoing indicates, the determination of the bargaining unit can influence the structural pattern of collective bargaining. Whether industrial or craft unions would prevail in a given industry could depend on the action of the NLRB. Or a unit might be determined in a manner that would relieve the employer of all responsibility to bargain collectively. Board decisions could be conclusive as to whether an industrial or a craft union would rule in a plant or within an industry. Finally, the manner in which the Board disposed of its duty to set up the bargaining unit determined whether certain classifications of workers were included in collective bargaining contracts.

Obviously, the NLRB was tackling a difficult job. There were no infallible standards for determining conclusively which groups of workers constituted appropriate bargaining units, given the complex and rapidly changing techniques of production in the American economy. Fundamentally, determination of the unit involved human judgment.

While the NLRB was setting up bargaining units under the Wagner Act, the American labor movement was expanding to unprecedented proportions. With a few notable exceptions, employers did not find great fault with the manner in which the agency set up units. Employers may have objected to the entire philosophy of the Wagner Act, but they were not unduly critical of the way in which the Board set up bargaining units. In short, collective bargaining progressed under the structural arrangement of unionism, which was influenced by Board bargaining-unit decisions. The record leads to the conclusion that the Board under the Wagner Act carried out the mandate of Congress. It set up bargaining units that insured employees "the full benefits of their right to self-organization and collective bargaining."

PRESSURE FOR BARGAINING-UNIT LIMITATIONS

When it enacted the 1947 Taft-Hartley Act, Congress restricted the power of the Board to set up units for collective bargaining. Before examining the character of those restrictions, it is necessary to discuss several groups agitating for enactment of such legislative control over Board authority.

In the first place, some employers did not agree with the Board's bargaining-unit policies. They did not find fault with the guides the Board utilized to determine bargaining units. Nor did they object to the manner in which the agency employed these standards. Rather, they objected to the policy of extending the protection of the law to certain classifications of workers. In particular, these employers objected to the policy of placing forepeople, plant guards, and partially organized plants into units for collective bargaining. As will be pointed out, the Board under the Wagner Act classified forepeople and plant guards as eligible for bargaining-unit status. Likewise it set up bargaining units of unionized workers that included only a small part of the organizable workers of a plant.

As noted previously, the AFL protested against the treatment of its unions by the NLRB. Hence this national federation constituted the second force that sought to limit the authority of the Board to establish bargaining units. The objective of the AFL was to influence the passage of legislation that would require favoritism for craft workers. Unions of the AFL desired the passage of legislation that would separate craft workers from industrial unions. The AFL position was that craft workers, wherever employed, should be classified in units for collective bargaining separate from production workers. They should not be lumped together with unskilled or semiskilled workers. Thus if four plumbers worked in a factory employing, say, two thousand unskilled and semiskilled workers, the plumbers should be classified in a separate unit for the purposes of collective bargaining. In this example, the AFL would have the four plumbers excluded from any labor agreement covering the unskilled and semiskilled workers and covered by a separate contract.

In addition to employers and the AFL, professional workers themselves agitated for restrictions on the Board's power to set up bargaining units. Similar to craft workers, professional workers wanted special consideration. Actually, under the Wagner Act, the Board frequently classified professional workers into special bargaining units by administrative ruling. The NLRB did this whenever it felt that collective bargaining would be advanced by the establishment of separate units for professional workers. However, this group was not satisfied with resolution of the problem by administrative ruling. It sought to fashion a law that would require the Board to separate the professional workers from others for purposes of collective bargaining. As in the case of craft workers, these employees wanted separate contracts covering the professional workers. If there were a few professional workers in a firm employing hundreds of nonprofessional workers, the position of the professionals was that they should not be affected by any collective bargaining contract covering the other workers, but that the terms of employment should be embodied into a special contract covering only the professional workers.

Greater detail regarding Board treatment of all the special-interest groups is required for a better understanding of the appropriate bargaining-unit problem. Special attention is now devoted to craft workers, forepeople, other managerial employees, plant guards, professionals, and the extent of organization. Finally, coordinated bargaining is treated as a special problem of unit determination.

TREATMENT OF CRAFT BARGAINING UNITS

Throughout the Wagner Act period, craft unions repeatedly alleged that the NLRB favored industrial unions. In weighing the contention of the AFL, we must look at the Board's record to determine whether or not the allegations made against it were valid. Some of the AFL antagonism undoubtedly springs from the results of NLRB elections where craft and industrial unions were opponents on the same ballot. Returns show that industrial unions won more of these elections than the AFL-affiliated craft unions. For example, during the period 1942–1945, the NLRB conducted 2,120 elections in which the sole contestants were AFL and CIO affiliates. In these elections, workers selected CIO units in 53.9 percent of the cases, AFL affiliates in 38.9 percent of the cases, and rejected both in 7.2 percent. To charge that the Board had been biased because the industrial unions had won more representation elections is to lose sight of the nature of the democratic process. The Board was not the cause of workers' selecting industrial units over craft representation. In this regard, one writer observing the 1935–36 period stated that the craft-union criticism leveled against the Board was comparable "to an attack on the use of the voting machines because they record the victory of the party with the largest number of votes."[8]

Another source of AFL antagonism arose from circumstances inherent in dealing with large numbers of workers in an industrial setting. It is obvious that if craft workers are grouped within a large industrial unit, they may have difficulties obtaining separate bargaining rights. To have their own union, the craft workers would have to be classified in a special bargaining unit. In practice, the Board frequently included craft workers in a wide industrial unit, thereby denying them any opportunity for special representation.

Action of AFL.   The objective of the AFL was to free the craft workers from the domination of industrial unions. To gain such an objective, the federation constantly sponsored amendments to the Wagner Act that would insure the autonomy of craft workers. These amendments required that when a craft composed of one or more employees existed, such craft should constitute an appropriate collective bargaining unit and could designate collective bargaining representatives. Despite the pressure of the AFL, Congress for twelve years refused to give additional protection to craft workers. Such amendments as those sponsored by the AFL were rejected.

Had Congress agreed to the craft-union position, the effect on industrial relations would have been profound. In the normal plant and industry, there is a variety of occupational groups. Some of the occupational groups fall within the jurisdiction of the craft unions affiliated with the AFL. Thus in, say, an auto parts firm, there would be a number of electricians, plumbers, tool-and-diemakers, painters, and carpenters, as well as other types of skilled craftsworkers. According to the craft-union viewpoint, each of these skilled groups should constitute a separate bargaining unit. Any union certified for the purpose of representing the semiskilled and unskilled workers would have no bargaining rights over the craft groups. Such an environment appears conducive to neither effective collective bargaining nor harmonious industrial relations. In each plant, there could be a number of labor unions with which the employer would be required to bargain collectively. Failure to reach an agreement with any one union could result in serious effects in the plant. It would indeed be incongruous for an entire plant to be shut down merely because no agreement could be reached with a small but vitally important group of craft workers. In addition, the setting up of a number of bargaining units in one plant would lead to a great deal of time diverted away from the production process. Suppose ten unions were certified for collective bargaining purposes within one factory. Other than the ten possibilities for interruptions to production, there would be ten different contracts to negotiate and ten separate grievance procedures. Each union grievance and negotiation committee would be composed of different workers, since each group would represent a different labor union. Under such conditions, management and unions would devote a disproportionate amount of time to union affairs. Production would inevitably suffer.

Apparently the craft organization did not give much attention to the implications and consequences of its proposals. The federation was merely concerned with building up its own membership. Congress was alert to the serious dangers inherent in the craft-unit proposal, and refused to act favorably on AFL-sponsored amendments. This meant that the NLRB was free to set up industrial units when it believed that the interests of effective collective bargaining and sound industrial relations indicated the appropriateness of such groupings.

Concessions to Craft Groups by NLRB.   However, the NLRB did make two major concessions to craft unions. In 1937, the Board established the *Globe* doctrine.[9] Under this doctrine the NLRB, under proper circumstances, afforded craft workers the opportunity to decide by secret ballot whether or not they desired to be included in an industrial unit before any bargaining unit was established. Thus the Board was conscious of the problem of the craft worker. It recognized that effective collective bargaining and sound industrial relations at times had to be balanced against the freedom of workers to select their own bargaining representatives. In practice, the Board ordered the "Globe election" when it appeared that a group of craft workers constituted a "true" craft, and that this group consisted of a substantial number of employees who had attempted to organize their own union. However, the Board reserved the right to deny craft workers the opportunity to select their own bargaining representatives. When the Board felt that a craft unit would retard effective collective bargaining or impair sound industrial relations, it refused to implement the *Globe* doctrine.

In 1944, the NLRB established the *General Electric* doctrine,[10] and therein made a second major concession to craft organizations. Previously, the Board had held that craft workers, once included in a larger industrial unit, would be frozen indefinitely in the industrial classification.[11] This doctrine, bitterly criticized by the AFL, was established in 1939 in *American Can.* Abandoning this rule in a wartime case, the NLRB decided that it would entertain a representation petition from craft members included in a larger industrial unit if it could be shown that (1) the craft employees involved constituted a "true" craft and not a mere dissident faction; and (2) the craft members had maintained their identity throughout the period of bargaining with a more comprehensive unit, and had protested their inclusion in such a larger bargaining unit.

When craft members were able to satisfy these prerequisites, the Board was prepared to authorize an election to determine whether the craft workers desired a separate unit, or chose instead to remain in the industrial unit. Should such an election take place, and if the craft workers voted for their own union, the Board would certify the craft group as an appropriate bargaining unit. Under these conditions, the craft group would be "carved out" of the wider industrial unit. The larger industrial unit would lose bargaining rights over the craft group, and the employer would be required to bargain with the new unit. Of course, the Board would not undertake to separate craft groups from an industrial unit when this would be inconsistent with effective collective bargaining and sound industrial relations.

Neither the *Globe* doctrine nor the principles that the NLRB established in the *General Electric* case satisfied the parent craft organization. In their 1944 convention, AFL officers once more denounced the Board. The old charge was repeated that the Board functioned in the interest of industrial unions.[12] Clearly, there is an appropriate place in the American economy for both the craft and the industrial labor organization. This fact was recognized by the NLRB. Under the Wagner Act, craft union membership almost doubled. But the liberty of craft workers to select their own unions had to be balanced against the setting up of an appropriate bargaining unit to insure effective collective bargaining for *all* workers. In addition, the interests of management could not be overlooked. Consider the plight of an employer who is required to bargain with a host of labor unions! As far as possible, the craft worker should be given freedom to choose her or his own union for representation purposes. However, this liberty should not be afforded at the expense of violating the basic principles of effective collective bargaining and sound industrial relations. It seems that the Board struck a justifiable balance in the *Globe* and *General Electric* doctrines.

CRAFT WORKERS UNDER TAFT-HARTLEY

Efforts of the AFL to win favor for the craft worker finally bore fruit in the Taft-Hartley Act. The 1947 labor law provided in Section 9 that the NLRB could not decide that any craft unit was inappropriate for collective bargaining on the ground that a different unit had been established by a prior Board determination, unless a majority of the employees in the proposed craft unit had voted against separate representation. This provision reflected the Board policy established in the *General Electric* case. Congress merely wrote into law an administrative ruling of the agency. The action of Congress is of prime significance. Personnel of administrative agencies change. With changing personnel, the policies of administrative agencies are often modified. By making the *General Electric* doctrine a matter of law, Congress prevented the abolition of the policy by the Board regardless of its future composition. In addition, the NLRB would be expected to "lean over backward" to comply with the mandate of Congress. A policy established by administrative ruling does not have the force of a doctrine created by statute. Actually, the Board has granted more elections of the *General Electric* variety since the enactment of Taft-Hartley than in a comparable period before the passage of the statute. This is, of course, an expected consequence of the law. The intent of Congress was to provide more freedom to the craft worker as long as the basic intent of national labor policy was not damaged. The NLRB must now pay full attention to the congressional objective in the administration of the statute.

Experience of NLRB with Craft-Union Provision.   Under the terms of Taft-Hartley, however, the Board had the right to deny to craft workers included in an industrial unit the opportunity to vote in a "self-determination" election. This point is illustrated in the *National Tube* case, which the Board decided in the spring of 1948.[13] The agency refused to permit a group of bricklayers in a steel mill to vote in a craft election on the grounds that inclusion of the bricklayers in the industrial unit was essential for the proper operation of the plant. It was pointed out that bricklaying operations are closely integrated into the steelmaking process. Separation of the bricklayers from the industrial unit, the Board concluded, would not be in the interest of sound industrial relations under collective bargaining. This decision underscored the fact that the Board membership considered it within its discretion to decide under what conditions a group of craft workers would be permitted to vote on the question of separate representation. The 1947 law was taken to mean that the NLRB could not deprive craft workers previously included in an industrial unit of the opportunity to vote in a craft election on the sole ground that the employees were classified in an industrial unit, but might deny the opportunity on other grounds.

On other occasions during the Truman years, the Board permitted workers previously included within an industrial unit to vote in special craft elections. In one case, the NLRB directed a craft election for a group of electricians employed in a West Coast aircraft plant. This case underscored the fact that even though a group of workers belonging to a specific craft could be denied the opportunity to vote in a craft election, the Board under different circumstances might permit other workers belonging to the same craft to vote in such elections. Previously, the NLRB had denied to a group of electricians employed in a locomotive works the privilege of voting in a self-determination election. In sharp contrast to that ruling, the opportunity *was* made available to a group of electricians employed in an aircraft plant. The election in the aircraft plant case was directed on the grounds that the electricians (1) performed highly skilled work; (2) engaged in no duties other than electrical work; and (3) worked under special supervision.

Upon another occasion, the Board directed a self-determination election in part because the craft workers involved (machinists and millwrights) underwent a four-year training period before obtaining journey worker status. In cases in which craft elections were ordered, the Board refused to heed the election opponents who argued that (1) the employer as well as the industrial union objected to the election; and (2) the industrial union had bargained for the craft workers for periods as long as ten years.

In 1954, with a different Board membership, the agency reversed its earlier *National Tube* decision with a new policy in the *American Potash* case.[14] The doctrine of integration established in *National Tube* had been limited only to those industries where the doctrine had previously been established. Craft severance on an industry-wide basis was denied in basic steel, aluminum, lumber, and wet milling. Denial in the industries mentioned was to continue because of the highly integrated production processes and the prevailing industrial pattern of bargaining. However, in the *American Potash* case the Board declared that in future cases, craft units would automatically be permitted to break out of the industrial unit irrespective of their importance to the total production process.

Concern over the new craft policy of the Board generated a common concern among many observers, generally expressed as follows:

> New uncertainty has been introduced by the Taft-Hartley Act which gives preference for craft bargaining units. This could threaten the industry-wide bargaining mechanism which has functioned so successfully in the industry as an instrument of industrial peace. In this complex industry as many as fifteen to twenty individual craft unions might become involved, each with its separate contract and possibly conflicting aspirations. Instead of single negotiations, there might be many negotiations to conduct jurisdictional rivalries, and greater possibilities of strikes.[15]

Two basic tests for craft severance were established. First, the employees had to constitute a true craft or departmental group. Second, the union seeking to carve out a craft or departmental unit had to be one that had traditionally devoted itself to the special problems of the group. In its interpretation of congressional intent in Section 9 (b) (2), the section dealing with craft severance, the Board was convinced that the interests of craft employees within larger industrial units should prevail. In this regard, it stated in *American Potash* that "it is not the province of this Board to dictate the course and pattern of labor organization in our vast industrial complex." The Board concluded that it did not have its traditional discretion to review all the facts and on the basis of findings to determine the appropriate unit for collective bargaining.

The Board remained firm in its *American Potash* decision despite a decision by the Fourth Circuit Court of Appeals.[16] In the *Pittsburgh Plate Glass* case, the employer argued before the circuit court that Board severance of crafts out of the industrial unit was discriminatory, since such a development was disallowed in *National Tube* industries, but permitted in his own. The employer wanted to bargain with only one union, not several. The circuit court agreed with the employer and denied craft severance because of the highly integrated nature of the production process. The Board, however, refused to abandon its *American Potash* decision, despite the court decision. The firmness of the Board was demonstrated in its *Kennecott Copper* case in 1962.[17] The agency ruled that it would not apply the integration doctrine to the copper industry. The force of the 1962 decision was that the Board, at least for the time, would continue to establish separate craft units in industries with integrated production processes.

The Mallinckrodt *Doctrine.*   The NLRB reviewed the *American Potash* construction of Taft-Hartley Section 9 (b) (2) in *Mallinckrodt*, a 1966 case.[18] The different composition of Board membership led to a reevaluation of congressional intent on the craft severance problem. The Board held that Congress had not intended to deprive it of discretionary authority to find craft unions inappropriate for collective bargaining purposes under all circumstances. In *Mallinckrodt,* the Board held that all relevant factors would be considered in each case. Not only would the interests of craft employees be considered, but also the effect that severance might have on the effectiveness of the industrial unit. In other words, the NLRB had repudiated *American Potash,* and would no longer permit craft employees to break away from an industrial unit on an automatic basis; they might or might not be permitted to do so, depending upon the particular circumstances of a case. On the other hand, unions representing craft employees gained a concession from the new policy. When appropriate, the Board would permit craft employees to break away from the industrial unit in the basic steel, aluminum, lumber, and wet milling industries. In other words, regardless of the industry, the Board would permit severance of skilled employees under appropriate circumstances.

In *Mallinckrodt,* the Board established some basic principles and standards to apply to all industries on a case-by-case basis, but it refused to restrict itself to the ones mentioned because of the inappropriateness of purely mechanistic rules. Considerations described by the Board as relevant to such a decision were (1) status of the employees as craftsworkers working at their craft, or as employees in a traditionally distinct department; (2) existing patterns of bargaining relationships, their stabilizing effect, and the possible effect of altering them; (3) separate identity of the employees within the broader unit; (4) the history and pattern of bargaining in the industry; (5) the degree of integration and interdependence of the production system; and (6) the qualifications and experience of the union seeking to represent the employees.

A few examples will demonstrate how the NLRB has applied the *Mallinckrodt* doctrine. In 1976, the Board refused to sever the "skilled trades" employees from a production unit.[19] To justify this decision, the agency pointed out that the craft employees were highly integrated in the employer's operation and that severance would probably have a disruptive effect on the operation of the business. On the other hand, in another case, the Board permitted a group of toolroom employees to break away from the industrial unit.[20] One of the chief reasons for the decision was the evidence that the industrial union did not represent the toolroom employees fairly in collective bargaining. Whether or not the industrial union represents craft employees effectively in collective bargaining and in the grievance procedure is one factor that the Board will consider in making the determination of severance.[21] Whenever craft employees receive equal treatment from their industrial union, it is not likely that separation will be permitted unless there are other compelling reasons for it. In another case, the Board denied powerhouse employees the opportunity to separate, partly on the basis of a long and stable collective bargaining experience in the company involved.[22] Here the agency pointed out that its decision in that case did not mean that units of powerhouse employees were inherently or presumptively inappropriate and could never be severed. In a later case, powerhouse employees were permitted to have their own union on the basis of special circumstances, including a relatively short bargaining history and the fact that the separation would not necessarily prove disruptive to labor relations.[23] In 1978, the Board refused separation of a group of tool-and-die employees from the industrial unit. Among its reasons, the agency pointed to the functional integration of the production process and the high degree of participation by the employees in contract negotiations.[24]

It is obvious from the new principles established to evaluate severance actions that the Board is attempting to evaluate the rights of all parties involved in such actions. The interests of craft employees are not controlling, and the impact of severance on the larger industrial unit will now be given consideration. In addition, the possible disruptive effect of severance on employer ability to maintain production will also be weighed. The Board further recognizes the effect that technological change has on collective bargaining. In this regard, what is relevant and appropriate for evaluating the collective bargaining process at one point in time may change rapidly enough to render mechanistic rules inappropriate at another point in time.

FOREPEOPLE UNDER THE WAGNER ACT

No legal barrier prevented forepeople from organizing into labor organizations. All employees, regardless of their status in the industrial hierarchy, have had the legal right to organize into associations for the purpose of collective bargaining ever since *Commonwealth* v. *Hunt*. However, labor history has demonstrated that this right could be impaired by employers interfering with the development of rank-and-file organizations. The character of such opposition was revealed in Chapter 7. Accordingly, forepeople had reason to believe that employers would similarly resist the development and operation of their labor organizations. Under these conditions it was expected that forepeople would seek the support of the NLRB to protect them in their organizational activities. As the Board had prevented interference with the growth and activities of rank-and-file unions, forepeople hoped that the Board would extend the same protection to their organizations.

There were two major reasons why forepeople employed throughout industry had reason to believe the Board would grant such protection. One was the fact that traditional forepeople unions had consistently received the full measure of the protection afforded by the Wagner Act. Hence the forepeople employed in, say, manufacturing, felt that the NLRB would certify their organization for the purpose of collective bargaining in the same manner as the agency was prepared to set up bargaining units of forepeople traditionally organized in labor unions.

In the second place, the NLRB did protect forepeople engaged in general industry from discharge caused by their union activities. One typical case involved a construction superintendent of a mining company who had joined a rank-and-file labor organization. After repeated warnings to drop out of the union, the supervisor was discharged. But inasmuch as the NLRB considered the supervisors as "employees" within the terms of the Wagner Act, the employer was directed to reinstate the supervisor. On this point, the NLRB stated that "it does not lie with the employer to advise his employees who happen to be foremen that they may not join unions or to discharge them if they do."[25] Hence, the Board held that it would direct the reinstatement of any supervisor who was discharged because of union activities. This ruling, it must be emphasized, was established *before* the Board was called upon to rule on whether it would set up bargaining units composed of supervisors employed throughout general industry. Since the Board was ready to protect any supervisor discriminated against because of union activities, it was expected that the Wagner Act would cover all forepeople who desired to be classified into bargaining units for collective bargaining purposes. According to this logic, supervisors could not be covered by the Wagner Act for one of its purposes but excluded for another purpose. At least this line of reasoning buoyed up the hopes of those who desired the general application of the Wagner Act to forepeople.

Original NLRB Position on "Foreman Unions."   On June 15, 1942, the NLRB held that forepeople employed throughout general industry could constitute units appropriate for the purpose of collective bargaining.[26] When certified by the NLRB, a "foreman union" would be a statutory bargaining agent and the employer would be required by law to recognize the organization and to bargain collectively with its representatives. The case decided by the NLRB on June 15, 1942, involved fifty-eight low level supervisors engaged in coal mining. The supervisors organized an independent union, called the Mine Officials Union of America.

The NLRB decision attracted the attention of other supervisors. Guaranteed protection of their bargaining rights, the supervisors' labor movement made rapid progress, spearheaded by the Foreman's Association of America (FAA). The number of collective bargaining contracts covering forepeople increased sharply. In general, the leadership of the young movement rested in efficient and militant hands. Actually, many of the officers of the "foreman union" movement were former officers of rank-and-file labor organizations. As noted, during the World War II period, an unprecedented number of rank-and-file workers were promoted to the foreperson level.

Reversal of Policy: The **Maryland Drydock** *Decision.*   Although supervisors were enthusiastic about the Board decision of June 1942, many employers were concerned over it. Employers contended that organized supervisors could not give management their undivided loyalty. One member of the NLRB, G. D. Reilly, supported the employer position. In fact, in the 1942 decision, Reilly dissented, and supervisors had obtained legal support of their bargaining rights by a 2–1 vote. In the spring of 1943, John M. Houston replaced William M. Leiserson as a member of the three-person NLRB. In 1942, Leiserson and the late Harry A.

Millis, wartime chair of the NLRB, had teamed up against Reilly, the effect being that forepeople employed throughout general industry could be classified in bargaining units for the purpose of collective bargaining.

Shortly after new member Houston took office, he voted with Reilly to deny to supervisors the opportunity to bargain collectively under the protection of the Wagner Act. The reversal of policy of the Board on "foreman union" policy was contained in the *Maryland Drydock* decision, handed down by the Board on May 11, 1943.[27] This decision prevented supervisors from obtaining statutory protection while exercising their right of collective bargaining. However, the NLRB ruling did not outlaw forepeople's labor organizations. In spite of the *Maryland Drydock* doctrine, forepeople continued to organize in large numbers. The Foreman's Association of America grew from one chapter and 350 members in September 1941 to 281 chapters and 28,240 members in 1945. Though the *Maryland Drydock* decision was handed down in 1943, the FAA increased its membership from seven chapters and 10,000 members at the end of 1942 to 148 chapters and 32,000 members at the end of 1944. As noted, its membership had dropped off considerably by the end of 1945.

Forepeople's Recognition Strikes.   Notwithstanding employer contentions, some supervisors still believed that collective bargaining offered a method for effectively adjusting their grievances. As they organized into unions, supervisors obviously wanted their associations to be recognized by top management. However, supervisors were not eligible to obtain relief from the National Labor Relations Board. Therefore, there was apparently but one available remedy to implement their right to collective bargaining—the utilization of the strike. By resorting to industrial warfare, forepeople's unions, as had rank-and-file labor organizations in the pre–Wagner Act years, might compel management to bargain collectively. Chair Millis warned his colleagues that forepeople's organizational strikes would be encouraged by their refusal to protect these workers' collective bargaining rights. Actually, such collective bargaining strikes, rendered unnecessary to other workers by the Wagner Act, did take place.

One strike resulting from an employer's refusal to bargain with a forepeople's union paralyzed the production of coal in the eastern mining area. To remedy this situation, the President of the United States seized many of the mines. Supervisors' organizational strikes that occurred in the Detroit industrial area also seriously disrupted war production in that region: "April 1944 . . . foremen in thirteen industrial plants of six corporations walked out. Within two weeks of the start of the strike, Packard with its 35,000 employees closed down [for a few days] because its production did not measure up to Army specifications."[28] Additional evidence indicates that forepeople, after the *Maryland Drydock* decision, made widespread use of the collective bargaining strike. The following table indicates the number of strikes for recognition purposes effected through industry in 1943 and 1944.[29]

Comparison of Recognition Strikes

	1943	*1944*
Total Number Recognition Strikes	92	202
Workers Involved	14,440	169,958
Worker-Days Lost to War Production	71,168	853,118

As noted, the *Maryland Drydock* decision was handed down by the NLRB in 1943. In explaining the great increase in the frequency of these strikes in 1944 as compared with 1943, the Bureau of Labor Statistics reports:

> Work stoppages over questions of union recognition and bargaining rights increased in 1944 both numerically and proportionately. This was due in part to strikes over bargaining rights for foremen and supervisory workers. There were at least 30 such strikes in 1944, involving about 130,000 workers and over 650,000 man-days of idleness.[30]

Supervisors' recognition strikes, apparently encouraged by the *Maryland Drydock* decision, appear to have disrupted war production in 1944. Whereas the total number of recognition strikes in 1943 was comparatively small, the number increased considerably in 1944. And as the Bureau of Labor Statistics concluded, the sharp increase in the number of workers involved in these strikes was largely attributable to forepeople's recognition strikes.

In the light of these considerations, it seems that many of the 1944 supervisors' recognition strikes would not have occurred had supervisors been afforded the opportunity to settle their collective bargaining disputes with the aid of the National Labor Relations Board. Legal protection of their right to self-organization and collective bargaining would have eliminated the causes of these work stoppages.

Final NLRB Position Under Wagner Act. On March 26, 1945, the NLRB decided the *Packard Motor Car Company* case.[31] Therein the agency shifted its ground once again on the supervisors' union problem. Board member Houston changed his viewpoint and voted with Millis to afford legal protection to all supervisors in the exercise of their right to collective bargaining. Supervisors throughout industry were again permitted to form labor organizations, and these unions would be designated as appropriate units for the purpose of collective bargaining. Employers who refused to negotiate with their representatives on an industry basis could be legally compelled to bargain collectively.

The consequences of the *Maryland Drydock* doctrine made the change in the supervisors' union policy of the NLRB almost inevitable. Bulking large as a causal factor in this change were the collective bargaining strikes engaged in by supervisors. In this connection Millis and Houston declared that they could not "shut [their] eyes to these developments."

An additional factor involved the Board's policy on protection of supervisors discriminated against for engaging in union activity. Even before the NLRB had issued its first ruling dealing with the appropriateness of bargaining units of forepeople, it held that supervisors discharged because of union activities would be reinstated by the NLRB. This policy remained unchanged despite the Board's position in the *Maryland Drydock* case. According to the Board, supervisors could not be discriminated against for participating in union activities, but neither could they be classified in units for purposes of collective bargaining.

Such a position is inherently inconsistent. Either supervisors should have been covered by the Wagner Act for all its purposes, or else they should have been stripped of all benefits of the law. In the *Maryland Drydock* case, the Board took the position that supervisors could not be classified into bargaining units under the Wagner Act because they did not fall within the law's definition of "employee." In other words, forepeople, for bargaining-unit purposes, were not employees, but actually fell in the employer category. However, when the issue of discrimination was involved, the Board held that these same forepeople were no longer employers but employees. Hence, in the *Packard* decision, the Board held that forepeople were covered by the Wagner Act for all its purposes. In the absence of strike activity of forepeople following the *Maryland Drydock* decision, it is possible that the Board would have held that supervisors had lost all rights under the statute. Consistency could have been achieved by forfeiture of all benefits of the Wagner Act. However, the Board could scarcely have invited more industrial conflict during the war years.

Events Following the **Packard** *Decision.*   Four important events followed in the wake of the doctrine the NLRB established in the *Packard Motor Car Company* case: (1) extension of the protection of the Wagner Act to supervisors exercising considerable authority within industry; (2) permission to forepeople to choose rank-and-file unions for bargaining representatives; (3) review of the *Packard* decision by the Supreme Court; and (4) agitation for congressional action. A brief discussion of each of these points follows.

After the *Packard* decision was handed down, the Board extended the protection of the Wagner Act to supervisors whose tasks involved a high degree of responsibility and discretion. In other words, the application of the Wagner Act was not to be limited to those forepeople occupying the lower strata of the supervisory hierarchy. Formerly, most of the cases involved forepeople who carried out comparatively minor and routine supervisory tasks and exercised only a slight degree of authority within the plant. At one time the Board called these forepeople the "traffic cops" of industry. Once the *Packard* doctrine was established, however, the Board declared that "we do not believe that the application of the Act to foremen can or arbitrarily should be made to depend upon the type of industry involved, whether mass production or non-mass production, or upon the variation in the duties and responsibilities of foremen from company to company."[32] To illustrate this development, the details of one case may be examined.[33] Such a case involved a group of chain-store managers who organized a supervisors' union. Under the policy established by the company, the store managers exercised the authority to (1) hire and discharge all employees under their supervision; (2) set rates of pay, vacations, and hours of employment of such ordinary workers; (3) establish merchandising policies of their local stores; and (4) exercise general supervision over all operational activities of their respective stores. Thus the NLRB was prepared to make available the protection of the Wagner Act to supervisors who assumed considerable responsibility and exercised much authority within industry.

The second major event following the *Packard* decision attaches to the willingness of the NLRB to certify supervisors' unions for collective bargaining, even though such organizations were associated with a parent union that represented production and maintenance workers. Actually, the Board had established this doctrine before it handed down the *Maryland Drydock* doctrine.[34] Consequently, no great surprise accompanied the NLRB reaffirmation of this policy. Controlling factors that prompted establishment of the doctrine included the following principles: (1) the freedom of choice of bargaining agents is guaranteed by the Wagner Act to all employees; and (2) supervisors are free to choose such a representative independent of the National Labor Relations Act. The NLRB pointed out that the Wagner Act provided full freedom to all employees to choose any labor organization as their bargaining agent. It further declared that supervisors could seek to establish such a bargaining agent through the peaceful and democratic machinery of the NLRB, or else attempt to achieve this recognition by engaging in economic warfare. Thus the NLRB stated:

> By closing the door to the first of these alternatives, the Board would simply turn the direction of the struggle for union recognition from the ballot box to the economic battlefield. We would thus find ourselves in the anomalous position of promoting strikes for union recognition, the very kind of strikes which the Act intended to diminish.[35]

Many people, particularly employers, denounced the Board doctrine. Independent supervisors' unions, they claimed, interfered with the ability of management to operate their facilities. Supervisors' unions affiliated with rank-and-file labor unions even more seriously impaired the management of the business enterprise. According to this view, supervisors could not be loyal to management when they were organized in unions affiliated with rank-and-file organizations. Under such conditions, employers claimed, supervisors would place the interests of the labor union members ahead of those of management.

The NLRB was aware of the different duties and interests of supervisors and of the rank-and-file. For this reason it refused to lump together supervisors and ordinary workers into one bargaining unit. It set up separate bargaining units for supervisors. However, once classified in such a unit, the NLRB held that forepeople and supervisors were free to elect the same bargaining agent as represented the rank-and-file workers of the plant. The fact that the Board made this distinction did not stop the storm of employer protest. Very few Board policies under the Wagner Act stimulated more controversy than the one authorizing supervisors, though classified into separate units, to choose rank-and-file unions as their bargaining agent.

Shortly after the *Packard* case was decided, the Packard Motor Car Company carried the forepeople's battle into the federal courts. It charged that forepeople could not be classified into units for collective bargaining purposes. The company contended that in ruling that they could, the Board had badly misinterpreted the Wagner Act. Actually, the Supreme Court, when it finally decided the case, had no legislative basis to determine the validity of the contention of management. Congress had failed to deal with the position of supervisors in the National Labor Relations Act. No mention of the problem had appeared in congressional committee hearings or in the debate on the floors of Congress. No representative, senator, witness before congressional hearings, or observer of labor relations had brought the supervisor problem to the attention of Congress before the passage of the Wagner Act. Accordingly, the Supreme Court could not refer to legislative intent to determine whether the *Packard* doctrine was consistent with the terms of the Wagner Act.

On March 10, 1947, the Supreme Court of the United States sustained the position of the Board.[36] In upholding the authority of the NLRB to compel an employer to bargain collectively with a union composed of forepeople, Justice Robert H. Jackson, speaking for the majority, stated that the fact that forepeople were employees for purposes of the NLRB "is too obvious to be labored," and that there was nothing in the Wagner Act to indicate that Congress intended to deny benefits. By no means was the Supreme Court decision in the *Packard* case unanimous. The Court was divided 5–4 in its decision, the majority consisting of Associate Justices Jackson, Murphy, Black, Reed, and Rutledge, and the minority including Chief Justice Vinson and Associate Justices Frankfurter, Douglas, and Burton. The minority opinion echoed the fears of employers that the organization of supervisors under the protection of the Wagner Act would "obliterate the line between management and labor."

The *Packard* decision focused the attention of Congress on the "foreman union" problem. Though the supervisors' union in the *Packard* case was independent and not affiliated with any production workers' union, many members of Congress felt that the organization of supervisors constituted a threat to the effective operation of American industry. Consequently, in 1946, congressional action was taken to strip forepeople of all legal protection of their right to self-organization and collective bargaining. In that year, Congress enacted the Case Bill, a law that provided for the general regulation of labor unions. Included in the law was the provision that a foreperson could not be considered as an "employee" for purposes of the Wagner Act. This meant the NLRB could not afford any protection to forepeople in the exercise of their collective bargaining rights. Though the Case Bill, including the foreperson provisions, passed both

Houses of Congress, President Truman vetoed the entire measure. Congress lacked the necessary votes to pass the legislation over the President's veto. With respect to the section of the Case Bill dealing with forepeople, President Truman in his veto message declared:

> This section would strip from supervising employees the right of self-organization and collective bargaining now guaranteed them under the National Labor Relations Act. I feel that this section would increase labor strife, since I have no doubt that supervising employees would resort to self-help techniques to gain the right now given them by law.[37]

SUPERVISORS UNDER TAFT-HARTLEY

When Congress enacted the 1947 labor law, forepeople were fully stripped of all protection of their collective bargaining rights. Taft-Hartley effectively removed forepeople from the jurisdiction of the NLRB. Under its terms the Board could not classify forepeople in units for collective bargaining purposes. This meant that employers had no legal obligation to bargain collectively with unions composed of supervisors. Although the Taft-Hartley law did not outlaw forepeople's labor organizations per se, the removal of legal protection limited the growth of the "foreman union" movement. The Foreman's Association of America rapidly felt the effects of the Taft-Hartley Act. Shortly after passage of the law, the Ford Motor Company declined to recognize the FAA and refused to renew the collective bargaining contract covering its forepeople. As a result, the FAA called an organizational strike. Although the strike lasted 47 days, the FAA lost it, and by this defeat suffered irreparable damage. Many other companies refused to renew contracts, the result being that the FAA membership declined sharply.

In addition to relieving employers of any legal duty to bargain collectively with forepeople's unions, the Taft-Hartley Act permitted them to discriminate against forepeople engaged in union activities. Thus employers can discharge or take any disciplinary action against supervisors because of union activities. In this connection, a federal circuit court declared, "It is clear that Congress intended by the enactment of the Labor Management Relations Act that employers be free in the future to discharge supervisors for joining a union, and to interfere with their union activities."[38] Subsequently, the Supreme Court sustained the decision of the lower federal court when it held that the supervisors' union provisions of Taft-Hartley were constitutional.[39]

In only one way does the NLRB find the discharge of supervisors illegal under Taft-Hartley—when such discharges directly interfere with employee union activities.[40] Before *Parker-Robb Chevrolet,* decided in 1982, the Board did reinstate discharged supervisors if their discharge had been part of a general pattern of employer unfair labor practices. For example, in *Sheraton Puerto Rico,* supervisors and employees wrote a letter to the employer's home office that complained about working conditions at the hotel and requested that the hotel's general manager be replaced. In retaliation, the general manager discharged the supervisor and the employees. Given those circumstances, the Board ruled that the discharge of the supervisors discouraged employee union activities, and ordered the reinstatement of the supervisors and employees.[41]

In *Parker-Robb Chevrolet*, a supervisor demanded an explanation from the employer about the discharge of employees who attended a union organizational meeting. For this conduct, the employer discharged the supervisor. Though the NLRB recognized the general pattern of unfair labor practices, it upheld the discharge of the supervisor, but ordered the reinstatement of the employees. It said:

> the discharge of supervisors as a result of their participation in union or concerted activity—either by themselves or when allied with rank-and-file employees is *not* unlawful for the simple reason that employees, but not supervisors, have rights protected by the Act.

Thus, under current law, only when the discharge of a supervisor *directly* interferes with employees' union rights will the Board order reinstatement. Direct interference, the Board said, will be found in such circumstances as where a supervisor gave testimony adverse to an employer's interest at an NLRB proceeding or during grievance procedure meetings or arbitration, and when the supervisor refused to commit unfair labor practices to prevent the unionization of the employees. Only under circumstances such as these may an employer not lawfully discharge the supervisor.

In any event, Taft-Hartley in effect wiped out the "foreman union" movement. This was the objective of the authors of the statute. Thus Hartley said, "No one had ever considered foremen and other types of supervisors as constituting proper personnel for union organizations."[42] However, the fact that about 30,000 supervisors had already elected to organize contradicts Hartley's viewpoint that *no one* had considered supervisors as individuals suitable for collective bargaining. Supervisors themselves apparently wanted to bargain collectively!

Some people contend that Taft-Hartley does not treat forepeople unfairly because the statute does not actually outlaw forepeople's unions. It is said that the statute merely deprives them of their right to organize and bargain collectively under the protection of the NLRB. This liberty proves of little actual value to supervisors who elect to engage in collective bargaining. Inherently, supervisors possess little bargaining strength. The chief reason for this is that they represent a rather small percentage of all workers in a plant. Thus, in the event of a strike, their jobs can be covered fairly well by top supervisors or even by the rank-and-file. The FAA lost its forty-seven day Ford strike as a result of these factors. The point is that without legal support, a supervisors' union movement cannot become effective. Supervisors cannot rely on their own economic strength to gain recognition. Even rank-and-file workers find this a difficult task in the absence of government protection. This is true even though the rank-and-file possess the necessary power to close down entire plants or important sections of firms. Supervisors do not possess this power. They have insufficient economic strength to make organizational strikes effective. Such strikes are lost before they are begun. Their success during World War II was based on the tight wartime labor market and the willingness of some companies to make major concessions in the interest of wartime production and profits. In peacetime, supervisors have not resorted to the organizational strike because they are aware of the slim chance of gaining recognition through the utilization of economic power.

On the basis of these considerations, the conclusion must be reached that Taft-Hartley removed supervisors from effective union activities. Actually, the law's position on supervisors' unions appears inconsistent. If supervisors' unions are deemed undesirable from the public's point of view, they should be outlawed. It is illogical for a statute to permit them to exist but to take away the only means of making them effective—legal support. Supervisors have the permission to organize, but as a result of institutional factors are unable to do so without positive government support.

Constant efforts since 1947 have been made to change the law and bring supervisors within the scope of its protective features. For example, in 1976, a bill was introduced into the 94th Congress to accomplish this objective. As in the past, Congress refused to adopt such a measure. The employer point of view still prevails, as expressed by a representative of the Chamber of Commerce of the United States, who testified:

> This bill is, therefore, objectionable and undesirable not only because it tends to break down the managerial structure of companies, but because it has the potential to work against the interest of individual employees, particularly those who do not choose to play an activist role in affairs of the labor organization—a right equally protected by the Act.
>
> Finally, it should be considered that an employer is entitled to continue operating during a strike. To permit the unionization of supervisors would make continued operations virtually impossible, thus unnecessarily prolonging strikes and depriving an employer of an economic weapon which he is entitled to use in an effort to end a strike.[43]

MANAGERIAL EMPLOYEES OTHER THAN SUPERVISORS

Unlike supervisors, other managerial employees are not excluded from Taft-Hartley by express language. Under the terms of the law, a foreperson or supervisor is defined as a person who has the authority to enforce the labor relations program of a company. It would include those who have the authority to hire, transfer, suspend, lay off, recall, promote, discharge, or discipline employees, or effectively to recommend such action, or those who adjust employees' grievances. Clearly, there are many managerial employees who do not perform these duties. They are managers, but they do not perform the duties of supervisors as such duties are spelled out in the law. In this light, it came as a shock to some observers of the labor relations scene when the U.S. Supreme Court in 1974 held that all managerial employees are excluded from the scope of Taft-Hartley.[44] Previously, the NLRB had held that managerial employees who were not supervisors were covered by the statute.[45] In the Board's view, managerial employees who did not execute the labor relations policy of their employer did not have any conflict of interest should they form a union. It stated that the "fundamental touchstone" in determining whether employees are to be excluded from coverage of the law as managerial personnel is whether their duties

> do or do not include determinations which should be made free of any conflict of interest which could arise if the person was a participating member of a labor organization.

Since the management personnel involved in that case, a group of buyers, did not perform the duties of supervisors, or execute labor relations policies of the company, the Board held that there could not be any conflict of interest. Therefore, it held that managerial employees as a group should not automatically be excluded from the law. In short, until 1974, the Board was prepared to exclude only those managerial employees who participate in "the formulation, determination, or effectuation of [management] policy *with respect to employee matters.*"[46]But in *Bell Aerospace* in 1974, the high court by a 5–4 decision held that no managerial employees are covered by the law, placing them in the same category as forepeople. The majority said that the legislative history of Taft-Hartley supported this decision. Thus

> the legislative history strongly suggests that there were other employees much higher in the managerial structure, who were likewise regarded so clearly outside the Act that no specific exclusionary provision was thought necessary.... We think the inference is plain that "managerial employees" were paramount among this impliedly excluded group.

In short, the Supreme Court ruled that all managerial employees are excluded from protection of the law, and not just those who hold positions susceptible to conflict of interest in labor relations, as the Board previously held.

Four members of the Court sharply dissented, arguing that neither the legislative history of the law, its actual statutory provisions, nor the precedents of the NLRB justified the exclusion of managerial employees. They argued that "there is no reason here to hamstring the Board and deny a broad category of employees the protection of the law."

One feature of the majority's decision requires additional discussion. In the final analysis, the majority held that there is no need for Congress to exclude managerial employees other than forepeople by express language because at one time the Board did exclude this group.[47] The majority reasoned that Congress had no need to exclude managerial employees by literal language, as it did in the case of forepeople, because the Board had already done that. However, we know that the NLRB frequently changes its policies on many features of the law. Congress was certainly aware of this when it adopted Taft-Hartley. To make sure that the Board would not again deny craft employees the right to self-determination elections because they were previously included in an industrial unit, Congress by express language told the Board that it no longer had the discretion to adopt such a policy. This matter was fully explained in the craft employees' section of this chapter. It would be difficult to defend the majority decision of the Court in *Bell Aerospace* on the basis that Congress believed that it is not necessary to exclude managerial employees expressly as a group because the Board had previously excluded them. To accept the majority's reasoning, one would have to assume that Congress was not aware that the Board shifts its policies in the construction of the statute. The conclusion appears inescapable that if Congress had intended to exclude all managerial employees from the coverage of the law, it would have adopted express language to accomplish this objective. Instead of this approach, it excluded only those supervisors who play a part in the execution of a company's labor relations program.

Though *Bell Aerospace* excludes all managerial employees from the scope of the statute, the Supreme Court in that decision did not define the category. Instead of doing that, it remanded the case to the Board to determine whether buyers, the group involved in this case, were managerial employees. In 1975, the Board held that buyers were not managerial employees and so had the protection of the law.[48] It said that buyers are not "true" managerial employees because they did not "formulate and effectuate management policies by expressing and making operative the decisions of the employer." The Board observed that buyers often had only to sign a purchase order or place a telephone call to perform their duties.

To confuse this matter, the persons excluded under *Bell Aerospace* were those who exercise decision-making power to effectuate management policies. These are "true" managerial employees, and they are denied legal protection in union organization and collective bargaining. On the other hand, there are those who are covered by the law because they do not "formulate and effectuate" management policies. It is up to the Board in a particular case to determine whether or not a group falls within the concept of "true" managerial employees.

In one case, it would seem that the Board had departed from its own definition of managerial employees.[49] Some management trainees tried to form a union and were discharged by their employer. Upon review of the case, the NLRB held that management trainees were managerial employees and refused to reinstate the discharged employees. It ruled that this group were managerial employees within the meaning of *Bell Aerospace,* even though they did not formulate and effectuate management policies.

PLANT GUARDS

During World War II, every plant of any significance employed a plant protection force. Before Pearl Harbor, plant-security employees were ordinarily under the direct control of private employers. However, when the United States entered the war, approximately 200,000 plant guards throughout the country became members of the civilian auxiliary to the military police. Many plant guards of both the militarized and nonmilitarized categories wanted to organize and bargain collectively under the protection of the National Labor Relations Board. Some employers, however, vigorously contended that plant guards had no standing under the Wagner Act. In general, employers argued that guards were not "employees" within the meaning of the Wagner Act because of the nature of their duties. Thus the Board was compelled to decide whether plant guards, whether militarized or nonmilitarized, could form appropriate units under the Wagner Act for collective bargaining purposes. It is reported that "few single questions have been contested in NLRB proceedings more often during [World War II] than union organization of plant guards."[50]

In a series of decisions, the NLRB held that plant guards, similar to production and maintenance workers, enjoyed the full protection of the National Labor Relations Act. Not only did the Board hold that nonmilitarized guards could select bargaining agents who did not represent production workers, but the NLRB also ruled that a plant guards' (nonmilitarized) union constituted an appropriate bargaining unit even though the union was affiliated with a production workers' union.

Principles established by the Board for the organization problem of nonmilitarized guards remained in force for guards who became members of the civilian auxiliary to the military police. Militarized guards' unions that were affiliated with production workers' labor organizations received as much protection from the Wagner Act as did independent militarized plant-protection unions. In a case in which the NLRB held that a production workers' labor organization could properly represent a unit of militarized guards, the Board declared: "Freedom to choose a bargaining agent includes the right to select a representative which has been chosen to represent the employees of the employer in a different bargaining unit."[51]

Though full protection of the Wagner Act was available to plant guards during World War II, the Board classified plant-protection employees in units separate from those that included rank-and-file workers. This distinction was deemed necessary because of the difference in functions of plant guards and production workers. Beyond this limitation, security employees, classified in separate units, were afforded the opportunity to choose any bargaining agent as their representative. Thus a number of militarized plant-protection employees of the Chrysler Corporation selected the United Automobile Workers of America as their bargaining agent.

The Supreme Court of the United States upheld the ruling of the National Labor Relations Board. On May 19, 1947, the high court held that the provisions of the National Labor Relations Act were applicable to the collective bargaining activities of plant-protection employees. The decision of the Supreme Court established that plant-protection employees, whether or not militarized or depu-

tized, could form labor organizations and bargain collectively under protection of the National Labor Relations Act. The Court held, moreover, that plant guards classified in separate bargaining units could select production and maintenance employees' labor organizations as their bargaining agents. In commenting on this issue, the Court declared that to prevent guards "from choosing a union which also represents production and maintenance employees is to make the collective bargaining rights of guards distinctly second class."[52]

The Supreme Court decisions were announced while a joint congressional committee was considering Taft-Hartley and directed immediate attention to the status of plant-protection employees. When the conference committee returned the bill to Congress, a provision was included that prevented the full application of the protective features of the Taft-Hartley Act to plant guards. Under the terms of the 1947 labor law, any union of plant guards affiliated with a rank-and-file organization could not be certified by the NLRB. Thus the Taft-Hartley Act nullified the decision of the Supreme Court that held that the NLRB could properly certify a single labor union as the appropriate bargaining agent for both plant guards and production workers.

In administering the plant-guard section of the Taft-Hartley Act, the Board adopted a literal interpretation. Shortly following the passage of the Act, the AFL chartered a union to represent plant guards and no other workers. But the NLRB refused to certify the plant guards' union on the ground that it was affiliated with the AFL, a parent body composed of production and maintenance workers' international unions.

The meaning of this decision for plant guards' unions is clear. To qualify for certification by the NLRB, a labor organization of plant-protection employees must have no affiliation or connection with labor unions admitting production and maintenance workers. As a result, the growth of plant guards' unions was limited. Denied the privilege of anchoring their unions to established production workers' labor organizations, plant guards' unions remained relatively isolated in attempts at collective bargaining.

In 1948, the Board expanded considerably the application of the definition of plant guards as contained in the Taft-Hartley Act. Thus it held in the *C. V. Hill* case that watchmen are guards within the meaning of the Act, regardless of whether they are armed, uniformed, or deputized.[53] In this case, the watchmen were hourly-rated employees and wore the same badges as other employees. Watchmen in some firms are used primarily to check for fires. The effect of this ruling was to deprive a sizable group of employees of the benefits of collective bargaining. Only one qualification was made by the Board with respect to watchmen. The Board originally directed that watchmen could be included in production and maintenance workers' units if not more than 50 percent of their time was devoted to watchman duties.[54] Subsequently, the critical figure dropped to 25 percent.[55] Under current policy, therefore, watchmen who spend at least 25 percent of their time in the enforcement of company rules fall within the definition of plant guards.

In 1966, the Board was again required to determine the employee status of individuals considered guards by an employer.[56] In the *American Telegraph* case, the status of guards as employees within the meaning of Taft-Hartley Section 9(b)(3) dealing with the problem had to be resolved, since the individuals performed protective services by means of electric, electronic, and electromagnetic devices they installed and maintained. The employer argued that the performance of protective services and the servicing and installation of devices classified all such employees as guards because of the integrated nature of the work brought about by new detection techniques. The Board disapproved the employer's argument and held that employees who merely worked on the installation and maintenance of protective equipment did not come within the statutory definition of guards. *Guards* are those individuals engaged in enforcing rules to protect property or the safety of persons on the employer's premises.

In any event, the Board has the continuing problem of determining whether or not certain classifications of employees constitute plant guards within the meaning of the law. Janitors are not considered guards, even though they may hold the keys to the plant and have the authority to admit people into the plant.[57] Because this group did not have the authority to enforce plant rules to protect property or persons on the premises, the Board rejected the employer's contention that his janitors were guards within the meaning of the law. Previously, the Board had held that to be considered a guard an employee must enforce against employees and other persons rules to protect the property of the employer's premises.[58] On the other hand, the Board held that security toll road employees are guards within the meaning of the law because they are empowered to enforce against persons seeking to use the toll roads, the state's rules to protect the property and the safety of users of the roads.[59]

To the extent that the Board broadens the definition of "guard," more employees will be denied statutory rights. In this respect, the Board has held that armored car and express delivery (Brinks and Purolator, for example) employees are guards within the meaning of the law.[60] In an article on this subject, one author states:

> The Board has deviated from the legislative intent that prompted the guard exclusion by enlarging the guard definition to cover "driver guards" and other employees in the armored car and express delivery industries. The law in this area has developed in an erratic fashion without providing any rational criteria for distinguishing guards from nonguards. The result has been an unjustified restriction of basic employee rights under the Act and a concomitant disruption of labor-management relations in the affected industries.[61]

In *Wells Fargo Armored Service,*[62] decided in 1984, the Board held it would not require employers to continue to bargain with a mixed unit containing guards and other employees that had previously been recognized on a voluntary basis. Apparently this policy is applicable regardless of the industry involved, and serves to seriously reduce the statutory protection offered by Taft-Hartley.

Plant-Guard Organization Problems
Under Taft-Hartley

The Taft-Hartley Act decreased the ability of plant guards to engage in collective bargaining. Standing alone, these workers possess very little bargaining strength. This condition results from two factors: (1) they are comparatively few in number in any one plant; and (2) plant guards perform tasks that can be learned rather readily by new employees or can be replaced entirely with guards supplied by a detective agency. As a result of these two conditions, management can easily replace plant-protection employees. Since they are readily replaceable, plant guards cannot employ the strike effectively. This means that plant-guard unions, separated from production employees' labor organizations, cannot make effective use of their economic strength to win concessions. However, plant guards can have their unions certified by the NLRB. Unlike supervisors, they may be reinstated by the NLRB when they are discharged because of union activities.

An independent plant-guard international union was established soon after the passage of Taft-Hartley. This organization has been rather ineffective in promoting the organization of plant guards. The reason for this lack of success, as stated, rests upon the inherently weak bargaining strength of plant-guard unions separated from the established labor organizations. In January 1976, the independent plant-guard union was composed of only 20,000 members, a fraction of the employees who perform plant-protection work.[63]

Employers who sponsored the plant-guard limitations in the 1947 labor law contended that organized guards affiliated with production workers' unions were unable to carry out their duties in an effective and loyal manner. Nothing that happened during World War II indicates that organized plant-protection employees, classified in units separate from production and maintenance workers affiliated with rank-and-file labor unions, could not perform their plant-security duties effectively. The Supreme Court dealt with this problem when it affirmed the position of the NLRB. It refused to regard as controlling the argument that unionized plant guards might be less loyal to management in the execution of their duties. Neither did the Court give much weight to the contention that rank-and-file labor organizations would make demands upon unionized plant guards or force agreements from management that would lessen the loyalty and efficiency of the guards. The Court stated that the process of collective bargaining is "capable of adjustment to accommodate the special function of plant guards." From this statement it appears that the Court would look with disfavor upon certification of a bargaining agent that interferes with the proper execution of duties of plant guards. In addition, it is clear that organized plant guards, discharged because of disloyalty to management, inefficiency, or failure to carry out their duties in an effective manner, would not be reinstated by the Board. The observations of the Supreme Court underscore the fact that if guard unions affiliated with AFL-CIO labor organizations, this would not result in the consequences portrayed by some employers.

Plant guards, similar to ordinary production workers, develop a set of employment grievances. To adjust such complaints, some guards desire to organize and bargain collectively. Such collective bargaining activities cannot be carried out effectively when guard unions are denied the right to affiliate with established labor organizations. Taft-Hartley restriction on plant-guard labor organizations, in the words of the Supreme Court of the United States, "makes the collective bargaining right of guards distinctly second class."

As with the case of supervisors, unsuccessful efforts have been made in the past to provide full protection to the organization and collective bargaining rights of plant guards. They received consideration again in the Labor Law Reform Act of 1977, supported, as mentioned earlier, by President Carter. As part of that law, passed by the House of Representatives in October 1977, the opportunity of plant guards to select a rank-and-file labor organization would have been made available. The measure would have removed the restriction that guards at a plant may be represented only by a union composed exclusively of guards. Had the law passed the Senate, guards could have selected any union to represent them, provided that the union did not represent the other employees in the plant being guarded.

As stated earlier, a filibuster in the Senate blocked passage of the Labor Law Reform Act.

PROFESSIONAL WORKERS

One section of Taft-Hartley provided that the NLRB may not set up a bargaining unit that contains both professional and nonprofessional employees unless a majority of the professional employees vote for inclusion in a combined unit.[64] As noted, agitation for this policy did not come from employers but from professional workers. This group felt that its interests would be served through the setting up of independent professional worker units. Actually, the NLRB under the Wagner Act provided a considerable degree of freedom to professional workers to select their own unions. When a group of workers fell into the professional category, the Board frequently gave them the opportunity to select their own bargaining representatives, provided they wanted separate representation.

Unlike the supervisor, the professional worker may be reinstated by the Board if discharged by an employer because of union activities. Contrary to the plant guard, the professional worker may be represented in collective bargaining by rank-and-file labor organizations. The only restriction on the collective bargaining activities of professional workers contained in Taft-Hartley is the prohibition against including them in the same bargaining unit with nonprofessional workers when a majority of the professional workers vote against inclusion.

The major problem confronting the Board in the administration of this section of the 1947 labor law is the task of deciding which employees are professional workers. Although the Taft-Hartley Act sets up general standards for professional workers, the NLRB must decide which specific groups of employees are professional workers.[65]

The Board has held in one case that to be classed as a "professional employee," a worker does not need a specialized college degree. Thus the NLRB directed that a group of noncollege-trained plant engineers of a telephone company be polled on the question of whether they desired special representation. The Board in another case held that it is not the individual qualifications of employees but rather the character of the work required of them as a group that determines professional status.[66]

Lawyers employed by an insurance company were also classified as professional workers. In this proceeding, the Board rejected the employer's contention that professional employees were removed by the Taft-Hartley Act from the Board's jurisdiction. In a case involving a number of time-study people employed by a pump and machinery company, the Board held that these employees were not supervisors, as the employer urged, but fell within the professional classification. An employer engaged in the designing and construction of office and industrial buildings contended that the "estimators" employed by the firm were not professional workers. The estimators of the company determine the amount of material to be required for the construction of a building and further compute the cost of the material. In rejecting the employer position, the NLRB held the estimators are included within the professional category on the ground that they must possess a high degree of intellectual ability and a substantial background of training, education, and experience. It was further decided that the estimators perform jobs that require the exercise of a considerable degree of judgment and discretion.

Four employees performing accounting work for a manufacturer of window glass were held by the Board as not falling within the professional classification. Three of the four employees performed cost analyses. Training for the job was attained at a local business school and supplemented by a special training course provided by the company. A fourth employee was engaged in appraising the employer's assets and surveying records with the objective of reorganizing the property record accounting system. Even though he had three years of college work and performed work requiring a high degree of intellectual ability, the Board held he was not a professional worker.

Upon another occasion, a group of editorial employees of a newspaper were held not to be professional workers. In reaching this decision, the NLRB declared that the work they performed did not "require knowledge of an advanced type in a field of learning customarily acquired by a course of specialized intellectual instruction in an institution of higher learning as distinguished from a general academic education."[67] Thus a person with a general college education does not because of this fact alone fall within the professional classification, according to the NLRB. In another case involving the newspaper industry, the Board refused to classify special editors, rewrite staff, and out-of-town reporters as professional workers. These groups, in the Board's opinion, perform essentially the same duties as regular newspaper reporters, who are a nonprofessional group. In 1976, the Board reaffirmed its policy that newspaper journalists are not professional employees, rejecting the employer's effort to change its longstanding policy on this matter.[68] In this case, the employer attempted to separate the journalists from the other newspaper employees. Commenting on this case, a representative of the Newspaper Guild stated that the 1976 case should

> mark the end of a publisher attempt to drive a wedge between newspersons and other newspaper employees . . . a tactic clearly designed to weaken the bargaining positions of both.[69]

Radio announcers, singers, and continuity writers are not professional workers within the meaning of the Taft-Hartley Act. Although it was conceded that these groups are trained and skilled personnel, the Board refused to classify them as professional workers. If a professionally trained worker does not perform the duties of his or her profession, he or she will not be treated as a professional worker. In a case involving a professional chemist, the Board held that he was not a professional worker for purposes of the Taft-Hartley Act, on the ground that his job in the plant was the carrying out of duties relating to maintenance electrical work. As a result, he was included in a bargaining unit of maintenance employees.

From the cases reviewed above, it can be seen that the problem of establishing which workers are professional employees for purposes of the Taft-Hartley Act is fraught with difficulty, since no objective standards are available to resolve the problem. The matter will be determined within the area of opinion. The Board has considerable latitude in deciding whether employees are professional or not. Once employees are given professional status, the Board must hold an election to determine if they desire to be included in a bargaining unit with nonprofessionals. The provision of Taft-Hartley requiring a poll of professionals will be enforced by the U.S. Supreme Court, despite another provision of the same law intended to restrict judicial review of Board representation certifications.[70]

Section 9 (d) of the Act provides that the Board "shall decide in each case . . . the unit appropriate for the purposes of collective bargaining." The intent of Congress in giving such authority to the Board was to prevent unions and management from using the courts to delay the initiation of collective bargaining. The long delays that accompany litigation have the effect of frustrating the basic purpose of the Taft-Hartley Act. In this respect, the Board argued in *Leedom* v. *Kyne* that it had exclusive jurisdiction in representation cases. In this case, the NLRB did not poll a group of employees who were apparently professional within the meaning of Taft-Hartley, and included them in a rank-and-file bargaining unit. When the Supreme Court heard the case, it held that the bargaining unit was defective and remanded the case to the NLRB. While reversing the NLRB, the U.S. Supreme Court stated it could not "lightly infer that Congress does not intend judicial protection of rights it confers against agency action taken in excess of delegated powers." As the law now stands, it seems possible that a party dissatisfied with a Board bargaining-unit decision may resort to the courts for relief. Bargaining-unit efforts may be frustrated because a party is not satisfied with Board determinations.

"Extent of Organization"

A labor union instituting an organizing campaign in a plant may fail to induce all the workers to join the union. The union may be successful in organizing only a portion of the workers. When the NLRB administered the Wagner Act, it frequently granted legal protection to the collective bargaining rights of those actually organized. For example, in 1941, the Board held that a group of cutters employed by a company was an appropriate unit, although a large unit comprising all production employees might likewise constitute an appropriate unit. In reaching its decision, the NLRB declared:

> Self-organization among the Company's employees . . . has not extended beyond the limits of the unit proposed by the Union, nor is any organization here seeking to represent employees of the Company other than the cutters. Under these circumstances, we are of the opinion that the unit sought by the Union herein is appropriate. To find otherwise would deprive the cutters of the benefits of collective bargaining until the remaining production employees had organized.[71]

Thus when a group of workers, corresponding to the extent of organization, by majority vote elected to be represented for collective bargaining, the Board under the Wagner Act would certify such a group for the purposes of collective bargaining. The employer was then under legal obligation to bargain collectively with the union representing this group of employees. As noted, the NLRB based this policy on the grounds that the organized workers should not be required to wait until a majority or more of all employees in the bargaining unit were unionized before enjoying the benefits of collective bargaining.

Under the terms of the Taft-Hartley Act, the NLRB may not consider the "extent of organization" as the controlling factor in the setting up of the appropriate bargaining unit. This means that the Board may not certify a union to represent a small group of workers of a large bargaining unit solely on the grounds that a union has been successful in organizing a portion of the larger unit.

The insurance industry has received considerable attention regarding the Section 9(c)(5) congressional change that the extent of union organization shall not be the controlling factor in establishment of the appropriate unit for collective bargaining. In a 1944 case, the Board ruled that only a statewide or company-wide unit of insurance employees was appropriate.[72] The inclusion of insurance employees in such an extensive unit was overruled in 1962 when the Board declared that a city-wide unit of insurance employees was more appropriate than the state- or company-wide situation.[73] It held that there was no longer a rational basis for applying different organizational rules to the insurance industry than are applied to other industries. For example, there has never been any requirement for a labor organization to organize all plants of a particular manufacturing firm operating within a particular state before a single plant of employees will be certified as a unit appropriate to bargain with an employer. In contrast, the insurance industry was treated differently when the Board required all offices within the state or within a particular company to be organized before bargaining would be permitted. Obviously, such a requirement made it virtually impossible for labor organizations to function. Some offices in distant cities might not want to organize, which would prohibit employees in another city from bargaining collectively.

In a series of cases involving the Metropolitan Life Insurance Company, the Board moved away from the statewide unit to both single district offices and various geographic groupings of district offices in establishing bargaining units. The company challenged the Board and argued in various circuit courts that the extent of organization controlled the agency decision in violation of Taft-Hartley. The First Circuit Court agreed with the employer, but the Third and Sixth Circuits Courts disagreed.[74] The Board appealed to the U.S. Supreme Court for a policy clarification.[75]

In its decision, the high court held that the NLRB may properly consider the extent of organization as one factor in the establishment of bargaining units, but not as the controlling factor. It stated:

> Although it is clear that in passing this amendment Congress intended to overrule Board decisions where the unit determined could only be supported on the basis of the extent of organization, both the language and legislative history of 9(c)(5) demonstrate that the provision was not intended to prohibit the Board from considering the extent of organization as one factor, though not the controlling factor, in its unit determination.

However, the Court refused to sustain the Board's order in *Metropolitan Insurance* because of the agency's "lack of articulated reasons" for its establishment of the smaller bargaining units. The case was remanded to the Board for this purpose, and subsequently the agency articulated its reasons. It explained that each of the insurance company's individual offices constituted an administrative entity, and, therefore, an individual citywide unit was appropriate for collective bargaining under Taft-Hartley. In other words, the controlling factor for the establishment of the smaller unit was its independence and autonomy from the parent company. The extent of organization was a subsidiary and not the controlling factor. So far, the administrative entity reason used as the basis for the Board's policy to establish smaller bargaining units has not been upset by the Supreme Court.[76]

Subsequently, the Board spelled out factors that would make a particular store, restaurant, or office of a parent company an administrative entity. In one case, a single restaurant in a chain operation constituted an appropriate bargaining unit because in the day-to-day operation of the restaurant, its manager ordered all of its supplies, contracted for major repairs, did about 60 percent of the hiring, fixed wage rates within the ranges established by central headquarters, trained employees, and had the authority to discharge employees.[77] In another instance, the Board held single stores of a drug chain to be a proper unit for bargaining primarily because of the relatively infrequent visits of representatives of the central management.[78] Later on, in a case involving Michigan Bell Telephone, the Board certified for collective bargaining one of the company's sixty-three commercial offices on the grounds that the office manager had the power to effectuate labor policy. It rejected the employer's position that only a statewide unit of all the commercial department employees should be appropriate. In the Board's view, a single office was appropriate because the manager had the authority and responsibility to recommend promotion and merit increases, to schedule overtime and vacations, to discharge and suspend employees for disciplinary reasons, to issue warnings, and to direct the work of the employees.[79] On the other hand, the Board refused to establish a single store as appropriate, on the grounds that the parent corporation placed sharp limitations on store managers in the matter of personnel policies; considerable employee interchange between stores occurred; and district supervisors of the central headquarters had direct supervision over store departments.[80]

In short, the key to the establishment of a store or office of a chain operation as a bargaining unit is the autonomy and independence of the unit from control of central headquarters. When this finding is made, the Board applies its administrative entity principle. Each case will be determined on its own merits, since multistore or office operations differ widely in the amount of control exerted by the parent company. In any event, the *Metropolitan Insurance* doctrine has facilitated more organization among white-collar and service employees. Union efforts can be concentrated on smaller units of these employees without the necessity of dealing with a large dispersed unit of identical workers of the same company. Thus, the task of organization is easier within industries such as insurance, chain drug, restaurants, supermarkets, banking, and in other kindred industries that operate on a multistore or office basis.

COORDINATED BARGAINING

Several labor organizations that deal separately with a single employer have found that their bargaining power might be enhanced if they are successful in establishing a joint bargaining relationship. That is, unions desire to confront management collectively at the same time on contractual issues of mutual interest. The term *coordinated* or *coalition bargaining* may also refer to the presence of other unions' delegates on a nonvoting basis in proceedings involving another union and the employer. The basic purpose is to prevent some bargaining units from approving settlements less desirable than those reached by some other units. This issue is critical when the labor movement is considered in its totality. For example, some firms such as General Electric bargain with a large number of unions representing workers in various parts of the country. The copper industry is still another example. All collective bargaining contracts may not be subject to negotiation at the same time. Because of the different expiration dates, a firm may successfully resist union demands in one plant located in one section of the country through its ability to increase output in another plant in a different region. This arrangement is especially convenient for management when unemployment rates are relatively high. This indicates that there may be considerable excess productive capacity within a firm. A decision to shift production from plant to plant is difficult to realize when there is relatively little excess capacity during periods of high demand for goods and services. Thus in the last half of the 1960s as the economy neared relative full employment, unions opened a drive to change the historical pattern of bargaining. They have achieved some successes from their efforts.

In 1968, in the *General Electric Company* case, the NLRB set a precedent for future coordinated bargaining by permitting a union to include representatives of other unions on its negotiating committee.[81] Representatives of other unions included in the negotiations do have to belong to labor organizations having contracts with the involved firm. Even though they may sit in during negotiations, they are denied voting privileges. The Board, however, did not rule on several important issues in deciding the case. One is whether a company may refuse to bargain if participating unions enter into an agreement on the circumstances under which they would sign a contract with the employer. Still another problem is involved if a company refuses to bargain when the unions continue to press their demand for joint bargaining.[82] The Board in a 1962 case upheld the legality of an interunion agreement that no single union would sign a contract providing less than the agreed-upon conditions without the consent of the other labor organizations.[83] Each union, however, was free to sign a collective bargaining agreement containing the common demands.

Essentially, the *General Electric* decision broadens the concept of bargaining-unit negotiations. Many decisions may now be made at interunion conferences and not at the bargaining table. This type of bargaining may be defended only on the basis that the problems and issues confronting one bargaining unit are the same as those that face all the others. Otherwise, the NLRB with the approval of the U.S. Court of Appeals of New York City has permitted external union influence to shape the content of labor agreements.[84] The federal court was aware of the possibility of damage that could be done to bargaining-unit boundaries, but declared that the facts of the case did not demonstrate a clear and present danger to the bargaining process.

The NLRB has held interunion agreements unlawful when they require that no labor organization will sign a contract until all other unions have been offered the common demands. In 1972, the Board was overruled on this issue among others in *Phelps Dodge*.[85] During the 1967–1968 negotiations, Phelps Dodge dealt with the United Steelworkers of America and at least twenty-five other international unions. The unions through the Industrial Union Department of the AFL-CIO set up the Nonferrous Industry Conference to establish coalition bargaining. The Industry Conference set up joint union negotiating committees for each company. Phelps Dodge charged that the unions' objective was to obtain company-wide master agreements and common contract termination dates in the industry. The NLRB upheld the Phelps Dodge charge that the committee's insistence on the two items and delay of strike settlement until other company units reached agreements amounted to the same thing as demanding company-wide bargaining. The contract had been submitted to the Nonferrous Industry Conference for approval. Such behavior was viewed by the Board as illegal because it lay outside the mandatory bargaining category.

The Third Circuit Court of Appeals disagreed with the Board. It ruled that since negotiations were conducted at separate locations, and since no bargaining in any unit involved discussion of terms and conditions of employment in other units, the unions' behavior was legal. The appeals court also established that a union can strike for a limited no-strike clause and a "most favored nation" clause. Thus, a union is permitted to strike in support of workers in other bargaining units of the same employer under certain circumstances.

The Supreme Court refused to review the decision. This does not mean that the high court will not deal with the coalition bargaining issue at some future date. In the meantime, union efforts to expand the scope of bargaining beyond established units have been strengthened. Renewed activity to coordinate bargaining in other industries can be expected to follow the procedure used in the copper industry.

SUMMARY

Under the Wagner Act, the NLRB had full authority to establish the unit appropriate for collective bargaining. Taft-Hartley placed limitations on its authority by forbidding the Board to establish supervisors' bargaining units or units of plant guards that are affiliated with a production workers' union. Also, the Board must provide professional employees with the opportunity to vote in a special election before it includes the union in a unit composed of other employees. In 1974, the U.S. Supreme Court held that no managerial employees, like forepersons, are covered by the statute.

Under current policy, the NLRB will determine whether craft employees may separate from an industrial bargaining unit on a case-by-case basis. With respect to the problem of the extent of organization, the Board will certify single stores or offices of an employer's business when it finds that the single unit is an administrative entity. In those cases, the Board held that the extent of organization is not the controlling factor in the establishment of the smaller unit. An employer violates the law by refusing to bargain with different unions on a coordinated or coalition basis.

DISCUSSION QUESTIONS

1. Appropriate bargaining-unit guidelines were established under the Wagner Act to make the collective bargaining process effective. Discuss the factors considered by the Board when units were established.

2. What was controversial about the bargaining-unit appropriateness of the following: craft workers in industrial units, supervisors, other managerial employees, plant guards, professionals, and the extent of organization? How did Taft-Hartley deal with each of the controversial areas?

3. When may craft workers be separated from an industrial unit into appropriate craft units?

4. Under what circumstances might supervisors receive Taft-Hartley protection from discharge?

5. How does a broader definition of what constitutes a plant guard affect the basic Taft-Hartley rights of the workers involved? How valid are arguments that plant guards must be organized separately from all rank-and-file affiliations in order to protect the employer's position?

6. What is the definition of a professional worker for bargaining unit purposes? What standards are used by the NLRB to classify workers as professionals?

7. Discuss the controversies surrounding coordinated bargaining.

NOTES

1   National Labor Relations Board, *First Annual Report,* U.S. Government Printing Office, Washington, D.C., 1936, p. 112.

2   2 NLRB 374 (1936).

3   National Labor Relations Board, *Fourth Annual Report,* U.S. Government Printing Office, Washington, D.C., 1939, p. 83.

4   National Labor Relations Board, *Twelfth Annual Report,* U.S. Government Printing Office, Washington, D.C., 1947, p. 87.

5   *Pittsburgh Plate Glass Company* v. *NLRB,* 313 U.S. 146 (1941). In this case, the Supreme Court held that the courts were forbidden to set aside a bargaining-unit determination by the NLRB as long as the NLRB had exercised its power to designate the unit in a reasonable manner and had supported its findings with evidence.

6   *American Rolbal Corporation,* 41 NLRB 907 (1942).

7   *General Steel Castings Corporation,* 41 NLRB 350 (1942).

8   R. R. R. Brooks, *Unions of Their Own Choosing* (New Haven: Yale University Press, 1937), p. 164.

9   *Globe Machine & Stamping Company,* 3 NLRB 294 (1937).

10   *General Electric Company,* 58 NLRB 57 (1944).

11   *American Can*, 13 NLRB 1252 (1939).

12   Bureau of National Affairs, *Labor Relations Reporter*, XV (December 4, 1944), p. 396.

13   *National Tube Company*, 76 NLRB 169 (1948).

14   *American Potash & Chemical Corporation*, 107 NLRB 290 (1954).

15   National Planning Association, *Causes of Industrial Peace Under Collective Bargaining*, Study No. 1, p. 15.

16   *NLRB v. Pittsburgh Plate Glass Company*, 270 F. (2d) 26 (1959).

17   *Kennecott Copper Company*, 138 NLRB 3 (1962).

18   *Mallinckrodt Chemical Works*, 162 NLRB 48 (1966).

19   *Firestone Tire & Rubber Co.*, 222 NLRB 1254 (1976).

20   *Buddy L. Corp.*, 167 NLRB 808 (1967).

21   *Trico Products Corp.*, 169 NLRB 287 (1968).

22   *Mobil Oil Corp.*, 169 NLRB 259 (1968).

23   *Towmotor Corp.*, 187 NLRB 1027 (1971).

24   *LA-Z-Boy Chair Co.*, 235 NLRB No. 11 (1978).

25   *Golden Turkey Mining Company*, 34 NLRB 779 (1941).

26   *Union Collieries Coal Company*, 41 NLRB 961 (1942).

27   *Maryland Drydock Company*, 49 NLRB 733 (1943).

28   *New York Times*, March 11, 1947.

29   U.S. Department of Labor, Bureau of Labor Statistics, *Monthly Labor Review*, LX, 5 (May 1945), p. 968; LVIII, 5 (May 1944), p. 937.

30   *Ibid.*, p. 967.

31   *Packard Motor Car Company*, 61 NLRB 4 (1945).

32   *L. A. Young Spring & Wire Corporation*, 65 NLRB 301 (1946).

33   *Great Atlantic & Pacific Tea Company*, 69 NLRB 463 (1946).

34   *Godchaux Sugar Company*, 44 NLRB 874 (1942).

35   *Jones & Laughlin Steel Corporation*, 66 NLRB 400 (1946).

36   *Packard Motor Car Company v. NLRB*, 67 S. Ct. 789 (1947).

37   Bureau of National Affairs, *Labor Relations Reporter*, June 17, 1946, p. 123.

38   *NLRB v. Budd Manufacturing Company*, 138 F. (2d) 86 (1948).

39   335 U.S. 908 (1949).

40   *Parker-Robb Chevrolet, Inc.*, 262 NLRB No. 58 (1982). Enf. *Food and Commercial Workers, Local 1095, Automobile Salesmen's Union v. NLRB*, CA-DC, No. 82-2264, June 30, 1983. For an excellent treatment of this general problem, see Gail Frommer Brod, "The NLRB Changes Its Policy on the Legality of an Employer's Discharge of a Disloyal Supervisor," *Labor Law Journal*, XXXIV, 1 (January 1983), p.13.

41   *Sheraton Puerto Rico*, 248 NLRB No. 113 (1980).

42   Fred Hartley, *Our New National Labor Policy* (New York: Funk & Wagnalls Company, 1948), p. 56.

43   *Oversight Hearings on the National Labor Relations Board*, Hearings Before Subcommittee on Labor-Management Relations, Committee on Education and Labor, House of Representatives, 94th Congress, 2nd sess., February 17, 1976, p. 14.

44   *NLRB v. Bell Aerospace Co.*, 416 U.S. 267 (1974).

45   *Bell Aerospace Co.*, 196 NLRB 827 (1972).

46   *North Arkansas Electric Cooperative*, 185 NLRB 550 (1970).

47   *Swift and Co.*, 115 NLRB 752 (1956).

48   *Bell Aerospace Co.*, 219 NLRB 384 (1975).

49   *Curtis Noll Corp.*, 218 NLRB 222 (1975).

50   *Labor Relations Reporter,* XV (January 1, 1945), p. 4.

51   *Chrysler Corporation,* 44 NLRB 886 (1942).

52   *NLRB* v. *Atkins & Company,* 331 U.S. 398 (1947); *NLRB* v. *Jones & Laughlin Steel Corporation,* 331 U.S. 416 (1947).

53   *C. V. Hill,* 76 NLRB 24 (1948).

54   *Steelweld Equipment Company,* 76 NLRB 116 (1948).

55   *Reynolds Metals Co.,* 198 NLRB 120 (1972).

56   *American District Telegraph Company,* 160 NLRB 1130 (1966).

57   *Meyer Manufacturing Co.,* 170 NLRB 509 (1968).

58   *Petroleum Chemicals, Inc.,* 121 NLRB 630 (1958).

59   *The Wackenhut Corp.,* 196 NLRB 278 (1972).

60   *Purolator Courier Corp.,* 268 NLRB No. 67 (1983). *Brinks, Inc.,* 226 NLRB 1182 (1976).

61   Kahn, Stephen, "The NLRB Misinterpretation of the Guard Provision," *Labor Law Journal,* XXXV, 6 (June, 1984), p. 328.

62   *Wells Fargo Armored Service Corp.,* 270 NLRB No. 106 (1984).

63   U.S. Department of Labor, Bureau of Labor Statistics, *Directory of National Unions and Employee Associations,* January 1976, p. 49.

64   Section 9 (b)(1).

65   Section 2 (12) defines a *professional employee* as follows:

> (a) any employee engaged in work (i) predominantly intellectual and varied in character as opposed to routine mental, manual, mechanical, or physical work;(ii) involving the consistent exercise of discretion and judgment in its performance;(iii) of such a character that the output produced or the result accomplished cannot be standardized in relation to a given period of time; (iv) requiring knowledge of an advanced type in a field of science or learning customarily acquired by a prolonged course of specialized intellectual instruction and study in an institution of higher learning or a hospital, as distinguished from a general academic education or from an apprenticeship or from training in the performance of routine mental, manual, or physical processes; or (b) any employee, who (i) has completed the courses of specialized intellectual instruction and study described in clause (iv) of paragraph (a), and (ii) is performing related work under the supervision of a professional person to qualify himself to become a professional employee as defined in paragraph (a).

66   *Ryan Aeronautical Company,* 132 NLRB 1160 (1962).

67   *Free Press Company,* 76 NLRB 152 (1948).

68   *Express-News Corp.,* 223 NLRB 97 (1976).

69   *AFL-CIO News,* April 17, 1976.

70   *Leedom* v. *Kyne,* 358 U.S. 184 (1958).

71   *Crescent Dress Company,* 29 NLRB 351 (1941).

72   *Metropolitan Life Insurance Company,* 56 NLRB 1635 (1944).

73   *Quaker City Life Insurance Company,* 134 NLRB 960 (1962).

74   *Metropolitan Life Insurance Company* v. *NLRB,* 327 F. (2d) 906 (CA 1) denying enforcement of 142 NLRB 491; *Metropolitan Life Insurance Company* v. *NLRB,* 328 F. (2d) 820 (CA 3) enforcing 141 NLRB 337; *Metropolitan Life Insurance Company* v. *NLRB,* 330 F. (2d) 62 (CA 6) enforcing 141 NLRB 1074.

75   *NLRB* v. *Metropolitan Life Insurance Company,* 380 U.S. 438 (1965).

76   Federal courts have at times reversed the Board when they have found that there was not sufficient autonomy of the single store or office. For example, see *NLRB* v. *Purity Foods*, 376 F. (2d) 497, cert. denied 389 U.S. 959 (1967). This case and the subsequent action of the Supreme Court, however, should not be regarded as a reversal of the administrative entity doctrine. Rather, it should be regarded as an instance where the courts have disagreed with the Board's finding that the smaller unit was autonomous from the parent operation.

77   *Haag Drug Company,* 169 NLRB 877 (1968).

78   *Walgreen Company,* 198 NLRB 1138 (1972).

79   *Michigan Bell Telephone Co.,* 216 NLRB 806 (1975).

80   *Star Market,* 172 NLRB 1393 (1968).

81   *General Electric Company,* 173 NLRB 46 (1968).

82   *Monthly Labor Review, op. cit.,* XLII, 4 (April 1969), pp. 56-58.

83   *Standard Oil Company,* 137 NLRB 690 (1962).

84   *General Electric Company* v. *NLRB,* 358 F. (2d) 292 (1969).

85   *AFL-CIO Joint Negotiating Committee for Phelps Dodge* v. *NLRB,* 459 F. (2d) 374 (CA 3, 1972).

CHAPTER FOURTEEN

CONTROLS ON
THE SUBSTANCE OF BARGAINING

Government control over collective bargaining involves more than restrictions placed on certain economic weapons that may be used to obtain the particular contractual provisions desired by either management or unions. Control is extended also to restrictions placed on particular provisions that may be included in the collective bargaining agreement. Some union-security provisions are prohibited by law whereas many other items, such as subcontracting, are subject to bargaining. Impasses on some items may justify strikes or lockouts. Other subjects must be abandoned if the parties fail to reach agreement on them. That is, bargaining may take place voluntarily on some issues, but in the absence of agreement the parties are forbidden from striking or locking out to influence the contractual result. This chapter focuses on the issues and forms of union security, checkoff provisions, and NLRB policy regarding good-faith bargaining. Under certain circumstances, the Board defers the task of determining whether employers have complied with their bargaining obligations to private arbitrators.

UNION SECURITY: A CONTROVERSIAL ISSUE

Union security is a primary aim of most labor organizations. It usually involves some form of compulsory membership as a condition of employment. Automatic checkoff of union dues is a usual feature of such arrangements. Very few issues of collective bargaining are more controversial than the problem of union security. Union-security objectives include protection against employer discrimination, worker defection, and rival union raiding tactics.[1]

Unions contend that compulsory membership as a condition of employment precludes the possibility of some workers receiving the benefits of unionism without bearing the risks and obligations of union activities. A union is the legal bargaining agent for all employees in the bargaining unit whether or not the employees are union members. This means that benefits that the union secures in collective bargaining apply to union members and nonunion employees. Also, the union has the legal obligation to represent all employees in the bargaining unit in the grievance procedure. Unions argue, therefore, that nonunion employees are "free riders" and secure the same benefits as union members. Even the courts have recognized the character of this union argument. In a case that involved the constitutionality of the union shop, William F. Buckley, the columnist and magazine editor, and M. Stanton Evans, the editor of the *Indianapolis News*, argued that compulsory union membership violates the constitutional right to free speech. For reasons to be made clear later on, the courts held that "free riders" were not required to be members of their union. However, it was held that the union had the right to levy

> mandatory dues on all employees who will reap the benefits of the union's representation of them in the contract negotiations with the employer.[2]

More recently, Congress also recognized the service function that unions perform for employees in the bargaining unit. In 1980, it enacted an amendment to Taft-Hartley that exempted from compulsory union membership employees who have bona fide religious beliefs against joining labor organizations or financially supporting them.[3] The law says a labor agreement may provide that such persons must make a contribution equal to the amount of dues to a nonlabor, nonreligious charity. More pertinent, however, to our discussion at this point is that the amendment provides that if the religious objector requests that a labor organization handle a grievance on his or her behalf, the union may charge the employee a reasonable cost for such a service.

It is also claimed that in the absence of some union-security arrangement, union leaders must devote a large share of their time to organizing activities, since there is of necessity a constant effort to enlist members. This means that there may be less time available for efforts to improve conditions of work in the bargaining unit. Unions also argue that worker morale is improved when union membership is required. Freedom to remain outside the labor organization leads to conflict between union and nonunion workers. Union workers have historically preferred not to work with nonunion workers. It is argued that the production process could be carried out more efficiently if conflicts between the two could be avoided.

It is further contended that union security permits union discipline. A labor organization may be in a better position to enforce contractual provisions if it is able to discipline workers for violating the terms of the collective bargaining agreement. Enforcement is simpler if it is well known that expulsion from the union carries with it loss of job. Thus union-security clauses place unions in a better position to enforce internal organizational rules and regulations that result in a more disciplined organization. Essentially, the claim is that union security provides a greater degree of union responsibility.

Arguments presented against compulsory union membership are several. One is that union security may make some union leaders unresponsive to the needs of members. Workers may receive less than the full amount of service they should receive from their union leaders.

Still another argument that is widely discussed in many public circles is that the requirement of union membership as a condition of employment deprives a person of the freedom to work. The influence of this argument on the general public is currently reflected in the "right-to-work" laws of twenty states, as will be discussed later in this chapter. The elimination of compulsory union membership is also advanced as one method of dealing with excessive union power.

Most debates over union security are largely emotional. Generalizations are made on the basis of limited and usually unrepresentative information. Until more adequate data are available, the debate will continue.

Forms of Union Security

Several union-security devices have come into being over the years. There are three primary arrangements that unions have used to fulfill the objective of union security: closed shop, union shop, and maintenance of membership. Although each arrangement has its own distinguishing characteristics, all are common in requiring continued union membership as a condition of employment. These forms differ, however, in the timing for the requirement of union membership and in the degree of freedom permitted workers to decide whether to join organizations.

The *closed shop* and *union shop* are dissimilar in that under the former, the worker must belong to the union before obtaining a job. The latter requires union membership within a certain time period after the worker is hired. Under a *maintenance-of-membership* arrangement, the worker is free to elect whether or not to join the union. Once the worker does join, however, she or he must maintain membership in the union for the duration of the contract period, or forfeit employment. However, toward the end of the contract, the employee may withdraw from the union and still hold the job should the same device be incorporated in the next contract. Usually this "escape period" is between 15 and 30 days prior to the termination of the contract.

The maintenance-of-membership device was utilized heavily by the National War Labor Board (NWLB) during World War II as a compromise device between the union-security demands of organized labor and the principle laid down by President Roosevelt that "the Government of the United States will not order nor will Congress pass legislation ordering a so-called closed shop."[4] The President's statement was interpreted as extending also to the union shop. The union movement was demanding an acceptable form of security in return for its wartime no-strike pledge. The NWLB struck a compromise with the maintenance-of-membership device. This arrangement required that all present and future members of the union had to remain members for the duration of the contract as a condition of employment. A fifteen-day escape period was provided union members.

The maintenance-of-membership arrangement is still legal, but utilized relatively infrequently. After appearing in about one-quarter of all contracts in 1946, it declined in importance in the 1950s. Currently about 81 percent of all collective bargaining contracts in the nation—there are approximately 190,000 in force—contain some form of union security. Only about 7 percent provide for maintenance of membership, the overwhelming number of which provide for the straight union shop or a variety of this form of compulsory union membership.

Another form of union security is called the *agency shop*. Under this arrangement, employees are never required to join the union. Instead, the agency shop requires nonunion employees in the bargaining unit to make a financial contribution equivalent to dues to the union in order to keep their jobs. In this way, the "free rider" objection advanced by unions is satisfied.

Although the straight union shop is the most popular form of union security, some employers and unions have negotiated variations of this type of compulsory union membership. For example, under some contracts, employees who are not union members when the union-shop agreement becomes effective are not required to join the union. Other agreements may exempt employees with comparatively long company service. In such agreements, newly hired workers are required to join, and must hold union membership as a condition of employment.

Taft-Hartley and the Closed Shop

Abuses of Closed Shop.   The *closed shop* is a system of union security that requires a worker to join a union before qualifying for a job. Union membership is the prerequisite for employment. Under the closed-shop arrangement, the right of management to select workers from the labor market is sharply restricted. The denial of a worker's right to join the organization is tantamount to preventing work in the occupation or plant covered by the closed shop. The *hiring hall* is commonly associated with the closed shop; this arrangement originated partially as a convenience for small employers unable to maintain permanent work crews adequately trained to perform the required tasks. Another reason for hiring halls was the desire on the part of unions to control entry into the craft or occupation and to spread available work equally among the entire membership. The maritime and construction industries illustrate the practice. Discrimination against some individuals and groups was widely publicized when such arrangements were permissible under the law.

The closed shop extended considerable power to labor unions to regulate the supply of labor. They could restrict the number of workers in a particular occupation to keep wage rates high relative to alternative occupations that did not have such an arrangement. Racketeering has also been associated with unions having a long tradition of requiring the closed shop. It was not at all uncommon for business agents to require excessive fees from individuals seeking the union cards required for work in occupations such as those associated with the printing and construction industries.

Unfair denial by unions of the opportunity of a worker to join a labor union constitutes an antisocial policy, which is properly amenable to public regulation. For example, it was reported in 1949 that thirty-two international unions, comprising about 2.5 million members, discriminated against black people.[5] It is not known precisely how much discrimination against this group persists in unions at this time. Union discrimination operates to deprive qualified workers of the freedom to enter an occupation. Factors such as religion, sex, national origin, and ancestry were likewise utilized by some labor unions to deprive workers of the chance to join their organizations. Unreasonable apprenticeship limitations also operate to deny union membership to qualified employees. When labor unions charged excessive initiation fees, the effect again was to close the door to union membership. Professor Taft of Brown University found that some labor unions charged initiation fees that would appear excessive to the average worker.[6] This action excluded from membership a number of individuals capable of performing the work required. As a result, union members were placed in a more favorable bargaining position because of the lesser supply of labor available to firms in the labor market.

Union control of the organized small-firm labor market is based on the closed shop and strict regulation of membership admission. Employers are often too small to maintain permanent work forces and thus worker identification is with the union or occupation. Workers usually move frequently from one job to another and are dependent upon the union for job information and protection. This permits local unions to control specific job territories for the benefit of members. Theoretically, a craftworker such as a union plumber could move from one local labor organization to another with the full job rights enjoyed by any other unionist. In practice, locals often discriminated against members of other locals if unemployment was prevalent in the territory subject to its control. Thus membership transfer from one local to another was abused, since it was restricted by some union business agents.

Closed Shop Declared Illegal.   Under the terms of the Wagner Act, the issue of the closed shop was left to the determination of the union-management negotiators. This law neither required nor forbade the closed shop. The Wagner Act's only element of control was that to be lawful, the arrangement had to be executed with a union representing a majority of bargaining-unit workers. An employer could not institute the closed shop when the labor union did not represent a majority of workers in the bargaining unit. However, employers and majority-designated labor unions had full freedom to reject or accept the closed-shop arrangement. In short, the Wagner Act provided that the closed-shop issue was to be resolved through collective bargaining. It was not permissible if the union had been dominated or assisted by the employer, or if the union did not represent a majority of a unit appropriate for collective bargaining.

The closed shop was agreed to in 33 percent of the nation's labor contracts in 1946.[7] As a result of its abuses, Congress outlawed the closed shop when it enacted Taft-Hartley.[8] Unions and employers violated the law where a closed-shop arrangement caused the discharge of workers, or where it prevented the hiring of a worker. The NLRB took an early position that it would not respect a contract that included a closed-shop provision. Such an agreement would be made unlawful by the mere inclusion of any provision requiring union membership as the prerequisite for the obtainment of a job. Moreover, strikes or picketing to obtain a closed shop were ruled illegal. In 1950, the NLRB ruled that peaceful picketing or even the threat of it to coerce employers into hiring only union members violated Taft-Hartley.[9] The federal courts have upheld both of these Board decisions.[10]

Congress legislated out of existence a pattern of collective bargaining that over the span of years had become firmly entrenched in American industry. Events soon proved, however, that the closed-shop principle was so deeply rooted in the industrial relations environment that the passage of a law could not cause its elimination. Working against the successful operation of the 1947 law on the closed-shop issue stood powerful institutional forces. At the time of the passage of the Taft-Hartley Act, millions of employees were working under closed-shop agreements. Some industries—such as printing, building, construction, and maritime—had operated under the closed shop for scores of years. An elaborate study of 1,716 collective bargaining contracts, conducted in 1954 by the Bureau of Labor Statistics, revealed that less than 5 percent of all agreements sampled contained such a provision.[11] No exhaustive investigation on the subject has been made since 1954, but there is reason to suspect that the closed shop's decline was somewhat exaggerated in the bureau's figures.

Many employers cooperated actively with unions to continue closed-shop arrangements after 1947. Companies refused to bring charges against unions when they demanded the closed shop. Instead, many employers simply agreed to continue closed-shop provisions in collective bargaining contracts executed subsequent to Taft-Hartley passage. In this connection, the Senate Committee on Labor and Public Welfare in 1949 reported that "notwithstanding the provisions of the Labor Management Relations Act, closed shop contracts continue to be observed over a wide area of industry."[12] This observation was supported in the Buffalo, New York, area by a careful study of the closed-shop experience. It was reported that "the most noteworthy fact of all presented by the experience in Buffalo is that the new labor law abolished the closed shop in neither form nor substance."[13] The NLRB deals with this illegal form of union security only when formal charges are filed dealing with the issue. The Board does not have the authority to seek out violators of the law.

Many other employers and labor unions, though not renewing closed-shop provisions outright, designed devices that in effect meant that only union members could be hired. Actually, these clauses were a subterfuge to avoid the closed-shop ban. One contract negotiated in 1948 provided that "the employers agree in the hiring of employees to prefer applicants who have previously been employed on vessels of one or more of the companies signatory to the contract."[14] Since the companies and the union, parties to the agreement, had operated under a closed-shop contract for a number of years before the passage of Taft-Hartley, all "previously" employed workers were union members. The contract insured the continuation of the closed shop since all employees hired under it belonged to the labor union. Another contract negotiated in 1948 provided that only workers who had successfully completed an apprentice training program conducted in a school sponsored by a labor organization were eligible for employment.[15] Such a contract clause effectively continued the closed-shop arrangement. In still another contract, the employer gave the labor union the inside track in filling job vacancies.[16] It specified that the employer would give the union forty-eight hours' advance notice before interviewing any new applicants. The implication was that the union would send a qualified union member to apply for the position. Such a tactic obviously precluded hiring of nonunion workers.

These illustrations underline the support of employers for continuation of the closed-shop principle. Why have employers agreed to the closed shop even though the arrangement has been outlawed? There are two possible answers to this question: either employers have been satisfied with the closed shop; or else they do not want to invite possible trouble, such as strikes, by denying union demands for the closed shop. This latter consideration is of considerable importance during periods of relatively high levels of economic prosperity, such as existed in the first few years after the passage of Taft-Hartley. In short, employers did not want to risk interruption to production in a period of high profits. The Buffalo study, previously noted, disclosed that in one industry, an employer association representative said in support of the closed shop that "relations had been good and the closed shop worked satisfactorily."[17] Undoubtedly, many employers were of the opinion that the device was the prerequisite to harmonious labor relations. For these reasons they actively cooperated with labor unions to avoid the closed-shop ban of Taft-Hartley. The law is still evaded in some industries.

Brown-Olds *Doctrine: A New Board Effort.*   Aware of these wholesale violations, the NLRB in 1956 attempted to enforce the law by imposing financial penalties on employers and unions that maintained the closed shop. The opportunity was provided in the *Brown-Olds* case involving a collective bargaining agreement that contained several of the union's bylaws, working rules, and regulations requiring employees to obtain union clearance before seeking employment.[18] The union constitution and bylaws required members to obtain a union work permit before accepting employment and gave the business agent power to remove members from the job for delinquency in paying dues and assessments.

The law judge ruled that the specific provisions constituted an unlawful closed-shop agreement. Upon review, the Board decided to use its remedial powers to correct abuse of the closed-shop prohibitions. Union dues were to be returned to members to correct violations. The Board held in *Brown-Olds* that "the remedy of reimbursement of all such monies is appropriate and necessary to expunge the illegal effects of the unfair labor practices found here." A 1943 Supreme Court case in which a company union was held illegal by its very existence in that it was not formed by employee free choice was used as a precedent. In that case, return of dues had been one means of disestablishing the union.[19] The Board in the *Brown-Olds* case established the rule that a union would be required to reimburse employees for dues and assessments collected under illegal closed-shop agreements during a period beginning six months prior to the date unfair labor practice charges were filed. The doctrine was to affect both unions and management executing illegal closed-shop provisions: When it was determined that the employer had been a willing ally to the illegal arrangement, the company was required to share the costs involved in the refund of dues.

Thus, labor and management were put on notice that they would jointly be held responsible to reimburse all members for dues and other assessments paid from the time a remedial order was issued extending to six months previous to the filing of the charge. For example, if there were five hundred union members, all would be reimbursed for all monies paid during this period of time. Financially, the cost could run into thousands of dollars. The doctrine was applied in many cases, but, as will be seen, not a penny was refunded because of the Supreme Court's review of the NLRB policy.

The Board later extended the remedy to hiring-hall arrangements, even if these were not connected with a closed shop. The Board justified the extension by arguing that these arrangements had a coercive influence on work applicants to join the union.[20] That is, if an employer obtained workers exclusively through a hiring hall, the worker's first point of contact would be with the union. Both tacit and overt pressure could be applied to force union membership before a job opening would be made available. The Board decided to eliminate these pressures on workers.

The U.S. Supreme Court reviewed the *Brown-Olds* doctrine in 1961.[21] The case involved a collective bargaining contract with Mechanical Handling Systems, Inc., of Indianapolis, Indiana. In it, the company agreed to provisions requiring it to abide by the union rules and regulations requiring employment of only union members. The case arose when two job applicants, members of another union, were denied employment because they could not obtain referral from the union. The Board upon review applied its *Brown-Olds* doctrine requiring reimbursement to all employees of all dues and assessments collected by the union starting from six months prior to the date unfair labor practice charges were filed.

Upon review, the Supreme Court ruled that the Board's *Brown-Olds* doctrine was punitive and not remedial in character. It found that the Board had thus exceeded its statutory powers. The Board had presented no evidence indicating that a single union member had been coerced to join or remain in the labor organization. Indeed, all the workers might have been union members for many years. Thus, the requirement to pay back all dues and assessments to members starting six months prior to the charge benefited union members, but did not provide a remedy to persons denied work in the first place. The Court held that the only power given the Board was that sufficient to remedy the harm done to persons denied work because of the illegal union-security provisions. It could only require a company to hire a worker who had been denied employment and order back pay concerning lost wages and benefits. Any other construction of the law was not within the province of the NLRB. The Court did not agree with the implicit reasoning of the Board that the very existence of a closed-shop arrangement diminishes the worker's freedom of choice to join or refrain from joining unions guaranteed by Taft-Hartley. Board remedial policy could not be justified solely on its deterrent qualities. Thus the punitive financial aspect of *Brown-Olds* was held illegal by the Supreme Court.

Hiring-Hall Regulations.   The key to the union-controlled and -administered hiring hall is the closed shop since, to take advantage of its services, a worker had to become a union member. A review of the legislative history of Taft-Hartley establishes the fact that its proponents meant to eliminate the union hiring hall. During debate on the law Senator Taft, in illustrating the scope of the prohibition of the closed shop, declared that its abolishment "is best exemplified by the so-called hiring halls in the west coast where shipowners cannot employ anyone unless the union sends him to them."[22]

Soon after Taft-Hartley passage, the NLRB ruled that this traditional method for the organization of the labor market within industries of intermittent and casual employment violated the terms of the 1947 law. In *National Maritime Union,* the controlling case on the hiring-hall issue, the NLRB held hiring halls unlawful because they resulted in unlawful discrimination against nonunion workers and provided illegal preference for union members.[23]

The union hiring hall was first outlawed in the maritime industry, but the rule applied throughout industry. While commenting on the scope of the prohibition, Mr. Denham, former General Counsel of the NLRB, declared that

> in the construction industry the matter of the union shop has been the source of much uneasiness ever since the Taft-Hartley Act went on the books. The union shop provision of the law definitely was designed to do away with the closed shop, under which a man was required to be a member of the contracting union before he could ever be considered for a job. Now, all of that is prohibited, as also is the use of the hiring hall, either directly or indirectly. There simply is no further such thing as the closed shop or the hiring hall, nor any legitimate way by which the employer can contract to prefer union members over non-union members in the matter of hiring.[24]

Despite the fact that the hiring-hall arrangement was at first considered per se illegal, the NLRB in a 1950 case held that the hiring-hall provisions of a labor contract did not violate the law.[25] The contract stated that hiring provisions would be administered without discrimination and that "no retention of membership is required in order for preference to be granted under the agreement." Essentially, the Board was attempting to preserve an arrangement that had a long history of accommodation in several industries. In 1958, the Board set forth rules to deal with hiring halls.

Mountain Pacific *Doctrine.*   The NLRB ruled in 1958 that hiring-hall arrangements were not per se illegal if the union and company had agreed to a number of specific safeguards. The agreement had to specifically provide that (1) selection of applicants for referral to jobs would be without regard to union membership requirements; (2) the employer would retain the right to reject any applicant referred by the union; and (3) standards would be posted in the hiring hall for employee inspection.

Essentially, the Board established that contractual hiring-hall arrangements without inclusion of the above safeguards would be subject to the *Brown-Olds* doctrine requiring reimbursement of all member dues and assessments from six months prior to the filing of unfair labor practice charges. The Supreme Court reviewed the Board's hiring-hall standards on the same day in 1961 that it reviewed the *Brown-Olds* doctrine.

In the case before the Court, a union and a group of employers had agreed that casual employees would be hired only by union hiring-hall referral.[26] It was also agreed that referral would be on the basis of seniority and without regard to an employee's union membership. The Board previously had ruled that the hiring arrangement was unlawful because it did not contain the *Mountain Pacific* safeguards.

The Supreme Court reversed the NLRB by holding again it had exceeded its allowable powers. An exclusive hiring-hall arrangement was not per se illegal under the Act, even if it lacked specific safeguards imposed by the Board. The Court held that discrimination in hiring could not be inferred from the face of the contract when the contract provided for nondiscriminatory action. Board authority was provided only for remedying cases where discrimination exists—to which Taft-Hartley is addressed. General categories do not permit a logical basis upon which the NLRB can properly remedy unfair labor practices.

In short, the NLRB is required to examine the discriminatory nature of each hiring-hall arrangement formally presented to it. It cannot hold such arrangements as illegal per se just because certain safeguards are not contained explicitly in the contract. The Supreme Court requires the Board to look at the administrative operation of each arrangement prior to reaching a decision. If the hiring hall reveals discriminatory hiring practices, each violation must be remedied separately and without broad remedial categories such as provided by the *Brown-Olds* doctrine. It is obvious that the Supreme Court tacitly gave approval to the traditional arrangements of some industries. It did not require a rigid adherence to Taft-Hartley if hiring halls are in fact free from restrictive practices.

Landrum-Griffin Changes.   Congress gave special treatment to the building construction industry in 1959 when it amended Taft-Hartley. Section 8 (f) of Landrum-Griffin permits *prehire agreements* in the construction industry, and permits compulsory union membership seven days after employment. In other industries, union membership may be required only after a worker is employed thirty days. The reason for special treatment for the construction industry involves its short and intermittent nature of employment.

Prehire contracts are valid even though the majority status of the union has not been established at the time they are negotiated. This means that a contract may be negotiated before any employee is hired; the result is that employees do not have the opportunity to vote for bargaining agents. Even so, such agreements are valid when they require union membership after the seventh day of employment; when the union must be notified of vacancies and must be given the opportunity to refer workers; and when priority in employment is based on specified objective criteria. Though the short-term character of construction employment may justify this feature of the 1959 law, it still tends to conflict with the general public policy of permitting employees to choose their own unions.

A Board majority in *Smith Construction Co.* attempted to reconcile the prehire agreement authorization with other sections of the law.[27] It was held that Congress as evidenced by the final proviso to Section 8 (f) intended to permit a test of majority status and unit appropriateness at any time during the contract, and that prehire agreements did not prohibit examination through litigation of refusal to bargain charges. Thus, an employer may break the prehire contract at will because the final proviso of the Landrum-Griffin section makes the company immune from unfair labor practice liability. If employers wish to break such contracts, they can do so merely by challenging the union's representative status. *Smith Construction Co.* could result in more instability in the industry because of growing competition between union and nonunion firms. The incidence of future unilateral revocation of such contracts depends on the organization in the industry. In January 1978, the U. S. Supreme Court sustained the NLRB position, saying in *NLRB* v. *Local 103, Iron Workers* that a prehire agreement is "voidable" by either the employer or the union.[28] This policy encourages contractors to operate on a so-called "double-breasted" basis where the unionized employer starts a new nonunion firm. In such cases, the contractor simply abandons the prehire contract and assigns the work to nonunion employees. Needless to say, construction unions have bitterly criticized the NLRB policy that permits the same contractor to operate on a double-breasted basis while also providing contractors with the right to repudiate prehire contracts at will. In a congressional hearing, leaders of construction unions stated:

> . . . with the acquiescence of the NLRB, employers can walk away from their agreements by going double-breasted or simply by repudiating it and declaring the firms non-union.[29]

In two comparatively recent decisions, however, federal courts supported the integrity of prehire contracts. In April 1983, the U.S. Supreme Court unanimously ruled that such a contract is enforceable until clearly repudiated by the contractor.[30] When an employer desired to work at union job sites, the company was required to sign the master prehire contract. One provision required employers to make monthly contributions to a health and pension benefit trust fund for the covered employees. Despite this mandate, the employer involved did not make such payments during the months the company was working on the job. After the job was completed, the labor organization sued the contractor for the amount of money due, $5,316. In the company's defense, the employer asserted that the prehire contract was not judicially enforceable because the union had not demonstrated its majority status as representative of the employees during the period of the job. Rejecting the employer's contention, the high court held that the terms of prehire contracts were fully enforceable in court prior to repudiation. It pointed out that the contractor had not repudiated the contract during the job when it had the opportunity to do so.

In a 1983 case, a federal appeals court held that an employer could not abandon a prehire contract unilaterally if the union had demonstrated its majority status.[31] After a union does that, a prehire contract attains the status of a regular collective bargaining contract not to be terminated by the employer in the absence of bargaining. Of considerable importance, the court stated that a union is not required to prove its majority status by an NLRB election. Majority support will be presumed if a majority of the employees on the job were referred from the union hiring hall even though, as noted earlier, union-operated hiring halls must be operated without reference to union membership. Majority support will also be presumed when the majority of employees voluntarily comply with a union security provision contained in a prehire contract. Other presumptions of majority status could be demonstrated by other circumstances on a case-by-case basis.

In addition to the legality of prehire contracts, Congress extended additional special privileges to employers and unions in the construction industry. Landrum-Griffin made it more sure—and, indeed, at times almost positive—that only union members would be employed on construction jobs over which a union has collective bargaining rights. In practice, Congress legalized the closed shop in the construction industry despite Taft-Hartley's general ban of the closed shop.

The 1959 law made lawful the following kinds of provisions contained in a labor agreement negotiated by a construction union and an employer:

1. Requires the employer to notify a union of employment opportunities.
2. Gives the union the opportunity to refer qualified employees to the employer.
3. Specifies minimum training or experience qualifications for employment.
4. Establishes a priority system for the referral of employees based upon the length of service with the employer in the construction industry or in the geographical area.

Should a labor agreement contain such provisions, clearly only union members are likely to be referred to a job. For example, suppose the labor agreement provided that only employees with two years or more of employment with the particular contractor may be hired; if the union has had a bargaining relationship with the employer over the years, and if the employer previously hired only union members, who else but union members would be eligible for employment?

It could be argued that a construction job covered by a collective bargaining contract should only be staffed by union members. In this way, the problem of strife between union and nonunion employees would be avoided, including the propensity of union members to strike when nonunion employees are hired. If this is sound public policy, Congress should legalize the closed shop in the construction industry, and not seek to accomplish this end by the sort of subterfuge that is now the case.

In 1977, the NLRB upheld the legality of a job referral plan in the construction industry contained in a labor agreement that gave preference to employees who had worked with the particular contractor for one or two years in the last four years. A majority of the Board said:

> As is clear . . . Section 8(f)(4) expressly exempts from the strictures of the act and makes lawful an exclusive referral system under which priority in job referrals may be "based on length of service with such employer."[32]

TAFT-HARTLEY AND THE UNION SHOP

Union-Shop Elections

The Taft-Hartley Act maintained the union-shop device as a permissible form of union security. The statute, however, controlled the circumstances under which the arrangement could be incorporated into collective bargaining contracts, and regulated its implementation. The only legal limitation contained in the Wagner Act was that the labor organization negotiating a union-security arrangement had to represent a majority of the bargaining unit. There was no other barrier to the type of agreement that could be included in the contract.

Under the terms of the 1947 law, employers and labor unions were permitted to execute a union-shop agreement requiring membership as a condition of continued employment on or after thirty days following their employment. Conditions, however, were attached to its legality.

Until 1951, the most demanding prerequisite for both the union shop and the maintenance-of-membership arrangement was that a special authorization election had to be held by the NLRB. The referendum was known as the *union-shop election.* This election should not be confused with the representation or certification election. It will be recalled that a certification election refers to a poll to determine whether a labor union represents a majority of workers for the purpose of collective bargaining. The union-shop election was a special referendum to determine whether a majority of bargaining-unit workers approved of their union negotiating an agreement making union membership a condition of employment after the required waiting period. The Board would not conduct a union-shop election unless the labor organization petitioning for such an election represented a majority of workers in the bargaining unit.

Another distinction between representation and union-shop elections concerned the concept of "majority." For purposes of representation, a labor union was required only to win a majority of the votes cast. But for the union shop, the union was required to receive the votes of a majority of those workers *eligible* to vote in the election.[33] This meant that a worker who did not cast a ballot actually voted against the union shop or the maintenance-of-membership provision. Any worker who did not choose to vote, who was laid off, or who failed to vote because of illness or any other reason was counted as voting against union security. It is obvious that Taft-Hartley went beyond normal election procedures to make it difficult for unions to obtain union-security provisions requiring membership as a condition of employment. Even if the union shop was authorized by a majority of the bargaining unit, there was no guarantee that it could be obtained. Authorization by union members merely gave the parties the right to negotiate on the issue.[34] Employers were often in a position to resist successfully the union-shop demand regardless of the outcome of the election.

Not only were elections required to authorize the parties to negotiate union-shop terms, but employees had the right to petition the NLRB to hold union shop *deauthorization elections.* A petition including a minimum of 30 percent of the bargaining unit was required. A union loss would mean that the union shop was no longer a valid provision in the collective bargaining agreement. As in union-shop elections, the law provides that to revoke a union shop a majority of the employees eligible to vote must vote in favor of deauthorization. When the employees vote against the union shop, the effect is to revoke immediately the contractual requirement that employees must hold union membership to work.[35] No other provision of the labor agreement is affected by such a poll. Though deauthorization elections are not frequent, unions lose most of those that do take place. In 1981, the Board conducted only 147 of these polls, with the union shop defeated in 66.7 percent, although these elections covered only 3,121 employees.[36] Most of the union losses were in small bargaining units with less than 50 employees.[37] Though, as noted below, the union-shop election requirement was repealed in 1951, the union-shop deauthorization election is still a part of national labor policy.

Repeal of Union-Shop Election Requirement.   The assumption of Taft-Hartley that workers would reject a proposal that required union membership as a condition of employment if given an opportunity to do so in a secret-ballot election was not realized in practice. In any case, the election requirement was repealed on October 22, 1951, by the Taft-Humphrey amendment of the Taft-Hartley law.[38]

During the four years and two months in which the union-shop election was required, the Board conducted 46,119 polls. Union-shop agreements were authorized in 44,795 of the referendums, or in 97 percent of those conducted. In the polls 6,542,564 workers were eligible to vote, of whom 5,547,478, or 84.8 percent, cast valid ballots. Of those voting, 5,071,988, or 77.5 percent of the workers, voted in favor of union security.[39] In signing the October 1951 amendment, President Truman stated that union-shop elections "have involved expenditures in excess of $3,000,000 of public funds. Experience has proved them to be not only costly, and burdensome, but unnecessary as well."[40]

A state, however, may require a union-shop election before employers and unions are allowed to negotiate arrangements requiring union membership as a condition of employment. At least at one time, Colorado, Kansas, and Wisconsin had such laws. In Wisconsin, a union could not lawfully negotiate a union shop unless two-thirds of the bargaining unit voted for it. Though Taft-Hartley no longer provides for union-shop elections, such state laws appear valid and do not violate Taft-Hartley. In 1949, the U.S. Supreme Court held the Wisconsin statute lawful.[41] In addition, as will be discussed later in this chapter, the high court in 1963 held that the states under the authority of Section 14(b) of Taft-Hartley may regulate union security provisions.[42]

Taft-Hartley on Nonpayment of Dues.   Section 8 (a) (3) of Taft-Hartley states that the only condition whereby a worker may lose his job for nonmembership in a union is for nonpayment of dues. It has been established by Board cases that unions do not have a right to prescribe rules that interfere with the relationship between employee and employer, except in the case of the nonpayment of dues.[43]

In 1955, the NLRB established a policy prohibiting discharge of a worker if, at any time before the discharge became effective, the employee made full and unqualified tender of dues to the union.[44] This rule was changed in 1962, when the Board held that employee delay of dues payment was at odds with the congressional purpose in permitting the parties to negotiate union-shop agreements.[45] An automatic determination was eliminated in that the Board decided to review the record to determine why an employee had delayed dues payment under a valid union-security agreement. In still another case, the Board held that a union had the duty to inform members upon their joining of what their obligations were.[46] If workers had been informed of their obligations when they became members, they had the responsibility to tender dues in accordance with union rules, or run the risk of discharge.

An employee who offered to pay dues, however, was not in violation of the Act even if the labor organization had expelled him or her for lack of conformity to internal union rules. Union-shop contracts, therefore, merely offer unions financial security. In short, Taft-Hartley permitted the union shop as a condition of employment and then proceeded to dilute its enforcement. The basic reason for this arrangement was to provide both employment rights for workers and financial security for unions. As early as 1949, the Board held that a worker does not have to join a union even though a union-shop arrangement exists. His or her only obligation under the law is his or her willingness to tender the dues and initiation fees required by the union. If a union imposed any other qualifications and conditions for membership with which an employee was unwilling to comply, the employee could be excluded from union membership, but not from his or her job.[47] Twenty-five years later, in 1974, the NLRB upheld the same principle of law.[48] A union member worked during a strike. He wrote the union that he would continue to pay dues under the new labor agreement without being a member. The new contract contained a union shop, and the employer discharged the employee at the request of the union. However, the NLRB held that the discharge of the employee was illegal because he had been willing to pay his dues. When a federal court of appeals upheld the Board, it stressed once again that under Taft-Hartley an employee does not have to be a union member to protect his or her job. All that he or she has to do is to tender the dues required of union members.[49] This feature of the law explains why the courts held, as mentioned earlier, that columnist Buckley and editor Evans were not required to join a union as a condition of employment. They were, however, required to pay the equivalent of union dues.

Thus, it is well established that a union may expel an employee for a violation of its rules, but it may not effect his or her discharge if the expulsion is for any reason other than the refusal to pay an amount equivalent to union dues and initiation fees. Despite a contractual provision requiring union membership as a condition of employment, the individual does not have to be a union member to hold a job. In short, though Taft-Hartley makes lawful a contract provision that requires "membership" in a union as a condition of employment, the word "membership" does not mean actual membership in a union. For purposes of Taft-Hartley, an employee is a "union member" if he or she is willing to pay dues.

To deal with union members who violate union rules governing their conduct, some unions attempted a different approach. Instead of expelling the disobedient members, unions fined them. Aware that expulsion from a union, despite the existence of a union shop, would not cause these members to lose their jobs, such unions sought to impose a monetary penalty for nonmembership. In this approach, unions relied upon the feature of Section 8 (b)(1) of Taft-Hartley that says, "this paragraph shall not impair the right of labor organizations to prescribe their own rules with respect to the acquisition or retention of membership therein."

Such fines are lawful. Of more particular significance, they may be collected through court action instituted by the union against the member. In one case, a union established a rule that limited the amount of incentive earnings that employees could earn through increased production. A member violated the rule, and the union fined him. In *Scofield* v. *NLRB*, the U.S. Supreme Court held in 1969 that the fine was lawful.[50] It said that a union is free to enforce a properly adopted rule which reflects a legitimate union interest, impairs no policy Congress has imbedded in the labor laws and is reasonably enforced against union members.

It said that the fine was imposed against the person as a "union member" and not as an "employee." In the Court's view, the fine did not disturb the relationship of the union member with his employer.

Despite the legality of such fines, their usefulness to unions in dealing with disciplined members is quite limited. As we will note in a following chapter, the U.S. Supreme Court held in 1972 that fines cannot be imposed if a union member resigns from a union before he or she violates a union rule.[51] Indeed, even in *Scofield,* the high court said that if union members were unhappy about the production ceilings they were free "to leave the union." If a union member withdraws from a union because of dissatisfaction with a union rule, he or she may not be discharged from the job. As stated, to hold the job, an employee need not be a union member, despite a union shop, provided he or she is willing to pay the union's dues.

It is clear from this discussion that the nonpayment-of-dues feature of Taft-Hartley undermines the union shop. At the same time, it weakens the ability of a union to enforce its internal rules in terms of union members. In a later chapter, we shall find out that Landrum-Griffin protects a union member against expulsion under unfair procedures. Despite this feature of the 1959 law, Congress left intact the provision of Taft-Hartley that forbids the discharge of an employee from a job because of loss of union membership for any reason other than refusal to pay dues. Either Congress failed to relate its 1959 action to that feature of Taft-Hartley, or it believed that Landrum-Griffin protection of union membership was not sufficient to deal with the problem of arbitrary and capricious expulsion of members from their unions.

Board Control Over Union-Security Clauses.   The NLRB established principles to guide it in determining the effect of union-security clauses on bargaining representation election petitions. The Board has consistently held that a valid collective bargaining contract will bar an election for at least a twelve-month period.

In 1958, the Board held that the existence of a contract would not stop it from holding an election if the agreement did not reflect the limitations placed on union security by Taft-Hartley.[52] However, the Supreme Court did not permit this rule to stand. In 1961, in two cases before it, the Court held that such a mechanistic approach presumed illegality and amounted to a prejudgment of the labor organization.[53] The Board was forced to revise its rules regarding union-security clauses as bars to representation elections.

Revised rules were established in the same year, 1961, in the *Paragon Products Corporation* case.[54] It was deemed necessary for a union-security clause to be clearly unlawful on its face to permit a representation election before the end of a twelve-month period. The forms of unlawful union security include those that expressly and without doubt require that employers give union members preference in hiring, layoffs, and seniority. Also, unlawful provisions exist if employees are given less than the thirty-day grace period provided for union membership in Taft-Hartley. Contracts that require employees to pay the union money other than the periodic dues and initiation fees required of all unionists are unlawful. Any other payments required as a condition of employment will not bar the holding of a representation election.

Ambiguous union-security clauses will not necessarily relax the twelve-month rule unless the provision is found illegal by the Board or a federal court. Each case must therefore be investigated and an appropriate remedy provided as a result of findings. Mechanical approaches to the problem of union security are discouraged by the U.S. Supreme Court.

SECTION 14 (b) AND RIGHT-TO-WORK LAWS

Right-to-work is a term normally used to describe state statutory or state constitutional provisions banning the requirement of union membership as a condition of employment. A significant feature of right-to-work laws is that they not only outlaw the execution of union-security arrangements in the area of intrastate commerce, but they also forbid the negotiation of compulsory union membership provisions within the area of interstate commerce. It will be recalled that Taft-Hartley outlawed the closed shop, but permitted the negotiation of union shops or maintenance-of-membership arrangements. However, Section 14 (b) of the Act permitted states to enact laws applying to the area of interstate commerce that not only outlawed the closed shop, but that made any form of union security illegal. This provision of the Taft-Hartley Act states:

> Nothing in this Act shall be construed as authorizing the execution or application of agreements requiring membership in a labor organization as a condition of employment in any State or Territory in which such execution or application is prohibited by State or Territorial law.

In this manner, the federal government invited the states to legislate in the area reserved by the Constitution of the United States to the federal government.

Action of the states to eliminate union-security arrangements began several years before the passage of the 1947 law. In 1944, Arkansas and Florida amended their constitutions to outlaw all agreements making union membership a condition of employment.[55] The Florida amendment provided that "the rights of persons to work shall not be denied or abridged on account of membership in any labor union or labor organization."

After Florida and Arkansas set the pattern, Arizona, Nebraska, and South Dakota in 1946 passed amendments to their constitutions to prohibit all species of union-security arrangements.[56] In 1947, state prohibition of union security became even more widespread. During early 1947, seven states banned all forms of union security.[57] In these states, the method of eliminating union security was the enactment of statutes rather than constitutional amendments. Thus at the time Taft-Hartley was passed, twelve states had already prohibited all types of union security.

Without Section 14 (b), no state could lawfully enact right-to-work legislation applying to the area of interstate commerce, since such laws would conflict with the doctrine of national supremacy. National supremacy in the area of interstate commerce was established by the U.S. Supreme Court in 1819.[58]

If it desired, Congress when it passed Taft-Hartley could have made such state action inoperative in the area of interstate commerce. Even so, a constitutional issue was advanced to test the ability of states to enact laws that in fact become superior to federal law in the area of interstate commerce. In 1949, the U.S. Supreme Court held that Section 14 (b) of Taft-Hartley and state right-to-work legislation enacted under its authority were compatible with the federal Constitution.[59] In 1976, unions won minor relief from right-to-work laws when the U.S. Supreme Court held that the Texas law did not apply to marine workers who spend the vast majority of their time on the high seas.[60] Five years earlier, the high court had also nullified a provision of the Georgia right-to-work law that permitted employees to revoke their checkoff authorizations for union dues at any time.[61] The Georgia statute was held to be in conflict with Taft-Hartley on that point because under the federal law, checkoff authorizations may be irrevocable for a maximum of one year. The Court said that if the Georgia law prevailed it would prevent employers and unions from negotiating a checkoff agreement as authorized by the federal law. Later on in this chapter, we will discuss the nature of the checkoff and Taft-Hartley controls. In 1982, a federal appeals court ruled that federal properties were exempt from right-to-work laws.[62] At issue was a union shop provision negotiated by an employer and union covering employees working at a U.S. Air Force base located in Florida. Holding that the Florida right-to-work law did not apply to federal "enclaves" located in states, the high court sustained the validity of the union shop by refusing to review the lower court decision. However, the U.S. Supreme Court held that it was not unconstitutional for Congress to authorize states to enact right-to-work laws. In effect, the high court told organized labor that if it desired to eliminate Section 14(b) of the law, the proper forum was Congress and not the courts.

Convinced that employees should not get a "free ride," a union attempted to assess nonunion employees for their portion of its collective bargaining costs. Such representation fees would be lower than full dues required of union members. Its effort failed, however, when a federal appeals court ruled that the Mississippi right-to-work law forbade such assessments.[63]

Twenty states now prohibit all forms of union security. They are Alabama, Arizona, Arkansas, Florida, Georgia, Iowa, Kansas, Louisiana, Mississippi, Nebraska, Nevada, North Carolina, North Dakota, South Carolina, South Dakota, Tennessee, Texas, Utah, Virginia, and Wyoming. In 1985, Idaho passed a right-to-work law, the state legislature overriding the governor's veto.[64] At this writing, however, a state court has blocked the implementation of the law, at least temporarily.[65] Should the law prevail, Idaho would be the twenty-first state to have enacted a right-to-work law. In 1957, Indiana passed a right-to-work law and gained the distinction of being the only northern industrial state to have enacted one. As a result of the election of 1964 and the pressure of the Indiana labor movement, this law was repealed in 1965 and never again raised as an issue in that state.[66] Where union membership is comparatively large, organized labor has successfully prevented the enactment of such laws. At one time in California, Ohio, and Washington, right-to-work laws were on the ballot for referendum by the public. By large majorities, the proposals were rejected by the voters of those states. In contrast, in November 1976, the citizens of Arkansas voted 387,084 to 192,124 to retain that state's right-to-work law.[67] More recently, between 1978 and 1985, proposed right-to-work laws were defeated in Colorado, Illinois, Kentucky, Maine, Maryland, Missouri, Montana, New Hampshire, Vermont, and West Virginia.[68] In 1979, the New Mexico legislature enacted a right-to-work law, but it was vetoed by the governor of the state. In Missouri, it was generally expected that the right-to-work law would be adopted in a public referendum. However, in 1978, it was decisively defeated (60 to 40 percent) by the voters, largely attributable to a massive public relations campaign mounted by organized labor.

Recognizing that it was futile to attempt to repeal so many laws on a state level, organized labor has sought to eliminate Section 14 (b) from Taft-Hartley. Indeed, in President Johnson's administration during 1965–1966, Congress came close to repealing Section 14 (b). The House voted twice for repeal, and a majority of the Senate was prepared to do the same. However, Senator Everett M. Dirksen of Illinois led a filibuster to prevent Senate action. Since then, the union movement has tried continuously to knock out Section 14 (b), but its efforts have not been successful. It seemed that repeal was assured when President Carter was elected in 1976 along with a large Democratic party majority in Congress. President Carter said he would not veto a measure to eliminate Section 14 (b), nor would he actively promote one. At this writing, Section 14 (b) remains in Taft-Hartley, and so do right-to-work laws in twenty states.

In the summer of 1977, the union movement almost abandoned its fight to eliminate Section 14 (b). Recall that at that time, Carter had agreed to support the Labor Law Reform Act of 1977, which organized labor desired. The character of the legislation was mentioned in previous chapters. To gain Carter's support, the union movement agreed not to press for the repeal of Section 14 (b). As the *Wall Street Journal* reported on July 11, 1977:

> To win Mr. Carter's support, and satisfy critical Democratic congressional leaders, the AFL-CIO in May agreed to drop from the bill a proposal to repeal Section 14B of the Taft-Hartley Act, the provision that allows states to ban labor contracts requiring all workers to join the union.

This concession on the part of the union movement, however, did not pay off: a Senate filibuster in the summer of 1978 blocked passage of the Labor Law Reform Act after it was enacted in the House of Representatives.

At the very least, Section 14 (b) has created unequal labor relations conditions among the several states. In states without right-to-work legislation, forms of union security are permitted that are outlawed in the states with restrictive legislation. These latter states are located primarily in the south and southwestern parts of the United States and use their restrictive laws on union security to support their competitive drives to attract industry from other sections of the country. The economic effect that these legal differences may have on industry location evades verification. But the Congress itself has imposed an atmosphere of potentially unequal competition for industry between the states. However, this is not the case in the railroad and airline industries, since, as we shall soon learn, Congress in 1951 nullified state right-to-work laws as they apply to these two industries.

Enforcement of Right-to-Work Laws

The issue arose as to whether the states or the NLRB had the authority to deal with violations of state right-to-work laws. For understandable reasons, unions argued that the NLRB should have exclusive jurisdiction. Under Taft-Hartley, violators of the federal law do not face imprisonment or fines. On the other hand, under state right-to-work laws, violators may be imprisoned or fined. By unanimous decision, the U.S. Supreme Court held that the states have the right to enforce their own laws.[69] The Court said:

> When Congress gives state policy that degree of overriding authority, we are reluctant to conclude that it is nevertheless enforceable by the NLRB.

In other words, since Congress permitted the states under Taft-Hartley to outlaw union-security arrangements in the area of interstate commerce, the Court held that the states have the corollary authority to punish violators of state right-to-work laws.

UNION SECURITY UNDER THE RAILWAY LABOR ACT

The Railway Labor Act was enacted in 1926 to regulate labor relations in the railroad industry. In 1936, it was amended to extend its coverage to air transportation. The act was amended in 1934, making all forms of compulsory union membership illegal and enforcing violations by imposing criminal penalties. The major support for prohibiting compulsory union membership came from the railway unions themselves. It was feared that any form of union security would diminish the ability of the railway unions to compete with company-supported labor organizations for members. By 1951, the contest between the two groups had been resolved sufficiently to change the attitude of railway unions toward compulsory union membership. Nearly 80 percent of railroad employees were members of labor unions free from company domination.

One amendment in 1951 to the Railway Labor Act provided that "union shop contracts could be entered into notwithstanding . . . any other statute or law . . . of any state."[70]

Some employees of the Union Pacific Railroad Company challenged the constitutionality of the Railway Labor Act's union-security provision in the Nebraska courts. Nebraska has a right-to-work provision in its constitution and the workers claimed that compulsory union membership was in violation of the state constitution. The labor contract signed by the company with the various railway unions required membership within sixty days that was to be maintained thereafter as a condition of continued employment.

The Nebraska trial court held that the union-shop agreement was a violation of the First Amendment to the U.S. Constitution, since it deprived employees of their freedom of association; and of the Fifth Amendment, since members were required to pay for many things besides the cost of collective bargaining. No valid federal law superseded the right-to-work provision of the Nebraska Constitution for these reasons. The decision was upheld by the Nebraska Supreme Court. The U.S. Supreme Court reviewed the decision upon appeal. [71]

In this case, known as the *Hanson* case, the U.S. Supreme Court by unanimous vote reversed the Nebraska courts and held that Congress had the authority to permit the union-shop arrangement, notwithstanding any state laws to the contrary. Federal supremacy over interstate commerce eliminates the ability of states to regulate in this area unless legislation specifically cedes authority to them. Also, the Court reasoned that the union-shop provision of the Railway Labor Act is only permissive. The parties were not compelled to reach agreement on these provisions. Should they desire to include the union shop in the collective bargaining contract, state right-to-work laws would not prevail over the will of Congress.

Thus Congress has established a dual standard regarding union security. The railway and airline industries are permitted to negotiate union-shop arrangements under the Railway Labor Act. Industry in general is prohibited from doing so where states enact restrictive laws in the form of right-to-work statutes or constitutional amendments. Political pressures account for these differences. There is no economic justification for or against the permissiveness extended railway and airline employees that could not be identically applied to employees under Taft-Hartley.

UNION SHOP AND UNION POLITICAL ACTIVITIES

The Supreme Court's decision in *Hanson* also dealt with the contention that compulsory union membership forced workers into ideological and political conformity. In this case, the Court held that the charge was not supported by the record. However, in another case, *Machinists* v. *Street,* the Georgia Supreme Court held that when a union shop was in effect, the use of dues to support political activities was a violation of the U.S. Constitution.[72] Either the union would have to give up its union shop or cease engaging in political activities.

Upon review, the U.S. Supreme Court agreed in *Machinists* v. *Street* that Congress had not intended to require workers to support union political activities to which they objected. However, the high court rejected the Georgia court's position that a union shop was illegal just because a union engaged in political activities. Instead, the remedy was either to refund to a complaining member the proportion of the individual's dues money expended on such activities, or to refund that proportion spent on activities to which the member advised the union he or she was opposed.[73]

The Court had occasion to deal with the matter again in 1963 under the Railway Labor Act. It then held that a member could "contract out" of all union political activities and need not specify only those that were objectionable.[74] Not only would the member receive a refund of the proportion of his or her dues money (the same proportion that union political expenditures were to total expenditures) spent on political matters, but his or her future dues would be reduced in the same proportion.

The remedy provided was for the purpose of eliminating the ideological and political conformity that a union shop might require if a member were not able to refrain from financial support of union political activities considered contrary to the belief of the individual. All members of the union were not granted the remedy, only those who actually objected to the use of funds for political purposes. Class-action suits were thus eliminated, so that actual drain on a union treasury resulting from a court decision would probably be very small. Though the dues rebate policy for political dissenters originally arose under the Railway Labor Act, it is fully applicable to unions covered by Taft-Hartley.

To comply with the new policy, unions tried to establish some practicable and lawful way to rebate that portion of dues that a union spends on political activities. This is not an easy problem, given the difficulty of isolating funds used only for political activities. Indeed, Justice Black, who dissented in *Machinists* v. *Street,* said it would be a "mathematical impossibility" to separate that amount of dues used for collective bargaining purposes from the amount used for political activities. In any event, unions have established a variety of dues rebate plans trying to satisfy the policy. In 1975, a union adopted a flat 5 percent rebate plan which it said covered the amount of dues it spends for political campaigns and lobbying.[75] Later, the United Steelworkers put its figure at 3.92 percent[76] and the United Automobile Workers at 4 percent.[77]

In 1986, however, the U.S. Supreme Court unanimously held in *Chicago Teachers Union* v. *Lee Hudson* (Docket No. 84-1503, March 4, 1986) that the union was required to provide a detailed explanation to nonunion employees as to how it arrived at the calculation separating collective bargaining and political activities. Previously, the union announced that 95 percent of its expenditures were related to collective bargaining activities and 5 percent for political matters. Though the case arose in the public sector, it is more than likely the same rule will apply to the private sector. Given this decision, it appears that unions may no longer establish arbitrarily the percentage of dues which is allocated to political activities. They must be prepared to demonstrate by competent evidence the amount spent for that purpose.

So far, the dues rebate requirement has not had much impact upon union treasuries. For example, in 1980, the UAW rebated dues to only 100 disgruntled union members. However, a more serious problem has surfaced, which could cause hardship to the labor movement. Sparked and financed by the National Right to Work Legal Defense Foundation, a well-known antiunion group, many employees have filed court suits demanding rebates covering much more than union political expenditures. These members have claimed a rebate for any expenditure that is not used for purely collective bargaining and grievance adjustments, such as for conventions, organization, publications, social and educational activities, and contributions to groups like the NAACP and United Fund.

In 1984, the U.S. Supreme Court addressed this problem in a case that arose under the Railway Labor Act.[78] Involved in this litigation were employees of Western Airlines who were required to pay agency shop fees in lieu of joining the union and paying union dues. They protested the use of their money for purposes other than collective bargaining and grievance procedure proceedings. In *Ellis* v. *Railway Clerks,* the high court established some standards governing the use of agency shop fees. It held these payments may properly be used (even if employees object) for conventions where union officers are elected and bargaining goals set; social activities; union publications, except for articles relating to political activity; and litigation expenses, provided they are incurred for purposes of negotiating and administering collective bargaining agreements. However, of critical significance, the court ruled dissenters' payments may not be used for general organizing purposes. In this respect, it rejected the union's assertion that the degree of organization within an industry or trade has a direct bearing on the ability of unions to negotiate improved wages and working conditions.

One other aspect of the case is of considerable importance. A union may not use agency shop fees for improper purposes and then later rebate that portion to dissenters. Such a procedure, the court held, amounted to a non-interest-bearing loan to the union. To comply, unions must place the dissenters' payments in an interest-bearing escrow account, or establish a system of reduced dues payments for them.

Though *Ellis* v. *Railway Clerks* arose under the Railway Labor Act, the principles that it established undoubtedly apply to Taft-Hartley. In addition, though agency shop fees were involved, dissenters required to join unions to hold their jobs are probably covered by the decision. In essence, no difference exists between being compelled to pay agency fees or union dues to hold a job. In any event, only time will disclose the full burden placed on unions by those who object to union expenditures.

THE AGENCY SHOP IN RIGHT-TO-WORK LAW STATES

The agency shop, along with the maintenance-of-membership arrangement, was first used during World War II when the National War Labor Board refused to extend closed-shop and union-shop arrangements to industries when these had not been negotiated prior to the war. National labor policy required unions to represent all bargaining-unit workers, even those who were not union members. For this reason, unions argued that there was an incentive for many workers to refrain from union membership, since they were entitled to union benefits without paying their share of the financial costs. Such workers are referred to as "free-riders." The agency shop appeared attractive to unions representing workers in right-to-work states. When the arrangement is successfully negotiated, an employee does not have to join a union but is required to pay a fee for union services as a condition of employment. The fee required is usually the equivalent of periodic dues and initiation fees required of members.

As events turned out, however, the effort of unions to obtain the agency shop in right-to-work law states proved unsuccessful. In ten of the states, the agency shop was expressly outlawed. In the other ten, the legislation or constitutional provisions were silent on the issue. In Indiana, the state courts held that the agency shop was legal because the law did not expressly forbid it.[79] However, the agency shop in Indiana became moot after the state repealed its right-to-work law in 1965. Unions that had negotiated the agency shop while the law was in effect went back to the union shop after it was repealed. In the other states, the agency shop was declared illegal by either the states' attorneys general or courts. As will be pointed out later in this chapter, the U.S. Supreme Court held that the states did not violate Taft-Hartley when they outlawed the agency shop.

THE AGENCY SHOP UNDER TAFT-HARTLEY

Whereas the state courts dealt with the legality of the agency shop in state right-to-work laws, the NLRB and the federal courts were called on to determine whether the agency shop was lawful under Taft-Hartley. Though the NLRB had voted the device to be lawful in 1952,[80] the issue surfaced again in a considerable amount of litigation. One problem dealt with the changing personnel of the NLRB.

In February 1961, the NLRB, then composed predominantly of Eisenhower appointees, ruled on the legality of the agency shop under the national law.[81] The case involved a General Motors plant located in Indiana. As stated, the agency shop was held to be lawful under the Indiana right-to-work law. The company refused to bargain over the agency shop as proposed by the union on the grounds that the agency shop was illegal under Taft-Hartley. The Board held that the agency shop was unlawful because it was different from a union shop. Under Taft-Hartley, unions may not force employees to engage in any union activity except to require membership as a condition of employment. Section 7 of the law states that employees have the right to refrain from any or all union activities, "except to the extent that such right may be affected by an agreement requiring membership in a labor organization as a condition of employment." Since the agency shop does not require union membership as a condition of employment, the Board held that the agency shop was illegal because it forced employees to engage in a union activity not authorized by the law. If the Eisenhower Board's decision prevailed, the agency shop would be illegal throughout the United States. Whether or not a state had a right-to-work law forbidding the agency shop, a union could not make such a demand on an employer.

By September of the same year, 1961, the NLRB was composed predominantly of Kennedy appointees. It reviewed the previous decision and held that the agency shop was in fact lawful under Taft-Hartley.[82] As opposed to the Eisenhower Board, the new Board held that the agency shop was like the union shop, saying that it was a lesser form of the union shop. However, in 1962, the Sixth Circuit Court of Appeals rejected the Board's position and held that the agency shop was illegal under Taft-Hartley.[83] Like the Eisenhower Board, the court said:

> We do not regard the "agency shop arrangement" as being something lesser than a "union shop." We believe it is entirely different. A Union security agreement is premised upon membership in a labor organization. An "agency shop" on the contrary is based upon an employee paying charges in lieu of union membership as a condition of employment.

In other words, the union and the agency shop were different for purposes of Taft-Hartley.

In June 1963, the U.S. Supreme Court had the final word on the matter. It held that the agency shop was lawful under national labor policy and could be negotiated in any state that had not outlawed the agency shop.[84] The Court said that for purposes of Taft-Hartley, the agency shop and the union shop are the same because under its terms, financial security is the maximum security that a union can achieve. As an earlier discussion demonstrated, under the nonpayment-of-dues provision, an employee can be discharged from a job only if he or she loses membership because of nonpayment of periodic dues and initiation fees. The Court held that under Taft-Hartley, payment of dues—as in agency shop—is the maximum kind of security that a union can obtain. As noted, an employee need not ever join a union despite a union shop, provided that he or she is willing to pay union dues. As the Court said in *General Motors:*

> The burdens of membership upon which employment may be conditioned are expressly limited to the payment of initiation fees and monthly dues.

On the same day it decided *General Motors,* the Supreme Court also determined whether or not a state could outlaw the agency shop under Section 14 (b) of Taft-Hartley.[85] In *Schermerhorn,* a union located in Florida, where the agency shop was illegal under the state's right-to-work law, argued that the states did not have the authority to outlaw the device under Section 14 (b). It said that under Section 14 (b), a state could only make illegal arrangements that require union membership as a condition of employment. Section 14 (b) says that a state may make illegal "agreements requiring membership in a labor organization as a condition of employment." Thus, unlike the union involved in *General Motors,* the Florida union argued that the union shop and the agency shop were different for purposes of Taft-Hartley. Clearly, the high court could not possibly have accepted the position of the Florida union because to do so, it would have applied the same language found in Section 7 and Section 14 (b)—"membership in a labor organization as a condition of employment"—in a highly inconsistent manner. The high court held that the union shop and the agency shop were the same for purposes of Section 14 (b), and that a state could make either device illegal under its state right-to-work law.

In short, the unions could not have possibly been successful in both the *General Motors* and *Schermerhorn* cases. They came out the best they could—the agency shop is lawful in any state in which it is not illegal under state law. The Supreme Court could not possibly have held on the very same day that the union shop and the agency shop were the same for purposes of Section 7 and then turn around and hold that they were different for purposes of Section 14 (b).

In summary, a consequence of the Supreme Court decisions on the agency shop is that the arrangement is lawful in any state that does not make it illegal. In addition, states may outlaw the agency shop under Section 14 (b) of Taft-Hartley. Thus, unions came out the best that they could, given the provisions of the law. Indeed, had the high court held that the agency shop violated Taft-Hartley, it would be illegal in all states and not just in states in which it is prohibited by state law.

LEGAL CONTROL OF THE CHECKOFF

Checkoff arrangements are included in the large majority of collective bargaining contracts. This dues-collection method, whereby the employer agrees to deduct monthly union dues from the employee's pay (and in some cases his or her initiation fees and special assessments as well) for transmittal to the union, has obvious advantages for labor organizations, not only in terms of time and money savings, but also because the union's institutional needs are further strengthened. For the same reasons, many managers are not enthusiastic about the checkoff, although some have preferred it to the constant visits of union dues collectors to the workplace. Once willing to grant the union shop, however, employers have rarely made a major bargaining issue of the checkoff per se. And the growth of this mechanism has been remarkably consistent with that of the union security measure: whereas in 1946, about 40 percent of all labor agreements provided for the checkoff system of dues collection, by 1954, this percentage had increased to about 75 percent, and the figure is approximately 80 percent today.[86]

As indicated, and contrary to popular notion, many employers favor the checkoff. As the vice-president of the Allis-Chalmers Manufacturing Company once remarked:

> We offered the checkoff to Local 248 because for selfish reasons we do not want a lot of collecting on the company premises.[87]

In other words, from the point of view of plant efficiency, management in large measure favors the checkoff, an important factor for the growth of the checkoff in collective bargaining.

The Checkoff Under the Railway Labor Act

Congress first gave attention to the problem of the checkoff when it enacted the Railway Labor Act of 1926. Under this law, the checkoff of union dues by railroad operators was forbidden. Such a prohibition was favored by organized labor and not opposed by the Railroad Brotherhoods. Likewise, the railway unions urged Congress to prohibit arrangements that required union membership as a condition of securing a job. Congress responded to these union requests and outlawed both the closed shop and the checkoff in the railroad industry.

Labor unions generally favored the closed shop and the checkoff, for these arrangements enhanced union security and increased the bargaining effectiveness of the organizations. Why then did the railroad unions adopt a program that appears inconsistent with overall union policy? The answer to this question is found in the history of railroad unionism. Elsewhere it was noted that the company-dominated union characterized the railroad industry. For many years, railroad employers attempted to forestall genuine collective bargaining by sponsoring company-dominated unions. These employers were so determined that such unions receive the support of the workers that membership in these organizations was frequently made a condition of employment. Likewise, railroad management checked off a sum from the wages of each worker and turned the money over to the company-dominated unions. In other words, railway employees were forced to join these company-sponsored unions, with no way to prevent the railroad employers from deducting from their wages a sum equivalent to the dues charged for "membership." In some railroads, membership in the company union was not made a condition of employment, but the management nevertheless deducted membership dues from the workers' paychecks.

The checkoff and the requirement of membership as a condition of employment precluded the establishment of regular labor unions. Accordingly, the railroad workers sought relief from Congress. Hence, the Railway Labor Act of

1926 stamped out the closed shop and the checkoff in the railroad industry. The policy of the Railway Labor Act with respect to the closed shop and the checkoff had a particular and limited origin. It was adopted to aid the collective bargaining efforts of workers.

The 1951 amendments to the Act legalized the checkoff arrangement. The status of standard railroad unions relative to company unions had changed, as mentioned elsewhere in this chapter. Unlike in Taft-Hartley, there is no de-authorization machinery available to rescind union-security arrangements, and therefore the checkoff holds a more certain position in railroading and in the airlines than in general industry.

The Checkoff Under Taft-Hartley

The reaction of organized labor to checkoff control legislation in general industry was quite different from that of the railway labor unions. Unions opposed the efforts of Congress and state legislatures to outlaw or regulate the device. When Taft-Hartley was being considered, many labor leaders spoke out against the checkoff's control. Despite their efforts, however, the 1947 labor law contained two important checkoff restrictions.[88] The effect is to control the ability of the union and management to negotiate checkoff arrangements. Certain basic conditions must be met before a checkoff agreement can become effective.

First, each individual union member must sign an agreement authorizing the employer to deduct union dues under the checkoff plan. In the absence of such an authorization, the employer may not deduct union dues despite the existence of a checkoff clause negotiated through the collective bargaining process. The second restriction applies to the length of time for which the authorization can be effective: no authorization of a worker can be irrevocable for more than one year, or beyond the termination date of the contract, whichever is shorter. To illustrate: An authorization by a worker signed on January 1, 1987, becomes ineffective on December 31, 1987, regardless of the desires of the union, management, or the worker. Section 302 (d) provided that any employer who deducted union dues from the wages of employees in violation of these restrictions could be imprisoned for one year and was subject to a fine of $10,000.

Soon after the Taft-Hartley law was enacted, the question arose as to the lawfulness of a collective bargaining provision under which an employer deducts initiation fees, special assessments, and fines as well as regular monthly membership dues. In addition, a question was raised as to whether it was required under the national law that each employee personally sign a new authorization card each year. On May 13, 1948, the Assistant Solicitor General of the United States issued an opinion that has served to clarify these questions somewhat.[89] He ruled that the term *membership dues,* as utilized in the law, includes initiation fees and assessments as well as regular periodic dues. On the other hand, he made no reference to fines assessed against union members for the violation of union rules. The Assistant Solicitor General further offered his opinion that checkoff arrangements providing an employee the annual opportunity to rescind a written authorization did not appear to be a "willful" violation of the Taft-Hartley law. This meant that arrangements between employers and unions were valid if they gave employees such an opportunity but that employees did not actually have to sign a new authorization each year.

As a result, many checkoff provisions now allow for the deduction of initiation fees and assessments as well as for regular monthly membership dues. In addition, it is a common practice in industry for employees to sign one authorization card. However, under the latter arrangement, both the collective bargaining contract and the authorization card clearly state that the employee has an annual opportunity, usually lasting for fifteen days, to rescind his or her written authorization. If the employee does not take this opportunity, the authorization card remains in force for another year.

When bargaining-unit employees have deauthorized a union-security provision in a collective bargaining contract, they have the option of revoking checkoff authorizations.[90] The Second Circuit Court enforced the Board's *Penn Cork* rule that an employer's refusal to honor employee requests to revoke the checkoff constituted support or assistance to the labor organization. The Board reasoned that employees who authorize a dues checkoff do so under the influence of union-security clauses; otherwise they would not find it necessary to do so. Employees, therefore, have the right to revoke their checkoff authorizations at any time after a union-security clause is de-authorized through a validly held election.[91] They are not required to adhere to the usual period of time provided each year to rescind authorization. However, de-authorization of a union-security clause does not automatically rescind the checkoff provision.[92] An employer cannot unilaterally change the checkoff provision, since some bargaining-unit workers may desire to remain union members and to take advantage of the checkoff convenience. Also, some arrangements contain provisions permitting new employees voluntarily to designate the checkoff as a method of paying union dues. Unilateral employer revocation of the checkoff would constitute a unilateral contractual change affecting both new and old employees desiring the arrangement.[93]

Another checkoff problem arises when an employee resigns from the union. The issue is whether resignation also cancels the employee's checkoff authorization even though the employee did not rescind it during the allowable escape period. The Board has been ambivalent on this issue, holding that under some circumstances, the employer must still deduct dues,[94] and in other circumstances that dues deduction would be unlawful.[95] At this writing, given the most recent available Board decisions, it would seem that dues deduction would be unlawful after the employee resigns from the union.[96] Since these changing decisions were reached by a split vote, a definitive court decision is necessary to resolve the problem.

From the foregoing, it appears clear that though the checkoff is an important issue of collective bargaining, it does not normally constitute a crucial point of controversy between employers and unions. It does not contain the features of conflicting philosophy involved in the union-security problem. It has rarely by itself become a major strike issue, since the stakes are not high. As a matter of fact, though the checkoff serves the institutional needs of the union, employers often find some gain from the incorporation of the device in the collective bargaining agreement. This is particularly true when the labor contract contains a union-security arrangement. Not only does the checkoff obviate the need of dues collection on company premises with the attendant impact upon the orderly operation of the plant, but it avoids the need of starting the discharge process for employees who are negligent in the payment of dues. Frequently, without a checkoff, an employee who must belong to a union as a condition of employment will delay paying dues, and the employer and union are then both faced with the task of instituting the discharge process, which is most commonly suspended as the employee, faced with loss of employment, pays dues at the last possible minute. The checkoff eliminates the need for this wasted and time-consuming effort of busy employer and union representatives.

Even when the union shop is not in effect, moreover, the checkoff need not necessarily be given permanent status. The employee is obligated to pay dues for one year only, and if he or she desires to stop the checkoff, this can be done during the escape period. The escape period is different when deauthorization elections have occurred, as mentioned. But, under any circumstances, if the management believes that the union is so irresponsible as not to deserve the checkoff, it need not agree to it. The mechanism is consequently also revocable from the company's point of view.

CONTROLS OVER GOOD-FAITH BARGAINING

The duty to bargain in good faith is a government requirement that predates the Wagner Act of 1935. However, "conclusions as to whether a given attitude or approach to collective bargaining constitutes 'good faith' will always have to be drawn."[97] The good-faith bargaining duty was advanced as early as 1921 in a case before the Railway Labor Board.[98] In its interpretation of requirements set forth in the Transportation Act of 1920, the Board held that the negotiating parties must make an honest effort to decide all issues in conference. "If they cannot decide all matters in dispute in conference, it is their duty to then decide all that is possible."[99]

The National Labor Board, established by executive order to administer the National Industrial Recovery Act of 1933, could not ignore the good-faith bargaining issue. It held that Section 7 (a) of the Wagner Act placed an implicit reciprocal duty on employers to bargain.[100] This duty involved more than merely meeting and conferring with labor unions. During the 1930s it was assumed that unions as bargaining institutions would deal in good faith at the conference table.

The Wagner Act required the same obligation of employers. Experiences under the 1935 law did not convince the public that unions proceeded in good faith at the conference table. This led to inclusion of a provision in Taft-Hartley that required the same set of standards from unions as were required of employers under the earlier laws.[101]

Congress incorporated the Board's good-faith bargaining requirements into Section 8 (d) of the 1947 law. These requirements originated under earlier attempts of government to regulate labor relations. Section 8 (d) requires that

> for the purpose of this section, to bargain collectively is the performance of the mutual obligation of the employer and the representative of the employees to meet at reasonable times and confer in good faith with respect to wages, hours, and other terms and conditions of employment, or the negotiation of an agreement, or any question arising thereunder, and the execution of a written contract incorporating any agreement reached if requested by either party, but such obligation does not compel either party to agree to a proposal or require the making of a concession.[102]

This requirement constitutes the congressional framework of good-faith bargaining. The NLRB and the courts took on the responsibility for giving substance to the broad legislative language.

Under the Wagner Act, as with Taft-Hartley, the major task for the Board in each case was to determine whether the parties entered into discussion "with an open and fair mind, and a sincere purpose to find a basis of agreement . . . and if found to embody it in a contract . . . which shall stand as a mutual guarantee of conduct, and as a guide for the adjustment of grievances."[103] Decisions are made after a review of the totality of bargaining conduct. Isolated behavior does not generally determine the finding of unfair labor practices.

Good-faith conduct in bargaining requires an assessment of the state of mind of the negotiating parties; all the circumstances in a case must be reviewed to determine their motives. Even though the Wagner Act did not provide for union unfair labor practices, union conduct was reviewed by the Board before holding an employer in violation of the good-faith bargaining requirement. In one Wagner Act case, for example, the NLRB ruled that "a union's refusal to bargain in good faith may remove the possibility of negotiation and thus preclude the existence of a situation in which the employer's own good faith can be tested. If it cannot be tested, its absence can hardly be found."[104]

An assessment of good-faith bargaining very often requires that the Board turn to circumstantial evidence to make a determination. Some circumstantial evidence, however, makes the intent of the party so evident that the lack of good faith may be logically inferred.

The Board and the courts, in their continuing quest to bring about statutory bargaining conformance, have built an enormous set of conditions for good-faith bargaining. Applying to employers and unions, these include the following standards:

1. There must be a serious attempt to adjust differences and to reach an acceptable common ground.

2. Counterproposals must be offered when another party's proposal is rejected. This must involve the "give and take" of an auction system.[105]

3. A position with regard to contract terms may not be constantly changed.[106]

4. Evasive behavior during negotiations is not permitted.[107]

5. There must be a willingness to incorporate oral agreements into a written contract.[108]

In the 1960s, the NLRB and the courts held that General Electric did not bargain in good faith because it practiced what is called "boulwarism," named after its creator Lemuel R. Boulware, a vice-president of the corporation. G.E. submitted a complete labor agreement to the union. It refused to change any of its terms unless the union could prove to its satisfaction that such a change was necessary. In other words, the union realistically had the option to "take it or leave it." At the same time, the corporation mounted a massive publicity campaign directed at its employees. The purpose was to induce the employees to put pressure on the union to accept G.E.'s offer. In 1969, within the context of a long strike, a federal appeals court upheld the Board decision that such a bargaining approach did not meet the good-faith requirement.[109] The court held that a "take it or leave it" approach was not of itself necessarily illegal. What made the G.E. conduct illegal was that at the same time, it had carried on the employee publicity campaign in the attempt to bypass the union. An employer is not permitted to deal with a union through employees. It is required to deal with employees through a union. In the 1973 contract negotiations, G.E. abolished "boulwarism" and no strike occurred.

Employer Bad-Faith Bargaining.   Some comparatively recent examples where an employer did not bargain in good faith are these: granting a wage increase to employees over the union's protest and before it bargained with the union to an impasse;[110] refusing to furnish information to a union pertaining to a wage increase granted to nonbargaining unit employees which the union needed to prepare its wage proposals for upcoming negotiations with the employer;[111] withdrawing from multiemployer bargaining during contract negotiations and refusing to sign and implement the new multiemployer collective bargaining contract;[112] and refusing to grant members of the union's negotiating committee uncompensated leave to permit them to engage in bargaining during working hours while at the same time refusing the union's request to bargain during nonworking hours.[113]

In order to bargain for the health and safety of employees, the Oil, Chemical & Atomic Workers Union demanded that employers disclose generic names of chemical substances used or produced, as well as the medical records of employees. The employers refused, claiming that disclosure would invade the privacy of employees and compromise trade secrets. With some limitations, the NLRB in 1982 held that employers did not bargain in good faith when they refused to divulge such information.[114] While upholding the union's request, the Board said few matters could be of greater concern to employees "than exposure to working conditions potentially threatening their health, well-being or their very lives." However, before turning over employees' medical records, employers may conceal their identity. Also, employers need not disclose the generic names of chemicals that constitute proprietary trade secrets. Thus, the NLRB attempted to strike a balance between conflicting interests—the employer's desire to protect workers' privacy and protect trade secrets, and the union's need for material information about potentially life-threatening work conditions.

Union Bad-Faith Bargaining.   Unions did not bargain in good faith under the following circumstances: The unions amended by-laws forbidding members to work overtime after they agreed in collective bargaining that employers may require employees to work overtime to meet production requirements;[115] refused to bargain unless there was a merger of two historically separate bargaining units;[116] forbade members to accept temporary supervisory positions when the labor agreement gave employers the right to assign bargaining unit employees to such jobs;[117] and insisted that persons designated by the union to serve as stewards be hired by the employer.[118]

Cases of No Agreement.   Though good-faith collective bargaining is a cornerstone of national labor policy, it does not mean that the parties must reach an agreement. Its purpose is to encourage the parties to reach an agreement, but the concept does not mean that a strike or lockout cannot occur if they fail to settle their contractual problems. Also, the NLRB is powerless to order the parties to incorporate a particular provision into a labor agreement. In *H. K. Porter,*[119] the NLRB directed the employer to grant the checkoff to the union and incorporate the dues collection device into the labor agreement. The Board felt that this remedy was justified because the company had refused to bargain over the checkoff and generally frustrated the bargaining process. However, the U.S. Supreme Court held that violation of the requirement to bargain in good faith did not authorize the NLRB to insert a provision into the labor agreement as a remedy for the violation.

Underscoring the right of employers and unions to negotiate labor agreements free of judicial control, the U.S. Supreme Court in 1982 in *United Mine Workers of America Health & Retirement Funds* v. *Robinson* (455 U.S. 562) held that the courts do not have the power to apply a reasonableness standard in reviewing the provisions of collective bargaining contracts. That is, the judiciary may not substitute its judgment for that of the parties as to what is reasonable.

Borg-Warner Categories

Probably Congress did not intend for the NLRB and the courts to interfere with the substance of collective bargaining. However, under the *Borg-Warner* doctrine, the Board with court approval plays an important role in determining what the parties may negotiate in their agreements. The *Borg-Warner* doctrine applies Section 8 (d) of Taft-Hartley to particular demands made by employers and unions during negotiations. It will be recalled that Section 8 (d) of Taft-Hartley requires the parties to confer on "wages, hours, and other terms and conditions of employment." But some terms and conditions of employment are outlawed by the Act. Many other items that might be of interest to unions or management might not fall within the bargaining items mentioned in Section 8 (d). The Board eventually resolved the question of what to do in such circumstances.

The *Borg-Warner* case, ultimately decided by the U.S. Supreme Court in 1958, involved "a 'ballot' clause calling for a pre-strike secret vote of employees (union and nonunion) as to the employer's last offer."[120] It also involved "a recognition clause which excluded, as a party to the contract, the International Union which had been certified by the National Labor Relations Board as the employees' exclusive bargaining agent, and substituted for it the agent's uncertified local affiliate."

The union refused to agree upon either of the company's demands as conditions of contract settlement. A strike resulted and the union did not prevail. Both clauses were subsequently included in the collective bargaining agreement. Prior to their inclusion, the international union filed refusal-to-bargain unfair labor practice charges against the company.

The Board held that the company had violated the refusal-to-bargain provisions of Taft-Hartley by insisting upon inclusion of these items in the contract. It classified bargaining demands into three major categories. In *Borg-Warner*, the U.S. Supreme Court held that the Board did have the power to establish these classifications. At times, however, the courts have upset the agency because they believed that the Board placed a particular demand in the wrong category. In any event, here are the three categories in which the Board will place a particular demand of an employer or a union:

Illegal Items. The first was the illegal category. If a demand was made by a negotiating party that was illegal under the Act, the Board would find it in violation of the refusal-to-bargain unfair labor practice provision.[121] For example, the Act prohibits the closed shop and compulsory dues checkoff. A demand for items such as these is prohibited by law. A refusal to bargain on them would not constitute an unfair labor practice. The Act itself withdrew certain subjects from the scope of bargaining.

Mandatory Items. The second category established by the Board and later the Court involved the mandatory group of items. It was in this category that the Board placed the Section 8 (d) items of "wages, hours, and other terms and conditions of employment."

Labor and management groups must bargain in good faith on items in the mandatory category, and they may be bargained to an impasse without violating the unfair labor practice provisions of Taft-Hartley. Unions may strike to obtain mandatory items in the contract. Employers are authorized to refuse to sign a contract unless their version of the mandatory items is included in the agreement. The NLRB and the courts must ultimately decide which items fall within the meaning of wages, hours, and other terms and conditions of employment. Many issues have been designated as mandatory subjects for collective bargaining. Some of these include subcontracting, [122] stock purchase plans, [123] profit-sharing plans,[124] pension and employee welfare plans,[125] rental of company housing,[126] Christmas bonuses,[127] work loads and production standards,[128] plant rules,[129] whether union members should be paid by the employer when negotiating a labor agreement during working hours,[130] and a successorship clause that would require a new owner of the business to assume the old employer's contractual obligation.[131] In a significant decision, the U.S. Supreme Court held that employers may lawfully demand that promotions, discipline, and work scheduling be a matter of exclusive management control, and not subject to arbitration.[132] In June 1981, in *NLRB* v. *Amax Coal,* (453 U.S. 323), the high court also held that a union may lawfully strike an employer who refuses to contribute to the union's industry-wide pension and welfare programs.

In a particularly interesting case, a hospital had required that employees submit to a polygraph (lie-detector) test as a condition of continuance of employment. Serious vandalism had occurred inside and outside the hospital during a strike. The hospital required such test as an act of determining which employees, if any, were responsible for the vandalism. However, the union refused to permit the hospital to test employees under such circumstances. Upon review of the case, the NLRB held that polygraph testing is a mandatory subject of collective bargaining since if an employee failed the test, he or she could be discharged.[133] The hospital was required to bargain with the union over this issue and could not institute such tests as a matter of managerial prerogative.

After considerable litigation in the lower federal courts, the U.S. Supreme Court in 1979 sustained the Board position that in-plant food services and prices were mandatory subjects of bargaining. Almost every plant has a cafeteria or vending machines where employees may purchase food. Normally the employer uses an outside vendor to provide such food services. In *Ford Motor Co.,* a unanimous court said:

> With all due respect to the courts of appeals that have held otherwise, we conclude that the Board's consistent view that in-plant food prices and services are mandatory bargaining subjects is not an unreasonable or unprincipled construction of the statute. . .[T]he availability of food during working hours and the conditions under which it is to be consumed are matters of deep concern to workers, and one need not strain to consider them to be among those "conditions" of employment that should be subject to the mutual duty to bargain. By the same token, where the employer has chosen, apparently in his own interest, to make available a system of in-plant feeding facilities for his employees, the prices at which food is offered and other aspects of this service may reasonably be considered among those subjects about which management and the union must bargain.[134]

Another important issue was resolved by the U.S. Supreme Court in 1981. Recall that it had held in the *Darlington* case, discussed in Chapter 9, that an employer can go completely out of business for whatever reasons it chooses, including the desire to avoid unionization and collective bargaining. At times, however, an employer shuts down a single plant or operation that it deems to be unprofitable. In such a situation, the motive cannot be antiunionism, since as *Darlington* tells us, a partial closing for that reason violates Taft-Hartley. In other words, here we are concerned with a partial closing because of strictly economic reasons.

Since 1966, the NLRB had held that an employer's decision to close a portion of its business and to lay off workers was a mandatory subject for collective bargaining.[135] This did not mean that an employer could not shut down a facility or operation that was losing money. Rather, the employer had to bargain with the union to an impasse before closing. Then the employer could shut down the facility without violating Taft-Hartley.

Some federal appeals courts, however, refused to sustain the Board policy.[136] As a result, in January 1981, the U.S. Supreme Court agreed to adjudicate the matter.[137] Unions, of course, hoped that the Court would approve the Board position. They did not contend that bargaining over the employer's decision would necessarily persuade it not to close the operation. Instead, they believed that collective bargaining could result in an agreement that might minimize the adverse effects on employees.

Whatever merit there might have been in the unions' position, however, did not persuade the U.S. Supreme Court. In June 1981, it held that an employer may lawfully close part of a business for economic reasons without prior bargaining over the decision.[138] While reversing the Board, the Court said in *First National Maintenance* that Congress never intended

> that the elected union representative would become an equal partner in the running of the business enterprise in which the union's members are employed. Management must be free from the constraints of the bargaining process to the extent essential for the running of a profitable business.

In a way, there is some irony in this decision. As we noted, unions have the right to bargain with employers over many conditions of employment. It appears somewhat ironic for the Court to hold that unions do not have the right to bargain over job security, which is often their members' most pressing need. On the other hand, *First National Maintenance* does not change the policy established in the *Darlington* case. Also, employers must still bargain over the effects of a partial closing, including the provision of severance pay, pension plans, vacation pay, and preferential hiring rights for laid off employees.

Voluntary Items.   The third voluntary category includes items not labeled illegal or mandatory. One example might be a union demand to ratify promotions to the supervisor ranks as well as the right to ask for the dismissal of these employees. Voluntary items may be discussed at the bargaining table, but they cannot be bargained to an impasse. Unions may not strike over the item. Employers cannot make the item a condition for signing a labor contract. If the NLRB finds that an item in the voluntary category is bargained to an impasse, it will hold that a per se violation of Section 8 (d) has taken place. No further inquiry will be made into the remaining bargaining conduct of the parties. It is a per se violation regardless of the other issues. Some union demands have been placed in the voluntary category. These include demanding that agricultural labor and supervision be included in the labor agreement;[139] requiring a company to contribute to an industry-wide promotion fund;[140] requiring a company to abandon strike insurance plans;[141] requiring a bank to continue a free investment counseling service for its employees that the bank had terminated;[142] and insisting that an employer association with which the union was negotiating abandon litigation concerning management of a trust fund.[143] In 1971, the U.S. Supreme Court held that unions have no right to bargain for pensions and other insurance programs for persons previously retired. It held that retired persons are not "employees" within the meaning of the law.[144] Previously, the NLRB had held that retired persons are employees under the law, and unions could bargain for them in the area of pension benefits.[145] By the subsequent decision, unions lost the opportunity to improve the living standards of millions of retired persons. In 1985, bills were introduced in Congress that would have explicitly made pension benefits for already-retired employees a mandatory issue of collective bargaining.[146] Not much hope, however, exists for their enactment into law.

In 1976, the NLRB reaffirmed its longstanding policy that a union could not demand that an employer post a performance bond as a guarantee for the payment of wages and fringe benefits, including pensions.[147] It rejected the union's contention that the Board should change its policy because of the enactment of the 1974 Employee Retirement Insurance Security Act, which provides for federal regulation of employee pension plans.

Employer demands have also been placed in the voluntary category by the NLRB and the courts. These include demanding that a union withdraw fines previously imposed upon members who have crossed picket lines during a strike in violation of union rules;[148] insisting that a labor federation be party to the contract when a local union affiliated with the larger body was the lawful and certified bargaining representative;[149] granting the employer the right to use the union label;[150] requiring a union to post a performance bond;[151] and insisting that nonunion employees should have the right to vote upon the provisions of the contract negotiated by the union.[152] Reversing a longstanding policy, the NLRB held that an employer may not demand that a court reporter transcribe contract negotiations as a condition for collective bargaining.[153] Of course, should a union demand the use of a court reporter, it would also be covered by the same policy. As stated previously in *Borg-Warner,* an employer demand that would require a strike vote election among employees before a strike occurs falls within the voluntary category.

Additional *Borg-Warner* "voluntary" cases are of particular significance. One dealt with "interest arbitration."[154] As opposed to "grievance arbitration," interest arbitration involves the process in which an arbitrator, by prior mutual agreement of the parties, determines the terms of a labor agreement after the parties have reached an impasse in bargaining. Grievance arbitration deals with the arbitration of a grievance under an existing labor agreement. A union demanded that the employer agree to a contract provision that, should a dispute arise in the negotiation of the subsequent contract, arbitration would be used to settle the dispute. The employer refused to agree to such an arrangement. When the union pressed the issue to an impasse, the Board held that the union had violated Taft-Hartley. In short, the Board held that interest arbitration is not a term or condition of employment within the meaning of Section 8 (d) of the law. It said that federal policy favors collective bargaining free from outside interference. Submitting an issue to arbitration would remove it from the control of the bargaining process. Murphy, former chief of the NLRB, dissented from her colleagues. In her view, interest arbitration is a mandatory issue of collective bargaining because it would affect the relationship between employer and employees concerning wages, hours, and other terms and conditions of employment.

Nor did the Board relent from this policy when an expiring contract provided for interest arbitration.[155] It rejected the labor union's contention that pressing the issue to impasse was lawful on the grounds that the employer had previously agreed to interest arbitration. In other words, the NLRB ruled that just because a party has once agreed to a nonmandatory provision, that party does not waive its unilateral right to refuse to bargain on that provision in subsequent negotiations.

Another such case involved newspaper publishing, but it could reasonably apply to any appropriate industry in which the employer might desire to establish a "code of ethics." The publisher of the *Capital Times* of Madison, Wisconsin, established a code of ethics forbidding its reporters and other news employees from accepting gifts, free tickets, trips, or meals from actual or potential subjects of news stories. It also required reporters to report to the management any personal activity that could create a "potential conflict of interest." The Newspaper Guild supported the goal of insuring higher ethics, but insisted that it wanted an effective input in drafting the code. It also argued that the code of ethics directly affected the wages and working conditions of its members. Therefore, the union believed that the code should be a mandatory subject of collective bargaining. However, the NLRB in a split decision held that the code of ethics fell into the voluntary category.[156] This meant that newspaper publishers have the managerial right to establish such codes for their news employees without bargaining with their unions. To justify its decision, the Board said that the code of ethics did not change wage and working conditions because "prohibition of employees from accepting such gifts won't change working conditions," since the newpaper paid for any meals, tickets, or trips deemed necessary for newsgathering by its reporters. The Board stated that loss of the gifts could not be construed as a cut in wages, because the gifts had come from outside the paper rather than from the reporters' employer.

Though the Board held that the publisher could unilaterally establish a code of ethics, the publisher was required to bargain over the penalties for violation of the code. Former Chair, Fanning, who dissented in *Capital Times,* said that the majority was wholly inconsistent because in his view, the substance of the code could not be separated from the penalties. On this point, the union agreed:

> The decision mystifies us. Apparently, we're [the union] supposed to design punishment to fit crimes, without ever mentioning the crimes.[157]

Reversing a previous policy, the Reagan NLRB in 1984 held that an employer's decision to transfer bargaining-unit work to another location is not a mandatory issue of bargaining.[158] During the term of a labor agreement, United Technologies merged its elevator research and development operations in Manway, New Jersey, with a larger operation in East Hartford, Connecticut, resulting in the layoff of office and technical employees. When the employer refused to bargain on the transfer, the NLRB held originally in 1981 that the company had engaged in an unfair labor practice.[159] To justify the abolishment of that policy, the Reagan Board said in *United Technologies:*

> Despite the evident effect on employees, the critical factor to a determination of whether the decision is subject to mandatory bargaining is the essence of the decision itself . . . i.e. whether it turns upon a change in the nature or direction of the business, or turns upon labor costs; not its effect on employees nor a union's ability to offer alternatives.

Thus, as long as an employer's decision to transfer work is not made to reduce labor costs, the company can unilaterally make the change without bargaining with the union. No longer is an employer required to bargain when the transfer of work involves the scope, direction, or nature of the business.

Another Reagan Board's reversal of former policy, however, did permit an employer to move operations to a nonunion plant to save on labor costs.[160] During the effective period of a collective bargaining contract, the employer attempted to negotiate a wage cut and reduction of employee benefits. After union members had voted against midterm contract concessions, the employer moved operations from Milwaukee to its nonunion facility in Illinois, resulting in considerable layoffs in the Milwaukee plant. Ruling that the employer's conduct amounted to an illegal unilateral modification of existing contract provisions, the previous NLRB had held the employer to have engaged in an unfair labor practice.[161] Unlike in *United Technologies,* the employer in *Milwaukee Spring* had bargained to an impasse. Nonetheless, the impact of both decisions was the same—under both decisions, the capability of unions to provide job security for employees was significantly reduced.

Significance of *Borg-Warner*

Thus, the NLRB has the authority to circumscribe and limit the area of free collective bargaining. As economic conditions change, employers and unions place greater emphasis upon some subjects and less on others. Some issues that may be of the utmost importance in the 1980s may have required little attention in the 1970s. The Board continues to have the authority to classify such items in either the mandatory or voluntary categories. If the decision is made to place a subject in the voluntary category, neither party has the authority to insist upon its inclusion in a collective bargaining contract. A flat rejection of the issue by one of the parties ends the matter. In other words, once a demand is classified in the voluntary category, it is not likely to be included in a collective bargaining contract. Thus, the NLRB controls the substantive content of labor agreements by placing an item in one category or the other.

It is obvious that the NLRB has the authority to change the results of free collective bargaining. This constitutes a situation that may not have been intended by Congress. Nevertheless, the *Borg-Warner* doctrine placed the Board and the courts in the position of policing the collective bargaining process. There is no express provision in Taft-Hartley to provide the Board with such enormous power. Under this doctrine, it is not a question of who may benefit from a particular decision. Employers and unions may be treated favorably or unfavorably, depending upon the decision in a given situation. However, they both lose, since under *Borg-Warner,* employers and unions have both lost the full capability to deal with changing conditions in a climate of free collective bargaining. The NLRB is prepared to serve as a police officer to determine what may be included in a collective bargaining contract. Free collective bargaining would be advanced should the Board and the courts hold that, when an employer or union demand is not expressly illegal under Taft-Hartley, the demand is a mandatory issue of collective bargaining.

Objective standards are not available to determine whether a demand should be placed in the voluntary or mandatory category. Indeed, only the subjective judgment of the Board and the courts stands as the basis of the determination. In no way is there a scientific or objective test for the classification of bargaining demands. That only subjective judgment is involved is manifested by the fact that the NLRB has reversed itself over the years in the determination of these categories. The courts have also reversed the Board's judgments. If scientific and objective standards could determine the classification of demands, these reversals would not occur.

However, given the entrenchment of the *Borg-Warner* doctrine in the nation's labor policy, it cannot be expected that the Board or the courts will ever eliminate the doctrine. It would take an act of Congress to do so, which is not now very likely. Though the doctrine has been with us for about thirty years, this does not necessarily make it right. As one writer put it:

The serious question that is left is whether the Board or the Courts should intervene to prevent an impasse over a voluntary subject when the bargaining is being conducted in good faith. The essence of the argument presented herein is that so long as the parties are in good faith, and the demand is legal, the Board and the Courts should keep their hands off.[162]

Fibreboard Doctrine: Employer's Duty to Bargain During Contract Period

Once an issue falls within the mandatory category, the employer has the duty to bargain with the union over the issue while a collective bargaining contract is in effect. Section 8 (d) of the law does not limit the obligation of the parties to bargain on the "terms and conditions of employment" only when a new contract is being negotiated. It also establishes an affirmative duty to bargain during the effective period of a collective bargaining contract. This problem arises when an employer desires to change employment conditions during a contract period. In order to promote efficiency or to reduce costs, the employer may desire to eliminate or modify a term or condition of employment.

The employer duty to bargain was established under Taft-Hartley when the U.S. Supreme Court decided the *Fibreboard* case.[163] In that dispute, the employer subcontracted certain maintenance work during the term of a labor agreement. He did so to save costs, and subcontracted without consulting or bargaining with the union. As a result of the subcontract, many employees lost their jobs. Upon its review of the case, the Supreme Court held that the employer had unlawfully refused to bargain collectively under Taft-Hartley. Not only did the Court find that subcontracting was a mandatory issue of collective bargaining, but also that the employer had violated the law by taking action without consulting or bargaining with the union. As to the latter issue, the Supreme Court stated:

> The facts of the present case illustrate the propriety of submitting the dispute to collective negotiation. The Company's decision to contract out the maintenance work did not alter the Company's basic operation. The maintenance work still had to be performed in the plant. No capital investment was contemplated; the Company merely replaced existing employees with those of an independent contractor to do the same work under similar conditions of employment. Therefore, to require the employer to bargain about the matter would not significantly abridge his freedom to manage the business.

After it had made this decision, the Court held that the NLRB had the authority to order the employer to resume the maintenance operation that the company had subcontracted, and to reinstate the laid-off employees with back pay. In other words, the Board was authorized to restore the status quo because the employer had failed to bargain with the union before it subcontracted the work. As to the power of the Board to direct such a remedy, the Court pointed to Section 10 (c) of Taft-Hartley, which empowers the NLRB "to take such affirmative action including reinstatement of employees with or without back pay, as will effectuate the policies of this Act."

To understand *Fibreboard*, it should be noted that the law does not forbid an employer to make a change in working conditions. A company may make the change after bargaining with the union to an impasse. After it appears that further bargaining would be fruitless, the employer may make the change. By bargaining to an impasse, a company has discharged its duty to bargain in good faith under the terms of the law. In other words, an employer who has exhausted the bargaining process has the authority to make the change in working conditions that was the subject of negotiations prior to the impasse.[164] Should the union believe that the employer violated the terms of a labor agreement, it then has the opportunity to submit the dispute to arbitration. (We will treat the nature of the arbitration process in full in the next chapter.)

Some employers at times have probably experienced difficulties under the *Fibreboard* doctrine. Before making a change, they had to wait until an impasse was reached. This prevented them from taking immediate advantage of the benefit that would result from the change. If the employer was faced with stiff economic competition, it is possible the doctrine was burdensome. Also, the employer faces a risk under *Fibreboard,* in that the NLRB might subsequently find that no impasse had been reached. Even if the employer waited to make the change after impasse had seemingly been reached, the Board might later find that an impasse had not been reached. Though these appear to be valid criticisms of *Fibreboard*, it would be difficult, if not impossible, to obtain objective evidence to show that this doctrine has been injurious to the business community. At times it is far easier to raise theoretical arguments against the NLRB policy than it is to obtain the economic data to evaluate the merits of a charge.

The NLRB frequently applied the *Fibreboard* doctrine. It decided unfair labor practice cases where the union alleged that the employer did not bargain before the terms and conditions were changed. This does not mean that the Board would find the union charge meritorious in all cases. If it was determined that the employer was authorized to make the change under the language of the labor agreement involved, the union's charge would be dismissed. The Board would consider the management rights clause of the labor agreement and other material provisions contained in it to determine whether the employer was authorized to make the change. In general, a management rights clause in a labor agreement authorizes an employer to make any decision regarding the labor force and the operation of the plant unless limited by any other provision of the contract. Such a clause would also apply relevant NLRB and court decisions to the case under consideration. In this type of case, the employer would argue that it had such power under the terms of the agreement. Thus, if the employer's position prevailed, the Board would dismiss the union's claim that it did not bargain in good faith. On the other hand, if the NLRB found that the contract did not authorize the employer to make the change in working conditions, it would hold that the employer had not complied with lawful bargaining obligations. Under these circumstances, as noted, it would direct the employer to restore the working condition and, where appropriate, require the employer to provide back pay to employees who were adversely affected by the unlawful change in working conditions.

THE *COLLYER* DOCTRINE: DEFERRAL TO ARBITRATION

In 1971, the NLRB changed the forum for the determination of this type of case by deferring certain unfair labor practice cases to arbitrators. Subject to some restrictions to be discussed below, the Board announced in *Collyer*[165] that it would defer such cases to a private arbitrator to determine whether the employer had violated its bargaining obligations under Taft-Hartley. Under *Collyer*, the Board does not determine the merits of the unfair labor practice charge filed by the union. This is one of the most controversial doctrines which the Board has established. Indeed, *Collyer* and its progeny whipped up such a storm of controversy that it has not subsided to this day. One advantage of the doctrine, as stressed by its advocates, is that it reduces the NLRB case load. However, two Board members have said that *Collyer* has resulted in an "insignificant reduction of the Board's workload."[166] In any event, even if the doctrine substantially decreases the work of the NLRB, it is still controversial, as the following discussion will show.

In the *Collyer* case itself, the employer changed the wage rates of skilled-trade workers as well as the incentive factors used in computing wage rates for certain other employees. It also reassigned job duties among employees. It made these changes unilaterally, without consulting or bargaining with the union. The employer believed that the action was authorized under the terms of the collective bargaining contract. The union filed unfair labor practice charges, alleging that the employer did not fulfill the bargaining obligations of Taft-Hartley. The Board, instead of determining whether the unfair labor practice charge had merit, deferred the matter to arbitration.

In the Board's view, the policy was justified because the arbitration would simultaneously determine the contractual issue and the unfair labor practice charge. It said:

> The contract clearly provides for the grievance and arbitration machinery; where the unilateral action taken is not designed to undermine the union and is not patently erroneous but rather is based on a substantial claim of contractual privilege, and it appears that the arbitral interpretation of the contract will resolve both the unfair labor practice issue and the contract interpretation issue in a matter compatible with the purposes of the Act, then the Board should defer to the arbitration clause conceived by the parties.

And:

> In our view, disputes such as these can better be resolved by arbitrators with special skill and experience in deciding matters arising under established bargaining relationships than by the application by this Board of a particular provision of our statute.

The Board deferred to arbitration despite Section 10 (a) of Taft-Hartley, which empowers the NLRB to enforce the unfair labor practice program of the statute and which says that

> this power shall not be affected by any other means of adjustment or prevention that has or may be established by agreement, law, or otherwise.

To justify its position, the Board majority pinned its decision to Section 203 (d) of Taft-Hartley, which states:

> Final adjustment by a method agreed upon by the parties is hereby declared to be the desirable method of settlement of grievance disputes arising over the application or interpretation of an existing collective-bargaining agreement.

It is material that this provision appears in the section of the law that establishes the Federal Mediation and Conciliation Service. To carry out the policy expressed in the provision, the Federal Mediation and Conciliation Service makes available to employers and unions the names of qualified private arbitrators to enable them to use arbitration as a method for the final adjustment of disputes arising over the application and interpretation of a labor agreement. Since the provision does not appear in those areas of the law that deal with unfair labor practices, however, it could be argued that Congress did not intend Section 203 (d) to be used to dilute the exclusive power of the NLRB to prevent unfair labor practices.

Collyer was not established by unanimous decision. In the majority were Miller, Kennedy, and Brown. Jenkins and Fanning constituted the minority. None of this group is a Board member any longer. With unusual vigor, the minority criticized the majority on the grounds that, in their view, the Board had abandoned its statutory duty to enforce the unfair labor practice provisions of Taft-Hartley. Jenkins and Fanning stated:

> Congress has said that arbitration and the voluntary settlement of disputes are the preferred method of dealing with certain kinds of industrial unrest. Congress has also said that the power of the Board to dispose of unfair labor practices is not to be affected by any other method of adjustment. Whatever else these two statements mean, they do not mean that this Board can abdicate its authority wholesale.
>
> . . . The majority is so anxious to accommodate arbitration that it forgets that the first duty of this Board is to provide a forum for the adjudication of unfair labor practices. We have not been told that arbitration is the only method; it is one method.

In short, the minority believed that private arbitrators should not decide unfair labor practice disputes and that the NLRB had improperly conferred this right upon them. They held that once an unfair labor practice was filed, it was the duty of the Board to handle the case and not defer to arbitration. As one study states:

> The Board's contention that it should encourage the use of arbitration is laudable and may very well reflect the rather general, as well as the Congressional, sentiment that the arbitral process is the preferred way to settle contractual disputes, particularly if the alternative is economic strife. However, nowhere in the functions of the Board as described in the collective National Labor Relations Act, as amended, is there mention of encouragement of arbitration as one of those functions either prior to or after entertaining a charge of an unfair labor practice. To be blunt, once the unfair labor practice charge has been filed by one of the parties (in preference to arbitration) the Board should attend to the statutory business which Congress assigned it and leave the determination of arbitrability of a contractual dispute to the arbitration, and review of the award to the courts.[167]

Despite the language contained in Section 10(a) of the statute, as cited above, federal circuit courts of appeals have upheld the Board's deferral policy.[168] As did the majority of the agency, these courts held that the deferral policy constitutes a legitimate exercise of the discretionary power of the NLRB. A majority of the Board believed that the U.S. Supreme Court has also upheld the Board policy.[169] It should be stressed, however, that though the courts held that the NLRB has the lawful discretion to defer to arbitration, they did not say that the Board must defer.

Cases Deferred and Not Deferred

In the *Collyer* case itself, the employer unilaterally raised the wage rates of skilled employees and reassigned certain job duties without consulting or bargaining with the union. Since that time, the NLRB has deferred many other kinds of disputes to arbitration, rejecting the union claim that the NLRB should have jurisdiction over the disputes because of a refusal of the employer to bargain over changed conditions of employment. These cases included such issues as the reduction in crew sizes by an employer, who also increased the age of apprentices, and required that they be high school graduates;[170] discontinuance of the distribution of "turkey" money at Thanksgiving and Christmas;[171] curtailment of the seniority unit for purposes of transfer and promotion;[172] establishment of a separate seniority list for part-time employees;[173] revoking of employee parking privileges;[174] lengthening of Saturday hours and elimination of paid lunch periods;[175] institution of a wage incentive system;[176] and cancellation of a union member's leave of absence to engage in union work.[177]

In each of these cases, the NLRB held that the employer's act was covered by some provision of the labor agreement and/or a past practice. Therefore, it deferred the case to a private arbitrator to determine whether the employer had violated the terms of the labor agreement. The arbitrator would also determine whether the employer had violated the bargaining obligations of Taft-Hartley.

Particularly controversial were those cases involving employees' allegations that they were discharged because of their union activities. As we know, discharge for union activities is strictly unlawful. At the outset, the NLRB deferred such cases to arbitration. Deferral of this kind of case was particularly offensive to the minority members of the Board, who stated:

> This case confirms our fears, and again illustrates the extent to which the majority is willing, by its policy of deferring to private tribunals, to abrogate the right of individual employees under the act we administer.[178]

When Murphy (no longer a member) was appointed to the Board by President Ford, she sided with Fanning and Jenkins and refused to defer discharge cases.[179] She believed that employees allegedly discharged or otherwise disciplined for union activities should receive the full safeguards of the National Labor Relations Act. With the advent of the Reagan Board, however, the NLRB currently defers such cases to arbitration.[180] In an exception to this policy, the NLRB will not defer to arbitration cases in which an employee has allegedly been discharged because of filing an unfair labor practice charge against an employer.[181]

Though the Board has deferred to arbitration in an increasing number of cases, it should not be concluded that it has done so in every case. A dispute will not be deferred if the labor agreement does not contain a final and binding arbitration provision, or the employer refuses to agree to final and binding arbitration.[182] Also, the changed working condition must arguably be covered by some provision of the labor agreement or by a past practice. Probably this is not an important limitation to deferral since, as the minority stated in the *Collyer* case:

> Most unfair labor practices can be connected somehow to contract terms or existing practices, by board construction of general clauses, by the necessary inquiry into existing practices, by "waiver," or otherwise.

In any event, before the NLRB defers, it must show that employer conduct is arguably based upon contractual provision or practice. If company action is not covered by any provision of the labor agreement or by a past practice, the Board will not defer to arbitration.

In addition, the Board will not defer to arbitration if the evidence shows that the bargaining history between a union and company has been marred by constant friction. In one case, a dispute was not deferred because of a considerable number of wildcat strikes, distrust for one another, and continual bickering. For example, in one year, the union had filed 301 grievances.[183] Also, the Board will not defer when the employer has engaged in serious unfair labor practices. In one case of this type, the evidence showed the employer's "complete rejection of the principles of collective bargaining" and utter disregard for the organizational rights of its employees.[184]

To understand the significance of *Collyer*, however, one should focus on the Board's desire to defer to arbitration rather than the limited number of times that it has refused to do so.

NLRB Holds Jurisdiction

When the NLRB does defer to arbitration, it maintains jurisdiction of the case until after the arbitration award is issued. It will take jurisdiction of a case after the award is issued where the arbitrator did not conduct a fair hearing; when the employer refuses to abide by the award should the arbitrator find against it; or if the arbitrator's decision is repugnant to the policies of the NLRB. These are the so-called *Spielberg* standards, which are also discussed in the next chapter.[185] Thus, the Board will take jurisdiction of a case that it deferred to arbitration should the arbitrator not comply with the standards contained in *Spielberg*.

In *Suburban Motor Freight*, decided by the Board in 1980, the Board also held that it would not honor an arbitration decision unless the unfair labor practice issue was expressly presented during the hearing and specifically treated in the arbitrator's decision.[186] The Reagan Board, however, considerably weakened this policy, holding in *Olin Corporation* that it would defer to an arbitrator's award provided the contractual issue was factually parallel to the unfair labor practice issue, and if the arbitrator was presented generally with the facts relevant to resolving the unfair labor practice.[187] No longer, therefore, must the unfair labor practice be expressly raised in the arbitration hearing or treated specifically in the arbitration award. Zimmerman, a holdover from the Carter Board and no longer a member, dissented, arguing that under the majority's policy, there was no effective requirement for an arbitrator to give any consideration to statutory protections because the Board would "presume" such consideration even in its total absence. Some arbitrators, however, concerned with the ambivalent policy of the NLRB, still require that the unfair labor practice be presented in the hearing, and specifically treat the unfair labor practice in their decisions.

Between May 1973 and December 1975, the Board deferred a total of 1,632 cases to arbitration.[188] Of this number, arbitration awards were issued in 473 cases. In 159 of the arbitration cases, the losing party requested the NLRB to review the decision of the arbitrator. In slightly over 30 percent of these cases, the Board revoked deferral and was prepared to decide the merits of the unfair labor practice charges. Where the Board revoked deferral, it held that the arbitrator did not meet the *Spielberg* standards, generally because his or her decision was repugnant to the policies of the NLRB. Thus, not all arbitrators are competent to decide a *Collyer*-type case because they lack the knowledge of NLRB policies.

This is a weakness of the doctrine, particularly since the NLRB may hold that though the arbitrator's decision was not exactly consistent with Board policies it was not altogether repugnant to them either. If the NLRB had determined the issue in the first place, without deferral to arbitration, the agency might have rendered a decision unlike the one of the private arbitrator. Recall that in a *Collyer*-type case, the arbitrator must not only apply the terms of a labor agreement, but must take into consideration NLRB policies that bear on the dispute. As Peter Nash, a former General Counsel of the NLRB, stated:

> Perhaps the most difficult requirement of *Spielberg* for the arbitrator, again magnified by prearbitration *Collyer* deferral, is that his award may not be repugnant to the purposes and policies of the National Labor Relations Act.
>
> In general terms, this requirement does not mean that the Board must necessarily agree with the arbitrator's final decision. Thus, he may make fact findings with which the Board might well disagree, but which disagreements will not prompt independent Board consideration of the merits of the case. However, the requirement generally does compel an arbitrator to apply correctly Board law upon the facts found, and failure to do so will result in no Board deferral.[189]

Here are some examples where the arbitrators' decisions were not honored. In one instance, the Board refused to sustain an arbitrator's award in which he had held that a Christmas bonus arrangement in effect for many years did not constitute "wages" and could, therefore, be unilaterally terminated at will by the employer. The Board found that the employer had violated Taft-Hartley, and that the arbitrator had "ignored a long line of Board and Court precedent" that clearly established that, as a matter of law, a Christmas bonus system such as that considered by the arbitrator to have existed, did constitute wages and could not be unilaterally terminated by the employer.[190] In another case, an unfair labor practice complaint was issued against an employer after an arbitrator erroneously found that an employer had not violated its collective bargaining obligations when the company unilaterally abolished a wage incentive system.[191] In another case, a group of employees was discharged for allegedly violating the labor agreement's no-strike clause. An arbitrator reduced the penalty to a one-year suspension without back pay. When the General Counsel determined that the employer had not fulfilled its obligations under the same no-strike clause, he issued a complaint seeking to recover from the employer the pay lost by the employees.[192]

While commenting on the instances in which the NLRB or the General Counsel refused to honor an arbitrator's award, Nash warned arbitrators that these examples

> indicate a need for arbitrators to apply Board law accurately; to guard against inconsistent conclusions in their decisions, which conclusions would render the award contrary to Board law; and to view carefully the remedies to ensure that employees' rights under the Act are protected by the arbitrator's award.[193]

Refusal to Enforce Arbitrator's Decision

Though the Board will review an arbitration decision under the *Spielberg* doctrine, it will not enforce an arbitrator's decision of cases in which it deferred to arbitration.[194] Once again, there was a bitter conflict among the members of the Board. As in *Collyer,* the Board split 3–2 on the issue. The majority held that if an employer refused to abide by an arbitrator's decision, the union had the opportunity to go to court for enforcement of the decision. This, of course, results in considerable delay and litigation expenses.

In contrast, the two minority members believed that the arbitrator's award should be enforced by the NLRB. They stressed that if the Board deferred to arbitration, it should enforce the award and not burden the union with court proceedings. In considering this issue, it should be noted that if the Board had not deferred to arbitration in the first place, it would direct a remedy under Taft-Hartley. On this basis, it would seem reasonable that when the Board defers to arbitration, it has the obligation to enforce the arbitrator's award. After all, it was the *Collyer* doctrine that forced the arbitration, and to complete matters, it would seem fair that the Board should enforce the arbitrator's award.

Impact on Labor Relations

One obvious result of the *Collyer* doctrine is that it stimulates more arbitration. Costs of arbitration are substantial. In 1984, the average charge by an arbitrator for services and expenses in a case amounted to $1,372.00.[195] At this writing, this is the most recent data available. By the time this volume is published, the figure will undoubtedly be higher. Normally unions and employers share equally the arbitrator's fees and expenses. Beyond the arbitrator's fee, other costs are involved, including at times the use of an attorney and the making of a stenographic transcript. When workers are used as witnesses, their time lost from the job must be made up, normally by the union involved in the arbitration. Such costs are burdensome to unions, particularly to the smaller unions. Some unions faced with these costs may not proceed to arbitration, with the result that employer conduct allegedly in violation of Taft-Hartley will not be contested. When an employer or union charges a violation of the statute, the charging party does not have to pay for the use of the services of the NLRB. In 1974, the Board took this problem into consideration, holding that it would not defer to arbitration when the expenses of arbitration were beyond the financial resources of the union.[196] When the NLRB in effect forces a union to arbitration, some unions, faced with the financial burden—even those that are not poverty-stricken—might not challenge the employer's decision. It seems somewhat incongruous that a party covered by a federal statute designed to protect its rights must plead poverty to receive the benefits of national labor policy.

In addition, the Board assumes a level of expertise among arbitrators that is not necessarily warranted. Arbitrators differ widely in terms of experience and professional ability. Unfortunately, some arbitrators, one hopes few in number, may decide cases on grounds other than the evidence presented to them. There are more uncertainties in arbitration than in NLRB proceedings. As demonstrated earlier, some arbitrators are not qualified to apply NLRB and court law, and when this is so, the process of settlement of the issue is prolonged. Considerable time is involved in processing a case to arbitration, about 162 days from the time that a request for arbitration is made until such time as the arbitrator decides the case.[197] Should the NLRB refuse to honor the award because the arbitrator did not follow the *Spielberg* standards, the case then moves through the normal Board procedures. Under these circumstances, the time and money expended in the arbitration were wasted.

Beyond causing more arbitration, the *Collyer* doctrine has additional consequences for the state of labor-management relations. With the knowledge that the Board will likely defer to arbitration, it follows that some employers may be more aggressive in their labor practices. They could engage in conduct that arguably violates the labor agreement more frequently. Such conduct, when it occurs, would not be conducive to harmonious labor relations.

Defenders of the *Collyer* doctrine argue that it encourages the collective bargaining process. They argue as follows: The employer makes a change in the terms and conditions of employment without consulting or bargaining with the union. The Board defers to arbitration. At this point, the parties have an opportunity to settle the dispute by themselves through the grievance procedure machinery contained in the labor agreement. If the Board did not defer to arbitration, this opportunity would not be available, since the agency would settle the dispute.

The trouble with this argument is that the employer makes the change without consulting and bargaining with the union. It is not likely that an employer will change a decision after making it, despite the wisdom of the union arguments. If the union's input is to have real meaning, it should be made before the employer makes the change in the terms and conditions of employment. In the absence of *Collyer,* the employer would be more apt to consult and bargain with the union before making the change, since the company would recognize that failure to do so could result in NLRB proceedings. Under *Collyer,* the employer is encouraged to make the change without bargaining because the risk of an arbitration is less predictable than of an NLRB proceeding. It could be argued on this basis that *Collyer* discourages collective bargaining rather than promoting it.

SUMMARY

This chapter demonstrated that Taft-Hartley limits the opportunities of employers and unions to negotiate a labor agreement free from government direction. Though the public policy involved in this approach is subject to fair debate, Congress has controlled the substance of the labor agreement. In the area of union security, employers and unions may not negotiate the closed shop, and the opportunity to adopt a union shop is limited. In the right-to-work law states, this opportunity has been extinguished.

The *Borg-Warner* voluntary category of bargaining subjects deprives the parties to collective bargaining of the ability to apply economic pressure to influence the outcome of collective bargaining agreements. Restrictions of this type tend to frustrate the purpose of national labor legislation envisioned in the Wagner Act. The basic purpose of that law and of subsequent amendments in 1947 and 1959 was to balance the powers of labor and management. A balance-of-power approach was supposed to insure that the parties would be permitted to bargain on issues of interest without undue influence from external forces.

Under *Fibreboard,* employers have an obligation to bargain to an impasse before changing the conditions of employment during the term of a labor agreement. After the company discharges its bargaining obligations, it may make the change, and the union may challenge the action in arbitration. Before *Collyer,* the NLRB would determine whether the action of the employer was authorized under the labor agreement. With the advent of *Collyer,* the Board often deferred this kind of case to arbitration. So controversial is the doctrine that it would not be much of a surprise if a different Board membership abolished it. The major argument against *Collyer* is that the NLRB should not permit private arbitrators to determine issues that fall under a national law, a duty that Congress entrusted exclusively to the Board.

DISCUSSION QUESTIONS

1. Why is union security such an important issue for American unions?

2. How successful has Congress been in eliminating the closed shop? Of what use were the *Brown-Olds* and *Mountain Pacific* doctrines in pursuit of a policy to do away with the closed shop?

3. Describe the prehire arrangement permitted in the construction industry. What are the implications of such provisions in light of the Supreme Court's *NLRB* v. *Local 103, Iron Workers* case?

4. What is the difference between the union-shop arrangement and the agency shop? May workers be discharged for failing to join unions when a valid union-shop clause has been negotiated?

5. What is the current legal status of right-to-work laws? How important are such laws to unions? To employers?

6. What is current law regarding dues rebates under union-shop arrangements? In agency shops?

7. Why is the dues checkoff considered a form of union security?

8. How did the Board and Supreme Court construct the Congressional language regarding good-faith bargaining in the *Borg-Warner* case? How has that doctrine been applied in specific bargaining situations?

9. What impact might the Board's *United Technologies* and *Milwaukee Spring* policies have on union ability to provide job security for bargaining-unit employees?

10. Does the *Collyer* doctrine advance or hinder the good-faith collective bargaining process?

11. Compare the Board's policy in *Suburban Motor Freight* to the one in *Olin Corporation*. What are the implications for adequate hearings on unfair labor practices?

NOTES

1   *Hearings before the Committee on Labor and Public Welfare,* 80th Congress, 1st sess., on S. 55 and S.J. Res. 22, Part III, p. 1204.

2   *Buckley, National Review, Inc. and Evans* v. *AFTRA, NLRB, and American Civil Liberties Union,* 496 F. (2d) 305 (CA 2, 1974); cert. denied 419 U.S. 1093 (1974).

3   Public Law 96-593, 96th Congress, effective December 24, 1980.

4   National War Labor Board, *Termination Report,* Washington, D.C., I, p. 80.

5   Joseph Shister, *Economics of the Labor Market* (Chicago: J. B. Lippincott Company, Philadelphia, 1949), p. 83.

6   Philip Taft, "Dues and Initiation Fees in Labor Unions," *Quarterly Journal of Economics,* February 1946, p. 22.

7   Theodore Rose, "Union Security Provisions in Agreements, 1954," *Monthly Labor Review,* U.S. Department of Labor, Bureau of Labor Statistics, LVIII, 6 (November 1979), p. 37.

8   Sections 8 (a) (3) and 8 (b) (2).

9   NLRB Release R-336, August 10, 1950.

10   NLRB v. *National Maritime Union,* 175 F. (2d) 686 (1949).

11   Rose, *op. cit.*

12   *National Labor Relations Act of 1949,* Report No. 99 to accompany S. 249, 81st Congress, 1st sess., p. 20.

13   Horace E. Sheldon, "Union Security and the Taft-Hartley Act in the Buffalo Area," New York State School of Industrial and Labor Relations, Cornell University Research Bulletin No. 4, p. 41.

14   Contract negotiated by the Sailors Union (AFL) with a number of shipping operators in 1948.

15   Contract between the New York Local of the International Typographical Union and publishers of that city (1948).

16   Contract between the Milk Wagon Drivers Union and the Milk Industry Association of New York (1948).

17   Sheldon, *op. cit.,* p. 43.

18   The plumbers' union was found in violation of Section 8 (b) (2) of Taft-Hartley, which prohibits a union from causing or attempting to cause an employer to discriminate against an employee in violation of subsection (a) (3) or to discriminate against an employee with respect to whom membership in such an organization has been denied or terminated on some ground other than his or her failure to tender the periodic dues and the initiation fees uniformly required as a condition of acquiring or retaining membership.

19   *Virginia Electric Company* v. *NLRB,* 319 U.S. 533 (1943).

20   *Los Angeles–Seattle Motor Express, Inc.,* 121 NLRB 1629 (1958).

21   *Carpenters, Local 60* v. *NLRB*, 365 U.S. 651 (1961).

22   93 *Congressional Record* 3952, April 23, 1947.

23   *NLRB* v. *National Maritime Union of America, CIO*, 175 F. (2d) 686 (1949), cert. denied 338 U.S. 955 (1950).

24   U.S. Congress, Hearings before the Senate Subcommittee on Labor-Management Relations, *Hiring Halls in the Maritime Industry*, 81st Congress, 2d sess., p. 168.

25   *National Union of Marine Cooks & Stewards*, 90 NLRB 1099 (1950).

26   *Local 357, International Brotherhood of Teamsters* v. *NLRB*, 365 U.S. 667 (1961).

27   *R. J. Smith Construction Company, Inc.* and *Local 150, Operating Engineers*, 191 NLRB 135 (1971).

28   434 U.S. 355 (1978).

29   *AFL-CIO News*, Washington, D.C., March 12, 1983.

30   *Jim McNess* v. *Todd*, 461 U.S. 260 (1983).

31   *NLRB* v. *Pacific Erectors*, 718 F. 2d 1459, CA-9, 1983.

32   *Interstate Electric Co. (IBEW Local 354)*, 227 NLRB 291 (1977); *Howard Electric Co. (IBEW Local 6)*, 227 NLRB 278 (1977).

33   Sections 8 (a) (3) and 9 (e) of Taft-Hartley.

34   *Paragon Products Corporation*, 134 NLRB 86 (1961).

35   James D. Dworkin and Marian M. Extejt, "The Union-Shop Deauthorization Poll: A New Look After 20 Years, "*Monthly Labor Review*, U.S. Department of Labor, Bureau of Labor Statistics, CII, 11 (November 1979), p. 37.

36   National Labor Relations Board, *Forty-sixth Annual Report*, 1981, p. 203.

37   Dworkin and Extejt, *op. cit.*, p. 39.

38   Public Law 189, 82d Congress, approved October 22, 1951.

39   National Labor Relations Board, *Sixteenth Annual Report*, U.S. Government Printing Office, Washington, D.C., 1951, p. 10.

40   U.S. Department of Labor, Bureau of Labor Statistics, *Monthly Labor Review*, December 1951, p. 682.

41   *Algoma Plywood & Veneer Company* v. *WERB*, 336 U.S. 301 (1949).

42   See below for the U.S. Supreme Court decision authorizing the states to outlaw the agency shop under Section 14(b) of Taft-Hartley.

43   *International Union, United Automobile, Aircraft, and Agricultural Implement Workers*, 137 NLRB 104 (1962).

44   *Aluminum Workers International Union, Local 135*, 112 NLRB 619 (1955).

45   *General Motors Corporation, Packard Electric Division*, 134 NLRB 1107 (1962).

46   *Philadelphia Sheraton Corporation*, 136 NLRB 888 (1962).

47   *Union Starch & Refining Company*, 87 NLRB 779 (1949); *Union Starch & Refining Co.* v. *NLRB*, 186 F. (2d) 1008 (CA 7, 1951); cert. denied 342 U.S. 815 (1951).

48   *Hershey Foods Corp.*, 207 NLRB 897 (1974).

49   *NLRB* v. *Hershey Foods Corp.*, CA 9, Case No. 74-2114, April 15, 1975.

50   394 U.S. 423 (1969).

51   *NLRB* v. *Granite State Joint Board*, 409 U.S. 213 (1972).

52   *Keystone Coat, Apron & Towel Supply Company*, 121 NLRB 880 (1958).

53   *NLRB* v. *News Syndicate Company, Inc., et al.*, 365 U.S. 645 (1961); *Local 357, Teamsters* v. *NLRB (Los Angeles–Seattle Motor Express)*, 365 U.S. 807 (1961).

54   *Paragon Products Corporation, op. cit.*

55   Arkansas Constitutional Amendment No. 34, November 7, 1944; Florida Constitutional Declaration of Rights, No. 12, as amended November 7, 1944.

56   Fred Witney, "Union Security," *Labor Law Journal*, IV, 2, February 1953, p. 118.

57   Georgia, Iowa, North Carolina, North Dakota, Tennessee, Texas, and Virginia.

58   *McCulloch* v. *Maryland,* 4 Wheat. 316 (1819).

59   *Lincoln Federal Labor Union* v. *Northwestern Iron & Metal Company,* 335 U.S. 525 (1949).

60   *Mobil Oil Corporation* v. *Oil, Chemical and Atomic Workers International Union,* U.S. Sup. Ct. Case No. 74-1254, June 14, 1976.

61   *Sea Pak* v. *Industrial, Technical and Professional Employees,* 400 U.S. 985 (1971).

62   *Lord* and *Local Union 2088, International Brotherhood of Electronics Workers,* 646 F. 2d 1057, 1981. Cert. denied U.S. Sup. Ct. No. 81–8060, June 28, 1982.

63   *Plumbers Locals* v. *NLRB,* CCA–DC No. 80–2393. April 18, 1982.

64   *Wall Street Journal,* February 1, 1985.

65   *Monthly Labor Review,* CVIII, 4 (April, 1985), p. 61.

66   Fred Witney, *Indiana Labor Relations Law* (Bloomington, Indiana: Bureau of Business Research, Indiana University, 1960), p. 85.

67   *AFL-CIO News,* Washington, D.C., November 6, 1976.

68   *AFL-CIO News,* Washington, D.C., November 18, 1978; February 24, 1979; August 8, 1980; April 11, 1981; May 23, 1981; April 24, 1982; May 11, 1985. *Wall Street Journal,* April 21, 1981.

69   *Retail Clerks, Local 1625* v. *Schermerhorn,* 375 U.S. 96 (1964).

70   68 Stat. 1238, 45 U.S.C. 152 Eleventh, Section 2.

71   *Railway Employees' Dept.* v. *Hanson,* 351 U.S. 225 (1956).

72   367 U.S. 740 (1961).

73   *Ibid.*

74   *Brotherhood of Railway and Steamship Clerks* v. *Allen,* 373 U.S. 113 (1963).

75   *Wall Street Journal,* November 23, 1975.

76   *Steelabor,* March 1980.

77   *Wall Street Journal,* April 20, 1981.

78   *Ellis* v. *Railway Clerks,* 466 U.S. 435 (1984).

79   *Meade Electric Company* v. *Hagberg,* Indiana Superior Court, Lake County, May 19, 1958, No. 158-121. On June 19, 1959, the Second Northern Indiana Division, Indiana Court of Appeals, upheld the decision of the Superior Court.

80   *American Seating Company,* 98 NLRB 800 (1952).

81   *General Motors Corporation,* 130 NLRB 481 (1961).

82   *General Motors Corporation,* 133 NLRB 21 (1961).

83   *General Motors Corporation* v. *NLRB,* 303 F. (2d) 428 (1962).

84   *NLRB* v. *General Motors Corporation,* 373 U.S. 734 (1963).

85   *Retail Clerks International Association, Local 1625* v. *Schermerhorn,* 373 U.S. 746 (1963).

86   Rose, *op. cit.,* p. 657.

87   *Hearings before the Committee on Labor and Public Welfare,* 80th Congress, 1st sess., on S. 55 and S. J. Res. 22, Part II, p. 839.

88   Section 302.

89   "Coverage of Checkoff Under Taft-Hartley Act," *Monthly Labor Review,* U.S. Department of Labor, Bureau of Labor Statistics, LXVII, 5 (July 1948), p. 42.

90   *Penn Cork & Closures,* 156 NLRB 411 (1965), enforced 376 F. (2d) 52 (1967).

91   *Bedford Can Manufacturing Corporation,* 162 NLRB 133 (1967).

92   *W. P. Ihrie & Sons, Division of Sunshine Biscuits,* 165 NLRB 2 (1967).

93   *Keller Ladders, Southern Subsidiary of Keller Industries,* 161 NLRB 21 (1966).

94   *Frito-Lay,* 243 NLRB No. 16 (1979).

95   *Campbell Industries,* 243 NLRB No. 17 (1979).

96   *United Steelworkers of America (Asarco, Inc.)*, 246 NLRB No. 139 (1979).

97   Robben W. Fleming, "The Obligation to Bargain in Good Faith," in *Public Policy and Collective Bargaining*, eds. Joseph Shister, Benjamin Aaron, and Clyde W. Summers (New York: Harper & Row, 1962), p. 61.

98   *International Association of Machinists*, 2 RLB 87 (1921).

99   *Ibid.*

100   Section 7 (a) required "that employees shall have the right to organize and bargain collectively through representatives of their own choosing."

101   Section 8 (b) (3) (5) of Taft-Hartley.

102   61 Stat. 142 (1947).

103   *Globe Cotton Mills* v. *NLRB*, 103 F. (2d) 91, 94 (1939).

104   *Times Publishing Company*, 72 NLRB 676 (1947).

105   *Majure Transport Company* v. *NLRB*, 198 F. (2d) 735 (1952).

106   *NLRB* v. *Norfolk Shipbuilding & Drydock Corporation*, 172 F. (2d) 813 (1949).

107   *Na-Mac Product Corporation*, 70 NLRB 298 (1946).

108   *Southern Saddlery Company*, 90 NLRB 1205 (1950).

109   *NLRB* v. *General Electric Company*, 418 F. (2d) 736 (1969).

110   *Winn-Dixie Stores*, 243 NLRB No. 151 (1978).

111   *Brazos Electric Power Co-Op*, 241 NLRB No. 160 (1979).

112   *Graham Paper Division, Div. of Jim Walter Paper*, 245 NLRB No. 180 (1979).

113   *Indiana & Michigan Electric Co.*, 229 NLRB No. 95 (1977).

114   *Minnesota Mining & Manfacturing Co.*, 261 NLRB No. 2 (1982).

115   *Hour Publishing*, 245 NLRB No. 53 (1979).

116   *Local Union 323, IBEW (Active Enterprises)*, 242 NLRB No. 41 (1979).

117   *Communication Workers of America, Local 1122 (New York Telephone Co.)*, 226 NLRB 97 (1977).

118   *Local Union 798 of Nassau County, New York (Nassau Div. of Master Painters Assn. of Nassau-Suffolk Counties, et al.)*, 212 NLRB No. 89 (1975).

119   *H. K. Porter Company* v. *NLRB*, 397 U.S. 99 (1970).

120   *NLRB* v. *Wooster Division of Borg-Warner Corporation*, 356 U.S. 342 (1958).

121   These are Sections 8 (a) (5) for employers, and 8 (b) (3) (5) for unions.

122   *Fibreboard Paper Products* v. *NLRB*, 379 U.S. 203 (1964).

123   *Richfield Oil*, 110 NLRB 356 (1954), enforced 231 F. (2d) 717, cert. denied 351 U.S. 909 (1956).

124   *Dicten & Masch Manufacturing*, 129 NLRB 112 (1960); *Kroger Company* v. *NLRB*, 399 F. (2d) 445 (1968).

125   *Inland Steel Company*, 77 NLRB 1, enforced 170 F. (2d) 247 (1948), cert. denied 336 U.S. 960 (1949).

126   *Lehigh Portland Cement*, 101 NLRB 1010 (1952).

127   *NLRB* v. *Niles-Bemont Pond Company*, 199 F. (2d) 713 (1952).

128   *Beacon Piece Dyeing & Finishing Company*, 121 NLRB 953 (1958).

129   *Miller Brewing Company*, 166 NLRB 90 (1967).

130   *Axelson, Subsidiary of U.S. Industries*, 234 NLRB No. 49 (1978).

131   *United Mine Workers (Lone Star Steel)*, 231 NLRB No. 88 (1977).

132   *NLRB* v. *American National Insurance*, 343 U.S. 395 (1952).

133   *Medicenter, Mid-South Hospital*, 221 NLRB 670 (1975).

134   441 U.S. 488 (1979).

135   *Ozark Trailers*, 161 NLRB 561 (1966).

136   *NLRB* v. *Transmarine Navigation Corp.*, 380 F. (2d) 933 (CCA 9, 1967). *NLRB* v. *Thompson Transport*, 406 F. (2d) 698 (CCA 10, 1969). *Royal Typewriter* v. *NLRB*, 533 F. (2d) 1030 (CCA 8, 1976).

137   *Wall Street Journal*, January 13, 1981.

138   *First National Maintenance Corp.* v. *NLRB*, 449 U.S. 1076 (1981).

139   *NLRB* v. *Retail Clerks International Association*, 203 F. (2d) 165 (1953).

140   *Daelyte Service*, 126 NLRB 63 (1960).

141   *Operating Engineers, Local No. 12 (Associated General Contractors of America)*, 187 NLRB 439 (1970).

142   *Seattle First National Bank* v. *NLRB*, 450 F. (2d) 353 (1971), reversing 176 NLRB 691 (1969).

143   *NLRB* v. *United Brotherhood of Carpenters, Local 964*, 447 F. (2d) 643 (1971).

144   *Allied Chemical Workers, Local 1* v. *Pittsburgh Plate Glass*, 404 U.S. 157 (1971).

145   177 NLRB 911 (1969).

146   Commerce Clearing House, *Labor Law Reports*, No. 674, January 28, 1985, p. 3.

147   *Columbus Printing Pressmen and Assistants Union 252 (R. W. Page Corp.)*, 219 NLRB 268 (1975). In December 1976 the decision of the NLRB was upheld by a federal circuit court of appeals. *NLRB* v. *Printing Union, Columbus Pressmen and Assistants Union 252*, CA 5, No. 75-3546, December 13, 1976.

148   *Universal Oil Products* v. *NLRB*, 445 F. (2d) 155 (1971).

149   *NLRB* v. *Taormina*, 207 F. (2d) 251 (1953), enforcing 94 NLRB 884 (1951).

150   *Kit Manufacturing*, 150 NLRB 662 (1964), enforcing 365 F. (2d) 829 (1966).

151   *Arlington Asphalt Company*, 136 NLRB 742 (1962).

152   *NLRB* v. *Corsicana Cotton Mills*, 178 F. (2d) 344 (1959).

153   *Bartlett-Collins Co.*, 237 NLRB No. 106 (1978).

154   *Lathers Local 42 of Wood, Wire & Metal Lathers International Union (Lathing Contractors Association of Southern California)*, 223 NLRB 37 (1976).

155   *Electrical Workers (IBEW) Local 135, LaCrosse Electrical Contractors Assn.*, 271 NLRB No. 36 (1984).

156   *Capital Times Co.*, 223 NLRB 651 (1976).

157   *Wall Street Journal*, April 9, 1976, p. 8.

158   *United Technologies, Otis Elevator*, 269 NLRB No. 162 (1984).

159   *United Technologies, Otis Elevator*, 255 NLRB No. 5 (1981).

160   *Illinois Coil Spring Co., Milwaukee Spring Division*, 268 NLRB No. 87 (1984).

161   *Illinois Coil Spring Co., Milwaukee Spring Division*, 265 NLRB No. 28 (1982).

162   Fleming, *op. cit.*, p. 84.

163   *Fibreboard Paper Products Corporation* v. *NLRB*, 379 U.S. 203 (1964).

164   *Television & Radio Artists* v. *NLRB*, 398 F. (2d) 319 (1968).

165   *Collyer Insulated Wire*, 192 NLRB 837 (1971).

166   National Labor Relations Board, *Forty-second Annual Report*, U.S. Government Printing Office, Washington, D.C. (1977), p. 36.

167   D. J. Johannesen and W. Britton Smith, Jr., "*Collyer:* Open Sesame to Deferral," *Labor Law Journal*, XXIII, 12 (December 1972), p. 741.

168   *International Association of Machinists (United Aircraft Corp.)* v. *NLRB*, 525 F. (2d) 237 (CA 2, 1975); *Nabisco, Inc.* v. *NLRB*, 479 F. (2d) 770 (CA 2, 1973); *Associated Press* v. *NLRB*, 492 F. (2d) 662, DC. Cir., 1974; *Provision House Workers Union Local 274 (Urban Patman, Inc.)* v. *NLRB*, 493 F. (2d) 1249 (CA 9, 1974); *Enterprise Publishing Co.* v. *NLRB*, 403 F. (2d) 1024 (CA 1, 1974).

169   *William E. Arnold Co.* v. *Carpenters District Council of Jacksonville,* 417 U.S. 12 (1974). It should be noted, however, in that case, dealing with other matters, the Court made a passing reference to the Board's deferral policy. Fanning and Jenkins said that the Court's reference "was nothing more than dicta in a Section 301 suit rather than an unfair labor practice proceeding." National Labor Relations Board, *Forty-second Annual Report,* 1977, p. 38.

170   *Atlantic Richfield,* 199 NLRB 1224 (1972).

171   *Radioear,* 199 NLRB 1161 (1972).

172   *Western Electric,* 199 NLRB 326 (1972).

173   *Southwestern Bell Telephone,* 198 NLRB 569 (1972).

174   *Great Coastal Express,* 196 NLRB 871 (1972).

175   *Coppus Engineering,* 195 NLRB 595 (1972).

176   *Peerless Pressed Metal,* 198 NLRB 561 (1972).

177   *Appalachian Power Company,* 198 NLRB 576 (1972).

178   *National Radio Co.,* 198 NLRB 527 (1972).

179   *General American Transportation Corp.,* 288 NLRB 102 (1977).

180   *United Technologies,* 268 NLRB No. 83 (1984).

181   *International Harvester Co., Columbus Plastics Operation,* 271 NLRB No. 101 (1984).

182   *Tulsa-Whisenhunt Funeral Homes,* 195 NLRB 106 (1972).

183   *Borden Inc., Dairy & Services Division,* 196 NLRB 1170 (1973).

184   *Mountain State Construction Company,* 203 NLRB 1085 (1973).

185   *Spielberg Manufacturing Co.,* 112 NLRB 1080 (1955).

186   247 NLRB No. 2 (1980).

187   *Olin Corp.,* 268 NLRB No. 86 (1984).

188   *General Transportation Corp., supra.*

189   Peter Nash, "NLRB and Arbitration: Effect of *Collyer* Policy," Proceedings of the Twenty-seventh Annual Meeting, National Academy of Arbitrators, Bureau of National Affairs, Inc. (Washington, D.C.: 1974), p. 119.

190   *Radio Television Technical School, Inc.,* 199 NLRB 570 (1972).

191   Nash, *op. cit.,* pp. 120–121.

192   *Ibid.,* p. 120.

193   *Ibid.,* p. 122.

194   *Malrite of Wisconsin,* 198 NLRB 241 (1972).

195   Federal Mediation and Conciliation Service, *Thirty-seventh Annual Report,* U.S. Government Printing Office, Washington, D.C., 1984, p. 20.

196   *Local No. 171, Pulp and Paper Workers (Boise Cascade Corp.),* 165 NLRB 971 (1974).

197   Federal Mediation and Conciliation Service, *op. cit.,* p. 22.

CHAPTER FIFTEEN

ENFORCEMENT OF
THE COLLECTIVE BARGAINING
AGREEMENT

INTERNAL ENFORCEMENT PROCEDURE:
THE GRIEVANCE PROCEDURE

After a labor agreement is executed, management and the labor union bargain collectively on a day-to-day basis. Such bargaining does not involve negotiations for the purpose of fashioning a new labor contract. Nor is daily bargaining directed at altering the particular terms of the existing agreement. Collective bargaining on the day-to-day level is the process whereby the labor contract is made a living organism. Many of the day-to-day relations between management and labor involve the settling of disputes alleging violations of the provisions of the contract. Such settlement is achieved through the *grievance procedure,* a mechanism for self-enforcement of the contract contained in practically every collective bargaining agreement.

So that the collective bargaining contract will be enforced properly, labor and management rely on the grievance procedure. Both unions and management are aware that charges of contract violation will arise during the contract period. Every day-to-day problem or question that might arise cannot be anticipated in the collective bargaining agreement. The complexities of labor-management relations preclude the drawing up of such a contract. In addition, the provisions in an agreement are subject to conflicting interpretations, just as are laws enacted by legislative bodies. In this connection, it should be emphasized that many charges involving contract violations arise merely because union and management representatives do not agree on the meaning of a particular contract provision. The grievance procedure provides management and unions with a mechanism to dispose of charges of contract violations in an orderly and equitable manner.

CONTROL OF THE GRIEVANCE PROCEDURE:
WAGNER ACT EXPERIENCE

Under the terms of the National Labor Relations Act, a labor union certified by the NLRB became the exclusive representative of all employees within the bargaining unit "for the purposes of collective bargaining in respect to rates of pay, wages, hours of employment, or other conditions of employment."[1] Consequently, an employer was in violation of the Wagner Act if he or she recognized the majority union as the representative of its members only. A certified labor organization negotiates for all workers within the unit regardless of their union membership status. Apart from conferring this exclusive status upon certified labor organizations, the Wagner Act provided that "any individual employee or a group of employees shall have the right at any time to present grievances to their employers."[2]

For several years, the NLRB had no occasion to render an interpretation of this portion of the Wagner Act. Early in World War II, however, the North American Aviation Company believed that Section 9 (a) of the Act gave employees the right to present and adjust grievances individually regardless of the existence of a collective bargaining agreement.[3] The company had previously executed a contract with a union certified by the NLRB. Shortly afterward, copies of the contract were distributed to the firm's employees. In addition, each worker received a notice signed by the company's president which outlined a grievance procedure unilaterally prepared by the company. Such a procedure was inconsistent with the one set forth in the collective bargaining agreement. On the ground that the employer's conduct indicated a refusal to grant exclusive bargaining rights to the certified union, the NLRB subsequently found that the company had engaged in an unfair labor practice. But when the company appealed the Board's decision, a federal circuit court ruled that the "grievance provision" of the Wagner Act conferred upon employers the right to hear and to adjust any grievance presented by individual employees, notwithstanding the existence of a collective bargaining agreement.[4] It is noteworthy that the court construed the grievance provision to include not only "small out-of-mind grievances," but all grievances employees might wish to adjust. The court apparently indicated that an employer may lawfully adjust individual grievances relating to all conditions of employment regardless of the terms of a collective bargaining contract.

Beyond reversing the Board's decision, the court's ruling stimulated the first formal NLRB interpretation of the grievance provision. In general, the Board's General Counsel took the position that the provision meant that an individual employee had the technical right to present grievances to an employer, but that representatives of the certified union must be present each time an employee makes such a presentation, and must negotiate the settlement of the grievance. Under this construction, the Wagner Act grievance provision extended to individual workers the mechanical right of presentation of grievances, but reserved to certified labor organizations the exclusive right to settle the grievances.

Notwithstanding the rule of the federal court in the *North American* case, the NLRB adopted the interpretation of its General Counsel and ruled in a subsequent case that employers must settle grievances presented by individual workers with the majority union. In one instance, the Board declared that the right of employees to present grievances was not an "empty one." Such a right, according to the Board, insured to the individual employee that his or her grievances would not be ignored by the majority union.[5] When the exclusive bargaining agent refused to participate in the adjustment of the grievances, the NLRB ruled that the employee could individually negotiate with the employer.

In another case, the Board reaffirmed its policy, even though the certified union involved in the controversy had not yet negotiated a contract. An unfair labor practice was found because the employer had ordered any individual with grievances to take them up directly with management. It is noteworthy that the National War Labor Board also ruled that final adjustment of grievances had to be made with majority unions and not upon an individual basis.[6]

GRIEVANCE PROCEDURE UNDER TAFT-HARTLEY

The Taft-Hartley Act nullified the NLRB doctrine established under the Wagner Act dealing with the presentation and adjustment of grievances on an individual worker basis. Under the terms of Taft-Hartley, grievance procedure structures must be broad enough to meet these standards: (1) the individual worker must be permitted to present grievances to the employer on an individual basis; (2) the employer must be permitted to make an adjustment of grievances so presented, provided the adjustment is not inconsistent with the terms of the collective bargaining agreement; and (3) the employer must provide a union official with the opportunity to be present at the time of adjustment.[7]

The first requirement does not greatly change the rulings of the NLRB established under the Wagner Act. Individual workers had previously had the opportunity to present grievances to employers. However, it had been necessary for employers to invite representatives of the bargaining agent to be present at the time individual workers presented grievances to their employers. Under Taft-Hartley, the labor union holding bargaining rights in the plant did not have to be involved in grievance adjustment, but only had to be given an opportunity to be present during the proceedings.

Actually, in this respect, Taft-Hartley did not greatly alter collective bargaining procedures. Many collective bargaining contracts negotiated long before Taft-Hartley was enacted provided that the individual worker could choose the method of presentation of his or her grievance. Scores of agreements gave the worker the freedom to (1) present a grievance on an individual basis; (2) elect to have a representative of the labor union present the grievance for him or her; or (3) go with a union representative to the proper management official for the presentation of the grievance. A comparatively small number of agreements went to the extremes of forbidding anyone but the union representative to present workers' grievances, or of requiring that the worker present the grievance on an individual basis.

On the other hand, the second grievance procedure standard of the 1947 law upset traditional collective bargaining relationships. By providing that the employer may make adjustment of a grievance with a worker on an individual basis, Taft-Hartley destroyed the policies developed by the NLRB under the Wagner Act. As noted, the NLRB had previously required that all grievances must be adjusted with the representatives of the workers' labor union. Only when the collective bargaining agency did not want to adjust a worker's grievance was it permissible for the employer to adjust grievances on an individual worker basis. Obviously, if a labor union refused to do anything about a worker's grievance, the worker and the employer should have the right to make the adjustment. Any adjustment made through this arrangement since the Taft-Hartley enactment must be consistent with the terms of an existing collective bargaining contract. If individuals were permitted to reach agreements inconsistent with the contract, the entire process of collective bargaining would disintegrate rapidly. Most unions do not encourage individual processing of grievances because of the apparent implication that the union is not capable of adequately functioning as bargaining agent. However, it should be recognized that some unions are much less than enthusiastic about processing nonmember grievances on a par with those raised by members. Regardless of attempts to discourage individual initiative in these matters, unions do not have legal authority to cause the discharge of employees for circumventing the labor organization and directly presenting grievances to employers.[8]

Should an employer adjust a worker's grievance in a fashion that violates the terms of the collective bargaining contract, unions may sue in the federal courts under Section 301 of Taft-Hartley. Generally, a union in such a position prefers to resolve the issue through the grievance procedure. Often, however, an employer who violates the contractual terms of the agreement is aware of the action and union efforts to deal informally with the situation are not heeded. As the law now stands, a dissatisfied union might submit an unresolved grievance to arbitration, to the NLRB in the form of an unfair labor practice charge, or to the federal courts. The method will depend upon both the terms of the contract and the general nature of union-management relations in the bargaining unit.

Duty of Fair Representation: Employee Recourse Through NLRB

If a union that holds the position of exclusive bargaining representative of employees declines to process the grievance of a member of the bargaining unit, it has refused representation. Such a refusal constitutes restraint and coercion of the worker in his or her right to representation.[9] As the NLRB stated in *Miranda:*

> . . . Section 7 . . . gives employees the right to be free from unfair or irrelevant or invidious treatment by their exclusive bargaining agent in matters affecting their employment. This right of employees is a statutory limitation on statutory bargaining representatives, and . . . Section 8 (b) (1) (A) of the Act accordingly prohibits labor organizations, when acting in a statutory representative capacity, from taking action against any employee upon considerations or classifications which are irrelevant, invidious, or unfair.

Grievance handling is one aspect of an employee's right to fair and impartial treatment by exclusive bargaining agents. Popularly this is called the *duty of fair representation.*

Grievance processing is a part of the union's bargaining function. Refusal to process a grievance could constitute a breach of the union's duty to bargain with the employer under the Act's provisions. Any employee who feels aggrieved by a union's refusal to process his or her complaint may appeal the case to the NLRB.[10] This means that the Board must judge the substantive aspects of the collective bargaining agreement regarding the rights of employees to fair representation within the unfair labor practice provisions of Taft-Hartley.[11] The Board must evaluate the merits of the grievance and the union's action, as well as the union's motives for disposing of a situation so as to dissatisfy the worker. Failure to convince the NLRB that a worker's grievance was treated in the same fashion as those of other workers could result in unfair labor practice remedies.

Some examples demonstrate how this doctrine has been applied. A union member complained to the international union about the local's violations of the union's bylaws, constitution, and labor agreement. After he was discharged, the local union refused to process his grievance protesting his discharge. It was evident that the grievance was not processed because the union member had evoked the displeasure of the local union when he complained about its transgressions to the international union. Under these circumstances, the Board held that the union had unlawfully refused to accord the union member his right to fair and proper representation.[12] In another case, though a union processed the grievance of a member, it did so without much enthusiasm or sincerity. Under these circumstances, a federal circuit court of appeals held that the less than vigorous support of the grievance violated the doctrine of fair representation.[13] Within a bargaining unit, a dissident group was opposed to the union. Two of its supporters were discharged. The union failed to investigate the circumstances of the discharge and did not otherwise pursue the grievance filed by the employees. Under these circumstances, the Board held that the union's conduct was arbitrary and capricious and violated its duty of fair representation.[14] In another case, a union informed a discharged employee that it would request her reinstatement with back pay. When the union, despite its promise to the employee, told the employer it would not seek her reinstatement, the NLRB held the union had violated its duty of fair representation.[15]

Failure to process grievances properly is not the only way in which unions can violate their duty of fair representation. A union representing clerical employees and warehouse workers insisted in contract negotiations that both groups receive the same wage increase. Previously, the clericals had requested they receive the same increase as the warehouse workers. However, during contract negotiations, the employer told the union that a wage increase of that magnitude for the clericals would lead to their permanent layoff. The union did not relay that information to the clerical group. After agreeing to the wage increase demanded for the clericals, the employer terminated their employment. Subsequently, the NLRB in *The Emporium* held that the union had violated its duty of fair representation to the clerical workers for its failure to inform that group that the wage increase would jeopardize their jobs.[16] This policy has great significance for the relationship between unions and their members. Under it, a union must inform its members of employer warnings made during contract negotiations. As the Board pointed out in *The Emporium,* it makes no difference that union representatives might believe an employer is only using a common negotiating scare technique. The union is still obligated to inform its members so they can make an intelligent reassessment of their bargaining demands.

Even nonunion employees are protected under the union's duty to afford all members of the bargaining unit fair and equal representation. In a right-to-work state, a union desired to charge nonunion employees a fee for the processing of grievances. Since the union could not negotiate a union shop or agency shop, it believed that these employees should pay the costs of the handling of their grievances. Despite the apparent equity of this argument, the Board stressed that the union's lawful duty is to represent all employees in the bargaining unit on the same basis. It held that the union had engaged in an unfair labor practice because it could not discriminate against employees in the bargaining unit based on union membership for purposes of the grievance procedure.[17]

In a similar situation, a union did not permit nonunion employees to vote on an employer proposal dealing with vacation scheduling. The employer had said that a system of either fixed or rotating vacation days would be agreeable. The employer was willing to be bound by the vote of the bargaining unit employees. When the union restricted the right to make the choice to union members alone, a federal appeals court, sustaining the Board, held that the union had breached its duty of fair representation.[18]

When the NLRB finds that a union did not provide fair representation, it will direct an appropriate remedy. The Board will order the union to cease and desist from breaches of the duty of fair representation.[19] Of more practical value to a discharged employee, under appropriate circumstances the Board will order reinstatement with full back pay and other contractual rights.[20] When, however, the Board has no jurisdiction over the employer and so cannot direct reinstatement, it will direct the union to pay back pay to the discharged employee. In one such case, a union failed to process a grievance of a discharged employee. The Board required the union to pay back pay from the date of the initial refusal to handle the grievance "until such time as union fulfills its duty of fair representation, or discharged employee obtains substantially equivalent employment, whichever is sooner."[21] In a more recent case, the NLRB in 1984 held that a union was liable for back pay because it had failed to interview discharged employees before it processed their grievances.[22] It directed the union to request the employer to reinstate the employees. If the employer refused, the union was required to pursue the grievance to arbitration. Should the union be unable to proceed to arbitration because of time limits (labor agreements require an appeal to arbitration to be made within a specified period of time) or for any other reason, the NLRB ruled that the union alone would be liable for back pay.

Under some circumstances, the Board has held that unions did not violate their statutory duties by refusing grievances. Two employees were suspended for fighting on the job, one for twenty-five days and the other for four days. Through the grievance procedure, the union managed to reduce the twenty-five day suspension to fourteen days. It refused to process a grievance for the employee who was suspended for four days. While dismissing the latter employee's complaint against the union, the Board held that the union's effort to equalize the penalties was reasonable. Apparently, the union believed that both employees deserved some discipline for their violation of plant rules against fighting on the job.[23] In another case, a union through negligence failed to process an employee's grievance in a timely manner, with the result that the employer denied the grievance on this basis. The affected employee filed unfair labor practice charges against the union, claiming its negligence had denied him the right to fair representation. The Board dismissed the claim on the grounds that negligence alone did not add up to a breach of the statutory obligations of the union. Though the union had been negligent, the Board held that this did not constitute arbitrary, discriminatory, or unfair conduct.[24] In other words, to show that a union has breached its duty of fair and equal representation in the handling of grievances, the evidence must indicate that the union discriminated unfairly against employees and has acted arbitrarily and capriciously. Each case must be determined under its particular set of facts and circumstances.

In order to cut down on the number of cases alleging breach of the duty of fair representation, the General Counsel of the NLRB in 1979 established guidelines.[25] Union conduct that is "inept, negligent, unwise, insensitive, or ineffectual" does not establish breach of the duty. Complaints will be issued against unions charged with failure to provide fair representation only where union conduct (1) was based upon improper motives such as fraud; (2) was arbitrary; (3) was grossly negligent; or (4) was improperly undercutting an employee's grievance. In this way, it was expected that the Board's case load would be reduced. The guidelines were also established to ease the burden on union representatives. Rather than face employee charges, unions frequently process trivial grievances and even those which are completely devoid of merit. Under the guidelines, union officials will probably be more selective in pursuing employee complaints.

Individual Suits in Federal Courts.   Still another avenue is open to employees when a union does not represent them fairly in the collective bargaining process. They have the right to sue unions and employers in federal and state court jurisdictions under Section 301 of Taft-Hartley.[26] Thus employees who feel their rights have been violated under collective bargaining agreements may choose to seek relief from the courts or the NLRB. Unions have both the right and responsibility to represent all bargaining-unit members fairly by evaluating the merits of grievances filed. There is no requirement, however, that a union must process a grievance throughout the entire range of grievance machinery provided by the contract, including arbitration. The labor organization is required to accept a complaint for unbiased investigation before declining to proceed to advanced grievance stages. The Supreme Court stated that "to remove or gag the union in these cases would surely weaken the collective bargaining and grievance processes."[27]

Financial liability of unions in cases where they may abandon a grievance prior to arbitration is not present merely because an employee may prove to the courts that it was a meritorious one. The test for holding labor organizations responsible in court suits is whether the employee can show, as the U.S. Supreme Court said in *Vaca* v. *Sipes,* "arbitrary or bad faith conduct on the part of the union in processing his grievance."[28] Unions have the authority to resolve issues with employers without having to obtain solutions no more advantageous to one employee than to another. Differences are inevitable within bargaining units. A suitable solution to one employee may well be unacceptable to another. Unions cannot bargain effectively with employers unless they can provide reasonable assurances that their actions will not be destroyed legally by dissidents. The Supreme Court has ruled:

> A wide range of reasonableness must be allowed a statutory bargaining representative in serving the unit it represents subject always to complete good faith and honesty of purpose in the exercise of its discretion.[29]

As a result of litigation costs, most employees would probably seek relief from the NLRB rather than the courts. In any event, where a court finds that a union has breached its duty of fair representation, it will direct an appropriate remedy under the circumstances of a particular case. The court may afford the injured employee injunctive relief, or where appropriate, compensatory damages in the form of back pay.[30] As a matter of fact, in one case a court ordered the union not only to pay the aggrieved employee back pay, but *future* lost earnings.[31] As a result of the union's failure to represent the employee involved fairly, the employer was able to phase out his job. Under these circumstances, the court held that the award of future damages was the only effective remedy. In 1981, the U.S. Supreme Court made it somewhat easier for union members to sue their organizations. A discharged employee, claiming unfair representation, was denied reinstatement and back pay. Since the employee could not get his job back through internal union procedures, the Court held that he was not required to use that procedure before suing the union.[32] In other words, where an intraunion procedure is not adequate to provide the employee with the relief sought, the union member need not exhaust that procedure as a prerequisite to sue the union.

In a 1983 case, *Bowen* v. *United States Postal Service,* the Supreme Court made it crystal clear that unions are liable for damages when they fail to carry out the duty of fair representation.[33] When a union refused to arbitrate one employee's discharge, the employee sued both the union and the employer. The high court held that the union had failed to comply with its statutory obligation when it did not arbitrate the employee's grievance. As a remedy, the union was directed to pay the lion's share of the back pay award, $30,000, and $23,000 by the employer. The Court rejected the union's argument that only the employer should be responsible for back pay. To avoid the consequences of *Bowen,* some unions may arbitrate cases that do not have merit. As one union officer said, the policy will "create a workload problem for the arbitration system."[34]

Without detracting from the significance of *Bowen,* the U.S. Supreme Court later provided some relief to unions when it held that employees must sue within six months after the union allegedly breached its duty of fair representation.[35] Before the court established this policy, some courts established time limits as short as 30 days and as long as several years. As the basis of the six-month rule, the high court noted that unfair labor practice charges must be filed under Taft-Hartley within that period of time. Thus, given current case law, an employee who files a lawsuit against a union after more than six months will not be entitled to relief even if the union did in fact fail to provide fair representation.

In their zeal to protect employees, some lower federal courts awarded employees punitive damages beyond the amount of money that they actually lost because of the union's illegal conduct. In 1979, however, the U.S. Supreme Court ruled in *Foust* that under no circumstances could a union be liable for such excess damages in fair representation cases.[36] It held that punitive damages are not consistent with the purposes of national labor policy. In that case, a lower federal court had assessed $75,000 punitive damages. While reversing the lower courts, the high court said punitive awards could

> deplete union treasuries, thereby impairing the effectiveness of unions as collective bargaining agents.

To protect against punitive damages, the court reasoned further, unions "might feel compelled to process frivolous claims or resist fair settlements." Although the issue arose under the Railway Labor Act, the policy also applies to Taft-Hartley. Even in the absence of punitive damages, unions have a sufficient financial incentive to do their best to provide fair representation to their members.

Like the NLRB, federal courts have often held that unions have *not* failed to provide fair representation as alleged by employees. Reversing a district court's decision, a federal appeals court ruled that a union was not obligated to pay strike benefits to employees who did not participate in strike activities.[37] Required to pay the equivalent of union dues under an agency shop, an employee was nonetheless denied strike benefits because he did not picket, refused to take a turn in the kitchen to feed picketers, and failed to perform other strike duties. Under these circumstances, the court held the union had not violated its duty of fair representation, limiting such suits to matters that involved an employee's relationship to the employer. Thus, the payment of strike benefits was ruled a purely intraunion matter subject only to the eligibility rules established by a union. In addition, the court noted that the union did not have to pay strike benefits to union members who had refused to participate in strike activities.

Even when a union failed to appeal a grievance to arbitration within the labor agreement's time limits, a federal appeals court held the Union had not violated its duty of fair representation.[38] The union had simply forgotten the date on which the appeal should have been filed. Forgetting the deadline, the court said, is not the same as a conscious decision to abandon the grievance. In short, the court held that the union's negligence was not arbitrary, discriminatory, or bad-faith conduct.

In a particularly important case, another federal appeals court held that a union had not failed to represent an employee fairly simply because it had refused to seek judicial review to vacate an award that upheld his discharge.[39] It said the union's obligation to the employee was limited to submitting the grievance to arbitration. Whereas collective bargaining contracts provide for arbitration of grievances, and place a fair representation duty upon unions to arbitrate, they do not require unions to appeal unfavorable arbitration awards to the courts for reversal. While denying the employee's charge, the court pointed out that the employee as an individual was free to petition a court for reversal of the arbitration decision. Under these circumstances, the employee and not the union would be liable for litigation and court costs.

Court Enforcement of Contracts.   The Taft-Hartley Act made it easier for parties to the collective bargaining process to sue each other in courts of law when alleged violations of the labor agreement occur. This is accomplished by expanding the jurisdiction of the federal court in labor contract violation cases.[40] Before the 1947 law was enacted, labor organizations could be sued for contract violations in the federal courts. However, two conditions had to prevail before the federal courts would assume jurisdiction of the case: (1) the parties involved were required to be citizens of different states; and (2) the amount of damages resulting from the breach of contract had to be at least $3,000. The Taft-Hartley Act removed both of these restrictions on the federal courts. Section 301 provides that "suits for violations of contract between an employer and a labor organization . . . may be brought in any district court of the United States having jurisdiction of the parties, without respect to the amount in controversy or without regard to the citizenship of the parties."

Proponents of this feature of the 1947 labor law argued that its effect would make labor unions more responsible in the discharge of their obligations under collective bargaining contracts—in particular, that unions would be more prone to respect their no-strike and no-slowdown obligations. In this respect, the National Association of Manufacturers declared: "Now there is less danger that [workers] will suddenly be called out on strike while the contract is in effect."[41] Fearful of being sued in court for damages resulting from strikes violating the collective bargaining agreement, labor unions, it was felt, would exercise caution to prevent such work stoppages.

The Taft-Hartley Act expands considerably the jurisdiction of the federal courts over labor-management disputes. In addition, it sets up a concept of union responsibility quite different from the one in the Norris–La Guardia Act. Before the passage of Norris–La Guardia, the common-law rules of agency applied to federal court proceedings in which labor unions found themselves defendants. Under the common law a principal is liable for the unlawful acts of his or her agents whether or not the principal has knowledge of, has ratified, or has authorized the agents' actions. For purposes of labor relations, the union, under the common-law doctrine of agency, was responsible for actions of its members and officers.

Although the common-law doctrine of agency may be justified in many areas of judicial proceedings, its application to labor matters works a considerable hardship upon labor organizations. The fundamental reason for this rests upon the nature of the labor union as a functioning institution. Labor unions are composed of large numbers of members. In many unions there are hundreds— in some cases, thousands—of officers, but the employer chooses the union's membership by deciding whom to hire. The union at best exercises a loose degree of discipline over its membership. The imposition of discipline by the union over union members and union officers is usually a difficult process. Union members are not "fired" out of the normal labor organization except after an elaborate procedure. This characteristic of the union movement is not criticized. On the contrary, adequate protection of a worker's union membership is necessary if democracy within the labor union is to be preserved. This merely highlights the fact that the status of union members and officers is well protected. Such insulation provides a basis for conduct that may be inconsistent with the terms of the labor contract.

Finally, it is pertinent to point out that the labor union does not have the control a business firm has in choosing its personnel. Agents of labor unions— such as union officers, stewards, and grievance committee members—are elected by the membership. In contrast with the method employed by the union in obtaining its leadership, the company normally carefully selects representatives of management on the basis of education, experience, aptitude tests, and recommendations.

Congress was aware of these considerations when it passed Norris–La Guardia. It recognized that the application of the common-law rule of agency to labor relations operated to the serious disadvantage of the labor union. The complexities of modern industrial life and a realistic view of the labor union as a living organism militated for a different approach to the problem of union responsibility. As a result, Section 6 of the Norris–La Guardia Act was adopted. This provision required actual authorization or ratification by labor organizations of agents' acts to establish union responsibility. Section 6 declared:

> No officer or member of any association or organization, and no association or organization participating or interested in a labor dispute, shall be held responsible or liable in any court of the United States for the unlawful acts of individual officers, members, or agents, except upon clear proof of actual participation in, or actual authorization of, such acts, or of ratification of such acts after actual knowledge thereof.

Thus, Norris–La Guardia prevented the application of the common-law rule of agency to labor disputes. Under its terms, a labor union, before it could be held liable for illegal action of its members or officers, must have authorized such conduct or ratified the action after it occurred. Proponents of Norris–La Guardia contended that this conception of union responsibility was made necessary by the contemporary industrial relations environment.

Union Responsibility Under Taft-Hartley.   Under the terms of the 1947 labor law, it appeared at first that the rules of agency developed in common law would once again govern the issue of union responsibility. The law provides that in determining whether or not any person is acting as an agent of a labor organization so as to make the union responsible for his or her acts, "the question of whether the specific acts performed were actually authorized or subsequently ratified shall not be controlling." By this language, the statute makes the labor union responsible for the activities of its members or officers, regardless of whether the union authorized or ratified the conduct. In this connection, the International Association of Machinists pointed out that Taft-Hartley "makes the union responsible for the actions of irresponsible 'agents' who act without authorization. And it subjects the union to legal liability for such unauthorized actions."[42]

The officers of labor organizations must react responsibly when contractual violations occur or else they must be willing to subject their organizations to court actions.

At times, strikes and other interruptions to production not authorized by the labor organization occur. These work stoppages, commonly known as *wildcat strikes,* are instigated by a group of workers, sometimes including union officers, without the sanction of the labor union. Under many labor agreements, the employer has the right to discharge such employees or otherwise to penalize them for such activities.

An employer may sue a union because of a wildcat strike even if the union has not authorized or ratified it. As a result, unions and employers have negotiated *nonsuability clauses.* Under these arrangements, the company agrees that it will not sue a labor union because of wildcat strikes, provided that the union fulfills its obligation to terminate the work stoppage. Frequently, the labor contract specifies exactly what the union must do in order to free itself from the possibility of damage suits. Thus, in some contracts containing nonsuability clauses, the union agrees to announce orally and in writing that it disavows the strike, orders the workers back to their jobs, and refuses any form of strike relief to the participants in such work stoppages.

Though an employer may sue a union for money damages under Section 301 when employees participate in a wildcat strike, the provision does not authorize employer suits against individual union members.[43] A labor agreement contained a no-strike clause that forbade work interruptions during the period of the contract. Despite this provision, employees went out on strike. The employer sued both the union and the individual employees for breach of contract and requested a federal court to assess money damages against the union and its members. The company argued that Section 301 had established the congressional intent that individual strikers, as well as the unions, be held responsible for damages suffered by employers as a result of unauthorized strikes. In rejecting the employer position in *Sinclair Oil Corp.,* a federal appeals court stated:

> The legislative history of the act indicates that the principal concern of Congress was with making unions, as parties to collective bargaining agreements, responsible for breaches of agreements and to avoid subjecting individual union members to fiscal ruin.

In this regard, it should also be noted that union members as individuals are not responsible for damages levied against labor organizations. Section 301 provides that "any money judgment against a labor organization in a district court of the United States shall be enforceable only against the organization as an entity and shall not be enforceable against any individual member or his assets." In 1962, the U.S. Supreme Court maintained the integrity of this language when it held that "when a union is liable for damages for violation of the no-strike clause, its officers and members are not liable for these damages."[44]

Despite the language of the law and the judicial precedent, the issue surfaced once more: an employer requesting the federal courts to assess damages against individual union members because of a wildcat strike. In 1981, the U.S. Supreme Court held again that individual union members are not financially liable for the losses suffered by employers resulting from wildcat strikes.[45] Once again the high court explained that Congress had exempted individual union members because it did not want a repetition of the *Danbury Hatters* situation discussed in Chapter 4. In that case, the U.S. Supreme Court had held that individual union members were liable for damages assessed against their unions.

What all this means is that union members and officers as individuals are not liable for money damages in the event of wildcat strikes. Action against individual employees is, therefore, limited to discharge or other forms of discipline. Employees who participate in a wildcat strike do lose their status as employees for purposes of Taft-Hartley.[46] Thus, if an employer discharges such employees the NLRB will not direct their reinstatement.

The rule relieving individual union members from the damages of a wildcat strike takes on added significance because of a 1979 U.S. Supreme Court decision.[47] In *Carbon Fuel*, a unanimous Court held that a national union is not responsible for damages when its local unions are involved in wildcat strikes. Since local unions normally do not have large treasuries, the employer sought damages from the national union. Between 1969 and 1973, local union affiliates of United Mine Workers of America engaged in 48 wildcat strikes. A federal district court held that the national union was liable and ordered it to pay $500,000 to Carbon Fuel.

Reversing the lower court, the U.S. Supreme Court said the national union was not liable because it did not provoke or encourage the wildcat strike. If it had, it would have been liable. The Court also pointed out that the labor agreement did not place an affirmative obligation on the national union to end unauthorized strikes. In other words, the high court said that a national union could be responsible for damages should a labor agreement expressly make the national union liable, or expressly impose an affirmative obligation on a national union to do everything reasonably possible to end wildcat strikes, such as fining or expelling wildcatting employees. Should a national union fail to comply with those contractual obligations, it would be liable for damages. However, it is extremely unlikely that national unions would agree to these kinds of provisions.

Thus, employers have not fared well with the U.S. Supreme Court in their efforts to obtain damages resulting from unauthorized strikes. Union members and officers as individuals are not liable for damages, and under most circumstances national unions are also exempt.

WHEN DIRECT NEGOTIATIONS FAIL: ARBITRATION

The vast majority of disputes involving labor contract violations are settled by representatives of management and labor by direct negotiation. At one step or another in the grievance procedure, union and company representatives usually find a workable solution for a dispute. However, some grievances are not resolved by direct negotiations. Both sides may feel that their positions are supported by the terms of the collective bargaining agreement. The question arises: What should be done about disputes in which labor and management cannot reach an agreement by direct negotiation?

A do-nothing policy would not serve the interests of sound labor relations. Unsettled contract violation disputes adversely affect plant morale and result in the general deterioration of labor-management relations. Ultimately, unresolved grievances could cause such serious tensions in the bargaining unit that effective implementation of the productive process would deteriorate. An accumulation of unsettled grievances could result in strikes and lockouts. All parties suffer from such work stoppages.

To avoid a breakdown in labor-management relations and to promote uninterrupted production during the life of a contract, a large number of unions and companies make use of a third party—called an "arbitrator" or an "umpire." The arbitrator makes the final settlement of disputes involving contract violations. His or her decision is binding on the two parties.

The method for selecting an arbitrator is normally provided for in the labor agreement. Both union and management must agree on the third party before the dispute is submitted to arbitration. Persons who serve as arbitrators are strictly impartial and well versed in the fine points of collective bargaining. The function of the arbitration is to resolve the dispute in the light of the existing collective bargaining contract. The arbitrator has no power to add to, subtract from, or modify any provision of the collective bargaining agreement. His or her task is to determine whether or not a particular pattern of conduct constitutes a violation of the labor contract as it is written at the time of the arbitration. In short, the arbitrator applies the existing contract to the facts of the case and determines whether or not a violation has occurred.

Typical arbitration resembles a regular court of law in that a third party decides the dispute. Contrary to regular judicial proceedings, however, an atmosphere of informality characterizes the usual arbitration. Rules of procedure applicable to regular court proceedings are frequently ignored. The arbitrator may ask pertinent and searching questions to clarify points not presented adequately by the parties. In many arbitration proceedings, each side will attempt to prove its case without using lawyers.

Each side is responsible for preparation of its own case. If the labor union charges that a company violated a collective bargaining agreement, union representatives must come prepared to prove to the arbitrator that a violation actually took place. Witnesses may be called, documents produced, and briefs submitted. Oral argument is effective, provided that the speaker confines his or her remarks to the particular dispute and attempts to win the point by utilizing facts, not emotion.

When the arbitration proceedings are terminated, the arbitrator hands down a so-called *award*. The award contains the judgment of the arbitrator. However the arbitrator rules, the decision is final and binding on both parties. Obviously, the arbitration process is valuable for the peaceful settlement of industrial disputes. Certainly, contract violation disputes are better settled by arbitration than by resort to industrial warfare. Arbitration provides an orderly and peaceful mechanism to resolve grievances when direct negotiations fail.

One additional factor militates for the inclusion of an arbitration clause in the typical labor agreement. Unions will not agree to a no-strike provision unless a mechanism provides for the final settlement of grievances arising during the life of the contract. Organized labor feels that if it surrenders its right to strike during the contract period, it must be assured that a third party will break deadlocks over contract violation disputes. If arbitration were not provided for in a collective bargaining contract that contains a no-strike clause, a labor union could not take any economic action to effect a final settlement of grievances arising under the contract. Management representatives agree with organized labor that a contract containing a no-strike clause should also make provision for arbitration.

At present some 95 percent of all U.S. labor agreements provide for arbitration as the final step in the grievance procedure. This national percentage is significantly greater than it was in the early 1930s, when fewer than 8 to 10 percent of all agreements contained such a clause. And even by 1944 arbitration provisions had been included in only 73 percent of all contracts.[48]

ARBITRATION AND THE SUPREME COURT: FROM WESTINGHOUSE TO LINCOLN MILLS

Congressional inclusion of Section 301 in Taft-Hartley did not immediately resolve the common-law problems of collective bargaining agreement enforcement. No clarification was made of the substantive law applicable to labor contracts brought before the courts. Were the courts to apply state laws as was the previous practice, or were they to be bound by some yet undetermined federal law? If a federal law was be applied, what would it be? Diverse court opinions were handed down dealing with the issue of state versus federal jurisdiction under Section 301. In addition, the question of whether issues could be arbitrated was one with which the courts had considerable difficulty. Could an arbitrator proceed to grant an award prior to court determination of the merits of the issue under the agreement? So long as these issues remained unresolved, the use of grievance arbitration was not likely to receive as much attention from the parties to contracts as might otherwise occur. There would be little incentive to utilize arbitration as the final step of grievance procedures if the courts continued to interfere with arbitration awards. Industrial warfare might have remained the alternative to peaceful resolution of contractual disagreements without action from the courts to lend prestige and strength to the arbitration process.

In a 1947 decision, a New York state court of appeals ruled that the court had to decide the merits of a grievance raised under a contract before an arbitrator had the authority to issue an award.[49] It held that

> if the meaning of the provision sought to be arbitrated is beyond dispute, there cannot be anything to arbitrate, and the contract cannot be said to provide for arbitration.[50]

This attitude characterized the thinking of the courts, state and federal, until the 1960s. Even the U.S. Supreme Court for a time was uncertain as to how collective bargaining contracts should be treated in the courts. The intent of Congress proved hard to determine in the light of the various laws involved.

In 1955, the Supreme Court reviewed the Taft-Hartley Act's Section 301.

The *Westinghouse* case dealt with the issue of how collective bargaining agreements were to be enforced.[51] This case provides the necessary background for appreciating the issues and results of arbitration questions before the courts. Indeed, it also provides a basis for understanding the Court's *Humphrey* v. *Moore* decision, which we previously discussed regarding individual employee rights to bring suit in the courts. The dilemma of common law remained despite the 1947 legislation.

The *Westinghouse* case resulted from a contractual provision for salaried employees to receive their full month's pay even if they missed working a day, unless they were on furlough or leave of absence. The company deducted a day's pay from the salaries of 4,000 employees who had missed work on a particular day of the month. The union contended that a violation of the contract had occurred and filed a suit in a federal district court under Section 301 of Taft-Hartley. The trial court dismissed the case because the union had not stated a reason for the absences in dispute. The union, however, was permitted to amend its complaint, and the lower court ruled that the union had authority to file suit under the Taft-Hartley law.

Upon appeal to a court of appeals, the case was dismissed. The appellate court held that the individual employees were the proper ones to file suit, not the union. The union was considered without authority to sue for the employees under Taft-Hartley. It could sue only if a provision of the agreement between the union and management affected its rights exclusive of those employees. Rights not pertaining to employees—regarding such matters as wages, hours, and other terms and conditions of employment—were within the particular rights of unions. The result of this rule was that unions as organizations could not usually acquire many rights apart from those dealing with the contractual conditions under which employees work.

The U.S. Supreme Court sustained the appeals court, but on the basis of different logic. Justice Frankfurter, speaking for the Court, was of the opinion that suits brought in the district courts under Section 301 were to be disposed of by common law as it prevailed in the states. Also, employees themselves, not unions, were to bring the suits against employers. If suits were initiated by employees, the Justice argued that they would have to be brought in the state courts unless there was a diversity of citizenship, in which case employees could use the federal courts. But the case implied even more. Employees in cases such as *Westinghouse* could not use the federal courts because Section 301 permitted only actions between employers and unions, not litigation between employers and employees. The collective bargaining contract itself was not considered a sufficient basis for a union suit against employers.[52]

All the Supreme Court justices—both those concurring and those dissenting, as well as Justice Frankfurter speaking for the majority—were obviously ill at ease with the decision. It was inevitable that a new approach to collective contract enforcement would be undertaken. The inconsistencies of the decision were pointed out by the justices. More study and thought would be required to establish a law dealing with the complexities of labor relations. Two years passed before the high court had the opportunity to deal again with the constitutional issues of Section 301.

Lincoln Mills.   Refusal to abide by arbitration contract provisions in a small number of cases kept the problem of collective bargaining contract enforcement before the federal courts. In June 1957, three separate Section 301 cases were decided by the U.S. Supreme Court.[53] The lower courts held in the *General Electric* and *Goodall-Sanford* cases that agreements to arbitrate grievance disputes were enforceable in the federal courts under the federal arbitration act. However, an appellate court reviewing the *Lincoln Mills* case ruled differently. It ruled that there was no authority in federal or state law to require adherence to a labor contract provision calling for arbitration of future disputes. The *Lincoln Mills* case provided the Supreme Court with an opportunity to provide answers to the issue of how to deal with labor contracts.

The Supreme Court decided in *Lincoln Mills,* contrary to the *Westinghouse* case in 1955, "that the substantive law to apply in suits under Section 301 (a) is federal law, which the courts must fashion from the policy of our national labor laws." Thus arbitration provisions were deemed enforceable in the federal courts under federal law. In practice, what *Lincoln Mills* meant was that when a labor agreement provides that arbitration must be used to determine grievance disputes, the employer must proceed to arbitration. Should the employer refuse, a federal court will issue an injunction to force arbitration.

It was decided that the Norris–La Guardia Act did not bar injunctive relief, since "the congressional policy in favor of the enforcement of agreements to arbitrate grievance disputes being clear, there is no reason to submit them to the requirements of Section 4 of the Norris–La Guardia Act." The existing law of the state in which the controversy arises is not to be used to resolve the dispute. However, the federal courts may use state law to resolve the issue if it "will best effectuate the federal policy." Such a pronouncement on the part of the Court meant that the federal courts would establish their own doctrine dealing with Section 301 as long as such doctrine remained consistent with national labor policies. It should be observed that the state courts are not excluded from deciding Section 301 suits. They have concurrent jurisdiction with the federal courts in most cases. When the state courts are utilized by the parties, however, they must apply federal law.[54]

This decision of the Supreme Court to enforce agreements to arbitrate grievance disputes constituted a major impetus for growth in the use of arbitration. Considerably more prestige was provided the entire process as a result of *Lincoln Mills.* However, the drive toward establishment of a body of law under Section 301 has not proved a simple task. A long series of cases followed *Lincoln Mills,* which together laid down some rules to guide the courts in enforcing both arbitration agreements and awards. These cases extended broad latitude to arbitrators under federal law, and for this reason it is unlikely that future suits dealing with arbitration will be filed in the state courts.

THE "TRILOGY" CASES

On June 20, 1960, the U.S. Supreme Court handed down three other decisions that gave even greater integrity to the arbitration process.[55] These decisions are commonly referred to as the "Trilogy" cases. Each involved the United Steelworkers of America, and each demonstrates that the system of private arbitration in the United States has received the full support of the highest court in the land.

In *Warrior & Gulf Navigation,* the Court held that in the absence of an express agreement excluding arbitration, it would direct the parties to arbitrate a grievance. To put this in other terms, the Court would not find a case nonarbitrable unless the parties specifically excluded a subject from the arbitration process. The Court stated that a legal order to arbitrate would thenceforth not be denied "unless it may be said with positive assurance that the arbitration clause is not susceptible to an interpretation that covers the asserted dispute. Doubts should be resolved in favor of coverage."

More precisely, the courts will not decide that a dispute is not arbitrable unless the parties have taken care to expressly remove an area of labor relations from the arbitration process. This could be accomplished by providing, for example, that "disputes involving determination of the qualifications of employees for promotion will be determined exclusively by the company and such decision will not be subject to arbitration."[56] But, needless to say, not many unions would agree to such a clause, since management would then have the unilateral right to make determinations on this vital phase of the promotion process.

The *Warrior & Gulf Navigation* decision eliminated a course of action that some companies had followed. When faced with union demands for arbitration, some employers had frequently gone to court and asked the judge to decide that the issue involved in the case was not arbitrable. On many occasions the courts had agreed with the company, sustaining the company position in the grievance and denying the union an opportunity to get a decision based on the merits of the case.

In the case at hand, the Warrior & Gulf Navigation Company employed forty-two men at its dock terminal for maintenance and repair work. After the company had subcontracted out some of the work, the number was reduced to twenty-three. The union argued in the grievance procedure that this action of the company violated certain areas of the labor agreement—the integrity of the bargaining unit, seniority rights, and other clauses of the contract that provided benefits to workers. The company claimed that the issue of subcontracting was strictly a management function and relied on the management rights clause in the contract, which stated that "matters which are strictly a function of management should not be subject to arbitration." When the Supreme Court handled the case, it ordered arbitration because the contract did not specifically exclude subcontracting from the arbitration process. It stated:

> A specific collective bargaining agreement may exclude contracting-out from the grievance procedure. Or a written collateral agreement may make clear that contracting-out was not a matter for arbitration. In such a case a grievance based solely on contracting-out would not be arbitrated. Here, however, there is no such provision. Nor is there any showing that the parties designed the phrase "strictly as a function of management" to encompass any and all forms of contracting-out. In the absence of any express provision excluding a particular grievance from arbitration, we think only the most forceful evidence of a purpose to exclude the claim from arbitration can prevail, particularly where, as here, the exclusion clause is vague and the arbitration clause quite broad.

One additional point must be stressed to understand the significance of this decision. Though the court may direct arbitration, it will not determine the merits of the dispute. A federal court only decides whether the grievance is arbitrable, but the private arbitrator has full authority to rule on its merits. As the Supreme Court stated in *Warrior & Gulf Navigation,* "Whether contracting out in the present case violated the agreement is the question. It is a question for the arbiter, not for the courts." This principle was stressed by the U.S. Supreme Court in a 1986 case, *AT & T Technologies v. Communication Workers* (Docket No. 84-1913, April 7, 1986). When the union filed a grievance protesting the layoff of 79 employees, the employer refused to submit the grievance to arbitration, contending that its decision to lay off due to a lack of work is not arbitrable. Lower federal courts held that an arbitrator should determine whether the issue was arbitrable. By a unanimous decision, the Supreme Court held the lower federal courts have the exclusive duty to establish whether the grievance was arbitrable, and not the private arbitrator. It said the question of arbitrability "is undeniably an issue of judicial determination," and remanded the case to the lower federal court to make that decision. At the same time, the Court admonished it "not to rule on the potential merits of the underlying claim" while deciding arbitrability. In other words, should the courts determine the grievance to be arbitrable, a private arbitrator would establish whether the employer violated the labor agreement when it laid off the employees.

In the second case, *American Manufacturing,* the issue of arbitrability was also involved, but in a somewhat different way than in *Warrior & Gulf Navigation.* The American Manufacturing Company argued before a lower federal court that an issue was not arbitrable because it did not believe the grievance had merit. Involved was a dispute on reinstatement of an employee to his job after it was determined that the employee was 25 percent disabled and was drawing worker's compensation. The lower federal court sustained the employer's position and characterized the employee's grievance as "a frivolous, patently baseless one, not subject to arbitration." When the U.S. Supreme Court reversed the lower federal court, it held that the federal courts are limited in determining whether the dispute is covered by the labor agreement and that they have no power to evaluate the merits of a dispute. It stated:

> The function of the court is very limited when the parties have agreed to submit all questions of contract interpretation to the arbitrator. It is then confined to ascertaining whether the party seeking arbitration is making a claim which on its face is governed by the contract. Whether the moving party is right or wrong is a question of contract construction for the arbitrator. In these circumstances the moving party should not be deprived of the arbitrator's judgment, when it was his judgment and all that it connotes that was bargained for.

Essentially, this means that the courts may not hold a grievance nonarbitrable even if a judge believes it is completely worthless. It is up to the private arbitrator to make the decision on the merits of a case. He or she may dismiss the grievance as being without merit, but this duty rests exclusively with the arbitrator and not with the courts.

In the third case, *Enterprise Wheel & Car Corporation,* a lower federal court reversed the decision of an arbitrator on the grounds that the judge did not believe his decision was sound under the labor agreement. The arbitrator's award directed the employer to reinstate certain discharged workers and to pay them back wages for periods both before and after the expiration of the collective bargaining contract. The company refused to comply with the award, and the union petitioned for enforcement. The lower court held that the arbitrator's award was unenforceable because the contract had expired. The U.S. Supreme Court reversed the lower court and ordered full enforcement. In upholding the arbitrator's award, the Court stated:

> Interpretation of the collective bargaining agreement is a question for the arbitrator. It is the arbitrator's construction which was bargained for; and so far as the arbitration decision concerns construction of the contract, the courts have no business overruling him because their interpretation of the contract is different from his.

The significance of this last decision should be perfectly clear. It shows that a union or a company may not use the courts to set aside an arbitrator's award. The decision cuts both ways: it applies both to employers and labor organizations. Whereas the other two decisions definitely favor labor organizations, this one merely serves to preserve the integrity of the arbitrator's award. Thus, even if a judge believes an arbitrator's award is unfair, unwise, or inconsistent with the contract, he or she has no alternative but to enforce the award.

On the other hand, despite *Enterprise Wheel & Car Corporation,* under limited circumstances, a court may reverse an arbitrator's decision. Reversal could occur because an arbitrator clearly exceeded his or her jurisdiction under a labor agreement, failed to conduct a fair hearing, or failed to disclose a conflict-of-interest relationship to one of the parties. These circumstances are infrequent as compared to the number of cases when a federal court is mandated under the doctrine to enforce an arbitrator's award. As treated below, however, the U.S. Supreme Court carved out conditions under which the court can upset awards when the basis for the reversal is not attributable to the conduct of the arbitrator.

Thus the Trilogy cases demonstrate that the private arbitration system has been strengthened by the judiciary. They establish the integrity of the arbitration process. As a result of these decisions, companies and unions must be more careful in the selection of arbitrators. This is one reason they have increasingly voiced a desire to use seasoned and experienced arbitrators.

For arbitrators, the decisions are equally meaningful. Private arbitrators bear an even greater degree of responsibility as they decide their cases. Not only are the posts ones of honor, in which the parties have confidence in arbitrators' professional competency and integrity, but arbitrators must recognize that for all intents and purposes, their decisions are completely final and binding upon the parties. Indeed, if the system of private arbitration is to remain a permanent feature of the American system of industrial relations, arbitrators must measure up to their responsibilities. Should they fail, companies and unions may simply delete the arbitration clause from the contract and resolve their disputes by strikes or by going directly to the courts. These are not pleasant alternatives, but the parties may choose these routes if they believe that arbitrators are not discharging their responsibilities in an honorable, judicious, and professional manner.

After the Trilogy

Several major cases dealing with arbitration were decided by the Supreme Court after the Trilogy. Some supported its basic purpose and philosophy, but others opened the door for court reversal of arbitration decisions.

In *Gateway Coal,* [57] a coal operator refused to suspend two supervisors who had failed to report the collapse of a ventilation structure that reduced the flow of air in the mine. The employees on all three shifts went out on strike, and the union refused to submit the suspension of the supervisors to arbitration in accordance with the National Bituminous Coal Wage Agreement. This agreement provided that local disputes will ultimately be settled by binding decision of an impartial arbitrator. It specifically provided arbitration for "any local trouble of any kind [arising] at the mine." Only matters of "national character" were excluded from the arbitration process by express contractual language. A federal district court ordered the union to stop the strike and to arbitrate the dispute. It also directed the employer to suspend the supervisors pending the arbitrator's decision. A court of appeals vacated the injunction, holding that the labor agreement might be construed as excepting safety matters from arbitration.

The Supreme Court reversed the appellate court and held that the arbitration clause covered safety issues. To support its decision, the court referred to

Warrior & Gulf Navigation, and particularly the following statement contained in it:

> An order to arbitrate the particular grievances should not be denied unless it may be said with positive assurance that the arbitration clause is not susceptible to an interpretation that covers the asserted dispute. Doubts should be resolved in favor of coverage.

Since the arbitration clause in the coal agreement did not expressly exclude local safety matters from its coverage, the Court concluded in *Gateway Coal:*

> We think these remarks are as applicable to labor disputes touching the safety of the employees as to other varieties of disagreement. Certainly industrial strife may as easily result from unresolved controversies on safety matters as from those on other subjects.

Squarely involved in *Nolde Bros.*[58] was the right of a union to arbitrate a dispute after the labor agreement had expired and the employer had gone out of business. As a prerequisite for a strike over new contractual issues, the union terminated the existing labor agreement. Under that contract, there was a provision calling for severance pay upon termination of employment for all employees with three or more years of service. Four days after the strike started, the company closed the bakery permanently. The union then claimed severance pay for all eligible employees. Not only did the company refuse to pay severance benefits, but it refused to arbitrate the dispute on the grounds that the labor agreement had expired. A federal court held that there was nothing to arbitrate because the right of employees to severance pay ended when the contract was terminated.

In 1977, however, the U.S. Supreme Court ruled that the employer was obligated to arbitrate the issue even though the labor agreement had expired. Fundamental to the decision were two major reasons. In the first place, the high court pointed out that the right to severance pay accrued to employees under the expired labor agreement and was vested in them. In addition, it stated that there was nothing in the broad arbitration clause that expressly excluded from its coverage disputes arising under the contract but based upon events occurring after its termination. Thus, the Court stated that termination of a labor agreement does not automatically extinguish "a party's duty to arbitrate grievances arising under the contract." Any other holding, the Court stated,

> would permit the employer to cut off all arbitration of severance pay claims by terminating an existing contract simultaneously with closing business operations.

In short, the duty to arbitrate survives the termination of a contract when the dispute is over rights created under a labor agreement before it expired.

In *W.R. Grace,*[59] a 1983 case, the U.S. Supreme Court in a unanimous decision again upheld the integrity of the arbitration process. The employer entered into an agreement with the Equal Employment Opportunities Commission in which he promised to maintain in the plant the same proportion of women to men when layoffs occurred. When a layoff took place, pursuant to the EEOC agreement, the company laid off male employees who had greater seniority than the retained women. Under the labor agreement, strict seniority governed layoffs, and laid-off male employees filed grievances that were eventually upheld in arbitration. A federal court vacated the arbitrator's award on the grounds that the employer would violate his agreement with the EEOC should he lay off women employees by following the terms of the labor agreement and the arbitrator's award. While reversing the lower court, the high court said the arbitrator's award had to be followed regardless of its conflict with the EEOC agreement. Though the Court recognized the employer's dilemma—to follow the contract and arbitration award would result in the violation of the EEOC agreement, and to follow the EEOC agreement would result in violation of the labor agreement and arbitration award—it said the dilemma was of "its own making" because the union had not been a party to the EEOC agreement. If the union had been a party to the EEOC agreement, probably the employer could lawfully have laid off the senior male employees. In any event, while upholding the arbitrator's decision, the high court stated:

> Regardless of what this Court's view of the correctness might be of the arbitrator's contractual interpretation, [the parties] bargained for that interpretation, and a federal court may not second-guess it.

In other cases, however, the high court provided the basis for judicial review of arbitrators' decisions. These decisions were inconsistent with the Trilogy. In *Gardner-Denver*,[60] to be treated more fully in a later chapter, the Supreme Court held that an arbitrator's decision is not final and binding should Title VII of the Civil Rights Act be involved in a dispute. Though an arbitrator upheld the discharge of a black employee, the case was remanded to the district court to determine whether or not the employee's discharge was motivated by racial considerations. *Anchor Motor Freight*[61] established the principle that an arbitrator's decision is subject to reversal by a court when a union does not provide fair representation of employees involved in the arbitration. An employer discharged eight truck drivers for allegedly submitting inflated motel receipts for reimbursement. The drivers' union took the discharges to arbitration but failed to heed the employee's request to investigate the motel employees. After the arbitration, in which their discharges were sustained, evidence turned up that a motel clerk was originally the guilty party. He had been making false entries in the motel register and pocketing the difference.

Thereupon, the employees sued the employer and the union. A lower federal court upheld the arbitrator's award on the basis of *Enterprise Wheel & Car Corporation*. Consistent with this doctrine, the lower court held the arbitrator's decision to be immune to court reversal. However, the U.S. Supreme Court ruled that when a union fails to provide fair representation to employees involved in arbitration, the employees are entitled to an appropriate remedy. In its decision, the Court held that the remedy would be paid for by both the employer and the union. Thus, any back pay due the employees would be shared equally between them because the employer in error had discharged them in the first place and the union had failed to provide the employees fair representation in the arbitration.

The problem with *Anchor Motor Freight* is not that the employees involved should not receive a remedy. Obviously, they were not discharged for just cause. Elementary fairness should demonstrate that they be returned to their jobs with full back pay. Instead, the real problem is how far the courts will go in applying the doctrine. If employees who lose a case in arbitration discover some evidence that the union may have overlooked, will the arbitrator's award be subject to reversal? Probably in many cases a union may not have dug up every scrap of evidence that may have favored the employees. In other words, if the courts do not use restraint and caution in applying *Anchor Motor Freight,* the integrity and finality of the arbitration process could be threatened. Promiscuous use of the doctrine would make a mockery of the clause invariably contained in an arbitration provision: "The arbitrator's award shall be final and binding." Apparently the Supreme Court recognized this problem when it stated in *Anchor Motor Freight* that

> the grievance process cannot be expected to be error free. The finality provision has sufficient force to surmount occasional instances of mistakes.

The decision puts the unions on notice. In effect, the high court has said that the courts have the authority to upset an arbitration award when a union commits a gross error in the representation of employees in arbitration or when a union is dishonest or shows bad faith in the arbitration process. Not many unions engage in such reprehensible conduct, and probably *Anchor Motor Freight* will not provide the basis for wholesale reversal of arbitration decisions.

Following the *Gardner-Denver* precedent, in April 1981 the U.S. Supreme Court held that an arbitrator's decision involving rights established by the Fair Labor Standards Act may be reviewed and reversed by the federal courts.[62]

Three years later, the high court once again determined that an employee's claim, based upon statutory rights, is not finally foreclosed by an arbitration award. In *McDonald* v. *City of West Branch, Michigan,*[63] a police officer, a union steward, was discharged for allegedly participating in a sexual assault on a minor. An arbitrator sustained the discharge, finding that McDonald was discharged for just cause. Asserting that his discharge was in reprisal for his activities as a union steward, the police officer sued in federal district court requesting that damages be assessed against the chief of police and other city officials. His suit alleged a violation of Section 1983 of the Civil Rights Act of 1871, claiming that his discharge violated his First Amendment rights of freedom of speech, association, and freedom to petition the government for redress of grievances. A federal district court permitted McDonald to proceed with his suit, and a jury eventually awarded him an $8,000 judgment against the police chief. On appeal by the city, however, a federal appeals court reversed the lower court's decision, finding that the First Amendment claim was an unwarranted attempt to litigate a matter already decided by the arbitrator.

In a unanimous decision, the U.S. Supreme Court reversed the federal appeals court, finding that arbitration was not the proper forum to address issues involving statutory and constitutional rights. Following its earlier decisions, the high court stated:

> . . . although arbitration is well suited to resolving contractual disputes, our decisions in *Barrentine* and *Gardner-Denver* compel the conclusion that it cannot provide an adequate substitute for a judicial proceeding in protecting the federal statutory and constitutional rights that sec. 1983 is designed to safeguard.

Finally, with respect to the integrity of arbitration awards as established by the Trilogy, there is the problem of these awards' relationship to matters of public policy. The specific issue is whether or not arbitration awards should be vacated by the courts when they conflict with public policy. In *W.R. Grace,* previously discussed, the U.S. Supreme Court held that arbitration awards would not be enforced when they directly violate public policy, stating:

> If the contract as interpreted by [the arbitrator] violates some *explicit* public policy, we are obliged to refrain from enforcing it. . . . Such a public policy, however, must be *well defined* and *dominant,* and is to be *ascertained by reference to the laws and legal precedents* and not from general considerations of supposed public interests. [Emphasis supplied]

Using that pronouncement as the guideline, federal appeals courts have reversed arbitration decisions when they appeared to conflict with public policy. For example, in one case an arbitrator reinstated a truck driver despite the fact that he was discharged for consuming alcoholic beverages on the job.[64]

A federal appeals court held that the arbitrator's decision violated the public policy directed against people who drive when drinking. While vacating the arbitrator's decision, the court stated the public policy of preventing people from "drinking and driving is established in the case law, the applicable regulations, statutory law, and pure common sense."

Another federal appeals court vacated an award reinstating a postal worker who had been discharged for embezzling postal money orders.[65] The court reversed the award even though the arbitrator held the employee had not been terminated for just cause because of his intent to repay, his unusual financial problems, and a previously spotless disciplinary record. To justify its decision, the court cited several statutes relating to the conduct and honesty of postal employees, and warned that the reinstatement of the employee would imply government condonation of dishonesty.

More cases exist demonstrating reversal of arbitration awards when these awards conflict with public policy.[66] Probably few would question that in principle, arbitration awards should be vacated when they directly violate public policy. Nonetheless, the danger exists that judges may undermine the integrity of the arbitration process based upon their judgments of the interpretation and application of public policy. At times, identification and interpretation of public policy are subject to the subjective judgment of the judiciary.

In sum, aside from judicial reversal resulting from arbitrators' conduct, under current case law, arbitration awards may be reversed when a union fails to provide fair representation to employees involved in arbitration; when statutory or constitutional guarantees are involved; and when arbitration decisions conflict with public policy. Though these exceptions to the Trilogy are, of course, significant, it is not a situation where exceptions make a rule meaningless. In the final analysis, *Warrior & Gulf Navigation, American Manufacturing,* and *Enterprise Wheel & Car Corporation* stand as effective barriers against promiscuous tampering with the arbitration process by the judiciary.

Norris–La Guardia Influence on No-Strike Provisions

Section 4 of the Norris–La Guardia Act was not immediately a problem at the time the Supreme Court handed down its *Lincoln Mills* decision and later the *Steelworkers* Trilogy. Section 4 prohibited the federal courts—and for that matter, state courts operating under little Norris–La Guardia acts—from issuing injunctions against unions engaged in strikes in violation of their contracts.

The *Lincoln Mills* and Trilogy cases established a *quid pro quo* approach to the enforcement of agreements. This was thought to have meant that an agreement to arbitrate disputes was entered into in exchange for a union agreement not to strike for the duration of the contract. These cases implied that the no-strike provision of labor contracts was subject to the same rules and treatment as any other contractual provision.[67] Previously, we explained that under *Lincoln Mills,* the employer must arbitrate when a labor agreement makes arbitration the final step in a grievance procedure. The question arose as to whether Section 301 of Taft-Hartley would also apply to a union that had struck in violation of a no-strike clause, instead of using arbitration to seek relief from an alleged employer violation of a contract.

In 1962, the Supreme Court decided *Sinclair,* which involved a suit for breach of a no-strike contract.[68] The high court refused to enjoin a strike engaged in by a union during a contractual period, despite the fact that the labor agreement contained no-strike and arbitration clauses. The union could have submitted the grievances that caused the strike to arbitration instead of striking. In its decision, the Court reasoned that it could not issue an injunction to stamp out the strike on the grounds that it was forbidden to do so under the Norris–La Guardia Act. Section 301 of Taft-Hartley had not repealed the Norris–La Guardia Act of 1932. Therefore the law discriminated against employers, since they had to arbitrate unresolved grievances, whereas a union could bypass arbitration and strike, free from fear that the courts would issue an injunction to stop the strike. It should be recognized, however, that most labor organizations would not strike over grievances rather than making use of the arbitration process.

In *Sinclair,* the high court pointed out that Congress did not make wildcat strikes an unfair labor practice when it established Taft-Hartley. Probably Congress believed that it was not necessary to do so, since such activity would be deterred by providing the employer the right to sue unions for damages under Section 301. Since such strikes are not an unfair labor practice, and since the Court held that they constitute a "labor dispute" within the meaning of Norris–La Guardia, it held that the federal courts were not authorized to issue an injunction to stop wildcat strikes. It rejected the employer's argument that an injunction under these circumstances would be compatible with Section 301 and would make that provision meaningful. To say the least, employers were very uphappy with the *Sinclair* decision.

The decision left intact the employer's right to sue unions for damages under Section 301 when a strike in violation of a no-strike provision took place. Also, the company could discharge workers who participated in such strikes, provided it did so without discrimination. However, employers believed that such remedies were not viable, since they would be implemented after the fact. Indeed, as a condition for ending a wildcat strike, unions frequently insisted that employers drop their suits and restore the employees to their jobs.[69] As a practical matter, some employers did so to restore production as quickly as possible. In short, what the employers desired was a legal remedy that would quickly terminate a wildcat strike. Such a remedy could be achieved only through the injunction.

SINCLAIR REVERSED BY BOYS MARKETS

In any event, unions generally remained in a favored position because they could refuse to honor their no-strike agreements without fear of court enjoinment of their actions. The Supreme Court, in *Sinclair,* had interpreted the use of injunctions in such cases to constitute a violation of Section 4 of the Norris–La Guardia Act. Yet three courses of possible action might provide employers with relief. The first involved a Supreme Court determination of state court authority to issue injunctions under the *American Dredging* rule.[70] The second involved congressional clarification of the issue. Congress could merely state that arbitration enforcement in the federal courts under federal law was not subject to the equity limitations of the Norris–La Guardia Act. The third approach depended upon the desire of unions and management to avoid industrial warfare. Collective bargaining agreements could have been constructed in a fashion that would subject both parties equally to the equity power of the courts. However, all these issues became moot in the light of the Supreme Court's decision in *Boys Markets* v. *Retail Clerks.*[71] On June 1, 1970, by a 5–2 vote, the Court reversed *Sinclair Refining* and held that employers could obtain injunctions from the federal courts to stop strikes in violation of a no-strike clause. The Supreme Court stated that *Sinclair Refining* was "a significant departure from our otherwise consistent emphasis upon the Congressional policy to promote the peaceful settlement of labor disputes through arbitration."

Though the 1970 decision may be defended on the grounds that employees and unions should not strike to settle their grievances when arbitration is available, the decision was nevertheless sharply criticized because Congress had not changed the 1962 policy, although many bills were introduced in Congress to nullify *Sinclair Refining*. As the *Wall Street Journal* observed on June 5, 1970:

> As a matter of fact such legislation was introduced, but Congress so far has not seen fit to act. Congressional action, of course, would have been much the better way. However desirable the result, the Supreme Court still should restrain itself from assuming the tasks that properly belong to the legislators.

Thus, the basis of the criticism of *Boys Markets* was the change in Supreme Court policy after an eight-year period during which Congress had not seen fit to reverse the *Sinclair Refining* doctrine. Black, writing the minority opinion, stated:

> Nothing at all has changed, in fact, except the membership of the Court and the personal view of one justice.

Nixon's first appointee to the Court, Burger, was Chief Justice at the time of *Boys Markets,* and Stewart was the Justice who changed his mind.

In any event, the Court has now provided employers with a potent weapon to stop strikes that violate no-strike agreements. Though objective data indicating the frequency of *Boys Markets* injunctions are not available, it is safe to say that employers have used them on a widespread basis to terminate wildcat strikes. When the decision was announced, there was speculation that unions would refuse to agree to no-strike and arbitration clauses to avoid injunctions. Unless there is a no-strike and arbitration clause in a labor agreement, an employer may not obtain an injunction. These speculations were not realized. There is no evidence that contracts now contain fewer no-strike and arbitration clauses than they did before *Boys Markets*.

Despite the advantage that employers receive from *Boys Markets,* federal courts have refused to issue injunctions under certain conditions. Before an injunction will be issued, the court must be satisfied that the issue is arbitrable under the labor agreement and that the employer will proceed to arbitration.[72] A federal appeals court refused to sustain an injunction issued by a district court because the employer refused to concede that certain work assignments were arbitrable under the labor agreement. Also, an injunction will not be issued when a strike took place before the parties agreed to a contract containing a no-strike and arbitration clause. In one case, the negotiating parties had agreed on economic terms, but not on the arbitration clause. By the time of the negotiations, the previous labor agreement containing an arbitration procedure had expired.[73] No injunction was issued. In another case, when an employer could not show that the wildcat strike was causing the company irreparable harm, a court refused to issue an injunction.[74] In a case involving safety in a coal mine, a federal court refused to issue an injunction because the employer did not comply with a contractual provision requiring the company to follow the recommendations of a safety committee to correct an imminently dangerous condition.[75] In this dispute, the court distinguished its circumstances from *Gateway Coal.*

In 1976, the U.S. Supreme Court placed a significant limitation on the employer's right to a *Boys Markets* injunction. In *Buffalo Forge,*[76] the same union represented the production workers and the office employees of the employer. The dispute arose when a strike occurred during the negotiation of the office employees' first labor agreement. Four days later, the production workers struck in sympathy with the office workers. The production workers' contract contained no-strike and arbitration provisions. The employer applied for an injunction after making it clear that it was willing to arbitrate the dispute under the production workers' arbitration clause.

Affirming lower federal courts' decisions, the U.S. Supreme Court by a vote of 5–4 held that a *Boys Markets* injunction was not proper. At the heart of the majority decision was the finding that the production workers' arbitration provision did not cover sympathy strikes. That is, the production workers' strike was not over a grievance which arose under their contract. Instead, the strike was undertaken to show sympathy with the office employees. Such an event, the majority held,

> was not *over* any dispute between the union and employer that was even remotely subject to the arbitration provisions of the contract.

To put it in other terms, the sympathy strike was not over an arbitrable issue under the production workers' contract. They had agreed only to arbitrate grievances which arose under the contract. They had not agreed to arbitrate the right to engage in sympathy strikes.

In a sharp dissent, the minority argued that the no-strike provision of the production workers' contract should be enforced by an injunction, without regard to whether the cause of the strike was subject to arbitration. In other words, the no-strike clause should be honored and subject to an injunction independent from the reason for the strike. While rejecting this argument, the majority stressed that the Court's decision in *Boys Markets* made a narrow and single exception to the prohibition of injunctions under the Norris–La Guardia Act. The exception is that a union shall not strike over an issue which is covered by a contract's arbitration provision. Otherwise, said the majority, any strike could be enjoined by a court.

Buffalo Forge marks an important restriction in the application of *Boys Markets,* serving to encourage unions to engage in sympathy strikes even if their contracts contain no-strike and arbitration provisions. Employers could defend against such conduct to the extent that they are successful in broadening the language of no-strike and arbitration provisions to cover sympathy strikes.

The Soviet Union's intervention in Afghanistan provided the background for the U.S. Supreme Court dealing with *Boys Markets* injunctions. After President Carter ordered trade restrictions, members of the Longshoremen's Union refused to handle cargo destined for or coming from the USSR. Harmed by the union's action, an employer requested a *Boys Markets* injunction and a judicial order directing the union to arbitrate the issue of whether the work stoppage violated the no-strike provisions of the labor agreement.

Although the high court recognized that the union's action was politically motivated, it held that an injunction could not be issued under the terms of the Norris–La Guardia Act because the work stoppage constituted a "labor dispute" within the meaning of the statute.[77] Nor could the employer obtain a *Boys Markets* injunction, because the issue that had caused the work stoppage was not arbitrable under the labor agreement. It was not arbitrable, the Court held, whether the work stoppage was regarded as protest of Soviet military policy or as expression of sympathy with the people of Afghanistan. Thus, as in *Buffalo Forge,* the U.S. Supreme Court held that a *Boys Markets* injunction may not be issued by the federal courts unless the issue giving rise to a work stoppage is arbitrable under the terms of a labor agreement.

In sum, though a *Boys Markets* injunction will not be issued under some circumstances, this should not detract from the importance of the doctrine. In the absence of some comparatively infrequent circumstances, employers may obtain an injunction to stamp out a strike that violates a no-strike provision. At times exceptions to a rule erase the viability of the rule. This has surely not been the case with respect to the *Boys Markets* injunction.

METROPOLITAN EDISON: DISCIPLINE OF UNION OFFICERS

To deal with unauthorized or wildcat strikes in violation of a no-strike clause, some employers impose stiffer penalties on local union officers, including stewards and grievance committee members, compared with rank-and-file employees who commit the same offense. Disparate discipline is justified because union officials have a greater obligation to comply with and enforce the no-strike clause.

In the *Metropolitan Edison* case of 1983, however, the U.S. Supreme Court held that employers may not impose more severe discipline on union officials who commit the same offense as rank-and-file employees.[78] If both, for example, instigate a wildcat strike, engage in picketing, or encourage other employees to join the strike, an employer may not discharge the union officials while only suspending the rank-and-file employees. Should a management desire to penalize union officials more severely, it must negotiate a contract provision that specifically authorizes disparate treatment by placing special obligations on the union officials. It is not likely, however, that many unions would agree to such a contractual provision.

Nonetheless, following *Metropolitan Edison,* a U.S. Chamber of Commerce representative stated:

> It is quite likely that employers are going to put some responsibility back where it belongs—on the union stewards and even higher up. Employers will insist during contract talks that the duty of union leaders be spelled out.[79]

At this writing, however, no evidence exists that clauses of that kind have been negotiated in collective bargaining. Thus, the decision tends to make it more difficult for employers to enforce no-strike clauses. Obviously, the NLRB has no choice except to follow the high court's policy on this issue. In one case, an arbitrator sustained the discharge of a union steward because the steward failed to end a wildcat strike. However, the NLRB refused to defer to the award because of its conflict with the Supreme Court's decision.[80] Reversing the arbitrator's decision, the NLRB pointed out that the steward had no contractual duty to end unlawful strikes. Though NLRB Chair Dotson was compelled to follow *Metropolitan Edison,* he said that if not for that decision, he would have deferred to the arbitrator's award.

DUAL JURISDICTION OF ARBITRATORS AND NLRB

Despite the existence of no-strike and arbitration clauses in a labor contract, there are situations in which an arbitrator's award might not put an end to a dispute. There is a possibility that some cases may be relitigated before the NLRB if one party is disappointed with the award. These are cases in which Taft-Hartley issues are either directly or indirectly involved. For example, a union may prefer to use arbitration rather than the NLRB in cases that involve Taft-Hartley matters. But under certain circumstances, the NLRB will hear the case if a union loses the arbitration award. Thus, the union could get two chances to win its case. However, with certain important exceptions to be noted below, the NLRB as a matter of general policy defers to arbitration for the resolution of conflicts.[81]

Recall that under the *Collyer* doctrine, treated in the previous chapter, an unfair labor practice is filed, but the NLRB instructs the parties to proceed to arbitration. Under certain circumstances, we learned that the Board might elect to upset the arbitrator's award and find that an unfair labor practice was committed. At this time, we are concerned with an arbitration undertaken by the parties *before* unfair labor practices are filed. The issue here is a determination of NLRB policies, as to whether it will subsequently honor the arbitrator's award, or upset it and find that unfair labor practices have been committed.

The U.S. Supreme Court has extended considerable prestige to the voluntary arbitration process through *Lincoln Mills* and the *Steelworkers* Trilogy, as demonstrated previously. In these cases, the Court recognized that Congress intended that "privately agreed-upon methods of settlement should be favored, the attempt being to restrict administrative supervision of bargaining as much as possible."[82] However, the NLRB may not honor an arbitrator's award if Taft-Hartley unfair labor practices are involved in the case.[83] Thus the Trilogy doctrine will not preserve an arbitrator's decision if it does not conform with Taft-Hartley and its construction by the NLRB.

Taft-Hartley granted the NLRB wide authority to deal with employer-employee relations. One federal court of appeals ruled that the NLRB has exclusive power over unfair labor practices and this authority "shall not be affected by any other means of adjustment or prevention that has been or may be established by agreement, law or otherwise."[84] The power of the Board in the context of existing law is greater than that of any other body in establishing employer and union regulations.[85] Indeed, when the NLRB takes a case after it has been arbitrated, it does so because statutory law is superior to a private labor agreement. In other words, Taft-Hartley takes precedence over any labor agreement, so that unions, employees, and employers do not forfeit any statutory rights under labor agreements. Therefore, the NLRB under certain circumstances will void an arbitrator's award if it finds that the arbitrator deprived someone of rights guaranteed by statute.

As in the *Collyer*-type case, the determination of whether or not the NLRB will defer to an arbitration award issued prior to the filing of unfair labor practice charges depends upon the application of the *Spielberg* standards.[86] To repeat, the NLRB will defer to an arbitration decision where the proceedings appear fair and regular; the parties are in agreement to be bound by the arbitration award; the decision is not clearly repugnant to the purpose and policies of the law; and, as the Reagan Board held—weakening considerably the previous policy—where the contractual issue is factually parallel to the unfair labor practice issue, if the arbitrator was generally presented with the facts relevant to resolving the unfair labor practice.

Arbitrators must take due care in rendering decisions. Not only are they subject to review by the courts, but by the NLRB as well. Both the courts and the NLRB attempt to give wide latitude to the process that provides a peaceful solution to labor disputes with a minimum of public interference. However, failure of an arbitrator to conform to Board guidelines could result in the reversal of his or her decision.

In any event, the NLRB has been criticized for its willingness to review cases that have been arbitrated. It is argued that such a policy undermines arbitration and is in conflict with stable labor relations. Indeed, from time to time, professional arbitrators have complained about the NLRB because it will review cases. Actually, like many other issues in labor law, there are two sides to the picture. On the one hand, there is some doubt that a party who has elected to arbitrate instead of going to the NLRB in the first place should be permitted to use the Board to upset an unfavorable arbitration award. The argument is that the party should not get two opportunities to win the same case. On the other hand, the fact is that statutory law takes precedence over private labor agreements. Therefore, the NLRB has the duty to reverse an arbitrator's award when that award deprives an employee, employer, or union of rights guaranteed by Taft-Hartley. Probably there is no satisfactory solution to the problem, and the accommodation between the NLRB and arbitration will have to be resolved on a case-by-case basis.

BARGAINING OBLIGATION OF SUCCESSOR EMPLOYER

In 1970, the NLRB issued a decision that required a successor employer to honor the collective bargaining agreement signed by the predecessor employer.[87] Lockheed Aircraft received security services from Wackenhut. The United Plant Guard Workers had prevailed in a Board-held election and was certified as bargaining agent for Wackenhut employees. A collective bargaining agreement was signed, but four months later, Lockheed awarded the Burns International Detective Agency the contract to provide security services. It was apprised of the collective bargaining relationship Wackenhut had with the United Plant Guard Workers. Burns employed forty-two men on the Lockheed job, of whom twenty-seven had previously worked for Wackenhut. Burns had a bargaining contract with a different union with an accretion clause that was applied to workers on the Lockheed job. Charges were filed against Burns because it did not recognize the United Plant Guard Workers and honor the Wackenhut contract.

In reaching its decision in the *Burns* case, the Board relied on the Supreme Court decision in *John Wiley and Sons* v. *Livingston.*[88] In *Wiley,* a small unionized company was merged into a larger nonunion organization. The union brought a Section 301 suit against the surviving firm to compel arbitration under the terms of agreement with the predecessor. The Supreme Court ordered arbitration, which left the question of applicability of other provisions of the labor contract to the surviving company. In the *Burns* case, the Board relied on the *Wiley* case to hold that Burns was obligated under Section 8 (a) (5) to honor the Wackenhut agreements. The Board reasoned that a collective bargaining agreement is not an ordinary contract, but is a generalized code binding on successors who continue essentially the same enterprise.

Burns appealed the case. The court of appeals upheld the Board on the order to recognize the union, but refused to enforce that part of the order requiring Burns to honor the labor contract of the predecessor.[89] The Supreme Court affirmed the appellate court decision.[90] The high court reasoned:

> A potential employer may be willing to take over a moribund business only if he can make changes in corporate structure, composition of the labor force, work, location, task assignment, and nature of supervision. Saddling such an employer with the terms and conditions of employment contained in the old [labor] contract may make these changes impossible and may discourage and inhibit the transfer of capital.[91]

Thus *Burns* tells us the successor employer must recognize the union, but has no obligation to accept the labor agreement negotiated with the employer.

SUCCESSOR EMPLOYER OBLIGATIONS

Burns did not resolve several issues that arose after the decision. Other questions required determination. For a successor employer to have an obligation to recognize the union, the company must continue the same product lines, departmental organization, employee identity, and job functions.[92] So if the new employer changes the business structure in a genuine and fundamental way, the company need not recognize the union. Also, recognition would depend upon the majority status of the union. Should the new employer hire a majority of the workers employed by the former owner, the successor employer must recognize the union. A successor employer may raise a good-faith doubt concerning the majority status of the union. However, it must present objective evidence to show that the union no longer represents a majority of the employees. In a 1985 case of this type, a successor employer voluntarily recognized the union and met with it in contract negotiation sessions.[93] Before a subsequently scheduled session, the employer received a petition signed by a majority of the employees stating they no longer desired union representation. At this point, the employer ceased recognizing the union and withdrew from bargaining. Under these circumstances, the NLRB held that the employer's conduct was lawful even though no one had verified the signatures on the petition. The Board held that the petition constituted a sufficient basis to support a good-faith doubt as to the union's majority status.

Also *Burns* did not resolve the issue of when a successor employer can unilaterally institute changes in working conditions. In one case, a union had never been certified by the Board, but had won an election supervised by the mayor of the town fourteen years prior to the change of employers. It had a one-year contract with the predecessor employer that was based on an automatic renewal provision.[94] The successor employer refused either to accept the contract in existence or to negotiate a new one. An unfair labor practice was filed by the union. The Board ordered the successor employer to honor the old contract and to recognize and bargain with the union.

A court of appeals overruled the Board order to honor the old contract, but did require the successor employer to bargain. It also determined the issue of when a successor employer loses the right to make unilateral decisions. This right is lost at the moment it becomes clear that most of the predecessor's employees will retain their jobs, and if the nature of the business remains unchanged. The court reasoned that although there was no obligation to honor the old contract, the employer was not free to make unilateral changes until the two sides had bargained to impasse. If a new employer intends to retain most of the previous employer's workers, the company cannot avoid an obligation to bargain about initial working conditions merely by making employment dependent upon acceptance of unilateral conditions.[95] If a company plans to take most of the employees, bargaining with the incumbent is required before employment conditions are fixed. For example, a former employer paid "year-end bonuses" to employees. Though the benefit was not contained in the labor agreement, it was paid as a matter of practice, and was based upon the employees' sales. Therefore, the payment was not really a "bonus," but more realistically a regular portion of the employees' wages. After the successor employer purchased the establishment, the company discontinued the payment without negotiations with the union. A federal appeals court sustained the Board's decision, which held that the successor employer could not end the payment before bargaining with the union.[96]

In June 1974, unions lost some ground in the successor employer controversy. At that time, in *Howard Johnson* v. *Hotel and Restaurant Employees,* the U.S. Supreme Court held that a successor employer did not have the obligation to arbitrate the refusal to hire employees of the seller's work force. In this case, the new employer discharged all supervisors and hired only a small number of the employees who had worked for the former employer.[97] On the other hand, in 1980, unions registered a significant victory. For many years, the Board and courts have held that when a new employer purchases a firm that owes back pay to employees for unfair labor practices, the successor employer becomes responsible for the payment.[98] The U.S. Supreme Court sustained this doctrine.[99] However, in *International Technical Products*[100] the original employer who owed back pay for committing an unfair labor practice went bankrupt. A bankruptcy court's order permitted the successor employer to purchase the firm "free and clear of all liens, claims, and encumbrances." Based upon these circumstances, the new employer refused to pay the back pay. Rejecting the new employer's position, the Board directed payment on the grounds that its orders may not be modified or eliminated by a bankruptcy court.

As in many other areas of its work, the NLRB deals with the successor employer problem on a case-by-case basis. Though *Burns* established the basic principle, it certainly did not settle all the issues.

SUMMARY

Enforcement of collective bargaining contracts has changed considerably since the Wagner Act era. Prior to the Taft-Hartley Act, unions generally had little legal recognition for entering into contracts with management. Individual employees obtained rights under collective bargaining contracts and as such were the appropriate ones to file suit in state courts under common law.

The 1947 labor law brought with it a recognition of union maturity and therefore recognition of their right to engage in collective bargaining contracts. Unions were permitted to sue and to be sued. Such suits are permitted in the federal courts as well as state courts, but federal law applies.

Given the statutory right to represent all employees in a bargaining unit, unions have the corollary duty of fair representation. Unions that fail to perform this duty face NLRB and court proceedings. Case law establishes the circumstances under which unions have failed, thereby meeting this obligation.

The U.S. Supreme Court is in the process of building a body of substantive law for the purpose of dealing with Section 301 suits. The *Lincoln Mills* and subsequent *Steelworkers* Trilogy cases brought substantial prestige to the arbitration process. Federal judges were instructed to stay away from the merits of arbitration cases and to sustain arbitrators unless clear violations of national labor policy occurred. At the same time, it must be realized that alleged violations must be reviewed by the courts and this means the merits of a particular case must be evaluated, although in a context different from the normal law of contracts. Subsequent to the Trilogy, the U.S. Supreme Court established that arbitration awards may not be honored when Title VII of the Civil Rights Act is involved and when the union fails to provide fair representation to employees in an arbitration.

Reversing *Sinclair,* the Supreme Court in *Boys Markets* held that federal courts may issue an injunction terminating a strike in violation of a no-strike clause. The 1970 decision occasioned some surprise because Congress did not act to nullify *Sinclair.* In any event, *Boys Markets* clarifies the complex situation that developed as a result of the courts' attempts to accommodate the Norris–La Guardia Act to violations of union agreements not to strike during the term of a labor agreement. Though congressional action would have been the better method to abolish the *Sinclair* doctrine, the result of *Boys Markets* is to provide employers with an effective method of making sure that unions will abide by their no-strike pledge when arbitration is available for the final settlement of contract disputes.

The NLRB has jurisdiction over unfair labor practices, and at times this opens the possibility for relitigating an arbitration case if a party is dissatisfied with the award. The Board attempts to accommodate the arbitration process. In so doing, it has decided to defer to arbitration if certain conditions are met. The proceedings must have been fair and regular, the parties must have agreed to accept awards as final and binding, the award must not be a clear contradiction of the purposes and policies of the Board, and the award must deal with the statutory rights of the parties. The NLRB has the authority to decide if these four conditions have been met. This means that the Board, like the federal courts, makes a review of cases presented to it to determine the merits of each case.

Despite *Burns,* the problem of the successor employer is far from resolved.

DISCUSSION QUESTIONS

1. In what way did a federal appeals court, in the *North American* case, influence the NLRB's Wagner Act policy concerning the right of an individual employee to present grievances directly to an employer? How did Taft-Hartley deal with the same issue?

2. Provide examples of a union's duty of fair representation. What remedies are available to employees when they feel that the duty of fair representation has been breached?

3. Discuss Section 301's intention of making the parties more responsible to their obligations under collective bargaining contracts. What weaknesses and strengths do you find in Section 301?

4. Describe the primary purpose of the arbitration process. How did the courts deal with the process originally?

5. What is the primary significance of the *Lincoln Mills* case? In what ways did the Trilogy cases amplify the *Lincoln Mills* decision? How have these cases affected the institution of arbitration?

6. How strict has the Supreme Court been in following its *Gardner-Denver* decision? Support your answer with appropriate cases.

7. Discuss the relative merits of the *Sinclair* and *Boys Markets* cases. How does *Buffalo Forge* relate to each case?

8. Evaluate the relative impact that the *Metropolitan Edison* decision may possibly have on the collective bargaining process.

9. To what circumstances does the Board apply the *Spielberg* standards? Does it have flexibility in those applications?

10. Under what circumstances might a successor employer have an obligation to a predecessor's collective bargaining agreement? Cite cases to support your answer.

NOTES

1   Section 9.
2   Section 9 (a).
3   *North American Aviation Company,* 44 NLRB 604 (1942).
4   *NLRB* v. *North American Aviation Company,* 136 F. (2d) 899 (1943).
5   *Hughes Tool Company,* 56 NLRB 981 (1944).
6   *Douglas Aircraft Company,* 25 War Labor Reports 57 (1944).

7   Section 9 (a).

8   *Lakeland Bus Lines, Inc.* v. *NLRB*, 287 F. (2d) 888 (1960).

9   *Miranda Fuel Company*, 140 NLRB 181 (1963).

10   *Hughes Tool Company*, 147 NLRB 166 (1964).

11   *Ibid.* Reference is made here to Section 8 (b) (3) of Taft-Hartley, which holds that a labor organization or its agent commits an unfair labor practice by refusing "to bargain collectively with an employer, provided it is the representative of his employees subject to the provisions of section 9 (a)."

12   *Sargent Electric Co.*, 209 NLRB 630 (1974).

13   *Kesner* v. *NLRB*, 532 F. (2d) 1169 (CA 7, 1976).

14   *General Motors Corp. Delco Moraine Div.*, 237 NLRB No. 167 (1978).

15   *Retail Clerks, Local 324, FED Mart Stores, Inc.*, 261 NLRB No. 156 (1982).

16   *Warehouse Union, Local 860, IBT (The Emporium)*, 237 NLRB No. 163 (1978).

17   *International Association of Machinists & Aerospace Workers, Local Union 697 (H. O. Canfield Rubber Co. of Va.)*, 223 NLRB 832 (1976).

18   *Branch 6000, Natl. Assn. of Letter Carriers* v. *NLRB*, 595 F. (2d) 808 (CCA DC, 1979).

19   *Cargo Handlers, Inc.*, 159 NLRB 321 (1966).

20   *Miranda Fuel Co.*, 140 NLRB 181 (1962).

21   *International Union of Electrical Workers, Local 485 (Automotive Plating Corp.)*, 170 NLRB No. 121 (1968).

22   *San Francisco Web Pressman and Platemakers' No. 4. San Francisco Newspaper Agency*, 272 NLRB No. 138 (1984).

23   *United Steelworkers of America, Local Union 2610 (Bethlehem Steel)*, 225 NLRB 54 (1976).

24   *General Truck Drivers, Chauffeurs & Helpers Union, Local 692, IBT (Great Western Unifreight System)*, 209 NLRB 446 (1974).

25   National Labor Relations Board, Office of the General Counsel, *Memorandum 79-55*, July 9, 1979.

26   *Humphrey* v. *Moore*, 375 U.S. 335 (1964).

27   *Ibid.*

28   *Vaca* v. *Sipes*, 386 U.S. 171 (1967).

29   *Ford Motor Company* v. *Huffman*, 345 U.S. 330 (1953).

30   *Cent. of Ga. Ry.* v. *Jones*, 229 F. (2d) 648 (CCA 5, 1956).

31   *Thompson* v. *BHD. of Sleeping Car Porters*, 367 F. (2d) 489 (CCA 4, 1966).

32   *Clayton* v. *Automobile Workers*, 451 U.S. 679 (1981).

33   *Bowen* v. *United States Postal Service*, 459 U.S. 212 (1983).

34   *AFL-CIO News*, Washington, D.C., January 15, 1983.

35   *Del Costello* v. *Teamsters*, 462 U.S. 151 (1983).

36   *Electrical Workers* v. *Foust*, 439 U.S. 892 (1979).

37   *Kolinske* v. *Lubbers*, CCA–DC No. 82–1203, June 17, 1983.

38   *Hoffman* v. *Lonza*, CCA–7 No. 80–2314, August 31, 1981.

39   *Freeman* v. *Teamsters, Local 135*, CCA–5, 746 F. (2d) 1316 (1984).

40   Section 301.

41   National Association of Manufacturers, *That New Labor Law*, p. 21.

42   International Association of Machinists, *The Truth About the Taft-Hartley Law and Its Consequences to the Labor Movement*, April 1948, p. 26.

43   *Sinclair Oil Corporation* v. *Oil, Chemical and Atomic Workers*, 452 F. (2d) 49 (1971).

44   *Atkinson* v. *Sinclair Refining Company*, 370 U.S. 238 (1962).

45   *Complete Auto Transit, Inc.* v. *Reis*, 451 U.S. 401 (1981).

46   Section 8 (d).

47   *Carbon Fuel* v. *United Mine Workers of America,* 444 U.S. 212 (1979).

48   "Arbitration Provisions in Collective Agreements, 1952," *Monthly Labor Review,* U.S. Department of Labor, Bureau of Labor Statistics, March 1953, pp. 261–266.

49   *Cutler-Hammer,* 271 App. Div. 917, 67 N.Y.S. (2d) 317 (1947).

50   *Ibid.*

51   *Association of Westinghouse Salaried Employees* v. *Westinghouse Electric Corporation,* 348 U.S. 437 (1955).

52   See Charles O. Gregory, *Labor and the Law,* 2nd ed., (New York: W.W. Norton & Co., Inc., 1961) pp. 457–466, for an excellent and perceptive treatment of the *Westinghouse* case.

53   These were *Textile Workers Union of America* v. *Lincoln Mills of Alabama,* 353 U.S. 448 (1957); *Goodall-Sanford, Inc.* v. *United Textile Workers of America,* 353 U.S. 550 (1957); and *General Electric Company* v. *United Electrical, Radio & Machine Workers of America,* 353 U.S. 547 (1957).

54   *Dowd Box* v. *Courtney,* 368 U.S. 502 (1962).

55   *United Steelworkers of America* v. *American Manufacturing Company,* 363 U.S. 564 (1960); *United Steelworkers of America* v. *Warrior & Gulf Navigation Company,* 363 U.S. 574 (1960); *United Steelworkers of America* v. *Enterprise Wheel & Car Corporation,* 363 U.S. 593 (1960).

56   For other examples of such limiting language, see *To Protect Management Rights* (Washington, D.C.: U.S. Chamber of Commerce, 1961), pp. 7–22.

57   *Gateway Coal Co.* v. *United Mine Workers,* 414 U.S. 368 (1974).

58   *Nolde Bros., Inc.* v. *Bakery & Confectionery Workers, Local 358,* 430 U.S. 243 (1977).

59   *W.R. Grace* v. *Rubber Workers, Local 759,* 103 Sup. Ct. 2177 (1983).

60   *Alexander* v. *Gardner-Denver,* 415 U.S. 36 (1974).

61   *Hines* v. *Anchor Motor Freight,* 96 Sup. Ct. 1048 (1976).

62   *Barrentine* v. *Arkansas-Best Freight System, Inc.,* 450 U.S. 728 (1981).

63   466 U.S. 284 (1984).

64   *Local 540* v. *Great Western Food Co.,* CA-5, No. 82-1207, August 1, 1983.

65   *U.S. Postal Service* v. *Postal Workers Union,* CA-1, No. 84-1094, June 19, 1984.

66   *Carpenters Local 1478* v. *Stevens,* CA-9, No. 83-6144, August 1, 1984. *Devine* v. *White,* CA-DC 697 F. (2d) 421 (1983).

67   Thomas J. McDermott, "Enforcing No-Strike Provisions via Arbitration," *Labor Law Journal,* XVIII, 10 (October 1967), pp. 579–587.

68   *Sinclair Refining Company* v. *Atkinson,* 370 U.S. 238 (1962).

69   McDermott, "Enforcing No-Strike Provisions via Arbitration," *op. cit.,* p. 2.

70   *American Dredging Company* v. *Local 25, Marine Division, Operating Engineers,* 338 F. (2d) 837 (1964), cert. denied, 380 U.S. 935 (1965).

71   398 U.S. 235 (1970).

72   *Parade Publications Inc.* v. *Philadelphia Mailers Union No. 14,* CA 3, Case No. 71-1107, May 1, 1972.

73   *Emery Air Freight Corporation* v. *Teamsters, Local 295,* 356 F. (2d) 974 (1971).

74   *Ciba-Geigy Corp.* v. *Local 2546, Textile Workers,* 391 F. Supp. 287 (1975).

75   *Jones & Laughlin Steel Corp.* v. *Mine Workers,* 519 F. (2d) 1154 (1976).

76   *Buffalo Forge* v. *United Steelworkers,* 428 U.S. 397 (1976).

77   *Jacksonville Bulk Terminals* v. *Longshoremen,* 457 U.S. 702 (1982).

78   *Metropolitan Edison Co.* v. *NLRB,* 460 U.S. 693 (1983).

79   *Wall Street Journal,* April 5, 1983.

80   *John Morrell & Co.,* 270 NLRB No. 1 (1984).

81   Jay W. Waks, "The 'Dual Jurisdiction' Problem in Labor Arbitration: A Research Report," *The Arbitration Journal*, XXIII, 4 (1968), p. 227.

82   Labor Management Relations Act, Section 203 (d), cited in Richard I. Bloch, "The NLRB and Arbitration: Is the Board's Expanding Jurisdiction Justified?" *Labor Law Journal*, XIX, 10 (October 1968), p. 646.

83   *NLRB* v. *Acme Industrial Company*, 385 U.S. 432 (1967).

84   *NLRB* v. *Walt Disney Productions*, 146 F. (2d) 44 (1945).

85   *Shoreline Enterprises* v. *NLRB*, 262 F. (2d) 933 (1959).

86   *Spielberg Manufacturing Company*, 112 NLRB 1080 (1955).

87   *William J. Burns International Detective Agency*, 182 NLRB 348 (1970).

88   376 U.S. 543 (1964).

89   *NLRB* v. *Burns International Detective Agency*, 441 F. (2d) 911 (1971).

90   406 U.S. 272 (1972).

91   *Ibid.*, pp. 287–288.

92   Robert E. Wachs, "Successorship: The Consequences of *Burns*," *Labor Law Journal*, XXIV, 4 (April 1973), p. 223.

93   *Harley-Davidson Transportation Co., Inc.*, 273 NLRB No. 192 (1985).

94   *NLRB* v. *Bachrodt Chevrolet Company*, 468 F. (2d) 963 (1972).

95   *Howard Johnson Company*, 198 NLRB 763 (1972).

96   *NLRB* v. *Pepsi-Cola Distributing Co.*, CCA 6, Case No. 79-1314, May 1, 1981.

97   417 U.S. 249 (1974).

98   *Perma Vinyl Corporation*, 164 NLRB 968 (1967).

99   *Golden State Bottling Company, Inc.* v. *NLRB*, 414 U.S. 168 (1973).

100   249 NLRB No. 183 (1980).

CHAPTER SIXTEEN

STRIKES, LOCKOUTS, AND PICKETING

RECAPITULATION

It was established in earlier chapters that courts frequently limited the right of labor organizations to strike. Judges ruled that certain strikes, such as those for union security, were unlawful. The injunction was the vehicle whereby strikes were stamped out when deemed unlawful. The social and economic predilections of judges provided the basis for the injunction. No action of the legislative branch of government branded these strikes as unlawful. Nevertheless, the judiciary determined the legality of strikes. As the Massachusetts Supreme Court once put it:

> Whether the purpose for which a strike is instituted is or is not a legal justification for it is a question of law to be decided by the court. To justify interference with the right of others the strikers must in good faith strike for a purpose which the court decides to be a legal justification for such interference.[1]

Organized labor protested against a policy that permitted the courts to exercise their equity power in labor disputes. Union leaders charged that the government via the courts sided with management in labor disputes. They claimed that the indiscriminate use of the labor injunction made it difficult—and at times impossible—for workers to obtain economic concessions from employers.

The legislative branch afforded relief to the nation's labor unions. This was accomplished by stripping the courts of their power to enjoin strikes. In short, judges lost their power to decide whether or not the purposes of strikes were lawful. Peacefully conducted strikes, regardless of objective, were immunized from the injunction. Such a public policy was established by Norris–La Guardia and by a number of state anti-injunction laws. Not only did the federal anti-injunction law protect strikes from the injunction, but it also largely relieved labor unions from prosecution under the antitrust laws. The Wagner Act added still more protection for labor's right to strike, outlawing a variety of strikebreaking practices engaged in from time to time by antiunion employers.

Thus Norris–La Guardia and the Wagner Act protected the right of employees to strike. Labor acclaimed these laws for the strike as the most effective of all of labor's economic weapons. After World War II, the legal status of the strike underwent a change. A number of states and the federal government regulated and outlawed certain types of strikes. Once again, labor was forbidden to engage in strikes calculated to gain certain objectives. This time, however, it was the legislative branch of government and not the judiciary that was responsible for the limitations on the exercise of the strike.

Our task in this chapter and the next three is to analyze Taft-Hartley and Landrum-Griffin changes regulating strike activity. How is this limitation accomplished? What enforcement techniques are provided in strike-control legislation? How do these laws affect the operation of collective bargaining? What forms of strikes are completely outlawed? Do these strike-control laws protect the basic interests of the public?

ECONOMIC STRIKER RIGHTS

The Taft-Hartley Act denied replaced economic strikers the right to vote in representation elections. Workers hired to replace economic strikers could vote, but economic strikers for whom the employer had found replacements were not eligible to cast ballots. Such a condition was established in a very short sentence in the law: "Employees on strike who are not entitled to reinstatement shall not be eligible to vote."[2] Organized labor immediately claimed that this fifteen-word phrase threatened the success of every economic strike. More important, union leaders charged that this policy of Taft-Hartley endangered the security of the entire union movement by providing employers with a potent antiunion weapon. In contrast, some people asserted that workers on an economic strike replaced by other employees had severed their employment relationship by the mere act of not reporting to work. Consequently, it was contended, these workers no longer had an interest in the outcome of representation elections.

Economic versus Unfair Labor Practice Strikes

So that the significance of the voting policy of Taft-Hartley may be fully understood, it is first necessary to distinguish between *economic strikes* and *unfair labor practice strikes.* Falling into the economic-strike category are strikes for higher wages, shorter hours, better working conditions, health and welfare plans, and so on. In contrast, an unfair labor practice strike is a work stoppage caused by employer tactics declared unlawful by national labor relations policy. In this classification fall such strikes as those concerning union recognition, discrimination against union members, refusal to bargain collectively, and interference by the employer with the right of workers to organize and bargain collectively. If members of a local union strike because some of their officers are discharged for union activity, they would not be classified as economic strikers. Such a strike falls within the unfair labor practice category. It results from employer action declared unlawful under national law. The strike would not have occurred if the employer had not engaged in an unfair labor practice.

Reinstatement Rights of Strikers

Reinstatement rights of strikers differ depending upon the cause of the strike. Employees engaging in an unfair labor practice strike have unlimited right to reinstatement. This means that the NLRB has full authority to order the reinstatement of workers, including back pay awards, when this category of strike occurs. Such strikers will be reinstated whether or not the employer replaced them with other workers. An employer must rehire these strikers even though their reinstatement results in the discharge of workers hired to take their jobs.

Indeed, in *Mastro Plastics* the U.S. Supreme Court held that employees are entitled to reinstatement even when they strike in violation of a no-strike clause in a labor agreement, if they strike because of employer unfair labor practices.[3] In this case, the Court, while upholding the NLRB, held that there is an

> inherent inequity in any interpretation that penalizes one party to a contract for conduct induced solely by the unlawful conduct of the other, thus giving advantage to the wrongdoer.

In the absence of such a policy, the employer unfair labor practice section of national law would be rendered meaningless. Assume that employers would not be required to rehire unfair labor practice strikers. Now suppose an employer refuses to bargain collectively with a majority union. A strike results. During the course of the strike, the employer permanently replaces the strikers with other workers. Under these conditions, a strike resulting from employer noncompliance with national labor policy could have the effect of eliminating unions. It appears therefore as a matter of industrial justice that unfair labor practice strikers have the unlimited right to reinstatement. However, workers out on strike are generally not entitled to reinstatement when they engage in violence or coercive misconduct. In such a case, it does not matter if an employer had committed unfair labor practices that either caused or prolonged the strike.[4]

As a matter of fact, resulting from a 1983 U.S. Supreme Court decision, employers are placed in a more vulnerable position should they commit unfair labor practices during a strike. In the *Belknap* v. *Hale* case,[5] following an impasse in contract negotiations, the employees struck. At this point, the strike was for economic reasons and the employer hired replacements, assuring them their jobs were permanent. However, during the strike, the employer committed an unfair labor practice by granting a wage increase for nonstriking employees. In a settlement of the strike and the unfair labor practice charge, approved by the NLRB, the employer agreed to reinstate the strikers and lay off the replacements. Asserting a breach of contract and misrepresentation, the "permanent" replacements sued the employer for a total of $6,000,000 damages in state court. The high court held that such suits could properly be adjudicated in state court. Under these circumstances, said the Court, federal preemption did not apply because

> we cannot believe that Congress determined that the employer must be free to deceive by promising permanent employment, knowing that [the employer] may choose to reinstate strikers or may be forced to do so by [the National Labor Relations Board].

Among the implications of this decision is that it will probably be more difficult to settle strikes calling for the reinstatement of the strikers and the discharge of the replacement strikebreakers.

In contrast with unfair labor practice strikers, employees who engage in economic strikes enjoy only a limited right to reinstatement. The NLRB will order their immediate reinstatement only when the employer does not fill their jobs with permanent replacements. In the event that economic strikers have been permanently replaced, the NLRB has no authority to direct their reinstatement. Hence, permanently replaced economic strikers have no absolute legal right to reinstatement.

This policy was established in a case decided by the U.S. Supreme Court in 1938.[6] In *NLRB* v. *Mackay Radio & Telegraph*, the Court ruled that an employer could hire permanent replacements for economic strikers. The Wagner Act was interpreted as not prohibiting companies from protecting and continuing business operations when workers went on strike for economic reasons. If an employer was concerned with business, the company could continue to operate as long as this was for economic reasons and not for the purpose of destroying unions.

Later the same year, 1938, the NLRB was faced with the issue of whether replaced economic strikers could vote in Board-held representation elections. The NLRB held that workers could be deprived of their jobs by replacement, but not of their right to vote in such elections.[7] Both strikers and their replacements were extended the franchise. The Board was not satisfied with its rule, however, and reconsidered its position in the same case (*Sartorius*) about two months later. Replaced economic strikers were permitted to vote, but their replacements were deprived of the right. The conflict of job interest of the two groups was offered as justification for changing the rule. The Board reasoned that two separate groups of employees should not be permitted to vote for representation or the lack of it within the same bargaining unit.

The Board was dissatisfied with its rule change and made still another revision in 1941. In the *Rudolph Wurlitzer Company* case, it returned to its original *Sartorius* position.[8] Both economic strikers and their replacements were viewed as holding legal claims to their jobs and the Board held that "both should have the same right to vote in a representation election." Considerable criticism was leveled at the Board for permitting replaced strikers to vote in representation elections. It was often argued that only replacements should be permitted to vote, since the strikers had no hope of returning to their jobs.

Taft-Hartley Act Innovation.   It is obvious that the policy on reinstatement rights of strikers was not first established in 1947 by the Taft-Hartley Act. It was originally set up by the NLRB under the Wagner Act. The innovation of the 1947 labor law was that replaced economic strikers were denied the right to vote in any representation election held during the course of the work stoppage. Under the final Wagner Act position, the opportunity to vote was extended to this group of strikers as well as to their replacements. It did not distinguish between the voting rights of economic and unfair labor practice strikers.

This aspect of the law generated substantial concern on the part of unions. The Taft-Harley Act did not completely alleviate those concerns. Suppose the workers of the XYZ Manufacturing Company strike for higher wages. This, of course, is an economic strike. The employer manages to find permanent replacements for the bulk of striking workers. The replacements eventually petition the NLRB for a bargaining election. Alternatively, they could have petitioned for a decertification election. A decertification election could provide the basis for eliminating the old bargaining-unit representative and for stabilizing replacement worker jobs. Even so, a normal election petition may be filed. The Board conducts the election but permits only the replacements to vote. The replaced strikers are not eligible to cast ballots. This means that the replacements would win the election. As a consequence, the strikers' union would lose bargaining rights and the employer would no longer need to recognize it or bargain with it. In fact, if the strikers now demand recognition, the strike becomes unlawful. A union may not lawfully strike for recognition under Taft-Hartley when another organization has been certified.[9] This means that the employees might have to give up the strike.

In short, the nationally affiliated union involved in such a situation would be frozen out of the plant. It could no longer demand recognition. The strike is lost and the union is broken. The striking employees could not expect to be rehired. After an economic strike is terminated, a union that maintains its bargaining position will invariably demand that all strikers be reinstated. Such a demand is made as one condition for ending the strike. However, in the illustration, the striking union has lost its status in the plant. It could not extend any protection whatsoever to the striking employees. The company would not be obligated to rehire any of the workers—even those with long years of service. The Board would not hold another election for at least one year. Periods marked by serious unemployment could have resulted in widespread union decline, since worker risk of replacement for striking could have become more pronounced. Small bargaining units were particularly vulnerable under Taft-Hartley because of the relatively greater possibility of replacement than in larger units.

LANDRUM-GRIFFIN REVISION

Prior to the 1959 amendments of Taft-Hartley, recommendations were made by several persons to either eliminate the Section 9 (c) (3) feature, or to modify it so as to provide replaced economic strikers with some opportunity to vote in representation elections. Among these recommendations were those by President Dwight D. Eisenhower in a speech as early as 1952, and by Senator Robert A. Taft, one of the authors of the 1947 law.

Section 702 of Title VII changed the language of the 1947 statute. Under the new voting policy

> employees engaged in an economic strike who are not entitled to reinstatement shall be eligible to vote under such regulations as the Board shall find are consistent with the purposes and provisions of this act in any election conducted within twelve months after the commencement of the strike.

Congress was of the opinion that replaced strikers would usually not be interested in the bargaining-unit representative after a period of twelve months. It may also have been the view of Congress that strikers would have obtained other employment after such a long period. Yet it must be considered that many replaced strikers did retain a substantial interest in recapturing their former jobs. This was particularly the case of workers with long seniority with a company. Even if replaced workers did not possess long service records, their ages may have precluded them from finding comparable employment. Thus, if an employer managed to keep a business operating for more than one year by the use of replacements, unions and employees were no better off than they were before the Landrum-Griffin change was made. In any event, unions received relief. It is probably true that not many employers could stand a work stoppage for more than a year.

For a time, after *Pioneer Flour Mills,* the NLRB permitted replaced economic strikers to vote in elections that were held more than twelve months after a strike started.[10] The basis for this decision in *Brooks Research* was that replaced strikers were employees, and entitled to vote for as long as they retained an expectation for future employment by the same employer. As noted later in this section, under the *Laidlaw-Fleetwood* doctrine, replaced economic strikers have a right to a job whenever a job becomes available for them. That is, they have permanent reinstatement rights.[11] The Board held that replaced economic strikers had permanent reinstatement rights, and that an employer could not limit this right to a specific time period. It stated: "We likewise reject the contention that a time limit should be placed on the reinstatement rights of economic strikers." On this basis, the NLRB had held in *Pioneer Flour Mills* that replaced economic strikers had the right to vote in elections regardless of when they were held. In 1972, however, the NLRB ruled that voting rights of replaced strikers were limited to one year.[12] It stated in *Wahl Clipper:*

> It seems to us the most reasonable course, as well as the most reasonable interpretation of the statutory language, is to hold that replaced strikers are not eligible to vote in elections held more than 12 months after the commencement of an economic strike.

By this decision, though reasonable under the language of the 1959 law and its legislative history, there is greater opportunity for a motivated employer to get rid of a union, with the resultant consequences to the employees.

In contrast to replaced economic strikers, the Board held that unreplaced economic strikers could vote in elections held more than twelve months after the strike began.[13] In its decision, the agency stressed that the original or amended law placed no restrictions on the voting rights of unreplaced strikers.

The Board was required to establish regulations to implement the economic striker provision of the 1959 law. In 1960, it provided some rules to govern the new policy. The voting eligibility of economic strikers was to be determined by certain tests.[14] Voting privileges were to be forfeited when (1) the striker obtains permanent employment elsewhere before the election; (2) the employer eliminates a striker's job for economic reasons; or (3) the striker is discharged or refused reinstatement for misconduct rendering him or her unsuitable for reemployment. These are not the only standards established to evaluate cases, as discussed below.

An economic striker must be on strike at the time of the election before he or she is entitled to vote.[15] But this does not mean that if a striker gets a new job, he or she automatically forfeits the right to vote. Forfeiture of voting rights occurs only if the new job is substantially equivalent to the struck job.[16] Substantial equivalency depends upon such factors as pay, seniority, and working conditions. Even if the new job is substantially equivalent to the struck job, a replaced economic striker does not automatically lose voting rights. The replaced striker may retain the franchise despite the new job if he or she continues to picket, or informs the new employer that he or she is on strike and intends to return to the struck job if given the opportunity.[17] Thus, it is apparent that the Board weighs the economic gains and losses of replaced strikers when their ballots are challenged in Board-held elections. There is a recognition that these workers may have a substantial economic interest in their struck jobs. Voting privileges may afford an opportunity to recover the struck job.

Ordinarily, the Board directs that elections be held within thirty days from the date of the direction of an election. The NLRB has determined that "permanent replacements for strikers are eligible to vote in elections even if they are employed [elsewhere] on the date of the election."[18] However, no more replacements than strikers are permitted to vote. This limitation is imposed despite any favorable changes in economic conditions between the time of replacement and the holding of the election. This rule is provided to eliminate any voting imbalance between the two groups competing for the same jobs. Furthermore, this restriction eliminates the possible creation of a situation whereby the union on strike can be placed at a voting disadvantage by a struck company. It would be a simple matter to hire a large number of workers for a short period in order to influence election results.

The election policies of the NLRB established to carry out the objectives of Landrum-Griffin provide some relief to unions and their members who engage in economic strikes. However, there is no certainty that strikers will prevail in elections should employers choose to continue operations after reaching bargaining impasses. Regardless of the administrative ruling or legislation prevailing at any given period of time, the issue of economic striker replacement will remain open to criticism. The position taken depends upon the economic gain or loss involved. Once a labor union loses an election under such conditions, the union is dissolved by law. Chance for job recovery is lost. The smaller the bargaining unit, the greater the chance that jobs will be lost permanently when economic strikes occur.

In 1968, the NLRB reversed its previous rule governing economic strikers. It held that those who had been permanently replaced still had to be reinstated if their jobs opened up again.[19] The new rule is based on a 1967 decision of the U.S. Supreme Court that requires a company to reinstate strikers not rehired at the termination of a strike because of the low level of production.[20] The Board, following the Supreme Court, reasoned that a striker remains an employee even though he or she is not reinstated immediately after the strike is concluded. This is called the *Laidlaw-Fleetwood* doctrine.

In 1971, the Board modified the scope of this doctrine. In *United Aircraft*, the union, as a condition of ending a long strike, "agreed" that reinstatement rights of the strikers would be limited to four and one-half months following the termination of the strike.[21] If they were reinstated after this time, they were to be treated as new employees. Under these circumstances, the employees would have lost their accumulated seniority and other contractual rights. As a matter of fact, 1,500 employees were not rehired at the end of the period. Under this agreement, they had lost reinstatement rights. In reviewing this situation, the NLRB, by this time dominated by Nixon appointees, held that the action of the employer in refusing to reinstate strikers after the four and one-half months, and to treat those rehired after this time as new hires, did not violate the law because the union had "agreed" to this arrangement. The Board took the position that an agreement reached under the pressures to end a strike stands as a waiver of employee rights established by federal law. If the scenario in *United Aircraft* is used on a wide scale, the *Laidlaw-Fleetwood* doctrine would not be of much practical value.

JURISDICTIONAL STRIKES: ILLEGAL UNDER TAFT-HARTLEY

A *jurisdictional strike* is a work stoppage resulting from a dispute between two or more unions over the assignment of work. At times, unions strike because of interunion conflict over the representation of workers. Such strikes do not fall within the jurisdictional strike category. These are representation and not jurisdictional strikes. As John T. Dunlop, a leading authority on labor relations, put it: "In the jurisdictional dispute proper the contending organizations are not seeking new members; they are demanding the work in dispute for existing members."[22] If the character of the jurisdictional strike is understood, it is not difficult to see why such strikes occur. Unions that extend their jurisdiction over new jobs increase their power. A jurisdictional strike does not increase the total amount of work available. It is merely a device to obtain work for one union at the expense of another.

The record reveals that jurisdictional strikes have been persistent features of the industrial environment. Despite this, they have accounted for only a minor fraction of all strikes. However, their effect on employers, workers, and the public has been much greater than the figures reveal. As late as 1981, the NLRB reported 401 alleged union violations of the Taft-Hartley provision making strikes against employer work assignments unfair labor practices.[23] Thus, it is obvious that the continuing trend of technological change generates increased friction between unions regarding which one should perform assigned tasks. New materials and new production methods, particularly those affecting the building trades, will promote continued interunion rivalry to obtain controversial work assignments for their own members.

Taft-Hartley outlaws the jurisdictional strike.[24] Unions may not strike against a work assignment of an employer. As noted, jurisdictional strikes in the construction industry are particularly harmful because contractors usually work under specified time limits.

Section 10(k): Settlement of Dispute by NLRB

Not only does Taft-Hartley outlaw the jurisdictional strike, but it also places an affirmative obligation on the NLRB to settle the dispute giving rise to the strike. It is one thing to outlaw such a strike, but a different matter to determine which of two unions has the jurisdiction over the work. Section 10(k) states that the Board "is empowered and directed to hear and determine the dispute" that gives rise to a jurisdictional strike unless the parties had adjusted the dispute within ten days, or have agreed upon a method for the voluntary adjustment of the dispute.

After the passage of Taft-Hartley, unions and employers in the construction industry established the National Joint Board for the Settlement of Jurisdictional Disputes. In 1973, that board was replaced by the impartial Jurisdictional

Disputes Board. In 1984, that agency was abolished, with the parties agreeing to resolve jurisdictional disputes through private arbitrators. These procedures were adopted to make unnecessary NLRB determination of such disputes.

To say the least, settlement of jurisdictional disputes in the construction industry is a very difficult and complex task. If decisions are to be workable and equitable, they must conform to a large body of precedent established over a long period of time. In addition, arbiters of these disputes must have a firm knowledge of the entire construction industry. Obviously, the parties intimately connected with the construction industry are much better qualified to settle jurisdictional disputes than the NLRB. In this connection, the General Counsel of the NLRB declared:

> We of the Board have plenty to do in the field with which we are familiar, and in which we are properly expected to serve as experts. We frankly do not want to be plunged into this new field that is strange territory to us, in which we would be compelled to become experts almost overnight, but we will do it if we must.[25]

The Board considered itself unqualified to deal with jurisdictional problems and thereby largely ignored such cases unless (1) an employer made a work assignment inconsistent with Board certification of a union or (2) the assignment was inconsistent with the terms of the collective bargaining contract. This NLRB attitude left the actual determination of work assignment in the hands of employers. The possibility of unilateral action in this regard was precisely one of the situations the national labor laws had intended to eliminate.

Supreme Court Intervention

Thus, the Board viewed its function under Section 10 (k) as merely that of determining whether a striking union was entitled to the work in dispute under a preexisting Board order or certification, or under a collective bargaining contract. If the striking union was not entitled to the work on the basis of the two criteria just mentioned, the employer's assignment of work was regarded as decisive. Very often, however, neither the certifications nor the agreements clearly assigned work. This type of problem could lead to constant disputes extending over a period of years. An employer forced to make an assignment would not be immune from work stoppages by dissatisfied labor organizations. A company would attempt to satisfy all the unions involved, but usually would end up satisfying none. A strike by one of the unions would leave an employer no recourse but to file an unfair labor practice charge with the NLRB.[26]

These circumstances were presented to the U.S. Supreme Court in a 1961 case.[27] The high court came down hard on the NLRB and explicitly informed it that it had not been carrying out its statutory duty to hear and resolve jurisdictional disputes in every case where the parties had not been able to resolve the problem themselves. The Board is required to decide any "underlying jurisdictional dispute on its merits and . . . make affirmative" awards of disputed work in every case before it if the parties have not set up their own machinery to do so within ten days.

The Board has responded in accordance with Supreme Court direction. The *Radio Engineers Union (Columbia Broadcasting System)* decision was fully justified under the law. The legislative history of Section 10 (k) makes it obvious that Congress did not intend to permit the Board to ignore such cases.

The Supreme Court in 1971 was presented with the problem of NLRB authority to impose a jurisdictional dispute settlement when an employer refused to accept an award agreed to by the unions.[28] The issue centered on whether the employer was a "party" to the "dispute" within the meaning of Section 10 (k). The Board has long held that a voluntary method of adjustment must include the employer as well as the unions to be valid. The two unions as members of the AFL-CIO's Building Trades Department were required to submit their dispute to the National Joint Board for Settlement of Jurisdictional Disputes. They did so and an award was made. The employers involved had contracts with the union losing the award and refused to accept the National Joint Board's determination. Picketing resulted, and the companies filed unfair labor practice charges with the NLRB. The NLRB accepted the case and made its own award to the Tile Setters and not the Plasterers, as did the National Joint Board. A lower federal court set aside the Board order and held that the employers were bound by the National Joint Board's decision even though they had not agreed to submit the dispute to it.[29] This meant that the NLRB was without authority to settle the dispute. The Supreme Court upheld the NLRB and stated in *Plasterers' Local 79* that "the LMRA requires that the Board defer only when all of the parties have agreed on a method of settlement." In other instances the Board must settle the dispute.

Thus, the U.S. Supreme Court held in *Plasterers' Local 79* that an employer is a "party" to a dispute within the meaning of Section 10 (k). If the employer refuses to submit a jurisdictional dispute to an outside party for determination, the NLRB is required to settle it.

When employers and unions agree by contract that they will take a jurisdictional dispute to a private forum for final determination, they are "parties" to the dispute within the meaning of Section 10 (k). They may not avoid this obligation in the effort to involve the NLRB in the settlement of the dispute. On the other hand, if they had not previously and affirmatively agreed, and refuse to be parties to such a submission, the NLRB under the *Plasterers' Local 79* doctrine must determine the dispute.

The Board has established criteria that it usually observes in making work assignments. These factors of evaluation are the bargaining agreements and union constitutions, skills and work involved, industry custom and practice, and employer's past practice. However, it should be noted that these factors do not always permit an assignment. Conflicting results may be obtained when these criteria are applied. This is particularly the case when "new work" is involved. The Board has on occasion relied upon novel factors to make work assignments.

In the *Philadelphia Inquirer* case, the NLRB applied "substitution of function" and "loss-of-jobs" tests in resolving a jurisdictional dispute.[30] Of critical concern to the Board was what would happen to a union's members if it assigned work to another organization. Another factor that impressed the Board was that one union had undertaken to retrain its members in the new technology. Yet similarity of the new techniques to prior processes would have required a different assignment of work.

Generally, however, the Board, when assigning disputed work, adheres to the tests of (1) bargaining agreements and union constitutions, (2) skills and work involved, (3) industry custom and practice, and (4) employer's past practice and preference. Use of these tests provides a greater degree of stability than would determinations made without guidelines. The Board relies upon its "experience and common sense" when established tests fail to be adequate. Such an approach is consistent with the Supreme Court's *Columbia Broadcasting System* rule. However, the Board's determination of a jurisdictional dispute may be upset by the courts should it be found that these factors are not applied in a consistent manner. A federal circuit court of appeals reversed a Board decision on the grounds that it applied its standards in an arbitrary and capricious manner. In particular, the court held that the Board did not give sufficient weight to employer preference, a standard that it frequently used in resolving jurisdictional disputes.[31]

Despite the standards established by the NLRB to resolve jurisdictional disputes, one study reveals that from *Columbia Broadcasting System* to the present, the employer's position is sustained in ninety percent of all work assignment disputes.[32] Given this record, the study concludes:

> the apparent routine acceptance of the employer's assignment can be said to be an unwillingness to use or an abdication by the Board of its statutory powers.[33]

Based upon this study, it appears that the situation essentially remains the same as was the case before the Supreme Court's decision in *Columbia Broadcasting System*.

STRIKES AGAINST NLRB CERTIFICATION

The Wagner Act was based on the principle of majority rule. Unions selected by the majority of workers in a bargaining unit were to represent all employees within the unit. Employers were required to recognize and bargain with the majority union and with no other organization. An employer violated the statute by granting any measure of recognition to a minority union. Some labor unions, however, violated the doctrine of majority rule. They refused to respect certifications awarded by the NLRB. Despite the evidence of the ballot box, a number of unions struck against certifications of the NLRB. These unions struck to force employers to violate their legal obligation to recognize majority-designated unions.

Such action resulted when unions were defeated in bargaining elections. Let us assume that Union A and Union B are rivals in a bargaining election. Union A polls a majority vote. Dissatisfied with the election returns, Union B strikes to force the employer to recognize it and not Union A, the majority-designated labor organization. Of course, the employer is under legal obligation to bargain with A. Under the Wagner Act, management would commit an unfair labor practice if it granted any recognition whatsoever to B, the defeated labor organization.

Such strikes are totally indefensible. They violate the most elementary principles of democracy. They are completely inconsistent with the spirit of the Wagner Act. The frequency of such strikes under the Wagner Act was not very great. In the vast majority of cases, unions defeated in elections accepted the results of the polls in good faith. Frequently, this meant that workers were required to change union affiliations. It is to the credit of the union movement that such changes occurred without serious impairment to the productive process.

Ultimate Position of NLRB

Despite their limited frequency, the fact remains that such strikes did take place in the Wagner Act era. When they did occur, employers and majority-designated unions were placed in an intolerable position. Ultimately, the NLRB did attempt to discourage strikes against its certifications. In the early part of 1947, the Board ruled that employees who participated in a strike with the purpose of compelling an employer to recognize and bargain with the union of the striking employees rather than with a certified labor organization, were not entitled to reinstatement or back pay.[34] Since the Board held the purpose of this form of strike to be unjustified, the strikers were stripped of all benefits of the Wagner Act. This ruling was handed down by the NLRB at about the time the Wagner Act was to expire. The agency had not seen fit to establish this policy earlier in the Wagner Act era.

Treatment Under Taft-Hartley

Even the ultimate position of the NLRB on minority strikes, however, was not sufficient to protect the principle of majority rule. At the very best, it merely had the effect of discouraging such strikes. Under the Wagner Act, the NLRB did not have the power to prevent them. In this respect, the law was defective. The Board certified majority unions, but it did not have the authority to protect its certifications against strike action.

The principle of majority rule was included in the Taft-Hartley Act. As in the Wagner Act, employers are required to bargain with majority-designated labor unions. However, when it passed the 1947 labor law, Congress overcame the shortcoming of the Wagner Act. It outlawed strikes for recognition when another union had been certified by the NLRB.[35]

Certification of a union as exclusive bargaining representative makes a primary strike for recognition by a union other than the one certified an unfair labor practice under Section 8 (b) (4) (C). Adequate enforcement procedures were adopted. Injunctions may be obtained against unions that engage in such strikes.

When strikes against NLRB certification occur, Section 10 (1) makes it mandatory for the Board to seek injunctions against the strikes. It must give priority to violations of this nature. In addition, whoever is injured by a minority recognition strike may sue the minority union for actual damages. Punitive damages are not permitted[36] under Section 301, which does permit damage suits in federal and state courts.[37] However, adequate provision is now available to protect the bargaining rights of certified majority unions in most situations likely to arise.

LOCKOUT RIGHTS OF EMPLOYERS

The right of unions to strike to influence the outcome of bargaining demands has generally been considered as balanced by the right of employers to lock out employees for the same reason. The NLRB has never upheld the lockout as a legal form of economic pressure when used as an antiunion weapon. Purposes other than to destroy a union may qualify the weapon for legal use.

Essentially, the Board has established two situations under which it permits lockouts. One provides that the weapon is permissible as a defensive device to protect the employer against a sudden strike that might result in unusual economic losses. The other involves a lockout to preserve the institution of multiemployer bargaining. Employers themselves, however, may withdraw from a multiemployer bargaining arrangement only if notice is given prior to contract renegotiations. Later on the company cannot withdraw, even if an impasse is reached. The impasse does not constitute an "unusual circumstance." The U.S. Supreme Court upheld this policy in 1982.[38] Finally, under proper circumstances an employer may use the lockout as an offensive weapon to put pressure upon a union to accept its position when a collective bargaining contract is being negotiated.

Unusual Economic Hardship

Unusual economic hardship might result for a company engaged in custom work that cannot afford to continue to operate on a day-to-day basis for an extended period after contract expiration. This is particularly the case when the timing of a possible work stoppage is not certain. Uncertainty regarding a work stoppage at a firm dealing with custom work could result in loss of considerable goodwill if it were caught with unexecuted orders on hand.

Unusual economic costs might also be involved for a firm that produces a perishable raw material. After a contract has expired, a company may lock out if it has no knowledge of the timing of an expected union strike. Such action is regarded as defensive by the Board, and as such would have nothing to do with an attempt to destroy a union.

Defense of Multibargaining Unit

The *Buffalo Linen* case was decided by the Supreme Court in 1956; the case involved a union, the Truck Drivers Local Union No. 449, and eight companies with which it bargained.[39] There was a history of multiemployer bargaining among the parties. The union struck one company and the remaining seven reacted by locking out their employees. The nonstruck companies reacted to prevent whipsawing. Whipsawing refers to successive strikes against one after another of the various members of an employers' association.

Whipsaw action can be highly beneficial to labor organizations in that they may strike one company while all the others continue operations. A single company cannot normally hold out for a long period of time if its competitors continue to supply the market for a particular product. Unions often strike the wealthiest companies first under these circumstances, and then pick off the others at their discretion until all agree to approximately the same contractual terms.

The Board ruled in *Buffalo Linen* that the employers had the right to preserve the traditional multiemployer collective bargaining relationship, which was being threatened by the whipsawing action. A circuit court reviewing the case overruled the NLRB on the basis that it had expanded its "hardship doctrine," which permitted lockouts only if unusual economic costs were likely to be incurred. The U.S. Supreme Court reversed the lower court and upheld Board action on the theory that the pattern of multiemployer bargaining had been established for all purposes. Actually, the doctrine established means that the lockout may be used to preserve a multiemployer bargaining arrangement, but only in cases where there is a history of it. The Board has had several occasions to implement the rule.

In a 1964 *A & P* case, a recently formed employer association used the lockout to attempt to force a change in the pattern of bargaining. Traditionally, bargaining took place on a single-employer basis. During negotiations, the association insisted upon a bargaining change from single units to a multiemployer unit. The union met with the group to discuss the issue and an impasse was reached in negotiations without agreement upon a change to a new procedure. The union struck one of the members whose contract had expired. The other employers locked out their employees as an offensive tactic to secure their objective. The Board held that the employer action was outside *Buffalo Linen* limits, since the lockout in such cases could be undertaken merely to preserve a multiemployer unit from attempted union destruction. This made the lockout an offensive weapon in the Board's view, and as such not permissible because of the effect it might have on unionism.

In another case, however, *Evening News Association*, the NLRB held that employer lockout action was protected within the *Buffalo Linen* principle, since the result was to preserve the existing bargaining arrangement.[40]

Supreme Court Expansion of Employer Right
to Lock Out and Continue Operations

The NLRB was persistent until 1965 in requiring a rigid interpretation regarding what constituted defensive employer lockout behavior. In a 1962 case, *Brown Food Store,* the Board held that in locking out their employees, nonstruck employers were exceeding the lawful defensive limits established in *Buffalo Linen* by continuing operations with temporary replacements.[41]

The Tenth Circuit Court of Appeals subsequently refused to enforce the Board's order and the Supreme Court agreed to hear the case. The high court rejected the Board's reasoning and held that it was not an unfair labor practice for the nonstruck members of a multiemployer unit to continue to operate by using temporary replacements.[42] The companies were permitted to do so as a response to a whipsaw strike against one of the association members. The Court reasoned that

> the continued operations . . . and their use of temporary replacements [no] more imply hostile motivation, nor [is it] inherently more destructive of employee rights, than is the lockout itself. Rather, the compelling inference is that this was all part and parcel [of the employers'] defensive measure to preserve the multi-employer groups in the face of the whipsaw strike.[43]

Thus multiemployer bargaining units have been extended considerable economic power to deal with labor organizations engaged in whipsaw action. They may lock out workers and replace them temporarily to preserve their bargaining-unit structure.

The Supreme Court was not entirely free to rule differently. It had already ruled in *Mackay Radio* that a struck employer could use replacements to keep a firm open.[44] Since the struck employer has such a right, then the other employers must also be entitled to do so, or they would be placed at a competitive disadvantage relative to the struck firms. Thus a union may engage in whipsaw action, but if it does, multiemployer unit firms do not have to suffer the economic consequences that would flow from a policy of permitting only a struck firm to continue its operations by replacing employees.

It should be noted, however, that the struck firm may permanently replace economic strikers, whereas the nonstruck firms may replace them only temporarily. Practically, this distinction means very little, since one of the conditions of restoring the bargaining unit to normalcy would be reinstatement of all replaced workers.

Lockout as an Offensive Weapon

The Supreme Court's *American Ship Building* case provided employers with the right to lock out as a counterweapon to a strike.[45] However, such action was permissible only after a deadlock has been reached on mandatory bargaining items. Lockouts were not legal economic weapons if intended to discourage union membership.

When the lockout was used to support the legitimate bargaining demands of single employers, temporary or permanent replacements seemingly could not be employed. Temporary replacements were permitted only to protect the integrity of multiemployer bargaining units where whipsaw action against the non-struck firms may result.[46]

The lockout is viewed in a different fashion under single-employer bargaining arrangements than it is in multiemployer units. When a single employer acts in its own self-interest, the lockout is distinguished from union strike action in that it merely deprives the labor organization of the exclusive power to determine when a work stoppage will occur and how long it will last. Determination of the timing and duration of work stoppages were not rights extended to unions under the national labor law.

The real question that must be answered involves to what extent the Court has balanced the strategic economic weapons that may be used by unions and employers in gaining desirable bargaining results. One construction of *American Ship Building* is that employers bargaining individually are only permitted to influence the timing and duration of work stoppages by use of lockouts. However, the issue arose as to whether a single employer who has locked out employees may use temporary replacements to operate while the lockout is in progress.

In *Inland Trucking,* an employer locked out employees after contract negotiations reached an impasse.[47] Temporary replacements were hired and the firm continued to operate. The Board and a federal appeals court held the employer in violation of Taft-Hartley. The court ruled that the lockout differed from *American Ship Building* and *Brown* because the use of temporary substitutes during a bargaining lockout was inherently destructive of employee statutory rights. In addition, an appeals court was of the opinion that the employer's motives or reasons for using substitutes were unimportant. The desire to avoid a strike that might be called during the busiest season was insufficient by itself to justify use of temporary replacements. An employer's actions cannot be inherently destructive of important employee rights. For example, a union has a statutorily protected right to take initiative with respect to strikes because the right to strike and to refrain from striking are equally guaranteed under Section 7 of Taft-Hartley. Thus, the employer could not use the lockout for the purpose of forcing agreement to a contract proposed by the employer, nor for the purpose of avoiding a strike that could be called during its busiest season.[48] In *U.S. Pipe,* the company unilaterally reduced benefits, and several weeks later, locked out its workers when they refused to agree to the company's changes. This action was considered illegal.

In 1972, despite the federal court's decision in *Inland Trucking,* the Board position on use of temporary replacements during lockouts started to change. It held by a split vote in *Ottawa Silica* that for a single firm to continue operation with temporary replacements was lawful as a means of getting locked-out workers to act on the company's bargaining proposals.[49] The same circumstances occurred in a subsequent Board decision during the same year.[50] In 1974, a federal circuit court of appeals upheld the right of an employer to use temporary replacements after a company had locked out employees as an offensive weapon. Unlike its sister federal court, it held that such conduct of the employer did not destroy the protected rights of either the employees or the union. It rejected the union's argument that, even in the absence of an antiunion motive, the use of replacements during a lockout was unlawful.[51] However, in 1976, the Board ruled that a lockout becomes illegal when the employer uses *permanent* replacements.[52]

The Board majority apparently interprets the Supreme Court's *Brown Food Store* decision as requiring an examination on a case-by-case basis, and the defensive nature of the lockout is one very relevant factor that permits use of temporary replacements. It appears that the NLRB has now started to expand employer use of temporary replacements after a bargaining impasse has been reached to include single-firm bargaining arrangements. As a consequence, legitimate employer objectives may be interpreted to outweigh employee rights under the Act, which in turn means that temporary replacements may be hired legally.[53] From this tendency a wave of complications should be expected to develop, with the Supreme Court ultimately having to review the permissiveness of temporary replacement use in light of its *American Ship Building* decision. It was in that case that the high court left the issue open when it stated that "we intimate no view whatever as to the consequences which would follow had the employer replaced its employees with permanent or even temporary help."

At this writing, the high court has not determined the issue. Should it do so, the fundamental problem is whether or not an employer should have the right not only to affect the time of the work stoppage and its duration by a lockout, but also to use temporary replacements to force the union to accept its terms and conditions of employment. The problem is not resolved merely by saying that if the union struck, the employer could lawfully replace the strikers. What is critical is a determination of whether or not the current Board policy destroys the protected rights of employees under national labor policy.

EMPLOYEE CONDUCT ON THE PICKET LINE

The Taft-Hartley Act also regulates the conduct of workers participating in the picketing process. During strikes, employees normally engage in picket-line activities. Hence the law on picketing cannot be divorced from that regulating strike action. One would look in vain for specific provisions of the law that deal with strike-related picketing. Nevertheless, the NLRB has inferred from particular sections of the law that certain picketing patterns are unlawful. What are these sections?

Section 7 of Taft-Hartley provides that

employees shall have the right to self-organization, to form, join or assist labor organizations, to bargain collectively through representatives of their own choosing, and to engage in mutual other concerted activities for the purpose of collective bargaining or other mutual aid or protection, *and shall have the right to refrain from any or all of such activities.* [54]

The italicized phrase did not appear in the Wagner Act. Although the Wagner Act guaranteed to workers the right to engage in collective bargaining activities, such as striking and picketing, free from employer interference, it did not protect workers in the right to refrain from such activities. The assumption of Taft-Hartley is that certain workers do not desire to bargain collectively, to strike, or to picket. Hence the law shields these workers from union tactics calculated to force them to participate in concerted employee activities.

Section 7 must be read in conjunction with another provision of Taft-Hartley to gain an understanding of the impact of the statute on picketing.[55] This additional section provides that it shall be unlawful for labor unions or their agents "to restrain or coerce employees in the exercise of the rights guaranteed in section 7." Thus, labor unions violate the law if they coerce or restrain employees in their right to refrain from union activities. However, the Act also provides that "the paragraph shall not impair the right of a labor organization to prescribe its own rules with respect to the acquisition or retention of membership therein."[56]

The NLRB has held that certain picketing conduct of labor unions operates to deny workers their right not to engage in union activities. What is the general character of such unlawful picketing? Picketing is illegal under Taft-Hartley when the effect of the picketing denies to employees the opportunity to work during a strike. In short, employees have the protected right to work in face of a strike. The Board declared in October 1948 that "employees have a guaranteed right to refrain from striking. That right includes the right to go to and from work without restraint or coercion while a strike is in progress."[57] The legislative history of Taft-Hartley fully supports this position of the NLRB. In this connection, Senator Taft declared that Taft-Hartley outlaws "such restraint and coercion as would prevent people from going to work if they wished to go to work."[58] Thus, picketing that prevents employees from working during a strike coerces and restrains workers in the exercise of their right not to engage in collective action.

Substance of Restraint and Coercion.   To establish the full effect of the statute on picketing, the NLRB is required to spell out the meaning of the terms *restraint* and *coercion.* What are the circumstances in which a picket line restrains and coerces employees within the meaning of the law? Specifically, what patterns of picketing conduct prevent employees from working during a strike? Actually, this is a much more difficult problem to resolve than the mere establishment of the general character of unlawful picketing. This is necessarily the case because restraint and coercion mean different things to different people.

After the enactment of Taft-Hartley, the Board declared that picketing that forcibly blocks ingress and egress to a struck plant violates the Taft-Hartley Act. For example, during one strike, a union organized a picket line of between two hundred and three hundred members. The workers massed in front of the driveway leading to the struck plant's parking lot. When cars carrying nonstriking employees reached the driveway, they were blocked by the crowd. Three cars successfully drove into the parking lot, but only through the assistance of local police officers. Two other automobiles started to drive through the picket line but, when instructed by the plant superintendent not to attempt to go through, they drove away. Such picketing, the NLRB held, was unlawful.[59]

A case involving the United Furniture Workers of America is particularly helpful in determining the unlawful area of picketing. In this case, the Board held unlawful a number of picketing tactics that operated to deny employees the right to work, free from restraint and coercion, during a strike. Such conduct included (1) the carrying of sticks by the pickets on the picket line; (2) the piling of bricks for use by the pickets; (3) the blocking of plant entrances by railroad ties, automobiles, raised gutter plates, and tacks; (4) the threat of violence toward nonstriking employees; (5) the warning given one nonstriking employee that "when we get in with the union, you old fellows won't have a job"; (6) the placing of pickets in such a manner as to prevent nonstrikers from carrying out their assigned work of loading cabinets into railroad boxcars on a railroad siding located about a quarter of a mile from the plant; (7) the "goon squad" mass assaults upon various nonstrikers; (8) the overturning of automobiles; and (9) the barring from the plant of a superintendent and a foreman by force and intimidation in full view of nonstriking employees.

Every one of the above acts of violence was held unlawful by the National Labor Relations Board.[60] This policy has been reaffirmed in subsequent cases.[61] However, a new philosophy toward picketing conduct has developed. Picket violence directed against employer property likewise constitutes unlawful coercion of employees. Thus, during one work stoppage, striking employees engaged in picketing broke more than 443 windows. This was accomplished by hurling stones, rocks, railroad tieplates, railroad spikes, clubs, and other objects through the windows. The union claimed its activities were not directed at employees but against the employer. Hence, it contended that this action did not coerce or restrain employees in their right not to engage in union activities. This contention was flatly rejected by the Board. It held that the "atmosphere of terror" created by the union in the destruction of the property constituted a threat to employees. The Board observed that nonstrikers would have to risk physical violence if they attempted to enter the struck plant.[62]

Name-Calling Lawful.   About a year after Taft-Hartley was enacted, the NLRB was called upon to decide whether or not pickets may lawfully abuse strikebreakers by calling them profane names. Pickets frequently call strikebreakers a variety of foul names as they come through the picket line. It was almost inevitable that the Board would be called upon to decide this problem. Its decision was handed down in a case that involved a number of pickets and strikebreakers. The facts indicate that six employees who had chosen to abandon the strike and return to work were met at the plant gate by a large group of pickets. The Board reports that "[the strikebreakers] were vilified and verbally abused as scabs—deserters from the strikers' ranks." Some of the pickets called the strikebreakers a variety of obscene epithets besides "scab" and "deserter."

The Board refused to find a violation of the Taft-Hartley Act, declaring that the abuse of the strikebreakers amounted only to name-calling.[63] Thus, vocal resentment by pickets directed against strikebreakers is considered a form of peaceful picketing. Such picketing tactics, according to the Board, do not constitute coercion and restraint of employees within the meaning of the 1947 labor law. To support its position, the Board pointed to the section of Taft-Hartley that provides that

> the expressing of any views, arguments, or opinions, or the dissemination thereof, whether in written, printed, graphic, or visual form, shall not constitute or be evidence of an unfair labor practice under the provisions of this Act, if such expression contains no threat of reprisal or force or promise of benefit.

Actually, this section, popularly termed the "free speech" clause, was inserted into the law to provide employers with greater opportunity to deliver speeches to employees.[64] It is noteworthy that the Board utilized this section to legalize name-calling on the picket line.

In June 1974, the opportunity to degrade nonmembers of a union was increased. At that time, in *Letter Carriers* v. *Austin,* the U.S. Supreme Court held that publication in a union's newsletter of nonmembers' names in a "list of scabs" that also carried a highly pejorative definition of the term "scab" was protected under federal labor laws. Noting that such laws encourage "uninhibited, robust, and wide-open discussion," the Court reversed the decision of the Supreme Court of Virginia, which had previously held that the publication was libelous under state law. State courts had found that under state law, the use of "scab" was libelous and had awarded listed nonmembers $165,000 in damages.[65]

Name-calling constitutes protected conduct. But the Reagan Board changed a previous policy when it ruled that employees who make threats of physical violence to nonstrikers may lawfully be discharged.[66] Previously the Board had held:

> Absent violence . . . a picket is not disqualified from reinstatement despite . . . making abusive threats against nonstrikers.[67]

Later, in *Clear Pine Mouldings, Inc.,* employees directed threats of physical violence against nonstrikers, including threats to break their hands, saying they were taking their lives in their hands by crossing the picket line, and saying: "I am going to kill you . . ." Reversing the previous policy, the Reagan Board rejected "the *per se* rule that words alone can never warrant a denial of reinstatement in the absence of physical acts." In a 1985 case, the NLRB also upheld an employer's decision to discharge two employees who threatened an employee with bodily harm if he continued to work during a strike.[68]

Nonviolent Mass Picketing Unlawful.   Picketing by large numbers of workers is commonly termed *mass picketing*. This form of union activity poses no great legal problem when the picket line engages in acts of violence. As noted, the Board ruled that forcible blocking of the entrance to plants constitutes unlawful picketing. This would be true regardless of the number of workers who are picketing.

The perplexing legal problem, however, involves picketing in a peaceful manner by large numbers of workers. Strikebreakers must be allowed entry into the struck plant without violence or threats of violence to their persons or property. What then is the legal status of mass picketing carried out in a peaceful manner?

In 1949, the Board dealt with this extremely difficult problem. The case involved a picket line of some one thousand to two thousand persons. The pickets marched back and forth in front of a plant involved in a strike. Apparently, they did not engage in overt acts of violence. However, the Board held that such picketing was unlawful, declaring that "realistically viewed, restraint and coercion were the effect of the mass picketing."[69] It further observed that the "necessary effect of the manner in which the demonstration was conducted was to deny nonstriking employees access to the plant."

The effect of the Board's position was to outlaw nonviolent mass picketing. The Board has not, however, dogmatically stated how many workers can compose lawful picket lines. It avoids this problem by declaring that one definition of mass picketing cannot possibly fit all cases. Hence, the substance of mass picketing must be determined by particular Board decisions. Each case will be decided on its own merits. For example, the Board did not find a violation in one case even though a picket line of about two hundred persons assembled near a plant during a strike. What is more, the pickets verbally denounced strikebreakers as they entered the plant. The Board pointed out that "there was no difficulty entering or leaving the plant."[70]

Despite its reluctance to set forth the exact number who may properly picket, the Board has regarded the number of workers on a picket line as relevant in determining the potential or calculated restraining effect of massed pickets in barring nonstrikers from entering or leaving the plant. It has held that some picket parades by mere force of numbers have the effect of coercing employees who want to enter a plant and work. The exact point at which peaceful picketing becomes "massed" and unlawful because of the number of pickets turns on the particular circumstances of each case.

Penalties for Unlawful Picketing.   Both unions and employees are subject to penalties for unlawful picketing. Unions that sponsor unlawful picketing face injunction proceedings. Employees who engage in unlawful picketing lose reinstatement rights. Employers have no legal obligation to reinstate a striker found to have engaged in picketing held unlawful under Taft-Hartley. For example, the NLRB has held that workers engaging in violent picketing can expect no relief from the NLRB when discharged. A Puerto Rican firm discharged eighteen strikers who engaged in various acts of violence, threats of force against nonstrikers, and destruction of plant property. The NLRB refused to order the reinstatement of these workers.[71] Actually, the NLRB established this principle under the Wagner Act and has consistently utilized it. In this case, it refused to order the reinstatement of workers who committed extreme acts of violence while on strike, workers found guilty of offenses such as assault and battery, dynamiting, and murder. Under Taft-Hartley, a worker engaging in any act of unlawful picketing loses reinstatement rights. The penalty is not reserved for extreme acts of violence. Thus, the principle of denial of reinstatement has much wider application under Taft-Hartley than was true under the Wagner Act.

The "Clean Hands" Problem

For many years, the NLRB held that unlawful picketing is not excusable because the employer has engaged in unfair labor practices. Even if company unfair labor practices provoked a strike, the Board has held that unions and employees still violate the 1947 labor law when they prevent strikebreakers from entering a plant during a strike. In 1949, the Board rejected the "clean hands" doctrine in the enforcement of the statute. In this connection, it declared:

> With respect to the "clean hands" defense, we find that the company's alleged unfair labor practices if established, do not lessen the need for vindicating and protecting employees rights under the Act, which the [union had] infringed.[72]

Some courts, however, did not approve the Board's position that employees should always lose reinstatement rights when they engage in unlawful picketing in the face of employer unfair labor practices. For example, during a long and bitter strike between the UAW and the Kohler Corporation, the employer engaged in serious unfair labor practices. Many strikers committed unlawful acts during the work stoppage. Adhering to its policy, the NLRB refused to direct reinstatement of those employees. However, the federal appeals court in the District of Columbia remanded the case to the Board to weigh the character of the employer's unfair labor practices against the misconduct of employees and determine on that basis whether employees were entitled to reinstatement.[73] Nonetheless, the Board clung to its traditional policy on this issue. Indeed, in *Clear Pine Mouldings,* as discussed earlier, the agency denied reinstatement to employees even though the employer had apparently committed serious unfair labor practices. In that case, the Board rejected the test that

> balanced the severity of the employer's unfair labor practices that provoked the strike against the gravity of the strikers' misconduct.

Strangely enough, to this day, the U.S. Supreme Court has not expressly adopted a rule establishing the extent to which employer unfair labor practices affect the reinstatement rights of employees who engage in unlawful strike activities. Given the importance of this issue, it would seem that the high court should address it.

FINES AGAINST UNION MEMBERS WORKING DURING A STRIKE

The NLRB held in 1964 that a union has the authority to impose fines against members who cross picket lines while they are on strike.[74] This Board position was rejected by the Seventh Circuit Court of Appeals, however, and was accepted for review by the U.S. Supreme Court. The high court sustained the Board's position in a close 5–4 decision in *Allis-Chalmers*.[75] In doing so, it stated that the "economic strike against the employer is the ultimate weapon in labor's arsenal for achieving agreement upon its terms and the power to fine or expel strike-breakers is essential if the union is to be an effective bargaining agent." The Court argued further, "that Congress did not propose any limitations with respect to the internal affairs of unions, aside from barring enforcement of a union's internal regulations to affect a member's employment status." Thus, rules are legal that impose fines on members for crossing picket lines, because unions have the right to preserve their integrity during a time of crisis. Section 7 does not insulate an employee from all consequences flowing from his or her choice of actions. The employee may legally cross a picket line to work during a strike, but he or she may have to pay a fine for doing so if it is administered without discrimination by a labor organization. The ability to deal with a worker as a union member is therefore established by law. Unions, on the other hand, are not to interfere with a worker's status as an employee. The difference between the two is often difficult to determine. Court suits may be initiated by unions to collect fines assessed against members. This authority is found in Section 8 (b) (1) which states that "this paragraph shall not impair the right of a labor organization to prescribe its own rules with respect to the acquisition or retention of membership therein." This language prompted five Supreme Court justices to hold that a fine for crossing a picket line was a legitimate union action. However, the other four were of the opinion that such union action forced employees to engage in union activities against their will.

Though the high court held that a union may fine union members who work during a strike and sue such members for the collection of the fines in state courts, it stated that the amount of the fines must be "reasonable." The question arose as to whether or not the NLRB has jurisdiction to determine the reasonableness of a fine. Thus, if the Board has authority over such a problem, it could hold that a union would commit an unfair labor practice if the fine was deemed unreasonable. However, in 1973, the Supreme Court held that the NLRB is without authority to determine the reasonableness of such fines.[76] What this decision means is that state courts have jurisdiction to establish whether a fine levied against a union member for strikebreaking is reasonable. If a union member feels that the fine levied is too high, he or she must seek relief from the state courts and not from the Board.

In June 1974, the *Allis-Chalmers* doctrine was applied to supervisors who were members of a union. At that time, the U.S. Supreme Court in *Florida Power and Light* v. *Electrical Workers* held that a union may properly fine supervisor-members who cross picket lines during a strike and perform bargaining-unit work.[77] However, such fines would not be lawful when supervisor-members represented their employer in collective bargaining or in the grievance procedure. To justify its decision, the Court reasoned that supervisor-members do not carry out their supervisory duties when during a strike they take over the jobs normally performed by striking employees.

However, the Board has had particular difficulty in applying the Supreme Court decision. In a dozen or so cases that followed the decision, the Board reached its decision by split votes.[78] A majority held that supervisor-members could not be fined if they performed only the following types of work: managerial work; a minimal amount of bargaining-unit work in connection with their managerial duties; or a large amount of bargaining-unit work if the supervisor-members had performed that amount of work prior to the strike. As long as the amount of such work did not increase during the strike, a fine could not be imposed. In practically every case, Fanning dissented on the grounds that the Board majority had not properly applied the *Florida Power & Light* doctrine. In his view, a supervisor-member could lawfully be fined regardless of the amount of bargaining-unit work he or she performed, or whether the amount increased during the strike. The situation became so confused that the U.S. Supreme Court agreed to review the problem.[79]

In *American Broadcasting Companies* v. *Writers Guild of America,* (437US411) decided in June 1978, the high court held that a union may not fine supervisor-members who cross a picket line and perform regular supervisory duties, including the adjustment of grievances. To permit fines when the supervisors' duties involve the handling of grievances, the court reasoned, meant that a supervisor "might be tempted to give the union side of a grievance a more favorable slant while the threat of discipline remained, or while his own appeal of a union sanction was pending." Thus, the U.S. Supreme Court said that under such circumstances, union-imposed fines unlawfully coerced employers in the selection of their grievance-adjustment representatives. On the other hand, it would appear that the decision authorizes fines should supervisor-members perform struck work. The high court stated that a union has "ample leeway" to discipline members, including supervisors, for performing tasks at issue under a union contract. In its decision, the court expressly noted that the supervisors did not perform any struck work. Fines, however, may not be levied against a supervisor-member when the bargaining unit work in question was traditionally performed by the employer's supervisory personnel.[80]

Severe criticism has been leveled at the *Allis-Chalmers* decision.[81] Since four Supreme Court justices believed that the majority was wrong, the criticisms obviously have a degree of validity. It was argued that union rules designed to prevent employees from crossing picket lines have an effect on their job status. To avoid a fine, employees may avoid work, and hence, lose wages. If employees do work, the union may fine them in the amount of the wages that they earned. Fines in this amount would probably be deemed reasonable by state courts. Under these circumstances, the union members would in effect work at their jobs without pay. On the other hand, the enforcement of a union rule against strike-breaking preserves the integrity of the union and the wishes of the majority during a strike.

In any event, the sharp criticisms against *Allis-Chalmers* probably prompted the Supreme Court in a subsequent case to undermine the policy. The question was whether a union may fine a union member who resigns from the union before he or she crosses the picket line. In determining this important issue, the high court held by an 8–1 majority in *Granite State Joint Board* that a fine under these circumstances violates Taft-Hartley.[82] Thus, a union member who desires to engage in strikebreaking may simply resign from the union before crossing the picket line, and the union may not levy fines for this activity. Justice Blackmun, the sole dissenter, stated in his opposition to the majority:

> I cannot join the Court's opinion, which seems to me to exalt the formality of resignation over the substance of the various interests and national labor policies that are at stake here. Union activity, by its very nature, is group activity, and is grounded on the notion that strength can be garnered from unity, solidarity, and mutual commitment. This concept is of particular force during a strike, where the individual members of the union draw strength from the commitments of fellow members, and where the activities carried on by the union rest fundamentally on the mutual reliance that inheres in the "pact."

One question, however, was not determined by the majority in *Granite State Joint Board.* The constitution of the union involved in that case did not expressly forbid resignations of members during a strike. It was silent on this issue. In its decision, the Court majority made special note of this omission. It stated: "We do not now decide to what extent the contractual relationship between union and member may curtail the freedom to resign." For a time it appeared that a union could lawfully place a reasonable restriction upon a member's right to resign. In *Dalmo Victor,*[83] the NLRB said a reasonable restriction would be a rule stating that a union member must wait 30 days after tendering a resignation notice before actually resigning. This limitation would apply regardless of whether there were a strike in progress. Members who violated this rule would be subject to fines.

Predictably, however, the Reagan NLRB upset this policy, holding that any restriction on a union member's right to resign unlawfully interfered with the right to refrain from union activities.[84] In the case *Neufeld Porsche-Audi,* the union's constitution held that resignation from the union would not relieve a member from the obligation to refrain from working during a legal strike or lockout. After a member tendered a letter of resignation and returned to work for the struck employer, the union imposed a fine of $2,250. Imposition of the fine after the employee had left the union and returned to work during the strike was an unfair labor practice.

By providing union members with the unfettered right to resign, despite restrictions contained in a union's constitution or bylaws, the NLRB had obviously ignored the portion of the law that states that the Section 7 rights of employees to refrain from union activities do not impair the right of a labor organization to adopt its internal rules. In addition, the Reagan Board did not recognize that the absolute right of members to resign interferes with the protected right of other employees to engage in a lawful strike. Obviously *Neufeld Porsche-Audi* will make it more difficult for unions to implement successful strikes, thereby interfering with the Section 7 right of employees to engage in "concerted activities for the purpose of collective bargaining or other mutual aid or protection." The current policy does not attempt to balance the right of employees to refrain from union activities with the corresponding right of employees to engage in concerted activities.

In any event, in *Pattern Makers' League,* the U.S. Supreme Court in 1985 by a 5–4 vote sustained the Board's policy permitting union members to resign at any time and under any circumstances, free from union fines.[85] The Court said it deferred to the Board's expert judgment, suggesting that if the NLRB had upheld reasonable restrictions against a union member's right to resign during a strike, it would also have sustained such a policy. Thus, whatever protection unions received in *Allis-Chalmers* has been eliminated by the high court's pronouncements in *Granite State Joint Board* and *Pattern Makers' League.*

CONCEPT OF "CONCERTED ACTIVITY": MEYERS INDUSTRIES

Aside from applying Taft-Hartley to strikes engaged in by employees, the NLRB addressed the problem involving a *single employee*'s refusal to work. The key to this problem involves Section 7 of the law, which states in part:

> Employees shall have the right . . . to engage in other concerted activities for the purpose of . . . mutual aid or protection.

For many years, the NLRB protected employees from discharge when a single employee refused to work for a purpose of group concern. For purposes of the law, a concerted activity existed, since other employees would presumably have supported the individual employee's refusal to work. For example, in *Alleluia Cushion Co.,*[86] an employee complained to the employer about safety matters. Not satisfied with the employer's response, the employee reported the employer to the California Occupational Safety and Health Administration (OSHA).

The employee had not expressly sought the support of other employees in the matter of safety. He did not request their help or advice in the drafting of the letter to OSHA. He acted by himself, not as part of any group. Despite the individual nature of his action, the NLRB held the discharge to be illegal on the premise that "safe working conditions are matters of great and continuing concern for all within the work place." That is, the employee *had* engaged in concerted activities within the meaning of Section 7 because other employees, also concerned with safety matters, would have supported his activities had they been requested to do so.

In *Meyers Industries,* [87] the Reagan Board reversed this concept of concerted activity. To be protected from discharge, an employee must expressly act in concert with other employees to protest employer conduct. The facts of the *Meyers* case demonstrate that the employer's mechanic failed to correct defects on a tractor-trailer truck assigned to the employee. When on the highway, the trailer's brakes malfunctioned. The driver stopped at an Ohio roadside inspection station where the vehicle was cited for several defects, including the brakes. The employee sent the citation to the company.

Subsequently, while in Tennessee, the employee, driving the same vehicle, had an accident caused by the defective brakes on the trailer. The employee then contacted the Tennessee Public Service Commission. Upon inspection of the vehicle, an official of the agency cited the vehicle, directing the employee not to move it until repairs had been made. Faced with this situation, the employer decided to sell the trailer for scrap.

When the employee returned to company headquarters, he was discharged, the employer telling him, "We can't have you calling the cops like this all the time."

Reversing *Alleluia Cushion,* the Reagan NLRB upheld the employee's discharge, ruling that he had not engaged in concerted activity within the meaning of Section 7 of Taft-Hartley because he had acted by himself and not with other employees when he had reported the defective vehicle to the state authorities. Although expressing "outrage" at the employer's conduct, the Board said that to be engaged in concerted activities for purposes of the law, and so to be protected from discharge, the employee must be "engaged in with or on the authority of other employees, and not solely by and behalf of the employee himself."

Subsequently, the Reagan NLRB applied its construction of concerted activities to other situations, sustaining the discharge of the employee in each instance. For example, in one case a truck driver refused to drive more hours than permitted by federal regulations. Upholding his discharge, the NLRB said that the employee had acted by himself and not with other employees, nor did he have their authorization when he had refused to drive the excess hours. [88]

At this writing, however, it is possible that the Reagan Board's construction of concerted activities may not be upheld by the federal courts. In 1985, a federal appeals court remanded *Meyers Industries* to the NLRB with instructions that its literal and narrow construction of concerted activities was not mandated by Taft-Hartley.[89] It said that the NLRB had erred when it decided that its new definition of "concerted activities" was mandated by the National Labor Relations Act. It suggested that the NLRB may lawfully apply the concept of concerted activities in a more broad and realistic manner so as to afford employees statutory protection.

In support of its decision, the federal appeals court made reference to the U.S. Supreme Court's decision in *City Disposal Systems.*[90] In that case, by a 5–4 vote, the high court held that an individual employee's refusal to drive what he believed to be an unsafe truck constituted concerted activity within the meaning of Section 7 of Taft-Hartley. However, a significant difference exists between *Meyers Industries* and *City Disposal Systems.* Unlike the former case, the latter involved a collective bargaining contract that provided employees with the right to refuse to drive unsafe vehicles. No union or collective bargaining contract had been involved in *Meyers Industries.* In *City Disposal Systems,* though the employee did not make specific reference to the labor agreement when he refused to drive, nor discuss his conduct with other employees, nor have their express support and authorization, the high court held that the employee had nonetheless engaged in concerted activity in the sense that he was attempting to enforce the labor agreement. It pointed out that as long as the nature of an employee's complaint is reasonably clear and refers to a reasonably perceived violation of a contract, the employee is engaged in the enforcement of the contract, and so in concerted activity under the statute. Other drivers are also concerned with the proper enforcement of the labor agreement.

In any event, given their differences, it is uncertain whether *City Disposal Systems* would apply to the circumstances of *Meyers Industries,* since a labor agreement was not involved in the latter case. It is very possible that the U.S. Supreme Court may use that distinction to sustain the Reagan Board's current construction of concerted activities.

RECOGNITIONAL AND ORGANIZATIONAL PICKETING

Recognitional picketing is undertaken to obtain bargaining recognition from employers, whereas *organizational picketing* is for the purpose of inducing workers to join the labor union. The history of organized labor makes it apparent that unions have long picketed nonunion employers as a means of organizing and obtaining bargaining recognition. Furthermore, although the primary aim has been to gain recognition and bargaining rights, unions have argued that they have been just as interested in maintaining union-established working standards. The economic interests of unions generally have required that they spread union organization throughout an entire industry to stabilize and protect working conditions in that industry. Failure to do so has usually resulted in a deterioration of unionization.

The recognitional and organizational efforts of unions were protected activities under the Norris–La Guardia Act provisions as well as under the free-speech doctrines of the United States Supreme Court. The Wagner Act as well as the 1947 Taft-Hartley amendments did not alter this right even when picketing was undertaken by a minority union. Minority unions could picket even though another labor organization had been certified by the NLRB as the choice of a majority of employees.[91]

The NLRB attempted to deal with picketing of this nature under Taft-Hartley Section 8(b)(4)(C). Under this provision, a union engages in an unfair labor practice if it forces an employer to recognize or bargain with a labor organization as the representative of its employees if another labor organization has been certified as the representative of its employees.[92]

The Board used this provision of Taft-Hartley in 1956 to outlaw strikes and picketing, even when there was no independent evidence available to show that the union had picketed for recognitional or organizational purposes. In *Lewis Food,* the Board found a violation when a union struck to force an employer to reinstate employees who had previously been discharged.[93] On the surface at least, the labor organization did not strike to force the employer to recognize it and bargain with it for all the employees in the bargaining unit. However, the Board ruled that recognition was in fact the purpose of union action. It rejected the argument that the union had merely acted to require reinstatement of discharged workers, since "the union's strike for such a purpose necessarily . . . is a strike to force or require the employer to recognize or bargain . . . as to this matter."

The NLRB attempted to utilize the broad language of Taft-Hartley to outlaw recognitional picketing.[94] Until it decided the *Curtis* case, peaceful picketing had not been considered coercive within the meaning of the union unfair labor practice provisions.[95] In *Curtis,* a union lost an election conducted by the NLRB and immediately established picketing around the employer's premises. The Board ruled that recognitional and organizational picketing would tend to coerce workers to join a union in violation of their Section 7 right not to join. The U.S. Supreme Court reviewed the case and held that the NLRB did not have the authority to curb minority-union picketing undertaken to achieve recognition or organization.[96] If the situation had been left unchanged, the Board would have been incapable of restricting this type of union activity.

Landrum-Griffin Changes

By 1959, the country was in the mood to change some of the picketing procedures used by unions. Attempts were made in the Landrum-Griffin Act to eliminate the weaknesses that had become apparent in the 1947 labor law.[97] Section 8 (b) (7) was created by Congress. This section makes it an unfair labor practice for a union to picket any employer for the purpose of either forcing or requiring an employer to recognize or bargain with a labor organization as the representative of his employees, or forcing or requiring an employee to accept or select such labor organization as their collective bargaining representative.

The restriction was designed to operate in three situations. They are: (1) when the employer has lawfully recognized another union and a representation question may not appropriately be raised; (2) when a valid election has been held by the NLRB within the preceding twelve months; or (3) when picketing has been conducted for a reasonable period of time, "not to exceed thirty days from the commencement of such picketing," without filing an election petition with the Board. These restrictions do not apply to unions that are the certified bargaining agents of employees.

The Act does not define a reasonable period of time; however, its language and legislative history indicate that a period of less than thirty days may be considered unlawful.[98]

In one case, the Board reviewed employee conduct of picketing to decide that twenty-six days was more than a reasonable period for filing an election petition.[99] Pickets were engaged in conduct such as threatening physical violence, using abusive and coercive language, and blocking ingress and egress to the struck premises.

Picketing at common construction sites may include the total picketing time, even if the employer and employees at whom the activity is directed are absent part of the time.[100] The thirty-day period was computed on the basis of the record presented the Board.

The reasonable time period extended unions to petition for elections is generally set at thirty days. Extenuating circumstances may result in a shorter period of time, but as a general rule, a fixed period of time is easier to administer than one that fluctuates.

Expedited Elections

Another important problem stimulated by the 1959 Taft-Hartley amendments involves the so-called "quickie" election. Expedited election procedure has practically no legislative history because of the circumstances under which it was adopted into the law. It came out of the Senate-House Conference Committee proceedings. When an election petition is filed under the terms of the recognitional and organizational picketing provisions, the Board is directed to process it under an expedited procedure. Essentially, this means that a prehearing election is held. The Board merely determines a unit appropriate for collective bargaining and holds the poll.

The NLRB ruled that labor unions should not be permitted to circumvent usual election procedures by maneuvering to obtain a prehearing election. It decided that it would direct a prehearing election under the recognitional and organizational picketing provisions only when a charge is filed alleging violation of the section. The General Counsel of the Board stated that

> any other interpretation would be deemed to have done by indirection what it [Taft-Hartley] refused to do directly—authorize pre-hearing elections generally. And picketing would be encouraged where it has not been used before.[101]

A federal district court in Michigan upheld the NLRB position and implemented it by refusing to direct a quickie election when an employee at the suggestion of his union filed an unfair labor practice charge against his own union. The court held that a charge for purposes of securing an expedited election is not valid when a union in effect files a charge against itself.[102]

Once the Board directs a quickie election, the union involved must be a party to the poll whether or not it wants to participate. Thus, a union petitioned a federal district court to stop an expedited election, arguing that it desired a hearing prior to the poll. The court denied the injunction request.[103]

The impact of expedited elections could be to force unions into premature polls. To the extent that this is so, an employer may be able to halt recognitional and organizational picketing for a period of twelve months. Alternatively, such elections could prove beneficial to labor organizations, since they could decrease the time lag between petitioning for an election and holding the actual vote. Less time is available to lose majority status, if indeed it has ever been attained. Many unions attempt to get 50 to 55 percent of bargaining-unit members to sign authorization cards before proceeding to polls under normal procedures. Expedited elections could permit some unions to prevail in representation proceedings with a minimum of authorization cards signed by employees.

When an election petition is filed under the terms of the provision, the law directs the Board to process the petition under an expedited procedure. The agency does not follow the general procedures that guide it in other elections. It does not require a showing that at least 30 percent of the bargaining unit supports the petitioning union as proof that it represents a substantial number of employees. However, the Board is required to make a rapid determination of bargaining-unit appropriateness for collective bargaining purposes. This is the so-called quickie election procedure required by Section 8 (b) (7).[104]

Landrum-Griffin does not prohibit all picketing beyond thirty days under all circumstances, even when an election petition has not been filed with the Board. A union may picket beyond thirty days for the purpose of truthfully advising the public, including consumers, that an employer does not employ members of, or have a contract with, the labor organization engaged in picketing. However, this picketing is prohibited when it has the effect of interfering with services or the flow of goods to and from the picketed company. The NLRB is required to obtain federal court injunctions when violations occur.

Soon after the passage of Landrum-Griffin, controversy arose in the construction of its terms regulating recognitional and organizational picketing. The problem areas included (1) picketing objectives, (2) informational picketing, and (3) employer unfair labor practices.

Picketing Objectives

Soon after Section 8 (b) (7) became effective, the NLRB applied the provisions to a series of cases. As discussed in a previous chapter, changing NLRB personnel often brings with it a change in important policy areas. Prior to a transition from Eisenhower appointees to Kennedy appointees, the Board dealt with the new Landrum-Griffin provisions.

In the *Calumet Contractors* case, a union contended that it had picketed to protest that an employer was not paying the prevailing wage rates of the area.[105] Another union had been certified by the Board, and refused to accept the picketing union's disclaimer of intent to obtain recognition as bargaining agent. The NLRB was of the opinion that picketing to protest the employer's wage rates was an attempt to force recognition of the minority union. This meant that employees were coerced to accept the union as their bargaining agent. Thus, the Board returned to its *Curtis* doctrine and the one established in the *Lewis Food* case. All picketing by minority unions was considered to be for recognitional and organizational purposes. For what other reason would a union picket when it represents only a minority of the bargaining unit?

Changes in Board personnel in 1961 led to a change in policy in another case involving the Calumet Contractors Association.[106] This time the Board refused to find a violation of Section 8 (b) (4) (C) wherein a union had picketed to advertise the fact that an employer was not paying wage rates equal to those prevailing in the area. It will be recalled that a primary strike for the purpose of requiring recognition of a union other than the one certified is an unfair labor practice under Section 8 (b) (4) (C). Another union held NLRB certification as bargaining agent for bargaining-unit employees. Even so, the newly constituted Board held that picketing for this purpose was not the same as that undertaken to obtain recognition. Picketing, taken by itself, did not prove that the minority union was in pursuit of such an objective. In this regard the Board ruled:

> A union may legitimately be concerned that a particular employer is undermining area standards of employment by maintaining lower standards. It may be willing to forego recognition and bargaining provided subnormal working conditions are eliminated from area considerations. As this objective could be achieved without the employer either bargaining with or recognizing the union, we cannot reasonably conclude that the union's objective in picketing the employer was to obtain recognition or bargaining.

The finding that picketing by a minority union was for an object other than recognition left the Board only a short distance from overturning the previous Board's rule that all picketing by minority unions was for recognitional purposes. In *Fanelli Ford Sales,* the new Board accomplished its objective under Section 8

(b) (7).[107] A minority union was permitted to picket for reinstatement of a discharged employee without at the same time seeking recognition within the meaning of the 1959 provisions. Reinstatement could be accomplished without consultation with the union. In still another case involving picketing to protest an employer's deviation from prevailing union standards, the Board held that "union standards" picketing is distinguished from that undertaken to force recognition.[108] The language on picket signs intended to inform the public of substandard working conditions is sufficient to permit minority unions to picket an employer's premises. Since picketing objectives are distinguishable, such picketing is protected from the restrictions imposed by the 1959 law.

Later on, the NLRB held that picketing to persuade an employer to keep a promise did not constitute recognition picketing.[109] A union had lost a regular representation election. Then the employer held meetings with a committee of employee representatives. When the company later failed to put into effect a pay raise that the employees believed it had promised, a number of employees struck, established a picket line, and were promptly discharged. The employer argued that the employees were properly discharged because they had engaged in recognition picketing within a year after the election was lost. However, the Board held that the picketing was caused by the employer's alleged broken promise, and not to establish any sort of continuing bargaining relationship. In other words, "broken promise" picketing is not the same as recognition picketing. As a result, the Board ruled that the employees on the picket line had engaged in protected activity and directed their reinstatement.

Realistically, it may be argued that any minority union that pickets an employer's premises is seeking bargaining rights. Otherwise it would not make the effort. In any event, if a union is successful in convincing the NLRB that it is not picketing for organizational or recognitional purposes, it may picket indefinitely.

Informational Picketing

A proviso to Section 8 (b) (7) (C) permits unions to picket for informational purposes. The expedited election procedure does not apply to picketing and other publicity undertaken to truthfully advise the public, including consumers, that an employer does not employ members of, or have a contract with, a labor organization. To this provision there is added an exception. Even if a union engages in publicity or informational picketing, it becomes illegal under the law if it has an effect of inducing "any individual employed by any other person in the course of his employment, not to pick up, deliver or transport any goods or not to perform any services."

In its first effort to deal with this section, the NLRB held that picketing is unlawful even when picket signs reflect the statutory language of the 1959 law, if the objective is recognition or organization.[110] Publicity picketing was held illegal because the Board decided that it was undertaken to achieve recognition from the employer or organization of employees. For picketing to fall within the protection of the publicity proviso, it had to be undertaken solely to inform the public that an employer did not employ members of the picketing union or have a contract with it. In the first *Crown* case, the union truthfully advised the public that the employer was nonunion. However, upon examination, the Board found that the union did not represent a majority of the employees and had picketed beyond a reasonable period of time without petitioning for an election. The employees of the picketed employer were neither represented by another union nor had they expressed their choice for representation in an NLRB poll within twelve months prior to the time picketing began. Dual-purpose picketing was considered illegal under the terms of the law. Informational or publicity picketing had to be completely divorced from any organizational or recognitional objective to be legal. Since recognition was viewed as one object of the action, it was held in violation of national labor policy. The decision in effect implied that all publicity picketing was undertaken for recognitional purposes. Also, the decision implied that all picketing undertaken to inform the public that an employer does not employ union members has the purpose of organizing the nonmember workers.

Different Board personnel dealt with the same issue in the *Crown Cafeteria* case in 1962.[111] New NLRB personnel granted the union request to reconsider the decision of the replaced Board majority. This time the Board ruled differently. It held that the law clearly permits informational picketing even though organization, recognition, or bargaining is an implied objective. Thus, even if recognition is an object of the picketing, the Board will not find a violation, provided that the picket-sign legends advise the public that the picketed employer does not employ members of the union engaged in the picketing or have a contract with it. In short, the 1962 *Crown Cafeteria* case declared picketing lawful after the thirty-day time period under two conditions. These were that (1) the picket-sign legends must inform the public only that the employer does not employ members of the picketing union and/or does not have a contract with it; and (2) such picketing must not unlawfully interfere with deliveries and services.

Informational picketing was therefore considered lawful as long as it did not stop pickups and deliveries of goods and services. In 1962, however, the Board held that when interference with deliveries or pickups is not sufficiently extensive to disrupt, interfere with, or curtail the employer's business, then it has no effect on the employer's business.[112] Thus, picketing will not be prohibited merely on the basis of a few isolated instances of drivers refusing to cross a picket line, or where an effect of the picketing resulted in one service stoppage or one temporary service delay.

The Board in the *Barker* case argued that a literal reading of the Act would render illusory the very protection Congress had conferred upon labor's right to disseminate information to the public by engaging in publicity picketing. Such a restriction, it argued, might raise a serious constitutional question and do a disservice to the Congress. Thus, the effect of publicity picketing is construed in "terms of the actual impact on the picketed employer's business." An employer must prove not only that delivery stoppages occurred, but also the extent to which such stoppages disrupted business.

The Ninth Circuit Court upheld the Board's decisions in both the *Barker Bros. Corporation* and *Crown Cafeteria* cases.[113] In *Barker Bros.*, the federal court ruled that a "quantitative test concerning itself solely with the number of deliveries not made and/or services not performed is an inadequate yardstick for determining whether to remove informational picketing from" the protection of the publicity section of the law. The *Crown Cafeteria* case also resulted in court approval of the Board action. The court reasoned that to rule that picketing undertaken to truthfully advise the public is illegal would render the publicity proviso meaningless.

Under current law, there is no presumption that an original recognitional or organizational motive continues as the basic motive of unions after picketing becomes informational. There must be proof that the original motive remains the basic aim.[114] Proof may be available if a picket line is shifted from, for example, the public entrance to a restaurant to the employee entrance. A shift of the picket line provides a signal to employees to leave their job. Thus, the Board will not protect picketing of this nature, which is viewed as an appeal to other union members as opposed to consumers. The mere shift is deemed unlawful, and the fact that employees do not leave their jobs does not control the decision.[115]

A minority union may picket indefinitely under the publicity proviso without filing an election petition. This means that the Board has construed the informational picketing provision so broadly that a union that does not represent a majority of bargaining-unit employees may picket for an indefinite period of time, resulting in the possibility of eventually becoming the majority representative. This could be the case particularly when the union engages in other organizational activities simultaneously with the picket-line activity. It is often argued that such action was not the intent of Congress. Under this view, the NLRB has taken on a legislative function in excess of its delegated authority.[116] On the other hand, the current Board policy can be defended on the grounds that Congress did not intend to prohibit informational picketing when such an activity does not seriously curtail an employer's business. A contrary policy could very well conflict with constitutional guarantees of free speech.

Employer Unfair Labor Practices

Shortly after the recognitional and organizational sections were enacted into law, the question was raised as to whether a union may picket toward this end, without violating the provisions, when employers commit unfair labor practices. Congress did not expressly permit a union to picket for recognitional or organizational purposes beyond thirty days without filing a representation petition, even when an employer engages in unfair labor practices. The Eisenhower Board searched the legislative history of the 1959 law and concluded that Congress had not intended to permit recognitional and organizational picketing beyond thirty days even should employer unfair labor practices occur.[117]

Alternatively, it should be recalled that the U.S. Supreme Court held in *Mastro Plastics* that the Taft-Hartley penalties against a union striking during a contractual period do not apply when it strikes against an employer unfair labor practice.[118] In February 1961, the Board addressed itself to this problem.

In the *Blinne* case, a union sought to represent three common laborers employed by a construction company.[119] All three had signed bargaining authorization cards. The employer allegedly transferred one worker to another building site in an effort to destroy the union's majority status. The labor organization afterward engaged in recognitional picketing for more than thirty days before it filed an election petition. Unfair labor practice charges were filed against the employer about three weeks after the picketing started. The union advanced the argument that the recognitional and organizational regulations should not be enforced when employer unfair labor practices were alleged.

The Board in its first consideration of *Blinne* held that the employer unfair labor practices did not legalize the union's picketing. Despite the merit of such charges, congressional intent was interpreted as being opposed to lifting organizational and recognitional picketing prohibitions under such circumstances.[120]

The *Blinne Construction* case was reconsidered in 1962 after a change in Board personnel.[121] The new rule was only slightly changed from the one set forth in 1961. A union may picket beyond the thirty-day limit without filing an election petition only when an employer is in violation of the refusal-to-bargain provision of Taft-Hartley. Election petitions must be filed within the thirty-day limit when other unfair labor practices are committed. The NLRB set forth the reason for the distinction between unfair labor practices when recognitional and organizational picketing are involved. The reason is based entirely on Board procedure. For unfair labor practice charges other than refusal to bargain, the Board holds a representation petition in abeyance until the allegations have been remedied or dismissed. Under these circumstances, the Board will accept an election petition and will not dismiss one already filed. However, the election will not be conducted until such time as the unfair labor practice charges have been resolved. Refusal-to-bargain charges are handled differently; an election petition will not be accepted or, if already submitted, will be dismissed. This distinction is based upon the idea that a representation petition assumes an unresolved question concerning representation. However, a refusal-to-bargain charge presupposes that no question of representation exists and that the employer is wrongfully refusing to recognize or bargain with a statutory bargaining representative.

SUMMARY

No rights extended to any of the parties to collective bargaining are absolute. Thus, the complicated task of the Board and courts is to weigh the relative rights of each. The decisions resulting from this process often appear conflicting to many viewers. Indeed they are, if the criteria for evaluation are on the basis of precedent stemming from Board and Supreme Court cases. Essentially, the rule of precedent is followed consistently by the high court in regulating Board implementation of national labor policy. The totality of conduct must be reviewed in each case in reaching a decision in accordance with the *Virginia Electric Power* doctrine. If the Board is required to review the totality of circumstances that exists in each case, then the courts must do so too. It would be a strange doctrine indeed to require the NLRB to take one course of action in arriving at decisions while the courts use another.

The changing rules and regulations that exist in labor cases involving replacement of economic strikers, strikes against Board certification, striker conduct on picketing lines, lockout rights of employers, and recognitional and organizational picketing actually reflect the changing conditions and problems of American industry. Evolutionary changes in industry practices evade constancy in resolving conflict, which inevitably arises among the parties concerned. Not all decisions are immediately conducive to eliminating warfare in favor of more peaceful procedures for obtaining solutions. But the ability to make decisions on the basis of total conduct without necessarily adhering strictly to past decisions makes it easier to move toward solutions that are equitable to all parties.

DISCUSSION QUESTIONS

1. What is the difference between economic strikers and unfair labor practice strikers? What rights do each have to reinstatement?

2. Discuss the significance and implications of *Belknap* v. *Hale* for economic striker reinstatement rights.

3. Trace the development of NLRB policy regarding the voting rights in representation elections of permanently replaced economic strikers. What changes were made by Taft-Hartley? By Landrum-Griffin?

4. What is NLRB policy for determining the voting eligibility of replaced economic strikers?

5. How important is the Taft-Hartley prohibition against jurisdictional strikes? In which industry are such strikes most likely to prove harmful?

6. How have construction industry unions responded to the Taft-Hartley requirement obliging the NLRB to settle jurisdictional strikes?

7. What is the significance of the U.S. Supreme Court's decision in *Plasterers' Local 79?* Is it likely to be stabilizing or destabilizing of collective bargaining in the construction industry?

8. Discuss the tests applied by the NLRB when it is required to assign disputed work. How well has the Board performed in this category?

9. How effective are Taft-Hartley and Board decisions in dealing with strikes against NLRB certification?

10. What are the current lockout rights of employers? Is the lockout in all circumstances inherently destructive of worker rights to engage in union activities?

11. What is the difference between a strike and a lockout? When may striker replacements be used by an employer?

12. Briefly outline the range of permissible and prohibited conduct on the picket line.

13. Do employees always lose reinstatement rights when they engage in illegal picketing, even when an employer commits unfair labor practices?

14. Does the authority of unions to impose fines against union members who continue to work during strikes provide a solution for labor organizations to discipline their members in favor of maintaining a solid front against employers? How may a member evade a fine?

15. Discuss the balancing problem facing the Board in weighing the right of employees to refrain from union activities against their right to engage in concerted activities.

16. What criticism can you provide of the Landrum-Griffin provisions restricting recognitional and organizational picketing?

17. What is the actual outcome of the informational provision to the recognitional and organizational picketing provisions?

NOTES

1   Edwin E. Witte, *The Government in Labor Disputes* (New York: McGraw-Hill Book Company, 1932), p. 20.

2   Section 9 (c) (3).

3   *Mastro Plastics Corporation* v. *NLRB,* 350 U.S. 270 (1956).

4   *NLRB* v. *Fansteel Metallurgical Company,* 306 U.S. 240 (1939).

5   *Belknap* v. *Hale,* 463 U.S. 591 (1983).

6   *NLRB* v. *Mackay Radio & Telegraph Company,* 304 U.S. 333 (1938).

7   *A. Sartorius & Company, Inc.,* 10 NLRB 493 (1938).

8   *Rudolph Wurlitzer Company,* 32 NLRB 163 (1941).

9   See section entitled "Strikes Against NLRB Certification," Chapter 16.

10   *Pioneer Flour Mills,* 174 NLRB 1202 (1969).

11   *Brooks Research & Manufacturing,* 202 NLRB 93 (1973).

12   *Wahl Clipper Corporation,* 195 NLRB 104 (1972).

13   *Gulf States Paper Corp., EZ Packaging Division,* 219 NLRB 147 (1975).

14   *W. Wilton Wood, Inc.,* 127 NLRB 1675 (1960).

15   *Bright Foods, Inc.,* 126 NLRB 553 (1960).

16   *National Gypsum Company,* 133 NLRB 1492 (1962).

17   National Labor Relations Board, *Twenty-seventh Annual Report,* 1962 (Washington, D.C.: Government Printing Office, 1963), p. 80.

18   *Tampa Sand & Material Company,* 47 LRRM 1166 (1961).

19   *Laidlaw Corporation,* 171 NLRB 175 (1968).

20   *NLRB* v. *Fleetwood Trailer Company,* 389 U.S. 375 (1967).

21   *United Aircraft Corporation,* 192 NLRB 62 (1971).

22   John T. Dunlop, "Jurisdictional Disputes," *Proceedings of New York University Second Annual Conference of Labor,* p. 479.

23   National Labor Relations Board, *Forty-sixth Annual Report,* U.S. Government Printing Office, Washington, D.C. (1981), p. 192.

24   Section 8 (b) (4).

25   Bureau of National Affairs, *Taft-Hartley After One Year* (1948), p. 101.

26   Section 8 (b) (4) (D) makes it an unfair labor practice for a union to strike or to refuse to perform services when the object is "forcing or requiring any employer to assign particular work to employees in a particular labor organization or in a particular trade, craft, or class rather than to employees in another labor organization or in another trade, craft, or class, unless such employer is failing to conform to an order or certification of the Board determining the bargaining representative for employees performing such work."

27   *NLRB* v. *Radio Engineers Union,* 364 U.S. 573 (1961).

28   *NLRB* v. *Plasterers' Local 79, Operative Plasterers (Texas State Tile and Terrazzo Company),* 404 U.S. 116 (1971).

29   *NLRB* v. *Plasterers' Local 79, Operative Plasterers (Texas State Tile and Terrazzo Company),* 440 F. (2d) 174 (1971).

30   *Philadelphia Typographical Union, Local No. 2 (Philadelphia Inquirer, Division of Triangle Publications, Inc.),* 142 NLRB 1 (1963).

31   *NLRB* v. *International Longshoremen's and Warehousemen's Union, Local 50 (Pacific Maritime Association),* 504 F. (2d) 1209 (CA 9, 1974).

32   Simmons, Bruce, "Jurisdictional Disputes: Does the Board Really Snub the Supreme Court?" *Labor Law Journal,* XXXVI, 3 (March 1985), p. 183.

33   *Ibid.,* p. 191.

34   *Thompson Products, Inc.,* 72 NLRB 887 (1947).

35   Section 8 (b) (4).

36   *United Mine Workers* v. *Patton,* 211 F. (2d) 742 (1954), cert. denied, 348 U.S. 824 (1954).

37   *Dairy Distributors, Inc.* v. *Western Conference of Teamsters,* 294 F. (2d) 348 (1961).

38   *Charles D. Bonanno Linen Supply* v. NLRB, 450 U.S. 979 (1982).

39   *NLRB* v. *Truck Drivers Local Union No. 449, et al. (Buffalo Linen Supply Company),* 353 U.S. 85 (1956).

40   *Evening News Assn., Owner and Publisher of Detroit News,* 145 NLRB 996 (1964).

41   *Brown Food Store,* 137 NLRB 73 (1962), enforcement denied 319 F. (2d) 7 (CA 10), cert. granted 375 U.S. 962 (1965).

42   *NLRB* v. *Brown et al. d/b/a/ Brown Food Store, et al.,* 380 U.S. 278 (1965).

43   The Supreme Court used the *Buffalo Linen* case to arrive at its conclusion. A temporary layoff can be offset by temporary replacements.

44   *NLRB* v. *Mackay Radio & Telegraph Company,* 304 U.S. 333 (1938).

45   *American Ship Building Company* v. *NLRB,* 380 U.S. 300 (1965).

46   This result is obtained from the *Buffalo Linen* and *NLRB* v. *Brown* cases, *op. cit.*

47   *Inland Trucking Company* v. *NLRB,* 440 F. (2d) 562 (1971).

48   *Local 155, International Molders and Allied Workers Union (U.S. Pipe and Foundry Company)* v. *NLRB,* 442 F. (2d) 742 (1971).

49   *Ottawa Silica Company,* 197 NLRB 53 (1972).

50   *Intercollegiate Press, Graphic Arts Division,* 199 NLRB 35 (1972).

51   *Intercollegiate Press, Graphic Arts Division* v. *NLRB,* 486 F. (2d) 837 (CA 8, 1974).

52   *Johns-Manville Products Corp.,* 223 NLRB 189 (1976).

53   *Laclede Gas Company,* 187 NLRB 32 (1971).

54   Italics added.

55   Section 8 (b) (1).

56   Section 8 (b) (1) (A).

57   *Sunset Line & Twine,* 79 NLRB 1487 (1948).

58   *Congressional Record,* XCIII, 4563.

59   *Sunset Line & Twine, op. cit.*

60   81 NLRB 138 (1949).

61   *Local 761, International Union of Electrical, Radio & Machine Workers, AFL-CIO (General Electric Company),* 126 NLRB 123 (1960).

62   *North Electric Manufacturing Company,* 84 NLRB 23 (1949).

63   *Sunset Line & Twine, op. cit.*

64   See section entitled "Employer Free Speech Under the Wagner Act" in chapter 12.

65   *Letter Carriers (Old Dominion Branch No. 496, National Association of Letter Carriers)* v. *Austin,* 418 U.S. 264 (1974).

66   *Clear Pine Mouldings, Inc.,* 268 NLRB 1044 (1984).

67   *Coronet Casuals,* 207 NLRB 304 (1973).

68   *Georgia Kraft Company, Woodcraft Division,* 275 NLRB No. 246 (1985).

69   *Cory Corporation,* 84 NLRB 110 (1949).

70   80 NLRB 47 (1948).

71   NLRB Release R-321, May 27, 1950.

72   84 NLRB 110 (1949).

73   *Local 833, United Automobile, Aircraft & Agricultural Implement Workers of America, UAW-CIO* v. *NLRB,* 300 F. (2d) 699 (1962), cert. denied 370 U.S. 911.

74   *Local 248, UAW (Allis-Chalmers Manufacturing Company),* 149 NLRB 67 (1964).

75   *NLRB* v. *Allis-Chalmers Manufacturing Company,* 388 U.S. 175 (1967), reversing 358 F. (2d) 656.

76   *NLRB* v. *Boeing,* 412 U.S. 473 (1973).

77   *Florida Power and Light* v. *Electrical Workers,* 417 U.S. 790 (1974).

78   National Labor Relations Board, *Fortieth Annual Report,* 1975 (Washington, D.C.: Government Printing Office), pp. 113, 115.

79   *Wall Street Journal,* April 26, 1977, p. 4.

80   *Teamsters, Local 296. Northwest Publications, Inc.,* 263 NLRB No. 104 (1982).

81   Hearings before the Subcommittee on Separation of Powers, *Congressional Oversight of Administrative Agencies (National Labor Relations Board),* Part II, U.S. Senate (Washington, D.C.: Government Printing Office, 1968), p. 1115.

82   409 U.S. 213 (1972).

83   *Machinists, Local 1327. Dalmo Victor,* 263 NLRB 984 (1982).

84   *Machinists, Local 1414. Neufeld Porsche-Audi, Inc.,* 270 NLRB No. 209 (1984).

85   *Pattern Maker's League* v. *NLRB,* 105 Sup. Ct. 3064 (1985).

86   21 NLRB 999 (1979).

87   268 NLRB No. 73 (1984).

88   *Moyer Trucking & Garage Service,* 269 NLRB No. 168 (1984).

89   *Prill* v. *NLRB,* CCA–DC No. 84–1064, February 26, 1985.

90   *NLRB* v. *City Disposal Systems, Inc.,* 460 U.S. 1050 (1984).

91   Herbert S. Thatcher, "A Look at Section 8 (b) (7) and Problems Arising Thereafter," in *Symposium on the Labor-Management Reporting and Disclosure Act of 1959,* ed. Ralph Slovenko (Baton Rouge, Louisiana: Claitor's Bookstore Publishers, 1961), pp. 939–940.

92   Section 8 (b) (4) (C) makes it unlawful for a union to force or require "any employer to recognize or bargain with a particular labor organization as the representative of his

employees if another labor organization has been certified as the representative of such employees under the provisions of Section 9."

93   *Lewis Food Company*, 115 NLRB 890 (1956).

94   The Board used Section 8 (b) (1) (A) of Taft-Hartley, which makes it an unfair labor practice for unions "to restrain or coerce employees" in the exercise of their right to engage in or refrain from concerted activities directed toward self-organization and collective bargaining.

95   *Curtis Bros.*, 119 NLRB 232 (1957).

96   *NLRB* v. *Drivers Local Union*, 362 U.S. 274 (1960).

97   Section 704 (c) of the Labor Management Reporting and Disclosure Act of 1959, 73 Stat. 519, 544.

98   National Labor Relations Board, *Twenty-eighth Annual Report*, U.S. Government Printing Office, Washington, D.C. (1963) p. 115.

99   *District 65, Retail, Wholesale & Department Store Union (Eastern Camera & Photo Corporation)*, 141 NLRB 85 (1963).

100   *IBEW, Local 113 (ICG Electric, Inc.)*, 142 NLRB 145 (1963).

101   Address of Stuart Rothman before the Section on Labor Law of the Association of the Bar of the City of New York, November 12, 1959.

102   *Reed* v. *Ronmell*, 46 LRRM 2565 (E.D. Mich., 1960).

103   *Local 1265, Dept. Store Employees* v. *Brown*, 45 LRRM 3101 (N.D. Col., 1960).

104   See Fred Witney, "NLRB Membership Cleavage: Recognition and Organizational Picketing," *Labor Law Journal*, XIV, 5 (May 1963), pp. 434–458.

105   *Calumet Contractors Association*, 130 NLRB 17 (1961).

106   *Calumet Contractors Association*, 133 NLRB 57 (1961).

107   *United Automobile Workers, Local 259 (Fanelli Ford Sales, Inc.)*, 133 NLRB 1468 (1961).

108   *Claude Everett Construction Company*, 136 NLRB 321 (1962). See also *Texarkana Construction Company*, 138 NLRB 102 (1962).

109   *National Packing, Inc.*, 155 NLRB 142 (1966).

110   *Crown Cafeteria*, 130 NLRB 570 (1961).

111   *Crown Cafeteria*, 135 NLRB 124 (1962).

112   *Retail Clerks, Locals 324 & 770 (Barker Bros.)*, 138 NLRB 54 (1962).

113   *Barker Bros. Corporation* v. *NLRB*, 328 F.(2d) 431 (1964); *Crown Cafeteria* v. *NLRB*, 327 F. (2d) 351 (1964).

114   *Retail Clerks International Association, Local 344*, 136 NLRB 1270 (1962).

115   *Atlantic Maintenance Company*, 136 NLRB 105 (1962).

116   Hearings before the Subcommittee on Separation of Powers, *Congressional Oversight of Administrative Agencies (National Labor Relations Board)*, Part I, *op. cit.*, pp. 34–35; U.S. Senate (Washington, D.C.: Government Printing Office, 1968), pp. 34–35.

117   *Legislative History of the Labor-Management Reporting and Disclosure Act of 1959*, II, 1383, 1384.

118   *Mastro Plastics Corporation* v. *NLRB*, 350 U.S. 270 (1956).

119   *C. A. Blinne Construction Company*, 130 NLRB 587 (1961).

120   Discussion of Elliott bill as reported by the House, H.R. 8342, 86th Congress, 1st sess., 1959, and Kennedy-Irvin bill in the Senate, S. 1555, 86th Congress, 1st sess., 1959.

121   *C. A. Blinne Construction Company*, 135 NLRB 121 (1962).

CHAPTER SEVENTEEN

SECONDARY
BOYCOTT PRESSURES

In earlier chapters, we investigated at considerable length the legal status of the secondary boycott strike under the antitrust laws. Reference was made to famous labor cases such as *Danbury Hatters, Duplex,* and *Bedford Cut Stone.* In all of these cases, the Supreme Court held union secondary boycott activities unlawful under the Sherman Act. This meant that a union could not call or induce a strike when the objective would be to force one employer to cease doing business with another. Frankfurter and Greene defined the device as "a combination to influence A by exerting some sort of economic or social pressure against persons who deal with A."[1] This definition of a secondary boycott is not nearly as simple as implied, as will be seen subsequently.

In discussing the relationship of unions to the antitrust laws, close attention was paid to the economic factors that caused labor unions to resort to the secondary boycott. Consequently, there is no need to review these aspects again, except to point out that employees involved in labor antitrust cases resorted to the secondary boycott to preserve the status of their labor unions. The alternative to the secondary boycott could have been the disintegration of labor unions.

Congress enacted the Clayton Act in 1914, but this legislation did not prove to be the Magna Charta it was hailed to be. The legal position of organized labor under the antitrust law of 1890 and the common law was not improved. It was not until the Norris–La Guardia Act was passed in 1932 that the union objective was realized. The law protected secondary boycott activities from prosecution under antitrust provisions. This protection remained until the Taft-Hartley Act was passed in 1947. Loopholes developed, however, because the NLRB and the courts were responsible for insuring rights spelled out in other parts of the Act. Congress attempted to solve the problem again in Landrum-Griffin.

LEGAL STATUS UNDER TAFT-HARTLEY

The legislative history of the Taft-Hartley Act makes it clear that the congressional objective was to protect neutral employers and neutral employees from economically injurious union pressures stemming from labor-management disputes. Protection was to be extended to these groups only when they were neutral parties to the dispute.

In the Taft-Hartley hearings in 1947, Congress determined that the secondary boycott—the union practice of striking, picketing, or otherwise boycotting one employer in order to exert pressure on another—was an unjustifiable technique and should be removed from the labor scene. Congress drew up the Section 8 (b) (4) language to accomplish its objective. In pertinent part the provision provided:

> It shall be an unfair labor practice for a labor organization or its agents—(4) to engage in, or to induce or encourage the employees of any employer to engage in, a strike, or a concerted refusal in the course of their employment to use, manufacture, process, transport, or otherwise handle or work on any goods, articles, materials, or commodities, or to perform any services, where an object thereof is: (A) forcing or requiring . . . any employer or any other person to cease using, selling, handling, transporting, or otherwise dealing in the products of any other producer, processor, or manufacturer, or to cease doing business with any other person.

The scope of the section was explained by Senator Taft during the debates. He stated:

> This provision makes it unlawful to resort to a secondary boycott to injure the business of a third person who is wholly unconcerned in the disagreement between an employer and his employees. . . . It has been set forth that there are good secondary boycotts and bad secondary boycotts. Our committee heard evidence for weeks and never succeeded in having anyone tell us any difference between different kinds of secondary boycotts. So we have so broadened the provision dealing with secondary boycotts as to make them an unfair labor practice.[2]

The intent of Congress in enacting the provision is clear. However, the NLRB in applying the law opened up a large number of loopholes by permitting unions to continue using secondary boycotts under certain circumstances. In the years after the 1947 law was passed, the NLRB and the courts had occasion to deal with several sections of the law that were somewhat confusing. By 1953, a congressional committee was reviewing loopholes that were considered so large that "a truck can be driven through them."[3] The loopholes included:

> 1. Direct coercion of employers to cease doing business with another person. Strikes were not used to accomplish this end.
> 2. "Hot-cargo" contracts whereby employers agreed not to do business with firms considered "unfair" by unions.

3. Exemption from the secondary boycott provision of "employers," "persons," and "employees" not considered as coming within the Act's definitions.

4. Union ability to influence the nonconcerted activities of employees. That is, the ability to deal with an employee as a single individual.

5. Union inducement to engage in consumer boycotts.

6. Union refusal to allow members to accept jobs from secondary employers.

7. Boycotts taking place at the location of the primary dispute.

8. Picketing trucks at secondary locations.

9. Boycotts of secondary employers who are allied with primary employers.[4]

One overwhelming difficulty that faced the Board and the courts in attempts to construct workable secondary boycott policies stemmed from conflicts with other sections of the Taft-Hartley Act. Section 13 protects the right of employees to strike[5] and Section 7 guarantees employees the right to engage in concerted activity.[6] These sections show that Congress did not intend to outlaw all strikes or primary concerted activity. Neither did it intend to eliminate all secondary actions. A determination of what is legal primary activity and what is illegal secondary activity has generated problems for the NLRB and the courts. Section 10 (1) of Taft-Hartley requires that the Board give priority to hearings dealing with secondary boycotts. Temporary injunctions may be obtained while the case is pending before the Board for determination. The Board is often reluctant to exercise its authority in this regard, however, because union action may subsequently be found legal. In such cases, when unions have not violated the law, the injunction damage usually evades remedy.

Congress reviewed the secondary boycott loopholes of Taft-Hartley during the Landrum-Griffin Act hearings. It reaffirmed its intention to outlaw a large percentage of secondary action. Senator John F. Kennedy, chairman of the Senate conferees on the Landrum-Griffin bill, explained the intent of the secondary boycott provision amendments as follows:

> The chief effect of the conference agreement, therefore, will be to plug loopholes in the secondary boycott provisions of the National Labor Relations Act. There has never been any dispute about the desirability of plugging these artificial loopholes.[7]

The loopholes that developed under Taft-Hartley were therefore supposedly closed by the 1959 amendments. Because of the complicated nature of the statutory language and of subsequent Board and court interpretations, the loopholes of Taft-Hartley and Landrum-Griffin are treated together by major category of secondary activity.

ALLY DOCTRINE

The legislative history of Taft-Hartley makes it clear that Congress intended to prohibit union inducement of work stoppages for the purpose of forcing B to cease doing business with A only when B was in fact neutral in the dispute. The assumption implicit in the language of the law was that the two employers were independent.[8] Senator Taft during a debate on the section remarked that it "is not intended to apply to a case where the third party is, in effect, in cahoots with or acting as a part of the primary employer."[9] That is, the secondary boycott provisions do not apply when the third party is not really neutral, but is in fact a willing *ally* of the primary employer.

The ally doctrine is applicable when a primary employer is struck and then subcontracts work to another company that is aware of the existence of the labor dispute.[10] Indeed, this form of boycott was often permitted under the common law even when other secondary activity was held unlawful. Unionists are permitted to protect themselves against such offensive employer actions. The primary employees have a self-interest in the work in dispute and do not have to sit idly by while their economic position deteriorates as a result of subcontracting. The NLRB ruled in the *Kable Printing Co.* case that an "orchestrated" maneuver by a firm to have its customers contract directly with other companies during a strike does not make them neutral to the dispute.[11] A decision to discontinue a given type of work during the strike did not alter the Board's position, because the decision was not irrevocable.

The secondary employer in such cases is not completely powerless to resolve the underlying dispute. Such a company could refuse to handle the struck work that is not handled by it under normal circumstances, with the result that significant economic pressure would be placed back on the first point of union concern. Since this is the case, the "secondary employer" is in fact treated as a primary employer by the Board. The ally doctrine has been consistently applied by the NLRB and was not a topic for 1959 remedial action by Congress. The ally doctrine is not and has never been a loophole of the secondary boycott provisions of Taft-Hartley. The intent of Congress was made clear by the Conference Committee Report revealing that "no language has been included with reference to struck work because the committee conference did not wish to change the existing law as illustrated by such decisions as *Douds* v. *Metropolitan Federation of Architects.*"[12]

Soviet Union Boycott Revisited

Earlier we noted that the U.S. Supreme Court had held that an injunction could not be issued to prevent members of the Longshoremen's union from refusing to load or unload ships hauling goods to or from the Soviet Union. The union's action was undertaken to protest the USSR mititary invasion of Afghanistan. The high court, however, held that the union's action constituted an illegal secondary boycott.[13] The high court reasoned as follows: The union's primary targets were shipping line firms whose vessels were hauling Soviet cargo. To stop the flow of goods between the United States and the USSR, the union wanted the shipping lines to cease hauling such products. An American importer of Soviet wood, Allied International, became entangled in the union's boycott. Union members refused to unload the wood destined for that firm. Thus, the union was pressuring Allied International for the purpose of forcing it to cease doing business with the shipping lines. The high court held that Allied International was a neutral employer that had been harmed by the union's action. Under the terms of the law, "whoever" is injured in business by an illegal secondary boycott may sue the responsible union. Allied International sued the union for $10,000,000.

While making its decision, the Supreme Court rejected the union's argument that it intended only to free its members from the morally repugnant duty of handling Soviet goods and did not intend to harm any employer. Additionally, it made no difference, said the Court, that the union's activity was fundamentally a political dispute with a foreign nation, and not a labor dispute with a primary employer. In any event, it is somewhat difficult to reconcile the two Supreme Court decisions in question. Why should the very same union conduct be lawful under the Norris–LaGuardia Act, but unlawful under Taft-Hartley? It would seem reasonable that if the union's activity could not be curbed by an injunction under the terms of the anti-injunction statute, it should logically follow that the same activity should not be illegal under a sister federal law.

DEFINITION OF PERSONS AND INDIVIDUALS

Under the 1947 law, for secondary boycott activity to be unlawful, there had to be union pressure to induce the employees of the neutral employer in the course of their employment to engage in a concerted refusal to perform services. The refusal had to be for the purpose of interfering with a business relationship between the secondary and primary employers. The basis for one loophole included the key phrases, "induce the employees" of the neutral employer, and "a concerted refusal" to perform services. Interpretation of this language had to be made within the statutory definition of *employer* under Taft-Hartley, which excluded such users of labor as agencies of federal, state, and municipal governments. In addition, nonprofit hospitals, railroads, and airlines were among the organizations not defined as employers. Consequently, unions were permitted to lawfully exert pressure on the employees of these organizations for the purpose of effecting a secondary boycott. It would have been highly inconsistent to have ruled that some sections of law applied to these organizations while other sections did not. The Board and the courts responded to the total public policy and not to fragmented parts of it.

It was also lawful to exert pressure upon the secondary employer him- or herself, upon a supervisor, and even upon individual key employees hired by the neutral employer.[14] This situation was made clear by the Supreme Court in 1951. In the *International Rice Milling* case, a union was seeking to organize a company's employees. The primary employer's premises were picketed. Two employees of a neutral employer, on a truck, refused to cross the picket line. The NLRB did not consider the action a secondary boycott forbidden by Taft-Hartley because picketing was limited to the situs of the primary employer. The Fifth Circuit Court of Appeals reversed the Board and held that the union had deliberately discouraged the employees of neutral employers from supplying the primary employer.[15] The impact of this decision, if it had prevailed, would have been to outlaw most primary picketing if any other employer's employees had refused to continue to perform their normal functions in the face of a picket line.

The U.S. Supreme Court ruled differently from both the Board and the lower court. The union action was deemed lawful since the refusal of two laborers to cross the picket line did not constitute "concerted activity" within the meaning of the Taft-Hartley Act. The two employees had behaved merely as individuals in the face of a picket line.

On the basis of this decision in 1951, it became possible for unions to pressure a key employee of a secondary employer, such as a purchasing agent, not to deal with a company with whom the union had a dispute. Key employees could be told not to buy from particular employers until further notice. In some situations this action of a key employee of another firm might have prevented a primary employer from resisting union demands. Assume, for example, that a purchasing agent of a neutral employer constituted a source of significant business for an employer involved in a labor dispute. The mere fact that this sole employee honored union demands might have been enough to force the primary employer to yield to these demands. In some situations, a union may be required to obtain the same cooperation from several key employees to secure the same result. Even so, the law did not forbid the labor organization from pursuing such a course of action, since it did not amount to concerted activity.

Pressure could also be applied directly to the secondary employer since such action did not constitute concerted activity.[16] Thus, unions could coerce a secondary employer not to buy struck work, in order to exert economic pressure on the primary employer. This tactic was particularly effective when the union involved had a collective bargaining contract with the neutral employer. The union could threaten that failure to do as requested could result in an especially hard time when its own contract was due for renegotiation. In many situations, this type of threat was enough to obtain the desired action from the neutral employer.

Additionally, the union was permitted to take other action. Because unions could legally pressure secondary employers, they could also effect a secondary consumption boycott.[17] Appeals to the public not to buy from a firm that had a business relationship with the primary employer were lawful, since the union pressure was considered not to have been executed against the employees of the neutral firm but against the firm itself. This type of action often proved successful even in cases where the union did not have a collective bargaining relationship with the neutral employer.

Landrum-Griffin Changes

The Congress was intent upon closing the loopholes generated by the 1947 statutory language. Two clauses were adopted to achieve this end. Clause

(i) of Section 8 (b) (4) of Landrum-Griffin forbids unions to strike or to induce or encourage strikes or work stoppages by any individual employed by any person engaged in commerce or in an industry affecting commerce. Clause (ii) makes it unlawful for a union to threaten, coerce, or restrain any person engaged in commerce or in an industry affecting commerce for a secondary boycott objective.

It was the intent of Congress to prohibit a union from inducing "any individual employed by any person" to engage in a secondary boycott. "Any person" was to refer to government agencies and other organizations not defined as employers by Taft-Hartley. Thus, such employers as railroads and airlines are now covered by the law, since they are "persons" even if they are not legally defined as employers. Also, the new language outlaws union pressure on secondary employers themselves, since now the pressure need not be exerted against the employees of an employer to fall within the unlawful area. It is now illegal when pressure is exerted either against the employees of the neutral employer or against employers themselves. The amendment also makes secondary consumer boycotts unlawful, since such union pressure is directed against the secondary employer.

In short, Landrum-Griffin was intended to plug the loopholes of permitting unions to put pressure (1) directly on management, (2) directly on key individuals, and (3) directly on organizations not considered employers under Taft-Hartley. We shall see, however, that the NLRB and the courts found some loopholes even in the new language. However, despite these new loopholes, the opportunity for unions to engage in secondary boycotts is far less than it was before the adoption of the Landrum-Griffin changes.

Landrum-Griffin Loopholes

The Landrum-Griffin ban against inducing managerial employees to refuse to handle products of another employer came before the Board in the *Carolina* and *Servette* cases. In the *Carolina Lumber* case, a union exerted pressure against the company's foreman by asking him not to buy from a nonunion shop.[18] The foreman held the job of project supervisor. The Board established two categories for interpreting the meaning of the two clauses added to the law in 1959. Clause (i) prohibits inducing an individual employed by persons. This aspect of the law was viewed by the Board as applying to low-level supervision. Since forepeople were considered low-level supervision, the Board held it unlawful to induce them to follow union advice under the terms of this clause. The basic purpose of congressional enactment was viewed in this fashion because construction forepeople are often union members and they may not be induced by the union. The foreman in the *Carolina* case was considered high-level management since he was solely responsible for the work being performed at the construction site. High-level management is covered by clause (ii). This clause permits unions to induce or encourage high-level management to assist them in obtaining objectives against primary employers, but they may not be coerced. That is to say, a union may approach high-level management and request it not to use nonunion products or labor since such action is detrimental to the union. It may not use coercion, however, since this would violate the terms of the provision.

The *Carolina* case generated considerable concern because a foreperson, for example, is an individual under clause (i) and a person under clause (ii). He or she may be induced under one interpretation but not under another. Since the foreman was considered top management in the instant case, he was a person. Board rejection of his inclusion under clause (i) means that he was not an individual. Thus, for purposes of the law, he was a person and not an individual. This distinction permits unions to bring economic pressure on employers with whom they have a dispute through those neutral to it. The pressure may be made through top-level management when it is obtained through requests for cooperation and not coercion.

The U.S. Supreme Court dealt with the same issue in the *Servette* case in 1964.[19] The case involved a union's right to induce supervisors to cease handling the products of another employer. The union had induced managers of chain stores to discontinue handling merchandise supplied by Servette. The Board drew a distinction between high-level and low-level supervisors, and held that store managers were high-level supervisors and not "individuals" as defined in the Act. Thus, unions could induce them to refuse to handle Servette products. The NLRB continued the doctrine established in its *Carolina* case. A distinction was made between high- and low-level management, and therefore between individuals and persons.

The Ninth Circuit Court of Appeals refused to accept the Board rule on the contention that the congressional purpose to ban such conduct was clear and unequivocal. The U.S. Supreme Court did not adopt the NLRB criteria for such cases, but did not ban such action either. It held that the crucial test for union action in approaching supervisors was whether the appeal was to the exercise of managerial discretion or was instead an appeal for them to cease performing employment services. An appeal to the exercise of managerial discretion is permissible action, but unions are not permitted to make appeals seeking neutral supervisors to cease performing employment services. It may well be that union "appeals" to management to pressure other employers, however politely stated, carry with them implicit threats of economic reprisal if refused. This is particularly the case if the union has a bargaining relationship with the supervisor to whom it makes an appeal.

In any event, *Servette* opens a new loophole in the secondary boycott bans provided by Congress in 1959. Appeals may be made to management to exercise their discretion to heed union requests not to deal with other employers. The result reached by the Court has the same effect as the one reached by the Board. The Court did not attempt to distinguish between individuals and persons, but went directly to an examination of permissible union behavior.

On the other hand, the Board construed the word "person" to limit boycott activities in a dispute involving two divisions of the same parent corporation. In a case that concerned the Hearst Corporation, the NLRB forbade the picketing of one division of the enterprise when a union had a dispute with another division of the same corporation. Hearst owns a TV and a newspaper division. The direct labor dispute concerned the TV operation. During the dispute the union picketed the offices of the newspaper. The Board held that the picketing of the newspaper was illegal under the secondary boycott provisions of the law, since it was calculated to solicit support of the newspaper employees to aid the union in its dispute with the TV station. In upholding the Board decision, a federal court stated that the two enterprises, though owned by the same parent corporation, were separate "persons" within the meaning of the law.[20]

On the basis of the record, the NLRB found that the divisions were separate and autonomous, with independent control vested in the officers of the respective divisions. Though the court acknowledged that the Hearst president could replace division heads, and had the power to approve large corporation expenditures, it also determined that in practice Hearst vested active control in the respective division heads. For example, the division heads set their own news policies, could reject news services offered by Hearst, handled collective bargaining on an independent basis, and established their own financial and accounting systems. In short, it was found that there was a sufficient degree of autonomous control to warrant their treatment as separate "persons" for purposes of the secondary boycott provision. In any event, the *Hearst* case has important implications for labor policy in these days of the conglomerate business enterprise. Though owned by the same parent corporation, different divisions of the same enterprise could be regarded as separate "persons" for purposes of the federal law.

COMMON-SITUS PICKETING

The phrase *common situs* refers to a location in labor dispute cases where employees of both primary and secondary employers perform their duties. For example, a construction site may consist of employees of ten to fifteen different employers. The term *common situs* is used to refer to an area where picketing occurs to place pressure on an employer with whom a labor dispute exists. Neutral employees are also present and working at the same location. The legislative history is void of any mention of this concept.[21]

In 1949, the NLRB dealt with the complex question of whether picketing at a common situs constitutes secondary boycott activity, since secondary employers unavoidably feel the impact. In the *Pure Oil* case, two oil companies operated refineries on adjacent premises.[22] They shared a common dock from which the employees of one of the companies originally performed shipment handling for both. Later, the companies agreed that each would perform its own shipment services on the same dock, using separate personnel. A union became entangled in a dispute with one of the employers and picketed the dock, with the result that the neutral employer's employees refused to cross the picket line to perform their usual duties.

The NLRB held that such action was primary picketing and not in violation of the secondary boycott provisions, despite the fact that the neutral employees refused to perform work for the neutral employers. The Board based its decision on a distinction between primary and secondary picketing with regard to the physical location of the site. The physical layout within which picketing occurs must be viewed before an equitable determination of legality may be made. If the NLRB had held this picketing in violation of the secondary restrictions of the Act, it would have had to place severe restrictions on primary union activity, which is protected under national labor policy. The union had no alternative for picket action but that which it engaged in at the dock site. The physical location, according to the Board, was the proper variable to review in deciding the legality of union action at sites where several employees perform work.

In the same year, 1949, the Board had a similar situation before it in the *Ryan Construction* case.[23] In this case, Ryan was performing construction work on the premises of a manufacturer against whom a strike occurred. The Board adhered to its use of physical situs as a criterion for deciding the legality of picketing the manufacturer. The primary employer established a separate entry and exit gate for the exclusive use of the neutral employees. The union on strike proceeded to picket the separate gate as well as the one used by employees of the primary employer. The neutral employees honored the picket line and refused to perform work for the neutral employer on the struck manufacturer's premises.

The Board refused to accept the argument that the area of dispute was enlarged due to picketing of the separate gate. The union action was deemed lawful picketing activity by the NLRB. Thus, the doctrine that the physical site of the picketing is the most important determinant of picketing legality was established in 1949. In addition, this Board interpretation seems to have been approved by Congress in 1959 when it added two provisos to the secondary boycott section. The first proviso requires that "nothing contained in this clause shall be construed to make unlawful, where not otherwise unlawful, any primary strike or primary picketing."[24] The Supreme Court dealt with this issue after Landrum-Griffin was enacted.

Denver Building Trades Council.   A somewhat confusing twist must now be viewed, since it is often taken that the Supreme Court reversed the Board doctrine established in The *Pure Oil* and *Ryan* cases. In 1951, the U.S. Supreme Court decided a case involving common-situs picketing of a secondary nature. In this situation, the high court had to deal with a union that had undertaken picketing action to force a general contractor to cease doing business with a nonunion employer at the same location with union employers. Picketing of the site brought about a refusal to work by union members. The Supreme Court ruled that the use of economic pressure by unions against neutral employers at sites under their control was a violation of the law.

The dissenting justices pointed out that the general contractor was not a neutral party to the dispute. He had employed a nonunion subcontractor to perform work alongside union members, and the attitude of building trades unions toward working with nonunion members was widely known. Nevertheless, the minority view did not prevail. The Court held that the fact that the primary employer was operating at the same construction site with neutral employers was of no consequence.

On the surface, it would appear that the doctrine set forth in 1949 by the Board had been overruled. This is not the situation, since in the *Pure Oil* and *Ryan* cases, the Board had not permitted common-situs picketing with the motive of pressuring neutral employers. Picketing was undertaken against the primary employers, and the secondary employees only incidentally honored the picket line. No attempt was made to place pressure on the primary employer through the neutral one. The *Denver Building Trades* case was held to constitute secondary action because the general contractor in control of the site was neutral. Had he been deemed primary, the Court most likely would have permitted picketing at the site to continue.

"Reserve Gate" Doctrine.   In the 1949 *Ryan* case, the NLRB did not distinguish between picketing at a manufacturer's gate for general employees and at a gate reserved for construction workers of a neutral employer. It made this distinction in 1959. In the *Virginia-Carolina Chemical* case, a union that represented the production and maintenance employees of the company went out on strike and picketed the plant. The company had employed an outside construction company to work within the plant, but the work had not started prior to the strike. After the strike started, the company erected a fence around the plant with four separate entrances. One of the gates was set aside for the exclusive use of the other company's employees, and this action was communicated to both the contractor and the union on strike. The union on strike ignored the reserved gate and picketed it anyway, with the result that the construction workers honored the picket line.

The NLRB found the union in violation of the secondary boycott provisions because of its action at the reserved gate. The District of Columbia Circuit Court of Appeals enforced the Board order for the union to cease and desist from picketing activity at the reserve gate.[25]

The U.S. Supreme Court dealt with the Board's "separate gate" doctrine in 1961 in a case involving General Electric Company, and in the 1964 *Carrier Corp.* case.[26] In the *General Electric* case, the local union picketed the premises of the company with whom it had a labor dispute. It engaged in picketing not only at the gates utilized by General Electric's employees, but also at a gate reserved exclusively for independent contractors and their employees. The independent contractors regularly performed work in the manufacturer's plant. The NLRB held that picketing at the reserve gate constituted illegal secondary activity, since it pressured the employees of neutral employers to join in the union action. This decision was sustained by a lower federal court.

The U.S. Supreme Court upheld the Board-established "reserve gate" doctrine, but qualified its position. It held that the "distinction between legitimate 'primary activity' and banned 'secondary activity' " is difficult to make. For this reason, there must be an accommodation between a "union's right to picket and the interest of the secondary employer in being free from picketing." The key to resolving this issue in reserve gate cases is "found in the type of work that is being performed by those who use the separate gate." If independent contractors perform tasks "unconnected to the normal operations of the struck employer," then the Board could hold picketing at reserve gates to be secondary. However, if the work performed by employees using reserve gates is of the kind carried out by the regular employees of the plant, picketing would fall within the primary classification and hence be lawful. Thus, the amount of bargaining-unit work performed while the strike is in process is the key to the legality of union picketing at the reserve gate. If employees of the outside contractor perform work that they would not normally carry out because of the strike, a union may lawfully picket the reserve gate. In addition, the reserve gate must be clearly marked as such, or it will not be distinguished from any other gate leading to the primary employer's premises.

However, the "work-related" test to determine the legality of picketing reserve gates of common building sites in the construction industry is not used by the Board. In the *Markwell and Hartz* case, it used the *Moore Dry Dock* standards (to be discussed) in deviating from the *General Electric* and *Carrier* tests to distinguish between primary and secondary activity.[27] Thus, the Board applies *Moore Dry Dock* standards to the construction industry and *General Electric* and *Carrier* to manufacturing. In establishing the difference, the Board noted that:

> the close working relations of various construction contractors on a common situs involved them in a common undertaking which destroyed the neutrality and thus the immunity of secondary employers and employees to appeals.

Once neutrality has been breached, lawful picketing of a reserve gate may be undertaken.[28] Any gate that is used to deliver materials essential to the primary employer's normal operations is subject to lawful picketing.

***Common Situs* and Moore Dry Dock.**   When primary and neutral employers work on common premises during labor disputes, the NLRB must strike a "balance between the union's right to picket and the interest of the secondary employer in being free from picketing." In *Moore Dry Dock*,[29] a union was involved in a labor dispute with a shipowner. It asked the dockowner for permission to enter the shipyard to picket the docksite where the primary employer operated, but the request was refused. The union established a picket line at the gate to the shipyard, despite the fact that employees of other employers used the gate to reach their places of work in the shipyard. A secondary boycott unfair labor practice was filed against the union for its action.

The Board established four criteria for permitting picketing to take place at a site controlled by a neutral employer. It was forced to do so because the striking union could not exert effective economic pressure if a rigid rule were established regarding the effect of such action on neutral employers. In establishing the criteria for permissible activity, the Supreme Court upon review observed that these tests constituted a shift in administrative policy involving common-situs problems. Physical location was no longer deemed the most important consideration to determine legality of union action. Now picketing is deemed legal at a neutral point if publicity is directed at the primary employer.

Thus, picketing at a common situs is regarded as legal if (1) the picketing is strictly limited to times when the situs of the dispute is located on the secondary employer's premises; (2) at the time of the picketing the primary employer is engaged in normal business at the situs; (3) the picketing is limited to places reasonably close to the location of the situs; and (4) the picketing clearly discloses that the dispute is with the primary employer. This test is applied to common-situs picketing in cases where other evidence does not clearly show the intent and purpose of union activity.

The *Moore Dry Dock* case established a situation whereby picketing at the common situs may be undertaken if the test conditions are met. Picketing may be undertaken even if the effect is that employees of neutral employers refuse to cross the picket line. The secondary boycott effects are incidental to the right of labor unions to engage in primary picketing. As mentioned, *Moore Dry Dock* marked a departure from the earlier emphasis placed on the geographic location of picketing to determine legality, to a new emphasis on publicity. Thus, an accommodation is established between the right of unions to engage in primary activity and that of secondary employers to be free from union pressure. Neither right is absolute.

Common-Situs Policy Shifts: 1953–1962.   A new Board membership achieved majority status in 1953 and immediately had the opportunity to review the common-situs rules of its predecessor. In the *Washington Coca-Cola* case, the Board altered the physical location rule of prior decisions.[30] It held that if a primary employer maintained a place of business that presented no physical obstacles to picketing, a union could not lawfully picket some other location at which secondary neutral employees worked. In such situations, picketing had to be confined to the easily accessible premises of the primary employer.

The Board meant that a union engaged in a labor dispute had to refrain from picketing the company at, say, an office building or some other facility at another place in the community. It did not matter if the office building was located ten miles away from the site where nonunion workers and union workers were engaged side by side in work. It was reasoned that the mere presence of a picket sign is a signal to members of building trades unions to leave the job. This doctrine of 1953 was meant to eliminate the use of the signal so as to relieve pressure on neutral employers in labor disputes.

The doctrine of *Washington Coca-Cola* was not destined for continued life;

it was reversed by a new Board majority in 1962. In the *Plauche Electric* case, a secondary neutral employer awarded a contract to the nonunion Plauche Electric Company to perform electrical work, along with other employers, on the premises of U.S. Tire, a manufacturing firm.[31] The nonunion contractor maintained an office to which its employees reported twice a day regardless of the project on which they were employed. The union did not choose to picket Plauche's place of business, as required under the *Washington Coca-Cola* doctrine, but elected to picket the plant premises of U.S. Tire instead. The new Board found no violation of the secondary boycott provisions of the law and consequently reversed *Washington Coca-Cola*. The revised position was justified on the ground that the standard established in 1953 was too rigid. Unions were viewed as unduly restricted in their efforts to picket employers that did not conform to union standards. There may be occasions when a primary employer's permanent place of business is adequate for a union to picket to seek its objective. However, a rigid rule requiring picketing only at permanent locations severely restricts the right of unions to engage in this action, as guaranteed by law. The place where work is performed is usually the only effective place where unions may exert economic pressure. Thus, the law now permits unions to picket the physical location where the labor dispute is concentrated, as opposed to a distant office maintained by an employer involved in a labor controversy. This policy permits unions to place the greatest economic pressure on a firm at the location where it is likely to have the greatest effect. The fact that neutral employers also work at the same location does not control the right of unions to engage in primary action. They must attempt to meet the tests provided in *Moore Dry Dock* unless other evidence clearly demonstrates to the Board the primary nature of union action. This aspect of Board policy may be considered a loophole in the law; however, it should be emphasized at this point that the NLRB has to balance the right of unions to strike with the right of neutral employers to be free from economic pressures when they have no power to influence the outcome of the dispute.

ROVING OR AMBULATORY SITUS

A deviation of the common-situs picketing standards involves union picketing of primary employer vehicles when they stop temporarily at neutral employer facilities to pick up or deliver commodities. In trucking, drivers spend most of their time delivering or picking up shipments at various employer premises. This makes these workers ambulatory employees. In 1949, the NLRB recognized the nature of this type of work and permitted a union to picket a primary employer's trucks even during the time they were at a secondary employer's site of operations.[32] During the 1950s, the Board adhered to its *Washington Coca-Cola* doctrine, whereby ambulatory picketing was almost totally eliminated.[33] Under this requirement, a union had to picket the permanent place of business of a primary employer, if such existed, and refrain from such activity at sites where neutral employers operated. Thus, the union tactic of truck following was not permissible unless the union could show that a permanent place of business did not exist.

This prohibition was eliminated in 1961 when the NLRB set forth its *Carrier Corporation* ruling.[34] In *Carrier,* a union picketed the company premises. The New York Central Railroad Company, a secondary employer, maintained a right of way on property next to Carrier Corporation property. The right of way was fenced in and trains moved through a gate to approach the Carrier plant to load and unload materials. The union picketed the gate to stop the secondary employer's workers from performing their usual jobs, the loading and unloading of Carrier Corporation products.

The NLRB held the picketing legal under secondary boycott provisions of the law, since the secondary employer's business activity was "related to the normal plant operations of the primary employer with whom the union is in dispute." The union that had the dispute with Carrier had a clear economic interest in attempting to halt the movement of its goods to market. For clarity regarding the economic significance of the decision, let us assume that the Carrier Corporation had maintained significantly high inventories at the time of the dispute. If its employees were unsuccessful in slowing down or stopping the company's ability to supply users with its product, the union might have been unable to exert adequate economic pressure to support its position. However, if the union was left free to peaceably induce employees of the other employer not to provide Carrier with their services, then it would be in a better position to require Carrier to bargain on items in dispute. This follows since the company would not be able to continue to supply other companies with its product, despite high levels of inventories. Thus, it is obvious that the railroad's employees were not neutral to the dispute, since their services had vital implications for bargaining-unit employees on strike. The U.S. Supreme Court sustained the NLRB.[35]

At the same time, it should be realized that the *Moore Dry Dock* rules apply to ambulatory picketing as well as to that at stationary common sites. Pickets must clearly identify on their signs that their dispute is with a primary employer and not with those who are neutral. Due care must be taken not to appeal to neutral employees for the purpose of enmeshing them in an existing dispute. If this occurs, the Board will outlaw picketing of vehicles as exceeding the permissible limits of primary picketing.[36]

These rules of *Moore Dry Dock* apply to ambulatory picketing cases, unless there is evidence to the contrary revealing union motives such as in the *Carrier Corporation* case. If there is no clear evidence of the secondary employer's business relationship with the primary employer's normal operations, a picketing union becomes subject to the four rules of *Moore Dry Dock* in determining ambulatory picketing legality. Once again it is obvious that the difference between primary and secondary union activity is unclear at best. The lack of clear delineation between the two types of activity places the Board and courts in the position of attempting to draw conclusions on the basis of information gathered during investigation of charges filed as well as that brought out during formal Board hearings.

A bill was passed by Congress in 1975 that would have allowed unions to picket all contractors at a common construction site as a result of a legal dispute with one of the contractors. President Ford vetoed the bill after he had first agreed to sign it. Organized labor was furious with the administration over the veto, and Secretary of Labor John T. Dunlop resigned because he was of the opinion that the action had destroyed prospects of labor-management cooperation in a depressed construction industry market.

CONSUMER SECONDARY BOYCOTTS

Prohibited secondary boycott action includes activity calculated to induce work stoppages or to coerce any persons engaged in commerce in order to obtain an illegal object. One example of prohibited action is the forcing of any person to cease doing business with any other person. The law, however, is not as simple as it may first appear. It contains a proviso that reads that

> for the purpose of this paragraph, only, nothing contained in such paragraph shall be construed to prohibit publicity, *other than picketing,* for the purpose of truthfully advising the public, including consumers and members of a labor organization, that a product or products are produced by an employer with whom a labor organization has a primary dispute and are distributed by another employer [emphasis added].[37]

Unions have the ability to publicize a dispute with a primary employer at retail outlets selling the goods in dispute by using such outlets as handbills, newspaper advertisements, and radio and television advertisements. The legality of picketing to induce customers not to buy "unfair" products is not entirely prohibited despite the language of the 1959 law. A consumer boycott depends mainly on publicity, but it is difficult to measure the effect of union efforts in most cases. Such activity is likely to be more successful in areas that are heavily populated with union members than in those with few if any members.

The NLRB held at first that Congress in 1959 had intended to outlaw all consumer picketing in front of a secondary store for the purpose of appealing to consumers not to buy the products in dispute.[38] Following its policy of holding all consumer picketing illegal, the Board held, in one highly important case destined for Supreme Court review, that union picketing was illegal when it picketed a retail outlet to appeal to customers on the grounds that it had a dispute with another employer whose product was sold by the retail store.[39]

The Court of Appeals for the District of Columbia reversed the Board and held that consumer picketing could not be found to "threaten, coerce or restrain the stores being picketed [without] affirmative proof that a substantial economic impact on the store had occurred, or was likely to occur as a result of the conduct." The case was remanded to the Board to look for this type of evidence. However, upon appeal, the U.S. Supreme Court established a different guideline for the Board to use when such cases came before it.

The Supreme Court ruled in the *Tree Fruits* case that the legislative history "does not reflect with the requisite clarity a congressional plan to proscribe all peaceful consumer picketing at secondary sites." The record merely revealed that such picketing was unlawful if the labor organization attempted to persuade customers not to buy any of the products on sale at the neutral store. Customers may be persuaded through picketing not to buy the struck product. Thus, picketing confined to persuading customers to cease buying the product of the primary employer with whom the dispute exists is not prohibited secondary action. In most cases, the Court reasoned, if secondary stores drop the item in dispute from their counters, they would not be hurt economically. This view of the Court may be correct in terms of grocery stores or department stores that handle a large range of goods. Presumably, the *Tree Fruits* doctrine rationale would not hold when specialty shops are involved. That is, a store that specializes in a particular good supplied by a single producer could easily be dealt a severe economic setback if consumer picketing were permitted in cases where suppliers were involved in labor disputes.

At the same time, however, it should be realized that unions may be legally within their rights to use forms of publicity other than picketing to appeal to customers not to patronize a secondary store at all. Consider this statement of the Court in *Tree Fruits:*

> Peaceful consumer picketing to shut off all trade with the secondary employer unless he aids the union in its dispute with the primary employer is poles apart from such picketing which only persuades his customer not to buy the struck product.

The Court said that picketing may not be used to stop all customer trade with a neutral employer, but that other forms of publicity may be used even if they accomplish this end. All that is required is that the information on handbills, for example, be truthful and not misleading to the public. Thus, the area of labor dispute in accordance with this implication extends to all situations involving a struck product, from a manufacturer, to distributors, and to retail outlets.

In short, the Supreme Court has held that all picketing of secondary employers is not per se illegal. This doctrine provides a basis for unions to exert secondary pressure and tends to create a loophole in the provisions of Landrum-Griffin. Carefully worded picket signs permit unions to effectuate consumer boycotts on particular goods.

In 1968, the District of Columbia Court of Appeals was faced with a consumer boycott issue that was somewhat less clear than the test provided by *Tree Fruits.* [40] A union had a primary dispute with a newspaper and picketed a restaurant that advertised regularly in the struck newspaper. The NLRB held the picketing to violate the secondary boycott provisions of Landrum-Griffin. Hand-bills were also passed out describing the union's dispute with the newspaper company in some detail. The question is: What part of the restaurant's product was the union permitted to ask customers not to buy?

The court of appeals upheld the NLRB rule in this case on the grounds that *Tree Fruits* did not apply to the *Honolulu* case. This position was taken because a newspaper advertisement actually becomes incorporated into every product sold by the restaurant. The court of appeals ruled that "the struck product has become part of the retailer's entire offering, so that the product boycott will of necessity encompass the entire business of the secondary employer."

The Supreme Court's *Tree Fruits* decision upholds a limited boycott and will not support a total boycott. A total boycott spreads to and disrupts a retailer's entire trade. The Act protects a neutral employer from a boycott of its entire business. The point of *Honolulu* became clearer after the NLRB and District of Columbia Circuit Court of Appeals disagreed on the application of the Supreme Court's 1964 *Tree Fruits* case: the court of appeals refused to enforce a Board order that found unlawful consumer picketing aimed at a product that constituted 90 percent of a retailer's business. The Board held that *Tree Fruits* did not control a union's picketing of six service stations for informational purposes seeking consumer boycotting of the gasoline refined by Dow Chemical Company. The Board reasoned that the impact on receipts of the six service stations selling the gasoline was more than minimal. The appellate court disagreed, holding that the lawfulness of consumer picketing, arguably protected by the First Amendment, cannot depend on the portion of revenues that the struck product constitutes of the neutral retailer's total business.[41] Apparently, the Supreme Court agreed with the NLRB, remanding the case to it to deal with unspecified intervening circumstances.[42]

It is clear that not all peaceful consumer picketing at secondary sites is illegal. *Tree Fruits* permits consumer secondary boycotts of a limited variety. *Steelworkers Local 14055* seems to have added the restriction of considering the impact that boycotting a single item might have on a neutral retailer's total receipts. A minimal impact, however "minimal" is interpreted, is required. Total boycotts against secondary retailers remain illegal even if the struck product is the only one sold by the store.

The Supreme Court placed limits on *Tree Fruits* in its *NLRB* v. *Retail Store Employees,* decided in 1980. This case, also called *Safeco,* brought considerable uncertainty to union decisions to picket secondary sites advocating boycotts of a primary product.[43] The economic impact or extent of loss that picketing would have on the secondary employer became a new standard that would have to be assessed when picketing was undertaken at secondary sites. The standard of extent of loss was not involved in *Tree Fruits,* where the standard was the identity of the boycotted product to the picketed firm. The new standard places greater limits on union boycotts of employers' products at secondary locations than was the trend prior to the 1980 decision. In addition to picketing Safeco's office, strikers also picketed and passed out handbills outside the offices of five land title companies. The five companies obtained 90 percent of their business from the sale of Safeco insurance policies. It will be recalled that the law permits a union to engage in consumer picketing at the site of a secondary employer if the picketing is directed only at the struck product. A union is not allowed to appeal to the public at the secondary site not to trade at all with the secondary employer. The fact that the five title companies depended on Safeco policies for 90 percent of their business led the Supreme Court to hold that "the union's secondary appeal against the central product sold by the title companies is reasonably calculated to persuade customers not to patronize the neutrals at all." Thus, a union that desires to picket a central product at a secondary site will be required to calculate whether the primary product makes up such a substantial proportion of the firm's business that the Board and courts will not approve of the action.

Unfair Lists

A union device often used to put economic pressure on employers with whom disputes exist is the *unfair list.* This list is circulated among the members of various local and national unions, urging them not to buy particular goods or services. The desired result is to induce consumers and secondary employers to cease doing business with struck employers so long as the dispute lasts. It is often asserted that unfair lists constitute secondary boycott activity, unless they clearly state that they are not designed to induce neutrals to cease all transactions with primary employers.[44]

As early as 1949, the NLRB held that the mere placing of a primary employer's name on an unfair list and circulating the list among other locals did not induce secondary employees to withhold labor from neutral employers. Even if some employees of other employers withhold their services, it cannot be deemed the intent of unions using unfair lists to accomplish this end.[45] Members of other locals are merely encouraged not to purchase a struck employer's product. Other items on sale in retail stores, for example, are not in question and as such the secondary employer may feel little if any economic pressure as a result of the list.

Unfair lists merely provide a means for unions to publicize labor disputes. The list is a traditional device for accomplishing this objective. Neither Taft-Hartley nor the subsequent 1959 amendments outlawed its use and, until specific language is provided by Congress to do so, the device is legal.[46]

There is no evidence to support any contention that unfair lists are very effective even among union members. Some ardent members may follow the advice given by unions not to purchase certain goods and services, but most may not. Further, it may well be that most individuals with longstanding union membership would be hard pressed to name even one unfair employer, with the possible exception of J. P. Stevens, identified on any union unfair list circulated at any time during the past twenty years. The NLRB has not opened a secondary boycott loophole by permitting unfair lists, since there is no evidence Congress intended to outlaw their use.

Products Produced Aspect of Publicity Exemption

Another aspect of the amended secondary boycott section provides that where the primary employer is the producer of a product, and that product is distributed by a secondary employer, the union may truthfully publicize that fact by means other than picketing, so long as the publicity does not affect the performance of services at the establishment of the secondary employer. The NLRB has construed this provision in such a manner that widespread criticism of the agency has resulted. The basis of the criticism is that the Board provides an economic construction of the term *products produced,* and does not regard it in the sense that the primary employer must produce a physical product, such as an automobile. Instead, the Board holds that the primary employer produces a product for purposes of the publicity section by providing a service to the secondary employer.

In 1961, the *Lohman Sales, Middle South Broadcasting,* and *Great Western* cases came before the Board for interpretation of this proviso.[47] All three cases resulted in a determination that unions had the statutory right to name neutral companies on handbills.

In *Lohman,* the primary employer with whom a labor dispute existed was Lohman Sales Company, a distributor. The Teamsters struck the company and then proceeded to pass out handbills in front of several drugstores to inform the public that these stores distributed items produced by a struck employer. The Board held that the wholesaler, Lohman, produced a product, and thus distributing handbills around the drugstores was lawful. The products produced by Lohman Sales were deemed the candy and cigarettes it distributed. Essentially, the NLRB took this position because the distributor applied its labor to the product, which added value to it. Services constitute a part of a product, since the national income accounts consider services at all stages of production and distribution in calculating final value.

This interpretation was carried over to the *Middle South Broadcasting* case. A union had a dispute with a radio station. A blacklist with the names of several firms that advertised over the station was circulated. One of the firms listed was an automobile agency that advertised over the Middle South station. The Board overruled an administrative law judge to hold that the radio station was a producer of the products it advertised. The Board justified its position by stating that

> as found in [Lohman Sales], labor is the prime requisite of one who "produces" and therefore an employer who applies his labor to a product, whether of an abstract or physical nature, or in the initial or intermediate stages of the marketing of the product, is one of the "producers" of the product.

Value is added at each stage of production, from supplying a firm through manufacturing a product, and ultimately to final sales.

The Board utilized this same argument to uphold a union's action in a case involving a television station. The same criteria for product produced were used. The NLRB position was not sustained when presented to the Ninth Circuit Court of Appeals in the *Servette* case, but was later adopted by the U.S. Supreme Court upon review.[48] In economic terms, the Board and the Supreme Court are correct. Value is added to a product at each stage of production and distribution. In this regard, there is no loophole in secondary boycott prohibitions, since the proper use of economic terms would logically lead to this conclusion. However, if Congress intended that "products produced" refers exclusively to physical products, it could be argued that the NLRB and the courts created a loophole in the 1959 amendment.

In another case involving the publicity exemption, the Supreme Court held that it was unlawful for a union to use handbills to persuade consumers to boycott products of all stores in a shopping mall just because a department store was being built there by a contractor that the union claimed was paying substandard wages.[49] The Court agreed with the union that the department store was distributing a product produced by the contractor. Reversing the NLRB and a federal appeals court, however, the high court held that other stores in the shopping mall were not distributing a product produced by the contractor. Previously the NLRB and the federal appeals court had ruled that the owner of the shopping mall and other stores would benefit from the construction of the department store in the sense that more consumers would be attracted to shop there. Since this was the case, the publicity provision covered all stores. Refusing to accept that reasoning, the Court said neither the owner nor the other stores had a business relationship to the contractor in the sense that they distributed a product produced by it.

HOT-CARGO AGREEMENTS

Section 8 (e) of the amended Taft-Hartley Act makes it an unfair labor practice for an employer and a union to enter into any contract or agreement, express or implied, whereby such employer ceases or refrains, or agrees to cease or refrain, from handling, using, selling, transporting, or otherwise dealing in any of the products of any other employer, or to cease doing business with any other employer, or to cease doing business with any other person. *Hot-cargo agreements* refer to those made by an employer and union whereby it is promised that goods declared as unfair by the labor organization will not be handled by the company. Usually, unfair goods refer to those produced by nonunion shops. These agreements are considered effective in union attempts to organize nonunion employers. The arrangement has been used by unions for a considerable period of time and is considered highly effective in invoking economic pressure on nonunionized companies.

Originally, the NLRB held that not only may a union and employer execute a contract wherein the firm agrees not to handle work declared unfair, but that the labor organization could also apply economic pressure to enforce it.[50] Such action was deemed permissible despite the secondary boycott prohibitions of Taft-Hartley. However, new Board personnel changed the prior position and ruled in 1955 that hot-cargo agreements could be executed, but that unions could not engage in prohibited secondary boycott activity to enforce the arrangement.[51] The Supreme Court upheld this position in 1958 in the *Sand Door* case.[52]

Landrum-Griffin amendments to Taft-Hartley make hot-cargo arrangements unlawful throughout all industry except clothing and construction. Such agreements may not be made—either written or oral.

Attempts to Circumvent the Law

Some unions have been very active in attempts to get around the provisions of the 1959 law. Soon after the Taft-Hartley amendments became effective on November 13, 1959, a union attempted to circumvent the restrictions by obtaining a "Refusal to Handle" clause in the labor agreement. This required an employer to agree that it would not discharge or discipline any employee because he refused to work on nonunion or struck goods. The Board held that such clauses were an attempt to evade the law, and as such were illegal.[53]

A "struck work" clause was also included in the case, which bound the employer not to assist or handle work from any employer on strike. This would have meant that any work of a struck employer, including that normally performed, would be prohibited. The Board held this language illegal because of its broad implications. The area of industrial conflict would be widened if such a clause had been permitted to stand.

In another case before the Board, a contractual clause forbade subcontracting to other employers of any work unless their employees "enjoy the same or greater wages" as the companies that were parties to the agreement paid.[54] The Board held the clause illegal because it went further than merely restricting subcontracting "for the purpose of the preservation of jobs and job rights of the unit employees." This type of clause was viewed as an attempt to prohibit an employer from doing business with another firm, and as such violated the law.

Thus, the NLRB has been steadfast in preventing unions from subverting the prohibitions against hot-cargo arrangements. It has carefully reviewed such clauses in the light of the intent of Congress and has repeatedly struck down subterfuges designed to circumvent the hot-cargo proscription. The ingenuity of unions has not been so sharp as to delude the Board into believing that violations did not exist.

CONSTRUCTION AND CLOTHING INDUSTRY EXEMPTION

Congress extended special privileges to labor unions operating in the construction and clothing industries. This policy was motivated by the peculiarities of these industries.

In a qualification to Section 8 (e), the anti–hot-cargo provision, the law states that "nothing in this section shall apply to an agreement between a labor organization and an employer in the construction industry relating to the contracting or subcontracting of work to be done at the site of the construction, alteration, painting, or repair of a building, structure or other work." Several important problems are involved in this exemption. One concerns the interpretation of the phrase "at the site." May an employer and a construction union lawfully execute a hot-cargo arrangement for work that could be done at the site, or does the exemption apply only to work actually done at the site of construction?

A source of the problem is that in the construction industry, certain work could be done either at the site, or in firms located off the construction site. These off-site shops are frequently owned by employers not involved in the actual construction of the building site. Some work—such as the threading, bending, or fabrication of pipe, for example—could be done either in the shop or at the construction site. One of the Senate members of the Conference Committee debating the Landrum-Griffin changes of Taft-Hartley stated that the exemption was meant to apply to any work that "could be" done at the construction site.[55] Against this position, however, there is substantial evidence that the exemption was to apply only to work actually done at the site.

In 1963, the Board gave attention to the issue. It ruled that the hot-cargo exemption applies only to work done at the site.[56] Otherwise, the NLRB held, a subcontractor that performs work away from the site would be effectively deprived of its contract to fulfill a work assignment. A supplier of materials to an employer at the site was deemed the primary target of the union's conduct, which constituted secondary action. Thus, nonunion labor may perform work off the site at lower wages, even though the work could be done at the site. Contract clauses that attempt to cover subcontractor operations away from the site were found unlawful. This policy reflects the intent of Congress when the exemption was granted to the construction industry. When this issue was being debated in the Senate, then Senator John Kennedy stated:

> It should be particularly noted that the proviso relates only to the contracting or subcontracting of work to be done at the site of construction. The proviso does not cover boycotts of goods manufactured in an industrial plant for installation at the job site, or suppliers who do not work at the job site.

On the other hand, in 1982, a unanimous U.S. Supreme Court held that it is lawful for construction unions and employers to negotiate a clause that required a general contractor to subcontract work at any of its sites only to employers who recognized the union.[57] Upholding an NLRB decision on this issue, the high court rejected the employer's argument that the exemption only applied to a particular job site where both union and nonunion workers may be employed. As long as the hot-cargo clause was adopted in the normal course of collective bargaining, such provisions may lawfully apply to all job sites of the general contractor. In this way the high court distinguished *Woelke & Romero Framing* from its *Connel* decision issued in 1975. Recall that in that case, the Supreme Court held unions violated the antitrust laws when they demanded a subcontract clause limiting work to employers who recognized the union. However, unlike *Woelke & Romero Framing,* the union in *Connel* did not have a bargaining relationship with the general contractor and did not seek to represent its employees.

Unions and employers in the clothing industry may lawfully negotiate a hot-cargo provision limiting subcontracts to employers who recognized the union. This exception was adopted to prevent clothing manufacturers from subcontracting work to so-called "sweat shops" where substandard labor conditions prevail.

Strikes to Obtain and Enforce Hot-Cargo Clauses

In addition, within the clothing industry, no doubt exists as to the right of unions to use economic force to secure and enforce hot-cargo provisions. Given the language of Section 8 (e), however, the right of construction unions to use strikes and picketing to obtain and enforce hot-cargo provisions remains somewhat unsettled. At the outset, the NLRB held that unions in the construction industry were forbidden to use economic pressure to obtain or enforce agreements to cease doing business with nonunion contractors.[58] However, federal appeals courts have consistently held that construction unions may strike and picket to secure hot-cargo provisions, though courts have also held that it is not legal to use economic pressure to enforce such provisions.[59] This principle was explained fully in a court case involving the issue:

> Secondary subcontracting clauses in the construction industry are lawful, under the proviso to Section 8 (e), and economic force may be used to obtain them notwithstanding Section 8 (b) (4) (A), because Section 8 (b) (4) (A) incorporates that proviso by reference. But under Section 8 (b) (4) (B) such secondary clauses may be enforced only through lawsuits, and not through economic action. . . .[60]

The language used by Congress in Section 8 (e) prompted the courts to construe the proviso as they did. Congress referred to the third qualification of the hot-cargo clause as "nothing in this Act shall prohibit the enforcement of any agreement that is within *the foregoing exception.*" The exception referred to has been interpreted to include the clothing industry, but not the construction industry.

At this writing, the Supreme Court has still not ruled whether construction unions may use force to secure hot-cargo provisions. In *Woelke & Romero Framing,* the employer argued that even if the subcontract clause in question was legal, unions could not strike or picket to force contractors to agree to such a provision. However, the high court refused to deal with this issue, saying that the employer involved did not raise the issue when the case was before the NLRB.

Preservation of Bargaining-Unit Work

The Board has long held with court approval that a union strike to preserve bargaining-unit work does not violate the secondary boycott prohibitions even though there may be consequences for neutral employers.[61] Work "historically and regularly" performed by employees is not involved in the secondary boycott proscription if a labor organization attempts to force an employer to abide by a contractual clause to preserve bargaining-unit work.[62]

In the *National Woodwork* case, the NLRB and Supreme Court sustained the right of unions to enforce work-preservation clauses.[63] The carpenters' union had a clause in its contract that provided that union members would not handle or install prefitted doors. That is, the labor agreement provided that only the carpenters on the site would fit the doors with the necessary hardware. Hence the union and the contractor agreed that such work fell under the jurisdiction of the union. It was a work-preservation clause. A strike was called to enforce the clause after the contractor purchased prefitted doors and the carpenters refused to install them.

The NLRB ruled in *National Woodwork* that a product boycott taken to enforce a work-preservation clause did not violate the hot-cargo or secondary boycott provisions of amended Taft-Hartley. The Board reasoned that union action was taken to preserve bargaining-unit work for members of the construction union, and was not aimed at the suppliers of the prefabricated product. This was deemed legal even though the effect was to force the contractor to boycott the products of suppliers.

The Supreme Court in a 5–4 decision upheld the NLRB position. Thus, the work-preservation doctrine of the Board and Supreme Court recognizes that a literal reading of the boycott prohibitions of Taft-Hartley would render unions helpless in attempts to protect bargaining-unit work at the job site. The Court reasoned that the clause was included in the contract for the sole benefit of bargaining-unit members, and was not directed against a secondary employer. The strike was provoked by the employer's unilateral decision to purchase prefabricated doors in violation of a collective bargaining agreement designed to protect the traditional job-site work of craft workers against the inherent danger of factory-fitted building materials. There is no doubt that this interpretation may well slow down efforts to utilize new and improved materials and methods of production. However, unions must also be given the opportunity to attempt by use of economic pressure to prevent unilateral decisions to subcontract traditional work. A failure to distinguish between primary and secondary activity could indeed lead to a demise of union action that other portions of the same law purport to protect. There is no absolute union right to preserve bargaining-unit work, but a labor organization's right should be protected in order to enable it to bargain effectively on problems vital not only to its existence, but to the jobs of members as well. The *National Woodwork* case permits strikes to preserve bargaining-unit work and as such, is an important exception to the secondary boycott and hot-cargo prohibitions found in the amended Taft-Hartley Act. Appropriately written work-preservation clauses are permissible in general industry as well as in construction.

Right-of-Control Test

The practical significance of *National Woodwork,* however, is related to the so-called "right-of-control" test that the NLRB stressed in the case. In the precedent case, the employer had the right to use either prefitted or unfitted doors. Thus, it controlled the kind of product that could be used. When the employer has no option as to the kind of product to be used, the NLRB has held that employees may not refuse to install the product called for by job specifications. In short, the right-of-control test establishes that if an employer controls the use of prefabricated products, union pressure tactics to stop use of the product are lawful. But if the owner of the building or general contractor specified a prefabricated product, the employer lacks control of its use and union pressures directed at it constitute illegal secondary boycott activity.

It is easy to see why the right-of-control test is significant in establishing the potential value of *National Woodwork.* To get around this decision, prefabricated materials could be specified in construction contracts. For example, the builder's architect could establish that prefitted doors be used. Under the right-of-control test, the employees assigned to the installation of the doors could not refuse to install them because their employer has no control over what kind of doors may be used. In fact, should the NLRB right-of-control test prevail, much of the protection that construction workers receive from *National Woodwork* would be lost. On the other hand, under this test, economies in construction could be realized by the use of prefabricated products. In this respect, an attorney for the Associated General Contractors warned that if the right-of-control test is abandoned, "You'll see housing costs go higher, since cheaper prefabricated material would be kept off the market."[64]

The Supreme Court approved the right-of-control doctrine for the first time in 1977, in *Plumbers, Local 638.*[65] In doing so, it limited the right of construction unions to enforce agreements containing work-preservation clauses. Furthermore, the decision makes it more difficult for construction unions and employers to negotiate solutions to disputes arising out of technological change, bringing with it greater reliance on prefabricated materials that might eliminate or diminish jobs at the site of construction. A negotiated work-preservation clause can be avoided by a subcontractor who merely permits a general contractor to specify that a different type of material or equipment must be used. Should a union refuse to install the equipment or use the material because it violates their agreement, such refusal is considered to be secondary, with the general contractor the illegal target. The *Plumbers* decision can be interpreted to mean that a union has a right to negotiate a work-preservation clause under *National Woodwork*, but it has only a limited right to enforce it, depending on how the Board and courts interpret the right-of-control doctrine.

Language Must Be Specific

For a work-preservation clause to be valid, the language must be specific, and not written in a way to accomplish objectives other than preserving work traditionally performed by employees. Also, a work-preservation clause will not protect union conduct if it is used in a manner other than to protect unit work. Two cases demonstrate these two conditions. In one case, the clause stated "all work . . . will be done on material, equipment, and apparatus owned by the Employer." The union argued that this clause preserved work for employees because ownership of the equipment would facilitate the contractor's control of the work assignments. In finding this provision invalid, the Board held that the language was too broad, aimed primarily at the ownership of equipment and not at work to be done at the job site.[66] In the second case, union conduct was held to be illegal in its use of the following clause: "All merchandise for resale which is delivered to a retail outlet owned by the Employer . . . shall be delivered from the warehouses of the Employer covered by the Collective Bargaining Agreement." The union involved used this clause to prevent retail outlets from purchasing soft drinks directly from a soft drink firm. In holding the union action illegal, the Board found that the provision was not being used to preserve work, but rather to force the employees of the soda pop companies to join the Teamsters union.[67] In the case, the Board was not impressed with the union's argument that its conduct did not cause the employer to terminate completely its business relationship with the soda pop company. By changing the point of delivery, the Board held that this would mean that the soda pop company would be required to reduce the number of its drivers. As the Supreme Court has held, Taft-Hartley does not require a union to demand a complete cessation of business before a secondary boycott violation can be found.[68]

In any event, the *National Woodwork* doctrine has been bitterly criticized in many circles. The criticisms became more intense as the doctrine was applied to several products. Work-preservation clauses protected employees against the installation of prefabricated fireplaces,[69] precut steel bands,[70] and prefitted boilers.[71] As stated, the controversy involves job protection as against economy in construction. Ignoring employee concern for their jobs, the *Wall Street Journal* remarked:

If the labor unions, with the labor board's help, continue successfully to plumb these depths of inefficiency, the outlook for even minor economies in construction seems very dim too. If their theories are sound, they ought to go all the way and come out foursquare for making things like nails by hand.[72]

SUMMARY

Considerable attention has been directed by the Board and the courts to the various secondary boycott issues that come before them. It is often charged that they have opened up loopholes in the secondary boycott sections of the Act that Congress clearly intended to close and prohibit. Close examination of the entire law does not support such a conclusion. The major problem facing the Board and the courts is to distinguish between primary and prohibited secondary pressures.

Congress did not intend to outlaw primary strikes and picketing, but this could be the actual result if all the secondary consequences that inevitably follow from pressures placed on employers with whom a dispute exists are prohibited.

The regulatory bodies must strike a balance between the right of unions to exert effective economic pressure to achieve their goals, and the right of neutral employers to escape incidental pressure, which may derive from the primary action. It appears that the publicity provisos to the secondary boycott section of the Act were constructed broadly enough by Congress to permit unions to continue to act in their own self-interest. It may well be that some of the decisions set forth by the Board have been somewhat unrealistic regarding the conditions that prevail in a particular industry. For example, the rule that unions in the construction industry may picket to obtain hot-cargo clauses, but may not do so to enforce them, does not appear reasonable. An exception to this policy is permissible when preservation of bargaining-unit work is an issue. Perhaps it would be more realistic to permit either both to occur, or neither.

Regardless of the merits of Board and court action, if there are inconsistencies between their decisions and the will of Congress, it was Congress that created a jungle of highly inconsistent provisions, and not the interpreting and enforcement authorities. Broad congressional language that is both workable and equitable must be developed. After all, the basic public policy continues to be to protect and encourage the institution of collective bargaining. The Board and the courts have the responsibility to do just that.

DISCUSSION QUESTIONS

1. Define a secondary boycott.

2. What did Congress intend in its secondary boycott language provided in the Taft-Hartley Act?

3. Discuss the secondary boycott loopholes that developed after the 1947 law was passed.

4. Why was the ally doctrine excluded from the secondary boycott provisions in 1947 and again in 1959?

5. Compare the loopholes of the *Carolina Lumber* and *Servette* cases.

6. When may unions picket at common sites, and when are they unable to legally do so?

7. Compare the permissible picketing rights provided by the *Tree Fruits* case to the limits imposed by the *Safeco* case.

8. Discuss the interpretation applied to the products produced aspect of the publicity exemption in the context of whether or not the interpretation opens a loophole that permits a greater range of secondary boycott activity.

9. Why do you think that Congress excepted the clothing and construction industries from its hot-cargo provision?

10. Compare the Supreme Court's decision in *Woelke & Romero Framing* to its *Connel* decision. What impact do you expect each to have on a union's ability to negotiate hot-cargo clauses?

11. What is the current policy on the right of construction unions to strike and picket to obtain and enforce hot-cargo provisions?

12. Use the *National Woodwork* and the *Plumbers, Local 638* cases to illustrate the extent to which unions may negotiate and enforce bargaining-unit work-preservation clauses.

NOTES

1   Felix Frankfurter and Nathan Greene, *The Labor Injunction* (New York: The Macmillan Company, 1930), p. 43.

2   *Legislative History,* Taft-Hartley Act, p. 1106.

3   *Hearings Before Committee on Education and Labor,* on H.R. 115, 83d Congress, 1st sess., 1953, p. 3441.

4   Melvin J. Segal, "Secondary Boycott Loopholes," *Labor Law Journal,* X, 3 (March 1959) p. 175.

5   61 Stat. 151 (1947).

6   61 Stat. 140 (1947).

7   *Legislative History,* Landrum-Griffin Act, p. 1431.

8   Section 8 (b) (4) (B) in part makes it an unfair labor practice for a union to induce a work stoppage in order to force a secondary employer to cease doing business with a primary employer.

9   95 Congressional Record 8709 (1947).

10   *AFL-CIO Brewery Workers Union (Adolph Coors Company),* 121 NLRB 35 (1958).

11   *Graphic Arts International Union and Kable Printing Co.,* 225 NLRB 186 (1976).

12   *Douds* v. *Metropolitan Federation of Architects,* 75 F. Supp. 672 (S. D. N. Y., 1948).

13   *Longshoremen* v. *Allied International, Inc.,* 454 U.S. 814 (1982).

14   *NLRB* v. *International Rice Milling Company,* 341 U.S. 665 (1951).

15   181 F. (2d) 21 (CA 5, 1950).

16   *Texas Industries,* 112 NLRB 923 (1955).

17   *NLRB* v. *Brewery Workers* 272 F. (2d) 817 (1959).

18   *Carolina Lumber Company*, 130 NLRB 148 (1961).

19   *NLRB* v. *Servette, Inc.*, 337 U.S. 46 (1964).

20   *Radio Artists, Washington-Baltimore Local* v. *NLRB*, CA DC No. 24, 641 (April 17, 1972).

21   Hearings before the Subcommittee on Separation of Powers, *Congressional Oversight of Administrative Agencies (National Labor Relations Board)*, Part II (1968), p. 1146.

22   *CIO-Oil Workers (Pure Oil Company, Toledo Refining Division)*, 84 NLRB 315 (1949).

23   *CIO-Electrical Workers (Ryan Construction Company)*, 85 NLRB 417 (1949).

24   Bernard Marcus, "Secondary Boycotts," in *Symposium on the Labor-Management Reporting and Disclosure Act of 1959*, ed. Ralph Slovenko (Baton Rouge, Louisiana: Claitor's Bookstore Publishers, 1961), pp. 826–827.

25   *Local 36, International Chemical Workers Union, AFL-CIO* v. *NLRB*, 47 LRRM 2493, cert. denied 366 U.S. 949 (1961).

26   *Local 761, I.U.E. (General Electric Co.)* v. *NLRB*, 366 U.S. 667 (1961); *United Steelworkers (Carrier Corp.)* v. *NLRB*, 376 U.S. 492 (1964).

27   *Building and Construction Trades Council of New Orleans (Markwell and Hartz)*, 155 NLRB 319 (1965), enf. 387 F. (2d) 79 (5th Cir. 1967), cert. denied 391 US 914 (1968).

28   *International Union of Operating Engineers, Local 450 (Linbeck Construction Corp.)*, 219 NLRB 997 (1975).

29   *Sailors' Union of the Pacific (Moore Dry Dock Company)*, 92 NLRB 547 (1950), 366 U.S. 667.

30   *AFL-Teamsters, Local 67 (Washington Coca-Cola Bottling Works, Inc.)*, 107 NLRB 299 (1953) enf. granted 220 F. (2d) 380 (CA DC, 1955).

31   *Plauche Electric*, 135 NLRB 250 (1963).

32   *Schultz Refrigerated Service*, 87 NLRB 502 (1949).

33   *AFL-Teamsters, Local 67, op. cit.*

34   *Carrier Corporation*, 132 NLRB 127 (1961).

35   *United Steelworkers of America* v. *NLRB*, 376 U.S. 492 (1964).

36   See, for example, *Highway Truck Drivers & Helpers, Local 107, IBT (Riss & Company)*, 130 NLRB 943 (1960).

37   29 U.S.C.S. 158 (b) (4).

38   *Upholsterers Frame & Bedding Workers Twin City Local 61 (Minneapolis House Furnishings Company)*, 132 NLRB 40 (1961).

39   *NLRB* v. *Fruit & Vegetable Packers & Warehousemen, Local 760, et al. (Tree Fruits, Inc.)*, 377 U.S. 58 (1964).

40   *Honolulu Typographical Union No. 37* v. *NLRB*, 167 NLRB 150 (CA DC, 1968).

41   *Steelworkers, Local 14055* v. *NLRB*, 524 F. (2d) 853 (1975).

42   *NLRB* v. *Steelworkers, Local 14055*, 429 U.S. 807 (1976).

43   *NLRB v. Retail Store Employees Union, Local 1001*, 444 U.S. 1011 (1980).

44   Hearings before the Subcommittee on Separation of Powers, *Congressional Oversight of Administrative Agencies (National Labor Relations Board)*, Part II (1968), p. 1151. The controversy deals with Section 8 (b) (4) (A).

45   *Grauman Company*, 87 NLRB 755 (1949).

46   *Western, Inc.*, 93 NLRB 336 (1951).

47   *Local 537, Teamsters (Lohman Sales Company)*, 132 NLRB 901 (1961); *Local 662, Electrical Workers (Middle South Broadcasting Company)*, 133 NLRB 1968 (1961); *Television & Radio Artists (Great Western Broadcasting Corporation)*, 134 NLRB 1617 (1961).

48   *Local 848, Wholesale Delivery Drivers & Salesmen (Servette, Inc.)*, 133 NLRB 1501, 310 F. (2d) 659 (9th Cir., 1962), 337 U.S. 46 (1964).

49   *DeBartolo Corp.* v. *NLRB*, 463 U.S. 147 (1983).

50   *Conway's Express*, 87 NLRB 972 (1949), affirmed, *Rabouin* v. *NLRB*, 195 F. (2d) 906 (2d Cir., 1952).

51   *Local 1976, United Brotherhood of Carpenters (Sand Door & Plywood Company)*, 113 NLRB 1211 (1955), enforced *NLRB* v. *Local 1976*, 241 F. (2d) 147 (9th Cir., 1957), affirmed 357 U.S. 93 (1958).

52   *United Brotherhood of Carpenters & Joiners* v. *NLRB*, 357 U.S. 93 (1958).

53   *Brown* v. *Local No. 17, Amalgamated Lithographers of America (Employing Lithographers Division)*, 180 F. Supp. 294 (DCN, Calif.), 1960.

54   *Meat & Highway Drivers, Local 710 (Wilson & Company)*, 143 NLRB 1221 (1964).

55   45 *Labor Relations Reporter* 132 (1959).

56   *Ohio Valley Carpenters District Council (Cardinal Industries)*, 144 NLRB 91 (1963).

57   *Woelke & Romero Framing* v. *NLRB*, 956 U.S. 645 (1982).

58   *Construction, Production & Maintenance Laborers Union Local 383 (Colson & Stevens Construction Company)*, 137 NLRB 1650 (1963).

59   323 F. (2d) 422 (1964).

60   *Building & Construction Trades Council of San Bernadino* v. *NLRB*, 328 F. (2d) 540 (1964).

61   The proviso to Section 8 (b) (4) (B) reads: "Provided, that nothing contained in this clause (B) shall be construed to make unlawful, where not otherwise unlawful, any primary strike or primary picketing." See *International Association of Heat & Frost Insulators (Houston Insulation Contractors Association)*, 148 NLRB 866, sustained 386 U.S. 664 (1967).

62   *Local 1332, ILA (Philadelphia Marine Trade Association)*, 151 NLRB 1447 (1965).

63   *National Woodwork Manufacturers Association* v. *NLRB*, 386 U.S. 612 (1967).

64   *Wall Street Journal,* June 26, 1972.

65   *Plumbers, Local 638* v. *NLRB*, 429 U.S. 507 (1977).

66   *IBEW, Local 1186 (Pacific General Contractors)*, 192 NLRB 254 (1971).

67   *Teamsters, Local 688 (Schnuck Markets)*, 193 NLRB 701 (1971).

68   *NLRB* v. *Operating Engineers, Local 825*, 400 U.S. 297 (1971).

69   *Bricklayers & Stone Masons, Local 8 (California Concrete Systems)*, 180 NLRB 43 (1969).

70   *Houston Insulation Contractors Association*, 148 NLRB 866 (1966).

71   *American Boiler Manufacturers Association*, 167 NLRB 602 (1967).

72   *Wall Street Journal,* October 27, 1967.

CHAPTER EIGHTEEN

STATE PICKETING POLICY
AND THE U.S. SUPREME COURT

Though we have considered in some detail the right of employees to picket under the Taft-Hartley Act, there is another feature of the law of picketing that warrants attention. This deals with the rights of the states to establish picketing policy either by legislation or through their courts. The crux of this problem is that the U.S. Constitution and its free-speech guarantees apply to all citizens of the United States. For this reason, the United States Supreme Court has frequently tested state picketing policy in the light of the federal Constitution.

As this chapter demonstrates, the Court has not been wholly consistent in discharging this task. The chief reason for this is the Court's desire to accommodate a state policy as far as possible. Thus, the Court has the difficult problem of viewing with sympathy state efforts to regulate picketing, while at the same time assuring that the standards of the federal Constitution are not breached by state action.

THE THORNHILL DOCTRINE: BASIC MEANING

In 1940, the Supreme Court of the United States handed down a picketing decision of momentous importance. It held that peaceful picketing is a form of free speech entitled to the protection of the federal Constitution. This doctrine at first seemed entirely different from the one reflecting the mature judgment of the Court that Congress and the states may regulate the use of the injunction in labor disputes. In the Norris–La Guardia cases, the Court had held that the legislative branch of government may properly shield the picketing process from injunctions. It fully approved the limitation of the authority of the Court in labor disputes, including those involving picketing. The 1940 innovation is that the free-speech guarantee of the Constitution also operates to protect the peaceful picketing process under certain circumstances from the effect of antipicketing laws fashioned by either the legislative or judicial branches of government. Now the Court seemingly was not only prepared to approve legislative action calculated to give protection to picketing, but was ready to strike down legislation that endeavored to unduly forbid or control picketing.

Picketing was identified with free speech by the Court in the celebrated *Thornhill* v. *Alabama* case.[1] The state of Alabama had passed a statute that outlawed all picketing. The statute did not distinguish between peaceful or violent picketing. It was not aimed at a particular form of picketing, such as the stranger or secondary boycott varieties. Rather, the provisions of the law applied to the general picketing process, outlawing completely this form of union activity. Violators of the statute were subject to fines and imprisonment.

In striking down this statute, the Court declared that

> freedom of speech and of the press guaranteed by the Constitution embraces at least the liberty to discuss publicly and truthfully all matters of public concern without previous restraint or fear of subsequent punishment. . . . In the circumstances of our times the dissemination of information concerning the facts of a labor dispute must be regarded as within that area of free discussion that is guaranteed in the Constitution.

Here indeed was a most significant pronouncement! It operated to shed constitutional doubt on all legislative action calculated to control the peaceful picketing process. Actually, considerable misinterpretation of the meaning of the *Thornhill* decision led to the immediate belief that the Court meant to invalidate every federal or state action regulating peaceful picketing. No such conclusion was warranted by the *Thornhill* decision. The Court held that picketing is a form of free speech. It did not say, however, that all picketing, regardless of form and objective, would be protected by the guarantees of the Constitution. In fact, the Court declared in the *Thornhill* case:

> The right of employers and employees to conduct their economic affairs and to compete with others for a share in the products of industry are subject to modification or qualification in the interests of the society in which they exist. This is but an instance of the power of the State to set the limits of permissible contest open to industrial combatants. It does not follow that the states in dealing with the evils arising from industrial dispute may impair the effective exercise of the right to discuss freely industrial relations which are matters of public concern.

This statement appears clear enough. Thus, the Court served notice that federal and state action restricting the picketing process must not infringe on the constitutional guarantee of free speech. At the same time, it conceded that states have the right to regulate the peaceful picketing process. To grasp subsequent picketing decisions of the Court, the basic meaning of the *Thornhill* doctrine must be kept in mind. In later cases, the Court allowed the regulation of peaceful picketing. Such action is not inconsistent with *Thornhill* v. *Alabama* if one understands the fundamental limitations of the decision.

STRANGER PICKETING AND THE FREE-SPEECH GUARANTEE

Subsequent to the *Thornhill* decision, the Supreme Court held that picketing was protected by the constitutional guarantee of free speech in several other cases. The first of these, the *Swing* case, was decided in 1941.[2] It so happened that an AFL labor union operating in Illinois claimed jurisdiction over beauty shops. It attempted to organize a particular beauty shop. Failing in its efforts, the union picketed Swing's shop. The picket line was of the stranger variety; that is, it included workers not employed by Swing. Displeased with these circumstances, Swing obtained an injunction from the Illinois courts to stamp out the picketing. The supreme court of the state upheld the injunction.

Upon review of the case, the Supreme Court of the United States declared that no court, state or federal, could suppress peaceful stranger picketing. Such restraint violated the free-speech guarantees of the federal Constitution. The injunction restraining stranger picketing was invalid because

> a state cannot exclude workingmen from peacefully exercising the right of free communication by drawing the circle of economic competition between employers and workers so small as to contain only an employer and those directly employed by him. The interdependence of economic interest of all engaged under the same industry has become commonplace.

Thus, in the *Swing* decision the Supreme Court shielded stranger picketing from the attack of legislative and court action. As a form of free speech, this type of picketing was privileged under the Constitution.

However, in 1957, the Supreme Court permitted the state of Wisconsin to enjoin peaceful stranger picketing contrary to its determined position of 1941.[3] In *Vogt,* a union picketed a gravel pit for the express purpose of organizing the employees. The workers indicated they did not want to join the union and a lower court enjoined the union action. The action was held unlawful under a state law prohibiting peaceful picketing from coercing employers to force workers to join unions.

The U.S. Supreme Court ruled therefore that a state may place a statutory ban on peaceful picketing that conflicts with its public policy. Both state courts and their legislatures may constitutionally declare stranger picketing a violation of public policy. Seemingly, the injunction may be used every time stranger picketing occurs. All that is necessary is for a court to declare it illegal when such cases arise, and to issue an injunction that specifically identifies the activity as contrary to public policy.

But, even in the absence of express legislative prohibition of picketing, state courts may take the initiative. The way is now paved for state courts dealing with cases under their jurisdictions to draw the circle of economic competition between employers and workers so small as to contain only an employer and those directly employed by him or her. Legislation at the state level would seemingly be required to control the courts in labor cases involved in intrastate commerce. They may also deal with cases rejected by administrative decree from coverage of the national labor laws. It will be recalled that this is permitted in accordance with the jurisdictional dollar guidelines of the NLRB.

It appeared for some time that specific enforcement of state public policy could lead to blanket prohibition of picketing, one situation at a time. Public policy would merely be established at the time a case reached the Court for its consideration. This direction in the high court's decisions seemed certain for a few years. Later in this chapter we shall see that this course was revised, apparently in the quest for equity in establishing constitutional rights of all parties involved in labor disputes.

THE NEW YORK CASES:
ABSENCE OF LABOR DISPUTE NOT CONTROLLING

In 1942 and 1943, the Supreme Court again utilized the constitutional guarantee of free speech to afford protection to the picketing process. The locale of both cases was the state of New York. The 1942 case, *Bakery & Pastry Drivers Union* v. *Wohl,* involved the picketing of a bakery drivers' union.[4] A number of employers of bakery wagon drivers engaged in activity calculated to decrease both their operating costs and the possibility of having to deal with unions. They wanted to avoid payment of social security taxes and worker's compensation as well as liability insurance and vehicle upkeep. To accomplish this objective, they forced some drivers to drop out of the union and to purchase the trucks that the employees were utilizing to make deliveries. The drivers were then expected to purchase the merchandise from their former employers and peddle the bakery goods on an independent basis. In effect, the tactics of the bakery owners made peddlers out of their employees. Experience soon proved that the "profits" that the newly created "businesspeople" earned by this arrangement fell far below the amount they had earned when they were mere "workers." Two of them, for example, earned only about $35 per week. In addition, they lost all protection of laws passed by Congress and the New York legislature calculated to protect the status of employees.

To prevent the spread of the peddler system, the bakery drivers' union conducted a widespread peaceful picketing campaign. The objective of the union was to stamp out this development before it undermined the economic standards of all the unionized employees. The union requested the peddlers to work only six days a week instead of seven and to hire an unemployed union member for the seventh day at wages of about $6 to $9 per day. Obviously, the peddlers could not afford to agree to the demands of their former union. They scarcely earned enough on a seven-day week to get along. When the peddlers refused to comply, the union picketed the area of the bakeries where two of the peddlers involved in the case purchased their bakery goods. The picketing placards bore the names of these peddlers and highlighted in an accurate fashion the nature of the controversy. At times, the union also ordered pickets to follow the trucks of the peddlers to induce customers not to buy from them. Actually, the peddlers felt the brunt of the union pressure, but the picketing tactics were fundamentally directed against the employers who for their own profit had introduced the peddler system.

The 1943 case, *Cafeteria Employees Union* v. *Angelos,* involved the peaceful picketing of two restaurants by a labor organization composed of cafeteria workers.[5] The owners of the restaurants ran their establishments without any union employees and were able to sell food at cheaper prices than the eating establishments hiring union employees. This was a situation that had to be rectified by the cafeteria workers' union lest the standards it had established in the organized restaurants be swept away. The objective of the picketing was to force the owners to hire union employees. The union appealed to the public to withhold patronage from the picketed restaurants.

In both of these cases, New York courts issued injunctions stamping out the picketing. The New York Court of Appeals, the highest court of the state, upheld the injunctions. It ruled that the New York anti-injunction act, patterned after Norris–La Guardia, did not protect the picketing from the injunction. The court held that no "labor dispute" existed within the meaning of the statute; therefore, the New York court could properly enjoin the picketing. The high court of New York rejected the union's argument that labor disputes did exist within the meaning of the state's anti-injunction statute.

Eventually, both cases were appealed to the Supreme Court of the United States. This Court did not quarrel with the state courts' interpretation of the New York anti-injunction law. The Supreme Court of the United States respected the interpretation placed on state laws by the state judiciary. However, the Supreme Court reversed both of the state courts' decisions on the ground that the picketing of the two unions was protected by the federal Constitution's guarantee of free speech. The employees obtained protection from the fundamental document of the nation, though the state courts felt that their picketing could be properly enjoined under state law. In short, the Supreme Court was not concerned with the manner in which the New York Court of Appeals construed the meaning of "labor dispute" for purposes of the state's anti-injunction law. It struck down the decisions because they infringed on guarantees contained in the federal Constitution.

The implications of the New York picketing cases were of crucial importance. The mere fact that a "labor dispute" prevailed under state law did not preclude the application of the free-speech guarantee to picketing. Once the Supreme Court holds the picketing to be protected by the Constitution, it is of no importance that under state law the activity can be restrained on the ground of the nonexistence of a labor dispute. Such picketing is protected under the immunities of free speech in the federal Constitution for, as the Court stated in the bakery drivers' case, "One need not be in a labor dispute as defined by state law to have a right under the Fourteenth Amendment to express a grievance in a labor matter unattended by violence, coercion, or conduct otherwise unlawful or oppressive." There is need to protect the union right to make known grievances to the public even if the cause is in accordance with law. The Court did not deny that states have the right to regulate peaceful picketing. It merely demonstrated its ability to decide when free speech is denied under the Fourteenth Amendment.

PEACEFUL PICKETING NOT PROTECTED BY THE GUARANTEE OF FREE SPEECH

Under certain circumstances, the Supreme Court will not utilize free-speech immunities to protect peaceful picketing from regulation by legislative and court action. Once again it must be stressed that this position of the Court is not inconsistent with the *Thornhill* doctrine. On the contrary, its refusal to hold all picketing beyond control supports the principle of the 1940 decision that the free-speech guarantee would not protect the picketing process under each and every circumstance that might arise.

Peaceful Picketing in a Context of Violence

On the same day that the Court handed down the *Swing* decision, it ruled that the free-speech guarantee of the Constitution is not available to protect picketing carried on in a context of violence.[6] The Chicago Milk Wagon Drivers' Union utilized violent tactics to prevent the Meadowmoor Dairies from utilizing the "vendor system" for the distribution of milk in the Chicago area. Under this system, milk was sold by the dairy companies to vendors, operating their own trucks, who sold to retailers. The vendors departed from the working standards achieved by the union for its members as dairy employees. To force the company to abandon the vendor system, the union instituted a campaign of terror that included window-smashing, bombing, arson, wrecking of trucks, shootings, and beatings. This violence was directed against the Meadowmoor Dairies and the retail outlets that handled its products. As part of its general program, the union also employed peaceful picketing in the vicinity of the stores handling Meadowmoor's products.

The Supreme Court of Illinois upheld an injunction that restrained all picketing conduct, peaceful or violent. All picketing, not merely the acts of violence, was enjoined. The milk wagon drivers' union appealed the case to the U.S. Supreme Court. The union argued that the state court had imposed a blanket denial of picketing, and contended further that the Illinois judiciary had denied the exercise of the right of free speech when it enjoined the peaceful picketing activities.

The union's position was rejected by the Supreme Court. It held that peaceful acts of picketing when enmeshed with concurrent violent conduct can be properly enjoined. The Court took due care to distinguish the instant case from the *Thornhill* and *Carlson*[7] decisions. It declared, "We do not qualify the *Thornhill* and *Carlson* decisions. We affirm them. They involved statutes boldly forbidding all picketing near an employer's place of business. Entanglement with violence was expressly out of those cases." Thus, peaceful picketing carried out in a general campaign of terror can be stamped out without violating the guarantee of free speech. Blanket injunctions may be issued to enjoin picketing undertaken in a context of violence.

In another case, a union official's photographing of persons crossing a picket line was not deemed coercive conduct equivalent to threatening physical violence.[8] In the *Newell* case, the Supreme Court referred to the free-speech doctrine of *Thornhill* in overturning a trial court decision that such photographing generated fear on the part of persons crossing the picket line that future violence would come to them. The context of violence was evidently not deemed sufficient to invoke the *Meadowmoor* doctrine as an exception to *Thornhill.*

In still another case, *Rainfair,* the Supreme Court was required to determine what was meant by *Meadowmoor*'s context of violence for the purpose of enjoining all future picketing. The *Rainfair* case involved both peaceful picketing at a plant engaged in interstate commerce and a segregated group of strikers involved in violent action.[9] The employer obtained a blanket injunction in an Arkansas court outlawing all future picketing on the grounds that violence was so enmeshed in peaceful picketing that no picketing at the plant could be free from violence.

The Supreme Court was not willing to permit the blanket enjoinment of all picketing. It found that the violence of the segregated group of strikers was not adequate justification for extending the injunction to the separate group of peaceful pickets. The state court was within its authority to deal specifically with illegal activity, but that did not include a blanket stoppage of all picketing. Furthermore, even if the violent action had warranted enjoinment of all future picketing, it could not be permanently stopped by a state court. That is because the NLRB preempts state courts from permanently enjoining any peaceful picketing unconnected with violence that is associated with some other group.

Thus, in the years after *Meadowmoor,* the Supreme Court has become more reluctant to permit blanket injunctions in cases involving peaceful picketing. There is greater reliance upon the *Thornhill* doctrine than seemed probable from the first few peaceful picketing cases immediately subsequent to its pronouncement.

The Area of the Industry

In 1942, the Supreme Court of the United States held that a state may confine peaceful picketing to the industry directly related to a labor dispute. This principle was established in *Carpenters & Joiners Union* v. *Ritter's Cafe.* [10] Even more than the *Meadowmoor* decision, the *Ritter* case demonstrates the fact that the legislative branch of government may regulate peaceful picketing. The carpenters' and painters' unions of Houston peacefully picketed the restaurant owned by a Mr. Ritter. The union had no dispute with Ritter in his role as proprietor of the café. No carpentry work was being performed at the restaurant at the time of the picketing. All of the restaurant employees were members of the Hotel and Restaurant Employees Union. There was no controversy between Ritter and his restaurant employees' union. Why then the picketing?

It so happened that Ritter had made an arrangement with a contractor named Plaster for the construction of a building. The contract gave Plaster the right to make his own arrangements regarding the hiring of employees. Plaster employed nonunion carpenters and painters. The new building was being constructed about a mile and a half from the picketed café, and was wholly unconnected with the business of Ritter as a café proprietor.

The reason for picketing the café should now be clear. By damaging Ritter's restaurant business, the union hoped to force him to make arrangements for the employment of union workers at the site of the other business. The facts show that the picketing was very effective. Union truck drivers refused to cross the picket line or deliver food or other supplies to the restaurant. The restaurant workers' union, out of sympathy with the carpenters' and painters' organizations, called Ritter's employees out on strike. In short, the picketing resulted in a curtailment of 60 percent of Ritter's restaurant business.

The Texas judiciary held that the peaceful picketing activities of the union were unlawful under state law. Accordingly, the union was enjoined from picketing Ritter's café. The injunction, however, forbade neither picketing elsewhere (including at the site of the new building under construction) nor communication of the facts of the dispute by any means other than the picketing of Ritter's restaurant.

Subsequently, the union appealed the matter to the Supreme Court of the United States. The union felt that its picketing activities were privileged under the free-speech guarantees of the federal Constitution. As such, state law could not be utilized to restrain the picketing of Ritter's café. It was not the task of the Supreme Court to determine whether the union had in effect violated Texas law. This question had already been answered in the affirmative by the Texas courts. As noted, the Supreme Court of the United States normally respects the construction that state courts place on state laws. This is a principle of constitutional law established early in the history of American jurisprudence. The problem facing the Supreme Court was to decide whether or not Texas law, as interpreted by the state judiciary, infringed on the free-speech guarantees of the Constitution.

The Court ruled that it did not. It held that free-speech immunities are not violated by a law that confines the peaceful picketing process to the industry directly involved in the dispute. Texas had the right to enjoin picketing of Ritter's restaurant because the picketing had been undertaken to win concessions in the construction industry. The union had improperly picketed beyond the area of the industry involved in the basic dispute. In short, the legislative branch of government could restrict peaceful picketing to the area of the industry in which a labor dispute arises.

The *Ritter* decision was criticized.[11] The basis of objection to the Court was the free-speech decision of *Thornhill* v. *Alabama.* Such criticism was not warranted, because the Court in the *Thornhill* decision did not state or imply that the legislative or judicial branch of government was without power to regulate peaceful picketing. *Ritter* would have been inconsistent if the Court had ruled in *Thornhill* v. *Alabama* that all peaceful picketing, regardless of form or objective, was entitled to the protection of the free-speech immunity. The fact is, however, that the Court did no such thing. It carefully pointed out in the *Thornhill* case that the state has the power "to set the limits of permissible contest open to industrial combatants." Among other things, a state may restrict peaceful picketing by requiring that it be undertaken with (1) a reasonable number of pickets, (2) quietness, and (3) truthful placards. Also, open ingress and egress to employer premises may be required, along with suitable hours for picketing action. It may be found, for example, that a union's right to publicize a labor dispute is not impaired by restricting the picketing to between the hours of 6:00 A.M. and 6:00 P.M.

Peaceful Picketing That Violates a State's Antitrust Law

In 1949, the Court again reaffirmed the principle that a state may regulate the peaceful picketing process.[12] The State Supreme Court of Missouri found that picketing by a labor union violated the state's antitrust laws. Unlike in the *Ritter* case, the picketing involved in the *Giboney* case took place in the area of the industry within which the labor dispute arose.

The Kansas City Ice and Coal Drivers Union undertook to organize all the peddlers of the city. The union claimed within its membership 160 of the 200 retail ice peddlers who drove their own trucks in selling ice from door to door in Kansas City. The objective of the union was to better the working conditions of all ice peddlers. However, most of the nonunion peddlers refused to join the organization.

To force them into the union, the organization attempted to obtain pledges from the Kansas City ice distributors not to sell ice to nonunion peddlers.

It obtained such agreement from all but one ice company, the Empire Storage and Ice Company. It was determined to sell ice to union and nonunion peddlers alike. As a result, the union picketed the premises of the company. Most of the truck drivers working for Empire's customers were members of the labor union. These union truck drivers refused to haul goods to or from Empire's place of business. Because of the picketing, Empire's business was reduced by about 85 percent. Faced with these circumstances, the company obtained an injunction under the provision of the state's antitrust laws to restrain the picketing.

The Supreme Court of Missouri held that the picketing was unlawful, and affirmed the injunction that stamped it out. The union appealed to the Supreme Court of the United States, claiming that its picketing activities were protected by the free-speech immunities of the federal Constitution. The Court rejected the union's position. It refused to apply the Constitution to shield the picketing from the application of the Missouri antitrust law. It pointed out that the picketing was part of an integrated plan calculated to violate a lawful purpose. Since the conduct was unlawful in objective, the constitutional guarantee of free speech could not be employed to legalize it. The Court declared that the pickets "were doing more than exercising a right of free speech or press. They were exercising their economic power together with that of their allies to compel Empire to abide by union rather than by state regulation of trade." Thus, unions cannot utilize the constitutional guarantee of free speech to protect picketing undertaken to violate the provision of a state's antitrust law.

It is a long-established principle of American jurisprudence that legislative action should be regarded as valid unless it is so bad on its face that there is no mistaking its unconstitutionality. Few would disagree with the inherent value of such a principle. Congress and state legislatures should have the utmost freedom in the shaping of public policy. In the field of labor relations, the courts should be particularly careful to allow the widest latitude to shape policy. The fundamental philosophy of Holmes should not be ignored. Likewise, one is impressed with the wisdom of Brandeis when he declared:

> The condition developed in industry may be such that those engaged in it cannot continue their struggle without danger to the community. But it is not for judges to determine whether such conditions exist, nor is it their function to set the limits of permissible conduct and to declare the duties which the new situation demands. This is the function of the legislature which, while limiting individual and group rights to aggression and defense, may substitute processes of justice for the more primitive method of trial by combat.[13]

For many years, the Supreme Court invalidated legislation passed by Congress and state legislatures calculated to improve the economic lot of the nation's workers. Statutes designed to protect the right to organize, to regulate the use of the injunction in labor disputes, and to impose minimum employment standards on industry failed to stand the test of constitutionality. These laws, however, are not prohibited by express provisions of the Constitution. The high court established their unconstitutionality only by resorting to their own ideas regarding how the economy should function. No provision of the Constitution denies to Congress or the states the right to pass legislation forbidding the discharge of a worker because of union activity. The Court therefore tends to permit the widest range of options to states when they deal with economic matters within their own jurisdictions.

In the case of antipicketing legislation, however, a different condition is attached. Specific constitutional provisions protect the right to free speech. Picketing transmits ideas, relays thoughts, and communicates concepts. As such, it falls within the embrace of the Constitution as a form of speech. Statutes that clearly and unmistakably suppress the picketing process transgress constitutional guarantees. Granting the unquestionable wisdom of a policy that allows the legislative arm of government wide freedom to determine the character of labor law, the fact remains that any statute, labor or otherwise, must necessarily fall if it is obviously prohibited by the express terms of the Constitution.

The Case of **Gazzam.**   The greatest point of significance resulting from the *Giboney* case was that peaceful picketing is not protected if it seeks an objective that is illegal under a valid state law. The *Gazzam* decision was based on this declaration involving the state of Washington's "little Norris–La Guardia Act."[14] This law makes it illegal for an employer to coerce employees in the designation of collective bargaining representatives.

A union organizer approached a small hotel operator and asked him to sign an agreement that would require his employees to join the labor organization. The request was refused; however, the employer did not interfere with the union's contacting workers. At a meeting of eleven workers with the union, nine voted against representation, one was neutral, and the other was not acceptable for membership. The union established a picket line to force the employer to yield to its demands. Since the hotel was small, it did not qualify for coverage under the National Labor Relations Act.

The employer in a Washington court filed a suit for damages and to obtain an injunction to halt picketing. The lower court granted the request. Subsequently, the Washington Supreme Court upheld the trial court decision. The U.S. Supreme Court was faced with the question of whether the First and Fourteenth Amendments permit a state to enjoin peaceful picketing on the basis of its own state policy.

The Court, as mentioned, relied upon the *Giboney* case to uphold the Washington Supreme Court. Prevention of peaceful picketing was held permissible if the injunction is "limited to the wrong being perpetrated, namely, 'an abusive exercise of the right to picket.' " Workers or organizations of workers have no more right to violate public policy than the judiciary has the right to interfere with certain worker rights. A specific violation of state law was enjoined, and there was no blanket attempt to ban all peaceful picketing. Thus, specific violations of peaceful picketing are enjoinable by injunctive use, but blanket restrictions constitute an undue violation of constitutional rights to free speech. The ability of states to regulate peaceful picketing is not restricted to legislation, but may be accomplished through common law.

Peaceful Picketing in Violation of Common Law

In 1950, the high court upheld the right of state courts to restrict peaceful picketing in violation of its public policy as established by common law.[15] A significant deviation was made from *Thornhill* in the *Hughes* case, which involved picketing of a grocery store by an association of black persons who requested the store to hire clerks of their race in proportion to the percentage that patronized the store. The store refused to honor the request, desiring to set hiring ratios by collective bargaining with the union with which it contracted. The black group picketed the Lucky Store and the operator went to court to obtain an injunction. It was granted, but peaceful picketing continued. The California Supreme Court upheld the trial court decision to issue a limited injunction covering a specific violation.

The U.S. Supreme Court upheld the decision of the California courts. It held that

> the fact that California's policy is expressed by the judicial organ of the state rather than by the legislature we have repeatedly ruled to be immaterial.

It is apparent that the high court permitted the California courts to establish their own policy to deal with peaceful picketing in a labor dispute. The *Giboney* case was used as a precedent for permitting the judges to behave as they did. But the *Swing* case was ignored. It will be recalled that it was established in this case that stranger picketing was protected by the federal Constitution. Evidently, hiring on the basis of quotas set by a union dominated by whites was permissible, but blacks could not picket peaceably to eliminate discrimination in hiring.[16] Nevertheless, judges were commissioned by the high court to set limits on peaceful picketing in accordance with their own views regarding how the economy should function.

Would the Supreme Court Return To Pre-Norris–La Guardia Picketing Objectives Policies?

Highly regarded legal scholars were concerned with the seeming return of the U.S. Supreme Court to its pre-1933 picketing doctrines.[17] There is no doubt that the courts have a constitutional responsibility to deal with changing socioeconomic problems as such problems come before the courts. By 1950, the country had not yet readjusted to union behavior that many citizens had considered economically abusive during and immediately after World War II. Perhaps the courts are often more in tune with current sentiment than the other two branches of government and constitutionally have authority to deal with problems that their coequals are too slow to recognize. It is certain that many problems that occur in the state of New York are not necessarily pressing in the states of Indiana and Arizona. The Supreme Court seemed almost determined in 1950 to uphold local courts when they were dealing with local policy of their own making. The particular reason for this remains open for speculation.

Two cases with identical issues were decided by the high court; both involved the policy of state of Washington courts. Hanke and Cline were self-employed used-car dealers in Seattle, Washington.[18] Both dealers were picketed by different unions because they refused to observe the hours of operation observed by organized dealers. Cline was requested additionally to hire a union member as sales agent and to compensate him with 7 percent of gross sales. Refusal to agree resulted in a loss of sales from peaceful picketing. The Washington Supreme Court upheld a lower court's order of a permanent injunction.

The two unions were clearly engaged in primary and not secondary picketing. The courts under common law have traditionally attempted to distinguish between the two in issuing injunctions. The Washington courts did not do so.

The high court seemed uneasy in upholding the Washington Supreme Court decision. It was not only forced to review its rule in *Hughes* permitting the judiciary to proclaim state policy, but it had to go further and stated:

> We cannot conclude that Washington, in holding the picketing in these cases to be for an unlawful object, has struck a balance so inconsistent with rooted traditions of a free people that it must be found an unconstitutional choice. . . . Nor does the Fourteenth Amendment require prohibition by Washington also of voluntary acquiescence in the demands of the union in order that it may choose to prohibit the right to secure submission through picketing. In abstaining from interference with such voluntary agreements a state may rely on self-interest. In any event, it is not for this Court to question a State's judgment in regulating only where an evil seems to it most conspicuous.

The most obvious interpretation of *Hanke* and *Cline* is that the state courts were turned loose to decide once again the desirability of union objectives sought through peaceful picketing. If, for example, judges consider the picketing of small employers an unjustifiable weapon for the purpose of forcing compliance with union standards in a particular area, they may stop it when requested to do so. The decision moved dangerously close to bringing about a new era of conflict between unions and the judiciary regarding what economic activity is legal and what is illegal.

A state may not, however, regulate peaceful picketing in a field where the federal government has legislated.[19] This issue was dealt with in two separate cases involving a Wisconsin law prohibiting strikes by unions representing employees in public utilities. The state employment relations board obtained injunctions to perpetually forbid work stoppages after unions went out on strike. The U.S. Supreme Court refused to allow the injunction because the National Labor Relations Act covers public utilities. A state is forbidden to regulate when Congress establishes federal law covering the same field. Thus, the marked decline of the *Thornhill* free-speech doctrine has greater relevance under state than under federal jurisdiction. A considerable body of federal legislation has been passed to restrict the freedom of the courts to deal with peaceful picketing. Many states, however, do not have adequate legislation in the labor field, and for this reason their courts have considerable freedom to establish public policy.

FREE-SPEECH AND PRIVATE PROPERTY RIGHTS

In 1967, the Supreme Court was faced with a major issue involving state public policy and the right to picket peaceably.[20] The *Logan Valley Plaza* case was first presented to the Blair County, Pennsylvania, Court of Common Pleas. A union was engaged in a labor dispute with a nonunion supermarket. Peaceful picketing was initiated on privately owned shopping center premises. This activity was undertaken by six individuals and was restricted almost entirely to the parcel pickup area immediately adjacent to a supermarket with whom the dispute existed. The signs publicized that the market was nonunion and that wages and fringe benefits were substandard. There was no violence, nor were there any threats involved in the action.

A trial court issued an injunction upon the request of the supermarket owner, prohibiting the union from picketing and trespassing on private property. Peaceful picketing was not enjoined, since the union still had the option of establishing its picket lines on public property off the shopping center premises. The union argued that the free-speech provision guaranteed by the First Amendment to the Constitution gave it the right to picket on shopping center grounds. The Pennsylvania Supreme Court denied this defense and upheld the injunction on the ground that state law prohibited trespassing on private property.

The U.S. Supreme Court reversed the Pennsylvania court. It held that owners of private property have the right to establish reasonable rules governing free-speech rights on private property. Regulations governing free speech on private property may be made through injunctions issued by state courts. However, limits were placed on the right of private property owners to restrict unions from peaceful picketing during labor disputes.

Absolute restriction of picketing on private property open to the public was held to infringe on that right. The Court distinguished between a private home and private property that is open and accessible to the public. Thus, state rules regarding trespass do not apply to property used for business because the right of privacy is clearly not an issue.

The Court in establishing guidelines indicated that the free-speech rights may be subject to alteration if private property owners assert that peaceful picketing restrictions are necessary to protect normal business operations. No such evidence was presented in the *Logan Valley Plaza* case. Thus, private shopping centers did not have access to the usual private property rights laws of homeowners to restrict normal union activities. In this regard, the Court stated:

The more an owner, for his advantage, opens up his property for use by the public in general, the more do his rights become circumscribed by the statutory and constitutional rights of those who use it.

State policy may not be used to place a blanket policy against all picketing. In this regard, the *Logan Valley Plaza* case was consistent with *Gazzam, Vogt,* and *Hughes.* However, it was inconsistent in that the Supreme Court has questioned the specific prohibition of peaceful picketing in accordance with state policy, which it had vowed not to do in *Hughes, Hanke, Cline, Gazzam,* and *Vogt.* However, in *Taggart* v. *Weinacker,* decided in 1970, Chief Justice Burger, in an unusual concurring opinion to dismiss the case, held the view that Congress had never undertaken to alter the power of states to protect private property.[21] His opinion gave insight into the direction the Chief Justice would lead the court in the confused area of state and federal control over the right of unions to picket. The issue centered on union rights to free speech and employer rights to protect private property from trespass.

One early step in the direction of giving states greater authority to control union picketing came in *Atlantic Coast Line.*[22] In a 5–2 decision, it was decided that a federal court does not have inherent power to enjoin state court proceedings merely because those proceedings interfere with a protected federal right. The Supreme Court relied on a 1793 law to hold that the lower federal courts cannot interfere with the state courts' proceedings. The only legal situations in which a lower federal court may enjoin a state court are to protect its judgments. When state and federal courts have concurrent jurisdiction, such as picketing rights, a party can simultaneously pursue claims in both court systems. Then if a state court issues an injunction to halt union picketing, a union must appeal through the state court system and ultimately to the U.S. Supreme Court. Lower federal courts cannot directly review the decisions of state courts in such matters.

Essentially, the high court decided to permit greater authority of state courts in the area of picketing if it is for the purpose of protecting the private property rights of employers from trespass. The National Labor Relations Act barred any court from enjoining peaceful picketing, provided it was not aimed at an illegal object. The basic problem with *Atlantic Coast* is that it opened up permission for state courts to interfere with the right to picket when union activity was arguably protected by federal law. The Court's 1978 *Sears, Roebuck, and Co.* v. *San Diego County District Council of Carpenters* declared there must be sufficient purpose to preempt a state's trespass law in favor of NLRB picketing policy dealing with private property.

In 1972, drifting even further from *Logan Valley Plaza,* the Court held in *Lloyd Corp., Ltd.,* that nonemployees had access to a private parking lot only if a union had no other means to reach employees or if nonunion forces were free to use the lot.[23] The Supreme Court decided *Central Hardware Company* concurrently with *Lloyd.*[24] The high court went back to *NLRB* v. *Babcock & Wilcox*[25] as the precedent to rule on union organizational rights in contrast to employer property rights. In *Central Hardware,* the company had a no-solicitation rule against nonemployees on company property and ordered union organizers from its parking lots. The Board relied on *Logan Valley* to order the company to permit solicitation on Central Hardware's parking lots. The order was enforced by the court of appeals, and the Supreme Court agreed to review the decision. Relying on its *Babcock* decision, the Court remanded the case to the circuit court of appeals to determine if there was "no reasonable means of communication with employees . . . other than solicitation in Central Hardware's parking lots." In essence, the Court was trying to balance union organizational rights with employer property rights.

The *Lloyd* and *Central Hardware* cases made it legal for a retail merchant or shopping center owner to prohibit speech or organizational activity in a shopping center or parking lot under three circumstances. Prohibition may occur (1) if the activity is not directly related in its purpose to the use to which the store or the shopping center property is being put; (2) if other reasonable opportunities to communicate with the intended audience are available; and (3) if the rule prohibiting such activity has been enforced without discrimination.

The Board concluded on the basis of *Central Hardware* that a store manager was lawfully protecting his employer's property rights when he caused the arrest of nonemployee organizers who were picketing and passing out handbills in a private shopping center parking lot.[26]

The ax fell hard in 1976 in the *Hudgens* v. *NLRB* case because it represented the first outright overturning of any Warren Court decisions.[27] Earlier, the NLRB ruled, and the Fifth Circuit Court of Appeals upheld the decision, that a shopping center owner had violated the law by prohibiting warehouse employees on strike against their employer from picketing the entrances to a retail store in the shopping center that was leased by the employer. The Board and Fifth Circuit Court of Appeals used the Supreme Court's *Logan Valley Plaza* and *Lloyd Corp.* v. *Tanner* cases to decide that the warehouse workers were entitled to picket in front of the store because it involved a labor dispute with a lessee of the shopping center and was related to the normal function of the center. The appellate court in *Hudgens* applied First Amendment rights as a basis for its decision after finding that alternatives to picketing the store's entrances in the shopping center were either unavailable or inadequate. Upon review in 1976, the Supreme Court ruled that employees of firms located in shopping malls and shopping centers do not have a constitutional right to picket in a privately owned shopping center. *Hudgens* requires a balance between strikers' rights and the private property rights of owners. The NLRB must balance rights under labor law, and not under the First Amendment guarantee of free speech.

SUMMARY

The U.S. Supreme Court attempts to yield as much authority as possible to state jurisdictions to establish policies that are peculiar to their own philosophies. The federal system of government makes it difficult for the Court to articulate an unchanging body of law in a category as complicated as that which deals with labor disputes. This means, however, that the free-speech concept pronounced in the *Thornhill* case has no definitive limits or content. Those skilled in the law have difficulties in understanding the free-speech protection of picketing and certainly have not defined it sufficiently to facilitate the understanding of others.

Peaceful picketing obviously is not exactly synonymous with free speech. This was made clear by Justice Douglas in the *Wohl* case when he stated that

> picketing by an organized group is more than free speech, since it involves patrol of a particular locality and since the very presence of a picket line may induce action of one kind or another quite irrespective of the nature of ideas which are being disseminated.[28]

It is obvious, therefore, that the Supreme Court has retreated somewhat from the *Thornhill* doctrine set forth in 1941. The chain of picketing cases since *Thornhill* makes it clear that the highest tribunal in the country continues to struggle with the problem of foregoing judicial legislation in order not to take exclusive control over matters that are of considerable local concern. This problem was best stated by Justice Frankfurter in the *Vogt* case when he wrote:

> It is inherent in the concept embodied in the Due Process Clause that its scope be determined by a gradual process of judicial inclusion and exclusion.

The process of gradual inclusion and exclusion is apparently the course of action that continues to dominate picketing cases reaching the Supreme Court. Precise definitions and limitations may not be logically set forth all at once.

DISCUSSION QUESTIONS

1. How has the U. S. Supreme Court reconciled federal and state picketing restrictions with the Constitutional guarantee of free speech? Compare *Thornhill* v. *Alabama* to *Hudgens* v. *NLRB*.

2. When is peaceful picketing not protected by the guarantee of free speech?

3. What flexibility was given to the state courts in the *Hanke* and *Cline* cases?

4. Are you more sympathetic toward the Supreme Court's *Logan Valley Plaza* decision, or to its decision in *Hudgens* v. *NLRB?*

NOTES

1   310 U.S. 88 (1940).
2   *AFL* v. *Swing,* 312 U.S. 321 (1941).
3   *International Brotherhood of Teamsters, Local 695, AFL* v. *Vogt, Inc.,* 354 U.S. 284 (1957).
4   315 U.S. 769 (1942).

5   *Cafeteria Employees' Union* v. *Angelos*, 320 U.S. 293 (1943).

6   *Milk Wagon Drivers Union* v. *Meadowmoor Dairies, Inc.*, 312 U.S. 287 (1941).

7   The Supreme Court decided the *Carlson* case (*Carlson* v. *California*, 310 U.S. 106) the same day on which it handed down its ruling in the *Thornhill* case. In the *Carlson* case, the court invalidated an antipicketing ordinance of Shasta County, California.

8   *Chauffeurs, Teamsters & Helpers Local Union 795* v. *Richard Newell, d/b/a El Dorado Dairy*, 356 U.S. 341 (1958).

9   *James E. Youngdahl* v. *Rainfair, Inc.*, 335 U.S. 131 (1957).

10   315 U.S. 722 (1942).

11   For example, see Charles O. Gregory, *Labor and the Law* (New York: W. W. Norton & Company, Inc., 1946), pp. 357–362. See also International Juridical Association, *Monthly Bulletin*, XI (1942), pp. 1–6.

12   *Giboney* v. *Empire Storage & Ice Company*, 336 U.S. 490 (1949).

13   *Duplex Printing Press Company* v. *Deering*, 254 U.S. 443 (1921).

14   *Building Service Employees Union* v. *Gazzam*, 339 U.S. 532 (1950).

15   *Hughes* v. *Superior Court of the State of California*, 339 U.S. 460 (1950).

16   Charles O. Gregory, *Labor and the Law*, 2d ed. (New York: W. W. Norton & Company, Inc., 1961), pp. 324–325.

17   *Ibid.*, pp. 325–329.

18   *International Brotherhood of Teamsters, Local 309* v. *Hanke; Automobile Drivers & Demonstrators Local 882* v. *Cline*, 339 U.S. 470 (1949).

19   *Amalgamated Association of Street, Electric Railway & Motor Coach Employees of America, Division 998* v. *Wisconsin Employment Relations Board; United Gas, Coke & Chemical Workers of America, CIO* v. *Wisconsin Employment Relations Board*, 340 U.S. 383 (1951).

20   *Amalgamated Food Employees Union Local 590* v. *Logan Valley Plaza, Inc.*, 391 U.S. 308 (1967).

21   *Taggart* v. *Weinacker*, 397 U.S. 223 (1970).

22   *Atlantic Coastline Railroad Company* v. *Locomotive Engineers*, 398 U.S. 281 (1970).

23   *Lloyd Corporation, Ltd.* v. *Tanner*, 407 U.S. 551 (1972).

24   *Central Hardware Company* v. *NLRB*, 407 U.S. 539 (1972).

25   *NLRB* v. *Babcock & Wilcox Company*, 351 U.S. 105 (1956).

26   *S. E. Nichols of Ohio, Inc.*, 200 NLRB 1130 (1973).

27   *Hudgens* v. *NLRB*, 424 U.S. 507 (1976).

28   *Bakery & Pastry Drivers & Helpers Local, etc.* v. *Wohl*, 315 U.S. 769 (1940).

CHAPTER NINETEEN

NATIONAL EMERGENCY LABOR DISPUTES

CHARACTERISTICS OF NATIONAL EMERGENCY DISPUTES

Strikes vary in their effect on the general public. A nationwide strike in the steel industry may cause more public concern than a work stoppage in a section of the garment industry. The effective functioning of the national economy may depend on the continuous operation of the nation's critical industries such as coal, oil, steel, ocean shipping, and transportation. Extensive strikes in these industries may or may not imperil the nation's health or safety.

Widespread union organization of the nation's critical industries focused attention on the problem of national emergency strikes just after World War II. The public viewed unions as having the power to shut down the nation's vital industries. As a result, Congress sought to protect the nation from such strikes by enacting the Taft-Hartley Act. Indeed, a fundamental aspect of this statute involves the procedures by which national emergency strikes are to be controlled. Such an attempt immediately raised fundamental questions. Are there strikes that actually constitute threats to the national health and safety? How effective are the national emergency strike provisions of Taft-Hartley? Are there alternative procedures available for the control of national emergency strikes?

This chapter deals with the economic effect of strikes in general industry, historical attempts to control strikes, legislation dealing with emergency disputes under Taft-Hartley, Railway Labor Act provisions, and alternatives that may be available to replace current laws. A national emergency dispute may be simply defined as a work stoppage that jeopardizes the health or safety of the general public. No general agreement exists on a precise workable definition of such disputes; however, broadly outlined procedures have been suggested from time to time to deal with national emergency disputes, however they are defined.

Difficulties in Identifying Emergency Disputes

It is easier to name the nation's critical industries and to define a national emergency strike than to spell out the circumstances that indicate that a strike imperils the nation's health and safety. In some of the critical industries, a national emergency is not caused at the moment a strike begins. Stockpiles of coal and steel, for example, invariably exist at any one time. Stockpiles cushion the public for a time from the shock of nationwide strikes involving the critical industries. On the other hand, strikes in critical service industries, such as railroads, might result in a national emergency coincident with the work stoppage. Even here, however, the result may be more of an inconvenience to the public than a threat to the national health or safety.

Actually, there are no statistical or infallible rules to follow in the determination of national emergency strikes. The issue is much too complex for such a simple solution. However, certain criteria may be referred to in the determination of whether or not a strike is of national emergency proportions. The status of existing stockpiles may be taken into account. Vanishing stocks of critical items might at least indicate that a strike approaches a national emergency stage. The condition of the industries that depend on the struck product for their operation is another standard. If inadequate stockpiling is present among firms using a particular good as an import, for example, a work stoppage in a key industry may force shutdowns among firms not directly involved in the labor dispute. Such an assessment is difficult to make in the short period of time available to a President when these decisions are necessary.

An industry affected by a strike may supply a product or service essential to the personal comfort of the public. Coal and rail service may fall within this category. Thus, the effect of a strike on the personal comfort of the general public is still another reference point in the determination of national emergency strikes. At a certain point during a strike involving a critical item, mere public inconvenience turns into public suffering. A national emergency does not exist when people do not have all the coal they would like to burn; this condition involves public inconvenience. However, the safety and health of the nation are imperiled when the people have little or no coal to warm their homes, schools, and hospitals. Consequently, the personal-comfort standard is perfectly valid, provided a distinction is drawn between public inconvenience and an actual threat to national health and safety. Several studies have been undertaken to determine whether national emergencies have ever actually resulted from strikes, and if so, to what extent. A review of a few of these studies is appropriate before discussing the specific provisions for dealing with national emergency strikes.

The dilemma facing the public is that it is made fully aware of the strikes that stem from the collective bargaining process, but is less informed of the essentially peaceful character of the total process. The basic reason for this circumstance involves the relative newsworthiness of strikes as compared to the lesser interest of industrial peace.

ECONOMIC EFFECT OF STRIKES

Contrary to public impression, the collective bargaining process in the overwhelming majority of cases results in the peaceful settlement of labor disputes. In 1946, the nation experienced the most serious strike wave in its history. Still, in that year, marked by significant postwar economic readjustments, there were about nine labor contracts renewed or revised peacefully for every one that resulted in a strike. The public was informed of the 4,985 work stoppages. What the public did not know, however, was that about 45,000 contracts were rewritten in whole or in part in 1946 without work stoppages. In 1968, there was a total of 4,950 work stoppages, resulting in only 0.27 percent of total working time lost as a consequence. In total stoppages, the record of 1946 was only slightly higher than 1968, and even this was the highest since 1953. The 1968 percent of total working time lost for the year was the highest since 1959, when it was 0.50.[1] In aggregate terms, the impact of strikes at the close of the 1960s was less than it was at the close of World War II. The same held for the 1970s. Even so, the public appears to remain unwilling to accept much inconvenience from work stoppages. It may well be that the inconveniences are more imagined than real, since the mere possibility of them is enough to threaten the normal preference patterns of a significant proportion of the adult population. If the period 1933–1948 is considered, omitting 1946, a thoroughly abnormal year, the record of industrial peace under collective bargaining seems impressive. In this period, the worker-days of production lost due to strikes averaged 15 million per year. This amounted to approximately one-half of 1 percent of the worker-days worked during this span of years. It is interesting to note that the worker-days lost to strikes from 1940 to 1947 were less than the loss from work injuries on the job. Worker-days of production lost from work injuries averaged 45 million per year. The average annual loss from strikes was 15 million.[2] Even so, the strike record of 1946 prompted Congress to include provisions to deal with strikes viewed by the President as threats to the national health or safety. After some experience with the law, several observers of the economy studied the impact of strikes in certain industries in an effort to evaluate the Taft-Hartley provisions.

Bituminous Coal Studies.   C. Lawrence Christenson examined the bituminous coal industry in two separate studies. In one study, it was shown that most output of coal supposedly lost due to strikes from 1933 to 1950 was offset before and after the stoppages.[3] This was possible because of excess capacity in the industry. Production of coal was moved from one operating period to another. The timing of production was shifted in two ways to offset the loss of production due to strikes. The one was anticipatory, the other was retroactive. That is, production was increased before strikes in anticipation of stoppages, as well as afterward to catch up on any orders that may have been unfilled. It was also concluded that output foregone might be totally and immediately neutralized simply by a shifting of orders from firms involved in the dispute to firms not on strike. The rise of unionism in the industry, however, tended to weaken the transfer of orders from union to nonunion firms, thus spreading disputes over a larger area.

The same author in a 1955 study analyzed the impact of strikes on coal consumption.[4] Three consumer groups were classified according to (1) purpose of use, (2) availability of supplies for use, and (3) continuity of use. It was found that over 85 percent of the time, the strikes that had occurred over the two decades actually coincided with either seasonally falling demand for coal or a business recession. No evidence was found to support the contention that the steel industry, the general public, or other users such as the utilities were forced to curtail production because of inadequate coal supplies. A part of the reason was stockpiling by the individual companies, but the railroads were also important. They increased reserves sharply prior to the major disputes. This enabled them to continue deliveries once strikes went into effect.

Still another study of the bituminous coal industry set forth three economic tests for defining the term *national emergency*.[5] These were: "First, the strike must have an actual as distinguished from a potential effect; second, it must impose hardship rather than inconvenience; and, finally, its impact must be national rather than local." These tests were compared to the findings obtained from an analysis of the ten coal strikes that took place during 1937–1950. Not only did the study analyze coal data, it also studied output trends of the industry's major customers. It then concluded that "none of the ten strikes studied created a national emergency." However, the two strikes that occurred in 1946 and 1949–1950 approached the emergency stage.[6]

Other Studies.   Fifty-one highly unionized industries were studied by another observer to evaluate their national emergency potential.[7] The working definition of a national emergency was the same as the economic tests just mentioned.[8] The potential for creating a crisis when strikes occur was evaluated in terms of six tests. These were:

1. The industry must be highly unionized.
2. Its product or service must be essential.
3. It must have a national product market.
4. Its employees must be represented by a single labor organization, by several unions whose strike policies are coordinated, or by one or more craft organizations with power to shut down the industry.
5. Bargaining must be on an industry-wide basis in fact or in effect.
6. The collective bargaining agreements in the industry must expire on the same date.[9]

The observer applied the tests just listed and concluded that

only three of fifty-one highly unionized industries in the United States have a national emergency potential: coal, steel, and railroads. In the nine years following World War II there was a total of eight nationwide strikes in these industries—four in coal, three in steel, and one in railways. By applying the criteria of a national emergency . . . two of the eight (one steel and one railroad) were emergencies, four (three coal and one steel) were serious but failed to satisfy the criteria, and two (one coal and one steel) caused little inconvenience. The results leave little doubt that the national emergency problem, in so far as it is economic in character, has been much exaggerated.[10]

Several other studies have been conducted dealing with such industries as steel and public utilities.[11] Strikes in these industries were not deemed as constituting national emergencies. The Livernash study of the impact of steel strikes concluded that the economic effects "are usually seriously exaggerated." Similar to the Christenson study, it found that excess capacity was an important factor to be considered in making any final judgment. An assessment of production foregone must be viewed "over a time span that encompasses a period prior to the strike, the period of the strike, and a period long enough following the strike to permit restoration of inventory." The secondary effects also had to be viewed in terms of "inventory accumulation at several stages beyond basic steel itself." In these terms, it was concluded that strikes generally can last much longer than is often believed before the economy is impaired.

Most studies that attempt to evaluate the effects of particular work stoppages reveal the difficulties associated with such tasks.[12] The major difficulty of assessing the impact of emergency strikes on the economy is the inability to find a fixed definition of emergency disputes. The lack of a standard leaves the question of legislative need open to continued debate. The provisions of the Taft-Hartley and the Railway Labor acts, and these acts' use, make it clear that the public continues to be concerned about strikes in key industries. It is to an examination of these provisions that we now turn.

TAFT-HARTLEY PROCEDURES

Sections 206 through 210 of the Act provide for government intervention in cases that can be interpreted as affecting the national health or safety. If the President of the United States believes that a threatened or actual strike affects "an entire industry or a substantial part thereof" in such a way as to "imperil the national health or safety," she or he is empowered to take certain carefully delineated action. There are several steps to the action that may be taken if all legal measures in the Act are implemented.

Appointment of Board of Inquiry

The President of the United States is required to appoint a board of inquiry before proceeding to deal with a situation that she or he believes will imperil the national health or safety. Since 1947, such a board has been assembled on thirty-five occasions. The board, composed of qualified and disinterested parties, must be given the opportunity to investigate the dispute. After conducting the investigation, it is required to submit a report to the President; this report is submitted in writing and within a period of time determined by the Chief Executive. The board is to find out and report the facts of the dispute. It is allowed subpoena authority and can thus compel the appearance of witnesses. It cannot, however, make recommendations for a settlement. National emergency measures may not be taken by a President without use of the board.

The very fact that a board of inquiry is required procedure, however, has received criticism. If a strike or strike threat were actually to threaten the national health or safety, the period of time required to investigate and report the findings could result in serious consequences. The President would be unable to respond as promptly to the threat as may be called for under emergency conditions.[13] It should also be recognized that the board has insufficient time to uncover all the information needed to support a decision to forego or to proceed with use of the national emergency provisions.

The board of inquiry is also restricted in what it may report to the President. As mentioned, it is unable to provide recommendations from its findings. This may be a weakness, in that the publication of recommendations could place public pressure on the parties to bargain within a particular framework whereby an acceptable solution could be found in a short period of time.

Neither does a board of inquiry have mediation authority. It appears that the framers of Taft-Hartley were concerned with the compulsory arbitration implication of such power.[14] The drawing of public attention to the mediation of disputes could have extended board power to approach that of binding arbitration of collective bargaining issues. Consequently, only the Federal Mediation and Conciliation Service has authority to mediate such disputes. The board of inquiry was viewed by Congress merely as a device for structuring public opinion. Public opinion was to be the force for effecting settlement. However, there have been but four occasions when the board has placed blame for a labor dispute on only one party to the proceedings. These have fallen exclusively on the coal and maritime industries.[15] Usually, the diverse positions of the parties are spelled out in the board's report, with no attempt made to identify a "guilty party." Failure to attach some blame may have the effect of dampening public opinion and in turn decreasing pressure on a single party for settlement.

It has been recognized, however, that some boards have played a mediation role and have been successful. This occurred, for example, in the 1961 maritime industry dispute, upon request of President John F. Kennedy. The same was done by the 1959 Basic Steel Industry Dispute Board under the chair of George W. Taylor.[16] Other board mediation activities are credited with settling the 1962–1963 Longshoremen's dispute and the 1967 Avco-UAW dispute.

Some other negative results are attributed to the very existence of boards of inquiry. One is that the bargaining parties relax their efforts to reach a settlement once a board has been appointed. Still another is the lack of respect held for such bodies by bargaining agents of labor and management. In short, the appointment of boards of inquiry before strikes actually occur may lead to a decline in efforts to reach agreement before a strike deadline.

As the law now stands, boards of inquiry may not be as effective as they could be. Criticism of board authority to deal effectively with bargaining parties is widespread. It is suggested that frequent use of Taft-Hartley machinery should be avoided.

After the Board Reports to the President

After the board of inquiry reports its findings, the President may decide the situation does not warrant intervention. Alternatively, he or she may direct the Attorney General of the United States to petition any U.S. district court having jurisdiction of the parties to enjoin a strike or lockout. An injunction may be issued for an eighty-day period.[17]

A district court is under no obligation to grant the request for an injunction. In November 1971, a federal district court refused to grant an eighty-day injunction request for the first time.[18] The court reviewed the facts presented to it and held that the Port of Chicago did not handle sufficient volume to fulfill the congressional intent that the dispute must affect "an entire industry or a substantial part thereof," and that the national health or safety had not been imperiled. It was concluded that the injunction request was made solely on an economic basis totally devoid of any threat to national defense or any war effort as such. In fact, in twenty-five situations, temporary restraining orders were issued by the courts for ten days, at which time reconsideration of the request would be made. The initial request was subsequently granted in twenty-three of these cases.

Eighty-day injunctions have been issued in twenty-nine cases. On five occasions, injunctions were not requested after receipt of board-of-inquiry reports. These involved the packing, telephone, and bituminous coal disputes of 1948 and 1978, and the atomic energy dispute of 1954. President Truman declined to proceed with the Taft-Hartley provisions on three occasions and President Eisenhower declined to do so on only one. In total, Truman appointed ten boards of inquiry; Eisenhower, seven; Kennedy, seven; Johnson, five; Nixon, five; and Carter, one. These presidents called for eighty-day injunctions on thirty-one occasions. On two of the occasions, injunctions were requested from three different district courts.

During the eighty-day period the injunction is in force, the parties are required to continue to bargain in good faith, making every effort to adjust and settle their differences. They are assisted by the Federal Mediation and Conciliation Service. In five cases, injunctions have been requested before strikes actually occurred. In a few instances, settlement was not reached until after the eighty-day injunction period, but without a strike. In six other cases, all of which involved the maritime industry, some agreements were reached during the injunction period, and some not until the injunction was lifted. On the west coast in 1972, the longshore workers struck after the eighty-day injunction period. Congress passed special legislation in that year that would have required workers to return while a special arbitration board resolved the dispute if the parties failed to agree by a given date. An agreement was reached. (In total, six strikes occurred after the eighty-day injunction period expired under the Taft-Hartley procedures.) This special legislation to resolve the dispute was the first time such action was taken by Congress, although President Truman requested seizure authority in 1950 after the coal industry failed to settle. Congress did not have to act on the coal dispute because of settlement, and the 1972 legislation never took effect because of agreement in longshoring before the date assigned by legislation.

The board of inquiry is reconvened by the President when an injunction is granted. If a settlement is not reached at the end of sixty days, the board is required to make a second public report to the President. This report does not carry with it recommendations for settlement. It includes the current status of the dispute, the positions of the parties, and "the employer's last offer of settlement."

Between the sixtieth and seventy-fifth day, the National Labor Relations Board is required to poll the employees to find out if they will accept the last offer of the employer. The results of the election are certified to the Attorney General within five days. By the close of eighty days, the Attorney General must ask the federal court to dissolve the injunction. When the request is granted, the President makes a report of the entire proceedings to Congress, together with any requests for legislation she or he may desire to make. Unless Congress acts, a strike may begin or resume because the emergency provisions of Taft-Hartley have been exhausted.

THE LAST-OFFER VOTE RECORD

Last-offer ballots have been cast on seventeen occasions under the Taft-Hartley provisions. In every reported case, employees have rejected the employer's last offer. The 1948 maritime dispute proved even more disastrous for the procedure. The International Longshoremen's and Warehousemen's Union boycotted the balloting and not a single vote was cast. Balloting was engaged in through mailed ballots by other west coast unions, but the NLRB was not able to complete the procedure with offshore personnel before the end of the eighty-day injunction period.[19]

It has often been charged that one difficulty with the last-offer vote is the inability to draft the language of the employer's offer so employees can understand it. Congress intended that union members be given the opportunity to show whether they preferred to take an employer's last offer or to strike. Even if workers vote to accept the last offer, there is no legal requirement for union officers to abide by the results of a secret-ballot poll. Such a result, however, would obviously place union leaders in the position either of going along with the vote or having their careers jeopardized when union elections are held.

Unions instruct their members to reject the last offer presented to them.

Experiences with Taft-Hartley Act National Emergency Provisions, 1947–1985

Board of Inquiry Number and Dates	Dispute	President	Injunction Issued	Number Per Board	Employer Final Offer Vote	Strike Before Injunction	Strike After Injunction	Settlement Reached During Injunction
1. 1948	Atomic Energy	Truman	Yes	1	Rejected	No	No	
2. 1948	Meatpacking	Truman	No		No Vote	No		
3. 1948	Bituminous—Coal	Truman	Yes	1	No Vote	Yes	No	Yes
4. 1948	Telephone	Truman	No		No Vote	No	No	
5. 1948	Maritime Industry	Truman	Yes	3	Rejected	No	Pacific Coast	Except Pacific Coast
6. 1948	Bituminous—Coal	Truman	No		No Vote	No		
7. 1948	Dockworkers	Truman	Yes	1	Rejected	No	Yes	No
8. 1949–1950	Bituminous—Coal	Truman	Yes	1	No Vote	Yes	No	Yes
9. 1951	Nonferrous Metals	Truman	Yes	1	Rejected	Yes	No	Yes
10. 1952	American Locomotive	Truman	Yes	1	No Vote	Yes	No	Yes
11. 1953	Longshoring	Eisenhower	Yes	1	No Vote	Yes	No	Yes
12. 1954	Atomic Energy	Eisenhower	Yes	1	Rejected	Yes	No	No
13. 1954	Atomic Energy	Eisenhower	No		No Vote	Yes	No	
14. 1956–1957	Longshoring	Eisenhower	Yes	1	Rejected	Yes	Yes	
15. 1957	Atomic Energy	Eisenhower	Yes	1	Rejected	Yes	No	Yes
16. 1959	Longshoring	Eisenhower	Yes	1	Rejected	Yes	No	Yes
17. 1959	Steel	Eisenhower	Yes	1	Rejected	Yes	No	Yes

No.	Year	Industry	President						
18.	1961	Maritime	Kennedy	Yes	1	Rejected	Yes	No	Yes
19.	1962	Maritime	Kennedy	Yes	1	No Vote	Yes	No	Yes
20.	1962	Aircraft (Republic)	Kennedy	Yes	1	No Vote	No	No	No
21.	1962	Longshoring	Kennedy	Yes	1	Rejected	Yes	Yes	No
22.	1962–1963	Aircraft (Lockheed)	Kennedy	Yes	1	No Vote	Yes	No	Yes
23.	1963	Aircraft (Boeing)	Kennedy	Yes	1	No Vote	No	No	No
24.	1964	Longshoring	Johnson	Yes	1	Rejected	Yes	No	No
25.	1966	General Electric Co.	Johnson	Yes	1	No Vote	Yes	No	Yes
26.	1966–1967	Union Carbide	Johnson	Yes	1	No Vote	Yes	No	Yes
27.	1967	West Coast Shipyards	Johnson	Yes	1	No Vote	Yes	No	Yes
28.	1967	AVCO Corporation UAW	Johnson	Yes	1	Rejected	Yes	No	Yes
29.	1968–1969	Atlantic and Gulf Coast Longshore	Nixon	Yes	1	Rejected	Yes	Yes	No
30.	1971–1972	Atlantic, Gulf and Pacific Coasts	Nixon	Yes	2 of 3 requested	Rejected	Yes	Yes	No
31.									
32.	1971–1972	Grain Elevators	Nixon	Yes	1 of 2 requested	Rejected	Yes	Yes	No
33.									
34.	1977–1978	Bituminous-Coal	Carter	No (Temporary Restraining Order)	1	No Vote	Yes	Yes	No

Source: Adapted from Federal Mediation and Conciliation Service, "Synopsis of Presidential Boards of Inquiry Created Under National Emergency Provisions of the Labor Management Relations Act, 1947," Washington, D.C., July 1973; and U.S. Department of Labor, Bureau of Labor Statistics, "National Emergency Disputes Under the Taft-Hartley Act, 1947–77," Report 542, Washington, D.C., 1978.

Actually, it is well known among workers that there is no reason to accept the employer's last offer. The offer may always be accepted on the last day of the injunction. A refusal at the time of the NLRB-conducted poll is seen as automatic, since employers may not make their best offer at that time. An early acceptance may also appear to be a repudiation of bargaining representatives engaged in negotiations with management. Union leaders and members are aware that employers know they will reject their last offer at the secret polls and for this reason, the last offer will probably not be the best one. Experience since 1948 has led to this realization by the three parties involved in the process. This aspect of Taft-Hartley is useless and no rational basis exists to continue it.[20] This result was predicted shortly after the law was passed.[21]

SETTLEMENT RECORD DURING THE INJUNCTION PERIOD

Strikes have not always been in progress at the time eighty-day injunctions were issued. It will be recalled that in four cases, the President did not choose to proceed to the injunction stage. Of the remaining thirty-one cases, strikes were in progress in only twenty-five when the injunction was granted. Only the United Mine Workers of America members refused to honor the injunction when it was issued during the 1949–1950 dispute. The union was subsequently found not guilty of ordering continuation of the strike. The miners themselves may have decided to continue the strike action despite the UMWA telegrams requesting them to return to work. During the 1977–1978 coal strike, workers refused to honor the temporary restraining order that had been issued prior to a court's determination regarding the U.S. Attorney General's request for an injunction. The court refused the petition for an injunction.

It has been charged that the entire procedure of dealing with national emergency disputes prolongs or delays serious bargaining.[22] The settlement record reveals that on fourteen of the twenty-nine occasions injunctions were issued, agreements were reached during the injunction period. In three other cases, partial agreement was reached during the eighty-day period. The maritime industry was involved in all these cases, in which some unions agreed to new collective bargaining contracts during the injunction period and others did not. The circumstances in all these cases were unusual in that the West Coast Longshoremen's Union has usually refused to settle before taking strike action after the injunction period.

In some cases, settlements were obtained prior to the last-offer ballot. Indeed, of the fourteen cases resolved during the eighty-day period, only a few proceeded to the point where ballots were cast. This may mean that when the atmosphere is right for settlement of issues, the parties resolve them without regard to maneuvers moving them close to the midnight hour when a strike may either begin or resume. The weight of the particular issues such as the problem of containerization among longshore workers no doubt influences the dispute duration. In such cases the eighty-day period may merely prolong settlement. In most cases, however, the data do not support a suggestion that the parties play cat-and-mouse games until the very end of the eighty-day period. Even so it may well be that, in the absence of the eighty-day cooling-off period, greater pressure would exist to reach settlement.

Still another criticism of the injunction period is that workers are placed at a disadvantage because of the requirement to proceed with production for an eighty-day period. The various studies previously reviewed point out that production is increased both prior to and after the eighty-day period for the purpose of accumulating inventories. The existence of excess capacity in a particular industry engaged in a labor dispute increases employer power to withstand bargaining pressures. The requirement of continued production for eighty days may have the effect of raising inventory levels still higher and consequently increasing the possibility of strike action after an injunction is lifted. This ability obviously depends a great deal on the nature of an industry's product. Some products, such as services, cannot be accumulated. To the extent that they may be accumulated, however, the balance of power is placed in the hands of employers and eventual agreement to a contract may be prolonged. No actual penalty is imposed on employers during the eighty-day period. Employees, however, must continue to work at prestrike wages and other conditions of employment. This provides an incentive for employers to wait until near the end of the period before agreeing to new contract terms. Employers may thus discontinue bargaining efforts in cases where there is a reasonable chance that the government will intervene in the dispute.[23] The cost of continued operation of an industry seems to fall most heavily upon labor.

Another criticism of the injunction period involves the issue of the threat to the public health or safety. If an actual threat is the reason the injunction was imposed in the first place, what is the situation after the eighty-day period? It will be recalled that six strikes have occurred after the injunction period. Taft-Hartley provides that the entire Congress may become involved at the close of the injunction. The President may submit recommendations to Congress regarding action such "as he [sic] may see fit to make for consideration and appropriate action." Congress may choose to deal with a particular situation on an ad hoc basis by enactment of specific legislation to alleviate the problem. Such legislation once materialized under Taft-Hartley. In 1969, some members of Congress desired to provide legislation to end the longshore workers strike, which resumed after the Taft-Hartley emergency injunction was lifted. President Nixon responded, however, by indicating a preference for avoiding a legislative solution.[24]

Even if desirable, not much confidence may be placed in Congress to deal with such matters. It may well be that any legislation suggested by a President would be forthcoming only after a considerable period of time. The strike may be concluded with a more lasting solution by that time. A settlement imposed by government may not actually lead to an acceptable solution for the parties. To the extent that this is so, a final solution is again deferred to a later period of time.

The possibility of further government intervention could retard the industry bargaining process. This is particularly the case if a government-imposed solution appears to one party as more desirable than one that might be reached without government involvement.

Evidence is not available to support any contention that the public health or safety has been impaired as a result of resumed strikes after emergency injunctions. Until such evidence exists, it may be premature to invoke legislation to continue government intervention into labor disputes.

Another possible weakness of the Taft-Hartley procedures is that the injunction is viewed by unions as evidence the government is taking antilabor action against them. This injunction psychology is a carryover from the pre–Norris–La Guardia Act period. It is often argued that good-faith collective bargaining ceases at the time it appears likely an injunction will be issued. Unions take the position that better terms may be obtained by holding out longer. Employers are aware that a union is restrained from strike action and will not grant a more favorable offer. To the extent that an injunction psychology is generated, this constitutes a major defect in Taft-Hartley emergency procedures.

Last, it is frequently argued that the Taft-Hartley procedures are inflexible, with the result that bargaining is adjusted to the next legal step and not to the critical issues in dispute.[25] A variety of approaches is viewed as unavailable, and this has the effect of gutting the objective of national emergency provisions. However, unsettled disputes might still be referred to Congress for specific action, and any specific legislation that might be forthcoming from that body could leave the parties in a state of uncertainty.

CONSTITUTIONALITY OF TAFT-HARTLEY PROVISIONS

The U.S. Supreme Court entertained the issue of constitutionality of the national emergency strike procedures in a 1959 case involving the steel industry.[26] The United Steelworkers of America Union argued that Section 208 of Taft-Hartley, which vests jurisdiction in federal district courts to grant the federal government a temporary injunction against a national emergency strike in the steel industry, exceeded the constitutional limitations placed on the courts. The Constitution prohibits courts from exercising powers of a legislative or executive nature. The union argued that the Court would be placed in the position of dual authority if the Act's provisions were permitted to stand. The Court would decide when to apply the law on the one hand, and on the other it would determine the legislative standards to apply in each case. The second part of the union argument contended that if the Court viewed the law as valid, the emergency provisions should not be applied to the 1959 steel dispute because the national health and safety were not in jeopardy. Less than 1 percent of steel production was for defense purposes. Why should the entire industry be penalized when less than 1 percent of it could be classed as affecting "national safety"?

The U.S. Supreme Court ruled that the district courts have the constitutional authority to issue injunctions despite the fact that the Act "does not set up any standard of lawful or unlawful conduct on the part of labor [and] management." The Court reasoned that the law recognized the public has certain rights "to have unimpeded for a time production in industries vital to the national health or safety." Thus, the Taft-Hartley law merely entrusts the courts with the power to decide on the basis of evidence if a national emergency dispute exists. The judiciary was viewed as functioning on the power extended it by Congress to implement one phase of the total procedure.

The second union argument that the total industry should not be placed under national emergency provisions was also rejected by the high court. It held that the statute did not require that

> the United States formulate a reorganization of the affected industry to satisfy its defense needs without the complete reopening of closed facilities.

The force of the Court's opinion was that an injunction against a part of an industry is not reasonable. The Court majority resolved the issue on the basis of national "safety," viewed broadly, and avoided the construction of national "health."

The Douglas Dissent

Justice Douglas dissented vigorously from the majority opinion. He reviewed the legislative history to determine the meaning Congress had intended to apply to the terms *health* and *safety*. It was argued that Congress had not intended that "national health" include the economic well-being or general welfare of the country. Senator Kennedy remarked in this regard that

> the proposal embraces two separate things, health and safety. Because the remedy is drastic these two, in my opinion are sufficient. I believe we should apply this remedy, when the strike affects health or safety, but not the welfare and interest, which may mean anything.

The Justice went further and argued that the word "welfare" should not be read into "health." In his opinion, however, the Court majority had done just that.

The 1959 steel strike had not met the condition of placing "the national health or safety" in peril. When the board of inquiry was appointed, President Eisenhower stated that

> the strike has closed 85 percent of the nation's steel mills, shutting off practically all new supplies of steel. Over 500,000 steel workers and about 200,000 workers in related industries, together with their families, have been deprived of their usual means of support. Present steel supplies are low and the resumption of full-scale production will require some weeks. If production is not quickly resumed, severe effects upon the economy will endanger the economic health of the nation.

Obviously, the President was concerned with economic health, which was contrary to the intent of Congress. Justice Douglas was concerned that this broad construction of the national emergency provisions would return the government to the strikebreaking role it had played in the pre–Norris–La Guardia era. This was especially possible in the 1959 *Steelworkers* case, since the mills that continued to operate accounted for at least 15 percent of the nation's steel production. Section 208 does not require that *all* strikers must be enjoined; this leaves the Court in the position to decide whether only a portion should be covered by the injunction. Furthermore, a grant of jurisdiction to issue injunctions does not impose an absolute duty to do so under all circumstances. Justice Douglas concluded by arguing that an injunction covering all steel workers, when less than 1 percent were needed to supply defense needs, constituted inequitable treatment of workers relative to employers.

RAILWAY LABOR ACT EMERGENCY PROVISIONS

The Railway Labor Act provides a set of procedures for resolving national emergency disputes involving railroad and airline companies. The basic emergency provisions of the 1926 law were developed by union and management groups before Congress reviewed them. There was no hasty attempt to pass this type of legislation in the mid-1920s, as when Taft-Hartley was debated about the time of 1946, the worst strike year in history.

The amended Railway Labor Act of 1926 provides several steps in dealing with emergency disputes in both the railroad and airline industries. First, when either the companies or unions desire to change existing contractual terms, and the private parties cannot agree upon terms, they may call for the mediation services of the National Mediation Board. Furthermore, the Board has the authority to enter the dispute without an invitation from either party. The National Mediation Board, contrary to Taft-Hartley board-of-inquiry authority, may make recommendations for the parties to consider for settlement. There is no requirement, however, that such recommendations be accepted.

Failure to end the dispute with mediation services moves the National Mediation Board to a second stage. It urges the parties to submit disputes to voluntary arbitration. Acceptance of this proposal is rare among all unions, in or outside of rail and air. Arbitration is commonplace for resolving existing contractual problems, but not for the fixing of new contractual terms. Once arbitration is refused, the Board notifies the parties in writing that mediation has failed. Once notification is given, unilateral changes in wages, rules, or working conditions are prohibited for thirty days. Strikes are not permissible during this period.

At this point the National Mediation Board takes the initiative in dealing with a possible emergency in the rail and air industries. At any time during the thirty-day period that the Board feels the dispute threatens to "deprive any section of the country of essential transportation service," it notifies the President of the United States. The President may then appoint an emergency board for the purpose of hearing the dispute and making recommendations for settlement. Within thirty days the Board must make a report to the President. During the thirty days, unilateral changes in the disputed issues are prohibited. Voluntary agreement is permitted, of course. Thus, the Railway Labor Act provides a sixty-day period for postponing strike activity. After this period the parties are supposedly free to strike or otherwise make unilateral changes in contractual terms. No provision for controlling the dispute is spelled out after the sixty days expire.

In a 1981 amendment to the Railway Labor Act, Congress, however, established a special procedure which applies to publicly funded and publicly operated carriers providing rail commuter service, including Amtrak.[27] Under its terms, a work stoppage is not allowed for 120 days from the creation of the emergency board. Should this period expire without settlement, the union, employer, or governor of any state through which the rail commuter service operates may request the President to establish another emergency board which serves to delay a strike for an additional 120 days. When such a request is made, the President is required to appoint the second emergency board. Within thirty days after the creation of this board, each party must present a final offer for the settlement of the dispute. Then the board selects the offer which it believes most reasonable. If the employees strike when the board selects the carrier's first offer, they are denied benefits under the Railroad Unemployment Act. Should the board select the union's final offer as most reasonable, and if a strike takes place because the carrier refuses to comply, the employer may not participate in any benefits of any agreement between carriers which is designed to provide monetary benefits to such carriers during a work stoppage.

The Railway Labor Act worked so well prior to 1941 that it was considered "model legislation." The airlines industry was placed under it in 1936. It has been estimated that emergency boards were appointed on twenty-one occasions in railroading between 1926 and 1941. During the entire period of the law's operation, approximately 190 emergency boards have been formed to deal with transportation crises, or an average of about four per year.[28]

Despite the rising incidence of strikes in rail and air transportation, the proportion of work time lost has been lower than for general industry.[29] A great deal of effort has been exerted by former presidents to "keep the rails operative." Seizure, use of injunctions, and requests for special legislation have been used by Roosevelt, Truman, and Kennedy. In the 1960s, work rules were so prevalent an issue that the number of strikes increased substantially. For example, twenty-seven railroad strikes occurred in 1964, accounting for the largest number recorded in the then thirty-eight-year history of the Railway Labor Act. On August 28, 1963, Congress approved a joint resolution requiring arbitration of two issues in a railroad dispute. Approval was based on a special message sent to Congress by the President seven days before a deadline was due to expire on July 29, 1963. The action by Congress constituted the first compulsory arbitration law ever passed by the federal government during a time of peace. In 1967, Congress again forbade a national rail strike and compelled the parties to arbitrate their differences. It has been suggested that this approach may have been largely responsible for breakdown of private negotiations.[30] The entire process of intervention has received widespread criticism.[31]

The courts have also intervened in railroad disputes. The Supreme Court held in *Chicago and Northwestern Railway Co.* that the Railway Labor Act requirement that every reasonable effort be made to reach agreement on wages and working conditions is enforceable by the courts.[32] As a consequence, the Norris–La Guardia Act will not prohibit injunctions under the Railway Labor Act if an employer or union alleges before a court that the other party bargained in bad faith. The threat of a strike and the economic pressure it may have in bringing agreement will be less effective in railway disputes from now on. The negative effect works on unions and management alike. Any party opposing change may now be less willing to compromise than before, with the result that more and more government intervention in railway disputes is inevitable.

The courts have upset established patterns of bargaining by permitting rail unions to conduct selective strikes for the purpose of obtaining a national contract agreement. Selective strikes and lockouts are permitted, provided the parties act in good faith.[33] Reasonable notice (defined as two weeks) of strikes and lockouts must be given. If national negotiations reach an impasse and all procedures of the act have been exhausted, a union may now whipsaw a few selected carriers in order to pressure the remainder to reach a national agreement. The result is that longstanding patterns of bargaining may now be unilaterally terminated after impasse and new patterns established. In September 1982, when the Brotherhood of Locomotive Engineers engaged in a four-day strike, the strike curtailed freight and passenger service throughout most of the nation.[34] Faced with this situation, Congress passed special legislation ending the strike.[35] Not only did the legislation stop the strike, but it also mandated some of the recommendations the emergency board had previously established to deal with the dispute.

GOVERNMENT POLICY IN THE RAILROAD INDUSTRY

Within the railroad industry, successful collective bargaining has been seriously impaired due to federal government policy that there will be no national work stoppages in this industry. In 1963, 1967, 1970, and 1982, the government prohibited stoppages in the railroad industry, and by such action has made it perfectly clear that widespread strikes or lockouts within the railroad industry will not be tolerated. Except under the circumstances of World War II, this was the first time the United States government had prohibited strikes.

Despite the lack of agreement on the justification of outlawing widespread strikes in the railroad industry, the fact remains that the carriers and organizations well understand that from this time forward there will be no national strikes within this industry. Such strikes will not be tolerated, and this is a fact the parties must accept. The government justifies this policy on the grounds that outlawing widespread railroad strikes serves the public interest. It could be argued that such a policy serves the public *convenience*, but not necessarily the public *interest*. The latter could be identified with the preservation of free collective bargaining, even though periodic railroad strikes would impose serious inconvenience to the public.

In short, consideration should be paid to the proposition that the genuine public interest is advanced to the extent to which employers and employees are permitted to strike and lock out. The railway experience has now established a precedent that could easily be applied to other critical industries of the nation. Is the public interest preserved when the government destroys the free collective bargaining process? Short-run gains in terms of public convenience could eventually result in the domination of working conditions by government. Once the government determines working conditions, it is only a short step to the determination of prices, profits, labor mobility, investment, and other critical features of the national economy. Granted that the public convenience is protected to the extent that the government outlaws important strikes, the question still arises as to whether the true public interest is promoted by a system of government domination of our economic life. Is security against strikes worth the loss of freedom? Where does the true public interest lie: in the preservation of free collective bargaining or in state domination of our economic life?

COMPULSORY ARBITRATION AND COLLECTIVE BARGAINING

When the government outlawed the railway strikes in 1963, 1967, and 1970, it required the parties to arbitrate their disputes. That is, compulsory arbitration rather than collective bargaining is the federal policy within the railroad industry. Some government representatives attempted to identify the procedure in 1967 in terms of mediation. It was called "mediation to finality"—a sheer euphemism to cloak a procedure that was absolute compulsory arbitration.

By outlawing the strike and establishing a system of compulsory arbitration, the federal government has destroyed the collective bargaining process in the railroad industry. True, up to this point Congress has not yet passed a general compulsory arbitration law. The railroad disputes were dealt with on an ad hoc basis. However, the federal government has made it very clear that any threat of a future national railroad strike or lockout will be dealt with in the same manner. What the policy means is that the parties will not bargain in good faith and in a realistic manner. Why should they compromise their position in eventual arbitration by making concessions at the bargaining table? If it is argued that the carriers and the organizations do not live up to their responsibilities, the fact is that government policy brought about this state of affairs. If there is one fixed principle of labor relations, and one that is underscored by incontrovertible evidence, it is that a system of compulsory arbitration is incompatible with genuine collective bargaining. Realistic compromises, concessions, and counterproposals designed to reach settlement are simply not made out of the fear that by such action a party will prejudice its position before the arbitrator. It is a matter of game-playing to cling to the original position in order to protect a position destined for arbitration.

These observations are proved by the relationship between the carriers and the labor organizations. Once the parties understood that the government would not tolerate a national railroad work stoppage, there was no realistic collective bargaining. True, the parties met, discussed, and went through the rituals, but once they understood that there would be no strike or lockout, they made no serious attempt to reach a settlement. To argue that they did not meet their "responsibilities" ignores the reality of the situation. They did not meet their obligations because the government had established an environment that produced the inevitable sterility in their negotiations. They understandably responded to a state of affairs that makes good-faith collective bargaining an impossibility. Why should the parties have bargained realistically when they were fully aware that failure to reach a settlement would not result in economic sanctions? Why should they make any genuine and serious effort to resolve their differences when they were aware that making concessions would serve to weaken their position in the eventual arbitration?

The events of the airline strike during the summer of 1966 and the 1970 dispute further establish proof that good-faith collective bargaining will not occur when the government makes it explicit that it will impose compulsory arbitration. Here was a wage dispute between the Machinists Union and most of the major airlines in the nation. Before the government made it clear that it would legislate compulsory arbitration, there was reason to believe that the parties would promptly reach an agreement. However, once the government in effect told the parties that compulsory arbitration was in the picture, realistic collective bargaining stopped. It may well be that the government prolonged the airline strike by its intervention.

If additional proof is needed, World War II experience with compulsory arbitration is quite relevant. It is true, of course, that during World War II, production had to go forward without interruption. No one quarrels with this point. However, it still remains true that the National War Labor Board was deluged with cases because the parties were aware that to bargain realistically would impair their position before the arbitration tribunal.

Not only does compulsory arbitration make genuine collective bargaining an impossibility, but the procedure also worsens the state of labor relations. This occurs because the parties may push to an impasse issues which they might have readily settled within the climate of free collective bargaining. Once again, it is the game-playing of the parties that produces this state of affairs. If the dispute is going to wind up before the arbitrator, it is a matter of strategy to send to the tribunal as many issues as possible. For several years, the state of Indiana had a compulsory arbitration law that applied to public utilities. In a study of the operation of the statute by one of the authors, the following observations were offered:

> Finally, in evaluating the operation of the Indiana law, it is quite plain that the parties submitted issues for decision in arbitration that they undoubtedly would have settled themselves within the climate of free collective bargaining. In general, in the absence of the requirement to arbitrate, there are ordinarily only a few issues remaining toward the close of negotiations. To avoid a strike, both parties normally make every effort to settle their differences and thereby eliminate all but a few particularly serious issues for final determination. However, under the Indiana law, great bulks of problems have been laid before the boards of arbitration. In one case, a board was required to make 30 separate decisions, and in others, arbitrators were called upon to decide cases involving from 10 to 18 separate problems. The smallest number of issues placed before a board was 7. Some of these items were quite insignificant, and would have been peacefully settled in one way or another without the compulsory arbitration statute.
>
> Companies and unions frequently and deliberately refuse to settle items when they recognize that compulsory arbitration is involved. This is done on the grounds that some of these demands may be granted by a board of arbitration. They have nothing to lose by such a procedure, since the worst that can happen is to have the board reject these issues. In addition, the board may decide the major issue in favor of a party on the grounds that it disposed of some minor items against it. Once the arbitration process is interjected into a collective bargaining relationship, the parties will adopt appropriate strategy procedures to maximize their position if the case goes before a board. Parties hold on to demands that they would quickly dispose of under free collective bargaining.[36]

The same state of affairs can be expected within any industry under a system of compulsory arbitration. Understandably, the parties will refuse to dispose of even minor issues, hoping that by this strategy their position in compulsory arbitration will be strengthened. It is a matter of game-playing between the parties under a system of compulsory arbitration.

SUGGESTED ALTERNATIVES TO EXISTING EMERGENCY PROCEDURES: LABOR-MANAGEMENT ADVISORY COMMITTEE PROPOSAL

Several suggestions for Taft-Hartley changes were reported to President Kennedy by his Advisory Committee on Labor-Management Policy in 1962.[37] One committee proposal subject to little criticism was the elimination of the last-offer vote conducted by the NLRB between the sixtieth and the seventy-fifth day of the injunction period.

More controversial, however, was the proposal to eliminate the eighty-day injunction and replace it with presidential authority to order the parties to negotiate during a similar eighty-day cooling-off period. This proposal would supposedly take away the psychological aspect of the injunction. The primary argument that may be advanced for this change is that the parties will comply with a presidential request. It will be recalled that the Railway Labor Act does not provide for an injunction.

Still another suggestion dealt with the power of "emergency dispute boards" to make recommendations when deemed desirable by the President. This proposal carried with it a name change from the current "board of inquiry." In addition, it was advanced that appointment of boards be broadened to extend to any situation that might develop into a dispute threatening the national health or safety. The boards could be appointed to make recommendations at any time during the eighty-day period. This proposal differs from the procedure under the Railway Labor Act, whereby recommendations are required at the beginning.

Essentially, the advisory committee sought to establish procedures making it easier to intervene in strikes and as a result increase the governmental role in the collective bargaining process. It has been suggested that the committee desired procedures similar to those of the Railway Labor Act to govern general industry.[38]

Some of the suggestions of the advisory committee have been tried at various times, both before and after the report was submitted to President Kennedy. Extralegal action was taken in the 1959 steel strike, in which the board of inquiry succeeded in clearly defining the positions of management and the union for the first time. In addition, recommendations for settlement were made privately by the board. Still another mediation function was provided by then Vice-President Nixon and Secretary of Labor Mitchell. Extralegal action was also taken during the 1962 Lockheed-machinist dispute, the 1962–1963 longshore workers' dispute, and the 1967 Avco Corporation–UAW dispute. The boards of inquiry made recommendations in all these cases. Thus, increasingly, boards take on a conciliation role by making recommendations for dispute settlement. Clearly, the Taft-Hartley Act does not provide for such action.[39] This expanded extralegal role has been assumed in order to encourage bargaining, which tends to degenerate as soon as a panel is appointed by the President.

Presidential appointment of boards responsible for making recommendations follows closely the example of the Railway Labor Act. Yet it has been noted that the procedure used for the rail and airlines industries has not resolved all the issues over the past twenty years. Various reasons account for this record. The most obvious is the featherbedding issue resulting from technological change. Related to this larger problem is the fact that the parties, particularly unions, have little respect for the boards. They have become routinely ignored. Unions have not fared so well from board recommendations since World War II. It may well be that the boards have been impressed with the alleged hardship pleas of the railroads and airlines. Continued governmental intervention has not provided the lasting solutions anticipated when the machinery was conceived. Public opinion was to be the factor that would force settlement, not the use of force by public officials.

STATUTORY STRIKES

The *statutory strike* is known by various synonyms. It is also referred to as a semistrike and a nonstoppage strike. This type of alternative to existing emergency dispute machinery requires that financial penalties be placed on unions, workers, and employers in lieu of strikes. Workers would be deprived of all or a part of their wages and benefits, unions would forego dues, and employers would lose all or part of their profits. Work would continue under this arrangement until settlement was reached.[40]

Various plans have been advanced to implement the proposal. The problems inherent in them, however, appear too formidable to result in a workable arrangement. Some suggest that workers may agree to strike, but a work stoppage is foregone in favor of a certain percentage deduction from wages which is matched by employers. All deductions would go to the public treasury and would be lost to the parties involved. The exact percentage deducted would be set by the President. In addition, a union treasury as well might be taxed—perhaps instead of workers. A more likely plan would be a tax on both workers and their unions. Periodic strike taxes would be collected. If settlement were obtained, for example, in between two collection periods, no further payment would be required. This has been held to provide an incentive to reach settlement.

Enforcement of all the conceived variations of the statutory strike would be most difficult. The heaviest penalty for unresolved disputes would fall on workers. Marginal firms might be an exception, but such firms would not likely be involved in a national emergency dispute. Income taxes, unemployment compensation, and other related adjustments would be involved in any such plan. No plan exists that would place an equal penalty on all parties to an emergency labor dispute. The impact that a payroll deduction of 40 percent might have on an individual worker may be reasonably calculated. But how does one impose an equal liability upon General Motors? Even if such a calculation can be made, there is no guarantee that workers will not engage in limited work stoppages such as slowdowns, or even resort to industrial sabotage. The end result of bargaining may be less equitable than if a strike were permitted, which would clear the air more completely.

SEIZURE

Government seizure of industry has occurred some seventy-one times in the history of the United States.[41] Sixty of these actions were taken under express statutory authority. The remaining eleven seizures were not supported by legislation. Seizure has been used by presidents either during or immediately before and after wars. Government behavior in the collective bargaining process varies widely in such cases. At times, unions have been extended a wage and benefit package until settlement was reached with the employer. In other cases, the government has merely taken measures to maintain production; no attempt has been made to influence the final package. Of course, unions lose their right to strike in such cases. President Truman used both seizures and injunctions to deal with the rail disputes in 1948, 1950, and 1951.

The last time seizure was used to deal with an emergency dispute was in the steel industry in 1952 during the Korean War. President Truman, believing that he had such authority under his war powers, directed the Secretary of Commerce to take possession of and operate most of the steel mills engaged in the labor dispute. The Secretary complied and called upon the various company presidents to serve as operating managers of their firms. The companies brought suit against the United States, charging that seizure was not authorized by either Congress or any constitutional provision.[42]

Upon review, the Supreme Court ruled in favor of the companies. It was made clear that if the other ten seizures without express legislative authority had been litigated, they would have been held unconstitutional. It is interesting to note that the steel crisis had passed by the time the Supreme Court handed down its decision in June 1952. Despite this fact, seizure since then has not been used by presidents even when they were convinced national emergencies existed.

Seizure and the States

Seven states at various times have passed seizure laws to deal with labor disputes.[43] Only five, however, actually used such laws and seized production facilities. Most of these laws dealt with strikes involving public utilities. The threat that these strikes may result in emergency situations is considerably less now than was the case immediately after World War II. Continued technological changes and the ability of supervisory personnel to operate facilities have contributed to diminishing the threat.

Most state laws designed to control strikes have been invalidated by the Supreme Court because of federal preemption in the area. This is the case with compulsory arbitration, strike-vote requirements, and fact-finding boards insofar as these devices apply to interstate commerce.[44]

The state of Missouri enacted legislation known as the King-Thompson Act to control public utility strikes. It provided that

> it shall be unlawful for any person, employer, or representative . . . to call, incite, support or participate in any strike or concerted refusal to work for any utility or for the state after any plant, equipment or facility has been taken over by the state . . . as a means of enforcing any demands against the utility or against the state.

Under this provision, the governor of Missouri seized the Kansas City Transit, Inc., on November 13, 1961, the same day that a strike had begun. A permanent injunction was later obtained barring the continuation of the strike "against the

State of Missouri." The union appealed the case to the Supreme Court of Missouri and argued that the King-Thompson Act conflicted with the National Labor Relations Act, which preempted the state in such matters. The Missouri court ruled in favor of the state.

The U.S. Supreme Court accepted the case for review and reversed the state court in 1962.[45] It held that

> neither the designation of the state statute as "emergency legislation" nor the purported "seizure" by the State could make a peaceful strike against a public utility unlawful in direct conflict with Section 7 of the National Labor Relations Act, which guarantees the right to strike against a public utility, as against any employer engaged in interstate commerce.

State-owned and -operated facilities are not covered by Taft-Hartley, and may be controlled by state law. However, firms that meet the NLRB's jurisdictional dollar standards are not subject to state control. States are prohibited from dealing with so-called state emergencies despite the fact that they may be closer to the source of difficulty than federal officials and thus in a better position to judge the possible effect on local economies. It is often feared that a change in national labor policy extending greater authority to state governments to deal with local disputes would result in widespread abuse. The first issue that must be resolved in dealing with emergency disputes is a more adequate definition of what constitutes an emergency dispute. The definition of Taft-Hartley precludes the states from dealing with most strikes, whether actual or threatened.

PARTIAL INJUNCTION

The partial injunction has been suggested by several as an alternate method of dealing with national emergency disputes.[46] It has been suggested that the judiciary take the initiative in making a decision on what part of production or services should be continued. As opposed to this view, the Attorney General would be required to satisfy the judiciary of the need for certain production. Once a determination has been made, the injunction would be lifted, permitting the remainder of workers to strike or the company to lock out. A great deal of precise information would be required to implement this type of arrangement, and a more workable definition of national emergency would have to be worked out. Assuming that some workable solution could be reached on this issue, other problems would still exist.

Some workers would enjoy full wages until the entire dispute was settled, whereas others would receive only strike benefits. Should employees supply the necessary labor on the basis of seniority, or should those who normally perform specific tasks remain on the job? Often it may be impossible to single out a specific division and operate it to the exclusion of other sections of the firm.

Still other difficulties would have to be resolved before an operational plan could be developed to change the existing emergency procedure. In any event, if it is ever decided that the present methods do not adequately deal with emergency labor disputes, partial operation may provide an equitable approach to the problem.

CHOICE OF PROCEDURES

No single one of the devices mentioned has complete acceptance from observers of the labor scene. The choice-of-procedures approach would give the President a variety of weapons from which to choose in dealing with any given situation. Basically, advocates of this approach argue that the parties would be uncertain how to promote settlement and would attempt to settle their problems through collective bargaining. Among the weapons from which the President can select are (1) the injunction, (2) compulsory arbitration, (3) mediation, and (4) seizure or partial seizure. In addition, other approaches have been suggested.

It is not at all certain that the choice-of-procedures approach would provide an incentive for the parties to settle disputes prior to intervention. Recent presidents have used—or have threatened to use—a wide range of methods for dealing with particular industries. This does not seem to diminish the periodic concern with strikes in certain key industries. New legislation of the choice-of-procedures variety may merely formalize what already takes place in practice.

The state of Massachusetts enacted a choice-of-procedures law after a study by a committee headed by the late Sumner H. Slichter, but in actual practice it has not proved as successful as many had hoped. It has been reported that in some cases when the Slichter law was invoked, the unions may have obtained a settlement in excess of what they were prepared to settle for earlier.[47] The Massachusetts law has been used sparingly by governors for political reasons. The law was passed without union backing by a Republican administration. Democratic governors have not generally favored its use. However, this may be a positive factor in that the law has not been overused, as may have been the case with the provisions of both the Taft-Hartley and Railway Labor acts.

SUMMARY

It seems feasible to remark that the emergency strike provisions of Taft-Hartley were enacted more for political purposes than for any other reason. Congress intended that a narrow construction be placed on the meaning of national health and safety. Both Taft-Hartley and the Railway Labor Act emergency provisions receive an economic interpretation. Threats that a strike may impose an economic inconvenience upon the public are likely to be met by presidential use of national emergency provisions. Past studies reveal that disputes that arise in key industries have political implications as opposed to economic ones.

Intervention into labor disputes to protect the public from inconveniences may result in a higher economic cost than would have occurred if the parties were permitted to strike or lock out without restraint. At the time that it appears that presidential action may be forthcoming, the parties cease bargaining in good faith. Political settlements are achieved that may well be higher than if good-faith bargaining had been present throughout the entire period of negotiations. Extralegal action is used to secure political settlements. That is, presidents instruct boards of inquiry to make settlement recommendations even though Taft-Hartley forbids such behavior.

Compulsory arbitration is the political response, but the cost may be the tendency to forego greater economic efficiency over time. Several alternative national emergency procedures have been offered from time to time, but none has yet been accepted by Congress. There is no overwhelming evidence that national emergency dispute provisions were necessary on the occasions when they were used in the past. It is unknown to what extent that workable machinery will be necessary in the future. Because of the uncertainty regarding future need, there is no reason to allow inadequate machinery to persist on the statute books. Before a new approach is accepted, however, there is need to study the available alternatives. The real purpose for such provisions should be clearly revealed. If the public is not to bear any inconvenience such as may be forthcoming from strikes in key industries, then there is no reason to deal with the matter under the guise of public health and safety. The new law should clearly state that the federal government is concerned with the national economic welfare, however that is defined. It may be that states have no more basis for dealing with so-called emergencies than the federal government. But if a level of government should move more into the strike arena, it should be the federal government. The probability is greater of a more balanced and uniform treatment of both parties at the federal rather than the state level.

DISCUSSION QUESTIONS

1. Why are there difficulties in identifying national emergency disputes?
2. Outline the Taft-Hartley procedure required to implement the national emergency dispute provisions.
3. How useful have the national emergency provisions been since 1947?
4. Discuss the record of final-offer votes and evaluate that method's usefulness to the purposes of the law.
5. How did the Supreme Court construct the constitutionality of Taft-Hartley national emergency provisions? How do you evaluate the dissent of Justice William O. Douglas?
6. Compare and evaluate the emergency provisions of Taft-Hartley in contrast to those of the Railway Labor Act.
7. Are national emergency strike provisions needed in either Taft-Hartley or the Railway Labor Act?

8. Evaluate the advisability of suggested alternatives to existing emergency procedures.

9. When may the courts deny a request for an 80-day injunction? Have the courts ever done so? When? Why?

NOTES

1   *Monthly Labor Review,* XCII, 3 (March 1969), p. 75.

2   Bureau of Labor Statistics, *Handbook of Labor Statistics* (Washington, D.C.: Government Printing Office, 1947), pp. 136, 163.

3   C. L. Christenson, "The Theory of the Offset Factor: The Impact of Labor Disputes upon Coal Production," *American Economic Review,* XLIII, 4 (September 1953), pp. 513–547.

4   C. Lawrence Christenson, "The Impact of Labor Disputes upon Coal Consumption," *American Economic Review,* XLV, 1 (March 1955), pp. 79–112.

5   Irving Bernstein and Hugh G. Lovell, "Are Coal Strikes National Emergencies?" *Industrial and Labor Relations Review,* VI, 3 (April 1953), p. 353.

6   *Ibid.,* p. 365.

7   Irving Bernstein, "The Economic Impact of Strikes in Key Industries," in *Emergency Disputes and National Policy,* eds. Irving Bernstein, Harold L. Enarson, and R. W. Fleming (New York: Harper & Bros., 1955), Chapter 2.

8   *Ibid.,* p. 25.

9   *Ibid.,* p. 27.

10   *Ibid.,* p. 44.

11   See, for example, E. Robert Livernash, *Collective Bargaining in the Basic Steel Industry,* U.S. Department of Labor (Washington, D.C.: Government Printing Office, 1961); and Robert R. France and Richard A. Lester, *Compulsory Arbitration of Utility Disputes in New Jersey and Pennsylvania* (Princeton, N.J.: Industrial Relations Section, Princeton University, 1951).

12   Donald E. Cullen, *National Emergency Strikes,* ILR Paperback No. 7 (Ithaca, N.Y.: New York School of Industrial and Labor Relations, Cornell University, 1968), p. 45.

13   Senator Wayne Morse, Senate Joint Resolution 180, *Congressional Quarterly Weekly Report,* No. 30 (July 29, 1966), pp. 1636–1637.

14   Arthur A. Sloane, "Presidential Boards of Inquiry in National Emergency Disputes, An Assessment After 20 Years of Performance," *Labor Law Journal,* XVIII (November 1967), p. 667.

15   *Ibid.,* p. 669.

16   *Ibid.,* p. 671.

17   Section 210.

18   *United States* v. *International Longshoremen's Association, Local 418,* D.C.—N.D. 111, No. 71 Civ. 2416 (November 3, 1971).

19   Cullen, *op. cit.,* p. 58.

20   Herbert Northrup and Gordon Bloom, *Government and Labor* (Homewood, Ill.: Richard D. Irwin, Inc., 1963), pp. 364–65.

21   Harry A. Millis and Emily Clark Brown, *From the Wagner Act to Taft-Hartley* (Chicago: The University of Chicago Press, 1950), p. 578.

22   *Ibid.,* pp. 581–582.

23   Richard B. Peterson, "National Emergency Dispute Legislation—What Next?" *University of Washington Business Review,* XXVIII, 1 (Autumn 1968), p. 39.

24   *Monthly Labor Review,* XCII, No. 3 (March 1969), p. 2.

25   Cullen, *op. cit.,* p. 64.

26   *United Steelworkers* v. *U.S.,* 361 U.S. 39 (1959).

27   95 Stat. 681, Section 1157. Public Law 97–35, 97th Congress, 1st Session, August 13, 1981.

28   Cullen, *op. cit.,* pp. 69–70.

29   Jacob J. Kaufman, *Collective Bargaining in the Railroad Industry* (New York: King's Crown Press, 1954), pp. 78–80.

30   Jacob J. Kaufman, "The Railroad Labor Dispute: A Marathon of Maneuver and Improvisation," *Industrial and Labor Relations Review,* XVIII, 2 (January 1965), p. 201.

31   *Ibid.,* pp. 211–212.

32   *Chicago and Northwestern Railway Company* v. *United Transportation Union,* 410 U.S. 917 (1971).

33   *Delaware and Hudson Railway Co.* v. *United Transportation Union,* 403 U.S. 911 (1971).

34   *Monthly Labor Review,* CV, 11 (November 1982), p. 47.

35   Public Law 97–262, 1982.

36   Fred Witney, *Indiana Labor Relations Law,* Indiana Business Report No. 30 (Bloomington, Indiana: Bureau of Business Research, Indiana University, 1960), pp. 72–73.

37   *Free and Responsible Collective Bargaining and Industrial Peace,* Report of the President's Advisory Committee on Labor-Management Policy (Washington, D.C.: Government Printing Office, 1962).

38   Northrup and Bloom, *op. cit.,* p. 429.

39   Sloane, *op. cit.,* pp. 671–672.

40   David B. McCalmont, "The Semi-Strike," *Industrial and Labor Relations Review,* XV, 2 (January 1962); Stephen H. Sosnick, "Non-Stoppage Strikes: A New Approach," *Industrial and Labor Relations Review,* XVIII, 1 (October 1964); also Cullen, *op. cit.,* pp. 102–106.

41   John L. Blackman, Jr., *Presidential Seizure in Labor Disputes* (Cambridge, Mass.: Harvard University Press, 1967).

42   *Youngstown Sheet & Tube Company* v. *Sawyer,* 353 U.S. 579 (1952).

43   These states are Hawaii, Maryland, Massachusetts, Missouri, New Jersey, North Dakota, and Virginia.

44   For example, see *International Union* v. *O'Brien,* 339 U.S. 454 (1950); *Amalgamated Association* v. *Wisconsin Employment Relations Board,* 340 U.S. 383 (1951); *Grand Rapids City Coach Lines* v. *Howlett,* 137 F. Supp. 667 (1956).

45   *Division 1287, Amalgamated Association of Street, Electric Railway & Motor Coach Employees of America et al.* v. *Missouri,* 374 U.S. 74 (1962).

46   Senator Javits, "A Bill . . . ," Senate of the United States, 89th Congress, 2d sess., January 20, 1966; Committee for Economic Development, *The Public Interest in National Labor Policy* (New York, 1961), pp. 101–103.

47   George P. Shultz, "The Massachusetts Choice-of-Procedures Approach to Emergency Disputes," *Industrial and Labor Relations Review,* X, 3 (April 1957), pp. 364–365.

LABOR-MANAGEMENT REPORTING AND DISCLOSURE ACT OF 1959

The Labor-Management Reporting and Disclosure Act of 1959, commonly referred to as the Landrum-Griffin Act, is concerned primarily with the internal practices of unions.[1] Its major purpose is to protect union members from improper union conduct. Still another purpose of the law is to eliminate arrangements between unions and employers that would deprive members of proper union representation. A few provisions of the Act are directed at management. The 1959 law was the direct outgrowth of Senate investigations revealing unsatisfactory internal practices of a small but strategically located minority of unions. The first six of seven titles in the statute introduce controls on the powers that union officials exercise over funds, internal union affairs, and the membership. This chapter reviews the background and treats the major areas of the 1959 law. They are (1) "the bill of rights," (2) reports to the Secretary of Labor, (3) union trusteeships, (4) conduct of union elections, and (5) financial safeguards.

In addition to an analysis of the provisions of the 1959 statute and its application by the courts, experience with it will be discussed to the extent that information is available. How the law operates in practice provides the necessary basis for its understanding and evaluation. Unfortunately, however, at this writing, the most recent data are for 1978. Attempts to obtain more up-to-date information from the federal government did not prove successful.

BACKGROUND OF REGULATION OF INTERNAL UNION AFFAIRS

Growth of the U.S. labor movement from a position of relative weakness in the early 1930s to one of relative strength by the 1950s led to greater public attention devoted to internal union practices. Union membership grew from about 9 million in 1941 to 17 million in the 1950s. The logical extension of concern with strikes and picketing was to the perceived power of those directing such actions. The war years and the period of adjustment thereafter did not represent the first period of time the public was conscious of internal union operations. Concern with internal union affairs was prevalent even before the period of government protection of the right to organize and bargain collectively as provided by the Wagner Act of 1935.

By 1900 racketeering was revealed in the building trades, longshore workers, and teamsters unions. Graft, violence, extortion, and mishandling of funds by union leaders are some practices reported in these organizations. Labor organizations were also criticized for improper use of trusteeships, discrimination against black people by barring them from membership or placing them in separate auxiliary locals, and lack of disciplinary protection of members.[2]

Scrutiny of union activities was intensified after World War II. In 1954, Congress began investigating the administration of employee benefit plans. Discovery of widespread abuses in the labor field led to the creation of the Senate Select Committee on Improper Activities in the Labor or Management Field, better known as the McClellan Anti-Racketeering Committee. Between 1957 and 1959, the McClellan committee held numerous hearings dealing with patterns of union behavior. Several findings and recommendations were presented as a result of the three-year effort. It should be noted that the committee concentrated its efforts on only five national unions of the 200 or so that operate in the nation. These were the International Brotherhood of Teamsters, Bakery and Confectionery Workers, United Textile Workers, Operating Engineers, and Allied Industrial Workers of America. Some attention was devoted to other unions, including those in the building trades, but the five mentioned accounted for the largest share of the committee's efforts. As a result of the inquiry, the Teamsters were expelled from the AFL-CIO, and, subsequently, its president, James Hoffa, was convicted and jailed for tampering with a jury and mail fraud. Prior to the 1972 national elections, President Nixon permitted Hoffa to leave prison, but he was forbidden to hold a union office until 1980. After being released from jail, Hoffa engaged in litigation to set aside the ban, and began a campaign to return as president of the Teamsters, a job then held by Frank Fitzsimmons. Ironically, Hoffa had hand-picked Fitzsimmons for the top job when he went to jail. However, once established in office, Fitzsimmons did not look with favor on Hoffa's effort to regain control of the union, to say the least. In 1976, Hoffa disappeared; allegedly, he was murdered by elements that opposed his efforts to gain control of the union. At this writing, no one has been indicted for the alleged crime committed against Hoffa.

McClellan Committee Findings and Recommendations

The labor movement anticipated government intervention into its internal affairs. In 1957, the AFL-CIO adopted a series of six codes of ethical practices to regulate the behavior of its affiliates. The codes dealt with paper locals, health and welfare funds, subversives and racketeers, business interests of union officials, union financial and proprietary activities, and union democratic processes.[3] The self-regulated effort proved too late. The McClellan committee, after many hearings and thousands of pages of testimony, uncovered these facts:

1. Rank-and-file members have no voice in union affairs, notably in financial matters, and frequently are denied secret ballot.
2. International unions have abused their right to place local unions under trusteeship by imposing the trusteeship merely to plunder the local's treasury or boost the ambitions of candidates for high office.
3. Certain managements have bribed union officials to get sweetheart contracts or other favored treatment.
4. Widespread misuse of union funds through lack of adequate inspection and audit.
5. Acts of violence to keep union members in line.
6. Improper practices by employers and their agents to influence employees in exercising the rights guaranteed them by NLRA.
7. Organizational picketing misused to extort money from employers or to influence employees in their selection of representation.
8. Infiltration of unions at high levels by criminals.
9. A no man's land in which employers and unions could not resort either to the NLRB or state agencies for relief.

On the basis of the findings, the McClellan committee recommended legislation to deal with abuses in five areas. They were:

1. Legislation to regulate and control pension, health, and welfare funds.
2. Legislation to regulate and control union funds.
3. Legislation to insure union democracy.
4. Legislation to curb activities of middlemen in labor-management disputes.
5. Legislation to clarify the no man's land in labor-management disputes.[4]

As presented in previous chapters, Title VII of the 1959 law dealt with amendments to Taft-Hartley. We are concerned here with the first six titles of the law; as will be disclosed, they were broad and ambitious.

BILL OF RIGHTS OF MEMBERS OF LABOR ORGANIZATIONS

Senator McClellan was largely responsible for the "bill of rights" section that was written into the 1959 law. He stated that "racketeering, corruption, abuse of power and other improper practices on the part of some labor organizations" could not be prevented

until and unless the Congress of the United States has the wisdom and the courage to enact laws prescribing minimum standards of democratic process and conduct for the administration of internal union affairs.[5]

The resulting bill of rights for union members is an ambitious and wide-sweeping one. It attempts to legislate into internal union constitutions and bylaws certain basic rights contained in the Bill of Rights of the United States Constitution. Title I provides for equality of rights concerning the nomination of candidates for union office, voting in elections, attendance at membership meetings, and participation in business transactions—all, however, "subject to reasonable union rules and regulations" as contained in constitutions and bylaws. It lays down strict standards to insure that increases in dues and fees are responsive to the desires of the union membership majority. It affirms the right of any member to sue the organization, once "reasonable" hearing procedures within the union have been exhausted. Provision is also made that no member may be fined, suspended, or otherwise disciplined by the union except for nonpayment of dues, unless the member has been granted such procedural safeguards as being served with written specific charges, given time to prepare a defense, and being afforded a fair hearing. And the provision obligates union officers to furnish each of their members with a copy of the collective bargaining agreement, as well as full information concerning the Landrum-Griffin Act itself.

Considerable controversy broke out almost immediately after passage of the 1959 law. The underlying premise of the bill of rights was that labor organizations should function in a democratic fashion. The question was, however, could such a standard be imposed on unions externally? Union members are often viewed as apathetic to internal operations as long as they remain reasonably satisfied with collective bargaining results. Revolt against the leadership may be forthcoming only when there is a widespread feeling that contractual terms obtained are less than could have been received. Furthermore, some allege that union responsibility and internal democracy are often in conflict within the context of collective bargaining.[6]

Congress intended to give individual members the right to assert themselves more fully in matters dealing with their employment relationships. At the same time, it recognized the union right to represent a majority of workers in collective bargaining matters. Unions must have authority to enforce a labor contract entered into with an employer. For this reason, the exercise of individual rights is subject to "reasonable" union rules. Members have some responsibilities to the labor organization to which they belong. Recognition of this fact prompted Congress to provide that nothing in this section of the law should be construed to

> impair the right of a labor organization to adopt and enforce reasonable rules as to the responsibility of every member toward the organization as an institution and to his refraining from conduct that would interfere with its performance of its legal or contractual obligations.

The application of particular Title I provisions is somewhat complicated and for this reason each will be considered in turn.

EQUAL RIGHTS

The law grants equal rights and privileges to every union member with regard to nomination of candidates, voting in elections and referendums, attendance at union meetings, and voting at such meetings. The section made no attempt, however, to regulate union admission standards. The procedural safeguards did not prohibit labor organizations from refusing membership or segregating members on the grounds of race, religion, color, sex, or national origin. This aspect was made clear by Representative Landrum when he stated that

> we do not seek in this legislation, to tell the labor unions of this country whom they shall admit to their unions.[7]

Congressman Powell attempted to remedy this defect in Title I, but was unsuccessful by a vote of 215 to 160. A partial remedy to the problem was not available until it was provided by Title VII of the Civil Rights Act of 1964.[8]

Race was not the only form of discrimination permissible under Title I. The practice of filial preference has also been recognized as a basis for closing the door to union membership.[9] Only sons and close relatives are admitted under this practice which has the blessing of the courts, including the New York Court of Appeals.[10] Thus, the law permits union action designed to restrict the supply of labor available under some circumstances. Union democracy is limited to the extent that membership may be denied to qualified applicants. The view is taken by many that unions are no longer voluntary associations, but quasi-public organizations. Prevailing technology, it is argued, does not lend itself to monopolistic control over labor supply. Thus, the internal restrictive membership practices are viewed as antisocial because they work against public attempts to achieve and sustain high levels of employment.[11] On the other hand, it should be realized that restrictive admission practices have been in response to excessive unemployment in the labor markets in which these unions operate. A public policy not committed to full employment through its monetary and fiscal policy cannot hope to attain it by changing union admission standards. Discrimination in any form, however, is unacceptable.

The Title I political rights of union members are closely connected with Title IV of Landrum-Griffin. Title I guarantees equal rights and privileges to nominate candidates and vote in union elections. Title IV extends members a reasonable opportunity to nominate candidates. It also provides that every member, subject to some qualifications, shall be eligible to hold office. The member also has the opportunity to support candidates and vote for them without interference or reprisals.

Benjamin Aaron reveals that the courts have given these titles narrow interpretations.[12] Title I rights may be enforced prior to the holding of elections, but Title IV rights are enforceable only after an election is held. After an election, only the Secretary of Labor has authority to seek relief in the courts. The full range of litigation required to secure member rights may take so long that the full term of office in dispute may be served out completely before a decision may be obtained. Little practical relief from a violation, therefore, may be forthcoming.

A union may deprive members of their equal rights to nominate, to vote, and to participate in internal affairs. It may do so by the way it frames its eligibility rules. A union may do as was done by the National Marine Engineers' Beneficial Association. The association constitution provided that a member could nominate only him or herself for office, but no one was eligible to hold office unless he or she had been a member of the national union for five years. Also, eligibility was conditioned by the requirement that a member had to have served at least 180 days at sea in two of the preceding three years prior to the election. Sea service had to be on ships covered by labor contracts with the national or its locals. The U.S. Supreme Court sustained a motion to dismiss the case filed against the union in *Calhoon* v. *Harvey*.[13]

Despite its authority to adopt reasonable rules, a federal appeals court held that a union may not deprive a laid-off union member of the right to vote and participate in union affairs.[14] Under a union constitution, laid-off union members were forbidden to pay dues. Since they could not pay dues, they were not members in good standing. So they were denied the opportunity to vote on an issue dealing with recall rights. Only actively employed union members were permitted to vote. Under those circumstances, the court held that the union had violated the equal rights section of Landrum-Griffin. It pointed out that the union's "good standing" provision permitted one group of union members to benefit and protect itself at the expense of laid-off members who were not permitted to vote, or even speak, on the recall issue.

FREEDOM OF SPEECH AND ASSEMBLY

Landrum-Griffin provides for both individual and organizational rights. Every member is granted the right to meet and assemble freely with other members to express views, arguments, and opinions. Such activity may be at union meetings or some other place. The rights of members are subject to two qualifications. One permits unions to apply their established and reasonable rules pertaining to the conduct of meetings. For example, time limits may be placed on debate and measures may be taken to maintain order. The ability to conduct business in an orderly fashion is necessary to efficient operation. Dissident members could call the tune at union meetings without this organizational safeguard. An inability to restrict member misbehavior could result in serious industrial strife. For example, wildcat strikes could be called by a vocal minority because of the inability of the majority to control normal union business.

The second limit placed on member rights to speech and assembly is that a union has the right "to adopt and enforce reasonable rules as to the responsibility of each member toward the organization as an institution and to his refraining from conduct that would interfere with its performance of its legal or contractual obligations." The union member therefore is extended the right to dissent from established or advocated union policies, but that right is not without limit.

It appears that the courts tend to rule in favor of individual speech and assembly rights as opposed to union rights. *Salzhandler* v. *Caputo* was a case posing the issue of whether a union member's allegedly libelous statements regarding the handling of union funds by union officers justified disciplinary action against the member.[15] The case also involved the issue of whether the union could exclude the member from any participation in union affairs for a period of five years, including speaking and voting at meetings, and even attending meetings. A district court ruled in favor of the union. Upon appeal, the Second Circuit Court of Appeals reversed the lower court and remanded the case for further proceedings.

In upholding individual over organization rights, the appeals court stated:

> We hold that the LMRDA protects the union member in the exercise of his right to make such charges without reprisal by the union; that any provisions of the union constitution which make such criticism, whether libelous or not, subject to union discipline are unenforceable; and that the Act allows redress for such unlawful treatment.

The court pointed out that libelous statements may be made the basis of civil suit between those concerned, but a union governing board may not subject a member to disciplinary action for his or her statements. Libelous statements do not stand outside the law merely because they were made within the context of internal union affairs. The court merely established that other remedial action is available through civil suits. This approach appears to enhance democratic action within labor organizations. At the same time the individual member is still responsible for any libelous statements he or she may utter.

Two more examples demonstrate that the courts lean toward supporting individual rights over union rights. A union member was expelled for publicly urging the membership to refuse to pay an assessment levied by the union. He claimed that the levy violated federal law. A federal appeals court directed his reinstatement in the union, holding that he was protected by the free speech section of Landrum-Griffin.[16] Some members who belonged to the union by virtue of a union-shop agreement were fined for supporting a rival union in a representation election. Even though they sought to destroy the bargaining rights of their union, courts held that their activities were protected by the free-speech provision.[17]

In 1973, the U.S. Supreme Court made it easier for union members to sue their organizations.[18] It held that a union is liable for the attorney's fees when a union member's suit prevails in court. It said that "to the extent that such lawsuits contribute to the preservation of union democracy," they benefit the entire membership. On these grounds, unions are responsible for attorneys' fees. Thus, union members are encouraged to sue their organizations. Lack of funds to engage an attorney need not be a deterrent. Of course, should a union's position prevail in court, union members would be required to pay their attorneys' fees.

DUES, INITIATION FEES, AND ASSESSMENTS

Certain democratic procedures must be followed by a union—procedures not applicable to federations of unions—in increasing dues, initiation fees, or assessments. This policy is intended to stop unscrupulous union officers from imposing higher dues upon members against their will. The McClellan committee hearings and reports had revealed such actions in a few unions.

A local union has different procedural requirements than an international union. A local union may raise dues, initiation fees, or assessments by secret ballots in two ways so long as the determination is based on a majority of those members voting who are in good standing. The vote may be (1) taken at a membership meeting after reasonable notice that the issue will be put to the members, or (2) in a membership referendum. Posted notices on bulletin boards in union halls and where work is performed, as well as an announcement at one regular monthly meeting that a vote on the issue will be held at the next regular monthly meeting, would meet the reasonable-notice requirement. There may be no better way to get a large membership turnout to a meeting than to announce that a vote will be taken on whether to increase union dues. Union leaders have to present valid reasons for desiring an increase in dues. Failure to do so will inevitably lead to a rejection of the proposal by the membership.

An international union may use one of three different ways to increase its income from members. It may require (1) a majority vote of the delegates voting at a regular convention, or at a special convention held upon thirty days' written notice to each local union, with delegates selected by secret vote of the local unions; (2) a majority vote of the members voting by secret ballot in a membership referendum; or (3) a majority vote of the members of the executive board or similar governing body, if they are expressly granted such authority by the union's constitution and bylaws. The latter approach is subject to repeal at the next regular convention, and for this reason may not be a politically feasible approach for increasing international union income.

Federations of national or international unions, AFL-CIO, for example, do not fall within the Landrum-Griffin prohibitions on increases of dues, initiation fees, and assessments.

In *American Federation of Musicians*, the U.S. Supreme Court was faced with the issue of whether the law prohibits the vote of delegates at a national convention of the union, in accordance with its constitution, to be weighed and counted according to the number of members in the local that the delegate represents.[19] The Court was of the opinion that the legislative history of the section makes it clear that weighted voting was not thought to be one of the abuses of union government found by the McClellan committee. Many large unions vary voting strength according to the size of the locals.

The Court held that full and active participation of the rank and file in union affairs is the basic aim of Landrum-Griffin. The argument that a delegate may not vote in the same fashion as would the members questions the validity of representative government. Congress did not intend to impose a town-hall type of government upon labor unions. They were merely required to guarantee membership participation in fair elections.

A union may not, however, impose an increase in dues and assessments unilaterally and then proceed to obtain member ratification after the fact.[20] Also, a local union's bylaws that in effect delegated to union officers the authority to increase dues was declared a violation of the statute.[21] In that case, the San Francisco federal appeals court stressed that under the statute, a majority vote of the union membership by secret ballot is required to increase membership dues. The court invalidated the bylaw, stating that where a bylaw essentially delegates control over increases in the rate of dues to union officers and not to members, depriving the membership of any meaningful ability to vote on dues increases, it violates Landrum-Griffin. A union in violation of the procedural safeguards concerning dues and assessments must return the excess of dues unlawfully collected. An employer is not responsible for union action in the absence of proof that it conspired with the labor organization to withhold illegally the increased dues via the checkoff. The union must account for its own actions.

PROTECTION OF THE RIGHT TO SUE

Unions are prohibited from limiting the right of a member to bring suit against a labor organization, even when the leaders may be involved. A member also has the right to petition a legislature or communicate with particular legislators without union-imposed limits. Congress, however, placed two qualifications on member rights to engage in such action. The first is that a member "may be required" to exhaust "reasonable hearing procedures (but not to exceed a four-month lapse of time) within such organization" before initiating action. The second qualification is as follows:

> No interested employer or employer association shall directly or indirectly finance, encourage, or participate in, except as a party, any such action, proceeding, appearance, or petition.

In June 1977, however, a federal district court held this provision to be unconstitutional.[22] The National Right to Work Legal Defense & Education Foundation solicited money from antiunion employers. These funds were used to support legal action by dissident union members against their unions. On these facts alone, the court held that the foundation violated the law. The judge declared that "by financing union members in litigation against their labor organizations, the foundation had violated" the 1959 law. He cited the foundation as "an agent and conduit" for employers seeking to weaken unions.

In other words, though the district court held that the employer-financed foundation violated the law based on the facts of the case, it said that the provisions of the law violated the First Amendment rights of the foundation and the employers who contributed to it. Later on, a federal appeals court sidestepped the constitutional issue and held that the foundation did not violate the law, since the statute is not intended to cover legitimate legal aid associations, even though they received money from interested employers.[23] As long as the employer contributors have no control over the litigation that the foundation seeks to pursue on behalf of union members, the statute is not violated. Unless reversed by the U.S. Supreme Court, this decision means unions can be expected to defend themselves from more lawsuits. Naturally unhappy about this state of affairs, a union attorney commented:

> Our entire American labor policy has been based on keeping employers out of union affairs. This decision reverses 80 years of history.[24]

With respect to the first qualification, the one dealing with the exhaustion of internal union procedures before a union member has the right to sue his or her union, the issue quickly arose as to how the courts would apply this limitation.

Typical union constitutions contain procedures that provide for an appeal of local decisions to the international and then ultimately to the international convention. The section provides that a member may be required to exhaust internal remedies available within a four-month period before permitting suit against a union or its officers. Some questions arose immediately after the law was enacted. Does a member have to exhaust all internal remedies available within a four-month period before initiating proceedings? Does a member have the right to bring suit after four months of internal effort?

The legislative history of the Act sheds light on the issue of the members' right to bring suit after four months of internal effort to deal with a problem. Senator Kennedy was of the opinion that the section did not automatically permit a suit after a four-month period. He stated:

> The purpose of the law [was not] to eliminate existing grievance procedures established by union constitutions for redress of alleged violation of their internal governing laws. Nor is it the intent or purpose of the provision to invalidate the considerable body of State and Federal court decisions of many years standing, which require, or do not require, the exhaustion of internal remedies prior to court intervention depending on the reasonableness of such requirements in terms of the facts and circumstances of a particular case. So long as the union member is not prevented by his union from resorting to the courts, the intent and purpose of the "right to sue" provision is fulfilled, and any requirements which the court may then

impose in terms of pursuing reasonable remedies within the organization to redress violation of his union constitutional rights will not conflict with the statute.[25]

The magnitude of the particular problem of a member and the appropriateness
of internal appeals machinery have a great deal to do with a court's judgment of
particular cases. Some courts may require an exhaustion of internal remedies
before allowing judicial relief, whereas others may permit a suit despite the
availability of internal procedures.

The issue of exhausting all internal remedies available within a four-month
period has been litigated on several occasions since 1959. Congress intended to
permit unions to correct their own wrongdoing by stimulating them to independently establish democratic appeal procedures.[26] A safeguard against union abuse
was provided by not requiring exhaustion of union remedies if the procedures
exceed four months in duration. As stated by Representative Griffin, "It should
be clear that no obligation is imposed to exhaust procedures where it would
obviously be futile or would place an undue burden on the union member."[27]

In 1961, an appellate court reversed a district court decision that imposed
upon a union member an absolute duty to exhaust union remedies before applying to the federal courts.[28] In so doing, it made a review of the legislative history
of the section and held:

> Taking due account of the declared policy favoring self-regulation by unions, we
> nonetheless hold that where the internal union remedy is uncertain and has not
> been specifically brought to the attention of the disciplined party, the violation of
> federal law clear and undisputed, and the injury to the union member immediate
> and difficult to compensate by means of a subsequent money award, exhaustion of
> union remedies ought not to be required. The absence of any of these elements
> might, in light of Congressional approval of the exhaustion doctrine, call for a
> different result.

In a case decided by the U.S. Supreme Court in 1968, *Industrial Union of
Marine & Shipbuilding Workers,* it was decided that the four-month period was not
a grant of authority to unions to require exhaustion of internal remedies.[29]
Instead, it was merely a statement of policy that the courts may refuse to intervene
for this period of time. Courts may prefer to consider whether a procedure is
reasonable and should be exhausted, or if they should entertain the complaint.
Each case therefore appears to revolve about the particular issues involved and
the particular procedures available to which members may appeal.

SAFEGUARDS AGAINST IMPROPER DISCIPLINARY ACTION

Landrum-Griffin provides that a union member may not be "fined, expelled, or
otherwise disciplined," except for nonpayment of dues, unless certain procedural
steps are taken to insure due process. The member must be "(A) served with

written specific charges; (B) given a reasonable time to prepare his or her defense; (C) afforded a full and fair hearing." When a union violates these standards, the union member has the right to challenge the action taken against him or her in the courts. In 1971, however, the U.S. Supreme Court held that the courts do not have the power to construe union rules to determine the offenses for which discipline may be imposed.[30] Previously, lower federal courts construed a union rule allowing expulsion of a union member for conduct against union interest so as to exclude expulsion for a personal altercation between a union member and a union official. When a union official did not refer a union member to an available job, the member struck the official. Subsequently, the union member was disciplined by his union, and the lower federal courts held that the union rule in question could not be used as the basis for expulsion. By its reversal of these decisions, the U.S. Supreme Court has held that unions may interpret union rules for which members may be disciplined. In other words, the law's protection is limited to the procedure for discipline and not to the substantive character of union rules and their interpretation by the organization. Should a court find that a union member was fined, expelled, or otherwise disciplined without due process, it will direct an appropriate remedy. For example, under appropriate circumstances, a court will direct reinstatement of an expelled member in the union and award damages.

Due-Process Rights for Whom? Early litigation dealing with the due-process rights of union members construed the section to apply only to the union-member relationship, not the employer-employee relationship with a union. A much more difficult problem arose concerning the relationship of unions to their officers. Thus, may a union summarily remove an officer from office without affording due process? As noted above, a union member may not be fined, expelled, or otherwise disciplined unless due process is afforded. Is a union officer "otherwise disciplined" when removed from office?

To resolve this problem, courts distinguish among the reasons why an officer is removed. If removal is caused by malfeasance, the officer is not entitled to due process. For example, in one case, a business agent was removed because he showed favoritism in work assignments. A federal appeals court upheld the removal, saying: ". . . it was the union-membership relationship not the union-officer relationship that is protected . . ." by the bill of rights section of Landrum-Griffin.[31]

In contrast, when a union officer exercises rights protected by the bill of rights section, a federal appeals court held that the union must comply with the due process requirements. A group of officials was summarily removed from their offices because they actively supported an unsuccessful candidate for union office.[32] A federal appeals court upheld the dismissed officers and ruled that:

> nothing in the statutory language excludes members who are officers. Nor is there any intimation in the legislative history that Congress intended these guarantees

of equal political rights and freedom of speech and assembly to be inapplicable to officer members.

In other words, due process depends upon the reason why an officer is removed. Due process need not be afforded when removal is the result of malfeasance. In contrast, due process must be afforded a union officer who is removed for exercising rights guaranteed by the bill of rights section. Under these circumstances, the union officer was entitled to the same protection as a rank-and-file union member. As a federal court pointed out:

> the statutory distinction between officers and members of a union organization seems to be, for the most part, confined to the summary discharge of officers for alleged malfeasance. However, by contrast, when rights are asserted under [the bill of rights], no member "may be fined, suspended, expelled, or otherwise disciplined" without observance of . . . the due process section.[33]

During May 1982, however, the U.S. Supreme Court in *Finnegan* v. *Leu* held that a union president lawfully dismissed appointed union officers (business agents). They supported the challenger who had unsuccessfully run against the incumbent union president. The Court pointed out that Landrum-Griffin is designed to protect the interests of rank and file union members, not the job security of appointed union officers or employees. It ruled that the statute does not preclude an elected union officer from selecting staff members who hold compatible views with his or her own. However, in a footnote, the Court left open the question of whether a different result might be reached in a case involving "a nonpolicymaking and nonconfidential" employee.

Following the high court's precedent, a federal appeals court held that a union could lawfully discharge a secretary employed in its office because of her perceived lack of loyalty to a newly elected union administration.[34] During the election campaign, the secretary remained neutral at least outwardly, supporting neither the incumbents nor the challengers. Her apparent neutral stance, however, did not provide her with a valid suit under the law. Since she had almost unlimited access to confidential and sensitive union information, she did not fall within the exemption expressed by the high court.

Another federal appeals court held that the removal of a dissident union member from an important union committee was lawful.[35] Noting that the operation of the group from which he was removed, the Nuclear Safety Committee, played a significant role in union affairs, the court held that the removed member did not fall within the "nonpolicymaking" exemption expressed in the precedent case.

Understand that *Finnegan* v. *Leu* dealt with appointed union officers and not persons who are elected to union office. Nothing in the decision appears to authorize the removal of elected union officers who exercise their rights established in the statute. Indeed, should the decision be interpreted to cover elected union officers, the result would deal a serious blow to internal union democracy. In the past, national union presidents defeated in elections almost always lost to officers serving under them. One example was the loss of the United Steelworkers presidency by MacDonald to I. W. Abel, former secretary-treasurer of the national union. Also, in 1969, Joseph Yablonski, a United Mine Workers official for twenty-seven years, challenged W. A. (Tony) Boyle for the presidency. Mr. Yablonski lost the election and later his life, along with the lives of his wife and daughter. The Secretary of Labor challenged the election after Mr. Yablonski's murder, which had been one of the most notorious blots on union history. The fact that Mr. Yablonski was successful in even running for the UMW presidency is considered almost miraculous and marks the first attempt in about 40 years to challenge the incumbent president of the UMW. In December 1972, Arnold R. Miller decisively defeated Boyle for the union presidency in an election ordered by the courts and supervised by the Department of Labor. Miller, a reform candidate, headed an insurgent group called "Miners for Democracy." Several UMW officials who had served under Boyle were convicted for the Yablonski murders, and subsequently Boyle was convicted for the crime. Miller was embroiled in considerable internal political problems during the 1978 bituminous coal strike, and subsequently resigned his office.

Nonetheless, two federal court of appeals' decisions permitted the removal of elected union officers. In 1984, the federal appeals court in New Orleans upheld the removal of eleven elected union officials.[36] In 1985, the Atlanta federal appeals court ruled that the removal of the union president did not violate Landrum-Griffin.[37] In these cases, however, the courts carefully pointed out that the removal of the elected officers did not impair the democratic integrity of the union. Given these two cases, and the courts' reasoning, it is safe to say that should the removal of union officers result in the abrogation of the right of the membership to select their own officers, such action would violate the statute. Indeed, in one case, the court stressed that no proof was provided to demonstrate that the officer's removal was part of an attempt to dismantle the union's election system.

ENFORCEMENT OF THE "BILL OF RIGHTS"

Civil actions may be brought by anyone whose rights have been affected by violations of the "bill of rights" provisions of Landrum-Griffin. In contrast, the Secretary of Labor has administrative and enforcement responsibilities in connection with Titles II, III, and IV. There is no public remedy for violations of Title I. Most members do not have the financial resources to bring legal proceedings against labor organizations violating their rights. Also, they may be subject to group pressure militating against their using court action.[38] In this way, the full benefits of the "bill of rights" section may not be available to union members. On the other hand, to permit the Secretary of Labor to intervene at the request of union members may result in an unreasonable amount of litigation, which could impair the effective operation of labor organizations. Dissident groups could use the section to harass union officers if union members did not bear the burden of enforcement. It was these considerations that prompted Congress to forbid the Secretary of Labor to enforce the "bill of rights" section.

Despite the difficulty of union member enforcement, however, the fact is that private suits alleging violations of the "bill of rights" section are filed in court. Between 1959 and 1974, 1,559 private suits were filed by union members against their unions or officers, and a majority of them alleged violations of the "bill of rights" section.[39] By 1977 the number had increased to 2,072,[40] or an average of about 188 per year since Landrum-Griffin was enacted. As noted above, the number should increase given the current court policy on the activities of the National Right to Work Legal Defense and Education Foundation.

In addition, an added incentive was provided union members to sue their unions. Earlier we pointed out that the Supreme Court had held under Taft-Hartley that punitive damages could not be assessed against a union that violated its members' right of fair representation. In contrast, under Landrum-Griffin, a federal appeals court held that punitive damages could be assessed when a union violates its members' rights protected by the "bill of rights" section of that statute.[41] However, the court restricted its own rights in this respect, saying that punitive damages should be awarded only in the most egregious cases, where the conduct involved is malicious; and the amount should not be so great as to financially cripple a union. In any event, unlike fair representation cases under Taft-Hartley, no blanket prohibition of punitive damages exists so far under Landrum-Griffin.

REPORTS TO SECRETARY OF LABOR

Landrum-Griffin requires every labor organization to report its financial and administrative practices. Under certain conditions imposed by the Act, labor relations consultants, employers, union officers and employees, and surety companies must also file reports of their activities. The reports become public information and available to anyone for examination. Administrative responsibility is vested in the Secretary of Labor, with most authority delegated to the Office of Labor-Management and Welfare-Pension Reports. The office is under the supervision of the Assistant Secretary for Labor-Management Services Administration.

The Secretary of Labor is authorized to establish regulations prescribing the form and publication of reports. The Act requires that all persons who file reports must maintain records for a period of five years from which the reports may be verified. Criminal sanctions are available to deal with persons who violate the reporting and disclosure provisions of the law. Civil enforcement is available to the Secretary of Labor.

Before 1959, unions were required to file certain reports with the National

Labor Relations Board. Failure to comply resulted in a denial of their right to use the NLRB. With the passage of Landrum-Griffin, unions are not required to file reports with the Board.

Reports by Unions

Every labor organization is required to file a copy of its constitution and bylaws with the Office of Labor-Management and Welfare-Pension Reports. A labor organization is defined as not only a union in the usual sense, but also as employee representation groups, committees, and industry councils affecting commerce.[42] Such organizations fall within the Act's provisions if they deal with employers over grievances, rates of pay, and other terms and conditions of employment. Effective January 1, 1970, unions composed of federal employees must also file reports.[43] State or local central bodies do not have to file reports because their membership is made up of local unions or other subordinate affiliates.

The Initial Report

Within ninety days of the time a union first becomes subject to the 1959 law, it must file an initial report. The report must be signed by the principal union officers such as the president and secretary and must include specific information on the following:

1. Union name and address and address where records are kept.
2. Names and titles of officers.
3. Initiation fees for new members or other fees for transferred members as well as for working permits.
4. Dues and fees required of members.

The union must also indicate where information may be found in documents filed that contain provisions and procedures for:

1. Membership qualifications.
2. Assessment levies.
3. Participation in insurance and other benefits.
4. Authorization for disbursement of funds.
5. Financial audits.
6. Calling of regular or special meetings.
7. Selection of officers and representatives.
8. Discipline or removal of officers or agents.
9. Imposition of fines, suspensions, and expulsion of members.
10. Authorization for bargaining demands.
11. Ratification of contract terms.
12. Strike authorization.
13. Issuance of work permits.

Any change in information filed in the initial report must be reported once a year when the annual financial report is filed. A union that is terminated for reasons such as merger or consolidation and dissolution must file a terminal report within thirty days after loss of identity or existence. The report must state (1) circumstances and effective date of termination; and (2) name and address of the union into which it was consolidated, merged, or absorbed.

Annual Financial Report

A labor organization is required to file an annual financial report within ninety days after the end of each fiscal year. The report must show:

1. Assets and liabilities at the beginning and end of the fiscal year.
2. Receipts of any kind and the sources thereof.
3. Salaries, allowances, and other direct or indirect payments to each officer, irrespective of amounts, and also to each employee who received a total of more than $10,000 during the year from the reporting organization and any other affiliated union.
4. Direct and indirect loans to any officer, employee, or member that aggregated more than $250 during the fiscal year, together with a statement of the purpose, security, and arrangements for repayment.
5. Direct and indirect loans to any business enterprise, together with a statement of the purpose, security, and arrangements for repayment.
6. Other disbursements made by it and the purposes thereof.

Simplified reports may be filed by small unions if (1) gross receipts total less than $30,000 per reporting year and (2) the union is not in trusteeship. Terminal financial reports are required within thirty days after dissolution or consolidation, as are annual reports.

The reporting requirement has not been really controversial. Though it imposed a heavy burden on union officers, they faced the inevitable and complied with the law. Between 1959 and 1977, the Secretary of Labor filed 115 civil court actions to compel compliance with the reporting sections of the law, or an average of only about six per year.[44] Most of these cases were filed against unions. Considering, however, that 53,265 unions were covered by the law in 1977,[45] compliance appears excellent. Friction still exists over the application of the reporting duty to small unions. They received some relief when the Secretary of Labor permitted them to file simplified reports.

Like large unions, small unions must file these reports in order to deal with corruption and racketeering if it should arise.

Availability of Information to Union Members

Section 201 (c) requires reporting unions to make information contained in reports available to all its members. The right of members to examine the union's books and records to verify the report is enforceable in any state court of competent jurisdiction or in an appropriate federal district court. The provision provides also that a union member successful in a court suit may be allowed to recover costs and reasonable attorney's fees. Thus, proper administration of union funds is advanced because of the provision.

CONFLICT-OF-INTEREST REPORTING

Every union officer or employee, other than those performing clerical or custodial services exclusively, is required to file an annual report within ninety days after the end of the fiscal year if he or she, a spouse, or a minor child had any specified financial transaction that might constitute a possible conflict of interest. The obvious reason for such a requirement was to discourage the kinds of transactions that might constitute a conflict of interest. Apparently not many union officers are involved in this kind of activity. Only one action has been brought against a union officer for refusal to file the necessary reports, and that occurred in 1964.[46] Union officers and employees who do engage in conflict-of-interest transactions must at least disclose their activity. Should the membership learn that an officer receives income from a company in which the union holds bargaining rights (one example of a conflict-of-interest transaction), such an officer would probably be defeated in the next election, or quickly removed pursuant to the internal rules of the organization.

Criminal Penalties under Landrum-Griffin

Union officers who willfully violate the reporting section of the law may be fined up to $10,000 and imprisoned for one year. A violation could involve a union officer who fails to report, files a false report, or withholds material information. Between 1959 and 1974, about 900,000 reports were filed by union officers. In 1977, they filed about 93,000 reports.[47]

To understand convictions for willful violations of the reporting sections, it should be noted that other areas of the law, as indicated later, also provide for criminal penalties. Also, it is necessary to understand that there are several hundred thousand union officers who are in a position to commit Landrum-Griffin violations. As noted earlier, in 1977 the law applied to about 53,000 labor organizations. Each union averages about seven officers, or a total of about 370,000. Beyond the reporting requirements, a union officer may be convicted under the law for many crimes, including failure to secure union bonds; embezzlement; bribery; making of union loans to union officers or employees in excess of $2,000; payment of any fine imposed on a union officer or employee convicted of violating the law; depriving union members of their rights by coercion or violence; wrongful transfer of funds of a local union to the national union under a trusteeship arrangement; and serving as a union official after being convicted for specified crimes.

Between 1959 and 1977, approximately 933 union officers were convicted for *any* criminal offense under the law.[48] This amounted to an average of 51 convictions per year. The most frequent offense involved embezzlement, theft, or conversion of union funds. Violation of the reporting requirements was the second most prevalent offense. Given the small number of convictions, it would appear that union officers have faithfully complied with their obligations under the law. This analysis provides objective evidence that the American labor movement is largely free from corrupt and undemocractic practices.

EMPLOYER REPORTS

Employers are also required to file reports. Willful violations call for fines up to $10,000 and a year in prison. In general, these reports must be filed when employers engage in activities or make expenditures that undermine the integrity of the collective bargaining process or interfere with employee rights protected by Taft-Hartley.

To be reported are any payments or loans made to any labor organization or union officer. One purpose is to prevent the negotiation of "sweetheart contracts," in which the employer pays off union officers to settle on cheap or obviously substandard labor agreements. This employer requirement is the counterpart of the obligation of union officers to report any receipt of money or things of value from an employer, and the obligation of union officers to report any conflict-of-interest transaction.

An employer must also report any payment to any of its employees for the purpose of persuading other employees not to exercise their right to organize and bargain collectively. So if an employer makes a payment to an employee, for example, to persuade other employees not to vote for a union, such an expenditure must be reported. Payments to the employer's regular officers or supervisors, however, would be exempt. So the employer would not be required to report the salary, for example, of its personnel manager or labor relations director who as part of their regular duties persuade employees not to join or vote for a union.

An employer must also report expenditures made to *anyone* hired from outside the company to interfere with lawfully protected employee rights or to obtain information about its employees or labor organization involved in a labor dispute with the employer. For example, such expenditures must be reported should the employer engage the services of so-called "consultants," who may or may not be attorneys, for the purpose of persuading employees not to vote for a union, or to decertify a union. (The issue of consultants will be discussed further.) Exempt would be payments to obtain information to be used in proceedings with a government agency, arbitration, or court proceedings. Also, an employer need not report payments made to any person engaged to represent it in collective bargaining negotiations or in arbitration, government agency, or court proceedings.

Curiously, the reporting requirements impose on the employer the responsibility for determining whether its actions violate the Taft-Hartley unfair labor practice provisions or whether they are protected by the free-speech provisions of the law. Indeed, the law requires an employer to report expenditures made to dissuade employees from joining unions or to affect the results of collective negotiations. A free-speech problem could arise when an employer makes a publicity expenditure during a union organizing campaign. As we learned in Chapter 12, some employer "publicity" during election campaigns has been held to be an unfair labor practice. An employer cannot always be certain of the legality of the company's actions until a decision is rendered by the NLRB. Activities protected by the free-speech provisions are not exempt from the reporting requirements for that reason alone.[49] The employer must merely report such expenditures. The number of actions against employers has been very small.

LABOR RELATIONS CONSULTANTS

The law imposes a duty on an employer to report any arrangement and payment made to an outside consultant for the reasons specified. It imposes the same duty on the consultant to report the arrangement and payment as well. Two separate reports are required of the consultant. One involves arrangements made with the employer, and the other is a report on receipts and disbursements it made as a result of the arrangements. The report on arrangements must be filed within thirty days after entering into an agreement. It must contain:

1. Name under which the person making the report is engaged in doing business and the address of the principal office.
2. Detailed statement of the terms and conditions of the agreement or arrangement.

The basic reason for this requirement is to obtain reports from those consultants who agree to try to (1) influence employees regarding their organizational and bargaining rights, or (2) supply an employer with information regarding union activities similar to those that employers are required to report.

When consultants provide such services to employers, they must report the following financial data:

1. Receipts of any kind from employers on account of labor relations advice or services, and the sources of the receipts.
2. Disbursements of any kind in connection with labor relations services and the purposes thereof.

Nothing in law, of course, forbids consultants from engaging in such activities. It is only that they must report the information. However, willful failure to report, or false reporting, could result in criminal penalties, a fine up to $10,000 and a year imprisonment. Regardless of whether the consultant is an attorney, a report must be filed should the consultant persuade employees not to exercise their organizational and collective bargaining rights protected by Taft-Hartley. A federal appeals court held that an attorney, however, must report such activities and financial data, and is not exempt from doing so on the basis of the attorney-client relationship.[50] In 1985, another federal appeals court ordered a law firm to report its persuasion activities, though the attorneys did not commit any violation of Taft-Hartley on behalf of their employer-clients.[51] The law firm contended reports are required only when a consultant engages in unfair labor practices, for example, industrial espionage or threatening employees should they vote for a union. Rejecting this position, the court stated:

> Congress did not distinguish between disclosed and undisclosed persuaders or between legitimate and nefarious persuasive activities.

Nor are consultants relieved from the reporting requirements because they may infringe upon the First Amendment rights of free speech, association, or privacy.[52] A trade association published a magazine and other documents "unabashedly anti-union," which were distributed to employer members and employees. Holding that the trade association was required to report such activities, the court said any encroachment on its free speech right was speculative and was not substantially breached. In other words, any infringement on the association's First Amendment right was outweighed by the public interest of protection of employees in the exercise of their union rights. It also rejected the argument that the reporting requirement constituted a prior restriction on free speech, observing that the association is free to publish and distribute whatever material it desired as long as it complied with the reporting requirements of the law.

In recent years, increased use of consultants by antiunion employers has generated growing attention.[53] As reported in the *Wall Street Journal:*

> The number of specialists—including lawyers, consultants and social scientists—who are on the companies' side in these fights has ballooned, though statistics are sketchy. Last year, the Labor Department chronicled the involvement of such specialists in 159 labor disputes, a 127% increase from 1975.[54]

More recently, an AFL-CIO study published in 1984 revealed that consultants were directing management antiunion strategy in 70 percent of organizing campaigns conducted in 1982–83.[55]

In a congressional investigation of the subject, an AFL-CIO official said:

> So let me turn now to examining the nature of union-busting in 1979.
> The fact is that today the phenomena of union-busting is very different from 1959. Unfair labor practices of all kinds have skyrocketed. Our records show that out of 6,000 organizing campaigns of 10 or more workers, two-thirds involve some form of outside anti-union expertise. By some estimates there are more than 1,000

firms directly and indirectly involved in union-busting activities with more than 1,500 individual practitioners engaged in the full-time activity of preventing unionization efforts. Union-busting is now a major American industry with annual sales well over $½ billion.

These firms and consultants have almost all emerged within the last ten years. The conclusion must be drawn that there is a direct link between the professionalization of union-busting and the skyrocketing abuse of the law. In fact, many consultants openly claim credit for the meteoric rise in decertification and deauthorization elections.

Union-busting is no longer as blatant as the blunt-end of a billyclub. It is a sophisticated science spanning the field of psychology, law, and personnel administration. The practice of union-busting, like any of these component professions, involves the dissemination of expertise for practical application. We have identified five principal delivery systems by which this union-busting technology is disseminated from the expert into the midst of the workplace. They are: (1) The seminar lecturer who gives companies a two or three day crash course in the art of antiunionism. (2) The consulting firm composed of psychologists and industrial relations experts. (3) The anti-union law firm which handles the legal strategies of union-busting, including delays, discharges, bargaining to impasse and decertification. (4) The industrial psychologist who develops and administers the surveys and psychological testing of anti-unionism. (5) The trade association which combines all of these functions and specifically tailors them to the labor relations of an industry.[56]

Though the AFL-CIO official may have been hyperbolic and not completely accurate, the statement nevertheless highlights the growing use of the consultant as part of an employer's antiunion campaign. It reveals organized labor's fear of this comparatively new employer tactic.

Should consultants merely give advice directly to employers, they have no obligation to report their activities or financial data. Landrum-Griffin states:

Nothing in this section shall be construed to require any employer or other person to file a report covering the services of such person by reason of his giving advice to such employer. . .

As long as the consultant does not deal directly with employees, but provides antiunion counsel directly to the employer and its supervisors, no reports need to be filed. Given the growing use of consultants, unions claim that this is a weakness in the law which should be corrected. Thus:

The House Subcommitee on Labor-Management Relations issued in March 1981, a report on labor relations consultants that was based on extensive hearings in 1979 and 1980. A key recommendation was that the Labor Department should be more diligent in enforcing the reporting requirements for consultants under the Landrum-Griffin Act. "Virtually every union is required to and does report its activities under the provisions of the Act," the report says. "It is inequitable that the Department does not require consultants, even in instances when they are clearly running management's anti-union campaign, to disclose their involvement."[57]

At least up to this writing, the Department of Labor is apparently not adequately enforcing the reporting requirements imposed by Landrum-Griffin on employers and consultants. One recent study on this issue states:

> That there has been general noncompliance with the Act's employer and consultant reporting provisions is agreed upon by all observers. Indeed, a report entitled *The Forgotten Law—Disclosure of Consultant and Employer Activity under the LMRDA* was issued by the Subcommittee on Labor-Management Relations of the House Education and Labor Committee in December 1984. It concluded that the Labor Department had "systematically dismantled its employer and consultant reporting enforcement program."[58]

CONTROL OF TRUSTEESHIPS

Trusteeships are normally used by national unions to prevent or eliminate malpractices in subordinate local unions. House Committee Report No. 741 explained the operation of trusteeships as follows:

> Constitutions of many international unions authorize the international officers to suspend the normal processes of government of local unions and other subordinate bodies, to supervise their internal activity and assume control of their property and funds. These "trusteeships" (or "receiverships" or "supervisorships," as they are sometimes called) are among the most effective devices which responsible international officers have to insure order within their organization. In general, they have been widely used to prevent corruption, mismanagement of union funds, violation of collective bargaining agreements, infiltration of Communists; in short, to preserve the integrity and stability of the organization itself.

The McClellan committee found, however, various misuses of the trusteeship arrangement. It was found that some national unions without justification imposed trusteeships. Some suppressed rank-and-file members who attempted to release their local from the national union. At times, a local was taken over and its officers removed because the local union officers were opposed to the national union officers. Some national unions used the device to plunder local treasuries. Also, the corrupt nature of the trusteeship arrangement was displayed in some instances wherein local union funds were diverted to national-union-appointed trustees for their personal use. Once the arrangement was imposed, some continued under national control for as long as thirty years.

The McClellan committee devoted a great deal of attention to the trusteeship abuses of three unions: the Bakery and Confectionery Union, the Operating Engineers, and the Teamsters Union. Widespread publicity was devoted to union trusteeship abuses. The result was that the 1959 Landrum-Griffin Act provided three types of regulation of trusteeships. The first permits the establishment of trusteeships only if they are to achieve certain specific aims. These are as follows:

1. To correct corruption.
2. To correct financial malpractices.
3. To assure the performance of union contracts.
4. To assure the performance of a bargaining representative's duty.
5. To restore democratic practices.
6. To carry out the legitimate objects of the labor organization.

The constitution and bylaws of a union imposing a trusteeship must establish the administrative procedure to be used. This requirement limits the freedom of a parent body to impose its own rules as it pleases.

The second statutory regulation prohibits a local under trusteeship to cast votes at an international convention, "unless the delegates have been chosen by secret ballot in an election in which all members in good standing . . . were eligible to participate." This restriction makes it more difficult for parent bodies to keep locals under their control to further their political objectives.

The third regulation is that parent unions are required to file reports on each trusteeship upon its imposition, periodically while it is in effect, and upon its termination. Once a labor organization imposes a trusteeship over a subordinate body, it must report the action within thirty days to the Secretary of Labor. Detailed information is required on the following items:

1. Name and address of the subordinate body.
2. Date the trusteeship was established.
3. Detailed statement of reasons for establishing the trusteeship.
4. Nature and extent that the subordinate body's membership participates in regular or special conventions or other policy-making sessions.
5. Full and complete account of the financial condition of the local at the time the trusteeship was established.

Much of the information listed must be filed every six months while the trusteeship remains in effect. A trusteeship imposed in accordance with a parent union's constitution and bylaws and the allowable purposes enumerated above are presumed to be valid for a period of eighteen months. However, if union officials feel the arrangement should continue beyond the eighteen-month period, the presumption of validity is reversed, if challenged, and the national officers must show "clear and convincing proof" for the need to continue the device.[59] Even before a trusteeship arrangement may be considered valid for eighteen months, it must be ratified "after a fair hearing before the executive board or before such other body as may be provided in accordance with its constitution or bylaws."[60]

A regular annual financial report is required of the national union president, the treasurer, and the trustee in order to account for the use of the funds of the seized local.

A third type of report is required under the trusteeship provisions. A financial report must be filed at the time a trustee arrangement is terminated, in order to protect the integrity of the finances of a trusteed organization. Violation of the provision dealing with transfer of funds is punishable by a maximum fine of $10,000 and one year of imprisonment.

A union may file a complaint with the Secretary of Labor alleging violation of the prohibitions regarding (1) transfer of funds, (2) delegate voting, or (3) improper imposition of the trusteeship. The Act requires an investigation when a complaint is filed alleging any violation of these three conditions. A civil suit is brought in a federal district court if the Secretary finds a violation.

A complaining union member or a trusteed labor organization apparently has the right to bring suit in a federal district court. Court cases are divided on the issue of whether a union member could choose between filing a complaint with the Secretary of Labor or filing suit in a district court. One court ruled that a review of trusteeship had to be made first through the Secretary of Labor as the primary remedy.[61] Another court, however, reasoned that a union member could seek relief from either source.[62] Remedies for trusteeship violations are available under state or local courts. However, if the Secretary of Labor files a complaint, his or her action takes precedence over one that may be pending in any other court.

Only on very infrequent occasions has the Secretary of Labor instituted civil actions to compel compliance with Landrum-Griffin trusteeship provisions. As of 1986, only five of these suits had been filed since the 1959 law was enacted.[63] One case was particularly noteworthy because it dealt with a subterfuge to cloak an illegal trusteeship. A federal court ruled that a trusteeship is considered to be in effect merely on the basis of someone showing a suspension of autonomy that would "otherwise [be] available to a subordinate body under its constitution and by-laws."[64] The court rejected a national union claim that a trusteeship was not in effect because a literal suspension of autonomy had not been imposed on the local. Undoubtedly, the court's judgment was influenced by the fact that the local had lost in fact its autonomy for twenty years. This decision would indicate that the courts will sweep aside subterfuges calculated to conceal violations of the trusteeship provisions.

In 1973, however, a federal appeals court held that the courts do not have the authority to terminate a trusteeship when the subordinate body is limited to state public employees.[65] The basis for the court's decision was its finding that the local union, composed solely of public employees, was not a "labor organization" within the meaning of the law. In one way, the decision seems somewhat strange because the national union itself, American Federation of State, County and Municipal Employees, is subject to the provisions of Landrum-Griffin.

It would appear that abuses involving the trusteeship arrangement have abated as a result of the legislation. In 1959, the year in which Landrum-Griffin was enacted, there were about 500 trusteeships in effect. It is quite possible that these involved abuses in at least some cases, since the locals had been placed in trusteeship prior to enactment of the law. By 1966, only 19 of the 500 were still under an active trusteeship arrangement.[66]

As noted, the law permits trusteeships for specified and legitimate purposes. Since the enactment of the law, national unions continue to place locals under this arrangement. Indeed, between 1959 and 1972, about 2,200 trustee-ships were reported to the Secretary of Labor. However, by June 1972, the most recent data available, only 351 of this number were still in effect.[67] This is not a large number when one considers that there were more than 50,000 local unions in the nation; and, further, since the trusteeships were put into effect under the stringent provisions of the law, the national unions probably acted lawfully.

CONDUCT OF UNION ELECTIONS

Landrum-Griffin deals with internal union elections as well. The relevant section establishes requirements concerning the frequency of elections, and sets forth minimum standards relating to such things as nomination and election proce-dures, candidate eligibility to vote, campaign rules, and fund expenditures. It also establishes provisions to enforce the requirements.

Background of Election Regulation

Concern with union officer election procedures predates the Taft-Hartley Act, although the interest was at the state level and not in Congress. Indeed, in 1943, five states passed laws with the purpose of regulating election of officers among other internal practices.[68] One state supreme court held the election provisions unconstitutional (Texas), and another held them to be valid (Colorado).[69] However, most "state legislatures and courts were reluctant" to regulate internal union procedures prior to 1959.[70]

Malpractices in union election procedures were disclosed by the Bureau of Labor Statistics, the National Industrial Conference Board, and the McClellan committee. The committee found various violations of democratic principles in union elections. These were:

1. Disregard for the [union] constitutional provisions regulating elections.
2. Prevention of members from participating in elections.
3. Prevention of opponents from nomination by violence and intimidation.
4. Use of checkoff system to disfranchise membership.
5. Giving no advance notice to membership of balloting.
6. Not using secret ballots.
7. Use of union money for the election of incumbent officers.
8. Rigging elections by stuffing ballot box.
9. Removal of duly elected officers without due process.[71]

Two studies found that only a small percentage of unions were in violation of democratic internal practices. The 1958 Bureau of Labor Statistics study re-vealed that only 5 percent of unions did not hold presidential elections at least every five years.[72]

A study by Philip Taft was far more devastating to unions. Taft found that during the period 1900–1948, 81 percent of 202 national union presidential elections were uncontested. The reason was either lack of membership interest or political strength of incumbents.[73] Membership apathy, therefore, was an element in lack of membership participation in internal union affairs. The federal government proceeded to deal with the election abuses with the aim of establishing democracy in the election procedures used by unions.

ELECTION PROVISIONS

Frequency of Elections.   Election provisions of Landrum-Griffin apply to national and international unions, intermediate bodies, and local unions. Federations and state or local central bodies were not included in its coverage. National or international unions are required to hold elections at least once every five years. Voting must be by secret ballot among members of good standing, or at a convention of delegates chosen by secret ballot.

Local union elections must be held at least every three years. Secret balloting must proceed among members in good standing. Intermediate bodies must hold elections at least every four years. Balloting is on the same basis as that required of national unions. The credentials of convention delegates and all election records must be preserved for one year.

Many union constitutions and bylaws may call for more frequent elections than are required under the statute. Labor organizations may also legally establish stricter requirements for the election of officers. Title IV merely provides minimum standards, not maximum. Also, it would appear that the states under the federal preemption doctrine are forbidden to impose requirements stricter than those in Landrum-Griffin. Greater uniformity of internal union behavior is provided by federal control as opposed to state control of elections. For example, the too-frequent holding of elections could generate uncertainty in the collective bargaining process.

Minimum Election Procedures.   A union's constitution and bylaws control elections if they are not in conflict with the following Landrum-Griffin standards:

1. An election notice must be mailed to the last known address of a member within at least fifteen days prior to an election.
2. Each member in good standing is entitled to one vote.
3. No member shall be ineligible to vote or to be a candidate because of alleged default or delay in payment of dues if his or her dues have been withheld by the employer pursuant to a voluntary dues checkoff established in the labor agreement.
4. Votes by members of each local union must be counted and the results published, separately.
5. Election records must be kept for at least one year.
6. Any candidate has a right to have an observer at the polls and at the counting of ballots.

7. A reasonable opportunity must be given to nominate candidates and every member in good standing is eligible to be a candidate and entitled to vote without fear of reprisal.

Exceptions to Right to Hold Office.   Congress prohibited some persons from holding office in Title V of the 1959 law. Persons are barred from holding most union offices and jobs for five years after the end of their imprisonment for such crimes as robbery, bribery, extortion, embezzlement, grand larceny, burglary, arson, violation of narcotics laws, murder, rape, assault with intent to kill, and assault that inflicts grievous bodily injury. The five-year ban on holding office runs from the date of prison sentence expiration, not from parole date.[74] A union office, however, may be held by a banned person prior to the end of the five-year period if either U.S. citizenship has been regained or a Certificate of Exemption has been issued by the Board of Parole, U.S. Department of Justice.

Originally disqualified from being a union officer was any individual who was also a member of the Communist Party, who was excluded for five years after Communist Party membership termination. The Landrum-Griffin anticommunist provision was intended to replace the provision of Taft-Hartley that required principal union officers to sign noncommunist oaths before they could use National Labor Relations Board facilities. The labor movement fought such a requirement and argued that it stigmatized union leaders as anti-American. Furthermore, some critics argue that Communists holding union offices could easily sign such an oath. Others, however, pointed out that refusal of known Communist union leaders to sign the oath prevented their unions from using NLRB facilities. This paved the way for noncommunist unions to raid their membership and therefore weaken the Communist hold on the labor movement.

In any event, the noncommunist oath requirement of Taft-Hartley was held constitutional by the U.S. Supreme Court in 1950.[75] The Court pointed out that Taft-Hartley merely denied the use of NLRB facilities to unions whose officers refused to sign the affidavit. The 1947 law did not deny them the right to hold office.

Landrum-Griffin, as mentioned, denied Communists the right to hold union office for a five-year period after termination of party membership. The U.S. Supreme Court, however, held the provision unconstitutional in 1965.[76] The high court admitted that Congress has power to deal with the problem of Communists occupying positions of power and trust in labor unions. It was not willing, however, to permit Congress to deal with Communist Party members under criminal sanctions through general legislation.

Thus, there are no longer prohibitions on a Communist holding union office. It should be recognized, however, that the number of Communists holding union offices has declined over the years. There is no apparent need for a statutory prohibition on such individuals. Should a threat arise, it appears that the Congress, despite the Supreme Court's decision, would have power to deal with specific abuses. As stated, the Court held the Landrum-Griffin anticommunist provision unconstitutional because the law dealt with Communists as a class. Legislation designed to prevent Communists or members of other political groups from holding union office would probably stand the test of constitutionality if a law established specific standards upon which to judge the fitness of such individuals to serve as union officers.

Qualifications to Run for Union Office

Under Landrum-Griffin, all union members in good standing are eligible to run for local and national office, subject "to reasonable conditions uniformly imposed." As noted earlier, the U.S. Supreme Court in 1964 held in *Calhoun* v. *Harvey* that the limitations placed on union members' quest for office were reasonable. Since the union covered the maritime industry, the requirements for a candidate to serve at sea and be a member for five years were held to be lawful. In two other cases, however, the high court invalidated qualifications placed upon the opportunity of union members to run for office. One case required a union member to have held prior office and the other required attendance at a certain number of meetings.

Local 6, Hotel, Motel and Club Employees Union, established a requirement that candidates for office had to be prior officeholders as a condition of eligibility.[77] A district court held the requirement an unreasonable restriction on the right of union members to hold office and as such a violation of the Act. It refused, however, to set aside the election and order a new one because of lack of evidence that the prior officeholding requirement affected the election outcome. The trial court merely enjoined the local from using the requirement for candidacy in future elections. An appellate court deemed the union-imposed requirement reasonable and reversed the lower court.

The Supreme Court reversed the prior decisions and held that an eligibility requirement that rendered 93 percent of the membership ineligible for office could hardly be deemed reasonable. Further, exclusion of candidates from the ballot was prima facie evidence that the violation "may have affected the outcome." Disqualified candidates might have won an election. Such a restriction was viewed as a deviation from the congressional model for democratic union elections. The members themselves were deemed the best judges of candidacy qualifications as expressed in their actions at the polls.

In 1977, the high court by a split vote upset a rule requiring candidates to have attended at least one-half of a local's regular meetings for the three years preceding the election.[78] Under the union's rule, 96.5 percent of the members of the local were disqualified from union office. In its decision, the Court stressed that the 1959 law was designed to promote union democracy without interfering unduly with union internal affairs. It said:

Applying these principles to this case, we conclude that . . . the anti-democratic effects of the meeting attendance rule outweigh the interests urged in its support. . . . An attendance requirement that results in the exclusion of 96.5 percent of the members from candidacy for union office hardly seems to be a "reasonable qualification" consistent with the goal of free and democratic elections. A requirement having that result obviously severely restricts the free choice of the membership in selecting their leaders.

The minority believed the attendance rule to be a reasonable qualification. It criticized the majority for using a statistical test. The rule was reasonable, said the minority, because it could encourage attendance at meetings; guarantee that candidates for office had a meaningful interest in the union; and assure that the candidates have a chance to become informed about union affairs.

During 1982, in *Marshall* v. *Illinois Education Association,* a federal appeals court held unlawful a union's bylaw reserving a bloc of seats on its board of directors for members of specified minority groups: American Indians, black people, Hispanics, and Asians. It said that the policy conflicted with the purpose of the statute.

In 1982, a federal appeals court protected the right of dissidents to run for office.[79] Attempts to discipline a dissident received widespread publicity throughout the union, the members gaining the impression that the dissident member was not eligible to run for office because disciplinary action had been taken against him. To correct this situation, the court directed the union to send a letter to each member stating that the dissident was a union member in good standing and the disciplinary action taken against him did not bar his candidacy for union office. The court, however, did not deal with the merits of the charges alleged against the dissident member.

Undoubtedly, other qualifications for union office will be reviewed by the courts. In this type of case, the question becomes the reasonableness of the rule in question, and the problem of balancing the right of the union to run its internal affairs against the right of union members to seek union office. Not all union rules are designed to limit unfairly the opportunity for union office. Some serve to maintain the integrity and viability of the organization. On the other hand, rules that are arbitrary and capricious should not be permitted, since they would be inconsistent with the general philosophy of the 1959 law assuring maximum participation of union members in the organization's affairs.

Conduct of Campaign.   A candidate for union office can be at a distinct disadvantage during a campaign if he or she does not have access to the membership on a par with all other candidates. The law therefore provides that within thirty days prior to an election, a candidate can inspect a list of the last-known addresses of the union's members. Discrimination in the use of such lists is forbidden. The list must be available to all candidates at a union's main office, and if one candidate is permitted to copy the membership list, then all must be afforded the same right.[80]

The distribution of campaign literature is treated in similar fashion. Unions subject to the Act must comply with any reasonable request by a candidate to distribute campaign literature. The candidate, however, must bear the expense. This applies to the incumbent officers as well as to those who may be challenging the present officers. Any distribution arrangement made on behalf of any candidate must be made available to all upon request.

Union funds and employer contributions cannot be used to promote any candidate for election. A labor organization, however, has authority to use its funds to operate election machinery. It may pay for such items as ballots and notices publicizing the election date, place, time, and candidates. It may even publish factual statements of election issues as long as the names of the candidates are not included.

On the basis of wholesale violations of these campaign standards, a federal court invalidated the 1969 United Mine Workers' election, in which the incumbent Boyle defeated Yablonski, the challenger. It was determined that the union journal, financed wholly out of union member dues, had given extensive and favorable coverage during the election campaign to Boyle and his slate, printing their speeches, statements, and pictures. The journal, sent to all union members, did not even note the candidacy of Yablonski, or credit him for his efforts to secure the enactment of mine safety legislation. Union funds were used in other ways to support the election of the incumbents. Salary increases were provided to persons on the union's payroll to secure their support of Boyle and his slate. It was expected that these salary increases out of union funds would be turned over to Boyle to finance his campaign. Yablonski was denied the right to have observers at polling places. These and other serious campaign irregularities prompted a federal district court to say:

> . . . to find for the union [Boyle] the court would be forced to swim upstream against the tide of evidence too strong to resist.[81]

Ironically, these were the same charges that Yablonski had made before the 1969 election took place. If the government had acted on these charges and had forbidden the election to take place, it is possible that the Yablonski murders would not have occurred. As it turned out, Yablonski was not alive to enjoy the fruits of victory when his supporters defeated Boyle in the 1972 court-ordered election. In any event, the law did provide the basis for the new election and the restoration of democracy in the union.

In a hotly contested election for international president of the United Steelworkers of America in 1977, the challenger, Edward Sadlowski, obtained substantial financial contributions from nonmembers of the labor organization. Though the incumbent, Lloyd McBride, won the election by about 80,000 votes, the union later amended its constitution forbidding a candidate to solicit or accept funds from anyone not a member of the organization. Sustaining a lower court, a federal appeals court held the restriction to violate Landrum-Griffin.[82] It said that the outside contribution restriction

> . . .unreasonably impinges on the right of free speech and association guaranteed by section 10 (a) (2). . .

of the bill of rights provision of the 1959 statute. On June 14, 1982, however, in *United Steelworkers of America* v. *Sadlowski,* the U.S. Supreme Court by 5-4 held that unions can bar candidates for union offices from accepting contributions from individuals or groups outside the union so that outside individuals and groups cannot influence union elections by giving cash contributions to challengers.

Removal of Officers.   Elected union officers may be removed for serious misconduct. If a union's constitution or bylaws do not provide an adequate procedure for removal, the Act provides a procedure. A union member may file a complaint with the Secretary of Labor. The Secretary then holds a hearing to determine the adequacy of internal union machinery for such matters. If inadequate procedures are found, proper notice must be given that a hearing will be held on the charges. If the hearing discloses that serious misconduct occurred, a secret-ballot election will be held. The Secretary can force such an election by a civil suit. If a court orders a vote, the Secretary certifies the results. The court will decide from the results whether or not an officer is removed.

Enforcement of Election Procedures.   There are three preliminary steps involved in the enforcement of election provisions based on a union member's complaint to the Secretary of Labor. The steps are as follows:

> 1. The complaining union member must have exhausted his or her internal union procedures, at local and parent union levels, or must have invoked them without a final decision within three calendar months from the time he or she invoked them.
> 2. The complaint must be filed within one calendar month thereafter.
> 3. The Secretary of Labor must investigate the complaint.

A challenged election is presumed valid unless found to the contrary. Elected officials perform their regular duties during the investigation. If the Secretary of Labor finds probable cause to believe a violation has occurred, he or she must file suit in a federal district court within sixty days after the complaint is filed. It is important to note that the union member must challenge an election through the Secretary of Labor and not through the courts. In 1973, a court held that regardless of wrongdoing by a union in election matters, the member may not directly solicit the courts for relief. The member must file charges with the Secretary of Labor, and the government will file suit in court on his or her behalf.[83]

In 1984 this policy was upheld by the U.S. Supreme Court in *Teamsters, Local 82.*[84] Union members alleged that an election was not held in conformance with the Landrum-Griffin standards. After the union dismissed the complaint, they successfully persuaded a district court to enjoin the election and direct a new poll to be conducted by an impartial arbitrator. Reversing a district and a federal appeals court, the high court held that the union members' exclusive remedy, after exhaustion of internal union procedures, was to file a complaint with the Secretary of Labor. Only the Secretary of Labor after an investigation has the authority to petition a federal district court to void an election and order a new one. Though the Supreme Court noted that union members may appeal directly to the courts for alleged violations of the "bill of rights" section of the statute, it held that election matters fall within the exclusive jurisdiction of the Secretary of Labor. Should a federal court direct a new election, it is to be held under the Secretary of Labor's supervision.

The question has also arisen whether a decision by the Secretary of Labor not to set an election aside could be reviewed by the courts. This was a particularly difficult issue, because under the 1959 law, the Secretary of Labor has wide and seemingly conclusive power to determine the circumstances under which he or she will challenge an election. Mindful of this congressional purpose, the U.S. Supreme Court held in 1975 that the courts do not have the authority to order a trial-type inquiry into the factual basis of the Labor Secretary's refusal to upset an election.[85] On the other hand, the high court rejected the contention of the Secretary of Labor that the courts have no authority whatsoever to review such a decision. It pointed out that nothing in the 1959 law explicitly makes such a decision immune from judicial review. In short, the high court said that a decision of the Labor Secretary not to challenge an election will not be disturbed unless the reasons which he or she offers are so "irrational as to be arbitrary and capricious." In other words, the Secretary of Labor must provide the court and the complaining union member with a statement of the supporting reasons for the refusal to challenge an election. If in a particular case the court determines that the Secretary acted capriciously or arbitrarily, it has the authority to direct the Secretary of Labor to run a new election.

A new election, if directed by the court, is held under the supervision of the Secretary of Labor. The court will void the challenged election and direct a new one if it is found that an election has not been held within the time period established by law, or if a violation may have affected the election outcome.

The Secretary will not bring suit in every case where violations are found, but only in cases where there is evidence that violations "may have affected the outcome of an election." The Department of Labor adopted this policy because a district court is required by law to make a similar finding before ordering a new election. An appeal of a district court's decision is available, but an ordered election must be held while the appeal is pending. Otherwise, the period required for final litigation could be—and usually is—longer than the term of office challenged.

The U.S. Supreme Court ruled that a district federal court must direct a new election when the Secretary of Labor has demonstrated that violations of Landrum-Griffin standards may have affected the outcome of an election. To assure compliance with the law, the Court also held that another election held by the union after the original one was challenged does not stay the Secretary of Labor's power to conduct one under his or her supervision. The Court stated:

> The intervention of an election in which the outcome might be as much a product of unlawful circumstances as the challenged election cannot bring the Secretary's action to a halt. Aborting the exclusive statutory remedy would immunize a proved violation from further attack and leave unvindicated the interests protected [by law].[86]

Thus, a union may not eliminate a pending Title IV action by conducting an unsupervised election of officers after the original one was challenged.

In still another case before the Supreme Court, it was held that the Secretary of Labor's investigative powers are not limited to the specifics of a union member's complaint. The Court stated:

> We reject the narrow construction adopted by the District Court and supported by respondent limiting the Secretary's complaint solely to the allegations made in the union member's initial complaint. Such a severe restriction upon the Secretary's powers should not be read into the statute without a clear indication of congressional intent to that effect . . . [when] the indications are quite clearly to the contrary.[87]

A union member may file a complaint based on incomplete information. The Secretary of Labor has machinery at his or her disposal to look at the totality of election conduct, and the Supreme Court upholds his or her right to do so. However, in 1971, the high court limited the power of the Secretary of Labor to police union elections.[88] It held that the Secretary can bring suit in court only against the union practices that a union member protests to his or her union before filing charges with the Department of Labor. While investigating a member's complaint, it was discovered that the union allegedly committed another violation of the law. However, the union member did not attempt to correct this condition through internal union procedures, but only through the complaint that was filed with the Labor Department. On this basis, the Supreme Court held that the district court could consider only that complaint that the union member had unsuccessfully attempted to correct through internal union procedures. Thus, it was the judgment of the high court that a union should be given the opportunity to correct undemocratic procedures before a court takes action. If the Secretary of Labor could file suit against union practices that the union itself had not been given the opportunity to correct, the court stated that union "self-government . . . would be needlessly" weakened.

Usage of Election Provisions

The election provisions of the 1959 law have been used far more frequently by union members than has any other feature of Landrum-Griffin. Between 1965 and 1974, union members filed 1,296 complaints alleging violations of the election standards contained in the law.[89] Though this number appears substantial, it should be noted that in that period, there were about 57,000 labor organizations covered by the law. Since local unions must conduct an election at least once every three years, intermediate bodies at least once every four years, and national unions at least once every five years, it follows that in this ten-year period, more than 150,000 elections were held. Actual violations of the law were found in only a small number of the cases alleging wrongdoing. Of the 1,296 complaints, the federal courts ordered only 165 new elections.[90] In 767 instances, complaints were dismissed because no violations were found, or because of the lack of evidence to demonstrate that alleged violations affected the outcome of the elections. In 239 of the cases, unions agreed to take corrective measures, such as recounting the ballots, amending the election provisions of their constitutions and bylaws, or installing winning candidates whom they had previously refused to install for some reason.

Essentially the same experience occurred between 1975 and 1977.[91] Of the 742 complaints filed by union members in those three years, 443 were dismissed because no violation had occurred, or because of lack of evidence to show that alleged violations had affected the outcome of the elections. Federal courts ordered new elections in only 70 instances.

In short, in the light of the large number of elections held by union groups, it appears that the vast number of labor organizations hold regular and fair elections. Undoubtedly, union members frequently challenge elections because of internal political differences rather than on the basis of genuine wrongdoing by incumbent union officials. On these grounds, it is understandable why the AFL-CIO remarked that Landrum-Griffin election investigations "produced only harassment and disruption, with justifiable bitterness against unnecessary governmental intrusion into internal union affairs."[92] In any event, on balance Landrum-Griffin election standards are salutory, because they provide an effective remedy whenever incumbent union officers fail to provide for a fair election. Also, the existence of the law serves as a deterrent to union officers who may be inclined to deprive members of the opportunity to elect officers of their own choice on a regular and fair basis.

FINANCIAL SAFEGUARDS FOR LABOR ORGANIZATIONS

Title V includes some of the most important provisions of Landrum-Griffin on internal union operations. It provides for (1) fiduciary responsibilities of union officers and employees; (2) general bonding; and (3) loan and payment-of-fines standards.

Fiduciary Responsibilities of Union Officers and Employees

Union officers and representatives occupy positions of trust in relation to the union and its members. Under Landrum-Griffin, they have a duty to use the union's money and property in accordance with its constitution and bylaws "solely for the benefit of the organization and its members."

A *fiduciary* may be defined as a person who undertakes to act in the interest of another person.[93] Congress codified the common law applicable to trust relations in Title V. Persons responsible for union funds must manage, invest, and expend such funds and property in strict accordance with a labor organization's constitution, bylaws, and governing body resolutions. They must refrain from (1) dealing with their own union as an adverse party, and (2) holding or acquiring pecuniary or personal interests that conflict with the union's interests. Also, such persons must account to the union for any profits received by them in any transaction conducted under their direction on behalf of the union. The prohibitions extend beyond money transactions, but include other deals, as well as some that could evolve out of the collective bargaining process. This basic language was intended "to aid members of labor organizations in their efforts to drive criminals from the trade union movement."[94] Judge Cardozo captured the primary fiduciary responsibility well when he stated:

> Many forms of conduct permissible in a workaday world for those acting at arm's length, are forbidden to those bound by fiduciary ties. A trustee is held to something stricter than the morals of the market place. Not honesty alone, but the punctilio of an honor the most sensitive, is then the standard of behavior. As to this there has developed a tradition that is unbending and inveterate. Uncompromising rigidity has been the attitude of courts of equity when petitioned to undermine the rule of undivided loyalty by the "disintegrating erosion" of particular exceptions. . . . Only thus has the level of conduct for fiduciaries been kept at a level higher than that trodden by the crowd.[95]

It is not at all strange in light of the attention that Congress devoted to the common law that a section was included preventing a union from freeing its personnel from liability of trust duties. Any attempt to do so by the inclusion of provisions in constitutions or bylaws is void because it is against public policy.

Congress made no attempt to tell unions how to spend their money. It merely intended that funds and assets be used in accordance with the direction of the membership. Senator Kennedy made this clear when he remarked that

> the bill wisely takes note of the need to consider the special problems and functions of a labor organization in applying fiduciary principles to their officers and agents.[96]

A local union, for example, may pass a resolution to use union funds to pay an officer's defense in court litigation. Should a local do so, however, the courts may enjoin the resolution as *ultra vires* in violation of the Act's purpose.[97] The resolution itself does not have the effect of relieving a person from his or her trust duties.

The fiduciary feature of the law becomes more meaningful when considered in the light of the reporting features discussed in the earlier part of this chapter. As noted, union officers must report all expenditures of union funds and specify the purpose. If a union officer does not report such expenditures, or reports falsely, he or she would be subject to criminal penalties. If he or she expends funds not in the interest of the union and reports the transaction, this information is available to union members. For example, suppose a union officer caused union funds to be spent for an item for his or her personal use, say a boat, and truthfully reports the expenditure. Under these circumstances, the union or its members can by suit in court force the union officer to return the money to the union treasury. The suit would be based upon the charge that the union officer breached fiduciary responsibilities. Unfortunately, there are no data available to demonstrate experience under this section of the law.

Recovery of Assets.   Landrum-Griffin provides that in the event a labor organization or its governing board of officers refuses or fails to proceed against union agents who violate their fiduciary responsibilities, a union member may file a civil suit in a federal or state court for appropriate relief under certain circumstances. A request must first be made of the officers. If they fail to correct the situation within a reasonable period of time, the member may file suit. An individual suit may be brought only "upon leave of the court obtained upon verified application and for good cause shown." If a court permits an individual suit, it may be for damages, an accounting of the assets in question, or "other appropriate relief" for the benefit of the labor organization. Upon request, a trial judge may allot to an individual the counsel fees and expenses incurred in the litigation. Recovery of such costs to the individual is usually allotted from any recovery of assets resulting from the action. However, the District of Columbia Circuit Court of Appeals has ruled that the Act does not limit the courts to the amount of assets recovered through litigation.[98] Thus, unions that become lax in maintaining internal control over officers could find themselves liable for litigation costs that far exceed the value of assets in question. In still another case, an appellate court held that the monetary recovery may constitute a source from which litigation costs of a member are paid.[99] The award of costs, in the court's view, should be based on the benefits realized by the union as a result of the suit.

A union member is not required to exhaust internal union remedies prior to bringing suit.[100] In *Giordani,* the union argued that it had not refused or failed to sue its officers within a reasonable time after being requested to do so. Nearly a year had passed from the time the member had requested union officials to proceed to obtain appropriate relief. In another case, *Purcell* v. *Keane,* a trial judge relying on the *Giordani* case ruled that "since exhaustion of remedies is not mandatory, a court does not have to find exhaustion in order to find good cause."[101]

It is still not known exactly what is meant by "within a reasonable period of time," but the courts in the *Giordani* and *Purcell* cases referred to about one year. The period of time, however, could depend largely upon the procedures initiated by particular unions after members request action of them. Many union officers, particularly those who remember the court proceedings during and prior to the 1930s, prefer to keep union affairs out of court. This may account for some reluctance to initiate action. Some officers may have convinced their members to forget violations of fiduciary responsibility. The courts have proved themselves less kind in such matters.

Embezzlement of Union Funds.   Under Landrum-Griffin, it is a federal crime for anyone to embezzle, steal, or unlawfully and willfully convert union assets to his or her own or to someone else's use. The section goes farther than placing a limit on union officers. Any officer or employee who siphons off union funds to third parties violates the law. It is no violation of the section for a nonmember to behave in such fashion. However, it is unlikely that a nonmember would be in a position to violate the law without assistance from a member. A person convicted of such a violation may receive a maximum sentence of $10,000 fine or five years' imprisonment, or both. The basic issue involved at an embezzlement trial is whether an official misused union funds, not whether personal benefit was gained from the assets.[102] The courts deal sharply with officials convicted of Section 501 (c) violations. For example, a New York federal district court in 1963 fined a union official $25,000 on two counts of embezzlement and one of absconding with union fund records.[103] A five-year prison sentence was also imposed. In 1977, a union business agent was imprisoned for two and one-half years because of embezzlement.[104]

General Bonding

All union personnel who "receive, handle, disburse, or otherwise exercise custody or control of the funds or other property of a labor organization or a trust in which a labor organization is interested" must be bonded. Union officers, agents, shop stewards or other representatives, and union employees are included in the requirement. Bonding is not required of personnel, however, if their union has property and annual financial receipts of less than $5,000. The amount of bond required of a person is not less than 10 percent of the funds handled by the person in the previous fiscal year. The law does not require any bond to exceed $500,000. If there is no previous fiscal-year experience upon which to calculate the bond, it shall be (1) not less than $1,000 in the case of a local union, and (2) not less than $10,000 in the case of any other kind of union.

Bonds must be obtained from a surety company authorized by the Secretary of the Treasury as a surety on federal bonds. They cannot be obtained from a broker or surety company in which any labor organization or any union representative has a direct or indirect interest. The bond can be either individual or schedule in form. An *individual* bond is a single bond covering a single named individual. A *schedule bond* covers particular positions. A single position may be involved, or the bond may designate several positions. Each position may carry quite different coverage in accordance with the amount of funds handled. Most unions prefer schedule bonds because under this system, they are relieved from the expense and trouble of obtaining a new bond each time a new officer is elected or appointed to a position.

The bonding enforcement provision makes any person who willfully violates the requirements subject to a fine of not more than $10,000 or imprisonment for not more than one year, or both. Unintentional violations may merely result in a prohibition on an individual's function in a capacity for which bonding is required.

Loans and Payment of Fines

Landrum-Griffin limits the amount of loans unions can make to their personnel. It also forbids both unions and employers from paying a fine for any officer or employee convicted of any willful violation of the Act.

Total indebtedness of union officers and employees cannot exceed $2,000. This safeguard was provided to eliminate the misuse of union assets under the guise of bona fide loans.

Willful violations are subject to fines up to $5,000 and imprisonment of up to one year.

SUMMARY

The basic aim of Landrum-Griffin is to assure fair treatment to union members, and guarantee to them rights that are expressed or implied by the United States Constitution. At this writing, the law has been in effect for about twenty-seven years. Despite the original protest of organized labor against the law, and its continued opposition in some respects, unions have learned to live with and adjust to the law. Its provisions have proved burdensome at times. Particularly with regard to the election standards, unions have often been burdened with defending themselves against false or trivial charges. However, when there is evidence of abuse and wrongdoing and the interests of people are placed in jeopardy, it is commonplace that government does intervene.

Certainly the vast number of union leaders are honest and have integrity. As in any large institution, however, there are those who would use the union movement for their personal aggrandizement and not in the interest of the members. In this light, the law fulfills a public purpose and constitutes a valuable feature of our social fabric. No law, of course, can possibly result in a utopian kind of democracy in which all participants are treated equally and fairly. Despite Landrum-Griffin, some corruption and undemocratic practices undoubtedly still exist in the union movement. Undoubtedly, some unions are dominated and controlled by organized crime. Based upon a congressional investigation, one writer put the figure at at least 300 local unions.[105] Even if that figure is accurate, it should be noted that at this writing, there are about 65,000 local unions in the nation.[106] By the same token, organized crime has also infiltrated and seized control of some business enterprises. To condemn all union and business leaders because of racketeering on the part of a portion of them clearly flies in the face of fairness and common sense. In any event, Landrum-Griffin has eliminated some of the more flagrant abuses, and has at least served to educate officers on their responsibilities to membership. Clearly, it has served as a deterrent to those unscrupulous union officers who would be inclined to treat the rights of members with contempt.

DISCUSSION QUESTIONS

1. Were internal union abuses sufficient to warrant passage of the Landrum-Griffin Act?

2. What were the findings and recommendations of the McClellan committee?

3. Explain the objectives sought by Congress as revealed in Title I of the 1959 law.

4. Discuss the apparent conflict between the Title I and Title IV guarantees.

5. How do the courts tend to deal with conflicts between the right of members to free speech and assembly and the right of unions to adopt and enforce rules about member responsibilities toward the labor organization?

6. What checks or controls were placed on unions regarding dues, initiation fees, and assessments?

7. What qualifications did Congress place on the right of members to bring suits against their unions? How have the courts construed this provision?

8. What due-process protections do members have against improper disciplinary action? What due-process rights are extended to appointed union officers or employees? To elected union officers?

9. Are there basic weaknesses in enforcement procedures available to union members who allege violations of the "bill of rights" provision of Landrum-Griffin?

10. When must attorneys file reports under Landrum-Griffin? How extensive are the reporting requirements? How vigorous is the Department of Labor in enforcing the reporting provisions concerning employees and consultants?

11. What relief has been provided to local unions from trusteeship abuses of national unions?

12. How have the courts interpreted union rights to impose qualifications on members who seek union offices?

13. If a union violates Landrum-Griffin election standards, what remedy is available to members who seek relief?

14. What financial safeguards were provided by Title V to protect unions from fiduciary violations on the part of officers and employees?

NOTES

1   73 Stat. 519.

2   Joel Seidman, "Emergence of Concern with Union Government and Administration," in *Regulating Union Government,* eds. Marten S. Estey, Philip Taft, and Martin Wagner (New York: Harper & Row, 1964), pp. 2–3.

3   Robert D. Leiter, "LMRDA and Its Setting," in *Symposium on the Labor-Management Reporting and Disclosure Act of 1959,* ed. Ralph Slovenko (Baton Rouge, Louisiana: Claitor's Bookstore Publishers, 1961), p. 13.

4   Interim Report of the Senate Select Committee on Improper Activities in the Labor or Management Field, Report No. 1417, 85th Congress, 1958.

5   105 Congressional Record 5806 (daily ed.), April 22, 1959.

6   C. Peter Magrath, "Democracy in Overalls: The Futile Quest for Union Democracy," *Industrial and Labor Relations Review,* XII (1959), p. 503.

7   105 Congressional Record 14389 (daily ed.), August 12, 1959.

8   Benjamin Aaron, "Employee Rights and Union Democracy," *Monthly Labor Review,* U.S. Department of Labor, Bureau of Labor Statistics, XCII, 3 (March 1969), p. 50.

9   *Ibid.,* p. 50.

10   *Ibid.*

11   *Phalen* v. *Theatrical Protective Union No. 1 International Alliance of Theatrical & Stage Employees, AFL-CIO,* 22 N.Y. (2d) 34 (1968).

12   Aaron, *op. cit.,* pp. 50–51.

13   *Calhoon* v. *Harvey,* 379 U.S. 134 (1964).

14   *Alvey* v. *General Electric Co.,* CCA 7, Case No. 79–1636, June 11, 1980.

15   *Salzhandler* v. *Caputo,* 316 F. (2d) 445 (1963).

16   *Farowitz* v. *Associated Musicians of Greater New York, Local 802,* CCA 2, Case No. 28434, April 29, 1964.

17   U.S, Department of Labor, Labor-Management Services Administration, *Compliance, Enforcement, and Reporting,* U.S. Government Printing Office, Washington, D.C. (1975), p. 49.

18   *Hall* v. *Cole,* 412 U.S. 1 (1973).

19   *American Federation of Musicians* v. *Wittstein,* 379 U.S. 171 (1964).

20   *Peck* v. *Associated Food Distributors of New England,* 237 F. Supp. 113 (1965).

21   *Burroughs* v. *Operating Engineers, Local 3,* CCA–9, No. 81–4145, July 2, 1982.

22   *Auto Workers* v. *National Right to Work Legal Defense & Education Foundation,* U.S. Dist. Ct. (D.C.), Case No. 839-73, June 2, 1977.

23   *Automobile Workers* v. *National Right to Work Legal Defense & Education Foundation,* CCA DC, Case No. 77–1739, November 17, 1978.

24   *Wall Street Journal,* June 3, 1977, p. 2.

25   105 Congressional Record 16414 (daily ed.), September 3, 1959.

26   Archibald Cox, "The Role of Law in Preserving Union Democracy," *Harvard Law Review,* LXXII (1959), pp. 609, 615.

27   105 Congressional Record A7915 (daily ed.), September 4, 1959.

28   *Detroy* v. *American Guild of Variety Artists,* 286 F. (2d) 75 (1961).

29   *NLRB* v. *Industrial Union of Marine & Shipbuilding Workers, AFL-CIO, Local 22,* 391 U.S. 418 (1968).

30   *Boilermakers* v. *Hardeman,* 401 U.S. 233 (1971).

31   *Sheridan* v. *United Brotherhood of Carpenters,* 306 F. (2d) 152 (1962).

32   *Grand Lodge of International Association of Machinists* v. *King,* 335 F. (2d) 340 (1962), cert. denied 379 U.S. 920 (1964).

33   *DeCampli* v. *Greeley* (November 1968); see *Monthly Labor Review,* U.S. Department of Labor, Bureau of Labor Statistics, XCII, 3 (March 1969), pp. 62–63.

34   *Hodge* v. *Teamsters,* CCA–7, No. 82–2555, May 25, 1983.

35   *Cotter* v. *Owens,* CCA–2, No. 84–7574, January 15, 1985.

36   *Adams-Lundy* v. *Association of Professional Flight Attendants*, CA–5 No. 84–1257, April 30, 1984.

37   *Dolan* v. *Transport Workers*, CCA–11, November 13, 1984.

38   Russell A. Smith, "The Labor-Management Reporting and Disclosure Act of 1959," *Virginia Law Review*, XLVI, 2 (March 1960), p. 210.

39   U.S. Department of Labor, Labor-Management Services Administration, *Compliance, Enforcement, and Reporting*, U.S. Government Printing Office, Washington, D.C. (1974), p. 43.

40   *Compliance, Enforcement, and Reporting*, 1977, *op. cit.*, p. 61.

41   *Quinn* v. *DiGiulian*, CCA–DC, No. 83–2065, July 13, 1984.

42   *NLRB* v. *Cabot Carbon Company*, 360 U.S. 203 (1959).

43   *Compliance, Enforcement, and Reporting*, 1977, *op. cit.*, p. 47.

44   *Ibid.*, p. 22.

45   *Ibid.*, p. 39.

46   *Compliance, Enforcement, and Reporting*, 1968, *op. cit.*, p. 11.

47   *Compliance, Enforcement, and Reporting*, 1977, *op. cit.*, p. 39.

48   *Ibid.*, p. 25.

49   Regulations of Secretary of Labor, Part CDV, Chapter 4, Title 29, December 27, 1963.

50   *Price, Nelson, & Sears* v. *Wirtz*, CCA–5, 412 F. (2d) 647 (1969).

51   *Humphrey, Hutchenson and Moseley* v. *Donovan*, CCA–6, No. 83–5564, February 20, 1985.

52   *Master Printers of America* v. *Donovan*, CCA–4, No. 82–1990, December 26, 1984.

53   *Hearings Before Subcommittee on Labor-Management Relations, Committee on Education and Labor, House of Representatives, 96th Congress, First Sess., Pressures in Today's Work Place*, I and II, October, December, 1979.

54   *Wall Street Journal*, November 19, 1979.

55   *AFL-CIO News*, February 11, 1984.

56   *Pressures in Today's Work Place, op. cit.*, I, p. 410.

57   AFL-CIO, Industrial Union Department, *Viewpoint* (Spring 1981), p. 6.

58   Bernstein, Jules A., "The Evolution of the Use of Management Consultants in Labor Relations: A Labor Perspective," *Labor Law Journal*, XXXVI, 5 (May 1985), p. 297.

59   Sar A. Levitan, "The Federal Law of Union Trusteeship," in *Symposium on the Labor-Management Reporting and Disclosure Act of 1959*, ed. Ralph Slovenko (Baton Rouge, Louisiana: Claitor's Bookstore Publishers, 1961), p. 453.

60   *Ibid.*

61   *Rizzo* v. *Ammond*, 182 F. Supp. 456 (1960).

62   *Local 28* v. *IBEW*, 184 F. Supp. 649 (1960).

63   *Compliance, Enforcement, and Reporting*, 1977, *op. cit.*, p. 22.

64   *Lavender* v. *United Mine Workers of America*, 285 F. (2d) 869 (1968).

65   *State, County, and Municipal Employees, New Jersey and Municipal Council 61* v. *State, County, and Municipal Employees*, 478 F. (2d) 1156 (CA 3, 1973); cert. denied 414 U.S. 975 (1973).

66   U.S. Department of Labor, *Summary of Operations, 1966, LMRDA*, pp. 15–17.

67   *Compliance, Enforcement and Reporting*, 1972, *op. cit.*, p. 5.

68   The states were Colorado, Florida, Kansas, Minnesota, and Texas.

69   See Julius Rezler, "Union Elections: The Background of Title IV of LMRDA," in Slovenko, ed., *op. cit.*, pp. 475–494.

70   *Ibid.*, p. 482.

71   *Ibid.*, pp. 485–486.

72   *Ibid.*, p. 483.

73   *Ibid.*, p. 483.

74   *Serio* v. *Liss,* 189 F. Supp. 358 (1960), affirmed 300 F. (2d) 386 (1961).

75   *American Communications Association* v. *Douds,* 339 U.S. 382 (1950).

76   *United States* v. *Archie Brown,* 381 U.S. 437 (1965).

77   *Wirtz* v. *Hotel, Motel & Club Employees Union, Local 6,* 391 U.S. 492 (1968).

78   *Local 3489, United Steelworkers* v. *Usery,* 429 U.S. 305 (1977).

79   *Rollison* v. *Hotel and Restaurant Employees, Local 879,* CCA–9, No. 80–3498, May 18, 1982.

80   *Conley* v. *Aiello,* 276 F. Supp. 614 (1967).

81   *Wall Street Journal,* April 3, 1972.

82   *United Steelworkers of America* v. *Sadlowski,* CA DC, Case No. 81–1174, March 31, 1981.

83   *Schonfeld* v. *Raferty,* U.S. District Court, Southern District of New York, No. 67 Civ. 3147, May 8, 1973.

84   *Teamsters, Local 82 Furniture & Piano Movers* v. *Crowley,* 104 Sup. Ct. 2557 (1984).

85   *Dunlop* v. *Backowski,* 421 U.S. 560 (1975).

86   *Wirtz* v. *Local 153, Glass Bottle Blowers Association of the United States & Canada, AFL-CIO,* 389 U.S. 463 (1968).

87   *Wirtz* v. *Local Union No. 125, Laborers International Union of North America, AFL-CIO,* 389 U.S. 477 (1968).

88   *Hodgson* v. *Steelworkers, Local 6799,* 403 U.S. 333 (1971).

89   *Compliance, Enforcement and Reporting,* 1974, *op. cit.,* p. 4.

90   *Ibid.,* p. 5.

91   *Compliance, Enforcement, and Reporting,* 1977, *op. cit.,* p. 8.

92   AFL-CIO, *American Federationist,* XXVII, 11 (November 1970), p. 21.

93   Albert B. Tarbutton, Jr., "The Fiduciary Responsibility of Officers of Labor Organizations Under the Common Law and LMRDA," in Slovenko, ed., *op. cit.,* p. 514.

94   Samuel Duker, "Fiduciary Responsibility of Union Officials," in Slovenko, ed., *op. cit.,* p. 521.

95   *Meinhard* v. *Salmon,* 249 N.Y. 464 (1928).

96   *History of the Labor-Management Reporting and Disclosure Act,* NLRB, II (1959), p. 1433.

97   *Local 107, Highway Truck Drivers & Helpers* v. *Cohen,* 182 F. Supp. 608 (1960), affirmed 284 F. (2d) 162 (1960), cert. denied 365 U.S. 833 (1961).

98   *Ratner* v. *Bakery Workers,* 394 F. (2d) 780 (1968).

99   *Local 92, Iron Workers* v. *Norris,* 383 F. (2d) 735 (1967).

100   *Giordani* v. *Hoffman,* 277 F. Supp. 722 (1967).

101   *Purcell* v. *Keane,* 277 F. Supp. 252 (1967).

102   *United States* v. *Harrelson,* 223 F. Supp. 869 (1963)

103   *United States* v. *Davis* (SD N.Y., September 12, 1963), Nos. 63 Criminal 164 and 293.

104   *Compliance, Enforcement, and Reporting,* 1977, *op. cit.,* p. 115.

105   Baker Armstrong Smith, "Landrum-Griffin After Twenty-One Years: Mature Legislation or Childish Fantasy," *Labor Law Journal,* XXXI, 5 (May 1980), p. 276.

106   Marten Estey, *The Unions, Structure, Development, and Management,* (New York: Harcourt Brace Jovanovich, Third Edition, 1981), p. 49.

CHAPTER TWENTY-ONE

LABOR RELATIONS
IN THE PUBLIC SECTOR

The issue of public employee collective bargaining reached unprecedented proportions in the decades of the sixties and seventies, primarily for two reasons. One was the rapid growth of government employment. The other was the issuance of Executive Order 10988 by President John F. Kennedy, as well as legislative action in many states. The Executive Order established the basic framework for collective bargaining in agencies under the executive branch of the federal government. All of these factors ushered in a new era of labor relations in the public sector. The new federal attitude toward employees prompted the states to reconsider many of their own employment practices. In fact, the federal government transferred employee bargaining rights from the executive orders to the Civil Service Reform Act of 1978.[1]

The public sector has experimented extensively with the issues, which have grown with the level of public-sector employment. This fact is revealed in the diverse pattern of treatment extended to workers in the fifty states and in the federal government. Twenty-one states have passed labor legislation to protect the collective bargaining rights of some state and local employees. Labor relations systems are generally governed by a wide variety of state laws, local ordinances, and federal statutes. For identical jobs, the collective bargaining rights of workers in the same locale are usually quite different for a state or local employee, a federal employee, and an employee in the private sector.

This chapter will focus on the diverse patterns of the states and the federal government for dealing with the employment conditions confronting workers in their jurisdictions.

627

BASIS OF DENIAL OF GOVERNMENT EMPLOYEE BARGAINING

The doctrine of sovereignty has been used by government bodies as a basis for denying the collective bargaining process to public employees. Sovereignty may be defined as the supreme, absolute, and uncontrollable power by which any independent state is governed. Unionization of government workers is still viewed in some jurisdictions as interference with sovereign authority because it could lead to joint determination of wages, hours, and terms and conditions of employment. But the sovereignty doctrine is no longer as important as it once was.

The extension to public employees of the right to join unions was traditionally viewed as a surrender of power and a dereliction of duty. President Franklin Roosevelt made a distinction between public and private bargaining rights in 1937. He has often been quoted:

> The employer is the whole people, who speak by means of laws enacted by their representatives in Congress. Accordingly, administrative officials, and employees alike, are governed and guided, and in many instances restrained, by laws which establish policy procedures or rules in personal matters.[2]

Both the Wagner Act and the Taft-Hartley Act deliberately excluded all government employees from coverage under their provisions. Public Law 330 (1955) made a felony of federal employee strike activity.[3]

It has been advanced in recent years that a government has the authority to abandon traditional approaches to public employee bargaining. This may be done either by the legislative or executive branches of government. One writer concluded that

> the [sovereignty] doctrine does not preclude the enactment of legislation specifically authorizing the government to enter into collective bargaining relationships with its employees.[4]

Indeed, the concept of sovereignty has not prevailed as a hard and fast political concept over time. The federal government has long deviated from a policy of absoluteness.

It is frequently argued that the public is deprived of essential services if strikes result from bargaining impasses. One member of the House Post Office and Civil Service Committee assessed the public-interest argument this way:

> The trouble with the "public interest" concept is that it is only triggered in time of crisis. There's no "public interest" generated ahead of time, no particular show of concern for meeting the genuine economic and social needs of the public employee—whether he's a teacher, a fireman, a policeman, a clerk or a laborer. It's not until there is a direct, adverse effect on the body politic that the "public interest" is invoked—and then, of course, it's invoked against the public employee and on the side of the public administrator.[5]

A second argument that is used to deny public employee collective bargaining is known as the special status concept. Such workers are viewed as virtually immune from unemployment imposed by business cycles. Furthermore, it is alleged that their pensions and other fringe benefits are superior to those available in the private sector. The late 1970s and early 1980's revealed that public employees were more susceptible to problems experienced in the private sector than had been so in earlier years.

The doctrine of sovereignty is no longer capable of generating acceptance of the denial of collective action in the public sector. Various approaches have been used to deal with the employment difficulties of public employees.

COLLECTIVE BARGAINING AMONG FEDERAL EMPLOYEES

Unionization of federal employees reportedly existed as early as 1800 in naval yards.[6] The Departments of Defense and Interior have a long history of collective bargaining. Wage-rate negotiation has occurred among various levels of TVA employees, ranging from those classed as production workers through the professional ranks. Negotiations have occurred despite the general understanding that wages are set by law.

Federal policy toward employee organizations dates back to 1883, when the Pendleton Act was passed. This Act is commonly known as the Civil Service Act. Under its terms, only Congress had the authority to regulate wages, hours, and other terms and conditions of employment.

President Theodore Roosevelt in 1902 banned federal employees from seeking legislation that would benefit them directly or indirectly through their association, except through the departments in which they were employed. A violation of the order was grounds for dismissal.[7] In 1906, President Roosevelt broadened the earlier order, stating that

> all officers and employees of the United States of every description, serving in or under any of the Executive Departments or independent Government establishments, and whether so serving in or out of Washington, are hereby forbidden, either directly or indirectly, individually or through associations, to solicit an increase of pay or to influence or attempt to influence in their own interest any other legislation whatever, either before Congress or its Committees, or in any way save through the heads of the Departments or independent Government establishments, in or under which they serve, on penalty of dismissal from the Government service.[8]

Congress took up the question of federal employee organization in 1912. It rejected the approach of President Theodore Roosevelt in the Lloyd-LaFollette Act.[9] The statute became the basis for the principle that federal employees in general had the right to join any organization that did not assert the right to strike against the government.[10] If a literal interpretation is made of it, the Act limited protection of union membership to postal employees. Despite that fact, other employees gained the right to organize on the basis of its language. The right to organize, however, is of limited value if procedures are not provided to guarantee an effective collective bargaining process. The Lloyd-LaFollette Act did not provide such machinery.

Construction of the Alaskan railroad, which began in 1914, provided another boon to federal employee bargaining. Most of the construction workers on the railroad had already been organized prior to the time work was to start. The government negotiated its first written labor agreement, with these workers, in 1920.[11]

The Boston police officer's strike slowed the drive toward more effective collective bargaining machinery among all public employees—federal, state, and local alike. However, instances of collective bargaining arrangements occurred throughout the period of the thirties despite the damage done by the Boston strike. Renewed efforts to obtain more favorable bargaining legislation started in the 1940s.

The Rhodes-Johnston Bill was introduced in 1949 as a measure to protect the right of unions to represent federal employees. It failed to pass in that year and was debated for fourteen years.[12] Essentially, the bill was designed primarily to provide for the resolving of grievances within the various federal agencies. A large number of weaknesses in the bill were partially responsible for its not being passed.

The Classification Act of 1949 contained a section that facilitates union influence on wages. It provides that wage board employees' compensation

> shall be fixed and adjusted from time to time as nearly as is consistent with the public interest in accordance with prevailing wages.

The provision makes it possible to affect wage rates by negotiating on the items that determine the outcome. These are (1) the geographic area to be covered, (2) the firms to be included or excluded in the survey, (3) key jobs to be used as a basis for gathering wage information, and (4) the number of jobs to be surveyed. The 1949 provisions therefore enhanced the power of some unions to influence the wage rates paid their members.

THE POSTAL SERVICE

The U.S. Postal Service is not subject to Title VII of the Civil Service Reform Act of 1978. It was removed from cabinet status to that of an independent government agency by the Postal Reorganization Act of 1970. Postal employees were removed from coverage under executive order labor policy and given collective bargaining rights comparable to those governing private industry.

The pay comparability principle covering federal workers was retained in the law, and progression through the pay grades was compressed from 21 to 8 years. The process of collective bargaining was designated to guide the operation of these provisions.

The National Labor Relations Board was authorized to determine the appropriateness of bargaining units, supervise representation elections, and enforce unfair labor practice provisions permitted in the 1970 law. Even though the Act authorized collective bargaining on wages and working conditions under laws that apply to private industry, it continued the prohibition against strikes. Final and binding arbitration could be utilized only after an impasse had persisted for 180 days after the start of bargaining.

Postal employees have never had a statutory right to strike, even though some have engaged in work stoppages. As a matter of fact, one federal court ruled that the right to strike could not be denied if the right had never existed in the first place.[13] There was a two-week strike by 225,000 postal workers in 1970. The 1975 and the 1981 National Postal Agreements were signed only after postal workers threatened strike action. The six-month delay on submitting issues to arbitration by virtue of law may not provide an adequate alternative to strike action. In 1978, the no-strike provision was again tested.

Union-shop arrangements are prohibited; in this regard the Postal Reorganization Act retained the basic union security limitations of the executive orders.

Overall, federal collective bargaining is evolving closer to private sector practices. Postal Service experiences will undoubtedly have some influence over practices adopted under the executive orders. On the other hand, state and local collective bargaining rights continue to remain varied, with no significant pattern in the relaxation of traditional restrictions.

FEDERAL RESERVE SYSTEM

The Federal Reserve System remains under its own bargaining system, separate from the Civil Service Reform Act of 1978. On May 9, 1969, the Board of Governors of the Federal Reserve System issued a statement of policies concerning employee-management relations within the system.[14] The statement was patterned after the executive order system, but took into account the special responsibilities of the system under the terms of the Federal Reserve Act and related statutes. It recognized the right of certain classes of employees to join or to refrain from joining labor organizations. Procedures were provided for recognition of labor organizations, bargaining-unit determinations, and elections. Grievance machinery was established, along with a list of unfair labor practice prohibitions.

The Board of Governors issued its "Policy on Unionization and Collective Bargaining for the Federal Reserve Banks," because of the exclusion of the system from both the Taft-Hartley Act and the Executive Order.

A few features of the policy require comment. Professional employees are given the right to organize, as long as they belong to bargaining units separate from those that represent the other bank employees. Bank guards also have the right to organize into separate labor organizations. Therefore, some of the NLRB policies dealing with bargaining units have been incorporated into the policy statement.

Exclusive recognition of a labor organization is available after an election is held. At least 30 percent of employees of an appropriate bargaining unit must sign representation request cards. Once this is achieved, an election is held under the auspices of the American Arbitration Association. A union will receive exclusive recognition if a majority of at least 60 percent of eligible bargaining-unit employees cast votes for representation. Discontinuance of a labor organization's exclusive status is determined by the same procedure; however, only one election may be held in any unit in a twelve-month period.

Unfair labor practice prohibitions are fashioned after those contained in Taft-Hartley. Both parties are required to bargain collectively and are prohibited from interfering with employee organizational rights guaranteed by the system's policy.

Administration of the provision is vested in a three-member Federal Reserve System Labor Relations Panel. The panel is fashioned after the Federal Labor Relations Council established by Executive Order 11491. Two of the panel members are from the Board of Governors and one is a public member. All three are selected by the Board of Governors. The panel is charged with the responsibility of establishing regulations and procedures similar to those applicable to unions and management in the private sector. The Board of Governors reserves the right to amend its labor relations policies without notice, provided that all labor organizations are informed of any changes. Amendments will not be applied retroactively.

The Federal Reserve System's labor relations policy has the strength of incorporating many of the essential features of both the Taft-Hartley Act and the Executive Order. The potentially most serious weakness is the possibility of considerable shifts in policy as the membership of the Board of Governors changes. It may be that pressures will continue to be placed upon Congress to provide statutory rights for Federal Reserve employee collective bargaining, as is the case with federal employees organized under executive order provisions.

CIVIL SERVICE REFORM ACT OF 1978: TITLE VII

The current framework within which collective bargaining is structured in federal agencies evolved from the initial Executive Order 10988 issued by President Kennedy in January 1962, through President Nixon's revision in 1970 (Executive Order 11491, entitled "Labor-Management Relations in the Federal Service"), and up to President Ford's further amendment in 1975 in Executive Order 11838.

The essential features of the executive order framework, procedures, and practices provided the basis for the Civil Service Reform Act of 1978. Title VII of the law superseded E.O. 11491 in January 1979. The State Department continued to operate under the Executive Order until the Foreign Service Act of 1980 was passed.

Administrative Structure

Title VII gave federal labor relations the stability of law. It organized the bargaining system into the Office of Personnel Management (OPM), the Merit System Protection Board (MSPB), and the Federal Labor Relations Authority (FLRA).

The Office of Personnel Management has delegated functions that are subject to further delegation to agency heads. Rule making of the OPM is subject to consultation with labor organizations over any substantive changes made in personnel regulations.

The Merit System Protection Board was granted authority to review Office of Personnel Management regulations and to invalidate them if in violation of the prohibited personnel practices detailed in Title I of the Civil Service Reform Act of 1978. A three-member board is empowered to obtain testimony and evidence to decide issues before it. It may order corrective action of any agency found in violation of the Act's provision. Also, the Merit System Protection Board may discipline federal employees prosecuted by the Special Counsel to the Board. Such actions may include removal, reduction in grade, or reprimands among others.

The Federal Labor Relations Authority took over the functions previously performed by the Federal Labor Relations Council under the former executive orders. The Authority was made independent from the executive branch by protecting tenure of its three members for five-year terms. In large measure, the Authority is modeled on the National Labor Relations Board, and includes a General Counsel to prosecute unfair labor practice complaints.

The Authority administers the law to meet the special needs of the federal system. It has somewhat the same powers as its predecessor, the Federal Labor Relations Council. The Council functioned under the executive orders and members were *ex officio* part time. Members were the Secretary of Labor, the Director of the Office of Management and Budget, and the Chair of the Civil Service Commission.

The Department of State remained under Executive Order 11636 until the Foreign Service Act of 1980 was passed. A Federal Labor Relations Board was established to administer labor relations in the State Department. Other employees covered by this law work in the International Communications Agency, the International Development Cooperation Agency, and the Departments of Commerce and Agriculture. The Foreign Service Relations Board has a connection with the Federal Labor Relations Authority through a common chair. Board decisions must by law be consistent with decisions of the Authority under the Civil Service Reform Act of 1978.

The Federal Service Impasse Panel's authority under Executive Order 11491 to "take any action it considers necessary to settle an impasse" remains virtually the same under the 1978 law. The Federal Mediation and Conciliation Service provides its services, and in practice it determines "under what circumstances and in what manner it shall proffer its services." Generally, the panel becomes involved in disputes only after the FMCS has bowed out of them.

The Assistant Secretary of Labor for Labor-Management Relations during the executive order era had authority to resolve disputes over the makeup of bargaining units and representation rights, to order and supervise elections, and to disqualify unions from recognition because of corrupt or undemocratic influences. The Assistant Secretary of Labor function was terminated in the 1978 law because the Federal Labor Relations Authority has its own staff.

Recognition and Elections

Exclusive recognition is the only form that is available to unions representing federal employees. Such recognition must be established in a secret ballot election by a majority of employees in an appropriate bargaining unit. The Authority may withhold exclusive recognition from a labor organization if it is subject to corrupt influences, fails to represent at least 30 percent of the unit, or if there is an election bar to such recognition. There are other comparatively minor circumstances when recognition may be withheld.

Unit Appropriateness

The Authority determines the appropriateness of a bargaining unit. It will consider several factors in arriving at a determination, such as extent of organization, an identifiable community of interest among employees, and whether a union will promote an effective relationship with the agency. National consultation rights provided by the Act were not available under the executive orders. If an organization with exclusive rights does not exist, then one that represents a substantial number of employees of the agency may obtain national consultation rights from the Authority. The Authority has the power to determine criteria for national consultation designation. Essentially, an exchange of views is provided for, with the agency involved obligated to inform the labor organization of reasons why a given action was finally undertaken.

Employee Categories In Unit Determinations

Managerial employees are not eligible for bargaining unit inclusion except in cases where they were represented by labor organizations that historically or traditionally represented management workers in private industry. Also, the specialized organization had to have held exclusive rights at the time the 1978 law became effective in 1979.

Confidential employees, or those in positions of trust with supervisors and management officials, are not to be placed into bargaining units. The fear is that the agency could be compromised by such inclusion. Professional employees may not be placed into units with any other employees unless they vote to be included with nonprofessionals.

Employees who administer any provisions of the labor relations law may join unions if such unions are separate from those that represent other workers. These unions may not even be indirectly affiliated with other organizations.

Employees who are engaged in work that directly affects national security or internal security are not eligible for membership in an appropriate bargaining unit. Guards do not fall within these general prohibitions. The excluded categories must be involved in administration of security matters, such as deciding whether duties are discharged honestly and with integrity.

Military personnel are forbidden from union membership in the United States by the Thurmond Act of 1979. The Teamsters and the American Federation of Government Employees once threatened to organize enlisted military personnel. Their motive, perhaps as much as anything else, could have been to influence the outcome of the Civil Service Reform Act, which was under consideration by the Congress at the time. The Thurmond Act makes it a felony for (1) enlisted personnel to join a union; (2) anyone to solicit enlisted personnel to join a union; (3) military officers or designees, to recognize or bargain with a union; and (4) a union to attempt to bargain for enlisted personnel.

Actually, the Department of Defense has a long history of bargaining with civilian employees, dating back to approximately 1830. Many civilians in the Department of Defense perform jobs comparable to some in the military, and these employees do have bargaining rights.

Consolidation of Units

In situations where there are two or more units in an agency for which a labor organization is the exclusive representative, consolidation into a larger single unit may be permitted by the Authority. The Authority may be petitioned for such by either the labor organization or the agency, or both. The Authority may permit the petition with or without an election if it considers the proposed larger unit appropriate.

Bars to Elections

The Act identifies three bars to elections. One is an election bar, which means that if an election has been held within the previous twelve months, a new one will not be approved.

A second is a certification bar to an election. This bar exists if exclusive rights have been granted to another labor organization through an election held within the previous twelve months.

The third bar to an election is a contract bar. The act defines a contract bar as a lawful written agreement in effect for less than three years.

Labor Organizations and Recognition

Agencies may only grant exclusive recognition to labor organizations that are "free from corrupt influences and influences opposed to basic democratic principals." In this respect, several Landrum-Griffin provisions applicable to unions in the private sector are prescribed for federal employee representatives. These include the holding of periodic elections, member rights to participate in internal organization affairs, and the filing of financial and other reports with the Assistant Secretary of Labor for Labor Management Relations.

A labor organization may not be extended exclusive bargaining status by the Authority if it is involved willfully or intentionally in a strike, slowdown, or work stoppage. It must take positive corrective action in such events, or be subject to the Authority rescinding exclusive status and legal representation rights. It is an unfair labor practice for a labor organization to call or participate in strikes, picketing, or work stoppages or slowdowns, or even to condone such activity.

In October 1981, the Federal Labor Relations Authority revoked the right of the Professional Air Traffic Controllers Organization (PATCO) to represent air traffic controllers. The reason for the decertification order was a strike called by the union in August 1981. Striking air controllers were dismissed by the Reagan Administration for violation of strike prohibitions in federal employment. The decertification order marked the first time that a union lost its status as legal representative of a group of federal workers. The permanently replaced strikers were denied reinstatement. Programs to train replacements were developed after the wholesale dismissals, in order to support the Administration's stated resolve not to recall strikers to duty or declare them eligible for alternative federal employment.

Union Conduct

The Civil Rights Act of 1964, Title VII, plus the 1972 amendments to it, establish Equal Employment Opportunity requirements for unions. Labor organizations representing government workers are prohibited from discriminating in their terms or conditions for membership on the basis of race, color, creed, sex, age, or national origin.

Communists are excluded from "office holding as are persons affiliated with other totalitarian movements." Persons identified with corrupt influences are also prohibited from office holding.

Scope of Bargaining

The parties must bargain in good faith on negotiable issues. The basic scope of bargaining remains about the same as it was under the executive orders. The 1978 law expanded labor organizations rights in this regard by permitting negotiations without regard to agency regulations. The Act specifies and clarifies management rights. Agency officials have the right to make unilateral decisions on items not subject to bargaining. These include determination of the agency's mission, budget, organization, number of employees, and internal security. Management is also given the full right to determine whether work will be performed within the unit or subcontracted out to personnel outside of the agency. Permissible items for bargaining are specified, and include methods, means, and technology of conducting agency operations.

Illegal items for bargaining are also covered. Some of these include retirement, life and health insurance, and suspension or removal for national security reasons.

Considerable concern developed over possible conflicts between internal agency regulations and conflicting bargaining proposals presented by unions. The 1975 Ford Order changes were designed to broaden the scope of permissible negotiations at local levels by restricting the regulatory authority of federal agencies. The view of the Federal Labor Relations Council in its recommendations to President Ford was that in many situations, higher-level agency regulations were not critical to effective agency management or to the public interest and, therefore, were unduly restrictive of negotiations.[15] After 1975, agency regulations would bar negotiations only if a compelling need for the regulations could be established. The council decided on a case-by-case basis whether a compelling need existed in the context of its rules outlining permissible limits. The overall effect was to broaden the scope of collective bargaining at the local agency levels. The 1978 law reaffirmed these developments.

Federal labor relations under the statute differ from those in the private sector in that some items may not be bargained on (e.g., budget, mission) under any circumstances. Management rights *may* be bargained, but management is not required *initially* to bargain on these issues. However, if bargaining on management rights *is* initiated, the defense that it is a management right is not controlling, and an unfair labor practice may result. Thus, some issues are mandatorily bargainable, some are mandatorily nonnegotiable, and some are, in effect, "optionally" bargainable.

The use of work time to negotiate agreements has been controversial. The 1962 order permitted a wide range of practices for allowing union negotiators to be paid while negotiating a contract. In 1969, union negotiators could not be paid at all for negotiating during working hours. The 1971 modification permitted the parties to agree to pay union representatives a maximum of forty hours of official time, or a maximum of one-half the total time spent in negotiations. The issue of whether or not to permit negotiators to be paid within the allowable limits of forty hours of official time required substantial negotiation time to determine and left little if any clock time to settle other matters. The law now requires that union representatives be on official time and be paid for time spent in negotiations equal to the offical time and compensation provided to management officials.

GRIEVANCE AND ARBITRATION PROCEDURES

From 1962 to 1970, the parties could negotiate a grievance procedure to apply the terms of an existing labor agreement. The capstone step, however, provided only for advisory arbitration, not for final and binding arbitration, as is common in the private sector. There was, therefore, no impartial procedure for breaking deadlocks in contract negotiations. The federal agency involved in the negotiations made the final decisions concerning all disputes.

In 1970, the amended order required that a grievance procedure must be negotiated by the parties. Applicable grievances were to be exclusively resolved through the negotiated device. Grievable issues were limited to interpretation or application of the contract. The order excluded matters from the negotiated grievance procedure which were subject to a statutory appeals system, as well as issues concerned with the application or interpretation of agency policy. The 1975 amendments retained only those matters subject to statutory appeals systems as exclusions to the one. Since 1975, grievances over agency policies and regulations have been processed through the negotiated system. The 1975 executive order amendments opened up considerably the range of potential coverage of a negotiated grievance procedure. Except for statutory appeals rights, the potential to negotiate was left to the parties.

In 1962, the Civil Service Commission issued standards limiting the procedures that could be negotiated by agencies and unions. Advisory arbitration was permitted, but only if the employee concerned gave approval, and even then it was limited to an interpretation or application of negotiated agreements or agency policy. Dual systems were permissible in that a negotiated grievance procedure and a separate agency grievance system could exist side by side. In 1970, dual grievance systems could be eliminated through negotiation. They remained permissible. Whichever system was negotiated, it had to conform to the requirements established by the Civil Service Commission. Since 1975, there were no restrictions on negotiated grievance procedures as long as they did not conflict with the statute or Executive Order. If, for example, the order did not specifically exclude an item from the bargaining process, it was a matter for determination through the negotiated grievance system, even if the issue involved an agency policy or regulation not contained in the collective bargaining contract.

The 1978 law says that negotiated grievance procedures must be the exclusive ones for resolving grievances available to bargaining unit employees, except in the case of adverse action and Equal Employment Opportunity (EEO) cases, when the employee may use either the negotiated procedure or the statutory appeals procedure—but not both. Employees not in the bargaining unit or employees eligible but not represented by a union have access only to the agency procedure. The applicability of *Alexander* v. *Gardner-Denver* (to be treated in the next chapter), which permits the use of both procedures in EEO cases, is uncertain as far as unrepresented employees are concerned.

Arbitration is the final step of negotiated grievance procedures. The process may be invoked by either the labor organization or the agency. The arbitrator's award may be appealed to the Authority for review, but it will not be overturned unless the award is

1. contrary to any law, rule, or regulation; or
2. inconsistent with federal court standards or those applied by the NLRB in its *Spielberg* standards.

Exceptions to an arbitrator's award must be taken within 30 days, or else the award will be final and binding.

Union Security

Title VII of the Civil Service Reform Act forbids arrangements requiring union membership as a condition of employment. Exclusive recognition requires that a union represent all employees in the bargaining unit, even if they do not hold membership in the labor organization. However, union security arrangements may be negotiated in the Postal Service, Government Printing Office, and the Tennessee Valley Authority. In the private sector, as we learned, federal law permits the union shop or lesser arrangements unless the states prohibit them.

Dues checkoff, a form of financial union security, is permitted if the employee has authorized the union as the exclusive representative. Once allowed, dues checkoff is not revocable for one year. No charge is assessed for the service. Unions in units with ten percent or more membership, but where no exclusive representative exists, also have dues checkoff rights.

UNFAIR LABOR PRACTICES AND THEIR RESOLUTION

Unfair labor practices largely reflected those established under the Taft-Hartley law. A government agency violates the terms of the order if it interferes with the right of employees to join unions; encourages or discourages membership in a union by discrimination in regard to hiring, tenure, promotion, or other conditions of employment; refuses to recognize a union qualified for recognition; or refuses to negotiate with a union that has secured exclusive bargaining rights. A union engages in an unfair labor practice if it interferes with the right of employees not to join a union; coerces or fines a member as punishment for the purpose of impeding his or her work performance, productivity, or duties as a government employee; engages in strikes or slowdowns or fails to take appropriate action to prevent or stop a strike; or refuses to bargain collectively.

Union unfair labor practices are expanded beyond those of Taft-Hartley in that a union cannot interfere with a member's performance as an employee. Unions also cannot discriminate on the basis of race, color, creed, national origin, sex, age, preferential or nonpreferential civil service status, political affiliation, marital status, or handicapping condition. To do so constitutes an unfair labor practice.

Informational picketing that does not interfere with an agency's operations is expressly eliminated from being an unfair labor practice. It is, however, an unfair labor practice to call, or to participate in, a strike, slowdown, or the picketing of an agency in a labor-management dispute if such picketing does interfere with an agency's operations.

Labor organizations have a right to set reasonable admission standards without committing an unfair labor practice if these standards are uniformly required and administered. Thus, a person may be denied membership if occupational standards for admission are not met, and may be denied membership or expelled for nonpayment of dues.

The Federal Labor Relations Authority interprets unfair labor practices that come before it in the same way that the NLRB interprets the Taft-Hartley law. Regional directors and administrative law judges are appointed by the Authority to apply its rules and policies in cases that come before them.

An unfair labor practice charge is investigated by the General Counsel's office. If a complaint is issued, then the case is set for a formal hearing. The labor organization or agency involved has a right to answer the complaint at the hearing. Informal methods of resolution are available in the Authority's regulations. Formal orders are issued to support the findings demanding corrective action.

Final orders of the Authority may be appealed to the appropriate court of appeals, and judicial enforcement may be requested by the Authority.

CONTRACT NEGOTIATION IMPASSES

Impasses between labor organizations and agencies are provided for in the 1978 statute. The Federal Mediation and Conciliation Service decides under which circumstances and in what manner it will provide services and assistance as it did under the former executive order. If other efforts also fail, either party may request that the Federal Service Impasse Panel consider the matter. Prior to this step, though, the parties may seek binding arbitration of the impasse, subject to Panel approval.

Once the Impasse Panel is involved, it holds a prehearing meeting and then may proceed along various courses of action to deal with the dispute. Fact finding, recommendations for settlement, and directed settlement may be required. The arsenal of weapons approach is utilized by the Federal Impasse Panel, the only federal dispute settlement agency that does so.

The Panel is able to settle most disputes prior to formal recommendations for settlement. So-called "informal settlements" are actually mandatory. Moreover, if the parties have not sought and secured mediation, this too will be directed and the recommendation followed. The Federal Services Impasse Panel is generally effective in its mission.

A special expedited procedure for most negotiability disputes is provided in the law to determine whether an item is subject to negotiation. The matter may be taken to the Authority to decide whether a compelling need exists for any rule or regulation of the agency. Impasses that occur in this category may be resolved quickly by the Authority, without General Counsel involvement in the procedure.

Assessment

Collective bargaining experience was gained in the federal sector under the executive orders. Periodic reviews made the system more viable. The Civil Service Reform Act of 1978 provided a statutory basis for the federal labor relations program. The Office of Personnel Management has estimated that approximately seventy percent of eligible federal employees are represented by labor organizations, whereas less than one-half of these are members. Collective bargaining practices in the federal sector have grown closer to those of the private sector, though there remain some sharp differences. In any event, the new law made a number of changes that have improved labor relations in general.

COLLECTIVE BARGAINING AT THE STATE AND LOCAL LEVELS

Whereas federal civilian employment has remained more or less constant for the last 35 years, state and local government employment has grown fourfold over the same period, from less than 7 million in 1945 to about 16 million in 1980.[16] In general, there are many more local government workers than at the state level. There is generally no uniform pattern to bargaining rights available through state and local governments. For example, some states have no policy whatever. At the local level, New York, Detroit, and San Francisco have had across-the-board bargaining for decades. It may well be that as many as eight million workers, or well over one-half of all state and local government employees, are represented by unions. They are represented by the National Education Association affiliates, American Federation of Teachers, Fraternal Order of Police, International Association of Fire Fighters, American Federation of State and Municipal Employees, County Laborers, Teamsters, and a large number of unaffiliated independent labor organizations. Many states dwell on collective bargaining controls through statutes, court pronouncements, or attorneys' general opinions, such as prohibitions on work stoppages.

In 1969, a federal court of appeals determined the right of public employees to join unions.[17] The issue presented to the appellate court in the *Woodward* case was whether public employees discharged because of union membership have a right to seek injunctions and sue for damages those public officials who discharged them. A solution to the basic issue required a determination of whether public employees have a constitutionally protected right to belong to a union.

The court ruled unanimously that union membership is protected by the right of association under the First and Fourteenth Amendments. The court quoted an earlier ruling that the right of assembly protects more than the right to attend a meeting. It includes "the right to express one's attitudes or philosophies by membership in a group or by affiliation with it or by other lawful means."[18]

Public officials who violate the public employees' constitutional right of association are subject to court action for damages. A different appellate court decision was quoted in reaching this conclusion. It stated:

> It is settled that teachers have the right of free association, and unjustified interference with teachers' associational freedom violates the Due Process clause of The Fourteenth Amendment . . . Public Employment may not be subjected to unreasonable conditions, and the assertion of First Amendment rights by teachers will usually not warrant their dismissal. . . . Unless there is some illegal intent, an individual's right to form and join a union is protected by the First Amendment.[19]

The guaranteed right to join a union may be important to a worker, but that right is not effective if there is no procedure to protect it—such as required recognition of a labor organization representing a majority of bargaining-unit workers and, thereafter, good-faith collective bargaining. Other courts will not necessarily rule the same as the Seventh and Eighth Circuit Courts of Appeals. Conflicting rules may eventually result in a Supreme Court decision on the issue. In the meantime, the states vary in their interpretation of public employee collective bargaining rights.

STATUS OF STATE LAWS

Some states require bargaining for all categories of public employees. A total of thirty-one states required the covered parties to bargain, until the Indiana Supreme Court voided its Act applicable to all workers except teachers. But only ten of those states adequately provided machinery to resolve questions of representation.[20] Teachers may receive favored treatment under some laws while other categories of workers have fewer bargaining rights. Despite the fact that most states prohibit strikes, many do not have methods to settle disputes.

Dispute settlement provisions vary. A few states, such as Maine, Nebraska, and Nevada, require compulsory arbitration if other methods fail. However, the requirement of compulsory arbitration is often limited to certain groups, such as police officers, teachers, and fire fighters in states such as Michigan, Pennsylvania, Wisconsin, and Wyoming. Some states permit voluntary, binding arbitration of interest items, including the states of Delaware, New York, and Vermont. Final and binding arbitration is authorized in some states, although some employee classifications are exempted and it is not unusual to limit arbitrable items. Wages and salaries are often subject to arbitration. Consequently, for the majority of states, there is no adequate dispute settlement machinery designed to deal with the economic issues that most trouble public employees.

Bargaining is authorized but not required in some states. There is no penalty, however, for refusals to bargain or for refusals to meet and confer. Usually the "meet and confer" laws are enforced by state lower courts rather than by a specialized labor agency. For employees in several states, as in Arkansas and Mississippi, there are no provisions whatever on either bargaining permissiveness or meeting and conferring. Obviously, some states, through silence, encourage power conflicts between public employers and employees. Work stoppages may thus force legislative action. Once meetings and conferences are forced by such pressures, it may be more difficult to establish conditions within which constructive negotiations can prevail.

Considerable uncertainty regarding bargaining rights faces public employees in a large number of states. In some cases, rights are spelled out for certain categories of workers, but not for others. Even if public employees are dealt with uniformly in a particular state or lesser political jurisdiction, the mere difference of treatment in other states is enough to create instability in employment relations. Union organizers supply the comparative information to workers. This situation may be termed a "demonstration effect." Public workers in a municipality, or in a state that does not protect collective bargaining, become malcontents when bargaining rights are observed for employees performing similar tasks in other states. Indeed, the ability of federal employees to engage in limited and growing bargaining activities within the same state serves also to frustrate state and local employees deprived of the same right.

Agitation for equal bargaining rights is likely to persist among public employees. Public pressure forces government agencies to maintain a constant flow of public services, and there is considerable pressure to expand and improve services when per capita income rises. It is difficult to adhere to traditional practices in the face of widespread employee dissatisfaction. Disruption of services could invoke the wrath of the general public, which in turn could lead to losses at the polls, and eventually to new public employers. These factors, including widespread strikes among public employees, will probably result in more and more recognition of public employee unions.

Selected categories of state and local treatment of collective bargaining are provided to permit comparisons with private and federal practices.

THE RIGHT TO STRIKE

There is no more explosive issue in the public sector than the right of public employees to strike. Thirty-nine states have outlawed strikes through legislation, court decisions, or attorney-general opinions. Fourteen states either permit a limited right to strike, or have relaxed strike penalties to the point that in effect, a deterrent does not exist. The states that permit a limited right to strike are Vermont, Montana, Pennsylvania, Hawaii, Alaska, Minnesota, Oregon, Rhode Island, and Wisconsin. Alaska permits strikes by employees in the nonessential category, and extends a limited right to semiessential workers. The problem is in the definition of which public employees are nonessential, and which are essential or semiessential. Hawaii extends a limited right to strike; strikes endangering public health and safety are prohibited. The determination of which strikes endanger public health and safety is made by the Public Employment Relations Board. Thus, in Hawaii, strike legality depends on the basic philosophy of Board personnel which, of course, can change over relatively short periods of time. Pennsylvania law also extends a limited right to strike to state and local employees. Many strikes have occurred, however, with minimal interference. The courts may prohibit strikes that they deem to constitute a clear and present danger or threat to health, safety, or welfare of the public.

It is obvious that the right to strike is not as liberal in those states that permit a limited version as might be thought on the face of the laws. Most public bodies with authority to decide strike legality will hold generally false conceptions of the effect that public employee strikes will have, and will prohibit them far beyond any real need to do so. In this respect, the politics of the moment may prevail over rational economic judgment. It has been demonstrated that because of technology, excess capacity, and the ability to substitute and postpone demand for services often performed by the public sector, most public employee strikes will impose little or no economic cost, only some inconvenience in substituting or in delay. State legislatures should spend more time developing strike safeguards instead of evading the problem by merely outlawing strikes.

An increasing number of unions and employee organizations are changing their traditional policy of no-strike pledges. In 1963, the American Federation of Teachers issued a policy statement supporting strikes under certain conditions. The American Federation of State, County, and Municipal Employees Union followed this example in 1966. In one study it was found that, of twenty unions composed primarily of public employees, eight had constitutional bans on strikes and eight others did not refer to the issue in their union constitutions.[21] In 1968, in federal employment, four unions representing federal employees dropped the no-strike pledge clauses from their constitutions. These were the National Association of Government Employees, the United Federation of Postal Clerks, the National Postal Union, and the International Association of Firefighters. As yet, however, none of the unions has formally asserted the right to strike because of the serious penalties against strikers and their unions in the federal government.

Public employee union leaders contend that without the right to strike employers will not negotiate in good faith. A former union official, speaking for the International Association of Firefighters, remarked:

Certain arbitrary public officials knowing that we cannot and will not strike because we voluntarily gave up the right in 1918 when we were founded, have certainly taken advantage of the professional firefighters across the land. As a matter of fact, the record will show we have been exploited by such arbitrary public officials who oft time dared us to strike, knowing that we would not.[22]

Various penalties have from time to time been imposed upon striking employees. In 1947, New York passed the Condon-Wadlin Act, which permitted reemployment of strikers but eliminated their pay increases for a period of three years. Reinstated strikers were also considered temporary employees for a period of five years. The 1967 New York Taylor Act eliminated the ban on pay raises, but provided instead for dismissal or fines. A labor organization is subject to loss of dues checkoff privileges for as long as eighteen months, plus fines, for engaging in strikes. In effect, strike activity is no longer subject to serious restraints in New York, although as a practical matter, any striker runs the risk of losing a job, whether in public or private employment.

In Michigan, state employees are subject to discharge or financial penalties for striking. Massachusetts provides that striking municipal workers may be fined $100. Most states reserve the right to discharge striking public employees, although this is not clearly spelled out in legislation.[23] In the 1970s, Wisconsin, Maine, and South Dakota either lowered or eliminated strike penalties.

Laws prohibiting public employee strikes have not been successful in their objective. In 1966, the first full year after Michigan amended its public employee relations act, there were twenty-three strikes in the public sector. This number of strikes was more than had occurred in the previous twenty years.[24] In the next year, 1967, the number of strikes in Michigan almost doubled. Other states have experienced increased strike threats even if actual work stoppages have not materialized. A part of the problem can be traced to the nature of bargaining structures, which delay agreements. Even if the parties come to agreement, the appropriate legislative body has to pass a law on the subject. If it does not, or the law is different, difficulties result.

Government employee strikes increased between 1960 and 1980. Over 90 percent of all government strikes occur at the local level. In 1960, there were 33 stoppages at the local level, but in 1980, there were 493. There was a substantial increase in strike activity after 1965, but by 1986, the level of strike activity had fallen dramatically. Days of idleness were 67.7 in 1960, but 2,240.6 in 1980. Teachers account for more than one-half of local government strikes.[25] Most strikes occur in public education. Local school boards tend not to resolve teacher employment problems, but merely discuss them without providing answers. Past practices of school boards will have to be altered if relative peace is to be achieved in public education. In general, public employees are expressing a growing dissatisfaction with their wages and conditions of work. States without adequate provisions for resolving disputes or establishing bargaining relationships should expect work stoppages caused by the lack of alternatives for dealing with employee problems.

UNION SECURITY PRACTICES

As noted earlier, union-security agreements are forbidden under the Civil Service Reform Act of 1978 for federal employees, except for dues checkoff. The states have a variety of practices. Alaska, Kentucky, Vermont, and Washington permit the union shop. In Washington, the agency shop is authorized for employees who object to union membership on religious grounds.

The states of Alaska, Hawaii, Massachusetts, Michigan, Montana, Oregon, Rhode Island, Vermont, and Wisconsin authorize the agency shop. As long as the fee paid to a union is not used for political activity in case the employee objects, the U.S. Supreme Court has authorized agency-shop clauses in public employee contracts.[26] New Mexico prohibits the arrangement. Only Pennsylvania law expressly permits maintenance of membership for state and local employees. There may, in fact, be many other forms of union security negotiated at the state and local level, but they probably take the form of tacit understandings as opposed to written agreements in a majority of cases. The union-security issue is, at times, an issue in long strikes involving public employees. It would seem, therefore, that the public interest would best be served if state legislatures would address themselves to the problem of union security and permit negotiation to resolve the issue.

RESOLUTION OF DISPUTES

One of the most significant issues facing the public sector is machinery for resolving disputes in the face of prohibitions on the right to strike. Thirty-four states have some limited provisions for dispute settlement. Some limit machinery to specific categories of workers, such as fire fighters or teachers. When legislation has been passed, it almost always states that there can be no conflict with civil service provisions or other statutes setting employment standards. The major difficulty seems to come from legislative bodies, even when economic issues are negotiable. These bodies have to appropriate funds to cover the agreements, and are usually unwilling to abide by decisions denied outside the traditional legislative processes.[27]

There are at least three types of disputes in the public employment field. The first, organizational, involves the issue of determining employee desires for union representation. Some states have labor relations boards to make bargaining-unit determinations.

The second type involves the terms and conditions of employment that are usually included in written collective bargaining agreements. Resolution may result from such devices as mediation or fact-finding boards with authority to offer recommendations.

The third type involves interpretation and enforcement of existing collective bargaining agreements. The usual method of resolving such disputes in private industry is an internal grievance procedure, with impartial third-party arbitration as a final step.

It seems probable that strikes in the public sector could be decreased if certain steps were clearly provided. Some possible steps that could result in better labor-management relations include:

1. The right of employee representation by a union of employees' own choice.
2. Independent third-party mediation and fact finding to deal with bargaining impasses.
3. Written contracts with detailed clauses dealing with wages and other working conditions.
4. Voluntary final and binding arbitration as the last step in a grievance procedure involving contractual interpretation.

Mediation and fact-finding boards are utilized by some states to resolve bargaining impasses. Connecticut made them available in its Municipal Employee Relations Act of 1965. Michigan also provides for fact finding and nonbinding recommendations by its State Labor Mediation Board to resolve bargaining impasses. Wisconsin utilizes the fact-finding approach, which may be initiated by its Employment Relations Board to break deadlocked negotiations. Generally, public employees tend to strike over wages and fringe benefits. Mediation and fact-finding boards are utilized by a large number of states to resolve bargaining impasses. Thirty-five states use mediation, thirty-two use fact finding, and twenty-seven use the arbitration process.

Fact finding is more formal than mediation. Fact finders hear the positions of both parties, informally collect information during hearings, and then make settlement recommendations. Massachusetts and Indiana use labor-management committees to deal with bargaining impasses. This process involves workers, but in Indiana, a committee may also include representatives from the legislative and executive branches, civil rights groups, and the general public. The labor management committee decides which impasse procedure is appropriate to deal with a dispute. It may call for a cooling-off period, fact finding, or arbitration, or even hold public hearings on the issues.

Referendums may be used to deal with disputes, but several problems are associated with this procedure. Delay and voter misunderstanding are primary problems that must be overcome if impasses are to be settled on election ballots.

ARBITRATION

Interest arbitration is different from grievance arbitration in that it involves determination of the content of contracts as opposed to interpretation and application of an existing agreement. In the private sector, the strike and other economic sanctions have been the preferred methods of determining contract content. Public employees in most jurisdictions are prohibited from using the strike for any purpose. Seven states have legalized some public employee strikes under controlled conditions.[28] Because of the widespread prohibition on strikes, alternatives for dispute settlement became important. Twenty-seven states have passed legislation permitting arbitration for settling unresolved issues as a substitute for strikes.

Compulsory arbitration of interest items or of rights items may frequently be restricted to a few units in the state, such as police and fire fighters in New York. Rhode Island makes the award advisory on wages. Oregon limits compulsory arbitration to units prohibited from striking. As a result, the use of arbitration is varied among the states as to its permissible coverage.

Final-offer arbitration refers to the process of limiting the third-party umpire to selection of the final offer of one party or the other, but not to a pick-and-choose of the best features from both positions. It has been tried in Michigan, Wisconsin, and Iowa. Each state has imposed its own peculiar description of guidelines that must be followed in selecting the final offer that will become the parties' contract. In Michigan, the arbitrator assumes the role of mediator in carrying out her or his function. Final-offer arbitration may have the effect of forcing unions and employers to deal with each other in good faith at the bargaining table. Failure to do so may result in selection of a final package, not a combination of the final offers, that would not have materialized from good-faith bargaining. Most of the twenty-four states with comprehensive collective bargaining legislation provide fact finding with recommendations as a final step in impasse procedure. Mediation is usually required before the fact-finding stage. One study concluded that the longer the fact-finding procedures required, the greater the probability that illegal strikes will occur.[29]

Voluntary binding arbitration is available in fourteen states, with four placing limits on the bargaining units involved, or on the issues subject to a binding award. Binding arbitration, where it was available, has been used more often than work stoppages to settle interest disputes.[30]

Another variation is "advisory arbitration" which actually means fact finding with recommendations. Several states take the position that judicial or legislative bodies are prohibited from delegating their powers to some other body. Hence, a negotiating team or tripartite arbitration group may only recommend to a city council any terms arrived at for inclusion into an agreement.

Mediation and arbitration combined places authority in a given third party to mediate and then to arbitrate, if mediation fails. The same person is empowered to function in both processes. The arbitrator will have greater familiarity with the case than if different persons are involved in the two processes. Wisconsin utilizes the combined mediation and arbitration form of dispute settlement. A final and binding arbitration award may be more agreeable to the parties because of the greater involvement of one person in the entire proceedings. If legislatures desire to avoid strikes, they will need to furnish acceptable substitutes. Binding arbitration seems to be strongly preferred over fact finding with recommendations.

State courts generally uphold the constitutionality of compulsory arbitration statutes, which makes this form available as a substitute to voluntary final and binding arbitration.[31] Compulsory arbitration on either interest items or interpretation of rights under existing agreements is more objectionable to some than is voluntary arbitration. Voluntary arbitration with minimal guidelines controlling the process is more consistent with the general development of collective bargaining in the United States. An economic package contained in an award can be made subject to ability of a jurisdiction to pay. A responsible arbitrator would take this factor into consideration even without a legislative charge.

Whatever pros and cons may be advanced, every dispute settlement mechanism (elections, mediation, fact finding, mediation-arbitration, final-offer arbitration) is growing due to growth in public-sector bargaining and to the consequent need for solutions to the resulting policy problems.

SUMMARY

Labor relations policies in the federal services are developing as experience is gained with the collective bargaining process. Changes were made in the executive orders and policies under them to facilitate changing conditions. Collective bargaining under the executive orders was superseded by passage of the Civil Service Reform Act of 1978. State and local practices vary from comprehensive statutes defining collective bargaining rights to outright prohibition of collective bargaining.

Unilateral determination of wages and employment conditions is increasingly being questioned by government employees. Employers are finding their decisions questioned not only by unions representing their employees, but also by associations that have traditionally been somewhat passive in the area of collective bargaining. Competition between unions and associations has resulted in the use of more aggressive tactics to obtain wages and other working conditions that more nearly approach those of the private sector. Experimentation with impasse procedures is necessary for the development of stability in public-sector collective bargaining.

Several years of sustained high levels of employment, coupled with increased demand for public services, have placed employers in a position whereby they must reevaluate their traditional management practices. The general public is intolerant of inconveniences resulting from stoppages in the flow of services performed by the various agencies of government. Placed between their employees and the general public, a growing number of state and local governments have been forced to spell out more clearly the collective bargaining rights of workers. Once the process begins, there is little possibility of reversing it. The rights established in one state may be expected to spill over into adjoining states, and then to spread still further. The process may be expected to continue for as long as relatively high levels of employment exist. Otherwise, work stoppages and high turnover rates may be expected to persist. The general public may react more against work stoppages than against the high turnover rates, although both are costly in terms of taxes. The public may not approve of government employee strikes and may therefore treat such workers in harsh fashion—but probably for a short period of time only. The greatest cost of a failure to provide a workable labor-management policy is likely to fall on the elected officeholders. Thus, there are incentives for state and local governments to deal with their employees on a basis more comparable with the private sector.

DISCUSSION QUESTIONS

1. Discuss the sovereignty doctrine in the context of essential services in the public sector. Compare services in the public sector to those in the private sector as to which sector's services are more essential.

2. Trace the development of collective bargaining in federal employment. How effective were the various laws in achieving their stated purposes?

3. Outline the structural framework of collective bargaining provided by Title VII of the Civil Service Reform Act of 1978.

4. How are bargaining impasses dealt with under the Civil Service Reform Act of 1978?

5. What was the statutory basis for discharge of striking air traffic controllers in 1981?

6. Discuss the range of permissible bargaining items under the 1978 law. How are management rights handled?

7. How important are negotiated grievance procedures in federal agencies as compared to statutory appeals procedures?

8. Discuss the unfair labor practice procedure used in federal employment compared to that of the NLRB in its interpretation of Taft-Hartley.

9. Do you detect any trends in the development of collective bargaining at the state and local levels?

10. To what extent is the strike permissible at the state and local levels? How important is the strike weapon to successful bargaining results in the public sector?

11. Which category of state or local public employee is most likely to resort to strikes as a method of resolving impasses? Why?

12. Identify and discuss the most popular methods used by state and local governments to resolve impasses. Do you prefer other methods? Why?

NOTES

1   Title VII of the Civil Service Reform Act of 1978 is provided in Appendix G.

2   Committee on Public Employer-Employee Relations, *Employee Organizations in the Public Service* (New York: National Civil Service, National Civil Service League, 1946), p. 16.

3   69 Stat. 624 (1955).

4   Wilson R. Hart, *Collective Bargaining in the Federal Civil Service* (New York: Harper & Row, 1961), p. 44.

5   *Collective Bargaining in the Public Sector, An Interim Report.* Prepared for Executive Board, AFL-CIO Maritime Trades Department, February 13, 1969.

6   H. Roberts, *A Manual for Employee-Management Cooperation in the Federal Service* (Honolulu, Hawaii: Industrial Relations Center, University of Hawaii, 1964), p. 4.

7   Sterling Denhard Spero, *Government as Employer* (New York: Remsen Press, 1948), p. 122.

8   Kurt L. Hanslowe, *The Emerging Law of Labor Relations in Public Employment,* ILR Paperback No. 4 (Ithaca, N.Y.: New York State School of Industrial and Labor Relations, Cornell University, 1967), p. 35.

9   5 U.S.C. 642 (1912).

10   Charles B. Craver, "Bargaining in the Federal Sector," *Labor Law Journal,* IX, 9 (September 1968), p. 570.

11   *Ibid.*

12   Hart, *op. cit.,* p. 168.

13   *Postal Clerks* v. *Blount,* 325 F. Supp. 879 (D-D.C.) (1971), affirmed 404 U.S. 802 (1971).

14   Federal Reserve Press Release, "Policy on Unionization and Collective Bargaining for the Federal Reserve Banks," May 9, 1969.

15   United States Federal Labor Relations Council, *Labor-Management Relations in the Federal Service* (Washington, D.C., 1975), p. 32.

16   U.S. Department of Labor, Bureau of Labor Statistics, *Monthly Labor Review,* CIV, 9 (1981) p. 65.

17   *American Federation of State, County, and Municipal Employees, AFL-CIO* v. *Woodward,* 406 F. (2d) 137 (1969).

18   *Ibid.,* p. 139.

19   *McLaughlin* v. *Tilendis,* 398 F. (2d) 287 (CA 7, 1968).

20   *IEERB* v. *Benton Community School Corp.,* 95 LRRM 3084 (1977).

21   James E. Young and Betty L. Brewer, *State Legislation Affecting Labor Relations in State and Local Government,* Labor and Industrial Relations Series No. 2 (Kent, Ohio: Kent State University Bureau of Economic and Business Research, 1968), p. 16.

22   William Buck, former president of the International Association of Fire Fighters, as quoted by Eric Polisor in "Strikes and Solutions," Public Employee Relations Report No. 7, Public Employee Personnel Association, 1968.

23   Anne M. Ross, "Public Employee Unions and the Right to Strike," *Monthly Labor Review,* XCII, 3 (March 1968), p. 15.

24   John Bloedorn, "The Strike and the Public Sector," *Labor Law Journal,* XX, 3 (March 1969), p. 157.

25   Richard C. Kearney, *Labor Relations in the Public Sectors* (New York: Marcel Dekker, Inc., 1984), p. 210.

26   *Abood* v. *Detroit Board of Education,* 431 U.S. 209 (1977).

27   *Collective Bargaining in the Public Sector,* Interim Report, Executive Board, AFL-CIO Maritime Trades Department, 1969, p. 42.

28   Robert E. Dunham, "Interest Arbitration in Non-Federal Public Employment," *The Arbitration Journal,* XXXI, 1 (March 1976), pp. 45–46. States that permit public-employee strikes are Alaska, Hawaii, Minnesota, Montana, Oregon, Pennsylvania, and Vermont. Others, as noted, have minimal penalties and therefore impose few constraints to strikes.

29   *Ibid.*

30   *Ibid.*

31   Paul D. Standohar, "Constitutionality of Compulsory Arbitration Statutes in Public Employment," *Labor Law Journal,* XXVII, 11 (November 1976), p. 675.

CHAPTER TWENTY-TWO

DISCRIMINATION AND EMPLOYMENT OPPORTUNITY

Title VII of the Civil Rights Act of 1964 started machinery into motion throughout the entire economy toward equal employment opportunities for all persons without regard to race, religion, sex, color, or national origin. Employers and unions fall under the jurisdiction of agencies and laws as well as those created by the Civil Rights Act of 1964 as amended in 1968 and 1972. This chapter will focus on the essential features of Title VII of the Civil Rights Act as amended, Landrum-Griffin, and the operations of the National Labor Relations Act, as administered respectively by the Equal Employment Opportunity Commission (EEOC) and the National Labor Relations Board. Policies, regulations, and remedies of both will be analyzed in the context of court decisions affecting them.[1] Discussed are EEOC guidelines and court construction of them; NLRB treatment of discrimination cases; and the economic impact that antidiscrimination laws may have on public and private employers, unions, and workers. The chapter closes with a discussion of the Age Discrimination Act of 1967.

EVOLUTION OF RACIAL DISCRIMINATION POLICY

Both employers and unions practiced discrimination in employment, reflecting society's general attitude toward women and minorities. The CIO recognized the need to include black persons in unions and courted them more so than did the AFL. Even so, few black people progressed through the ranks to better union positions after the right to represent the bargaining units was achieved. Indeed, the government participated in racial discrimination under both the Railway Labor Act of 1926 and the National Labor Relations Act of 1935. The National

Mediation Board certifies unions under the Railway Labor Act and, in this function, certified unions that expressly prohibited black people from membership. It did so until the Civil Rights Act was passed in 1964.

The NLRB, prior to 1964, generally took the position that the Taft-Hartley Act did not contain a mandate from Congress to deal with union discrimination practices. The duty to represent fairly all workers in the bargaining unit was a vehicle made available by the U.S. Supreme Court in *Syres* v. *Oil Workers Union*, 1955.[2] The Court ruled that a union certified by the NLRB could not engage in racial discrimination. The Board did not move quickly to use the power to certify and decertify unions practicing racial discrimination. As was often the case during the 1950s and part of the 1960s, the Court was running well ahead of other institutions in society in attempts to provide fundamental rights to all citizens. The judiciary has rarely taken the initiative in providing such rights because of the web of rules developed for its own purposes. Not even the Thirteenth and Fourteenth Amendments to the U.S. Constitution deterred the Supreme Court from applying its rules of precedent until 1954, when in *Brown* v. *Board of Education*[3] it held that its separate-but-equal rule of 1896 for public education no longer applied.[4] The landmark case of 1954 slowly led to changes in the racially discriminatory practices of other institutions, but in the face of their reluctance. The NLRB was no exception.

The Duty of Fair Representation

The U.S. Supreme Court declared in the 1944 *Steele* and *Wallace Corporation* cases that Section 9(a) of the Wagner Act imposed upon unions the duty to provide "fair representation" of all employees in an exclusive bargaining unit.[5] Neither the Wagner Act nor Taft-Hartley mentioned the duty of fair representation. Since a union is the legal bargaining agent, however, the Court held that it could not discriminate against any employee in the bargaining unit. Enforcement of this duty was treated as if it fell within the exclusive jurisdiction of the courts until 1962, when the Board considered that it had the responsibility to employees and union members to assure them of fair representation in all aspects of collective bargaining. As mentioned, the Second Circuit Court of Appeals disagreed with the Board and denied enforcement.

The Board was not deterred by the adverse treatment it received in *Miranda,* and in a 1964 case involving racial discrimination, ruled that the union had by discrimination, refused to bargain, since a majority union has the statutory obligation to represent fairly *all* employees in a collective bargaining unit.[6] The *Hughes Tool Company* case arose when a local union comprised of only white employees refused to consider a grievance filed by a member of a jointly certified local union comprised entirely of black workers. Refusal to process an employee's grievance was solely for reasons of race. Refusal to consider the grievance for processing was held to be, in effect, a situation where the local had acted for the benefit of only its white members. But the local had the statutory duty to represent all employees in the bargaining unit, irrespective of membership. The Board held further that there was no statutory language limiting a union's bargaining obligation as owed only to employers.[7] The obligation to bargain was a duty owed equally to employees. The Board decision was not controlled by the *Miranda* reversal in the court of appeals, but by the Supreme Court opinion handed down after that case. Determination of the question of the duty of fair representation as redressable by unfair labor practice charges was held open by the Supreme Court.[8] The Board interpreted this as granting it the authority to rule on the issue. It was suggested in the case that the employer owed an obligation under Section 8(a)(5) not to enter into contracts permitting invidious discrimination.

The Board further declared in a later case that perpetuation of discriminatory provisions in a collective bargaining agreement was "ground upon the irrelevant, invidious, and unfair considerations of race or union membership." Such a situation was adjudged in violation of union responsibility under the Act, in that the labor organization was in effect causing an employer to discriminate against employees in violation of Section 8(a)(3). It was clear that the Board did not intend to free employers from responsibility for attempting to alleviate racial injustice in employment.

In 1966, the Fifth Circuit Court of Appeals reviewed a determination by the NLRB that a labor union had engaged in unfair labor practices when it refused to process grievances of black workers in the bargaining unit.[9] Local 12 had been the exclusive bargaining agent for employees of a Goodyear Alabama plant since 1943. Three separate seniority lists had been maintained until 1962. Separate rolls were provided for white males, black males, and females. It was the custom that black employees with greater seniority had no rights over white employees with less seniority with respect to promotions, transfers, layoffs, and recalls. Separate facilities were also maintained on the basis of race. Eight black workers approached the president of Local 12 and requested grievance action to remedy their being laid off while white workers with less seniority remained on the job. Additionally, it was alleged that new employees were being hired while the black workers were still on layoff status. The black employees asked for back pay. The local union refused to process the grievances, which the Board held was an unfair labor practice. The issue before the court of appeals was to determine whether a breach of the duty of fair representation in itself constituted an unfair labor practice within the framework of the Taft-Hartley Act.

The Fifth Circuit Court of Appeals, contrary to the Second Circuit Court of Appeals, held that "the duty of fair representation was implicit in the exclusive representation requirement of Section 9(a) of the act . . . as guaranteed in Section 7." As such, remedial action was considered available to the Board through the unfair labor practice provisions of national labor laws. Also, the Fifth Circuit Court argued that breaches of the duty to provide fair representation were within the primary jurisdiction of the Board.[10]

It is significant that the Fifth Circuit Court upheld the Board requirement that the employer in the *Rubber Workers* case should incorporate provisions in the collective bargaining contract aimed at prohibiting continued racial discrimination in terms and conditions of employment. It is obvious that the Board had invoked unfair labor practice charges against both unions and employers for the purpose of dealing with racial discrimination. The unfair labor practices of refusal to bargain and discrimination with regard to hire and tenure were to be utilized to achieve the goal of racial justice in collective bargaining relations. It had taken the Board nearly thirty years to move forcibly into this area. In a 1969 case, the District of Columbia Circuit Court of Appeals upheld and went beyond a Board decision that the existence of racial discrimination was a proper subject for bargaining.[11] The federal court also ruled that discrimination may be an unfair labor practice in and of itself. The Supreme Court refused to review the decision. As noted above, the NLRB has long held that racial discrimination by unions violates the Taft-Hartley Act. The *Farmers' Cooperative Compress* case meant that both employer and union racial discrimination cases could be decided by the NLRB.[12]

An example of this is contained in a Supreme Court decision handed down in 1975, ruling that employees cannot bypass their exclusive bargaining representative to present grievances to an employer separate from the prescribed contractual grievance procedure.[13] If minority workers picket for separate recognition along racial lines, they may be discharged under Taft-Hartley. Justice Thurgood Marshall, writing the 8–1 majority opinion, stated that the whole concept of collective bargaining would be negated if a dissident handful of workers were able to compel employers to bargain only with them and not with the union charged with the statutory responsibility of representing the entire bargaining unit. However, as the Supreme Court majority pointed out in *Emporium*, a basis for discharge under Taft-Hartley might not be the end of the matter, because remedies against discrimination on the job are available through a variety of orderly means. Instead of picketing, the black workers could have taken action through the NLRB's unfair labor practice procedures, used Title VII machinery, or ultimately sued in court. The remedial provisions of Section 704(a) of Title VII provide the means by which discharged workers in the case might recover their jobs with back pay.[14] This decision, plus others of kindred types, has provided the basis for union liability in discrimination cases under Title VII. When a union is a codefendant in fair representation cases, and the evidence demonstrates that the union has violated the principle of fair representation, the courts have held that unions and employers are jointly liable for damages.

Once discrimination is proved under the Equal Pay Act of 1963 and Title VII of the Civil Rights Act of 1964, an employer cannot force a union to share back pay liability under a "right to contribution" doctrine available under other statutes. Congress did not permit this means of enforcement as a remedy available to workers under the two laws. Arguments before the Court in *Northwest Airlines* generally were along the lines that liabilities of employers and unions should be kept separate to encourage vigorous antidiscriminatory bargaining.[15]

Equal Rights Under Landrum-Griffin

In a previous chapter, we dealt extensively with the first six titles of Landrum-Griffin. Some of the provisions relate to the material of this chapter and should be stressed at this point. We learned that Title I of the 1959 law, the "bill of rights" provision, grants equal rights and privileges to every union member with regard to nomination of candidates, voting in elections and referendums, attendance at union meetings, and voting at such meetings. The section made no attempt, however, to regulate union admissions standards. The procedural safeguards did not prohibit labor organizations from refusing membership or segregating members on the grounds of race, religion, color, sex, or national origin. Representative Adam Clayton Powell attempted to remedy this defect in Title I, but was unsuccessful by a vote of 215 to 160. A remedy to the problem was not available until Title VII of the Civil Rights Act of 1964.[16]

Racial discrimination was permissible under Title I of Landrum-Griffin, but not under the Civil Rights Act. Other forms of discrimination under Title I involved the practice of filial preference, which was a basis for closing the door to union membership. Only sons and close relatives are admitted under this practice, which has the blessing of the courts. The practice has been approved by the New York Court of Appeals. Thus, the law permits union action designed to restrict the supply of labor available under some circumstances. Many take the view that unions are no longer voluntary associations, but quasi-public organizations. Internal restrictive membership practices are viewed as antisocial because they may work against public attempts to achieve and sustain high levels of employment.[17] On the other hand, it should be realized that restrictive admission practices have been responses to excessive unemployment in labor markets in which these unions operate, as well as attempts to protect wage rates and to pass on high skill levels to relatives. A public policy not committed to full employment cannot hope to attain it by changing union admission.

EQUAL EMPLOYMENT OPPORTUNITY: ESSENTIAL FEATURES OF TITLE VII

Title VII of the Civil Rights Act of 1964, as amended in 1968 and 1972, is designed to prohibit discrimination in hiring, firing, wages, terms, and conditions or privileges of employment. The law covers employers, employment agencies, and labor unions whose activities affect interstate commerce. The protected classes of Title VII are race, sex, religion, and national origin.

Coverage under Title VII is broader than that of Taft-Hartley because the employer for its purposes includes individuals, state and local governments, government agencies, political subdivisions, labor unions, partnerships, associations, corporations, legal representatives, mutual companies, joint-stock companies, trusts, unincorporated organizations, trustees, and trustees in bankruptcy, or receivers. The enforcement agency (Equal Employment Opportunity Commission) has not established dollar guidelines eliminating certain categories from coverage, as has the NLRB. Agricultural workers, supervisors, and state and local government employees also fall within the Civil Rights law. Successor employers may be liable to remedy past discrimination on the same basis as these employers assume the bargaining duties of succeeded employers under Taft-Hartley.

Educational institutions since 1972 face all of the same provisions of law as do private employers. The only exception is that religious institutions are not covered by the prohibition on religious discrimination, which means, for example, that preference in employment may be given to a member of a given denomination over others. (Religious organizations are exempt only from the Act's prohibition on religious discrimination, but must comply with other provisions of the law, such as race or sex discrimination.)

Employers who are covered by Taft-Hartley are also covered by Title VII. Federal civil service employees fall under the provisions of the Act, but enforcement of the law against discrimination based on race, color, religion, sex, or national origin is in the hands of the U.S. Civil Service Commission. State and local governments on the other hand are covered on the same basis as employees in the private sector. Indian tribes and elected officials, along with their personnel and policy-making staffs, do not come under the Act.

Enforcement and Procedure of Title VII Complaints

The Equal Employment Opportunity Commission consists of five members charged with responsibility for administering the law. Regional or state offices have been established to administer the Act, in addition to the commission's main location in Washington, D.C. In 1972, the office of General Counsel, similar to the office created by Taft-Hartley, was created. The General Counsel is responsible for all cases before the courts except those in the U.S. Supreme Court, which are handled by the Attorney General. The commission may assign other duties to the General Counsel, and the office shares responsibility with the commission chair for appointing and supervising regional attorneys.

An Equal Employment Opportunity Coordinating Council was established by the 1972 amendments. It consists of the Secretary of Labor, EEOC chair, Attorney General, chair of the U.S. Civil Service Commission, and chair of the U.S. Civil Rights Commission. The council is required to coordinate the operations, functions, and jurisdictions of the various departments. An annual report to the President and Congress is required by July 1 of each year, and should include recommendations for administrative or legislative changes.

The commission has issued rules and regulations to guide compliance with the law. Those covered by the Act must keep records and file any reports that might be required by the EEOC. A notice must be posted by those covered containing information and summaries of the law that have been prepared and approved by the commission.

Enforcement Procedures.   In general, the procedure followed in fair employment practice cases is as follows: A charge must first be filed with an approved state or local agency if the state in which the alleged violation occurs has a fair employment practice law. After a specified time, a written charge may be filed with the EEOC by a person who claims discrimination, or since the 1972 amendments, by someone else who may file on behalf of the person aggrieved. A member of the commission may file a charge if there is reasonable cause to believe a violation has occurred. Within ten days, the commission must inform an employer, union, or employment agency that a charge has been filed against them. The public is not informed of the charge at this time. Under certain circumstances, the EEOC will defer to a state or local fair employment practices law if there is an agency to deal with discrimination in employment practices.

A state or local fair employment practices agency operating under legislation approved by the EEOC may request what is known as a "706 agency" designation. If EEOC requirements are met, the EEOC will defer charges to the state or local agency and give substantial weight to its findings and final order. An agency that does not meet EEOC standards will merely be advised that a complaint has been filed in its jurisdiction. The state agency must keep the information confidential, whether it merely receives notice or has the complaint deferred to it.

PROCEDURE IN NON-DEFERRAL STATES. The procedure used when there is no comparable state agency is as follows:

1. The charge must be filed with the EEOC within 180 days following the incidence of an unlawful employment practice.
2. After the charge has been filed, the EEOC must serve notice of the charge on the company within 10 days.
3. An investigation must be made within 120 days, if practicable, to determine whether there is reasonable cause to believe that the charge is true.
4. If it is found that there is no reasonable cause, the EEOC must dismiss the charge. If reasonable cause is found, the EEOC will attempt to conciliate the case.

PROCEDURE IN DEFERRAL STATES. In states with their own agencies, the following procedure is used:

1. The charge may be filed with the EEOC first, but then it is automatically deferred to the state agency for 60 days.
2. If the initial charge is filed with a state agency, it must be filed within 240 days of the unlawful practice.
3. The state agency has at least 60 days to act on the charge, but the charge must be filed with the EEOC within 300 days.
4. The EEOC procedure then progresses from step 2 in the nondeferral state procedure.

The following chart shows the essential ingredients of the procedure.

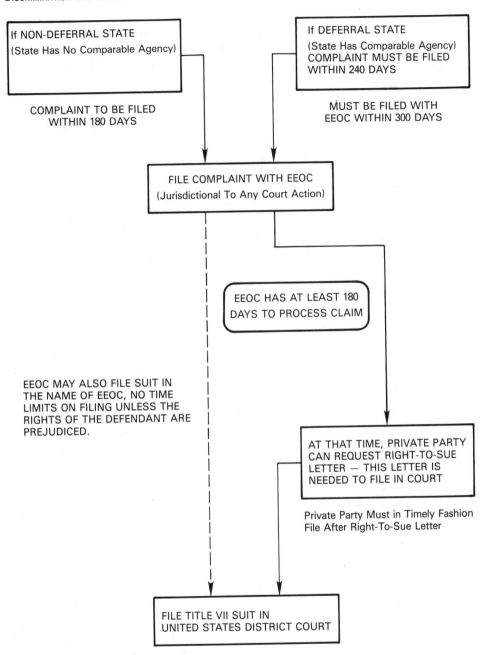

If NON-DEFERRAL STATE
(State Has No Comparable Agency)

If DEFERRAL STATE
(State Has Comparable Agency)
COMPLAINT MUST BE FILED
WITHIN 240 DAYS

COMPLAINT TO BE FILED
WITHIN 180 DAYS

MUST BE FILED WITH
EEOC WITHIN 300 DAYS

FILE COMPLAINT WITH EEOC
(Jurisdictional To Any Court Action)

EEOC HAS AT LEAST 180
DAYS TO PROCESS CLAIM

EEOC MAY ALSO FILE SUIT IN
THE NAME OF EEOC, NO TIME
LIMITS ON FILING UNLESS THE
RIGHTS OF THE DEFENDANT ARE
PREJUDICED.

AT THAT TIME, PRIVATE PARTY
CAN REQUEST RIGHT-TO-SUE
LETTER — THIS LETTER IS
NEEDED TO FILE IN COURT

Private Party Must in Timely Fashion
File After Right-To-Sue Letter

FILE TITLE VII SUIT IN
UNITED STATES DISTRICT COURT

CIVIL SUITS. The EEOC can file a suit in federal district court if it is unable to obtain voluntary compliance within thirty days after a charge is filed. The U.S. Attorney General must initiate any legal action that is taken against a government, government agency, or political subdivision. The aggrieved person has a right to intervene.

There is no time limit on the EEOC's right to sue, which is likewise not affected by any statute of limitations that may be written into federal or state laws.[18] The individual may bring suit after 180 days if the EEOC has not done so, but the commission may also bring suit of its own later. As noted, the EEOC is required to engage in conciliation efforts, and a time limit might frustrate those efforts.

The commission or the Attorney General must notify individuals filing charges within 180 days of the filing that a conciliation settlement has not been made or a suit filed. The individual then has ninety days after receipt of the notice to bring court action on his or her own. Suits are brought in the most appropriate U.S. district court.

Three standards are applied by the courts in deciding Title VII discrimination cases.

Individual Disparate Treatment.   Under this standard, one person has been treated differently than others merely for being a member of a protected class. For example, if five employees are habitually late to work, but only the black person is fired, this constitutes discrimination under this standard. However, an intent to discriminate must be shown.

Systematic Disparate Treatment.   The employment system as a whole must have treated a protected class differently under this standard. For example, if Hispanics or blacks are only rarely promoted from blue-collar to white-collar jobs, this constitutes discrimination under this standard. Statistics may be used to prove discrimination in these cases; intent to discriminate need not be shown.

Adverse Impact.   In this classification, an employment policy may be neutral on its face, but in application have an adverse impact on the protected classes. For example, height and weight restrictions may appear to be neutral, but in practice eliminate women from consideration for certain jobs. Intent to discriminate does not need to be proven under this standard.

REMEDIES. The EEOC can seek court enforcement of its orders. Remedial action may be quite varied, depending on the nature of the violation. Reinstatement or hiring of employees, or other appropriate affirmative action may be ordered. Back pay less interim earnings may be a part of the remedy.

The courts have determined that punitive damages are not allowed in Title VII suits. Punitive damages are allowed in civil rights cases under section 1983 and private suits.[19]

A discriminating party may be required to proceed through more than one forum on the same issue. An employer might go through arbitration or NLRB unfair labor practice procedures, and then through state machinery. In rare but conceivable circumstances, the same action could advance through the EEOC and ultimately to the courts.

The U.S. Supreme Court in 1977 decided two cases that set forth procedures for using statistics in Title VII suits that allege a pattern or practice of illegal discrimination.[20] A person bringing suit has to show that comparative general population figures are drawn from the relevant labor market area. In addition, general statistics would have to demonstrate that the discriminatory behavior was "long-lasting and gross." The burden of proof to show discriminatory motive is on the one bringing action.

Though discrimination problems have been handled by the NLRB, civil rights legislation endorsed by Congress constitutes the cornerstone of national policy calculated to provide equal opportunity in employment and union membership. The Civil Rights Act of 1964 was passed to deal with a variety of discriminations in employment. Title VII of the 1964 law was at first not very effective because of the lack of enforcement machinery.

The Equal Employment Opportunity Act of 1972 was passed to correct some of the deficiencies of the original law. The Equal Employment Opportunity Commission was reorganized along the lines of the NLRB. An independent General Counsel was named and made responsible for litigation. Three new groups of employers were also brought under the law. These were (1) public and private educational institutions, (2) state and local governments, and (3) employers and unions with fifteen or more members, and unions as employers without regard to numbers.

The Equal Employment Opportunity Commission set forth guidelines in 1965 to deal with discriminatory employment practices. These guidelines became far more meaningful because of the 1972 amendments to Title VII; they are used in all of the commission's deliberations. Some of the more controversial guidelines are discussed.

Recruitment, Selection, and Conditions of Employment Advertisements.   Title VII enjoins any advertisement that indicates a preference, limitation, specification, or discrimination based on sex. The EEOC holds it a violation for Help Wanted advertisements to indicate a sex unless sex is a bona fide occupational qualification for the particular job involved. A preference for race can never be a bona fide occupational qualification, but on occasion the law permits such a qualification concerning religion, sex, or national origin.

However, newspapers are not employment agencies within the meaning of the law and therefore may publish classified ads under "Male" and "Female" columns.[21] Employers must publish in both columns or in only one labeled "Help Wanted—Male or Female." Otherwise the employer is considered to have expressed a preference, limitation, specification, or discrimination based on sex.

Employment Records.   At first, the EEOC held it discriminatory even to indicate on employment records a person's race, sex, or marital status. Later, it was realized that such information was necessary in order to develop statistical evidence of discrimination. Now such questions may be asked when a person fills out the initial employment application.

Physical Examinations and Business Necessity.   A requirement that a job applicant pass a physical examination is not discriminatory per se. For example, if 20/20 vision is required, an employer must show that the requirement is necessary for the person to perform a job, or that it is a reasonable safety requirement. Physical requirements must be justified on the basis of the particular job to be performed. Disqualification must be made on a case-to-case basis, because some women might be able to perform a given job, even though a majority of them might not.[22] The same restriction applies to stereotyped views of certain jobs traditionally labeled "men's work" or "women's work."

Height and weight requirements for jobs must be shown to be related to the task to be performed. The Supreme Court in *Dothard* held that such requirements posed unnecessary barriers to employment.[23] The decision eliminated women from employment as prison guards in men's prisons in Alabama, however, on the sex bona fide occupational qualification (BFOQ) provision of Title VII. The majority felt that the job itself posed a threat to women in general.

Justices Brennen and Marshall disagreed with the majority on the BFOQ rule, because any attack on a guard of either sex should require immediate punitive action. Justice White disagreed with the height and weight decision because he was not convinced that a large percentage of females would fail to meet the requirements set by Alabama law, which were a height of between 5'2" and 6'10" and a weight of between 120 and 300 pounds.

The Court emphasized that physical requirements would be considered on a case-to-case basis, and that they could be established.

"Sex-Plus" Qualifications.   A rule to hire unmarried women is only discriminatory if there is no rule against hiring married men. Any rule that affects married women but not married men is discriminatory. The fact that such a rule does not affect all women does not eliminate sex as a factor in the employment decision. Sex plus some other factor, whether it is marital status or family responsibility, is an unlawful hiring restriction. An employer may, however, have a rule against hiring any relative of an employee, as long as the rule is applied without sex discrimination. For example, newlyweds in a plant could be given the right to decide who would quit his or her job, or employment policy could require the one with the least seniority to quit.[24]

Testing and Educational Requirements.   Regarding testing and educational requirements, the basic case for guiding equal employment actions is *Griggs* v. *Duke Power Company,* a U.S. Supreme Court decision.[25] In it, the Court held that the requirement to successfully pass an unvalidated ability test or to require a high school education as a condition of employment or a prerequisite for promotion was in violation of Title VII, because such requirements discriminated against black people and were not job-related.

Extension of coverage of Title VII to government employees in 1972 led to substantial revision of civil service examinations. In fact, the Federal Service Entrance Examination was eliminated by the Civil Service Commission, largely because of a court case charging that the test discriminated against black people.[26]

More females than males have high school diplomas, which raises the question of whether such a requirement discriminates against males. Another question is involved: Do such requirements perpetuate discrimination that started in the past?

The EEOC developed its guidelines on testing after conducting a study on their uses and obtaining a report from a panel of psychologists. The guidelines issued in 1970 were revised in 1978. General agreement on the Uniform Guidelines was reached with the Office of Personnel Management, the EEOC, the Justice Department, and the Department of Labor. The U.S. Supreme Court in the *Griggs* case held that not only tests, but any employment practice "which operates to exclude [minority groups] and cannot be shown to be related to job performance," is prohibited. The employer must prove that a test is job-related in any action brought contesting its validity.

Validation studies that show a given test to be valid for minority groups as well as for nonminorities may be required of employers. The EEOC makes every effort to require equal opportunity for employment, and if a test's validity is questionable, an employer may be required to seek some alternative method of selection. Unions that desire to examine test scores of individual employees are not entitled to do so without the written consent of the persons involved, according to the U.S. Supreme Court in *Detroit Edison.* The 1979 decision may make it more difficult for unions and workers to pursue complaints of discriminatory tests. Companies have increasingly turned to aptitude and *skill* tests as substantial factors in hiring and promotions, in order to protect themselves from Title VII liability if statistical data show inadequate minority representation.[27] The cloud of secrecy provided by the Court over union access to these data was to protect test access.

Business necessity can justify employment practices that have discriminatory impact, but demonstrating the business necessity basis for tests is not an easy task. About the most that can be said in this regard is that if serious consequences result from hiring an unqualified applicant, an employer bears a correspondingly lighter burden to show that employment criteria are job-related.[28] In one case, the District of Columbia Court of Appeals declined to consider the validity of tests that were used by a company to refuse to hire a black person because his commitment to a career in its sales force was doubted.[29]

The *Griggs* case also held that educational requirements were subject to the same scrutiny as tests. They must be job related and the employer must prove it.

Minorities placed into lower paid jobs and departments as a result of past discrimination cannot be locked into those positions by imposing tests for promotion or transfer. The *Griggs* case makes it clear that when majority employees had a chance at better-paying jobs without tests, then even nondiscriminatory tests could not be used as a basis for promotion after the illegal discrimination had ended. Tests may be used by employers only if they apply equally to everyone.

THE EQUAL PAY ACT AND COMPARABLE WORTH

The Equal Pay Act of 1963 requires equal pay for equal work. The only protected class under this act is sex. The Act permits wage differentials if based on (1) seniority, (2) merit, (3) quantity or quality of production, or (4) any other factor except sex.[30] An employer cannot pay different rates of pay for the same job on the basis of sex or race. Violations of this standard transgress the Equal Pay Act of 1963 as well as Title VII of the Equal Employment Opportunity Act. The Wage and Hour Division enforces the Equal Pay Act of 1963, taking the position that the work need only be substantially the same in order to require equal pay. The EEOC guideline with respect to wages states that the commission will give appropriate consideration to the interpretation of the Wage and Hour Division, but it will not be bound thereby, even though Section 703(h) of the Civil Rights law states that wage differentials between sexes are not illegal if they are authorized by the Equal Pay Law.

Comparable Worth.   It was thought that the Equal Pay Act would solve the problems of pay differentials between men and women. Instead, most suits under the Act involve questions of whether the work is equal. It is legal under the Equal Pay Act for employers to pay differentially to employees if they perform different work. Title VII of the Civil Rights Act of 1964 forbids discrimination in any of the terms and conditions of employment as well as pay that may have comparable worth to the firm.

Pay differentials exist in part because of occupational segregation, whereby women are concentrated in lower paying jobs. The average wage differential between women and men hovers around 60 per cent. The concept of comparable worth was born out of concern over the persistence of the pay differential over time. The assumption of comparable worth is that women should be paid wages comparable to men for work that is comparable. Implementing this principle would eliminate wage differentials based on occupational segregation of the sexes, so that the wage structure would reflect the worth of jobs to the firm.

In 1981, the Supreme Court in a 5–4 decision gave women more grounds to challenge pay discrimination than had been provided under the Equal Pay Act of 1963. The question of comparable worth was raised in the case *County of Washington* v. *Alberta Gunther.*[31] Four female prison guards brought suit against the county under Title VII of the Civil Rights Act of 1964. Part of their claim was that since they received less pay than did males performing a similar job, they were being discriminated against due to their gender.

During the court proceedings, it was made clear that although the jobs the female guards performed were similar to those of the male guards, the positions and duties were not equal. According to past court decisions and interpretations of the amendment to the Civil Rights Act of 1964, commonly called the Bennett Amendment, the matrons appeared to have a good case.

The Bennett Amendment had been interpreted in the past as simply incorporating the affirmative defenses of the Equal Pay Act into Title VII. The *Gunther* decision, however, interpreted the amendment quite differently. The Court determined that the amendment insured that the equal pay standard specified in the Equal Pay Act would also apply to wage compensation claims filed under Title VII, but would not limit discriminatory wage suits to the equal pay for equal work standard of the Equal Pay Act. In *Gunther,* the Court held that an action for wage discrimination can be brought under Title VII even if the work is not equal. The "equal work" standard of the Equal Pay Act will not apply to Title VII wage discrimination suits. Though the high court held in *Gunther* that wage discrimination suits may be filed under Title VII, it did not hold that discrimination may be proved based upon comparable worth. To prevail under Title VII, a successful suit must demonstrate intentional discrimination against women.

At this writing, it appears clear that Title VII suits filed by women on the basis of comparable worth will not be successful. Based upon a 1983 job evaluation of 15,000 public sector employees in the State of Washington, it was determined that on the average, job classifications dominated by women were paid 20 percent less than those classifications in which men dominated though both classes of jobs were given the same number of points in the study. Faced with this situation, and to reduce the disparity, the state legislature appropriated funds to be paid to women-dominated jobs. However, given the pace of the projected legislative action, the inequity would not be corrected until 1993. State officials admitted the pay inequity, but claimed lack of financial ability to correct the situation at a faster rate. A Washington State federal district court in 1983 held that the state's plan to eliminate the inequity was much too slow. Rejecting the state's position, the court held that cost and ability to pay is not a valid defense for a Title VII violation. In *AFSCME* v. *State of Washington* (578 F. Supp. 846 (DC-Wash)), the court directed the state to pay almost a billion dollars to wipe out the inequity. Thus, the district court upheld comparable worth valid to prove a Title VII violation.

No money was paid, however, while the case was appealed. In 1985, a federal appeals court in a case involving the same parties, reversed the district court's decision. (770 F. 2d 1401 (CA-9) 1985) It specifically rejected comparable worth for purposes of Title VII. As long as an employer can hire women at lower rates than men for comparable jobs, it does not violate Civil Rights statutes. In other words, the free labor market system prevails over matters of equity. The federal appeals court said:

> . . . Neither law nor logic deems the free market system a suspect enterprise
> . . . The State of Washington's initial reliance on a free market system in which

employees in male-dominated jobs are compensated at a higher rate than employees in dissimilar female-dominated jobs is not in and of itself a violation of Title VII, notwithstanding that the [job evaluation] study deemed the positions of comparable worth.

Despite its failure in the judiciary, women's groups, including their unions, press comparable worth in collective bargaining and state legislatures. After a prolonged strike at Yale University, which completely disrupted the campus for several months, the union successfully used comparable worth to obtain substantial wage increases for jobs held predominantly by women. Indeed, unions increasingly have made comparable worth a bargaining goal. Sparked by women's groups, several states and their political subdivisions have enacted comparable worth statutes. By no means is comparable worth dead just because it has not met the judicial test.

Sexual Harrassment.   Courts were initially reluctant to view sexual harassment as actionable under Title VII, but later recognized that it was because of a person's sex that she—or he—was being harassed. Not until 1976 was the first case involving sexual harassment found actionable under Title VII. This was in *Williams* v. *Saxbe*.[32] The EEOC defines sexual harassment as unwelcome sexual advances, requests for sexual favors, and any other verbal or physical conduct of a sexual nature, under the following guidelines:

1) when submission is a term or condition of employment;
2) when sexual conduct is used as a basis for employment decisions, such as hiring or promotion;
3) when the conduct has the purpose or effect of interfering with the work environment.

An adverse job reaction such as termination of employment was often necessary in order to prove sexual harassment. In *Fisher* v. *Flynn,* a college professor was required to show that she had been fired because she rejected the department chair's sexual advances.[33] Since she had no proof that she had been terminated because of the advances, the advances were deemed merely an "unsatisfactory personal encounter."

Sexual harassment was found to exist under Title VII for the first time in *Bundy* v. *Jackson*[34] without the requirement of proof that employment or job benefits were lost by rejecting the overtures. It is important to note that if a supervisor or manager sexually harasses an employee, the company or agency is absolutely liable under Title VII. If an employee views behavior as sexually harassing, it is actionable under Title VII even if the supervisor lacked intent. Men may also be sexually harassed by a member of the same sex or by women and obtain relief under Title VII.

A work environment made hostile because of sexual harassment is judged on the totality of circumstances. Some behavior such as vulgar language may be merely annoying, but insufficient to create a hostile work environment in violation of the law. Teasing and touching, comparisons of the person to nude pictures, and requests that a person strip have been held as sufficient to find an employer guilty of providing a hostile work environment. Once again, the employer is responsible for providing a work climate that is free from sexual harassment. Immediate and appropriate corrective action must be taken by employers to protect themselves from liability.

Homosexuals.   While homosexual advances are subjects for remedy as sexual harassment under Title VII, homosexuals themselves may be discriminated against by employers on the basis of affectional preference. A court of appeals ruled in *DeSantis* v. *Pacific Telephone and Telegraph Co., Inc.* that Title VII's prohibition of "sex" discrimination applies only to discrimination on the basis of gender.[35] In *DeSantis,* it was charged that the employer refused to hire or promote a person who preferred sexual partners of the same sex. The Court ruled that homosexuals are not a protected class within the meaning of the civil rights statute. It also ruled that employment discrimination because of effeminacy, like discrimination because of homosexuality or transsexualism, is not protected by the law.

Pregnancy.   The treatment of pregnancy as unlawful discrimination on the basis of sex has developed in stages. The EEOC guideline is that pregnancy must be treated as any other temporary disability. It states that

> disabilities caused or contributed to by pregnancy, miscarriage, abortion, childbirth, and recovery therefrom, for all job-related purposes, are temporary disabilities and should be treated as such under any health or temporary disability insurance or sick leave plan available in connection with employment. Written and unwritten employment policies and practices involving matters such as the commencement and duration of leave, the availability of extensions, the accrual of seniority and other benefits and privileges, reinstatement, and payment under any health or temporary disability insurance or sick leave plan, formal or informal, shall be applied to disability due to pregnancy or childbirth on the same terms and conditions as they are applied to other temporary disabilities.

Thus, the EEOC guideline was that pregnancy would require the collecting of sick leave pay; therefore, it did not really matter when the leave started or how long it lasted. However, the length of the leave can determine whether or not disability pay will be available, since some employers have little or no short-term disability coverage. The U.S. Supreme Court has hinted that a woman with the advice of her physician will decide when to leave a job due to pregnancy and when to return after childbirth.[36] The Court also decided that a state could not deprive all women of unemployment compensation for a prescribed period of time under the assumption that they are unable to work due to pregnancy.[37] Some are able to work much longer than are others prior to delivery, and some return to work earlier.

In 1976, in *General Electric Co.* v. *Gilbert,* the U.S. Supreme Court voided the essential part of the EEOC guideline.[38] The exclusion of pregnancy from an employer's disability insurance plan was not viewed as sex discrimination. The *Gilbert* ruling was similar to the Court's earlier decision that a state disability insurance law could exclude disabilities arising from pregnancy.[39] The Court's *Gilbert* decision was overturned when Congress amended Title VII by the 1978 Pregnancy Amendment. Now, according to the EEOC, pregnancy must be treated as any other disability. The best policy appears to be a maximum number of weeks for employee coverage under a disability plan. This limit would apply to all physical disabilities, including pregnancy.

Fringe Benefits in General.   Fringe benefits include medical, hospital, accident, life insurance, and retirement benefits. In addition, profit-sharing and bonus plans, leaves, and other terms, conditions, and privileges of employment are included in EEOC guidelines. The EEOC makes it an unlawful employment practice for an employer to discriminate between men and women with regard to fringe benefits. This means that when an employer makes benefits conditional on whether the employee is head of a household, or the principal wage earner in the family unit, it is assumed that the benefits tend to be available primarily to male employees and their families. As such, there is discrimination against the rights of female employees. Further, it is held that the head of household or principal wage earner status bears no relationship to job performance and, consequently, such conditions discriminate against females. It is also an unlawful employment practice for an employer to make benefits available to wives and families of male employees if the same benefits are not made available to the husbands and families of female employees. In addition, the EEOC will not permit an employer to defend a practice under Title VII when charged with sex discrimination on the basis that the cost of such benefits is greater with respect to one sex than the other.

Maternity is not grounds for termination, but must be treated as a leave of absence. Reinstatement poses a different situation. The problem is whether a woman is entitled to exactly the same job she held when she left, or only to the vacancies that exist at the time of reinstatement. The particular circumstances of each case arising under the guidelines should determine each answer without a mechanistic approach.

Pension and Retirement Plans.   Pension and retirement plans pose critical difficulties for employers. The problem with them is that, in fact, men and women are not "equal," because women live longer. The Wage and Hour Division takes the position, under the Equal Pay Act, that there is no violation if the employer contribution for both sexes is equal, or if the benefits paid are equal even though the cost is different. However, the Wage and Hour Division has not prohibited different retirement ages for men and women. The EEOC operates differently. It states: "It shall be an unlawful employment practice for an employer to have a pension or retirement plan which establishes different optional or compulsory retirement ages based on sex, or which differentiates in benefits on the basis of sex." So far, the courts have agreed.[40]

A critical problem in pension discrimination cases is that normally the number of female employees covered by such plans is comparatively small. To extend additional benefits to male employees has the effect of increasing benefits to a very high level. Because of the high cost involved in these benefit cases, employers faced with pension litigation seek to bring unions in as codefendants. Understandably, unions do not want to be involved in these cases, despite the fact that they, along with employers, may have negotiated a pension plan favoring women. In any event, discrimination in pension plans more favorable to women is not permitted under EEOC guidelines.

State workers' compensation laws are forbidden from differentiating death benefits based on sex.[41] The laws of seven states—Missouri, Pennsylvania, Michigan, Indiana, Georgia, Idaho, and Mississippi—gave automatic death benefits to widows in job-related deaths, but no benefit was given to the widowers.

The problems with pensions and retirement plans are of such magnitude that Congress may eventually have to clarify its intent with additional legislation. The other guidelines range from relatively simple to extremely difficult to implement. In most cases, there will be substantial changes in the labor market if the EEOC becomes more active in enforcement.

Reverse Discrimination

Male employees have filed many complaints alleging sex discrimination under Title VII. For example, the EEOC has held that an employer hiring females with long hair may not discriminate against males with long hair.[42] A very controversial type of case involves pension and profit-sharing plans, as mentioned above. These plans usually provide for different retirement ages for female and male employees. A circuit court of appeals held in *Rosen* v. *Public Service Electric Company* that males who were penalized by reduction in pension, if retiring before sixty-five, were entitled to recover the amounts necessary to equalize them with females, who were permitted to retire at age sixty-two on full pension without actuarial reductions.[43]

ARBITRATION AND TITLE VII RIGHTS

In 1972, in *Rios* v. *Reynolds Metals Company*,[44] a circuit court of appeals ruled that federal courts may defer to arbitration cases involving employees' rights protected by Title VII of the Civil Rights Act. The conditions set by the court of appeals for accepting arbitration awards for cases involving Title VII rights are more specific and demanding than the NLRB's.[45] These are as follows:

. . . First, there may be no deference to the decision of the arbitrator unless the contractual right coincides with rights under Title VII.

Second, it must be plain that the arbitrator's decision in no way violates the private rights guaranteed by Title VII, nor of the public policy which inheres in Title VII. In addition, before deferring, the District Court must be satisfied that (1) the factual issues before it are identical to those decided by the arbitrator; (2) the arbitrator had power under the collective agreement to decide the ultimate issue of discrimination; (3) the evidence presented at the arbitral hearing dealt adequately with all factual issues; (4) the arbitrator actually decided the factual issues presented to the Court; and (5) the arbitration proceeding was fair and regular and free of procedural infirmities. The burden of proof in establishing these conditions of limitation will be upon the respondent as distinguished from the claimant.

A question also raised in *Rios* involved whether an aggrieved employee could seek relief under Title VII without first invoking or exhausting available alternative legal or contractual remedies. That is, could an aggrieved employee submit a grievance to arbitration and also take it before the court? It was decided in *Caldwell* v. *National Brewing Company* that employees may seek relief under Title VII without invoking or exhausting available alternative legal or contractual remedies.[46] Further, in *Hutchins* v. *United States Industries, Inc.* it was held that even where an employee does pursue an alternative remedy, such as arbitration in cases involving Title VII rights, the federal court is the final arbiter.[47] In *Rios*, however, the circuit court stated that

it does not follow, however, that the policies of Title VII require that an employee who has submitted his claim to binding arbitration must always be given an opportunity to relitigate his claim in court. In some instances such a requirement would not comport with elementary notions of equity for it would give the employee but not the employer a second chance to have the same issue resolved.

In February 1974, the U.S. Supreme Court resolved the inconsistency created by the lower courts in *Rios* and *Hutchins.* At that time, in *Alexander* v. *Gardner-Denver,* the high court held that an arbitrator's decision is not final and binding when an employee claims that he or she was discharged because of racial reasons in violation of Title VII of the Civil Rights Act. An arbitrator sustained the discharge of a black employee on the grounds that the employee had been terminated for just cause. A district court upheld the arbitrator's decision, and did not inquire into the question of whether the discharge was in violation of the Civil Rights Act. However, the U.S. Supreme Court remanded the case to the lower court with instructions that it determine whether the employee's rights under Title VII had been violated. What *Gardner-Denver* means, therefore, is that even if an employee loses a case in arbitration, appeal for relief may be made from the courts provided that Title VII rights are involved; as stated, the employee has two bites at the apple. In other words, the finality of an arbitrator's award as established under *Enterprise Wheel,* discussed in an earlier chapter, does not apply.

RELIGIOUS DISCRIMINATION

The problem of direct discrimination because of an individual's religion has taken several forms. It has involved outright refusal to hire, segregation after employment, and job classification and assignment according to religion. Special problems have also been observed, such as observance of religious holidays and the Sabbath that differ from the majority observances.

The 1972 amendments to the Civil Rights Act accepted the position of the EEOC guidelines, which was that "the term 'religion' includes all aspects of religious observance and practice, as well as belief, unless an employer demonstrates that he [or she] is unable to reasonably accommodate to an employee's or prospective employee's religious observance or practice without undue hardship on the conduct of the employer's business." The Fifth Circuit Court of Appeals ruled that the 1972 amendments endorsed EEOC's guidelines on relitigation.[48]

The EEOC has a wide range of standards regarding its construction of what is meant by "reasonable accommodation" and "undue hardship." It has held, among many decisions, that a company could not (1) discharge a Saturday Sabbath observer without proving that rotation of other employees would result in an undue hardship to the firm; (2) apply a rule that vacations had to be taken at a certain time for a worker who had requested leave to attend a compulsory religious convention, even though other employees would be discontented; and (3) apply a policy of a whole weekend of overtime or none at all to a person whose religion prohibited working on one of the two days. The burden of proof is on the employer to show that accommodation to one's religious beliefs would impose an undue hardship on the firm.

Collective bargaining agreements combine the dimension of conflict and the need for accommodation of the Taft-Hartley law and the Equal Employment Opportunity Act of 1972. In 1977, the U.S. Supreme Court ruled that an employer was not obligated to go very far in seeking to accommodate a worker's religious beliefs.[49] In *TWA,* it held that Title VII does not require an employer to violate a collective bargaining agreement so that a few employees may observe their Sabbath. The seniority system protects the rights of all employees; therefore, an employer does not have to put up with the cost of being shorthanded or pay overtime to accommodate an employee's religious beliefs. It was held that the Civil Rights law was designed to eliminate discrimination against the majority as well as minorities. To pay overtime to some employees in order to give others the days off they wanted, when no such costs were required for the majority of workers, was viewed as unequal treatment of employees on the basis of religion.

Justices Marshall and Brennen, in dissent, argued that the Court majority had gutted the Civil Rights Act without declaring it illegal.

Still another troublesome area is found in union-security arrangements. Union-shop agreements provide that an employee can be discharged for nonpayment of dues. Circuit courts have taken the position in several cases, with *Gray* denied Supreme Court review, that workers may be discharged under Taft-Hartley for failure to pay union dues even if the refusal is due to religious objections to unions.[50] The EEOC has ruled that both a company and union violate Title VII if they discharge a worker for refusing to pay union dues for religious reasons.[51] An attempt to accommodate the employee's belief is required before discharge is permissible.

The *TWA* decision of the Supreme Court in 1977 has essentially said that not much of an accommodation for religious beliefs is required under Title VII. It did not say, however, that the provision was unconstitutional.

It was pointed out in Chapter 14 that Congress amended Taft-Hartley in 1980 and exempted from compulsory union membership employees who have bona fide religious beliefs against joining or financially supporting labor organizations.

NATIONAL ORIGIN

Discrimination based on national origin is unlawful. The national origin provision of Title VII does not apply to aliens unless a firm's employment policy applies only to aliens of certain national origins, or if it is used to refuse jobs to certain nationalities.[52] A rule that employees must be U.S. citizens is not in violation of the law.

EEOC guidelines require that violations occur when (1) employment tests are given in English to persons whose native language is not English and whose language skill has nothing to do with job performance, (2) height and weight requirements are applied that have nothing to do with job performance and certain groups fall outside the national norms, and (3) rules are instituted against persons who belong to organizations identified with national groups.

The U.S. Supreme Court ruled in *Espinoza* v. *Farah Manufacturing Co.*[53] that the term "national origin" does not mean citizenship. An employer has the right to deny employment to noncitizens. Discrimination in hiring noncitizens may occur where employment policies are based on whether employees are U.S. citizens. If a firm hired noncitizens from one national origin, but refused to hire the same of some other ancestry, that would be a violation of the law. But the Civil Rights Act of 1964 does not make it illegal to formulate a hiring policy based on citizenship.

Justice Douglas entered a vigorous dissent from the majority opinion, which construed the Congressional interpretation of "national origin" to exclude citizenship. Douglas noted that legal permanent resident aliens are most vulnerable to discrimination and exploitation, and chided the court for its inconsistency with other cases. He viewed citizenship as much an artificial, arbitrary, and unnecessary barrier to equal employment opportunity as those barriers addressed in *Griggs* v. *Duke Power Co.*

AFFIRMATIVE ACTION PROGRAMS

Affirmative action means active efforts toward voluntarily redressing any racial, sexual, or other minority imbalances that may exist in an employee work force. Executive Orders 11246 and 11375, along with related regulations of the Office of Federal Contract Compliance (OFCC), brought affirmative action programs into existence. The Civil Rights Act does not contain language that requires a program of affirmative action. The OFCC affirmative action program requirements apply to all employers, contractors, and subcontractors of the federal government, whether the contract is direct, or is only financed or assisted by federal funds. Employers are not under a strict obligation to seek racial balance for its own sake. Neither must future job openings be necessarily reserved for minority groups. However, affirmative action requires employers to evaluate their work forces, analyze their employment needs, and actively solicit to obtain more minority employees. The primary requirement is a written stipulation of good-faith efforts to achieve more rapid change than would occur from Title VII alone. At a minimum, such efforts must include (1) an analysis of deficiencies in the utilization of minorities; (2) a timetable for correcting such deficiencies, together with their expected goals; and (3) a coherent and reasonable plan for achieving these goals.

The analysis of the work force should include an analysis of all major job categories, by establishment, to determine where minorities are being underutilized, along with an explanation of why they are being underutilized and a further explanation of how this can be corrected. Goals and timetables must be couched in terms of actual commitment. Also, they must be cast in terms of correcting identifiable conditions, and support data must be furnished to show that the goals and timetables are realistic. Specific means set forth in a plan for reaching equal employment goals must include internal and external dissemination. Internally, the company should publicize its commitment to equal employment by placing appropriate notices on company bulletin boards, by setting forth its goals in company newspapers, and by verbal expression during meetings held with company employees. Externally, a company must actively recruit employees from minority groups. After a contractor with the federal government has established an affirmative action policy, he or she must then disseminate that policy.

In 1971, the OFCC set up a number of factors that have to be considered in order to determine whether an employer is guilty of underutilization. These considerations are (1) minority population of the labor area in the plant locale; (2) size of the minority unemployment force in that locale; (3) percentage of minority work force compared with the total work force of that locale; (4) general availability of minorities with the necessary skills, both in the immediate location and within a reasonable recruiting radius; (5) availability of promotable minorities within the employer's work force; (6) existence of training institutions capable of training minorities with the requisite skills; and (7) amount of training that the contractor is reasonably able to undertake to make all job classifications available to minorities.

Later on in this chapter, several U.S. Supreme Court decisions will be presented dealing with affirmative action within a context of negotiated seniority provisions contained in labor agreements.

Negotiated Consent Decree

In employment discrimination cases, the parties to a court action may enter into a negotiated consent decree for purposes of working toward affirmative action plan objectives. If a labor organization is not a named party to the action, it is nevertheless usually given an opportunity to intervene in proceedings to protect its interests. Failure to do so within the time frame allowed by a court may exclude it from input in the initial proceedings before a negotiated consent decree is approved.

The negotiated consent decree approach is a temporary remedy designed to end when the targeted racial or sex imbalances have been corrected. At this writing, specific statistical promotion and hiring goals and ratios are permissible elements of the plan. The future of such goals and ratios depends upon the continued support of the Chief Executive, and could be altered or eliminated by executive order. In the meantime, a consent decree of this nature has certain court-imposed restrictions placed on its content.

In order to approve a negotiated consent decree, the trial court must find that several ingredients are present, namely, that it is *reasonable,* which means that it provides a fair and adequate solution to the complaints raised. The solution must also be fair and reasonable to nonminorities affected by it. Reverse discrimination challenges to the solution are viewed as impermissible secondary attacks if the consent decree is found to be reasonable. For a decree to be found reasonable, the court must consider all objections to the decree, as well as alternative approaches to secure equal employment opportunity.

The court maintains jurisdictional administration over reasonable consent decrees and is empowered to issue further orders to achieve the statistical goals and ratios of the order as they may be necessary over the life of the agreement. These bargained affirmative action decrees may be terminated when the court is convinced that the objectives of the agreement have been achieved. At that time, the essence of employment relations is returned to the original parties to collective bargaining agreements.

The Secretary of Labor has extensive powers to enforce the nondiscrimination policy of the executive orders. A failure to develop an affirmative action program can lead to possible cancellation of existing contracts and debarment from future contracts. The OFCC will grant a conference to a contractor who has not developed an acceptable affirmative action program. The purpose of the conference is to make every effort to assist in developing an acceptable affirmative action program. If the contractor remains in noncompliance, the OFCC will move to set a hearing date that will serve to make the contractor ineligible for future contracts and subcontracts. If there is no program at all, or one that is unacceptable, the agency can issue notice, giving the contractor thirty days to show cause why enforcement proceedings should not be instituted. If the situation is not corrected within the thirty days, the compliance agency, with authorization, will commence formal proceedings leading to the cancellation or termination of existing contracts or subcontracts. In reality, very few contract terminations have occurred.

If an employer's discrimination is caused by union practices in referral or membership, the Secretary of Labor can refer union violations to the EEOC or the Attorney General for action. It is the employer who contracts directly with the government, not the unions.

PREFERENTIAL TREATMENT

The issue of preferential treatment or reverse discrimination has been narrowly constructed by the U.S. Supreme Court. In the celebrated *Bakke* case,[54] it was ruled that the University of California had practiced reverse discrimination against Bakke by denying admission to him and at the same time declaring that race could be taken into account in establishing the medical school's special admissions program. In another case involving selection of workers, the Court in *Weber* ruled that voluntary affirmative action agreements could be reached through collective bargaining.[55] As such, race-conscious affirmative action plans were permissible to correct or eliminate conspicuous racial imbalance in traditionally segregated job categories. The Court refused to distinguish between lawful and unlawful voluntary affirmative action plans. It stressed that voluntary collective bargaining accords well reflected the intent of Equal Employment Opportunity.

The United Steelworkers and Kaiser Aluminum and Chemical Corp. agreed to require one black worker for every white worker to enter into a new job training program. The intent was to increase minority representation in craft jobs. There was no constitutional question in *Weber,* and because there was no state action involved, there was no possible violation of the Equal Protection Clause of the U.S. Constitution. The negotiated plan was to continue in force only until the target percent of black people in skilled jobs equaled the percentage of black people in the local labor force. Thus, the Supreme Court reasoned, white people were not unduly harmed, since they were not locked out of job training programs. The EEOC issued a policy statement in 1980 that voluntary union-management efforts should be the preferred solution. However, if only one party is willing to advocate measures to deal with discrimination, the EEOC would recognize the good faith efforts of that party in any subsequent discrimination actions.

Title VII does not require employers to hire women and racial minority members just because they are as qualified as white men competing for the same jobs.[56] Employers do not have to restructure employment practices to maximize the number of minorities and women hired.

EQUAL EMPLOYMENT OPPORTUNITY AND LABOR UNIONS

Labor unions are covered by the fair employment practices provisions of the Civil Rights Act of 1964, as amended in 1968 and 1972, if they are in an industry affecting commerce. A union is deemed to affect commerce if (1) it operates a hiring hall, or (2) has fifteen or more members. The EEOC has ruled that a union is covered by the law regarding its own employees, even though it may have fewer than fifteen members. The Act in Section 703(c) prohibits a union from excluding or expelling from its membership or otherwise discriminating against any individual because of race, color, religion, sex, or national origin. Thus, EEOC has ruled that the Act's language is broad enough to prohibit a union from discriminating against its employees without regard to numbers. In addition, a union must meet one of several additional requirements to be covered by the Act. In essential part, the possibilities are (1) the union must be certified under the NLRA or Railway Labor Act; (2) if not certified, the union must represent employees of an employer covered by the Act; (3) the union has chartered a local or subsidiary that represents or seeks to represent employees falling under (1) or (2) above; (4) the organization has been chartered by a union that represents or seeks to represent employees falling under (1) or (2) above; or (5) the group is a conference, general committee, joint or system board, or joint council subordinate to a national or international union that includes a union covered under any of the tests set out in (1) to (4) above.

Discrimination Under NLRA and Equal Employment Opportunity

As noted, a union is guilty of an unfair labor practice under Taft-Hartley if it causes or attempts to cause an employer to discriminate against an employee who has been denied union membership on any ground other than nonpayment of dues. The Civil Rights Act prohibits a union from causing or attempting to cause an employer to discriminate against any person because of race, color, religion, national origin, or sex. Thus, a union may be in violation of both the NLRA and Civil Rights Act if it causes or attempts to cause discrimination for any reason other than nonpayment of dues.

Unions as employers are covered under the same provisions of equal employment opportunity as employers generally. Selected categories have been identified below to provide information on how labor unions are affected by the Civil Rights Act.

Seniority

The law provides that "it shall not be an unlawful employment practice for an employer to apply different standards of compensation, or different terms, conditions or privileges of employment pursuant to a bona fide seniority . . . system . . . provided that such differences are not the result of an intention to discriminate because of race, color, religion, sex, or national origin." Any collective bargaining contractual clause that conflicts with the Act is void.[57] The seniority system itself cannot be discriminatory. Both unions and employers are held responsible when discriminatory seniority practices are found.

Seniority systems that maintain the results of past discrimination can place some unions in serious situations. If an employer attempts to champion the cause of the minority worker and proposes to revise long established discriminatory seniority systems, unions may face a dilemma, depending on the nature, severity, and timing of the practices as discussed below.

Title VII prohibits seniority clauses in labor agreements that perpetuate discrimination against minorities where a history of discrimination has been shown. In *Griggs,* it was held that Title VII required the removal of any artificial, arbitrary, and unnecessary barriers to employment. The Court stated that such barriers included not only those that were overtly discriminatory, but also those that were fair in theory but discriminatory in practice. With respect to construction industry union employment barriers, the courts have indicated a willingness to require affirmative action in any situation where a deliberately discriminatory employment practice has been discovered.[58]

It is intended that employees keep all benefits of their seniority. However, a problem of substantial proportions arises in attempts to correct seniority systems that had been discriminatory in the past. Congressional debate shows that the 1964 law was not intended to permit the firing of whites to hire blacks, or to grant blacks special seniority rights at the expense of whites with longer years of service.[59] One court has held that this point was not controlling over remedies to systems containing past discrimination, because the debate took place before the Act's seniority provision was introduced to the Senate.[60] The possibility of reverse discrimination and, indeed, charges of such have been popular in recent years. Reverse discrimination seems to be prohibited by Section 703(j), which says in brief: "Nothing in this title . . . [shall require the granting] of preferential treatment to any individual or group because of race, color, religion, sex, or national origin . . . on account of an imbalance which may exist with respect to the total number or percentage of [such] persons."

Several theories for remedying the effects of past discriminatory systems have been advanced. The "status quo" approach is one usually called for by some union leaders, who argue that employers today follow fair employment practices and may even prefer minorities when federal or state contracts are involved. Thus, the negative effects of past discrimination should be ignored. Others at the opposite end of the "status quo" argument advanced a "freedom now" proposition, that all remains of past discrimination should be eradicated immediately. The Fifth Circuit Court of Appeals took a position between the "status quo" and "freedom now" positions, advancing its "rightful place" theory.[61] Some lower courts accepted the "status quo" and "freedom now" theories, but most found the "rightful place" theory more acceptable.[62]

The "rightful place" theory provides that future awarding of vacant jobs based on a seniority system that locks in past discrimination is unlawful. White employees should not lose positions held, however, even though minorities continued at a disadvantage. The Fifth Circuit Court of Appeals held, "Where a seniority system has the effect of perpetuating discrimination, and concentrating or 'telescoping' the effect of past years of discrimination against Negro employees into the *present* placement of Negroes in an inferior position for promotion and other purposes, the present result is prohibited, and a seniority system which operates to produce that present result must be replaced with another system." The court argued further that the fact that Title VII of the Act referred to an effective date was no defense for expanding a discriminatory, departmental seniority system into a plantwide system. White employees were not deprived of seniority accrued before passage of the Act. Black employees would no longer be locked into dead end departments, but would become eligible for promotion into better jobs on a par with white workers on a plantwide basis.

Precisely how far a remedy may go under particular circumstances depends upon the court ordering the remedy. For example, a federal district court in Virginia ordered that *all* nonsupervisory jobs must be opened for bidding, with the only qualifications for a position being a willingness to learn the job and seniority.[63] The court ordered this remedy because vacancies seldom occurred in the tobacco industry, plagued by static employment because of automation. Any incumbent employees demoted as a result of the remedy, however, were not to have their wages reduced. Demotions were ordered because the details of the case revealed that future job openings would probably not occur in sufficient number to correct past practices. Employers maintain that such orders can seriously affect the financial welfare of businesses.

The Fifth Circuit Court of Appeals introduced still another dimension into seniority cases evidencing past discrimination with present effects.[64] It set forth a twofold test: (1) Does the present policy perpetuate the past discrimination? (2) Is the present policy justified by a showing of business necessity?

The question then becomes, what constitutes justifiable business necessity? It means more than attempting to avoid inconvenience or additional costs. An employment policy must be related to job performance before a business necessity policy that affects any group adversely will be acceptable.[65] Employee preferences for a given policy will not justify an employer's discriminatory practice.[66] A medical examination for the purpose of determining the ability of a person to physically perform a job is justifiable under the business necessity doctrine if the standard used is in fact essential for attaining the goals of the specific job. A physical standard not necessary for the specific job, such as a minimum height requirement, is considered discriminatory.

Any seniority clause in a collective bargaining agreement that had a negative effect on minorities prior to 1965 is unlawful at present. Employers are generally held responsible for training minorities to qualify them for advancement to higher level jobs in nondiscriminatory seniority systems. While a "business necessity" exception to discriminatory practices exists, it is not often accepted by the courts.

Section 703(l) outlaws seniority systems that perpetuate past discrimination, but Section 703(j) prohibits reverse discrimination when remedies are required.

In 1976, the U.S. Supreme Court in *Franks* v. *Bowman Transportation* utilized the "rightful place" theory in dealing with a make-whole remedy for rectifying the victims of unlawful employment discrimination.[67] Seniority was ordered from the date that employment was wrongfully refused. Thus, the blacks involved got seniority from the date of discrimination and would jump ahead of whites who were hired after that date and who had actually worked, whereas those discriminated against did not actually work. The Court held that Section 706(g) provided for an award of seniority as a remedy even though the court of appeals reasoned that Section 703(l) prohibited tampering with a bona fide seniority system. Section 703(g) provides that the courts could

> order such affirmative action as may be appropriate which may include, but is not limited to, reinstatement or hiring of employees, with or without backpay . . ., or any other relief as the court deems appropriate.

The Supreme Court went on to say that a refusal to provide seniority relief on the grounds that it would diminish the expectations of other employees would frustrate the objective of Title VII. Majority employees must share the burden of past discrimination, even when it requires a modification of their expectations arising from a seniority system agreement. The Court then dampened the inclusiveness of the decision by granting trial courts initial control over the remedy required in seniority cases. General tampering with the seniority system was not required.

Majority employees may therefore expect to have their seniority rights modified in cases where discrimination in employment has been found in the past with present and future implications.

T.I.M.E.-D.C. and Alteration of *Griggs*

In 1977, the U.S. Supreme Court handed down a decision on bona fide seniority systems which runs counter to thirty decisions by six federal courts of appeals on similar issues.[68] The Court ruled that it is *not* unlawful for a bona fide seniority system to perpetuate the effects of Title VII discrimination. Retroactive seniority after the law became effective may be ordered in appropriate cases under the *Franks* v. *Bowman Transportation Co.* case.[69] However, the *T.I.M.E.-D.C.* case addressed itself to discrimination in seniority systems that occurred prior to the effective date of Title VII. Employees who suffered from pre-Act discrimination are not entitled to relief, and retroactive seniority cannot be awarded to a date earlier than the effective date of Title VII. Discriminatory intent in negotiating or administering seniority systems is required to win suits.

It is recalled that *Griggs* made any employment practice that was "fair in form, but discriminatory in operation," unlawful. As such, then, any practice that perpetuated the effects of past discrimination was governed by *Griggs*. *T.I.M.E.-D.C.* released bona fide seniority systems in existence before Title VII from the *Griggs* doctrine because of the language of Section 703(h) of the Act protecting bona fide seniority systems.

The Court was convinced that Section 703(h) prevented the courts from outlawing existing seniority lists and tampering with the vested rights of workers simply because their employer had engaged in discrimination prior to passage of the Civil Rights Act. Blacks and Chicanos had been hired for years by a Texas trucking firm, the subject of the *T.I.M.E.-D.C.* case, only for local hauls; they were excluded from the higher-paying hauls between cities. When the minority workers were finally accepted to drive the intercity routes, they were not permitted to take their intracity seniority to the other division. The result was that blacks and Chicanos received the less desirable routes and were more vulnerable to layoffs than were whites.

Justices Marshall and Brennen dissented from the majority view that workers suffering from pre–Title VII discrimination should be denied relief. They argued that Congress did not intend this result, because it did not overturn the courts of appeals decisions on the issue when Title VII was amended in 1972. Thus, a system that contains pre–Title VII discrimination can nevertheless continue to be bona fide, with no relief available. Past discrimination, if committed prior to the effective date of the Civil Rights Act, cannot lead to relief for workers who suffered from the system.

More Recent Supreme Court Decisions

In a series of decisions issued between 1984 and 1986, the U. S. Supreme Court continued to address the problem of affirmative action and negotiated seniority programs contained in collective bargaining agreements. In *Firefighters* v. *Stotts* (467 U.S. 561 (1984)), the high court held an affirmative action program may not be used to lay off senior white employees and retain junior service black workers. Under a federal court decree, the City of Memphis was required to increase the number of black firefighters from 4 to 11 percent. Subsequently, the city laid off senior white employees ahead of junior service black employees to maintain the balance between white and black firefighters. Reversing a federal appeals court which sustained the layoff procedure, the U.S. Supreme Court held that Title VII was violated by such preferential treatment afforded black employees. As in *T.I.M.E.-D.C.,* the high court held the seniority system as it applies to layoffs was bona fide and not intended for discrimination against black employees.

In May 1986, the high court again held that junior service black employees may not be retained and senior white employees laid off. (*Wygant* v. *Jackson Board of Education,* U.S. Sup. Ct. Case No. 84-1340, May 19, 1986) In Jackson, Michigan, the board of education negotiated a labor agreement with the teachers' union which stipulated that junior service black teachers would be kept on while senior white teachers would be laid off. Such a system was negotiated to keep black teachers as "role models." By a 5-4 majority, the high court held that the white teachers were denied equal protection of the law, ruling the affirmative action program to maintain black teachers as role models could not alone justify laying off the senior white teachers. That the Court found the issue to be perplexing and highly controversial is demonstrated by the fact that five separate opinions were written, none of them joined by more than three justices. Nonetheless, the Court did not slam the door on all aspects of affirmative action as the following two 1986 cases will demonstrate. As a matter of fact, even in the matter of layoffs, it hinted in *Wygant* that under special circumstances white employees senior to minority employees may be laid off. Apparently there was sufficient agreement among the justices that such a condition might prevail should the facts of a case prove the employer historically discriminated against minority group employees.

In 1980, a group of black firefighters sued the City of Cleveland contending discrimination because only 4.5 percent of the lieutenants and higher officers were black while nearly one-half of the city's population was black. Subsequently, lower federal courts approved a voluntary settlement of the suit calling for promotion of black firefighters on a one-to-one ratio with white firefighters. That is, 50 percent of the promotions were to be filled by blacks regardless of their seniority and test scores compared with whites.

By a 6-3 vote, the United States Supreme Court on July 2, 1986 upheld the promotion system which obviously provided affirmative action for black employees. (*Local 98, International Association of Firefighters* v. *City of Cleveland,* U.S. Supreme Ct. Case No. 84-1999, July 2, 1986) It rejected the Firefighters Union position that the plan was illegal under Title VII. Differentiating the case from *Stotts,* the high court pointed out that case dealt strictly with layoffs and not with voluntary affirmative action programs providing preference to black employees for promotion purposes. Justice Brennan, who wrote the majority opinion, observed the Memphis case involved the integrity of a bona fide seniority system governing layoffs, and nothing in that decision prevented federal courts from ordering race-conscious programs "to dismantle prior patterns of employment discrimination and to prevent discrimination in the future."

On the same day, July 2, 1986, the high court, this time by a 5-4 vote, upheld a federal court order establishing a 29 percent minority membership goal for a sheet metal workers' union in New York which for many years had excluded non-white applicants. (*Local 28, Sheet Metal Workers' International Association* v. *EEOC,* U.S. Sup. Ct. Case No. 84-1656, July 2, 1986) Justice Brennan, again writing the majority opinion, stated:

> A court may have to resort to race-conscious affirmative action when confronted with an employer or labor union that has engaged in persistent or egregious discrimination. Or such relief may be necessary to dissipate the lingering effects of pervasive discrimination.

Of course, the final word on affirmative action has not been written. Given the controversy on this problem, and the divided court (no less than nine opinions were issued in the July 1986 cases), only time will tell as to its ultimate outcome. Nonetheless, at this writing, it would be safe to say that affirmative action programs may not supersede negotiated seniority systems governing layoffs. It appears equally safe to say that affirmative action is alive and well when the program deals with hiring, promotions, and apprenticeship programs.

Indeed, the July 1986 decisions dealt a stinging rebuke to the Reagan Department of Justice. Starting in 1981, the Department of Justice contended that only actual victims of discrimination may prevail in civil rights suits. It denounced race-conscious remedies and numerical goals as morally wrong. Throughout the nation, the Department of Justice attempted to nullify programs in which state and local governments agreed to use employment goals to undo the effects of discrimination against black employees, Hispanic workers, and women. Given the July 1986 Supreme Court pronouncements, the Reagan administration has not been successful—at least not as of this time.

Remedies

Remedies for seniority cases are up to the courts. The more popular ones include carryover of seniority from one department to another, rate retention from one department to another, leapfrogging, retroactive seniority, fictional seniority, and back pay. As mentioned, the courts may fashion a remedy to fit each set of circumstances and do not seem to be inhibited by Section 703(j) regarding the reverse discrimination prohibition. It is argued that restoring a person to his or her rightful place does not discriminate against those who were in superior positions because of the practice.

Seniority carryover, rate retention, and leapfrogging refer most often to remedies devised to correct departmental seniority systems that impede transfers to other departments in plants evidencing effects of discriminatory policies. Seniority carryover has been ordered where minorities would have to give up substantial seniority and start at the bottom in departments with better jobs. In order to encourage transfers, some courts have permitted retention of seniority rights in former departments as protection against layoffs.[70] Still others have ordered seniority in the new department to date from the time the person would have been eligible for transfer without a discriminatory policy.[71]

Rate retention has been ordered in cases where transfer to a better job in another department might carry a lower rate of pay until the individual could work up the pay scale. A decrease in pay would discourage transfers to better jobs. Some courts, as mentioned, have ordered no pay reduction as a result of transfer to departments that previously discriminated against minorities.[72]

Leapfrogging refers to permitting minorities to leap over employees already in a department in bidding for higher jobs. It also refers to leaping over jobs in between the one held and higher ones, such as an entry-level job compared to one higher in the scale.[73] In a departmental system, those with higher overall plant seniority may be permitted to leap over those in the department with less plantwide seniority. The courts have justified the practice by arguing that majority employee expectations resulted from an illegal system in the first place, or by arguing that any seniority system is subject to modification through the collective bargaining process. A business necessity defense against leapfrogging may be appropriate if the firm can demonstrate that the needs of safety and efficiency require experience on one job before moving up to the next one.

Retroactive seniority that affects the right to full fringe benefits, layoffs, rehires, and promotions is available through the Supreme Court's *Bowman* decision.[74]

Fictional seniority may be made available to minorities on the basis of the *Bowman* decision, even though the courts of appeals prohibited its use prior to 1974. They did so on the basis of their interpretation of the Act's description of what constitutes a bona fide seniority system. Thus, fictional or retroactive seniority can be granted by the courts. At present, it is not known if an absolute quota system can be used to govern layoffs, such as was ordered by a federal district court in Louisiana.[75] The Fifth Circuit Court of Appeals reversed the decision, but on the grounds that Title VII prohibited retroactive seniority. Even so, the Supreme Court has interpreted the Title VII barrier of bona fide seniority system and now permits majority workers to bear the burden of past discrimination through layoffs, but limits the remedy to the date Title VII became effective.

It does not appear that a Taft-Hartley Section 301 breach-of-contract suit will be interpreted in a manner that would place employers in a dilemma over these court-ordered remedies. That is, should a seniority clause provide that the "last hired would be the first fired," and because a discriminatory system is found retroactive seniority is granted, then majority workers may be laid off instead of minority workers. The question is, may majority workers who held superior expectations under the seniority system prior to the court-ordered remedy be allowed to seek relief under another law? What is not permitted in the courts under Title VII of the Civil Rights Act cannot be used as a basis for breach of contract under Taft-Hartley. To hold otherwise would absolve a union and its members from all blame for illegal seniority clauses. The point is that unions express majority-rule principles and approval of the past practice. The Supreme Court has recognized this and will undoubtedly not force an employer to hire more labor than is deemed necessary for production because of the conflict in laws.

Hiring-Hall Arrangements

The hiring-hall arrangements in building trades labor agreements limit employers to hiring individuals referred by the union. As noted in a previous chapter, Taft-Hartley requires unions to refer people for jobs without discriminating between members and nonmembers, and further requires employers to hire those referred without discrimination. We also learned that it stipulates that it shall not be an unfair labor practice for a construction industry collective bargaining agreement to specify minimum training or experience qualifications for employment. As a result, some construction industry collective bargaining agreements have set up referral preference categories based on the extent of worker qualifications. These usually include the number of years of experience that a journey worker must have as a condition of employment. Such provisions have long been known to be discriminatory against black people and other minority groups. Courts have struck down these rules for black people and other minority workers who were unable to obtain experience because of illegal practices, and in some cases the same was done even when discrimination practices occurred before enactment of Title VII.[76] The Supreme Court's *T.I.M.E.-D.C.* decision in 1977, however, has eliminated the pre–Title VII violations to nonremedial forms.

The Philadelphia Plan, the Washington Plan, and "home town" plans focus directly on federal construction project contractors. These plans require the contractor to use good-faith efforts to meet specific minority hiring goals. They were designed to circumvent union control of federal construction employment by requiring the employer to insure adequate minority worker representation. The employer cannot meet the requirements merely because the union has refused to refer minority workers.

In 1970, the Office of Federal Contract Compliance announced that the Philadelphia Plan solutions would be imposed in nineteen cities unless those cities developed acceptable home town solutions.

The elimination of discriminatory hiring patterns has presented difficult enforcement problems under Title VII of the Civil Rights Act. It prohibits discriminatory exclusion from union membership and precludes discriminatory classifications in the use of referral categories, such as those traditionally employed by construction unions. It also prohibits discriminatory training in apprenticeship programs.

The effectiveness of Title VII in removing employment barriers is, however, limited by a section that permits employers to vary the terms and conditions of employment pursuant to a bona fide seniority or merit system. Normally, courts have not invalidated this exception unless a past history of discrimination has been established, but remedies are not available if the offense occurred prior to Title VII's effective date. Also, admission to a training program can be refused because of religion, sex, or national origin if one of these categories constitutes a bona fide occupational qualification under the law. An example of religion constituting a bona fide occupational qualification might involve a company that sells religious books and insists that salespersons belong to the religion involved. Sex and national origin as bona fide occupational qualifications are more difficult to define. The U.S. Supreme Court ruled in *Dothard* v. *Rawlinson* that women could be excluded from prison guard jobs because of violence and the fact that sex offenders live in the same dormitories with other prisoners. A female's "very womanhood" would undermine her ability to perform a guard's job effectively.[77]

The Supreme Court's *Griggs* doctrine and EEOC decisions are available to remove employment barriers that restrict minority employment on the basis of apprentice age restrictions, excessive formal educational requirements, and testing, unless there is a direct correlation between scores and the ability to perform the job, and restrictions on the size of union membership based on a projection of employment prospects and residence requirements.[78] Attacks on the duration of apprenticeship training as being excessive may also be sustained in the courts.

AGE DISCRIMINATION

The Age Discrimination Act of 1967 protects workers from the ages of 40 to 70. It applies to employers, labor organizations, and employment agencies. Coverage of the Act extends to federal employees. Age discrimination is the only type of discrimination that all workers face at some point. The Act prohibits an employer to fail or refuse to hire, to fire any individual, or otherwise to discriminate with respect to pay, terms, conditions, or privileges of employment because of age. Mandatory retirement before age 70 is unlawful. It is permissible for an employer to make it attractive for an individual to retire before age 70. Thus, voluntary retirement plans are acceptable. However, the Act provides an exception "where age is a bona fide occupational qualification reasonably necessary to the normal operation of the particular business."

The U.S. Supreme Court in *Western Airlines* v. *Criswell*[79] dealt with whether an airline could require mandatory retirement in the interest of public safety. The Court ruled that the idea that persons above a given age lacked the qualifications for a position had to be proved. Western Airlines argued that a "rational basis" standard should be used to establish a BFOQ, because it would be highly impractical to deal with each person on an individualized basis to determine whether each had the ability to perform the job. The Court rejected the argument and held that individual evaluation is required before a person can be forced to retire before age 70.

Under the Age Discrimination Act, employers are to evaluate employees between the ages of 40 and 70 on their merits and not on their age. If employers are to discriminate on the basis of age, they must validate that discrimination as "reasonably necessary to the normal operation of the particular business." The rationale for a particular retirement age chosen under age 70 must be justified.

Summary

Various categories of equal employment opportunity pose difficult problems of interpretation for both the EEOC and the courts. The procedures required under the law often result in long delays from the time of the infraction until final resolution. The EEOC cannot enforce its own orders after a decision is reached.

Legal behavior under some statutes such as the National Labor Relations Act may be illegal under Title VII. In other cases, Title VII may not apply if other statutes prohibit the behavior. Considerably more experience with Title VII will be required before an accommodation can be reached among the various laws dealing with employment rights. In the meantime, expensive and uncertain courses of action will be involved in attempts to determine the employment opportunities of the various groups in American society.

Discussion Questions

1. Prior to 1964, could the NLRB have used national labor legislation or Supreme Court decisions to deal with employment discrimination against women and minorities? What was available for use in such cases prior to 1964? After 1964?

2. Explain the procedures necessary to file Title VII complaints. Distinguish between nondeferral and deferral states.

3. Three standards are applied by the courts in deciding Title VII discrimination cases. How might each standard affect the outcome of a case?

4. Explain how the Equal Employment Opportunity Commission deals with classified ads seeking job applicants.

5. What might constitute a bona fide occupational qualification (BFOQ) based on sex? Religion? Race?

6. In which important areas do you think that *Griggs* v. *Duke Power Co.* has had the most impact?

7. If the Equal Pay Act of 1963 was designed to deal with the issue of equal pay for equal work, how did the concept of comparable worth develop? Explain the concept of comparable worth, and discuss the impact that it might have on internal and external markets.

8. How does *Bundy* v. *Jackson* differ from *Fisher* v. *Flynn?* How might employers protect themselves from liability under *Bundy?*

9. Do you agree with the decision in *De Santis?* Why or why not?

10. The treatment of pregnancy as any other disability is still a subject for debate and experimentation. What do you think should be included in a model policy on the issue?

11. What are the major economic problems associated with nondiscriminatory pension plans?

12. A protected class under Title VII is national origin. Evaluate the *Espinoza* case in the context of that objective.

13. Evaluate affirmative action programs with respect to reverse discrimination and the integrity of collective bargaining agreements. Hint: *Bakke* and *Stotts* may provide useful information.

14. Which theory do you consider most important to apply as a remedy to the effects of past discriminatory seniority systems? What effect would each have on all of the impacted parties?

15. The Age Discrimination Act of 1967 generally prohibits mandatory retirement before age 70. When might an employer require retirement before age 70? On what grounds other than retirement might an employer discriminate on the basis of age?

NOTES

1   See Appendix H for the text of Title VII, as amended by the Equal Employment Opportunity Act of 1972.

2   350 U.S. 892 (1955).

3   347 U.S. 483 (1954).

4   *Plessy* v. *Ferguson*, 163 U.S. 537 (1896).

5   *Wallace Corporation* v. *NLRB*, 323 U.S. 248 (1944); *Steele* v. *Louisville and Nashville Railroad*, 323 U.S. 197 (1944).

6   *Independent Metal Workers (Hughes Tool Company)*, 147 NLRB 166 (1964).

7   *Humphrey* v. *Moore*, 375 U.S. 335 (1964).

8   *Local 1367, International Longshoremen's Association (Galveston Maritime Association)*, 148 NLRB 897 (1965), enf. 368 F. (2d) 1010 (CA 5, 1966), cert. denied 389 U.S. 837 (1967).

9   *Local 12, Rubber Workers* v. *NLRB*, 368 F. (2d) 12 (CA 5, 1966), cert. denied 389 U.S. 837 (1967).

10   See *San Diego Building Trades Council* v. *Garman*, 359 U.S. 236 (1959), whereby the U.S. Supreme Court held that "when an activity is arguably subject to sections 7 or 8 of the Act, the states as well as the federal courts must defer to the exclusive competence of the National Labor Relations Board."

11   *Farmers' Cooperative Compress* v. *United Packinghouse, Food and Allied Workers Union*, 416 F. (2d) 1126 (1969), cert. denied 396 U.S. 903 (1969).

12   *Farmers' Cooperative Compress*, 194 NLRB 185 (1972).

13   *Emporium Capwell Co.* v. *Western Addition Community Organization*, 420 U.S. 50 (1975).

14   420 U.S. 72.

15   *Northwest Airlines, Inc.* v. *Air Line Pilots and Transport Workers*, 447 U.S. 920 (1981).

16   Benjamin Aaron, "Employee Rights and Union Democracy," *Monthly Labor Review*, XCII, 3 (March 1969), p. 50.

17   *Phalen* v. *Theatrical Protective Union No. 1, International Alliance of Theatrical & Stage Employees, AFL-CIO*, 22 N.Y. (2d) 34 (1968).

18   *Occidental Life Ins. Co.*, 14 FEP Cases 1718 (1977).

19   *EEOC and Hugh Stone III* v. *Gladdis*, 733 F. (2d) 1373 (1984): *EEOC* v. *Detroit Edison Co.*, 515 F. (2d) 301 (1975).

20   *Teamsters* v. *United States*, 431 U.S. 324 (1977) and *Hazelwood School District* v. *United States*, 433 U.S. 299 (1977); See J.P. McGuire, "The Use of Statistics in Title VII Cases," *Labor Law Journal*, XXX, 6, June, 1979, p. 361.

21   *Brush v. San Francisco Newspaper Printing Co.*, (N D Calif.) 315 F. Supp. 577, 1970, aff'd. (9 Cir.), 469 F. (2d) 89, 1972.

22   *Weeks* v. *Southern Bell Telephone and Telegraph Co.*, 409 F. (2d) 228 (CA 5, 1969).

23   *Dothard* v. *Rawlinson*, 433 U.S. 321 (1977).

24   *Harper* v. *TWA, Inc.*, 525 F. (2d) 409 (CA 8, 1975).

25   401 U.S. 424 (1971).

26   *Douglas* v. *Hampton*, CDC CA, February 27, 1975, Case No. 72–1376 (case remanded to Civil Service Commission).

27   *Detroit Edison Co.* v. *NLRB*, 440 U.S. 301 (1979).

28   *Spurlock* v. *United Airlines, Inc.*, 475 F. (2d) 216 (CA 10, 1972).

29   *Kinsey* v. *First Regional Securities, Inc.* (DC CA), No. 75-1224, April 18, 1977. EEOC Decision No. 71-1504, March 25, 1971.

30   Unpublished paper by Karen S. Koziara, David A. Pierson, and Russell E. Johannesson, "The Comparable Worth Issue: Current Status and New Directions," Department of Industrial Relations and Organizational Behavior, Temple University, 1985.

31   *Washington County* v. *Alberta Gunther*, 452 U.S. 161 (1981).

32   *Williams* v. *Saxbe*, 413 F. Supp. 654 (D.C. 1976), reversed on other grounds *Williams* v. *Bell*, 587 F. (2d) 1240 (D.C. Cir. 1978).

33   *Fisher* v. *Flynn*, 598 2d 663 (1st Cir. 1979).

34   *Bundy* v. *Jackson*, 641 F. (2d) 934 (D.C. Cir. 1981).

35   *DeSantis* v. *Pacific Telephone and Telegraph Co., Inc.*, 608 F (2d) 327 (1979).

36   *Cleveland Board of Education* v. *La Fleur*, 414 U.S. 632 (1974).

37   *Turner* v. *Department of Employment Security*, 423 U.S. 44 (1975).

38   *General Electric Co.* v. *Gilbert*, 429 U.S. 881 (1976).

39   *Geduldig* v. *Aiello*, 94 U.S. 2485 (1974).

40   See *Bortmess* v. *Drewry's U.S.A., Inc.*, 444 F. (2d) 1186 (1971), cert. denied, 92 U.S. 274 (1971); *Rosen* v. *Public Service Electric and Gas Co.*, 477 F. (2d) 90 (CA 3, 1973).

41   *Wengler* v. *Druggists Mutual Insurance Co.*, 446 U.S. 142 (1980).

42   EEOC Decision No. 6-8-6654, M EPG Section 6021 (1969).

43   409 F. (2d) 775 (1969).

44   467 F. (2d) 54 (1972).

45   In Chapter 14, there is discussion of the circumstances under which the NLRB defers to arbitration under the *Collyer, Spielberg,* and *Banyard* doctrines.

46   443 F. (2d) 1044 (1971).

47   428 F. (2d) 303 (1970).

48   *Riley* v. *Bendix Corp.*, 464 F. (2d) 1113 (CA 5, 1972).

49   *Trans World Airlines, Inc.*, v. *Hardison*, 432 U.S. 63 (1977).

50   *Gray* v. *Gulf, Mobile and Ohio Railroad Co.*, 429 F. (2d) 1064 (CA 5, 1970), cert. denied 401 U.S. 1001 (1971).

51   EEOC Decision No. 74-107, April 2, 1974.

52   *Espinoza* v. *Farah Manufacturing Co., Inc.*, 94 U.S. 334 (1973), affirming 462 F. (2d) 1331 (CA 5, 1972).

53   *Espinoza v. Farah Manufacturing Co.*, 414 U.S. 86 (1973).

54   *Regents of the University of California* v. *Bakke*, 438 U.S. 265 (1978).

55   *United Steelworkers of America* v. *Weber*, 440 U.S. 193 (1979).

56   *Texas Department of Community Affairs* v. *Burdine*, 450 U.S. 248 (1981).

57   *U.S.* v. *Local 189, Papermakers,* 416 F. (2d) 980 (5th Cir., 1969), cert. denied 397 U.S. 919 (1970).

58   *Heat, Frost and Asbestos Workers, Local 53* v. *Vogler,* 407 F. (2d) 1047 (1969).

59   *Congressional Record,* April 8, 1964, p. 6992.

60   *Watkins* v. *United Steelworkers,* 369 F. Supp. 1221 (1974).

61   *U.S.* v. *Local 189, United Papermakers and Paperworkers,* 282 F. Supp. 39 (ED La., 1968), affirmed 416 F. (2d) 980 (5th Cir., 1969), cert. denied (U.S. S. Ct.) 397 U.S. 919 (1970).

62   Irving Kovarsky, *Discrimination in Employment* (Iowa City: Center for Labor and Management, 1976), pp. 84–85.

63   *Patterson* v. *The American Tobacco Co.* (ED Va., September 26, 1974), No. 104-73-R.

64   *Bing* v. *Roadway Express, Inc.,* 444 F. (2d) 245 (1970), cert. denied 401 U.S. 954 (1971).

65   *Johnson* v. *Pike Corp. of America,* 332 F. Supp. 490 (1971).

66   EEOC Decision, Case No. CL-68-431 EU, December 16, 1969.

67   *Franks* v. *Bowman Transportation Co.,* 424 U.S. 747 (1976).

68   *International Brotherhood of Teamsters* v. *U.S.; T.I.M.E.-D.C., Inc.* v. *U.S.,* 431 U.S. 324 (1977).

69   424 U.S. 747 (1976).

70   See, for example, *U.S.* v. *St. Louis–San Francisco Railway Co.,* 464 F. (2d) 301 (8th Cir., 1972), cert. denied 409 U.S. 1107 (1973).

71   For example, see *Rodriquez* v. *East Texas Motor Freight,* 505 F. (2d) 40 (5th Cir., 1974).

72   See, for example, *U.S.* v. *Bethlehem Steel Corp.,* 446 F. (2d) 652 (2d Cir., 1971).

73   *Ibid.*

74   *Franks* v. *Bowman Transportation Co.,* 424 U.S. 747 (1976).

75   *Watkins* v. *United Steelworkers,* 369 F. Supp. 1221 (1974), reversed 516 F. (2d) 41 (5th Cir., 1975).

76   *U.S.* v. *Sheet Metal Workers Local 36,* 416 F. (2d) 123 (CA 8, 1969).

77   *Dothard* v. *Rawlinson,* 433 U.S. 321 (1977).

78   EEOC decisions include Nos. 71-2229 (1971); 72-0265 (1971); 72-0495 (1971).

79   *Western Air Lines, Inc.* v. *Criswell,* 105 Sup. Ct. 2743 (1985).

CHAPTER TWENTY-THREE

EVOLUTION AND PROBLEMS
OF LABOR RELATIONS LAW

From the inception of unionism in the United States until the advent of the New Deal era, organized labor operated in a legal environment that had not accepted unionism as a permanent and responsible institution. As a result, unions played a minor role in the affairs of the nation. Union membership was small. With few exceptions, the bargaining power of unions was weak. The basic industries were essentially nonunion. By 1932, unions were freed from the effects of the conspiracy doctrine as developed in the pre–*Commonwealth* v. *Hunt* period. However, the courts were still heavily utilizing the injunction. By use of the injunction, the courts stamped out union economic activities calculated to influence and expand the collective bargaining process. Unions that engaged in secondary boycott activities risked prosecution under the Sherman Act, a statute ostensibly enacted to curb the growth of big business. The yellow-dog contract was still enforceable in the courts, owing to the pronouncement of the Supreme Court in the *Hitchman* decision.

While the courts blocked the progress of unions and collective bargaining, the legislative branch of government made some attempts to encourage the growth of unionism. Congress and some states passed laws calculated to prevent the employer from interfering with the right of employees to self-organization and collective bargaining. Congress limited its action to the railroad industry, though some states passed union protection legislation that applied to general industry. These laws forbade employers to discharge workers because of their membership in labor unions. To check abusive use of the labor injunction, Congress and some states attempted to curb the power of the judiciary. The injunction provided the means whereby government aided management at the most crucial points of industrial relations conflicts.

It is noteworthy that the legislative branch of government was more favorable to organized labor than were the courts. This condition resulted from the often more responsive character of the legislative branch to social change. Protected in tenure, the judiciary was more concerned with legal formalism and precedent than with social and economic realities. For many years, the legislative and judicial branches of government were in sharp conflict over the labor issue. The employees of the nation stood by, hoping for a favorable outcome to the struggle so that they might realize a better socioeconomic existence. But for decades, the courts refused to confirm legislation calculated to promote unions or, for that matter, any laws which promoted the welfare of the working population. Social legislation was blocked by a Supreme Court that ignored the most obvious facts of economic life. As late as 1937, there was substantial reason to doubt that the Court would change its views on social legislation and approve the Wagner Act.

However, the period 1929–1937 was characterized by sweeping changes in the attitude of the American people relative to the proper role of government in the area of economic activity. Stimulated by the effects of the Great Depression, the climate of opinion of the nation underwent great change. Many people came to believe that government had an important part to play if the national economy was to be restored to conditions of relatively full employment. Previously, only a small group held this view, the majority having faith in the operation of "natural" economic laws to maintain a healthy industrial environment. Indeed, prior to the Great Depression, the nation generally believed that "the government governs best that governs least." The depression changed this attitude, and great segments of the people welcomed government intervention in the economic sphere. The people saw in this approach the cure for many of the problems of the national economy. In short, the people became government-minded, supporting government efforts to restore the national economy to a relatively higher level of operation.

This change in the climate of opinion had great implications for organized labor. If weak unions had not prevented a depression, there was reason to believe that a strong and widespread union movement might contribute to economic recovery. A strong and growing union movement depended on the action of government. It was necessary to establish a legal framework in which the collective bargaining process could function effectively. This produced the logic underlying the Norris–La Guardia and Wagner acts, the laws that set the tone of the labor policy of the New Deal. These laws were products of the Great Depression. They rested not only on the assumption that effective unionism would insure workers a greater measure of social justice, but on the idea that an effective and growing labor movement would promote economic stability. In short, a strong union movement would fit nicely into the scheme of New Deal economics; hence, the unqualified support of legislation calculated to protect the right of employees to self-organization and collective bargaining.

Since 1937, the Supreme Court has permitted the legislative branch the widest latitude to shape labor policy. Congress and state legislatures are judicially free to determine the elements of the framework of labor law. Only upon rare occasions has the Court invalidated labor legislation on the ground of unconstitutionality. Actions of the legislative branch are struck down only when the statute clearly and unmistakably violates the terms of the Constitution.

Such was the status of organized labor in 1947. In that year, Taft-Hartley became the law of the land, and many changes occurred in the character of national labor policy. A variety of factors produced this legislation, but not the least important was the fact that society felt that the power of unionism was excessive. The law was an effort to provide collective bargaining balance between unions and management. Unions were to be made more responsible.

The Carter administration proposed considerable changes in Taft-Hartley to Congress in 1977. Among the proposals were the acceleration of NLRB elections; immediate reinstatement of employees discharged for union activity during an organizational campaign; financial penalties against the employer who refuses to bargain in good faith; loss of federal contracts to employers who flaunt NLRB and court orders; and increasing the number of NLRB members. Though the Carter program was passed in the House, action in the Senate was forestalled because of filibustering during the summer of 1978.

The demand for more union responsibility did not end with the Taft-Hartley Act. Between 1957 and 1959 the McClellan Anti-Racketeering Committee held numerous hearings dealing with patterns of union behavior. Several findings and recommendations were presented to Congress as a result of the three-year effort. The Labor-Management Reporting and Disclosure Act was enacted in 1959. Its primary concern is with the internal practices of unions. The law attempts to protect union members from improper union conduct. Proper union representation is the vehicle by which labor organizations are expected to respond to the desires of members. The election provisions of Title IV have been utilized more heavily than other sections seeking to regulate internal union affairs. The loose organizational structure of the AFL-CIO resulted in government intervention into union internal affairs. Its adoption of six codes of ethical practices to regulate the behavior of its affiliates in 1957 proved to be too little, too late.

Continued public concern with the general operation of economic institutions is reflected in efforts other than Landrum-Griffin. President Kennedy issued Executive Order 10988 in 1962. This event touched off a wave of reexaminations of traditional attitudes toward public employee organization. President Nixon took advantage of experiences under the Kennedy order in Executive Order 11491. Attempts were made to make federal bargaining more effective. The Civil Service Reform Act of 1978 was passed which superseded the executive orders. State and local jurisdictions continue their efforts to define the collective bargaining rights of their employees.

Repeated examination of government regulation of the collective bargaining process is evident from the changes discussed in this book. The policies forthcoming depend, and have depended, largely upon the public's view of the type of economic system it desires. Changing views of the economic system change the costs and benefits that may be associated with particular policies in the labor relations field.

Should national labor policy shift from private reliance upon statutory and administrative law to one that relies more upon informal pressure? Perhaps a shift toward informal pressure is attractive. The particular answers that one might come up with depend upon the objectives posed for the economic system. Various management groups have gone on record as desiring to change the basic national labor policy. They would radically change the laws of the past thirty years; the NLRB would be eliminated and replaced by special labor courts. Others would call for evolutionary changes from time to time as the old laws prove inadequate on particular issues. Indeed, changing views on how the economy should operate have led recent political figures to rely increasingly upon informal pressures to deal with labor-management disputes. For example, the wage-price guidelines were set forth in 1962 by the Council of Economic Advisors, which implied a policy shift from private to public interests when economic matters arise during collective bargaining negotiations. Certainly the guidelines went beyond union-management matters, but they do represent a general policy shift at the national level on collective bargaining matters. Of course, the wage-price controls between August 15, 1971, and April 30, 1974, underscore this proposition.

Various pressures exist that illustrate the subtle debate over how the economy and collective bargaining should work. Brief mention of just a few will make the point more clear.

ISSUES WITH POLICY IMPLICATIONS

Categories for Bargaining

The ability of the government to limit and circumscribe the content of collective bargaining contracts is nowhere made as obvious as by the NLRB authority to decide the mandatory and voluntary items of bargaining. Employers and unions have upon occasion attacked the NLRB for some of its bargaining orders. Pressures to eliminate or modify Board policies on bargainable items will undoubtedly accelerate over time. The search for a proper balance between worker and management rights will keep the issue of bargainable items active in the future. The NLRB has ruled, for example, that a company must bargain, if requested, on the level of benefits received by retired workers. The novel aspect of the ruling was that the order concerned workers who were not active members of the bargaining unit. The Board justified its decision partly by stating that active employees have considerable concern about retirement benefit adequacy. Actually, the basic concern of active employees regarding the general welfare of retirees reflects the economic welfare concerns of the general public. Since negotiated insurance plans often are set for postretirement enjoyment, the Board ruled that the terms of such benefits relate back to active employment. The Board found that collective bargaining is a suitable medium for resolving health and welfare questions affecting retired workers. However, the Supreme Court reversed this policy.

The issue of bargaining rights for retired workers serves as an example of government authority to control the content and coverage of collective bargaining agreements. We believe the public interest would be served if Congress would mandate that bargaining issues not expressly declared unlawful by Taft-Hartley constitute mandatory issues.

Integrity of the NLRB

Greater public control over private interests is called for by most groups. Various tactics are deployed in attempts to influence results. Several employer groups attacked the NLRB fiercely during the Johnson and Kennedy years. It is not that employers—or unions either, for that matter—deplore public control of issues; it is merely that each attempts to direct that control to suit its own economic ends. Thus, during the Nixon years, organized labor believed that the Board had treated employees unfairly. To avoid changes in national labor policy based upon political considerations of the moment, we believe that permanent tenure for NLRB members would be in the national interest. The Reagan administration has been severely criticized by organized labor as being antiunion in most categories.

The current NLRB has overturned more precedents than has any other Board in its fifty-year history. Such a large number of new policies has made unions more reluctant to pursue their claims before the Board. This situation could lead to an accumulation of cases that will be deferred until a newly constituted Board is in place. Greater instability in collective bargaining could result because of perceptions of partiality. The integrity of the Board may be in question more than in any previous period. If so, alternatives to NLRB policymaking may become more viable. For example, there may be renewed pressure to take labor cases to special labor courts if Congress can be persuaded to go along with that concept.

The pressures applied to change national labor policy can be expected to continue. Involved in the struggle is the basic issue of how the economy should function. The outcome of the battle will influence many of the basic economic decisions made in society—how the economy should function and for whom.

EQUAL EMPLOYMENT OPPORTUNITY

Basic laws dealing with equal employment opportunity for covered classes have led to significant new problems. First, affirmative action programs have sparked new implications for collective bargaining contracts. A collective bargaining contract can be altered for a limited period of time on the basis of a negotiated consent decree, which seeks to achieve the objectives of affirmative action goals. In this regard, there are charges of reverse discrimination when uncovered classes are laid off, for example, in order to maintain gains of the covered classes. The impact that negotiated consent decrees are likely to have will be more weighty with generally declining employment opportunities. State and local workers may also become more involved in these problems as revenues decline. The Reagan Administration has gone on record as being opposed to affirmative action programs. The ultimate outcome will be subject to considerable debate and court tests.

Second, sexual harassment is a growing problem since the courts have given it more attention. Prior to 1976, sexual harassment was not deemed actionable under Title VII. The problem can be particularly onerous to employers when supervisory personnel are involved. Their involvement makes employers liable for damages. More litigation on the matter is likely, and new preventive company policies are already being designed. Failure to take early preventive action could expose employers to new unexpected liabilities.

Comparable Worth

The concept of comparable worth has grown out of the interaction between the Equal Pay Act and Title VII of the Equal Employment Opportunity Act. Even though the courts have not displayed an overwhelming desire to further the doctrine, it will nevertheless continue to receive a great deal of attention from legislatures and from unions in the collective bargaining process. Indeed, should unions refuse to pursue comparable worth as a bargaining item, they may become vulnerable to charges of violating their duty of fair representation.

GENERAL VIEWS

The citizen should become more informed on the operation of trade unions and collective bargaining. Since he or she will determine the ultimate status of unions, judgment as to their merits should be based on accurate information and sound analysis. Too many people judge the overall program and functioning of unions by information purveyed by sources of doubtful reliability. The citizen owes it to the nation to gain the sound knowledge that will place him or her in a position to intelligently appraise the operation of unions and collective bargaining.

Such a search will not lead to the conclusion that legal curbs on unions are undesirable. On the contrary, some limitations on union activities are perfectly compatible with strong and militant unionism. However, the quest for accurate knowledge, if faithfully carried out, will lead to one obvious conclusion: In the modern profit economy, characterized by institutional forces not contemplated or given adequate weight by the classical or neoclassical school of economics, collective bargaining offers the American worker an effective means whereby he or she can realize social and industrial justice. This factor underlies the nation's labor union movement. It is the major justification for unions.

Unions themselves can do much to influence the climate of opinion and thereby the character of the law of labor relations. Acts of social irresponsibility on the part of unions will result in the enactment of restrictive measures. In some areas of organized labor, the growth of union power has not been matched by the development of social responsibility. Unions that are socially responsible do not have to be servile or weak. Rather, union responsibility means the orientation of collective bargaining and union practices for the public good. Responsible unions are democratic unions. They scrupulously adhere to the letter and spirit of collective bargaining contracts. Such unions are vitally concerned with the overall prosperity of the firm, the industry, and the national economy. They recognize and understand the problems of management, and they expect management to recognize and understand the problems of the union and its members. Within the framework of effective collective bargaining, responsible unions are a force for national progress. In short, the responsible union is social-minded.

If this attitude of organized labor prevails, and if employers accept in good faith the principle of collective bargaining, the reliance upon law to enforce a viable and responsible collective bargaining system would decrease. If past history is any guide, however, it is doubtful that such a desirable change of attitude on the part of unions and management will take place. At this writing, therefore, the safe prediction is for increasing government intervention in labor relations and the growing complexity of labor relations law.

APPENDIX A

THE SHERMAN ANTITRUST ACT

Act of July 2, 1890, 26 Stat. 209, as Amended.

An Act

To protect trade and commerce against unlawful restraints and monopolies.

Be it enacted by the Senate and House of Representatives of the United States of America in Congress assembled,

CONTRACT, COMBINATION OR CONSPIRACY IN RESTRAINT OF INTERSTATE COMMERCE. SEC. 1. That every contract, combination in the form of trust or otherwise, or conspiracy, in restraint of trade or commerce among the several States, or with foreign nations, is hereby declared to be illegal: *Provided,* That nothing herein contained shall render illegal, contracts or agreements prescribing minimum prices for the resale of a commodity which bears, or the label or container of which bears, the trade mark, brand, or name of the producer or distributor of such commodity and which is in free and open competition with commodities of the same general class produced or distributed by others, when contracts or agreements of that description are lawful as applied to intrastate transactions, under any statute, law, or public policy now or hereafter in effect in any State, Territory, or the District of Columbia in which such resale is to be made, or to which the commodity is to be transported for such resale, and the making of such contracts or agreements shall not be an unfair method of competition under section 5, as amended and supplemented, of the Act entitled "An Act to create a Federal Trade Commission, to define its powers and duties, and for other purposes," approved September 26, 1914: *Provided further,* That the preceding proviso shall not make lawful any contract or agreement, providing for the establishment or maintenance of minimum resale prices on any commodity herein involved, between manufacturers, or between producers, or between wholesalers, or between brokers, or between factors, or between retailers, or between persons, firms, or corporations in competition with each other. Every person who shall make any contract or engage in any combination or conspiracy hereby declared to be illegal shall be deemed guilty of a misdemeanor, and, on conviction thereof, shall be punished by fine not exceeding $5,000, or by imprisonment not exceeding one year, or by both said punishments, in the discretion of the court.

697

MONOPOLIZING TRADE. SEC. 2. Every person who shall monopolize or attempt to monopolize, or combine or conspire with any other person or persons, to monopolize any part of the trade or commerce among the several States, or with foreign nations, shall be deemed guilty of a misdemeanor, and, on conviction thereof, shall be punished by fine not exceeding five thousand dollars, or by imprisonment not exceeding one year, or by both said punishments, in the discretion of the court.

TRUST IN TERRITORIES OF DISTRICT OF COLUMBIA. SEC. 3. Every contract, combination in form of trust or otherwise, or conspiracy, in restraint of trade or commerce in any Territory of the United States or of the District of Columbia, or in restraint of trade or commerce between any such Territory and another, or between any such Territory or Territories and any State or States or the District of Columbia, or with foreign nations, or between the District of Columbia and any State or States or foreign nations, is hereby declared illegal. Every person who shall make any such contract or engage in any such combination or conspiracy, shall be deemed guilty of a misdemeanor, and, on conviction thereof, shall be punished by fine not exceeding five thousand dollars, or by imprisonment not exceeding one year, or by both said punishments, in the discretion of the court.

EQUITY CASES. SEC. 4. The several district courts of the United States are hereby invested with jurisdiction to prevent and restrain violations of this act; and it shall be the duty of the several district attorneys of the United States, in their respective districts, under the direction of the Attorney General, to institute proceedings in equity to prevent and restrain such violations. Such proceedings may be by way of petition setting forth the case and praying that such violation shall be enjoined or otherwise prohibited. When the parties complained of shall have been duly notified of such petition the court shall

proceed, as soon as may be to the hearing and determination of the case; and pending such petition and before final decree, the court may at any time make such temporary restraining order or prohibition as shall be deemed just in the premises.

ADDING PARTIES IN EQUITY CASES. SEC. 5. Whenever it shall appear to the court before which any proceeding under section four of this act may be pending, that the ends of justice require that other parties should be brought before the court, the court may cause them to be summoned, whether they reside in the district in which the court is held or not; and subpoenas to that end may be served in any district by the marshal thereof.

PROPERTY IN TRANSIT. SEC. 6. Any property owned under any contract or by any combination, or pursuant to any conspiracy (and being the subject thereof) mentioned in section one of this act, and being in the course of transportation from one State to another, or to a foreign country, shall be forfeited to the United States, and may be seized and condemned by like proceedings as those provided by law for the forfeiture, seizure and condemnation of property imported into the United States contrary to law.

TREBLE DAMAGE SUITS. SEC. 7. Any person who shall be injured in his business or property by any other person or corporation by reason of anything forbidden or declared to be unlawful by this act, may sue therefor in any district court of the United States in the district in which the defendant resides or is found, without respect to the amount in controversy, and shall recover threefold the damages by him sustained, and the costs of suit, including a reasonable attorney's fee.

DEFINITIONS. SEC. 8. The word "person," or "persons," wherever used in this act shall be deemed to include corporations and associations existing under or authorized by the laws of either the United States, the laws of any of the Territories, the laws of any State, or the laws of any foreign country.

APPENDIX B

THE CLAYTON ACT

SECTIONS 6 AND 20

Act of Oct. 15, 1914, 38 Stat. 731, as Amended.

An Act

To supplement existing laws against unlawful restraints and monopolies, and for other purposes.

Be it enacted by the Senate and House of Representatives of the United States of America in Congress assembled,

LEGITIMATE ACTIVITIES OF LABOR. SEC. 6. That the labor of a human being is not a commodity or article of commerce. Nothing contained in the antitrust laws shall be construed to forbid the existence and operation of labor, agricultural, or horticultural organizations, instituted for the purposes of mutual help, and not having capital stock or conducted for profit, or to forbid or restrain individual members of such organizations, from lawfully carrying out the legitimate objects thereof; nor shall such organizations, or the members thereof, be held or construed to be illegal combinations or conspiracies in restraint of trade, under the antitrust laws.

STATUTORY RESTRICTION. SEC. 20. That no restraining order or injunction shall be granted by any court of the United States, or a judge or the judges thereof, in any case between an employer and employees, or between employers and employees, or between employees, or between persons employed and persons seeking employment, involving, or growing out of, a dispute concerning terms or conditions of employment, unless necessary to prevent irreparable injury to property, or to a property right, of the party making the application, for which injury there is no adequate remedy at law, and such property or property right must be described with particularity in the application, which must be in writing and sworn to by the applicant or by his agent or attorney.

And no such restraining order or injunction shall prohibit any person or persons, whether singly or in concert, from terminating any relation of employment, or from ceasing to perform any work or labor, or from recommending, advising or persuading others by peaceful means so to do; or from attending at any place where any such person or persons may lawfully be, for the purpose of peacefully obtaining or communicating information, or from peacefully persuading any person to work or to abstain from working; or from ceasing to patronize or to employ any party to such dispute, or from recommending, advising, or persuading others by peaceful and lawful means so to do; or from paying or giving to, or withholding from, any person engaged in such dispute, any strike benefits or other moneys or things of value; or from peaceably assembling in a lawful manner, and for lawful purposes; or from doing any act or thing which might lawfully be done in the absence of such dispute by any party thereto; nor shall any of the acts specified in this paragraph be considered or held to be violations of any law of the United States.

APPENDIX C

THE NORRIS–LA GUARDIA ACT

Act of March 23, 1932, 47 Stat. 70

An Act

To amend the Judicial Code and to define and limit the jurisdiction of courts sitting in equity, and for other purposes.

JURISDICTION OF FEDERAL COURTS IN LABOR DISPUTES. SEC. 1. *Be it enacted by the Senate and House of Representatives of the United States of America in Congress assembled,* That no court of the United States, as herein defined, shall have jurisdiction to issue any restraining order or temporary or permanent injunction in a case involving or growing out of a labor dispute, except in a strict conformity with the provisions of this Act; nor shall any such restraining order or temporary or permanent injunction be issued contrary to the public policy declared in this Act.

DECLARATION OF PUBLIC POLICY IN LABOR CONTROVERSIES. SEC. 2. In the interpretation of this Act and in determining the jurisdiction and authority of the courts of the United States, as such jurisdiction and authority are herein defined and limited, the public policy

of the United States is hereby declared as follows:

Whereas under prevailing economic conditions, developed with the aid of governmental authority for owners of property to organize in the corporate and other forms of ownership association, the individual unorganized worker is commonly helpless to exercise actual liberty of contract and to protect his freedom of labor, and thereby to obtain acceptable terms and conditions of employment, wherefore, though he should be free to decline to associate with his fellows, it is necessary that he have full freedom of association, self-organization, and designation of representatives of his own choosing, to negotiate the terms and conditions of his employment, and that he shall be free from the interference, restraint, or coercion of employers of labor, or their agents, in the designation of such representatives or in self-organization or in other concerted activities for the purpose of collective bargaining or other mutual aid or protection; therefore, the following definitions of, and limitations upon, the jurisdiction and au-

701

thority of the courts of the United States are hereby enacted.

NONENFORCEABILITY OF UNDERTAKINGS IN CONFLICT WITH DECLARED POLICY—"YELLOW DOG" CONTRACTS. SEC. 3. Any undertaking or promise, such as is described in this section, or any other undertaking or promise in conflict with the public policy declared in section 2 of this Act, is hereby declared to be contrary to the public policy of the United States, shall not be enforceable in any court of the United States and shall not afford any basis for the granting of legal or equitable relief by any such court, including specifically the following:

Every undertaking or promise hereafter made, whether written or oral, express or implied, constituting or contained in any contract or agreement of hiring or employment between any individual, firm, company, association, or corporation, and any employee or prospective employee of the same, whereby

(a) Either party to such contract or agreement undertakes or promises that he will withdraw from an employment relation in the event that he joins, becomes, or remains a member of any labor organization or of any employer organization.

DENIAL OF INJUNCTIVE RELIEF IN CERTAIN CASES. SEC. 4. No court of the United States shall have jurisdiction to issue any restraining order or temporary or permanent injunction in any case involving or growing out of any labor dispute to prohibit any person or persons participating or interested in such dispute (as these terms are herein defined) from doing, whether singly or in concert any of the following acts:

(a) Ceasing or refusing to perform any work or to remain in any relation of employment;

(b) Becoming or remaining a member of any labor organization or of any employer organization, regardless of any such undertaking or promise as is described in section 3 of this act;

(c) Paying or giving to, or withholding from, any person participating or interested in such labor dispute, any strike for unemployment benefits or insurance, or other moneys or things of value;

(d) By all lawful means aiding any person participating or interested in any labor dispute who is being proceeded against in, or is prosecuting, any action or suit in any court of the United States or of any State:

(e) Giving publicity to the existence of, or the facts involved in, any labor dispute, whether by advertising, speaking, patrolling, or by any other method not involving fraud or violence;

(f) Assembling peaceably to act or organize to act in promotion of their interests in a labor dispute;

(g) Advising or notifying any person of an intention to do any of the acts heretofore specified;

(h) Agreeing with other persons to do or not to do any of the acts heretofore specified; and

(i) Advising, urging, or otherwise causing or inducing without fraud or violence the acts heretofore specified, regardless of any such undertaking or promise as is described in section 3 of this act.

DENIAL OF INJUNCTIVE RELIEF FROM CONCERTED ACTIONS. SEC. 5. No court of the United States shall have jurisdiction to issue a restraining order or temporary or permanent injunction upon the grounds that any of the persons participating or interested in a labor dispute constitute or are engaged in an unlawful combination or conspiracy because of the doing in concert of the acts enumerated in section 4 of this act.

RESPONSIBILITY FOR ACTS. SEC. 6. No officer or member of any association or organization, and no association or organization participating or interested in a labor dispute, shall be held responsible or liable in any court of the United States for the unlawful acts of individual officers, members, or agents, except upon clear proof of actual participating in, or actual authorization of, such acts, or of ratification of such acts after actual knowledge thereof.

ISSUE OF INJUNCTIONS—WHEN PERMISSIBLE.

SEC. 7. No court of the United States shall have jurisdiction to issue a temporary or permanent injunction in any case involving or growing out of a labor dispute, as herein defined, except after hearing the testimony of witnesses in open court (with opportunity for cross-examination) in support of the allegations of a complaint made under oath, and testimony in opposition thereto, if offered, and except after findings of fact by the court, to the effect—

(a) That unlawful acts have been threatened or will be committed unless restrained or have been committed and will be continued unless restrained, but no injunction or temporary restraining order shall be issued on account of any threat or unlawful act excepting against the person or persons, association, or organization making the threat or committing the unlawful act or actually authorizing or ratifying the same after actual knowledge thereof:

(b) That substantial and irreparable injury to complainant's property will follow;

(c) That as to each item of relief granted greater injury will be inflicted upon complainant by the denial of relief than will be inflicted upon defendants by the granting of relief;

(d) That complainant has no adequate remedy at law; and

(e) That the public officers charged with the duty to protect complainant's property are unable or unwilling to furnish adequate protection.

Such hearing shall be held after due and personal notice thereof has been given, in such manner as the court shall direct, to all known persons against whom relief is sought, and also to the chief of those public officials of the county and city within which the unlawful acts have been threatened or committed charged with the duty to protect

complainant's property: *Provided, however,* That if a complainant shall also allege that, unless a temporary restraining order shall be issued without notice, a substantial and irreparable injury to complainant's property will be unavoidable, such a temporary restraining order may be issued upon testimony under oath, sufficient, if sustained, to justify the court in issuing a temporary injunction upon a hearing after notice. Such a temporary restraining order shall be effective for no longer than five days and shall become void at the expiration of said five days. No temporary restraining order or temporary injunction shall be issued except on condition that complainant shall first file an undertaking with adequate security in an amount to be fixed by the court sufficient to recompense those enjoined for any loss, expense, or damage caused by the improvident or erroneous issuance of such order or injunction, including all reasonable costs (together with a reasonable attorney's fee) and expense of defense against the order or against the granting of any injunctive relief sought in the same proceeding and subsequently denied by the court.

The undertaking herein mentioned shall be understood to signify an agreement entered into by the complainant and the surety upon which a decree may be rendered in the same suit or proceeding against said complainant and surety, upon a hearing to assess damages of which hearing complainant and surety shall have reasonable notice, the said complainant and surety submitting themselves to the jurisdiction of the court for that purpose. But nothing herein contained shall deprive any party having a claim or cause of action under or upon such undertaking from electing to pursue his ordinary remedy by suit at law or in equity.

EFFORT TO SETTLE DISPUTES.

SEC. 8. No restraining order or injunctive relief shall be granted to any complainant who has failed to comply with any obligation imposed by law which is involved in the labor dispute in question, or who has failed to make every reasonable effort to settle such dispute either by negotiation or with the aid of any available governmental machinery of mediation or voluntary arbitration.

ISSUANCE OF INJUNCTIONS BASED ON FINDINGS OF FACT. SEC. 9. No restraining order or temporary or permanent injunction shall be granted in a case involving or growing out of a labor dispute, except on the basis of findings of fact made and filed by the court in the record of the case prior to the issuance of such restraining order or injunction; and every restraining order or injunction granted in a case involving or growing out of a labor dispute shall include only a prohibition of such specific act or acts as may be expressly complained of in the bill of complaint or petition filed in such case and as shall be expressly included in said findings of fact made and filed by the court as provided herein.

APPEALS—SECURITY FOR COSTS. SEC. 10. Whenever any court of the United States shall issue or deny any temporary injunction in a case involving or growing out of a labor dispute, the court shall, upon the request of any party to the proceedings and on his filing the usual bond for costs, forthwith certify as in ordinary cases the record of the case to the circuit court of appeals for its review. Upon the filing of such record in the circuit court of appeals, the appeal shall be heard and the temporary injunctive order affirmed, modified, or set aside with the greatest possible expedition, giving the proceedings precedence over all other matters except older matters of the same character.

JURY TRIAL IN CASES OF INDIRECT CONTEMPT. SEC. 11. In all cases arising under this act in which a person shall be charged with contempt in a court of the United States (as herein defined), the accused shall enjoy the right of a speedy and public trial by an impartial jury of the State and district wherein the contempt shall have been committed: *Provided,* That this right shall not apply to contempts committed in the presence of the court or so near thereto as to interfere directly with the administration of justice or to apply to the misbehavior, misconduct, or disobedience of any officer of the court in respect to the writs, orders, or process of the court.

REMOVAL OF JUDGE IN INDIRECT CONTEMPT CASES. SEC. 12. The defendant in any proceeding for contempt of court may file with the court a demand for the retirement of the judge sitting in the proceeding, if the contempt arises from an attack upon the character or conduct of such judge and if the attack occurred elsewhere than in the presence of the court or so near thereto as to interfere directly with the administration of justice. Upon the filing of any such demand the judge shall thereupon proceed no further, but another judge shall be designated in the same manner as is provided by law. The demand shall be filed prior to the hearing in the contempt proceeding.

DEFINITIONS. SEC. 13. When used in this act, and for the purposes of this act—

(a) A case shall be held to involve or to grow out of a labor dispute when the case involves persons who are engaged in the same industry, trade, craft, or occupation; or have direct or indirect interests therein; or who are employees of the same employer; or who are members of the same or an affiliated organization of employers or employees; whether such dispute is (1) between one or more employers or associations of employers and one or more employees or associations of employees; (2) between one or more employers or associations and one or more employers or associations of employers or; (3) between one or more employees or associations of employees and one or more employees or associations of employees; or, when the case involves any conflicting or competing interests in a "labor dispute" (as hereinafter defined) of "persons anticipating or interested" therein (as hereinafter defined).

(b) A person or association shall be held to be a person participating or interested in a labor dispute if relief is sought against him or it, and if he or it is engaged in the same industry, trade, craft, or occupation in which such dispute occurs, or has a direct or indirect interest therein, or is a member, officer, or agent of any association composed in whole or in part of employers or employees engaged in such industry, trade, craft, or occupation.

(c) The term "labor dispute" includes any controversy concerning terms or conditions of employment, or concerning the association or representation of persons negotiating, fixing, maintaining, changing, or seeking to arrange terms or conditions of employment, regardless of whether or not the disputants stand in the proximate relation of employer and employee.

(d) The term "court of the United States" means any court of the United States whose jurisdiction has been or may be conferred or defined or limited by Act of Congress, including the courts of the District of Columbia.

SEPARABILITY PROVISION. SEC. 14. If any provision of this Act or the application thereof to any person or circumstance is held unconstitutional or otherwise invalid, the remaining provisions of the Act and the application of such provisions to other persons or circumstances shall not be affected thereby.

REPEAL OF CONFLICTING ACTS. SEC. 15. All Acts and parts of Acts in conflict with the provision of this Act are hereby repealed.

THE WAGNER ACT

Act of July 5, 1935, 49 Stat. 449

An Act

To diminish the causes of labor disputes burdening or obstructing interstate and foreign commerce, to create a National Labor Relations Board, and for other purposes.

Be it enacted by the Senate and House of Representatives of the United States of America in Congress assembled.

FINDINGS AND POLICY. SEC. 1. The denial by employers of the right of employees to organize and the refusal by employers to accept the procedure of collective bargaining lead to strikes and other forms of industrial strife or unrest, which have the intent or the necessary effect of burdening or obstructing commerce by (a) impairing the efficiency, safety, or operation of the instrumentalities of commerce; (b) occurring in the current of commerce; (c) materially affecting, restraining, or controlling the flow of raw materials or manufactured or processed goods from or into the channels of commerce, or the prices of such materials or goods in commerce; or (d) causing diminution of employment and wages in such volume as substantially to impair or disrupt the market for goods flowing from or into the channels of commerce.

The inequality of bargaining power between employees who do not possess full freedom of association or actual liberty of contract, and employers who are organized in the corporate or other forms of ownership association substantially burdens and affects the flow of commerce, and tends to aggravate recurrent business depressions, by depressing wage rates and the purchasing power of wage earners in industry and by preventing the stabilization of competitive wage rates and working conditions within and between industries.

Experience has proved that protection by law of the right of employees to organize and bargain collectively safeguards commerce from injury, impairment, or interruption, and promotes the flow of commerce by removing certain recognized sources of industrial strife and unrest, by encouraging practices fundamental to the friendly adjustment of industrial disputes arising out of differences as to wages, hours, or other working conditions, and by restoring equality of bargaining power between employers and employees.

It is hereby declared to be the policy of the United States to eliminate the causes of certain substantial obstructions to the free flow of commerce and to mitigate and eliminate these obstructions when they have occurred by encouraging the practice and procedure of collective bargaining and by protecting the exercise by workers of full freedom of association, self-organization, and designation of representatives of their own choosing, for the purpose of negotiating the terms and conditions of their employment or other mutual aid or protection.

DEFINITIONS. SEC. 2. When used in this Act—

(1) The term "person" includes one or more individuals, partnerships, associations, corporations, legal representatives, trustees, trustees in bankruptcy, or receivers.

(2) The term "employer" includes any person acting in the interest of an employer, directly or indirectly, but shall not include the United States, or any State or political subdivision thereof, or any person subject to the Railway Labor Act, as amended from time to time, or any labor organization (other than when acting as an employer), or anyone acting in the capacity of officer or agent of such labor organization.

(3) The term "employee" shall include any employee, and shall not be limited to the employees of a particular employer, unless the Act explicitly states otherwise, and shall include any individual whose work has ceased as a consequence of, or in connection with any current labor dispute or because of any unfair labor practice, and who has not obtained any other regular and substantially equivalent employment, but shall not include any individual employed as an agricultural laborer, or in the domestic service of any family or person at his home or any individual employed by his parent or spouse.

(4) The term "representatives" includes any individual or labor organization.

(5) The term "labor organization" means any organization of any kind, or any agency or employee representation committee or plan, in which employees participate and which exists for the purpose, in whole or in part, of dealing with employers concerning grievances, labor disputes, wages, rates of pay, hours of employment, or conditions of work.

(6) The term "commerce" means trade, traffic, commerce, transportation, or communication among the several States, or between the District of Columbia or any Territory of the United States and any State or other Territory, or between any foreign country and any State, Territory, or the District of Columbia, or within the District of Columbia or any Territory, or between points in the same State but through any other State or any Territory or the District of Columbia or any foreign country.

(7) The term "affecting commerce" means in commerce, or burdening or obstructing commerce or the free flow of commerce, or having led or tending to lead to a labor dispute burdening or obstructing commerce or the free flow of commerce.

(8) The term "unfair labor practice" means unfair labor practice listed in section 8.

(9) The term "labor dispute" includes any controversy concerning terms, tenure, or conditions of employment, or concerning the association or representation of persons in negotiating, fixing, maintaining, changing, or seeking to arrange terms or conditions of employment, regardless of whether the disputants stand in the proximate relation of employer and employee.

(10) The term "National Labor Relations Board" means the National Labor Relations Board, created by section 3 of this Act.

(11) The term "old Board" means the National Labor Relations Board established by Executive Order Numbered 6763 of the President on June 29, 1934, pursuant to Public Resolution Numbered 44, approved June 19, 1934 (48 Stat. 1183), and reestab-

lished and continued by Executive Order Numbered 7074 of the President of June 15, 1935, pursuant to Title I of the National Industrial Recovery Act (48 Stat. 195) as amended and continued by Senate Joint Resolution 133 approved June 14, 1935.

NATIONAL LABOR RELATIONS BOARD

SEC. 3. (a) There is hereby created a board, to be known as the "National Labor Relations Board" (hereinafter referred to as the "Board"), which shall be composed of three members, who shall be appointed by the President, by and with the advice and consent of the Senate. One of the original members shall be appointed for a term of one year, one for a term of three years, and one for a term of five years, but their successors shall be appointed for terms of five years each, except that any individual chosen to fill a vacancy shall be appointed only for the unexpired term of the member whom he shall succeed. The President shall designate one member to serve as the chairman of the Board. Any member of the Board may be removed by the President, upon notice and hearing, for neglect of duty or malfeasance in office, but for no other cause.

(b) A vacancy in the Board shall not impair the right of the remaining members to exercise all the powers of the Board, and two members of the Board shall, at all times, constitute a quorum. The Board shall have an official seal which shall be judicially noticed.

(c) The Board shall at the close of each fiscal year make a report in writing to Congress and to the President stating in detail the cases it has heard, the decisions it has rendered, the names, salaries, and duties of all employees and officers in the employ or under the supervision of the Board, and an account of all moneys it has disbursed.

SEC. 4. (a) Each member of the Board shall receive a salary of $10,000 a year, shall be eligible for reappointment, and shall not engage in any other business, vocation, or employment. The Board shall appoint, without regard for the provisions of the civil-service laws but subject to the Classification Act of 1923, as amended, an executive secretary, and such attorneys, examiners, and regional directors, and shall appoint such other employees with regard to existing laws applicable to the employment and compensation of officers and employees of the United States, as it may from time to time find necessary for the proper performance of its duties and as may be from time to time appropriated for by Congress. The Board may establish or utilize such regional, local, or other agencies, and utilize such voluntary and uncompensated services, as may from time to time be needed. Attorneys appointed under this section may, at the direction of the Board, appear for and represent the Board in any case in court. Nothing in this Act shall be construed to authorize the Board to appoint individuals for the purpose of conciliation or mediation (or for statistical work), where such service may be obtained from the Department of Labor.

(b) Upon the appointment of the three original members of the Board and the designation of its chairman, the old Board shall cease to exist. All employees of the old Board shall be transferred to and become employees of the Board with salaries under the Classification Act of 1923, as amended, without acquiring by such transfer a permanent or civil-service status. All records, papers, and property of the old Board shall become records, papers, and property of the Board, and all unexpended funds and appropriations for the use and maintenance of the old Board shall become funds and appropriations available to be expended by the Board in the exercise of the powers, authority, and duties conferred on it by this Act.

(c) All of the expenses of the Board, including all necessary traveling and subsistence expenses outside the District of Columbia incurred by the members or employees of the Board under its orders, shall be allowed and paid on the presentation of itemized vouchers therefor approved by the Board or by any individual it designates for that purpose.

SEC. 5. The principal office of the Board shall be in the District of Columbia, but it may meet and exercise any or all of its powers at any other place. The Board may, by one or more of its members or by such agents or agencies as it may designate, prosecute any inquiry necessary to its functions in any part of the United States. A member who participates in such an inquiry shall not be disqualified from subsequently participating in a decision of the Board in the same case.

SEC. 6. (a) The Board shall have authority from time to time to make, amend, and rescind such rules and regulations as may be necessary to carry out the provisions of this Act. Such rules and regulations shall be effective upon publication in the manner which the Board shall prescribe.

RIGHTS OF EMPLOYEES

SEC. 7. Employees shall have the right to self-organization, to form, join, or assist labor organizations, to bargain collectively through representatives of their own choosing, and to engage in concerted activities, for the purpose of collective bargaining or other mutual aid or protection.

SEC. 8. It shall be an unfair labor practice for an employer—

(1) To interfere with, restrain, or coerce employees in the exercise of the rights guaranteed in section 7.

(2) To dominate or interfere with the formation or administration of any labor organization or contribute financial or other support to it: *Provided,* That subject to rules and regulations made and published by the Board pursuant to section 6(a), an employer shall not be prohibited from permitting employees to confer with him during working hours without loss of time or pay.

(3) By discrimination in regard to hire or tenure of employment or any term or condition of employment to encourage or discour-

age membership in any labor organization: *Provided,* That nothing in this Act, or in the National Industrial Recovery Act (U.S.C., Supp. VII, title 15, secs. 701–712), as amended from time to time, or in any code or agreement approved or prescribed thereunder, or in any other statute of the United States, shall preclude an employer from making an agreement with a labor organization (not established, maintained, or assisted by any action defined in this Act as an unfair labor practice) to require, as a condition of employment, membership therein, if such labor organization is the representative of the employees as provided in section 9 (a), in the appropriate collective bargaining unit covered by such agreement when made.

(4) To discharge or otherwise discriminate against an employee because he has filed charges or given testimony under this Act.

(5) To refuse to bargain collectively with the representatives of his employees, subject to the provisions of section 9 (a).

REPRESENTATIVES AND ELECTIONS. SEC. 9. (a) Representatives designated or selected for the purposes of collective bargaining by the majority of the employees in a unit appropriate for such purposes, shall be the exclusive representatives of all the employees in such unit for the purposes of collective bargaining in respect to rates of pay, wages, hours of employment, or other conditions of employment: *Provided,* That any individual employee or a group of employees shall have the right at any time to present grievances to their employer.

(b) The Board shall decide in each case whether, in order to insure to employees the full benefit of their right to self-organization and to collective bargaining, and otherwise to effectuate the policies of this Act, the unit appropriate for the purposes of collective bargaining shall be the employer unit, craft unit, plant unit, or subdivision thereof.

(c) Whenever a question affecting commerce arises concerning the representation of employees, the Board may investigate such controversy and certify to the parties, in writing, the name or names of the representatives that have been designated or selected. In any such investigation, the Board shall provide for an appropriate hearing upon due notice, either in conjunction with a proceeding under section 10 or otherwise, and may take a secret ballot of employees, or utilize any other suitable method to ascertain such representatives.

(d) Whenever an order of the Board made pursuant to section 10 (c) is based in whole or in part upon facts certified following an investigation pursuant to subsection (c) of this section, and there is a petition for the enforcement or review of such order, such certification and the record of such investigation shall be included in the transcript of the entire record required to be filed under subsections 10 (e) or 10 (f), and thereupon the decree of the court enforcing, modifying, or setting aside in whole or in part the order of the Board shall be made and entered upon the pleadings, testimony, and proceedings set forth in such transcript.

PREVENTION OF UNFAIR LABOR PRACTICES. SEC. 10. The Board is empowered, as hereinafter provided, to prevent any person from engaging in any unfair labor practice (listed in section 8) affecting commerce. This power shall be exclusive, and shall not be affected by any other means of adjustment or prevention that has been or may be established by agreement, code, law, or otherwise.

(b) Whenever it is charged that any person has engaged in or is engaging in any such unfair labor practice, the Board, or any agent or agency designated by the Board for such purposes, shall have power to issue and cause to be served upon such person a complaint stating the charges in that respect, and containing a notice of hearing before the Board or a member thereof, or before a designated agent or agency, at a place therein fixed, not less than five days after the serving of said complaint. Any such complaint may be amended by the member, agent, or agency conducting the hearing or the Board in its discretion at any time prior to the issuance of an order based thereon. The person so complained of shall have the right to file an answer to the original or amended complaint and to appear in person or otherwise and give testimony at the place and time fixed in the complaint. In the discretion of the member, agent, or agency conducting the hearing or the Board, any other person may be allowed to intervene in the said proceeding and to present testimony. In any such proceeding the rules of evidence prevailing in courts of law or equity shall not be controlling.

(c) The testimony taken by such member, agent, or agency or the Board shall be reduced to writing and filed with the Board. Thereafter, in its discretion, the Board upon notice may take further testimony or hear argument. If upon all the testimony taken the Board shall be of the opinion that any person named in the complaint has engaged in or is engaging in any such unfair labor practice, then the Board shall state its findings of fact and shall issue and cause to be served on such person an order requiring such person to cease and desist from such unfair labor practice, and to take such affirmative action, including reinstatement of employees with or without back pay, as will effectuate the policies of this Act. Such order may further require such person to make reports from time to time showing the extent to which it has complied with the order. If upon all the testimony taken the Board shall be of the opinion that no person named in the complaint has engaged in or is engaging in any such unfair labor practice, then the Board shall state its findings of fact and shall issue an order dismissing the said complaint.

(d) Until a transcript of the record in a case shall have been filed in a court, as hereinafter provided, the Board may at any time, upon reasonable notice and in such manner as it shall deem proper, modify or set aside, in whole or in part, any finding or order made or issued by it.

(e) The Board shall have power to petition any circuit court of appeals of the United States (including the Court of Appeals of the District of Columbia), or if all the circuit courts of appeals to which application may be made are in vacation, any district court of the United States (including the Supreme Court of the District of Columbia), within any circuit or district, respectively, wherein the unfair labor practice in question occurred or wherein such person resides or transacts business, for the enforcement of such order and for appropriate temporary relief or restraining order, and shall certify and file in the court a transcript of the entire record in the proceeding, including the pleadings and testimony upon which such order was entered and the findings and order of the Board. Upon such filing, the court shall cause notice thereof to be served upon such person, and thereupon shall have jurisdiction of the proceeding and of the question determined therein, and shall have power to grant such temporary relief or restraining order as it deems just and proper, and to make and enter upon the pleadings, testimony, and proceedings set forth in such transcript a decree enforcing, modifying, and enforcing as so modified, or setting aside in whole or in part the order of the Board. No objection that has not been urged before the Board, its member, agent, or agency, shall be considered by the court, unless the failure or neglect to urge such objection shall be excused because of extraordinary circumstances. The findings of the Board as to the facts, if supported by evidence, shall be conclusive. If either party shall apply to the court for leave to adduce additional evidence and shall show to the satisfaction of the court that such additional evidence is material and that there were reasonable grounds for the failure to adduce such evidence in the hearing before the Board, its member, agent, or agency, the court may order such additional evidence to be taken before the Board, its member, agent, or agency, and to be made a part of the transcript. The Board may modify its findings as to the facts, or make new findings, by reason of additional evidence so taken and filed, and it shall file such modified or new findings, which, if supported by evidence shall be conclusive, and shall file its recommendations, if any, for the modification or setting aside of its original order. The jurisdiction of the court shall be exclusive and its judgment and decree shall be final, except that the same shall be subject to review by the appropriate circuit court of appeals if application was made to the district court as hereinabove provided, and by the Supreme Court of the United States and upon writ of certiorari or certification as provided in sections 239 and 240 of the Judicial Code, as amended (U.S.C., title 28, secs. 346 and 347).

(f) Any person aggrieved by a final order of the Board granting or denying in whole or in part the relief sought may obtain a review of such order in any circuit court of appeals of the United States in the circuit wherein the unfair labor practice in question was alleged to have been engaged in or wherein such person resides or transacts business, or in the Court of Appeals of the District of Columbia, by filing in such a court a written petition praying that the order of the Board be modified or set aside. A copy of such petition shall be forthwith served upon the Board, and thereupon the aggrieved party shall file in the court a transcript of the entire record in the proceeding, certified by the Board, including the pleading and testimony upon which the order complained of was entered and the findings and order of the Board. Upon such filing, the court shall proceed in the same manner as in the case of an application by the Board under subsection (e), and shall have the same exclusive jurisdiction to grant to the Board such temporary relief or restraining order as it deems just and proper, and in like manner to make and enter a decree enforcing, modifying, and enforcing as so modified, or setting aside in whole or in part the order of the Board; and the findings of the Board as to the facts, if supported by evidence, shall in like manner be conclusive.

(g) The commencement of proceedings under subsection (e) or (f) of this section shall not, unless specifically ordered by the court, operate as a stay of the Board's order.

(h) When granting appropriate temporary relief or a restraining order, or making and entering a decree enforcing, modifying, and enforcing as so modified or setting aside in whole or in part an order of the Board, as provided in this section, the jurisdiction of courts sitting in equity, shall not be limited by the Act entitled "An Act to amend the Judicial Code and to define and limit the jurisdiction of courts sitting in equity, and for other purposes," approved March 23, 1932 (U.S.C., Supp. VII, title 29, secs. 101–115).

(i) Petitions filed under this act shall be heard expeditiously, and if possible within ten days after they have been docketed.

INVESTIGATORY POWERS

SEC. 11. For the purpose of all hearings and investigations, which, in the opinion of the Board, are necessary and proper for the exercise of the powers vested in it by section 9 and section 10—

(1) The Board, or its duly authorized agents or agencies, shall at all reasonable times have access to, for the purpose of examination, and the right to copy any evidence of any person being investigated or proceeded against that relates to any matter under investigation or in question. Any member of the Board shall have power to issue subpenas requiring the attendance and testimony of witnesses and the production of any evidence that relates to any matter under investigation or in question, before the Board, its member, agent, or agency conducting the hearing or investigation. Any member of the Board, or any agent or agency designated by the Board for such purposes, may administer oaths and affirmations, examine witnesses, and receive evidence. Such attendance of witnesses and the production of such evidence may be required from any place in the United States or any Territory or possession thereof, at any designated place of hearing.

(2) In case of contumacy or refusal to obey a subpena issued to any person, any District Court of the United States or the United States courts of any Territory or possession, or the Supreme Court of the District of Columbia, within the jurisdiction of which the inquiry is carried on or within the jurisdiction of which said person guilty of contumacy or refusal to obey is found or resides or transacts business, upon application by the Board shall have jurisdiction to issue to such person an order requiring such person to appear before the Board, its member, agent, or agency, there to produce evidence if so ordered, or there to give testimony touching the matter under investigation or in question; and any failure to obey such order of the court may be punished by said court as a contempt thereof.

(3) No person shall be excused from attending and testifying or from producing books, records, correspondence, documents, or other evidence in obedience to the subpena of the Board, on the ground that the testimony or evidence required of him may tend to incriminate him or subject him to a penalty or forfeiture; but no individual shall be prosecuted or subjected to any penalty or forfeiture for or on account of any transaction, matter, or thing concerning which he is compelled, after having claimed his privilege against self-incrimination, to testify or produce evidence, except that such individual so testifying shall not be exempt from prosecution and punishment for perjury committed in so testifying.

(4) Complaints, orders, and other process and papers of the Board, its member, agent, or agency, may be served either personally or by registered mail or by telegraph or by

leaving a copy thereof at the principal office or place of business of the person required to be served. The verified return by the individual so serving the same setting forth the manner of such service shall be proof of the same, and the return post office receipt or telegraph receipt therefor when registered and mailed or telegraphed as aforesaid shall be proof of service of the same. Witnesses summoned before the Board, its member, agent, or agency, shall be paid the same fees and mileage that are paid witnesses in the courts of the United States, and witnesses whose depositions are taken and the persons taking the same shall severally be entitled to the same fees as are paid for like services in the courts of the United States.

(5) All process of any court to which application may be made under this Act may be served in the judicial district wherein the defendant or other person required to be served resides or may be found.

(6) The several departments and agencies of the Government, when directed by the President, shall furnish the Board, upon its request, all records, papers, and information in their possession relating to any matter before the Board.

SEC. 12. Any person who shall willfully resist, prevent, impede, or interfere with any member of the Board or any of its agents or agencies in the performance of duties pursuant to this act shall be punished by a fine of not more than $5,000 or by imprisonment for not more than one year, or both.

LIMITATIONS

SEC. 13. Nothing in this Act shall be construed so as to interfere with or impede or diminish in any way the right to strike.

SEC. 14. Wherever the application of the provisions of section 7(a) of the National Industrial Recovery Act [U.S.C., Supp. VII, title 15, sec. 707 (a)], as amended from time to time, or of section 77B, paragraphs (l) and (m) of the Act approved June 7, 1934, entitled "An Act to amend an Act entitled 'An Act to establish a uniform system of bankruptcy throughout the United States' approved July 1, 1898, and Acts amendatory thereof and supplementary thereto" 48 Stat. 922, pars. (l) and (m), as amended from time to time, or of Public Resolution Numbered 44, approved June 19, 1934 (48 Stat. 1183), conflicts with the application of the provisions of this Act, this Act shall prevail: *Provided,* That in any situation where the provisions of this Act cannot be validly enforced, the provisions of such other Acts shall remain in full force and effect.

SEC. 15. If any provision of this Act, or the application of such provision to any person or circumstance, shall be held invalid, the remainder of this Act, or the application of such provision to persons or circumstances other than those as to which it is held invalid, shall not be affected thereby.

SEC. 16. This Act may be cited as the "National Labor Relations Act."

Approved, July 5, 1935.

APPENDIX E

LABOR MANAGEMENT RELATIONS ACT, 1947

Act of June 23, 1947, 61 Stat. 136, as Amended by Act of September 14, 1959, 73 Stat. 519*

KEY TO AMENDMENTS

Portions of the Act which have been eliminated by the Labor-Management Reporting and Disclosure Act of 1959, Public Law 86–257, are enclosed by black brackets; provisions which have been added to the Act are in italics, and unchanged portions are shown in roman type.

---

*Section 201 (d) and (e) of the Labor-Management Reporting and Disclosure Act of 1959 which repealed Section 9 (f), (g), and (h) of the Labor Management Relations Act, 1947, and Section 505 amending Section 302(a), (b), and (c) of the Labor Management Relations Act, 1947, took effect upon enactment of Public Law 86–257, September 14, 1959. As to the other amendments of the Labor Management Relations Act, 1947, Section 707 of the Labor-Management Reporting and Disclosure Act provides:

The amendments made by this title shall take effect sixty days after the date of the enactment of this Act and no provision of this title shall be deemed to make an unfair labor practice, any act which is performed prior to such effective date which did not constitute an unfair labor practice prior thereto.

An Act

To amend the National Labor Relations Act, to provide additional facilities for the mediation of labor disputes affecting commerce, to equalize legal responsibilities of labor organizations and employers, and for other purposes.

Be it enacted by the Senate and House of Representatives of the United States of America in Congress assembled,

SHORT TITLE AND DECLARATION OF POLICY

Sec. 1. (a) This Act may be cited as the "Labor Management Relations Act, 1947."

(b) Industrial strife which interferes with the normal flow of commerce and with the full production of articles and commodities for commerce, can be avoided or substantially minimized if employers, employees, and labor organizations each recognize under law one another's legitimate rights in their relations with each other, and above all recognize under law that neither party has any right in its relations with any other to engage in acts or practices which jeopardize the public health, safety, or interest.

It is the purpose and policy of this Act, in order to promote the full flow of commerce, to prescribe the legitimate rights of both employees and employers in their relations affecting commerce, to provide orderly and peaceful procedures for preventing the interference by either with the legitimate rights of the other, to protect the rights of individual employees in their relations with labor organizations whose activities affect commerce, to define and proscribe practices on the part of labor and management which affect commerce and are inimical to the general welfare, and to protect the rights of the public in connection with labor disputes affecting commerce.

TITLE I

AMENDMENT OF NATIONAL LABOR RELATIONS ACT

SEC. 101. The National Labor Relations Act is hereby amended to read as follows:

FINDINGS AND POLICIES

SEC. 1. The denial by some employers of the right of employees to organize and the refusal by some employers to accept the procedure of collective bargaining lead to strikes and other forms of industrial strife or unrest, which have the intent or the necessary effect of burdening or obstructing commerce by (a) impairing the efficiency, safety, or operation of the instrumentalities of commerce;

(b) occurring in the current of commerce; (c) materially affecting, restraining, or controlling the flow of raw materials or manufactured or processed goods in commerce; or (d) causing diminution of employment and wages in such volume as substantially to impair or disrupt the market for goods flowing from or into the channels of commerce.

The inequality of bargaining power between employees who do not possess full freedom of association or actual liberty of contract, and employers who are organized in the corporate or other forms of ownership association substantially burdens and affects the flow of commerce, and tends to aggravate recurrent business depressions, by depressing wage rates and the purchasing power of wage earners in industry and by preventing the stabilization of competitive wage rates and working conditions within and between industries.

Experience has proved that protection by law of the right of employees to organize and bargain collectively safeguards commerce from injury, impairment, or interruption, and promotes the flow of commerce by removing certain recognized sources of industrial strife and unrest, by encouraging practices fundamental to the friendly adjustment of industrial disputes arising out of differences as to wages, hours, or other working conditions, and by restoring equality or bargaining power between employers and employees.

Experience has further demonstrated that certain practices by some labor organizations, their officers, and members have the intent or the necessary effect of burdening or obstructing commerce by preventing the free flow of goods in such commerce through strikes and other forms of industrial unrest or through concerted activities which impair the interest of the public in the free flow of such commerce. The elimination of such practices is a necessary condition to the assurance of the rights herein guaranteed.

It is hereby declared to be the policy of

the United States to eliminate the causes of certain substantial obstructions to the free flow of commerce and to mitigate and eliminate these obstructions when they have occurred by encouraging the practice and procedure of collective bargaining and by protecting the exercise by workers of full freedom of association, self-organization, and designation of representatives of their own choosing, for the purpose of negotiating the terms and conditions of their employment or other mutual aid or protection.

DEFINITIONS. SEC. 2. When used in this Act—

(1) The term "person" includes one or more individuals, labor organizations, partnerships, associations, corporations, legal representatives, trustees, trustees in bankruptcy, or receivers.

(2) The term "employer" includes any person acting as an agent of an employer, directly or indirectly, but shall not include the United States or any wholly owned Government corporation, or any Federal Reserve Bank, or any State or political subdivision thereof, or any corporation or association operating a hospital, if no part of the net earnings inures to the benefit of any private shareholder or individual, or any person subject to the Railway Labor Act, as amended from time to time, or any labor organization (other than when acting as an employer), or anyone acting in the capacity of officer or agent of such labor organization.

(3) The term "employee" shall include any employee, and shall not be limited to the employees of a particular employer, unless the Act explicitly states otherwise, and shall include any individual whose work has ceased as a consequence of, or in connection with, any current labor dispute or because of any unfair labor practice, and who has not obtained any other regular and substantially equivalent employment, but shall not include any individual employed as an agricultural laborer, or in the domestic service of any family or person at his home, or any individual employed by his parent or spouse, or any individual having the status of an independent contractor, or any individual employed as a supervisor, or any individual employed by an employer subject to the Railway Labor Act, as amended from time to time, or by any other person who is not an employer as herein defined.

(4) The term "representatives" includes any individual or labor organization.

(5) The term "labor organization" means any organization of any kind, or any agency or employee representation committee or plan, in which employees participate and which exists for the purpose, in whole or in part, of dealing with employers concerning grievances, labor disputes, wages, rates of pay, hours of employment, or conditions of work.

(6) The term "commerce" means trade, traffic, commerce, transportation, or communication among the several States, or between the District of Columbia or any Territory of the United States and any State or other Territory, or between any foreign country and any State, Territory, or the District of Columbia, or within the District of Columbia or any Territory, or between points in the same State but through any other State or any Territory or the District of Columbia or any foreign country.

(7) The term "affecting commerce" means in commerce, or burdening or obstructing commerce or the free flow of commerce, or having led or tending to lead to a labor dispute burdening or obstructing commerce or the free flow of commerce.

(8) The term "unfair labor practice" means any unfair labor practice listed in section 8.

(9) The term "labor dispute" includes any controversy concerning terms, tenure or conditions of employment, or concerning the association or representation of persons in negotiating, fixing, maintaining, changing, or seeking to arrange terms or conditions of employment, regardless of whether

the disputants stand in the proximate relation of employer and employee.

(10) The term "National Labor Relations Board" means the National Labor Relations Board provided for in section 3 of this Act.

(11) The term "supervisor" means any individual having authority, in the interest of the employer, to hire, transfer, suspend, lay off, recall, promote, discharge, assign, reward, or discipline other employees, or responsibly to direct them, or to adjust their grievances, or effectively to recommend such action, if in connection with the foregoing the exercise of such authority is not of a merely routine or clerical nature, but requires the use of independent judgment.

(12) The term "professional employee" means—

(a) any employee engaged in work (i) predominantly intellectual and varied in character as opposed to routine mental, manual, mechanical, or physical work; (i) involving the consistent exercise of discretion and judgment in its performance; (iii) of such a character that the output produced or the result accomplished cannot be standardized in relation to a given period of time; (iv) requiring knowledge of an advanced type in a field of science or learning customarily acquired by a prolonged course of specialized intellectual instruction and study in an institution of higher learning or a hospital, as distinguished from a general academic education or from an apprenticeship or from training in the performance of routine mental, manual, or physical processes; or

(b) any employee, who (i) has completed the courses of specialized intellectual instruction and study described in clause (iv) of paragraph (a), and (ii) is performing related work under the supervision of a professional person to qualify himself to become a professional employee as defined in paragraph (a).

(13) In determining whether any person is acting as an "agent" of another person so as to make such other person responsible for his acts, the question of whether the specific acts performed were actually authorized or subsequently ratified shall not be controlling.

(14) The term "health care institution" shall include any hospital, convalescent hospital, health maintenance organization, health clinic, nursing home, extended care facility, or other institution devoted to the care of sick, infirm, or aged persons.

NATIONAL LABOR RELATIONS BOARD

SEC. 3. (a) The National Labor Relations Board (hereinafter called the "Board") created by this Act prior to its amendment by the Labor Management Relations Act, 1947, is hereby continued as an agency of the United States, except that the Board shall consist of five instead of three members, appointed by the President by and with the advice and consent of the Senate. Of the two additional members so provided for, one shall be appointed for a term of five years and the other for a term of two years. Their successors, and the successors of the other members, shall be appointed for terms of five years each, excepting that any individual chosen to fill a vacancy shall be appointed only for the unexpired term of the member whom he shall succeed. The President shall designate one member to serve as Chairman of the Board. Any members of the Board may be removed by the President, upon notice and hearing, for neglect of duty or malfeasance in office, but for no other cause.

(b) The Board is authorized to delegate to any group of three or more members any or all of the powers which it may itself exercise. *The Board is also authorized to delegate to its regional directors its powers under section 9 to determine the unit appropriate for the purpose of collective bargaining, to investigate and provide for hearings, and determine whether a question of representation exists, and to direct an election or take a secret ballot under subsection (c) or (e) of section 9 and certify the results thereof, except that upon the filing of a request therefor with the Board by any interested person, the Board may review any action of a regional director delegated to him under this paragraph, but such a review shall not, unless specifically ordered by the Board, operate as a stay of any action taken by the regional director.* A vacancy in the Board shall not impair the right of the remaining members to exercise all of the powers of the Board, and three members of the Board shall, at all times, constitute a quorum of the Board, except that two members shall constitute a quorum of any group designated pursuant to the first sentence hereof. The Board shall have an official seal which shall be judicially noticed.

(c) The Board shall at the close of each fiscal year make a report in writing to Congress and to the President stating in detail the cases it has heard, the decisions it has rendered, the names, salaries, and duties of all employees and officers in the employ or under the supervision of the Board, and an account of all moneys it has disbursed.

(d) There shall be a General Counsel of the Board who shall be appointed by the President, by and with the advice and consent of the Senate, for a term of four years. The General Counsel of the Board shall exercise general supervision over all attorneys employed by the Board (other than trial examiners and legal assistants to Board members) and over the officers and employees in the regional offices. He shall have final authority, on behalf of the Board, in respect of the investigation of charges and issuance of complaints under section 10, and in respect of the prosecution of such complaints before the Board, and shall have such other duties as the Board may prescribe or as may be provided by law. *In case of a vacancy in the office of the General Counsel the President is authorized to designate the officer or employee who shall act as General Counsel during such vacancy, but no person or persons so designated shall so act (1) for more than forty days when the Congress is in session unless a nomination to fill such vacancy shall have been submitted to the Senate, or (2) after the adjournment sine die of the session of the Senate in which such nomination was submitted.*

SEC. 4. (a) Each member of the Board and the General Counsel of the Board shall receive a salary of $12,000* a year, shall be eligible for reappointment, and shall not engage in any other business, vocation, or employment. The Board shall appoint an executive secretary, and such attorneys, examiners, and regional directors, and such other employees as it may from time to time find necessary for the proper performance of its duties. The Board may not employ any attorneys for the purpose of reviewing transcripts of hearings or preparing drafts of opinions except that any attorney employed for assignment as a legal assistant to any Board member may for such Board member review such transcripts and prepare such drafts. No trial examiner's report shall be reviewed, either before or after its publication, by any person other than a member of the Board or his legal assistant, and no trial examiner shall advise or consult with the Board with respect to exceptions taken to his findings, rulings, or recommendations. The Board may establish or utilize such regional, local, or other agencies, and utilize such voluntary and uncompensated services, as may from time to time be needed. Attorneys appointed under this section may, at the direction of the Board, appear for and represent the Board in any case in court. Nothing in this Act shall be construed to authorize the Board to appoint individuals for the purpose of conciliation or mediation, or for economic analysis.

(b) All of the expenses of the Board, including all necessary traveling and subsistence expenses outside the District of Columbia incurred by the members or employees of the Board under its orders, shall be allowed and paid on the presentation of itemized vouchers therefor approved

---

*AUTHOR'S NOTE: All salaries quoted in this Act are now increased periodically as a result of the Government Employees Salary Reform Act of 1964, 88th Congress, Public Law 88–426. 78 Stat. 400.

by the Board or by any individual it designates for that purpose.

SEC. 5. The principal office of the Board shall be in the District of Columbia, but it may meet and exercise any or all of its powers at any other place. The Board may, by one or more of its members or by such agents or agencies as it may designate, prosecute any inquiry necessary to its functions in any part of the United States. A member who participates in such an inquiry shall not be disqualified from subsequently participating in a decision of the Board in the same case.

SEC. 6. The Board shall have authority from time to time to make, amend, and rescind, in the manner prescribed by the Administrative Procedure Act, such rules and regulations as may be necessary to carry out the provisions of this Act.

RIGHTS OF EMPLOYEES. SEC. 7. Employees shall have the right to self-organization, to form, join, or assist labor organizations, to bargain collectively through representatives of their own choosing, or to engage in other concerted activities for the purpose of collective bargaining or other mutual aid or protection, and shall also have the right to refrain from any or all of such activities except to the extent that such right may be affected by an agreement requiring membership in a labor organization as a condition of employment as authorized in section 8(a)(3).

UNFAIR LABOR PRACTICES. SEC. 8. (a) It shall be an unfair labor practice for an employer—

(1) to interfere with, restrain, or coerce employees in the exercise of the rights guaranteed in section 7;

(2) to dominate or interfere with the formation or administration of any labor organization or contribute financial or other support to it: Provided, That subject to rules and regulations made and published by the Board pursuant to section 6, an employer shall not be prohibited from permitting employees to confer with him during working hours without loss of time or pay;

(3) by discrimination in regard to hire or tenure of employment or any term or condition of employment to encourage or discourage membership in any labor organization: Provided, That nothing in this Act, or in any other statute of the United States, shall preclude an employer from making an agreement with a labor organization (not established, maintained, or assisted by any action defined in section 8[a] of this Act as an unfair labor practice) to require as a condition of employment membership therein on or after the thirtieth day following the beginning of such employment or the effective date of such agreement, whichever is the later, (i) if such labor organization is the representative of the employees as provided in section 9(a), in the appropriate collective-bargaining unit covered by such agreement when made [and has at the time the agreement was made or within the preceding twelve months received from the Board a notice of compliance with section 9 (f), (g), (h)], and (ii) unless following an election held as provided in section 9 (e) within one year preceding the effective date of such agreement, the Board shall have certified that at least a majority of the employees eligible to vote in such election have voted to rescind the authority of such labor organization to make such an agreement: Provided further, That no employer shall justify any discrimination against an employee for nonmembership in a labor organization (A) if he has reasonable grounds for believing that such membership was not available to the employee on the same terms and conditions generally applicable to other members, or (B) if he has reasonable grounds for believing that membership was denied or terminated for reasons other than the failure of the employee to tender the periodic dues and the initiation fees uniformly required as a condition of acquiring or retaining membership;

(4) to discharge or otherwise discriminate against an employee because he has filed charges or given testimony under this Act;

(5) to refuse to bargain collectively with

the representatives of his employees, subject to the provisions of section 9 (a).

(b) It shall be an unfair labor practice for a labor organization or its agents

(1) to restrain or coerce (A) employees in the exercise of the rights guaranteed in section 7: Provided, That this paragraph shall not impair the right of a labor organization to prescribe its own rules with respect to the acquisition or retention of membership therein; or (B) an employer in the selection of his representatives for the purposes of collective bargaining or the adjustment of grievances;

(2) to cause or attempt to cause an employer to discriminate against an employee in violation of subsection (a)(3) or to discriminate against an employee with respect to whom membership in such organization has been denied or terminated on some ground other than his failure to tender the periodic dues and the initiation fees uniformly required as a condition of acquiring or retaining membership;

(3) to refuse to bargain collectively with an employer, provided it is the representative of his employees subject to the provisions of section 9 (a);

(4) (i) to engage in, or to induce or encourage [the employees of any employer] *any individual employed by any person engaged in commerce or in an industry affecting commerce* to engage in, a strike or a [concerted] refusal in the course of [their] *his* employment to use, manufacture, process, transport, or otherwise handle or work on any goods, articles, materials, or commodities or to perform any services [,]; *or (ii) to threaten, coerce, or restrain any person engaged in commerce or in an industry affecting commerce,* where in *either case* an object thereof is:

(A) forcing or requiring any employer or self-employed person to join any labor or employer organization or [any employer or other person to cease using, selling, handling, transporting, or otherwise dealing in the products of any other producer, proces-

sor, or manufacturer, or to cease doing business with any other person] *to enter into any agreement which is prohibited by section 8 (e);*

(B) *forcing or requiring any person to cease using, selling, handling, transporting, or otherwise dealing in the products of any other producer, processor, or manufacturer, or to doing business with any other person, or* forcing or requiring any other employer to recognize or bargain with a labor organization as the representative of his employees unless such labor organization has been certified as the representative of such employees under the provisions of section 9 [;]: *Provided, That nothing contained in this clause (B) shall be construed to make unlawful, where not otherwise unlawful, any primary strike or primary picketing;*

(C) forcing or requiring any employer to recognize or bargain with a particular labor organization as the representative of his employees if another labor organization has been certified as the representative of such employees under the provisions of section 9;

(D) forcing or requiring any employer to assign particular work to employees in a particular labor organization or in a particular trade, craft, or class rather than to employees in another labor organization or in another trade, craft, or class, unless such employer is failing to conform to an order or certification of the Board determining the bargaining representative for employees performing such work:

Provided, That nothing contained in this subsection (b) shall be construed to make unlawful a refusal by any person to enter upon the premises of any employer (other than his own employer), if the employees of such employer are engaged in a strike ratified or approved by a representative of such employees whom such employer is required to recognize under this Act [;]: *Provided further, That for the purposes of this paragraph (4) only, nothing contained in such paragraph shall be construed to prohibit publicity, other than picketing, for the purpose of truthfully advising the public, including consumers and members of a labor organization, that a product or products are produced by an employer with whom the labor organization has a primary dispute and are distributed by another employer, as long as such publicity does not have an effect of inducing any individual employed by any person other than the primary employer in the course of his employment to refuse to pick up, deliver, or transport any goods, or not to perform any services, at the establishment of the employer engaged in such distribution;*

(5) to require of employees covered by an agreement authorized under subsection (a)(3) the payment, as a condition precedent to becoming a member of such organization, of a fee in an amount which the Board finds excessive or discriminatory under all the circumstances. In making such a finding, the Board shall consider, among other relevant factors, the practices and customs of labor organizations in the particular industry, and the wages currently paid to the employees affected; [and]

(6) to cause or attempt to cause an employer to pay or deliver or agree to pay or deliver any money or other thing of value, in the nature of an exaction, for services which are not performed or not to be performed [.]; *and*

(7) *to picket or cause to be picketed, or threaten to picket or cause to be picketed, any employer where an object thereof is forcing or requiring an employer to recognize or bargain with a labor organization as the representative of his employees, or forcing or requiring the employees of an employer to accept or select labor organization as their collective bargaining representative, unless such labor organization is currently certified as the representative of such employees:*

(A) *where the employer has lawfully recognized in accordance with this Act any other labor organization and a question concerning representation may not appropriately be raised under section 9 (c) of this Act,*

(B) *where within the preceding twelve months a valid election under section 9 (c) of this Act has been conducted, or*

(C) *where such picketing has been conducted without a petition under section 9 (c) being filed within a rea-*

sonable period of time not to exceed thirty days from the commencement of such picketing: Provided, That when such a petition has been filed the Board shall forthwith, without regard to the provisions of section 9 (c)(1) or the absence of a showing of a substantial interest on the part of the labor organization, direct an election in such unit as the Board finds to be appropriate and shall certify the results thereof: Provided further, That nothing in this subparagraph (C) shall be construed to prohibit any picketing or other publicity for the purpose of truthfully advising the public (including consumers) that an employer does not employ members of, or have a contract with, a labor organization, unless an effect of such picketing is to induce any individual employed by any other person in the course of his employment, not to pick up, deliver or transport any goods or not to perform any services.

Nothing in this paragraph (7) shall be construed to permit any act which would otherwise be an unfair labor practice under this section 8 (b).

(c) The expressing of any views, argument, or opinion, or the dissemination thereof, whether in written, printed, graphic, or visual form, shall not constitute or be evidence of an unfair labor practice under any of the provisions of this Act, if such expression contains no threat of reprisal or force or promise of benefit.

(d) For the purposes of this section, to bargain collectively is the performance of the mutual obligation of the employer and the representative of the employees to meet at reasonable times and confer in good faith with respect to wages, hours, and other terms and conditions of employment, or the negotiation of an agreement, or any question arising thereunder, and the execution of a written contract incorporating any agreement reached if requested by either party, but such obligation does not compel either party to agree to a proposal or require the making of a concession: Provided, That where there is in effect a collective-bargaining contract covering employees in an industry affecting commerce, the duty to bargain collectively shall also mean that no party to such contract shall terminate or modify such contract, unless the party desiring such termination or modification—

(1) serves a written notice upon the other party to the contract of the proposed termination or modification sixty days prior to the expiration date thereof, or in the event such contract contains no expiration date, sixty days prior to the time it is proposed to make such termination or modification;

(2) offers to meet and confer with the other party for the purpose of negotiating a new contract or a contract containing the proposed modifications;

(3) notifies the Federal Mediation and Conciliation Service within thirty days after such notice of the existence of a dispute, and simultaneously therewith notifies any State or Territorial agency established to mediate and conciliate disputes within the State or Territory where the dispute occurred, provided no agreement has been reached by that time; and

(4) continues in full force and effect, without resorting to strike or lockout, all the terms and conditions of the existing contract for a period of sixty days after such notice is given or until the expiration date of such contract, whichever occurs later.

Whenever the collective bargaining involves employees of a health care institution, the provisions of this section 8 (d) shall be modified as follows:

(A) The notice of section 8 (d) (1) shall be ninety days; the notice of section 8 (d) (3) shall be sixty days; and the contract period of section 8 (d) (4) shall be ninety days.

(B) Where the bargaining is for an initial agreement following certification or recognition, at least thirty days' notice of the existence of a dispute shall be given by the labor organization to the agencies set forth in section 8 (d) (3).

(C) After notice is given to the Federal Mediation and Conciliation Service under either clause (A) or (B) of this sentence, the Service shall

promptly communicate with the parties and use its best efforts, by mediation and conciliation, to bring them to agreement. The parties shall participate fully and promptly in such meetings as may be undertaken by the Service for the purpose of aiding in a settlement of the dispute.

The duties imposed upon employers, employees, and labor organizations by paragraphs (2), (3), and (4) shall become inapplicable upon an intervening certification of the Board, under which the labor organization or individual, which is a party to the contract, has been superseded as or ceased to be the representative of the employees subject to the provisions of section 9 (a), and the duties so imposed shall not be construed as requiring either party to discuss or agree to any modification of the terms and conditions contained in a contract for a fixed period, if such modification is to become effective before such terms and conditions can be reopened under the provisions of the contract. Any employee who engages in a strike within the sixty-day period specified in this subsection shall lose his status as an employee of the employer engaged in the particular labor dispute, for the purposes of sections 8, 9, and 10 of this Act, as amended, but such loss of status for such employee shall terminate if and when he is reemployed by such employer.

(e) It shall be an unfair labor practice for any labor organization and any employer to enter into any contract or agreement, express or implied, whereby such employer ceases or refrains or agrees to cease or refrain from handling, using, selling, transporting or otherwise dealing in any of the products of any other employer, or to cease doing business with any other person, and any contract or agreement entered into heretofore or hereafter containing such an agreement shall be to such extent unenforceable and void: Provided, That nothing in this subsection (e) shall apply to an agreement between a labor organization and an employer in the construction industry relating to the contracting or subcon-

tracting of work to be done at the site of the construction, alteration, painting, or repair of a building, structure, or other work: Provided further, That for the purposes of this subsection (e) and section 8 (b) (4) (B) the terms "any employer," "any person engaged in commerce or an industry affecting commerce" and "any person" when used in relation to the term "any other producer, processor, or manufacturer," "any other employer," or "any other person" shall not include persons in the relation of a jobber, manufacturer, contractor, or subcontractor working on the goods or premises of the jobber or manufacturer or performing parts of an integrated process of production in the apparel and clothing industry: Provided further, That nothing in this Act shall prohibit the enforcement of any agreement which is within the foregoing exception.

(f) It shall not be an unfair labor practice under subsections (a) and (b) of this section for an employer engaged primarily in the building and construction industry to make an agreement covering employees engaged (or who upon their employment, will be engaged) in the building and construction industry with a labor organization of which building and construction employees are members (not established, maintained, or assisted by any action defined in section 8 [a] of this Act as an unfair labor practice) because (1) the majority status of such labor organization has not been established under the provisions of section 9 of this Act prior to the making of such agreement, or (2) such agreement requires as a condition of employment, membership in such labor organization after the seventh day following the beginning of such employment or the effective date of the agreement, whichever is later, or (3) such agreement requires the employer to notify such labor organization of opportunities for employment with such employer, or gives such labor organization an opportunity to refer qualified applicants for such employment, or (4) such agreement specifies minimum training or experience qualifications for employment or provides for priority in opportunities for employment based upon length of service with such employer, in the industry or in the particular geographical area: Provided, That nothing in this subsection shall set aside the final proviso to section 8 (a) (3) of this Act: Provided further, That any

agreement which would be invalid, but for clause (1) of this subsection, shall not be a bar to a petition filed pursuant to section 9 (c) or 9 (e).*

(g) A labor organization before engaging in any strike, picketing, or other concerted refusal to work at any health care institution shall, not less than ten days prior to such action, notify the institution in writing and the Federal Mediation and Conciliation Service of that intention, except that in the case of bargaining for an initial agreement following certification or recognition the notice required by this subsection shall not be given until the expiration of the period specified in clause (B) of the last sentence of section 8 (d) of this Act. The notice shall state the date and time that such action will commence. The notice, once given, may be extended by the written agreement of both parties.

REPRESENTATIVES AND ELECTIONS. SEC. 9. (a) Representatives designated or selected for the purpose of collective bargaining by the majority of the employees in a unit appropriate for such purposes, shall be the exclusive representatives of all the employees in such unit for the purpose of collective bargaining in respect to rates of pay, wages, hours of employment, or other conditions of employment: Provided, That any individual employee or a group of employees shall have the right at any time to present grievances to their employer and to have such grievances adjusted, without the intervention of the bargaining representative, as long as the adjustment is not inconsistent with the terms of a collective-bargaining contract or agreement then in effect: Provided further, That the bargaining representative has been given

---

*Section 8 (f) is inserted in the Act by subsection (a) of Section 705 of Public Law 86–257. Section 705 (b) provides:

Nothing contained in the amendment made by subsection (a) shall be construed as authorizing the execution or application requiring membership in a labor organization as a condition of employment in any State or Territory in which such execution or application is prohibited by State or Territorial law.

opportunity to be present at such adjustment.

(b) The Board shall decide in each case whether, in order to assure to employees the fullest freedom in exercising the rights guaranteed by this Act, the unit appropriate for the purposes of collective bargaining shall be the employer unit, craft unit, plant unit, or subdivision thereof: Provided, That the Board shall not (1) decide that any unit is appropriate for such purposes if such unit includes both professional employees and employees who are not professional employees unless a majority of such professional employees vote for inclusion in such unit; or (2) decide that any craft unit is inappropriate for such purposes on the ground that a different unit has been established by a prior Board determination, unless a majority of the employees in the proposed craft unit vote against separate representation; or (3) decide that any unit is appropriate for such purposes if it includes, together with other employees, any individual employed as a guard to enforce against employees and other persons rules to protect property of the employer or to protect the safety of persons on the employer's premises; but no labor organization shall be certified as the representative of employees in a bargaining unit of guards if such organization admits to membership, or is affiliated directly or indirectly with an organization which admits to membership, employees other than guards.

(c) (1) Whenever a petition shall have been filed, in accordance with such regulations as may be prescribed by the Board—

(A) by an employee or group of employees or any individual or labor organization acting in their behalf alleging that a substantial number of employees (i) wish to be represented for collective bargaining and that their employer declines to recognize their representative as the representative defined in section 9 (a), or (ii) assert that the individual or labor organization, which has been certified or is being currently recognized by their employer as the bargaining representative, is no longer a representative as defined in section 9 (a); or

(B) by an employer, alleging that one or more individuals or labor organizations have presented to him a claim to be recognized as the representative defined in section 9 (a);

the Board shall investigate such petition and if it has reasonable cause to believe that a question of representation affecting commerce exists shall provide for an appropriate hearing upon due notice. Such hearing may be conducted by an officer or employee of the regional office, who shall not make any recommendations with respect thereto. If the Board finds upon the record of such hearing that such a question of representation exists, it shall direct an election by secret ballot and shall certify the results thereof.

(2) In determining whether or not a question of representation affecting commerce exists, the same regulations and rules of decision shall apply irrespective of the identity of the persons filing the petition or the kind of relief sought and in no case shall the Board deny a labor organization a place on the ballot by reason of an order with respect to such labor organization or its predecessor not issued in conformity with section 10 (c).

(3) No election shall be directed in any bargaining unit or any subdivision within which, in the preceding twelve-month period, a valid election shall have been held. Employees [on] *engaged in an economic* strike who are not entitled to reinstatement shall [not] be eligible to vote [.] *under such regulations as the Board shall find are consistent with the purposes and provisions of this Act in any election conducted within twelve months after the commencement of the strike.* In any election where none of the choices on the ballot receives a majority, a run-off shall be conducted, the ballot providing for a selection between the two choices receiving the largest and second largest number of valid votes cast in the election.

(4) Nothing in this section shall be construed to prohibit the waiving of hearings by stipulation for the purpose of a consent election in conformity with regulations and rules of decision of the Board.

(5) In determining whether a unit is appropriate for the purposes specified in subsection (b) the extent to which the employees have organized shall not be controlling.

(d) Whenever an order of the Board made pursuant to section 10 (c) is based in whole or in part upon facts certified following an investigation pursuant to subsection (c) of this section and there is a petition for the enforcement or review of such order, such certification and the record of such investigation shall be included in the transcript of the entire record required to be filed under section 10 (e) or 10 (f), and thereupon the decree of the court enforcing, modifying, or setting aside in whole or in part the order of the Board shall be made and entered upon the pleadings, testimony, and proceedings set forth in such transcript.

(e)(1) Upon the filing with the Board, by 30 per centum or more of the employees in a bargaining unit covered by an agreement between their employer and a labor organization made pursuant to section 8 (a) (3), of a petition alleging they desire that such authority be rescinded, the Board shall take a secret ballot of the employees in such unit and certify the results thereof to such labor organization and to the employer.

(2) No election shall be conducted pursuant to this subsection in any bargaining unit or any subdivision within which, in the preceding twelve-month period, a valid election shall have been held.

[(f) No investigation shall be made by the Board of any question affecting commerce concerning the representation of employees, raised by a labor organization under subsection (c) of this section, and no complaint shall be issued pursuant to a charge made by a labor organization under subsection (b) of

section 10, unless such labor organization and any national or international labor organization of which such labor organization is an affiliate or constituent unit (A) shall have prior thereto filed with the Secretary of Labor copies of its constitution and bylaws and a report, in such form as the Secretary may prescribe, showing—

(1) the name of such labor organization and the address of its principal place of business;

(2) the names, titles, and compensation and allowances of its three principal officers and of any of its other officers or agents whose aggregate compensation and allowances for the preceding year exceeded $5,000, and the amount of the compensation and allowances paid to each such officer or agent during such year;

(3) the manner in which the officers and agents referred to in clause (2) were elected, appointed, or otherwise selected;

(4) the initiation fee or fees which new members are required to pay on becoming members of such labor organization;

(5) the regular dues or fees which members are required to pay in order to remain members in good standing of such labor organization;

(6) a detailed statement of, or reference to provisions of its constitution and bylaws showing the procedure followed with respect to, (a) qualification for or restrictions on membership, (b) election of officers and stewards, (c) calling of regular and special meetings, (d) levying of assessments, (e) imposition of fines, (f) authorization for bargaining demands, (g) ratification of contract terms, (h) authorization for strikes, (i) authorization for disbursement of union funds, (j) audit of union financial transactions, (k) participation in insurance or other benefit plans, and (l) expulsion of members and the grounds therefor;

and (B) can show that prior thereto it has—

(1) filed with the Secretary of Labor, in such forms as the Secretary may prescribe, a report showing all of (a) its receipts of any kind and

the sources of such receipts, (b) its total assets and liabilities as of the end of its last fiscal year, (c) the disbursements made by it during such fiscal year, including the purposes for which made; and

(2) furnished to all of the members of such labor organization copies of the financial report required by paragraph (1) hereof to be filed with the Secretary of Labor.]

[(g) It shall be the obligation of all labor organizations to file annually with the Secretary of Labor, in such form as the Secretary of Labor may prescribe, reports bringing up to date the information required to be supplied in the initial filing by subsection (f) (A) of this section, and to file with the Secretary of Labor and furnish to its members annually financial reports in the form and manner prescribed in subsection (f) (B). No labor organization shall be eligible for certification under this section as the representative of any employees, and no complaint shall issue under section 10 with respect to a charge filed by a labor organization unless it can show that it and any national or international labor organization of which it is an affiliate or constituent unit has complied with its obligation under this subsection.]

[(h) No investigation shall be made by the Board of any question affecting commerce concerning the representation of employees, raised by a labor organization under subsection (c) of this section, and no complaint shall be issued pursuant to a charge made by a labor organization under subsection (b) of section 10, unless there is on file with the Board an affidavit executed contemporaneously or within the preceding twelve-month period by each officer of such labor organization and the officers of any national or international labor organization of which it is an affiliate or constituent unit that he is not a member of the Communist Party or affiliated with such party, and that he does not believe in, and is not a member of or supports any organization that believes in or teaches, the overthrow of the United States Government by force or by any illegal or unconstitutional methods. The provisions of section 35A of the Criminal Code shall be applicable in respect to such affidavits.]

PREVENTION OF UNFAIR LABOR PRACTICES. SEC. 10. (a) The Board is empowered, as hereinafter provided, to prevent any person from engaging in any unfair labor practice (listed in section 8) affecting commerce. This power shall not be affected by any other means of adjustment or prevention that has been or may be established by agreement, law, or otherwise: Provided, That the Board is empowered by agreement with any agency of any State or Territory to cede to such agency jurisdiction over any cases in any industry, (other than mining, manufacturing, communications, and transportation except where predominantly local in character) even though such cases may involve labor disputes affecting commerce, unless the provision of the State or Territorial statute applicable to the determination of such cases by such agency is inconsistent with the corresponding provisions of this Act or has received a construction inconsistent therewith.

(b) Whenever it is charged that any person has engaged in or is engaging in any such unfair labor practice, the Board, or any agent or agency designated by the Board for such purposes, shall have power to issue and cause to be served upon such person a complaint stating the charges in that respect, and containing a notice of hearing before the Board or a member thereof, or before a designated agent or agency, at a place therein fixed, not less than five days after the serving of said complaint: Provided, That no complaint shall issue based upon any unfair labor practice occurring more than six months prior to the filing of the charge with the Board and the service of a copy thereof upon the person against whom such charge is made, unless the person aggrieved thereby was prevented from filing such charge by reason of service in the armed forces, in which event the six-month period shall be computed from the day of his discharge. Any such complaint may be amended by the member, agent, or agency conducting the hearing or the Board in its discretion at any time prior to the issuance of an order based thereon. The person so complained of shall have the right to file an answer to the original or amended complaint and to appear in person or otherwise and give testimony at the place and time fixed in the complaint. In the discretion of the member, agent, or agency conducting the hearing or the Board, any other person may be allowed to intervene in the said proceeding and to present testimony. Any such proceeding shall, so far as practicable, be conducted in accordance with the rules of evidence applicable in the district courts of the United States under the rules of civil procedure for the district courts of the United States, adopted by the Supreme Court of the United States pursuant to the Act of June 19, 1934 (U.S.C., title 28, secs. 723-B, 723-C).

(c) The testimony taken by such member, agent, or agency or the Board shall be reduced to writing and filed with the Board. Thereafter, in its discretion, the Board upon notice may take further testimony or hear argument. If upon the preponderance of the testimony taken the Board shall be of the opinion that any person named in the complaint has engaged in or is engaging in any such unfair labor practice, then the Board shall state its findings of fact and shall issue and cause to be served on such person an order requiring such person to cease and desist from such unfair labor practice, and to take such affirmative action including reinstatement of employees with or without back pay, as will effectuate the policies of this Act: Provided, That where an order directs reinstatement of an employee, back pay may be required of the employer or labor organization, as the case may be, responsible for the discrimination suffered by him: And provided further, That in determining whether a complaint shall issue alleging a violation of section 8 (a) (1) or section 8 (a) (2), and in

deciding such cases, the same regulations and rules of decision shall apply irrespective of whether or not the labor organization affected is affiliated with a labor organization national or international in scope. Such order may further require such person to make reports from time to time showing the extent to which it has complied with the order. If upon the preponderance of the testimony taken the Board shall not be of the opinion that the person named in the complaint has engaged in or is engaging in any such unfair labor practice, then the Board shall state its findings of fact and shall issue an order dismissing the said complaint. No order of the Board shall require the reinstatement of any individual as an employee who has been suspended or discharged, or the payment to him of any back pay, if such individual was suspended or discharged for cause. In case the evidence is presented before a member of the Board, or before an examiner or examiners thereof, such member, or such examiner or examiners, as the case may be, shall issue and cause to be served on the parties to the proceeding a proposed report, together with a recommended order, which shall be filed with the Board, and if no exceptions are filed within twenty days after service thereof upon such parties, or within such further period as the Board may authorize, such recommended order shall become the order of the Board and become effective as therein prescribed.

(d) Until the record in a case shall have been filed in a court, as hereinafter provided, the Board may at any time, upon reasonable notice and in such manner as it shall deem proper, modify or set aside, in whole or in part, any finding or order made or issued by it.

(e) The Board shall have power to petition any court of appeals of the United States, or if all the courts of appeals to which application may be made are in vacation, any district court of the United States, within any circuit or district, respectively, wherein the unfair labor practice in question occurred or wherein such person resides or transacts business, for the enforcement of such order and for appropriate temporary relief or restraining order, and shall file in the court the record in the proceedings, as provided in section 2112 of title 28, United States Code. Upon the filing of such petition, the court shall cause notice thereof to be served upon such person, and thereupon shall have the jurisdiction of the proceeding and of the question determined therein, and shall have power to grant such temporary relief or restraining order as it deems just and proper, and to make and enter a decree enforcing, modifying, and enforcing, as so modified, or setting aside in whole or in part the order of the Board. No objection that has not been urged before the Board, its member agent, or agency, shall be considered by the court, unless the failure or neglect to urge such objection shall be excused because of extraordinary circumstances. The findings of the Board with respect to questions of fact if supported by substantial evidence on the record considered as a whole shall be conclusive. If either party shall apply to the court for leave to adduce additional evidence and shall show to the satisfaction of the court that such additional evidence is material and that there were reasonable grounds for the failure to adduce such evidence in the hearing before the Board, its member, agent, or agency, the court may order such additional evidence to be taken before the Board, its member, agent, or agency, and to be made a part of the record. The Board may modify its findings as to the facts, or make new findings, by reason of additional evidence so taken and filed, and it shall file such modified or new findings, which findings with respect to questions of fact if supported by substantial evidence on the record considered as a whole shall be conclusive, and shall file its recommendations, if any, for the modification or setting aside of its original order. Upon the filing of the record with it the jurisdiction of the court shall be exclusive and its judgment and decree shall be final, except

that the same shall be subject to review by the appropriate United States court of appeals if application was made to the district court as hereinabove provided, and by the Supreme Court of the United States upon writ of certiorari or certification as provided in section 1254 of title 28.

(f) Any person aggrieved by a final order of the Board granting or denying in whole or in part the relief sought may obtain a review of such order in any circuit court of appeals of the United States in the circuit wherein the unfair labor practice in question was alleged to have been engaged in or wherein such person resides or transacts business, or in the United States Court of Appeals for the District of Columbia, by filing in such court a written petition praying that the order of the Board be modified or set aside. A copy of such petition shall be forthwith transmitted by the clerk of the court to the Board, and thereupon the aggrieved party shall file in the court the record in the proceeding, certified by the board, as provided in section 2112 of title 28, United States Code. Upon the filing of such petition, the court shall proceed in the same manner as in the case of an application by the Board under subsection (e) of this section, and shall have the same jurisdiction to grant to the Board such temporary relief or restraining order as it deems just and proper, and in like manner to make and enter a decree enforcing, modifying, and enforcing as so modified, or setting aside in whole or in part the order of the Board; the findings of the Board with respect to questions of fact if supported by substantial evidence on the record considered as a whole shall in like manner be conclusive.

(g) The commencement of proceedings under subsection (e) or (f) of this section shall not, unless specifically ordered by the court, operate as a stay of the Board's order.

(h) When granting appropriate temporary relief or a restraining order, or making and entering a decree enforcing, modifying, and enforcing as so modified, or setting aside in whole or in part an order of the Board, as provided in this section, the jurisdiction of courts sitting in equity shall not be limited by the Act entitled "An Act to amend the Judicial Code and to define and limit the jurisdiction of courts sitting in equity, and for other purposes," approved March 23, 1932 (U.S.C., Supp. VII, title 29, secs. 101–115).

(i) Petitions filed under this Act shall be heard expeditiously, and if possible within ten days after they have been docketed.

(j) The Board shall have power, upon issuance of a complaint as provided in subsection (b) charging that any person has engaged in or is engaging in an unfair labor practice, to petition any district court of the United States (including the District Court of the United States for the District of Columbia), within any district wherein the unfair labor practice in question is alleged to have occurred or wherein such person resides or transacts business, for appropriate temporary relief or restraining order. Upon the filing of any such petition the court shall cause notice thereof to be served upon such person, and thereupon shall have jurisdiction to grant to the Board such temporary relief or restraining order as it deems just and proper.

(k) Whenever it is charged that any person has engaged in an unfair labor practice within the meaning of paragraph (4) (D) of section 8 (b), the Board is empowered and directed to hear and determine the dispute out of which such unfair labor practice shall have arisen, unless, within ten days after notice that such charge has been filed, the parties to such dispute submit to the Board satisfactory evidence that they have adjusted, or agreed upon methods for the voluntary adjustment of the dispute. Upon compliance by the parties to the dispute with the decision of the Board or upon such voluntary adjustment of the dispute, such charge shall be dismissed.

(l) Whenever it is charged that any person has engaged in an unfair labor practice within the meaning of paragraph (4) (A), (B), or (C) of section 8 (b), *or section 8 (e) or section 8 (b)(7)*, the preliminary investigation of such charge shall be made forthwith and given priority over all other cases except cases of like character in the office where it is filed or to which it is referred. If, after such investigation, the officer or regional attorney to whom the matter may be referred has reasonable cause to believe such charge is true and that a complaint should issue, he shall, on behalf of the Board, petition any district court of the United States (including the District Court of the United States for the District of Columbia) within any district where the unfair labor practice in question has occurred, is alleged to have occurred, or wherein such person resides or transacts business, for appropriate injunctive relief pending the final adjudication of the Board with respect to such matter. Upon the filing of any such petition the district court shall have jurisdiction to grant such injunctive relief or temporary restraining order as it deems just and proper, notwithstanding any other provision of law: Provided further, That no temporary restraining order shall be issued without notice unless a petition alleges that substantial and irreparable injury to the charging party will be unavoidable and such temporary restraining order shall be effective for no longer than five days and will become void at the expiration of such period [.]: Provided further, That such officer or regional attorney shall not apply for any restraining order under section 8 (b)(7) if a charge against the employer under section 8 (a) (2) has been filed and after the preliminary investigation, he has reasonable cause to believe that such charge is true and that a complaint should issue. Upon filing of any such petition the courts shall cause notice thereof to be served upon any person involved in the charge and such person, including the charging party, shall be given an opportunity to appear by counsel and present any relevant testimony: Provided further, That for the purposes of this subsection district courts shall be deemed to have jurisdiction of a labor organization (1) in the district in which such organization maintains its principal office, or (2) in any district in which its duly authorized officers or agents are engaged in promoting or protecting the interests of employee members. The service of legal process upon such officer or agent shall constitute service upon the labor organization and make such organization a party to the suit. In situations where such relief is appropriate the procedure specified herein shall apply to charges with respect to section 8 (b) (4) (D).

(m) Whenever it is charged that any person has engaged in an unfair labor practice within the meaning of subsection (a) (3) or (b) (2) of section 8, such charges shall be given priority over all other cases except cases of like character in the office where it is filed or to which it is referred and cases given priority under subsection (1).

INVESTIGATORY POWERS

SEC. 11. For the purpose of all hearings and investigations, which, in the opinion of the Board, are necessary and proper for the exercise of the powers vested in it by section 9 and section 10—

(1) The Board, or its duly authorized agents or agencies, shall at all reasonable times have access to, for the purpose of examination, and the right to copy any evidence of any person being investigated or proceeded against that relates to any matter under investigation or in question. The Board, or any member thereof, shall upon application of any party to such proceedings, forthwith issue to such party subpenas requiring the attendance and testimony of witnesses or the production of any evidence in such proceeding or investigation requested in such application. Within five days after the service of a subpena on any person requiring the production of any evidence in his possession or under his control, such person may petition the Board to revoke, and the Board shall revoke, such subpena if in its opinion

the evidence whose production is required does not relate to any matter under investigation, or any matter in question in such proceedings, or if in its opinion such subpena does not describe with sufficient particularity the evidence whose production is required. Any member of the Board, or any agent or agency designated by the Board for such purposes, may administer oaths and affirmations, examine witnesses, and receive evidence. Such attendance of witnesses and the production of such evidence may be required from any place in the United States or any Territory or possession thereof, at any designated place of hearing.

(2) In case of contumacy or refusal to obey a subpena issued to any person, any district court of the United States or the United States courts of any Territory or possession, or the District Court of the United States for the District of Columbia, within the jurisdiction of which the inquiry is carried on or within the jurisdiction of which said person guilty of contumacy or refusal to obey is found or resides or transacts business, upon application by the Board shall have jurisdiction to issue to such person an order requiring such person to appear before the Board, its member, agent, or agency, there to produce evidence if so ordered, or there to give testimony touching the matter under investigation or in question; and any failure to obey such order of the court may be punished by said court as a contempt thereof.

(3) [Repealed.]

(4) Complaints, orders, and other process and papers of the Board, its member, agent, or agency, may be served either personally or by registered mail or by telegraph or by leaving a copy thereof at the principal office or place of business of the person required to be served. The verified return by the individual so serving the same setting forth the manner of such service shall be proof of the same, and the return post office receipt or telegraph receipt therefor when registered and mailed or telegraphed as aforesaid shall

be proof of service of the same. Witnesses summoned before the Board, its member, agent, or agency, shall be paid the same fees and mileage that are paid witnesses in the court of the United States, and witnesses whose depositions are taken and the persons taking the same shall severally be entitled to the same fees as are paid for like services in the courts of the United States.

(5) All process of any court to which application may be made under this Act may be served in the judicial district wherein the defendant or other person required to be served resides or may found.

(6) The several departments and agencies of the Government, when directed by the President, shall furnish the Board, upon its request, all records, papers, and information in their possession relating to any matter before the Board.

SEC. 12. Any person who shall willfully resist, prevent, impede, or interfere with any member of the Board or any of its agents or agencies in the performance of duties pursuant to this Act shall be punished by a fine of not more than $5,000 or by imprisonment for not more than one year, or both.

LIMITATIONS

SEC. 13. Nothing in this Act, except as specifically provided for herein, shall be construed so as either to interfere with or impede or diminish in any way the right to strike, or to affect the limitations or qualifications on that right.

SEC. 14. (a) Nothing herein shall prohibit any individual employed as a supervisor from becoming or remaining a member of a labor organization, but no employer subject to this Act shall be compelled to deem individuals defined herein as supervisors as employees for the purpose of any law, either national or local, relating to collective bargaining.

(b) Nothing in this Act shall be construed as authorizing the execution or application of agreements requiring membership in a labor organization as a condition of employment in any State or Territory in which such execution or application is prohibited by State or Territorial law.

(c) (1) The Board, in its discretion, may, by rule of decision or by published rules adopted pursuant to the Administrative Procedure Act, decline to assert jurisdiction over any labor dispute involving any class or category of employers, where, in the opinion of the Board, the effect of such labor dispute on commerce is not sufficiently substantial to warrant the exercise of its jurisdiction: Provided, That the Board shall not decline to assert jurisdiction over any labor dispute over which it would assert jurisdiction under the standards prevailing upon August 1, 1959.

(2) Nothing in this Act shall be deemed to prevent or bar any agency or the courts of any State or Territory (including the Commonwealth of Puerto Rico, Guam, and the Virgin Islands), from assuming and asserting jurisdiction over labor disputes over which the Board declines, pursuant to paragraph (1) of this subsection, to assert jurisdiction.

SEC. 15. Wherever the application of the provisions of section 272 of chapter 10 of the Act entitled "An Act to establish a uniform system of bankruptcy throughout the United States," approved July 1, 1898, and Acts amendatory thereof and supplementary thereto (U.S.C., title 11, sec. 672), conflicts with the application of the provisions of this Act, this Act shall prevail: Provided, That in any situation where the provisions of this Act cannot be validly enforced, the provisions of such other Acts shall remain in full force and effect.

SEC. 16. If any provision of this Act, or the application of such provision to any person or circumstances, shall be held invalid, the remainder of this Act, or the application of such provision to persons or circumstances other than those as to which it is held invalid, shall not be affected thereby.

SEC. 17. This Act may be cited as the "National Labor Relations Act."

SEC. 18. No petition entertained, no investigation made, no election held, and no certification issued by the National Labor Relations Board, under any of the provisions of section 9 of the National Labor Relations Act, as amended, shall be invalid by reason of the failure of the Congress of Industrial Organizations to have complied with the requirements of section 9 (f), (g), or (h) of the aforesaid Act prior to December 22, 1949, or by reason of the failure of the American Federation of Labor to have complied with the provisions of section 9 (f), (g), or (h) of the aforesaid Act prior to November 7, 1947: Provided, That no liability shall be imposed under any provision of this Act upon any person for failure to honor any election or certificate referred to above, prior to the effective date of this amendment: Provided, however, That this proviso shall not have the effect of setting aside or in any way affecting judgments or decrees heretofore entered under section 10 (e) or (f) and which have become final.

INDIVIDUALS WITH
RELIGIOUS CONVICTIONS

SEC. 19. Any employee of a health care institution who is a member of and adheres to established traditional tenets or teachings of a bona fide religion, body, or sect which has historically held conscientious objections to joining or financially supporting labor organizations shall not be required to join or financially support any labor organization as a condition of employment; except that such employee may be required, in lieu of periodic dues and initiation fees, to pay sums equal to such dues and initiation fees to a nonreligious charitable fund exempt from taxation under section 501 (c) (3) of the Internal Revenue Code, chosen by such employee from a list of at least three such funds, designated in a contract between such institution and a labor organization, or if the contract fails to designate such funds, then to any such fund chosen by the employee.

EFFECTIVE DATE OF CERTAIN
CHANGES*

SEC. 102. No provision of this title shall be deemed to make an unfair labor practice any act which was performed prior to the date of the enactment of this Act which did not constitute an unfair labor practice prior thereto, and the provisions of section 8 (a)(3) and section 8 (b) (2) of the National Labor Relations Act as amended by this title shall not make an unfair labor practice the performance of any obligation under a collective-bargaining agreement entered into prior to the date of the enactment of this Act, or (in the case of an agreement for a period of not more than one year) entered into on or after such date of enactment, but prior to the effective date of this title, if the performance of such obligation would not have constituted an unfair labor practice under section 8 (3) of the National Labor Relations Act prior to the effective date of this title, unless such agreement was renewed or extended subsequent thereto.

SEC. 103. No provisions of this title shall affect any certification of representatives or any determination as to the appropriate collective-bargaining unit, which was made under section 9 of the National Labor Relations Act prior to the effective date of this title until one year after the date of such certification or if, in respect of any such certification, a collective-bargaining contract was entered into prior to the effective date of this title, until the end of the contract period or until one year after such date, whichever first occurs.

*The effective date referred to in Sections 102, 103, and 104 is August 22, 1947.

SEC. 104. The amendments made by this title shall take effect sixty days after the date of the enactment of this Act, except that the authority of the President to appoint certain officers conferred upon him by section 3 of the National Labor Relations Act as amended by this title may be exercised forthwith.

TITLE II

CONCILIATION OF LABOR DISPUTES IN INDUSTRIES AFFECTING COMMERCE: NATIONAL EMERGENCIES

SEC. 201. That it is the policy of the United States that—

(a) sound and stable industrial peace and the advancement of the general welfare, health, and safety of the Nation and of the best interest of employers and employees can most satisfactorily be secured by the settlement of issues between employers and employees through the processes of conference and collective bargaining between employers and the representatives of their employees;

(b) the settlement of issues between employers and employees through collective bargaining may be advanced by making available full and adequate governmental facilities for conciliation, mediation, and voluntary arbitration to aid and encourage employers and the representatives of their employees to reach and maintain agreements concerning rates of pay, hours, and working conditions, and to make all reasonable efforts to settle their differences by mutual agreement reached through conferences and collective bargaining or by such methods as may be provided for in any applicable agreement for the settlement of disputes; and

(c) certain controversies which arise between parties to collective bargaining agreements may be avoided or minimized by making available full and adequate governmental facilities for furnishing assistance to employers and the representatives of their employees in formulating for inclusion within such agreements provision for adequate notice of any proposed changes in the terms of such agreements, for the final adjustment of grievances or questions regarding the application or interpretation of such agreements, and other provisions designed to prevent the subsequent arising of such controversies.

SEC. 202. (a) There is hereby created an independent agency to be known as the Federal Mediation and Conciliation Service (herein referred to as the "Service," except that for sixty days after the date of the enactment of this Act such term shall refer to the Conciliation Service of the Department of Labor). The Service shall be under the direction of a Federal Mediation and Conciliation Director (hereinafter referred to as the "Director"), who shall be appointed by the President by and with the advice and consent of the Senate. The Director shall receive compensation at the rate of $12,000* per annum. The Director shall not engage in any other business, vocation, or employment.

(b) The Director is authorized, subject to the civil-service laws, to appoint such clerical and other personnel as may be necessary for the execution of the functions of the Service, and shall fix their compensation in accordance with the Classification Act of 1923, as amended, and may, without regard to the provisions of the civil service laws and the Classification Act of 1923, as amended, appoint and fix the compensation of such conciliators and mediators as may be necessary to carry out the functions of the Service. The Director is authorized to make such expenditures for supplies, facilities, and services as he deems necessary. Such expenditures shall

---

*AUTHORS' NOTE: All salaries quoted in this Act are now increased periodically as a result of the Government Employees Salary Reform Act of 1964, 88th Congress, Public Law 88–426, 78 Stat. 400.

be allowed and paid upon presentation of itemized vouchers therefor approved by the Director or by any employee designated by him for that purpose.

(c) The principal office of the Service shall be in the District of Columbia, but the Director may establish regional offices convenient to localities in which labor controversies are likely to arise. The Director may by order, subject to revocation at any time, delegate any authority and discretion conferred upon him by this Act to any regional director, or other officer or employee of the Service. The Director may establish suitable procedures for cooperation with State and local mediation agencies. The Director shall make an annual report in writing to Congress at the end of the fiscal year.

(d) All mediation and conciliation functions of the Secretary of Labor or the United States Conciliation Service under section 8 of the Act entitled "An Act to create a Department of Labor," approved March 4, 1913 (U.S.C., title 29, sec. 51), and all functions of the United States Conciliation Service under any other law are hereby transferred to the Federal Mediation and Conciliation Service, together with the personnel and records of the United States Conciliation Service. Such transfer shall take effect upon the sixtieth day after the date of enactment of this Act. Such transfer shall not affect any proceedings, pending before the United States Conciliation Service or any certification, order, rule, or regulation theretofore made by it or by the Secretary of Labor. The Director and the Service shall not be subject in any way to the jurisdiction or authority of the Secretary of Labor or any official or division of the Department of Labor.

FUNCTIONS OF THE SERVICE

SEC. 203. (a) It shall be the duty of the Service, in order to prevent or minimize interruptions of the free flow of commerce growing out of labor disputes, to assist parties to labor disputes in industries affecting commerce to settle such disputes through conciliation and mediation.

(b) The Service may proffer its services in any labor dispute in any industry affecting commerce, either upon its own motion or upon the request of one or more of the parties to the dispute, whenever in its judgment such dispute threatens to cause a substantial interruption of commerce. The Director and the Service are directed to avoid attempting to mediate disputes which would have only a minor effect on interstate commerce if State or other conciliation services are available to the parties. Whenever the Service does proffer its services in any dispute, it shall be the duty of the Service promptly to put itself in communication with the parties and to use its best efforts, by mediation and conciliation, to bring them to agreement.

(c) If the Director is not able to bring the parties to agreement by conciliation within a reasonable time, he shall seek to induce the parties voluntarily to seek other means of settling the dispute without resort to strike, lockout, or other coercion, including submission to the employees in the bargaining unit of the employer's last offer of settlement for approval or rejection in a secret ballot. The failure or refusal of either party to agree to any procedure suggested by the Director shall not be deemed a violation of any duty or obligation imposed by this Act.

(d) Final adjustment by a method agreed upon by the parties is hereby declared to be the desirable method for settlement of grievance disputes arising over the application or interpretation of an existing collective-bargaining agreement. The Service is directed to make its conciliation and mediation services available in the settlement of such grievance disputes only as a last resort and in exceptional cases.

SEC. 204. (a) In order to prevent or minimize interruptions of the free flow of commerce growing out of labor disputes, employers and employees and their representatives, in any industry affecting commerce, shall—

(1) exert every reasonable effort to make and maintain agreements concerning rates of pay, hours, and working conditions, including provision for adequate notice of any proposed change in the terms of such agreements;

(2) whenever a dispute arises over the terms or application of a collective-bargaining agreement and a conference is requested by a party or prospective party thereto, arrange promptly for such a conference to be held and endeavor in such conference to settle such dispute expeditiously; and

(3) in case such dispute is not settled by conference, participate fully and promptly in such meetings as may be undertaken by the Service under this Act for the purpose of aiding in a settlement of the dispute.

SEC. 205. (a) There is hereby created a National Labor-Management Panel which shall be composed of twelve members appointed by the President, six of whom shall be selected from among persons outstanding in the field of management and six of whom shall be selected from among persons outstanding in the field of labor. Each member shall hold office for a term of three years, except that any member appointed to fill a vacancy occurring prior to the expiration of the term for which his predecessor was appointed shall be appointed for the remainder of such term, and the terms of office of the members first taking office shall expire, as designated by the President at the time of appointment, four at the end of the first year, four at the end of the second year, and four at the end of the third year after the date of appointment. Members of the panel, when serving on business of the panel, shall be paid compensation at the rate of $25 per day, and shall also be entitled to receive an allowance for actual and necessary travel and subsistence expenses while so serving away from their places of residence.

(b) It shall be the duty of the panel, at the request of the Director, to advise in the avoidance of industrial controversies and the manner in which mediation and voluntary adjustment shall be administered, particularly with reference to controversies affecting the general welfare of the country.

NATIONAL EMERGENCIES

SEC. 206. Whenever in the opinion of the President of the United States, a threatened or actual strike or lockout affecting an entire industry or a substantial part thereof engaged in trade, commerce, transportation, transmission, or communication among the several States or with foreign nations, or engaged in the production of goods for commerce, will, if permitted to occur or to continue, imperil the national health or safety, he may appoint a board of inquiry to inquire into the issues involved in the dispute and to make a written report to him within such time as he shall prescribe. Such report shall include a statement of the facts with respect to the dispute, including each party's statement of its position but shall not contain any recommendations. The President shall file a copy of such report with the Service and shall make its contents available to the public.

SEC. 207. (a) A board of inquiry shall be composed of a chairman and such other members as the President shall determine, and shall have power to sit and act in any place within the United States and to conduct such hearings either in public or in private, as it may deem necessary or proper, to ascertain the facts with respect to the causes and circumstances of the dispute.

(b) Members of a board of inquiry shall receive compensation at the rate of $50 for each day actually spent by them in the work of the board, together with necessary travel and subsistence expenses.

(c) For the purpose of any hearing or inquiry conducted by any board appointed under this title, the provisions of sections 9 and 10 (relating to the attendance of witnesses and the production of books, papers, and documents) of the Federal Trade Commission Act of September 16, 1914, as amended (U.S.C. 19, title 15, secs. 49 and 50, as amended), are hereby made applicable to the powers and duties of such board.

Sec. 208. (a) Upon receiving a report from a board of inquiry the President may direct the Attorney General to petition any district court of the United States having jurisdiction of the parties to enjoin such strike or lockout or the continuing thereof, and if the court finds that such threatened or actual strike or lockout—

(i) affects an entire industry or a substantial part thereof engaged in trade, commerce, transportation, transmission, or communication among the several States or with foreign nations, or engaged in the production of goods for commerce; and

(ii) if permitted to occur or to continue, will imperil the national health or safety, it shall have jurisdiction to enjoin any such strike or lockout, or the continuing thereof, and to make such other orders as may be appropriate.

(b) In any case, the provisions of the Act of March 23, 1932, entitled "An Act to amend the Judicial Code and to define and limit the jurisdiction of courts sitting in equity, and for other purposes," shall not be applicable.

(c) The order or orders of the court shall be subject to review by the appropriate circuit court of appeals and by the Supreme Court upon writ of certiorari of certification as provided in sections 239 and 240 of the Judicial Code, as amended (U.S.C., title 29, secs. 346 and 347).

Sec. 209. (a) Whenever a district court has issued an order under section 208 enjoining acts or practices which imperil or threaten to imperil the national health or safety, it shall be the duty of the parties to the labor dispute giving rise to such order to make every effort to adjust and settle their differences, with the assistance of the Service created by this Act. Neither party shall be under any duty to accept, in whole or in part, any proposal of settlement made by the Service.

(b) Upon the issuance of such order, the President shall reconvene the board of inquiry which has previously reported with respect to the dispute. At the end of a sixty-day period (unless the dispute has been settled by that time), the board of inquiry shall report to the President the current position of the parties and the efforts which has (sic) been made for settlement, and shall include a statement by each party of its position and a statement of the employer's last offer of settlement. The President shall make such report available to the public. The National Labor Relations Board, within the succeeding fifteen days, shall take a secret ballot of the employees of each employer involved in the dispute on the question of whether they wish to accept the final offer of settlement made by their employer as stated by him and shall certify the results thereof to the Attorney General within five days thereafter.

Sec. 210. Upon the certification of the results of such ballot or upon a settlement being reached, whichever happens sooner, the Attorney General shall move the court to discharge the injunction, which motion shall then be granted and the injunction discharged. When such motion is granted, the President shall submit to the Congress a full and comprehensive report of the proceedings, including the findings of the board of inquiry and the ballot taken by the National Labor Relations Board, together with such recommendations as he may see fit to make for consideration and appropriate action.

Compilation of Collective-Bargaining Agreements, Etc. Sec. 211. (a) For the guidance and information of interested representatives of employers, employees, and the general public, the Bureau of Labor Statistics of the Department of Labor shall maintain a file of copies of all available collective-bargaining agreements and other available agreements and actions thereunder settling or adjusting labor disputes. Such file shall be open to inspection under appropriate conditions prescribed by the Secretary of Labor, except that no specific information submitted in confidence shall be disclosed.

(b) The Bureau of Labor Statistics in the Department of Labor is authorized to furnish upon request of the Service, or employers, employees, or their representatives, all available data and factual information which may aid in the settlement of any labor dispute, except that no specific information submitted to confidence shall be disclosed.

Exemption of Railway Labor Act. Sec. 212 The provisions of this title shall not be applicable with respect to any matter which is subject to the provisions of the Railway Labor Act, as amended from time to time.

CONCILIATION OF LABOR DISPUTES IN THE HEALTH CARE INDUSTRY

Sec. 213 (a) If, in the opinion of the Director of the Federal Mediation and Conciliation Service a threatened or actual strike or lockout affecting a health care institution will, if permitted to occur or to continue, substantially interrupt the delivery of health care in the locality concerned, the Director may further assist in the resolution of the impasse by establishing within 30 days after the notice to the Federal Mediation and Conciliation Service under clause (A) of the last sentence of section 8 (d) [which is required by clause (3) of such section 8 (d)], or within 10 days after the notice under clause (B), an impartial Board of Inquiry to investigate the issue involved in the dispute and to make a written report thereon to the parties within fifteen (15) days after the establishment of such a Board. The written report shall contain the findings of fact together with the Board's recommendations for settling the dispute.

Each such Board shall be composed of such number of individuals as the Director may deem desirable. No member appointed under this section shall have any interest or involvement in the health care institutions or the employee organizations involved in the dispute.

(b) (1) Members of any board established under this section who are otherwise employed by the Federal Government shall serve without compensation but shall be reimbursed for travel, subsistence, and other necessary expenses incurred by them in carrying out its duties under this section.

(2) Members of any board established under this section who are not subject to paragraph (1) shall receive compensation at a rate prescribed by the Director but not to exceed the daily rate prescribed for GS-18 of the General Schedule under section 5332 of title 5, United States Code, including travel for each day they are engaged in the performance of their duties under this section and shall be entitled to reimbursement for travel, subsistence, and other necessary expenses incurred by them in carrying out their duties under this section.

(c) After the establishment of a board under subsection (a) of this section and for 15 days after any such board has issued its report, no change in the status quo in effect prior to the expiration of the contract in the case of negotiations for a contract renewal, or in effect prior to the time of the impasse in the case of an initial bargaining negotiation, except by agreement, shall be made by the parties to the controversy.

TITLE III

SUITS BY AND AGAINST LABOR ORGANIZATIONS

Sec. 301. (a) Suits for violation of contracts between an employer and a labor organization representing employees in an industry affecting commerce as defined in this Act, or between any such labor organizations, may be brought in any district court of the United States having jurisdiction of the parties, without respect to the amount in controversy or without regard to the citizenship of the parties.

(b) Any labor organization which represents employees in an industry affecting commerce as defined in this Act and any employer whose activities affect commerce as defined in this Act shall be bound by the acts of its agents. Any such labor organization may sue or be sued as an entity and in behalf of the employees whom it represents in the courts of the United States. Any money judgment against a labor organization in a district court of the United States shall be enforceable only against the organization as an entity and against its assets, and shall not be enforceable against any individual member or his assets.

(c) For the purposes of actions and proceedings by or against labor organizations in the district courts of the United States, district courts shall be deemed to have jurisdiction of a labor organization (1) in the district in which such organization maintains its principal office, or (2) in any district in which its duly authorized officers or agents are engaged in representing or acting for employee members.

(d) The service of summons, subpena, or other legal process of any court of the United States upon an officer or agent of a labor organization, in his capacity as such, shall constitute service upon the labor organization.

(e) For the purposes of this section, in determining whether any person is acting as an "agent" of another person so as to make such other person responsible for his acts, the question of whether the specific acts performed were actually authorized or subsequently ratified shall not be controlling.

RESTRICTIONS ON PAYMENTS TO EMPLOYEE REPRESENTATIVES. SEC. 302. (a) It shall be unlawful for any employer *or association of em-* *ployers or any person who acts as a labor relations expert, adviser, or consultant to an employer or who acts in the interest of an employer* to pay, *lend,* or deliver, or [to] agree to pay, *lend,* or deliver, any money or other thing of value—

(1) to any representative of any of his employees who are employed in an industry affecting commerce [.]; *or*

(2) to any labor organization, or any officer or employee thereof, which represents, seeks to represent, or would admit to membership, any of the employees of such employer who are employed in an industry affecting commerce; or

(3) to any employee or group or committee of employees of such employer employed in an industry affecting commerce in excess of their normal compensation for the purpose of causing such employee or group or committee directly or indirectly to influence any other employees in the exercise of the right to organize and bargain collectively through representatives of their own choosing; or

(4) to any officer or employee of a labor organization engaged in an industry affecting commerce with intent to influence him in respect to any of his actions, decisions, or duties as a representative of employees or as such officer or employee of such labor organization.

(b) (1) It shall be unlawful for any [representative of any employees who are employed in an industry affecting commerce] *person* to *request, demand,* receive, or accept, or [to] agree to receive or accept, [from the employer of such employees] *any payment, loan, or delivery* of any money or other thing of value[.] *prohibited by subsection* (a).

(2) It shall be unlawful for any labor organization, or for any person acting as an officer, agent, representative, or employee of such labor organization, to demand or accept from the operator of any motor vehicle (as defined in part II of the Interstate Commerce Act) employed in the transportation of property in commerce, or the employer of any such operator, any money or other thing of value payable to such organization or to an officer, agent, representative or employee thereof as a fee or charge for the unloading, or in connection with the unloading,

of the cargo of such vehicle: Provided, That nothing in this paragraph shall be construed to make unlawful any payment by an employer to any of his employees as compensation for their services as employees.

(c) The provisions of this section shall not be applicable (1) [with] in respect to any money or other thing of value payable by an employer *to any of his employees whose established duties include acting openly for such employer in matters of labor relations or personnel administration or* to any representative *of his employees, or to any officer or employee of a labor organization* who is *also* an employee or former employee of such employer, as a compensation for, or by reason of, his service [s] as an employee of such employer; (2) with respect to the payment or delivery of any money or other thing of value in satisfaction of a judgment of any court or a decision or award of an arbitrator or impartial chairman or in compromise, adjustment, settlement, or release of any claim, complaint, grievance, or dispute in the absence of fraud or duress; (3) with respect to the sale or purchase of an article or commodity at the prevailing market price in the regular course of business; (4) with respect to money deducted from the wages of employees in payment of membership dues in a labor organization: Provided, That the employer has received from each employee, on whose account such deductions are made, a written assignment which shall not be irrevocable for a period of more than one year, or beyond the termination date of the applicable collective agreement, whichever occurs sooner; [or] (5) with respect to money or other thing of value paid to a trust fund established by such representative, for the sole and exclusive benefit of the employees of such employer, and their families and dependents (or of such employees, families, and dependents jointly with the employees of other employers making similar payments, and their families and dependents): Provided, That (A) such payments are held in trust for the purpose of paying, either from principal or income or both, for the benefit of employees, their families and de-

pendents, for medical or hospital care, pensions on retirement or death of employees, compensation for injuries or illness resulting from occupational acitivity or insurance to provide any of the foregoing, or unemployment benefits or life insurance, disability and sickness insurance, or accident insurance; (B) the detailed basis on which such payments are to be made is specified in a written agreement with the employer, and employees and employers are equally represented in the administration of such fund, together with such neutral persons as the representatives in the administration of such fund, together with such neutral persons as the representatives of the employers and the representatives of [the] employees may agree upon and in the event the employer and employee groups deadlock on the administration of such fund and there are no neutral persons empowered to break such deadlock, such agreement provides that the two groups shall agree on an impartial umpire to decide such dispute or in event of their failure to agree within a reasonable length of time an impartial umpire to decide such dispute shall, on petition of either group, be appointed by the district court of the United States for the district where the trust fund has its principal office, and shall also contain provisions for an annual audit of the trust fund, a statement of the results of which shall be available for inspection by interested persons at the principal office of the trust fund and at such other places as may be designated in such written agreement; and (C) such payments as are intended to be used for the purpose of providing pensions or annuities for employees are made to a separate trust which provides that the funds held therein cannot be used for any purpose other than paying such pensions or annuities [.]; *or (6) with respect to money or other thing of value paid by any employer to a trust fund established by such representative for the purpose of pooled vacation, holiday, severance or similar benefits, or defraying costs of apprenticeship or other training programs; Provided, That the requirements of clause (B) of the proviso to clause (5) of this subsection shall apply to such trust funds. [; or]* (7) With respect to money or other thing of value paid by any employer to a pooled or individual trust fund established by such representative for the purpose of (A) scholarships for the benefit of employees, their families, and dependents for study at educational institutions, or (B) child care centers for preschool and school age dependents of employees: Provided, That no labor organization or employer shall be required to bargain on the establishment of any such trust fund, and refusal to do so shall not constitute an unfair labor practice: Provided further, That the requirements of clause (B) of the proviso to clause (5) of this subsection shall apply to such trust funds; or (8) with respect to money or any other thing of value paid by any employer to a trust fund established by such representative for the purpose of defraying the costs of legal services for employees, their families, and dependents for counsel or plan of their choice: Provided, That the requirements of clause (B) of the proviso to clause (5) of this subsection shall apply to such trust funds: Provided further, That no such legal services shall be furnished: (A) to initiate any proceeding directed (i) against any such employer or its officers or agents except in workman's compensation cases, or (ii) against such labor organizations, or its parent or subordinate bodies, or their officers or agents, or (iii) against any other employer or labor organization, or their officers or agents, in any matter arising under the National Labor Relations Act, as amended, or this Act; and (B) in any proceeding where a labor organization would have been prohibited from defraying the costs of legal services by the provisions of the Labor-Management Reporting and Disclosure Act of 1959.

(d) Any person who willfully violates any of the provisions of this section shall, upon conviction thereof, be guilty of a misdemeanor and be subject to a fine of not more than $10,000 or to imprisonment for not more than one year, or both.

(e) The district courts of the United States and the United States courts of the Territories and possessions shall have jurisdiction, for cause shown, and subject to the provisions of section 17 (relating to notice to opposite party) of the Act entitled "An Act to supplement existing laws against unlawful restraints and monopolies, and for other purposes," approved October 15, 1914, as amended (U.S.C., title 28, sec. 381), to restrain violations of this section, without regard to the provisions of sections 6 and 20 of such Act of October 15, 1914, as amended (U.S.C. title 15, sec. 17, and title 29, sec. 52), and the provisions of the Act entitled "An Act to amend the Judicial Code and to define and limit the jurisdiction of courts sitting in equity, and for other purposes," approved March 23, 1932 (U.S.C., title 29, secs. 101–115).

(f) This section shall not apply to any contract in force on the date of enactment of this Act, until the expiration of such contract, or until July 1, 1948, whichever first occurs.

(g) Compliance with the restrictions contained in subsection (c) (5) (B) upon contributions to trust funds, otherwise lawful, shall not be applicable to contributions to such trust funds established by collective agreement prior to January 1, 1946, nor shall subsection (c) (5) (A) be construed as prohibiting contributions to such trust funds if prior to January 1, 1947, such funds contained provisions for pooled vacation benefits.

BOYCOTTS AND OTHER UNLAWFUL COMBINATIONS. SEC. 303. (a) It shall be unlawful, for the purpose [s] of this section only, in an industry or activity affecting commerce, for any labor organization to engage in [, or to induce or encourage the employees of any employer to engage in, a strike or a concerted refusal in the course of their employment to use, manufacture, process, transport, or otherwise handle or work on any goods, articles, materials, or commodities or to perform any services, where an object thereof is—]

[(1) forcing or requiring any employer or self-employed person to join any labor or employer organization or any employer or other person to cease using, selling, handling, transporting, or otherwise dealing in the products of any other producer, processor, or manufacturer, or to cease doing business with any other person;]

[(2) forcing or requiring any other employer to recognize or bargain with a labor organization as the representative of his employees unless such labor organization has been certified as the representative of such employees under the provisions of section 9 of the National Labor Relations Act;]

[(3) forcing or requiring any employer to recognize or bargain with a particular labor organization as the representative of his employees if another labor organization has been certified as the representative of such employees under the provisions of section 9 of the National Labor Relations Act;]

[(4) forcing or requiring any employer to assign particular work to employees in a particular labor organization or in a particular trade, craft, or class rather than to employees in another labor organization or in another trade, craft, or class unless such employer is failing to conform to an order or certification of the National Labor Relations Board determining the bargaining representative for employees performing such work. Nothing contained in this subsection shall be construed to make unlawful a refusal by any person to enter upon the premises of any employer (other than his own employer), if the employees of such employer are engaged in a strike ratified or approved by a representative of such employees whom such employer is required to recognize under the National Labor Relations Act.]

any activity or conduct defined as an unfair labor practice in section 8 (b) (4) of the National Labor Relations Act, as amended.

(b) Whoever shall be injured in his business or property by reason of any violation of subsection (a) may sue therefor in any district court of the United States subject to the limitations and provisions of section 301 hereof without respect to the amount in controversy, or in any other court having jurisdiction of the parties, and shall recover the damages by him sustained and the cost of the suit.

RESTRICTION ON POLITICAL CONTRIBUTIONS

SEC. 304. Section 313 of the Federal Corrupt Practices Act, 1925 (U.S.C., 1940 edition, title 2, sec. 251; Supp. V, title 50, App., sec. 1509), as amended, is amended to read as follows:

SEC. 313. It is unlawful for any national bank, or any corporation organized by authority of any law of Congress, to make a contribution or expenditure in connection with any election to any political office, or in connection with any primary election or political convention or caucus held to select candidates for any political office, or for any corporation whatever, or any labor organization to make a contribution or expenditure in connection with any election at which Presidential and Vice Presidential electors or a Senator or Representative in, or a Delegate or Resident Commissioner to Congress are to be voted for, or in connection with any primary election or political convention or caucus held to select candidates for any of the foregoing offices, or for any candidate, political committee, or other person to accept or receive any contribution prohibited by this section. Every corporation or labor organization which makes any contribution or expenditure in violation of this section shall be fined not more than $5,000; and every officer or director of any corporation, or officer of any labor organization, who consents to any contribution or expenditure by the corporation or labor organization, as the case may be, in violation of this section shall be fined not more than $1,000 or imprisoned for not more than one year, or both. For the purposes of this section "labor organization" means any organization of any kind, or any agency or employee representation committee or plan, in which employees participate and which exists for the purpose, in whole or in part, of dealing with employers concerning grievances, labor disputes, wages, rates of pay, hours of employment, or conditions of work.

STRIKES BY GOVERNMENT EMPLOYEES

SEC. 305. It shall be unlawful for any individual employed by the United States or any agency thereof including wholly owned Government corporations to participate in any strike. Any individual employed by the United States or by any such agency who strikes shall be discharged immediately from his employment, and shall forfeit his civil-service status, if any, and shall not be eligible for reemployment for three years by the United States or any such agency.

TITLE IV

CREATION OF JOINT COMMITTEE TO STUDY AND REPORT ON BASIC PROBLEMS AFFECTING FRIENDLY LABOR RELATIONS AND PRODUCTIVITY

SEC. 401. There is hereby established a joint congressional committee to be known as the Joint Committee on Labor-Management Relations (hereafter referred to as the committee), and to be composed of seven Members of the Senate Committee on Labor and Public Welfare to be appointed by the President pro tempore of the Senate, and seven Members of the House of Representatives Committee on Education and Labor, to be appointed by the Speaker of the House of

Representatives. A vacancy in membership of the committee shall not affect the powers of the remaining members to execute the functions of the committee, and shall be filled in the same manner as the original selection. The committee shall select a chairman and a vice chairman from among its members.

SEC. 402. The committee, acting as a whole or by subcommittee, shall conduct a thorough study and investigation of the entire field of labor-management relations including but not limited to—

(1) the means by which permanent friendly co-operation between employers and employees and stability of labor relations may be secured throughout the United States.

(2) the means by which the individual employee may achieve a greater productivity and higher wages, including plans for guaranteed annual wages, incentive, profit-sharing and bonus systems;

(3) the internal organization and administration of labor unions, with special attention to the impact on individuals of collective agreements requiring membership in unions as a condition of employment;

(4) the labor relations policies and practices of employers and associations of employers;

(5) the desirability of welfare funds for the benefit of employees and their relation to the social-security system;

(6) the methods and procedures for best carrying out the collective-bargaining processes, with special attention to the effects of industry-wide or regional bargaining upon the national economy;

(7) the administration and operation of existing Federal laws relating to labor relations; and

(8) such other problems and subjects in the field of labor-management relations as the committee deems appropriate.

SEC. 403. The committee shall report to the Senate and the House of Representatives not later than March 15, 1948, the results of its study and investigation, together with such recommendations as to necessary legislation and such other recommendations as it may deem advisable and shall make its final report not later than January 2, 1949.

SEC. 404. The committee shall have the power, without regard to the civil-service laws and the Classification Act of 1923, as amended, to employ and fix the compensation of such officers, experts, and employees as it deems necessary for the performance of its duties, including consultants who shall receive compensation at a rate not to exceed $35 for each day actually spent by them in the work of the committee, together with their necessary travel and subsistence expenses. The committee is further authorized, with the consent of the head of the department or agency concerned to utilize the services, information, facilities, and personnel of all agencies in the executive branch of the Government and may request the governments of the several States, representatives of business, industry, finance, and labor, and such other persons, agencies, organizations, and instrumentalities as it deems appropriate to attend its hearings and to give and present information, advice, and recommendations.

SEC. 405. The committee, or any subcommittee thereof, is authorized to hold such hearings; to sit and act at such times and places during the sessions, recesses, and adjourned periods of the Eightieth Congress; to require by subpoena or otherwise the attendance of such witnesses and the production of such books, papers, and documents; to administer oaths; to take such testimony; to have such printing and binding done; and to make such expenditures within the amount appropriated therefor; as it deems advisable. The cost of stenographic services in reporting such hearings shall not be in excess of 25 cents per one hundred words. Subpoenas shall be issued under the signature of the chairman or vice chairman of the

committee and shall be served by any person designated by them.

SEC. 406. The members of the committee shall be reimbursed for travel, subsistence, and other necessary expenses incurred by them in the performance of the duties vested in the committee, other than expenses in connection with meetings of the committee held in the District of Columbia during such times as the Congress is in session.

SEC. 407. There is hereby authorized to be appropriated the sum of $150,000, or so much thereof as may be necessary, to carry out the provisions of this title, to be disbursed by the Secretary of the Senate on vouchers signed by the chairman.

TITLE V

DEFINITIONS

SEC. 501. When used in this Act—

(1) The term "industry affecting commerce" means any industry or activity in commerce or in which a labor dispute would burden or obstruct commerce or tend to burden or obstruct commerce or the free flow of commerce.

(2) The term "strike" includes any strike or other concerted stoppage of work by employees (including a stoppage by reason of the expiration of a collective-bargaining agreement) and any concerted slow-down or other concerted interruption of operations by employees.

(3) The terms "commerce," "labor disputes," "employer," "employee," "labor organization," "representative," "person," and "supervisor" shall have the same meaning when used in the National Labor Relations Act as amended by this Act.

SAVING PROVISION. SEC. 502. Nothing in this Act shall be construed to require an individual employee to render labor or service without his consent, nor shall anything in this Act be construed to make the quitting of his labor by an individual employee an illegal act; nor shall any court issue any process to compel the performance by an individual employee of such labor or service, without his consent; nor shall the quitting of labor by an employee or employees in good faith because of abnormally dangerous conditions for work at this place of employment of such employee or employees be deemed a strike under this Act.

SEPARABILITY. SEC. 503. If any provision of this Act, or the application of such provision to any person or circumstance, shall be held invalid, the remainder of this Act, or the application of such provision to persons or circumstances other than those as to which it is held invalid, shall not be affected thereby.

APPENDIX F

THE LANDRUM-GRIFFIN ACT

73 Stat. 519

Labor-Management Reporting and Disclosure Act of 1959

An Act

DECLARATION OF FINDINGS, PURPOSES, AND POLICY. SEC. 2. (a) The Congress finds that, in the public interest, it continues to be the responsibility of the Federal Government to protect employees' rights to organize, choose their own representatives, bargain collectively, and otherwise engage in concerted activities for their mutual aid or protection; that the relations between employers and labor organizations and the millions of workers they represent have a substantial impact on the commerce of the Nations; and that in order to accomplish the objective of a free flow of commerce it is essential that labor organizations, employers, and their officials adhere to the highest standards of responsibility and ethical conduct in administering the affairs of their organizations, particularly as they affect labor-management relations.

(b) The Congress further finds, from recent investigations in the labor and management fields, that there have been a number of instances of breach of trust, corruption, disregard of the rights of individual employees, and other failures to observe high standards of responsibility and ethical conduct which require further and supplementary legislation that will afford necessary protection of the rights and interests of employees and the public generally as they relate to the activities of labor organizations, employers, labor relations consultants, and their officers and representatives.

(c) The Congress, therefore, further finds and declares that the enactment of this Act is necessary to eliminate or prevent improper practices on the part of labor organizations, employers, labor relations consultants, and their officers and representatives which distort and defeat the policies of the Labor Management Relations Act, 1947, as amended, and the Railway Labor Act, as amended, and have the tendency or necessary effect of burdening or obstructing commerce by (1) impairing the efficiency, safety, or operation of the instrumentalities of commerce; (2) occurring in the current of commerce; (3) materially affecting, restraining, or controlling the flow of raw materials or manufactured or processed goods into or from the channels of commerce, or the

745

prices of such materials or goods in commerce; or (4) causing diminution of employment and wages in such volume as substantially to impair or disrupt the market for goods flowing into or from the channels of commerce.

DEFINITIONS. SEC. 3. For the purposes of titles I, II, III, IV, V (except section 505), and VI of this Act—

(a) "Commerce" means trade, traffic, commerce, transportation, transmission, or communication among the several States or between any State and any place outside thereof.

(b) "State" includes any State of the United States, the District of Columbia, Puerto Rico, the Virgin Islands, American Samoa, Guam, Wake Island, the Canal Zone, and Outer Continental Shelf lands defined in the Outer Continental Shelf Lands Act (43 U.S.C. 1331–1343).

(c) "Industry affecting commerce" means any activity, business, or industry in commerce or in which a labor dispute would hinder or obstruct commerce or the free flow of commerce and includes any activity or industry "affecting commerce" within the meaning of the Labor Management Relations Act, 1947, as amended, or the Railway Labor Act, as amended.

(d) "Person" includes one or more individuals, labor organizations, partnerships, associations, corporations, legal representatives, mutual companies, joint-stock companies, trusts, unincorporated organizations, trustees, trustees in bankruptcy, or receivers.

(e) "Employer" means any employer or any group or association of employers engaged in an industry affecting commerce (1) which is, with respect to employees engaged in an industry affecting commerce, an employer within the meaning of any law of the United States relating to the employment of any employees or (2) which may deal with any labor organization concerning grievances, labor disputes, wages, rates of pay, hours of employment, or conditions of work, and includes any person acting directly or indirectly as an employer or as an agent of an employer in relation to an employee but does not include the United States or any corporation wholly owned by the Government of the United States or any State or political subdivision thereof.

(f) "Employee" means any individual employed by an employer, and includes any individual whose work has ceased as a consequence of, or in connection with, any current labor dispute or because of any unfair labor practice or because of exclusion or expulsion from a labor organization in any manner or for any reason inconsistent with the requirements of this Act.

(g) "Labor dispute" includes any controversy concerning terms, tenure, or conditions of employment, or concerning the association or representation of persons in negotiating, fixing, maintaining, changing, or seeking to arrange terms or conditions of employment, regardless of whether the disputants stand in the proximate relation of employer and employee.

(h) "Trusteeship" means any receivership, trusteeship, or other method of supervision or control whereby a labor organization suspends the autonomy otherwise available to a subordinate body under its constitution or bylaws.

(i) "Labor organization" means a labor organization engaged in an industry affecting commerce and includes any organization of any kind, any agency, or employee representation committee, group, association, or plan so engaged in which employees participate and which exists for the purpose, in whole or in part, of dealing with employers concerning grievances, labor disputes, wages, rates of pay, hours, or other terms or conditions of employment, and any conference, general committee, joint or system board, or joint council so engaged which is subordinate to a national or international labor organization, other than a State or local central body.

(j) A labor organization shall be deemed to be engaged in an industry affecting commerce if it—

1. is the certified representative of employees under the provisions of the National Labor Relations Act, as amended, or the Railway Labor Act, as amended; or
2. although not certified, is a national or international labor organization or a local labor organization recognized or acting as the representative of employees of an employer or employers engaged in an industry affecting commerce; or
3. has chartered a local labor organization or subsidiary body which is representing or actively seeking to represent employees or employers within the meaning of paragraph (1) or (2); or
4. has been chartered by a labor organization representing or actively seeking to represent employees within the meaning of paragraph (1) or (2) as the local or subordinate body through which such employees may enjoy membership or become affiliated with such labor organization; or
5. is a conference, general committee, joint or system board, or joint council, subordinate to a national or international labor organization, which includes a labor organization engaged in an industry affecting commerce within the meaning of any of the preceding paragraphs of this subsection, other than a State or local central body.

(k) "Secret ballot" means the expression by ballot, voting machine, or otherwise, but in no event by proxy, of a choice with respect to any election or vote taken upon any matter, which is cast in such a manner that the person expressing such choice cannot be identified with the choice expressed.

(l) "Trust in which a labor organization is interested" means a trust or other fund or organization (1) which was created or established by a labor organization, or one of more of the trustees or one or more members of the governing body of which is selected or appointed by a labor organization, and (2) a primary purpose of which is to provide benefits for the members of such labor organization or their beneficiaries.

(m) "Labor relations consultant" means any person who, for compensation, advises or represents an employer, employer organization, or labor organization concerning employee organizing, concerted activities, or collective bargaining activities.

(n) "Officer" means any constitutional officer, any person authorized to perform the functions of president, vice president, secretary, treasurer, or other executive functions of a labor organization, and any member of its executive board or similar governing body.

(o) "Member" or "member in good standing," when used in reference to a labor organization, includes any person who has fulfilled the requirements for membership in such organization, and who neither has voluntarily withdrawn from membership nor has been expelled or suspended from membership after appropriate proceedings consistent with lawful provisions of the constitution and bylaws of such organization.

(p) "Secretary" means the Secretary of Labor.

(q) "Officer, agent, shop steward, or other representative," when used with respect to a labor organization, includes elected officials and key administrative personnel, whether elected or appointed (such as business agents, heads of departments or major units, and organizers who exercise substantial independent authority), but does not include salaried nonsupervisory professional staff, stenographic, and service personnel.

(r) "District court of the United States" means a United States district court and a United States court of any place subject to the jurisdiction of the United States.

TITLE I

BILL OF RIGHTS OF MEMBERS OF LABOR ORGANIZATIONS

BILL OF RIGHTS. SEC. 101. (a)(1) EQUAL RIGHTS.—Every member of a labor organization shall have equal rights and privileges within such organization to nominate candidates, to vote in elections or referendums of the labor organization, to attend membership meetings, and to participate in the deliberations and voting upon the business of such meetings, subject to reasonable rules and regulations in such organization's constitution and bylaws.

(2) FREEDOM OF SPEECH AND ASSEMBLY. –Every member of any labor organization shall have the right to meet and assemble freely with other members; and to express any views, arguments, or opinions; and to express at meetings of the labor organization his views, upon candidates in an election of the labor organization or upon any business properly before the meeting, subject to the organization's established and reasonable rules pertaining to the conduct of meetings: *Provided,* That nothing herein shall be construed to impair the right of a labor organization to adopt and enforce reasonable rules as to the responsibility of every member toward the organization as an institution and to his refraining from conduct that would interfere with its performance of its legal or contractual obligations.

(3) DUES, INITIATION FEES, AND ASSESS-MENTS.–Except in the case of a federation of national or international labor organizations, the rates of dues and initiation fees payable by members of any labor organization in effect on the date of enactment of this Act shall not be increased, and no general or special assessment shall be levied upon such members, except—

A. in the case of a local labor organization, (i) by majority vote by secret ballot of the members in good standing voting at a general or special membership meeting, after reasonable notice of the intention to vote upon such question, or (ii) by majority vote of the members in good standing voting in a membership referendum conducted by secret ballot; or
B. in the case of a labor organization, other than a local labor organization or a federation of national or international labor organizations, (i) by majority vote of the delegates voting at a regular convention, or at a special convention of such labor organization held upon not less than thirty days' written notice to the principal office of each local or constituent labor organization entitled to such notice, or (ii) by majority vote of the members in good standing of such labor organization voting in a membership referendum conducted by secret ballot, or (iii) by majority vote of the members of the executive board or similar governing body of such labor organization, pursuant to express authority contained in the constitution and bylaws of such labor organization: *Provided,* That such action on the part of the executive board or similar governing body shall be effective only until the next regular convention of such labor organization.

(4) PROTECTION OF THE RIGHT TO SUE. –No labor organization shall limit the right of any member thereof to institute an action in any court, or in a proceeding before any administrative agency, irrespective of whether or not the labor organization or its officers are named as defendants or respondents in such action or proceeding, or the right of any member of a labor organization to appear as a witness in any judicial, administrative, or legislative proceeding, or to petition any legislature or to communicate with any legislator: *Provided,* That any such member may be required to exhaust reasonable hearing procedures (but not to exceed a four-month lapse of time) within such organization, before instituting legal or administrative proceedings against such organizations or any officer thereof: *And provided further,* That no interested employer or employer association shall directly or indirectly finance, encourage, or participate in, except as a party, any such action, proceeding, appearance, or petition.

(5) SAFEGUARDS AGAINST IMPROPER DISCI-PLINARY ACTION.–No member of any labor organization may be fined, suspended, expelled, or otherwise disciplined except for nonpayment of dues by such organization or by any officer thereof unless such member has been (A) served with written specific

charges; (B) given a reasonable time to prepare his defense; (C) afforded a full and fair hearing.

(b) Any provision of the constitution and bylaws of any labor organization which is inconsistent with the provisions of this section shall be of no force or effect.

CIVIL ENFORCEMENT. SEC. 102. Any person whose rights secured by the provisions of this title have been infringed by any violation of this title may bring a civil action in a district court of the United States for such relief (including injunctions) as may be appropriate. Any such action against a labor organization shall be brought in the district court of the United States for the district where the alleged violation occurred, or where the principal office of such labor organization is located.

RETENTION OF EXISTING RIGHTS. SEC. 103. Nothing contained in this title shall limit the rights and remedies of any member of a labor organization under any State or Federal law or before any court or other tribunal, or under the constitution and bylaws of any labor organization.

RIGHT TO COPIES OF COLLECTIVE BARGAINING AGREEMENTS. SEC. 104. It shall be the duty of the secretary or corresponding principal officer of each labor organization, in the case of a local labor organization, to forward a copy of each collective bargaining agreement made by such labor organization with any employer to any employee who requests such a copy and whose rights as such employee are directly affected by such agreement, and in the case of a labor organization other than a local labor organization, to forward a copy of any such agreement to each constituent unit which has members directly affected by such agreement; and such officer shall maintain at the principal office of the labor organization of which he is an officer copies of any such agreement made or received by such labor organization, which copies shall be available for inspection by any member or by any employee whose

rights are affected by such agreement. The provisions of section 210 shall be applicable in the enforcement of this section.

INFORMATION AS TO ACT. SEC. 105. Every labor organization shall inform its members concerning the provisions of this Act.

TITLE II

REPORTING BY LABOR ORGANIZATIONS, OFFICERS AND EMPLOYEES OF LABOR ORGANIZATIONS, AND EMPLOYERS

REPORT OF LABOR ORGANIZATIONS. SEC. 201. (a) Every labor organization shall adopt a constitution and bylaws and shall file a copy thereof with the Secretary, together with a report, signed by its president and secretary or corresponding principal officers, containing the following information—

1. the name of the labor organization, its mailing address, and any other address at which it maintains its principal office or at which it keeps the records referred to in this title;
2. the name and title of each of its officers;
3. the initiation fee or fees required from a new or transferred member and fees for work permits required by the reporting labor organization;
4. the regular dues or fees or other periodic payments required to remain a member of the reporting labor organization; and
5. detailed statements, or references to specific provisions of documents filed under this subsection which contain such statements, showing the provision made and procedures followed with respect to each of the following: (A) qualifications for or restrictions on membership, (B) levying of assessments, (C) participation in insurance or other benefit plans, (D) authorization for disbursement of funds of the labor organization, (E) audit of financial transactions of the labor organization, (F) the calling of regular and special meetings, (G) the

selection of officers and stewards and of any representatives to other bodies composed of labor organizations' representatives, with a specific statement of the manner in which each officer was elected, appointed, or otherwise selected, (H) discipline or removal of officers or agents for breaches of their trust, (I) imposition of fines, suspensions, and expulsions of members, including the grounds for such action and any provision made for notice, hearing, judgment on the evidence, and appeal procedures, (J) authorization for bargaining demands, (K) ratification of contract terms, (L) authorization for strikes, and (M) issuance of work permits. Any change in the information required by this subsection shall be reported to the Secretary at the time the reporting labor organization files with the Secretary the annual financial report required by subsection (b).

(b) Every labor organization shall file annually with the Secretary a financial report signed by its president and treasurer or corresponding principal officers containing the following information in such detail as may be necessary accurately to disclose its financial condition and operations for its preceding fiscal year—

1. assets and liabilities at the beginning and end of the fiscal year;
2. receipts of any kind and the sources thereof;
3. salary, allowances, and other direct or indirect disbursements (including reimbursed expenses) to each officer and also to each employee who, during such fiscal year, received more than $10,000 in the aggregate from such labor organization and any other labor organization affiliated with it or with which it is affiliated, or which is affiliated with the same national or international labor organization;
4. direct and indirect loans made to any officer, employee, or member, which aggregated more than $250 during the fiscal year, together with a statement of the purpose, security, if any, and arrangements for repayment;
5. direct and indirect loans to any business enterprise, together with a statement of the purpose, security, if any, and arrangements for repayment; and

6. other disbursements made by it including the purposes thereof;

all in such categories as the Secretary may prescribe.

(c) Every labor organization required to submit a report under this title shall make available the information required to be contained in such report to all of its members, and every such labor organization and its officers shall be under a duty enforceable at the suit of any member of such organization in any State court of competent jurisdiction or in the district court of the United States for the district in which such labor organization maintains its principal office, to permit such member for just cause to examine any books, records, and accounts necessary to verify such report. The court in such action may, in its discretion, in addition to any judgment awarded to the plaintiff or plaintiffs, allow a reasonable attorney's fee to be paid by the defendant, and costs of the action.

(d) Subsections (f), (g), and (h) of section 9 of the National Labor Relations Act, as amended, are hereby repealed.

(e) Clause (i) of section 8(a)(3) of the National Labor Relations Act, as amended, is amended by striking out the following: "and has at the time the agreement was made or within the preceding twelve months received from the Board a notice of compliance with sections 9 (f), (g), (h)".

REPORT OF OFFICERS AND EMPLOYEES OF LABOR ORGANIZATIONS. SEC. 202. (a) Every officer of a labor organization and every employee of a labor organization (other than an employee performing exclusively clerical or custodial services) shall file with the Secretary a signed report listing and describing for his preceding fiscal year—

1. any stock, bond, security, or other interest, legal or equitable, which he or his spouse or minor child directly or indirectly held in, and any income or any other benefit with monetary

value (including reimbursed expenses) which he or his spouse or minor child derived directly or indirectly from, an employer whose employees such labor organization represents or is actively seeking to represent, except payments and other benefits received as a bona fide employee of such employer;

2. any transaction in which he or his spouse or minor child engaged, directly or indirectly, involving any stock, bond, security, or loan to or from, or other legal or equitable interest in the business of an employer whose employees such labor organization represents or is actively seeking to represent;

3. any stock, bond, security, or other interest, legal or equitable, which he or his spouse or minor child directly or indirectly held in, and any income or any other benefit with monetary value (including reimbursed expenses) which he or his spouse or minor child directly or indirectly derived from, any business a substantial part of which consists of buying from, selling or leasing to, or otherwise dealing with, the business of an employer whose employees such labor organization represents or is actively seeking to represent;

4. any stock, bond, security, or other interest, legal or equitable, which he or his spouse or minor child directly or indirectly held in, and any income or any other benefit with monetary value (including reimbursed expenses) which he or his spouse or minor child directly or indirectly derived from, a business any part of which consists of buying from, or selling or leasing directly or indirectly to, or otherwise dealing with such labor organization;

5. any direct or indirect business transaction or arrangement between him or his spouse or minor child and any employer whose employees his organization represents or is actively seeking to represent, except work performed and payments and benefits received as a bona fide employee of such employer and except purchases and sales of goods or services in the regular course of business at prices generally available to any employee of such employer; and

6. any payment of money or other thing of value (including reimbursed expenses) which he or his spouse or minor child received directly or indirectly from any employer or any person who acts as a labor relations consultant to an employer, except payments of the kinds referred to in section 302(c) of the Labor Management Relations Act, 1947, as amended.

(b) The provisions of paragraphs (1), (2), (3), (4), and (5) of subsection (a) shall not be construed to require any such officer or employee to report his bona fide investments in securities traded on a securities exchange registered as a national securities exchange under the Securities Exchange Act of 1934, in shares in an investment company registered under the Investment Company Act of 1940, or in securities of a public utility holding company registered under the Public Utility Holding Company Act of 1935, or to report any income derived therefrom.

(c) Nothing contained in this section shall be construed to require any officer or employee of a labor organization to file a report under subsection (a) unless he or his spouse or minor child holds or has held an interest, has received income or any other benefit with monetary value or a loan, or has engaged in a transaction described therein.

REPORT OF EMPLOYERS. SEC. 203. (a) Every employer who in any fiscal year made—

1. any payment or loan, direct or indirect, of money or other thing of value (including reimbursed expenses), or any promise or agreement therefor, to any labor organization or officer, agent, shop steward, or other representative of a labor organization, or employee of any labor organization, except (A) payments or loans made by any national or State bank, credit union, insurance company, savings and loan association or other credit institution and (B) payments of the kind referred to in section 302(c) of the Labor Management Relations Act, 1947, as amended;

2. any payment (including reimbursed expenses) to any of his employees, or any group or committee of such employees, for the purpose of causing such employee or group or committee of employees to persuade other employees to

exercise or not to exercise, or as the manner of exercising, the right to organize and bargain collectively through representatives of their own choosing unless such payments were contemporaneously or previously disclosed to such other employees;

3. any expenditure, during the fiscal year, where an object thereof, directly or indirectly, is to interfere with, restrain, or coerce employees in the exercise of the right to organize and bargain collectively through representatives of their own choosing, or is to obtain information concerning the activities of employees or a labor organization in connection with a labor dispute involving such employer, except for use solely in conjunction with an administrative or arbitral proceeding or a criminal or civil judicial proceeding;

4. any agreement or arrangement with a labor relations consultant or other independent contractor or organization pursuant to which such person undertakes activities where an object thereof, directly or indirectly, is to persuade employees to exercise or not to exercise, or persuade employees as to the manner of exercising, the right to organize and bargain collectively through representatives of their own choosing, or undertakes to supply such employer with information concerning the activities of employees or a labor organization in connection with a labor dispute involving such employer, except information for use solely in conjunction with an administrative or arbitral proceeding or a criminal or civil judicial proceeding; or

5. any payment (including reimbursed expenses) pursuant to an agreement or arrangement described in subdivision (4);

shall file with the Secretary a report, in a form prescribed by him, signed by its president and treasurer or corresponding principal officers showing in detail the date and amount of each such payment, loan, promise, agreement, or arrangement and the name, address, and position, if any, in any firm or labor organization of the person to whom it was made and a full explanation of the circumstances of all such payments, including the terms of any agreement or understanding pursuant to which they were made.

(d) Every person who pursuant to any agreement or arrangement with an employer undertakes activities where an object thereof is, directly or indirectly—

1. to persuade employees to exercise or not to exercise, or persuade employees as to the manner of exercising, the right to organize and bargain collectively through representatives of their own choosing; or

2. to supply an employer with information concerning the activities of employees or a labor organization in connection with a labor dispute involving such employer, except information for use solely in conjunction with an administrative or arbitral proceeding or a criminal or civil judicial proceeding;

shall file within thirty days after entering into such agreement or arrangement a report with the Secretary, signed by its president and treasurer or corresponding principal officers, containing the name under which such person is engaged in doing business and the address of its principal office, and a detailed statement of the terms and conditions of such agreement or arrangement. Every such person shall file annually, with respect to each fiscal year during which payments were made as a result of such an agreement or arrangement, a report with the Secretary, signed by its president and treasurer or corresponding principal officers, containing a statement (A) of its receipts of any kind from employers on account of labor relations advice or services, designating the sources thereof, and (B) of its disbursements of any kind, in connection with such services and the purposes thereof. In each such case such information shall be set forth in such categories as the Secretary may prescribe.

(c) Nothing in this section shall be construed to require any employer or other person to file a report covering the services of such person by reason of his giving or agreeing to give advice to such employer or representing or agreeing to represent such employer before any court, administrative agency, or tribunal of arbitration or engaging or agreeing to engage in collective bargaining on behalf of such employer with respect to wages, hours, or other terms or conditions of employment or the negotiation of an agreement or any question arising thereunder.

(d) Nothing contained in this section shall be construed to require an employer to file a report under subsection (a) unless he has made an expenditure, payment, loan, agreement, or arrangement of the kind described therein. Nothing contained in this section shall be construed to require any other person to file a report under subsection (b) unless he was a party to an agreement or arrangement of the kind described therein.

(e) Nothing contained in this section shall be construed to require any regular officer, supervisor, or employee of an employer to file a report in connection with services rendered to such employer nor shall any employer be required to file a report covering expenditures made to any regular officer, supervisor, or employee of an employer as compensation for service as a regular officer, supervisor, or employee of such employer.

(f) Nothing contained in this section shall be construed as an amendment to, or modification of the rights protected by, section 8(c) of the National Labor Relations Act, as amended.

(g) The term "interfere with, restrain, or coerce" as used in this section means interference, restraint, and coercion which, if done with respect to the exercise of rights guaranteed in section 7 of the National Labor Relations Act, as amended, would, under section 8(a) of such Act, constitute an unfair labor practice.

ATTORNEY-CLIENT COMMUNICATIONS EXEMPTED. SEC. 204. Nothing contained in this Act shall be construed to require an attorney who is a member in good standing of the bar of any State, to include in any report required to be filed pursuant to the provisions of this Act any information which was lawfully communicated to such attorney by any of his clients in the course of a legitimate attorney-client relationship.

REPORTS MADE PUBLIC INFORMATION. SEC. 205. (a) The contents of the reports and documents filed with the Secretary pursuant to sections 201, 202, and 203 shall be public information, and the Secretary may publish any information and data which he obtains pursuant to the provisions of this title. The Secretary may use the information and data for statistical and research purposes, and compile and publish such studies, analyses, reports, and surveys based thereon as he may deem appropriate.

(b) The Secretary shall by regulation make reasonable provision for the inspection and examination, on the request of any person, of the information and data contained in any report or other document filed with him pursuant to section 201, 202, or 203.

(c) The Secretary shall by regulation provide for the furnishing by the Department of Labor of copies of reports or other documents filed with the Secretary pursuant to this title, upon payment of a charge based upon the cost of the service. The Secretary shall make available without payment of a charge, or require any person to furnish, to such State agency as is designated by law or by the Governor of the State in which such person has his principal place of business or headquarters, upon request of the Governor of such State, copies of any reports and documents filed by such person with the Secretary pursuant to section 201, 202, or 203, or of information and data contained therein. No person shall be required by reason of any law of any State to furnish to any officer or agency of such State any information included in a report filed by such person with the Secretary pursuant to the provisions of this title, if a copy of such report, or of the portion thereof containing such information, is furnished to such officer or agency. All moneys received in payment of such charges fixed by the Secretary pursuant to this subsection shall be deposited in the general fund of the Treasury.

RETENTION OF RECORDS. SEC. 206. Every person required to file any report under this title shall maintain records on the matters required to be reported which will provide in sufficient detail the necessary basic information and data from which the documents filed with the Secretary may be verified, explained or clarified, and checked for accuracy and completeness, and shall include vouchers, worksheets, receipts, and applicable resolutions, and shall keep such records available for examination for a period of not less than five years after the filing of the documents based on the information which they contain.

EFFECTIVE DATE. SEC. 207. (a) Each labor organization shall file the initial report required under section 201(a) within ninety days after the date on which it first becomes subject to this Act.

(b) Each person required to file a report under section 201(b), 202, 203(a), or the second sentence of 203(b) shall file such report within ninety days after the end of each of its fiscal years; except that where such person is subject to section 201(b), 202, 203(a), or the second sentence of 203(b), as the case may be, for only a portion of such a fiscal year (because the date of enactment of this Act occurs during such person's fiscal year or such person becomes subject to this Act during its fiscal year) such person may consider that portion as the entire fiscal year in making such report.

RULES AND REGULATIONS. SEC. 208. The Secretary shall have authority to issue, amend, and rescind rules and regulations prescribing the form and publication of reports required to be filed under this title and such other reasonable rules and regulations (including rules prescribing reports concerning trusts in which a labor organization is interested) as he may find necessary to prevent the circumvention or evasion of such report-

ing requirements. In exercising his power under this section the Secretary shall prescribe by general rule simplified reports for labor organizations or employers for whom he finds that by virtue of their size a detailed report would be unduly burdensome, but the Secretary may revoke such provision for simplified forms of any labor organization or employer if he determines, after such investigation as he deems proper and due notice and opportunity for a hearing, that the purposes of this section would be served thereby.

CRIMINAL PROVISIONS. SEC. 209. (a) Any person who willfully violates this title shall be fined not more than $10,000 or imprisoned for not more than one year, or both.

(b) Any person who makes a false statement or representation of a material fact, knowing it to be false, or who knowingly fails to disclose a material fact, in any document, report, or other information required under the provisions of this title shall be fined not more than $10,000 or imprisoned for not more than one year, or both.

(c) Any person who willfully makes a false entry in or willfully conceals, withholds, or destroys any books, records, reports, or statements required to be kept by any provision of this title shall be fined not more than $10,000 or imprisoned for not more than one year, or both.

(d) Each individual required to sign reports under sections 201 and 203 shall be personally responsible for the filing of such reports and for any statement contained therein which he knows to be false.

CIVIL ENFORCEMENT. SEC. 210. Whenever it shall appear that any person has violated or is about to violate any of the provisions of this title, the Secretary may bring a civil action for such relief (including injunctions) as may be appropriate. Any such action may be brought in the district court of the United States where the violation occurred or, at the option of the parties, in the United States District Court for the District of Columbia.

TITLE III

TRUSTEESHIPS

REPORTS. SEC. 301. (a) Every labor organization which has or assumes trusteeship over any subordinate labor organization shall file with the Secretary within thirty days after the date of the enactment of this Act or the imposition of any such trusteeship, and semiannually thereafter, a report, signed by its president and treasurer or corresponding principal officers, as well as by the trustees of such subordinate labor organization, containing the following information: (1) the name and address of the subordinate organization; (2) the date of establishing the trusteeship; (3) a detailed statement of the reason or reasons for establishing or continuing the trusteeship; and (4) the nature and extent of participation by the membership of the subordinate organization in the selection of delegates to represent such organization in regular or special conventions or other policy-determining bodies and in the election of officers of the labor organization which has assumed trusteeship over such subordinate organization. The initial report shall also include a full and complete account of the financial condition of such subordinate organization as of the time trusteeship was assumed over it. During the continuance of a trusteeship the labor organization which has assumed trusteeship over a subordinate labor organization shall file on behalf of the subordinate labor organization the annual financial report required by section 201(b) signed by the president and treasurer or corresponding principal officers of the labor organization which has assumed such trusteeship and the trustees of the subordinate labor organization.

(b) The provisions of section 201(c), 205, 206, 208, and 210 shall be applicable to reports filed under this title.

(c) Any person who willfully violates this section shall be fined not more than $10,000 or imprisoned for not more than one year, or both.

(d) Any person who makes a false statement or representation of a material fact, knowing it to be false, or who knowingly fails to disclose a material fact, in any report required under the provisions of this section or willfully makes any false entry in or willfully withholds, conceals, or destroys any documents, books, records, reports, or statements upon which such report is based, shall be fined not more than $10,000 or imprisoned for not more than one year, or both.

(e) Each individual required to sign a report under this section shall be personally responsible for the filing of such report and for any statement contained therein which he knows to be false.

PURPOSES FOR WHICH A TRUSTEESHIP MAY BE ESTABLISHED. SEC. 302. Trusteeships shall be established and administered by a labor organization over a subordinate body only in accordance with the constitution and bylaws of the organization which has assumed trusteeship over the subordinate body and for the purpose of correcting corruption or financial malpractice, assuring the performance of collective bargaining agreements or other duties of a bargaining representative, restoring democratic procedures, or otherwise carrying out the legitimate objects of such labor organization.

UNLAWFUL ACTS RELATING TO LABOR ORGANIZATION UNDER TRUSTEESHIP. SEC. 303. (a) During any period when a subordinate body of a labor organization is in trusteeship, it shall be unlawful (1) to count the vote of delegates from such body in any convention or election of officers of the labor organization unless the delegates have been chosen by secret ballot in an election in which all the members in good standing of such subordinate body were eligible to participate, or (2) to transfer to such organization any current receipts or other funds of the subordinate body except the normal per capita tax and assessments payable by subordinate bodies not in trusteeship: *Provided,* That nothing herein contained shall prevent the distribution of the assets of a labor organization in accordance with its constitution and bylaws upon the bona fide dissolution thereof.

(b) Any person who willfully violates this section shall be fined not more than $10,000 or imprisoned for not more than one year, or both.

ENFORCEMENT. SEC. 304. (a) Upon the written complaint of any member or subordinate body of a labor organization alleging that such organization has violated the provisions of this title (except section 301) the Secretary shall investigate the complaint and if the Secretary finds probable cause to believe that such violation has occurred and has not been remedied he shall, without disclosing the identity of the complainant, bring a civil action in any district court of the United States having jurisdiction of the labor organization for such relief (including injunctions) as may be appropriate. Any member or subordinate body of a labor organization affected by any violation of this title (except section 301) may bring a civil action in any district court of the United States having jurisdiction of the labor organization for such relief (including injunctions) as may be appropriate.

(b) For the purpose of actions under this section, district courts of the United States shall be deemed to have jurisdiction of a labor organization (1) in the district in which the principal office of such labor organization is located, or (2) in any district in which its duly authorized officers or agents are engaged in conducting the affairs of the trusteeship.

(c) In any proceeding pursuant to this section a trusteeship established by a labor organization in conformity with the procedural requirements of its constitution and bylaws and authorized or ratified after a fair hearing either before the executive board or before such other body as may be provided in accordance with its constitution or bylaws shall

be presumed valid for a period of eighteen months from the date of its establishment and shall not be subject to attack during such period except upon clear and convincing proof that the trusteeship was not established or maintained in good faith for a purpose allowable under section 302. After the expiration of eighteen months the trusteeship shall be presumed invalid in any such proceeding and its discontinuance shall be decreed unless the labor organization shall show by clear and convincing proof that the continuation of the trusteeship is necessary for a purpose allowable under section 302. In the latter event the court may dismiss the complaint or retain jurisdiction of the cause on such conditions and for such period as it deems appropriate.

REPORT TO CONGRESS. SEC. 305. The Secretary shall submit to the Congress at the expiration of three years from the date of enactment of this Act a report upon the operation of this title.

COMPLAINT BY SECRETARY. SEC. 306. The rights and remedies provided by this title shall be in addition to any and all other rights and remedies at law or in equity: *Provided,* That upon the filing of a complaint by the Secretary the jurisdiction of the district court over such trusteeship shall be exclusive and the final judgment shall be res judicata.

TITLE IV

ELECTIONS

TERMS OF OFFICE; ELECTION PROCEDURES. SEC. 401. (a) Every national or international labor organization, except a federation of national or international labor organizations, shall elect its officers not less often than once every five years either by secret ballot among the members in good standing or at a convention of delegates chosen by secret ballot.

(b) Every local labor organization shall elect its officers not less often than once every three years by secret ballot among the members in good standing.

(c) Every national or international labor organization, except a federation of national or international labor organizations, and every local labor organization, and its officers, shall be under a duty, enforceable at the suit of any bona fide candidate for office in such labor organization in the district court of the United States in which such labor organization maintains its principal office, to comply with all reasonable requests of any candidate to distribute by mail or otherwise at the candidate's expense campaign literature in aid of such person's candidacy to all members in good standing of such labor organization and to refrain from discrimination in favor of or against any candidate with respect to the use of lists of members, and whenever such labor organizations or its officers authorize the distribution by mail or otherwise to members of campaign literature on behalf of any candidate or of the labor organization itself with reference to such election, similar distribution at the request of any other bona fide candidate shall be made by such labor organization and its officers, with equal treatment as to the expense of such distribution. Every bona fide candidate shall have the right, once within 30 days prior to an election of a labor organization in which he is a candidate, to inspect a list containing the names and last known addresses of all members of the labor organization who are subject to a collective bargaining agreement requiring membership therein as a condition of employment, which list shall be maintained and kept at the principal office of such labor organization by a designated official thereof. Adequate safeguards to insure a fair election shall be provided, including the right of any candidate to have an observer at the polls and at the counting of the ballots.

(d) Officers of intermediate bodies, such as general committees, system boards, joint boards, or joint councils, shall be elected not less often than once every four years by secret ballot among the members in good standing or by labor organization officers representative of such members who have been elected by secret ballot.

(e) In any election required by this section which is to be held by secret ballot a reasonable opportunity shall be given for the nomination of candidates and every member in good standing shall be eligible to be a candidate and to hold office (subject to section 504 and to reasonable qualifications uniformly imposed) and shall have the right to vote for or otherwise support the candidate or candidates of his choice, without being subject to penalty, discipline, or improper interference or reprisal of any kind by such organization or any member thereof. Not less than fifteen days prior to the election notice thereof shall be mailed to each member at his last known home address. Each member in good standing shall be entitled to one vote. No member whose dues have been withheld by his employer for payment to such organization pursuant to his voluntary authorization provided for in a collective bargaining agreement shall be declared ineligible to vote or be a candidate for office in such organization by reason of alleged delay or default in the payment of dues. The votes cast by members of each local labor organization shall be counted, and the results published, separately. The election officials designated in the constitution and bylaws or the secretary, if no other official is designated, shall preserve for one year the ballots and all other records pertaining to the election. The election shall be conducted in accordance with the constitution and bylaws of such organization insofar as they are not inconsistent with the provisions of this title.

(f) When officers are chosen by a convention of delegates elected by secret ballot, the convention shall be conducted in accordance with the constitution and bylaws of the labor organization insofar as they are not inconsistent with the provisions of this title. The officials designated in the constitution and bylaws or the secretary, if no other is designated, shall preserve for one year the credentials of the delegates and all minutes and other records of the convention pertaining to the election of officers.

(g) No moneys received by any labor organization by way of dues, assessment, or similar levy, and no moneys of an employer shall be contributed or applied to promote the candidacy of any person in an election subject to the provisions of this title. Such moneys of a labor organization may be utilized for notices, factual statements of issues not involving candidates, and other expenses necessary for the holding of an election.

(h) If the Secretary, upon application of any member of a local labor organization, finds after hearing in accordance with the Administrative Procedure Act that the constitution and bylaws of such labor organization do not provide an adequate procedure for the removal of an elected officer guilty of serious misconduct, such officer may be removed, for cause shown and after notice and hearing, by the members in good standing voting in a secret ballot conducted by the officers of such labor organization in accordance with its constitution and bylaws insofar as they are not inconsistent with the provisions of this title.

(i) The Secretary shall promulgate rules and regulations prescribing minimum standards and procedures for determining the adequacy of the removal procedures to which reference is made in subsection (h).

ENFORCEMENT. SEC. 402. (a) A member of a labor organization—

1. who has exhausted the remedies available under the constitution and bylaws of such organization and of any parent body, or
2. who has invoked such available remedies without obtaining a final decision within three calendar months after their invocation,

may file a complaint with the Secretary within one calendar month thereafter alleging the violation of any provision of section 401 (including violation of the constitution and bylaws of the labor organization pertaining to the election and removal of officers). The challenged election shall be presumed valid pending a final decision thereon (as hereinafter provided) and in the interim the affairs of the organization shall be conducted by the officers elected or in such other manner as its constitution and bylaws may provide.

(b) The Secretary shall investigate such complaint and, if he finds probable cause to believe that a violation of this title has occurred and has not been remedied, he shall, within sixty days after the filing of such complaint, bring a civil action against the labor organization as an entity in the district court of the United States in which such labor organization maintains its principal office to set aside the invalid election, if any, and to direct the conduct of an election or hearing and vote upon the removal of officers under the supervision of the Secretary and in accordance with the provisions of this title and such rules and regulations as the Secretary may prescribe. The court shall have power to take such action as it deems proper to preserve the assets of the labor organization.

(c) If, upon a preponderance of the evidence after a trial upon the merits, the court finds—

1. that an election has not been held within the time prescribed by section 401, or
2. that the violation of section 401 may have affected the outcome of an election,

the court shall declare the election, if any, to be void and direct the conduct of a new election under supervision of the Secretary and, so far as lawful and practicable, in conformity with the constitution and bylaws of the labor organization. The Secretary shall promptly certify to the court the names of the persons elected, and the court shall thereupon enter a decree declaring such persons to be the officers of the labor organization. If the proceeding is for the removal of officers pursuant to subsection (h) of section 401, the Secretary shall certify the results of the vote and the court shall enter a decree declaring whether such persons have been removed as officers of the labor organization.

(d) An order directing an election, dismissing a complaint, or designating elected officers of a labor organization shall be appealable in the same manner as the final judgment in a civil action, but an order directing an election shall not be stayed pending appeal.

APPLICATION OF OTHER LAWS. SEC. 403. No labor organization shall be required by law to conduct elections of officers with greater frequency or in a different form or manner than is required by its own constitution or bylaws, except as otherwise provided by this title. Existing rights and remedies to enforce the constitution and bylaws of a labor organization with respect to elections prior to the conduct thereof shall not be affected by the provisions of this title. The remedy provided by this title for challenging an election already conducted shall be exclusive.

EFFECTIVE DATE. SEC. 404. The provisions of this title shall become applicable—

1. ninety days after the date of enactment of this Act in the case of a labor organization whose constitution and bylaws can lawfully be modified or amended by action of its constitutional officers or governing body, or
2. where such modification can only be made by a constitutional convention of the labor organization, not later than the next constitutional convention of such labor organization after the date of enactment of this Act, or one year after such date, whichever is sooner. If no such convention is held within such one-year period, the executive board or similar governing body empowered to act for such labor organization

between conventions is empowered to make such interim constitutional changes as are necessary to carry out the provisions of this title.

TITLE V

SAFEGUARDS FOR LABOR ORGANIZATIONS

FIDUCIARY RESPONSIBILITY OF OFFICERS OF LABOR ORGANIZATIONS. SEC. 501. (a) The officers, agents, shop stewards, and other representatives of a labor organization occupy positions of trust in relation to such organization and its members as a group. It is, therefore, the duty of each such person, taking into account the special problems and functions of a labor organization, to hold its money and property solely for the benefit of the organization and its members and to manage, invest, and expend the same in accordance with its constitution and bylaws and any resolutions of the governing bodies adopted thereunder, to refrain from dealing with such organization as an adverse party or in behalf of an adverse party in any matter connected with his duties and from holding or acquiring any pecuniary or personal interest which conflicts with the interests of such organization, and to account to the organization for any profit received by him in whatever capacity in connection with transactions conducted by him or under his direction on behalf of the organization. A general exculpatory provision in the constitution and bylaws of such a labor organization or a general exculpatory resolution of a governing body purporting to relieve any such person of liability for breach of the duties declared by this section shall be void as against public policy.

(b) When any officer, agent, shop steward, or representative of any labor organization is alleged to have violated the duties declared in subsection (a) and the labor organization or its governing board or officers refuse or fail to sue or recover damages or secure an accounting or other appropriate relief within a reasonable time after being requested to do so by any member of the labor organization, such member may sue such officer, agent, shop steward, or representative in any district court of the United States or in any State court of competent jurisdiction to recover damages or secure an accounting or other appropriate relief for the benefit of the labor organization. No such proceeding shall be brought except upon leave of the court obtained upon verified application and for good cause shown, which application may be made ex parte. The trial judge may allot a reasonable part of the recovery in any action under this subsection to pay the fees of counsel prosecuting the suit at the instance of the member of the labor organization and to compensate such member for any expenses necessarily paid or incurred by him in connection with the litigation.

(c) Any person who embezzles, steals, or unlawfully and willfully abstracts or converts to his own use, or the use of another, any of the moneys, funds, securities, property, or other assets of a labor organization of which he is an officer, or by which he is employed, directly or indirectly, shall be fined not more than $10,000 or imprisoned for not more than five years, or both.

BONDING. SEC. 502. (a) Every officer, agent, shop steward, or other representative or employee of any labor organization (other than a labor organization whose property and annual financial receipts do not exceed $5,000 in value), or of a trust in which a labor organization is interested, who handles funds or other property thereof shall be bonded for the faithful discharge of his duties. The bond of each such person shall be fixed at the beginning of the organization's fiscal year and shall be in an amount not less than 10 per centum of the funds handled by him and his predecessor or predecessors, if any, during the preceding fiscal year, but in no case more than $500,000. If the labor organization or the trust in which a labor organization is interested does not have a preceding fiscal year, the amount of the bond shall be, in the case of a local labor organization, not less than $1,000, and in the case of any other labor organization or of a trust in which a labor organization is interested, not less than $10,000. Such bonds shall be individual or schedule in form, and shall have a corporate surety company as surety thereon. Any person who is not covered by such bonds shall not be permitted to receive, handle, disburse, or otherwise exercise custody or control of the funds or other property of a labor organization or of a trust in which a labor organization is interested. No such bond shall be placed through an agent or broker or with a surety company in which any labor organization or any officer, agent, shop steward, or other representative of a labor organization has any direct or indirect interest. Such surety company shall be a corporate surety which holds a grant of authority from the Secretary of the Treasury under the Act of July 30, 1947 (6 U.S.C. 6-13), as an acceptable surety on Federal bonds.

(b) Any person who willfully violates this section shall be fined not more than $10,000 or imprisoned for not more than one year, or both.

MAKING OF LOANS; PAYMENT OF FINES. SEC. 503. (a) No labor organization shall make directly or indirectly any loan or loans to any officer or employee of such organization which results in a total indebtedness on the part of such officer or employee to the labor organization in excess of $2,000.

(b) No labor organization or employer shall directly or indirectly pay the fine of any officer or employee convicted of any willful violation of this Act.

(c) Any person who willfully violates this section shall be fined not more than $5,000 or imprisoned for not more than one year, or both.

PROHIBITION AGAINST CERTAIN PERSONS HOLDING OFFICE. SEC. 504. (a) No person who is or has been a member of the Communist Party or who has been convicted of, or served any part of a prison term resulting from his conviction of, robbery, bribery, extortion, embezzlement, grand larceny, burglary, arson, violation of narcotics laws, murder, rape, assault with intent to kill, assault which inflicts grievous bodily injury, or a violation of title II or III of this Act, or conspiracy to commit any such crimes, shall serve—

1. as an officer, director, trustee, member of any executive board or similar governing body, business agent, manager, organizer, or other employee (other than as an employee performing exclusively clerical or custodial duties) of any labor organization, or
2. as a labor relations consultant to a person engaged in an industry or activity affecting commerce, or as an officer, director, agent, or employee (other than as an employee performing exclusively clerical or custodial duties) of any group or association of employers dealing with any labor organization,

during or for five years after the termination of his membership in the Communist Party, or for five years after such conviction or after the end of such imprisonment, unless prior to the end of such five-year period, in the case of a person so convicted or imprisoned, (A) his citizenship rights, having been revoked as a result of such conviction, have been fully restored, or (B) the Board of Parole of the United States Department of Justice determines that such person's service in any capacity referred to in clause (1) or (2) would not be contrary to the purposes of this Act. Prior to making any such determination the Board shall hold an administrative hearing and shall give notice of such proceeding by certified mail to the State, county, and Federal prosecuting officials in the jurisdiction or jurisdictions in which such person was convicted. The Board's determination in any such proceeding shall be final. No labor organization or officer thereof shall knowingly permit any person to assume or hold any office or paid position in violation of this subsection.

(b) Any person who willfully violates this section shall be fined not more than $10,000 or imprisoned for not more than one year, or both.

(c) For the purposes of this section, any person shall be deemed to have been "convicted" and under the disability of "conviction" from the date of the judgment of the trial court or the date of the final sustaining of such judgment on appeal, whichever is the later event, regardless of whether such conviction occurred before or after the date of enactment of this Act.

AMENDMENT TO SECTION 302, LABOR MANAGEMENT RELATIONS ACT, 1947. SEC. 505. Subsections (a), (b), and (c) of section 302 of the Labor Management Relations Act, 1947, as amended, are amended to read as follows:

"SEC. 302. (a) It shall be unlawful for any employer or association of employers or any person who acts as a labor relations expert, adviser, or consultant to an employer or who acts in the interest of an employer to pay, lend, or deliver, or agree to pay, lend, or deliver, any money or other thing of value—

"1. to any representative of any of his employees who are employed in an industry affecting commerce; or
"2. to any labor organization, or any officer or employee thereof, which represents, seeks to represent, or would admit to membership, any of the employees of such employer who are employed in an industry affecting commerce; or
"3. to any employee or group or committee of employees of such employer employed in an industry affecting commerce in excess of their normal compensation for the purpose of causing such employee or group or committee directly or indirectly to influence any other employees in the exercise of the right to organize and bargain collectively through representatives of their own choosing; or

"4. to any officer or employee of a labor organization engaged in an industry affecting commerce with intent to influence him in respect to any of his actions, decisions, or duties as a representative of employees or as such officer or employee of such labor organization.

"(b) (1) It shall be unlawful for any person to request, demand, receive, or accept, or agree to receive or accept, any payment, loan, or delivery of any money or other thing of value prohibited by subsection (a).

"(2) It shall be unlawful for any labor organization, or for any person acting as an officer, agent, representative, or employee of such labor organization, to demand or accept from the operator of any motor vehicle (as defined in part II of the Interstate Commerce Act) employed in the transportation of property in commerce, or the employer of any such operator, any money or other thing of value payable to such organization or to an officer, agent, representative or employee thereof as a fee or charge for the unloading, or in connection with the unloading, of the cargo of such vehicle: *Provided,* That nothing in this paragraph shall be construed to make unlawful any payment by an employer to any of his employees as compensation for their services as employees.

"(c) The provisions of this section shall not be applicable (1) in respect to any money or other thing of value payable by an employer to any of his employees whose established duties include acting openly for such employer in matters of labor relations or personnel administration or to any representative of his employees, or to any officer or employee of a labor organization, who is also an employee or former employee of such employer, as compensation for, or by reason of, his service as an employee of such employer; (2) with respect to the payment or delivery of any money or other thing of value in satisfaction of a judgment of any court or a decision or award of an arbitrator or impartial chairman or in compromise, adjustment, settlement, or release of any claim, complaint, grievance, or dispute in the absence of fraud or duress; (3) with respect to the sale or purchase of an article or commodity at the prevailing market price in the regular course of business; (4) with respect to money deducted from the wages of employees in payment of membership dues in a labor organization: *Provided,* That the employer has received from each employee, on whose account such deductions are made, a written assignment which shall not be irrevocable for a period of more than one year, or beyond the termination date of the applicable collective agreement, whichever occurs sooner; (5) with respect to money or other thing of value paid to a trust fund established by such representative, for the sole and exclusive benefit of the employees of such employer, and their families and dependents (or of such employees, families, and dependents jointly with the employees of other employers making similar payments, and their families and dependents): *Provided,* That (A) such payments are held in trust for the purpose of paying, either from principal or income or both, for the benefit of employees, their families and dependents, for medical or hospital care, pensions on retirement or death of employees, compensation for injuries or illness resulting from occupational activity or insurance to provide any of the foregoing, or unemployment benefits or life insurance, disability and sickness insurance, or accident insurance; (B) the detailed basis on which such payments are to be made is specified in a written agreement with the employer, and employees and employers are equally represented in the administration of such fund, together with such neutral persons as the representatives of the employers and the representatives of employees may agree upon and in the event the employer and employee groups deadlock on the administration of such fund and there are no neutral persons empowered to break such deadlock, such agreement provides that the two groups shall agree on an impartial umpire to decide such dispute, or in event of their failure to agree within a reasonable length of time, an impartial umpire to decide such dispute shall, on petition of either group, be appointed by the district court of the United States for the district where the trust fund has its principal office, and shall also contain provisions for an annual audit of the trust fund, a statement of the results of which shall be available for inspection by interested persons at the principal office of the trust fund and at such other places as may be designated in such written agreement; and (C) such payments as are intended to be used for the purpose of providing pensions or annuities for employees are made to a separate trust which provides that the funds held therein cannot be used for any purpose other than paying such pensions or annuities; or (6) with respect to money or other thing of value paid by any employer to a trust fund established by such representative for the purpose of pooled vacation, holiday, severance or similar benefits, or defraying costs of apprenticeship or other training programs: *Provided,* That the requirements of clause (B) of the proviso to clause (5) of this subsection shall apply to such trust funds."

TITLE VI

MISCELLANEOUS PROVISIONS

INVESTIGATIONS. SEC. 601. (a) The Secretary shall have power when he believes it necessary in order to determine whether any person has violated or is about to violate any provision of this Act (except title I or amendments made by this Act to other statutes) to make an investigation and in connection therewith he may enter such places and inspect such records and accounts and question such persons as he may deem necessary to enable him to determine the facts relative thereto. The Secretary may report to interested persons or officials concerning the facts required to be shown in any report required by this Act and concerning the reasons for failure or refusal to file such a report or any other matter which he deems to be appropriate as a result of such an investigation.

(b) For the purpose of any investigation provided for in this Act, the provisions of sections 9 and 10 (relating to the attendance of witnesses and the production of books, papers, and documents) of the Federal Trade Commission Act of September 16, 1914, as amended (15 U.S.C. 49, 50), are hereby made applicable to the jurisdiction, powers, and duties of the Secretary or any officers designated by him.

EXTORTIONATE PICKETING. SEC. 602. (a) It shall be unlawful to carry on picketing on or about the premises of any employer for the purpose of, or as part of any conspiracy or in furtherance of any plan or purpose for, the personal profit or enrichment of any individual (except a bona fide increase in wages or other employee benefits) by taking or obtaining any money or other thing of value from such employer against his will or with his consent.

(b) Any person who willfully violates this section shall be fined not more than $10,000 or imprisoned not more than twenty years, or both.

RETENTION OF RIGHTS UNDER OTHER FEDERAL AND STATE LAWS. SEC. 603. (a) Except as explicitly provided to the contrary, nothing in this Act shall reduce or limit the responsibilities of any labor organization or any officer, agent, shop steward, or other representative of a labor organization, or of any trust in which a labor organization is interested, under any other Federal law or under the laws of any State, and, except as explicitly provided to the contrary, nothing in this Act shall take away any right or bar any remedy to which members of a labor organization are entitled under such other Federal law or law of any State.

(b) Nothing contained in titles I, II, III, IV, V, or VI of this Act shall be construed to supersede or impair or otherwise affect the provisions of the Railway Labor Act, as amended, or any of the obligations, rights, benefits, privileges, or immunities of any carrier, employee, organization, representative, or person subject thereto; nor shall anything contained in said titles (except section 505) of this Act be construed to confer any rights, privileges, immunities, or defenses upon employers, or to impair or otherwise affect the rights of any person under the National Labor Relations Act, as amended.

EFFECT ON STATE LAWS. SEC. 604. Nothing in this Act shall be construed to impair or diminish the authority of any State to enact and enforce general criminal laws with respect to robbery, bribery, extortion, embezzlement, grand larceny, burglary, arson, violation of narcotics laws, murder, rape, assault with intent to kill, or assault which inflicts grievous bodily injury, or conspiracy to commit any of such crimes.

SERVICE OF PROCESS. SEC. 605. For the purposes of this Act, service of summons, subpena, or other legal process of a court of the United States upon an officer or agent of a labor organization in his capacity as such shall constitute service upon the labor organization.

ADMINISTRATIVE PROCEDURE ACT. SEC. 606. The provisions of the Administrative Procedure Act shall be applicable to the issuance, amendment, or rescission of any rules or regulations, or any adjudication, authorized or required pursuant to the provisions of this Act.

OTHER AGENCIES AND DEPARTMENTS. SEC. 607. In order to avoid unnecessary expense and duplication of functions among Government agencies, the Secretary may make such arrangements or agreements for cooperation or mutual assistance in the performance of his functions under this Act and the functions of any such agency as he may find to be practicable and consistent with law. The Secretary may utilize the facilities or services of any department, agency, or establishment of the United States or of any State or political subdivision of a State, including the services of any of its employees, with the lawful consent of such department, agency, or establishment; and each department, agency, or establishment of the United States is authorized and directed to cooperate with the Secretary and, to the extent permitted by law, to provide such information and facilities as he may request for his assistance in the performance of his functions under this Act. The Attorney General or his representative shall receive from the Secretary for appropriate action such evidence developed in the performance of his functions under this Act as may be found to warrant consideration for criminal prosecution under the provisions of this Act or other Federal law.

CRIMINAL CONTEMPT. SEC. 608. No person shall be punished for any criminal contempt allegedly committed outside the immediate presence of the court in connection with any civil action prosecuted by the Secretary or any other person in any court of the United States under the provisions of this Act unless the facts constituting such criminal contempt are established by the verdict of the jury in a proceeding in the district court of the United States, which jury shall be chosen and empaneled in the manner prescribed by the law governing trial juries in criminal prosecutions in the district courts of the United States.

PROHIBITION ON CERTAIN DISCIPLINE BY LABOR ORGANIZATION. SEC. 609. It shall be unlawful for any labor organization, or any officer, agent, shop steward, or other representative of a labor organization, or any employee thereof to fine, suspend, expel, or otherwise discipline any of its members for exercising any right to which he is entitled under the provisions of this Act. The provisions of section 102 shall be applicable in the enforcement of this section.

DEPRIVATION OF RIGHTS UNDER ACT BY VIOLENCE. SEC. 610. It shall be unlawful for any person through the use of force or violence, or threat of the use of force or violence, to restrain, coerce, or intimidate, or attempt to restrain, coerce, or intimate any member of a labor organization for the purpose of interfering with or preventing the exercise of any right to which he is entitled under the provisions of this Act. Any person who willfully violates this section shall be fined not more than $1,000 or imprisoned for not more than one year, or both.

SEPARABILITY PROVISIONS. SEC. 611. If any provision of this Act, or the application of such provision to any person or circumstances, shall be held invalid, the remainder of this Act or the application of such provision to persons or circumstances other than those as to which it is held invalid, shall not be affected thereby.

TITLE VII

AMENDMENTS TO THE LABOR MANAGEMENT RELATIONS ACT, 1947, AS AMENDED

FEDERAL-STATE JURISDICTION. SEC. 701. (a) Section 14 of the National Labor Relations Act, as amended, is amended by adding at the end thereof the following new subsection:

"(c)(1) The Board, in its discretion, may, by rule of decision or by published rules adopted pursuant to the Administrative Procedure Act, decline to assert jurisdiction over any labor dispute involving any class or category of employers, where, in the opinion of the Board, the effect of such labor dispute on commerce is not sufficiently substantial to warrant the exercise of its jurisdiction: *Provided,* That the Board shall not decline to assert jurisdiction over any labor dispute over which it would assert jurisdiction under the standards prevailing upon August 1, 1959.

"(2) Nothing in this Act shall be deemed to prevent or bar any agency or the courts of any State or Territory (including the Commonwealth of Puerto Rico, Guam, and the Virgin Islands), from assuming and asserting jurisdiction over labor disputes over which the Board declines, pursuant to paragraph (1) of this subsection, to assert jurisdiction."

(b) Section 3(b) of such Act is amended to read as follows:

"(b) The Board is authorized to delegate to any group of three or more members any or all of the powers which it may itself exercise. The Board is also authorized to delegate to its regional directors its powers under section 9 to determine the unit appropriate for the purpose of collective bargaining, to investigate and provide for hearings, and determine whether a question of representation exists, and to direct an election or take a secret ballot under subsection (c) or (e) of section 9 and certify the results thereof, except that upon the filing of a request therefor with the Board by any interested person, the Board may review any action of a regional director delegated to him under this paragraph, but such a review shall not, unless specifically ordered by the Board, operate as a stay of any action taken by the regional director. A vacancy in the Board shall not impair the right of the remaining members to exercise all of the powers of the Board, and three members of the Board shall, at all times, constitute a quorum of the Board, except that two members shall constitute a quorum of any group designated pursuant to the first sentence hereof. The Board shall have an official seal which shall be judicially noticed."

ECONOMIC STRIKERS. SEC. 702. Section 9(c)(3) of the National Labor Relations Act, as amended, is amended by amending the second sentence thereof to read as follows: "Employees engaged in an economic strike who are not entitled to reinstatement shall be eligible to vote under such regulations as the Board shall find are consistent with the purposes and provisions of this Act in any election conducted within twelve months after the commencement of the strike."

VACANCY IN OFFICE OF GENERAL COUNSEL. SEC. 703. Section 3(d) of the National Labor Relations Act, as amended, is amended by adding after the period at the end thereof the following: "In case of a vacancy in the office of the General Counsel the President is authorized to designate the officer or employee who shall act as General Counsel during such vacancy, but no person or persons so designated shall so act (1) for more than forty days when the Congress is in session unless a nomination to fill such vacancy shall have been submitted to the Senate, or (2) after the adjournment sine die of the session of the Senate in which such nomination was submitted."

BOYCOTTS AND RECOGNITION PICKETING. SEC. 704. (a) Section 8(b)(4) of the National Labor Relations Act, as amended, is amended to read as follows:

"4. (i) to engage in, or to induce or encourage any individual employed by any person engaged in commerce or in an industry affecting commerce to engage in, a strike or a refusal in the course of his employment to use, manufacture, process, transport, or otherwise handle or work on any goods, articles, materials, or commodities or to perform any services; or (ii) to threaten, coerce, or restrain any person engaged in commerce or in an industry affecting commerce, where in either case an object thereof is—

"A. forcing or requiring any employer or self-employed person to join any labor or employer organization or to enter into any agreement which is prohibited by section 8(e);

"B. forcing or requiring any person to cease using, selling, handling, transporting, or otherwise dealing in the products of any other producer, processor, or manufacturer, or to cease doing business with any other person, or forcing or requiring any other employer to recognize or bargain with a labor organization as the representative of his employees unless such labor organization has been certified as the representative of such employees under the provisions of section 9: *Provided,* That nothing contained in this clause (B) shall be construed to make unlawful, where not otherwise unlawful, any primary strike or primary picketing;

"C. forcing or requiring any employer to recognize or bargain with a particular labor organization as the representative of his employees if another labor organization has been certified as the representative of such employees under the provisions of section 9;

"D. forcing or requiring any employer to assign particular work to employees in a particular labor organization or in a particular trade, craft, or class rather than to employees in another labor organization or in another trade, craft, or class, unless such employer is failing to conform to an order or certification of the Board determining the bargaining representative for employees performing such work:

Provided, That nothing contained in this subsection (b) shall be construed to make unlawful a refusal by any person to enter upon the premises of any employer (other than his own employer), if the employees of such employer are engaged in a strike ratified or approved by a representative of such employees whom such employer is required to recognize under this Act: *Provided further,* That for the purposes of this paragraph (4) only, nothing contained in such paragraph shall be construed to prohibit publicity, other than picketing, for the purpose of truthfully advising the public, including consumers and members of a labor organization, that a product or products are produced by an employer with whom the labor organization has a primary dispute and are distributed by another employer, as long as such publicity does not have an effect of inducing any individual employed by any person other than the primary employer in the course of his employment to refuse to pick up, deliver, or transport any goods, or not to perform any services, at the establishment of the employer engaged in such distribution;".

(b) Section 8 of the National Labor Relations Act, as amended, is amended by adding at the end thereof the following new subsection:

"(e) It shall be an unfair labor practice for any labor organization and any employer to enter into any contract or agreement, express or implied, whereby such employer ceases or refrains or agrees to cease or refrain from handling, using, selling, transporting or otherwise dealing in any of the products of any other employer, or to cease doing business with any other person, and any contract or agreement entered into heretofore or hereafter containing such an agreement shall be to such extent unenforceable and void: *Provided,* That nothing in this subsection (e) shall apply to an agreement between a labor organization and an employer in the construction industry relating to the contracting or subcontracting of work to be done at the site of the construction, alteration, painting, or repair of a building, structure, or other work: *Provided further,* That for the purposes of this subsection (e) and section 8(b) (4) (B) the terms 'any employer', 'any person engaged in commerce or an industry affecting commerce', and 'any person' when used in relation to the terms 'any other producer, processor, or manufacturer', 'any other employer', or 'any other person' shall not include persons in the relation of a jobber, manufacturer, contractor, or subcontractor working on the goods or premises of the jobber or manufacturer or performing parts of an integrated process of production in the apparel and clothing industry: *Provided further,* That nothing in this Act shall prohibit the enforcement of any agreement which is within the foregoing exception."

(c) Section 8(b) of the National Labor Relations Act, as amended, is amended by striking out the word "and" at the end of paragraph (5), striking out the period at the end of paragraph (6), and inserting in lieu thereof a semicolon and the word "and," and adding a new paragraph as follows:

"7. to picket or cause to be picketed, or threaten to picket or cause to be picketed, any employer where an object thereof is forcing or requiring an employer to recognize or bargain with a labor organization as the representative of his employees, or forcing or requiring the employees of an employer to accept or select such labor organization as their collective bargaining representative, unless such labor organization is currently certified as the representative of such employees:

"A. where the employer has lawfully recognized in accordance with this Act any other labor organization and a question concerning representation may not appropriately be raised under section 9(c) of this Act.

"B. where within the preceding twelve months a valid election under section 9(c) of this Act has been conducted, or

"C. where such picketing has been conducted without a petition under section 9(c) being filed within a reasonable period of time not to exceed thirty days from the commencement of such picketing: *Provided,* That when such a petition has been filed the Board shall forthwith, without regard to the provisions of section 9(c)(1) or the absence of a showing of a substantial interest on the part of the labor organization, direct an election in such unit as the Board finds to be appropriate and shall certify the results thereof: *Provided further,* That nothing in this subparagraph (C) shall be construed to prohibit any picketing or other publicity for the purpose of truthfully advising the public (including consumers) that an employer does not employ members of, or have a contract with, a labor organization, unless an effect of such picketing is to induce any individual employed by any other person in the course of his employment, not to pickup, deliver or transport any goods or not to perform any services.

"Nothing in this paragraph (7) shall be construed to permit any act which would otherwise be an unfair labor practice under this section 8(b)."

(d) Section 10(1) of the National Labor Relations Act, as amended, is amended by adding after the words "section 8(b)," the words "or section 8(e) or section 8(b)(7)," and by striking out the period at the end of the third sentence and inserting in lieu thereof a colon and the following: *"Provided further,* That such officer or regional attorney shall not apply for any restraining order under section 8(b)(7) if a charge against the employer under section 8(a)(2) has been filed and after the preliminary investigation, he has reasonable cause to believe that such charge is true and that a complaint should issue."

(e) Section 303(a) of the Labor Management Relations Act, 1947, is amended to read as follows:

"(a) It shall be unlawful, for the purpose of this section only, in an industry or activity affecting commerce, for any labor organization to engage in any activity or conduct defined as an unfair labor practice in section 8(b)(4) of the National Labor Relations Act, as amended."

BUILDING AND CONSTRUCTION INDUSTRY. SEC. 705. (a) Section 8 of the National Labor Relations Act, as amended by section 704(b) of this Act, is amended by adding at the end thereof the following new subsection:

"(f) It shall not be an unfair labor practice under subsections (a) and (b) of this section for an employer engaged primarily in the building and construction industry to make an agreement covering employees engaged (or who, upon their employment will be engaged) in the building and construction industry with a labor organization of which building and construction employees are members (not established, maintained, or assisted by any action defined in section 8(a) of this Act as an unfair labor practice) because (1) the majority status of such labor organization has not been established under the provisions of section 9 of this Act prior to the making of such agreement, or (2) such agreement requires as a condition of employment, membership in such labor organization after the seventh day following the beginning of such employment or the effective date of the agreement, whichever is later, or (3) such agreement requires the employer to notify such labor organization of opportunities for employment with such employer, or gives such labor organization an opportunity to refer qualified applicants for such employment, or (4) such agreement specifies minimum training or experience qualifications for employment or provides for priority in opportunities for employment based upon length of service with such employer, in the industry or in the particular geographical area: *Provided,* That nothing in this subsection shall set aside the final proviso to section 8(a)(3) of this Act: *Provided further,* That any agreement which would be invalid, but for clause (1) of this subsection, shall not be a bar to a petition filed pursuant to section 9(c) or 9(e)."

(b) Nothing contained in the amendment made by subsection (a) shall be construed as authorizing the execution or application of agreements requiring membership in a labor organization as a condition of employment in any State or Territory in which such execution or application is prohibited by State or Territorial law.

PRIORITY IN CASE HANDLING. SEC. 706. Section 10 of the National Labor Relations Act, as amended, is amended by adding at the end thereof a new subsection as follows:

"(m) Whenever it is charged that any person has engaged in an unfair labor practice within the meaning of subsection (a)(3) or (b)(2) of section 8, such charge shall be given priority over all other cases except cases of like character in the office where it is filed or to which it is referred and cases given priority under subsection (1)."

EFFECTIVE DATE OF AMENDMENTS. SEC. 707. The amendments made by this title shall take effect sixty days after the date of the enactment of this Act and no provision of this title shall be deemed to make an unfair labor practice, any act which is performed prior to such effective date which did not constitute an unfair labor practice prior thereto.

APPENDIX G

CIVIL SERVICE REFORM ACT OF 1978

TITLE VII

FEDERAL SERVICE LABOR—MANAGEMENT RELATIONS

Federal Service Labor-Management Relations

Sec. 701. So much of subpart F of part III of title 5, United States Code, as precedes subchapter II of chapter 71 thereof is amended to read as follows:

SUBPART F—LABOR-MANAGEMENT AND EMPLOYEE RELATIONS

CHAPTER 71—LABOR-MANAGEMENT RELATIONS

Subchapter I—General Provisions

Sec.
7101. Findings and purpose.
7102. Employees' rights.
7103. Definitions; application.
7104. Federal Labor Relations Authority.
7105. Powers and duties of the Authority.
7106. Management rights.

Subchapter II—Rights and Duties of Agencies and Labor Organizations

Sec.
7111. Exclusive recognition of labor organizations.
7112. Determination of appropriate units for labor organization representation.
7113. National consultation rights.
7114. Representation rights and duties.
7115. Allotments to representatives.
7116. Unfair labor practices.
7117. Duty to bargain in good faith; compelling need; duty to consult.
7118. Prevention of unfair labor practices.
7119. Negotiation impasses; Federal Service Impasses Panel.
7120. Standards of conduct for labor organizations.

Subchapter III—Grievances, Appeals, and Review

Sec.
7121.   Grievance procedures.
7122.   Exceptions to arbitral awards.
7123.   Judicial review; enforcement.

Subchapter IV—Administrative and Other Provisions

Sec.
7131.   Official time.
7132.   Subpoenas.
7133.   Compilation and publication of data.
7134.   Regulations.
7135.   Continuation of existing laws, recognitions, agreements, and procedures.

Subchapter I—General Provisions

§ 7101. Findings and purpose

(a) The Congress finds that—

(1) experience in both private and public employment indicates that the statutory protection of the right of employees to organize, bargain collectively, and participate through labor organizations of their own choosing in decisions which affect them—

(A) safeguards the public interest,

(B) contributes to the effective conduct of public business, and

(C) facilitates and encourages the amicable settlements of disputes between employees and their employers involving conditions of employment; and

(2) the public interest demands the highest standards of employee performance and the continued development and implementation of modern progressive work practices to facilitate and improve employee performance and the efficient accomplishment of the operations of the Government. Therefore, labor organizations and collective bargaining in the civil service are in the public interest.

(b) It is the purpose of this chapter to prescribe certain rights and obligations of the employees of the Federal Government and to establish procedures which are designed to meet the special requirements and needs of the Government. The provisions of this chapter should be interpreted in a manner consistent with the requirement of an effective and efficient Government.

§ 7102. Employees' rights

Each employee shall have the right to form, join, or assist any labor organization, or to refrain from any such activity, freely and without fear of penalty or reprisal, and each employee shall be protected in the exercise of such right. Except as otherwise provided under this chapter, such right includes the right—

(1) to act for a labor organization in the capacity of a representative and the right, in that capacity, to present the views of the labor organization to heads of agencies and other officials of the executive branch of the Government, the Congress, or other appropriate authorities, and

(2) to engage in collective bargaining with respect to conditions of employment through representatives chosen by employees under this chapter.

§ 7103. Definitions; application

(a) For the purpose of this chapter—

(1) 'person' means an individual, labor organization, or agency;

(2) 'employee' means an individual—

(A) employed in an agency; or

(B) whose employment in an agency has ceased because of any unfair labor practice under section 7116 of this title and who has not obtained any other regular and substantially equivalent employment, as determined under regulations prescribed by the Federal Labor Relations Authority; but does not include—

(i) an alien or noncitizen of the United States who occupies a position outside the United States;

(ii) a member of the uniformed services;

(iii) a supervisor or a management official;

(iv) an officer or employee in the Foreign Service of the United States employed in the Department of State, the Agency for International Development, or the International Communication Agency; or

(v) any person who participates in a strike in violation of section 7311 of this title;

(3) 'agency' means an Executive agency (including a nonappropriated fund instrumentality described in section 2105(c) of this title and the Veterans' Canteen Service, Veterans' Administration), the Library of Congress, and the Government Printing Office, but does not include—

(A) the General Accounting Office;

(B) the Federal Bureau of Investigation;

(C) the Central Intelligence Agency;

(D) the National Security Agency;

(E) the Tennessee Valley Authority;

(F) the Federal Labor Relations Authority;

(G) the Federal Service Impasses Panel;

(4) 'labor organization' means an organization composed in whole or in part of employees, in which employees participate and pay dues, and which has as a purpose the dealing with an agency concerning grievances and conditions of employment, but does not include—

(A) an organization which, by its constitution, bylaws, tacit agreement among its members, or otherwise, denies membership because of race, color, creed, national origin, sex, age, preferential or nonpreferential civil service status, political affiliation, marital status, or handicapping condition;

(B) an organization which advocates the overthrow of the constitutional form of government of the United States;

(C) an organization sponsored by an agency; or

(D) an organization which participates in the conduct of a strike against the Government or any agency thereof or imposes a duty or obligation to conduct, assist, or participate in such a strike;

(5) 'dues' means dues, fees, and assessments;

(6) 'Authority' means the Federal Labor Relations Authority described in section 7104(a) of this title;

(7) 'Panel' means the Federal Service Impasses Panel described in section 7119(c) of this title;

(8) 'collective bargaining agreement' means an agreement entered into as a result of collective bargaining pursuant to the provisions of this chapter;

(9) 'grievance' means any complaint—

(A) by any employee concerning any matter relating to the employment of the employee;

(B) by any labor organization concerning any matter relating to the employment of any employee; or

(C) by any employee, labor organization, or agency concerning—
   (i) the effect or interpretation, or a claim of breach, of a collective bargaining agreement; or
   (ii) any claimed violation, misinterpretation, or misapplication of any law, rule, or regulation affecting conditions of employment;

(10) 'supervisor' means an individual employed by an agency having authority in the interest of the agency to hire, direct, assign, promote, reward, transfer, furlough, layoff, recall, suspend, discipline, or remove employees, to adjust their grievances, or to effectively recommend such action, if the exercise of the authority is not merely routine or clerical in nature but requires the consistent exercise of independent judgment, except that, with respect to any unit which includes firefighters or nurses, the term 'supervisor' includes only those individuals who devote a preponderance of their employment time to exercising such authority;

(11) 'management official' means an individual employed by an agency in a position the duties and responsibilities of which require or authorize the individual to formulate, determine, or influence the policies of the agency;

(12) 'collective bargaining' means the performance of the mutual obligation of the representative of an agency and the exclusive representative of employees in an appropriate unit in the agency to meet at reasonable times and to consult and bargain in a good-faith effort to reach agreement with respect to the conditions of employment affecting such employees and to execute, if requested by either party, a written document incorporating any collective bargaining agreement reached, but the obligation referred to in this paragraph does not compel either party to agree to a proposal or to make a concession;

(13) 'confidential employee' means an employee who acts in a confidential capacity with respect to an individual who formulates or effectuates management policies in the field of labor-management relations;

(14) 'conditions of employment' means personnel policies, practices, and matters, whether established by rule, regulation, or otherwise, affecting working conditions, except that such term does not include policies, practices, and matters—
   (A) relating to political activities prohibited under subchapter III of chapter 73 of this title;
   (B) relating to the classification of any position; or
   (C) to the extent such matters are specifically provided for by Federal statute;

(15) 'professional employee' means—
   (A) an employee engaged in the performance of work—
      (i) requiring knowledge of an advanced type in a field of science or learning customarily acquired by a prolonged course of specialized intellectual instruction and study in an institution of higher learning or a hospital (as distinguished from knowledge acquired by a general academic education, or from an apprenticeship, or from training in the performance of routine mental, manual, mechanical, or physical activities);

(ii) requiring the consistent exercise of discretion and judgment in its performance;

(iii) which is predominantly intellectual and varied in character (as distinguished from routine mental, manual, mechanical, or physical work); and

(iv) which is of such character that the output produced or the result accomplished by such work cannot be standardized in relation to a given period of time; or

(B) an employee who has completed the courses of specified intellectual instruction and study described in subparagraph (A)(i) of this paragraph and is performing related work under appropriate direction or guidance to qualify the employee as a professional employee described in subparagraph (A) of this paragraph;

(16) 'exclusive representative' means any labor organization which—

(A) is certified as the exclusive representative of employees in an appropriate unit pursuant to section 7111 of this title; or

(B) was recognized by an agency immediately before the effective date of this chapter as the exclusive representative of employees in an appropriate unit—

(i) on the basis of an election, or

(ii) on any basis other than an election, and continues to be so recognized in accordance with the provisions of this chapter;

(17) 'firefighter' means any employee engaged in the performance of work directly connected with the control and extinguishment of fires or the maintenance and use of firefighting apparatus and equipment; and

(18) 'United States' means the 50 states, the District of Columbia, the Commonwealth of Puerto Rico, Guam, the Virgin Islands, the Trust Territory of the Pacific Islands, and any territory or possession of the United States.

(b) (1) The President may issue an order excluding any agency or subdivision thereof from coverage under this chapter if the President determines that—

(A) the agency or subdivision has as a primary function intelligence, counterintelligence, investigative, or national security work, and

(B) the provisions of this chapter cannot be applied to that agency or subdivision in a manner consistent with national security requirements and considerations.

(2) The President may issue an order suspending any provision of this chapter with respect to any agency, installation, or activity located outside the 50 States and the District of Columbia, if the President determines that the suspension is necessary in the interest of national security.

§ 7104.   Federal Labor Relations Authority

(a) The Federal Labor Relations Authority is composed of three members, not more than 2 of whom may be adherents of the same political party. No member shall engage in any other business or employment or hold another office or position in the Government of the United States except as otherwise provided by law.

(b) Members of the Authority shall be appointed by the President by and with the advice and consent of the Senate, and may be removed by the President only upon notice and hearing and only for inefficiency, neglect of duty, or malfeasance in office. The President shall designate one member to serve as Chairman of the Authority.

(c) (1) One of the original members of the Authority shall be appointed for a term of 1 year, one for a term of 3 years, and the Chairman for a term of 5 years. Thereafter, each member shall be appointed for a term of 5 years.

    (2) Notwithstanding paragraph (1) of this subsection, the term of any member shall not expire before the earlier of—

        (A) the date on which the member's successor takes office, or

        (B) the last day of the Congress beginning after the date on which the member's term of office would (but for this subparagraph) expire. An individual chosen to fill a vacancy shall be appointed for the unexpired term of the member replaced.

(d) A vacancy in the Authority shall not impair the right of the remaining members to exercise all of the powers of the Authority.

(e) The Authority shall make an annual report to the President for transmittal to the Congress which shall include information as to the cases it has heard and the decisions it has rendered.

(f) (1) The General Counsel of the Authority shall be appointed by the President, by and with the advice and consent of the Senate, for a term of 5 years. The General Counsel may be removed at any time by the President. The General Counsel shall hold no other office or position in the Government of the United States except as provided by law.

    (2) The General Counsel may—

        (A) investigate alleged unfair labor practices under this chapter,

        (B) file and prosecute complaints under this chapter, and

        (C) exercise such other powers of the Authority as the Authority may prescribe.

    (3) The General Counsel shall have direct authority over, and responsibility for, all employees in the office of General Counsel, including employees of the General Counsel in the regional offices of the Authority.

§ 7105. Powers and duties of the Authority

(a) (1) The Authority shall provide leadership in establishing policies and guidance relating to matters under this chapter, and, except as otherwise provided, shall be responsible for carrying out the purpose of this chapter.

    (2) The Authority shall, to the extent provided in this chapter and in accordance with regulations prescribed by the Authority—

        (A) determine the appropriateness of units for labor organization representation under section 7112 of this title;

        (B) supervise or conduct elections to determine whether a labor organization has been selected as an exclusive representative by a majority of the employees in an appropriate unit and otherwise administer the provisions of section 7111 of this title relating to the according of exclusive recognition to labor organizations;

        (C) prescribe criteria and resolve issues relating to the granting of national consultation rights under section 7113 of this title;

        (D) prescribe criteria and resolve issues relating to determining compelling need for agency rules or regulations under section 7117(b) of this title;

(E) resolve issues relating to the duty to bargain in good faith under section 7117(c) of this title;

(F) prescribe criteria relating to the granting of consultation rights with respect to conditions of employment under section 7117(d) of this title;

(G) conduct hearings and resolve complaints of unfair labor practices under section 7118 of this title;

(H) resolve exceptions to arbitrator's awards under section 7122 of this title; and

(I) take such other actions as are necessary and appropriate to effectively administer the provisions of this chapter.

(b) The Authority shall adopt an official seal which shall be judicially noticed.

(c) The principal office of the Authority shall be in or about the District of Columbia, but the Authority may meet and exercise any or all of its powers at any time or place. Except as otherwise expressly provided by law, the Authority may, by one or more of its members or by such agents as it may designate, make any appropriate inquiry necessary to carry out its duties wherever persons subject to this chapter are located. Any member who participates in the inquiry shall not be disqualified from later participating in a decision of the Authority in any case relating to the inquiry.

(d) The Authority shall appoint an Executive Director and such regional directors, administrative law judges under section 3105 of this title, and other individuals as it may from time to time find necessary for the proper performance of its functions. The Authority may delegate to officers and employees appointed under this subsection authority

to perform such duties and make such expenditures as may be necessary.

(e) (1) The Authority may delegate to any regional director its authority under this chapter—

(A) to determine whether a group of employees is an appropriate unit;

(B) to conduct investigations and to provide for hearings;

(C) to determine whether a question of representation exists and to direct an election; and

(D) to supervise or conduct secret ballot elections and certify the results thereof.

(2) The Authority may delegate to any administrative law judge appointed under subsection (d) of this section its authority under section 7118 of this title to determine whether any person has engaged in or is engaging in an unfair labor practice.

(f) If the Authority delegates any authority to any regional director or administrative law judge to take any action pursuant to subsection (e) of this section, the Authority may, upon application by any interested person filed within 60 days after the date of the action, review such action, but the review shall not, unless specifically ordered by the Authority, operate as a stay of action. The Authority may affirm, modify, or reverse any action reviewed under this subsection. If the Authority does not undertake to grant review of the action under this subsection within 60 days after the later of—

(1) the date of the action; or

(2) the date of the filing of any application under this subsection for review of the action; the action shall become the action of the Authority at the end of such 60-day period.

(g) In order to carry out its functions under this chapter, the Authority may—

(1) hold hearings;

(2) administer oaths, take the testimony or deposition of any person under oath, and issue subpoenas as provided in section 7132 of this title; and

(3) may require an agency or a labor organization to cease and desist from violations of this chapter and require it to take any remedial action it considers appropriate to carry out the policies in this chapter.

(h) Except as provided in section 518 of title 28, relating to litigation before the Supreme Court, attorneys designated by the Authority may appear for the Authority and represent the Authority in any civil action brought in connection with any function carried out by the Authority pursuant to this title or as otherwise authorized by law;

(i) In the exercise of the functions of the Authority under this title, the Authority may request from the Director of the Office of Personnel Management an advisory opinion concerning the proper interpretation of rules, regulations, or policy directives issued by the Office of Personnel Management in connection with any matter before the Authority.

§ 7106. Management rights

(a) Subject to subsection (b) of this section, nothing in this chapter shall affect the authority of any management official of any agency—

(1) to determine the mission, budget, organization, number of employees, and internal security practices of the agency; and

(2) in accordance with applicable laws—

(A) to hire, assign, direct, layoff, and retain employees in the agency, or to suspend, remove, reduce in grade or pay, or take other disciplinary action against such employees;

(B) to assign work, to make determinations with respect to contracting out, and to determine the personnel by which agency operations shall be conducted;

(C) with respect to filling positions, to make selections for appointments from—

(i) among properly ranked and certified candidates for promotion; or

(ii) any other appropriate source; and

(D) to take whatever actions may be necessary to carry out the agency mission during emergencies.

(b) Nothing in this section shall preclude any agency and any labor organization from negotiating—

(1) at the election of the agency, on the numbers, types, and grades of employees or positions assigned to any organizational subdivision, work project, or tour of duty, or on the technology, methods, and means of performing work;

(2) procedures which management officials of the agency will observe in exercising any authority under this section; or

(3) appropriate arrangements for employees adversely affected by the exercise of any authority under this section by such management officials.

SUBCHAPTER II—RIGHTS AND DUTIES OF AGENCIES AND LABOR ORGANIZATIONS

§ 7111. Exclusive recognition of labor organizations

(a) An agency shall accord exclusive recognition to a labor organization if the organization has been selected as the representative, in a secret ballot election, by a majority of the employees in an appropriate unit who cast valid ballots in the election.

(b) If a petition if filed with the Authority—

  (1) by any person alleging—

    (A) in the case of an appropriate unit for which there is no exclusive representative, that 30 percent of the employees in the appropriate unit wish to be represented for the purpose of collective bargaining by an exclusive representative, or

    (B) in the case of an appropriate unit for which there is an exclusive representative, that 30 percent of the employees in the unit allege that the exclusive representative is no longer the representative of the majority of the employees in the unit; or

  (2) by any person seeking clarification of, or an amendment to, a certification then in effect or a matter relating to representation; the Authority shall investigate the petition, and if it has reasonable cause to believe that a question of representation exists, it shall provide an opportunity for a hearing (for which a transcript shall be kept) after reasonable notice. If the Authority finds on the record of the hearing that a question of representation exists, the Authority shall supervise or conduct an election on the question by secret ballot and shall certify the results thereof. An election under this subsection shall not be conducted in any appropriate unit or in any subdivision thereof within which, in the preceding 12 calendar months, a valid election under this subsection has been held.

(c) A labor organization which—

  (1) has been designated by at least 10 percent of the employees in the unit specified in any petition filed pursuant to subsection (b) of this section;

  (2) has submitted a valid copy of a current or recently expired collective bargaining agreement for the unit; or

  (3) has submitted other evidence that it is the exclusive representative of the employees involved may intervene with respect to a petition filed pursuant to subsection (b) of this section and shall be placed on the ballot of any election under such subsection (b) with respect to the petition.

(d) The Authority shall determine who is eligible to vote in any election under this section and shall establish rules governing any such election, which shall include rules allowing employees eligible to vote the opportunity to choose—

  (1) from labor organizations on the ballot, that labor organization which the employees wish to have represent them; or

  (2) not to be represented by a labor organization. In any election in which no choice on the ballot receives a majority of the votes cast, a runoff election shall be conducted between the two choices receiving the highest number of votes. A labor organization which receives the majority of the votes cast in an election shall be certified by the Authority as the exclusive representative.

(e) A labor organization seeking exclusive recognition shall submit to the Authority and the agency involved a roster of its officers and representatives, a copy of its constitution and bylaws, and a statement of its objectives.

(f) Exclusive recognition shall not be accorded to a labor organization—

  (1) if the Authority determines that the labor organization is subject to corrupt influences or influences opposed to democratic principles;

  (2) in the case of a petition filed pursuant to subsection (b)(1)(A) of this section, if there is not credible evi-

dence that at least 30 percent of the employees in the unit specified in the petition wish to be represented for the purpose of collective bargaining by the labor organization seeking exclusive recognition;

(3) if there is then in effect a lawful written collective bargaining agreement between the agency involved and an exclusive representative (other than the labor organization seeking exclusive recognition) covering any employees included in the unit specified in the petition, unless—

    (A) the collective bargaining agreement has been in effect for more than 3 years, or

    (B) the petition for exclusive recognition is filed not more than 105 days and not less than 60 days before the expiration date of the collective bargaining agreement; or

(4) if the Authority has, within the previous 12 calendar months, conducted a secret ballot election for the unit described in any petition under this section and in such election a majority of the employees voting chose a labor organization for certification as the unit's exclusive representative.

(g) Nothing in this section shall be construed to prohibit the waiving of hearings by stipulation for the purpose of a consent election in conformity with regulations and rules or decisions of the Authority.

§ 7112. Determination of appropriate units for labor organization representation.

(a) (1) The Authority shall determine the appropriateness of any unit. The Authority shall determine in each case whether, in order to ensure employees the fullest freedom in exercising the rights guaranteed under this chapter, the appropriate unit should be established on an agency, plant, installation, functional, or other basis and shall determine any unit to be an appropriate unit only if the determination will ensure a clear and identifiable community of interest among the employees in the unit and will promote effective dealing with, and efficiency of the operations of, the agency involved.

(b) A unit shall not be determined to be appropriate under this section solely on the basis of the extent to which employees in the proposed unit have organized, nor shall a unit be determined to be appropriate if it includes—

(1) except as provided under section 7135(a)(2) of this title, any management official or supervisor;

(2) a confidential employee;

(3) an employee engaged in personnel work in other than a purely clerical capacity;

(4) an employee engaged in administering the provisions of this chapter;

(5) both professional employees and other employees, unless a majority of the professional employees vote for inclusion in the unit;

(6) any employee engaged in intelligence, counterintelligence, investigative, or security work which directly affects national security; or

(7) any employee primarily engaged in investigation or audit functions relating to the work of individuals employed by an agency whose duties directly affect the internal security of the agency, but only if the functions are undertaken to ensure that the duties are discharged honestly and with integrity.

(c) Any employee who is engaged in administering any provision of law relating to labor-management relations may not be represented by a labor organization—

(1) which represents other individuals to whom such provision applies; or

(2) which is affiliated directly or indirectly with an organization which represents other individuals to whom such provision applies.

(d) Two or more units which are in an agency and for which a labor organization is the exclusive representative may, upon petition by the agency or labor organization, be consolidated with or without an election into a single larger unit if the Authority considers the larger unit to be appropriate. The Authority shall certify the labor organization as the exclusive representative of the new larger unit.

§ 7113. National consultation rights

(a) (1) If, in connection with any agency, no labor organization has been accorded exclusive recognition on an agency basis, a labor organization which is the exclusive representative of a substantial number of the employees of the agency, as determined in accordance with criteria prescribed by the Authority, shall be granted national consultation rights by the agency. National consultation rights shall terminate when the labor organization no longer meets the criteria prescribed by the Authority. Any issue relating to any labor organization's eligibility for, or continuation of, national consultation rights shall be subject to determination by the Authority.

(b) (1) Any labor organization having national consultation rights in connection with any agency under subsection (a) of this section shall—
  (A) be informed of any substantive change in conditions of employment proposed by the agency, and
  (B) be permitted reasonable time to present its views and recommendations regarding the changes.

(2) If any views or recommendations are presented under paragraph (1) of this subsection to an agency by any labor organization—
  (A) the agency shall consider the views or recommendations before taking final action on any matter with respect to which the views or recommendations are presented; and
  (B) the agency shall provide the labor organization a written statement of the reasons for taking the final action.

(c) Nothing in this section shall be construed to limit the right of any agency or exclusive representative to engage in collective bargaining.

§ 7114. Representation rights and duties

(a) (1) A labor organization which has been accorded exclusive recognition is the exclusive representative of the employees in the unit it represents and is entitled to act for, and negotiate collective bargaining agreements covering, all employees in the unit. An exclusive representative is responsible for representing the interests of all employees in the unit it represents without discrimination and without regard to labor organization membership.

(2) An exclusive representative of an appropriate unit in an agency shall be given the opportunity to be represented at—
  (A) any formal discussion between one or more representatives of the agency and one or more employees in the unit or their representatives concerning any grievance or any personnel policy or practices or other general condition of employment; or
  (B) any examination of an employee in the unit by a repre-

sentative of the agency in connection with an investigation if — (i) the employee reasonably believes that the examination may result in disciplinary action against the employee; and

(ii) the employee requests representation.

(3) Each agency shall annually inform its employees of their rights under paragraph (2)(B) of this subsection.

(4) Any agency and any exclusive representative in any appropriate unit in the agency, through appropriate representatives, shall meet and negotiate in good faith for the purposes of arriving at a collective bargaining agreement. In addition, the agency and the exclusive representative may determine appropriate techniques, consistent with the provisions of section 7119 of this title, to assist in any negotiation.

(5) The rights of an exclusive representative under the provisions of this subsection shall not be construed to preclude an employee from—

(A) being represented by an attorney or other representative, other than the exclusive representative, of the employee's own choosing in any grievance or appeal action; or

(B) exercising grievance or appellate rights established by law, rule, or regulation; except in the case of grievance or appeal procedures negotiated under this chapter.

(b) The duty of an agency and an exclusive representative to negotiate in good faith under subsection (A) of this section shall include the obligation—

(1) to approach the negotiations with a sincere resolve to reach a collective bargaining agreement;

(2) to be represented at the negotiations by duly authorized representatives prepared to discuss and negotiate on any condition of employment;

(3) to meet at reasonable times and convenient places as frequently as may be necessary, and to avoid unnecessary delays;

(4) in the case of an agency, to furnish to the exclusive representative involved, or its authorized representative, upon request and, to the extent not prohibited by law, data—

(A) which is normally maintained by the agency in the regular course of business;

(B) which is reasonably available and necessary for full and proper discussion, understanding, and negotiation of subjects within the scope of collective bargaining; and

(C) which does not constitute guidance, advice, counsel, or training provided for management officials or supervisors, relating to collective bargaining; and

(5) if agreement is reached, to execute on the request of any party to the negotiation a written document embodying the agreed terms, and to take such steps as are necessary to implement such agreement.

(c) (1) An agreement between any agency and an exclusive representative shall be subject to approval by the head of the agency.

(2) The head of the agency shall approve the agreement within 30 days from the date the agreement is executed if the agreement is in accordance with the provisions of this chapter and any other applicable law, rule, or regulation (unless the agency has granted an exception to the provision).

(3) If the head of the agency does not approve or disapprove the agree-

ment within the 30-day period, the agreement shall take effect and shall be binding on the agency and the exclusive representative subject to the provisions of this chapter and any other applicable law, rule, or regulation.

(4) A local agreement subject to a national or other controlling agreement at a higher level shall be approved under the procedures of the controlling agreement or, if none, under regulations prescribed by the agency.

§ 7115. Allotments to representatives

(a) If an agency has received from an employee in an appropriate unit a written assignment which authorizes the agency to deduct from the pay of the employee amounts for the payment of regular and periodic dues of the exclusive representative of the unit, the agency shall honor the assignment and make an appropriate allotment pursuant to the assignment. Any such allotment shall be made at no cost to the exclusive representative or the employee. Except as provided under subsection (b) of this section, any such assignment may not be revoked for a period of 1 year.

(b) An allotment under subsection (a) of this section for the deduction of dues with respect to any employee shall terminate when—

(1) the agreement between the agency and the exclusive representative involved ceases to be applicable to the employee; or

(2) the employee is suspended or expelled from membership in the exclusive representative.

(c) (1) Subject to paragraph (2) of this subsection, if a petition has been filed with the Authority by a labor organization alleging that 10 percent of the employees in an appropriate unit in an agency have membership in the labor organization, the Authority shall investigate the petition to determine its validity. Upon certification by the Authority of the validity of the petition, the agency shall have a duty to negotiate with the labor organization from the pay of the members of the labor organization who are employees in the unit and who make a voluntary allotment for such purpose.

(2) (A) The provisions of paragraph (1) of this subsection shall not apply in the case of any appropriate unit for which there is an exclusive representative.

(B) Any agreement under paragraph (1) of this subsection between a labor organization and an agency with respect to an appropriate unit shall be null and void upon the certification of an exclusive representative of the unit.

§ 7116. Unfair labor practices

(a) For the purpose of this chapter, it shall be an unfair labor practice for an agency—

(1) to interfere with, restrain, or coerce any employee in the exercise by the employee of any right under this chapter;

(2) to encourage or discourage membership in any labor organization by discrimination in connection with hiring, tenure, promotion, or other conditions of employment;

(3) to sponsor, control, or otherwise assist any labor organization, other than to furnish, upon request, customary and routine services and facilities if the services and facilities are also furnished on an impartial basis to other labor organizations having equivalent status;

(4) to discipline or otherwise discriminate against an employee because the employee has filed a complaint, affidavit, or petition, or has given any information or testimony under this chapter;

(5) to refuse to consult or negotiate in good faith with a labor organization as required by this chapter;

(6) to fail or refuse to cooperate in impasse procedures and impasse decisions as required by this chapter;

(7) to enforce any rule or regulation (other than a rule or regulation implementing section 2302 of this title) which is in conflict with any applicable collective bargaining agreement if the agreement was in effect before the date the rule or regulation was prescribed; or

(8) to otherwise fail or refuse to comply with any provisions of this chapter.

(b) For the purpose of this chapter, it shall be an unfair labor practice for a labor organization—

(1) to interfere with, restrain, or coerce any employee in the exercise by the employee of any right under this chapter;

(2) to cause or attempt to cause any agency to discriminate against any employee in the exercise by the employee of any right under this chapter;

(3) to coerce, discipline, fine, or attempt to coerce a member of the labor organization as punishment, reprisal, or for the purpose of hindering or impeding the member's work performance or productivity as an employee or the discharge of the member's duties as an employee;

(4) to discriminate against an employee with regard to the terms or conditions of membership in the labor organization on the basis of race, color, creed, national origin, sex,

age, preferential or nonpreferential civil service status, political affiliation, marital status, or handicapping condition;

(5) to refuse to consult or negotiate in good faith with an agency as required by this chapter;

(6) to fail or refuse to cooperate in impasse procedures and impasse decisions as required by this chapter;

(7) (A) to call, or participate in, a strike, work stoppage, or slow-down, or picketing of an agency in a labor-management dispute if such picketing interferes with an agency's operations, or

(B) to condone any activity described in subparagraph (A) of this paragraph by failing to take action to prevent or stop such activity; or

(8) to otherwise fail or refuse to comply with any provision of this chapter. Nothing in paragraph (7) of this subsection shall result in any informational picketing which does not interfere with an agency's operations being considered as an unfair labor practice.

(c) For the purpose of this chapter it shall be an unfair labor practice for an exclusive representative to deny membership to any employee in the appropriate unit represented by such exclusive representative except for failure—

(1) to meet reasonable occupational standards uniformly required for admission, or

(2) to tender dues uniformly required as a condition of acquiring and retaining membership. This subsection does not preclude any labor organization from enforcing discipline in accordance with procedures under its constitution or bylaws to the extent consistent with the provisions of this chapter.

(d) Issues which can properly be raised under an appeals procedure may not be raised as unfair labor practices prohibited under this section. Except for matters wherein, under section 7121 (e) and (f) of this title, an employee has an option of using the negotiated grievance procedure or an appeals procedure, issues which can be raised under a grievance procedure may, in the discretion of the aggrieved party, be raised under the grievance procedure or as an unfair labor practice under this section, but not under both procedures.

(e) The expression of any personal view, argument, opinion or the making of any statement which—

    (1) publicizes the fact of a representational election and encourages employees to exercise their right to vote in such election,

    (2) corrects the record with respect to any false or misleading statement made by any person, or

    (3) informs employees of the Government's policy relating to labor-management relations and representation, shall not, if the expression contains no threat of reprisal or force or promise of benefit or was not made under coercive conditions, (A) constitute an unfair labor practice under any provision of this chapter, or (B) constitute grounds for the setting aside of any election conducted under any provisions of this chapter.

§ 7117. Duty to bargain in good faith; compelling need; duty to consult

(a) (1) Subject to paragraph (2) of this subsection, the duty to bargain in good faith shall, to the extent not inconsistent with any Federal law or any Government-wide rule or regulation, extend to matters which are the subject of any rule or regulation only if the rule or regulation is not a Government-wide rule or regulation.

    (2) The duty to bargain in good faith shall, to the extent not inconsistent with Federal law or any Government-wide rule or regulation, extend to matters which are the subject of any agency rule or regulation referred to in paragraph (3) of this subsection only if the Authority has determined under subsection (b) of this section that no compelling need (as determined under regulations prescribed by the Authority) exists for the rule or regulation.

    (3) Paragraph (2) of the subsection applies to any rule or regulation issued by any agency or issued by any primary national subdivision of such agency, unless an exclusive representative represents an appropriate unit including not less than a majority of the employees in the issuing agency or primary national subdivision, as the case may be, to whom the rule or regulation is applicable.

(b) (1) In any case of collective bargaining in which an exclusive representative alleges that no compelling need exists for any rule or regulation referred to in subsection (a)(3) of this section which is then in effect and which governs any matter at issue in such collective bargaining, the Authority shall determine under paragraph (2) of this subsection, in accordance with regulations prescribed by the Authority, whether such a compelling need exists.

    (2) For the purpose of this section, a compelling need shall be determined not to exist for any rule or regulation only if—

        (A) the agency, or primary national subdivision, as the case may be, which issued the rule or regulation informs the Authority in writing that a compelling need for the rule or regulation does not exist; or

(B) the Authority determines that a compelling need for a rule or regulation does not exist.

(3) A hearing may be held, in the discretion of the Authority, before a determination is made under this subsection. If a hearing is held, it shall be expedited to the extent practicable and shall not include the General Counsel as a party.

(4) The agency, or primary national subdivision, as the case may be, which issued the rule or regulation shall be a necessary party at any hearing under this subsection.

(c) (1) Except in any case to which subsection (b) of this section applies, if any agency involved in collective bargaining with an exclusive representative alleges that the duty to bargain in good faith does not extend to any matter, the exclusive representative may appeal the allegation to the Authority in accordance with the provisions of this subsection.

(2) The exclusive representative may, on or before the 15th day after the date on which the agency first makes the allegation referred to in paragraph (1) of this subsection, institute an appeal under this subsection by—

(A) filing a petition with the Authority; and

(B) furnishing a copy of the petition to the head of the agency.

(3) On or before the 30th day after the date of the receipt by the head of the agency of the copy of the petition under paragraph (2)(B) of this subsection, the agency shall—

(A) file with the Authority a statement—

(i) withdrawing the allegation; or

(ii) setting forth in full its reasons supporting the allegation; and

(B) furnish a copy of such statement to the exclusive representative.

(4) On or before the 15th day after the date of the receipt by the exclusive representative of a copy of a statement under paragraph (3)(B) of this subsection, the exclusive representative shall file with the Authority its response to the statement.

(5) A hearing may be held, in the discretion of the Authority, before a determination is made under this subsection. If a hearing is held, it shall not include the General Counsel as a party.

(6) The Authority shall expedite proceedings under this subsection to the extent practicable and shall issue to the exclusive representative and to the agency a written decision on the allegation and specific reasons therefore at the earliest practicable date.

(d) (1) A labor organization which is the exclusive representative of a substantial number of employees, determined in accordance with criteria prescribed by the Authority, shall be granted consultation rights by any agency with respect to any Government-wide rule or regulation issued by the agency effecting any substantive change in any condition of employment. Such consultation rights shall terminate when the labor organization no longer meets the criteria prescribed by the Authority. Any issue relating to a labor organization's eligibility for, or continuation of, such consultation rights shall be subject to determination by the Authority.

(2) A labor organization having consultation rights under paragraph (1) of this subsection shall—

(A) be informed of any substantive change in conditions of employment proposed by the agency, and

(B) shall be permitted reasonable time to present its views and recommendations regarding the changes.

(3) If any views or recommendations are presented under paragraph (2) of this subsection to an agency by any labor organization—

(A) the agency shall consider the views or recommendations before taking final action on any matter with respect to which the views or recommendations are presented; and

(B) the agency shall provide the labor organization a written statement of the reasons for taking the final action.

§ 7118. Prevention of unfair labor practices

(a) (1) If any agency or labor organization is charged by any person with having engaged in or engaging in an unfair labor practice, the General Counsel shall investigate the charge and may issue and cause to be served upon the agency or labor organization a complaint. In any case in which the General Counsel does not issue a complaint because the charge fails to state an unfair labor practice, the General Counsel shall provide the person making the charge a written statement of the reasons for not issuing a complaint.

(2) Any complaint under paragraph (1) of this subsection shall contain a notice—

(A) of the charge;

(B) that a hearing will be held before the Authority (or any member thereof or before an individual employed by the authority and designated for such purpose); and

(C) of the time and place fixed for the hearing.

(3) The labor organization or agency involved shall have the right to file an answer to the original and any amended complaint and to appear in person or otherwise and give testimony at the time and place fixed in the complaint for the hearing.

(4) (A) Except as provided in subparagraph (B) of this paragraph, no complaint shall be issued based on any alleged unfair labor practice which occurred more than 6 months before the filing of the charge with the Authority.

(B) If the General Counsel determines that the person filing any charge was prevented from filing the charge during the 6-month period referred to in subparagraph (A) of this paragraph by reason of—

(i) any failure of the agency or labor organization against which the charge is made to perform a duty owed to the person, or

(ii) any concealment which prevented discovery of the alleged unfair labor practice during the 6-month period, the General Counsel may issue a complaint based on the charge if the charge was filed during the 6-month period beginning on the day of the discovery by the person of the alleged unfair labor practice.

(5) The General Counsel may prescribe regulations providing for informal methods by which the alleged unfair labor practice may be resolved prior to the issuance of a complaint.

(6) The Authority (or any member thereof or any individual employed by the Authority and designated for such purpose) shall conduct a hearing on the complaint not earlier than 5 days after the date on which the complaint is served. In the discretion of the individual or individuals conducting the hearing, any person involved may be allowed to intervene in the hearing and to present testimony. Any such hearing shall, to the extent practicable, be conducted in accordance with the provisions of subchapter II of chapter 5 of this title, except that the parties shall not be bound by rules of evidence, whether statutory, common law, or adopted by a court. A transcript shall be kept of the hearing. After such a hearing the Authority, in its discretion, may upon notice receive further evidence or hear argument.

(7) If the Authority (or any member thereof or any individual employed by the Authority and designated for such purpose) determines after any hearing on a complaint under paragraph (5) of this subsection that the preponderance of the evidence received demonstrates that the agency or labor organization named in the complaint has engaged in or is engaging in an unfair labor practice, then the individual or individuals conducting the hearing shall state in writing their findings of fact and shall issue and cause to be served on the agency or labor organization an order—

(A) to cease and desist from any such unfair labor practice in which the agency or labor organization is engaged;

(B) requiring the parties to renegotiate a collective bargaining agreement in accordance with the order of the Authority and requiring that the agreement, as amended, be given retroactive effect;

(C) requiring reinstatement of an employee with backpay in accordance with section 5596 of this title; or

(D) including any combination of the actions described in subparagraphs (A) through (C) of this paragraph or such other actions as will carry out the purpose of this chapter.

If any such order requires reinstatement of an employee with backpay, backpay may be required of the agency (as provided in section 5596 of this title) or of the labor organization, as the case may be, which is found to have engaged in the unfair labor practice involved.

(8) If the individual or individuals conducting the hearing determine that the preponderance of the evidence received fails to demonstrate that the agency or labor organization named in the complaint has engaged in or is engaging in an unfair labor practice, the individual or individuals shall state in writing their findings of fact and shall issue an order dismissing the complaint.

(b) In connection with any matter before the Authority in any proceeding under this section, the Authority may request, in accordance with the provisions of section 7105(i) of this title, from the Director of the Office of Personnel Management an advisory opinion concerning the proper interpretation of rules, regulations, or other policy directives issued by the Office of Personnel Management.

§ 7119. Negotiation impasses; Federal Service Impasses Panel

(a) The Federal Mediation and Conciliation Service shall provide services and assistance to agencies and exclusive representatives in the resolution of negotiation impasses. The Service shall determine under what circumstances and in what manner it shall provide services and assistance.

(b) If voluntary arrangements, including the services of the Federal Mediation and Conciliation Service or any other third-party mediation, fail to resolve a negotiation impasse—

  (1) either party may request the Federal Service Impasses Panel to consider the matter, or

  (2) the parties may agree to adopt a procedure for binding arbitration of the negotiation impasse, but only if the procedure is approved by the Panel.

(c) (1) The Federal Service Impasses Panel is an entity within the Authority, the function of which is to provide assistance in resolving negotiation impasses between agencies and exclusive representatives.

  (2) The Panel shall be composed of a Chairman and at least six other members, who shall be appointed by the President, solely on the basis of fitness to perform the duties and functions involved, from among individuals who are familiar with Government operations and knowledgeable in labor-management relations.

  (3) Of the original members of the Panel, 2 members shall be appointed for a term of 1 year, 2 members shall be appointed for a term of 3 years,

and the Chairman and the remaining members shall be appointed for a term of 5 years. Thereafter each member shall be appointed for a term of 5 years, except that an individual chosen to fill a vacancy shall be appointed for the unexpired term of the member replaced. Any member of the Panel may be removed by the President.

  (4) The Panel may appoint an Executive Director and any other individuals it may from time to time find necessary for the proper performance of its duties. Each member of the Panel who is not an employee (as defined in section 2105 of this title) is entitled to pay at a rate equal to the daily equivalent of the maximum annual rate of basic pay then currently paid under the General Schedule for each day he is engaged in the performance of official business of the Panel, including travel time, and is entitled to travel expenses as provided under section 5703 of this title.

  (5) (A) The Panel or its designee shall promptly investigate any impasse presented to it under subsection (b) of this section. The Panel shall consider the impasse and shall either—

    (i) recommend to the parties procedures for the resolution of the impasse; or

    (ii) assist the parties in resolving the impasse through whatever methods and procedures, including factfinding and recommendations, it may consider appropriate to accomplish the purpose of this section.

  (B) If the parties do not arrive at a settlement after assistance by the Panel under subparagraph (A) of this paragraph, the Panel may—

(i) hold hearings;

(ii) administer oaths, take the testimony or deposition of any person under oath, and issue subpoenas as provided in section 7132 of this title; and

(iii) take whatever action is necessary and not inconsistent with this chapter to resolve the impasse.

(C) Notice of any final action of the Panel under this section shall be promptly served upon the parties, and the action shall be binding on such parties during the term of the agreement, unless the parties agree otherwise.

§ 7120.   Standards of conduct for labor organizations

(a) An agency shall only accord recognition to a labor organization that is free from corrupt influences and influences opposed to basic democratic principles. Except as provided in subsection (b) of this section, an organization is not required to prove that it is free from such influences if it is subject to governing requirements adopted by the organization or by a national or international labor organization or federation of labor organizations with which it is affiliated, or in which it participates, containing explicit and detailed provisions to which it subscribes calling for—

(1) the maintenance of democratic procedures and practices including provisions for periodic elections to be conducted subject to recognized safeguards and provisions defining and securing the right of individual members to participate in the affairs of the organization, to receive fair and equal treatment under the governing rules of the organization, and to receive fair process in disciplinary proceedings;

(2) the exclusion from office in the organization of persons affiliated with communist or other totalitarian movements and persons identified with corrupt influences;

(3) the prohibition of business or financial interests on the part of organization officers and agents which conflict with their duty to the organization and its members; and

(4) the maintenance of fiscal integrity in the conduct of the affairs of the organization, including provisions for accounting and financial controls and regular financial reports or summaries to be made available to members.

(b) Notwithstanding the fact that a labor organization has adopted or subscribed to standards of conduct as provided in subsection (a) of this section, the organization is required to furnish evidence of its freedom from corrupt influences or influences opposed to basic democratic principles if there is reasonable cause to believe that—

(1) the organization has been suspended or expelled from, or is subject to other sanction, by a parent labor organization, or federation of organizations with which it had been affiliated, because it has demonstrated an unwillingness or inability to comply with governing requirements comparable in purpose to those required by subsection (a) of this section; or

(2) the organization is in fact subject to influences that would preclude recognition under this chapter.

(c) A labor organization which has or seeks recognition as a representative of employees under this chapter shall file financial and other reports with the Assistant Secretary of Labor for Labor Management Relations, provide for bonding of officials and employees of the organization, and comply with trusteeship and election standards.

(d) The Assistant Secretary shall prescribe such regulations as are necessary to carry out the purposes of this section. Such regulations shall conform generally to the principles applied to labor organizations in the private sector. Complaints of violations of this section shall be filed with the Assistant Secretary. In any matter arising under this section, the Assistant Secretary may require a labor organization to cease and desist from violations of this section and require it to take such actions as he considers appropriate to carry out the policies of this section.

(e) This chapter does not authorize participation in the management of a labor organization or acting as a representative of a labor organization by a management official, a supervisor, or a confidential employee, except as specifically provided in this chapter, or by an employee if the participation or activity would result in a conflict or apparent conflict of interest or would otherwise be incompatible with law or with the official duties of the employee.

(f) In the case of any labor organization which by omission or commission has willfully and intentionally, with regard to any strike, work stoppage, or slowdown, violated section 7116(b)(7) of this title, the Authority shall, upon an appropriate finding by the Authority of such violation—

    (1) revoke the exclusive recognition status of the labor organization, which shall then immediately cease to be legally entitled and obligated to represent employees in the unit; or

    (2) take any other appropriate disciplinary action.

SUBCHAPTER III—GRIEVANCES

§ 7121. Grievance procedures

(a) (1) Except as provided in paragraph (2) of this subsection, any collective bar-gaining agreement shall provide procedures for the settlement of grievances, including questions of arbitrability. Except as provided in subsections (d) and (e) of this section, the procedures shall be the exclusive procedures for resolving grievances which fall within its coverage.

    (2) Any collective bargaining agreement may exclude any matter from the application of the grievance procedures which are provided for in the agreement.

(b) Any negotiated grievance procedure referred to in subsection (a) of this section shall—

    (1) be fair and simple.

    (2) provide for expeditious processing, and

    (3) include procedures that—

        (A) assure an exclusive representative the right, in its own behalf or on behalf of any employee in the unit represented by the exclusive representative, to present and process grievances;

        (B) assure such an employee the right to present a grievance on the employee's own behalf, and assure the exclusive representative the right to be present during the grievance proceeding; and

        (C) provide that any grievance not satisfactorily settled under the negotiated grievance procedure shall be subject to binding arbitration which may be invoked by either the exclusive representative or the agency.

(c) The preceding subsections of this section shall not apply with respect to any grievance concerning—

    (1) any claimed violation of subchapter III of chapter 73 of this title (relating to prohibited political activities);

(2) retirement, life insurance, or health insurance;

(3) a suspension or removal under section 7532 of this title;

(4) any examination, certification, or appointment; or

(5) the classification of any position which does not result in the reduction in grade or pay of an employee.

(d) An aggrieved employee affected by a prohibited personnel practice under section 2302(b)(1) of this title which also falls under the coverage of the negotiated grievance procedure may raise the matter under a statutory procedure or the negotiated procedure, but not both. An employee shall be deemed to have exercised his option under this subsection to raise the matter under either a statutory procedure or the negotiated procedure at such time as the employee timely initiates an action under the applicable statutory procedure or timely files a grievance in writing, in accordance with the provisions of the parties' negotiated procedure in no manner prejudices the right of an aggrieved employee to request the Merit Systems Protection Board to review the final decision pursuant to section 7702 of this title in the case of any personnel action that could have been appealed to the Board, or, where applicable, to request the Equal Employment Opportunity Commission.

(e) (1) Matters covered under sections 4303 and 7512 of this title which also fall within the coverage of the negotiated grievance procedure may, in the discretion of the aggrieved employee, be raised either under the appellate procedures of section 7701 of this title or under the negotiated grievance procedure, but not both. Similar matters which arise under other personnel systems applicable to employees covered by this chapter may, in the discretion of the aggrieved employee, be raised either under the appellate proce-

dures, if any, applicable to those matters, or under the negotiated grievance procedure, but not both. An employee shall be deemed to have exercised his option under this subsection to raise a matter either under the applicable appellate procedures or under the negotiated grievance procedure at such time as the employee timely files a notice of appeal under the applicable appellate procedures or timely files a grievance in writing in accordance with the provisions of the parties' negotiated grievance procedure, whichever event occurs first.

(2) In matters covered under sections 4303 and 7512 of this title which have been raised under the negotiated grievance procedure in accordance with this section, an arbitrator shall be governed by section 7701(c)(1) of this title, as applicable.

(f) In matters covered under sections 4303 and 7512 of this title which have been raised under the negotiated grievance procedure in accordance with this section, section 7703 of this title pertaining to judicial review shall apply to the award of an arbitrator in the same manner and under the same conditions as if the matter had been decided by the Board. In matters similar to those covered under sections 4303 and 7512 of this title which arise under other personnel systems and which an aggrieved employee has raised under the negotiated grievance procedure, judicial review of an arbitrator's award may be obtained in the same manner and on the same basis as could be obtained of a final decision in such matters raised under applicable appellate procedures.

§ 7122.   Exceptions to arbitral awards

(a) Either party to arbitration under this chapter may file with the Authority an exception to any arbitrator's award pursuant to the arbitration (other than an award relating to a matter described in section 7121(f) of this title). If upon review the Authority finds that the award is deficient—

(1) because it is contrary to any law, rule, or regulation; or

(2) on other grounds similar to those applied by Federal courts in private sector labor-management relations; the Authority may take such action and make such recommendations concerning the award as it considers necessary, consistent with applicable laws, rules, or regulations.

(b) If no exception to an arbitrator's award is filed under subsection (a) of this section during the 30-day period beginning on the date of such award, the award shall be final and binding. An agency shall take the actions required by an arbitrator's final award. The award may include the payment of backpay (as provided in section 5596 of this title).

§ 7123. Judicial review; enforcement

(a) Any person aggrieved by any final order of the Authority other than an order under—

(1) section 7122 of this title (involving an award by an arbitrator), unless the order involves an unfair labor practice under section 7118 of this title, or

(2) section 7112 of this title (involving an appropriate unit determination), may, during the 60-day period beginning on the date on which the order was issued, institute an action for judicial review of the Authority's order in the United States court of appeals in the circuit in which the person resides or transacts business or in the United States Court of Appeals for the District of Columbia.

(b) The Authority may petition any appropriate United States court of appeals for the enforcement of any order of the Authority and for appropriate temporary relief or restraining order.

(c) Upon the filing of a petition under subsection (a) of this section for judicial review or under subsection (b) of this section for enforcement, the Authority shall file in the court the record in the proceedings, as provided in section 2112 of title 28. Upon the filing of the petition, the court shall cause notice thereof to be served to the parties involved, and thereupon shall have jurisdiction of the proceeding and of the question determined therein and may grant any temporary relief (including a temporary restraining order) it considers just and proper, and may make and enter a decree affirming and enforcing, modifying and enforcing as so modified, or setting aside in whole or part the order of the Authority. The filing of a petition under subsection (a) or (b) of this section shall not operate as a stay of the Authority's order unless the court specifically orders the stay. Review of the Authority's order shall be on record in accordance with section 706 of this title. No objection that has not been urged before the Authority, or its designees, shall be considered by the court, unless the failure or neglect to urge the objection is excused because of extraordinary circumstances. The findings of the Authority with respect to questions of fact, if supported by substantial evidence on the record considered as a whole, shall be conclusive. If any person applies to the court for leave to adduce additional evidence and shows to the satisfaction of the court that the additional evidence is material and that there were reasonable grounds for the failure to adduce the evidence in the hearing before the Authority, or its designee, the court may order the additional evidence to be taken before the Authority, or its designee, and to be made a part of the record. The Authority may modify its findings as to the facts, or make new findings by reason of additional evidence so taken and filed. The Authority shall file its modified or new findings, which, with respect to questions of fact, if supported by substantial evidence on the record considered as a whole, shall be conclusive. The Authority shall file its recommendations, if any, for the modification or setting aside of its original order. Upon the filing of the record with the court, the jurisdiction of the court shall be exclusive and its judgment and decree shall be final, except that the judgment and decree shall be subject to review by the Supreme Court of the United States upon writ of certiorari or certification as provided in section 1254 of title 28.

(d) The Authority may, upon issuance of a complaint as provided in section 7118 of this title charging that any person has engaged in or is engaging in an unfair labor practice, petition any United States district court within any district in which the unfair labor practice in question is alleged to have occurred or in which such person resides or transacts business for appropriate temporary relief (including a restraining order). Upon the filing of the petition, the court shall cause notice thereof to be served upon the person, and thereupon shall have jurisdiction to grant any temporary relief (including a temporary restraining order) it considers just and proper. A court shall not grant any temporary relief under this section if it would interfere with the ability of the agency to carry out its essential functions or if the Authority fails to establish probable cause that an unfair labor practice is being committed.

Subchapter IV-Administrative and Other Provisions

§ 7131. Official time

(a) Any employee representing an exclusive representative in the negotiation of a collective bargaining agreement under this chapter shall be authorized official time for such purposes, including attendance at impasse proceeding, during the time the employee otherwise would be in a duty status. The number of employees for whom official time is authorized under this subsection shall not exceed the number of individuals designated as representing the agency for such purposes.

(b) Any activities performed by any employee relating to the internal business of a labor organization (including the solicitation of membership, elections of labor organization officials, and collection of dues) shall be performed during the time the employee is in a non-duty status.

(c) Except as provided in subsection (a) of this section, the Authority shall determine whether any employee participating for, or on behalf of, a labor organization in any phase of proceedings before the Authority shall be authorized official time for such purpose during the time the employee otherwise would be in a duty status.

(d) Except as provided in the preceding subsections of this section—
    (1) any employee representing an exclusive representative, or
    (2) in connection with any other matter covered by this chapter, any employee in an appropriate unit represented by an exclusive representative, shall be granted official time in any amount the agency and the exclusive representative involved agree to be reasonable, necessary, and in the public interest.

§ 7132. Subpoenas

(a) Any member of the Authority, the General Counsel, or the Panel, any administrative law judge appointed by the Authority under section 3105 of this title, and any employee of the Authority designated by the Authority may—

(1) issue subpoenas requiring the attendance and testimony of witnesses and the production of documentary or other evidence from any place in the United States; and

(2) administer oaths, take or order the taking of depositions, order responses to written interrogatories, examine witnesses, and receive evidence. No subpoena shall be issued under this section which requires the disclosure of intramanagement guidance, advice, counsel, or training within an agency or between an agency and the Office of Personnel Management.

(b) In the case of contumacy or failure to obey a subpoena issued under subsection (a)(1) of this section, the United States district court for the judicial district in which the person to whom the subpoena is addressed resides or is served may issue an order requiring such person to appear at any designated place to testify or to produce documentary or other evidence. Any failure to obey the order of the court may be punished by the court as a contempt thereof.

(c) Witnesses (whether appearing voluntarily or under subpoena) shall be paid the same fee and mileage allowances which are paid subpoenaed witnesses in the courts of the United States.

§ 7133. Compilation and publication of data

(a) The Authority shall maintain a file of its proceedings and copies of all available agreements and arbitration decisions, and shall publish the texts of its decisions and the actions taken by the Panel under section 7119 of this title.

(b) All files maintained under subsection (a) of this section shall be open to inspection and reproduction in accordance with the provisions of sections 552 and 552a of this title.

§ 7134. Regulations

The Authority, the General Counsel, the Federal Mediation and Conciliation Service, the Assistant Secretary of Labor for Labor Management Relations, and the panel shall each prescribe rules and regulations to carry out the provisions of this chapter applicable to each of them, respectively. Provisions of subchapter II of chapter 5 of this title shall be applicable to the issuance, revision, or repeal of any such rule or regulation.

§ 7135. Continuation of existing laws, recognitions, agreements, and procedures

(a) Nothing contained in this chapter shall preclude—

(1) the renewal or continuation of an exclusive recognition, certification of an exclusive representative, or a lawful agreement between an agency and an exclusive representative of its employees, which is entered into before the effective date of this chapter; or

(2) the renewal, continuation, or initial according of recognition for units of management officials or supervisors represented by labor organizations which historically or traditionally represent management officials or supervisors in private industry and which hold exclusive recognition for units of such officials or supervisors in any agency on the effective date of this chapter.

(b) Policies, regulations, and procedures established under and decisions issued under Executive Orders 11491, 11616, 11636, 11787, and 11838, or under any other Executive order, as in effect on the effective date of this chapter, shall remain in full force and effect until revised or revoked by President, or unless superseded by specific provisions of this chapter or by regulations or decisions issued pursuant to this chapter."

Backpay In Case Of Unfair Labor Practices And Grievances

Sec. 702. Section 5596(b) of title 5, United States Code is amended to read as follows:

(b) (1) An employee of an agency who, on the basis of a timely appeal or an administrative determination (including a decision relating to an unfair labor practice or a grievance) is found by appropriate authority under applicable law, rule, regulation, or collective bargaining agreement, to have been affected by an unjustified or unwarranted personnel action which has resulted in the withdrawal or reduction of all or part of the pay, allowances, or differentials of the employee—

(A) is entitled, on correction of the personnel action, to receive for the period for which the personnel action was in effect—

(i) an amount equal to all or any part of the pay, allowances, or differentials, as applicable which the employee normally would have earned or received during the period if the personnel action had not occurred, less any amounts earned by the employee through other employment during that period; and

(ii) reasonable attorney fees related to the personnel action which, with respect to any decision relating to an unfair labor practice or a grievance processed under a procedure negotiated in accordance with chapter 71 of this title, shall be awarded in accordance with standards established under section 7701(g) of this title; and

(B) for all purposes, is deemed to have performed service for the agency during that period, except that—

(i) annual leave restored under this paragraph which is in excess of the maximum leave accumulation permitted by law shall be credited to a separate leave account for the employee and shall be available for use by the employee within the time limits prescribed by regulations of the Office of Personnel Management, and

(ii) annual leave credited under clause (i) of this subparagraph but unused and still available to the employee under regulations prescribed by the Office shall be included in the lump-sum payment under section 5551 or 5552(1) of this title but may not be retained to the credit of the employee under section 5552(2) of this title.

(2) This subsection does not apply to any reclassification action nor authorize the setting aside of an otherwise proper promotion by a selecting official from a group of properly ranked and certified candidates.

(3) For the purpose of this subsection, 'grievance' and 'collective bargaining agreement' have the meanings set forth in section 7103 of this title, 'unfair labor practice' means an unfair labor practice described in section 7116 of this title, and 'personnel action' includes the omission or failure to take an action or confer a benefit."

Technical And Conforming Amendments

Sec. 703.

(a) Subchapter II of chapter 71 of title 5, United States Code, is amended—
   (1) by redesignating sections 7151 (as amended by section 310 of this Act), 7152, 7153, and 7154 as sections 7201, 7202, 7203, and 7204, respectively;
   (2) by striking out the subchapter heading and inserting in lieu thereof the following:

CHAPTER 72—
ANTIDISCRIMINATION; RIGHT TO PETITION CONGRESS

Subchapter I—Antidiscrimination in Employment

Sec.
7201. Antidiscrimination policy; minority recruitment program.
7202. Marital status.
7203. Handicapping condition.
7204. Other prohibitions.

Subchapter II—Employees' Right to Petition Congress

7211 Employees' right to petition Congress."; and
   (3) by adding at the end thereof the following new subchapter:

Subchapter II—Employees' Right To Petition Congress

§ 7211. Employees' right to petition Congress
    The right of employees, individually or collectively, to petition Congress or a Member of Congress, or to furnish information to either House of Congress, or to a committee or Member thereof, may not be interfered with or denied."

(b) The analysis for part III of title 5, United States Code, is amended by striking out—

Subpart F—Employee Relations

71. Policies 7101;
   and inserting in lieu thereof—

Subpart F—Labor-Management and Employee Relations

71. Labor-Management Relations 7101
72. Antidiscrimination; Right to Petition Congress 7201

(c) (1) Section 2105(c)(1) of title 5, United States Code, is amended by striking out "7152, 7153" and inserting in lieu thereof "7202, 7203".
   (2) Section 3302(2) of title 5, United States Code, is amended by striking out "and 7154" and inserting in lieu thereof "and 7204".
   (3) Sections 4540(c), 7212(a), and 9540(c) of title 10, United States Code, are each amended by striking out "7154 of title 5" and inserting in lieu thereof "7204 of title 5".
   (4) Section 410(b)(1) of title 39, United States Code, is amended by striking out "chapters 71 (employee policies)" and inserting in lieu thereof the following: "chapters 72 (antidiscrimination; right to petition Congress)".
   (5) Section 1002(g) of title 39, United States Code, is amended by striking out "section 7102 of title 5" and inserting in lieu thereof "section 7211 of title 5".

(d) Section 5315 of title 5, United States Code, is amended by adding at the end thereof the following clause:

(124) Chairman, Federal Labor Relations Authority.".

(e) Section 5316 of such title is amended by adding at the end thereof the following clause:

(145) Members, Federal Labor Relations Authority (2) and its General Counsel.".

Sec. 704.   (a) Those terms and conditions of employment and other employment benefits with respect to Government prevailing rate employees to whom section 9(b) of Public Law 92-392 applies which were the subject of negotiation in accordance with prevailing rates and practices prior to August 19, 1972, shall be negotiated on and after the date of the enactment of this Act in accordance with the provisions of section 9(b) of Public Law 92-392 without regard to any provision of chapter 71 of title 5, United States Code (as amended by this title), to the extent that any such provision is inconsistent with the paragraph.

(b) The pay and pay practices relating to employees referred to in paragraph (1) of this subsection shall be negotiated in accordance with prevailing rates and pay practices without regard to any provision of—

(A) chapter 71 of title 5, United States Code (as amended by this title), to the extent that any such provision is inconsistent with this paragraph;

(B) subchapter IV of chapter 53 and subchapter V of chapter 55 of title 5, United States Code; or

(C) any rule, regulation, decision, or order relating to rates of pay or pay practices under subchapter IV of chapter 53 or subchapter V of chapter 55 of title 5, United States Code.

APPENDIX H

EQUAL EMPLOYMENT OPPORTUNITY ACT AMENDING CIVIL RIGHTS ACT OF 1964: TITLE VII— EQUAL EMPLOYMENT OPPORTUNITY ACT OF 1972

86 Stat. 235

DEFINITIONS

[10,401 Title—Sec. 1] This Act may be cited as the "Equal Employment Opportunity Act of 1972."

[10,402 Definitions] Sec. 701. For the purpose of this title—

[10,403 "Person"] [S701] (a) The term "person" includes one or more individuals, governments, governmental agencies, political subdivisions, labor unions, partnerships, associations, corporations, legal representatives, mutual companies, joint-stock companies, trusts, unincorporated organizations, trustees, trustees in bankruptcy, or receivers.

[10,404 "Employer"] [S701] (b) The term "employer" means a person engaged in an industry affecting commerce who has fifteen or more employees for each working day in each of twenty or more calendar weeks in the current or preceding calendar year, and any agent of such a person, but such term does not include (1) the United States, a corporation wholly owned by the Government of the United States, an Indian tribe, or any department or agency of the District of Columbia subject by statute to procedures of the competitive service (as defined in section 2102 of title 5 of the United States Code), or (2) a bona fide private membership club (other than a labor organization) which is exempt from taxation under section 501(c) of the Internal Revenue Code of 1954, except that during the first year after the date of enactment of the Equal Employment Opportunity Act of 1972, persons having fewer than twenty-five employees (and their agents) shall not be considered employers.

[10,405 "Employment agency"] [S701] (c) The term "employment agency" means any person regularly undertaking with or without compensation to procure employees for an employer or to procure for employees opportunities to work for an employer and includes an agent of such a person.

[10,406 "Labor organization"] [S701] (d) The term "labor organization" means a labor organization engaged in an industry affecting commerce, and any agent of such an organization, and includes any organization of any kind, any agency, or employee representation committee, group, association, or plan so engaged in which employees participate and which exists for the purpose, in whole or in part, of dealing with employers concerning grievances, labor disputes, wages, rates of pay, hours, or other terms or conditions of employment, and any conference, general committee, joint or system board, or joint council so engaged which is subordinate to a national or international labor organization.

[10,407 "Labor organization affecting commerce"] [S701] (e) A labor organization shall be deemed to be engaged in an industry affecting commerce if (1) it maintains or operates a hiring hall or hiring office which procures employees for an employer or procures for employees opportunities to work for an employer, or (2) the number of its members (or, where it is a labor organization composed of other labor organizations or their representatives, if the aggregate number of the members of such other labor organization) is (A) twenty-five or more during the first year after the date of enactment of the Equal Employment Opportunity Act of 1972, or (B) fifteen or more thereafter, and such labor organization—

(1) is the certified representative of employees under the provisions of the National Labor Relations Act, as amended, or the Railway Labor Act, as amended;

(2) although not certified, is a national or international labor organization or a local labor organization recognized or acting as the representative of employees of an employer or employers engaged in an industry affecting commerce; or

(3) has chartered a local labor organization or subsidiary body which is representing or actively seeking to represent employees within the meaning of paragraph (1) or (2); or

(4) has been chartered by a labor organization representing or actively seeking to represent employees within the meaning of paragraph (1) or (2) as the local or subordinate body through which such employees may enjoy membership or become affiliated with such labor organization; or

(5) is a conference, general committee, joint or system board, or joint council subordinate to a national or international labor organization, which includes a labor organization engaged in an industry affecting commerce within the meaning of any of the preceding paragraphs of this subsection.

[10,408 "Employee"] [S701] (f) The term "employee" means an individual employed by an employer, except that the term "employee" shall not include any person elected to public office in any State or political subdivision of any State by the qualified voters thereof, or any person chosen by such officer to be on such officer's personal staff, or an appointee on the policy making level or an immediate adviser with respect to the exercise of the constitutional or legal powers of the office. The exemption set forth in the preceding sentence shall not include employees subject to the civil service laws of a State government, governmental agency or political subdivision.

[10,409 "Commerce"] [S701] (g) The term "commerce" means trade, traffic, commerce, transportation, transmission, or communication among the several States; or between a State and any place outside thereof; or within the District of Columbia, or a possession of the United States; or between points in the same State but through a point outside thereof.

[10,410 "Industry affecting commerce"] [S701] (h) The term "industry affecting commerce" means any activity, business, or industry in commerce or in which a labor dispute would hinder or obstruct commerce or the free flow of commerce and includes any activity or industry "affecting commerce" within the meaning of the Labor-Management Reporting and Disclosure Act of 1959, and further includes any governmental industry, business, or activity.

[10,411 "State"] [S701] (i) The term "State" includes a State of the United States, the District of Columbia, Puerto Rico, the Virgin Islands, American Samoa, Guam, Wake Island, the Canal Zone, and Outer Continental Shelf lands defined in the Outer Continental Shelf Lands Act.

[10,412 "Religion"] [S701] (j) The term

"religion" includes all aspects of religious observance and practice, as well as belief, unless an employer demonstrates that he is unable to reasonably accommodate to an employee's or prospective employee's religious observance or practice without undue hardship on the conduct of the employer's business.

EXEMPTION

[10,413 "Exemption"] Sec. 702. This title shall not apply to an employer with respect to the employment of aliens outside any State, or to a religious corporation, association, educational institution, or society with respect of the employment of individuals of a particular religion to perform work connected with the carrying on by such corporation, association, educational institution, or society of its activities.

DISCRIMINATION BECAUSE OF RACE, COLOR, RELIGION, SEX, OR NATIONAL ORIGIN

[10,414 Unlawful employment practices by employers]
SEC. 703. (a) It shall be an unlawful employment practice for an employee—
[10,414.1 Discrimination] [S703 (a)] (1) to fail or refuse to hire or to discharge any individual, or otherwise to discriminate against any individual with respect to his compensation, terms, conditions, or privileges of employment, because of such individual's race, color, religion, sex, or national origin; or
[10,414.2 Segregation] [S703(a)] (2) to limit, segregate, or classify his employees or applicants for employment in any way which would deprive or tend to deprive any individual of employment opportunities or otherwise adversely affect his status as an employee, because of such individual's race, color, religion, sex, or national origin.

[10,415 Unlawful employment practices by employment agencies] [S703] (b) It shall be an unlawful employment practice for an employment agency to fail or refuse to refer for employment, or otherwise to discriminate against any individual because of race, color, religion, sex, or national origin, or to classify or refer for employment any individual on the basis of his race, color, religion, sex or national origin.
[10,416 Unlawful employment practices by labor organizations] [S703] (c) It shall be an unlawful employment practice for a labor organization—
[10,416.1 Discrimination] [S703(c)] (1) to exclude or to expel from its membership, or otherwise to discriminate against, any individual because of his race, color, religion, sex, or national origin;
[10,416.2 Segregation] [S703(c)] (2) to limit, segregate, or classify its membership or applicants for membership or to classify or fail or refuse to refer for employment any individual, in any way which would deprive or tend to deprive any individual of employment opportunities, or would limit such employment opportunities or otherwise adversely affect his status as an employee or as an applicant for employment, because of such individual's race, color, religion, sex, or national origin; or
[10,416.3 Causing employers to discriminate] [S703 (c)] (3) to cause or attempt to cause an employer to discriminate against an individual in violation of this section.
[10,417 Discrimination in apprenticeship programs] [S703] (d) It shall be an unlawful employment practice for any employer, labor organization, or joint labor-management committee controlling apprenticeship or other training or retraining, including on-the-job training programs to discriminate against any individual because of his race, color, religion, sex, or national origin in admission to, or employment in, any program established to provide apprenticeship or other training.
[10,418 Exceptions to unlawful employ-

ment practices] [S703] (e) Notwithstanding any other provision of this title,

[10,418.1 Occupational qualifications] [S703 (e)] (1) it shall not be an unlawful employment practice for an employer to hire and employ employees, for an employment agency to classify, or refer for employment any individual, for a labor organization to classify its membership or to classify or refer for employment any individual, or for an employer, labor organization, or joint labor-management committee controlling apprenticeship or other training or retraining programs to admit or employ any individual in any such program, on the basis of his religion, sex, or national origin in those certain instances where religion, sex, or national origin is a bona fide occupational qualification reasonably necessary to the normal operation of that particular business or enterprise, and

[10,418.2 Religiously affiliated educational institutions] [S703 (e)] (2) it shall not be an unlawful employment practice for a school, college, university, or other educational institution or institution of learning to hire and employ employees of a particular religion if such school, college, university, or other educational institution or institution of learning is, in whole or in substantial part, owned, supported, controlled, or managed by a particular religion or by a particular religious corporation, association, or society, or if the curriculum of such school, college, university, or other educational institution or institution of learning is directed toward the propagation of a particular religion.

[10,419 Communists] [S703] (f) As used in this title, the phrase "unlawful employment practice" shall not be deemed to include any action or measure taken by an employer, labor organization, joint labor-management committee, or employment agency with respect to an individual who is a member of the Communist Party of the United States or of any other organization required to register as a Communist-action or Communist-front organization by final order of the Subversive Activities Control

Board pursuant to the Subversive Activities Control Act of 1950.

[10,420 Security requirements] [S703] (g) Notwithstanding any other provision of this title, it shall not be an unlawful employment practice for an employer to fail or refuse to hire and employ any individual for any position, for an employer to discharge any individual from any position, or for an employment agency to fail or refuse to refer any individual for employment in any position, or for a labor organization to fail or refuse to refer any individual for employment in any position, if—

(1) the occupancy of such position, or access to the premises in or upon which any part of the duties of such position is performed or is to be performed, is subject to any requirement imposed in the interest of the national security of the United States under any security program in effect pursuant to or administered under any statute of the United States or any Executive order of the President; and

(2) such individual has not fulfilled or has ceased to fulfill that requirement.

[10,421 Seniority, merit systems, pay differentials, etc.] [S703] (h) Notwithstanding any other provision of this title, it shall not be an unlawful employment practice for an employer to apply different standards of compensation, or different terms, conditions, or privileges of employment pursuant to a bona fide seniority or merit system, or a system which measures earnings by quantity or quality of production or to employees who work in different locations, provided that such differences are not the result of an intention to discriminate because of race, color, religion, sex, or national origin, nor shall it be an unlawful employment practice for an employer to give and to act upon the results of any professionally developed ability test provided that such test, its administration or action upon the results is not designed, intended, or used to discriminate because of race, color, religion, sex or national origin. It shall not be an unlawful employment practice under this title for any employer to differentiate upon the basis of sex in determining the amount of the wages or compensation paid or to be paid to employees of such employer if such differentiation is authorized by the provisions of section 6(d) of the Fair Labor Standards Act of 1938, as amended [29 U.S.C. 206(d)].

[10,422 Indians] [S703] (i) Nothing contained in this title shall apply to any business or enterprise on or near an Indian reservation with respect to any publicly announced employment practice of such business or enterprise under which a preferential treatment is given to any individual because he is an Indian living on or near a reservation.

[10,423 Existing Imbalances] [S703] (j) Nothing contained in this title shall be interpreted to require any employer, employment agency, labor organization, or joint labor-management committee subject to this title to grant preferential treatment to any individual or to any group because of the race, color, religion, sex, or national origin of such individual or group on account of an imbalance which may exist with respect to the total number or percentage of persons of any race, color, religion, sex, or national origin employed by any employer, referred or classified for employment by any employment agency or labor organization, admitted to membership or classified by any labor organization, or admitted to, or employed in, any apprenticeship or other training program, in comparison with the total number or percentage of persons of such race, color, religion, sex, or national origin in any community, State, section, or other area, or in the available work force in any community, State, section, or other area.

OTHER UNLAWFUL EMPLOYMENT PRACTICES

[10,424 Persons participating in investigations, proceedings, or hearings] Sec. 704. (a) It shall be an unlawful employment practice for an employer to discriminate against any of his employees or applicants for employment, for an employment agency, or joint labor-management committee controlling apprenticeship or other training or retraining, including on-the-job training programs, to discriminate against any individual, or for a labor organization to discriminate against any member thereof or applicant for membership, because he has opposed any practice made an unlawful employment practice by this title, or because he has made a charge, testified, assisted, or participated in any manner in an investigation, proceeding, or hearing under this title.

[10,425 Employment advertisements] [S704] (b) It shall be an unlawful employment practice for an employer, labor organization, employment agency, or joint labor-management committee controlling apprenticeship or other training or retraining, including on-the-job training programs, to print or publish or cause to be printed or published any notice or advertisement relating to employment by such an employer or membership in or any classification or referral for employment by such a labor organization, or relating to any classification or referral for employment by such an employment agency, or relating to admission to, or employment in, any program, established to provide apprenticeship or other training by such a joint labor-management committee indicating any preference, limitation, specification, or discrimination based on race, color, religion, sex, or national origin, except that such a notice or advertisement may indicate a preference, limitation, specification, or discrimination based on religion, sex, or national origin when religion, sex, or national origin is a bona fide occupational qualification for employment.

EQUAL EMPLOYMENT OPPORTUNITY COMMISSION

[10,426 Creation of the Commission] Sec. 705. (a) There is hereby created a Commission to be known as the Equal Employment Opportunity Commission, which shall be composed of five members, not more than three of whom shall be members of the same political party. Members of the Commission shall be appointed by the President by and with the advice and consent of the Senate for a term of five years. Any individual chosen to fill a vacancy shall be appointed only for the unexpired term of the member whom he shall succeed, and all members of the Commission shall continue to serve until their successors are appointed and qualified except that no such member of the Commission shall continue to serve (1) for more than sixty days when the Congress is in session unless a nomination to fill such vacancy shall have been submitted to the Senate, or (2) after the adjournment sine die of the session of the Senate in which such nomination was submitted. The President shall designate one member to serve as Chairman of the Commission, and one member to serve as Vice Chairman. The Chairman shall be responsible on behalf of the Commission for the administrative operations of the Commission, and, except as provided in subsection (b), shall appoint, in accordance with the provisions of title 5, United States Code, governing appointments in the competitive service, such officers, agents, attorneys, hearing examiners, and employees as he deems necessary to assist it in the performance of its functions and to fix their compensation in accordance with the provisions of chapter 51 and subchapter III of chapter 53 of title 5, United States Code, relating to classification and General Schedule pay rates: Provided, That assignment, removal, and compensation of hearing examiners shall be in accordance with sections 3105, 3344, 5362, and 7521 of title 5, United States Code.

[10,427 General Counsel] [S705] (b) (1) There shall be a General Counsel of the Commission appointed by the President, by and with the advice and consent of the Senate, for a term of four years. The General Counsel shall have responsibility for the conduct of litigation as provided in sections 706 and 707 of this title. The General Counsel shall have such other duties as the Commission may prescribe or as may be provided by law and shall concur with the Chairman of the Commission on the appointment and supervision of regional attorneys. The General Counsel of the Commission on the effective date of this Act shall continue in such position and perform the functions specified in this subsection until a successor is appointed and qualified.

(2) Attorneys appointed under this section may, at the direction of the Commission, appear for and represent the Commission in any case in court, provided that the Attorney General shall conduct all litigation to which the Commission is a party in the Supreme Court pursuant to this title.

[10,428 Vacancies] [S705] (c) A vacancy in the Commission shall not impair the right of the remaining members to exercise all the powers of the Commission and three members thereof shall constitute a quorum.

[10,429 Seal] [S705] (d) The Commission shall have an official seal which shall be judicially noticed.

[10,430 Fiscal reports] [S705] (e) The Commission shall at the close of each fiscal year report to the Congress and to the President concerning the action it has taken; the names, salaries, and duties of all individuals in its employ and the moneys it has disbursed; and shall make such further reports on the cause of and means of eliminating discrimination and such recommendations for further legislation as may appear desirable.

[10,431 Amendments to Federal Executive Pay Act of 1956] [Repealed]

[10,432 Principal office] [S705] (f) The principal office of the Commission shall be in or near the District of Columbia, but it may meet or exercise any or all its powers at any other place. The Commission may establish such regional or State offices as it deems necessary to accomplish the purpose of this title.

[10,433 Powers] [S705] (g) The Commission shall have power—

[10,433.1 Cooperation with State, local and other agencies] [S705(g)] (1) to cooperate with and, with their consent, utilize regional, State, local, and other agencies, both public and private, and individuals;

[10,433.2 Payments to witnesses] [S705(g)] (2) to pay to witnesses whose depositions are taken or who are summoned before the Commission or any of its agents the same witness and mileage fees as are paid to witnesses in the courts of the United States;

[10,433.3 Technical assistance] [S705(g)] (3) to furnish to persons subject to this title such technical assistance as they may request to further their compliance with this title or an order issued thereunder;

[10,433.4 Assistance to effectuate Act's provisions] [S705(g)] (4) upon the request of (i) any employer, whose employees or some of them, or (ii) any labor organization, whose members or some of them, refuse or threaten to refuse to cooperate in effectuating the provisions of this title, to assist in such effectuation by conciliation or such other remedial action as is provided by this title;

[10,433.5 Technical studies] [S705(g)] (5) to make such technical studies as are appropriate to effectuate the purposes and policies of this title and to make the results of such studies available to the public;

[10,433.6 Intervention in civil actions] [S705(g)] (6) to intervene in a civil action brought under section 706 by an aggrieved party against a respondent other than a government, governmental agency or political subdivision.

[10,434 Commission's attorneys appearing in court [S705] [Repealed]

[10,435 Cooperation with other departments] [S705] (h) The Commission shall, in any of its educational or promotional activities, cooperate with other departments and agencies in the performance of such educational and promotional activities.

[10,436 Applicability of Hatch Act] [S705] (i) All officers, agents, attorneys, and employees of the Commission shall be subject to the provisions of section 9 of the Act of August 2, 1939, as amended (the Hatch Act), notwithstanding any exemption contained in such action.

PREVENTION OF UNLAWFUL EMPLOYMENT PRACTICES

[10,437 Prevention of unlawful practices] SEC. 706 (a) The Commission is empowered, as hereinafter provided, to prevent any person from engaging in any unlawful employment practice as set forth in section 703 or 704 of this title.

[10,438 Charges and investigations] [S706] (b) Whenever a charge is filed by or on behalf of a person claiming to be aggrieved, or by a member of the Commission, alleging that an employer, employment agency, labor organization, or joint labor-management committee controlling apprenticeship or other training or retraining, including on-the-job training programs, has engaged in an unlawful employment practice, the Commission shall serve a notice of the charge (including the date, place and circumstances of the alleged unlawful employment practice) on such employer, employment agency, labor organization, or joint labor-management committee (hereinafter referred to as the "respondent") within ten days, and shall make an investigation thereof. Charges shall be in such form as the Commission requires. Charges shall not be made public by the Commission. If the Commission determines after such investigation that there is not reasonable cause to believe that the charge is true, it shall dismiss the charge and promptly notify the person claiming to be aggrieved and the respondent of its action. In determining whether reasonable cause exists, the Commission shall accord substantial weight to final findings and orders made by State or local authorities in proceedings commenced under State or local law pursuant to the requirements of subsections (c) and (d). If the Commission determines after such investigation that there is reasonable cause to believe that the charge is true, the Commission shall endeavor to eliminate any such alleged unlawful employment practice by informal methods of conference, conciliation, and persuasion. Nothing said or done during and as a part of such informal endeavors may be made public by the Commission, its officers or employees, or used as evidence in a subsequent proceeding without the written consent of the persons concerned. Any person who makes public information in violation of this subsection shall be fined not more than $1,000 or imprisoned for not more than one year, or both. The Commission shall make its determination on reasonable cause as promptly as possible and, so far as practicable, not later than one hundred and twenty days from the filing of the charge or, where applicable under subsection (c) or (d) from the date upon which the Commission is authorized to take action with respect to the charge.

[10,439 State and local action on individuals' charges] [S706] (c) In the case of an alleged unlawful employment practice occurring in a State, or political subdivision of a State, which has a State or local law prohibiting the unlawful employment practice alleged and establishing or authorizing a State or local authority to grant or seek relief from such practice or to institute criminal proceedings with respect thereto upon receiving notice thereof, no charge may be filed under subsection (a) by the person aggrieved before the expiration of sixty days after proceedings have been commenced under the State or local law, unless such proceedings have been earlier terminated, provided that such sixty-day period shall be extended to one hundred and twenty days during the first year after the effective date of such State or local law. If any requirement for the commencement of such proceedings is imposed by a State or local authority other than a requirement of the filing of a written and signed statement of the facts upon which the proceeding is based, the proceeding shall be deemed to have been commenced for the purposes of this subsection at the time such statement is sent by registered mail to the appropriate State or local authority.

[10,440 State and local action on Commissioners' charges] [S706] (d) In the case of any charge filed by a member of the Commission alleging an unlawful employment practice occurring in a State or political subdivision of a State, which has a State or local law prohibiting the practice alleged and establishing or authorizing a State or local authority to grant or seek relief from such practice or to institute criminal proceedings with respect thereto upon receiving notice thereof, the Commission shall, before taking any action with respect to such charge, notify the appropriate State of local officials and, upon request, afford them a reasonable time, but no less than sixty days (provided that such sixty-day period shall be extended to one hundred and twenty days during the first year after the effective day of such State or local law), unless a shorter period is requested, to act under such State or local law to remedy the practice alleged.

[10,441 Time to file charges] [S706] (e) A charge under this section shall be filed within one hundred and eighty days after the alleged unlawful employment practice occurred and notice of the charge (including the date, place and circumstances of the alleged unlawful employment practice) shall be served upon the person against whom such charge is made within ten days thereafter, except that in a case of an unlawful employment practice with respect to which the person aggrieved has initially instituted proceedings with a State or local agency with authority to grant or seek relief from such practice or to institute criminal proceedings with respect thereto upon receiving notice thereof, such charge shall be filed by or on behalf of the person aggrieved within three hundred days after the alleged unlawful employment practice occurred, or within thirty days after receiving notice that the State or local agency has terminated the proceedings under the State or local law, whichever is earlier, and a copy of such charge shall be filed by the Commission with the State or local agency.

[10,442 Civil action] [S706] (f)(1) If within thirty days after a charge is filed with the Commission or within thirty days after expiration of any period of reference under subsection (c) or (d), the Commission has been unable to secure from the respondent a conciliation agreement acceptable to the Commission, the Commission may bring a civil action against any respondent not a government, governmental agency, or political subdivision named in the charge. In the case of a respondent which is a government, governmental agency, or political subdivision, if the Commission has been unable to secure from the respondent a conciliation agreement acceptable to the Commission, the Commission shall take no further action and shall refer the case to the Attorney General who may bring a civil action against such respondent in the appropriate United States district court. The person or persons aggrieved shall have the right to intervene in a civil action brought by the Commission or the Attorney General in a case involving a government, governmental agency, or political subdivision. If a charge filed with the Commission pursuant to subsection (b) is dismissed by the Commission, or if within one hundred and eighty days from the filing of such charge or the expiration of any period of reference under subsection (c) or (d), whichever is later, the Commission has not filed a civil action under this section or the Attorney General has not filed a civil action in a case involving a government, governmental agency, or political subdivision, or the Commission has not entered into a conciliation agreement to which the person aggrieved is a party, the Commission, or the Attorney General in a case involving a government, governmental agency, or political subdivision, shall so notify the person ag-

grieved and within ninety days after the giving of such notice a civil action may be brought against the respondent named in the charge (A) by the person claiming to be aggrieved or (B) if such charge was filed by a member of the Commission, by any person whom the charge alleges was aggrieved by the alleged unlawful employment practice. Upon application by the complainant and in such circumstances as the court may deem just, the court may appoint an attorney for such complainant and may authorize the commencement of the action without the payment of fees, costs, or security. Upon timely application, the court may, in its discretion, permit the Commission, or the Attorney General in a case involving a government, governmental agency, or political subdivision, to intervene in such civil action upon certification that the case is of general public importance. Upon request, the court may, in its discretion, stay further proceedings for not more than sixty days pending the termination of State or local proceedings described in subsections (c) or (d) of this section or further efforts of the Commission to obtain voluntary compliance.

[10,442.1 Injunctions] [S706(f)] (2) Whenever a charge is filed with the Commission and the Commission concludes on the basis of a preliminary investigation that prompt judicial action is necessary to carry out the purposes of this Act, the Commission, or the Attorney General in a case involving a government, governmental agency, or political subdivision, may bring an action for appropriate temporary or preliminary relief pending final disposition of such charge. Any temporary restraining order or other order granting preliminary or temporary relief shall be issued in accordance with rule 65 of the Federal Rules of Civil Procedure. It shall be the duty of a court having jurisdiction over proceedings under this section to assign cases for hearing at the earliest practicable date and to cause such cases to be in every way expedited.

[10,442.2 Jurisdiction of courts] [S706(f)]

(2) Each United States district court and each United States court of a place subject to the jurisdiction of the United States shall have jurisdiction of actions brought under this title. Such an action may be brought in any judicial district in the State in which the unlawful employment practice is alleged to have been committed, in the judicial district in which the employment records relevant to such practice are maintained and administered, or in the judicial district in which the aggrieved person would have worked but for the alleged unlawful employment practice, but if the respondent is not found within any such district, such an action may be brought within the judicial district in which the respondent has his principal office. For purposes of sections 1404 and 1406 of title 28 of the United States Code, the judicial district in which the respondent has his principal office shall in all cases be considered a district in which the action might have been brought.

[10,442.3 Assigning cases] [S706(f)] (4) It shall be the duty of the chief judge of the district (or in his absence, the acting chief judge) in which the case is pending immediately to designate a judge in such district to hear and determine the case. In the event that no judge in the district is available to hear and determine the case, the chief judge of the district, or the acting chief judge, as the case may be, shall certify this fact to the chief judge of the circuit (or in his absence, the acting chief judge) who shall then designate a circuit judge of the circuit to hear and determine the case.

[10,442.4 Expediting cases] [S706(f)] (5) It shall be the duty of the judge designated pursuant to this subsection to assign the case for hearing at the earliest practicable date to cause the case to be in every way expedited. If such judge has not scheduled the case for trial within one hundred and twenty days after issue has been joined, that judge may appoint a master pursuant to rule 53 of the Federal Rules of Civil Procedure.

[10,443 Courts' remedial authority] [S706] (g) If the court finds that the respondent has intentionally engaged in an unlawful employment practice charged in the complaint, the court may enjoin the respondent from engaging in such unlawful employment practice, and order such affirmative action as may be appropriate, which may include, but is not limited to, reinstatement or hiring of employees, with or without back pay payable by the employer, employment agency, or labor organization, as the case may be, responsible for the unlawful employment practice, or any other equitable relief as the court deems appropriate. Back pay liability shall not accrue from a date more than two years prior to the filing of a charge with the Commission. Interim earnings or amounts earnable with reasonable diligence by the person or persons discriminated against shall operate to reduce the back pay otherwise allowable. No order of the court shall require the admission or reinstatement of an individual as a member of a union, or the hiring, reinstatement, or promotion of an individual as an employee, or the payment to him of any back pay, if such individual was refused admission, suspended, or expelled or was refused employment or advancement or was suspended or discharged for any reason other than discrimination on account of race, color, religion, sex, or national origin or in violation of section 704(a).

[10,444 Applicability of 29 U.S.C. 101–115] [S706] (h) The provisions of the Act entitled "An Act to amend the Judicial Code and to define and limit the jurisdiction of courts sitting in equity, and for other purposes," approved March 23, 1932 (29 U.S.C. 101–115), shall not apply with respect to civil actions brought under this section.

[10,445 Enforcement of court orders] [S706] (i) In any case in which an employer, employment agency, or labor organization fails to comply with an order of a court issued in a civil action brought under this section, the Commission may commence proceedings to compel compliance with such order.

[10,446 Appeals] [S706] (j) Any civil action brought under subsection (e) and any proceedings brought under this section shall be subject to appeal as provided in sections 1291 and 1292, title 28, United States Code.

[10,447 Attorney's fees] [S706] (k) In any action or proceeding under this title the court, in its discretion, may allow the prevailing party, other than the Commission or the United States, a reasonable attorney's fee as part of the costs, and the Commission and the United States shall be liable for costs the same as a private person.

[10,448 Civil actions by the Attorney General] SEC. 707. (a) Whenever the Attorney General has reasonable cause to believe that any person or group of persons is engaged in a pattern or practice of resistance to the full enjoyment of any of the rights secured by this title, and the pattern or practice is of such a nature and is intended to deny the full exercise of the rights herein described, the Attorney General may bring a civil action in the appropriate district court of the United States by filing with it a complaint (1) signed by him (or in his absence the Acting Attorney General), (2) setting forth facts pertaining to such pattern or practice, and (3) requesting such relief, including an application for a permanent or temporary injunction, restraining order or other order against the person or persons responsible for such pattern or practice, as he deems necessary to insure the full enjoyment of the rights herein described.

[10,449 Court handling of suits by the Attorney General] [S707] (b) The district courts of the United States shall have and shall exercise jurisdiction of proceedings instituted pursuant to this section, and in any such proceeding the Attorney General may file with the clerk of such court a request that a court of three judges be convened to hear and determine the case. Such request by the Attorney General shall be accompanied by a certificate that, in his opinion, the case is of general public importance. A copy of the certificate and request for a three-judge court shall be immediately furnished by such clerk to the chief judge of the circuit (or in his absence, the presiding circuit judge of the circuit) in which the case is pending. Upon receipt of such request it shall be the duty of the chief judge of the circuit or the presiding circuit judge, as the case may be, to designate immediately three judges in such circuit, of whom at least one shall be a circuit judge and another of whom shall be a district judge of the court in which the proceeding was instituted, to hear and determine such case, and it shall be the duty of the judges so designated to assign the case for hearing at the earliest practicable date, to participate in the hearing and determination thereof, and to cause the case to be in every way expedited. An appeal from the final judgment of such court will lie to the Supreme Court.

In the event the Attorney General fails to file such a request in any such proceeding, it shall be the duty of the chief judge of the district (or in his absence, the acting chief judge) in which the case is pending immediately to designate a judge in such district to hear and determine the case. In the event that no judge in the district is available to hear and determine the case, the chief judge of the district, or the acting chief judge, as the case may be, shall certify this fact to the chief judge of the circuit (or in his absence, the acting chief judge) who shall then designate a district or circuit judge of the circuit to hear and determine the case.

It shall be the duty of the judge designated pursuant to this section to assign the case for hearing at the earliest practicable date and to cause the case to be in every way expedited.

[10,450 Transfer of functions to Commission] [S707] (c) Effective two years after the date of enactment of the Equal Employment Opportunity Act of 1972, the functions of the Attorney General under this section shall be transferred to the Commission, together with such personnel, property, records, and unexpended balances of appropriations, allocations, and other funds employed, used, held, available, or to be made available in connection with such functions unless the President submits, and neither House of Congress vetoes, a reorganization plan pursuant to chapter 9 of title 5, United States Code, inconsistent with the provisions of this subsection. The Commission shall carry out such functions in accordance with subsections (d) and (e) of this section.

[10,451 Suits pending] [S707] (d) Upon the transfer of functions provided for in subsection (c) of this section, in all suits commenced pursuant to this section prior to the date of such transfer, proceedings shall continue without abatement, all court orders and decrees shall remain in effect, and the Commission shall be substituted as a party for the United States of America, the Attorney General, or the Acting Attorney General, as appropriate.

[10,452 Commission's authority] [S707] (e) Subsequent to the date of enactment of the Equal Employment Opportunity Act of 1972, the Commission shall have authority to investigate and act on a charge of pattern or practice of discrimination, whether filed by or on behalf of a person claiming to be aggrieved or by a member of the Commission. All such actions shall be conducted in accordance with the procedures set forth in section 706 of this act.

EFFECT ON STATE LAWS

[10,453 State law] Sec. 708. Nothing in this title shall be deemed to exempt or relieve any person from any liability, duty, penalty, or punishment provided by any present or future law of any State or political subdivision of a State, other than any such law which purports to require or permit the doing of any act which would be an unlawful employment practice under this title.

INVESTIGATIONS, INSPECTIONS, RECORDS, STATE AGENCIES

[10,454 Right to evidence during investigation] Sec. 709. (a) In connection with any investigation of a charge filed under section 706, the Commission or its designated representative shall at all reasonable times have access to, for the purposes of examination, and the right to copy any evidence of any person being investigated or proceeded against that relates to unlawful employment practices covered by this title and is relevant to the charge under investigation.

[10,455 Agreements with, and payments to, other agencies] [S709] (b) The Commission may cooperate with State and local agencies charged with the administration of State fair employment practices laws and, with the consent of such agencies, may, for the purpose of carrying out its functions and duties under this title and within the limitation of funds appropriated specifically for such purpose, engage in and contribute to the cost of research and other projects of mutual interest undertaken by such agencies, and utilize the services of such agencies and their employees, and, notwithstanding any other provision of law, pay by advance or reimbursement such agencies and their employees for services rendered to assist the Commission in carrying out this title. In furtherance of such cooperative efforts, the Commission may enter into written agreements with such State or local agencies and such agreements may include provisions under which the Commission shall refrain from processing a charge in any cases or class of cases specified in such agreements or under which the Commission shall relieve any person or class of persons in such State or locality from requirements imposed under this section. The Commission shall rescind any such agreement whenever it determines that the agreement no longer serves the interest of effective enforcement of this title.

[10,456 Reports and records] [S709] (c) Every employer, employment agency, and labor organization subject to this title shall (1) make and keep such records relevant to the determinations of whether unlawful employment practices have been or are being committed, (2) preserve such records for such periods, and (3) make such reports therefrom as the Commission shall prescribe by regulation or order, after public hearing, as reasonable, necessary, or appropriate for the enforcement of this title or the regulations or orders thereunder. The Commission shall, by regulation, require each employer, labor organization, and joint labor-management committee subject to this title which controls an apprenticeship or other training program to maintain such records as are reasonably necessary to carry out the purpose of this title, including, but not limited to, a list of applicants who wish to participate in such program, including the chronological order in which such applications were received, and to furnish to the Commission upon request, a detailed description of the manner in which persons are selected to participate in the apprenticeship or other training program. Any employer, employment agency, labor organization, or joint labor-management committee which believes that the application to it of any regulation or order issued under this section would result in undue hardship may apply to the Commission for an exemption from the application of such regulation or order, and, if such application for an exemption is denied, bring a civil action in the United States district court for the district where such records are kept. If the Commission or the court, as the case may be, finds that the application of the regulation or order to the employer, employment agency, or labor organization in question would impose an undue hardship, the Commission or the court, as the case may be, may grant appropriate relief. If any person required to comply with the provisions of this subsection fails or refuses to do so, the United States district court for the district in which such person is found, resides, or transacts business, shall, upon application of the Commission, or the Attorney General in a case involving a government, governmental agency or political subdivision, have jurisdiction to issue to such person an order requiring him to comply.

[10,457 Reports and records required by other agencies] [S709] (d) In prescribing requirement pursuant to subsection (c) of this section, the Commission shall consult with other interested State and Federal agencies and shall endeavor to coordinate its requirements with those adopted by such agencies. The Commission shall furnish upon request and without cost to any State or local agency charged with the administration of a fair employment practice law information obtained pursuant to subsection (c) of this section from any employer, to the jurisdiction of such agency. Such information shall be furnished on condition that it not be made public by the recipient agency prior to the institution of a proceeding under State or local law involving such information. If this condition is violated by a recipient agency, the Commission may decline to honor subsequent requests pursuant to this subsection.

[10,458 Criminal provisions for releasing confidential information] [S709] (e) It shall be unlawful for any officer or employee of the Commission to make public in any manner whatever any information obtained by the Commission pursuant to its authority under this section proper to the institution of any proceeding under this title involving such information. Any officer or employee of the Commission who shall make public in any manner whatever any information in violation of this subsection shall be guilty of a misdemeanor and upon conviction thereof, shall be fined not more than $1,000, or imprisoned not more than one year.

INVESTIGATORY POWERS

[10,459 Investigations; obtaining evidence] Sec. 710. For the purpose of all hearings and investigations conducted by the Commission or its duly authorized agents or agencies, section 11 of the National Labor Relations Act (49 Stat. 455; 29 U.S.C. 161) [10,511] shall apply.

NOTICES TO BE POSTED

[10,460 Notices] Sec. 711. (a) Every employer, employment agency, and labor organization, as the case may be, shall post and keep posted in conspicuous places upon its premises where notices to employees, applicants for employment, and members are customarily posted a notice to be prepared or approved by the Commission setting forth excerpts from or, summaries of, the pertinent provisions of this title and information pertinent to the filing of a complaint.

[10,461 Penalties for not posting notices] [S711] (b) A willful violation of this section shall be punishable by a fine of not more than $100 for each separate offense.

VETERANS' PREFERENCE

[10,462 Veterans' preference] Sec. 712. Nothing contained in this title shall be construed to repeal or modify any Federal, State, territorial, or local law creating special right or preference for veterans.

RULES AND REGULATIONS

[10,463 Rules and regulations] Sec. 713. (a) The Commission shall have authority from time to time to issue, amend, or rescind suitable procedural regulations to carry out the provisions of this title. Regulations issued under this section shall be in conformity with the standards and limitations of the Administrative Procedure Act.

[10,464 Defenses; good faith] [S713] (b) In any action or proceeding based on any alleged unlawful employment practice, no person shall be subject to any liability or punishment for or on account of (1) the commission by such person of an unlawful employment practice if he pleads and proves that the act or omission complained of was in good faith, in conformity with, and in reli-

ance on any written interpretation or opinion of the Commission, or (2) the failure of such person to publish and file any information required by any provision of this title if he pleads and proves that he failed to publish and file such information in good faith, in conformity with the instructions of the Commission issued under this title regarding the filing of such information. Such a defense, if established, shall be a bar to the action or proceeding, notwithstanding that (A) after such act or omission, such interpretation or opinion is modified or rescinded or is determined by judicial authority to be invalid or of no legal effect, or (B) after publishing or filing the description and annual reports, such publication or filing is determined by judicial authority not to be in conformity with the requirements of this title.

FORCIBLY RESISTING THE COMMISSION OR ITS REPRESENTATIVES

[10,465 Applicability of 18 U.S.C. 111] Sec. 714. The provisions of sections 111 and 1114, title 18, United States Code, shall apply to officers, agents, and employees of the Commission in the performance of their official duties. Notwithstanding the provisions of sections 111 and 1114 of title 18, United States Code, whoever in violation of the provisions of section 1114 of such title kills a person while engaged in or on account of the performance of his official functions under this Act shall be punished by imprisonment for any term of years or for life.

EQUAL EMPLOYMENT OPPORTUNITY COORDINATING COUNCIL

[10,466 Coordinating Council] Sec. 715. There shall be established an Equal Employment Opportunity Coordinating Council (hereinafter referred to in this section as the Council) composed of the Secretary of Labor, the Chairman of the Equal Employment Opportunity Commission, the Attorney General, the Chairman of the United States Civil Service Commission, and the Chairman of the United States Civil Rights Commission, or their respective delegates. The Council shall have the responsibility for developing and implementing agreements, policies and practices designed to maximize effort, promote efficiency, and eliminate conflict, competition, duplication and inconsistency among the operations, functions and jurisdictions of the various departments, agencies, and branches of the Federal Government responsible for the implementation and enforcement of equal employment opportunity legislation, orders, and policies. On or before July 1 of each year, the Council shall transmit to the president and to the Congress a report of its activities, together with such recommendations for legislative or administrative changes as it concludes are desirable to further promote the purposes of this section.

NONDISCRIMINATION IN FEDERAL GOVERNMENT EMPLOYMENT

[10,467 Nondiscrimination] SEC. 717. (a) All personnel actions affecting employees or applicants for employment (except with regard to aliens employed outside the limits of the United States) in military departments as defined in section 102 of title 5, United States Code, in executive agencies (other than the General Accounting Office) as defined in section 105 of title 5, United States Code (including employees and applicants for employment who are paid from nonappropriated funds), in the United States Postal Service and the Postal Rate Commission, in those units of the Government of the District of Columbia having positions in the competitive service, and in those units of the legislative and judicial branches of the Federal Government having positions in the competitive service, and in the Library of Congress shall be made free from any discrimination based on race, color, religion, sex, or national origin.

[10,468 Civil Service Commission] [S717] (b) Except as otherwise provided in this subsection, the Civil Service Commission shall have authority to enforce the provisions of subsection (a) through appropriate remedies, including reinstatement or hiring of employees with or without back pay, as will effectuate the policies of this section, and shall issue such rules, regulations, orders and instructions as it deems necessary and appropriate to carry out its responsibilities under this section. The Civil Service Commission shall—

[10,468.1 Annual Review] [S717(b)] (1) be responsible for the annual review and approval of a national and regional equal employment opportunity plan which each department and agency and each appropriate unit referred to in subsection (a) of this section shall submit in order to maintain an affirmative program of equal employment opportunity for all such employees and applicants for employment;

[10,468.2 Semiannual Reports] [S717(b)] (2) be responsible for the review and evaluation of the operation of all agency equal employment opportunity programs, periodically obtaining and publishing (on at least a semiannual basis) progress reports from each such department, agency, or unit; and

[10,468.3 Consultation] [S717(b)] (3) consult with and solicit the recommendations of interested individuals, groups, and organizations relating to equal employment opportunity.

[10,468.4 Heads of Agencies] [S717(b)] (4) The head of each such department, agency, or unit shall comply with such rules, regulations, orders, and instructions which shall include a provision that an employee or applicant for employment shall be notified of any final action taken on any complaint of discrimination filed by him thereunder. The plan submitted by each department, agency, and unit shall include, but not be limited to —

(1) provision for the establishment of training and education programs designed to provide a maximum opportunity for employees to advance so as to perform at their highest potential; and

(2) a description of the qualifications in terms of training and experience relating to equal employment opportunity for the principal and operating officials of each such department, agency, or unit responsible for carrying out the equal employment opportunity program and of the allocation of personnel and resources proposed by such department, agency, or unit to carry out its equal employment opportunity program.

[10,468.5 Librarian of Congress] [S717(b)] (5) With respect to employment in the Library of Congress, authorities granted in this subsection to the Civil Service Commission shall be exercised by the Librarian of Congress.

[10,469 Civil Actions] [S717] (c) Within thirty days of receipt of notice of final action taken by a department, agency, or unit referred to in subsection 717 (a), or by the Civil Service Commission upon an appeal from a decision or order of such department, agency, or unit of a complaint of discrimination based on race, color, religion, sex or national origin, brought pursuant to subsection (a) of this section, Executive Order 11478 or any succeeding Executive orders, or after one hundred and eighty days from the filing of the initial charge with the department, agency, or unit or with the Civil Service Commission on appeal from a decision or order of such department, agency, or unit until such time as final action may be taken by a department, agency, or unit, an employee or applicant for employment, if aggrieved by the final disposition of his com-

plaint, or by the failure to take final action on his complaint, may file a civil action as provided in section 706, in which civil action the head of the department, agency, or unit, as appropriate, shall be the defendant.

[10,470 Applicability of other sections] [S717] (d) The provisions of section 706 (f) through (k), as applicable, shall govern civil actions brought hereunder.

[10,471 Responsibility under Executive Order] [S717] (e) Nothing contained in this Act shall relieve any Government agency or official of its or his primary responsibility to assure nondiscrimination in employment as required by the Constitution and statutes or of its or his responsibilities under Executive Order 11478 relating to equal employment opportunity in the Federal Government.

SPECIAL PROVISION WITH RESPECT TO DENIAL, TERMINATION, AND SUSPENSION OF GOVERNMENT CONTRACTS

[10,472 Hearings required] Sec. 718. No Government contract, or portion thereof, with any employer, shall be denied, withheld, terminated, or suspended, by any agency or officer of the United States under any equal employment opportunity law or order, where such employer has an affirmative action plan which has previously been accepted by the Government for the same facility within the past twelve months without first according such employer full hearing and adjudication under the provisions of title 5, United States Code, section 554, and the following pertinent sections: Provided, That if such employer has deviated substantially from such previously agreed to affirmative action plan, this section shall not apply: Provided further, That for the purposes of this section an affirmative action plan shall be deemed to have been accepted by the Government at the time the appropriate compliance agency has accepted such plan unless within forty-five days thereafter the Office of Federal Contract Compliance has disapproved such plan.

MISCELLANEOUS PROVISIONS UNDER 1964 LAW

[10,473 Effective date] (a) This title shall become effective one year after the date of its enactment.

(b) Notwithstanding subsection (a), sections of this title other than sections 703, 704, 706, and 707 shall become effective immediately.

[10,474 Presidential conferences] (c) The President shall, as soon as feasible after the enactment of this title, convene one or more conferences for the purpose of enabling the leaders of groups whose members will be affected by this title to become familiar with the rights afforded and obligations imposed by its provisions, and for the purpose of making plans which will result in the fair and effective administration of this title, when all of its provisions become effective. The President shall invite the participation in such conference or conferences of (1) the members of the President's Committee on Equal Employment Opportunity, (2) the members of the Commission on Civil Rights, (3) representatives of State and local agencies engaged in furthering equal employment opportunity, (4) representatives of private agencies engaged in furthering equal employment opportunity, and (5) representatives of employers, labor organizations, and employment agencies who will be subject to this title.

MISCELLANEOUS PROVISION UNDER 1972 LAW

[10,475 Effective date] The amendments made by this Act to section 706 of the Civil Rights Act of 1964 shall be applicable with respect to charges pending with the Commission on the date of enactment of this Act and all charges filed thereafter.

BIBLIOGRAPHY

Books

BARNES, JAMES A., *Wealth of the American People.* Englewood Cliffs, N.J.: Prentice-Hall, Inc., 1949.

BEARD, CHARLES A. AND MARY BEARD, *The Rise of American Civilization.* New York: The Macmillan Company, 1927.

BENT, SILAS, *Justice Oliver Wendell Holmes.* New York: Vanguard Press, 1932.

BERMAN, EDWARD, *Labor and the Sherman Act.* New York: Harper & Bros., 1930.

BLACKMAN, JOHN L., JR., *Presidential Seizure in Labor Disputes.* Cambridge, Mass.: Harvard University Press, 1967.

BOWMAN, D. O., *Public Control of Labor Relations.* New York: The Macmillan Company, 1942.

BROOKS, R. R., *Unions of Their Own Choosing.* New Haven: Yale University Press, 1937.

————, *When Labor Organizes.* New Haven: Yale University Press, 1937.

CHRISTENSON, CARROLL L. AND RICHARD A. MYREN, *Wage Policy Under the Walsh-Healey Public Contracts Act: A Critical Review.* Bloomington, Ind.: Indiana University Press, 1966.

COCHRAN, THOMAS C. AND WILLIAM MILLER, *The Age of Enterprise.* New York: The Macmillan Company, 1943.

COMMONS, JOHN R. AND ASSOCIATES, *History of Labour in the United States.* New York: The Macmillan Company, 1926.

COMMONS, JOHN R. AND EUGENE A. GILMORE, *A Documentary History of American Industrial Society.* Cleveland: The Arthur H. Clark Company, 1910.

DOUGLAS, PAUL A. AND AARON DIRECTOR, *The Problem of Unemployment.* New York: The Macmillan Company, 1931.

ESTEY, MARTEN S., PHILIP TAFT, AND MARTIN WAGNER, eds., *Regulating Union Government.* New York: Harper & Row, 1964.

815

EVANS, HYWELL, *Government Regulation of Industrial Relations.* New York: Cornell University, New York State School of Industrial and Labor Relations, 1961.

FALCONE, NICHOLAS S., *Labor Law.* New York: John Wiley & Sons, Inc., 1963.

FRANCE, ROBERT R. AND RICHARD A. LESTER, *Compulsory Arbitration of Utility Disputes in New Jersey and Pennsylvania.* Princeton, N.J.: Industrial Relations Section, Princeton University, 1951.

FRANKFURTER, FELIX AND NATHAN GREENE, *The Labor Injunction.* New York: The Macmillan Company, 1930.

FREY, J. P., *The Labor Injunction.* Cincinnati: Equity Publishing Company, 1927.

HANDLER, MILTON, *Cases and Materials on Trade Regulations.* Chicago: The Foundation Press, 1937.

HART, WILSON R., *Collective Bargaining in the Federal Civil Service.* New York: Harper & Row, 1961.

HARTLEY, FRED, *Our New National Labor Policy.* New York: Funk & Wagnalls Company, 1948.

HERON, ALEXANDER R., *Beyond Collective Bargaining.* Stanford, Calif.: Stanford University Press, 1948.

HOWARD, SIDNEY AND ROBERT DUNN, *The Labor Spy.* New York: The Republic Publishing Company, 1921.

Interchurch World Movement's Study of the Steel Strike of 1919.

KAUFMAN, JACOB J., *Collective Bargaining in the Railroad Industry.* New York: King's Crown Press, 1954.

KEARNEY, RICHARD C., *Labor Relations in the Public Sectors,* New York: Marcel Dekker, Inc., 1984.

KILLINGSWORTH, CHARLES C., *State Labor Relations Acts.* Chicago: The University of Chicago Press, 1948.

KOVARSKY, IRVING, *Discrimination in Employment.* Iowa City: Center for Labor and Management, The University of Iowa, 1976.

LANDIS, JAMES M. AND MARCUS MANOFF, *Cases on Labor Law.* Chicago: The Foundation Press, 1942.

LEVINSON, EDWARD, *I Break Strikes: The Technique of Pearl L. Bergoff.* New York: R. M. McBride and Company, 1935.

LORWIN, LEWIS L. AND ARTHUR WUBNIG, *Labor Relations Boards.* New York: Brookings Institution, 1935.

MASON, A. T., *Brandeis: A Free Man's Life.* New York: The Viking Press, 1946.

——, *Organized Labor and the Law.* Durham, N.C.: Duke University Press, 1925.

McCULLOCH, FRANK N. AND TIM BORNSTEIN, *The National Labor Relations Board.* New York: Frederick A. Praeger, Inc., 1974.

MILLER, GLENN W., *American Labor and the Government.* Englewood Cliffs, N.J.: Prentice-Hall, Inc., 1948.

MILLIS, HARRY A. AND ROYAL E. MONTGOMERY, *Organized Labor.* New York: McGraw-Hill Book Company, 1945.

NATIONAL CIVIL SERVICE LEAGUE, Committee on Public Employer-Employee Relations, *Employee Organizations in the Public Service.* New York, 1946.

PALMER, FRANK, *Spies in Steel: An Exposé of Industrial Warfare.* Denver, Colo.: The Labor Press, 1928.

PETERSON, FLORENCE, *American Labor Unions.* New York: Harper & Bros., 1935.

POWDERLY, T. V., *The Path I Trod.* New York: Columbia University Press, 1940.

Public Papers and Addresses of Franklin D. Roosevelt. New York: Random House, 1938–1950.

REES, ALBERT, *The Economics of Trade Unions.* Chicago: The University of Chicago Press, 1962.

SEIDMAN, JOEL, *The Yellow Dog Contract.* Baltimore: Johns Hopkins Press, 1932.

SHISTER, JOSEPH, BENJAMIN AARON, AND CLYDE W. SUMMERS, eds., *Public Policy and Collective Bargaining.* New York: Harper & Row, 1962.

———, *Economics of the Labor Market.* Chicago: J. B. Lippincott Company, 1949.

SLESINGER, REUBEN E., *National Economic Policy: The Presidential Reports.* Princeton, N.J.: D. Van Nostrand Company, Inc., 1968.

SLOVENKO, RALPH, ed., *Symposium on the Labor-Management Reporting and Disclosure Act of 1959.* Baton Rouge, La.: Claitor's Bookstore, 1960.

SPERO, STERLING DENHARD, *Government as Employer.* New York: Remsen Press, 1948.

TAYLOR, BENJAMIN J., *Arizona Labor Relations Law,* Occasional Paper No. 2. Tempe: Arizona State University, Bureau of Business and Economic Research, College of Business Administration, 1967.

———, *The Operation of the Taft-Hartley Act in Indiana,* Indiana Business Bulletin No. 58. Bloomington, Ind.: Bureau of Business Research, 1967.

TWENTIETH CENTURY FUND, INC., *Labor and Government.* New York: McGraw-Hill Book Company, 1953.

UNITED STATES DEPARTMENT OF LABOR, *Growth of Labor Law in the United States.* Washington, D.C.: Government Printing Office, 1967.

WITNEY, FRED, *Indiana Labor Relations Law.* Bloomington, Ind.: Indiana University, Bureau of Business Research, 1960.

———, *Wartime Experiences of the National Labor Relations Board.* Urbana, Ill.: University of Illinois Press, 1949.

WITTE, EDWIN E., *The Government in Labor Disputes.* New York: McGraw-Hill Book Company, 1932.

WRIGHT, CHESTER W., *Economic History of the United States.* New York: McGraw-Hill Book Company, 1949.

YOUNG, JAMES E. AND BETTY L. BREWER, *State Legislation Affecting Labor Relations in State and Local Government.* Kent, Ohio: Kent State University Bureau of Economic and Business Research, 1968.

ARTICLES

AARON, BENJAMIN, "Employee Rights and Union Democracy," *Monthly Labor Review,* v. 92, No. 3, March 1969.

ABNER, WILLOUGHBY, "The FMCS and Dispute Mediation in the Federal Government," *Monthly Labor Review,* v. 92, No. 5, May 1969.

AMERICAN ASSOCIATION OF UNIVERSITY PROFESSORS. "The *Yeshiva* Decision," *Academe,* Bulletin of the AAUP, v. 66, May 1980.

"Arbitration Provisions in Collective Agreements, 1952," *Monthly Labor Review,* March 1953.

"Bargaining in Agriculture: Current Trends in Labor Management Relations," Speech before the Fifteenth New Jersey Marketing Institute, November 30, 1972.

BERNSTEIN, IRVING, HAROLD L. ENARSON, AND R. W. FLEMING, eds., "The Economic Impact of Strikes in Key Industries," *Emergency Disputes and National Policy.* New York: Harper & Bros., 1955.

———— AND HUGH G. LOVELL, "Are Coal Strikes National Emergencies?" *Industrial and Labor Relations Review,* v. 6, No. 3, April 1953.

BERNSTEIN, JULES A., "The Evolution of the Use of Management Consultants in Labor Relations: A Labor Perspective," *Labor Law Journal,* v. 36, No. 5, May 1985.

BLOCH, RICHARD I., "The NLRB and Arbitration: Is the Board's Expanding Jurisdiction Justified?" *Labor Law Journal,* v. 19, No. 10, October 1968.

BLOEDORN, JOHN, "The Strike and the Public Sector," *Labor Law Journal,* v. 20, No. 3, March 1969.

BOK, DEREK C., "The Regulation of Campaign Tactics in Representation Elections under the National Labor Relations Act," *Harvard Law Review,* v. 78, No. 1, November 1964.

BRISSENDEN, P. F. AND C. O. SWAYZEE, "The Use of Injunctions in the New York Needle Trades," *Political Science Quarterly,* v. 44, 1929.

BROD, GAIL FROMMER, "The NLRB Changes its Policy on the Legality of an Employer's Discharge of a Disloyal Supervisor," *Labor Law Journal,* v. 34, No. 1, January 1983.

BUREAU OF NATIONAL AFFAIRS, "Report and Recommendations of the Panel," *War Labor Reports,* v. 26.

CHRISTENSON, C. L., "The Impact of Labor Disputes upon Coal Consumption," *American Economic Review,* v. 45, No. 1, March 1955.

————, "The Theory of the Offset Factor: The Impact of Labor Disputes upon Coal Production," *American Economic Review,* v. 43, No. 4, September 1953.

COOKE, WILLIAM N. and FREDERICK H. GAUTSCHI III, "Political Bias in NLRB Unfair Labor Practice Decisions," *Industrial and Labor Relations Review,* v. 35, No. 4, July 1982.

COUNCIL ON LABOR LAW AND LABOR RELATIONS, "Federal Bar Association Task Force I Report—E. O. 11616," *Labor Law Journal,* July 1972.

"Coverage of Checkoff Under Taft-Hartley Act," *Monthly Labor Review,* v. 67, July 1948.

COX, ARCHIBALD, "Rights Under a Labor Agreement," *Harvard Law Review,* v. 69, 1956.

————, "The Role of Law in Preserving Union Democracy," *Harvard Law Review,* v. 72, 1959.

CRAVER, CHARLES B., "Bargaining in the Federal Sector," *Labor Law Journal,* v. 19, No. 9, September 1968.

DONIAN, HARRY A., "A New Approach to Setting the Pay of Federal Blue-Collar Workers," *Monthly Labor Review,* v. 92, No. 4, April 1969.

DOTSON, DONALD L. "Processing Cases at the NLRB," *Labor Law Journal,* v. 35, No. 1, January 1984.

DROTNING, JOHN E., "Employer Free Speech: Two Basic Questions Considered by the NLRB and Courts," *Labor Law Journal,* v. 16, No. 3, March 1965.

DUNHAM, ROBERT E., "Interest Arbitration in Non-Federal Public Employment," *The Arbitration Journal,* v. 31, No. 1, March 1976.

DUNLOP, JOHN T., "Jurisdictional Disputes," *Proceedings of New York University Second Annual Conference of Labor.*

DWORKIN, JAMES D. AND MARIAN EXTEJT, "The Union-Shop Deauthorization Poll: A New Look After 20 Years, *"Monthly Labor Review,* v. 102, No. 11, November 1979.

FLEMING, R. W., "Title VII: The Taft-Hartley Amendments," *Northwestern University Law Review,* v. 54, No. 6, January-February 1960.

Fox, Milden J. Jr., Robert H. C. Even, and John G. Hamilton, "Product Boycotts in the Construction Industry and the NLRB 'Right of Control' Doctrine," *Labor Law Journal*, v. 27, No. 4, April 1976.

Gercacz, John William and Charles E. Krider, "NLRB v. Yeshiva University: The End of Faculty Unions?", *Wake Forest Law Review*, v. 16, No. 6, December 1980.

Glasgow, John M., "The Right-to-Work Law Controversy Again," *Labor Law Journal*, v. 18, No. 2, February 1967.

Glass, Ronald W., "Work Stoppages and Teachers: History and Prospect," *Monthly Labor Review*, v. 90, No. 8, August 1967.

Goldberg, Stephen B., "Coordinated Bargaining: Some Unresolved Questions," *Monthly Labor Review*, v. 92, No. 4, April 1969.

Hall, John T. Jr., "Work Stoppages in Government," *Monthly Labor Review*, v. 91, No. 7, July 1968.

Hilgert, Raymond L. and Jerry D. Young, "Right-to-Work Legislation—Examination of Related Issues and Effects," *Personnel Journal*, December 1963.

Hunter, Robert P., "Conair: Minority Bargaining Orders Usher in 1984 at NLRB," *Labor Law Journal*, v. 33, No. 9, September 1982.

Isaacson, William J., "Discernible Trends in the 'Miller' Board—Practical Considerations for the Labor Counsel," *Labor Law Journal*, v. 13, No. 9, 1962.

Johannesen, D. J. and W. Britton Smith, Jr., "*Collyer:* Open Sesame to Deferral," *Labor Law Journal*, v. 23, No. 12, December 1972.

Jones, Dallas L., "The Enigma of the Clayton Act," *Industrial and Labor Relations Review*, v, 10, No. 2, January 1957.

Kahn, Stephen, "The NLRB Misinterpretation of the Guard Provision," *Labor Law Journal*, v. 35, No. 6, June 1984.

Kapp, Robert W., "Management's Concern with Recent Civil Rights Legislation," *Labor Law Journal*, v. 16, No. 2, February 1965.

Kaufman, Jacob J., "The Railroad Labor Dispute: A Marathon of Maneuver and Improvisation," *Industrial and Labor Relations Review*, v. 18, No. 2, January 1965.

Kirkwood, John H., "The Enforcement of Collective Bargaining Contracts," *Labor Law Journal*, v. 15, No. 2, February 1964.

Kovarsky, Irving, "Union Security, Hiring Halls, Right-to-Work Laws and the Supreme Court," *Labor Law Journal*, v. 15, No. 10, October 1964.

Koziara, Karen S., "Agricultural Labor Relations in Four States—A Comparison," *Monthly Labor Review*, May 1977.

Koziara, Karen S., David A. Pierson and Russell E. Johannesson, "The Comparable Worth Issue: Current Status and New Directions," unpublished manuscript, Temple University, Department of Industrial Relations and Organizational Behavior, 1985.

Krislov, Joseph, "The Increase in Union Decertification Elections," *Monthly Labor Review*, v. 102, No. 11, November 1979.

Krupman, William A. and Gregory I. Rasin, "Decertification: Removing the Shroud," *Labor Law Journal* v. 30, No. 4, April 1979.

McCalmont, David B., "The Semi-Strike," *Industrial and Labor Relations Review*, v. 15, No. 2, January 1962.

McDermott, Thomas J., "Arbitrability: The Courts Versus the Arbitrator," *The Arbitration Journal*, v. 23, No. 4, 1968.

———, "Enforcing No-Strike Provisions via Arbitration," *Labor Law Journal*, v. 18, No. 10, October 1967.

McGuire, J.P., "The Use of Statistics in Title VII Cases," *Labor Law Journal,* v. 30, No. 6, June 1979.

McLennan, Kenneth and Michael H. Moskow, "Multilateral Bargaining in the Public Sector," *Monthly Labor Review,* v. 92, No. 4, April 1969.

McNatt, E.B., "Labor Again Menaced by the Sherman Act," *The Southern Economic Journal,* v. 6, No. 2, October 1939.

Magrath, C. Peter, "Democracy in Overalls: The Futile Quest for Union Democracy," *Industrial and Labor Relations Review,* v. 12, 1959.

Mulcahy, Robert W. and Dennis W. Rader, "Trends in Hospital Labor Relations," *Labor Law Journal,* v. 31, No. 2, February 1980.

Nash, Peter, "NLRB and Arbitration: Effect of Collyer Policy," *Proceedings of the Twenty-seventh Annual Meeting, National Academy of Arbitrators,* Bureau of National Affairs, Inc., Washington, D.C., 1974.

Peterson, Richard B., "National Emergency Dispute Legislation—What Next?" *University of Washington Business Review,* v. 27, No. 1, Autumn 1968.

Phelps, Orme W., "Compulsory Arbitration: Some Perspectives," *Industrial and Labor Relations Review,* v. 18, No. 1, October 1964.

Rezler, Julius and S. John Insalatta, "Doctrine of Mutuality: A Driving Force in American Labor Legislation," *Labor Law Journal,* v. 18, No. 5, May 1967.

Rose, Theodore, "Union Security and Checkoff Provisions in Major Union Contracts," *Monthly Labor Review,* v. 82, No. 12, December 1959.

———, "Union Security Provisions in Agreements, 1954," *Monthly Labor Review,* v. 78, No. 6, June 1955.

———, "Union Security Provisions in Agreements, 1954," *Monthly Labor Review,* v. 78, No. 6, November 1979.

Ross, Anne M., "Public Employee Unions and the Right to Strike," *Monthly Labor Review,* v. 92, No. 3, March 1969.

Rummell, Charles A., "Current Developments in Farm Labor Law," *Labor Law Journal,* v. 19, No. 4, April 1968.

Samoff, Bernard, "The Case of the Burgeoning Load of the NLRB," *Labor Law Journal,* v. 22, No. 10, October 1971.

Schultz, George P., "The Massachusetts Choice-of-Procedures Approach to Emergency Disputes," *Industrial and Labor Relations Review,* v. 10, No. 3, April 1957.

Segal, Melvin J., "Secondary Boycott Loopholes," *Labor Law Journal,* v. 10, No. 3, March 1959.

Segur, W. H. and Varden Fuller, "California's Farm Labor Elections: An Analysis of the Initial Results," *Monthly Labor Review,* December 1976.

Simmons, Bruce, "Jurisdictional Disputes: Does the Board Really Snub the Supreme Court?" *Labor Law Journal,* v. 36, No. 3, March 1984.

Sloane, Arthur A., "Presidential Boards of Inquiry in National Emergency Disputes, An Assessment After 20 Years of Performance," *Labor Law Journal,* v. 18, No. 11, November 1967.

Smith, Baker Armstrong, "Landrum-Griffin After Twenty-One Years: Mature Legislation or Childish Fantasy," *Labor Law Journal,* v. 31, No. 5, May 1980.

Smith, Russell A., "The Labor-Management Reporting and Disclosure Act of 1959," *Virginia Law Review,* v. 46, No. 2, March 1960.

Sonsnick, Stephen H., "Non-Stoppage Strikes: A New Approach," *Industrial and Labor Relations Review,* v. 18, No. 1, October 1964.

Spelfogel, Evan J., "Enforcement of No-Strike Clause by Injunction, Damage Action and Discipline," *Labor Law Journal,* v. 17, No. 2, 1966.

Standohar, Paul D., "Constitutionality of Compulsory Arbitration Statutes in Public Employment," *Labor Law Journal,* v. 27, No. 11, November 1976.

Stessin, Lawrence, "A New Look at Arbitration," *The New York Times Magazine,* November 17, 1963.

Stevens, Carl M., "Is Compulsory Arbitration Compatible with Bargaining?" *Industrial Relations,* v. 6, No. 2, February 1966.

Stochaj, John M., "Free Speech Policies," *Labor Law Journal,* v. 8, No. 8, August 1957.

Taft, Philip, "Dues and Initiation Fees in Labor Unions," *Quarterly Journal of Economics,* February 1946.

Truesdale, John C., "From *General Shoe* to *General Knit:* A Return to *Hollywood Ceramics,*" *Labor Law Journal,* v. 30, No. 2, February 1979.

Wacks, Robert E., "Successorship: The Consequences of *Burns,*" *Labor Law Journal,* v. 24, No. 4, April 1973.

Waks, Jay W., "The Dual Jurisdiction Problem in Labor Arbitration: A Research Report," *The Arbitration Journal,* v. 23, No. 4, 1968.

Watkins, Myron W., "Trusts," *Encyclopedia of Social Sciences,* v. 15.

Weisenfeld, Allen, "Public Employees Are Still Second Class Citizens," *Labor Law Journal,* v. 20, No. 3, March 1969.

White, Harold C. and William Gibney, "The Arizona Farm Labor Law: A Supreme Court Test," *Labor Law Journal,* v. 31, No. 2, February 1980.

Witney, Fred, "NLRB Jurisdictional Policies and the Federal-State Relationship," *Labor Law Journal,* v. 6, No. 1, January 1955.

———, "NLRB Membership Cleavage: Recognition and Organizational Picketing," *Labor Law Journal,* v. 14, No. 5, May 1963.

———, "Union Security," *Labor Law Journal,* v. 4, No. 2, February 1953.

Witte, E.E., "Early American Labor Cases," *Yale Law Journal,* v. 35, 1926.

Wortman, Max S., Jr., and Nathaniel Jones, "Remedial Actions of the NLRB in Representation Cases: An Analysis of the *Gissel* Bargaining Order," *Labor Law Journal,* v. 30, No. 5, May 1979.

Zander, Arnold S., "Trends in Labor Legislation for Public Employees," *Monthly Labor Review,* v. 83, No. 12, December 1960.

Zimmerman, Don A., "Trends in NLRB Health Care Industry Decisions," *Labor Law Journal,* v. 32, No. 1, January 1981.

Pamphlets And Booklets

AFL-CIO Maritime Trades Department, *Collective Bargaining in the Public Sector, An Interim Report.* Washington, D.C.: Executive Board AFL-CIO Maritime Trades Department, 1969.

Bureau of National Affairs, *Taft-Hartley After One Year, 1948.*

Cullen, Donald E., *National Emergency Strikes,* ILR Paperback No. 7. Ithaca, N.Y.: Cornell University, New York State School of Industrial and Labor Relations, 1968.

Estey, Marten, *The Unions, Structure, Development and Management.* New York: Harcourt Brace Jovanovich, Third Edition, 1981.

HANSLOWE, KURT L., *The Emerging Law of Labor Relations in Public Employment,* ILR Paperback No. 4. Ithaca, N.Y.: Cornell University, New York State School of Industrial and Labor Relations, 1967.

INTERNATIONAL ASSOCIATION OF MACHINISTS, *The Truth About the Taft-Hartley Law and Its Consequences to the Labor Movement,* April 1948.

LIVERNASH, E. ROBERT, *Collective Bargaining in the Basic Steel Industry.* Washington, D.C.: Government Printing Office, 1961.

NATIONAL PLANNING ASSOCIATION, *Causes of Industrial Peace under Collective Bargaining.* Washington, D.C., 1948–1950.

POLISOR, ERIC, "Strikes and Solutions," Public Employee Relations Report No. 7, Public Personnel Association, 1968.

ROBERTS, H., *A Manual for Employee-Management Cooperation in the Federal Service.* Honolulu, Hawaii: Industrial Relations Center, University of Hawaii, 1964.

SHELDON, HORACE E., "Union Security and the Taft-Hartley Act in the Buffalo Area." Ithaca, N.Y.: Cornell University, New York State School of Industrial and Labor Relations Research Bulletin 4.

SHERIFF, DON R. AND VIOLA M. KUEBLER, eds., *NLRB in a Changing Industrial Society,* Conference Series No. 2. Iowa City: College of Business Administration, The University of Iowa, 1967.

UNITED AUTO WORKERS, *A More Perfect Union.* Detroit: UAW Publications Department, 1958.

U.S. CHAMBER OF COMMERCE, *To Protect Management Rights.* Washington, D.C., 1961.

YOUNG, JAMES E. AND BETTY L. BREWER, *State Legislation Affecting Labor Relations in State and Local Government,* Labor and Industrial Relations Series No. 2. Kent, Ohio: Kent State University, Bureau of Economic and Business Research, 1968.

GOVERNMENT DOCUMENTS AND PUBLICATIONS

BUREAU OF LABOR STATISTICS, *Analysis of Work Stoppages 1965,* Bulletin No. 1525. Washington, D.C.: Government Printing Office, 1966.

——, *Characteristics of Company Unions,* Bulletin No. 634. Washington, D.C.: Government Printing Office, 1938.

——, *Employment and Earnings Statistics in the United States.* Washington, D.C.: Government Printing Office, 1980.

——, *Handbook of Labor Statistics.* Washington, D.C.: Government Printing Office, 1968.

——, *Union Membership and Collective Bargaining by Foremen,* Bulletin No. 745. Washington, D.C.: Government Printing Office.

——, *Union Security Provisions in Collective Bargaining,* Bulletin No. 908. Washington, D.C.: Government Printing Office, 1947.

——, *Work Stoppages in Government,* 1978. Report 582 Washington, D.C.: Government Printing Office, 1980

Congressional Quarterly Weekly Report, No. 30, July 29, 1966.

Congressional Record, various volumes. Washington, D.C.: Government Printing Office.

FEDERAL MEDIATION AND CONCILIATION SERVICE, *Annual Reports,* 1947–1979.

LA FOLLETTE COMMITTEE, *Private Police Systems,* Report No. 6, Part II, 76th Cong., 1st sess.

——, *Report on Industrial Espionage,* Report No. 46, Part III, 75th Cong.

———, *The Chicago Memorial Day Incident,* Report No. 46, Part II, 75th Cong.

National Labor Relations Board, *Annual Reports,* v. 1–47. Washington, D.C.: Government Printing Office, 1936–1982.

———, Office of the General Counsel, "Arbitration Deferral Policy Under Revised Guidelines," *Collyer,* May 10, 1973.

———, Office of the General Counsel, *Memorandum 79–55.*

———, Office of the General Counsel, *"NLRB General Counsel's Monthly Report on Health Care Institution Cases," Release 1385, March 27, 1975.*

———, Office of The General Counsel, *Summary of Operations for Fiscal Year 1984,* January 28, 1985.

———, *Decisions and Orders of the National Labor Relations Board.*

———, *History of the Labor-Management Reporting and Disclosure Act,* I, II. Washington, D.C.: Government Printing Office, 1959.

———, *Interim Report and Recommendations of the Chariman's Task Force of the NLRB for 1976,* 1976.

———, *Legislative History of the Labor-Management Relations Act, 1947,* I, II. Washington, D.C.: Government Printing Office, 1948.

———, *Rules and Regulations and Statements of Procedure.* Washington, D.C.: Government Printing Office, 1973.

———, *Statistical Services Staff,* Letter, June 24, 1981.

NATIONAL WAR LABOR BOARD, *Report, April 1918 to May 1919.*

———, *Termination Report.* Washington, D.C.: I (1946).

———, *War Labor Reports,* 1942–1945.

Presidential Report, *A Policy for Employee-Management Cooperation in the Federal Service,* Report of the President's Task Force on Employee-Management Relations in the Federal Service. Washington, D.C.: Government Printing Office, 1961.

———, *Free and Responsible Collective Bargaining and Industrial Peace,* Report of the President's Advisory Committee on Labor-Management Policy. Washington, D.C.: Government Printing Office, 1962.

Report of the Industrial Commission on Labor Legislation. Washington, D.C.: Government Printing Office, 1900.

Report of the U.S. Commission on Industrial Relations, 11 vols. Washington, D.C.: Government Printing Office, 1916.

U.S. CONGRESS, *Document No. 669,* 72d Cong., 1st sess.

———, Committee on Government Operations, "Delay, Slowness in Decisionmaking, and the Case Backlog at the NLRB," 98th Congress, 2nd Session, House Report 98–1141, October 4, 1984.

———, *Hearings Before the Committee on Education and Labor on H.R. 115,* 83d Cong., 1st sess., 1953.

———, *Hearings Before the Committee on Labor and Public Welfare,* U.S. Senate, 80th Cong., 1st sess. on S. 55 and S.J. Res. 22, Part I and Part II, 1947.

———, *Hearings Before the Senate Subcommittee on Labor-Management Relations, Hiring Halls in the Maritime Industry,* 81st Cong., 2nd sess., 1950.

———, *Heartings Before Subcommittee on Labor-Management Relations, Committee on Education and Labor,* 96th Cong., 1st sess., *Pressures in Today's Work Place,* v. 1 and v. 2, October, December 1979.

————, *Hearings Before the Subcommittee on Separation of Powers of the Committee on the Judiciary, Congressional Oversight of Administrative Agencies (National Labor Relations Board),* United States Senate, Parts I and II. Washington, D.C.: Government Printing Office, 1968.

————, *Hearings on a National Labor Relations Board,* 74th Cong., 1st sess., 1935.

————, *Hearings on H.R. 6288 Before the House Committee on Labor,* 74th Cong., 1st sess., 1935.

————, *Hearings on S. 1958 Before the House Committee on Labor,* 74th Cong., 1st sess., Part III, 1935.

————, *Hearings on S. 249 (Labor Relations),* III, Senate Committee on Labor and Public Welfare, 81st Cong., 1st sess., 1949.

————, *House Report No. 1147,* 86th Cong., 1st sess., 1959.

————, *House Report No. 245 on H.R. 3020,* 80th Cong., 1st sess., 1947.

————, *Intermediate Report, House Report No. 1902,* House of Representatives, Special Committee to Investigate the National Labor Relations Board, 76th Cong., 3d sess., Part I, 1940.

————, *Oversight Hearings on National Labor Relations Board, Hearings Before the Subcommittee on Labor-Management Relations, Committee on Education and Labor,* House of Representatives, 94th Cong., 1st, 2d sess., 1976.

————, *Oversight Hearings Before the Subcommittee on Labor-Management Relations, Committee on Education and Labor,* "Pressures in Today's Workplace", 96th Cong., 1st sess.

————, *Report No. 99 to Accompany S. 249, National Labor Relations Act of 1949,* 81st Cong., 1st sess., 1949.

————, *Senate Report No. 1417, Interim Report of the Senate Select Committee on Improper Activities in the Labor or Management Fields,* 85th Cong., 2d sess., 1958.

————, *Senate Report No. 105 on Senate 1126,* 80th Cong., 1st sess., 1947.

————, *Senate Report No. 986, Report of the Joint Committee on Labor-Management Relations,* Part I, March 15, 1948.

U.S. DEPARTMENT OF LABOR, *Compliance, Enforcement and Reporting,* 1968–1977. Washington, D.C.: Government Printing Office.

————, *Directory of National Unions and Employee Associations,* January 1976.

————, "Government Work Stoppages, 1960, 1969, and 1971," Summary Report, November 1971.

U.S. DEPARTMENT OF LABOR, LABOR-MANAGEMENT SERVICES ADMINISTRATION, *Union Elections under the LMRDA, 1966–1970.*

U.S. FEDERAL LABOR RELATIONS COUNCIL, *Labor-Management Relations in the Federal Service.* Washington, D.C.: Government Printing Office, 1975.

WISCONSIN EMPLOYMENT RELATIONS BOARD. *First Annual Report,* 1938.

NEWSPAPERS AND PERIODICALS

AFL-CIO, *American Federationist*

AFL-CIO, Industrial Union Department, *Viewpoint,* Spring 1981.

AFL-CIO News

American Arbitration Association, "News and Views," No. 1, January-February 1976.

BUREAU OF NATIONAL AFFAIRS, *Labor Relations Reference Manual*

Business Week

Commerce Clearing House, *Labor Law Reports,* No. 211, August 21, 1976.

Congress of Industrial Organizations, Department of Education and Research, "Economic Outlook," v.16, No. 2, February 1955.

National Association of Manufacturers Law Digest

New York Times

Steelabor, March 1980.

Wall Street Journal

INDEX OF CASES

For cases in which the United States or the NLRB is the moving party, the name of the other party is listed first. Thus, in NLRB v. *Smith,* the case is listed as *Smith* (NLRB v.). In addition, the full name of a union is reduced to show the industry or craft of the union. Thus, in a case involving the international Association of Machinists and Aerospace Workers, the union's name is listed as *Machinists* v. NLRB

A

A & P, 1964, **479**
Abilities & Goodwill, 241 NLRB No. 5 (1979), **187**
Abood v. Detroit Board of Education, 431 U.S. 209 (1977), **646**
Acme Industrial Co. (NLRB v.) 385 U.S. 432 (1967), **456**
Adair v. United States, 208 U.S. 161 (1908), **35, 138, 139, 141, 142, 143, 147–48, 166**
Adams-Lundy v. Association of Professional Flight Attendants, CA-5 No. 84-1257, April 30, 1984, **597**
Adkins v. Children's Hospital, 261 U.S. 525 (1923), **139**
Agler (United States v.), 62 Fed. 24 (1897), **43–44**
Agricultural Labor Relations Board v. Superior Court, 546 P. (2d) 687 (1976), **276**

Aiello Dairy Co., 110 NLRB 1365 (1954), **307**
Al Long, Inc., 173 NLRB 447 (1968), **289**
Alameda Medical Group, Inc., 195 NLRB 312 (1972), **258**
Alexander v. Gardner-Denver, 415 U.S. 36 (1974), **447, 448, 449, 639, 670**
Algoma Plywood & Veneer Co. v. Wisconsin Employment Relations Board, 336 U.S. 301 (1949), **380**
Alleluia Cushion Co., 21 NLRB 999 (1979), **491–92**
Allen-Bradley Co. v. Local Union 3, IBEW, 325 U.S. 797 (1945), **107, 109, 113**
Allied Chemical Workers, Local 1 v. Pittsburgh Plate Glass, 177 NLRB 911 (1969), **403**
Allied Chemical Workers, Local 1 v. Pittsburgh Plate Glass, 404 U.S. 157 (1971), **403**
Allis-Chalmers Manufacturing Co. (NLRB v.) 388

Allis-Chalmers Manufacturing Co. (NLRB v. (cont.) U.S. 175 (1967); reversing 358 F. (2d) 656, **488, 490, 491**

Aluminum Workers International Union, Local 135, 112 NLRB 619 (1955), **380**

Alvey v. General Electric Co., CCA 7, Case No. 79-1636, June 11, 1980, **589**

Amalgamated Association v. Wisconsin Employment Relations Board, 340 U.S. 383 (1951), **583**

American Boiler Manufacturers Assn., 167 NLRB 602 (1967), **533**

American Broadcasting Companies v. Writers Guild of America, U.S. Sup. Ct., Case No. 76-1121, June 21, 1978, **489**

American Can, 13 NLRB 1252 (1939), **333**

American Communications Assn. v. Douds, 339 U.S. 382 (1950), **611**

American District Telegraph Co., 160 NLRB 1130 (1966), **352**

American Dredging Co. v. Local 25, Marine Div., Operating Engineers, 338 F. (2d) 837 (1964); cert. denied 380 U.S. 935 (1965), **463–64**

American Hoist & Derrick Co., Industrial Brownhoist Div., 184 NLRB 551 (1970), **297**

American League of Professional Baseball Clubs, 180 NLRB 190 (1970), **263**

American National Insurance (NLRB v.) 343 U.S. 395 (1952), **401**

American News Co., 55 NLRB 1302 (1944), **181**

American Newspaper Publishers Assn. v. NLRB, 345 U.S. 100 (1952), **216**

American Potash & Chemical Corp., 107 NLRB 290 (1954), **335–36, 337**

American Rolbal Corp., 41 NLRB 907 (1942), **329**

American Seating Co., 98 NLRB 800 (1952), **390**

American Ship Building Co. v. NLRB 380 U.S. 300 (1965), **480–81, 482**

American Steel Foundries v. Tri-City Central Trades Council, 257 U.S. 312 (1921), **74–75, 82–83, 119**

American Telecommunications Corp., 249 NLRB No. 149 (1980), **294**

American Tobacco Co. (United States v.) 221 U.S. 106 (1911), **52–53**

American Tube Bending (NLRB v.), 134 F. (2d) 993 (1943); cert. denied 320 U.S. 768 (1943), **285–86**

Amex Coal Co. (NLRB v.) U.S. Sup. Ct. Case No. 80-692, June 29, 1981, **401**

Ann Lee Sportswear, Inc. v. NLRB, CA 5, Case No. 75-1719, October 29, 1976, **315**

Apex Hosiery Co. v. Leader, 310 U.S. 409 (1940), **105–8**

Appalachian Power Co., 198 NLRB 576 (1972), **411**

Apple Tree Chevrolet, 237 NLRB No. 103 (1979), **312**

Arlington Asphalt Co., 136 NLRB 742 (1962), **403**

Arnold, William E., & Co. v. Carpenters District Council of Jacksonville, 417 U.S. 12 (1974), **411**

Associated Press v. NLRB, 492 F. (2d) 662, D.C. Cir. (1974), **411**

Association of Hebrew Teachers of Metropolitan Detroit, 210 NLRB 1053 (1974), **262**

Atkins & Co. (NLRB v.), 331 U.S. 398 (1947), **351**

Atkinson v. Sinclair Refining Co., 370 U.S. 238 (1962), **436**

Atlantic Coastline Railroad Co. v. Locomotive Engineers, 398 U.S. 281 (1970), **552**

Atlantic Maintenance Co., 136 NLRB 105 (1962), **500**

Atlantic Richfield, 199 NLRB 1224 (1972), **411**

AT&T Technologies v. Communication Workers (Docket No. 84-1913, April 7, 1986), **443**

Auto Workers v. National Right to Work Legal Defense & Education Foundation, U.S. Dist. Ct. (D.C.), Case No. 839-73 June 2, 1977, **592**

Automobile Drivers & Demonstrators, Local 882 v. Cline, 339 U.S. 470 (1949), **550, 552**

Automobile Workers Union, Local 248 (Allis-Chalmers Manufacturing Co.), 149 NLRB 67 (1964), **488**

Automobile Workers Union, Local 259 (Fanelli Ford Sales, Inc.), 133 NLRB 1468 (1961), **497–98**

Automobile Workers Union, Local 833 v. NLRB, 300 F. (2d) 699 (1962); cert. denied 370 U.S. 911, **487**

Automobile Workers Union v. NLRB, CA DC, Case No. 79-2539, March 3, 1981, **240**

Automobile Workers Union v. National Right to Work Legal Defense & Education Foundation, CCA DC, Case No. 877-1739, November 17, 1978, **593**

Axelson, Subsidiary of U.S. Industries, 234 NLRB No. 49 (1978), **401**

B

Babcock & Wilcox Co., 77 NLRB 577 (1948), **300**

Babcock & Wilcox Co. (NLRB v.), 251 U.S. 145 (1956), **552, 553**

Babcock & Wilcox Co. (NLRB v.), 351 U.S. 105 (1956), **302**

Bachrodt Chevrolet Co. (NLRB v.), 468 F. (2d) 963 (1972), **458–59**

Bailey v. Drexel Furniture, 259 U.S. 20 (1922), **139**

Bakery & Pastry Drivers & Helpers, Local, etc. v. Wohl, 315 U.S. 769 (1942), **554**

Bakery & Pastry Drivers Union v. Wohl, 315 U.S. 769 (1942), **541**

Bakke (Regents of University of California v.) 438 U.S. 265 (1978), **675**

Baltimore Transit Co. (NLRB v.), 321 U.S. 796 (1944), **196n**

Baptist Hospital (NLRB) v.), 99 S. Ct. 2598 (1979), **268**

Barber-Scotia College, Inc., 245 NLRB No. 48 (1979), **262**

Barker Bros. Corp. v. NLRB, 328 F. (2d) 431 (1964), **500**

Barnert Memorial Hospital Center, 217 NLRB 775 (1975), **265**

Barrentine v. Arkansas-Best Freight System, Inc., 450 U.S. 728 (1981), **448**

Bartlett-Collins Co., 237 NLRB No. 106 (1978), **403**

Bausch & Lomb, Inc., 185 NLRB 262 (1970), **290**

Beacon Piece Dyeing & Finishing Co., 121 NLRB 953 (1958), **401**

Bedford Can Manufacturing Corp., 162 NLRB 133 (1967), **395**

Bedford Cut Stone Co. v. Journeyman Stonecutters Assn., 274 U.S. 37 (1927), **52, 61–64, 73, 100, 101, 105**

Belknap v. Hale, 463 U.S. 591 (1983), **467–68**

Bell Aerospace Co., 219 NLRB 384 (1975) **349**

Bell Aerospace Co., (NLRB v.), 416 U.S. 267 (1974), **348–49**

Benton Community School Corp. (Indiana Education Employment Relations Board v.), 95 LRRM 3084 (1977), **642**

Bernal Foam Products Co., 146 NLRB 1277 (1964), **307–8**

Beth Israel Hospital v. NLRB, 98 S. Ct. 2463 (1978), **268**

Bethlehem Steel Corp. v. New York State Relations Board, 330 U.S. 767 (1947) **252, 254**

Bethlehem Steel Corp. (United States v.) 446 F. (2d) 652 (2d Cir., 1971), **683**

Big Three Industries, 201 NLRB 197 (1973), **317**

Bildisco (NLRB v.), 682 F. 2d 72, CA-3, 1982, **270**

Bildisco and Bildisco, 255 NLRB No. 154 (1981), **269, 270–71, 272–73**

Bildisco and Bildisco (NLRB v.), 465 U.S. 513 (1984), **270**

Bing v. Roadway Express, Inc., 444 F. (2d) 245 (1970); cert. denied 401 U.S. 954 (1971), **678**

Bitte Medical Properties d/b/a/ Medical Center Hospital, 168 NLRB 52 (1967), **263–64**

Blinne, C. A., Construction Co., 130 NLRB 587 (1961), **501**

Blinne, C. A., Construction Co., 135 NLRB 121 (1962), **501**

Blue Flash Express, Inc., 109 NLRB 391 (1954), **295**

Bodle, Fogel, Julber, Reinhardt & Rothchild, 206 NLRB 512 (1973), **260**

Boeing (NLRB v.), 412 U.S. 473 (1973), **488–89**

Boilermakers v. Hardeman, 401 U.S. 233 (1971), **595**

Bonanno, Charles D., Linen Service, Inc., v. NLRB,

U.S. Sup. Ct., Case No. 80–931, January 12, 1982, **115**

Bonanno, Charles D., Linen Supply v. NLRB, 450 U.S. 979 (1982), **478**

Bonwit Teller, Inc., 96 NLRB 608 (1951), **300**

Bonwit Teller, Inc., v. NLRB, 197 F. (2d) 640 (CA 2, 1952), **301**

Borden Manufacturing Co., 193 NLRB 1028 (1971), **297**

Bordon Inc., Dairy & Services Division, 196 NLRB 1170 (1973), **412–13**

Borg-Warner Corp., Wooster Div. (NLRB v.), 356 U.S. 342 (1958), **399–407**

Bortmess v. Drewry's U.S.A., Inc., 444 F. (2d) 1186 (1971); cert. denied 92 U.S. 274 (1971), **669**

Bowen v. United States Postal Service, 459 U.S. 212 (1983), **432**

Boys Markets, Inc., v. Retail Clerks, 398 U.S. 235 (1970), **452–54**

Brazos Electric Power Co-OP, 241 NLRB No. 160 (1979), **398**

Brewery Workers Union, AFL-CIO (Adolph Coors Co.), 121 NLRB 35 (1958), **510**

Brewery Workers Union (NLRB v.), 272 F. (2d) 817 (1959), **512**

Bricklayers and Masons Union Local 8 (California Concrete Systems), 180 NLRB 43 (1969), **533**

Bright Foods, Inc., 126 NLRB 553 (1960), **471**

Brinks, Inc., 226 NLRB 1182 (1976), **352**

Brooks Research & Manufacturing, 202 NLRB 93 (1973), **470**

Brotherhood of Railway and Steamship Clerks v. Allen, 373 U.S. 113 (1963), **388**

Brown, Archie (United States v.), 381 U.S. 437 (1965), **611**

Brown v. Amalgamated Lithographers of America, Local No. 17 (Employing Lithographers Div.), 180 F. Supp. 294 (DCN, Calif.), 1960, **528**

Brown v. Board of Education, 347 U.S. 483 (1954) **653**

Brown et al. d/b/a Brown Food Store (NLRB v.), 380 U.S. 278 (1965), **480**

Brown Food Store, 137 NLRB 73 (1962); enf. denied 319 F. (2d) 7 (CA 10); cert. granted 375 U.S. 962 (1965), **480, 481, 482**

Brown v. Hotel and Restaurant Employees, Local 54, 104 Sup. Ct. 3179 (1984), **255**

Brush v. San Francisco Newspaper Printing Co., (N D Calif.) 315 F. Supp. 577, 1970; aff'd. 19 Cir., 469 F. 2d 89, 1972, **661**

Buckley, National Review, Inc., and Evans v. AFTRA, NLRB, and American Civil Liberties Union, 496 F. (2d) 305 (CA 2, 1974); cert. denied 419 U.S. 1093 (1974), **367**

Buckley v. Voleo, U.S. Sup. Ct., Case Nos. 75–436, 75–437, January 30, 1976, **238**

Budd Manufacturing Co. (NLRB v.), 138 F. (2d) 86 (1948), **153, 245**

Buddy L. Corp., 167 NLRB 808 (1967), **337**

Burger King v. NLRB, 725 F. 2d 1053 (1984), **173**

Buffalo Forge v. United Steelworkers, 428 U.S. 397 (1976), **453, 454**

Building and Construction Trades Council of New Orleans (Markwell & Hartz), 155 NLRB 319 (1965); enfd. 387 F. 2d 79 (5th Cir. 1967); cert. denied 391 U.S. 914 (1968), **518**

Building & Construction Trades Council of San Bernadino v. NLRB, 328 F. (2d) 540 (1964), **530**

Building Service Employees Union v. Gazzam, 339 U.S. 532 (1950), **548, 552**

Bundy v. Jackson, 641 F. 2d 934 (D.C. Cir. 1981), **666**

Burns, William J., International Detective Agency, 182 NLRB 348 (1970), **457, 458**

Burns, William J., International Detective Agency (NLRB v.) 406 U.S. 272 (1972), **458**

Burroughs v. Operating Engineers, Local 3, CCA-9, No. 814145, July 2, 1982, **592**

C

Cabot Carbon Co. (NLRB v.), 360 U.S. 203 (1959), **599**

Cadillac Overall Supply Co., 148 NLRB 1133 (1964), **297**

Cafeteria Employees Union v. Angelo, 320 U.S. 293 (1943), **542**

Caldwell v. National Brewing Co., 443 F. (2d) 1044 (1971), **670**

Calhoon v. Harvey, 379 U.S. 134 (1964), **589, 612**

Calumet Contractors Assn., 130 NLRB 17 (1961), **497**

Calumet Contractors Assn., 133 NLRB 57 (1961), **497**

Campbell Industries, 243 NLRB No. 17 (1979), **395**

Capital Times Co., 223 NLRB 651 (1976) **404–5**

Carbon Fuel v. United Mine Workers of America, 444 U.S. 212 (1979), **437**

Cargo Handlers, Inc., 159 NLRB 321 (1966) **429**

Carlson v. California, 310 U.S. 106 (1940), **544**

Carolina Lumber Co., 130 NLRB 148 (1961), **513–14**

Carpenters and Joiners Union v. Ritter's Cafe, 315 U.S. 722 (1942), **85, 545–46**

Carpenters, Local 60 v. NLRB, 365 U.S. 651 (1961), **373**

Carpenters Local 1478 v. Stevens, CA-9, No. 83-6144, August 1, 1984, **450**

Carpenters Union, Local 964 (NLRB v.), 447 F. (2d) 643 (1971), **403**

Carpenters Union, Local 1976 (Sand Door & Plywood Co.), 113 NLRB 1211 (1955) enforced NLRB v. Local 1976, 241 F. (2d) 147 (9th Cir. 1957); affirmed 357 U.S. 93 (1958), **528**

Carpenters Union V. NLRB, 357 U.S. 93 (1958), **528**

Carrier Corp., 132 NLRB 127 (1961), **521**

Carter v. Carter Coal Co., 298 U.S. 238 (1936), **167–68**

Catholic Bishop of Chicago, 220 NLRB 359 (1975), **261**

Catholic Bishop of Chicago (NLRB v.), 440 U.S. 490 (1979), **262**

Cedars-Sinai Medical Center, 223 NLRB 251 (1976), **266–67**

Cent. of Ga. Ry. v. Jones, 229 F. (2d) 648 (CCA 5, 1956), **431**

Centenial Turf Club, Inc., 192 NLRB 698 (1971), **258**

Central Dispensary and Emergency Hospital (NLRB v.), 324 U.S. 847 (1945), **196n**

Central Hardware Co. v. NLRB, 407 U.S. 539 (1972), **552–53**

Chauffeurs, Teamsters & Helpers Local Union 795 v. Richard Newell, d/b/a El Dorado Dairy, 356 U.S. 341 (1958), **544**

Chemical Workers Union, Local 36, AFL-CIO v. NLRB, 47 LPRM 2493, cert. denied 366 U.S. 949 (1961), **517**

Chicago Lighthouse for the Blind, 225 NLRB 46 (1976), **260**

Chicago and Northwestern Railway Co. v. United Transportation Union, 410 U.S. 917 (1971), **572**

Chicago Teachers Union v. Lee Hudson (Docket No. 84-1503, March 4, 1986), **388–89**

Chrysler Corp., 44 NLRB 886 (1942), **350**

Ciba-Geigy Corp. v. Local 2546, Textile Workers, 391 F. Supp. 287 (1975), **453**

City Disposal Systems, Inc. (NLRB v.) 460 U.S. 1050 (1984), **493**

Clark Brothers Co., Inc., 70 NLRB 802 (1946), 163 F. (2d) 373 (1947), **285**

Claude Everett Construction Co., 136 NLRB 321 (1962), **498**

Clayton v. Automobile Workers, 451 U.S. 679 (1981), **432**

Clear Pine Mouldings, Inc., 268 NLRB 1044 (1984), **485–86, 487**

Cleveland Board of Education v. La Fleur 414 U.S. 632 (1974), **667**

Collyer Insulated Wire, 192 NLRB 837 (1971), **409–16**

Columbia University, 97 NLRB 424 (1951), **258**

Columbus Printing Pressmen and Assistants Union 252 (R. W. Page Corp.), 219 NLRB 268 (1975), **403**

Commonwealth v. Hunt, **690**

Commonwealth of Massachusetts v. Hunt, 4 Metcalf 3 (1842), **16–20, 118, 136, 338**

Communication Workers, Local 1122 (New York Telephone Co.), 226 NLRB 97 (1977), **399**

Complete Auto Transit, Inc. v. Reis, 451 U.S. 401 (1981), **436**

Conair Corp., 261 NLRB No. 178, **311**

Conley v. Aiello, 276 F. Supp. 614 (1967), **613**

Connell Construction Co., Inc. v. Plumbers, Local 100, 421 U.S. 616 (1975), **107, 108, 113, 114**

Consolidated Edison Co. v. NLRB, **305** U.S. 197 (1938), **196***n*

Construction, Production & Maintenance Laborers Union, Local 383 (Colson & Stevens Construction Co.), 137 NLRB 1650 (1963), **530**

Contris Packing Co., 268 NLRB No. 7 (1983), **177**

Conway's Express, 87 NLRB 972 (1949), **528**

Cooper Union for the Advancement of Science and Art, 273 NLRB No. 214 (1985), **259**

Coppage v. Kansas, 236 U.S. 1 (1915), **35, 138, 139, 141–42**

Coppus Engineering, 195 NLRB 595 (1972), **423**

Cornell University, 183 NLRB 329 (1970), **258**

Coronado Coal Co. v. United Mine Workers of America, 268 U.S. 295 (1925), **56–61, 105–7**

Corsicana Cotton Mills (NLRB v.) 178 F. (2d) 244 (1959), **403**

Cory Corp., 84 NLRB 110 (1949), **486**

Cotter v. Owens, CCA-2, No. 84-7574, January 15, 1985, **596**

Crescent Dress Co., 29 NLRB 351 (1941), **357**

Crown Cafeteria, 130 NLRB 570 (1961), **498**

Crown Cafeteria, 135 NLRB 124 (1962), **498**

Crown Cafeteria v. NLRB, 327 F. (2d), 351 (1964), **500**

Cumberland Shoe Corp., 144 NLRB 1268 (1964), **313**

Curtis Bros., 119 NLRB 232 (1957), **494**

Curtis Noll Corp., 218 NLRB 222 (1975), **349**

Cutler-Hammer, 271 App. Div. 971, 67 N.Y.S. (2d) 317 (1947), **439**

C. V. Hill, 76 NLRB 24 (1948), **351**

D

Daelyte Service, 126 NLRB 63 (1960), **403**

Dairy Distributors, Inc. v. Western Conference of Teamsters, 294 F. (2d) 348 (1961), **478**

Davis (United States v.), (SD N.Y. September 12, 1963), Nos. 63 Criminal 164 and 293, **621**

De Bartolo Corp. v. NLRB, 463 U.S. 147 (1983), **527**

Debs, Petitioner, In re, 158 U.S. 564 (1895), **26–27, 28, 43–44, 135, 139**

DeCampli v. Greeley (November 1968), **596;** for additional informational see *Monthly Labor Review v. 92,* No. 3 (March, 1969), pp. **62–63**

Del Costello v. Teamsters, 462 U.S. 151 (1983), **432**

Delaware & Hudson Railway Co. v. United Transportation Union, 400 U.S. 911 (1971), **572**

Dept. Store Employees, Local 1265 v. Brown, 45 LRRM 3101 (N.D. Col., 1960), **496**

DeSantis v. Pacific Telephone and Telegraph Co., Inc. 608 F. 2d 327 (1979), **667**

Detroit Edison Co. v. NLRB 440 U.S. 301 (1979), **663**

Detroy v. American Guild of Variety Artists, 286 F. (2d) 75 (1961), **594**

Devine v. White, CA-DC 697 F. 2d 421 (1983), **450**

Dic-Amco, Inc., 163 NLRB 1019 (1967), **298**

Dicten & Masch Manufacturing, 129 NLRB 112 (1960), **401**

Dolan v. Transport Workers, CCA-11, November 13, 1984, **597**

Dominican Santa Cruz Hospital, 218 NLRB No. 182 (1975), **265**

Donn Products, Inc., and American Metals Corp., 229 NLRB 7 (1977), **294**

Dothard v. Rawlinson, 433 U.S. 321 (1977), **662, 685**

Douds v. Metropolitan Federation of Architects, 75 F. Supp. 672 (S.D.N.Y., 1948), **510**

Douglas Aircraft Co., 25 War Labor Reports 57 (1944), **426**

Douglas v. Hampton, CDC CA, February 27, 1975, Case No. 72-1376 (case remanded to Civil Service Commission), **663**

Dowd Box v. Courtney, 368 U.S. 502 (1962), **441**

Dresser Industries, Inc., 264 NLRB No. 145 (1982), **318**

Drivers Local Union (NLRB v.), 362 U.S. 274 (1960), **494**

Dunlop v. Backowski, 421 U.S. 560 (1975), **616**

Duplex Printing Press Co. v. Deering, 254 U.S. 443 (1921), **54, 55–56, 63, 73, 74, 100, 101, 102, 105, 547**

E

East Oakland Community Alliance, 248 NLRB 1270 (1975), **265**

Eastex Inc. v. NLRB, 437 U.S. 556 (1978), **239–40**

Economic Machinery Co., 111 NLRB 947 (1955), **288**

El Cid, Inc., 222 NLRB 1315 (1976), **317**

El Dorado, Inc., 151 NLRB 579 (1965), **263**

Electrical Contractors Assn. v. Ordman, 366 F. (2d) 776 (CA 2, 1966); cert. denied 385 U.S. 1026 (1966), **222**

Electrical, Radio & Machine Workers, Local 761, AFL-CIO (General Electric Co.), 126 NLRB 123 (1960), **484**

Electrical Workers v. Foust, 439 U.S. 892 (1979), **432**

Electrical Workers Union (Local 28 v.), 184 F. Supp. 649 (1960), **608**

Electrical Workers Union, Local 113 (ICG Electric, Inc.) 142 NLRB 145 (1963), **495**

Electrical Workers (IBEW) Local 135, La Crosse Electrical Contractors, Assn., 271 NLRB No. 36 (1984), **404**

Electrical Workers Union, Local 323 (Active Enterprises), 242 NLRB No. 41 (1979), **399**

Electrical Workers Union, Local 485 (Automotive Plating Corp.), 170 NLRB No. 121 (1968), **430**

Electrical Workers Union, Local 662 (Middle South Broadcasting Co.), 133 NLRB 1968 (1961), **526–27**

Electrical Workers Union, Local 761 (General Electric Co.) v. NLRB 366 U.S. 667 (1961), **517, 518**

Electrical Workers Union, Local 1186 (Pacific General Contractors), 192 NLRB 254 (1971), **533**

Electrical Workers, CIO (Ryan Construction Co.), 85 NLRB 419 (1949), **516**

Electro-Wire Products, 242 NLRB No. 144 (1979), **289**

Elliot (United States v.), 64 Fed. 27 (1898), **44**

Ellis v. Railway Clerks, 466 U.S. 435 (1984), **389**

Elson Bottling, 155 NLRB 714 (1965), **303**

Emery Air Freight Corp. v. Teamsters, Local 295, 356 F. (2d), 974 (1971), **453**

Emporium Capwell Co. v. Western Addition Community Organization, 420 U.S. 50 (1975), **655**

Enterprise Publishing Co. v. NLRB, 403 F. (2d) 1024 (CA 1, 1974), **411**

Equal Employment Opportunity Commission (EEOC) v. Detroit Edison Co., 515 F. 2d 301 (1975), **660**

Equal Employment Opportunity Commission (EEOC) and Hugh Stone III v. Gladdis, 733 F. 2d. 1373 (1984), **660**

Espinoza v. Farah Manufacturing Co., 414 U.S. 86 (1973), **672**

Espinoza v. Farah Manufacturing Co. Inc., 94 U.S. 334 (1973), affirming 462 F. (2d) 1331 (CA 5 1972), **672**

Evening News Assn., Owner and Publisher of Detroit News, 145 NLRB 996 (1964), **479**

Ex-Cell-O, 185 NLRB 107 (1970), **231, 232**

Excelsior Underwear, Inc., 156 NLRB 1236 (1966), **290, 305**

Express-News Corp., 223 NLRB 97 (1976), **356**

F

Fainblatt (NLRB v.), 306 U.S. 601 (1939), **196n, 247**

Fansteel Metallurigical Co., (NLRB v.) 360 U.S. 240 (1939), **467**

Farmers' Cooperative Compress, 194 NLRB 185 (1972), **655**

Farmers' Cooperative Compress v. United Packinghouse, Food and Allied Workers Union, 416 F. (2d) 1126 (1969), cert. denied 396 U.S. 903 (1969), **655**

Farowitz v. Associated Musicians of Greater New York, Local 802, CCA 2, Case No. 28434, April 29, 1964, **596**

Federal Election Commission v. National Conservative Political Action Committee, No. 83-1032, March 18, 1985, **239**

Fibreboard Paper Products v. NLRB, 379 U.S. 203 (1964), **401**

Fibreboard Paper Products Corp. v. NLRB, 379 U.S. 203 (1964), **407–9**

Finnegan v. Leu, U.S. Sup. Ct., Case No. 80–2150, May 17, 1982, **596–97**

Firefighters, Local 98, v. City of Cleveland, U.S. Supreme Ct. Case No. 84–1999, July 2, 1986, **681**

Firefighters v. Stotts (467 U.S. 561 (1984), **680–81**

Firestone Tire & Rubber Co., 222 NLRB 1254 (1976), **337–38**

First Church of Christ Scientist in Boston, 194 NLRB 1006 (1972), **261**

First National Maintenance Corp. v. NLRB, 449 U.S. 1079 (1981), **402**

Fisher v. Flynn, 598 2d 663 (1st cir. 1979), **666**

Fleetwood Trailer Co. (NLRB v.) 389 U.S. 375 (1967), **472**

Florida Hotel of Tampa, 124 NLRB 261 (1959), **257**

Florida Power & Light v. Electrical Workers, 417 U.S. 790 (1974), **489**

Foley Hoag & Eliot, 229 NLRB 80 (1977), **260**

Food & Commercial Workers, Local 1095, Automobile Salesmen's Union v. NLRB, CA-D of C, No. 82-2264, June 30, 1983, **345**

Food & Commercial Workers (NLRB v.) (Docket No. 84-1493, February 26, 1986), **236**

Food Employees Union, Local 590 v. Logan Valley Plaza, Inc., 391 U.S. 308 (1967), **551, 552, 553**

Ford Motor Co. v. Huffman, 345 U.S. 330 (1953), **431**

Ford Motor Co. v. NLRB, 114 F. (2d) 905 (1940), **284**

Ford Motor Co. (NLRB v.) 441 U.S. 488 (1979), **401**

Fordham University, 193 NLRB 134 (1971), **258**

Fort Apache Timber, 226 NLRB 63 (1976), **263**

Franks v. Bowman Transportation Co., 424 U.S. 747 (1976), **679, 680, 683**

Free Press Co., 76 NLRB 152 (1948), **355**

Freeman v. Teamsters, Local 135, CCA-5, 746 F. (2d) 1316 (1984), **433**

Frito-Lay, 243 NLRB No. 16 (1979), **395**

Fruit & Vegetable Packers & Warehousemen, Local 760, et al. (Tree Fruits, Inc.) (NLRB v.) 377 U.S. 58 (1964), **522–24**

G

Garner v. Teamsters Union, 246 U.S. 485 (1953), **254, 255**

Gate of Spain Restaurant, 192 NLRB 1091 (1971), **313**

Gateway Coal Co. v. United Mine Workers, 414 U.S. 368 (1974), **445–46, 453**

Gazzam case, **548–49**

Geduldig v. Aiello, 94 U.S. 2485 (1974), **668**

General American Transportation Corp., 288 NLRB 102 (1977), **412**

General Electric Co., 58 NLRB 57 (1944), **333, 334**

General Electric Co., 167 NLRB 618 (1966), **289**

General Electric Co., 173 NLRB 46 (1968), **360**

General Electric Co., 215 NLRB 520 (1975) **293**

General Electric Co. v. Gilbert, 429 U.S. 881 (1976), **668**

General Electric Co. v. NLRB, 358 F. (2d) 292 (1969), **360**

General Electric Co. (NLRB v.), 418 F. (2d) 736 (1969), **398**

General Electric Co. v. United Electrical, Radio, Machine Workers of America, 353 U.S. 547 (1957), **441**

General Knit of California, 229 NLRB No. 101 (1978), **292**

General Motors Corp., 130 NLRB 481 (1961), **390–91**

General Motors Corp., 133 NLRB 21 (1961), **391**

General Motors Corp. v. NLRB, 303 F. (2d) 428 (1962), **391**

General Motors Corp. (NLRB v.), 373 U.S. 734 (1963), **391**

General Motors Corp., Delco Moraine Div., 237 NLRB No. 167 (1978), **428**

General Motors Corp., Packard Electric Div., 134 NLRB 1107 (1962), **380**

General Shoe Corp., 77 NLRB 124 (1948), **287–92**

General Steel Castings Corp., 41 NLRB 350 (1942), **329**

General Truck Drivers, Chauffeurs, Helpers Union, Local 692, IBT (Great Western Uni-freight System), 209 NLRB 446 (1974), **430**

Georgia Kraft Co., Woodcraft Division 275 NLRB No. 246 (1985), **486**

Giboney v. Empire Storage & Ice Co., 336 U.S. 490 (1949), **546, 548, 549**

Giordani v. Hoffman, 277 F. Supp. 722 (1967), **620**

Gissel Packing Co. (NLRB v.), 395 U.S. 575 (1969), **293, 309, 311, 312, 314**

Globe Cotton Mills v. NLRB, 103 F. (2d), 91, 94 (1939), **397**

Globe Machine & Stamping Co., 3 NLRB 294 (1937) **1, 333**

Godchaux Sugar Co., 44 NLRB 874 (1942), **343**

Golden State Bottling Co., Inc. v. NLRB, 414 U.S. 168 (1973), **459**

Golden Turkey Mining Co., 34 NLRB 779 (1941), **339**

Goldfarb v. Virginia State Bar. 421 U.S. 773 (1975), **260**

Gompers v. Bucks Stove & Range Co., 221 U.S. 418 (1911), **47–48, 54, 59, 101, 105**

Goodall-Sanford, Inc. v. United Textile Workers of America, 353 U.S. 550 (1957), **441**

Gornet Casuals, 207 NLRB 304 (1973), **485**

Gourmet Foods, 270 NLRB No. 113 (1984), **311**

Grace, W. R., v. Rubber Workers, Local 759, 103 Sup. Ct. 2177 (1983), **446–47, 449**

Graham Paper Division, Div. of Jim Walter Paper, 245 NLRB No. 180 (1979), **398**

Grand Rapids City Coach Lines v. Howlett, 137 F. Supp. 667 (1956), **578**

Granite State Joint Board, 409 U.S. 213 (1972), **382, 490**

Graphic Arts Intl. Union and Kable Printing Co., 225 NLRB 186 (1976), **510**

Grauman Co., 87 NLRB 755 (1949), **525**

Gray v. Gulf Mobile & Ohio Railroad Co., 429 F. (2d) 1064 (CA 5, 1970), cert. denied 401 U.S. 1001 (1971), **671–72**

Great Atlantic & Pacific Tea Co., 69 NLRB 463 (1946), **343**

Great Atlantic & Pacific Tea Co., 166 NLRB 27 (1967), **297**

Great Coastal Express, 196 NLRB 871 (1972), **411**

Great Northern Railway Co. v. Brosseau, 286 Fed. 416 (1923), **33**

Great Southern Construction, Inc., 266 NLRB No. 69 (1983), **316**

Great Western Food Co. (Local 540 v.) CA-5 No. 82-1207, August 1, 1983, **449**

Griggs v. Duke Power Co., 401 U.S. 424 (1971), **662–64, 672, 677, 680, 685**

Gulf States Paper Corp., EZ Packaging Division, 219 NLRB 147 (1975), **471**

Guss v. Utah Labor Relations Board, 353 U.S. 1 (1957), **255–56**

H

Haag Drug Co., 169 NLRB 877 (1968), **359**

Hall v. Cole, 412 U.S. 1 (1973), **596–97**

Hammer v. Dagenhart, 247 U.S. 251 (1918), **139**

Harley-Davidson Transportation Co., Inc., 273 NLRB No. 192 (1985), **458**

Harper v. TWA, Inc., 525 F. (2d) 409 (CA 8, 1975), **662**

Harrelson (United States v.) 223 F. Supp. 869 (1963), **621**

Hazelwood School District v. United States, 433 U.S. 299 (1977), **661**

Heat, Frost and Asbestos Workers, Local 53 v. Vogler, 407 F. (2d) 1097 (1969), **677**

Heinz, H. J., Co. v. NLRB, 311 U.S. 514 (1941), **180**

Hendricks County Rural Electric Membership Corp. (NLRB v.) U.S. Sup. Ct., Case No. 80–885, December 2, 1981, **261**

Herbert and Meisel Trunk Co. v. United Leather Workers International Union, 268 Fed. 662 (1920), **60–61**

Hershey Foods Corp., 207 NLRB 897 (1974), **381**

Hershey Foods Corp. (NLRB v.) CA. 9, case No. 74–2114, April 15, 1975, **381**

Highway Trailer Co., 3 NLRB 591 (1936), **173**

Highway Truck Drivers & Helpers, Local 107 v. Cohen, 182 F. Supp. 608 (1960), aff. 284 F (2d) 162 (1960), cert. denied 365 U.S. 833 (1961), **619**

Highway Truck Drivers & Helpers, Local 107, IBT (Riss & Co.), 130 NLRB 943 (1960), **521**

Hill v. Florida, 325 U.S. 538 (1945), **252**

Hineline's Meat Plant, Inc., 193 NLRB 867 (1971), **297**

Hines v. Anchor Motor Freight, 96 S. Ct. 1048 (1976), **447–48**

Hitchman Coal Co. v. Mitchell, 245 U.S. 229 (1917), **34–37, 73, 85, 139**

H. K. Porter Co. v. NLRB, 397 U.S. 99 (1970), **232**

Hodge v. Teamsters, CCA-7, No. 82-2555, May 25, 1983, **596**

Hodgson v. Steelworkers, Local 6799, 403 U.S. 333 (1971), **617**

Hoffman v. Lonza, CCA-7 No. 80-2314, August 31, 1981, **433**

Hollywood Ceramics, 140 NLRB 221 (1962), **290**

Honeywell, Inc., 225 NLRB 79 (1976), **293**

Honolulu Typographical Union No. 37 v. NLRB, 167 NLRB 150 (CA DC, 1968), **523, 524**

Hospital & Healthcare Employees, District 1199, 222 NLRB 212 (1976), **268**

Hotel Employees Local 255 v. Leedom, 358 U.S. 99 (1958), **257**

Hotel & Restaurant Employees, Local 11, CA-9, No. 84-7353, May 18, 1985, **296**

Hour Publishing, 245 NLRB No. 53 (1979), **399**

Houston Insulation Contractor's Assn., 148 NLRB 866 (1966), **533**

Howard Electric Co. (IBEW Local 6), 227 NLRB 278 (1977), **378**

Howard Johnson Co., 198 NLRB 763 (1972), **459**

Howard Johnson v. Hotel & Restaurant Employees, 417 U.S. 249 (1974), **459**

Hudgens v. NLRB, 424 U.S. 507 (1976), **553**

Hudson, J. L., Co. (NLRB v.) 135 Fed. (2d) 380 **196**n

Hughes v. Superior Court of California U.S. Supreme Court, May 8, 1950, **99**n

Hughes v. Superior Court of the State of California, 339 U.S. 460 (1950), **549, 552**

Hughes Tool Co., 56 NLRB 981 (1944) **426**

Hughes Tool Co., 147 NLRB 166 (1964), **428**

Humble Oil & Refining Co., 15 War Labor Reports 380 (1974), **208**

Humphrey, Hutchenson & Mosely v. Donovan, CCA-6, No. 83-5564, February 20, 1985, **604**

Humphrey v. Moore, 375 U.S. 335 (1964), **431, 440, 654**

Hurley Co., 130 NLRB 282 (1961), **288**

Hutcheson (United States v.), 321 U.S. 219 (1941), **100, 102, 103, 105, 108, 111**

Hutchins v. United States Industries, Inc., 428 F. (2d) 303 (1970), **670**

I

IBEW, 325 U.S. 797 (1945), **107–8, 115**

Ihrie, W. P., & Sons, Div. of Sunshine Biscuits, 165 NLRB 2 (1967), **395**

Illinois Coil Spring Co., Milwaukee Spring Div., 265 NLRB No. 28 (1982), **405**

Illinois Coil Spring Co., Milwaukee Spring Div., 268 NLRB No. 87 (1984), **405**

Independent Metal Workers (Hughes Tool Co.), 147 NLRB 166 (1964), **653**

Indiana & Michigan Electric Co., 229 NLRB No. 95 (1977), **398**

Industrial Union of Marine and Shipbuilding Workers of America (NLRB v.) 391 U.S. 418 (1968), **318**

Inland Steel Co., 77 NLRB 1, enf. 170 F. (2d) 247 (1948); cert. denied 336 U.S. 960 (1949), **401**

Inland Trucking Co., v. NLRB, 440 F. (2d) 562 (1971), **481**

Intercollegiate Press, Graphic Arts Div., 199 NLRB 35 (1972), **482**

Intercollegiate Press, Graphic Arts Div., v. NLRB, 486 F. (2d) 837 (CA 8, 1974), **482**

International Harvester, 15 War Labor Reports 84 (1944), **209**

International Harvester Co., Columbus Plastics Operation, 271 NLRB No. 101 (1984), **412**

International Molders & Allied Workers Local No. 125, 178 NLRB 25 (1969), **318**

International Rice Milling Co., (NLRB v.) 181 F. (2d) 21 (CA 5, 1950), **512**

International Rice Milling Co., NLRB v.) 341 U.S. 665 (1951), **511**

International Technical Products, 249 No. 183 (1980), **459**

International Union v. O'Brien, 339 U.S. 454 (1950), **583**

International Union, United Automobile, Aircraft and Agricultural Implement Workers, 137 NLRB 104 (1962), **380**

Interstate Electric Co., (IBEW Local 354) 227 NLRB 291), **378**

Iron Workers, Local 92, V. Norris, 383 F. (2d) 735 (1967), **620**

Iron Workers, Local 103 (NLRB v.), **376**

J

Jackson Engineering Co., 265 NLRB No. 175 (1982), **174**

Jacksonville Bulk Terminals v. Longshoremen, 457 U.S. 702 (1982), **454**

John Morrell & Co., 270 NLRB No. 1 (1984), **455**

Johns-Manville Products Corp., 223 NLRB 189 (1976), **482**

Johnson v. Pike Corp. of America, 332 F. Supp. 490 (1971), **678**

Jones & Laughlin Steel Corp., 66 NLRB 400 (1946), **343**

Jones & Laughlin Steel Corp. v. Mine Workers, 519 F. (2d) 1154 (1976), **453**

Jones & Laughlin Steel Corp. (NLRB v.), 301 U.S. 1 (1937), **130, 168–71, 195, 247**

Jones & Laughlin Steel Corp. (NLRB v.), 331 U.S. 416 (1947), **351**

Jou-Jou Designs, Inc., v. Garment Workers, ILGWU, 643 F. (2d) 905 (1981), **113**

Joy Silk Mills, Inc., 85 NLRB 1236 (1949) 185 F. (2d) 732 (1950); cert. denied 341 U.S. 914 (1951), **307, 308**

K

Keller Ladders, Southers Subsidiary of Keller Industries, 161 NLRB 21 (1966), **395**

Kennecott Copper Co., 138 NLRB 3 (1962), **336**

Kesner v. NLRB, 532 F. (2d) 1169 (CA 7, 1976), **428**

Keystone Coat, Apron & Towel Supply Co., 121 NLRB 880 (1958), **382**

Keystone Pretzel Bakery, Inc. (NLRB v.) CA 3. No. 81-2067, December 29, 1982, **313**

Kinsey v. First Regional Securities, Inc., (DC CA), No. 75-1224, April 18, 1977; EEOC Decision No. 71-1504, March 25, 1971, **663**

Kit Manufacturing, 150 NLRB 662 (1964); enf. 365 F. (2d) 829 (1966), **403**

Kleinberg, Kaplan, Wolf, Cohen, & Burrows, P.C., 253 NLRB No. 54 (1980), **260**

Knight, E. C. (United States v.), 156 U.S. 1 (1895), **52, 167**

Kolinske v. Lubbers, CCA-DC No. 82-1203 June 17, 1983, **433**

Kono-TV-Mission Telecasting, 163 NLRB 1005 (1967), **317**

Kroger Co. v. NLRB, 399 F. (2d) 445 (1968), **401**

L

La Crosse Telephone Corp. v. Wisconsin Employment Relations Board, 336 U.S. 18 (1948), **253, 254**

Lakeland Bus Lines, Inc. v. NLRB, 287 F. (2d) 888 (1960), **427**

Lavender v. United Mine Workers of America, 285 F. (2d) 869 (1968), **608**

LA-Z-Boy Chair Co., 235 NLRB No. 11 (1978), **338**

Laborers, Local 1057 v. NLRB, CCA DC, Case Nos. 75-1854, 75-1859, November 23, 1977, **268**

Laclede Gas Co., 187 NLRB 32 (1971), **482**

Laidlaw Corp., 171 NLRB 175 (1968), **472**

Lathers Union, Local 42 of Wood, Wire & Metal Lathers International Union (Lathing Contractors Association of Southern California), 223 NLRB 37 (1976), **404**

Lau Industries, 210 NLRB 182 (1974), **298**

Lauf v. Shinner & Co., 303 U.S. 323 (1938), **93–94**

Leather Workers International Union v. Herbert and Meisel Truck Co., 284 Fed. 446 (1922), **61**

Leather Workers International Union v. Herbert and Meisel Trunk Co., 285 U.S. 457 (1925), **61**

Leedom v. Kyne, 358 U.S. 184 (1958), **356**

Lees, James, & Sons Co., 130 NLRB 1290 (1961), **289**

Lehigh Portland Cement, 101 NLRB 1010 (1952), **401**

Letter Carriers Union, Branch 6000 v. NLRB, 595 F. (2d) 808 (CCA DC, (1979), **429**

Letter Carriers (Old Dominion Branch No. 496, National Association of Letter Carriers) v. Austin, 418 U.S. 264 (1974), **485**

Levi Strauss Co., 172 NLRB 57 (1968), **313**

Lewis Food Co., 115 NLRB 890 (1956), **494, 497**

Lincoln Federal Labor Union v. Northwestern Iron & Metal Co., 335 U.S. 525 (1949), **384**

Little Steel Cases, 1 War Labor Reports 324 (1942), **208–9**

Livingston Shirt, 107 NLRB 400 (1953), **301–2, 305, 306**

Lloyd Corp., Ltd. v. Tanner, 407 U.S. 551 (1972), **552–53**

Loewe v. Lawlor (Danbury Hatters), 208 U.S. 274 (1908), **44–47, 54, 55, 59, 101, 105, 139, 436**

Lof Glass, Inc., 249 NLRB No. 57 (1980), **290**

Logan, S. S., Packing Co. (NLRB v.), 386 F. (2d) 562, CCA 4, 1967, **313**

Long v. Bricklayers Union, 17 Pa. Dist. R. 984 (1929), **33**

Longshoremens Union v. Allied International, Inc., 454 U.S. 814 (1982), **510**

Longshoremens Union (Galveston Maritime Assn.), 148 NLRB 897 (1965); enf. 368 F. (2d) 1010 (CA 5, 1966); cert. denied 389 U.S. 837 (1967), **654**

Longshoremens Union, Local 50 (Pacific Maritime Assn.) (NLRB v.), 504 F. (2d) 1209 (CA 9, 1974), **476**

Longshoremens Union, Local 1332, ILA (Philadelphia Marine Trade Assn.), 151 NLRB 1447 (1965), **531**

Longshoremens Union, Local 418 (United States v.), D.C.-N.D. III, No. 71 Civ. 2416 (November 3, 1971), **562**

Lord & Local Union 2088, International Brotherhood of Electronics Workers, 646 F. (2d) 1057, 1981; cert. denied U.S. Sup. Ct. No. 81-8060, June 28, 1982, **384**

Los Angeles-Seattle Motor Express, Inc., 121 NLRB 1629 (1958), **373**

Ludwig Motor Corp., 222 NLRB 635 (1976), **297**

Lyons Restaurant, 234 NLRB No. 10 (1978), **296**

M

Machinists, 2 NLRB 87 (1921), **396**

Machinists v. King, 335 F. (2d) 340 (1962); cert. denied 379 U.S. 920 (1964), **595**

Machinists v. Street, 367 U.S. 740 (1961), **388**

Machinists, Local 697 (H.O. Canfield Rubber Co. of Va.), 223 NLRB 832 (1976), **429**

Machinists, Local 1327 Dalmo Victor, 263 NLRB 984 (1982), **490**

Machinists, Local 1414, Neufeld Porsche-Audi, Inc., 270 NLRB No. 209 (1984), **490–91**

Machinists, Lodge No. 76 v. Wisconsin Employment Relations Commission, 96 S. Ct. 2548 (1976), **254**

Machinists (United Aircraft Corp.) v. NLRB, 525 F. (2d) 237, (CA 2, 1975), **411**

Mackay Radio & Telegraph Co. (NLRB v.) 304 U.S. 323 (1938), **468**

Mackay Radio & Telegraph Co. (NLRB v.) 304 U.S. 333 (1938), **480**

Majure Transport Co. v. NLRB, 198 F. (2d), 735 (1952), **398**

Mallinckrodt Chemical Works, 162 NLRB 48 (1966), **336–37**

Maple Flooring Manufacturers Assn. v. United States, 268 U.S. 563 (1925), **53**

Marine Cooks & Stewards, 90 NLRB 1099 (1950), **374–75**

Marine & Shipbuilding Workers, Local 22, AFL-CIO (NLRB v.), 391 U.S. 418 (1968), **594**

Maritime Union, CIO (NLRB v.), 175 F. (2d) 686 (1949); cert. denied 338 U.S. 955 (1950), **371, 374**

Marriott Corp. v. Great America Service Trades Council, AFL-CIO, No. 76-1453 (CA 7, 1977), **84**

Maryland Drydock Co., 41 NLRB 961 (1942), **339–42**

Master Printers of America v. Donovan, CCA-4, No. 82-1990, December 26, 1984, **604**

Mastro Plastics Corp. v. NLRB, 350 U.S. 270 (1956), **467, 501**

Matrite of Wisconsin, 198 NLRB 241 (1972), **415**

McCulloch v. Maryland, 4 Wheat, 316 (1819), **384**

McDonald v. City of West Branch, Michigan, 466 U.S. 284 (1984), **448–49**

McEwen Manufacturing Co., 172 NLRB 990 (1968), **313**

McLaughlin v. Tilendis, 398 F. (2d) 287 (CCA 7, 1968), **642**

McNess, Jim v. Todd, 461 U.S. 260 (1983), **377**

Meade Electric Co. v. Hagberg, Indiana Superior Court, Lake County, May 19, 1958, No. 158–121, **390**

Meat Cutters Union, AFL-CIO, Local 189 v. Jewel Tea Co., Inc., 381 U.S. 676 (1965), **108–9, 114**

Meat & Highway Drivers, Local 710 (Wilson Co.), 143 NLRB 1221 (1964), **528**

Medicenter, Mid-South Hospital, 221 NLRB 670 (1975), **401**

Meinhard v. Salmon, 249 N.Y. 464 (1928), **619**

Meir's Wine Cellars, Inc., 188 NLRB 153 (1971), **297**

Mercy Hospitals of Sacraments, 217 NLRB 765 (1975), **265**

Metropolitan Auto Parts, 99 NLRB 401 (1952), **301**

Metropolitan Edison Co. v. NLRB, 460 U.S. 693 (1983), **455**

Metropolitan Life Insurance Co., 56 NLRB 1635 (1944), **357**

Metropolitan Life Insurance Co. v. NLRB, 327 F. (2d) 906 (CA 1), **358**

Metropolitan Life Insurance Co., v. NLRB, 328 F. (2d) 820 (CA 3), **358**

Metropolitan Life Insurance Co. v. NLRB, 330 F. (2d) 62 (CA 6), **358**

Metropolitan Life Insurance Co. (NLRB v.), 380 U.S. 438 (1965), **358**

Meyer Manufacturing Co., 170 NLRB 509 (1968), **352**

Meyers Industries, 268 NLRB No. 73 (1984), **492–93**

Michigan Bell Telephone Co., 216 NLRB 806 (1975), **359**

Mid-Continent Refrigerated Service Co., 228 NLRB 649 (1977), **317**

Midland National Life Insurance Co., 263 NLRB No. 24 (1982), **292**

Milk Wagon Drivers Union v. Lake Valley Farm Products, 108 F. (2d) 436 (1939), **102–3, 105**

Milk Wagon Drivers Union v. Lake Valley Farm Products, 311 U.S. 91 (1940), **103**

Milk Wagon Drivers Union v. Meadowmoor Dairies, Inc., 312 U.S. 287 (1941), **543–44, 545**

Miller Brewing Co., 166 NLRB 90 (1967), **401**

Mine Workers v. Coronado Coal Co., 259 U.S. 344 (1922), **57**

Mine Workers v. Patton, 211 F. (2d) 742 (1954); cert. denied, 348 U.S. 824 (1954), **478**

Mine Workers v. James M. Pennington, 381 U.S. 657 (1965), **109–10, 113–14**

Mine Workers Health & Retirement Funds v. Robinson, U.S. Sup. Ct., Case No. 81-61, January 13, 1982, **399**

Mine Workers (Lone Star Steel), 231 NLRB No. 88 (1977), **401**

Ming Quong Children's Center & Social Services Union, Local 535, 210 NLRB 899 (1974), **259**

Minnesota Mining & Manufacturing Co., 261 NLRB No. 2 (1982), **398–99**

Miranda Fuel Co., 140 NLRB 181 (1962); enf. denied 326 F. (2d) 172 (1963), **427–28, 429, 653, 654**

MMIC, Inc., 270 NLRB No. 51 (1984), **312**

Mobil Oil Corp., 169 NLRB 259 (1968), **337**

Mobil Oil Corp. v. Oil, Chemical & Atomic Workers International Union, U.S. Sup. Ct. Case No. 74–1254, June 14, 1976, **384**

Molders and Allied Workers Local 155 (U.S. Pipe & Foundry Co.), v. NLRB, 442 F. (2d) 742 (1971), **481, 482**

Monmouth Medical Center v. NLRB, CCA 3, Case No. 78-1832, August 20, 1979, **291**

Montefiore Medical Center, 235 NLRB No. 29 (1978), **265**

Montgomery Ward & Co., Inc., 145 NLRB 846 (1946), **302**

Montgomery Ward Co., Inc., (NLRB v.), 339 F. (2d) 889 (CA 6, 1965), **302**

Mountain State Construction Co., 203 NLRB 1085 (1973), **413**

Moyer Trucking & Garage Service, 269 NLRB No. 168 (1984), **492–93**

Musicians v. Stein, 218 F. (2d) 679 (1954), **101**

Musicians v. Wittstein, 379 U.S. 171 (1964), **591–92**

My Store, Inc. (NLRB v.), 345 F. (2d) 494 (CA 7, 1965), **298–99**

N

Nabisco, Inc. v. NLRB, 479 F. (2d) 770 (CA 2, 1973), **411**

Na-Mac Product Corp., 70 NLRB 298 (1946), **398**

National Gypsum Co., 133 NLRB 1492 (1962), **471**

National Packing, Inc., 155 NLRB 142 (1966), **498**

National Radio Co., 198 NLRB 527 (1972), **412**

National Tube Co., 76 NLRB 169 (1948), **335–36**

National Woodwork Manufacturers Assn. v. NLRB, 328 U.S. 612 (1967), **531, 533**

New Negro Alliance v. Sanitary Grocery Co., 303 U.S. 552 (1938), **94–96**

Newington Children's Hospital, 217 NLRB No. 134 (1975), **265**

Newport News Shipbuilding & Dry Dock Co. v. Schauffler, 303 U.S. 54 (1938), **196n**

News Syndicate Co., Inc., et al. (NLRB v.) 365 U.S. 645 (1961), **382**

Nichols, S. E. of Ohio, Inc., 200 NLRB 1130 (1973), **553**

Niles-Bemont Pond Co. (NLRB) v.), 199 F. (2d) 713 (1952), **401**

Nolde Bros., Inc., v. Bakery & Confectionery Workers, Local 358, 430 U.S. 243 (1977), **446**

Norfolk Shipbuilding & Drydock Corp. (NLRB v.), 172 F. (2d) 813 (1949), **398**

North American Aviation Co., 44 NLRB 604 (1943), **425**

North American Aviation Co., (NLRB v.), 136 F. (2d) 899 (1943), **425, 426**

North Arkansas Electric Cooperative, 185 NLRB 550 (1970), **348**

North Electric Manufacturing Co., 84 NLRB 23 (1949), **484**

Northern Securities Co. v. United States, 193 U.S. 199 (1904), **52, 53**

Northwest Airlines, Inc. v. Air Line Pilots & Transport Workers, 447 U.S. 920 (1981), **655**

NVF Co. Hartwell Div., 210 NLRB 663 (1974), **288**

O

Occidental Life Ins. Co., 14 FEP Cases 1718 (1977), **660**

Office Employees International Union, Local 11 v. NLRB, 353 U.S. 313 (1957), **263**

Ohio Valley Carpenters District Council (Cardinal Industries), 144 NLRB 91 (1963), **529**

Ohmite Manufacturing Co., 217 NLRB 435 (1975), **294**

Oil Workers, CIO (Pure Pil Co., Toledo Refining Div.), 84 NLRB 315 (1949), **516**

Olin Corp., 268 NLRB No. 86 (1904), **413**

Onondaga Pottery Co., 100 NLRB 1143 (1953), **301**

Operating Engineers, Local No. 12 (Associated General Contractors of America), 187 NLRB 439 (1970), **403**

Operating Engineers, Local 450 (Linbeck Construction Corp.), 219 NLRB 997 (1975), **518**

Operating Engineers, Local 825, (NLRB v.), 400 U.S. 297 (1971), **533**

Ottawa Silica Co., 197 NLRB 53 (1972), **481–82**

Ozark Trailers, 161 NLRB 561 (1966), **402**

P

Pacific Erectors (NLRB v.) 718 F. 2d 1459, CA-9 1983, 377 Section 8(f)(4), **378**

Pacific Molasses Co. v. NLRB, 577 F. (2d) 1172 (CCA 5, 1978), **314**

Packard Motor Car Co., 61 NLRB 4 (1945), **340, 341, 342–45**

Packard Motor Car Co. v. NLRB, 67 S. Ct. 789 (1947), **344**

Painters, Local 798 (Nassau Div. of Master Painters Assn. of Nassau-Suffolk Counties, et al.) 212 NLRB No. 89 (1975), **399**

Pandol & Sons v. Agricultural Labor Relations Board of California, 429 U.S. 802 (1976), **276**

Papermakers, Local 189 (United States v.) 416 F. (2d) 980 (5th Cir., 1969), cert. denied 397 U.S. 919 (1970), **677**

Papermakers, Local 189 (United States v.) 282 F. Supp. 39 (ED La., 1969), cert. denied (U.S. S Ct) 397 U.S. 919 (1970), **678**

Parade Publications Inc. v. Philadelphia Mailers Union No. 14, CA 3, Case No. 71-1107, May 1, 1972, **453**

Paragon Products Corp., 134 NLRB 86 (1961), **379, 382**

Parker-Robb Chevrolet, Inc., 262 NLRB No. 58 (1982), **345, 346**

Pattern Maker's League v. NLRB, 105 Sup. Ct. 3064 (1985), **491**

Patterson v. The American Tobacco Co. (ED Va., September 26, 1974), No. 104, 73-R, **678**

Peck v. Associated Press Distributors of New England, 237 F. Supp. 113 (1965), **592**

Peerless Plywood Co., 107 NLRB 427 (1953), **288–89, 302**

Peerless Pressed Metal, 198 NLRB 561 (1972), **411**

Penn Cork & Closures, 156 NLRB, 411 (1965), enf. 376 F. (2d) 52 (1967), **395**

Pennington v. United Mine Workers, 257 F. Supp. 815 (1966), **109–10, 111, 113–14**

Pepsi-Cola Distributing Co. (NLRB v.) CCA 6, Case No. 79-1314, May 1, 1981, **459**

Performance Measurements Co., Inc., 148 NLRB 1657 (1964), **297**

Perma Vinyl Corp., 164 NLRB 968 (1967), **459**

Petroleum Chemicals, Inc., 121 NLRB 630 (1958), **352**

Phalen v. Theatrical Protective Union No. 1 International Alliance of Theatrical & Stage Employees, AFL-CIO, 22 N.Y. (2d) 34 (1968), **588, 656**

Phelps Dodge (AFL-CIO Joint Negotiating Committee) v. NLRB, 459 F. (2d) 374 (CA 3, 1972), **361**

Philadelphia Sheraton Corp., 136 NLRB 888 (1962), **380**

Philadelphia Typographical Union, Local No. 2 (Philadelphia Inquirer, Division of Triangle Publications, Inc.), 142 NLRB 1 (1963), **476**

Phillips Manufacturing Co., 148 NLRB 1420 (1964), **298–99**

Physicians National House Staff Assn. v. Fanning, CCA DC, Case No. 78-1209, July 11, 1980, **267**

Pioneer Flour Mills, 174 NLRB 1202 (1969), **470–71**

Pipefitters, Local Union 562 v. United States, 407 U.S. 385 (1972), **238–40**

Pittsburgh Plate Glass (NLRB v.) 270 F. (2d) 26 (1959), **336**

Pittsburgh Plate Glass Co. v. NLRB, 313 U.S. 146 (1941), **327**

Plankinton Packing Co. v. WERB, 338 U.S. 953 (1950), **254**

Plant City Welding & Tank Co., 119 NLRB 962 (1957), **288**

Plasterers Union, Local 79, Operative Plasterers (Texas State Tile & Terrazzo Co.) (NLRB v.) 404 U.S. 116 (1971), **475**

Plasterers Union, Local 79, Operative Plasterers (Texas State Tile & Terrazzo Co.) (NLRB v.) 440 F. (2d) 174 (1971), **475**

Plauche Electric, 135 NLRB 250 (1963), **520**

Plessy v. Ferguson, 163 U.S. 537 (1896), **653**

Plumbers, Local 638 v. NLRB, 97 S. Ct. 891 (1977), **531**

Plumbers Locals v. NLRB, CCA-DC No. 80-2393, April 18, 1982, **384**

Polish National Alliance v. NLRB, 322 U.S. 643 (1944), **196n**

Ponn Distributing, Inc., 203 NLRB 482 (1973), **299**

Porter, H. K. Co. v. NLRB, 397 U.S. 99 (1970), **399**

Postal Clerks v. Blount, 325 F. Supp. 879 (D-D.C.) (1971) affirmed 404 U.S. 802 (1971), **631, 879**

PPG Industries, 251 NLRB 1146 (1980), **295**

Prescott Industrial Products Co., 205 NLRB 51 (1973), **304**

Price, Nelson & Sears v. Wirtz, CCA-5, 412 F. (2d) 647 (1969), **604**

Prill v. NLRB, CCA-DC No. 84-1064, February 26, 1985, **493**

Printing Union, Columbus Pressmen & Assistants Union 252 (NLRB v.) CA 5, No. 75-3546, December 13, 1976, **403**

Provision House Workers Union Local 274 (Urban Patmar, Inc.) v. NLRB, 493 F. (2d) 1249 (CA 9, 1974), **411**

Pulp & Paper Workers, Local 171 (Boise Cascade Corp.), 165 NLRB 971 (1974), **415**

Purcell v. Keane, 277 F. Supp. 252 (1967) **620**

Purity Foods (NLRB v.) 376 F. (2d) 497, cert. denied 389 U.S. 959 (1967), **358**

Purolator Courier Corp., 268 NLRB No. 67 (1983), **352**

Q

Quaker City Life Insurance Co., 134 NLRB 960 (1962), **357–58**

Quinn v. DiGiulian, CCA-DC, No. 83-2065, July 13, 1984, **598**

R

Rabouin v. NLRB, 195 F. (2d) 906 (2d Cir., 1952), **528**

Radio Artists, Washington-Baltimore Local v. NLRB, CA DC No. 24, 641 (April 17, 1972), **515**

Radio Engineers Union (NLRB v.) 364 U.S. 573 (1961), **474–75**

Radio Television Technical School, Inc., 199 NLRB 570 (1972), **414**

Radioear, 199 NLRB 1161 (1972), **411**

Railway Employees Dept. v. Hanson, 351 U.S. 225 (1956), **387–88**

Ramsey v. Mineworkers, U.S. Sup. Ct., No. 88 (February 24, 1971), **111–12**

Ratner v. Bakery Workers, 394 F. (2d) 780 (1968), **620**

Redmond Plastics, Inc., 187 NLRB 487 (1970), **308**

Reed v. Ronmell, 46 LRRM 2565 (E.D. Mich., 1960), **496**

Republic Aviation Corp. v. NLRB, 324 U.S. 105 (1956), **300**

Retail Clerks, Local 324, FED Mart Stores, Inc., 261 NLRB No. 156 (1982), **428**

Retail Clerks, Local 344, 136 NLRB 1270 (1962), **500**

Retail Clerks, Local 1001 (NLRB v.), 444 U.S. 1011 (1980), **524–25**

Retail Clerks, Local 1625 v. Schermerhorn, 373 U.S. 726 (1963), **392**

Retail Clerks, Local 1625 v. Schermerhorn, 375 U.S. 96 (1964), **386**

Retail Clerks, Locals 324 & 770 (Barker Bros.), 138 NLRB 54 (1962), **449, 450**

Retail Clerks (NLRB v.), 203 F. (2d) 165 (1953), **403**

Retail, Wholesale & Department Store Union, District 65 (Eastern Camera & Photo Corp.), 141 NLRB 85 (1965), **495**

Reynolds Metals Co., 198 NLRB 120 (1972), **351**

Rhode Island Catholic Orphan Asylum, 224 NLRB 70 (1976), **259, 260**

Richfield Oil, 110 NLRB 356 (1954), enf. 231 F. (2d) 717; cert. denied 351 U.S. 909 (1956), **401**

Riecke Metal Products Co., 40 NLRB 872 (1942), **125, 172**

Riley v. Bendix Corp., 464 F. (2d) 1113 (CA-5, 1972), **671**

Rios v. Reynolds Metals Co., 467 F. (2d) 54 (1972), **669**

Rizzo v. Ammond, 182 F. Supp. 456 (1960), **608**

Rodriquez v. East Texas Motor Freight, 505 F. (2d) 40 (5th Cir., 1974), **682**

Rollison v. Hotel & Restaurant Employees, Local 879, CCA-9, No. 80–348, May 18, 1982, **613**

Roney Plaza Apartments (NLRB v.), CCA 5, Case No. 77-3481, July 2, 1979, **314**

Rosen v. Public Service Electric Co., 409 F. (2d) 775 (1969), **669**

Rosen v. Public Service Electric & Gas Co., 477 F. (2d) 90 (CA 3, 1973), **669**

Rossmore House, 269 NLRB No. 198 (1984), **295–96**

Royal Typewriter v. NLRB, 533 F. (2d) 1030 (CCA 8, 1976), **402**

Rubber Workers, Local 12 v. NLRB, 368 F. (2d) 12 (CA 5, 1966), cert. denied 384 U.S. 837 (1967), **654, 655**

Rudolph Wurlitzer Co., 32 NLRB 163 (1941), **469**

Ryan Aeronautical Co., 132 NLRB 1160 (1962), **355**

S

Safeco case, **524–25**

Sailors' Union of Pacific (Moore Dry Dock Co.), 92 NLRB 547 (1950), 366 U.S. 667, **518**

St. Elizabeth Community Hospital v. NLRB, CA-9, No. 82-7098, June 22, 1983, **262**

St. Elizabeth Community Hospital, 259 NLRB No. 156 (1981), **262**

St. Francis Hospital, 277 NLRB No. 160 (1984), **266**

St. John's Hospital v. NLRB, CCA 10, Case No. 76-1130, July 14, 1977, **267**

St. Johns Hospital & School of Nursing, Inc., 222 NLRB 1150 (1976), **267, 268**

St. Joseph of the Peace, 217 NLRB No. 135 (1975), **265**

St. Louis Christian Home, 251 NLRB No. 195 (1980), **262**

St. Louis Christian Home (NLRB v.), CA-8, No. 80-2031, November 11, 1981, **262**

St. Louis-San Francisco Railway Co. (United States v.), 464 F. (2d) 301 (8th Cir. 1972), cert. denied 409 U.S. 1107 (1973), **682**

Salvation Army of Massachusetts Dorchester Day Care Center, 271 NLRB No. 37 (1984), **262**

Salzhandler v. Caputo, 316 F. (2d) 445 (1963), **590**

San Diego Building Trades Council v. Garman, 359 U.S. 206 (1959), **654, 687n**

San Francisco Web Pressman & Platemakers' No. 4 San Francisco Newspaper Agency, 272 NLRB No. 138 (1984), **430**

Sands Corrugated Paper Machinery Co., 89 NLRB 1363 (1950), **300**

Santa Cruz Fruit Packing Co. v. NLRB, 303 U.S. 453 (1938), **196n**

Sargent Electric Co., 209 NLRB 630 (1974), **428**

Sartorius, A. & Co., Inc., 10 NLRB 493 (1938), **468, 469**

Savair Manufacturing Co., 414 U.S. 270 (1970), **298**

Schapiro & Whitehouse, Inc., (NLRB v.), 356 F. (2d) 675 (1966), **290**

Schecter Poultry Corp. v. United States, 295 U.S. 495 (1935), **157, 247**

Schonfeld v. Raferty, U.S. District Court, Southern District of New York, No. 67 Civ. 3147, May 8, 1973, **615**

Schultz Refrigerated Service, 87 NLRB 502 (1949), **520**

Sciosa Home & Industrial Disposal Service, 266 NLRB No. 22 (1983), **296**

Scofield v. NLRB, 394 U.S. 423 (1969), **381–82**

Sea Pak v. Industrial, Technical & Professional Employees, 400 U.S. 985 (1971), **384**

Sears, Roebuck, & Co. v. San Diego County District Council of Carpenters, 436 U.S. 180 (1978), **552**

Seattle First National Bank v. NLRB, 450 F. (2d) 353 (1971), reversing 176 NLRB 691 (1969), **403**

Senn v. Tile Layers, 301 U.S. 468 (1937), **91–93**

Serio v. Liss, 189 F. Supp. 358 (1960) affirmed 300 F. (2d) 386 (1961), **611**

Serv-Air, Inc. v. NLRB, 401 F. 2d 363 (1968), **316**

Servette, Inc., (NLRB v.) 337 U.S. 46 (1964), **514**

Sewell Manufacturing, 138 NLRB 66 (1962), **290**

Sheet Metal Workers, Local 28 v. EEOC, U.S. Sup. Ct. Case No. 84-1656, July 2, 1986, **682**

Sheet Metal Workers, Local 36 (United States v.) 416 F. (2d) 123 (CA 8, 1969), **684**

Sheraton Puerto Rico, 248 NLRB No. 113 (1980), **345–46**

Sheridan v. United Brotherhood of Carpenters, 306 F. (2d) 152 (1962), **595**

Shopping Kart Food Market, 228 NLRB 190 (1977), **291–92**

Shoreline Enterprises v. NLRB, 262 F. (2d) 933 (1959), **456**

Sinclair Oil Corp. v. Oil, Chemical & Atomic Workers, 452 F. (2d) 49 (1971), **436**

Sinclair Refining Co. v. Atkinson, 370 U.S. 238 (1962), **450, 451, 452**

Smith Co., 192 NLRB 1098 (1972), **297**

Smith, R. J., Construction Co., Inc., & Local 150, Operating Engineers, 191 NLRB 135 (1971), **376**

Snow, Fred A., & Co., 41 NLRB 1292 (1942), **125, 308**

Somismo, Inc., 133 NLRB 131 (1961), **293**

Southern Saddlery Co., 90 NLRB 1205 (1950), **398**

Southwest Latex Corp., 175 NLRB 1 (1969), **291**

Southwestern Bell Telephone, 198 NLRB 569 (1972), **411**

Spielberg Manufacturing Co., 112 NLRB 1080 (1955), **413–15, 416, 456**

Spurlock v. United Airlines, Inc., 475 F. (2d) 216 (CA 10, 1972), **663**

Standard-Cossa-Thatcher Co., 85 NLRB 1358 (1949), **295**

Standard Knitting Mills, Inc., 172 NLRB 1122 (1968), **292–93**

Standard Oil Co., 137 NLRB 690 (1962), **360**

Standard Oil Co. of New Jersey v. United States, 221 U.S. 1 (1911), **52–53**

Star Market, 172 NLRB 1393 (1968), **359**

State Bank of India, 229 NLRB 137 (1977), **260–61**

State, County, and Municipal Employees, AFL-CIO v. Woodward, 406 F. (2d) 137 (1969), **641–42**

State, County, & Municipal Employees v. State of Washington, 578 F. Supp. 846 (DC-Wash), 1983, **665**

State, County, & Municipal Employees, New Jersey & Municipal Council 61 v. State, County, & Municipal Employees, 478 F. (2d) 1156 (CA 3, 1973), cert. denied 414 U.S. 975 (1973), **608**

State of Minnesota, 219 NLRB 1095 (1976), **252**

State of New Jersey v. Donaldson, 32 NLRB 151 (1867), **18**

Steel-Fab, 212 NLRB 363 (1974), **314**

Steele v. Louisville & Nashville Railroad, 323 U.S. 197 (1944) **653**

Steelweld Equipment Co., 76 NLRB 116 (1948), **351**

Steelworkers v. American Manufacturing Co., 363 U.S. 564 (1960), **442, 443–44, 450**

Steelworkers v. Enterprise Wheel & Car Corp., 363 U.S. 593 (1960), **442, 444, 447, 450, 670**

Steelworkers v. NLRB, 145 NLRB 846 (1964), **302**

Steelworkers v. NLRB, 376 U.S. 492 (1964), **521**

Steelworkers v. Sadlowski, CA DC Case No. 81-1174, March 31, 1981, **614**

Steelworkers v. U.S., 361 U.S. 39 (1959), **568, 570**

Steelworkers v. Warrior & Gulf Navigation Co., 363 U.S. 574 (1960), **442–43, 446, 450**

Steelworkers v. Weber, 440 U.S. 193 (1979), **675**

Steelworkers (Asarco, Inc.), 246 NLRB No. 139 (1979), **395**

Steelworkers (Carrier Corp.) v. NLRB, 376 U.S. 492 (1964), **517, 518**

Steelworkers (Nutone, Inc.) (NLRB v.) 357 U.S. 357 (1958), **302**

Steelworkers, Local Union 2610 (Bethlehem Steel), 225 NLRB 54 (1976), **430**

Steelworkers, Local 3489 v. Usery, 429 U.S. 305 (1977), **612**

Steelworkers, Local 14055, (NLRB v.) 429 U.S. 807 (1976), **524**

Steelworkers, Local 14055 v. NLRB, 524 F. (2d) 853 (1975), **524**

Stevens, J. P., & Co., 245 NLRB No. 20 (1979), **303**

Stevenson, J. R., Corp., 212 NLRB 968 (1974), **216**

Street, Electric Railway & Motor Coach Employees of America, Division 998 v. Wisconsin Employment Relations Board, 340 U.S. 383 (1951), **550**

Street, Electric Railway & Motor Coach Employees of America et al., Division 1287 v. Missouri, 374 U.S. 74 (1962), **579**

Struksnes Construction Co., Inc., 165 NLRB 1062 (1967), **299**

Suburban Motor Freight, 247 NLRB No. 2 (1980), **413**

Summer & Co., Linden Lumber Division, 190 NLRB 718 (1971), NLRB, Section 8 (a)(5), **309**

Summer & Co., Linden Lumber Division v. NLRB, 419 U.S. 301 (1974), **309**

Sunset Line & Twine, 79 NLRB 1487 (1948), **483, 484, 485**

Sure-Tan, Inc., v. NLRB, 460 U.S. 1021 (1984), **263**

Swift & Co., 115 NLRB 752 (1956), **348**

Swift & Co., 162 NLRB 6 (1967), **305**

Syres v. Oil Workers Union, 350 U.S. 892 (1955), **653**

T

Taggart v. Weinacker, 397 U.S. 223 (1970), **552**

Tampa Sand & Material Co., 47 LRRM 1166 (1961), **471**

Taormina (NLRB v.), 207 F. (2d) 251 enf. 94 NLRB 884 (1951), **403**

Teamsters Union v. United States, 431 U.S. 324 (1977), **661, 679**

Teamsters Union, Local 67, AFL (Washington Coca-Cola Bottling Works, Inc.), 107 NLRB 299 (1953) enf. granted 220 F. (2d) 380 (CA DC, 1955), **519–21**

Teamsters Union, Local 82 Furniture & Piano Movers v. Crowley, 104 Sup. Ct. 2557 (1984), **615**

Teamsters Union, Local 115 & Flavor Delight, Inc., v. NLRB, 640 F. 2d 1054, cert. denied 102 Sup. Ct. 141 (1981), **311**

Teamsters Union, Local 296, Northwest Publications, Inc., 263 NLRB No. 104 (1982), **489**

Teamsters Union, Local 309 v. Hanke, 339 U.S. 470 (1949), **550, 552**

Teamsters Union, Local 357 v. NLRB, 365 U.S. 667 (1961), **375**

Teamsters Union, Local 357 v. NLRB (Los Angeles-Seattle Motor Express), 365 U.S. 807 (1961), **382**

Teamsters Union, Local 537 (Lohman Sales Co.), 132 NLRB 901 (1961), **526**

Teamsters Union, Local 688 (Schnuck Markets) 193 NLRB 701 (1971), **533**

Teamsters Union, Local 695, AFL v. Vogt, Inc., 354 U.S. 284 (1957), **540, 552**

Telautograph Corp., 199 NLRB 892 (1972) **318**

Television & Radio Artists (Great Western Broadcasting Corp.), 134 NLRB 1617 (1961), **526**

Television & Radio Artists v. NLRB, 398 F. (2d) 319 (1968), **408**

Tennessee Auger Co., 169 NLRB 914 (1968), **297**

Testing Service Corp., 193 NLRB 332 (1971), **294**

Texarkana Construction Co., 138 NLRB 102 (1962), **498**

Texas Department of Community Affairs v. Burdine, 101 S. Ct. 1089 (1981), **676**

Texas Industries, 112 NLRB 923 (1955), **512**

Texas & New Orleans Railroad v. Brotherhood of Railroad Clerks, 281 U.S. 548 (1930), **147, 148–49, 166, 169, 170**

Textile Workers Union v. Darlington Mfg. Co., 380 U.S. 263 (1965), **176, 402**

Textile Workers Union v. Lincoln Mills of Alabama, 353 U.S. 448 (1957), **441–42, 450, 456**

Textile Workers Union v. NLRB (J. P. Stevens), CADC No. 71-1469, February 1, 1973, **232**

30 Sutton Place Corp., 240 NLRB No. 94 (1979), **258**

Thompson v. BHD of Sleeping Car Porters, 367 F. (2d) 489 (CCA 4, 1966), **431**

Thompson Products, Inc., 72 NLRB 887 (1947), **477**

Thompson Products, Inc., 72 NLRB 888 (1947), **181**

Thompson Transport (NLRB v.) 406 F. (2d) 698 (CCA 10, 1969), **402**

Thornhill v. Alabama, 310 U.S. 88 (1940), **284, 539–40, 546**

Tiidee Products, 194 NLRB 1234 (1972), **232**

T.I.M.E.-D.C., Inc. v. U.S., 431 U.S. 324 (1977), **679, 684**

Times Publishing Co., 72 NLRB 676 (1947), **180–81, 397**

Towmotor Corp., 187 NLRB 1027 (1971), **338**

Trading Port, 219 NLRB 298 (1975), **315**

Trans World Airlines, Inc. v. Hardison, 432 U.S. 63 (1977), **671, 672**

Transmarine Navigation Corp. (NLRB v.), 380 F. (2d) 933 (CCA 9, 1967), **402**

Transportation Management Corp. (NLRB v.), 426 U.S. 393 (1983), **177**

Tri-County Medical Center, 222 NLRB 1089 (1976), **267**

Trico Products Corp., 169 NLRB 287 (1968), **337**

Truax v. Corrigan, 257 U.S. 312 (1921), **75, 92**

Truck Drivers Local Union No. 449, et al. (Buffalo Linen Supply Co. (NLRB v.) 353 U.S. 85 (1956), **479**

TRW, Inc., 169 NLRB 21 (1968), **293**

Tulsa Whisenhunt Funeral Homes, 195 NLRB 106 (1972), **412**

Turner v. Department of Employment Security, 423 U.S. 44 (1975), **667**

U

Union Collieries Coal Co., 41 NLRB 961 (1942), **339**

Union Starch & Refining Co., 89 NLRB 779 (1949), **381**

Union Starch & Refining Co. v. NLRB, 186 F. (2d) 1008 (CA 7, 1951), cert. denied 342 U.S. 815 (1951), **381**

United Aircraft Corp., 192 NLRB 62 (1971), **472**

United Dairy Farmers Cooperative v. NLRB, 663 F. 2d 1054, CA 3 (1980), **311**

United Dairy Farmers Cooperative Assn., 242 NLRB No. 179 (1979), **310**

United Farm Workers National Union v. Babbit, 449 F. Supp. 449 (DC Ariz 1978), **274**

United Gas, Coke & Chemical Workers of America, CIO v. Wisconsin Employment Relations Board, 340 U.S. 383 (1951), **550**

United Shoe Machinery Co. (United States v.), 227 U.S. 32 (1913), **53, 64**

United States Steel Corp. (United States v.), 251 U.S. 417 (1920), **53, 64**

United Technologies, 268 NLRB No. 83 (1984), **412**

United Technologies, Otis Elevator, 255 NLRB No. 5 (1981), **405**

United Technologies, Otis Elevator, 269 NLRB No. 162 (1984), **405**

United Welding Co., 72 NLRB 954 (1947), **286**

Universal Oil Products v. NLRB, 445 F. (2d) 155 (1971), **403**

University Nursing Home, 168 NLRB 53 (1967), **264**

U.S. Postal Service v. Postal Workers Union, CA-1, No. 84-1094, June 19, 1984, **449**

Upholsterers Frame & Bedding Workers Twin City Local 61 (Minneapolis House Furnishings Co.), 132 NLRB 40 (1961), **522**

V

Vaca v. Sipes, 386 U.S. 171 (1967), **431**

Virginia-Carolina Chemical case, **517**

Virginia Electric Co. v. NLRB, 319 U.S. 533 (1943), **373**

Virginia Electric & Power Co. (NLRB v.) 314 U.S. 469 (1941), **285, 305**

W

Wackenhut Corp., 196 NLRB 278 (1972), **352**

Wahl Clipper Corp., 195 NLRB 104 (1972), **471**

Walgreen Co., 198 NLRB 1138 (1972), **359**

Wall Colmonoy Corp., 173 NLRB 40 (1968), **299**

Wallace Corp. v. NLRB, 323 U.S. 248 (1944), **653**

Walt Disney Productions (NLRB v.) 146 F. (2d) 44 (1945), **456**

Warehouse Union, Local 860, IBT (The Emporium), 237 NLRB No. 163 (1978), **429**

Washington County v. Alberta Gunther, 452 U.S. 161 (1981), **664, 665**

Waterhouse v. Comer, 55 Fed. 149 (1893), **43**

Watkins v. United Steelworkers, 369 F. Supp. 1221 (1974), **677**

Watkins v. United Steelworkers, 369 F. Supp. 1221 (1974), reversed 516 F. (2d) 41 (5th Cir., 1975), **683**

Weeks v. Southern Bell Telephone & Telegraph Co., 409 F. (2d) 228 (CA 3, 1969), **662**

Weirton Steel Co., **153**

Wells Fargo Armored Service Corp., 272 NLRB No. 106 (1984), **352**

Wengler v. Druggists Mutual Insurance Co., 446 U.S. 142 (1980), **669**

West Coast Hotel v. Parrish, 300 U.S. 391 (1937), **148**

Western, Inc., 93 NLRB 336 (1951), **525**

Western Air Lines, Inc. v. Criswell, 105 Sup. Ct. 2743 (1985), **685**

Western Cartridge Co. v. NLRB, 134 F. (2d) 240 (CA 7, 1943), **296**

Western Electric, 199 NLRB 326 (1972), **411**

Westinghouse Electric Corp. v. Westinghouse Salaried Employees, 348 U.S. 437 (1955), **440**

Wholesale Delivery Drivers & Salesmen (Servette, Inc.), Local 848, 133 NLRB 1501, 310 F. (2d) 659 (9th Cir., 1962) 337 U.S. 46 (1964), **527**

Wickwire Brothers, 16 NLRB 16 (1936), **284**

Wilder Manufacturing, 185 NLRB 175 (1970), **308**

Wiley, John, & Sons v. Livingston, 376 U.S. 543 (1964), **457**

Williams v. Bell, 587 F. (2d) 1240 (D.C. Cir. 1978), **666**

Williams v. Saxbe, 413 F. Supp. 654 (D.C. 1976), **666**

Window Glass Manufacturers v. United States, 263 U.S. 403 (1923), **55**

Winn-Dixie Stores, 243 NLRB No. 151 (1978), **398**

Wirtz v. Glass Bottle Blowers Assn. of United States & Canada, Local 153, AFL-CIO, 389 U.S. 463 (1968), **617**

Wirtz v. Hotel, Motel & Club Employees Union, Local 6, 391 U.S. 492 (1968), **612**

Wirtz v. Laborers International Union of North America, Local 125, AFL-CIO, 389 U.S. 477 (1968), **617**

Wisconsin Department of Industry, Labor & Human Relations v. Gould, CA-7, Nos. 84-1115 & 84-2075, December 13, 1984, **230**

Woelke & Romero Framing v. NLRB, 956 U.S. 645 (1982), **530, 531**

Wood, W. Wilton, Inc., 127 NLRB 1675 (1960), **471**

Workmen's Amalgamated Council (United States v.), 54, Fed 994 (1893), **42–43**

Wright Line, Inc., 251 NLRB 1083 (1980), **177**

Wygant v. Jackson Board of Education, U.S. Sup. Ct. Case No. 84-1340, May 19, 1986, **681**

Wyman-Gordon (NLRB v.), 394 U.S. 759 (1969), **306–7**

Y

Yellow Cab & Baggage Co., 17 NLRB 469 (1939), **247**

Yeshiva University (NLRB v.), 44 U.S. 672 (1980), **259, 262**

Young, L.A., Spring & Wire Corp., 65 NLRB 301 (1946), **342**

Youngdahl, James E., v. Rainfair, Inc., 335 U.S. 131 (1957), **544**

Youngstown Sheet & Tube Co. v. Sawyer, 353 U.S. 579 (1952), **578**

GENERAL INDEX

A

Aaron, Benjamin, **588**
Abel, I. W., **597**
Abuse(s) of labor injunctions, **29–34**
  blanket injunction as, **29–30**
  judges as legislators as, **29**
  quality of evidence in injunction proceedings as, **33–34**
  status quo in labor disputes as, **30–31**
  time lags in injunction proceedings as, **31–33**
Affirmative action programs, **673–75**
Age discrimination, **685**
Age Discrimination Act of 1967, **652, 685**
Agency shop, **369**
  in right-to-work law state, **390**
  under Taft-Hartley, **390–92**
Agricultural workers, Taft-Hartley Act and, **273–76**
  Arizona law on, **273–74**
  California law on, **275–76**
Allied Industrial Workers of America, **585**
"Ally" doctrine, **509–10**
Altgeld, Peter, **135**
Amalgamated Association of Iron, Steel and Tin Workers, **152–53, 154**
Ambulatory situs picketing, **520–22**

American Federation of Labor (AFL), **19**
  bargaining units and, **328, 332–33**
  legislative campaign of, on labor injunctions, **70–72**
  political activity of, **47, 48**
  Taft-Hartley Act and, **201–2**
  Wagner Act and, **157–58**
American Federation of State, County, and Municipal Employees Union, **608, 644**
American Federation of State and Municipal Employees, **641**
American Federation of Teachers, **263, 641**
American Liberty League, National Lawyer's Committee of, **164–65**
American Manufacturing Company, **443–44**
American Railway Union, **135**
American Steel Foundries, **74, 75, 82, 83**
American Sugar Refining Company, **52**
American Tobacco Company, **53**
Antitrust laws
  Clayton Act and, **48, 49–51**
  prosecution of, since Norris-La Guardia, **100–16**
  Sherman Act as, **41–44**. *See also* Sherman Antitrust Act
  state, peaceful picketing violating, **546–49**
  struggle for, **40–65**
Antiunion conduct, patterns of, **120–29**

845

Antiunion conduct *(cont.)*
   attack on union leadership as, **122–25**
   company unions as, **128–29**
   industrial espionage as, **120–22**
   need for public control and, **129–33**
   strike-breaking tactics as, **125–29**
Apex Company, **105**
Arbitration, **437–50**
   advisory, **648**
   Anchor Motor Freight and, **447–48**
   Civil Rights Act of 1964 and, **669–70**
   Collyer doctrine and, **409–16.** *See also Collyer*
      doctrine
   compulsory, **648–49**
      in national emergency labor disputes,
      573–75
   deferral to, *Collyer* doctrine and, **409–16**
   final-offer, **648**
   function of, **438**
   Gateway Coal and, **445–46**
   "grievance," **404**
   "interest," **404**
   McDonald v. City of West Branch, Michigan and,
      448–49
   mediation and, **648**
   no-strike clause and, **438–39**
   Nolde Bros. and, **446**
   for public employees, **638–39**
   for state and local employees, **647–49**
   Supreme Court and, **439–42**
   "Trilogy" cases and, **442–50**
   voluntary binding, **648**
   W. R. Grace and, **446–47**
Arbitrators, dual jurisdiction of, NLRB and,
   455–57
Arizona Agricultural Employment Relations
   Board, **274**
Assembly, freedom of, Landrum-Griffin Act and,
   589–91
Assessments, Union, Landrum-Griffin Act and,
   591–92
Authorization cards
   bargaining on basis of, **307–10**
   NLRB and, **307–14**
   validity of, **313–14**

B

Bache-Denman Coal Company, **56–59**
Bakery and Confectionery Workers, **585**
Ball, Joseph H., **201**
Bankruptcy, Taft-Hartley Act and, **269–72**
   congressional response to, **272–73**
Bargaining, collective. *See* Collective bargaining
Bargaining orders, retroactivity of, **314–15**
Bargaining unit(s), **325–62**
   AFL and, **328, 330–31**
   Civil Service Reform Act of 1978 and, **630–31,**

   632–38. *See also* Civil Service Reform Act
      of 1978
coordinated bargaining and, **359–61**
craft, **328, 330–38**
   AFL and, **332–33**
   Mallinckrodt doctrine and, **336–38**
   NLRB and, **333–34**
   Taft-Hartley and, **334–38**
   treatment of, **331–34**
discrimination and, **654**
establishment of, **326–30**
   controversial issues in, **327–39**
   NLRB guides for, **326–37**
   weight of evidence in, **329–30**
extent of organization of, **357–59**
in Federal Reserve System, **631–32**
forepeople and, **329, 338–45**
industrial, **328, 330–31**
limitations on, pressure for, **330–31**
for managerial employees, **347–49**
nature of, **325**
for plant guards, **349–54**
for professional workers, **329, 354–57, 364***n*
Taft-Hartley Act and, **330**
Wagner Act and, **326–30**
work of, preservation of, **531–32**
in World War II, **328–29**
Basic Steel Industry Dispute Board, **561**
Bedford-Bloomington quarry, **62–63**
Bedford Stone doctrine, **61–64**
Benefits, announcement of, elections and,
   296–98
Biemiller, A. J., **203**
"Bill of Rights" of union members, **586–87**
   enforcement of, **597–98**
Bituminous coal industry, economic effect of
   strikes in, **558–59**
Black, Hugo L., **344, 388, 452**
Blanket injunction, **29–30**
   Norris-La Guardia Act and, **88**
Bonding, general, of union personnel, **621–22**
Bonwit Teller doctrine, **299–301**
Borg-Warner doctrine, **399–407**
   allegal category of bargaining demands and,
      400
   mandatory category of bargaining demands
      and, **400–402**
   significance of, **406–7**
   voluntary category of bargaining demands
      and, **402–7**
Boulware, Lemuel R., **398**
"Boulwarism," **398**
Boycotts
   Clayton Act and, **50–51**
   Danbury Hatters doctrine and, **45–46**
   secondary. *See* Secondary boycotts
   Sherman Act and, **48, 51**
   Taft-Hartley Act and, **214–15**
   Truax case and, **75–76**

Boyle, W. A. (Tony), **597, 614**
Brandeis, Louis B., **36–37, 52, 64, 76–78, 92–93, 102, 168**
Breads, Gerald, **123–24**
Brennan, William, **259, 262, 671, 680, 682**
Brotherhood of Locomotive Engineers, **572**
Brotherhood of Railroad Clerks, **147**
Brown, Edmund G., **275**
Brown, Gerald, **410**
Brown-Olds doctrine, **372–74, 375**
Buckley, William F., **367**
Bucks Stove and Range Company, **47–48**
Budd Manufacturing Company, **152**
Bureau of Labor Statistics, **609**
Burger, Warren E., **240, 262, 452**
Burns Detective Agency, **457–58**
    labor spies from, **121**
Burton, Harold H., **344**
Business, "rule of reason" doctrine and, **52–54**
Butchers Union, **93–94**
Butler, Pierce, **95, 166, 168–69**

C

California Agricultural Labor Relations Board, **275–76**
California Occupational Safety and Health Administration, **491–92**
Calumet Contractors Association, **497**
Captive-audience problem in elections, **289, 299–304**
    Bonwit Teller doctrine and, **299–301**
    current policy on, **301–2**
    employee questions and, **303–4**
    equal opportunity doctrine and, **301–2**
    equal time and, **302–3**
    Labor Law Reform Act of 1977 and, **304**
    Livingston Shirt and, **301–2**
    unfair labor practices and, **302–3**
Cardozo, Benjamin N., **168, 619**
Carnegie-Illinois Steel Corporation, **325**
Carter, Jimmy, **221, 228, 230, 236, 239, 304, 354, 385, 562, 692**
Chamber of Commerce, **234–35**
Chamberlain, Neil, **233**
Chavez, Caesar, **274**
Chicago Lighthouse for the Blind, **259–60**
Chicago Milk Wagon Drivers' Union, **543**
Christenson, C. Lawrence, **558**
Civil Rights Act of 1964, **636, 652**
    Title VII of, **656–72, 675–85**
        arbitration and, **669–70**
        Equal Employment Opportunity Commission, **447, 652**. *See also* Equal Employment Opportunity Commission (EEOC)
        equal pay and, **664–66**
        fringe benefits and, **668**
        homosexuals and, **667**

national origin and, **672**
        pension and retirements and, **668–69**
        pregnancy and, **667–68**
        religious discrimination and, **671–72**
        reverse discrimination and, **669**
        sexual harrassment and, **666–67**
        unions and, **676–85**
Civil Rights Act of 1871, Section 1983 of, **448–49**
Civil Service Commission, **638**
Civil Service Reform Act of 1978, **627, 630, 631, 632–38, 641, 692, 769–96**
    administrative structure of, **633–34**
    bargaining unit appropriateness and, **634–35**
    bars to elections and, **635–36**
    consolidation of units and, **635**
    elections and, **634**
    employee categories in unit determinations and, **634–35**
    labor organizations and recognition and, **636**
    recognition and, **634**
    scope of bargaining and, **637–38**
    union conduct and, **636**
Clarke, John H., **36**
Classification Act of 1949, **630**
Clayton Act, **48, 49–51, 699–700**
    Duplex case and, **55–56**
    labor injunction and, **71–73, 74, 75, 78, 82**
    picketing and, **72**
    secondary boycotts and, **101–2, 507**
"Clean hands" doctrine, **487–88**
Cleveland, Grover, **135**
Closed shop, **368**
    abuses of, **369–70**
    Brown-Olds doctrine and, **372–74**
    "hiring hall" and, **369, 374–75**
    illegality of, **370–72**
    Landrum-Griffin Act and, **376–78**
    Mountain Pacific doctrine and, **375–78**
    National Labor Relations Board and, **371–78**
    National War Labor Board and, **207–8**
    racketeering and, **370**
    Taft-Hartley Act and, **369–78**
    Wagner Act and, **370–72**
Clothing industry, hot-cargo provision and, **530–31**
Clothing and Textile Workers, **232**
Coercion in picketing, **483–84**
Cohen, Sam "Chowderhead," **126–27**
Collective bargaining, **88–89**
    agency shop and, **390–92**
    arbitration in, **437–39**
        Supreme Court in, **439–42**
    authorization cards and, **307–10**
    bad-faith
        employer, **398–99**
        union, **399**
    bargaining obligation of successor employer in, **457–58**
    "boulwarism" and, **398**

Collective bargaining *(cont.)*
  categories for, policy implications of, **693–94**
  checkoff and, **392–96.** *See also* Dues, checkoff
  Civil Service Reform Act of 1978 and, **632–38.**
    See also Civil Service Reform Act of 1978
  "code of ethics" and, **404–5**
  company unions and, **128–29**
  in contract period, employer's duty in, **407–9**
  coordinated, **359–61**
  Danbury Hatters doctrine and, **44**
  deferral to arbitration and, **409–16**
  definition of, **1**
  discipline of union officers in, **454–55**
  dual jurisdiction of arbitrators and, NLRB and,
    455–57
  employee rights in, **216–17**
  employer rights in, **217–18**
  enforcement of, **424–61**
  extent of, **5–6**
  fair representation and, **427–37.** *See also* Fair
    representation, duty of
  federal employees, **629–30**
  for foremen and women, **252–53**
  good-faith, **396–409.** *See also* Good-faith bar-
    gaining
  government protection of, logic of, **118–33.** *See
    also* Antiunion conduct, patterns of
  grievance procedure and, **424–57.** *See also*
    Grievance procedure
  hospital employees and, **265–66**
  and individual suits in federal courts, **431–33**
  industrial peace and, **163**
  industry-wide, **110**
  issues for, **1–2**
  legal climate of, **6–8**
  legislative action on
    early, **136–38**
    judiciary and, **138–42**
    World War I and, **142–46**
  limitations of, **2**
  lockout and, **1**
  in national emergency labor disputes, **573–75**
  National Labor Relations Board and, **156**
  nature of, **1–3**
  Norris-La Guardia influence on no-strike
    provisions in, **450–51**
  obligation of successor employer for, **457–58**
  in postal service, **630–31**
  potential of, **2**
  power of NLRB to order, **310–15**
  public employee, **627, 629–30**
  Railway Labor Act and, **146–47, 148**
  right-to-work laws and, **383–86**
  Sherman law and, **68**
  significance of, **5–6**
  Sinclair reversed by boys markets in, **451–54**
  state laws on, status of, **642–43**
  at state and local levels, **641–42**
  strike and, **1**

  substance of, controls on, **366–417**
  successor employer obligations in, **458–59**
  summary on, **8, 460–61**
  Trading Port doctrine and, **314–15**
  "Trilogy" cases in, **442–50**
  union security and, **366–78, 386–88.** *See also*
    Union security
  union shop and, **378–83, 387–90.** *See also*
    Union shop
  unions and, **3–5**
  units for, **325–62.** *See also* Bargaining unit(s)
  Wagner Act and, **158, 161–62, 178–80**
  World War I and, **142–44**
Colleges, private, NLRB jurisdiction and, **258–59**
Collyer doctrine, **409–16, 455–56**
  cases deferred and not deferred in, **411–13**
  impact of, on labor relations, **415–16**
  NLRB jurisdiction in, **413–14**
  refusal to enforce arbitrator's decision in, **415**
Common law, peaceful picketing in violation of,
  549
Common-situs picketing, **515–20**
  Denver Building Trades Council and, **516–17**
  Moore Dry Dock and, **518–19, 520**
  policy shifts on, **519–20**
  "reserve gate" doctrine and, **517–18**
Commons, John R., **10**
Communist Party membership, union office-
  holding and, **611–12**
Company unions, **128–29**
  Railway Labor Act and, **147**
  Wagner Act and, **173–74**
Comparable worth, **695**
Condon-Wadlin Act, **645**
Conflict-of-interest reporting, **601–2**
Congress of Industrial Organizations (CIO), **145**
  bargaining units and, **328**
  on NLRB, **234**
  on Taft-Hartley Act, **201**
Consent-stipulated elections, **226**
Conspiracy doctrine, **11–19**
  Norris-La Guardia Act and, **83–84**
  unions and, **11–12**
Construction industry, hot-cargo provision and,
  529–30, 531–34
Consultants, labor relations, **603–6**
Consumer secondary boycotts, **522–27**
  products produced aspects of publicity exemp-
    tion and, **526–27**
  unfair lists and, **525–26**
Contempt of court, Norris-La Guardia Act and,
  89–90
Coronado Coal Mine, **56–60**
Coronado Doctrine
  apex doctrine and, **105–7**
  "rule of reason" doctrine, **56–61**
Corporation Auxiliary Company, labor spies
  from, **121**
Council of Economic Advisors, **693**

County Laborers, **641**
Crane, **238**
Curtis doctrine, **497**

D

Danbury Hatters doctrine, economic issues in, **44–46**
Darlington doctrine, **176–77**
Debs, Eugene V., **27**
Decertification elections, **316–18**
Denham, Robert, **374**
Denver Building Trades Council, **516–17**
Department of Agriculture, **633**
Department of Commerce, **633**
Department of Defense, **629, 635**
Department of Interior, **629**
Department of Justice, **682**
Department of Labor, **606, 616, 617**
Department of State, **633**
Depression of 1930's, labor and, **69–70**
Directed elections, **226–27**
Dirksen, Everett M., **383**
Disciplinary action, improper, safeguards against, **594–97**
Discrimination
  affirmative action programs and, **673–75**
  against unions
    Erdman Act and, **137–38**
    Wagner Act and, **174–78**
  age, **685**
  Civil Rights Act of 1964 and, **656–64**. *See also* Civil Rights Act of 1964
  employment opportunity and, **652–86**
  "hiring halls" and, **684–85**
  preferential treatment and, **675–76**
  racial
    Norris-La Guardia Act and, **95–96**
    policy on, evolution of, **652–56**
  religious, **671–72**
  reverse, **669, 675–76**
  seniority and, **677–82**
  sexual, **664–68**
  under NLRB and equal employment opportunity, **676**
Dotson, Donald, **235, 236**
Douglas, William O., **109, 110, 111, 112, 114, 344, 569–70**
Doyle, Charles, **123**
Dues
  checkoff, legal control of, **392–96**
    under Railway Labor Act, **393–94**
    under Taft-Hartley, **394–96**
  membership, **394**
  nonpayment of, Taft-Hartley Act on, **380–82**
  union, Landrum-Griffin Act and, **591–92**
Dunlop, John T., **473, 522**
Duplex Printing Press Co., **54–56**

E

Economic issues
  in *Danbury Hatters* doctrine, **44–46**
  labor injunctions and, **69–70**
  in unionism, **3–6**
Economic striker rights, **466–70**
Economic strike(s)
  participants in, rights of, **470–72**
  versus unfair labor practice strikes, **466–67**
Educational institutions, NLRB jurisdiction and, **258–59**
Eisenhower, Dwight D., **234, 248, 256, 301, 391, 470, 562**
Election(s)
  announcement of benefits and, **296–98**
  campaigning in, **613–15**
  captive-audience problem and, **289, 299–304**. *See also* Captive-audience problem in elections
  Civil Service Reform Act of 1978 and, **634, 635–36**
  consent-stipulated, **226**
  de-authorization, **379**
  decertification, **316–18**
  directed, **226–27**
  employer free speech and, **284–87**
  employer petitions for, **315–16**
  employer poll and, **298–99**
  Excelsior doctrine and, **305–7**
  expedited, picketing and, **495–97**
  frequency of, **610**
  General Shoe doctrine and, **287–92**
  names-and-addresses policy and, **305–7**
  NLRB policies on, **283–319**
  no-solicitation rule and, **300–302**
  procedures for
    enforcement of, **615–18**
    minimum, **610–11**
  provisions for, **610–18**
    usage of, **617–18**
  racial discrimination and, **289–90**
  runoff, **318–19**
  setting aside, reasons for, **298–99**
  surveillance and, **299**
  "Third-party" principle and, **289**
  threats and, **292–96**
  "totality-of-conduct" doctrine and, **285–86**
  "truth in campaign" doctrine and, **290–92**
  unfair labor practices and, **286, 287–88, 302–3**
  union, conduct of, **609–10**
  union-shop, **378–80**
  Wagner Act and, **284–87**
Embezzlement of union funds, **621**
Empire Storage and Ice Company, **547**
Employees, fiduciary responsibilities of, **618–20**
Employer bad-faith bargaining, **398–99**
Employer reports, **602–3**

Employment Relations Board, **647**

Equal employment opportunity
essential features of, **656–64**
policy implications of, **694–95**

Equal Employment Opportunity Act, **636, 638–39**

Equal Employment Opportunity Commission (EEOC), **447, 652**
civil suits and, **660**
employment records and, **661–62**
enforcement procedures of, **658–60**
equal pay and, **664–66**
fringe benefits and, **668**
homosexuals and, **667**
national origin and, **672**
pension and retirement plans and, **668–69**
physical examinations and business necessity in, **662**
pregnancy and, **667–68**
on recruitment and selection advertisements, **661**
religious discrimination and, **671–72**
remedies of, **660–61**
reverse discrimination and, **669, 675–76**
"sex-plus" qualifications and, **662**
sexual harrassment and, **666–67**
testing and educational requirements and, **662–64**
unions and, **676–85**

Equal Employment Opportunity Coordinating Council, **657**

Equal Pay Act of 1963, **655, 664–66**

Equal rights
under Landrum-Griffin, **656**
for union members, **588–89**

Equity courts, labor injunctions and, **23–24**

Erdman Act, **137–38, 140**

Ervin, Sam, J., **235**

Espionage, industrial, **120–22**

Evans, M. Stanton, **367**

Evidence, quality of, in injunction proceedings, **33–34**

Excelsior doctrine, **305–7**

Executive branch of government, labor relations law and, **7**

Executive Order 10988, **627, 632, 692**

Executive Order 11491, **632**

Executive Order 11636, **633**

Executive Order 11838, **632**

F

Fair representation, duty of, **427–37, 653–54**
court enforcement of contracts and, **433–35**
enforcement of, **429–30**
grievance processing and, **427–28**
individual suits on, in Federal Courts, **431–33**
informing members and, **429**

nonunion employees and, **429**
Taft-Hartley and, **435–37**

Fanning, John H., **405, 410, 412, 489**

Farmer, Guy, **114, 248**

Favorito, Vincent, **123**

Featherbedding, Taft-Hartley Act and, **216**

Federal Corrupt Practices Act of 1925, **237**

Federal Election Campaign Act of, 1971, **238–40**

Federal employees
arbitration and, **638–39**
bargaining unit for, **634–35**
Civil Rights Act of 1964 and, **636**
Civil Service Reform Act of 1978 and, **630–31, 632–38.** *See also* Civil Service Reform Act of 1978
classification Act and, **630**
collective bargaining among, **629–30**
Department of Agriculture and, **633**
Department of Commerce and, **633**
Department of Defense and, **629, 735**
Department of Interior and, **629**
elections and, **635–36**
Executive Order 10988 and, **627, 632**
Executive Order 11491 and, **632**
Executive Order 11838 and, **632**
Federal Labor Relations Authority and **633–34, 636**
Federal Labor Relations Council and, **633, 637**
Federal Reserve System, **631–32**
Foreign Service Act of 1980 and, **633**
Government Printing Office and, **639**
grievance procedures for, **638–39**
impasses and, **640–41**
Lloyd- La Follette Act and, **629–30**
Merit System Protection Board and, **633**
Office of Personnel Management and, **633**
Postal Service, **630–31, 639**
Public Law 330 and, **628**
Rhodes-Johnston Bill and, **630**
scope of bargaining and, **637–38**
strikes of, **628**
Tennessee Valley Authority and, **639**
Thurmond Act and, **635**
unfair labor practices and, **639–40**
union recognition and, **634**
union security and, **639**

Federal Labor Relations Authority (FLRA), **633–34, 636, 640**

Federal Labor Relations Council, **633, 637**

Federal Mediation and Conciliation Service, **410, 640**

Federal Reserve System, **631–32**

Federal Services Impasse Panel, **634, 640, 641**

Fees, initiation, of unions, **591–92**

Fibreboard doctrine, **407–9**

Fiduciary responsibilities of union officers and employees, **618–20**

Financial safeguards for unions, **618–22**

Fines

against union members working during strike, **488–491**
payment of, by unions, **622**
Fitzsimmons, Frank, **585**
Ford, Gerald, **236, 522, 632**
Ford Order, 1975, **637**
Foreign Service Act of 1980, **633**
Foreign Service Relations Board, **633**
Foreman's Association of America (FAA), **339,
  340, 346**
Forepeople
  bargaining units for, **329, 338–45**
  under Wagner Act, **338–45**
    final NLRB position on, **341–42**
    following *Packard* decision, **342–45**
    Maryland Drydock decision and, **339–40**
    original NLRB position on, **339**
    recognition strikes and, **340–41**
Frankfurter, Felix, **31–32, 33, 104, 236–37, 344,
  440, 507**
Fraternal Order of Police, **641**
Fringe benefits, EEOC and, **668**

G

General Shoe doctrine, **287–92, 316**
Gissel doctrine, **307–10**
Globe doctrine, **333, 334**
Goldberg, Arthur, **114, 201**
Gompers decision, **47–48, 50**
Gompers, Samuel, **48, 49, 50**
Good-faith bargaining
  assessment of, **397**
  Borg-Warner doctrine and, **399–407**
  cases of no agreement and, **399**
  controls over, **396–409**
  employer bad-faith bargaining and, **398–99**
  Fibreboard doctrine and, **407–9**
  union bad-faith bargaining and, **399**
  Wagner Act and, **396–97**
Goodwill Industries, 260
Goodyear Alabama plant, **654**
Gould, Jay, **18**
Government employees, **627–50.** *See also* Federal
  employees; Public employees; and State
  and local employees
Government protection, logic of, **118–33.** *See also*
  Antiunion conduct, patterns of
  need for public control and, **129–33**
Government seizure of industry in national
  emergency labor disputes, **577–79**
Great America Service Trades Council (AFL-
  CIO), **84**
Great Northern Railway, **52**
Green, William, **201–2, 205**
Greene, Nathan, **31–32, 33, 507**
Grievance procedure(s), **424–57**
  arbitration and, **437–50.** *See also* Arbitration

control of, **425–26**
fair representation duty of union and, **427–37**
for public employees, **638–39**
Taft-Hartley and, **426–27**
Wagner Act and, **425–26**
Guards, plant, bargaining units for, **349–54**

H

Hamilton, Alexander, **11, 16**
Hansen, **238**
Harrassment, sexual, EEOC and, **666–67**
Hartley, Fred, **346**
Hearst Corporation, **515**
"Hiring hall," **369, 684–85**
  regulations on, **374–75**
Hitchman Coal Company, **73**
  "yellow-dog contract," **35–37**
Hitchman decision, **690**
Hoffa, James, **585**
Holmes, Oliver Wendell, Jr., **36, 46, 76–77,
  141–42**
Homestead strike of 1892, **19**
Homosexuals, EEOC and, **667**
Hoover, Herbert, **79**
Hospital industry, NLRB and, **263–69**
  bargaining units in, **265–66**
  interns and resident physicians in, **266–67**
  problems of applications of, **265**
  special rules for, **267–69**
Hot-cargo agreements, **527–28**
  strikes to obtain and enforce, **530–31**
Hotel, Motel and Club Employees Union, **612**
House Post Office and Civil Service Committee,
  628
Houston, John M., **339–40, 341**
Hughes, Charles Evans, **168, 169–70**

I

Industrial Adjustment Act, **155–56**
Industrial democracy, Wagner Act and, **189–
  90**
Industrial espionage, **120–22**
Informational picketing, **498–500**
Initiation fees, union, Landrum-Griffin Act and,
  591–92
Insurance industry, **357–59**
International Association of Fire Fighters, **641,
  644**
International Association of Machinists (IAM),
  54–55, 56, 103
International Brotherhood of Electrical Workers,
  328
International Brotherhood of Teamsters, **585**
  farm labor law and, **275–76**
International Communications Agency, **633**

International Cut Stone & Quarryers Association, **62**
International Development Cooperation Agency, **633**
International Ladies Garment Workers Union, **235**
International Longshoremen's and Warehousemen's Union, **563**
Interns, hospital, NLRB and, **266–67**
Interstate commerce
   federal supremacy in labor relations and, **252–55**
   NLRB jurisdiction in, **249–52**

J

Jackson, Andres, **16**
Jackson, Robert H., **344**
Jefferson, Thomas, **16**
Jenkins, Howard, **224, 410, 412**
Jewel Tea Company, **108–9**
Johnson, Hugh S., **154**
Johnson, Lyndon B., **219, 305, 562, 694**
Joint Committee on Labor Management Relations, **201**
Joint Resolution No. 44, **155–57**
Jones & Laughlin Steel Company, **168**
Journeymen Stone Cutters Association, **62–63**
Judges as legislators in labor injunctions, **29**
Judiciary, labor relations law and, **6–7**
Juridictional Disputes Board, **473–74**
Jurisdictional strikes, **473–76**
   settlement of, by NLRB, **473–74**
   and Supreme Court, intervention of, **474–96**

K

Kansas City Ice and Coal Drivers Union, **546**
Kansas City Transit, Inc., **578–79**
Kennedy, John F., **305, 509, 529, 561, 562, 570, 575, 576, 593–94, 619, 627, 632, 692, 694**
Kennedy, Ralph, **410**
King-Thompson Act, **578–79**
Kirkland, Lane, **235**
Knights of Labor, **18–19**

L

La Follette, Robert, **119–20**
La Follette Committee, **119–20**
   on attack on union leadership, **123–24**
   on industrial espionage, **120**
   on need for public control, **131–32**
   on strikebreaking tactics, **126–27**
Labor dispute
   absence of, not controlling, **541–43**

concept of, in Norris-La Guardia Act, **84**
national emergency, **556–81.** *See also* National emergency labor disputes
Labor injunction(s)
   abuses of, **29–34.** *See also* Abuses of labor injunctions
   "blanket," **29–30**
   Boys Markets, **452–54**
   Clayton Act and, **71**
   control of, **68–97**
      early, **70–73**
   Debs case and, **26–27, 28**
   early use of, **38–39**n
   economic scene and, **69–70**
   emergence of, **18–19**
   equity courts and, **23–24**
   evidence in, quality of, **33–34**
   forms of, **24–26**
   industrial freedom and, **81–84**
   in labor disputes, **26–27**
   legislation on
      early court attitudes toward, **73–74**
      unconstitutionality of, **75–76**
   in national emergency labor disputes, **566–68**
   partial, **579–80**
   nature of, **23–24**
   Norris-La Guardia Act and, **78–81.** *See also* Norris-La Guardia Act
   permanent, **26**
   political scene and, **69–70**
   procedural limitations on, **85–90**
      elimination of blanket injunction as, **88**
      promotion of collective bargaining process as, **88–89**
      temporary and permanent injunction as, **87–88**
      temporary restraining orders as, **85–86**
      violations of injunctions as, **89–90**
   "property" concept and, **27–28**
   strikes and, **31**
   temporary, **25–26**
   temporary restraining order as, **24–25**
   time lags in, **31–33**
   "yellow-dog contract" and, **34–37, 84–85**
Labor Law Reform Act of 1977, **221, 228, 229–30, 233, 354, 385–86**
   captive audience problem and, **304**
Labor-Management Advisory Committee proposal for national emergency labor disputes, **575–76**
Labor Management Relations Act, **235, 345, 714–15**
   Section 203 (d), **456**
Labor-Management Reporting and Disclosure Act of 1959, **584–623, 692.** *See also* Landrum-Griffin Act
Labor relations consultants, **603–6**
Labor relations law, evolution and problems of, **690–96**

Labor unions. *See* Union(s)
Laidlaw-Fleetwood doctrine, **470, 471, 472**
Landrum, **588**
Landrum-Griffin Act, **240, 246, 584–623, 745–68**
  background of, **584–86**
  closed shop and, **376–78**
  conflict-of-interest reporting in, **601–2**
  criminal penalties under, **601–2**
  elections and, **306**
  embezzlement of union funds and, **621**
  employer reports in, **602–3**
  equal rights under, **656**
  financial safeguards for unions in, **618–22**
  freedom of speech and assembly in, **589–91**
  general bonding of union personnel and, **621–22**
  hot-cargo agreements and, **527–28**
  labor relations consultants in, **603–6**
  picketing and, **494–95**
  recovery of union assets in, **620–21**
  reports to Secretary of Labor in, **598–99**
  safeguards against improper disciplinary action in, **594–97**
  secondary boycotts and, **507, 512–15**
  Section 8(b)(4) of, **513**
  Section 8(b)(7) of, **494–95**
  Section 14(c), **256**
  strikes and, **470–72**
  union assessments in, **591–92**
  union dues in, **591–92**
  union elections and, **609–18**
  union initiation fees in, **591–92**
  union loans and fine payments in, **622**
  union members "bill of rights" in, **586–87**
    enforcement of, **597–98**
  union members due process in, **595–97**
  union members equal rights in, **588–89**
  union members right to sue in, **592–94**
  union membership protection under, **382**
  union reports and, **599–601**
  union trusteeships in, **606–9**
"Last-Offer" vote record in national emergency labor disputes, **563–66**
Leadership, union, attack on, **122–25**
Legal climate of collective bargaining, **6–8**
Legislators, judges as, in labor injunctions, **29**
Legislature, labor relations law and, **7**
Leiserson, William M., **339–40**
Lewis, John L., **205**
Lists, unfair, secondary boycotts and, **525–26**
Lloyd-La Follette Act, **629–30**
Loans, union, **622**
Lockheed Aircraft, **457**
Lockout(s), **478–82**
  collective bargaining and, **1**
  economic hardship from, **478–79**
  multibargaining unit and, **479**
    as offensive weapon, **480–82**
  rights of employers on, **478–82**
    Supreme Court expansion of, **480**
Loewe & Company, union organizing attempt in, **45–46**

M

MacDonald, David, **597**
"Maintenance-of-membership" arrangement, **208–10, 368–69**
"Majority principle," **153–54**
Majority rule in Wagner Act, **181–82**
"Make-Whole" controversy, **231–33**
Mallinckrodt doctrine, **336–38**
Managerial employees, bargaining units for, **347–49**
Manufacturing, Wagner Act and, **167–68, 169–70**
Marshall, Thurgood, **671, 680**
Maryland Drydock decision, **339–40, 341–42**
McBride, Lloyd, **614**
McClellan Anti-Racketeering Committee, **585, 591–92, 606, 609, 692**
  findings and recommendations, **585–86**
McNatt, E. B., **105–6**
McReynolds, James, **95, 166, 168–69**
Mechanical Handling Systems, Inc., **373**
Membership dues, **394**
Merit System Protection Board (MSPB), **633**
Milk Wagon Drivers Union, **102–3**
Miller, Arnold R., **597**
Miller, Edward B., **410**
Milliken, Deering, **176, 177**
Millis, Harry A., **339–40, 341**
Mitchell, James, **576**
"Mohawk Valley Formula," **127–28**
Molders' Union, "yellow-dog contract" and, **35**
Mondale, Fritz, **239**
Moore Dry Dock and common situs, **518–19**
Mountain Pacific doctrine, **375–78**
Multibargaining unit, defense of, **479**
Municipal Employee Relations Act of 1865, **647**
Murphy, Betty Southard, **190, 225, 228, 309–10, 412**
Murphy, Frank, **344**
Murray, Philip, **205**

N

Name-calling in picketing, **484–86**
Names-and-addresses policy, **305–7**
National Association of Manufacturers, **234–35, 286**
  work stoppages and, **434**
National Association of Window Glass Manufacturers, **55**
National Bituminous Coal Wage Agreement, **445**

National Coal Wage Agreement of 1950, **109,
111–12**
National Corporation Service, labor spies from,
121
National Defense Mediation Board, **208**
National Education Association, **641**
National emergency labor disputes, **556–81**
  board of inquiry in, **560–62**
  characteristics of, **556**
  choice of procedures in, **580**
  collective bargaining in, **573–75**
  compulsory arbitration in, **573–75**
  economic effects of strikes and, **558–60**
  identifying, difficulties in, **557**
  labor injunctions and, **562–63, 566–68**
    partial, **579–80**
  "last-offer" vote record in, **563–66**
  in railroad industry, government policy in,
    572–73
  Railway Labor Act provisions for, **570–72**
  seizures in, **577–79**
  settlement record during injunction period in,
    566–68
  statutory strikes in, **577**
  Taft-Hartley procedures for, **560–63**
    constitutionality of, **568–70**
    suggested alternatives to, **575–76**
National Industrial Recovery Act (NIRA), **150–
  57, 247, 396**
  collective bargaining and, **150, 151**
  National Labor Board and, **151–55**
  National Labor Relations Board and, **155–57**
  purpose of, **150**
  Section 7(a) of, **151–55**
  union membership and, **150–51**
  wages and, **150**
National Joint Board for Settlement of Jurisdictional Disputes, **473–74**
National Labor Board
  automobile strike and, **154**
  "majority principle" and, **153–54**
  National Industrial Recovery Act and, **151–
    55**
  "Reading Formula" of, **152–54**
  in strike settlements, **152**
  weakening of, **152–53, 154–55**
National Labor Relations Act, **158, 161, 237, 652**
National Labor Relations Board (NLRB), **652**
  agency shop and, **390–92**
  agricultural workers and, **273–76**
  authorization card bargaining and, **307–10**
  authorization cards and, **307–14**
  bankruptcy code and, **269–72**
  bargaining units and, **325–62.** *See also* Bargain-
    ing unit(s)
  Brown-Olds doctrine and, **372–74**
  case load of, **222–23, 247–48**
  Catholic schools and, **261–62**
  certification by, strikes against, **476–78**

church-operated commercial enterprises and,
  261
"clean hands" doctrine and, **487–88**
closed shop and, **371–78**
collective bargaining and, **156, 178–80**
Collyer doctrine and, **409–16**
confidential employees and, **261**
congressional response and, **272–73**
criticism of, **233–34**
decertification elections of, **316–18**
dual jurisdiction of arbitrators and, **455–57**
educational institutions and, **258–59**
Eisenhower, agency shop and, **391**
election policies of, **283–319.** *See also* Elec-
  tion(s)
employer election petitions and, **315–16**
enforcement problems of, **156–57**
fair representation duty of union and, **427–37**
Fibreboard, doctrine and, **407–9**
first, **155–57**
foreign banks and, **260–61**
General Shoe doctrine and, **287–92**
Globe doctrine of, **333–34**
Guss case and No Man's Land in, **255–56**
hospital employees and, **263–69.** *See also* Hospital industry, NLRB and
illegal alliens and, **263**
Indian tribes and, **263**
industrial democracy and, **189–90**
injunctive attack on, **164–65**
integrity of, policy implications of, **694**
interstate commerce and, **849–52**
Joint Resolution No. 44 and, **155–57**
jurisdiction of, **246–77**
  congressional policy on, **256–58**
jurisdictional standards of, publication of,
  248–49
jurisdictional strikes and, **473–74**
Kennedy, agency shop and, **391**
labor injunctions and, **27**
Landrum-Griffin Act and, **256–58**
law firms and, **280**
legislative aspects of Taft-Hartley and, **249–52**
"make-whole" remedy of, **231–33**
membership on, **234**
Mountain Pacific doctrine, **375**
names-and-addresses policy of, **305–7**
Nixon, bargaining rights without election and,
  308–9
nonprofit organizations and, **259–60**
personnel and policies of, changing, **233–37**
plant guards and, **349–54**
power of, to order bargaining, **310–15**
professional employees and, **354–57, 364***n*
Reagan, **235–36, 266**
  bargaining orders of, **312**
  coercion in elections and, **295–96**
  "concerted activity" concept and, **492–
    93**

name-calling in picketing and, **485–86**
on job security and, **405**
remedial orders by, **228**
reorganization of, under Taft-Hartley Act, **221–22**
representation elections and, **187–89**
runoff elections and, **318–19**
secondary boycotts and, **508–9**
self-imposed restrictions on, **247–49**
settlement of unfair labor practices cases by, **184–85**
Supreme Court and, **252–63**
time delays in, **223–26**
union responsibilities and, **180–81**
union security clauses and, **382–83**
World War II and, **172, 190–92**
"yellow-dog" contracts and, **137**
National Lawyer's Committee of the American Liberty League, **164–65**
National Mediation Board, **149, 570–71**
National origin, discrimination by, **672**
National Postal Agreements, **631**
National Right to Work Legal Defense & Education Foundation, **592–93, 598**
National Right to Work Legal Defense Foundation, **389**
National Tea Company, **108**
National Trades Union, **15–16**
National War Labor Board (NWLB)
  coal strikes and, **205**
  collective bargaining and, **142–43**
  labor peace and, **206**
  "maintenance-of-membership" arrangement of, **208–10, 268–69**
  World War I, **142–43, 144**
Negotiated consent decree, **674–75**
New Deal
  climate for unions and, **691**
  collective bargaining and, **161–62**
  National Industrial Recovery Act and, **150–57.** *See also* National Industrial Recovery Act (NIRA)
  unions and, **6**
New Jersey Casino Control Act, 1977, **255**
New Negro Alliance, **95–96**
New York State Labor Relations Act, **252–53**
Newspaper Guild, **356**
Newspaper industry, **355–56**
Nixon, Richard M., **234, 236, 239, 563, 567, 576, 585, 632, 682**
No-strike clause, discipline of union officers and, **454–55**
Nonsuability clauses, **435–36**
Norris-La Guardia Act, **78–81, 691, 701–5**
  antitrust prosecution since, **100–116**
  blanket injunctions and, **88**
  "clear proof" doctrine and, **111–12**
  collective bargaining and, **88–89**
  conspiracy doctrine and, **83–84**

contempt provisions of, **89–90**
impact of, **96–97**
influence of, on no-strike provisions, **450–51**
judicial construction of, **90–96**
judicial reaction to, **102–4**
"labor dispute" definition and, **84, 100–102**
labor injunctions and, **23**
labor protection and, **100**
Lauf doctrine and, **93–94**
New Negro Alliance and, **94–96**
permanent injunctions and, **87–88**
picketing and, **82**
purpose of, **80–81**
recognitional and organizational picketing and, **494**
secondary boycotts and, **103–4, 507**
Section 4 of, **81–84, 441, 450–51**
Section 6 of, **435**
strike-relief funds and, **82**
strikes and, **81–84, 466**
temporary injunctions and, **87–88**
temporary restraining orders and, **85–86**
underlying theory of, **79–80**
union responsibility and, **434–45**
"union town" and, **87**
"yellow-dog contracts" and, **84–85, 137**
North American Aviation Company, **425**
Northern Pacific Railway, **52**
Northern Securities Company, **52**
No-strike provisions
  arbitration and, **438–39**
  Norris-La Guardia and, **450–51**

O

Office of Federal Contract Compliance (OFCC), **673–75, 684**
Office of Labor-Management and Welfare Pension Reports, **598, 599**
Office of Personnel Management (OPM), **633, 641**
Ohl, Henry, **203**
Oil, Chemical & Atomic Workers Union, **398–99**
Operating Engineers, **585**
Organizational picketing, **493–501**
  employer unfair labor practices and, **500–501**
  expedited elections and, **495–97**
  Landrum-Griffin Act and, **494–95**
  objectives of, **497–98**
Organizational strikes
  legislative approach to, **130–31**
  Wagner Act and, **162–63, 165–66, 169–70, 192–93**

P

Packard decision, events following, **342–45**
Peddler system, picketing against, **541–42, 546–47**

Pennsylvania Labor Relations Act, **254**
Pensions, EEOC and, **668–69**
Perlman, Selig, **15**
Permanent injunction, **26**
    Norris-La Guardia Act and, **87–88**
Physicians, resident, NLRB and, **266–67**
Picket line, employee conduct on, **482–88**
    coercion and, **483–84**
    name-calling and, **484–86**
    nonviolent mass picketing and, **486**
    restraint and, **483–84**
    unlawful penalties for, **486–88**
Picketing, **482–88, 493–501**
    in absence of labor dispute, **541–43**
    ambulatory situs, **520–22**
    Clayton Act and, **74**
    common-situs, **515–20.** *See also* Common-situs
        picketing
    free speech and, **539–53**
        private property rights and, **551–53**
    by hospital employees, **268–69**
    informational, **498–500**
    labor injunctions and, **542**
    Norris-La Guardia Act and, **82**
    "one picket per entrance" and, **74–75**
    organizational, **493–501.** *See also* Organiza-
        tional picketing
    "patrolling" and, **82**
    peaceful
        in context of violence, **543–45**
        free speech and, **543–51**
        industry specificity of, **545–56**
        in violation of common law, **549**
    peddler system and, **541–42, 546–47**
    recognitional, **493–501**
        employer unfair labor practices and, **500–
            501**
        expedited elections and, **495–97**
        Landrum-Griffin Act and, **494–95**
        objectives of, **497–98**
    roving situs, **520–22**
    state policy on, U.S. Supreme Court and,
        538–54
    "stranger," free-speech guarantee and,
        540–41
    Thornhill doctrine and, **538–40, 543, 544–45,
        549**
    unlawful, penalties for, **486–88**
    Wisconsin Anti-injunction law and, **91**
Pinkerton Detective Agency, labor spies from,
    121, 122
Plant guards
    bargaining units for, **349–54**
    organization of, problems of, under Taft-Hart-
        ley, **353–54**
Political scene, labor injunctions and, **69–70**
Postal Reorganization Act of 1970, **630–31**
Postal service, **630–31**
Preferential treatment, **675–76**

Pregnancy, EEOC and, **667–68**
Prehire agreements, **376**
Private property rights, free-speech and, **551–53**
Products produced aspect of publicity exemption
    in secondary boycott, **526–27**
Professional Air Traffic Controllers Organization
    (PATCO), **636**
Professional strikebreakers, **126–27**
Professional workers, bargaining units for, **354–
    57, 364**n
"Property," concept of, in labor injunction cases,
    27–28
Public employees
    collective bargaining of, denied of, basis of,
        628–29
    Executive Order 10988 and, **627, 632**
    grievance and arbitration procedures for,
        638–39
Public Employment Relations Board, **644**
Public Law 330, **628**
Public sector, labor relations in, **627–50.** *See also*
    Federal employees; Public employees; and
    State and local employees
Pullman strike
    injunction against, **26–27, 43**
    breaking of, **135**
    Erdman Act and, **137**

R

Racial discrimination
    duty of fair representation and, **653–54**
    Landrum-Griffin Act and, **656**
    policy on evolution of, **652–56**
Railroad Administration, **143**
Railroad industry
    collective bargaining in, **163**
    government policy in, **572–73**
    Railroad Administration and, **143**
    Railway Labor Act and, **146–49.** *See also* Rail-
        way Labor Act
Railroad Unemployment Act, **571**
Railway Labor Act, **146–49, 163, 237, 652,
    653**
    agency shop fees and, **389**
    amendments to, **148–49**
    arbitration and, **146**
    checkoff under, **393–94**
    collective bargaining and, **146–47, 148**
    company union and, **147**
    emergency provisions of, **570–72, 576**
    mediation and, **146**
    punitive damages and, **432**
    purpose of, **146**
    union security under, **386–87**
    Wagner Act and, **149, 166**
Rand, James H., Jr., **121**
"Reading Formula," **152–54**

Reagan, Ronald, **223, 228, 235, 236, 239, 266, 292**
Recognitional picketing, **493–501**
  employer unfair labor practices and, **500–501**
  expedited elections and, **495–97**
  Landrum-Griffin Act and, **494–95**
  objectives of, **497–98**
Recognitional strike
  forepeople's, **340–41**
  Wagner Act and, **178–80**
Reed, Stanley F., **344**
Rehnquist, William H., **240**
Reilly, G. D., **339**
Reinstatement rights of strikers, **467–70**
Religious discrimination, **671–72**
Representation elections, procedure for, **187–89**
"Reserve gate" doctrine, **517–18**
Restraint in picketing, **483–84**
Retirement plans, EEOC and, **668–69**
Reverse discrimination, **669, 675–76**
Rhodes-Johnston Bill, **630**
Richberg, Donald R., **154**
Right-of-control test in secondary boycott, **532–33**
Right to sue, protection of, **592–94**
"Right-to-work" laws, **216–17**
  enforcement of, **386**
  states with, agency shop in, **390**
  Taft-Hartley Act and, **383–96**
Roberts, Owen J., **103–4, 168**
Roosevelt, Franklin Delano, **150, 151, 153, 154, 155–56, 158, 168, 205–6, 207, 211, 368, 571, 628**
Roosevelt, Theodore, **629**
Rough shadowing of union leadership, **124**
Roving situs picketing, **520–22**
"Rule of reason" doctrine, **51–61**
  application of
    to business, **52–54**
    to labor organizations, **54–56**
  Coronado doctrine and, **56–61**
Runoff elections, **318–19**
Rutledge, Wiley B., **344**

S

Sadlowski, Edward, **614**
Safeguards against improper disciplinary action, **594–97**
Sanitary Grocery Company, **95**
Secondary boycott(s), **507–34**
  "ally" doctrine and, **509–11**
  bargaining unit preservation in, **531–32**
  in *Bedford Stone,* case, **63**
  Clayton Act and, **101–2, 507**
  clothing industry exemption and, **529–34**
  common-situs picketing and, **515–20.** *See also* Common-situs picketing

construction industry exemption and, **529–34**
  consumer, **522–27**
  Danbury Hatters doctrine and, **46**
  definitions in, **510–11**
  Duplex case and, **55, 56**
  hot-cargo agreements and, **527–28, 530–31**
  Landrum-Griffin Act and, **507, 512–15**
  Norris-La Guardia Act and, **103–4, 507**
  "persons" and "individuals" in, **511–15**
  "right-to-control" test and, **532–33**
  roving or ambulatory situs picketing and, **520–22**
  Soviet Union, **510–11**
  Taft-Hartley Act and, **508–9**
Secretary of Labor, **608–9, 615–17, 674**
  reports to, **598–99**
Security, union. *See* Union security
Seizure
  government, in national emergency labor disputes, **577–79**
  and states, **578–79**
Senate Committee on Labor and Public Welfare, **371**
Senate Select Committee on Improper Activities in labor or Management Field, **585**
Seniority, **677–82**
  remedies for, **682–83**
  Supreme Court decisions on, **680–82**
  T.I.M.E.-D.C. and alteration of Griggs in, **679–80**
"Separate gate" doctrine, **517–18**
Settlement record during injunction period for national emergency labor disputes, **566–68**
Sexual harrassment, EEOC and, **666–67**
Shadowing, rough, of union leadership, **124**
Shanker, Albert, **263**
Shaw, Lemuel, **16–17**
Sherman Antitrust Act, **697–98**
  Bedford Stone decision and, **64**
  Clayton Act and, **48, 49–51**
  collective bargaining and, **68**
  Coronado case and, **57–59**
  Debs case and, **43–44**
  earliest union conviction under, **42–43**
  penalties of, **42**
  "rule of reason" doctrine and, **51–61.** *See also* "Rule of reason" doctrine
  strikes and, **108–7**
  unions and, **41–44**
    present applications of, **108–13**
Shop
  agency, **369**
  closed, **368, 369–78.** *See also* Closed shop
  union, **368.** *See also* Union shop
Smith, Adam, **166–67**
Smith & Wesson Arms Company, **143**
Socioeconomic content of early union movement, **9–11**

Soviet Union boycott, **510–11**
Speech, free
  employer rights to, Wagner Act and, **284–87**
  Landrum-Griffin Act and, **589–91**
  peaceful picketing and, **543–51**
  picketing and, **539–53**
  private property rights and, **551–53**
  stranger picketing and, **540–41**
Standard Oil Company, **52–53**
State Labor Mediation Board, **647**
State laws on collective bargaining, status of, **642–43**
State and local employees, **641–49**
  arbitration and, **647–49**
  collective bargaining for, **641–42**
  Condon-Wadlin Act and, **645**
  fact-finding boards and, **647**
  mediation for, **647**
  resolution of disputes and, **646–67**
  right to strike of, **643–45**
  strikes and, **643–45**
  Taylor Act and, **645**
  union security and, **646**
Statutory strikes in national emergency labor disputes, **577**
Stetin, Sol, **229, 230, 304**
Stevens, J. P., **230, 232, 303, 304, 525**
Stewart, Potter, **452**
Stone, Harlan F., **168**
Stranger picketing, free-speech guarantee and, **540–41**
Strike(s), **465–78, 488–93**
  against NLRB certification, **476–78**
  Apex case and, **106–7**
  collective bargaining and, **1**
  "concerted activity" concept and, **491–93**
  Coronado Mine, **57–60**
  economic, **466–70**
    versus unfair labor practice, **466–67**
  economic effect of, **558–60**
  Federal employees, **628**
  fines against union members working during, **488–91**
  by hospital employees, **268–69**
  jurisdictional, **473–76**
  Landrum-Griffin Act and, **470–72**
  national emergency, **218–19**
  nonorganizational, Wagner Act and, **193–94**
  Norris-La Guardia Act and, **81–84**
  to obtain and enforce hot-cargo clauses, **530–31**
  organizational
    legislative approach to, **130–31**
    Wagner Act and, **162–63, 165–66, 169–70, 192–93**
  Pullman Car Company, **26–27**. *See* Pullman strike
  recognitional

  forepeople's, **340–41**
    Wagner Act and, **178–80**
  record of, in 1946, **211**
  reinstatement rights after, **467–70**
    Taft-Hartley Act innovation on, **469–70**
  Sherman Act and, **106–7**
  state legislation on, **643–45**
  statutory, in national emergency labor disputes, **577**
  "strikebreaking" tactics for, **125–27**
  Taft-Hartley Act and, **214–15**
  unfair labor practice, versus economic strikes, **466–67**
  wildcat, **435–37**
    discipline of union officers and, **454–55**
Strikebreaking tactics, **125–29**
Strike-relief funds, Norris-La Guardia Act and, **82**
Successor employer obligations, **458–59**
Sue, right to, protection of, **592–94**
Supervisors under Wagner Act, **338–45**. *See also* Forepeople under Wagner Act
Supreme Court
  affirmative action and, **680–82**
  antitrust prosecution and, **113–15**
  arbitration and, **439–42**
  Bedford Stone decision of, **61–64**
  Brown-Olds doctrine and, **373–74**
  collective bargaining and, **138–42**
  Coronado case and, **57**
  Danbury Hatters doctrine and, **44, 45–46**
  economic social philosophy of, **139–40**
  Federal supremacy in labor relations and, **252–55**
  Gompers decision and, **48**
  judicial restraint and, **76–77, 141–42**
  jurisdictional strikes and, **474–76**
  labor legislation and, **137–38**
  liberty to contract and, **140–41**
  lockout rights and, **480**
  NLRB and, **252–63**
    Guss case and "No Man's Land in, **255–56**
    jurisdictional problems of, **258–63**
    Landrum-Griffin and, **256–58**
    "rule of reason" doctrine of, **51–61**. *See also* "Rule of reason" doctrine
  Sherman Act and, **42, 43–44, 139**
  state picketing policy and, **538–54**
  on state police power, **141**
  validation of Wagner Act by, **166–71**
Sutherland, George, **166, 168–69**
Swanton, Milo R., **203–4**

T

Taft, Philip, **370, 610**
Taft, Robert A., **470, 508**
Taft, William Howard, **74, 75, 119**

Taft-Hartley Act, **199–241, 246, 248, 249, 692**
  agency shop under, **390–92**
  agricultural workers and, **273–76**
  amendments to, **240**
  announcements of benefits and, **296–98**
  bankruptcy code and, **269–72**
    congressional response to, **272–73**
  bargaining units and, **330**
  changes in, existing labor contracts and, **220**
  checkoff under, **394–96**
  closed shop and, **369–78.** *See also* Closed shop
  controversy over, **199–202**
  craft workers under, **334–38**
  decertification elections and, **316–18**
  election cases in, **226–28**
  employer election petitions and, **316**
  enforcement procedures of, **228–33**
  fines and imprisonment and, **229**
  General Shoe doctrine and, **287–92**
  grievance procedure under, **426–27**
  injunctions and, **228–29**
  innovation of, **187**
  international union affairs and, **219–20**
  jurisdictional strikes and, **473–76**
  labor injunctions and, **23, 27**
  legislative aspects of, **249–52**
  loss of employee rights and, **229**
  managerial employees and, **347–49**
  national emergency strike provisions of, **218–19**
  NLRB reorganization under, **221–22**
  NLRB responsibilities and, **183**
  nonpayment of dues, **380–82**
  operations of, **221–28**
  opponents of, **201–7**
  passage of, factors resulting in, **202–13**
    developments in World War II as, **205–10**
    misconceptions of Wagner Act as, **204–5**
    perennial opposition to Wagner Act as, **202–4**
    strike record of 1946 as, **211–13**
    union abuses as, **210–11**
  picketing and, **482–88**
  plant guards and, **344–54**
    organization problems of, **353–54**
  procedures of, for national emergency labor disputes, **560–63**
    constitutionality of, **568–70**
    suggested alternatives to, **575–76**
  professional workers and, **354–57, 364***n*
  proponents of, **200–201**
  provisions of, **213–20**
    construction of, **287–99**
  reinstatement rights of strikers and, **469–70**
  remedial orders by NLRB and, **228**
  restraining orders and, **228–29**
  "right-to-work" laws and, **216–17, 383–86**
  rights of employees as individuals and, **216–17**

  rights of employers and, **217–18**
  runoff elections and, **318–19**
  secondary boycotts and, **508–9**
  Section 2 (12) of, **355**
  Section 7 of, **391, 392, 482–83, 491–93**
  Section 8 (a)(3), **263, 379, 380**
  Section 8 (a)(5) of, **400, 457**
  Section 8 (b)(1) of, **381, 483**
  Section 8 (b)(1)(1) of, **483, 494**
  Section 8 (b)(3) of, **428**
  Section 8 (b)(3)(5) of, **397**
  Section 8 (b)(4), **215, 473, 477**
  Section 8 (b)(4)(c) of, **478, 494, 497**
  Section 8 (b)(4)(D) of, **474**
  Section 8 (b)(7) of, **494–95, 496–98**
  Section 8 (b)(7)(c) of, **497**
  Section 8 (c) of, **286, 292, 298**
  Section 8 (d) of, **397, 400, 437**
  Section 8 (e), **527**
  Section 9 (a) of, **426, 428**
  Section 9 (b)(2), **336–37**
  Section 9 (b)(3) of, **352**
  Section 9 (c)(1)(A) of, **316**
  Section 9 (c)(3) of, **466**
  Section 9 (c)(5) of, **357**
  Section 9 (d) of, **356**
  Section 9 (e) of, **379**
  Section 10 (a), **250–52, 410**
  Section 10 (K) of, **473–74, 475**
  Section 14 of, Landrum-Griffin ammendments to, **256–58.** *See also* Landrum-Griffin Act
  Section 14 (b) of, **380, 392**
  Section 14 (b) of controversy over, **385–86**
  Section 203 (d) of, **410**
  Section 301 of, **433, 436, 439–41, 450–51, 457**
  Section 302 (d) of, **394**
  Section 304 of, **237–38**
  Section 610 of, **238**
  setting aside elections in, **298–99**
  shift in government policy and, **199–202**
  as "slave labor law," **201**
  state authority under, **249–52**
  strikes and, **466**
    against NLRB certification and, **477–78**
  suits for violations of contracts and, **220**
  supervisors under, **345–47**
  threats and, **292–96**
  time delay and, **223–26**
  unfair labor practice cases under, **186, 222–23**
  union political activities under, **237–40**
  union responsibility under, **435–37**
  union security and, **366–78.** *See also* Union security
  union shop and, **378–83.** *See also* Union shop(s)
  union unfair labor practices and, **213–16**
Taylor, George W., **561**
Taylor Act, **645**
Teamsters, **641.** *See* International Brotherhood of Teamsters

Temporary injunction(s), **25–26**
　Norris-La Guardia Act and, **87–88**
Temporary restraining orders, **24–25**
　Clayton Act and, **72**
　hearings on, **32**
　Norris-La Guardia Act and, **85–86**
　strikes and, **30–31**
Tennessee Valley Authority (TVA), **110–11**
Texas & New Orleans Railroad, **147**
Textile Workers of America, **304**
Textile Workers Union, **176, 230**
Thornhill doctrine, **538–40, 543, 544–45, 549**
Thurmond Act of, 1979, **635**
Tile-laying industry case, **90–93**
Time lags in injunction proceedings, **31–33**
T.I.M.E.D.C. and alteration of *Griggs,* **679–80**
"Totality-of-conduct" doctrine, **285–86**
Trading Port doctrine, **314–15**
Transportation Act of 1920, **396**
"Trilogy" cases, **442–50, 456**
Truman, Harry S., **212–13, 345, 380, 562, 563,**
　571, 578
Trusteeships, union, control of, **606–9**

U

Unfair labor practices
　bargaining orders and, **310–15**
　　for first category, **310–12**
　　for second category, **312**
　　for third category, **313**
　boycotts as, **214–15**
　cases on, processing of, under Taft-Hartley
　　Act, **222–23**
　collective bargaining and, **171–72, 178–80**
　company union and, **173–74**
　complaint of, **185–86**
　discharge for union activity, **175, 177**
　discrimination in hiring and, **174–75**
　discrimination in tenure and, **174–75**
　discrimination by union membership, **214**
　discrimination in working conditions and, **175**
　dues/fees as, **215–16**
　elections and, **286, 287–88**
　employer
　　elections and, **302–3**
　　recognitional and organizational picketing
　　　and, **500–501**
　featherbedding as, **216**
　filing charges of, **183–85**
　formal proceedings for, **185–86**
　hearing on, **186**
　industrial spies and, **171**
　informal settlement of, **184–85**
　investigation of, **184**
　layoffs and, **175–76**
　Mohawk Valley Formula and, **171–72**
　procedure for, **183**

　public employees and, **639–40**
　refusal to bargain as, **308**
　　by employer, **178–80**
　　by union, **214**
　restraint or coercion of employees as, **214**
　shutdowns and, **176–77**
　strikebreakers and, **171**
　strikes as, **214–15**
　strikes for, versus economic strikes, **466–67**
　Taft-Hartley Act and, **213–16**
　time delays in, **223–26**
　union, **213–16**
　union responsibilities and, **180–81**
　violence and, **171–72**
　Wagner Act and, **171–81**
　World War II and, **172**
Unfair lists, secondary boycotts and, **525–26**
Union(s), **9–20**
　abuses of, **210–11**
　activity of, in hospitals, restrictions on, **267–69**
　antisocial practices of, **210–11**
　bad-faith bargaining by, **399**
　before *Commonwealth v. Hunt,* 15–16
　"Bill of Rights" of, **586–87**
　　enforcement of, **597–98**
　bootmakers, **12**
　case against, **13–14**
　Clayton Act and, **49–51**
　company, **128–29.** *See* Company unions
　conduct of, Civil Rights Act and, **636**
　Congress and, **7**
　conspiracy doctrine, **11–19**
　decertification elections statistics of, **317–18**
　defense of, **14–15**
　depression of 30s and, **144–46**
　discipline in, improper safeguards against,
　　594–97
　due process for members of, **595–97**
　dues, initiation fees, and assessments of,
　　591–92
　early history of, **3–5, 9–20**
　economic influence of, **6**
　economic prerequisites for, **3–5**
　elections in, conduct of, **609–10**
　English Common Law and, **13–14**
　equal rights for members of, **588–89**
　fair representation duty of, **427–37**
　financial safeguards for, **618–22**
　fine payments by, **622**
　forepeople's, **329, 338–45.** *See also* Forepeople
　　under Wagner Act
　funds of, embezzlement of, **621**
　general bonding of personnel of, **621–22**
　government protection of, logic of, **118–33.** *See*
　　also Antiunion conduct, patterns of
　growth and development of, **4–5**
　hospital industry, **263–69**
　internal affairs of, regulation of, **584–86**
　international affairs of, **219–20**

labor injunctions and, **18–19, 22–38.** *See also*
    Labor injunctions
leadership of, attack on, **122–25**
legal climate and, **6–8**
legal environment of, **690**
legalization of, **16–17**
legislative support of, beginnings of, **135–36**
legislature and, **691**
loans of, **622**
mainsprings of, **3–5**
national policy on, **690–96**
NLRB-certified, strikes against, **476–78**
no-strike pledge of, in WW II, **206**
officers of
    discipline of, **454–55**
    fiduciary responsibilities of, **618–20**
    prohibitions for, **611–12**
    qualifications for, **612–17**
    removal of, **615**
political activities of
    under Taft-Hartley Act, **237–40**
    union shop and, **387–90**
recovery of assets of, **620–21**
reports by, **599–601**
responsibility of
    NLRB and, **180–81**
    in WW II, **209**
right to hold office in, exceptions to, **611–
    12**
"rule of reason" doctrine and, **54–56**
Sherman Act and, **41–44**
    present application of, **108–13**
shoemakers, **12**
Supreme Court and, **7**
tactics of, effect of, on completion of double
    standard, **61–64**
trusteeships of, **606–9**
unfair labor practices of, **213–16**
World War I and, **142–44**
Union security
  agency shop for, **369**
  clauses on, NLRB control over, **382–83**
  closed shop for, **368.** *See also* Closed shop
  controversial nature of, **366–78**
  forms of, **368–69**
  "hiring halls" and, **369**
  "maintenance-of-membership" and, **208–10,
    368–69**
  in national law, **249–50**
  National War Labor Board and, **207–8**
  for public employees, **639**
  for state and local employees, **646**
  under Railway Labor Act, **386–87**
  union shop for, **368.** *See also* Union shop
  in World War II, **208–10**
Union shop(s), **368, 369**
  elections of, **378–80**
  National War Labor Board and, **207–8**
  representation, **378–79**

Taft-Hartley and, **378–83**
union political activities and, **387–90**
United Brotherhood of Carpenters and Joiners
    of America, **103**
United Farm Workers of America, **274**
United Furniture Workers of America, **484**
United Hatters of North America, **44–46**
United Leather Workers Union, **60**
United Mine Workers (UMW), **111–12, 205, 566**
  in *Coronado* case, **56–60**
  Hitchman case and, **36–37**
  Welfare and Retirement Fund of, **109–10**
United Plant Guard Workers, **457**
United Shoe Machinery Company, **53**
United States Chamber of Commerce, **200**
United States Postal Service, **630–31**
United States Steel Corporation, **53**
United Steelworkers of America, **325, 328, 568,
    597, 614**
United Textile Workers, **585**
Universities, private, NLRB jurisdiction and,
    258–59

V

Van Devanter, Willis, **166, 168–69**
Vinson, Fred M., **344**
Virginia Electric Power doctrine, **502**

W

Wage and Hour Division, **668**
Wages, World War II and, **172**
Wagner, Robert, **155, 157, 161**
Wagner Act, **161–95, 247, 585, 691, 706–13**
  bargaining unit and, **326–30**
  board-developed union responsibilities of,
    180–81
  closed shop and, **370–72**
  collective bargaining and, **158, 161–62,
    178–80**
  discrimination under, **676**
  due process and, **170**
  elections and, **284–87**
  employer election petitions and, **315**
  employer free speech under, **284–87**
  forepeople under, **338–45.** *See also* Forepeople
    under Wagner Act
  industrial democracy and, **189–90**
  majority rule and, **181–82**
  manufacturing and, **167–68, 169–70**
  "no man's land" of, **255–56**
  nonorganizational strikes and, **193–94**
  opposition to, **164–65**
    Taft-Hartley Act passage and, **202–4**
  organizational strikes and, **162–63, 165–66,
    169–70, 192–93**

Wagner Act *(cont.)*
  passage of, **157–58**
  philosophy of, **163–64**
  precursors of, **135–59**
  purpose of, **161**
  Railway Labor Act and, **149, 166**
  record of, **186–87**
  results of, **192–94**
  Section 2 (7) of, **247**
  Section 7 (a) of, **396**
  Section 8 (a)(1) of, **171–73**
  Section 8 (a)(2) of, **173–74**
  Section 8 (a)(3) of, **174–78**
  Section 8 (a)(4) of, **178**
  Section 8 (a)(5) of, **178–80, 654**
  Section 9 (a) of, **425, 653, 654**
  Section 10 (a) of, **255, 258**
  socioeconomic rationale of, **161–65**
  state of affairs of, before *Jones and Laughlin,*
    165–68
  strike record of 1946 and, **211–13**
  strikes and, **466, 468**
  "totality-of-conduct" doctrine and, **285–86**
  unfair labor practices and, **171–81.** *See also* Un-
    fair Labor practices
  union certification and, **425**
  union membership and, **194**
  validation of, by Supreme Court, **166–71**
  in World War II, **190–92**
Wagner Labor Disputes Act, **155, 205, 206**
Walsh-Healey Act, **110**

Warrior & Gulf Navigation Company, **442–43**
Washington Coca-Cola doctrine, **519–21**
Weirton Steel Company, **152–53, 154**
Western Airlines, **489**
Western Union Telegraph Company, **143**
Wildcat strikes, **435–37**
  discipline of union officers and, **454–55**
Wilson, Woodrow, **48, 49–50, 142, 143**
Wisconsin Anti-Injunction Law, **90–93**
Wisconsin Employment Relations Board, **253–54**
Wisconsin Federation of Labor, **203**
Wisconsin Labor Relations Act, **254–55**
Wisconsin Public Utility Anti-Strike Law, **253–55**
Witte, Edwin E., **18, 27, 32**
Worth, comparable, **695**

Y

Yablonski, Joseph, **597, 614**
"Yellow-dog" contract(s)
  Erdman Act and, **137–38**
  labor injunction and, **34–57, 68**
  molders union and, **35**
  "Norris-La Guardia Act and, **84–85**
  outlawing of, **136–38, 149**

Z

Zimmerman, Donald, **235–36, 296**